2022 Licensing & Surplus Lines Laws

For The 50 States, District of Columbia, Territories, and Possessions

Christine G. Barlow, CPCU

International Standard Serial Number: 0-742-5120

International Standard Book Number: 978-1-954096-20-2

The National Underwriter Company
a division of ALM Media, LLC.
4157 Olympic Blvd., Suite 225
Erlanger, KY 41018
1-800-543-0874
www.nationalunderwriter.com

Printed in the United States of America

ABOUT THE NATIONAL UNDERWRITER COMPANY
A DIVISION OF ALM MEDIA, LLC

For over 110 years, The National Underwriter Company has been the first in line with the targeted tax, insurance, and financial planning information you need to make critical business decisions. Boasting nearly a century of expert experience, our reputable Editors are dedicated to putting accurate and relevant information right at your fingertips. With *Tax Facts*, *Tools & Techniques*, *Field Guide*, *FC&S®*, *FC&S Legal*, and other resources available in print, eBook, CD, and online, you can be assured that as the industry evolves National Underwriter will be at the forefront with the thorough and easy-to-use resources you rely on for success.

The National Underwriter Company
Update Service Notification

This National Underwriter Company publication is regularly updated to include coverage of developments and changes that affect the content. If you did not purchase this publication directly from The National Underwriter Company and you want to receive these important updates sent on a 30-day review basis and billed separately, please contact us at (800) 543-0874. Or you can mail your request with your name, company, address, and the title of the book to:

The National Underwriter Company
a division of ALM Media, LLC
4157 Olympic Boulevard
Suite 225
Erlanger, KY 41018

If you purchased this publication from The National Underwriter Company directly, you have already been registered for the update service.

National Underwriter Company Contact Information

To order any National Underwriter Company title, please

- call 1-800-543-0874, 8-6 ET Monday – Thursday and 8 to 5 ET Friday
- online bookstore at www.nationalunderwriter.com, or
- mail to The National Underwriter Company, Orders Department, 4157 Olympic Blvd, Suite 225, Erlanger, KY 41018

ABOUT THE EDITORS

Editor

Christine G. Barlow, CPCU, is Managing Editor of FC&S, a division of National Underwriter Company and ALM. Christine has over thirty years' experience in the insurance industry, beginning as a claims adjuster then working as an underwriter and underwriting supervisor handling personal lines. Before joining FC&S, Christine worked as an Underwriting Supervisor for Maryland Auto Insurance Fund, and as Senior Underwriter/Underwriter for companies Montgomery Mutual, Old American, Charter Group, and Nationwide.

The publications Christine has written or edited include *Personal Lines Unlocked: The Key to Personal Lines Underwriting*, *Personal Lines Endorsements Coverage Guide*, *Commercial Flood Insurance Coverage Guide*, *Personal Flood Insurance Coverage Guide*, *Homeowners Personal Lines Coverage Guide* 5th Edition, *Personal Umbrella Coverage Guide* 2nd Edition, and *Condominium Coverage Guide* 2nd Edition, all published by the National Underwriter Company. Christine regularly writes for *Claims Magazine* and *National Underwriter Magazine*. Christine regularly presents and moderates webinars on a variety of topics and is an experienced presenter.

Christine graduated cum laude from Towson University, Maryland, with a degree in Sociology/Psychology with a concentration in Gerontology.

Contributor

Kelly Helton, J.D. is an Assistant Editor for FC&S Coverage Interpretation. She received a BA in psychology and a BS in professional writing from Taylor University and her juris doctor from Salmon P. Chase College of Law.

Legal Research Assistants

Jasmyne Shaw is a second year student at Salmon P. Chase College of Law.

Editorial Services

Connie L. Jump, Senior Manager, Editorial Operations.

Emily Brunner, Editorial Assistant.

TABLE OF CONTENTS

Surplus Lines States — Alphabetical

INTRODUCTION

The listings in this book include licensing rules and requirements for producers (agents and brokers) as well as other insurance practitioners—managing general agents, solicitors, consultants, claims adjusters, public adjusters, service representatives, reinsurance intermediaries, and viatical settlement brokers/providers—who, in various states, must also be licensed and their activities subject to insurance department regulation. Each state's listing includes the requirements for property and casualty insurance, as well as for life and accident and health.

This book includes general information on the surplus lines laws of the various states. Among the information discussed: licensing requirements and restrictions; filing and tax provisions; listings of those lines of insurance that, in various jurisdictions, may not be placed with nonadmitted insurers; any required notice to the insured; independently procured coverage rules; and reports on the individual state's implementation of the Non-admitted and Reinsurance Reform Act (NRRA). Stamping fees and surplus lines associations contact information are included if applicable; not every state has a surplus lines association.

All charts have been updated with current information. Charts include licensing requirements for CAT duty for adjusters, class and exam exemptions for licensing, fraud chart, fraud division contacts, insurance department contacts, and many others.

The editors of this book have reviewed state statutes, regulations, and insurance division web pages. Normally, we ask the various state insurance departments to review our files before we go to print. With the burdens on staffing due to COVID-19 restrictions, we did not make that request of the departments this year. While we do our best to provide the most accurate information, we are aware that at times we make an error. We will make any corrections online if we discover a mistake.

This book is designed to provide accurate and authoritative about the subject matter covered. As many states have made temporary exceptions and rules in response to COVID-19, please check with the departments directly for that information. A list of insurance department contacts is provided online. This book is offered with the understanding that the writer is not engaged in rendering legal, accounting, or other professional service. If legal advice or other expert assistance is required, the services of a competent professional should be sought. We are not the final authority on the information in this text.

Comments or suggestions about this book may be addressed to the editor at 800-543-0874, or via email: fcspublic@alm.com. We welcome new ideas for content you may find useful.

ALABAMA

Commissioner of Insurance
201 Monroe St., Suite 502
Montgomery, AL 36104
Telephone: 334-269-3550; Fax: 334-241-4192;
Licensing & Examinations: 334-241-4126
https://www.aldoi.gov

I. Licensing Requirements: Sales Personnel—Producers, Limited Lines Producers, Managing General Agents, Service Representatives. Other Insurance Professionals—Adjusters, Reinsurance Intermediaries, Title Producers, Apprentice Adjusters or Business Entity Adjusters. (Ala. Code §27-7-1).

A. Applicability: No person shall sell, solicit, or negotiate insurance for any class or classes of insurance unless the person is then licensed for that line of authority. No producer shall act on behalf of any insurer for which an appointment is not held. (Ala. Code §27-7-4).

B. Licenses Required of Residents: Each of the following must be licensed in Alabama. Except as shown otherwise, all licenses expire on the last day of the licensee's birth month. All licenses renew biennially for $70 for individuals and $100 for business entities. Licensees born in odd numbered years renew in the odd years and licensees born in even numbered years renew in the even years. (Ala. Code §§27-4-2, 27-8A-9, and Ala. Admin. Code r. 482-1-110-.04(2)).

Sales Personnel

1. *Producers.* Producers must be appointed by each insurer represented; appointments are procured and renewed annually (due by December 31) through the insurer. Producers may be licensed in the lines of authority listed in c below.

   a. Fee: first year, $80 for individuals and $130 for business entities; biennial renewal, $70 for individuals, $100 for business entities. Application process is mandatory online.
   Licenses expire in the licensee's birth month biennially based on the producer's birth year. There is a grace period of thirty days during which time the producer may renew with a late fee of $50. If not renewed within that thirty-day period, license expires and all appointments are canceled. Notice of Appointment Fee - $40. Appointment Renewal Fee - $25 annually. Appointment invoice late payment fee - $250. (Ala. Code § 27-4-2).

   b. License term: biennial.

c. Lines of authority:

(1) Life—including annuities.
(2) Accident and health or sickness (commonly known as disability)—may include benefits for disability income.
(3) Property—covering direct or consequential loss or damage to property of every kind.
(4) Casualty—coverage against legal liability, including that for death, injury, or disability or damage to real or personal property, and surety.
(5) Variable life and variable annuity products—coverage provided under variable life insurance contracts and variable annuities.
(6) Personal lines—property and casualty insurance coverage sold to individuals and families for primarily noncommercial purposes.
(7) Credit—limited line credit insurance.
(8) Bail bond.
(9) Rental vehicle. (Ala. Code §27-7-5.1).
(10) Crop—coverage providing protection against damage to crops from unfavorable weather conditions, fire, or lightning, flood, hail, insect infestation, disease, or other yield-reducing conditions or peril provided by the private insurance market, or that is subsidized by the Federal Crop Insurance Corporation, including Multi-Peril Crop Insurance.
(11) Portable electronics. (Ala. Code §27-22A-1, 7).
(12) Travel. (Ala. Code §27-7-5.2).
(13) Any other line of insurance permitted under state laws or regulations.

Note: Alabama also has a temporary producer license for anyone who has not passed the exam but is otherwise qualified. Fee: $30 application fee; $50 license fee; $40 appointment fee. Application process is mandatory online. Temporary license is valid for six months. During that time the licensee must finish the required prelicensing course, pass the exam and be fingerprinted in order for the license to convert to a permanent producer's license. All insurers using temporary licenses shall have a prospective temporary licensee sign a disclosure form (ALDOI Form T-1) before application is made for the license. This applies to both new applicants and individuals who previously held a temporary license and are seeking a license and appointment for the unused six month period. A copy of the signed disclosure form shall be furnished to the applicant and the original signed form shall be retained by the insurer and made available to the Alabama Department of Insurance upon request or incident to an examination. (ALDOI Bulletin No. 2012-01 and Ala. Code §27-7-23 and Ala. Admin. Code r. 482-1-147-.08).

Note: Business entities may also be licensed as producers or Managing General Agents (MGAs). For MGA licensing see Section 3 *infra*. Business entities include corporations, associations, partnerships, limited liability companies, and limited liability partnerships. In addition to its entity producer license, a business entity must hold an appointment from each insurer for which the entity acts. Entities must apply online using the NAIC Uniform Business Entity Application. Corporations and partnerships must pay an initial filing fee of $130 for a producer license. The license is subject to a biennial renewal fee of $100 per line. (Ala. Code §27-7-5(b), Ala. Admin. Code r. 482-1-110-.04).

2. *Limited Lines Producers.*

   a. License fee: Initial license, $80; Biennial renewal: $70.
   b. Appointments: Initial appointment fee: $40 per insurer; annual continuation of appointment, $25. Sponsorship by an insurer is required. Appointment invoice late payment fee - $250. (Ala.Code § 27-4-2).

   Limited line credit producers are licensed to sell the limited lines of credit insurance (https://www.aldoi.gov/pdf/legal/111r-2014.pdf):

   (1) Limited line credit insurance.
   (2) Credit life.
   (3) Credit disability.
   (4) Credit property.
   (5) Credit unemployment.
   (6) Creditor-placed (also known as forced-placed).
   (7) Nonfiling, involuntary unemployment.
   (8) Involuntary Unemployment
   (9) Mortgage life.
   (10) Mortgage guaranty.
   (11) Mortgage disability.
   (12) Guaranteed automobile protection, guaranteed asset protection (GAP).
   (13) Family and medical leave insurance.
   (14) Any other form of insurance offered in connection with an extension of credit. (Ala. Code §27-7-1).
   (15) Travel insurance (Ala Code §27-7-5.2).
   (16) Crop insurance (Ala Code §27-7-14.1).
   (17) Portable electronics insurance (Ala Code §§ 27-22A-1).
   (18) Self Service Storage Facility (Ala Code §27-7-5.3).

   c. Insurance on rental vehicles.
      (1) Personal accident insurance covering the risks of travel.
      (2) Liability insurance, including uninsured and underinsured motorist coverage.

(3) Personal effects insurance.
(4) Roadside assistance and emergency sickness protection programs.
(5) Any other travel or auto-related coverage that a rental company offers in connection with and incidental to the rental of vehicles.
These lines are sold by car rental companies or their employees. (Ala. Code §27-7-5.1).

3. *Managing General Agents.* Initial total application fee per appointing insurer: $355. Application fee: $30 per insurer. Initial license fee: $125 per insurer. Application audit and examination fee: $200 per insurer. Retaliatory fees may also apply. Annual continuation fee: $75 per insurer, due by December 31 and must include a copy of the MGA's audited financial statement prepared by an independent CPA. An MGA must be licensed for each insurer represented and for each class of insurance handled. The MGA must maintain a bond or commercial crime policy, minimum amount of $100,000 with a deductible not to exceed $10,000. MGA must also maintain an E&O policy of $1 million or 25 percent of gross amount of direct premium, whichever is greater. Both the bond/commercial crime policy and the E&O policy must be issued by companies licensed in the State of Alabama. Documentation of these coverages and accompanying forms must be filed within thirty days of appointment. Application form is AL-MGA-1. Renewal form is AL-MGA-4. (Ala. Code §27-6A-3; Ala. Admin. Code r. 482-1-106-.04 and https://www.aldoi.gov/PDF/Licensing/FormALMGA1.pdf).

4. *Service Representatives.* Total Initial license fees: $70. Biennial License Renewal Fee - $70; annual appointment renewal fee: $40; late fee: $50. Must be a salaried employee of an insurer/MGA and authorized to work for or through producers in soliciting and negotiating insurance for such insurers/MGAs. License renews in the licensee's birth month. Initial and renewal processes are mandatory online. (Ala. Code §27-8A-9 and Ala. Code § 27-4-2).

5. *Bail Bonds.* Producers must furnish a bond in the amount of $25,000 ($10,000 in Cullman County) to the probate judge of each county in which such person engages in business. (Ala. Code §15-13-22).

Other Insurance Professionals

1. *Adjusters.* Examination fee not to exceed $100; Initial license fee and each biennial renewal on or before expiration date: Individuals $80; Business entities $200 Late renewal within the first thirty days after expiration: $120; Business entities — $300. Late fee after the first thirty days but before twelve months later: Individuals — $160 All independent adjusters must be licensed, but not staff adjusters. Public adjusters are not allowed in Alabama. Firms and corporations may

be licensed as adjusters. Initial and renewal licenses are mandatory online. In the event of a state emergency, a person who is not already licensed as an independent adjuster in this state, but who is otherwise qualified to adjust claims, may act as an emergency independent adjuster and may adjust claims for an insurer in this state. The insurer must file with the commissioner a registration of each person that will act as an emergency independent adjuster within five days of deployment. An independent adjuster's registration shall remain effective for a period not to exceed ninety days and at the time of registration, the insurer shall submit to the commissioner a fee not exceeding $50 for each emergency adjuster. In order to determine license eligibility, the commissioner may require fingerprints and a criminal history record check of all applicants. (Ala. Code §§ 27-9A-17, 27-4-2; Ala. Admin. Code r. 482-1-151-.09 482-1-151-.10).

2. *Pre-Need Sales Agent*. Any individual who offers preneed contracts to the public, or who execute preneed contracts on behalf of a certificate holder, shall be registered with the Commissioner as a preneed sales agent. Initial fee $25; annual renewal fee $25 (Ala. Code §27-17A-18).

3. *Reinsurance Intermediaries*. Reinsurance intermediaries must be licensed as producers in Alabama. Intermediary managers must file a bond in the amount of $100,000 for each reinsurer represented with the commissioner. Intermediary brokers must maintain an E&O policy. Initial fee: $170 ($30 application and $140 license); annual renewal fee: $100.

   Business entities may be licensed as reinsurance intermediaries.

   All residents should use Reinsurance Intermediary License Application —Form AL-RI-1 (2/2004). (Ala. Code §§27-5A-3, 27-4-2).

C. **Appointments:** Each insurer appointing a producer in this state shall file with the commissioner, in a format approved by the commissioner, a notice of appointment within fifteen days from the date the agency contract is executed or the first insurance application is submitted, whichever occurs first. An insurer may also elect to appoint a producer to all or some insurers within the insurer's holding company system or group by the filing of a single appointment request. Appointments renew effective January of each year. All insurance producers, service representatives, and title insurance agents who are appointed with an insurer on December 31 will be renewed for the next year, and an invoice for the appointment renewal fees is issued on or about January 12. All appointments are handled on-line through NIPR. NIPR may charge additional fees.

Initial appointment fee: producers — $40 for producers, service representatives, and business entities; $30 for title agents; temporary producers — $40 + $80 license fee;

service representatives — $40 + $70 license fee. Producers may also place insurance with companies with whom they do not have an appointment (brokers). Appointments and terminations are mandatory online. (Ala. Admin. Code r. 482-1-147-.10 and https://www.aldoi.gov/Licensing/Appointments.aspx).

D. **Licenses Required of Nonresidents:** The same licenses are required of nonresidents to sell or service insurance on Alabama property. Fees for P&C and L/A&H licenses are the same as for residents. A nonresident acting as an MGA for an Alabama-based insurer must be licensed as an Alabama MGA.

   Nonresident application process is the same mandatory online process as that of a resident. Nonresident producers must be appointed with the insurers for whom they write business in Alabama.

   Multi-State Exposures: A license is not required for a nonresident insurance producer who sells, solicits, or negotiates a contract of insurance for commercial property and casualty coverage when risks that are to be insured under that contract are located in more than one state. This exception applies only if the nonresident is licensed to sell, solicit, or negotiate that insurance in the state where the insured maintains its principal place of business and the contract of insurance insures risks located in that state. (Ala. Code §27-7-42; Ala. Code § 27-4-2 and Act 2001-702, p. 1509, §19).

E. **Prelicensing Examination and Education Requirements:**

   1. *Residents.* Producers: Twenty hour study course in each major line to be licensed or forty hour combined courses; exam, and once the exam is passed— fingerprinting. Producer Examination fee payment in the amount of $50. Producer combined life and health exam: $75. Producer combined property and casualty exam: $75.

      Service representatives have no exam requirement, but must complete the forty hour P&C course.

   2. *Adjusters.* Twenty hour study course for P&C excluding Workers Comp and Crop; forty hour study course for P&C including Workers Comp and Crop; twenty hours for Workers Comp Only; or twenty hours for Crop Only exam. (Ala. Code §27-9A-8). Examination fee payment in an amount not to exceed $100. Independent adjuster exam fee: $75. After the exam is passed, residents are required to be fingerprinted before applying for a license.

Exams are given through the University of Alabama. The various types of exams are:

a. life and/or health;
b. property and/or casualty;
c. personal lines;
d. bail bonds;
e. Adjuster worker's compensation;
f. Adjuster property & casualty excluding worker's compensation;
g. Adjuster crop;
h. Adjuster property & casualty including compensation & crop; and
i. Title.

(https://www.aldoi.gov/Licensing/ExamOutlines.aspx).

Fee must be PREPAID to the University of Alabama when registering for the exam online. Please refer to the Alabama DOI Web site for registration instruction at https://www.aldoi.gov/licensing/examsites.aspx.

After failing an exam twice, the applicant will have to wait ninety days. If the applicant then fails twice more, the applicant will have to wait 180 days to retake the exam. For limitations on repeat examinations see https://www.aldoi.gov/Licensing/RepeatExamLimits.aspx.

Applicants for limited lines licenses (credit, motor club, legal service, travel, portable electronics, dental, variable annuity, and rental car) are exempt from both the education and examination requirements. Holders of the CPCU or CIC designation are exempt from the property & casualty prelicensing, but must pass the exam; and holders of the CLU designation are exempt from the life and accident and health prelicensing, but must pass the exam. They must apply for prelicense certificate using paper process and by contacting ALDOI at 334-241-4126. (Ala. Code § 27-7-5 and https://www.aldoi.gov/Licensing/CourseExemptions.aspx).

For partnerships or corporations: each person with authority to act for the applicant must meet the education and examination requirements.

3. *Nonresidents.* Producer Examination requirement is reciprocal with applicant's home state. However, Independent Adjusters whose home state is California, Hawaii, and New York must take the appropriate prelicensing course and pass the Alabama exam. Nonresidents choosing Alabama as their Home State for an

Independent Adjuster license must take the appropriate prelicensing course and pass the Alabama exam. (https://www.aldoi.gov/Licensing/AdjusterReq.aspx).

F. Continuing Education Requirements:

Number of Hours Required: Twenty-four classroom hours biennially three hours of which shall be on the topic of insurance producer ethics or business practices for producers. Service representatives and producers who do no outside sales and who are not licensed in any other state only need twelve hours biennially, two hours of which shall be on the topic of insurance producer ethics or business practices. The courses may be classroom or self-study. Licensees may take any approved courses without regard to the type of license held. Teaching a class qualifies an instructor for the same number of hours. (Ala. Code §27-8A-1; https://www.aldoi.gov/ContinuingEd/).

Proof of Completion: Course will be electronically uploaded by provider in ten days.

Excess Hours: Carryover of excess hours is no longer permitted.

Final Exam: Must be monitored if a self-study course. Monitor cannot be a friend, relative or coworker in the same line of supervision above or below the individual.

Requirements **Not** *Applicable to:*

1. Newly licensed producers and service representatives for twelve months following the effective date of their license.

2. Licensees in lines of insurance for which no examination is required.

3. Anyone licensed only for the limited lines. Note: The following exemptions are only available to those qualified for the exemption as of December 31, 2012. (Ala. Code §27-8A-1(e)). Producers and service representatives licensed in Alabama for fifteen years and at least sixty years of age.

4. Holders of the following professional designations: CPCU, CIC, CLU, ChFC, CFP, RHU, REBC, CHC, or ARM if designation has been held since December 31, 2012 and is still in good standing.

5. Producers who hold a temporary license pending passage of the written examination for that line.

6. Officers of insurers who are not engaged in the active sale of products if held since December 31, 2012.

7. Persons who are active members of the Alabama Legislature during any portion of the biennial reporting period if held since December 31, 2012. (Ala. Code §27-8A-1).

Renewal Procedure:

1. The course provider electronically notifies the Department of Insurance of course completions within ten days and provides certificate of completion to the licensee.

2. Nonresidents are exempt from the CE requirement on a reciprocal basis, except as previously mentioned for Adjusters license in CA, HI and NY.

Long-Term Care CE Requirements: Only for those producers who write LTC products—eight hour one time course and then a four hour refresher every twenty-four months thereafter to continue to write LTC products.

Annuity CE Requirements: Only for those producers who write annuity products—Must complete a four-hour one time course in annuities or annuity suitablity. (per Ala. Ins. Dept., 2/10/2020).

G. **Cancellation of Agency Contracts/Producer Appointments:** Subject to the producer's contract rights, insurers may terminate a producer's contract at any time. Prompt notice must be given to the agent and thirty-days notice to the commissioner on Form AL-3A or AL-3B. The insurer must also file a statement of the facts relative to the termination with the commissioner. There is no fee requirement for appointment termination(s). (Ala. Code §27-7-30).

H. **Rules for Risk Retention and Purchasing Groups:** Alabama regulates risk retention groups in accordance with the Federal Liability Risk Retention Act of 1986. Policies issued by risk retention groups must contain the following notice on the front and declaration page in ten-point type:

NOTICE

"This policy is issued by your risk retention group. Your risk retention group may not be subject to all of the insurance laws and regulations of your state. State insurance insolvency guaranty funds are not available for your risk retention group." (Ala. Code §27-31A-4).

Each risk retention group shall be liable for the payment of premium taxes and taxes on premiums of direct business for risks resident or located within this state, and shall report to the commissioner the net premiums written for risks resident or located within this state.

To the extent licensed agents or brokers are utilized, they shall report to the commissioner the premiums for direct business for risks resident or located within this state which the licensees have placed with or on behalf of a risk retention group not chartered in this state. These records shall, for each policy and each kind of insurance provided thereunder, include the following:

1. The limit of liability.

2. The time period covered.

3. The effective date.

4. The name of the risk retention group which issued the policy.

5. The gross premium charged.

6. The amount of return premiums, if any.

The Alabama law does not apply to self-insurance funds established by counties.

Purchasing groups must be licensed as producers. (Ala. Code §27-31A-4).

I. Other License Rules, Requirements, or Restrictions:

Applications are available for download at https://www.aldoi.gov/Licensing/Forms.aspx.

NOTE: The previous link that we got from the Alabama website showed .org; this is incorrect and leads you into a ransomware situation; do NOT go to aldoi.org for any reason. We have advised the department of what we found.

Unlicensed nonresidents may not solicit or inspect in state. Solicitation in state includes mail or telephone or other electronic communication into the state from the outside, as well as physical presence in the state.

J. **Policy Countersignature Requirements:** Countersignature not required. (Ala. Code § 27-31A-6).

K. **Portable Electronics Insurance:** Alabama created a new class of license to take effect in 2013 for the sale of portable electronics insurance. The statutes are in Title 27, Chapter 22A of the Alabama Code. Any vendor of portable electronic devices who desires to sell insurance policies to cover those devices must hold a limited lines insurance producer license. The license of the vendor also authorizes any employee or authorized representative to offer insurance policies. To obtain a license, a vendor must pay an initial fee of up to $1,000 and a renewal fee of up to $500 for each biennial renewal. The amount of the fees is dependent on the number of locations that the vendor operates. If the vendor operates ten or fewer locations the fee shall not exceed $100 whether the initial fee or a renewal. Late fee is $50 and must be paid within 30 days of expiration. Portable electronic insurance is intended to cover electronic devices that are portable in nature, their accessories and services related to the use of the device such as cellphones, smartphones, tablet computers and similar items. (Ala. Code §27-22A-2 to7).

II. Commissions, Fees, Commingling of Funds, and Suitability in Annuity Transactions:

A. **Commissions:** No commission may be paid, under any circumstances, to an unlicensed resident or nonresident. Rebating of commissions is not allowed.

B. **Fees:** Producers who are not appointed with an insurer may charge a fee for services apart from the commission received from the sale of insurance. The Alabama Administrative Code does not permit persons to charge an additional fee for services that are customarily associated with the solicitation, negotiation or servicing of policies (Ala. Admin. Code r. 482-1-132-.06).

C. **Disclosure Requirements:** An advertisement shall not use as the name or title of an annuity contract any phrase that does not include the word "annuity" unless accompanied by other language clearly indicated it is an annuity. An annuity advertisement shall not refer to an annuity as a CD annuity, or deceptively company an annuity to a certificate of deposit. (Ala. Admin. Code r. 482-1-132-.06).

D. **Commingling of Funds:** All premiums or funds that belong to others are trust funds and received by the licensee in a fiduciary capacity. If a licensee diverts or appropriates such funds for his or her own use, the licensee is guilty of embezzlement. (Ala. Code §27-7-36).

E. **Suitability in Annuity Transactions:** In recommending to a consumer the purchase of an annuity or the exchange of an annuity that results in another insurance transaction or series of insurance transactions, the insurance producer must have reasonable grounds for believing that the recommendation is suitable for the consumer on the basis of the facts disclosed by the consumer as to his or her investments and other insurance products and as to his or her financial situation and needs. (Ala. Admin. Code r. 482-1-137-.06).

Alabama has adopted the 2006 NAIC Suitability in Annuity Transactions Model.

Annuity CE Requirements: Listed above under Section F – Continuing Ed. Requirements.

III. **Statutory References:** Ala. Code §§ 15-13-22; 27-4-2; 27-5A-3; 27-6A-3; 27-7-1, -4, -4.2, -5, -5.1 to -5.3, -14.1, -23, -28, -30, -36; 27-8A-1, -9; 27-9A-17; 27-17A-18; 27-22A-1 to -7; 27-31A-4, -6. Ala. Admin. Code r. 482-1-106-.04; 482-1-110-.04: 482-1-132-.06; 482-1-137-.06; 482-1-147-.08, -.10.

ALASKA

Department of Commerce, Community and Economic Development
Division of Insurance
333 Willoughby Ave., 9th Floor
Juneau, AK 99801-1770(for couriers);
P.O. Box 110805
Juneau, AK 99801-0805(for US mail)
Telephone: 907-465-2515; Fax: 907-465-3422
https:// www.commerce.alaska.gov/web/ins/

I. **Licensing Requirements:** Sales Personnel—Producers, Limited Line Insurance Producers, Managing General Agents. Other Insurance Professionals—Attorneys-in-Fact, Independent Adjusters, Reinsurance Intermediaries, Third-Party Administrators, Trainees, Viatical Settlement.

A. **Applicability:** A person may not act as or represent to be an insurance producer, managing general agent, reinsurance intermediary broker, reinsurance intermediary manager, surplus lines broker, or independent adjuster to a subject resident, located, or to be performed in Alaska unless he is licensed and is an appointed agent of the admitted insurer. A person may not act as or represent to be a managing general agent, reinsurance intermediary broker, or reinsurance intermediary manager representing an insurer domiciled in this state regarding a risk located outside this state unless licensed by this state. (Alaska Stat. §21.27.010).

B. **Licenses Required of Residents:** Each of the following renews biennially on the last day of an individual's birth month. If the individual licensee's birth year is an odd number, the license will renew on the last day of the individual's birth month every odd-numbered year. If the individual licensee's birth year is an even number, the license will renew on the last day of the individual's birth month every even-numbered year; on the anniversary of licensing for a firm. Business Entity (Firm) licenses include one designated compliance officer per class of authority. Alaska accepts the National Association of Insurance Commissioners (NAIC) Uniform application for residents and nonresidents. In addition, Alaska encourages electronic applications from residents or nonresidents for most license classes via the National Insurance Producer Registry (NIPR) from a person seeking to obtain, renew, amend, or reinstate a license under Alaska Stat. §21.27. Accordingly, Alaska will impose an additional $50 fee for paper filings when the filing can be submitted electronically. (https://www.commerce.alaska.gov/web/ins/Producers/PaperApplications.aspx).

Applications not completed within 120 days from the date filed will be withdrawn and a new application and application fees will be required. (Alaska Stat. §21.27.040(f)).

Fingerprint card and fee required for initial licensure. If an individual moves to Alaska from another state and holds an active nonresident Alaska license, that individual must notify the Alaska Division of Insurance by completing all of the requirements of the Change Form 08-1261, which includes submitting a fingerprint card and a $48.25 background check fee made payable to the State of Alaska. Notification of the change in residency must be filed within thirty days of the date the change in resident state occurred. (Alaska Stat. §21.27.025).

Sales Personnel

1. *Insurance Producers.*

    a. License Fee: $75 for individuals or firms, resident or nonresident, all lines.
    b. License Term: Biennial.
    c. Lines of Authority:

        (1) Life, including annuities and accidental death or dismemberment.
        (2) Health, including disability income.
        (3) Property.
        (4) Casualty, including surety and marine.
        (5) Variable life and variable annuity products.
        (6) Personal lines property and casualty for primarily noncommercial services.
        (7) Limited lines credit insurance.
        (8) Any insurance for which a limited license may be issued under Alaska Stat. §21.27.150. (Alaska Stat. §21.27.115; 3 Alaska Admin. Code 31.020).
        Licensees that include variable contracts require that the licensee must either be registered with the SEC as a broker-dealer, or personally take and pass tests of knowledge and competence of securities, to the satisfaction of the director. (Alaska Stat. §21.27.530).

2. *Limited Lines Insurance Producers.* The following classes are available.

    a. License Fee: $75.
    b. License Term: Biennial.
    c. Limited Lines of Authority:

        (1) Travel—lost baggage and personal effects, trip cancellation, trip interruption, damage to accommodations or rental vehicles or sickness, accident, disability or death occurring during travel: $75 for individuals or firms, resident or nonresident, all lines.
        (2) Title—individual: $75 for individuals or firms, any line(s).

(3) Bail Bond: $75 for individuals or firms, any line(s).

(4) Motor vehicle rental agency: $75 for individuals or firms, resident or nonresident, all lines. May only sell the following lines to renters of automobiles:

Liability.
Uninsured or underinsured motorist coverage.
Medical and disability.
Personal effects.
Towing and roadside assistance.

(5) Credit—$75 for individuals or firms, resident or nonresident, all lines.

A Limited Lines Credit Producer may sell the following:
Credit life.
Credit disability.
Credit property.
Credit unemployment.
Involuntary unemployment.
Mortgage life.
Mortgage guaranty.
Mortgage disability.
Guaranteed automobile protection (GAP).
(Alaska Stat. §§21.27.150, 990; 3 Alaska Admin. Code 31.020).

(6) Portable Electronics Limited Producer—individual or firms, resident or nonresident: $75 fee.
Insurance offered, issued for delivery, delivered, or renewed by a vendor engaged in the business of selling, leasing, or servicing portable electronic devices to cover the loss, theft, mechanical failure, malfunction, damage, repair, or replacement of a small electronic device including a cell phone, laptop computer, electronic tablet, GPS device, radio, portable music player, or associated accessory. (Alaska Stat. §§21.27.150, 21.36.515(h); 3 Alaska Admin. Code 31.020). Does not include a service contract under Alaska Stat. §21.03.021; a policy covering a seller's or manufacturer's obligations under a warranty; or a homeowner's, renter's, private passenger auto, commercial multiperil, or similar policy that covers loss or theft of portable electronics.

(7) Crop Insurance Limited Producer License: $75. (Alaska Stat. § 21.27.150).

3. *Managing General Agents.* Fees: $75 for individuals or firms, resident or nonresident, all lines. Submit form 08-226. If business is transacted with an Alaska-domiciled insurer, a copy of the contract must be filed with and approved by the insurance division at least thirty days prior to the transaction of business. The director of insurance may require an MGA to carry a bond and an E&O policy. (Alaska Stat. §§21.27.590, 21.27.620(a)(4)(K); 3 Alaska Admin. Code 31.020).

4. *Appointments.* The following appointments are required:

   a. An admitted insurer appointing a managing general agent.
   b. A managing general agent appointing an insurance producer as its subagent.
   c. A domestic reinsurer appointing a reinsurance intermediary manager.
   d. A reinsurance intermediary manager appointing an insurance producer as its subagent.
   e. An admitted insurer appointing an in-surance producer as its agent. (Alaska Stat. §21.27.100(a, b))
   Insurers, managing general agents (MGAs), and producers are required to maintain a current list of all their appointments that identifies the licensee's name, licensee's mailing address, license number, and effective date of appointment. An insurer, managing general agent, or insurance producer shall reply in writing within three working days to an inquiry made by the director regarding an appointment. (Alaska Stat. §21.27.100(c)).

Other Insurance Professionals

1. *Public Adjusters.* Alaska currently has no scheme to recognize or license public adjusters. Please consult an attorney for further advice.

2. *Resident Attorneys-in-Fact* (Reciprocal Insurers). Initial and annual renewal: $200.

3. *Nonresident Attorneys-in-Fact* (Reciprocal Insurers). Initial and annual renewal: $500. (3 Alaska Admin. Code 31.060(16, 17)).

4. *Independent Adjusters.* Fees: $75 for individuals or firms, any line(s). Adjusters must have at least six months experience in the previous two years; special education; or training in claims handling. License not required of adjusters who are employees of an insurer. (Alaska Stat. §21.27.830).

5. *Reinsurance Intermediary Brokers, Managers.* Fees: $75 for individuals or firms, any line(s). If business is transacted with an Alaska-domiciled insurer, a copy of the contract must be filed with and approved by the insurance division at least thirty days prior to the transaction of business. The director of insurance may

require reinsurance intermediaries to carry a bond and E&O policy. (Alaska Stat. §§21.27.670, 730).

6. *Third-Party Administrators.* Specific to life, health, and annuities and must be registered with the State of Alaska, unless the entity can qualify for an exemption. The director of insurance may require a TPA to carry a bond and E&O policy. Fees: For individual or firm; $300. Exemption fees are $100. (Alaska Stat. §21.27.640).

7. *Trainee Licenses.* This license may be issued to individuals who do not meet the experience requirement for a specific class of license. Trainee independent adjusters must submit specific passing exam results after four months (minimum score, 60 percent) and eight months of initial licensure (minimum score, 70 percent) to maintain the trainee license. Fee: $75 for individuals. Anyone with a trainee license must obtain an independent adjuster license within one year from the date of the issuance of the trainee license. (Alaska Stat. §21.27.840).

8. *Viatical Settlement Licenses.* Alaska licenses viatical settlement brokers, representatives, and providers. Director may require examination. Fees: individual: $100; firms: $100; viatical settlement providers: $300. (Alaska Stat. §21.96.110).

9. *Independent Portable Electronics Adjuster.* An employee of a licensed independent adjuster or an employee of an affiliate of a licensed independent adjuster with not more than twenty-five people under the supervision of one licensed independent adjuster or licensed producer who collects or furnishes claim information for portable electronic insurance is not required to be individually licensed if the person enters claim information in a preprogrammed computer system designed for the collection, data entry, calculation, and final resolution of portable electronic insurance claims. (Alaska Stat. §21.27.010).

10. *Motor Vehicle Service Contract Provider.* Firms only $300. A person that is contractually obligated to provide motor vehicle services to a service contract holder under the terms of a motor vehicle service contract. (Alaska Stat. §21.59.110).

13. *Motor Vehicle Service Contract Administrator.* Firms, $75. A person who is responsible for the administration of a motor vehicle service contract or the motor vehicle service contract plan. Must register the following with the director: name, business address, and other info as required by the director; names of providers for whom the person is acting as an administrator. (Alaska Stat. §21.59.160).

Firms must designate a compliance officer to be responsible for the firm's compliance with insurance statutes and regulations.

Surplus Lines. Individuals and entities seeking resident licensure for surplus lines broker authority must also hold an Alaska license as a producer or managing general agent with property and casualty lines of authority and, if required by the director, maintain both a bond acceptable to the director and an E&O policy. (Alaska Stat. §21.27.790).

Individuals seeking licensure for surplus lines, managing general agent, reinsurance intermediary manager or reinsurance intermediary broker authority are no longer required to meet a minimal experience requirement to obtain the license. These changes were made to comply and to be consistent with the Gramm-Leach-Bliley Act and other national standards.

Expired/lapsed licenses may be reinstated within one year from the date of expiration, without retesting. Reinstatement one to sixty days after expiration/lapse date, $100 plus renewal fee. Must meet all requirements and submit a notarized Business Transaction Form identifying whether or not any Alaska business has been transacted. If the license has been expired/lapsed more than sixty days, $200 plus renewal fee and application forms.

Alaska accepts electronic applications from residents or nonresidents for all license classes via the National Insurance Producer Registry (NIPR) from a person seeking to obtain, renew, amend, or reinstate a license under Alaska Stat. §21.27. Electronic filings are available through NIPR at www.nipr.com, then select Electronic Licensing, or through one of its authorized business partners at http://www.nipr.com/general/business-partners.htm. Electronic filings will occur within twenty-four to forty-eight hours of submission once all application requirements have been received. Adding a line or class of authority electronically is permitted, but if a licensee wishes to delete a line or class of authority, or cancel a license, it must be filed directly with the division, not electronically. (https://www.commerce.alaska.gov/web/ins/Producers/MakeChangestoaLicense.aspx).

Application forms may be downloaded from https://www.insurance.alaska.gov.

C. **Appointments:** A person may not act as or represent to be a representative of, authorized or appointed agent of, or other term implying a contractual relationship with a particular admitted insurer, or accept applications on behalf of an admitted insurer, unless the person is licensed as an insurance producer and is or becomes an appointed agent of the admitted insurer. Insurers, Managing General Agents (MGAs), and producers are required to maintain a list of all of their appointments and must be able to respond within three working days to an inquiry made by the director regarding an appointment. The Division does not maintain active records of any appointments. (Alaska Stat. §§21.27.550, 100(c)). Anyone selling variable annuities must hold a license as a life producer and submit a FINRA registration number. (https://www.commerce.alaska.gov/web/ins/Producers/LicensesWithSpecialRequirements.aspx).

D. Licenses Required of Nonresidents: Nonresidents may be licensed for any of the following:

1. *Insurance Producers.* Fee: $75 for individuals or firms, all line(s).

2. *Managing General Agents.* Fee: $75 for individuals or firms, all line(s).

3. *Independent Adjusters.* Fee: $75 for individuals or firms, all line(s).

4. *Reinsurance Intermediaries.* Individual: All individual in a firm license types were eliminated July 1, 2011. Fee: $75 for individuals or firms, all line(s).

5. *Third-Party Administrators.* Fee: $300 for individuals or firms. Only the individual designated as compliance officer for the business entity is required to be registered. A person who is an employee of a third-party administrator and who acts within the course and scope of that employment and within the scope of the written contract required under Alaska Stat. §21.27.650(a)(4).

6. *Attorney-in-Fact.* Initial and annual renewal: $500. (3 Alaska Admin. Code 31.060).

7. *Limited Lines.* Bail bond, motor vehicle rental agency, travel, portable electronics, credit, crop: For individuals or firms, any line(s): $75.

8. *Surplus Lines.* Fee: $300 for individuals or firms. May be required to have and maintain a bond in an amount acceptable to the director that requires the surplus lines broker to conduct business under this title, promptly remit taxes and fees required by law, return premiums promptly when due, and pay proper losses promptly. (Alaska Stat. § 21.27.270(b)).

9. *Independent Portable Electronics Adjuster.* Must be licensed as an independent adjuster in good standing in home state or have a designated home state.

10. *Viatical Settlement Licenses.* Alaska licenses viatical settlement brokers, representatives and providers. Individual: $100; firms: $100; viatical settlement providers: $300.

11. *Motor vehicle service contract provider:* $300 for firms.

12. *Motor vehicle service contract administrator:* $75 for firms.

Verification of nonresident travel, bail bond, and credit applicants: verification of licensure in home state will be obtained automatically via the state producer licensing database; a certificate of license status will only be required if verification cannot be obtained electronically.

NAIC Uniform Application forms may be downloaded from the department's Web site at: https://www.insurance.alaska.gov.

An electronic application may be submitted via the National Insurance Producer Registry (NIPR) Web site at http://www.nipr.com. Applicants who succeed in applying electronically should have a license issued within approximately twenty-four hours.

Multi-State Exposures: A license is not required for a nonresident insurance producer who sells, solicits, or negotiates a contract of insurance for commercial property and casualty coverage when risks that are to be insured under that contract are located in more than one state. This exception applies only if the nonresident is licensed to sell, solicit, or negotiate that insurance in the state where the insured maintains its principal place of business and the contract of insurance insures risks located in that state. (Alaska Stat. §21.27.010).

E. Prelicensing Examination or Education Requirements:

1. *Residents.* Applicants must pass a qualifying examination initially to obtain a license. The exam contains general insurance questions and questions about the specific section or sections of the Alaska Code. Additionally, one fingerprint card must be submitted with the application including a background check fee of $48.25.

   a. Insurance Producers:

      (1) Life.
      (2) Health.
      (3) Property.
      (4) Casualty.

   b. Independent/Portable Electronics adjusters.
   c. MGAs.
   d. Reinsurance intermediaries.
   e. Limited line bail bond.
   f. Limited line title.
   g. Limited line credit.
   h. Personal lines.

i. Surplus lines.
(Alaska Stat. §§21.27.115, 060, 080).

Exams are taken electronically using a computer. The test is scored immediately with results available. Exam fee: $89 due at time of reservation. Candidates testing at the Anchorage test center may pay a $15 fee to be digitally fingerprinted on site. This appointment is a separate appointment from examination, but should be made at the same site/same time as the examination. The exam appointment must be scheduled prior to scheduling the fingerprint appointment. Candidates who fail one part of the exam and pass the other need only retake the portion failed. Repeat examinees of the same examination level: $89. The exam requirement does not apply to: limited lines producers for travel, and motor vehicle rental; resident applicants who were licensed as a resident within one year of date of application; applicants for licensure as a nonresident producer, agent, broker, adjuster, certain limited lines, insurance producers, surplus lines brokers, MGAs, or reinsurance intermediaries who are properly licensed in their home state; and applicants moving to Alaska whose license is in good standing for the same lines and classes of authority and apply for licensure within 90 days of cancelling the applicant's prior home state license.

(https://home.pearsonvue.com/getattachment/3f3dfe05-153f-4f18-bb89-d8e3982189bc/Alaska%20Insurance%20Licensing%20Candidate%20Handbook.aspx). Anyone selling variable annuities must hold a license as a life producer and must pass the FINRA exam for qualification as a registered representative; or pass the SEC exam.

The following licenses require passing both general insurance material and Alaska specific material: producers for life, health, property, casualty, and personal lines.

Separate examinations are required for independent adjusters, independent portable electronics adjusters, managing general agents, reinsurance intermediary managers, reinsurance intermediary brokers, surplus lines brokers, limited lines title producer, limited lines bail bond producer, and limited lines credit producer. (https://www.commerce.alaska.gov/web/ins/Producers/LicensesWithSpecialRequirements.aspx).

Pearson VUE contact: Phone (800) 274-5993; Email pearsonvuecustomerservice@pearson.com

2. *Nonresidents.* Same fees as resident.

F. Continuing Education Requirements:

Number of Hours Required: Twenty-four hours, biennially. This requirement to all licensees, unless the licensee is exempt from CE under Alaska Stat. §21.27.020(f), or is seeking a temporary license under Alaska Stat. §25.27.244 or the renewal of a temporary license (Alaska Stat. §21.27.390) or limited lines license (Alaska Stat. §21.17.150).

The director will not approve more than eight continuing education credit hours in the general subject area of management, marketing, and sales training during the two-year license period. (3 Alaska Admin. Code 23.100(a), 105(b)).

A person renewing an insurance license who is subject to the twenty-four continuing education credit hour requirement must have taken and reported at least three hours of insurance ethics training as part of the continuing education credit hour requirement before the expiration date of the license. (3 Alaska Admin. Code 23.100(b)).

Submitting Proof of Completion: Provider will issue a certificate of completion upon successful completion of a course and report those credits to the Department within ten days of completion.

Excess Hours: Up to eight hours may be carried into the next renewal period. (3 Alaska Admin. Code 23.105).

Final Exam: Not addressed.

*Requirements **Not** Applicable to the Following:*

1. An individual holding only a limited lines license issued under Alaska Stat. § 21.27.150.
2. A license that was first issued before January 1, 1980.
3. If you are licensed as a nonresident. (https://www.commerce.alaska.gov/web/ins/Producers/ContinuingEducation.aspx).

Renewal Procedure: The Alaska Division of Insurance will approve providers and any courses that are advertised or offered for continuing education in Alaska. Once the course has been completed, the continuing education provider must submit course rosters to the director within ten days. Any licensee is able to view all course completions by accessing their education transcript available through State Based Systems. (3 Alaska Admin. Code 23.168).

Licensees shall include a notarized affidavit of compliance by the license renewal date, which may be subject to an audit, at the director's discretion. (3 Alaska Admin. Code 23.150, 155).

The licensee must maintain records of such completion and make them available to the director of insurance upon request. (3 Alaska Admin. Code 23.150).

Nonresidents are exempt from the CE requirements. (Alaska Stat. §21.27.020(f)).

If a licensee is unable to meet the CE requirements due to reasonable cause or excusable neglect, the licensee may submit a written request for an extension of time at least ninety days prior to the licensee's renewal date. (3 Alaska Admin. Code 23.100(d)).

Online course banking is required. The continuing education provider is required to submit course rosters for all attendees that have successfully completed the course. All credit hours will be banked and available for viewing through State Based Systems (SBS) at http://www.statebasedsystems.com. (3 Alaska Admin. Code 23.164).

Licensees should verify credit hours through SBS, pursuant to changes made to 3 Alaska Admin. Code 23.100 to 23.208.

G. **Cancellation of Agency Contracts/Producer Appointments:** If an appointment is terminated for cause because the appointee has engaged in an activity identified in Alaska Stat. §21.27.410, the director must be notified promptly.

Within fifteen days after providing notification, the insurer, reinsurer, or authorized representative shall mail a copy of the notification to the appointee at the last address on record with the insurer, reinsurer, or authorized representative. The notice must be provided by certified mail, return receipt requested, postage prepaid, or by overnight delivery using a nationally recognized mail carrier.

If the termination is for cause, within thirty days after the appointee receives notification, the appointee may file written comments concerning the substance of the notification. The written comments filed with the director must be included with each report distributed concerning the reason for termination of the appointment. (Alaska Stat. §21.27.110).

H. Rules for Risk Retention and Purchasing Groups: Alaska regulates risk retention groups in accordance with the Federal Liability Risk Retention Act of 1986. A risk retention group (RRG) shall apply for initial registration on forms prescribed by the director. Risk retention groups must be registered with the state as a liability insurance company, file an annual service of process filing fee continuation of $200 due December 31. RRG's must file a premium tax report and pay a premium tax of 2.7 percent on premiums written during the calendar year on or before March 1 of the following tax year. The filing of an annual report, as prescribed by 15 U.S.C.S. §3902(d)(3), is required pursuant to Alaska Stat. §21.09.200. (3 Alaska Admin. Code 24.015 to 24.290).

Failure to submit the continuation form and fee by January 31 of the year for which registration is sought will result in discontinuation of registration as of the prior December 31. A registrant who submits the continuation form and fee after January 31 will be required to reapply as a new registrant and pay the initial registration fee of $1,000 as required by 3 Alaska Admin. Code 31.060(a)(11).

A person acting as an agent or broker for insurance written or placed with an RRG for a risk located or to be performed in Alaska must be a properly licensed property/casualty producer or surplus lines broker.

All policies issued by a risk retention group must contain the following notice in ten-point type (3 Alaska Admin. Code 25.120):

NOTICE

This policy is issued by your risk retention group. Your risk retention group may not be subject to all of the insurance laws and regulations of your state. State insurance insolvency funds are not available for your risk retention group.

Purchasing Groups: Alaska regulates purchasing groups in accordance with the Federal Liability Risk Retention Act of 1986. A purchasing group shall apply for initial registration on forms prescribed by the director. Payment of a $500 registration fee shall be submitted with the application. Purchasing groups must register with the state; file an annual continuation form and pay an annual continuation fee of $200 due December 31. Failure to submit the continuation form and fee by January 31 of the year for which registration is sought will result in discontinuation of registration as of the prior December 31. A registrant who submits the continuation form and fee after January 31 will be required to reapply as a new registrant and pay the initial registration fee of $500 as required by 3 Alaska Admin. Code 31.060. (3 Alaska Admin. Code 24.320 to .590).

Annual Continuation Forms and Premium Tax Reports with attachments may be filed via the Online Premium Tax for Insurance (OPTins) application along with the tax payment at www.optins.org, which is preferred by the Alaska Division of Insurance. They can also be mailed to:

Alaska Division of Insurance

PO Box 110805

Juneau, AK 99811-0805.

Or, if by courier:

Alaska Division of Insurance

333 Willoughby Avenue, 9th Floor Juneau, AK 99801-1770

Annual filing and premium tax forms are available at https://www.commerce.alaska.gov/web/ins/insurers/annualfilingpremiumtaxforms.aspx.

I. **Other License Rules, Requirements, or Restrictions:** Note that Alaska Stat. § 21.27.010 sets out licensing exemption provisions in Alaska Stat. §21.27.010, which should be reviewed prior to submitting an application for licensure or transacting Alaska insurance business. In general, unlicensed nonresidents may not enter the state to solicit or inspect and are prohibited from writing in-state properties or exposures, even when no solicitation or service is performed in state. In-state solicitation includes mail or telephone or other electronic communication into the state from the outside, as well as physical presence in the state. Insurers may not accept business from any unlicensed person. For surplus lines transactions, a license is not required unless the home state of the insured is Alaska.

J. **Policy Countersignature Requirements:** None.

II. Commissions, Fees, Commingling of Funds, and Suitability in Annuity Transactions:

A. **Commissions:** There are no restrictions on the distribution of commissions among licensed producers, MGAs, reinsurance intermediaries, or surplus lines brokers. However, an insurer or insurance producer may not pay a commission, service fee, brokerage fee, or other valuable consideration to a person for selling, soliciting, or negotiating insurance in Alaska if that person is not required to be licensed and is not properly licensed. Further, a licensee or insurer may compensate a firm or another person if that person does not transact the business of insurance in Alaska as long as the payment does not violate Alaska

Stat. §§21.27.370, 21.36.100, or 21.36.120. A person who is no longer licensed in Alaska may be paid renewal or other deferred compensation for selling, soliciting, or negotiating insurance if the person was properly licensed at the time of the sale, solicitation, or negotiation. Rebating of commissions is not allowed. (Alaska Stat. §§21.27.100, 370).

B. **Fees:** Licensed insurance producers acting as brokers may only charge a broker's fee once a consumer has signed a written contract. See Bulletin 04-14 and 16-02 for additional compliance information. (Alaska Stat. §21.27.560; https://www.commerce.alaska.gov/web/portals/11/pub/Bulletins/B04-14.pdf).

C. **Disclosure Requirements:** None.

D. **Commingling of Funds:** A licensee acting as a fiduciary may only commingle funds for the purpose of advancing, reserving, or establishing a reserve of premiums. (Alaska Stat. §21.27.360).

E. **Suitability in Annuity Transactions:** In recommending to a consumer the purchase or exchange of an annuity contract that results in another insurance transaction or series of insurance transactions, an insurance producer or an insurer must have reasonable grounds for believing that the recommendation is suitable for the consumer, based on the facts disclosed by the consumer as to the consumer's financial situation, needs, investments, and other insurance products. (3 Alaska Admin. Code 26.775).

A person who desires to sell annuity products must obtain a life insurance line of authority and complete a one-time minimum four credit-hour annuity training course. The course must cover the types of and various classifications of annuities; identification of the parties to an annuity; how fixed, variable, and indexed annuity contract provisions affect the consumer; the application of income taxation of qualified and nonqualified annuities; the primary uses of an annuity; the appropriate sales practices, replacement, and disclosure requirements that are required. (3 Alaska Admin. Code 26.778).

A producer meets Alaska's general annuity training requirements under 3 Alaska Admin. Code 26.778(b) if the producer has satisfied substantially similar training requirements of another state.

Alaska has adopted the NAIC Suitability in Annuity Transactions Model Regulation. (3 Alaska Admin. Code 26.770 to 789).

F. **Long-Term Care:** Long-term care policies may not be sold unless the person is a licensed health or life insurance producer and has successfully completed a one-time course that must be at least eight credit hours and consist of topics related to long-term insurance and related care services. Producers holding an active health authority license who desire to sell long-term care, the required one-time training course must be completed before the producer sells, solicits, or negotiates long-term care insurance in Alaska. Training taken by the producer to comply with another state's requirements would satisfy our requirements as long as the one-time training course meets the requirements in Alaska Stat. §21.53.066(d). In addition, a producer licensed for health authority who sells, solicits, or negotiates long-term care insurance must complete an ongoing training course of at least four credit hours every twenty-four months. (Alaska Stat. §21.53.066).

G. **Insurance Employment Contracts (between a business entity (firm) and individuals representing the firm):** If an individual is affiliated with or represents a firm, an insurance employment contract is required. The contract must be in writing and must specify the lines (e.g., life, health, property, casualty, credit, etc.) and classes of authority (e.g., producer, surplus lines broker, adjuster, etc.) for the individual and firm. Both parties must retain a copy of the contract and reply in writing within three working days to an inquiry of the director regarding any business transacted by the individual and the firm. (Alaska Stat. §21.27.215).

III. References:

Alaska Stat. §21.	17.15
	27.010, 020, 025, 040, 060, 080, 100, 110, 115, 150, 215, 270, 370, 390, 530, 550, 560, 590, 620, 640, 640, 670, 730, 790, 830, 840, 990
	36.515
	53.066
	59.110, 160
	96.11

3 Alaska Admin. Code	23.100 to 208
	24.015 to 290, 320 to 590
	25.12
	26.770 to 789
	31.020, 060

ALASKA

Web References:

https://www.commerce.alaska.gov/web/ins/Producers/PaperApplications.aspx.

https://www.commerce.alaska.gov/web/ins/Producers/MakeChangestoaLicense.aspx.

https://www.insurance.alaska.gov.

https://www.commerce.alaska.gov/web/ins/Producers/LicensesWithSpecialRequirements.aspx.

https://home.pearsonvue.com/getattachment/3f3dfe05-153f-4f18-bb89-d8e3982189bc/Alaska%20Insurance%20Licensing%20Candidate%20Handbook.aspx.

https://www.commerce.alaska.gov/web/portals/11/pub/Bulletins/B04-14.pdf.

ARIZONA

Department of Insurance; 100 N. 15th Ave., Ste 102;
Phoenix, AZ 85007-2624
Telephone (Licensing): 602-364-4457 or (877) 660-0964
(In AZ but outside the Phoenix area)
Email: licensing@azinsurance.gov
https://insurance.az.gov/

I. **Licensing Requirements:** Insurance Professionals—Producers, Surplus Lines Brokers, Mexican Insurance Surplus Lines Brokers, Self-service Storage Agents, Rental Car Agents (business entities only), Portable Electronics Adjusters, Portable Electronics Agents, Limited Lines Travel Agents, Adjusters, Bail Bond Agents, Risk Management Consultants (individuals only), Life Settlement Brokers. Miscellaneous licensees—Life and Health Administrators, Reinsurance Intermediaries (broker or manager).

A. **Applicability:** Laws apply to all insurers and insurance professionals except as exempted by Arizona Revised Statutes (A.R.S.) or as preempted by federal law. Arizona Revised Statutes are available from the Legislative Council menu option on the Arizona State Legislature Web site at http://www.azleg.gov. Information provided in this publication focuses on basic license application and renewal requirements. Other requirements, restrictions and prohibitions may apply.

B. **Licenses Required:** A person shall not sell, solicit or negotiate insurance in this state for any class or classes of insurance unless the person is licensed for that line of authority. (A.R.S. §20-282).

Sales Personnel

License applications for producers and other insurance personal are available at https://insurance.az.gov/producers. License application and renewal fee is $120 unless otherwise stated. Late renewal fee is $100, unless otherwise stated. (https://insurance.az.gov/sites/default/files/documents/files/Fee_Schedule_20200131.pdf). FBI fingerprint processing fee is $22 per card. Applicants must submit fingerprints if any of the following apply: (1) Applicant is an Arizona resident who does not already hold an Arizona license for which fingerprints must be furnished; (2) Applicant is relocating to Arizona from another state; or (3) Applicant is a resident of a state that does not issue the type of license sought in Arizona. (https://insurance.az.gov/producers/producer-agentbroker/producer-agentbroker-license-application-individual).

1. *Major and Limited Lines Producers.*

   a. Arizona Revised Statutes enable the Director of Insurance to require a person to submit a set of fingerprints to be processed by the Arizona Department of Public Safety ("DPS") and the FBI, who use the fingerprints to conduct criminal records checks. (https://insurance.az.gov/producers/producer-agentbroker/producer-agentbroker-license-application-individual).
   b. License term: A license that is issued or renewed expires quadrennially, on the last day of the month of the licensee's birthday, but not less than three years and not more than four years after the last day of the month in which the license is issued or is required to be renewed. (A.R.S. §20-289).
   c. Lines of Authority:

      (1) Life.
      (2) Accident and health or sickness.
      (3) Property.
      (4) Casualty.
      (5) Variable life and variable annuity products.
      (6) Personal lines.
      (7) Limited line credit.
      (8) Limited line crop.
      (9) Any other line of insurance allowed under state law or adopted by the director. (A.R.S. §20-286).

2. *Managing General Agents.*

   a. A managing general agent (MGA) must be licensed as a producer.

      1. A person shall not act in the capacity of a managing general agent for an insurer licensed in Arizona with respect to the risks located in Arizona unless the person is licensed as an insurance producer by the director.
      2. A person shall not act in the capacity of a managing general agent for an insurer domiciled in this state with respect to risks located outside of Arizona unless the person is licensed as an insurance producer by the director. (A.R.S. §20-311.01).

   b. An insurer shall require the managing general agent to obtain and maintain a surety bond for the protection of the insurer. The amount of the surety bond shall be 10 percent of the managing general agent's total annual written premium nationwide produced by the managing general agent for the insurer in the prior calendar year, except that the surety bond shall not be in an amount less than $100,000 or more than $500,000. The insurer shall make the bond available for inspection by the director.

c. Within thirty days of entering into or terminating a contract with a managing general agent, provide to the director written notification of the appointment or termination. A notice of appointment of a managing general agent shall include a statement of the duties that the applicant shall perform on behalf of the insurer, the lines of insurance for which the applicant shall be authorized to act and any other information the director may request. (A.R.S. §20-311.02).

3. *Self-Service Storage Agents.* Self-service storage agent licenses are issued to operators who have been authorized to offer or to sell insurance in connection with and incidental to the rental of space at a self-service storage facility. Applications should specify all locations at which the self-service storage agent may conduct business under the license. A self-service storage agent is not required to have an individual licensee in each self-service storage facility or place where insurance is transacted. The self-service storage agent must notify the director within thirty days after commencing business under the license of any additional locations or locations that cease to do business under the license in Arizona. Each self-service storage agent must provide a training program that gives employees and agents of the self-service storage agent basic instruction about the kinds of insurance that are being offered. (A.R.S. §20-332).

4. *Rental Car Agents.* Rental car agents' licenses are issued to rental companies who are authorized to offer or sell insurance in connection with and incidental to rental agreements. A rental car agent is not required to have an individual licensee in each office or other rental site or place where insurance is transacted. Licensees must provide the director at least thirty days prior notice before conducting business under the license at any additional location. A rental car agent is not subject to the continuing education requirements. A rental car agent may offer or sell insurance at the rental company office or other rental site or process a preselection of coverage in a master, corporate, group or individual rental agreement for any of the following types of insurance, separately or in combination:

(1) Accident and health or sickness.
(2) Liability.
(3) Personal property.
(4) Vehicle breakdown.
(5) Physical damage. (A.R.S. §20-331).

5. *Title Agents.*

a. License term: Licenses of title insurance agents expire quadrennially at midnight on the last day of the same month four years after the license was issued or renewed. (A.R.S. §20-1580).

6. *Life Settlement Providers and Brokers.* A person may not use any form of life settlement contract in this state unless it is filled with and, if required, approved by the director in a manner that conforms with the filing procedures and any time restrictions or deeming provisions for life insurance forms, policies or contracts. (A.R.S. §20-3203). Individuals and business entities submitting an application should look to https://insurance.az.gov/producers/life-settlement-broker for more information.

   Fee for adding a life settlement broker authority to a license that expires in two years or more: $500.

   Fee for adding a life settlement broker authority to a license that expires in less than two years: $250.

   Fee for adding a life settlement provider: $1,000. (https://insurance.az.gov/sites/default/files/documents/files/Fee_Schedule_20200131.pdf).

   Arizona licensed producers with a life line of authority who meet the requirements for a life settlement license may act as a broker as long as they apply for the life settlement license within the first thirty days of operating as a broker.

   Attorneys and certified public accountants who are retained by the policy owner and are not paid by the provider or purchaser may negotiate a life settlement contract without having a life settlement broker license. Insurers that issue the policies are not responsible for any acts or omission of brokers or providers unless the insurer is compensated by the provider or broker in connection with the transaction. (A.R.S. §20-3202).

Other Insurance Professionals

1. *Adjusters.* Arizona requires that adjusters be licensed. Resident applicants as well as nonresidents who reside in states that do not issue adjuster licenses must take and pass the Arizona adjuster exam and submit fingerprints and the FBI fingerprint processing fee. (https://insurance.az.gov/producers/adjuster/adjuster-license-application-individual). Adjuster licensing and renewal fee: $120. Late renewal fee: $100. (https://insurance.az.gov/sites/default/files/documents/files/Fee_Schedule_20200131.pdf). Nonresident Portable Electronics adjusters who reside in states that do not issue licenses are not required to pass the Arizona adjuster exam. Arizona is not reciprocal with Adjuster Designated Home State Licenses. Applicants who reside in states that do not issue adjuster licenses must comply with all Resident Licensing Standards. (A.R.S. §20-321.01).

2. *Bail Bond Agents.* Applicants must pass a prelicensing examination and submit fingerprints and the FBI fingerprint processing fee. The license is withheld until the background check is complete and the applicant is qualified for licensure. Applicants must provide an affidavit that they have resided in Arizona for at least one year immediately preceding the date of application. Applicants must submit Form L-195 along with a $10,000 surety bond, which must be maintained throughout the term of the license. Each bail bond agent must maintain an office in Arizona that is accessible to the public where bail bond records are maintained. Each agent must also be licensed as a casualty producer in order to transact civil bonds. As a minimum requirement for permanent office records, each bail bond agent and general lines agent who is engaged in the bail bond business shall maintain a daily bond register. Each record shall state the following: (1) number of the power of attorney form; (2) date of bond execution; (3) Name of the principal; (4) amount of the bond; (5) premium charged; (6) premium reported to the surety company; (7) security or collateral received; (8) date the security/collateral was received and date of release; (9) indemnity agreements; (10) disposition of the bond; and (11) date of disposition. (A.R.S. §20-340.01; 20-340.02).

3. *Risk Management Consultants.* An employee of a political subdivision that is in a county with more than 1 million persons and whose governing body includes members of a county board of supervisors may be licensed as a risk management consultant. These employees will be licensed in the same manner as insurance producers. The examination requirement may be waived for a risk management consultant license. Applicants must submit an authorization letter from the political subdivision. The license automatically expires when the employee terminates employment with the political subdivision. (A.R.S. §20-331.01).

4. *Portable Electronics Insurance.* Vendors who sell portable electronic devices must obtain a limited lines license which authorizes employees and authorized representatives to sell coverage on the devices. The applicant must submit a license application form (L-LTD). Visit https://insurance.az.gov/producers/portable-electronics-vendoragent for more information. Portable Electronics Insurance is intended to cover electronic devices that are portable in nature, their accessories and services related to the use of the device such as cellphones, smartphones, tablet computers and similar items. (A.R.S. §20-1693 et seq.).

5. *Life and Health Insurance and Annuity Administrators.* Applications must be completed online at https://insurance.az.gov/producers/third-party-administrator-lifehealth. An annual report is due by March 1 for the preceding year's activity. (A.R.S. §§20-485.03).

6. *Reinsurance Intermediaries.* Both reinsurance intermediary brokers and reinsurance intermediary managers must be licensed in compliance with A.R.S. §§20-486 to 20-486.11. The Director of Insurance may require filing a bond or maintaining an E&O policy. (A.R.S. §§20-486.01).

C. **Appointments:** Insurers are not required to report producer appointments or terminations to the department. (Confirmed by Arizona Dept. of Insurance and Financial Institutions, 4/22/2021).

A title agent business entity must submit with each license and renewal application a letter of authorization from the Arizona-admitted title insurance company that the agent will represent. A title insurer shall, within thirty days of entering or terminating a contract with a managing general agent, provide the director with written notice. (A.R.S. §20-311.02).

D. **Licenses Required of Nonresidents:** Arizona laws generally apply to nonresidents the same as they apply to residents except:

1. *Exams:* A nonresident applying for a producer license in this state who was previously licensed for the same lines of authority in another state is exempt from examination if either (1) the applicant is currently licensed in the other state, or (2) the application is received within ninety days after the cancellation of the resident license that the applicant held in another state and the other state issues a certification that, at the time of cancellation, the applicant was in good standing in that state, or other reliable information available to the director indicates that the applicant is or was licensed in good standing for the line of authority requested. (A.R.S. § 20-288).

2. *Fingerprints:* A nonresident with evidence of resident-state licensure in good standing for the license authority sought in Arizona is exempt from the fingerprint requirement on a reciprocal basis with the resident state, unless the application is for an adjuster's license. (A.R.S. §20-287; confirmed, DIFI, 4/23/2021).

3. *Organizational Documents:* Organizational documents do not need to be submitted to the department by nonresident business entity applicants; however, nonresidents may need to satisfy the requirements of other Arizona state agencies, such as the Arizona Corporation Commission or Arizona Secretary of State.

4. *Multi-State Exposures:* A person who is not a resident of this state and who sells, solicits or negotiates a contract of insurance for commercial property and casualty

risks to an insured with risks that are located in more than one state insured under that contract, if that person is otherwise licensed as an insurance producer to sell, solicit or negotiate that insurance in the state where the insured maintains its principal place of business and the contract of insurance insures risks located in that state. (A.R.S. §20-283(B)(6)).

5. *Emergency Adjuster:* A license is not required for a person licensed or authorized to act as an adjuster in the person's home state in order for an insurer to send the person to investigate or adjust a particular loss under an insurance policy or a series of losses resulting from a catastrophe common to all those losses A.R.S. §20-321.01(D).

E. Prelicensing Examination or Education Requirements: Exams are administered by Prometric, 800-853-5448; http://www.prometric.com/arizona. Arizona does not prescribe prelicensing education requirements. Arizona law limits applicants to four attempts to pass an exam for a particular line of authority within a one-year period. After a fourth unsuccessful attempt, you will have to wait one year from the date of the last attempt to retake the exam. Furthermore, Arizona treats failing an examination that covers more than one line of license authority the same as failing the examination for each individual line of license authority. (A.R.S. §20-284(H)). Additionally, once you pass an exam, you must apply for the corresponding license within one year. (A.R.S. §20-284(A)). Although limited line producers are generally not required to take an examination, limited line crop insurance producers are not exempt from examination. (A.R.S. §20-288(B)).

1. *Resident Producers.* An Arizona resident applicant must pass an exam for the following producer and surplus lines broker authority prior to applying for the following license authority:

   a. Life Producer. Fee: $38.
   b. Accident and Health or Sickness Producer. Fee: $38.
   c. Life, Accident and Health or Sickness Producer. Fee: $49.
   d. Property and Casualty Producer. Fee: $49.
   e. Property Producer. Fee: $38.
   f. Casualty Producer. Fee: $38.
   g. Personal Lines Producer. Fee: $38.
   h. Surplus Lines Broker. Fee: $35.
   (Arizona Insurance Licensing Information Bulletin, page 23, found at https://www.prometric.com/sites/default/files/2020-08/AZINS%20LIB%202020%20Revised.pdf).

2. *Nonresident Producers.* Exam requirements for a nonresident producer is reciprocal with the licensee's resident state. Every attempt will be made to verify resident state licensure through the National Insurance Producer Registry. If the department is unable to verify resident state licensure, applicants must forward a letter of certification from their home state. (A.R.S. §20-288. https://insurance.az.gov/producers/producer-agentbroker/producer-agentbroker-license-application-individual).

3. *Adjusters and Bail Bond Agents.* Nonresident adjuster applicants who reside in states that do not issue adjuster licenses must pass the exam prior to applying for the license authority. Resident adjuster and bail bond applicants must pass the exam prior to applying. Arizona no longer licenses nonresidents as bail bond agents. Applicants must have been a resident of Arizona for at least one year immediately preceding the date of the license application.

   a. Adjuster. Fee: $49.
   b. Bail Bond Agent. Fee: $35.
   (Arizona Insurance Licensing Information Bulletin, page 23, found at https://www.prometric.com/sites/default/files/2020-08/AZINS%20LIB%20 2020%20Revised.pdf).

F. **Continuing Education (CE) Requirements:** Nonproducers who only hold a license as an adjuster or bail bond agent do not have an insurance continuing education requirement. A nonresident licensed in good standing in the resident state is not required to complete Arizona-approved continuing education courses to be eligible to renew the Arizona insurance license if the resident state has a continuing education requirement for its resident insurance producers and if the home state recognizes insurance continuing education credits earned in Arizona by Arizona residents. (A.R.S. §§20-2901 to 20-2904).

The Arizona Department of Insurance has recently created a new tool to help insurance professionals determine their continuing education requirements available at https://www.surveymonkey.com/r/adoi_ce.

1. *Number of Hours Required:* Limited line only producer licenses no longer require continuing education to renew. If the term of the license that you are renewing began before January 1, 2014, forty hours of insurance continuing education must be completed during the license term if a nonresident insurance producer license in another state was held at any time during the Arizona-resident license term. If the term of the license that you are renewing began on or after January 1, 2014, forty-eight hours of Arizona-approved insurance continuing education must be completed, with at least six of those hours being ethics training unless you are

exempt from the insurance continuing education requirement by having all the following apply and continue to apply:

a. You have been "continuously licensed" in Arizona as an insurance agent, broker, or producer since January 1, 1995.
b. You have not held a nonresident insurance producer license in another state at any time since January 1, 1995.
c. You have never been the subject of an order of the Director of Insurance for a violation of Arizona Insurance Laws (A.R.S. Title 20) that resulted in your license being suspended, revoked, denied or not renewed; or, that required you to cease and desist from unlawful activity; or, that required you to pay restitution or a civil penalty. (A.R.S. §20-2902(B)).

2. *Recordkeeping:* Licensees are required to maintain continuing education records (certificates of compliance) until the second renewal date after the license period during which the continuing education credits were earned. (A.R.S. §§20-2902, 20-2903).

3. *General procedures:*

a. Licensee should consult the list of approved courses from Prometric's Web site at https://www.prometric.com/en-us/clients/ce/Pages/azceprod.aspx, then select "CE Online services" and select the "Approved Courses Inquiry" link. After selecting Arizona and clicking submit you will be provided with the inquiry screen, and the list of courses matching the criteria you entered will display. Licensees should call or visit the Web site of Arizona-approved CE providers for information concerning the prices of courses, when the courses are available, and other information needed concerning courses.
b. Course provider will provide a certificate of compliance to each licensee and will report course completions to Prometric.
c. Prometric will post course completions to each licensee's transcript. If a course you completed does not appear on your transcript contact the course provider to remind them to send the information to Prometric.
d. Licensees should view their CE transcripts before applying to renew the Arizona license.
e. If renewing with a paper application, the licensee must submit a printout of the CE transcript or signed certificates of compliance with the renewal application.

G. **Cancellation of Agency Contracts/Producer Appointments:** Arizona has no law governing insurer cancellations of agency contracts. (Confirmed, DIFI, 4/22/2021).

H. Rules for Risk Retention and Purchasing Groups: A.R.S. §§20-2401 to -2414 regulate risk retention and risk purchasing groups operating or offering coverage on risks in Arizona. Risk retention groups not domiciled in Arizona must submit reports to the Arizona Director of Insurance in accordance with A.R.S. §20-2403(B). These groups and all resident and nonresident producers participating in them must comply with all Arizona insurance laws, including licensing and solicitation requirements or restrictions.

RPG's are to designate only insurers that are admitted in Arizona to provide coverage to Arizona members per 15 U.S.C.S. §3901 *et seq.* All policies issued by risk retention groups must contain the following notice in ten-point type on the face of the policy: (A.R.S. § 20-2403).

NOTICE

"This policy is issued by your risk retention group. Your risk retention group may not be subject to all of the insurance laws and regulations of your state. State insurance insolvency guaranty funds are not available for your risk retention group."

I. Other License Rules, Requirements, or Restrictions

In April 2017 the Arizona Department of Insurance changed all license numbers to match the National Producer Number (NPN). Arizona has created a crosswalk between old and new numbers available at https://insurance.az.gov/insurance-professional-license-number-crosswalk.

J. Policy Countersignature Requirements: None. The name of the licensed producer must be on the policy declaration page or endorsement. (A.R.S. §20-229).

K. Portable Electronics Insurance: The director may issue, and a vendor who intends to sell or offer insurance coverage under a portable electronics insurance policy is required to obtain, a limited lines license that authorizes the vendor to offer or sell insurance coverage under a portable electronics insurance policy. A limited lines license issued under this section authorizes an employee or authorized representative of the vendor to sell or offer coverage under a portable electronics insurance policy to a customer at each location at which the vendor engages in portable electronics transactions. An applicant for a portable electronics insurance license shall file with the director a written application that is in a form prescribed by the director and that is signed by the designated representative of the vendor who is the person responsible for the vendor's compliance with the requirements of this article. (A.R.S. § 20-1693.01).

II. Commissions, Fees, Commingling of Funds, and Suitability in Annuity Transactions

A. Commissions: There is no restriction on distribution of commissions between countersigning agent and any Arizona-licensed producer, except that Arizona is retaliatory as to producers of Arizona-domiciled insurers. No unlicensed resident or nonresident may be paid commissions except vested renewal commissions of formerly licensed life producers. An active license is required at the time of the transaction. Rebating of commissions is not allowed. (A.R.S. §20-298).

B. Fees: Producers cannot charge or receive any fee or service charge in addition to the premium in connection with the transaction of insurance, unless both of the following apply:

1. The fee or service charge and the specific services for which it is charged are disclosed and agreed to in writing by the insured.

2. The amount of the fee or service charge is reasonably related to the cost of the service rendered and does not duplicate or increase any fee or service charge included in the insurer's rate filing pursuant to this title.

This does not restrict insurance producers from charging and collecting fees included in the insurer's rate filing. Notwithstanding the above, an insurance producer cannot charge or receive any fee or service charge in connection with the transaction of life, annuity, long-term care or Medicare supplement insurance.

This does not apply to insurance producers transacting commercial insurance. "Commercial insurance" means insurance that insures against the risks arising from business and commercial activity other than insurance maintained by a transportation network company driver under a private passenger automobile insurance policy.

This does not apply to surplus lines brokers transacting surplus lines insurance. (A.R.S. §20-465).

C. Disclosure Requirements: Producers cannot charge or receive any fee or service charge in addition to the premium in connection with the transaction of insurance, unless both of the following apply:

1. The fee or service charge and the specific services for which it is charged are disclosed and agreed to in writing by the insured.

2. The amount of the fee or service charge is reasonably related to the cost of the service rendered and does not duplicate or increase any fee or service charge included in the insurer's rate filing pursuant to this title. (A.R.S. §20-465).

D. **Commingling of Funds:** Arizona has no restriction on agency commingling of agency and insurer funds in general.

However, a title insurance agent egnaged in handling escrows of real property transactions must maintain a separate record of all receipts and disbursements of escrow funds and must not commingle such funds with its own funds or with funds held in any other capacity. (A.R.S. §20-1581).

E. **Suitability in Annuity Transactions:** In recommending to a consumer the purchase of an annuity or the exchange of an annuity that results in another insurance transaction or series of insurance transactions, the insurance producer must have reasonable grounds for believing that the recommendation is suitable for the consumer of the basis of the facts disclosed by the consumer as to his investments and other insurance products and as to his financial situation and needs. An insurance producer may not solicit the sale of an annuity product unless the insurance producer has adequate knowledge of the product to recommend the annuity and the insurance producer is in compliance with the insurer's standards for product training. An insurance producer may rely on insurer-provided product specific training standards and materials to comply with this. Before selling, soliciting or negotiating an annuity, an insurance producer with a life insurance line of authority must complete a one-time four credit-hour training course approved under A.R.S. § 20-2904 and by an education provider who is also approved under A.R.S. § 20-2904. An insurer must verify that an insurance producer has completed the annuity training course before allowing the producer to sell an annuity product for that insurer. (A.R.S. §20-1243.03).

Similar to the NAIC Suitability in Annuity Transactions Model Regulation, Arizona has adopted A.R.S. §§20-1243 to 1243.07.

III. References:

A.R.S. §§	229, 282 to 284, 286 to 289, 298
	311.01, 311.02, 331, 331.01, 332, 340.01, 340.02
	465, 485 to 485.12, 486.01
	1243 to 1243.07, 1580, 1581, 1693 to 1693.06
	2401 to 2414, 2901 to 2904
	3203
15 U.S.C.S. §3901	

Web References:

https://insurance.az.gov/sites/default/files/documents/files/Fee_Schedule_20200131.pdf.

https://insurance.az.gov/producers/producer-agentbroker/producer-agentbroker-license-application-individual.

https://insurance.az.gov/producers/adjuster/adjuster-license-application-individual.

https://insurance.az.gov/producers/third-party-administrator-lifehealth.

https://www.prometric.com/sites/default/files/2020-08/AZINS%20LIB%202020%20Revised.pdf.

https://www.prometric.com/en-us/clients/ce/Pages/azceprod.aspx.

ARKANSAS

Insurance Commissioner
1200 W. 3rd St., 3rd & Cross
Little Rock, AR 72201-1904
Telephone: (501) 371-2600; Licensing: 501-371-2750; Fax: 501-683-2604
Legal: 501-371-2820; Fax: 501-371-2639
http://www.insurance.arkansas.gov

I. Licensing/Registration Requirements: Sales Personnel—Producers, Limited Lines Producer, Managing General Agents. Other Insurance Professionals—Adjusters, Third-Party Administrators, Consultants, Reinsurance Intermediaries; Surplus Lines Producers.

A. Applicability: A person shall not sell, solicit, or negotiate insurance in Arkansas for any class or classes of insurance unless the person is licensed for that line of authority. (A. C. A. § 23-64-503). A license is not required of an employee not individually engaged in the sale, a person who is not a resident of Arkansas who sells, solicits, or negotiates insurance in multiple states provided the person is licensed in their principal place of business, any salaried full-time employee who counsels or advises his or her employer relative to the insurance interests of the employer; or of the subsidiaries or business affiliates of the employer provided that the employee does not sell or solicit insurance or receive a commission; or employees of an insurer or of an insurance producer who respond to requests from existing policyholders on existing policies provided that those employees are not directly compensated based on the volume of premiums that may result from these services and provided those employees do not sell, solicit, or negotiate insurance. (A.C.A. §23-64-504).

B. Licenses Required of Residents: Each of the following must be licensed to conduct insurance activities in Arkansas; all licenses are continuous until terminated; renewal fees are payable biennially on the producer's date of birth. In addition to fees listed below, there is a small fee for using the NIPR system for both residents and nonresidents.

Sales Personnel

1. *Producers.* Individuals and business entities. Arkansas handles all producer licensing through PSI Services.

    a. License fee: Variable depending on the number of lines of authority. Single line: $70 ($50 exam –and $24 background Applications may be done online at www.NIPR.com There is also a $5 NIPR fee.

b. License term: Biennial, subject to renewal: $70. If late, $140 late fee for a total of $210. CE fees also apply at renewal. See Continuing education section. (http://insurance.arkansas.gov/License/Fees.pdf).

c. Lines of Authority:

 (1) Life.
 (2) Accident and Health or Sickness.
 (3) Property.
 (4) Casualty.
 (5) Variable life and variable annuity products.
 (6) Personal Lines Property and Casualty primarily for noncommercial services.
 (7) Credit limited line credit insurance.
 (8) Any other line of insurance which is permitted under state laws or regulations. (A.C.A. §23-64-507).

2. *Limited Lines Producers.*

 a. License fee: $70.
 b. License term: Biennially, subject to renewal. Late fee $140. CE fees also apply.
 c. Limited lines of authority:

  (1) Credit (see A.C.A. §23-64-502(7) for full list).
  (2) Crop hail.
  (3) Prepaid legal.
  (4) Bail bonds. Bail bond licenses are not handled by the Arkansas DOI. Please refer to the Bail Bond Board, 501-682-9050.
  (5) Any other line of insurance that the commissioner deems necessary.

 d. Car rental limited line license. Car rental companies must obtain a car rental limited line license. Each rental company shall conduct a training program in which employees being trained shall receive basic instruction about the kinds of coverage offered for purchase by prospective renters of rental vehicles. Insurance may not be issued by a limited licensee unless the rental period of the rental agreement does not exceed ninety consecutive days, and at every location where the rental agreements are executed, brochures and other literary materials are made available to the prospective renter regarding the material terms of the coverage being offered. (A.C.A. §23-64-202(a-d)). **Note**: As of October 1, 2019 Ark. Code Ann. 23-64-202 has been repealed by Acts 2019, No. 689 Section 4.
 Please refer to the link below for car rental limited line license details. https://insurance.arkansas.gov/uploads/finalrules/rnr14.pdf.

(1) License fee: $35.
(2) License term: annual.
(3) Lines of authority for a Car Rental Limited licensee:
  (a) Personal accident insurance covering the risks of travel.
  (b) Liability insurance, including uninsured and underinsured motorist coverage.
  (c) Personal effects insurance.
  (d) Roadside assistance and emergency sickness protection programs.
  (e) Any other travel or auto-related coverage that a rental company offers in connection with and incidental to the rental of vehicles. (A.C.A. §23-64-202(d)). **Note:** As of October 1, 2019 Ark. Code Ann. 23-64-202 has been repealed by Acts 2019, No. 689 Section 4. Please refer to the link below for car rental limited line license details. https://insurance.arkansas.gov/uploads/finalrules/rnr14.pdf.

(4) Other Requirements: Employees in the car rental location can solicit insurance without a license as long as the car rental company is licensed. If the location is a franchise of a car rental company, the franchise must be licensed.

3. *Title*. Only a title insurance agent licensed under A.C.A. § 23-64-101 shall issue title insurance policies, reports, or otherwise transact title insurance business. Such an agent shall not issue closing protection or issue a title insurance policy as an insurer. (A.C.A. § 23-103-403).

   a. *Fees.* Renewal will be on or before the individual agent's birthday each year after the first year of issue. Administrative and regulatory fee required from first-time applicants, for each and every original title license: $35. Background check fee required of new applicants: $22. Renewal fee, paid for each and every title agent license renewal: $35. Late renewal penalty: $105. CE filing fee: $10. Certigication of license fee: $10. (054.00 CARR 088)

4. *Managing General Agents.* Must be licensed and must also secure producer or business entity license. The commissioner requires the MGA to post bond in an amount acceptable to the commissioner for the protection of the insurer. MGAs may be individuals, firms, associations, limited liability companies, or corporations. Initial application, $1,500; annual renewal, $500. Late fee $1000. (A.C.A. §23-64-403).

Other Insurance Professionals

1. *Adjusters.* Adjuster's initial license fee: $120. Renewal fee: $120 due biennially on the last day of the licensee's birth month. Late fee $240. CE fees also apply. Initial license fee is included in fee for the exam (see A.C.A. § 23-61-401). Adjusters may be individuals, firms, LLCs, or corporations, but only individuals may hold the limited adjuster license. Arkansas licenses independent adjusters and does not license public adjusters. (A.C.A. §23-64-209).

2. *Administrators.* Third-Party Administrators (L&H only) must have a certificate of registration, pay a $25. A third-party administrator may only act in such capacity if the administrator has a written agreement with a self-insured plan or trust. Said agreement shall be maintained by the third-party administrator, subject to review by the commissioner. Workers' Compensation Commission phone number is 501-682-3930. (A.C.A. §§ 23-92-202 to 204).

3. *Insurance Consultants.* Insurance consultants must be licensed; initial fee: $120; biennial renewal: $120. Late fee: $240. Consultants may be licensed for life and health; property, casualty, and marine; and/or both. Insurance consultants may be individuals, firms, LLCs, or corporations. (A.C.A. §§23-64-207; and 23-61-401).

4. *Reinsurance Intermediaries.* Managers and brokers must be licensed. Intermediary managers must file a bond. Intermediary-Managers: initial fee: $500; renewal: $100 annually. Intermediary-Brokers: initial fee: $300; renewal: $75 annually. Insurance commissioner may require a bond or an E&O policy. $75 fee for designation of Commissioner as agent for service of process for both managers and brokers. (A.C.A. §§ 23-62-404; 054 00 CARR 057).

All resident applicants must complete an ASP-122 form and pay a $24 fee for a background check. Full instructions for the applications and a New Candidate Handbook are available on the license division Web site.

The commissioner may suspend, revoke, refuse to continue, or place on probation any license issued by the commissioner if, after notice to the licensee and a hearing, the commissioner finds any of the following:

(1) For a producer or broker, any of the causes under 23-64-512.

(2) For adjusters or consultants,

  a. Providing incorrect or materially untrue information on the license application;

b. Violating any insurance law, regulation, subpoena, or order of a state or out-of-state insurance commissioner;
c. Attempting or succeeding in getting a license through fraud;
d. Improperly withholding money or property received in the course of business;
e. Intentionally misrepresenting the terms of an insurance contract or insurance application;
f. Being convicted of a felony
g. Committing any unfair insurance trade practice or fraud;
h. Using dishonest practices or demonstrating untrustworthiness in business practice in this state or elsewhere;
i. Having a producer, consultant, or adjuster license revoked or suspended in any other state.
j. Forging a name on any document related to an insurance transaction;
k. Cheating on a licensing exam;
l. Knowingly accepting insurance business from an unlicensed individual;
m. Failing to comply with court-ordered child support; or
n. Failing to pay state income taxes.
o. Refusing to be examined or to produce any accounts, records, or files for examination; or
p. Failing to cooperate with the commissioner in an investigation when required by the commissioner.

C. **Appointments:** Producers acting as agents must be appointed in Arkansas as an agent of an insurer. Annual appointment fee: $20 for residents and $60 for nonresidents annually. The carrier must file a notice of appointment with the insurance department within fifteen days after the appointment contract is executed or after receipt of the first application for coverage. An insurer may also elect to appoint a producer to all or some insurers within the insurer's holding company system or group by the filing of a single appointment request. There is no restriction of the payment of commissions during this period. (A.C.A. §23-64-514).

D. **Licenses Required of Nonresidents:** Each of the following nonresidents must be licensed to sell or service insurance on Arkansas property or exposures:

1. *Nonresident Producers.* Producers may be licensed as agents or brokers if the producer is currently a producer in good standing in their home state, the producer has submitted the proper fees and licensure request, the producer has submitted their application to the commissioner, and the producer's home state awards nonresident producer licenses to producers from this state. The commissioner may verify the producer's licensing status through the producer database maintained by the National Association of Insurance Commissioners, its affiliates, or its subsidiaries. (A.C.A. §23-64-508(b)(1)).

License fee: $70. Must have an Arkansas appointment for each company represented. Appointment fee: $60. Nonresidents may be licensed without an appointment and the company can accept business, but must appoint the producer within fifteen days from the date of contact or receipt of the first piece of business. (A.C.A. §23-64-514(b)). The commissioner may summarily suspend the nonresident producer's nonresident producer license if at any time the nonresident producer has his or her home state producer license suspended, revoked, or terminated. Such suspension shall be lifted upon receipt of sufficient evidence that the nonresident producer's home state license is active and in good standing. (A.C.A. §23-64-508(b)).

2. *Nonresident Adjusters.* Nonresident adjuster's license, biennial fee: $120, due on the last day of the licensee's birth month. A nonresident sent into Arkansas to adjust claims for an insurer resulting from a catastrophe is not required to hold an Arkansas license if, within 10 days, the adjuster notifies the Commissioner in writing of the adjuster's activities. Within ninety days of such notification, the adjuster must stop activities or obtain an Arkansas license. Adjusters may apply for an additional ninety day extension but this is at the discretion of the commissioner. Nonresident adjusters must hold an independent adjuster license in their resident state. If the adjuster's state of residence does not license adjusters the individual may become licensed as an adjuster in Arkansas by meeting the same requirements as a resident of Arkansas. Arkansas will not license public adjusters. A nonresident independent adjuster whose home state does not license adjusters can designate a home state where the adjuster took the adjuster exam and is currently licensed. (A.C.A. §23-64-209).

3. *Nonresident Firms and Corporations.* Thirty-five dollars (includes one qualifying individual). Each additional individual, $30. Corporations and limited liability companies must register as a foreign corporation doing business in Arkansas prior to submitting application for business entity (agency) license. The business entity is not required to register with the Arkansas Secretary of State prior to licensure but is still required by law to register with Arkansas Secretary of State as a foreign corporation. (A.C.A. § 23-64-210).

4. *Border Agents (Producers).* Agents (Producers) in communities or trade areas within five miles of the Arkansas border in states with reciprocal agreements with Arkansas (currently Oklahoma) may be licensed as Arkansas resident agents (producers).

Arkansas will accept the uniform application for nonresidents using the National Insurance Producer Registry found at www.NIPR.com.

Arkansas will accept electronic applications for nonresident individuals who are licensed in their state of residence.

Multi-State Exposures: A license is not required for a nonresident insurance producer who sells, solicits, or negotiates a contract of insurance for commercial property and casualty coverage when risks that are to be insured under that contract are located in more than one state. This exception applies only if the nonresident is licensed to sell, solicit, or negotiate that insurance in the state where the insured maintains its principal place of business and the contract of insurance insures risks located in that state. (A.C.A. §23-64-504(b)(6)).

Note: Public adjusters are prohibited from adjusting claims in Arkansas. (insurance.arkansas.gov/pages/industry-regulation/licensing/).

E. Prelicensing Examination or Education Requirements:

1. *Residents.* An Arkansas resident must pass a qualifying examination to obtain a producer's or adjuster's license. The examinations are administered by PSI, 800-733-9267.

   The following PSI testing fees apply for exams (not including $22 background check fee):

Producer – Agent Application (1 Exam)	$66
(2 Exams)	$117
Producer – Broker Application (1 Exam)	$114
Producer – Broker Application (2 Exams)	$126
Producer – Life and Health Exam	$117
Consultant Application (1 Exam)	$124
Consultant Application (2 Exams)	$136
Adjuster Application (1 Exam)	$98.50
Adjuster Application (2 Exams)	$142.00
Adjuster Application (3 Exams)	$185.50
Surplus Lines Broker/Producer	$1,101 ($1035 fee + $66 exam)

Application fees for residents:

Producer - $15 State fee + $5 NIPR surcharge ($20 total)

Adjuster - $55 state fee + $5 NIPR surcharge ($60 total) [per the Arkansas Insurance Dept., 4/15/2020]

No exam is required for the following licenses: Credit; Accident Insurance Ticket Policies or Baggage Insurance; Temporary Licenses; Funeral Expense Insurance; or Farmer's Mutual Aid. (A.C.A. § 23-64-202(c)).

Auto rental companies must conduct training for their employees in the lines of insurance authorized.

For exam information contact PSI at 800-733-9267. Exams in the following areas are available: Life; Health, Multi-Line (Property & Casualty); Personal Lines-Property Casualty (no commercial lines); General Adjuster; Property Adjuster; Casualty Adjuster; Workers Comp. Adjuster; Title; Surplus Lines; and Crop Hail.

2. *Nonresidents.* Examination requirement is reciprocal with nonresident's home state. There is no classroom instruction requirement for nonresidents. (A.C.A. §§ 23-64-202 (c)(4), 23-64-302(6, 8).

3. *Retake Requirements.*

   a. Candidates must retake the examination within ninety days of the date of issuance of the original examination permit.
   b. Candidates may take the examination(s) a maximum of three times within the ninety day permit period.
   c. Candidates who fail the examination on the third attempt must wait four weeks before retaking the examination, regardless of the status of their examination permit. This waiting period applies after every third unsuccessful attempt.
   d. Candidates who do not pass the examination within thirty days, or who do not pass the examination after three attempts, must send a new application and application fees to Pearson VUE. (A.C.A. § 23-64-205).

F. Continuing Education Requirements:

Number of Hours Required: Producers, agents (including title agents) and brokers, and adjusters are required to complete twenty-four hours of continuing education biennially. This includes three hours of ethics every two years. Instructors receive the same number of credit hours as do students. Resident adjusters and nonresident adjusters, whose home states or designation home states do not require continuing education, must complete a total of twenty-four hours continuing education of which three must be in ethics. The continuing education is due every two years. The adjusters can only take courses approved for adjusters and cannot take courses approved for title agents or producers. (A.C.A. § 23-64-301; 054 00 CARR 050-4-A).

Submit Proof of Completion by: The provider of continuing education will report continuing education completion within ten business days of the completion of the course. Providers can file information on completed continuing education hours electronically. The cost for the filing is $1 for the course and $1 for each individual who is listed on the roster. The continuing education provider can pass along this cost of electronic filing to the licensee. (054 00 CARR 050-4-F).

Excess Hours: Excess hours may be carried into the next reporting period, not to exceed the number required for renewal (except for ethics hours).

Final Exam: Must be monitored. Correspondence course exam proctors must be disinterested third parties having no family relationship, or financial relationship to the exam taker. (054 00 CARR 050-8)

The continuing education is due biennially on the licensee's birth date. Adjusters can only take courses approved for adjusters and cannot take courses approved for title agents or producers. (054 00 CARR 050-4). Title agents must complete six hours of continuing education annually, one of which must be in ethics. (054 00 CARR 087-6).

C.E. Requirements **Not** *Applicable to the following:*

1. Any person holding a license for any kind of insurance for which an examination is not required in Arkansas.

2. Limited or restricted licensees.

3. Licensees who are at least sixty years of age.*

4. Those licensed for at least fifteen consecutive years.*

5. Firms, limited liability companies or corporations. This exception does not apply to individuals unless otherwise exempted.

6. Nonresident Producers.

7. Licensed Insurance Consultants.

8. Nonresident Agents or Brokers in their first full year as a resident.

9. Any licensee subject to continuing education requirements who is called to active duty in any branch of the United States military services during the entire period of active duty service.

   * These sections are not applicable to individual producers who allowed their license to lapse and have become relicensed. (054 00 CARR 050-3).

Renewal Procedure:

1. Course provider will submit an appendix H to the Department within ten business days of completion.

2. Licensee will be billed a $10 CE filing fee in addition to annual renewal fee on license renewal statement.

3. On or before their birthdate each biennial renewal period, Arkansas resident producers must pay $20 CE filing fee simultaneously with the other fees required. CE late fees range from $25-$150 depending on how late. The commissioner may grant an extension for good cause. (054 00 CARR 50-8).

Nonresidents are exempt from this requirement on a reciprocal basis, if the nonresident's home state also has a CE requirement. (054 00 CARR 050-3)

G. **Cancellation of Agency Contracts:** Submit a $10 fee for each terminated appointment through insurance.arkansas.gov. If an insurer terminates the appointment of a producer with cause, it must notify the insurance department within thirty days following the effective date of the termination; and it must notify the producer within fifteen days after notifying the department. The Arkansas statute allows termination "with cause" for the following actions of a producer:

   1. Providing incorrect, misleading, incomplete, or materially untrue information in the license application.

   2. Violating any insurance laws, or violating any regulation, subpoena, or order of the commissioner or of another state's commissioner.

   3. Obtaining or attempting to obtain a license through misrepresentation or fraud.

   4. Improperly withholding, misappropriating or converting any monies or properties received in the course of doing insurance business.

   5. Intentionally misrepresenting the terms of an actual or proposed insurance contract or application for insurance.

   6. Having been convicted of a felony.

   7. Having admitted or been found to have committed any insurance unfair trade practice or fraud.

8. Using fraudulent, coercive, or dishonest practices, or demonstrating incompetence, untrustworthiness or financial irresponsibility in the conduct of business in this state or elsewhere.

9. Having an insurance producer license, or its equivalent, denied, suspended, or revoked in any other state, province, district, or territory.

10. Forging another's name to an application for insurance or to any document related to an insurance transaction.

11. Improperly using notes or any other reference material to complete an examination for an insurance license.

12. Knowingly accepting insurance business from an individual who is not licensed.

13. Failing to provide a written response after receipt of a written inquiry from the commissioner or his representative as to transactions under the license within thirty days after receipt thereof, unless the timely written response is knowingly waived in writing by the commissioner.

14. Failing to comply with an administrative or court order imposing a child support obligation; or

15. Failing to pay state income tax or comply with any administrative or court order directing payment of state income tax.

16. Refusing to be examined or to produce any accounts, records, or files for examination.

17. Failing to cooperate with the commissioner in an investigation when required by the commissioner.

Termination without cause requires a thirty day notice to the commissioner. In either case, the producer must then be notified within fifteen days after the commissioner has been notified. The producer may file written comments concerning the substance of the notification with the commissioner within thirty days after the producer has received the original or additional notification. (A.C.A. §§ 23-64-515,-512).

H. Rules for Risk Retention and Purchasing Groups: The producer licensing laws are applicable to anyone acting or offering to act as an agent (producer) for a risk retention group or a broker for a purchasing group covering risks in Arkansas. (A.C.A §23-94-213). A foreign risk retention or purchasing group operating in Arkansas must be licensed as a liability insurer in its domiciliary state, have a certificate of registration from the Arkansas Insurance Department, and comply with Arkansas laws, rules, and regulations as provided in A.C.A §23-94-201, *et seq.* Annual reports are due on or before March 1, including payment of a 4 percent tax on the previous calendar year's Arkansas premiums. Fees: RRGs—initial registration fee: $250, renewal: $100, filing annual statement: $50; RPGs—initial registration fee: $150, renewal: $100. (054 00 CARR 057-10, -11; and A.C.A §§ 23-94-205, -210).

Agents and brokers must report to the commissioner the premiums for direct business written for risks resident or located within Arkansas that the licensees have placed with or on behalf of a risk retention group that is not chartered in Arkansas.

All applications and policies issued by a risk retention groups must contain the following notice in ten point type on its front page and on the declaration page:

NOTICE

> "This policy is issued by your risk retention group. Your risk retention group may not be subject to all of the insurance laws and regulations of your state. State insurance insolvency guaranty funds are not available for your risk retention group." (A.C.A. §23-94-205).

Arkansas has adopted the NAIC model law. For agent/broker record keeping requirements, refer to the discussion of Risk Retention Groups in the introduction.

Beginning July 1, 2018, an existing risk retention group shall comply with the governance standards in subsections (e)–(j) of this section. A risk retention group applying for initial licensure in this state shall comply with the governance standards in this section at the time of licensure. Subsections (e) – (j) require that the board of directors of risk retention groups have a majority of independent directors, require that the terms of material service providers do not exceed five years, require that the board adopt a written policy in the plan of operations, require an audit committee of at least 3 independent members, and require that the board disclose its governance standards, including a code of ethics, electronically. (A.C.A. §23-94-204(d)).

I. **Other License Rules, Requirements, or Restrictions:** For nonresident producers, evidence of current license in home state and affidavit that Arkansas business will be placed only with insurers admitted in Arkansas are required.

J. **Countersignature Requirements:** None.

K. **Portable Electronic Device Insurance:** Vendors of portable electronic devices are required to hold a limited lines license in order to offer or sell coverage of the devices. If the vendor has ten or fewer locations, including Web sites and/or call centers, then the license fee is $100 for a two-year license, and the vendor must complete form AID-LI-PEI-Limited. For vendors with more than ten locations the license fee is $1,000 for a two-year license, and the vendor must complete form AID-LI-PEI. Forms and instructions may be accessed at the Arkansas Department of Insurance Web site at http://www.insurance.arkansas.gov/License/forms.htm. Portable electronic insurance is intended to cover electronic devices that are portable in nature, their accessories and services related to the use of the device such as cellphones, smartphones, tablet computers and similar items. (A.C.A. §§23-88-504, -507).

II. Commissions, Fees, Commingling of Funds, and Suitability in Annuity Transactions

A. **Commissions:** A producer cannot share commissions with someone who should be licensed as an agent but is not; a producer can share commissions with someone who is not licensed, and does not have to be, unless doing so would violate some other law. Rebating of commissions is not allowed. (A.C.A. §§23-64-513; 23-66-308).

B. **Fees:** Property and casualty agents (producers) may charge interest on premiums after thirty days at rates permitted by state constitution; may collect membership dues for plans where organization membership is required for coverage, and may charge fees for services not customarily associated with soliciting, negotiating, or servicing an insurance policy, within certain parameters. A fee in excess of the premiums is permitted if the fee is separately disclosed on the insured's invoice or billing statement and the aggregate sum of the fees and all producers' commissions or other compensation due and owing for that policy or contract does not exceed 20 percent of the total gross premium charged by the insurer for that policy or contract. (A.C.A. §23-66-310).

C. **Disclosure Requirements:** Charging fees other than commissions by an insurance producer requires a written agreement that is signed by the party to be charged in advance of the performance of the services under the agreement.

1. A copy of the agreement must be provided to the party to be charged at the time the agreement is signed.

2. The agreement must specifically state the services for which the fee is to be charged and the amount of the fee to be charged or how it will be determined or calculated.

3. The agreement must state that the client is under no obligation to purchase any insurance product through the insurance producer.

4. A copy of the agreement must be kept for three years after completion of services.

5. A copy must be available to the insurance commissioner upon request.

(A.C.A.§23-66-206).

D. Commingling of Funds: All premiums collected must be kept as trust funds by the agent or broker (producer), but there is no prohibition as to commingling funds.

E. Suitability in Annuity Transactions: In recommending to a consumer the purchase of an annuity or the exchange of an annuity that results in another insurance transaction or series of insurance transactions, the insurance producer, or the insurer where no producer is involved, shall have reasonable grounds for believing that the recommendation is suitable for the consumer on the basis of the facts disclosed by the consumer as to his or her investments and other insurance products and as to his or her financial situation and needs. (054 00 CARR 082-6).

Insurers are responsible for ensuring that producers marketing their products have received a minimum of 4 hours of training annually where the training covers Arkansas suitability requirements and the mechanics of annuity products. (054 00 CARR 082-9)

III. Statutory References: A.C.A. §§ 23-61-401; 23-62-101, -202, -205, -207, -209, -210, 216, 302, -403, -502 to -504, -507, - 508, -512 to -515; 23-66-206, 308, 310; 23-88-504, 507; 23-94-201 to -215; 23-103-403. 054 00 CARR 050, 057, 082, 087, 088.

CALIFORNIA

Producer Licensing Bureau
300 Capitol Mall; 17th Fl.; Sacramento, CA 95814
Mailing Address for Fees for Resident documents:
P.O. Box 1139; Sacramento 95812-1139
Mailing address for Fees and Nonresident Applications:
P.O. Box 1139; Sacramento 95812-1139
Telephone, Commissioner: 916-492-3500; Fax: 916-327-6907
WATS: 800-967-9331; M-F; 7:00am-5:30pm, excluding State Holidays
Other Offices: 300 S. Spring St., 9th Fl.; Los Angeles CA 90013
1901 Harrison St., 6th Fl.; Oakland, CA 94612
Email:
http://www.insurance.ca.gov

I. **Licensing Requirements:** Sales Personnel—Casualty Broker-Agents, Property Broker-Agents, Personal Lines Broker-Agents, Bail Agents, Bail Permittees, Bail Solicitors, Cargo Shippers Agents, Fraternal Agents, Motor Club Agents, Life-Only Agents, Accident and Health Agents, MGAs, Rental Car Agents, Stock Agents, Limited Lines Travel Insurance Agents, Credit Agents, Portable Electronics Insurance Agent. Other Insurance Professionals—Adjusters, Registered Administrators, Life and Disability Insurance Analysts, Public Adjusters, Interim Public Adjusters, Reinsurance Intermediaries, Surplus Lines Brokers, Special Lines Surplus Lines Broker, Limited Lines Automobile Insurance Agents.

A. **Applicability:** A person shall not solicit, negotiate, or effect contracts of insurance, unless the person holds a valid license from the commissioner authorizing the person to act in that capacity. (Cal. Ins. Code §1631).

B. **Licenses Required of Residents:** Each of the following must be licensed in California. All licenses are biennial, expiring according to year-round expiration provisions, except as otherwise noted. (Cal. Ins. Code § 1630). Most individual and business entity insurance producers and applicants must submit their filings to the California Department of Insurance ("CDI") electronically. Specifically, this requirement applies to individuals renewing or applying for licenses. Individuals may, for good cause shown, request an exemption to the electronic filing requirements. (Cal. Ins. Code § 1655). Such requests may be made by contacting the toll-free producer licensing hotline 800-967-9331. For renewals, these requests should be made several weeks prior to the license expiration date to ensure a timely renewal. Also, license applicants must provide the email address to which the applicant wants the commissioner to direct all license-related correspondence. Visit insurance.ca.gov/0200-industry/ for more information.

Sales Personnel

1. *Casualty Broker-Agents.* A casualty broker-agent licensee is a person authorized to act as an insurance agent, broker, or solicitor, and a casualty broker-agent license is a license so to act. Licenses to act as a casualty broker-agent include the type casualty, which entitles the licensee to transact insurance coverage against legal liability, including that for death, injury, disability, or damage to real or personal property. (Cal. Ins. Code §1625(a) and (c)). Authority to act is required on one of the following ways: Form 417-5, a $10,000 bond for brokers; an Action of Notice of Appointment; or Form 417-31, an Appointment of Insurance Solicitor; Form 411-8A to be endorsed to a licensed organization. License Filing Fee: $94. Renewal Fee: $94, annually. Late Renewal: $705; $849 for each individual month. License fees remain the same when applying for a property broker and casualty broker license at the same time. To act as an insurance broker, a $10,000 bond (Form 417-5) must be filed, no fee required when submitted with a new license application, otherwise $29 per submitted bond. (Cal. Ins. Code §1665). All applicants must also submit fingerprints. Fee: $59 at CDI's examination sites, $68.95 at PSI's test centers. Fingerprinting services are also available for varying fees at DOJ approved Live Scan fingerprinting vendors throughout the state. All fingerprint services must include form LIC 442-39A. Fingerprinting can be done prior to taking the licensing test, or may be completed the day of the test at the PSI test center. California requires all applicants to pass the examination before submitting an application. All licensing tests are scheduled through PSI and include a $55 test fee as well as a $33 convenience fee if taken at a PSI test center. (insurance.ca.gov/0200-industry/0050-renew-license/0600-fees/index.cfm).

2. *Personal Lines Broker-Agents.* A personal lines broker-agent may transact the following lines of business: automobile insurance, residential property insurance (including earthquake and flood insurance), personal watercraft insurance, inland marine insurance covering personal property, and umbrella or excess liability insurance. (Cal. Ins. Code § 1625.5). Fee is $94. Renewal: $94 annually. Late fee: $776; $934 for each additional month. 255. Exam: $55, additional $33 convenience fee applies for testing at PSI test center. Application form for individuals: 441-9. For broker authority a $10,000 bond is required on Form 417-5. The bond must be executed by a California admitted surety in the name of the applicant and signed by the applicant. Fingerprints must be submitted. Fee: $59 at CDI examination sites and $68.95 at PSI test centers. Cash payments not accepted. The term of the license begins on the date of issue and expires on the last calendar day of the month in which the initial license was issued. (Cal. Ins. Code §1625.5; insurance.ca.gov/0200-industry).

3. *Property Broker-Agent.* A property broker-agent licensee is a person authorized to act as an insurance agent, broker, or solicitor. Licenses to act as a property

broker-agent include the type of property, which entitles the licensee to transact insurance coverage on the direct or consequential loss or damage to property of every kind. Authority to act is required in one of the following ways: Form 417-5, a $10,000 bond for brokers; an Action Notice of Appointment; or Form 417-31, an Action Notice of Solicitor; or Form 411-8A to be endorsed to a licensed organization. License Filing Fee: $94. Renewal Fee: $94 annually. License fees remain the same when applying for a property broker and casualty broker license at the same time. Late fee: $776. Exam: $55, $83 at PSI test center. To act as an insurance broker, a $10,000 bond (Form 417-5) must be filed, no fee required. All applicants must also submit fingerprints. Fee: $59 at CDI examination sites, $68.95 at PSI test centers, and fingerprinting services are also available for varying fees at DOJ approved Live Scan Fingerprinting vendors throughout the state. All fingerprint services must include form LIC 442-39A. Fingerprinting can be done prior to taking the licensing test, or may be completed the day of the test at the PSI test center. California requires all applicants to pass the examination before submitting an application. (Cal. Ins. Code §1625 to §1625.55).

4. *Life-Only Agents.* A life-only agent is authorized to transact insurance on human lives including benefits of endowment and annuities, and may include benefits in the event of death or dismemberment by accident and benefits for disability income. Fee is $94 license and renewal, annually. When applying with the accident & health license on the same application, the total fee for both licenses is $94. Late fee: Renewal plus fifty percent. Exam: $55, additional $33 convenience fee for testing at a PSI test center. They must also submit fingerprints; fee: $59 at CDI examination sites and $68.95 at PSI test centers. In order to sell variable insurance contracts, the licensee must pass the FINRA exam and furnish proof that he or she is registered to sell securities in accordance with the rules of the FINRA and be appointed by a life carrier that is also approved to sell variable contracts. California does not issue life brokers licenses. (Cal. Ins. Code §1626; insurance.ca.gov/0200-industry).

5. *Life Limited to Funeral and Burial Expenses.* A life-only license limited to the payment of funeral and burial expenses which is limited by the terms of a written agreement with an insurer which has filed on that life-only agent's behalf a notice of appointment with the commissioner to transact only specific life insurance policies or annuities having an initial face amount of twenty thousand dollars ($20,000) or less that are designated by the purchaser for the payment of funeral and burial expenses. Fee is $94 new license and renewal, annually. California requires all resident applicants to pass the examination before submitting an application. All licensing examinations are administered by CDI or PSI and require a $55 examination fee and, if taking the examination at a PSI location, an additional $33 convenience fee for a total fee of $85.

Late fee: Renewal plus fifty percent. They must also submit fingerprints. Fee: $59 at CDI test centers and $68.95 at PSI's test centers. (Cal. Ins. Code § 1676(c)).

6. *Accident and Health Agents.* This license is authorized to transact insurance coverage for sickness, bodily injury, or accidental death and may include benefits for disability income and is also authorized to transact twenty-four hour care coverage. The fee is $94 for new license and renewal, annually when applying with the life only license on the same application, the total fee for both of these licenses is $94. Late fee: Renewal plus fifty percent, plus filing new company appointments and/or endorsements. Exam: $55 at PSI test centers, $85 at CDI test centers. Fingerprinting is required, fee is $59 at CDI test centers, $68.95 at PSI test centers. (Cal. Ins. Code §1626).

7. *Bail Agents.* Must have continuously resided in California for two years. Must be licensed to solicit, negotiate, or effect undertakings of bail on behalf of any surety insurer. (Cal. Ins. Code §1802). Must be appointed by the surety, form 437-23 and file a $1,000 bond on Form 437-9, executed by a California admitted surety and signed by the principal along with Action Notice of Appointment Form 437-23 and Action Notice Statement of Employing Bail Agent Form 438. First Time Applicant: $622, Two-year term. Corporation: $622, Two-year term. Individual renewal: $188, Two-year term. Corporation renewal: $188, Two-year term. Late renewal: reapply and pay double the application fee. Renewal $170 per company (two-year term). Corporations use application form 431-2 submitted with a $1,000 bond on Form 437-9 and Action Notice of Appointment Form 438. Individuals must submit fingerprints; processing fee: $59 at CDI examination sites and $68.95 at PSI test centers. Exam: $62 at a PSI test center. For business entity licensees: each officer, director, stockholder, and employee must hold an individual bail agent license. (Cal. Ins. Code §1811).

   Prelicensing and CE requirements apply. See Sections E and F.

8. *Bail Permittees.* A bail permittee is a person permitted to solicit, negotiate, issue and deliver bail bonds. Must have continuously resided in California for two years. Must be licensed to solicit, negotiate, issue, or deliver bail bonds. Must file a bond of bail permittee form 437-10 for $5,000 executed by a California admitted surety and signed by the principal along with application for bail license form 431-1. First Time Applicants: $1,248 (two-year term). Renewal is $788 (two-year term). Late renewal: reapply and pay two times the application fee. Exam: $62, $89 at a PSI test center. Must submit fingerprints; fee, $59 at CDI examination sites and $68.95 at PSI test centers. For business entity licensees: each officer, director, stockholder, and employee must hold an individual bail agent license. A corporation may not employ a bail permittee. (Cal. Ins. Code §§ 1802.5, 1811).

Prelicensing and CE requirements apply. See Sections E and F.

9. *Bail Solicitors.* A bail solicitor is a person who transacts bail on behalf of and as the employee of the holder of a bail license. Must have continuously resided in California for two years. Must file a $1,000 bond of bail solicitor Form 437-11 executed by a California admitted surety and signed by the principal along with application for bail license Form 431-1. Initial fee: $622 per employer (two-year term). Renewal $188, per employer (two year term). Late renewal: reapply and pay two times the application fee. Employer must file form 438. Must also submit fingerprints; processing fee, $59 at CDI examination sites and $68.95 at PSI test centers. Exam: $62 at a PSI test center. A corporation may not employ a bail solicitor. (Cal. Ins. Code §§ 1803, 1811).

   For business entity licensees: each officer, director, stockholder, and employee must hold an individual bail agent license. Prelicensing and CE requirements apply. See Sections E and F.

10. *Cargo Shippers' Agent.* License may be issued to those who act as an agent on behalf of cargo owners or shippers, or both. This limited license authorizes the cargo owners' or shippers' agent to procure cargo insurance only on behalf of a cargo owner or shipper for whom the agent is also arranging for the carriage of goods. License fee: $64, Two-year term. Renewal: $64, Two-year term. Late fee: Renewal plus fifty percent, plus filing new appointments and/or endorsements. Application forms: Individuals, 441-9; Business Entities, 441-11. The application and Bond of Cargo Shippers Agent Form 447-70 for $10,000 executed by a California admitted surety completed in the name of the applicant and signed by the applicant, or the Organization Endorsement Form 411-8A completed by the sponsoring California licensed organization. Fingerprints are required for unlicensed applicants; Fee: $59 contacting Accurate Biometrics (866) 361-9944 and bringing completed Live Scan Request, from LIC 442-39A. Entities must also pay an Organization Endorsement Fee of $29 with Form 411-8A. (Cal. Ins. Code §1757.1 to 1757.3).

    There are no prelicensing or CE requirements.

11. *Part-Time Fraternal Agents.* Issued on a part-time basis only. "A part time fraternal license holder is person who is affiliated with a fraternal benefit society or association, selling the society's or association's insurance to the membership on a substantially less than full-time basis, which is interpreted as twenty hours or less per week." (Cal. Ins. Code §11101 to 11103).

License Filing: $188 (two-year term); Application for insurance license form 441-9. Renewal fee: $188 (two-year term). Late fee: Renewal plus fifty percent, plus filing new appointments. Unlicensed applicants must also submit fingerprints. Fee: $59 by contacting Accurate Biometrics (866) 361-9944 and bringing completed Live Scan Request, form LIC 442-39A. Part time fraternal agents must submit their renewal filings to CDI electronically. There are no prelicensing or CE requirements. (insurance.ca.gov/0200-industry/0050-renew-license/0200-requirements/part-time-fraternal.cfm).

12. *Motor Club Agents.* A motor club agent acts or aids in the solicitation, delivery, or negotiation of any membership or service contract on behalf of the appointing motor club. (Cal. Ins. Code §12143).

    Biennial fee: $188, application forms: Individuals, 441-9 along with Action Notice of Appointment Form 447-54A; Business Entities, 441-11. Late fee: Renewal plus fifty percent, plus filing new appointments. Action Notice Fee: $29. Must also submit fingerprints; Fee: $59, contact Accurate Biometrics (866) at 361-9944 and bring completed Live Scan Request, form LIC 442-39A. There are no prelicensing or CE requirements.

13. *Rental Car Agents and Endorsees.* A rental car agent is authorized to offer or sell those types of insurance incidental to rental car agreements on behalf of an insurer authorized to write those types of insurance in California. An endorsee is an unlicensed employee of a rental car agent who has been properly trained. Application forms: Individuals, 441-9; Business Entities, 441-11. In addition, the insurer must file a Rental car agent Notice of Appointment, RCA-3. Form RCA-3 certifies that the insurer is satisfied that the applicant is capable of acting on its behalf in the sale of rental car insurance. The applicant then files Form RCA-1 confirming that its employees have undergone the proper training. Biennial fees for Individuals and Business Entities are $509 (two-year term), new and renewal. Late fee: Renewal plus fifty percent, plus filing new company appointments or endorsements.

    A Rental Car Agent-Employer must do the following:

    a. Annually update the list of its employees certified to sell the coverage and maintain this list for three years.
    b. Complete certification RCA-1 and file annual certification RCA-2.
    c. Submit any changes in its training materials thirty days in advance.
    d. Conduct periodic retraining of its employees.
    e. Pay enforcement costs.
    f. Renew its license every two years.

g. Employers must provide training on ethical sales practices, personal accident insurance, liability insurance and personal effects as they pertain to renters and rental vehicles. Training in roadside assistance insurance and emergency sickness insurance may also be included. The endorsee training is described in form RCA 4.

Employees of rental car agents must:

a. Be eighteen years of age or older.
b. Be on a list of authorized employees (Form RCA 5) maintained by the rental car company.
c. Undergo mandatory training (form RCA 4). In addition, the rental car company must identify the authorized employee (Form RCA 5) who is the manager or supervisor at each location maintained by the company.

(Cal. Ins. Code §§ 1758.8 to 1758.89; insurance.ca.gov/0200-industry/0050-renew-license/0200-requirements/rental-car/index.cfm).

14. *Stock Agents.* License is issued only to California resident individuals employed by an insurer or broker who sell any security. License filing fee: $150. Expires each July 1. These licenses are not renewed. Rather, a new application must be submitted each year. There are no prelicensing or continuing education requirements. Application for Certificate to Sell Securities as Agent, form LIC 441-1. . Issued to individuals only. Must also submit fingerprints; fee: $59 at CDI exam sites, $68.95 at PSI test centers. (Cal Ins. Code § 825; insurance.ca.gov/0200-industry/0050-renew-license/0200-requirements/stock-agent.cfm).

15. *Limited Lines Travel Insurance Agents.* A limited license may be issued to any organization engaged in transacting travel insurance through travel retailers. Written application is to be completed using form 441-11 with a fee of $4,540 for a two-year license period beginning on the date the license is issued and expires the last day of that same calendar month two years later. License renewal fees are $4,540 for a two-year period. (Cal. Ins. Code § 1754(a)(3) and (5)). Insurer Notice of Appointment is required completing Form LIC TA 1 and a fee of $29. Initial certification of authorized travel retailers to be completed on form LIC TA 2. Submit training material in accordance with form LIC TA 3.

Limited Lines Travel Insurance Agent must do the following:

a. The limited lines travel insurance agent and its designated responsible employee shall hold property and casualty and/or life-only and accident/health agent licenses based upon the types of insurance transacted by the licensee. From a practical standpoint, the Property and Casualty Broker-Agent and Life-Only and Accident & Health are required as all of these license types will be needed by both the licensed business entity and its designated responsible employee, as it is expected that the policies offered for sale by all limited lines travel insurance agents will include property, casualty, life and health provisions.

b. At the time of licensure and thereafter maintain a list of its travel retailers certified to sell the coverage.
c. Complete initial certification LICTA-2 and file annual certification LICTA-4.
d. Submit any changes in its training materials thirty days in advance.
e. Conduct periodic retraining of its employees.
f. Pay enforcement costs.
g. Renew its license every two years.
h. Employers must provide training on ethical sales practices, types of insurance offered and disclosures to prospective insurance customers. The endorsee training is described in form TA 3.
i. The limited lines travel insurance agent must be appointed by an authorized insurer. An officer or managing agent of the insurer must sign a Notice of Appointment, Limited Lines Travel Insurance Agent, form LICTA 1 certifying that the named applicant is trustworthy and competent to act as its limited lines travel insurance agent and that the insurer will appoint the applicant to act as its agent if the limited lines travel insurance agent license applied for is issued by the commissioner. (Cal. Ins. Code § 1755(a)(2)).

16. *Credit Insurance Agents.* A credit insurance agent is a person authorized by and on behalf of an insurer to transact credit insurance and receive a commission without having to be licensed as a life agent and/or property and casualty broker agent. Application forms: Individuals, 441-9; Business Entities, 441-11. Licensing fee: $449 plus a $45 fee for each endorsee. Renews annually: $410 + $8 per endorsee. Late fee: $776. The term begins the date the license is issued and ends the last day of that same calendar month in the subsequent year. Must also submit fingerprints; contact Accurate Biometrics at (866) 361-9944. Applicants must bring a copy of form LIC 442-39A with them to fingerprinting site; fee is $59.

17. *Portable Electronic Insurance Agent.* A portable electronics insurance agent is a person authorized to sell insurance to cover the loss, theft, mechanical failure, or malfunction of or damage to portable electronics equipment. No portable electronics equipment vendor shall offer or sell any form of portable electronics equipment insurance unless that person is licensed as an insurance agent or broker. Portable electronics includes all of the following: personal, self-contained, easily carried by an individual, battery-operated electronic communication, viewing, listening, recording, gaming, computing, or global positioning devices, including cell or satellite phones, pagers, personal global positioning satellite

units, portable computers, portable audio listening, video viewing or recording devices, digital cameras, video camcorders, portable gaming systems, docking stations, automatic answering devices, their accessories, service related to the use of those devices, and any other portable electronic device approved by the commissioner. Application forms: Individuals, 441-9; business entities, 441-11. Application Fee: $321. Biennial Renewal Fee: $321. Late fee: Renewal plus fifty percent. A portable electronics insurance agent Notice of Appointment Form LIC PE 1 must be completed by an authorized insurer, or its managing agent, certifying that the insurer has satisfied itself that the named applicant is trustworthy and competent to act as its insurance agent limited to this purpose. The insurer will appoint the applicant to act as its agent to transact portable electronics insurance. The applicant must submit a list of all locations in California for which the licensee offers coverage under a policy of portable electronics insurance on Form LIC PE 2. (Cal. Ins. Code §§ 1758.62, 1758.69).

Portable Electronics Insurance Agent-Employers must:

a. Maintain and update annually, a list of all locations in California for which the licensee offers coverage under a policy of portable electronics insurance on Form LIC PE 2.b. Establish and update, when appropriate, training materials. Training materials must include instruction about the types of insurance that may be offered for sale; instruction on ethical sales practices; and instruction on the required disclosures to be given to prospective consumers.
b. Retraining of endorsees at least every three years and whenever there is a material change in the insurance products sold that requires modification of the training materials.
c. Provide training to employees who are to be endorsed to the license.

Portable Electronics Agent-Employees must:

a. Be eighteen years of age or older.
b. Go through mandatory training.

(Cal. Ins. Code §1758.6-1758.692).

18. *Surplus Line Broker*. A Surplus Line Broker is a person who places insurance with nonadmitted insurers, covering risks other than aircraft and certain marine and transportation risks. License filing and renewal fees $1,296 for individuals that have a $50,000 bond on file; $646 for an individual broker who only transacts on behalf of a business entity. Late fee: Renewal plus fifty percent. $1,296 is the fee for a surplus line broker business entity license. Prelicensing experience: California residents must hold a Property Broker-Agent and a Casualty

Broker-Agent license. Nonresident applicants must hold the equivalent of a Surplus Line Broker license in their resident state. (Cal. Ins. Code §1761).

Note: Applicants applying for both a Surplus Line Broker and a Special Lines' Surplus Line Broker license need only submit one filing fee.

19. *Special Lines' Surplus Line Broker.* A Special Lines' Surplus Line Broker is a person who places aircraft and certain marine and transportation insurance risks with nonadmitted insurers. License filing and renewal fees $1,296 for individuals that have a $10,000 bond on file. $646 for a special lines' surplus line broker who only transacts on behalf of a business entity; $1,296 for a special lines' broker business entity license. Late fee: Renewal plus fifty percent. Prelicensing experience: California residents must hold a Property Broker-Agent and a Casualty Broker-Agent license. Nonresident applicants must hold the equivalent of a Surplus Lines' Surplus Lines Broker license in their resident state. (Cal. Ins. Code §1760.5).

    Note: Applicants applying for both a Surplus Line Broker and a Special Lines' Surplus Line broker license need only submit one filing fee.

20. *Self Service Storage Agent.* A licensed Self-Service Storage facility or its franchisee may act as a Self-Service Storage agent authorized to offer or sell hazard insurance coverage to renters for the loss of, or damage to, tangible personal property in storage or in transit during the rental period. This coverage may be offered only with, and incidental to, self-service-storage rental agreements. Application forms: Individuals, 441-9; business entities, 441-11. Application Fee: $323. Biennial Renewal Fee: $323. Late fee: Renewal plus fifty percent. A portable electronics insurance agent must be appointed by an insurer evidenced from an Insurer Notice of Appointment Form SSA 2. This form must be completed by an authorized insurer, or its managing agent, certifying that the insurer has satisfied itself that the named applicant is trustworthy and competent to act as its insurance agent limited to this purpose. The insurer will appoint the applicant to act as its agent to transact portable electronics insurance. The applicant must submit a list of all locations in California for which the licensee offers coverage under the policy. (Cal. Ins. Code §1758.75).

License Requirements for Employers

A. Provide training to each self-service storage agent.

B. Annually update the list of employees certified to sell insurance and retain that list for three years, Form LIC SSA 1.

C. Submit modifications to training materials thirty days prior to their use by licensee.

D. Renew license every two years.

E. Pay enforcement costs.

License Requirements for Employees

A. Must be eighteen years of age or older.

B. Must be listed as an authorized endorsee on form LIC SSA 1 maintained by the self-storage company.

C. Must complete mandatory training.

Other Insurance Professionals

1. *Independent Adjusters.* An adjuster is a person other than a private investigator who, for any consideration whatsoever, engages in the business of making an investigation for the purpose of obtaining information in the course of adjusting or participating in the disposal of any claim in connection with a policy of insurance or engages in soliciting insurance adjustment business. (Cal. Ins. Code §14021). Requires two years' experience adjusting claims; 2,000 hours of compensated time equals one year's experience. Must file a $2,000 surety bond in accordance with form 31A-14. The person in charge of the business (the qualified manager) must pass a qualifying licensing exam. Application fee: $311 two-year term. Late fee: $355. Examination fee: $79. Branch Office Certificate: $52. Re-examination: $29. Additional delinquency fee required if license renewed more than thirty days after expiration. If taken at a PSI examination site there is an additional $33 convenience fee. **Do not include the examination fee with the license filing fee when you submit your adjuster application.** You will submit payment at the time that you schedule your examination. License fee (new and renewal): $311 per Qualified Manager named on the license. License must be renewed biennially. The term of the license begins the date the license is issued and ends the last day of that same calendar month two years later. Application forms: individuals, 041-A; business entities, 042-A. Must also submit fingerprints; fee, $59 at CDI's examination sites and $68.95 at PSI's test centers.

2. *Crop Insurance Adjuster.* A crop insurance adjuster means a person who investigates, negotiates, or settles crop insurance claims. The same requirements as an Independent Insurance Adjuster with the exception of the license exam requirement. An applicant must provide evidence that he or she has satisfactorily completed the loss adjustment training curriculum and competency testing required by the

Federal Crop Insurance Corporation Standard Reinsurance Agreement. Call (916) 492-3085 for more crop insurance adjuster licensing information. (Cal. Ins. Code §14085).

3. *Registered Administrators.* A Certificate of Registration as an administrator is issued to a person who collects any charge or premium from, or who adjusts or settles claims on, residents of this state in connection with life or health insurance coverage or annuities or coverage described in Section 740 of the California Insurnace Code. Biennial fee, $188 (expires last day of month issued, two years later). Renewal fee: $188. Late fee: Renewal plus fifty percent. Administrators must submit their renewal filings to CDI electronically. Administrators are subject to the regulation of the insurance commissioner as described in California Insurance Code Section 1759. Application Form for individuals: LIC CDI-182. Application Form for entities: 441-12. Must also submit fingerprints; processing fee, $59 at CDI exam sites, $68.95 at PSI test centers; bring completed Live Scan form 442-39A. There are no prelicensing or CE requirements for this license. (Cal. Ins. Code §§740 and 1759).

4. *Life and Disability Analysts.* A Life and Disability Insurance Analyst is a person who, for a fee or compensation of any kind, paid by or derived from any person or source other than an insurer, advises, purports to advise, or offers to advise any person insured under, named as beneficiary of, or having any interest in, a life or disability insurance contract, in any manner concerning that contract or his or her rights in respect thereto. (Cal. Ins. Code §1848). Minimum age of licensure: twenty-three years or older. Must be licensed as both a life-only (LO) and accident and health (AH) licensee for five years prior to taking the qualifying examination. Biennial fee: $622, two-year term. Late fee: Renewal plus fifty percent. Exam fee: $155, paid when licensing exam is scheduled. **Please do not include the examination fee when you are submitting your application.** Individual Life and Disability Insurance Analysts must submit their renewal filings to CDI electronically. Business Entities licensed as Life and Disability Insurance Analysts will continue to renew with form LIC 448-29B. Application forms: individuals, 441-9; business entities, 441-11. Must also submit fingerprints; fee, $59 at CDI examination sites and $68.95 at PSI test centers. Analyst's authority does not include employment by an insurer or sale of insurance of any kind, and analyst may also be licensed to sell insurance. There are no continuing education requirements for this license.

5. *Public Adjusters.* A public insurance adjuster is a person who, for compensation, acts on behalf of or aids in any manner, an insured in negotiating for or effecting the settlement of a claim or claims for loss or damage under any policy of insurance covering real or personal property or any person who advertises, solicits business,

or holds himself or herself out to the public as an adjuster of those claims and any person who, for compensation, investigates, for those losses on behalf of any public insurance adjuster. (Cal. Ins. Code §15007). Requires two-years' experience adjusting claims; 2,000 hours of compensated time equals one year of experience. One year as a licensed apprentice public adjuster will satisfy the requirement. California residents must complete a twenty-hour prelicensing education course, pass a qualifying exam and post a $20,000 bond (form 94A). The prelicensing education and exam requirement are waived for nonresidents who hold a valid resident or designated home state license. Application Fee: $264. Renewal: $264. Late fee: $302. Examination Fee: $68 at a CDI exam site, $101 at a PSI exam site. Re-examination: $25. **Do not include the application fee with the examination fee when you submit your adjuster application.** You will submit payment at the time that you schedule your examination. Applicants must complete a $20,000 bond. Authorization application: $56. Application forms: individuals, CDI-180; business entities, LIC CDI-181. Must also submit fingerprints. Fee; $59 at CDI examination sites, $68.95 at PSI test centers. License expires two years on the last day of the month the original license was issued. CE Requirements: twenty-four hours, including three hours of ethics, during two-year license term.

6. *Apprentice Public Adjuster.* A license as an apprentice public adjuster is available to a person employed by a public adjuster for the purpose of training. (Cal. Ins. Code §15016). Must post a $20,000 bond on Form 94A. Public Adjuster Authorization Application Form 0100A must be completed by employer. License filing fee, one year term: $264 plus $62 application fee, plus $62 employer authorization. Fingerprints are required. Fee; $59 at CDI exam sites, $68.95 at PSI test centers, and bring a completed Live Scan Request form 442-39A. License is not renewable. After fulfilling the experience requirements, an apprentice public adjuster licensee may file for a Public Insurer Adjuster license; see Public Insurance Adjuster licensing requirements. The apprentice public adjuster is authorized to adjust claims only in California. There are no prelicensing or continuing education requirements for this license.

7. *Reinsurance Intermediaries.* A Reinsurance Intermediary Broker is any person, other than an officer or employee of the ceding insurer, firm, association, or corporation, who solicits, negotiates, or places reinsurance cessions or retro-cessions on behalf of a ceding insurer without the authority or power to bind reinsurance on behalf of that insurer. A reinsurance intermediary-manager is any person, firm, association, or corporation that has the authority to bind, or manages all or part of the assumed reinsurance business of, a reinsurer and acts as an agent for the reinsurer whether known as a reinsurance intermediary-manager, manager, or similar term. (Cal. Ins. Code § 1781.2). License Fee: $411. If filing for both the

reinsurance intermediary-broker and the reinsurance intermediary-manager, only one application and fee are required. **No exam required.** Application forms: Individuals, LIC 441-14; Business Entities, LIC 441-15. The license is perpetual. Intermediary managers may be required to carry a fidelity bond or E&O insurance. There are no prelicensing or continuing education requirements for this license.

8. *Life Settlements Broker.* California viatical settlement statutes were repealed and replaced by life settlements statutes now contained in Cal. Ins. Code §§ 10113.1 to 10113.3. Under the terms of these statutes, life settlement brokers and providers are required to obtain a license from the California Insurance Commissioner to transact life settlement business in California and are subject to both licensing and consumer disclosure requirements in Cal. Ins. Code § 10113.2(d).

   a. Life Settlement Notifications—[Individuals transacting life settlements that have been licensed as life agents for more than one year.] These individuals are required to notify CDI within ten days of the first day transacting life settlements using Form LIC 441-20N found on the CDI website. The cost for life producer notification is $188 and is required to be renewed every two years at the same time that the individual's life license is to be renewed. (10 CCR 2548.21). The notification must be renewed on the same date the life agent license expires.
   b. Life Settlement Broker License—[Individuals who have not been licensed life agents for at least one year who intend to transact life settlements must first obtain a Life Settlement Broker license.] This license is a one year license at a cost of $188. Unlicensed applicants or applicants who have had a life agent license for less than one year must complete fifteen hours of life settlement education. The renewal fee for this license is $188. Application forms are to be submitted via the CDI online application service. (10 California Code of Regulations 2548.21; https://www.insurance.ca.gov/0200-industry/0045-lic-fees/). Fingerprint impressions are required for unlicensed applicants and can be submitted at any time, including prior to submitting the life settlement broker license application. Fee: $59 at CDI exam sites, $68.95 at PSI test centers, and bring completed Live Scan Service Request form 442-39A.

9. *Life Settlement Provider.* A life settlement provider is a person, other than an owner, who enters into or effectuates a life settlement contract with an owner. (Cal. Ins. Code § 10113.1). An applicant for a Life Settlement Provider license must submit an Application for a Life Settlement Provider, form LIC 441-19, including an application fee of $4,656. Once the Life Settlement Provider application is completely filled out, applicant may upload a copy of the application utilizing the Department's OASIS (Online Assistance System for Insurer Submittals). Prior to using OASIS, applicants must contact CDI for an Entity Identifying

Number (EID). The provider applicant shall upload as attachments to its provider application all forms the applicant intends to use to transact California life settlement business. The term for the Life Settlement Provider license is one year. The annual renewal fee is $292. The licensee shall file with the department a copy of all life settlement forms used in this state. No licensee may use any life settlement form in this state unless it has been provided in advance to the commissioner. Life settlement providers shall file such forms by filling out and submitting a Life Settlement Form Filing Cover Sheet, form LIC 441-20C, along with a copy of the forms to be filled with the Commissioner. The cover letter and a copy of the forms shall be submitted to the Commissioner by uploading the documents utilizing the OASIS.

10. *Limited Lines Automobile Insurance Agent.* A limited lines automobile insurance agent is a person authorized to transact automobile insurance, as defined in Section 660. A limited lines automobile insurance agent license is a license to so act. (Cal. Ins. Code § 1625.55). Licenses are issued as individual or business entities. The two-year license fee is $188. Examination Fee: $55 at a California Department of Insurance examination site or $88 at a PSI examination site. Late fee: $282. Applications are to be submitted electronically. Biennial license renewals are to be submitted electronically.

    License and renewal fees are $188.

11. *Title Marketing Representative.* A natural person employed by a title insurer, underwritten title company or controlled escrow company whose primary duty is to market, offer, solicit, negotiate or sell title insurance. Fingerprint impressions are required for unlicensed applicants and can be filed prior to submitting the certificate application. Impressions may be taken at the licensing examination site. (Cal. Ins. Code § 12418). At CDI exam sites, fee is $59; at PSI test centers, fee is $68.95. A completed Live Scan Request, form LIC 442-39A is required at the time your fingerprint impressions are made. Applications for an insurance certificate are accepted online through Sircon.com; instructions for such applications may be found on the CDI website, under the "Agents and Brokers" tab. Application fee is $261 for a three-year certificate term. Renewal fee: $276. Late renewal fee: $64.

12. *Vehicle Service Contract Provider.* An entity legally obligated under a terms of a vehicle service contract to repair, replace, or maintain a motor vehicle or watercraft, or to indemnify repairs of the same due to defective material or workmanship or normal wear-and-tear is required to have a Vehicle Service Contract Provider's license. (Cal. Ins. Code §§ 12800, 12815). Application fee is: $5,443 for a two-year term. Renewal fee: $932 for a two-year term. Late fee: Renewal plus fifty percent. Fingerprints are required for unlicensed

applicants. Fee: $59. To schedule your fingerprint impressions using CDI's contracted fingerprint vendor; Accurate Biometrics at (866) 361-9944 to find a fingerprint location near you to have your fingerprints taken. When you go to have your fingerprint impressions made, please bring with you a completed Live Scan Request, form LIC 442-39A.

A Vehicle Service Contract Provider (VSCP) must provide the following additional information:

1. Specimens of all VSCP forms that you intend to use in California. The CDI will be reviewing the forms in order to ensure they are compliant with state insurance law.
2. Either a copy of your VSCP license or your application. (Cal. Ins. Code § 12815(a)).
3. A copy of the insurance policy that will insure your California vehicle service contracts. Include a copy of the declaration page showing you as the insured, and showing the policy's effective date and expiration date. The Department will be reviewing the policy in order to ensure compliance with state insurance law.
4. If you will be contracting with another administrator, you will need to submit a copy of the contract.
5. Evidence that your back up insurer complies with state insurance law that it is rated B++ or better by A.M. Best.
6. Proof that the audited financial statement has been filed with the commissioner. The Department may contact you for further information if it is unable to determine whether the requirements of Cal. Ins. Code § 12830(a) are met by your back up insurer.
7. A copy of any agreement between yourselves and the sellers.
8. A statement about how your firm will ensure compliance with state insurance law.
9. Copies of all agreements that your firm or any of its officers, directors, or shareholders has with any insurer of the firm's service contract program, or with any general agent of that insurer. Including the language, formula, or chart used to calculate the amount your company must remit to the insurer for various types and terms of service contracts.
10. Copies of any other agreements, besides those submitted in response to item 3, between your firm and any other company concerning the marketing, premium collection and remittance, reserving, claim administration, or any other aspect of the proposed California third party obligor service contract program.
11. The name, title, address and phone number of a contact person at your insurer. (Please provide the name of an insurer employee, not the name of a nonemployee agent.)

12. The full, legal name, address, and phone number of each individual who will be marketing your firm's vehicle service contract program to California dealers. Please also provide the corporate name or fictitious business name of any company with which any of these individuals are associated or by whom they are employed.
13. The names, addresses, and phone numbers of all California dealers that currently issue your firm's vehicle service contracts.
14. The number of vehicle service contracts sold by your firm to California residents in the past twelve months.
15. The Web address (URL) of your firm's Web site, if you have a Web site.

(Cal. Ins. Code § 12830).

C. Appointments: Life, Limited Lines, Travel, Property Casualty, Accident and Health, Life-Limited to the Payment of Funeral & Burial Expenses, Limited Lines Auto Insurance, Cargo Shipper, Credit Insurance, Personal Lines Motor Club, and Part Time Fraternal agents shall not act as an agent of an insurer unless the insurer has filed with the commissioner a notice of appointment, executed by the insurer, appointing the licensee as the insurer's agent. Insurance companies are required to submit all appointments and terminations in an electronic format. A person acting as a licensee under this chapter shall not act as an agent of an insurer unless the insurer has filed with the commissioner a notice of appointment, executed by the insurer, appointing the licensee as the insurer's agent. Every property broker-agent, casualty broker-agent, personal lines broker-agent, or limited lines automobile insurance agent acting in the capacity of an insurance solicitor shall have filed on his or her behalf with the commissioner a notice executed by an insurance agent or insurance broker appointing and agreeing to employ the solicitor as an employee within this state. (Cal. Ins. Code §1704).

D. Licenses Required of Nonresidents: Similar licenses are required of nonresidents who are licensed to transact more than one class of insurance, other than life insurance, disability insurance, title insurance, or life and disability insurance, under the laws of the state, territory of the United States, or province of Canada a resident license to transact insurance is maintained. Nonresidents who desire broker authority must post a $10,000 bond. Nonresidents may not be licensed as life and disability insurance analysts, cargo shippers' agents, fraternal agents, motor club agents, stock agents, and bail licensees. (Cal. Ins. Code §§ 1638 to 1639).

Licensing filing fee, two-year term: $5,433. Renewal fee, two-year term: $932. Nonresident licensees who were fingerprinted as a condition of receiving their resident licenses are no longer required to be fingerprinted as a condition of obtaining an insurance producer license. Appointment in California is required for each insurer the agent wishes to represent. Appointment fee, $29; form 447-54A. However, nonresident licensees who were not fingerprinted as a condition of receiving their resident license must be fingerprinted. (insurance.ca.gov/0200-industry/0045-lic-fees/index.cfm).

For nonresident licensees, contact Accurate Biometrics at (866) 361-9944 to schedule a fingerprinting appointment; please bring a completed Live Scan Request, form LIC 442-39A. Fees are $59 at a CDI exam site and $68.95 at a PSI exam site. Payment may be made by check, money order, cashier's check, or credit/debit card. Cash not accepted. (insurance.ca.gov/0200-industry/0050-renew-license/0200-requirements).

Nonresident business entities will be able to endorse California resident individuals on their license. License filing fee, two-year term: $5,433; Renewal fee, two-year term: $932. Also, nonresident business entities will not be required to endorse an individual from the business entity's resident state. They do need to endorse at least one individual from a state other than California. (insurance.ca.gov/0200-industry/0050-renew-license/0200-requirements/property/app-proc-org-nonres.cfm#:~:text=Non-resident%20business%20entities%20will%20be%20able%20to%20endorse,one%20individual%20from%20a%20state%20other%20than%20California.).

Multi-State Exposures. Nonresident licensure is required if the insurance transaction takes place in California by physical or a virtual presence.

E. Prelicensing Examination and Education Requirements:

Important: Applicants who fail an exam ten times within twelve months will have to wait twelve months from the date of the last failed exam to retake an exam.

1. *Residents.* Requirements for the following:

   a. Casualty Broker-Agent. When applying for the Casualty Broker-Agent license and the Property Broker-Agent license jointly: Twenty hours of approved study, plus an additional twelve hours of approved study in ethics and the California Insurance Code. A new California resident applicant currently licensed as a state nonresident, or an applicant holding one of the following designations—Accredited Advisor in Insurance (AAI), Charter Property Casualty Underwriter (CPCU), Certified Insurance Counselor (CIC), or Associate in Risk Management (ARM)—is exempt from the twenty hours of prelicensing education. The Casualty Broker-Agent license exam before submitting the application. Fee: $55.
   b. Personal Lines Broker-Agents. Twenty hours of approved study. A new state resident applicant who is designated as an AAI, CPCU, CIC, or ARM is

exempt from the twenty hours of prelicensing education. Also, twelve hours of approved study on ethics and the California Insurance Code. If an applicant is applying for both the broker-agent and the life license, he/she needs only complete one twelve-hour ethics/California Insurance Code course. Exam fee: $55.

c. Property Broker-Agent. Twenty hours of approved study, plus twelve hours of approved study in ethics and the California Insurance Code. A new California resident applicant currently licensed as a state nonresident, or an applicant holding one of the following designations—AAI, CPCU, CIC, or ARM—is exempt from the twenty hours of prelicensing education. If an applicant is applying for both the broker-agent and the life license, he/she needs only complete one twelve-hour ethics/California Insurance Code course. Must also pass an exam. Fee: $55.

d. Life-Only Agents. A minimum of twenty hours of prelicensing study plus twelve hours of approved study in ethics and the California Insurance Code. A new state resident applicant who had a current Life-Only license in another state within the last ninety days and has a current state nonresident license, or an applicant holding any of the following designations—Life Underwriter Training Council Fellowship (LUTCF), Chartered Life Underwriter (CLU), Certified Insurance Counselor (CIC), Certified Employee Benefit Specialist (CEBS), Chartered Financial Consultant (ChFC), Certified Financial Planner (CFP), or Fellow, Life Management Institute (FLMI)—is exempt from the twenty hours of prelicensing education. When an applicant seeks both the Property and Casualty Broker-Agent license and the Life-Only agent license, he or she need only complete one twelve-hour ethics/California Insurance Code course. Must also pass an exam; exam fee, $55.

e. Accident and Health. Twenty hours of approved prelicensing study plus twelve hours of approved instruction in ethics and the California Insurance Code. A new state resident applicant who had a current Accident and Health license in another state within the last ninety days and has a current state nonresident license, or an applicant holding any of the following designations—LUTCF, CLU, CIC, CEBS, FLMI, HIA, REBC, or RHU—is exempt from the twenty hours of prelicensing education. When an applicant is applying for both the Property and Casualty Broker-Agent and the Accident and Health agent license, he or she need only complete one twelve-hour ethics/California Insurance Code course. Exam fee: $55.

f. Bail Agents, Permittees, Solicitors. Twenty hours of approved study in pertinent subjects, including but not limited to related laws and regulations, rights of the accused, and ethics. Must also pass an exam; exam fee: $62.

g. Cargo Shippers' Agent, Fraternal Agents, Motor Club Agents. Not required.

h. Rental Car Agents and Endorsees. Employer must provide training on personal accident insurance, liability insurance and personal effects insurance as they pertain to renters and rental vehicles. Training in roadside assistance insurance and emergency sickness insurance must also be included. Refer to form LIC RCA-4 for endorsee training requirements.

i. Stock Agents. Not required.

j. Limited Lines Travel Insurance Agents. Requires twenty hours of approved prelicensing study plus twelve hours of approved prelicensing study on ethics. (Cal. Ins. Code §1749.32). All limited lines travel insurance agents shall provide training as stated in the Required Training Elements—Limited Lines Travel Insurance Agent, form LIC TA 3, to all employees of its travel retailers who will be transacting travel insurance under its license. "Transact" as defined for purposes of the limited lines travel insurance agent license means, the following activities when engaged in by a travel retailer:

   (1) Offering and disseminating information to a prospective or current policyholder on behalf of a limited lines travel insurance agent, including brochures, buyer guides, descriptions of coverage and price.
   (2) Referring specific questions regarding coverage features and benefits from a prospective or current policyholder to a limited lines travel insurance agent.
   (3) Disseminating and processing applications for coverage, coverage selection forms or other similar forms in response to a request from a prospective or current policyholder.
   (4) Collecting premiums from a prospective or current policyholder on behalf of a limited lines travel insurance agent.
   (5) Receiving and recording information from a policyholder to share with a limited lines travel insurance agent.

   Training materials, at a minimum, should contain instruction on the types of insurance offered, ethical sales practices and disclosures to prospective insurance customers; see form LIC TA 3 for more details. Training should be provided whenever there is a material change that requires a modification to the training materials, but in no event less frequently than every three years. (Cal. Ins. Code §1754(a)(6)).

k. Independent Insurance Adjusters. The person in charge of the business must satisfy the following requirements: Two years of certified field experience adjusting claims; 2,000 hours of compensated time in the field equates one year of experience. Must also pass an exam; exam fee: $79.

l. Crop Insurance Adjuster. Must (1) obtain an insurance adjuster license, with the exception of the exam required under Cal. Ins. Code § 14026, and (2) provide evidence that the applicant has satisfactorily completed the loss adjustment training curriculum and competency testing required under the Federal Crop Insurance Corporation Standard Reinsurance Agreement. (Visit insurance.ca.gov/0200-industry/0050-renew-license/0200-requirements for more information.)

m. Registered Administrators. Not required.
n. Life and Disability Analysts. Must be licensed as both a life-only (LO) and an accident and health (AH) licensee for five years before taking the qualifying exam. Must pass an exam; exam fee: $155.
   All licensing examinations are administered by CDI or PSI and require a $155 examination fee and, if taking the examination at a PSI location, an additional $33 convenience fee.
o. Public Insurance Adjuster. Requires two years of certified experience adjusting claims. 2,000 hours of compensated time in the field equates one year of experience. Public adjusters must also complete twenty hours of prelicensing education. Applicants residing in another state that does not license public insurance adjusters may designate California as their home state; such applicants must complete the prelicensing education requirements, pass the public insurance adjust exam, and satisfy all other application requirements before such license will be issued. Nonresident applicants with a current public insurance adjuster license are exempt from this twenty hour requirement if, at the time of application, the out-of-state license is current or was canceled within ninety calendar days. (Cal. Ins. Code § 15009.1). California requires all individual applicants to pass the examination before submitting an application. All licensing examinations are administered by CDI or PSI; fee is $68 per scheduled exam at CDI exam sites, and $101 per scheduled exam at PSI exam sites. Do not include the exam fee when submitting the adjuster application.
p. Reinsurance Intermediary. Not required.
q. Life Settlement Provider. Person with authority to bind the provider must certify they have reviewed Cal. Ins. Code §§ 10113.1 to 10113.3 and 10 CCR §§ 2548.1 to 2548.32, and understand the provisions in Cal. Ins. Code §§ 10113.1(g)(2)(D) and 10113. 2(b).
r. Life Settlement Brokers. Applicants who have been licensed as a life agent for at least one year must certify they have reviewed Cal. Ins. Code §§ 10113.1 to 10113.3 and 10 CCR §§ 2548.1 to 2548.32, and understand the provisions in Cal. Ins. Code §§ 10113.1 and 10113.2. Applicants who have not been licensed as a life agent, or those holding the license for less than one year must submit a complete form LIC 441-20 to operate as a life settlement broker; must also certify they have reviewed Cal. Ins. Code §§ 10113.1 to 10113.3 and 10 CCR §§ 2548.1 to 2548.32, and understand the provisions in Cal. Ins. Code §§ 10113.1 and 10113.2.
s. Credit Agents. Must be appointed by an authorized insurer. Insurer must sign a form LIC CI 20 certification that the applicant is trustworthy and competent to act as an insurance agent for this purpose; insurer will appoint applicant as an agent to transact credit insurance.

t. Portable Electronics Agents. Require in-house retraining at least once every three years and whenever there is a material change in the insurance products sold that requires modification of the training materials. Training materials must include instruction about the types of insurance that may be offered for sale; instruction on ethical sales practices; and instruction on the required disclosures. (Cal. Ins. Code § 1758.63).

u. Limited Lines Automobile Insurance Agent. Requires a minimum of twenty hours of prelicensing study as a prerequisite for qualification for a limited lines automobile insurance agent license, plus twelve additional hours of approved instruction in ethics and the CIC. A new state resident applicant who had a current Limited Lines Auto agent license in another state within the last ninety days and has a current non-resident California license, or an applicant designated as an Accredited Advisor in Insurance (AAI), a Chartered Property Casualty Underwriter (CPCU), or a Certified Insurance Counselor (CIC) is exempt from the twenty hours of prelicensing education. Exam fee: $55 per scheduled exam at a CDI examination site or $88 at a PSI examination site.

v. Surplus Lines Broker and Special Lines' Surplus Line Broker. Must be licensed as a Property and Casualty Broker-Agent (residents and nonresidents). Nonresident applicants must hold a Special Lines' Surplus Line Broker license in their state of residence.

w. Self-Service Storage Agent. Employers must provide training to employees in compliance with CIC § 1758.72(a). Establish a list of trained endorsees, using form LIC SSA 1; update and maintain list annually, retain list for three years; submit modifications to training materials thirty days in advance of implementation; renew license on or before the two year expiration date.

x. Title Marketing Representative. The employer will be required to appoint the applicant by providing the applicant's ID number on form LIC 447-54A and provide a statement certifying that the applicant either has completed or will complete within sixty days, the required Title Marketing Representative Training that has been provided by the employer. Prelicensing experience or education is not required.

y. Vehicle Service Contract Provider. Not required.

Certificates of completion expire three years from completion of the course, whether a license is issued or not.

For those selling Long-Term Care products or California Partnership for Long-Term Care products: eight hours of specific partnership LTC courses and eight other hours of approved coursework in LTC, prior to selling the product are required.

For life only licensees selling annuity products, California law requires agents to complete eight hours of California specific annuities training prior to soliciting individual customers in order to sell annuities. In addition, if a life-only agent sells an annuity product in a subsequent license term the agent must complete an eight or four hour California specific annuity training course during that license term.

No prelicensing education required of life applicants who only sell funeral/burial insurance policies or annuities with a face value of $20,000 or less. Must pass the qualifying license exam before submitting application. Exam fee is $55 per scheduled exam at CDI sites, and $88 per scheduled exam at PSI sites.

Applicants may find information about providers of prelicensing education at http://www.insurance.ca.gov/0200-industry/0030-seek-pre-lic/.

Applicants are encouraged to review Prelicensing Educational and Exam Objectives bulletins, which are available at http://www.insurance.ca.gov/0200-industry/0030-seek-pre-lic/prelicensing-educational-objectives.cfm.

2. *Nonresidents.* Nonresident applicants who are currently licensed in another state and who have completed the equivalent of the number of California required hours of prelicensing education are only required to take the twelve hours of California Insurance Code and ethics course. In addition, applicants for certain types of licenses who are currently licensed as nonresident in this state are required to complete only the course of study on ethics and California code, even if they have not completed the equivalent of the number of California required hours of prelicensing education. Check with the California Insurance Department to see if you will be able to use one of these exemptions. Any nonresident applicant with a license holding one or more of the following designations or the specified number of hours shall be exempted from any requirement for courses in general insurance that would otherwise be a condition of issuance of a license: more than twenty-six hours of the LUTCF program, more than thirty hours of the CLU program, more than twenty-five hours of the AAI program, or more than thirty hours of the CPCU program. The following designations exempt applicants for certain licenses from prelicensing education except for the twelve hour course on ethics and the California code: LUTCF, CLU, AAI, CPCU, CIC, CEBS, ChFC, CFP, FLMI, HIA, REBC, RHU, ARM. For a full list of licenses subject to these designations, visit insurance.ca.gov/0200-industry/0050-renew-license/0200-requirements/. (Cal. Ins. Code §1749).

PSI Services, LLC, a California-based company providing state-based regulatory licensure services, handles the scheduling of examinations for individuals licensed by the California Department of Insurance's Producer Licensing Bureau. Instructions for scheduling examinations are posted on PSI's Web site at https://www.psiexams.com. Individuals may schedule their examinations with PSI either online or by telephone.

F. Continuing Education Requirements:

Number of Hours Required:

1. *Casualty Broker-Agent.* When licensed for the Casualty Broker-Agent license and the Property Broker-Agent license jointly or separately: Twenty-four hours during two-year license period, including at least three hours of ethics instruction. Anyone seventy years of age or older and who has been licensed for thirty continuous years in California as a licensee in good standing in this state may be exempted from the continuing education requirements; does not apply to those licensed for the first time on or after 1 January 2010. (Cal. Ins. Code § 1749.3).

2. *Personal Lines Broker-Agents.* Twenty-four hours of instruction during each two-year license term including at least three hours of ethics instruction. Anyone seventy years of age or older and who has been licensed for thirty continuous years in California as a licensee in good standing in this state may be exempted from the continuing education requirements; does not apply to those licensed for the first time on or after 1 January 2010. (Cal. Ins. Code § 1749.3).

3. *Property Broker-Agent.* When licensed for the Casualty Broker-Agent license and the Property Broker-Agent license jointly or separately: Twenty-four hours biennially with at least three hours of ethics instruction. Anyone seventy years of age or older and who has been licensed for thirty continuous years in California as a licensee in good standing in this state may be exempted from the continuing education requirements; does not apply to those licensed for the first time on or after 1 January 2010. (Cal. Ins. Code § 1749.3).

4. *Life-Only Agents (also licensed as accident and health agents).* Twenty-four hours of instruction for each two-year license term, including at least three hours of ethics training. Every life agent who sells annuities shall satisfactorily complete four hours of annuity training every two years prior to license renewal. For resident licensees, this requirement shall count toward the licensee's continuing education requirement, but may result in completing more than the minimum number of continuing education hours. Any accident and health agent who wishes to sell twenty-four hour care coverage, shall complete a course, program of instruction, or seminar of an approved continuing education provider on workers' compensation and general principles of employer liability, which shall be completed

by examination approved by the commissioner as part of the continuing education course prior to selling this coverage. The required number of instruction hours shall be equal to but no greater than that required by the curriculum board for the prelicensing education requirements of a casualty broker-agent. For resident licensees, this requirement shall count toward the licensee's continuing education requirement, but may still result in completing more than the minimum number of continuing education hours set forth in this section. Anyone seventy years of age or older and who has been licensed for thirty continuous years in California as a licensee in good standing in this state may be exempted from the continuing education requirements; does not apply to those licensed for the first time on or after 1 January 2010. (Cal. Ins. Code §1749.3).

5. *Bail Agents, Permittees, Solicitors.* Twelve hours of approved continuing education within each two-year license period.

6. *Cargo Shippers' Agent.* Not required.

7. *Fraternal Agents.* Not required.

8. *Motor Club Agents.* Not required.

9. *Rental Car Agents and Endorsees.* Employers must provide training on ethical sales practices, personal accident insurance, liability insurance, and personal effects as they pertain to renters and rental vehicles. Training in roadside assistance insurance and emergency sickness insurance may also be included. The endorsee training is described in form LIC RCA 4.

10. *Stock Agents.* Not required.

11. *Limited Lines Travel Insurance Agents.* Training should be provided whenever there is a material change that requires a modification to the training materials, but no less than every three years (Cal. Ins. Code §1754(a)(6)).

12. *Adjusters.* Insurance adjusters and public insurance adjusters are required to complete twenty-four hours of continuing education, including three hours of ethics, during each two-year license term. For nonresident licensees, if the declared resident state insurance regulator requires completion of continuing education in its jurisdiction, California continuing education requirements are waived. (Cal. Ins. Code § 14090.1(b)).

13. *Crop Insurance Adjuster.* Same requirements as Independent Insurance Adjusters; see sec. 12 above.

14. *Administrators.* Not required.

15. *Life and Disability Analysts.* Not applicable.

16. *Public Insurance Adjusters.* Required to complete twenty-four hours of continuing education, including three hours of ethics, during each two-year license term. For nonresident licenses, if the declared resident state insurance regulator requires completion of continuing education in its jurisdiction, California continuing education requirements are waived. (Cal. Ins. Code § 15059.1(b)).

17. *Reinsurance Intermediaries.* Not required.

18. *Life Settlement Brokers.* Not required.

19. *Life Settlement Provider.* Not required.

20. *Portable Electronics Insurance.* Retraining of endorsees at least every three years and whenever there is a material change in the insurance products sold that requires modification of the training materials.

21. *Credit Agents.* Periodic retraining of employees, form LIC CI 30.

22. *Limited Lines Automobile Insurance Agent.* Satisfactorily complete approved courses or programs of instruction or attend seminars equivalent to twenty hours of instruction during each two-year license period, including at least three hours of ethics training. Anyone seventy years of age or older and who has been licensed for thirty continuous years in California as a licensee in good standing in this state may be exempted from the continuing education requirements; does not apply to those licensed for the first time on or after 1 January 2010. (Cal. Ins. Code § 1749.3).

23. *Surplus Lines Broker and Special Lines' Surplus Line Broker.* As a licensed Property and Casualty Broker-Agent, twenty-four hours during each two-year license term including three hours of ethics training.

24. *Self Service Storage Agent.* Retraining of the endorsees whenever there is a change or modification of the training materials.

25. *Title Marketing Representative.* Not required.

26. *Vehicle Service Contract Provider.* Not required.

Excess Hours: Hours earned only in the second half of a biennial reporting period may be carried over to the next reporting period

Final Exam: Does not have to be monitored.

Renewal Procedure:

1. Course provider reports credits to the DOI within thirty days of course completion.

2. Licensee should keep completion certificate for five years for personal records.

Nonresidents. Are exempt on a reciprocal basis, except for the requirement of twelve hours of approved study of the California Insurance Code and ethics. However, the LTC requirement still applies.

Note: If filing for renewal for one of the following licenses, you must use the CDI Online Renewal Service: Life-Only Agent; Accident and Health Agent; Property Broker-Agent; Casualty Broker-Agent; Person Lines Broker-Agent; Special Lines Surplus Line Broker; Surplus Line Broker; Limited Lines Auto Insurance Agent; Independent Insurance Adjuster; Public Insurance Adjuster; Motor Club; Administrator; Cargo Shippers' Agent; Portable Electronics Insurance Agent; Credit Insurance Agent; Life and Disability Insurance Analyst; Life Limited to Payment of Funeral and Burial Expenses; Part-Time Fraternal Agent; Rental Car Agent; Self-Service Storage Agent; or Title Marketing Representative.

Note: All property and casualty broker-agents and personal lines broker-agents, who have not already completed a similar homeowner's insurance valuation course, must complete three hours of approved study on estimating replacement value. This requirement is part of and not in addition to other continuing education requirements. The homeowner's insurance valuation course only needs to be taken once to satisfy the requirement. If the course is completed prior to June 27, 2011, the requirement may also be satisfied. (10 CCR § 2188.65).

G. **Cancellation of Agency Contracts/Producer Appointments:** After a written agency contract has been in effect for at least one year, insurers must give agents 120 days advance written notice of termination or amendment of the contract, except by mutual agreement. Advance notice does not apply if the broker-agent has committed of any of the following seven agent violations:

1. Exceeded his or her binding authority under the agency contract.

2. Violated the written underwriting rules or regulations of the insurer, a copy of which has been provided to the agent, which misleads the insurer concerning the nature or extent of a risk.

3. Failed to comply with the fiduciary requirements set forth in Cal. Ins. Code §§ 1733 to 1735.

4. Failure, within ten days after written notice of failure to remit funds under the contract or within thirty days of a written demand if the contract does not set a time limit, to remit funds due and owing to the insurer.

5. Had his or her agency license suspended or revoked by the commissioner.

6. Engaged in fraudulent acts affecting his or her relationship with the insurer or its insureds.

7. Transferred ownership, control, or servicing of policies written with the insurer to another insurer or other specified entities.

If the agent, after termination of the contract, cannot place a risk, the insurer must renew it for one policy period or one year, whichever is shorter. (Cal. Ins. Code §769(b, d)).

H. Rules for Risk Retention and Purchasing Groups: Risk retention groups licensed in states other than California must file a notice of operation with the commissioner at least sixty days prior to commencing operations in this state. This notice must include a designation of the commissioner as the group's agent for service of process. Filing fee: $1,196. Risk retention groups must register annually by December 31. The annual filing shall include the following: (1) annual reporting statement; (2) the annual renewal fee, to be set by the commissioner but not in excess of is $300; and (3) any other information require by commissioner to determine compliance with the CIC. The group shall notify the commissioner of any changes within thirty days of the change being made. All policies issued by risk retention groups must contain the following notice on the front page in ten-point type:

NOTICE

"This policy is issued by your risk retention group. Your risk retention group may not be subject to all of the insurance laws and regulations of your state. State insurance insolvency guaranty funds are not available for your risk retention group." (Cal. Ins. Code §132).

Purchasing groups must supply the commissioner with a notice containing the following information:

1. The state in which the group is domiciled.

2. The lines and classifications of liability insurance to be purchased.

3. The names and domiciles of the insurance company or companies from which the group intends to purchase.

4. The methods by which and the persons through whom, the insurance will be offered to the group's members whose risks are located in this state.

5. The principal place of business of the group.

6. Provide other information that may be required by the commissioner to verify qualification.

Purchasing groups must designate the commissioner as their agent for the receipt of legal documents or process. Purchasing groups must reregister annually by December 31. The following documents must be filed with the commissioner on or before January 31 of each year: (1) annual reporting statement; (2)The annual renewal fee, to be set by the commissioner but not to exceed is $200; and (3) any other information required by the commissioner to determine compliance with the CIC. (Cal. Ins. Code §134).

I. **Other License Rules, Requirements, or Restrictions:** No unlicensed person, other than salaried employees of insurers may engage in any insurance activity in California. Unlicensed nonresidents may not enter California to solicit, inspect, or service but are not prohibited from soliciting insurance outside of California on California property or operation. Solicitation in state includes mail or telephone or other electronic communication into the state from the outside, as well as physical presence in the state.

Any licensee failing to provide the federal identification number or social security number at the time of issuance or renewal of any license shall be reported by the commissioner and, if failing to provide after notification, the licensee shall be subject to a $100 penalty. (Cal. Ins. Code §1666.5).

J. **Policy Countersignature Requirements:** All policies issued by incorporated insurers shall be subscribed by the president, vice president, chairman, chief executive officer, or, in case of the death, absence, or disability of those officers, by any two of the directors, and countersigned by the secretary of the corporation. All such policies are as binding and obligatory upon the corporation as if executed over the corporate seal. (Cal. Ins. Code §386).

K. **Portable Electronics Insurance Licensing:** To apply for a portable electronics insurance agent license an applicant must submit a written application for licensure, signed by the applicant, a certificate by the insurer stating that the named applicant is trustworthy and competent to act as the insurer's insurance agent, and an application fee. An application fee, and, for each license period thereafter, a renewal fee, of two hundred ninety-two dollars ($292). (Cal. Ins. Code § 1758.62).

L. **Flood InsuranceTraining:** All California licensed resident insurance producers that sell flood insurance policies must comply with the minimum training requirements of Section 207 of the Flood Insurance Reform Act of 2004. (42 U.S.C.S. § 4011). An insurance producer that sells flood insurance may satisfy the minimum training and education requirements by completing a three hour course related to the National Flood Insurance Program (NFIP) which was approved by CDI's Curriculum and Officer Review Bureau's Curriculum Review Section (Education Unit). Any questions can be directed to the Education Unit at 916-492-3064. In addition, the Federal Emergency Management Agency (FEMA) has prepared NFIP Advanced Training Topics and Objectives to be followed by education providers when developing advanced flood training courses.

II. Commissions, Fees, Commingling of Funds, and Suitability in Annuity Transactions

A. **Commissions:** There are no restrictions on the distribution of commissions other than in the Cal. Ins. Code §§ 10140, 1490 and 11628 (a) and the Unruh Civil Rights Act. Rebating of commissions is now allowed for all lines. (Cal. Ins. Code § 750(d)). While acting under the authority of a contract described in Cal. Ins. Code § 15027, a public adjuster may not receive any fees or other consideration from either the insured or any other source, in excess of the amount provided in the contract. (Cal. Ins. Code § 15027.5).

B. **Fees:** Fees for service may be charged provided:

1. The consumer agrees to the fee in advance of the agreement, as required by 10 CCR §2189.3(e), after full disclosure of material facts surrounding the fee.

2. The fee is not being charged directly or indirectly for services related to procuring coverage from the California Automobile Assigned Risk Plan or the California FAIR Plan and is not prohibited by statute or regulation.

3. The broker is not an appointed agent of the insurer with which the coverage is or will be placed.

4. The broker provides the consumer with the Standard Broker Fee Disclosure (available at http://www.insurance.ca.gov/0250-insurers/0500-legal-info/0500-gen-legal-info/0100-brkr-fee-reg-summ/index.cfm).

5. The broker has an in-force broker bond on file with the Department as required by the Insurance Code. (10 CRR § 2189.3).

C. **Disclosure Requirements:** When a broker-agent charges fees:

1. The disclosure and agreement shall be printed in English and in any other language principally used by the broker to advertise, solicit or negotiate the sale and purchase of insurance.

2. The disclosure and agreement, signed or initialed by the consumer, shall be retained by a broker for eighteen months following the latest expiration of any policy to which the disclosure and agreement apply. (10 CCR §2189.4).

D. **Commingling of Funds:** Fiduciary funds must be maintained, at all times, in a trust account in a bank or savings and loan association in any of the United State so long as the account is insured by the Federal Deposit Insurance Corporation (FDIC) and licensed by any state government or the federal government, separate from any other account, in the manner prescribed by Section 1734 of the CIC. Interest-paying deposits or securities may be used with interest accruing to the agency only if written agreements to this practice are obtained from all insurers involved. (Cal Ins. Code §§ 1734, 1734.5).

E. **Suitability in Annuity Transactions:** Brokers and agents selling variable products must comply with suitability standards. Such standards obligate the agent to make certain that there are reasonable grounds for believing that a variable contract recommended to a customer is suitable for that customer. It is expected that due diligence will be given to the consideration of suitability by brokers and agents licensed to sell variable contracts in California.

A variable annuity shall be considered to have hazardous operations when the variable annuity contract, viewed as a whole, and from the viewpoint of a reasonably prudent investor, is so risky an investment that it seriously jeopardizes the retirement expectations of the investor. If the investor's reasonable retirement expectations are in jeopardy of remaining substantially unfulfilled, the presumption could arise that the contact is hazardous. (10 CCR §2534.44).

All California resident and nonresident life agents who sell annuity products must satisfactorily complete eight hours of annuity training prior to soliciting individual consumers to sell annuities. In addition, upon completing the eight hour training, life agents who sell annuity products must also satisfactorily complete an additional four hours of annuity training every two years prior to their license renewal. For resident agents, this requirement is part of, and not in addition to, their continuing education requirements. (Cal. Ins. Code §10509.915).

III. Statutory References: Cal. Ins. Code §§ 132; 134; 386; 750; 769; 1625 to 1625.55; 1626; 1630 to 1631; 1638 to 1639; 1665; 1666.5; 1676; 1704; 1734 to 1734.5; 1749; 1749.3 to 1749.32; 1754 to 1755; 1757.1 to 1757.3; 1758.62, .63, .69; 1758.8 to 1758.89; 1802.5; 1803; 1811; 10113.1; 10509.915; 11101 to 11103; 12143; 12800; 12815; 12820; 12830; 14090.1; 15009.1; 15027.5; 15059.1.

10 CCR 2188.65; 2189.3, .4; 2534.44; 2548.21.

42 U.S.C.S. § 4011

insurance.ca.gov/0200-industry/.

insurance.ca.gov/0200-industry/0050-renew-license/0200-requirements/index.cfm.

COLORADO

Commissioner of Insurance
1560 Broadway, Suite 850; Denver, CO 80202
Telephone: (303) 894-7499; Toll free: 1800-930-3745
Licensing(Pearson VUE): 1800-275-8247
Licensing(D.O.R.A.): 303-894-7855 or 1-800-886-7675
https://doi.colorado.gov/
Email: dora_insurance@state.co.us
Online chat 10-4 M-F: http://www.dora.state.co.us/pacific/chat/chat_test_edo.html

I. Licensing Requirements: Sales Personnel—Producers, Bail Bonding Agents, Other Insurance Professionals—Public Adjusters, Reinsurance Intermediaries.

A. Applicability: No person shall act as or hold oneself out to be an insurance producer unless duly licensed as an insurance producer in accordance with the laws of Colorado. Every insurance producer who solicits or negotiates an application for insurance of any kind on behalf of an insurer shall be regarded as representing the insurer and not the insured or any beneficiary of the insured in any controversy between the insurer and such insured or beneficiary. A person shall not sell, solicit, or negotiate insurance in Colorado for any class or classes of insurance unless the person is licensed for that line of authority. (C.R.S. §10-2-401).

B. Licenses Required of Residents: Each of the following must be licensed in Colorado:

Sales Personnel

1. *Producers.* A producer license is required in Colorado of anyone who holds oneself out to be an insurance producer. (C.R.S. §10-2-401). The code of Colorado defines an insurance producer as a person who solicits, negotiates, effects, procures, delivers, renews, continues, or binds insurance. (C.R.S. §10-2-103).

   a. Resident License Initial & Reinstatement fee: $47 per line of authority; Renewal fee: $27 per line of authority. (3 CCR 702-1:1-2-10-12).
   b. License term: License expires biennially on the last day of the licensee's birthday month.
   c. Lines of authority:

      (1) Life.
      (2) Variable life and variable annuity products.

(3) Accident and health.
(4) Property.
(5) Casualty.
(6) Personal lines.

2. *Limited Lines Producers.*

(1) Credit.
(2) Title.
(3) Attorney title (must show proof of attorney license for Colorado; no exam required).
(4) Travel ticket.
(5) Crop/Hail.
(C.R.S. §10-2-407).

Two different bail bonding licenses are available:

a. *Surety Bonding Agent:* One who writes surety bonds for the insurer.
b. *Professional Cash Bail Agent:* A person who furnishes bail for compensation in any court or courts in Colorado in connection with judicial proceedings and by posting a bond with the division in lieu of being appointed by a bail insurance company. A professional cash bail agent is neither a full time salaried officer or employee of an insurer nor a person who pledges United States currency, a United States postal money order, a cashier's check, or other property in connection with a judicial proceeding, whether for compensation or otherwise. (C.R.S. §10-23-101).
Must have been licensed as a bail agent for four years, take a registered bail recovery training course as required by statute, and post a bond of $50,000. Must also be fingerprinted by local law enforcement, or any third party approved by the Colorado Bureau of Investigation, and pay fees for fingerprinting and background check. (C.R.S. §§10-23-103; 10-23-105).
An individual who applies for original registration must:

1. Complete the required application form.
2. Meet the minimum requirements for registration as a Professional Cash-Bail Agent.
3. Pay a registration fee of $183.00.
4. Submit the Qualification Bond.
5. Register any fictitious, former or trade names with the division. (3 CCR 702-7: 7-1-1-5(A)).

Registration renewal notices are generally mailed ninety days before the registration expiration date. An individual who applies to renew a registration must complete the required renewal application form and submit a renewal fee of $183. Likewise, an individual who applies for reinstatement of a registration must complete the required application form and pay the renewal fee of $183. A registrant whose registration has been expired or inactive for more than one year shall be required to apply in the same manner as is required for original registration, including satisfying the requirement that the individual be licensed as an insurance producer who furnishes bail bonds in Colorado for four years before making an application. (3 CCR 702-7:7-1-1-5(B), (C) and (D)).

All registrations are biennial and expire on the first day of January each year. New registrants will be given an initial registration expiration date that is no earlier than twelve months from the original registration date. Registrations that are expired but renewed within grace period will be given an initial expiration date that is no earlier than twelve months from the original registration date. Registrations that are reinstated outside of the grace period and within one year of the expiration date will be given a renewal date that is no earlier than twelve months from the reinstatement date. A registrant who does not renew his registration within the grace period shall be treated as having an expired registration and shall be prohibited from acting as Cash Bonding-Agent or Professional Cash-Bail Agent until and unless such registration is reinstated. (3 CCR 702-7:7-1-1-6).

The insurance department will consider release of the Qualification bond in the following situations:

1. On or after the seventh anniversary of the inactivation date of the license of the Cash-Bonding Agent or a Professional Cash-Bail Agent.

    a. On or after the third anniversary of the death of the registrant provided the heir has provided a copy of the registrant's death certificate, and a written request for release of the bond including the name and address of the appropriate heir to receive a copy of the order.
    b. If three years since the registrants death have not passed, the heir must provide a copy of the registrant's death certificate, a list of all Colorado municipal courts in which the registrant posted bail bonds, an original affidavit from each court clerk of the courts listed as well as the Denver County court clerk that no bail bond liability exists for the registrant, and an affidavit stating that all collateral held by the registrant have been released.

2. Upon request of a former Registrant within the seven-year period specified in C.R.S. § 10-23-105(5) if the request for relief:

    a. Is in writing and signed and notarized by the Registrant.
    b. Includes the date the Registrant registration was no longer effective.
    c. Includes a list of every Colorado municipal court in which the Registrant posted bail bonds.
    d. Includes an original affidavit by each court clerk for the municipal courts listed in (c) above and by the Denver County court clerk that attests that there exists no bail bond liability in said court for the Registrant.
    e. Includes an original affidavit by the Registrant that all collateral taken as security on a bail bond has been returned or released. Prior to registration, the cash bail agent must produce the documentation listed below. Likewise, those previously licensed and currently registered with the division who have posted qualification bonds that complied with 3 CCR 702-7:7-1-2 must provide verification that the qualification bond satisfies the following statutory requirements:

1. The qualification bond form that is attached as Appendix A of 3 CCR 702-7:7-1-2.
2. A copy of the bank account application, certificate of deposit, or commercial instrument or actual deposit of other security that evidences that the qualification bond is solely owned and in the legal name of the cash-bonding agent, division and commissioner. The division and commissioner must also be authorized signatories on the bank account, certificate of deposit, commercial instrument, or other security with a right of survivorship as described in C.R.S. §10-23-105(3).
3. A statement from the bank or other financial institution where the qualification bond is held that the bank or financial institution shall not release such funds unless upon prior written approval or order by the Division or Commissioner.
4. If the monies that fund the qualification bond consist of proceeds from a loan, promissory note or other financial arrangement, the terms of the loan, promissory note, or financial arrangement must be submitted to the division for review of their compliance with C.R.S. §10-23-105.

A professional cash-bail agent who fails to alter the qualification bond in compliance with this regulation prior to the registration renewal date shall have their registration renewal denied on grounds that the professional cash-bail agent has not satisfied the requirements of registration. Once information is on file with the division as satisfying the requirements of this regulation, the professional cash bail agent shall not be required to submit information related to the qualification bond on future renewal applications unless specifically requested by the division. After the professional cash-bail agent complies with C.R.S. § 10-23-105, and this regulation, the professional cash-bail agent must notify the division within twenty days of any change to the qualification bond that results in noncompliance. (3 CCR 702-7:7-1-2).

Each cash bonding-agent and professional cash bail-agent must file a complete premium fee statement for the reporting period with the division, as applicable, by January 15 each year. If a cash-bonding agent or professional-cash bail agent did not write any bail bonds during the reporting period, the individual still must file a completed Statement of No Premium by the same date. Both Premium Fee Statements and Statements of No Premium must be filed electronically using the division's Web-based application, which is available on the division's Web site. Any premium fee must be received by the division no later than January 15 and must be paid via check or money order. (3 CCR 702-7:7-1-2).

3. *Business Entities.* Must request trade name be added to their license. Sole proprietorships and limited partnerships must call Taxpayer Service, 303-534-1208, for procedures to register the assumed name with the Department of Revenue. (3 CCR § 702-1:1-2-10; C.R.S. § 10-2-701).

4. *Managing General Agents.* Must be licensed in Colorado as an insurance producer and must have a contract with the insurer(s) for which one is acting as a managing general agent. A bond shall be kept on file with each insurer with which the managing general agent has a contract. The insurer shall have on file an independent audited annual financial statement. All Colorado domiciled insurers contracting with a managing general agent shall submit to the Division of Insurance a completed Colorado Managing General Agent questionnaire with its annual statement. (3 CCR 702-1:1-2-7).

Other Insurance Professionals

1. *Public Adjusters.* Colorado requires that public adjusters be licensed as such in this state. A public adjuster is defined as a representative of an insurance claimant in situations only where an adjuster can act for an insurance company or any insured. Fees: initial, $47; renewal: $27. License expires on last day of birth month. Nonresident fees: initial, $71; renewal: $43. Must have a bond of at least $20,000, or more if the commissioner specifies an additional amount. (C.R.S. §§ 10-2-417, and 10-2-103; 3 CCR 702-1:1-2-10; https://home.pearsonvue.com/getattachment/9df8c6db-f2e3-4d14-a674-f07ba560388c/Colorado%20Division%20of%20Insurance%20Licensing%20Candidate%20Handbook.aspx, Candidate Handbook, page 13).

2. *Reinsurance Intermediaries.* Intermediary-producer requires five years of responsible insurance experience; intermediary-manager requires ten years. Managers must also file an E&O policy and a bond. They do not need to be licensed as producers. Fee: $200, new and renewal.

   All licenses expire biennially on the licensee's birthday. Individuals, corporations, and partnerships are licensed and each producer in a firm must be licensed. (3 CCR 702-1:1-2-6).

3. *Bail Bonding Agent:* A licensed insurance producer who is appointed by a bail insurance company to act as its agent to write bail bonds in accordance with C.R.S. § 10-2-415.5. (3 CCR 702-1:1-2-16).

   License available for Colorado residents only; initial fee is $183; biennial fee is $183. Examination fee $41. License is renewed biennially on January 1. All applicants for a bail bond agent license must submit their completed fingerprint card directly to the Colorado Bureau of Investigation (CBI), (or have digital prints taken via a third party approved by the CBI who will transmit them), prior to sitting for the examination. The division shall not license law enforcement or judicial officers as bonding agents. The nonrefundable fingerprinting fee is $39.50.

Bail bond agent applicants must not:

a. Have been convicted of a felony or any crime within ten years of the date of application.
b. Have served a jail sentence for conviction of a felony or any other crime involving moral turpitude; or have been under the supervision of the division of parole or any probation department within the last ten years from the date of completion or release. (C.R.S. §10-23-103).

4. To be eligible for a temporary license the applicant must make a reservation within the appropriate lead time period, pass the examination, meet the minimum licensing requirements as set forth in the candidate handbook (available in the licensing section of the Division of Insurance website) and pay the appropriate fees.

5. Resident producers applying for, renewing, or continuing the variable life and variable annuity products line of authority, in addition to holding the life authority, must furnish evidence that they have passed the test to be registered and are

currently registered with a Financial Industry Regulatory Authority (FINRA) member firm, broker or dealer with a FINRA membership.

6. Any person holding a Colorado resident or nonresident surplus lines license, or the equivalent issued by another state or territory that offers Colorado surplus lines producers a nonresident license on a reciprocal basis can be licensed as a surplus lines producer so long as the resident producer conducts business in accordance with the provisions of Colorado's statutes and the resident or nonresident surplus lines producer promptly remits the taxes required by C.R.S. § 10-5-111.Applicants must also hold a Property and Casualty license. (Candidate Handbook).

C. **Appointments:** Colorado only requires appointments for bail bond agents. Bail insurance companies must notify the commissioner of insurance of each bail bonding appointment or termination. Moreover, bail insurance companies are encouraged to verify appointment or termination with the National Insurance Producer Registry at https://nipr.com/products-and-services/nipr-gateway/appointment-renewals. Bail insurance companies are required to mail termination notices to the department of insurance and to bail bonding agents by certified mail within fifteen days of termination. (C.R.S. §§ 10-2-415.5, -.7).

A bail insurance company shall complete the following prior to appointing an insurance producer as a bail bonding agent:

1. Confirm that the insurance producer's identity, residence, licensure and instruction as recorded with the division is accurate.

2. Obtain documentation that the insurance producer has completed the training required by C.R.S. §10-2-415.5(2)(c). Moreover, the bail insurance company shall maintain these documents for the duration of the insurance producer's appointment and for three years thereafter and shall provide these documents to the division upon written request.

3. Be satisfied that the bail bonding agent is trustworthy and qualified to act as its agent and that the bail bonding agent will hold herself out in good faith to the general public as the bail insurance company's bail bonding agent.

Additionally, all appointments must be effectuated by the bail insurance company using the division's online licensing and appointment system. A nonrefundable appointment fee of $95 will be collected at the time the initial appointment is entered into the online licensing and appointment system. Prior to October 1 of each year, the division will provide each bail insurance company a listing of its active insurance producer appointments and a renewal invoice. Renewal fee is $95.

The insurance division is required to issue credentials to each insurance producer who is appointed by a bail insurance company. (C.R.S. § 10-2-418). All credentials issued will be valid for one year. These credentials will be issued by the division during the month following the birth month of the producer. (3 CCR 702-1:1-2-16).

D. **Licenses Required of Nonresidents:** The same licenses are required of nonresidents wishing to conduct insurance activities in connection with Colorado property or operations. Nonresidents must do the following:

1. Complete an NAIC Uniform Nonresident Application Form from www.nipr.com or www.sircon.com/colorado.

2. Pay an initial fee of $71 per line of authority or a renewal fee of $43 per line of authority. For surplus lines, the initial nonresident fee is $294 the renewal fee is $284.

3. Nonresident producers applying for, renewing or continuing the variable life and variable annuity products line of authority must meet the requirements of their resident state and have a current registration with a FINRA member firm, broker or dealer with a FINRA membership and must show exam scores from series 6, 63, or 7 type securities exams.

All licensed producers working for an agency must be licensed in Colorado as a resident or nonresident producer and be registered to the agency if they are servicing a Colorado policy and receiving commissions on behalf of that agency. The application for a nonresident license automatically appoints the commissioner as agent for the service of process. (3 CCR 702-1:1-2-10).

Applicants must submit electronic applications through www.sircon.com/colorado or www.nipr.com. Paper applications will only be accepted on an exceptional basis where an electronic application cannot be submitted. Nonownership of a computer is not considered an exception.

Multi-State Exposures: A license is not required for a nonresident insurance producer who sells, solicits, or negotiates a contract of insurance for commercial property and casualty coverage when risks that are to be insured under that contract are located in more than one state. This exception applies only if the nonresident is licensed to sell, solicit, or negotiate that insurance in the state where the insured maintains its principal place of business and the contract of insurance insures risks located in that state. (C.R.S. § 10-2-105).

E. Prelicensing Examination and Education Requirements:

The Colorado Division of Insurance uses only electronic process for new license and renewal applications, agency registrations, letter of certification requests, address changes and CE course tracking. Paper applications/requests for these transactions will be returned, unprocessed, if received.

1. *Residents.*

   a. Producer applicants must complete the following prelicensing education, prior to taking and passing the exam: fifty hours for life; fifty for health; fifty for property; fifty for casualty; or fifty for combined property and casualty; and fifty for personal lines. Three hours of the fifty required hours must be on insurance industry ethics. Three hours of the fifty required hours must be on Colorado insurance laws and regulations that are general in nature and not related to the specific line of business. Four hours of the fifty required hours must be on Colorado insurance laws and regulations that are specifically related to the line of business. Individuals applying for more than one line of authority, the three hours of ethics need only be taken once. (C.R.S. § 10-2-201).
   Fee for all exams is $41 due at time of reservation. Fees are not accepted at the test center. To change or cancel a reservation call (800) 274-2616 at least 48 hours prior to the exam or you will forfeit any chance of a refund. (Candidate Handbook, p.15).
   Passing score is 70 percent or higher.
   Prelicensing certificates of completion shall be valid for a period of one year from the date of completion. Prelicensing certificates of completion that are more than one year old will not be accepted by the division and students will be required to take an approved prelicensing course. (3 CCR 702-1:1-2-5).

   b. Applicants for a variable products license must show proof of current FINRA registration and exam scores for series 6, 63, or 7 type securities exams. (3 CCR 702-1:1-2-10).

   c. As a condition of initial licensure, an applicant must provide evidence to the commissioner that the applicant has satisfactorily completed an approved prelicensing course as follows: ... An applicant seeking a producer license for property or casualty insurance or both shall complete at least fifty hours of an approved course for certification for property or casualty insurance, or both. At least three of the fifty total hours must pertain to industry ethics.
   An applicant seeking a producer license to include life, sickness and accident, property, or casualty lines or any combination of them shall not be eligible to sit for the written exam described in C.R.S. § 10-2-402 until the above

prelicensing education requirements described above have been satisfied. (C.R.S. § 10-2-201).

d. Bail bond applicants must complete the following:

   (1) Complete the bail bond prelicense education course (total of eight hours): two hours on the criminal court system; two hours on bail recovery industry ethics; and four hours on the laws relating to bail bonds.
   (2) Complete the bail training recovery course (total of up to sixteen hours): Introduction to Bail Recovery, three hours; Principles of Criminal Culpability, three hours; Colorado Criminal Code, three hours; Firearms and Weapons, three hours; Seizure and Entry, two hours. (C.R.S. §10-2-415.5).
   (3) Pass the Pearson VUE exam.

e. Credit applicants must pass the credit exam.
f. Title applicants must pass the title exam.
g. An individual holding a current and valid AAI, ARM, CIC or CPCU designation is exempt from prelicensing education for property and casualty lines of authority. An individual holding a current and valid RHU, CEBS, REBC or HIA designation is exempt from prelicensing education for accident and health or sickness lines of authority. An individual holding a CEBS, ChFC, CIC, CFP, CLU, FLMI or LUTCF designation is exempt from prelicensing education for the life line of authority. (3 CCR 702-1:1-2-5).
   Also exempt is the holder of a bachelors degree with a major in insurance. Applicants for credit authority who already hold life, health, property, or casualty authority are authorized to write credit insurance under their major line authority. Colorado residents wanting only a limited lines credit authority must take and pass the credit exam. Applicants for crop hail authority who already hold the property or casualty lines of authority are authorized to write crop/hail under their major line property and casualty authorities. Colorado residents wanting only a limited lines crop/hail authority must take and pass the crop/hail exam. Attorneys currently licensed with the Colorado Bar Association are exempt from the title exam requirement for title authority. No exam is required of applicants for travel ticket authority. Pearson VUE handles prelicensing for Colorado, 800-275-8247.

2. *Nonresidents.* Nonresidents are exempt from Colorado prelicensing education requirements if they are licensed in their home state and have met the educational requirements of that state. Nonresident producer new license fee is $71.00 per authority. Renewal fee is $43.00 per authority. (Candidate Handbook, p. 13).

3. *Exemptions.* The following types of applicants are exempt from the prelicensing education requirements outlined above:

   (a) Applying to reinstate a cancelled or expired resident producer license in this state when said license has been inactive for one year or less.
   (b) Applying for temporary licensing authority pursuant to C.R.S. § 10-2-410.
   (c) Applying for a nonresident license in this state pertaining to the lines of authority held in the applicant's home state.

F. Continuing Education Requirements:

Number of Hours Required: Applicable to producers. Twenty-four hours of self-study or classroom instruction, biennially (eighteen hours must be in licensee's active lines). Also applies to HMOs and to nonprofit lines of authority. A maximum of six of the twenty-four credit hours shall be in approved courses on subjects designated by the commissioner whenever the commissioner determines that continuing education in such subjects is needed to protect insurance consumers. At least three of the twenty-four hours must be in an ethics course. In no instance, may a producer count as part of the twenty-four hours, a course taught by an immediate supervisor or employee of the producer acting in the capacity of supervisor or employee. Those individuals licensed as reinsurance intermediary brokers must complete the required continuing education through professional seminars or curriculum within the reinsurance field. Producers may accumulate no more than twelve carryover credit hours during the 120 days before the licensing continuation date, which may be applied to the next continuing education period. (C.R.S. § 10-2-301).

Any person who engages in solicitation or enrollment of membership in a health maintenance organization (HMO) or nonprofit hospital, medical-surgical and health service corporation is considered a producer and must be licensed by the commissioner of insurance. A license for HMO or nonprofit issued on or before January 1, 2002 may be renewed or continued until the licensee fails to meet the continuation requirements. Please note, there will be no new licenses issued for these lines of authority on or after January 1, 2002. (3 CCR 702-1:1-2-10).

In meeting the aforementioned CE requirements, producers must comply with the following:

1. In determining the number of credit hours to be counted toward meeting the required hours, the instructor shall qualify for the same number of hours of continuing education as the person attending and successfully completing the

course or program. A qualified instructor may not count instruction hours for the same course more than once during a twenty-four month period.

2. A producer who successfully completes an approved course may not repeat the course within a two-year period and count it toward the required hours, except for courses dealing with statutory updates.

3. If a producer works for a company with a qualified home office located in Colorado and that company provides a course of study for their producers, this will satisfy the continuing education requirement. The company must produce a certification letter attesting to successful completion of the company's course of study. This certification letter must be signed by the producer and endorsed by the company's licensing official. (3 CCR 702-1:1-2-4).

It is the responsibility of the producer to maintain records sufficient to document successful completion of twenty-four credit hours on a biennial basis. This information shall be maintained for a period of five years from licensing continuation and shall be made available for audit. (3 CCR 702-1:1-2-4).

Nonresidents. If a nonresident producer has satisfied the continuing education requirements of his or her home state, this will constitute satisfaction of Colorado's continuing education requirements so long as the nonresident producer's home state recognizes the satisfaction of its continuing education requirements imposed upon producers from Colorado on the same basis. Nonresident producers, whose home state does not recognize satisfaction of Colorado's continuing education requirement, must comply with the Colorado continuing insurance education requirements. (3 CCR 702-1:1-2-4). Nonresident public adjusters are exempt from the Colorado exam requirement if their license is active and they have met all requirements of their resident state. (C.R.S. § 10-2-403). Nonresident producer license fee is $71.00 per authority. Renewal fee is $43.00 per authority. (Candidate Handbook, p. 13).

For those producers marketing long-term care (LTC) insurance: the one-time training required shall be no less than sixteen hours. Eight hours of which shall consist of general long-term care which may be completed as a self-study, online, or classroom course and eight hours of which shall be specific to long-term care partnerships in a classroom setting. The ongoing training required by this section shall be no less than five hours in a classroom setting. (C.R.S. § 10-19-113.6).

Nonresident LTC Agents. Group long-term-care coverage may not be offered to Colorado residents under a group policy issued in another state to a group under C.R.S.

§ 10-19-103(4)(d) unless this state, or another state having substantially similar statutory and regulatory long-term care policy requirements to those adopted in this state, has determined that such requirements have been met. (C.R.S. § 10-19-105).

For those producers marketing claims-made policies, a one-time course of two hours is required. Courses may not be repeated for two years. Colorado will consider nonresidents in compliance with the CE requirements if they have satisfied the continuing education requirements of their home state.

Submit proof of completion by biennial license renewal date.

Those individuals licensed as reinsurance intermediary brokers must complete the required continuing education through professional seminars or curriculum within the reinsurance field. Producers may accumulate no more than twelve carryover credit hours during the 120 days before the licensing continuation date, which may be applied to the next continuing education period. (3 CCR 702-1:1-2-4).

Excess Hours: A maximum of twelve hours may be carried into the next reporting period. Excess hours are only those hours earned within the 120 days immediately preceding renewal date.

Final Exam: must be monitored for self-study courses.

Renewal Procedure:

1. Course providers give the licensee a copy of Colorado Course Completion Certificate (CE-03). The licensee must keep this certificate for five years. In the event the producer allows his or her license to lapse for more than one year, they will be required to provide a copy of this certificate for reinstatement or they will be required to complete a new prelicensing education course.

2. Submit application online at Sircon.com for renewal along with renewal fee. Nonresidents are exempt on a reciprocal basis. They must submit a license renewal and appropriate fees.

G. **Cancellation of Agency Contracts/Producer Appointments:** Group long-term-care coverage may not be offered to Colorado residents under a group policy issued in another state to a group under C.R.S. § 10-19-103(4)(d) unless this state, or another state having substantially similar statutory and regulatory long-term care policy requirements to those adopted in this state, has determined that such requirements have been met. (C.R.S. § 10-19-105).

H. **Rules for Risk Retention and Purchasing Groups:** Domestic risk retention groups must be licensed as liability insurance companies and submit a plan of operation to the commissioner. A group from out of state must submit a copy of the plan it submitted within its own state. For a full list of documentation that every risk retention group must submit, consult 3 CCR 702-2:2-1-8, or contact the Division of Insurance. Every application form for insurance from a risk retention group, and every policy (on its front and declaration pages) issued by a risk retention group, shall contain in ten point type the following notice:

NOTICE

"NOTICE THIS POLICY IS ISSUED BY YOUR RISK RETENTION GROUP. YOUR RISK RETENTION GROUP MAY NOT BE SUBJECT TO ALL OF THE INSURANCE LAWS AND REGULATIONS OF YOUR STATE. STATE INSURANCE INSOLVENCY GUARANTY FUNDS ARE NOT AVAILABLE FOR YOUR RISK RETENTION GROUP." (3 CCR 702-2:2-1-8).

I. **Other License Rules, Requirements, or Restrictions:** All license applications are electronic and can be accessed at www.sircon.com/colorado or www.NIPR.com. Licensing assistance can be obtained by contacting Pearson VUE at 800-275-8247 or Email PVColoradoInsurance@pearson.com.

Nonresidents must be certified by their home state insurance department for the lines for which Colorado license is desired. Licensed nonresidents may enter Colorado to solicit, inspect, and service. (C.R.S. §§ 10-2-501 to -503). Unlicensed nonresidents may not enter the state for any of these purposes. Entering the state includes mail or telephone or other electronic communication into the state from the outside, as well as physical presence in the state.

Colorado Division of Insurance offers a paperless license process with no paper licenses mailed. Producers are afforded the ability to print out a license certificate through Sircon Compliance Express located at www.sircon.com/colorado. Print function is free within the first thirty days following the initial or renewal issuance of the license. A fee of $5 will be charged for printing a license outside of this thirty-day period. This change affects all licenses issued by the Division of Insurance, except bail bond licenses which will continue to be provided on paper.

Email Notification. Producers who provide a valid email address will receive notifications of renewal/continuation approximately ninety days prior to the expiration date of the license. Approximately ninety days prior to renewal date, producers will receive a renewal notice through the U.S. Postal Service from the Division of Insurance. This notice will provide detailed information regarding the on-line renewal process. All licensed producers are reminded that the continuation of their license is their responsibility and should take care when authorizing licensing services or employers to continue their license. Errors made by employers and/or licensing services are not excluded should a license lapse. (3 CCR 702-1:1-2-10).

The following regulations were effected by House Bill 12-1266: 3 CCR 702-1:1-2-14, 702-7, 702-1:1-2-16, 702-1:1-2-5, 702-1:1-2-10, 702-1:1-2-4, and 702-1:1-2-15. Furthermore, the Colorado Insurance Division issued Emergency Regulations 12-E-01 to 12E-11 to effect the legislative changes of Bill 12-1266. SB17-236, Section 1 and 2 of the bill continue the regulation of cash bonding and professional cash bail agents until September 1, 2026.

The following rules are applicable to insurance producers authorized to write bail bonds in Colorado:

1. *Annual Report*. The annual report must be filed by October 1st of the calendar year following the conclusion of the reporting year. For example, if the reporting year is July 1, 2014, through June 30, 2015, then the annual report is due by October 1, 2015. An annual report must be filed by every insurance producer who was at any time during the reporting year appointed by a bail insurance company. The report must be filed regardless of the producer's license status on the due date, or appointment status on the due date or whether the producer wrote any bail bond business during the reporting year. It must be filed by October 1st of the calendar year following the conclusion of the reporting year. For example, if the reporting year is July 1, 2014, through June 30, 2015, then the annual report is due by October 1, 2015. Additionally, the annual report must be filed electronically using the division's Web-based application, which is available on the division's Web site. The division will not accept filings in any other format or manner. (The above still applies due to 3 CCR 702-1:1-2-14).

2. *Disclosure Statement*. The disclosure statement must not be altered and must be issued in the format contained in Appendix A of Emergency Regulation 12-E-05. It must be signed and dated by the producer and the defendant or third party indemnitor. Furthermore, a disclosure statement must be provided to each defendant who provides consideration, pays premium or pledges collateral and to each third party indemnitor who provides consideration, pays premium or pledges collateral. (3 CCR 702-1:1-2-14, 1-2-20; C.R.S. § 10-2-705).

J. Policy Countersignature Requirements: None.

K. Portable Electronics Insurance: Vendors of portable electronic devices who want to offer insurance policies to cover those devices must obtain a limited lines license. The vendor's license will cover employees and authorized representatives of the vendor to sell such insurance policies. If a vendor offers portable electronics insurance to customers, he or she must make available brochures or other written information that includes the following:

(1) Disclosure that such insurance may be duplicative of coverage under an existing homeowner's or renter's policy.

(2) State that enrollment in such a policy is not required to purchase or lease portable electronics.

(3) Summarize the material terms of the coverage.

(4) Summarize the process of filing a claim.

(5) State that the customer may cancel the policy at any time, and that the person paying the premium will receive a refund of any unearned premium.

The licensing procedure is the same as for all other lines of authority. Training must be provided for each employee or authorized representative before they are authorized under the vendor license to sell insurance products. Portable electronic insurance is intended to cover electronic devices that are portable in nature, their accessories and services related to the use of the device such as cellphones, smartphones, tablet computers and similar items. (C.R.S. §§ 10-4-1502 to -1504).

II. Commissions, Fees, Commingling of Funds, and Suitability in Annuity Transactions

A. Commissions: No insurer or insurance producer shall pay, directly or indirectly, any commission, service fee, brokerage, or other valuable consideration to any person selling, soliciting, or negotiating insurance in Colorado unless, at the time such services were performed, such person was a duly licensed insurance producer. No person, other than a person appropriately licensed by the state as an insurance producer at the time such services were performed, shall accept any such consideration; except that any person duly licensed under this article may pay or assign such person's commissions to, or direct that such person's commissions be paid to, a partnership of which the person is a member, employee, or agent or to a corporation of which the person is an officer, employee, or agent. This shall not prevent payment or receipt of renewal or other deferred commissions to or by any person entitled thereto.

Except for individuals or entities writing bail, an insurer or insurance producer may pay or assign commissions, service fees, brokerages, or other valuable consideration to an insurance agency, business entity, or persons who do not sell, solicit, or negotiate insurance in this state, unless the payment would violate section C.R.S. § 10-3-1104(1)(g). (C.R.S. § 10-2-702).

B. **Fees:** Insurance producers may not charge separate fees in addition to those contemplated in the rate filings and included in their commissions for the solicitation and procurement of insurance products and for servicing existing insurance policyholders. Fees may be charged for specific services that are beyond the scope of services pertaining to acquiring and/or maintaining specific insurance policies. Any such fees charged must be agreed to in advance by the client and the appropriate disclosure statement must be signed.

Colorado permits "wholesale intermediaries" to charge fees provided they give notice to the agent of the insured in writing that "the cost of the insurance coverage provided herein includes a fee to a wholesale intermediary in addition to the premium charge"The Colorado Insurance Department defines a wholesale intermediary as an independent office procuring surplus lines insurance on behalf of a retailer. (3 CCR 702-1:1-2-9).

C. **Disclosure Requirements:** Fees may be charged when the client signs a disclosure statement in advance of the performance of the specific services, which states that the client is under no obligation to purchase any insurance product through the insurance producer in exchange for receiving the specific services. This requirement may be met by including the disclosure language in any disclosure statement required by federal or state securities law. Additionally, fees may be charged in those cases where it is clear from the outset that no insurance product sale related to the specific services rendered will occur through the insurance producer. (3 CCR 702-1:1-2-9).

D. **Commingling of Funds:** No insurance producer shall commingle premiums belonging to insurers and returned premiums belonging to insureds with the producer's personal funds or with any other funds except those directly connected with the producer's insurance business. Upon receipt, the insurance producer or agency shall treat all premiums and returned premiums in a fiduciary capacity. Producers, including nonresidents collecting Colorado premiums, must maintain a trust fund for premiums collected on behalf of insurers, separate from any other agency funds. (C.R.S. §10-2-704).

E. **Suitability in Annuity Transactions:** Producers who hold a life insurance line of authority prior to April 1, 2011 must complete a one-time four-hour annuity training course by October 1, 2011. Individuals who obtain a life insurance line of authority on or after April 1, 2011 may not engage in the sale of annuities until they have completed the training. The training requirement applies to both resident and nonresident producers. A substantially similar course completed in another state will meet this requirement. (3 CCR 702-4).

Colorado has adopted the NAIC Suitability in Annuity Transactions Model Regulation. (standard.com/financial-professional/annuities/naic-suitability-state).

III. Statutory References: C.R.S. §§ 10-2-103, -105; 10-2-201; 10-2-301; 10-2-401, -403, -407, -410, -415.5 to -418; 10-2-501 to -503; 10-2-701, -702, -704, -705; 10-3-1104; 10-4-1502 to -1504; 10-5-111; 10-19-103, -105; 10-23-101, -103, -105. 3 CCR 702-1:1-2-4 to 1-2-7, 1-2-9, 1-2-10, 1-2-14, 1-2-16; 702-2-2-1-8; 702-4; 702-7:7-1-1, 7-1-2. Candidate Handbook pp. 13, 15.

CONNECTICUT

Insurance Department
PO Box 816; Hartford, CT 06142-0816
Physical Address: 153 Market St. (960 Main Bldg.),
Fl 7, Hartford, CT 06103
Main Telephone: 860-297-3800
Toll-free Number: 1 (800) 203-3447
Main Fax: 860-566-7410
Licensing Telephone: 860-297-3845
Licensing Fax: 860-297-3978
Email: cid.licensing@ct.gov
https://www.ct.gov/cid

I. Licensing Requirements: Producers (Standard Lines and Limited Lines); Fraternal Agents; Rental Car Companies; Surplus Lines Brokers; Title Insurance Agents. Other Insurance Professionals—Casualty Claim Adjusters; Certified Insurance Consultants; Life Settlement Brokers, Motor Vehicle Physical Damage Appraisers; Premium Finance Companies; Public Adjusters; Reinsurance Intermediary Brokers; Reinsurance Intermediary Managers; and Third-Party Administrators.

A. Applicability: A person shall not sell, solicit or negotiate insurance in Connecticut for any class or classes of insurance unless the person is licensed for that line of authority. (Conn. Gen. Stat. § 38a-702b).

B. Licenses Required of Residents: Each of the following must be licensed in Connecticut:

Producers

1. *Standard Lines Producers.*

   a. License fee: Initial fee, individuals: $140. Initial fee, Business Entities: $130. Amendment and reinstatement fee: $130. Applications: NAIC Uniform Application for Individual Insurance Producer License and Uniform Application for Business Entity Insurance License/Registration or online as shown below.
   b. License term: Individuals–Biennial. Individuals $160; renews on licensee's birthday, providing that resident licensees holding major lines of authority have satisfied their continuing education requirements and nonresident licensees continue to be licensed in good standing in their resident license state. Late fee: $320 within twelve months of license lapse. Business entities $160; renew on January 31 of every even-numbered year, providing that nonresident licensees continue to be licensed in their resident state.

Late fee: $320. (cidverifylicense.ct.gov/CLIC/LicenseType.html; Conn. Gen. Stat. § 38a-784).

c. An insurance producer may receive qualification for a license in one or more of the following lines of authority:

(1) Life
(2) Accident & Health or sickness
(3) Property
(4) Casualty
(5) Variable life and variable annuity products
(6) Personal Lines
(7) Credit
(8) Any other line of insurance permitted under this state's laws or regulations (cidonline.ct.gov/lit/inq/).

2. *Limited Lines Producers.*

a. License term and fees are the same as for standard lines producers.
b. Lines of Authority:

(1) *Credit Limited Line:* including credit life; credit accident and health; credit disability; credit property; credit unemployment; involuntary unemployment; mortgage life; mortgage guaranty; mortgage disability; and guaranteed automobile protection (GAP), and any other insurance offered in connection with an extension of credit.
(2) *Travel Limited Line:* including travel accident and baggage; and trip cancellation.

Authority to sell credit and travel limited lines coverage is automatically included in all standard lines producer licenses. Absent a standard lines producer license, a separate credit and/or travel limited line producer license is required for each. (Conn. Gen. Stat. §§ 38a-702a; 38a-398).

3. *Fraternal Agents.* License expires December 31 of odd-numbered years. Initial fee: $130; biennial renewal fee: $80; amendment and reinstatement fee: $130.00. Application: Individual Fraternal Agent's License/Appointment. Variable Contracts applicants must have life authority and a current Series 6 or 7 FINRA registration. Acts as an agent for a fraternal society and sells life, accident & health, or annuities only. Only individuals can be licensed in this capacity. Applications must be submitted by licensed fraternal societies only. (Conn. Gen. Stat. §§ 38a-764; 38a-800).

4. *Rental Car Companies.* All rental car companies that offer insurance in connection with the rental of a vehicle must obtain a permit to transact business in this limited capacity. Permit expires February 31 of each even-numbered year. Initial fee: $80; biennial renewal fee: $80. (Conn. Gen. Stat. § 38a-799(h); Conn. Gen. Stat. § 38a-11) Contact the department for a licensing/information packet. (cid.verifylicense.ct.gov/CLIC/LicenseType.html)

   The lines of insurance are:

   a. Personal accident insurance covering the risks of travel, including accident and health insurance, that provides coverage to renters and other rental vehicle occupants for accidental death or dismemberment and reimbursement for medical expenses resulting from an accident that occurs during the rental period.
   b. Liability insurance, including uninsured and underinsured motorist coverage whether offered separately or in combination with other liability insurance that provides coverage to renters and other authorized drivers of rental vehicles for liability arising from the operation of the rental vehicle.
   c. Personal effects insurance that provides coverage to renters and other vehicle occupants for the loss of, or damage to, personal effects that occurs during the rental period.
   d. Roadside assistance and emergency sickness protection programs.

   Each rental car company shall provide a training program to all employees who will be marketing insurance products to potential car renters. The training program must be in accordance with Conn. Gen. Stat. §38a-799 and supporting regulations. (Conn. Gen. Stat. § 38a-799(d)).

5. *Title Insurance Agents.* License requirement was repealed June 3, 1996. However, to solicit, negotiate, or sell title insurance, one must be a commissioner of the Connecticut Superior Court in good standing, except any individual holding a valid title agent license on or before June 12, 1984. (Conn. Gen. Stat. § 38a-402(13)).

Other Insurance Professionals

1. *Casualty Claim Adjusters.* License expires June 30th of odd-numbered years. Initial fee: $130; biennial renewal fee: $80. Applications: Individual Casualty Claim Adjuster License and Business Entity Casualty Claim Adjuster License. Lines of authority are: All lines, all lines except Workers' Compensation, Workers' Compensation only, and auto only. This license is required for any person who will investigate property or casualty claims and negotiate settlement of or subrogation of such claims arising under policies of insurance on behalf of insurers under such

policies or who advertises or solicits business from insurers as an adjuster before engaging in the adjusting of any claims. A casualty claim adjuster all lines or all lines except workers compensation license is required to adjust pet insurance claims. (cid.verifylicense.ct.gov/CLIC/LicenseType.html; Conn. Gen. Stat. § 38a-792).

a. A casualty claim adjuster license is not required to adjust fire, life, or accident and health claims.
b. A licensed producer with an agent appointment settling property damage claims of $1,500 or less, on behalf of the appointing insurer, does not require a casualty claim adjuster license.
c. Any member of the Connecticut Bar, in good standing, who is engaged in the general practice of law, does not require a casualty claim adjuster license. (Conn. Gen. Stat. §38a-792).

2. *Certified Insurance Consultants.* License expires September 30th of odd-numbered years. Initial fee: $300; biennial renewal fee: $250. Application: individual certified insurance consultant and business entity certified insurance consultant. Lines of authority include life/accident & health and property/casualty. (cid.verifylicense.ct.gov/CLIC/LicenseType.html; Conn. Gen. Stat. § 38a-786).

3. *Life Settlement Brokers.* License expires March 31st each year. Initial fee: $66; annual renewal fee: $40. Applications: Individual Life Settlement Broker and Business Entity Life Settlement Broker. Effective October, 1, 2008, life settlement broker means any person who, on behalf of a policy owner and for a fee, commission or other valuable consideration, offers or attempts to negotiate life settlement contracts between a policy owner and one or more life settlement providers. If a business entity is involved, only the business entity requires licensure as a life settlement broker. The business entity is required to submit biographical affidavits for all individuals acting on its behalf. (cid.verifylicense.ct.gov/CLIC/LicenseType.html; Conn. Gen. Stat. § 38a-465a).

   A licensed resident producer who has held life authority in this state for at least one year is not required to obtain a separate license to act in the capacity of a life settlement broker. A licensed nonresident producer who has held life authority in their home state for at least one year and holds a nonresident life producer license in Connecticut is not required to obtain a separate license to act in the capacity of a life settlement broker. In both cases, however, the Life Producer Registration to Act as a Life Settlement Broker form and $26 registration fee must be completed and submitted to the department within thirty days of acting as a life settlement broker in this state. If approved an amended producer license will be issued that includes life settlement authority. Business entities are not required to register, but must either meet above eligibility requirements or must apply for a life settlement broker business entity license. (Conn. Gen. Stat. § 38a-465a).

4. *Motor Vehicle Physical Damage Appraisers.* (auto physical damage). License expires June 30th of odd-numbered years. Initial and reinstatement fee: $130; biennial renewal fee: $80. Applications: Individual Motor Vehicle Physical Damage Appraiser and Business Entity Motor Vehicle Physical Damage Appraiser. Any person who has been engaged in the business of motor vehicle physical damage appraising for a period of two consecutive years immediately prior to July 1, 1968, shall be granted a license upon application with no further qualifications. The commissioner may waive the examination requirements, in the case of an applicant who at any time within two years next preceding the date of application has been licensed in this state under a license of the same type as the license applied for. (cid.verifylicense.ct.gov/CLIC/LicenseType.html; Conn. Gen. Stat. § 38a-790).

5. *Premium Finance Companies.* License expires June 30th of each year. Initial fee: $100; annual renewal fee: $50. Applications: Insurance Premium Finance Company Licensure Application. (cid.verifylicense.ct.gov/CLIC/LicenseType.html; Conn. Gen. Stat. § 38a-162).

6. *Public Adjusters.* License expires April 30th of even-numbered years. Initial fee: $300; biennial renewal fee; $250. Applications: Individual Public Adjuster and Business Entity Public Adjuster. Lawyers settling claims for their clients are not considered public adjusters. (cid.verifylicense.ct.gov/CLIC/LicenseType.html; Conn. Gen. Stat. § 38a-723).

7. *Reinsurance Intermediary Brokers.* License expires December 31st of even-numbered years. Initial and reinstatement fee: $675; biennial renewal fee: $625. Applications: Individual Reinsurance Intermediary and Business Entity Reinsurance Intermediary. Power of Attorney forms are required for nonresident applicants. Separate applications are required for broker and manager. (cid.verifylicense.ct.gov/CLIC/LicenseType.html; Conn. Gen. Stat. § 38a-760b).

8. *Reinsurance Intermediary Managers.* License expires December 31st of even-numbered years. Initial and reinstatement fee: $675; biennial renewal fee: $625. Applications: Individual Reinsurance Intermediary and Business Entity Reinsurance Intermediary. Power of Attorney forms are required for nonresident applicants. Separate applications are required for broker and manager. (cid.verifylicense.ct.gov/CLIC/LicenseType.html; Conn. Gen. Stat. § 38a-760b).

9. *Third-Party Administrators (TPAs).* An applicant for a TPA license must submit to the Connecticut Insurance Department an electronic application through the

National Insurance Producer Registry (NIPR) at www.nipr.com. Applicants applying for a TPA license must include with their application evidence that a surety bond has been executed in an amount determined by the commissioner sufficient to protect insurers and other persons utilizing the services of the TPA, but in no event less than the penal sum of $500,000. The surety bond requirement may be waived for applicants who submit the two most recent annual audited financial statements proving the applicant has a positive net worth.

TPAs that administer self-insured governmental or church plans in this state are required to provide evidence of an additional surety bond, which will not be waived, in the greater of $100,000 or 10 percent of the aggregate total amount of self-funded coverage under the governmental or church plans handled in this state and all additional states in which the TPA is authorized to conduct business. License expires September 30th of each year. Initial fee: $500; Renewal fee: $450. TPA Annual Report due July 1st each year. Report fee: $100. (cid.verifylicense.ct.gov/CLIC/LicenseType.html; Conn. Gen. Stat. § 38a-720j; Conn. Gen. Stat. § 38a-11).

C. **Appointments (Producers only):** A producer becomes an agent and requires an agent appointment when acting on behalf of an insurer and its products. An electronic appointment must be submitted to the department, within fifteen business days after the date the agency contract is executed or the first insurance application is submitted. The appointment is valid unless the commissioner determines otherwise. Continuation of appointments is contingent upon receipt of renewal fees, where applicable, payable by each appointing insurer by May 1st of even-numbered years. (Conn. Gen. Stat. §38a-702m).

Domestic Companies: Filing fee: $50; Appointment fee: $100. Appointment fees are billed quarterly for new appointments issued in the prior quarter. A renewal fee of $100 is billed April 30th of even-numbered years for all active appointments.

Foreign companies in reciprocal states (Alaska, Arizona, Colorado, Hawaii, Illinois, Indiana, Maryland, Missouri, Montana, New York, Oregon, and Rhode Island): No filing fee. No appointment fee. Appointment expires April 30th of each even-numbered year.

Foreign Companies in Nonreciprocal States: No filing fee. Appointment fee is $80 if premium tax rate in company's state of domicile is equal to or greater than Connecticut's 1.75 percent. Appointment fee is $20 if premium tax rate in company's state of domicile is less than Connecticut's 1.75 percent. Appointment fees are billed quarterly for new appointments issued in the prior quarter. Renewal fees are equal to appointment fees and are billed April 30th of every even-numbered year for all active appointments. (portal.ct.gov/CID/Licensing/Company-Appointment-Fee-Update-Process; Conn. Gen. Stat. § 38a-784).

D. **Licenses Required of Nonresidents:** The same licenses are required for nonresidents as are required for Connecticut residents. The same renewal dates, terms, and fees apply. The following licenses are reciprocal for nonresidents: casualty claim adjuster (except New York), certified insurance consultant, fraternal agent, life settlement broker, motor vehicle physical damage appraiser, producer, public adjuster, reinsurance intermediary broker, reinsurance intermediary manager, and surplus lines broker. (Conn. Gen. Stat. § 38a-769).

Multi-State Exposures: A license is not required for a nonresident insurance producer who sells, solicits, or negotiates a contract of insurance for commercial property and casualty coverage when risks that are to be insured under that contract are located in more than one state. This exception applies only if the nonresident is licensed to sell, solicit, or negotiate that insurance in the state where the insured maintains its principal place of business and the contract of insurance insures risks located in that state. (Conn. Gen. Stat. § 38a-702c).

E. **Prelicensing Examination and Education Requirements (Producers only):**

Producer: All individual applicants for a resident producer license for standard lines of authority must complete a course approved by the insurance commissioner, requiring not less than forty hours for each line of authority, or equivalent experience asdetermined by the commissioner; and must pass the equivalent examination administered by Prometric. (Conn. Gen. Stat. § 38a-702e).

Prelicensing education requirement is waived for:

1. *Life:* For any applicant who has been awarded the professional designation of CEBS, ChFC, CIC, CFP, CLU, FLMI and/or LUTCF and provides a current Letter of Designation.

2. *Accident/Health:* For any applicant who has been awarded the professional designation of CEBS, CLU, HIA, REBC and/or RHU and provides a current Letter of Designation.

3. *Property, Casualty and Personal Lines:* For any applicant who has been awarded the professional designation of AAI, ARM, CIC and/or CPCU and provides a current Letter of Designation.

4. *Nonresident Applicants:* Nonresident applicants must hold an equivalent license in their "home" state. An individual who applies for an insurance producer license in this state and who was previously licensed for the same lines of authority in another state shall not be required to complete any prelicensing education or examination if the application is received within ninety days after the cancellation of the applicant's previous license and if the applicant was in good standing in that state at the time of cancellation. (Conn. Gen. Stat. § 38a-702h).

Prelicensing examination requirement is waived for:

1. *Life:* For any applicant who has been awarded the professional designation of CLU and provides a current Letter of Designation.

2. *Accident / Health:* For any applicant who has been awarded the professional designation of CLU and provides a current Letter of Designation.

3. *Property, Casualty and Personal Lines:* For any applicant who has been awarded the professional designation of CPCU and provides a current Letter of Designation. (Conn. Licensing Handbook, p. 9).

All examinations for personal lines, property, and casualty will include questions related to Federal Flood requirements, guidelines and coverages. Letter of Designation must accompany producer application and fee. Applicants for a resident producer license must have their principal place of residence or principal place of business in Connecticut. Licensure will be verified on the NAIC Producer Database. All applicants for a nonresident Producer license must hold equivalent licensure in their resident state. All applicants for variable life and variable annuities authority must provide their current FINRA CRD (Central Registration Depository) number when applying. Registration will be verified on FINRA.

1. *Casualty Claim Adjuster.* All individual applicants must pass the qualifying examination administered by Prometric. Examination is waived if applicant holds an equivalent license in any other state. Connecticut is not reciprocal with New York.

2. *Certified Insurance Consultant.* All individual applicants who hold a CLU designation in good standing are exempt from prelicense requirements for life/accident & health and those who hold CPCU, AAI, or CIC designation in good standing are exempt from prelicense requirements for property/casualty, by providing a current letter of designation from the applicable society or organization. All other individual applicants must pass the qualifying examination administered by Prometric. Examination is also waived if applicant holds an equivalent license in any other state.

3. *Motor Vehicle Physical Damage Appraiser.* All individual applicants must pass the qualifying examination administered by Prometric. Examination is waived if applicant holds an equivalent license in any other state. Resident applicant must also pass a practical examination.

4. *Public Adjuster.* All individual applicants must complete a forty hour property course approved by the insurance commissioner and must pass the qualifying examination administered by Prometric. Education and examination are waived if applicant holds an equivalent license in any other state.

5. *Surplus Lines Broker.* All resident individual applicants for a surplus lines broker license must pass the qualifying examination administered by Prometric. Prerequisite: Active Connecticut producer license with property and casualty authority. All applicants for a nonresident surplus lines broker license must hold an equivalent licensure in their resident state.

6. *Others.* There is no prelicense education or exam requirement for fraternal agent, limited lines producer, premium finance company, reinsurance intermediary broker, reinsurance intermediary manager, or life settlement broker; however, each insurance company that solicits, negotiates, or sells any form of credit insurance shall provide to each individual, whose duties will include soliciting, negotiating or selling credit insurance, a program of instruction. (Conn. Licensing Handbook, p. 9).

Pursuant to Conn. Gen. Stat. §38a-771, if a Connecticut licensee has a change in license information (name, business or residence address regardless of state of residence, employer, bankruptcy, conviction, or administrative action), licensee must submit such information to the department, in writing, within thirty days of change. Go to www.ct.gov/cid, select *How to Change License Information* under *Industry*. You may Verify and Print licenses and license changes twenty-four hours after processing online. There is no charge. Go to www.ct.gov/cid and select the Verify and Print License under Industry.

F. **Continuing Education Requirements (Resident Producers only):** All resident individual standard lines producer licensees must fulfill continuing education requirements. Reciprocity will be accepted for nonresidents of all states that have a continuing education requirement and will be verified on the NAIC producer database.

Note: There is no CE requirement for Property & Casualty Claim Adjusters, Certified Insurance Consultants, Fraternal Agents, Motor Vehicle Physical Damage Appraisers, Portable Electronic, Public Adjusters, Reinsurance Intermediary Brokers and Managers, Surplus Lines Brokers and Surety Bail Bond Agents.

Number of Hours Required: Standard lines producers require twenty-four credit hours for the period ending on their license expiry/birth date biennially.

Mandatory Credits: Twenty-four credit hour requirement—at least three credit hours in Connecticut Law/Regulations/Ethics; a minimum of six credit hours per major line of authority which the producer held at the beginning of their compliance period and the balance in any approved CE course or combination. Make sure all requirements outlined on the transcript are completed. The "status" must read "Compliant" for all categories.

Major Lines of Authority:

1. Property/casualty (includes personal lines);

2. Life/accident & health (includes Variable Life and Variable Annuities).

All resident producers, licensed with property, casualty or personal lines authority are required to complete a one-time three credit course on federal flood requirements. The three credits can be applied toward licensee's property/casualty six credit requirement. Credits may be obtained from seminars, classes or self-study courses approved for CE credit by the department. Course instructors earn the same number of credit hours as do students, presuming that course is counted only once in a license period.

Proof of Completion: Per Regulation, all approved CE providers are required to post course completion information through Sircon/Vertafore within fifteen calendar days of course completion. Licensees are not responsible for filing their certificate(s); however, it is strongly recommended to retain certificate(s) in the event that a discrepancy occurs. If you have completed your CE course(s) and the information is not showing on your transcript, contact the CE provider you took the course with directly. (Connecticut CE Handbook).

Excess Hours: May not be carried into the next reporting period.

Courses with Exam: Proctors are required.

Requirements: Standard lines producers only. (Connecticut CE Producer Handbook).

The insurance department will mail renewal notices to all residents and nonresidents holding active producer licenses approximately sixty days prior to the producer's birth month. Therefore, it is imperative that the insurance department is notified of changes of address, in writing, within thirty days of change, pursuant to Conn. Gen. Stat. §§ 38a-702f and 38a-771. Report all name and address changes to the Insurance Department at https://portal.ct.gov/CID/Licensing/Online-Change-in-License-Information--Individual--Business-Entity-All-License-Types.

All CE requirements must be completed by the producer's license expiration date. Once resident producer has completed their CE requirement, they will receive a compliance letter from Prometric.

If you have not satisfied your continuing education requirements by the expiration date, the department will cancel your producer license and all company appointments. Your license will only be reinstated upon completion of your continuing education requirements and a payment of double the renewal fee has been received. (Connecticut CE Producer Handbook).

Individuals serving in the U.S. military on active duty outside the state of Connecticut during a substantial part of the compliance period and other emergency situations may be waived. You must send in a request for waiver to the insurance department, with documentation of the military orders.

G. **Cancellation of Agency Contracts/Producer Appointments:** Any property/casualty insurer terminating a producer's agent/agency contract and appointment shall do so in accordance with Conn. Gen. Stat. § 38a-709. Any insurer terminating a producer's agent/agency appointment is required to furnish facts relative to the termination and cause of termination to the insurance department and must notify the producer within thirty days of notifying the department. (Conn. Gen. Stat. § 38a-784).

H. **Rules for Risk Retention and Purchasing Groups:** Connecticut regulates risk retention and purchasing groups operating or offering coverage on risks in Connecticut. As required under Conn. Gen. Stat. § 38a-250, risk retention groups domiciled in Connecticut must be chartered and licensed as liability insurers, while groups not domiciled in Connecticut must register with the insurance commissioner and submit reports as described in Conn. Gen. Stat. §§ 38a-252 and 38a-253. Purchasing groups must also register with the insurance commissioner and submit reports as required in Conn. Gen. Stat. §§ 38a-260 and 38a-261. All groups and all resident and nonresident producers participating in them must comply with all Connecticut laws, including licensing and solicitation requirements or restrictions. All risk retention group policies must show the following notice in at least ten-point type on the front page and on the declarations page of the policy:

NOTICE

"This policy is issued by your risk retention group. Your risk retention group may not be subject to all of the insurance laws and regulations of your state. State insurance insolvency guaranty funds are not available for your risk retention group." (Conn. Gen. Stat. § 38a-255).

I. Other License Rules, Requirements, or Restrictions:

1. All names must be licensed in Connecticut before soliciting, negotiating or selling, or entering the state to solicit, negotiate, or sell, insurance coverage in Connecticut. Entering the state includes mail or telephone or other electronic communication into Connecticut from the outside, as well as a physical presence in the state. Producer licensees only: "Assumed Names" must be registered, as indicated under licensing requirements/applicability, above. (Conn. Gen. Stat. § 38a-702i).

   "Employer Group Benefit Plan"—No producer license is required of a person whose activities are limited to securing and furnishing information for the purpose of group life insurance, group annuities, group or blanket accident and health insurance, or for the purpose of enrolling individuals under such plans or administering such plans. This exemption is only applicable for true group insurance plans in which an employer sponsors such plan and employees are provided the option of enrolling in that plan. To solicit, negotiate or sell insurance coverage in addition to the group benefits offered by the employer, a producer license is required. (Conn. Gen. Stat. § 38a-702c).

2. Applications for business entities shall be made electronically through nipr.com. The following information is required:

   a. The name, social security number and Connecticut license number of at least one owner, officer, director, or partner of the entity, or in the case of a producer applicant, at least one designated/responsible individual producer.
   b. Authorization or signature of an owner, officer, director, or partner, of the entity.
   c. If applying electronically, be sure that the designee is licensed first; otherwise, the business entity application will be rejected.

3. Applicants for any of the above licenses, who have been convicted of any crime other than an infraction of Connecticut motor vehicle laws, are subject to insurance department qualifications at the time of application and on an ongoing basis.

Resident individuals and business entities can apply, amend, or reinstate a Connecticut producer license electronically at https://portal.ct.gov/CID/Licensing/Producer-Renewal-Information. or by going to *www.nipr.com.*

Nonresident individuals and business entities must apply for, amend, or reinstate a Connecticut producer license electronically at www.nipr.com.

All licensees can view and update their demographic information at www.ct.gov/cid by selecting the *How to Change License Information* link under *Industry.* Business entities can view and update their licensed responsible parties/designees using this same feature. Individual and business entity producers can also review and update assumed names.

J. **Policy Countersignature Requirements:** None.

K. **Portable Electronics Insurance:** If an individual only collects or furnishes claim information from or to insureds or claimants, and conducts data entry into an automated claims system, a license is not required, provided that individual is an employee of a casualty insurance company licensed in Connecticut that doesn't supervise more than twenty-five individuals. (Conn. Gen. Stat. § 38a-792).

II. Commissions, Fees, Commingling of Funds, and Suitability in Annuity Transactions

A. **Commissions:** An insurance company or insurance producer shall not pay a commission, service fee, brokerage or other valuable consideration to a person selling, soliciting or negotiating insurance in this state if the person is required to be licensed under §§ 38a-702(a) to 38a-702(r), inclusive, and is not so licensed. A person shall not accept a commission, service fee, brokerage or other valuable consideration for selling, soliciting or negotiating insurance in this state if the person is required to be licensed under §§ 38a-702(a) to 38a-702(r), inclusive, and is not so licensed. Renewal or other deferred commissions may be paid to a person, or an heir or assignee of the person, for selling, soliciting or negotiating insurance in this state if the person was required to be licensed under §§ 38a-702(a) to 38a-702(r), inclusive, at the time of the sale, solicitation or negotiation and was so licensed at that time. An insurer or insurance producer may pay or assign commissions, service fees, brokerages or other valuable consideration to an insurance agency or to persons who do not sell, solicit or negotiate insurance in this state, unless the payment would violate § 38a-825. (Conn. Gen. Stat. § 38a-702l).

B. **Fees:** Producers may charge a fee in addition to policy commissions, for insurance-related services only in full compliance with Conn. Gen. Stat. § 38a-707 and supporting regulations governing this subject, and only in accordance with a service fee agreement signed by the insured setting out the fees to be charged and the services to be provided. These provisions do not apply to insurance producers who are advisor representatives of a registered investments adviser registered pursuant to the Investment Advisory Act of 1940, 15 USC 80b-1, et seq., provided that the insurance producer makes a full disclosure in a written memorandum, signed by the party to be charged. (Conn. Gen. Stat. § 38a-707(d)).

Compensation from a customer excludes commissions that are deductible from the customer's premium payment and fees agreed to in writing for certain administrative services authorized by current regulation. Compensation from the insurer means payments, commissions, fees, awards, overrides, bonuses, contingent commissions, loans, stock options, gifts, prizes, or other valuable consideration, whether agreed to in writing or not.

Certified Insurance Consultants may charge fees based on the provisions of an insurance consulting contract with the client specifying the amount of fees to be charged and the services to be performed and meeting all other statutory requirements. Certified Insurance Consultants may not receive commission or compensation from any insurer or agent of an insurer in connection with any services provided under the contract for consulting.

In addition to the scheduled fees, a producer or surplus lines broker may charge as reimbursement any moneys expended by him for any:

(1) Inspection report fees.

(2) Motor vehicle department reports.

(3) Police reports.

(4) Credit card service fees.

(5) Regulatory fees from other jurisdictions, such as licensing fees, necessary for the placement of Connecticut risks with out-of-state exposure.

(6) Costs for overnight mail.

(7) Telegrams or telephone calls necessary for the placement of the risk under consideration. The insurance commissioner may establish a reasonable schedule

of maximum fees. Statute also allows the commissioner to allow such fees on an individual basis. (Regs., Conn. State Agencies § 38a-707-1).

The same policy may be assessed a service fee by both an insurance producer and a surplus lines broker. The total of such fees shall not exceed 5 percent of the applicable premium or $500, in the aggregate. (Regs., Conn. State Agencies § 38a-707-7).

C. **Disclosure Requirements:** No insurance producer or surplus lines broker shall charge any service fee without first obtaining a written memorandum, signed by the party to be charged and specifying and clearly defining the premium applicable to the policy and the amount or extent of any service fees assessed. Such memorandum shall be kept by the producer or surplus lines broker in such manner as to be easily subject to audit or inspection by the insurance commissioner or the commissioner's agents.

The customer's acknowledgement must be in writing, but if the transaction occurs over the telephone or electronically and written consent cannot reasonably be obtained, the producer can document the acknowledgement. (Regs., Conn. State Agencies §38a-707-9).

D. **Commingling of Funds:** Connecticut does not prohibit agents' commingling of insurer's premiums with other agency funds. (Regs., Conn. State Agencies §§ 38a-707-1, 38a-707-7 to 38a-707-9).

E. **Suitability in Annuity Transactions:**

Connecticut has adopted the NAIC Suitability in Annuity Transactions Model Regulation. Regs., Conn. State Agencies § 38a-432a-5.

Effective February 18, 2012, producers holding license on effective date who engage in sale of annuity products shall complete a one-time, four-CE credit training course within six months of effective date. Producers licensed on or after effective date may not engage in the sale of annuities until this training requirement has been met. The satisfaction of the training requirements of another state that are substantially similar shall be deemed to satisfy the requirement.

III. Statutory References:

Conn. Gen. Stat. §§ 38a-167, 250, 252 to 253, 255, 260 to 261, 398, 402, 465a, 702a to 702r, 707, 723, 731, 760b, 764, 769, 771, 782, 784, 790, 792, 799 to 800. Regs., Conn. State Agencies §§ 38a-432a-5, 707-1, 707-7 to 707-9.

IV. Other References:

Connecticut CE Producer Handbook.

Connecticut Licensing Handbook

Connecticut CE Producer Handbook

cidverifylicense.ct.gov/CLIC/LicenseType.html

cidonline.ct.gov/lit/inq/portal.ct.gov/CID/Licensing/Company-Appointment-Fee-Update-Process

DELAWARE

Insurance Commissioner
1351 West North St.
Suite 101; Dover, DE 19904 and
1007 Orange St., Suite 1010
Wilmington, DE 19801
Telephone (Licensing): 302-674-7390
https://insurance.delaware.gov/
licensing@delaware.gov

I. Licensing Requirements: Sales Personnel—Producers, Limited Lines Producers, Surplus Lines Brokers, Fraternal Producer and Misc. Limited Lines Producers. Other Insurance Professionals—Adjusters, Public Adjusters, Apprentice Adjusters, Apprentice Appraisers, Motor Vehicle Physical Damage Appraisers, Reinsurance Intermediaries, Temporary Licenses, Discount Medical Plan Organizations, Rental Car Insurance Producer, Portable Electronic Producer, and Viatical Settlement Provider.

A. Applicability: A person shall not transact insurance in Delaware for any class or classes of insurance unless the person is licensed for that line of authority business of insurance. (18 Del. C. § 1703).

B. Licenses Required of Residents: Each of the following must be licensed in Delaware. All licenses are permanent and are required to be renewed biennially. Apprentice adjuster and apprentice appraiser licenses are valid for one year.

Sales Personnel

1. *Producers.*

   a. License fee: initial fee: $100; and one-time $50 appointment fee paid by each insurer represented; applicants must apply online at www.nipr.com. (18 Del. C. § 701(23)).

   b. License Term: Resident licenses renew biennially by February 28 of even numbered years. Resident license renewal fee: $100. Nonresident licenses renew biennially by February 28 of odd numbered years. Nonresident license renewal fee: $100. Not subject to first renewal fee if initially licensed within ninety days prior to renewal date. (18 Del. C. § 701(23)(b) and (d)).

   c. Lines of Authority:

      (1) Life.

      (2) Accident and health or sickness.

(3) Property.
(4) Casualty.
(5) Variable life and variable annuity.
(6) Noncommercial personal and casualty lines.
(7) Surety and fidelity.
(8) Marine and transportation.
(9) Title.
(10) Any other line permitted under state laws or regulations. (18 Del. C. § 1707(a)(1)-(10)).

2. *Limited Lines Insurance Producer.* Licensed to sell any of the limited lines of credit insurance, prefunded funeral arrangements, title, and travel insurance, and automobile club. Fee: $100 plus one-time $50 appointment fee for each insurer represented. Resident licenses renew biennially by February 28 of even numbered years. Resident license renewal fee: $100. Nonresident licenses renew biennially by February 28 of odd numbered years. Nonresident renewal fee: $100. Not subject to first renewal fee if initially licensed within 90 days prior to renewal date. (18 Del. C. § 701(23)(a) and (c)).

3. *Rental Car Insurance Limited Producer.* Licensed to sell insurance only in connection with and incidental to the rental of vehicles, whether at the rental office or by preselection of coverage in master, corporate, group rental, or individual agreements. Annual fee: $300 per year per company. (18 Del. C. §§ 2003, 2006). Application available at https://insurance.delaware.gov/wp-content/uploads/sites/15/2020/10/RentalCarApp.pdf.

4. *Business Entities.* Initial license: $100 with a one-time appointment fee of $50. Resident licenses renew biennially by February 28 of even numbered years. Resident license renewal fee: $100. Nonresident licenses renew biennially by February 28 of odd numbered years. Nonresident license renewal fee: $100. Not subject to first renewal fee if initially licensed within ninety days prior to renewal date. (18 Del. C. § 701(23)(b) and (d)).

5. *Managing General Agents.* Any person, firm, association or corporation who negotiates and binds ceding reinsurance contracts on behalf of an insurer or manages all or part of the insurance business of an insurer (including the management of a separate division, department or underwriting office). Must be licensed as producers. (18 Del. C. §§ 1802 and 3).

Other Insurance Professionals

1. *Adjusters.* Initial license: $100. May be licensed in the following lines: property; casualty; fidelity and surety; motor vehicle; marine and transportation; crop; workers compensation. (18 Del. C. § 1707(27)). Resident licenses renew biennially by February 28 of even numbered years. Resident license renewal fee: $100. Nonresident licenses renew biennially by February 28 of odd numbered years. Nonresident license renewal fee: Not subject to first renewal fee if initially licensed within 90 days prior to renewal date. $100. (18 Del. C. § 701(27)).

2. *Motor Vehicle Damage Appraiser.* Initial license: $100. Resident licenses renew biennially by February 28 of even numbered years. Resident license renewal fee: $100. Nonresident licenses renew biennially by February 28 of odd numbered years. Nonresident license renewal fee; $100. Not subject to first renewal fee if initially licensed within ninety days prior to renewal date. (18 Del. C. §701(28)).

3. *Apprentice Adjusters and Appraisers.* "Apprentice" means a licensee of the Department who is qualified in all respects as an adjuster or appraiser, except as to experience, education and/or training. (18 Del. C. §1702). License is 180 days maximum. $50. (18 Del. C. §§ 701(29), 1711, 1722).

4. *Reinsurance Intermediaries.* Initial license: $250. Annual continuation: $100. May be required to file a bond and/or E&O policy. (18 Del. C. §701(12)).

5. *Viatical Settlement Provider.* Initial license: $250. Resident licenses renew biennially by February 28 in even numbered years. Resident license renewal fee: $250. Nonresident licenses renew biennially by February 28 in odd numbered years. Nonresident license renewal fee: $250. Not subject to first renewal fee if initially licensed within 90 days prior to renewal date. (18 Del. C. §701(30)).

6. *Discount Medical Plan Organization.* Initial license: $500. $50,000 surety bond required. Resident licenses renew biennially by February 28 in even numbered years. Resident license renewal fee: $250. Nonresident licenses renew biennially by February 28 in odd numbered years. Nonresident license renewal fee: $250 (18 Del. C. §§ 7604, 701(36)).

7. *Portable Electronic Producer.* Initial license: fee prescribed by commissioner not to exceed $1,000. Resident licenses renew biennially by February 28 in even numbered years. Resident license renewal fee: prescribed by commissioner not to exceed $500. Nonresident licenses renew biennially by February 28 in odd numbered years. Nonresident license renewal fee: $500. (18 Del. C. §§2052, 2057(e)).

8. *Limited Lines Travel Insurance Producer.* Initial license: $1,000. Renewal $500. Resident license renewal due biennially February 28 in even years. Nonresident license renewal due biennially February 28 in odd years. Not subject to first renewal fee if initially licensed within ninety days prior to renewal date. (18 Del. C. §701(37)).

Applicants, residents and nonresidents are required to apply online, and all renewal fees must be paid online at: www.nipr.com.

1. *Producers.* The applicant must submit an examination report from Pearson VUE, (800)-274-0455, and is subject to a criminal background check.

2. *Fraternal Representatives.* Applicants must submit a criminal background check; $75 fee.

3. *Adjusters and Motor Vehicle Physical Damage Appraisers.* Applicants must submit an examination report from Pearson VUE if they have tested with Delaware, and a criminal background check.

C. Appointments: An insurance producer shall not act as an agent of an insurer unless the insurance producer becomes an appointed agent of that insurer. An insurance producer who is not acting as an agent of an insurer is not required to become appointed. (18 Del. C. §1715(a)).

Appointments are permanent until cancelled by the insurer or the agent. Appointments are not necessary prior to being licensed. New appointments are obtained subsequent to licensing and must be in place within fifteen days of the date the producer signs a contract to represent an insurance company or submits an application for a policy to the insurance company. (18 Del. C. § 1715(b)).

D. Licenses Required of Nonresidents: Nonresidents serving as each of the above must also be licensed in Delaware. Nonresidents must be certified by home-state insurance department or must pass Delaware examination. (18 Del. C. §1708). The nonresident license must be renewed biennially by February 28 in odd numbered years. (18 Del. C. §701). Not subject to first renewal fee if initially licensed within ninety days prior to renewal date.

Multi-State Exposures. A license is not required for a nonresident insurance producer who sells, solicits, or negotiates a contract of insurance for commercial property and casualty coverage when risks that are to be insured under that contract are located in more than one state. This exception applies only if the nonresident is licensed to sell, solicit, or negotiate that insurance in the state where the insured maintains its principal place of business and the contract of insurance insures risks located in that state. (18 Del. C. §1704(6)).

E. Prelicensing Examination or Education Requirements:

1. *Residents.* All resident licensees must pass a qualifying examination initially to obtain any of the above licenses. (18 Del. C. §1705). Examinations are administered by Pearson VUE, 800-274-0455; https://home.pearsonvue.com/de/insurance. fee: $90.

   The following major lines exams are available:

   a. Life producer.
   b. Accident and health producer.
   c. Property producer.
   d. Casualty producer.
   e. Personal lines producer.

   The following limited lines exams are available:

   a. Surety producer.
   b. Title producer.
   c. Motor vehicle producer.
   d. Marine transportation producer.
   e. Property adjuster.
   f. Casualty adjuster.
   g. Motor vehicle appraiser.
   h. Marine and transportation adjuster.
   i. Surety adjuster.
   j. Motor vehicle adjuster.
   k. Bail Agent producer.
   l. Crop producer.
   m. Workers' comp adjuster.
   n. Public adjuster.

   The following are exempt from the examination requirement:

   a. Attorneys who are licensed to practiced law in Delaware applying for the title line. (18 Del. C. §1709).
   b. Fraternal representatives.

c. Individuals previously licensed for the same line in another state if still in good standing and if application is made within ninety days of cancellation of previous license.
d. Travel insurance license applicants.
e. Auto club license applicants.

2. *Nonresidents.* Examination requirement is reciprocal with applicant's home state. (18 Del. C. §1705).

F. Continuing Education Requirements:

Number of Hours Required: Twenty-four hours biennially, three hours must be in ethics; resident and public adjusters and fraternal agents—twelve hours biennially, three hours must be in ethics. (CDR 18-500-504).

Resident producers holding a health license and who solicit long term care policies must complete at least three hours of training in Delaware long term care insurance that consists of product knowledge, laws, rules and regulations. Since the Delaware Health Examination includes long term care knowledge, the long term care continuing education requirement does not need to be met prior to solicitation of the product. The requirement must be met during the biennium that the long term care policy was solicited.

All Delaware licensed resident insurance producers authorized to write homeowners or personal lines coverage shall be required to complete a two hour continuing education course related to flood insurance and the National Flood Insurance Program as part of the twenty-one general credit hours necessary to maintain a Delaware resident license. The requirement must be fulfilled during the licensee's biennial continuing education reporting period. The failure to comply with this continuing education requirement may jeopardize the producer's authority to write insurance through the NFIP and their Delaware state producer license. (CDR 18-500-504).

If continually licensed for twenty-five years, an automatic credit of twelve hours applies. Licensees with approved professional designations that require annual CE receive an automatic credit of twelve hours. However, these automatic hours may not be used to satisfy the ethics requirement or other specific requirements (flood insurance and long term care insurance.). The hours may be classroom or self-study and are not limited to the lines in which an agent is licensed. Submit proof of completion by February 28 of every even numbered year.

Excess Hours: Up to five hours may be carried over into the next reporting period. Excess hours apply to the general credit requirement only. (CDR 18-500-504).

Final Exam: Does not have to be monitored.

Requirements **Not** *Applicable to the following:*

1. Agents who hold authority for title, credit crop/hail, surety or car rental insurance.

2. New licensees in their first biennium.

3. Resident adjusters for the lines of surety or marine and transportation.

4. Waivers may be granted by the Department if good cause is shown (such as long-term illness or active military duty).

Renewal Procedure:

Course provider gives licensee a copy of the certificate of completion (form CE-4.) The licensee keeps the original on file for three years; the course provider, for three years. (CDR 18-500-504).

G. **Cancellation of Agency/Producer Contracts:** Subject to the terms of the agency agreement, the appointment may be terminated at any time. The commissioner must receive a notice within thirty days after the effective date of the termination. The producer must be notified within fifteen days after notifying the commissioner. (18 Del. C. §1716).

H. **Rules for Risk Retention and Purchasing Groups:** Delaware has a Risk Retention Act, modeled after the Federal Risk Retention Act. Every policy issued by such a group must contain the following notice in ten point type on its front and declarations pages:

> This policy is issued by your risk retention group.Your risk retention group may not be subject to all of the insurance laws and regulations of your state. State insurance insolvency guaranty funds are not available for your risk retention group. (18 Del. C. §8004(7)).

I. **Other License Rules, Requirements, or Restrictions:** License applications must be submitted online at: www.nipr.com. A Delaware-licensed nonresident may enter Delaware to solicit, inspect, or service, but an unlicensed nonresident may not, and may not write instate properties or exposures even when no solicitation is performed in state. Entering the state includes mail or telephone or other electronic communication into the state from the outside, as well as physical presence in the state. All licensees authorized for property, casualty, surety, or marine and transportation insurance must maintain a premium trust account for all premiums they handle, and retain policy, premium, and claim records for three years. (18 Del. C. §§ 1106, 1107).

J. **Policy Countersignature Requirements:** None. (18 Del. C. § 8006).

K. **Portable Electronics Insurance:** Portable electronic insurance is intended to cover electronic devices that are portable in nature, their accessories, and services related to the use of the device such as cellphones, smartphones, tablet computers and similar items. Vendors of such devices are required to hold a limited lines license to sell or offer coverage under a policy of portable electronics insurance. The limited lines license will authorize the employees of the vendor to sell policies on the devices without obtaining an individual license themselves. (18 Del. C. § 2052). License applications and fees are to be determined by the insurance commissioner. The license is to be valid for two years and will expire on February 28 of the renewal year assigned by the commissioner. License fees are limited to no more than $1,000 for the initial license, and $500 for each renewal. (18 Del. C. § 2057(d) and (e)).

II. Commissions, Fees, Commingling of Funds, and Suitability in Annuity Transactions

A. **Commissions:** An insurer shall not pay a commission or other consideration to a person for selling insurance if that person does not have the proper license. Neither shall such a person accept a commission or other compensation. An insurer may pay deferred commissions if the person, at the time of the sale, had the proper license. No producer may accept any fee from an insurer if the producer will receive a fee from the producer's client. Insurers may not pay commissions to a nonappointed producer if an appointment is required. (18 Del. C. § 1714). An insurer or other entity may provide commission or other compensation to an agent or other representative for the sale of a long-term care insurance policy or certificate which shall not exceed 35 percent of the total premium paid for that policy year. No entity shall provide compensation to its agents or other producers and no agent or producer shall receive compensation greater than 25 percent of the total premium paid for that policy year for the sale of a replacement long-term care insurance policy or certificate. Rebating of commissions is not allowed. (CDR 18-1400-1404). An unlicensed person who refers a customer or potential customer to an insurer and who does not discuss terms and conditions or give opinions or advice regarding insurance may be compensated for the referral, if the compensation:

(1) For each referral is:

(a) Nominal;

(b) On a 1-time basis; and

(c) Fixed in amount by referral;

(2) Does not depend on whether the customer purchases the insurance;

(3) Is not contingent on the volume of insurance transacted. (18 Del. C. §1714(g)).

B. **Fees:** Producers acting as agents of insurers may not charge fees for insurance services either in addition to or instead of commissions. Producers acting as agents of the insured (brokers) and consultants may charge a fee provided it is stated in advance and agreed upon with the client. Consultants may not receive commissions. (18 Del. C. §1714).

C. **Disclosure Requirements:** All fees, other than commissions for financial planning by an insurance producer, shall be based upon a written agreement signed by the party to be charged in advance of the performance of the services under the agreement. A copy of the agreement shall be provided to the party to be charged at the time the agreement is signed by the party. The person furnishing the agreement shall retain a copy for at least three years after completion of services. A copy shall be available to the commissioner upon request. The agreement shall specifically state:

1. The services for which the fee is to be charged.

2. The amount of the fee to be charged or the manner in which it will be determined.

3. The client shall not be required to purchase an insurance product through the person furnishing the agreement.

D. **Commingling of Funds:** Producers that make immediate remittance of collections to their entities need not maintain separate bank accounts for these collections. To constitute immediate remittance, remittance shall occur within five business days. Producers that have the express written consent of their entities to mingle premium moneys with their own funds may do so if the following exists: monies held in a fiduciary capacity are reasonably ascertainable from the books of accounts and records of the producers; and, amounts due entities are equal to or less than the combined accounts receivable and current bank balances. A producer that does not have the express consent of his entities to commingle moneys with his personal funds shall hold the premium moneys separate from other funds in accordance with the guidelines in CDR 18-500-505, § 8.1. (CDR 18-500-505, § 8).

E. **Suitability in Annuity Transactions:** An insurer must establish and maintain a system to supervise the insurer's, and the insurer's insurance producers' recommendations to senior consumers that is reasonably designed to ensure that the recommendations are suitable by instituting written procedures and periodic reviews. (CDR 18-1200-1214).

Delaware has not adopted the NAIC Suitability in Annuity Transactions Model Regulation.

III. **Statutory References:** 18 Del. C. §§ 701; 1106, 1107; 1702 to 1705; 1707 to 1709; 1711; 1714 to 1716; 1803; 2003; 2006; 2052; 2057; 7604; 8004; 8006. CDR 18-500-504; 500-505; 1200-1214; 1400-1404.

DISTRICT OF COLUMBIA

Commissioner,
Department of Insurance, Securities, and Banking
1050 First Street, NE, 801
Washington, DC 20002
Telephone: (202) 727-8000; FAX: (202) 535-1196; Email: disb@dc.gov
http://disb.dc.gov

I. Licensing Requirements: Producers.

A. Applicability: A person shall not sell, solicit, or negotiate insurance in the District for any class of insurance unless the person is licensed for that line of authority in accordance with this chapter. The license itself shall not create any authority in the licensee to represent or commit an insurance carrier. (DC Code § 31-1131.03(a)).

B. License Required of Residents: An individual applying for a resident insurance producer license shall pass a written examination unless the individual is (1) applying for a limited lines insurance producer license or a license in the surplus line of authority, or (2) exempt under DC Code §§ 31-1131.05b or 31-1131.09. (DC Code § 31-1131.05(a)). The renewal fee varies depending on the lines of authorities being held by the producer and the license group. An individual insurance producer license initially issued after May 13, 2008, and the first renewal after May 13, 2008 of an individual insurance producer initially issued before May 13, 2008, shall expire on the last day of the birth month of the producer that falls not less than eighteen months and not more than twenty-nine months after the effective date of the license. An initial business entity insurance producer license issued after May 13, 2008, shall expire on the May 31 that falls not less than eighteen months and not more than twenty-nine months after the effective date of the license. A renewal of an existing license shall expire two years after the expiration date of the license period. (DC Code § 31-1131.07a; disb.dc.gov/sites/default/files/dc/sites/disb/publication/attachments/DISBIBProducersFees022014.pdf).

An applicant may qualify as a resident if he resides in the District or maintains his principal place of business in the District. A person who maintains either, but not both, his or her principal place of residence or principal place of business in the District shall apply for a nonresident insurance producer license if the person is licensed as a resident insurance producer in another state; or a resident insurance producer license if the person is not licensed as a resident insurance producer in another state. (DC Code § 31-1131.03).

Applicants for bail bonding authority must take the bail bondsmen exam in addition to the property and casualty exam. A producer may receive qualification for one or more of the following lines: life, accident and health or sickness, variable life and variable annuity products, property, casualty, personal lines, bail bonds or surplus lines. A license may be issued for limited lines coverage. (DC Code § 31-1131.07).

Managing General Agents (MGAs) and reinsurance intermediaries must be licensed as producers. The mayor may require them to carry a bond or errors and omissions (E&O) policy. (DC Code § 31-1502).

Sales Personnel

The following fees shall apply to producer initial, renewal and reinstatement applications per licensee group:

1. One hundred dollars ($100) for Life, Accident and Health or sickness, and Variable Life and Variable Annuity Products.
2. One hundred dollars ($100) for Property, Casualty, Personal lines and Bail bonds.
3. One hundred dollars ($100) for Limited lines—credit, car rental, crop, surety and travel, or a limited line of insurance established by the commissioner by rule.
4. Two hundred dollars ($200) for qualifications as a surplus lines producer.
5. The renewal fee is the same as the initial license fee; and if applicable, a late fee is double the initial fee.
6. The reinstatement fee is double the initial fee.
7. A $100 processing fee is applied to paper applications. (CDCR 26-A105).

   An insurance producer shall not act as an agent of an insurer unless the producer becomes an appointed agent of that insurer. An Insurance Producer who is not acting as an agent of an insurer shall not be required to be appointed. Upon receipt of the notice of appointment, the Commissioner shall verify, within ten days, that the producer is eligible for appointment. If not eligible the Commissioner shall notify the insurer within five days of the determination. (DC Code § 31-1131.14) Producers with variable contracts authority must maintain an NASD series 6 or 7 license.

   There is no solicitor license.

   There is no salaried company employee license.

   An applicant who claims DC residency for licensing purposes may not claim to be a resident of any other jurisdiction.

Other Insurance Professionals

1. *Public Insurance Adjusters.* Must be licensed. Those not eligible for licensure by reciprocity shall pass a public insurance adjuster examination. (DC Code § 31-1631.04). Term of license: Two years. Producer license of an individual shall expire on the last day of the producer's birth month. Business entity licenses expire on May 31. (DC Code § 31-1131.07a).

   A surety bond in the amount of $20,000 is required to be maintained as well as accurate books and records of all transactions, retained for not less than five years. The records shall contain (1) the insured's name, (2) the date, location, and amount of the loss, (3) a copy of the contract, (4) the name of the insurer, amount, expiration date, and number of each policy, (5) itemized statement of recoveries, and (6) itemized statement of compensation received by the adjuster. (DC Code §§ 31-1631.05, 1631.06).

C. **Appointments:** An insurance producer shall not act as an agent of an insurer unless the insurance producer becomes an appointed agent of that insurer. An insurance producer who is not acting as an agent of an insurer shall not be required to become appointed. (DC Code § 31-1131.14(a)).

D. **Licenses Required of Nonresidents:** A person may request a nonresident license if the person is licensed as a resident insurance producer in good standing, in his or her home state, the person has submitted the proper request for license and paid fees, has submitted or transmitted to the Commissioner a completed NAIC Uniform Application. (DC Code § 31-1131.08).

   D.C. accepts electronic submission of the license application through the National Insurance Producers Registry (NIPR) at www.nipr.com.

   Multi-State Exposures: A license is not required for a nonresident insurance producer who sells, solicits, or negotiates a contract of insurance for commercial property and casualty risks to an insured with risks located in more than one state insured under that contract; provided, that the person is otherwise licensed as an insurance producer to sell, solicit or negotiate that insurance in the state where the insured maintains its principal place of business and the contract of insurance insures risks located in that state. (DC Code § 31-1131.04).

E. **Prelicensing Examination or Education Requirements:** Pre-Licensing is no longer required in this State for a title insurance producer's license. All other applicants may be required to complete prelicensing education before taking an examination or applying for a producer license.

Insurers that sell, solicit, or negotiate a limited line of insurance in the District are required to provide each individual whose duties will include selling, soliciting, or negotiating the insurer's limited line of insurance in the District a program of instruction which has been approved by the commissioner. The insurer shall provide the program of instruction to the individual prior to the individual's application for licensure as a limited lines insurance producer. (DC Code § 31-1131.05a(b)).

Fingerprinting: An individual applying for a resident insurance producer license (except for an individual applying only for a limited lines insurance producer license) and each officer, director, partner of, and owner of a controlling interest in, a business entity applying for a resident insurance producer license under this chapter shall submit to the commissioner the individual's fingerprints along with the individual's name, address, and written consent to the performance of a criminal history record background check. (DC Code § 31-1131.06a).

F. Continuing Education Requirements/Insurance Producers:

Number of Hours Required: A minimum of twenty-four hours biennially. Of the twenty-four hours, three hours are required in ethics; four hours of flood insurance training is required of all property and casualty producers. (CDCR 26-A106).

Excess Hours: May not be carried over.

Final Exam: The final exam for a self-study course must be monitored by the sponsor.

Renewal Procedure: Licensees must submit renewal application within sixty days prior to expiration of their licenses. Nonresidents must meet home state requirements. CE requirements must be taken within fifteen business days of expiration of the DC producers' insurance license in order to qualify for license renewal. Failure to do so may result in the expiration of the license. A waiver from continuing education courses may be requested for any of the following reasons:

1. Long-term illness or incapacity (physicians' certificate required).

2. Active duty in the Armed Forces of the United States outside of the Washington Metropolitan area.

3. Any other emergency deemed sufficient by the commissioner. (CDCR 26-A106).

For more information, visit disb.dc.gov/sites/default/files/dc/sites/disb/publication/attachments/continuing_education_faqs_012010.pdf.

G. **Cancellation of Agency Contracts/Producer Appointments:** Upon termination of employment appointment, contract or other insurance business relationship with an insurance producer. An insurer shall notify the commissioner within thirty days after the effective date of the termination, the reason for termination along with any additional information, documents, records or other data pertaining to the termination. (DC Code § 31-1131.15).

H. **Rules for Risk Retention and Purchasing Groups (RRGs):** Resident RRGs must file a plan of operation with the commissioner. Nonresident RRGs may also be licensed in the District. Filing fee: Determined by Commissioner. (D.C. Code §§ 31-4102, 4103, 4107).

a. A purchasing group may not purchase insurance from a risk retention group that is not chartered in a state or from an insurer not admitted in the state in which the purchasing group is located, unless the purchase is affected through a licensed agent or broker acting pursuant to the surplus lines laws and regulations of such a state.

b. A purchasing group which obtains liability insurance from an insurer not admitted in the District or a risk retention group shall inform each of the members of the group that has a risk resident or located in the District that such a risk is not protected by an insurance insolvency guaranty fund in the District, and that the risk retention group or the insurer may not be subject to all the insurance laws and regulations of the District.

c. No purchasing group may purchase insurance providing for a deductible or self-insured retention applicable to the group as a whole; however, coverage may provide for a deductible or self-insured retention applicable to individual members.

d. Purchases of insurance by purchasing groups are subject to the same standards regarding aggregate limits which are applicable to all purchases of group insurance. (DC Code § 31-4108).

Every application form for insurance from a risk retention group on its front and declaration page issued by a risk retention group, shall contain 10-point type the following notice:

NOTICE

This policy is issued by your retention group. Your risk retention group may not be subject to all of the insurance laws and regulations of your state. State insurance insolvency guaranty funds are not available for your risk retention group. (DC Code § 31-4103(7)).

Risk purchasing groups must also register with the commissioner.

I. **Other License Rules, Requirements, or Restrictions for an Insurance Producer License:** The Uniform Licensing applications may be processed online at http://www.nipr.com/state_district_of_columbia.htm. Unlicensed nonresidents may not enter the District of Columbia to solicit, inspect, or service. Mailing or telephoning into the District is not considered entering the District.

An individual insurance producer who allows his or her license to lapse may, within one year after the expiration date of the license, reinstate the same license without the necessity of passing a written examination; provided, that the producer shall pay a penalty in the amount of twice the unpaid renewal fee. (DC Code § 31-1131.07a).

J. **Policy Countersignature Requirement:** None. (D.C. Code § 31-4105).

K. **Portable Electronics Insurance:** A vendor is required to hold a limited-lines license to sell or offer coverage under a policy of portable electronics insurance. A limited-lines license authorizes any employee or authorized representative of the vendor to sell or offer coverage under a portable electronics insurance policy. Employees and authorized representatives of vendors who are engaged in selling or offering portable electronics insurance must be trained according to requirements listed in D.C. Code § 31-5051.02.

II. Commissions, Fees, Commingling of Funds, and Suitability in Annuity Transactions

A. **Commissions:** An insurer or insurance producer shall not pay or receive a commission, service fee, brokerage fee, or other variable consideration to a person for selling, soliciting or negotiating insurance in the District if that person is not licensed and is required to be licensed. (DC Code § 31-1131.13).

B. **Fees:** Fees may not be charged in lieu of or in addition to commissions.

C. **Disclosure Requirements:** All fees, other than commissions for financial planning by an insurance producer, shall be based upon a written agreement signed by the party to be charged in advance of the performance of the services under the agreement. A copy of the agreement shall be provided to the party to be charged at the time the agreement is signed by the party. The agreement shall specifically state:

(1) The services for which the fee is to be charged.

(2) The amount of the fee to be charged or the manner in which it will be determined.

(3) The client shall not be required to purchase an insurance product through the person furnishing the agreement.

(4) The person furnishing the agreement shall retain a copy for at least three years after completion of services.

(5) A copy shall be available to the commissioner upon request. (DC Code § 31-2231.15).

D. **Commingling of Funds:** The District of Columbia Insurance Code says that agents who collect premiums for their insurers are deemed to hold such premium in trust for the insurer. (DC Code § 31-4329).

E. **Suitability in Annuity Transactions:** An insurance producer shall not solicit the sale of an annuity product unless the insurance producer has adequate knowledge of the product to recommend the annuity and the insurance producer is in compliance with the insurer's standards for product training. An insurance producer who holds a life insurance line of authority and engages in the sale of annuity products shall complete a one-time four (4) credit training course approved by the Department. (CDCR § 26-A8404).

Washington, D.C. has adopted the NAIC Suitability in Annuity Transactions Model Regulation.

III. Statutory References:

DC Code §§ 31-1131.03 to 1131.05, 1131.13 to 1131.15; 31-1502; 31-1631.04 to 1631.06; 31-2231.15; 31-3102; 31-4102, 4103, 4105, 4107, 4108; 31-4329; 31-5051.02. CDCR 26-A105; 26-A106; 26- A8404.

FLORIDA

Chief Financial Officer
Department of Financial Services
200 E. Gaines St., Tallahassee, FL 32399-0301
Telephone: 850-413-3137; Fax: 850-413-3291
https://www.myfloridacfo.com/Division/Agents
AgentLicensing@MyFloridaCFO.com

I. Licensing Requirements: Sales Personnel—Agents, Managing General Agents (MGAs), Service Representatives, Insurance Agencies. Other Insurance Professionals—Adjusters, Customer Representatives, Administrators, Home Warranty, Automobile Warranty, Service Warranty, Reinsurance Intermediaries and Portable Electronics.

A. Applicability: Licensing laws apply to all insurers and all types of insurance.

B. Licenses Required of Residents:

Sales Personnel

1. *Licenses.* Florida issues the following agent licenses:

a. Life (Including Annuities and Variable Contracts).
b. Health and Life (Including Annuities and Variable Contracts).
c. Health.
d. General lines (property & casualty).
e. Personal lines (noncommercial property and casualty).
f. Industrial fire or burglary.
g. Surplus lines.
h. Travel insurance.
i. Credit insurance (includes: credit life/disability, credit property, credit insurance, and mortgage guaranty).
j. In-transit and storage personal property.
k. Motor vehicle rental insurance.
l. Legal expense.
m. Title agent.
n. Limited surety agent (bail bond agent); A temporary limited surety agent license is required to be held for one year prior to obtaining a permanent license.
o. Professional bail bond agent; a temporary limited surety agent license is required to be held for one year prior to obtaining a permanent license.
p. Crop, hail, and multiperil crop.
q. Portable electronics.

Note: Florida does not license brokers. Any individual soliciting or transacting insurance must be licensed as an insurance agent. (Fla. Stat. § 626.112(1)(a)).

2. *Agents.* Individuals required to pass an examination prior to licensure must apply for the examination with PearsonVUE and the examination fee of $44 must be paid directly to PearsonVUE https://www.myfloridacfo.com/Division/Agents/Licensure/Examinations/default.htm. Once the individual passes the examination, the individual must apply for licensure on the Department's website at www.myfloridacfo.com/Division/Agents/ within one year of passing the examination. Failure to apply for licensure within one year from the date the examination was taken and passed results in an invalid pass score. The following licensing fees are required to be paid online: $50 application filing fee ($10 for title agents), $5 license identification fee, and appointment fee is $60. Temporary appointments cost less depending on the length. See https://www.myfloridacfo.com/Division/Agents/Licensure/Agents-Adjusters/fees.htm for a complete list. Credit card convenience fee of $2.45 for licensure and education courses, and 3 percent of transaction for appointments if paying with a credit card. Members of the Armed Forces and veterans are exempt from application fees. Email AgentLicensing@MyFloridaCFO.com for a refund of the filing fee.

   Note: Applicants who pass the examination may still be denied a license if the applicant does not meet all qualification and eligibility requirements. All individuals applying for licensure must be fingerprinted. Fingerprinting is available through IdentoGo by Idemia (https://fl.ibtfingerprint.com/?RESTART&DFSORI=DFS-1-FL921060Z). The cost of fingerprinting is $45.80 (plus local Florida county sales tax). (Fla. Stat. Ann. § 626.202).

3. *Managing General Agents (MGAs).* Effective July 1, 2018, the MGA license is no longer available. Those individuals wanting to be a MGA must get a MGA Appointment by an insurer under a General Lines (P&C), Life, Health or Limited Surety (Bail Bond) agent license. Managing General Agents may only engage in assisting agents in negotiating and effecting contracts of insurance when accompanied by a resident general lines agent duly licensed and appointed. The appointment fee is $60 and 3 percent of transaction for appointments if paying with a credit card. Late fee for initial appointment: $250. Late fee for renewal $25.

   An agency/firm may obtain a MGA-Agency appointment by an insurance carrier who will verify the insurer's statutory prerequisites to appoint the agency.

4. *Service Representatives.* Must be licensed by the state and appointed by the insurer. Service representatives must also be accompanied by a licensed and appointed resident general lines agent when assisting agents in negotiating and effecting contracts of insurance. The license application fee is $50, license ID fee is $5,

fingerprinting processing fee is $45.80 (plus local Florida county sales tax), and the appointment fee is $60. Late fee for initial appointment: $250. Late fee for renewal $25.

5. *Insurance Agencies.* Insurance agencies must file an application for licensure. Effective January 1, 2015, agency branch locations are not required to be licensed separately if transacting business under the same name and federal identification number; however, a designated agent in charge of each location, location address and telephone number must be furnished to the department within thirty days after the branch location begins transacting business. The agency must apply online at the Department's website at www.myfloridacfo.com/Division/Agents/. Fingerprints are required of each of the following:

   a. A sole proprietor.
   b. Each owner, partner, officer, director, president, senior vice-president, secretary, treasurer, and limited liability company member who directs or participates in the management or control of the insurance agency, whether through ownership of voting securities, by contract, by ownership of any agency bank account or otherwise.
   c. Each individual who directs or participates in the management or control of an incorporated agency whose shares are not traded on a securities exchange.

   The fingerprinting processing fee is $45.80 (plus local Florida county sales tax). However, fingerprints need not be filed for an individual who is currently licensed and appointed under Chapter 626. No application filing fees or license identification fees are required for insurance agency licensure or registration.

   Licensure: Effective January 1, 2015, a license must be obtained by agencies that are transacting Florida insurance business. However, an insurance agency that is owned and operated by a single licensed agent conducting business in his or her individual name and not employing or otherwise using the services of or appointing other licensees are exempt from the agency licensing requirements.

   For additional information regarding insurance agency licensure and requirements access the Florida Department of Financial Services website at https://www.myfloridacfo.com/Division/Agents/.

   The Department may disapprove the use of any true or fictitious name, other than a bona fide natural name of an individual, by an insurance agency for the following reasons:

   1. The name interferes with or is too similar to a name already filed and in use by another agency or insurer.

2. The use of the name may mislead the public in any respect.
3. The name states or implies that the agency is an insurer, motor club, hospital service plan, state or federal agency, charitable organization, or entity that primarily provides advice and counsel rather than sells or solicits insurance, or is entitled to engage in insurance activities not permitted under licenses held or applied for. If the name is unacceptable, the agency will be notified and such agency will be provided the opportunity to change the name of the agency. (Fla. Stat. Ann. § 626.602).

A fictitious name, or as more commonly known, doing business as (DBA), must be properly registered with the Department of State, Division of Corporations; however, the Department has determined that the use of multiple fictitious names (DBAs) is misleading to the public. Accordingly, no insurance, bail bond, or title agency, adjusting firm, or any other business entity regulated by the Department of Financial Services, Division of Insurance Agent and Agency Services may use more than one DBA per business entity.

Other Insurance Professionals

1. *Adjusters.* Florida issues the following types of adjuster licenses:

   a. All lines adjuster. For an individual applying for the all lines adjuster license, the applicant must either pass the state's examination or be exempted from the examination by completing one of the designation courses identified by statute: Accredited Claims Adjuster (ACA), Certified Adjuster (CA) or Certified Claims Adjuster (CCA) American Institute for Chartered Property Casualty Underwriters - Chartered Property Casualty Underwriter (CPCU), HurriClaim Training Academy - Professional Property Insurance Adjuster (PPIA), Insurance Institute of America - Associate in Claims (AIC) Professional Career Institute - Professional Claims Adjuster (PCA), Claims and Litigation Management Alliance (CLM) - Universal Claims Certification (UCC), WebCE, Inc. - Claims Adjuster Certified Professional (CACP) designation (Fla. Stat. Ann. § 626.8651). There is a fingerprinting processing fee: $45.80 (plus local Florida county sales tax); license application fee: $50; license identification fee: $5; and an appointment fee: $60.
   b. Public adjuster. Public adjusters must pass the examination created specifically for public adjusters as described in Fla. Stat. Ann. § 626.241(6) in order to be licensed and are also required to post a $50,000 bond. (Fla. Stat. Ann. § 626.865).

   In order to qualify to become licensed as a public adjuster an individual must obtain a resident all lines adjuster license and have been appointed on a continual basis for the previous six months as a public adjuster apprentice under Fla Stat. Ann. § 626.8561, as an independent adjuster under § 626.855 or as a company employee adjuster under § 626.856, prior to being eligible for licensure as a public adjuster, and file an original fifty thousand-dollar surety bond, using a bond form provided by the Department on their website at https://www.myfloridacfo.com/Division/Agents/.

The Public Adjuster license may not be issued until the state examination is passed. License application fee: $50; license identification fee: $5; fingerprinting processing fee: $45.80 (plus local Florida county sales tax); unless currently licensed as an all lines adjuster with fingerprints already completed within the previous four years; appointment fee: $60. Please see the Department's website for more information on this new law as it becomes available.

2. *Customer Representatives.* A customer representative is an individual at least eighteen years of age, employed by a general lines agent or agency to assist the agent in his/her office and can only be appointed by one general lines agent or agency. A customer representative cannot maintain a separate office for conducting insurance activities. Only one customer representative appointment may be held and the individual may not be licensed as an agent, service representative, or managing general agent. Customer representatives must be salaried employees whose compensation is not primarily based on commissions or the production of applications, insurance, or premiums. Prior to applying for the Customer Representative license, the applicant must have obtained one of the industry specific designations listed in Fla Stat. Ann. § 626.7351. License application fee: $50; license identification fee: $5; fingerprint processing fee: $45.80 (plus local Florida county sales tax); appointment fee: $60.

3. *Administrators.* Third-party administrators must obtain a certificate of authority from the commissioner and file annual reports as prescribed by Florida law to maintain certificate of authority in effect. Administrators must maintain a fidelity bond of at least 10 percent of the amount of total funds handled or managed annually by the administrator (maximum $500,000). Filing fee is $100. Fingerprinting fee is $45.80 (plus local Florida county sales tax). Nonresident third-party administrators must meet the same requirements as residents. The Office of Insurance Regulation is responsible for issuing this type of license. Please access the web site at www.floir.com/. (Fla. Stat. Ann. §§ 626.8805, 626.8809).

   Note: Certificates of Authority are issued for life/health administrators only.

4. *Consultants.* Florida does not issue a consultant's license. In order to consult in the state for a fee, commission, or other compensation, the individual must be

licensed as a life and health or general lines agent or both and be appointed as an unaffiliated agent. For additional information, please visit the Department's website at https://www.myfloridacfo.com/Division/Agents/.

Unaffiliated agents—this is not a license, but is based on self-appointment—Fla Stat. Ann. § 626.112(18). "Unaffiliated insurance agent" means a licensed insurance agent, except a limited lines agent, who is self-appointed and who practices as an independent consultant in the business of analyzing or abstracting insurance policies, providing insurance advice or counseling, or making specific recommendations or comparisons of insurance products for a fee established in advance by written contract signed by the parties. An unaffiliated insurance agent may not be affiliated with an insurer, insurer-appointed insurance agent, or insurance agency contracted with or employing insurer-appointed insurance agents.

5. *Home Warranty.* License may be issued to individuals or entities.

6. *Automobile Warranty.* License may be issued to entities or sole proprietors only.

7. *Service Warranty.* License may be issued to individuals or entities.

8. *Reinsurance Intermediaries.* Licensure for reinsurance intermediaries is broken into two categories: brokers and managers. No exam is required of individual or firm reinsurance intermediary applicants. Both individual and firm applicants may apply for licensure at the Department's website.

   A reinsurance intermediary broker is a person other than an officer or employee of the ceding insurer, who solicits, negotiates, or places reinsurance cessions or retro cessions on behalf of a ceding insurer without the authority or power to bind reinsurance on behalf of the ceding insurer. (Fla. Stat. Ann. § 626.7492(f)). Brokers must be licensed and appointed in the same manner as other representatives. Application filing and license fee: $50; license identification fee: $5; original appointment and biennial appointment renewal fee: $60. Fingerprinting fee: $45.80 (plus local Florida county sales tax).

   A reinsurance intermediary manager is a person who has authority to bind, or manages all or part of the assumed reinsurance business of a reinsurer, including the management of a separate division, department, or underwriting office, and act as an agent for reinsurer whether known as a reinsurance intermediary manager, manager, or other similar term. (Fla. Stat. Ann. §626.7492(g)). Each majority owner, partner, officer and director of the agency must be fingerprinted. Fingerprinting fee is $45.80 (plus local Florida county sales tax); Application filing $50, and license identification fee $5; Original appointment and biennial appointment renewal fee: $60.

In addition to the general application qualifications, reinsurance intermediary managers must maintain errors and omissions insurance in an amount of 20 percent of the estimated premium volume subject to a minimum of ten million dollars (the reinsurance intermediary manager must furnish a copy of the declaration page of the policy); furnish character and credit reports for each person who is applying for a license for the first time for a five-year period immediately prior to the date of application for license. The report must be completed by an established and reputable reporting service; and list on the application for license an estimate of the premium volume for the first twelve months of licensure.

A license is not required for reinsurance intermediary managers or brokers if the person is:

1. Licensed as a resident or nonresident "producer" in Florida.
2. Domiciled in Florida and is licensed as a resident or nonresident "producer" in Florida.
3. Domiciled outside Florida, has an office in Florida and is a licensed "producer" in Florida.
4. A person domiciled outside Florida, has an office located outside of Florida and is licensed by Florida as a nonresident agent.
5. A licensed "producer" in a state with a substantially similar reinsurance intermediary law.
   (https://www.myfloridacfo.com/division/agents/licensure/general/docs/0-61-64.htm).

C. **Appointments:** Resident and nonresident insurance representatives (individuals and firms) may transact insurance only after appointment by an insurer or appointing entity as specified under Florida Statute. (Fla. Stat. Ann. § 626.451). The appointment of appointed licensee continues in force until suspended, revoked, or otherwise terminated. However, appointment continuation is subject to a renewal request filed by the appointing entity in the appointee's birth month as to natural persons or the month the original appointment was issued as to entities. Thereafter, the appointment is subject to renewal every twenty-four months. Compliance with continuing education requirements is a condition precedent to the issuance, continuation, reinstatement, or renewal of any appointment. (Fla. Stat. Ann. § 626.381).

Resident and nonresident all lines adjusters must be appointed as independent all lines adjusters with a self-appointment or by an independent adjusting firm, or company employee all lines adjusters appointed by an insurer or group of insurers. The appointment fee for adjusters is $60.

Appointment fees are as follows: Residents and nonresidents $60; additional per county $6 tax must be paid for every county in which a nonresident agent intends to physically transact insurance. Bail Bonds/Surety Agents $80; surplus lines $150; military registration certificate $20. Late fees for appointments: original/initial $250 per appointment; renewal $25 per appointment.

The fee schedule for all appointments may be reviewed at Fla. Stat. Ann. §624.501 or by accessing the following website: https://www.myfloridacfo.com/division/agents/licensure/agents-adjusters/fees.htm.

Examinations shall not be required for the renewal or appointment of the following lines: an agent, customer representative, or adjuster; an applicant for a limited license as agent for travel insurance, motor vehicle rental insurance, credit insurance, in-transit and storage personal property insurance. (Fla. Stat. Ann. § 626.221).

Note: Insurance agencies are not appointed.

D. **Licenses Required of Nonresidents:** Florida licenses the following nonresident agents:

1. Title agency.
2. Life (Including Annuities and Variable Contracts).
3. Health and Life (Including Annuities and Variable Contracts).
4. Health.
5. Credit insurance (Includes: credit life/disability, credit property, credit insurance, and mortgage guaranty.)
6. General lines (property and casualty).
7. Industrial fire or burglary.
8. Legal expense.
9. Personal lines (Noncommercial property and casualty).
10. Title agent (Applicants for nonresident title insurance agent's license must pass the Florida insurance examination and complete the Florida continuing education

requirement in the same manner as resident title agents). (https://myfloridacfo.com/Division/Agents/Licensure/General/).

11. Surplus Lines. (Please see the Surplus Lines section for additional information).

Florida also licenses the following nonresident adjusters:

1. All lines adjuster.

2. Public adjuster.

Florida licenses the following miscellaneous nonresident categories:

1. Reinsurance broker or manager.

2. Insurance agency.

Nonresident general lines agents, life and health agents, and insurance company adjusters must be licensed and appointed to conduct insurance operations in connection with Florida property or operations.

Nonresident public adjusters must be self-appointed or appointed by a public adjusting firm. Attorneys duly licensed to practice law in the courts of Florida, and in good standing with the Florida Bar are exempt from having to obtain a license to adjust or participate in the adjustment of any claim, loss, or damage arising under policies or contracts of insurance. However, this does not exempt attorneys from the state examination if an adjuster license is applied for. (Fla. Stat. Ann. § 626.8732).

Certificates from home state insurance departments are only required by those applicants whose home state does not utilize the National Association of Insurance Commissioners' (NAIC) Producer Database (PDB). The applicant must give power of attorney to the Chief Financial Officer for service of process. Any nonresident offering, soliciting, selling, purchasing, administering, or servicing of risks in Florida for any purchasing or risk retention group must hold a Florida nonresident general lines agent's license, a surplus lines agent license in the individual's home state, and post a $50,000 surety bond. Applicants must use the Department's automated application process. An Internet application program guides an applicant through a series of questions that results in qualification. The application is accepted or terminated and information regarding why qualification criteria were not met is listed. Applicants who qualify for licensure may pay all fees via credit card. Note, appointments may be paid for using a credit card or Electronic check.

Multi-State Exposures. A person who is not a resident of Florida who sells, solicits, or negotiates a contract of insurance for commercial or residential property and casualty risks to an insured with risks located in more than one state insured under that contract, provided that the person is otherwise licensed as an insurance producer to sell, solicit or negotiate that insurance in the state where the insured maintains its principal place of business or residency and the contract of insurance insures risks located in that state, is not required to be licensed as a producer in Florida. (Fla. Stat. Ann. § 626.901).

E. Prelicense Examination or Education Requirements:

Proof of prerequisites should be emailed to:
AgentLicensing@MyFloridaCFO.com.

Questions may be emailed to Education@MyFloridaCFO.com.

1. *Residents.* Unless exempt from the license examination by holding one of the designations listed in the Florida statutes or by having current experience or by transfer of license from another state as prescribed by statute, applicants for the following resident licenses must satisfactorily complete an approved qualification course and pass the state examination:

   a. *General Lines Agent* (includes limited licenses for: industrial fire and burglary). Within four years prior to filing an application for license, the applicant must have taught or successfully completed a 200-hour course (three hours of which must be on ethics) in property, casualty, surety, health, and marine insurance approved by the Department or any of the following:

      (1) One year experience in insurance duties as a full-time employee in all lines of property and casualty insurance.
      (2) A degree in insurance from an accredited institution of higher learning approved by the Department with a minimum of eighteen credit hours of insurance instruction, including specific instruction in the areas of property, casualty, health, and commercial insurance.
      (3) Complete at least one year of responsible insurance duties as a licensed and appointed customer representative, service representative, or personal lines agent and forty hours of coursework approved by the Department covering the areas of property, casualty, surety, health, and marine insurance.
      (4) Holding the CPCU designation. Applicant must submit an original letter from the American Institute for Property and Casualty Underwriters

that certifies his or her status as the holder of a CPCU. The designation exempts the required coursework and the required state examination.

(5) Having held an active general lines insurance agent's license in another state that grants reciprocal treatment to licensees formerly licensed in Florida. (Fla. Stat. Ann. § 626.732)

b. *Limited General Lines Licenses:* Industrial fire and burglary applicants must complete a twenty-hour department approved course and pass the state examination.

c. *Life Agent, Including Annuities & Variable Contracts.* Within the last four years prior to filing an application for license, the applicant must satisfactorily teach or complete forty-hours of coursework in life insurance, annuities, and variable contracts as approved by the department, three hours of which shall be on the subject matter of ethics. Courses must include instruction on the subject matter of unauthorized entities engaging in the business of insurance or successful completion of any one of the following:

(1) Earned or maintained an active designation as a Chartered Financial Consultant (ChFC) from the American College of Financial Services; or Fellow, Life Management Institute (FLMI) from the Life Management Institute.

(2) Earned a degree from an accredited institution of higher learning approved by the Department. Qualifying degrees must indicate a minimum of nine credit hours of insurance instruction, including specific instruction in the areas of life insurance, annuities, and variable insurance products. The qualifying degree exempts the required prelicensing course work and the required state examination.

(3) Holding the Chartered Life Underwriter (CLU) designation. Applicant must submit an original letter from the American College of Life Underwriters that certifies his or her status as the holder of a CLU. The designation exempts the required prelicensing coursework and the required state examination.

(4) Having held an active life or life and health insurance agent's license in another state that grants reciprocal treatment to licensees formerly licensed in Florida. (Fla. Stat. § 626.7851).

Note: Variable annuity authority is only granted along with life authority. Employees of the U.S. Veterans Administration or its State Service Office may not obtain a life agent license in Florida.

Florida does not license viatical settlement brokers. Individuals performing the functions of a viatical settlement broker must obtain a license as a life agent and appoint themselves by filing an appointment form and fee of $60.

Credit applicants for license are not required to complete a course or take the state examination. The application must be filed and the required fees must be paid.
(Fla. Stat. Ann. §§ 626.785 and 626.7851).

d. *Health Agent.* Within the last four years prior to filing an application for license, the applicant must have satisfactorily completed forty-hours of course work in health insurance approved by the Department, three hours of which shall be on the subject matter of ethics. Courses must include instruction on the subject matter of unauthorized entities engaging in the business of insurance, to include the Florida Nonprofit Multiple-Employer Welfare Arrangement Act and the Employee Retirement Income Security Act, 29 U.S.C. §§. 1001 *et seq.*, as it relates to the provision of health insurance by employers to their employees and the regulation thereof or any of the following requirements:

(1) Earned or maintained an active designation as a Registered Health Underwriter (RHU), Chartered Healthcare Consultant (ChHC), or Registered Employee Benefits Consultant (REBC), from the American College of Financial Services; Certified Employee Benefit Specialist (CEBS) from the Wharton School of the University of Pennsylvania; or the Health Insurance Associate (HIA) from America's Health Insurance Plans.

(2) Earned a degree from an accredited institution of higher learning approved by the Department. Qualifying degrees must indicate a minimum of nine credit hours of insurance instruction, including specific instruction in the area of health insurance products. The qualifying degree exempts the required prelicensing coursework and the required state examination.

(3) Holding the Chartered Life Underwriter (CLU) designation Applicant must submit an original letter from the American College of Life Underwriters that certifies his/her status as the holder of a CLU. The designation exempts the required prelicensing coursework and the required state examination.

(4) Having held an active health or life and health insurance agent's license in another state that grants reciprocal treatment to licensees formerly licensed in Florida. (Fla. Stat. § 626.8311).

Note: Employees of the U.S. Veterans Administration or its State Service Office may not obtain a health insurance agent license in Florida. (Fla. Stat. Ann. § 626.833). Applicant cannot be licensed for motor vehicle physical damage and mechanical breakdown or credit insurance simultaneously.

e. *Health & Life (Including Annuities & Variable Contracts).* Within the last four years prior to filing an application for license, the applicant must satisfactorily complete sixty-hours of coursework in multiple areas of insurance, which include life insurance, annuities, variable contracts and health insurance approved by the department three hours of which shall be on the subject matter of ethics. Individuals who completed the forty hour course prior to the statutory change 7/1/2015 are eligible to use that forty-hour course to satisfy the prelicensing course work requirement. Courses must include instruction on the subject matter of unauthorized entities engaging in the business of insurance or successful completion of any one of the following:

(1) Earned a degree from an accredited institution of higher learning approved by the Department. Qualifying degrees must indicate a minimum of eighteen credit hours of insurance instruction, including specific instruction in the areas of life insurance, annuities, variable insurance products and health insurance products. The qualifying degree exempts the required prelicensing coursework and the required state examination.
(2) Holding the Chartered Life Underwriter (CLU) designation Applicant must submit an original letter from the American College of Life Underwriters that certifies his or her status as the holder of a CLU. The designation exempts the required prelicensing coursework and the required state examination.
(3) Having held an active life and health insurance agent's license in another state that grants reciprocal treatment to licensees formerly licensed in Florida.

Note: Variable annuity authority is only granted along with life authority. Employees of the U.S. Veterans Administration or its State Service Office may not obtain a life agent license in Florida. (Fla. Stat. Ann. § 626.833).

f. *Customer Representative.* Must be employed by an agent or agency and supervised by a general lines agent. Within the last four years prior to filing an application for license, the applicant must meet one of the following requirements:

(1) Earned the designation of Accredited Advisor in Insurance (AAI), Associate in General Insurance (AINS), or Accredited Customer Service Representative (ACSR) from the Insurance Institute of America; the designation of Certified Insurance Counselor (CIC) from the Society of Certified Insurance Services Counselors; the designation of Certified Professional Service Representative (CPSR) from the National Foundation for CPSR; the designation of Certified Insurance

Service Representative (CISR) from the Society of Certified Insurance Representatives; the designation of Certified Insurance Representative (CIR) from All-Lines Training; the designation of Professional Customer Service Representative (PCSR) from the Professional Career Institute; Chartered Property and Casualty Underwriters (CPCU) from the American Institute for Chartered Property Casualty Underwriters; the designation of Registered Customer Service Representative (RCSR) from a regionally accredited postsecondary institution in the state whose curriculum is approved by the Department and includes comprehensive analysis of basic property and casualty lines of insurance and testing which demonstrates mastery of the subject. The Certified Customer Service Representative (CCSR) from the Florida Association of Insurance Agents is no longer accepted as of July 1, 2015.

(2) Earned a degree from an accredited institution of higher learning approved by the Department when the degree includes a minimum of nine credit hours of insurance instruction, including specific instruction in the areas of property, casualty, and inland marine insurance. (Fla. Stat. Ann. § 626.7351).

Note: No new limited customer representative (limited to private passenger motor vehicle insurance) license may be issued.

g. *Personal Lines Agent.* Within the last four years prior to filing an application, the applicant must satisfactorily complete sixty-hours of coursework in property, casualty, and inland marine insurance approved by the department, three hours of which must be on the subject matter of ethics, or meet any of the following requirements:

(1) Six months of responsible insurance duties as a substantially full time employee in the area of property and casualty insurance sold to individuals and families for noncommercial purposes, but without the prelicensing education requirement.

(2) Six months of responsible insurance duties as a licensed and appointed customer representative, limited customer representative, or service representative in property and casualty insurance.

(3) A degree which includes at least nine semester hours in property, casualty, and inland marine insurance from an accredited college or university.

(4) A letter certifying that you hold a CPCU designation.

h. *Title Agent.* Within four years prior to the date of filing the application for license, must successfully complete forty hours of approved coursework in title insurance; or have twelve months' experience in title insurance duties as a substantially full-time, bona fide employee of a title agency, title agent, title insurer, or attorney who conducts real estate closing transactions and issues title insurance policies. (Fla. Stat. Ann. §626.8417) For questions email AgentLicensing@MyFloridaCFO.com.

i. *Temporary Limited License as Limited Surety Agent or Professional Bail Bond Agent.* Within four years of applying for the license, the applicant must complete a basic certification course in criminal justice (minimum 120 classroom hours) with a passing grade of 80 percent or higher and complete an approved correspondence course for bail bond agents. In addition, the applicant must do all of the following:

(1) Be employed at the time of application, and remain employed during the term of the temporary license. The employment must be by only one licensed and appointed supervising bail bond agent, MGA, or authorized insurer. The employer is to supervise the work of the applicant and be responsible for the licensee's conduct in the bail bond business. Supervisor and applicant must file an affidavit under oath verifying this on the form available online at: https://www.myfloridacfo.com/Division/Agents/Licensure/Forms/documents/DFS-H2-1509.pdf.

(2) Be a person of high character and approved integrity. The licensee may never have been convicted of, or pleaded guilty, or no contest to: a felony crime that involves moral turpitude; or a crime punishable by imprisonment of one year.

(3) Submit live scan fingerprints taken by the Department's approved vendor.

(4) Supply a recent credential-sized, full-face photograph.

(5) Furnish a certificate of employment and a report as to the applicant's integrity and moral character. This certificate must be executed by the employer.

(6) Submit with the application, notarized statements by at least three residents of the same counties who will recommend the applicant as a bail bond agent.

(7) Not have been licensed as a temporary bail bond agent licensee in Florida within the previous two years.

(8) Pay $90 fee and submit form available online at: https://www.myfloridacfo.com/Division/Agents/Licensure/Forms/documents/DFS-H2-1544Term.pdf.

(Fla. Stat. Ann. § 648.355).

The temporary license is effective for eighteen months.

j. *Bail Bond Agent.* (Professional Bail Bond Agent or Limited Surety Agent). Obtaining this license is a two-step process. The applicant must first obtain a temporary limited license for a limited surety or Professional Bail Bond agent and have worked full time under the license for at least twelve months prior. Then, he or she may apply for a regular bail bond agent license. (Fla. Stat. Ann. § 648.355). Applicants may not be any of the following: A jailer or person employed in any jail; a police officer or employee of any police department or law enforcement agency; a committing magistrate, employee of a court, or employee of the Clerk of Court; a sheriff and deputy sheriff or employee of any sheriff's department; an attorney; or a person having the power to arrest or person who have authority over or control of federal, state, county, or municipal prisoners.
k. *Bail Bond Agent.* (Professional Bail Bond Agent or Limited Surety Agent): Phase 2. At the time the applicant submits his/her application to the DFS, the applicant must have been licensed for at least one year as a temporary limited bail bond agent. He must also meet numbers 2, 3, and 6, as described under the temporary license, above. Finally, the applicant must pass the required bail bond agent examination. A person who fails an examination three times must retake the 120-hour classroom course and obtain a grade of 80 percent or higher before sitting for the examination again. (Fla. Stat. Ann. § 648.381). Questions for the Division of Insurance can be emailed to BailBond@MyFloridaCFO.com.
l. *Adjuster.* All lines adjuster licenses are available for insurance company employee adjusters, independent adjusters, and public adjusters. Public adjuster applicants must have previously held an all-lines public adjusters or all-lines adjuster license or satisfy the public adjuster apprentice employment requirement per Fla. Stat. Ann. § 626.8541, and file a $50,000 surety bond with the application for a license.

Applicants must successfully take and pass the state examination. Applicants for insurance company and independent adjuster licenses who hold one of the following designations are exempt from the examination requirement: Chartered Property and Casualty Underwriter (CPCU) from the American Institute for Chartered Property Casualty Underwriters, Professional Claims Adjuster (PCA) from the Professional Career Institute, Professional Property Insurance Adjuster (PPIA) from the HurriClaim Training Academy, Certified Claims Adjuster (CCA) from AE21 Incorporated, Universal Claim Certification (UCC) from Claims and Litigation Management Alliance (CLM), Certified Adjuster (CA) from All Lines Training or Accredited Claims Adjuster (ACA) from a regionally accredited postsecondary institution in this state.

Florida resident applicants must pass a qualifying examination for each of the above licenses unless otherwise noted.

Designated Home State (DHS) adjuster license is available to individuals who are residents of a state that does not license adjusters and wants to designate Florida as their home state. Meaning, the adjuster will qualify and maintain the DHS adjuster license as a Florida resident would and maintain Florida's bi-annual continuing education requirement.

F. Continuing Education Requirements:

Required Licenses: The following licensees, resident and nonresident, are subject to satisfying the Florida CE requirement:

1. Adjusters (All-lines and public).

2. Customer representatives including limited customer representatives.

3. General lines (property & casualty) agents.

4. Health agents.

5. Industrial fire insurance or burglary agents.

6. Life and health agents.

7. Life (Including Annuities & Variable Contracts) agents.

8. Health & Life (Including Annuities & Variable Contracts) agents.

9. Life only agents.

10. Limited surety and professional bail bond agents.

11. Title agents.

12. Personal lines agents.

This section does not apply to an individual who only holds a license for the sale of any line of insurance for which an examination is not required by the laws of this state or who only holds a limited license as a crop or hail and multiple-peril crop insurance agent. Licensees who are unable to comply with the continuing education requirements due to active duty in the military may submit a written request for a waiver to the Department.

Non-Title License CE Requirement, Types and Hours:

Update Course Requirement (five hours). Each licensee, except a title agent, subject to meeting the Florida CE requirement must complete an approved five-hour law and ethics update course every two years which is specific to the license held by the licensee. The content of the course must address all lines of insurance for which examination and licensure are required and include the following subject areas: insurance law updates, ethics for insurance professionals, disciplinary trends and case studies, industry trends, premium discounts, determining suitability of products and services, and other similar insurance-related topics the Department determines are relevant to legally and ethically carrying out the responsibilities of the license granted. A licensee who holds multiple insurance licenses must complete an update course that is specific to at least one of the licenses held; holding more than one license does not require the individual to take more than one law and ethics update course during any two-year compliance cycle. (Fla. Stat. Ann. § 626.2815).

Elective Courses (hours may vary by license type and experience). The remaining CE requirements for each licensee, except a title agent, subject to meeting the Florida CE requirement will consist of elective courses. Except for public adjusters, elective course requirements may be satisfied by completing any Florida approved CE course. Elective continuing education courses for public adjusters must be specifically designed for public adjusters and approved by the Department.

The required number of elective hours will vary. If not specifically mentioned below as an exception, each licensee must also complete 19 hours of elective continuing education courses, approved by the Department, every two years.

Except that:

1. A licensee who has been licensed for six or more years must also complete a minimum of fifteen hours of elective continuing education every two years.

2. A licensee who has been licensed for twenty-five years or more and is a CLU or a CPCU or has a Bachelor of Science degree in risk management or insurance with evidence of eighteen or more semester hours in upper-level insurance-related courses must also complete a minimum of 5 hours of elective continuing education courses every two years.

3. An individual who holds a license as a customer representative, limited customer representative, motor vehicle physical damage and mechanical breakdown insurance agent, or an industrial fire insurance or burglary insurance agent

and who is not a licensed life or health agent, must also complete a minimum of five hours of continuing education courses every two years.

4. An individual who holds a license as a bail bond agent must also complete a minimum of nine hours of elective continuing education courses every two years.

   Title License Continuing Education requirement, Types and Hours:

   A resident and nonresident title insurance agent must complete a minimum of ten hours of continuing education credit every two years in title insurance and escrow management specific to this state and approved by the Department, which shall include at least three hours of continuing education on the subject matter of ethics, rules, or compliance with state and federal regulations relating specifically to title insurance and closing services.

   Title agents who hold multiple licenses requiring continuing education must complete the requirements for the title license in addition to the continuing education requirements for other licenses held.

Enforcement of Continuing Education

Continuing education hours are due the last day of the licensee's birth month, after the licensee has held the license for twenty-four months. The compliance cycle runs every twenty-four months thereafter as long as there is an active license. Excess hours accumulated during any two-year compliance period may be carried forward to the next compliance period. Compliance with continuing education requirements is a condition precedent to the issuance, continuation, reinstatement, or renewal of any appointment subject to this section. The number of hours required varies by type of license (Fla. Stat. Ann. § 626.2815).

Non-resident adjusters and public adjusters can satisfy their Florida CE requirement by meeting the CE requirements of their home state or a reciprocal state in which they are also licensed. Otherwise, they must complete Florida CE requirements as resident adjusters or public adjusters respectively. For list of reciprocal states click the following link: https://www.myfloridacfo.com/division/agents/Licensure/Agents-Adjusters/recip_nonres.htm

Nonresident agents can satisfy their Florida CE requirement by meeting the CE requirements of their home state. Otherwise, they must complete Florida CE requirements as resident agents.

Proof of compliance must be verified either by the Department searching the producer database, or by the licensee submitting a letter of certification. Nonresident title agent must meet Florida continuing education requirements. (Fla. Stat. Ann. §§ 626.2815 and 626.869).

Reduction in Hours Guideline Information

CLUs, CPCUs, and those with a degree in risk management or insurance with eighteen semester hours or more in insurance related courses and who have twenty-five years of experience, qualify for a reduction of elective course hour requirements. This reduction is based upon approval following submission of the Reduction of Continuing Education requirements application (form DFS-H2-1109). https://www.myfloridacfo.com/division/agents/licensure/forms/documents/DFS-H2-1109.pdf.

Applicability of Courses Taken by Licensees for CE Credit. All courses must be approved by the Department prior to being offered. Candidates should verify courses have been approved by visiting the Department's website prior to taking a course. Credit for approved courses can be given one time in a two-year period from the date the course was completed. Approved instructors can receive credit for CE courses that have been approved by the Department for the number of hours they teach. The instructor's name must be submitted on the roster as a student.

Each person or entity sponsoring a course for continuing education credit must furnish, within twenty-one days after completion of the course, in a form satisfactory to the Department or its designee, a roster showing the name and license number of all persons successfully completing such course and requesting credit.

Licensees may securely monitor their continuing education records and requirements by logging in to their MyProfile account at https://dice.fldfs.com/public/pb_index.aspx. Noncompliance with continuing education requirements will result in the issuance of a preliminary notice of noncompliance posted to the licensee's MyProfile account and a notice sent to licensee's email address on record with the Department. Failure to properly respond to the preliminary notice may result in the termination of appointments.

G. **Cancellation of Agency Contracts:** Subject to an appointee's contract rights, insurers must give agents sixty days' advance written notice of termination of the appointment of an appointee or MGA; any general lines agent terminating the appointment of a customer representative, or a crop hail or multiple-peril crop insurance agent; and any employer terminating the appointment of an adjuster or customer service representative, except when termination is for grounds for suspension or revocation of the appointee's license. Notice must also be filed with the Department of Financial Services within thirty days after the termination, including the reasons and facts involved in the termination. (Fla. Stat. Ann. § 626.471).

H. Risk Retention and Purchasing Groups: Fla. Stat. Ann. §§ 627.941 to 627.955. The purpose of this part is to set out rules for the information or operation of purchasing groups and risk retention groups in Florida.

Any person offering, soliciting, selling, purchasing, administering, or servicing risks in Florida for any purchasing or risk retention group must hold a Florida resident general lines agent license and a resident surplus lines agent license. Or if not a resident of this state, one must hold a nonresident general lines agent license and a nonresident surplus lines agent's license.

All policies issued by risk retention groups must contain the following wording in ten-point type on the front page and the declarations page:

NOTICE

"The risk retention group issues this policy. Your risk retention group may not be subject to all of the insurance laws and regulations of your state. State insurance insolvency guaranty funds are not available for your risk retention group."

I. Other License Rules, Requirements, or Restrictions: Unlicensed nonresidents may not enter or send mail or telephone into the state to solicit, inspect service, or otherwise transact. Nonresident agents are not required to maintain an insurance agency in this state. If a nonresident does maintain or have a financial interest in an insurance agency in this state, the agency is subject to the same requirements that apply to agencies of resident agents in this state. Life and Health agents may place excess or rejected business with insurers for whom they are not appointed, if they are appointed for the same class of business which is excess or rejected.

All applications for insurance policies or annuities must show the name of the agent and the agent's Florida license identification number.

It is imperative that licensees submit all address changes, as required by statute, within thirty days. (Fla. Stat. Ann. § 626.551). Address changes may be made online by logging in to their MyProfile account at https://dice.fldfs.com/public/pb_index.aspx.

Every agent transacting any insurance policy must maintain in his or her office, or have readily accessible by electronic or photographic means, such records of policies transacted by him or her as to enable the policyholders and department to obtain all necessary information, including daily reports, applications, change endorsements, or documents signed or initialed by the insured concerning such policies. Agents are required to keep these records for at least five years after policy expiration. (Fla. Stat. Ann. §626.748).

J. **Policy Countersignature Requirements:** Required except for:

1. Contracts of reinsurance.

2. Policies of insurance on the rolling stock of railroad companies doing a general freight and passenger business.

3. United States Customs surety bonds that are issued by a corporate surety approved by the United States Department of Treasury and that name the US as the beneficiary.

4. Policies of insurance issued by insurers whose agents represent only one company or group of companies under common ownership if ownership of a company within one group is transferring policies to another company within the same group and the agent of record remains the same.

5. Policies of insurance issued by insurers whose agents represent, as to property, casualty, and surety insurance, only one company or group of companies under common ownership and for which the application has been lawfully submitted to the insurer. (Fla. Stat. Ann. § 624.426).

K. **Portable Electronics Insurance:** Portable electronics insurance claims may only be resolved if used by a licensed independent adjuster, licensed agent, or supervised individual, complying with claims payment requirements of the insurance code, who is certified as a compliant with the law by an officer of a licensed business entity. (Fla. Stat. Ann. § 626.8685).

II. Commissions, Fees, Commingling of Funds, Rebating Commissions, and Suitability in Annuity Transactions

A. **Commissions:** No commission may be paid to anyone who does not hold a valid current resident or nonresident license.

Rebating of commissions is allowed in some situations. The agent must file a rebate schedule with each of the insurers represented and must make rebates available to all insureds in the same actuarial class. The agent is to apply the rebate schedule uniformly, so that all who purchase a policy from an agent will receive the same percentage rebate. The agent may not discriminate as to who receives a rebate—nor as to the amount of the rebate—based on the age, sex, residence, race, nationality, ethnic origin, marital status, or occupation of the insured. The agent may not condition the granting of a rebate on the purchase of a collateral coverage. (Fla. Stat. Ann. § 626.572).

B. Fees: No person licensed as an insurance agent may receive any fee or commission or any other thing of value in addition to the rates filed pursuant to Chapter 627 of the Florida Statutes for examining any health insurance or any health benefit plan for the purpose of giving or offering advice, counsel, recommendation, or information in respect to terms, conditions, benefits, coverage or premium of any such policy or contract unless such compensation is based upon a written contract signed by the party to be charged and specifying or clearly defining the amount or extent of such compensation and informing the party to be charged that any commission received from the insurer will be rebated to the party within thirty days after receipt of such commission by the insurance agent. (Fla. Stat. Ann. § 626.593).

A managing general agent may charge a per-policy fee not to exceed $25. In no instance shall the aggregate of per-policy fees for a placement of business when combined with any other per-policy fee charged by the insurer, result in per-policy fees which exceed the aggregate amount of $25. The per-policy fee shall be a component of the insurer's rate filing and shall be fully earned. (Fla. Stat. Ann. § 626.7451(11)).

A licensed general lines agent may charge a per-policy fee not to exceed $10 to cover the administrative costs of the agent associated with selling the motor vehicle insurance policy if the policy covers only personal injury protection coverage and property damage liability coverage and no other insurance is sold or issued in conjunction with or collateral to the policy. The fee is not considered part of the premium.

Trustees of a self-insured medical malpractice trust fund may obtain a professional consultant's services fee for loss prevention and claims coordination under a risk management program or employ a licensed Risk Manager acceptable to the Department. These services may be provided by a service agent or employees who are not licensed Risk Managers who demonstrate to the Department adequate experience and expertise in the areas of loss prevention and claims coordination under a medical malpractice risk management program. (Fla. Admin. Code Ann. r. 69O-187.005).

C. Disclosure Requirements: In general, consulting fees must be negotiated in advance and in writing if the services to be performed by the agent are completely outside the normal duties an agent would engage in to underwrite or otherwise procure coverage on behalf of a proposed insured. All compensation being paid to the insurance agent must be disclosed in the contract. A copy of every such contract must be retained by the licensee for not less than three years after such services have been fully performed. (Fla. Stat. Ann. §626.593). This law does not address service-based fee contracts.

D. Commingling of Funds: Florida law prohibits the commingling title insurance of premiums with other agency funds. Attorneys must deposit into a separate trust account all funds received in connections with transactions in which an attorney is serving as a title or real estate settlement agent.

E. **Suitability in Annuity Transactions:** Insurance agents and insurers prior to executing a purchase or transfer of an annuity resulting from a recommendation to a consumer, must make reasonable efforts to obtain information concerning the suitability of the recommendation. (Fla. Stat. Ann. § 627.4554 (5)(a-e)).

Disclosure In annuity replacement or exchanges – Before executing a replacement or exchange of an annuity contract resulting from a recommendation, the agent must provide on form DFS-H1-1981, which is hereby incorporated by reference, information that compares the differences between the existing annuity contract and the annuity contract being recommended in order to determine the suitability of the recommendation and its benefit to the consumer. A true and correct executed copy of this form must be provided by the agent to the insurer, or to the person or entity that has contracted with the insurer to perform this function as authorized by this section, within ten days after execution of the form, and must be provided to the consumer no later than the date of delivery of the contract or contracts. (Fla. Stat. Ann. §627.4554(5)(f)).

III. **Statutory References:** Florida Statutes Annotated §§624.10-426; 626.011 through 626.711; 626.726 through 626.754; 626.776 through 626.798; 626.826 through 626.839; 626.841 through 626.8473; 626.851 through 626.878; 626.88 through 626.899; 626.991 through 626.992; 626.995; 648.355 through 648.385; 69O-187.005.

GEORGIA

Insurance Commissioner, Agents Licensing Division
No. 2 Martin Luther King Jr., Drive West Tower, Suite 702; Atlanta, GA 30334
Telephone: 404-656-2070, 800-656-2298;
Fax: 404-657-8542
Email: Agents@oci.ga.gov
https://www.oci.ga.gov/

I. Licensing Requirements: Sales Personnel—Agents, Agencies, Limited Subagents, Managing General Agents. Other Insurance Professionals—Adjusters, Counselors, Field/ Marketing Representatives, Reinsurance Intermediaries, Public Adjusters, Third-Party Administrators.

A. Applicability: A person shall not sell, solicit, or negotiate insurance in Georgia for any class or classes of insurance unless the person is licensed for that line of authority. Any individual who sells, solicits, or negotiates insurance in Georgia shall be licensed as an agent. Any business entity that sells, solicits, or negotiates insurance in Georgia shall be licensed as an agency. Any individual defined as an adjuster who for a fee, commission, salary, or other compensation investigates, settles, or adjusts claims arising under insurance contracts on behalf of the insurer or the insured shall be licensed as either an independent adjuster or a public adjuster. A license as an insurance agent is not required of attorneys collecting insurance premiums and advising clients or adjusting losses incidental to the practice of law. Salaried employees of credit reporting agencies, employers who make salary deductions for employee's premiums, and people who serve the master policy holder of a group plan also do not need to be licensed as agents. (Ga. Code Ann. § 33-23-4).

B. Licenses Required of Residents: Each of the following must be licensed in Georgia.

Sales Personnel

1. *Agents.* Agents may be licensed in the following lines:

   a. Life, accident, and sickness.
   b. Property, marine, and transportation.
   c. Casualty.
   d. Surety.
   e. Title.
   f. Health Maintenance Organization.
   g. Life.

h. Accident and sickness.
i. Property.
j. Variable products.
k. Fraternal.
l. Personal lines.
m. Credit.

Each group (a) through (f) constitutes a class of insurance. (Ga. Code Ann. § 33-3-5 and Ga. Comp. R. & Regs. 120-2-3-.06).

License Fee: Unless specifically provided otherwise, for each certificate of authority, original license, renewal of a certificate of authority, or renewal of a license: agent, subagent, counselor, adjuster, or principal office of an insurance agency (new license) the fee will be $100; biennial license renewal fee will be $100. Application fee: $15. Each branch office of an insurance agency other than the principal office (new license), the fee will be $20; biennial license renewal will be $20. (Ga. Code Ann. § 33-8-1). For a copy of all agent licensing and renewal forms see https://www.oci.ga.gov/other/Forms.aspx?P5ctOUrkESbR4nnc8qOlXKnkuHpO8skp7s7j5PlZvzEsfZ3m4DnG8yFgfbXyF3oy.

Resident agent, limited subagent, adjuster, and counselor licenses may be renewed upon receipt by the commissioner of evidence of such continuing education as the commissioner may establish by rule or regulation and payment of such fees as are provided by law.

A late renewal fee of $15 and penalty of $150 applies to renewals more than fifteen days late. If a licensee fails to complete the reinstatement process within six months of their expiration date, electronic fingerprinting is required.

If the reinstatement process is not completed within twelve months of the expiration date of the license, all prelicensing requirements must be met if the applicant wishes to be licensed again. (https://www.oci.ga.gov/agents/home.aspx).

Renewal of the license on forms prescribed by rule or regulation must be made prior to the last day of the licensee's birth month and biennially thereafter. Renewals may be done at https://www.oci.ga.gov/Agencies/OnLineRenewals.aspx. (Ga. Code Ann. § 33-23-18).

As of July 1, 2002, Georgia adopted producer licensing. However, the term "producer" only applies to nonresidents who hold that title in their home state. Georgia still licenses residents as "agents."

2. *Agencies.* All agencies must be licensed. New and renewal fee: $100 (biennial) for the principal office of an agency; $20 (biennial) for each branch office. Complete form GID 130 (available at https://www.oci.ga.gov/ExternalResources/Forms/AllForms/GID-130-AL.pdf (Ga. Code Ann. § 33-8-1).

3. *Limited Lines.* Georgia offers the following limited licenses:

   a. Credit life and credit accident and sickness insurance.
   b. Credit casualty insurance.
   c. Credit property insurance.
   d. Credit unemployment insurance.
   e. Accidental death and dismemberment insurance.
   f. Nonfiling or nonrecording insurance.
   g. Vendors' single interest insurance.
   h. Rental car insurance.
   i. Portable electronics insurance. (Ga. Code Ann. § 33-23-12).

4. *Managing General Agents.* New certification, $600; renewal, $500. Must hold a producers license and an agency license. May be required to maintain a surety bond or an E&O policy. (Ga. Code Ann. § 33-8-1).

Other Insurance Professionals

1. *Counselors.* May be licensed for either P&C or life/accident and sickness. Must have a $5,000 bond. Biennial fee: $100. (Ga. Code Ann. § 33-23-7, Ga. Comp. R. & Regs. 120-2-3-.06, 120-2-3-.18).

2. *Adjusters, Including Public Adjusters.* Public adjuster, workers compensation, and crop hail adjusters must be licensed. All new applicants must complete a forty-hour prelicensing course. Public adjusters must be licensed and have a $5,000 bond. (Ga. Comp. R. & Regs. r. 120-2-3-.06, .25).

3. *Reinsurance Intermediaries.* Must be licensed as producers. The commissioner may require intermediary-managers to file a bond and carry an E&O policy. (Ga. Code Ann. § 33-49-3).

4. *Third-Party Administrators.* New, $500; renewal, $400. Must file a bond and have an E&O policy, in an amount of at least $100,000. (Ga. Code Ann. § 33-23-102, 33-8-1; Ga. Comp. R. & Regs. r. 120-2-49-.07).

All licenses are continuous, based on agents, adjusters, and counselors completing continuing education requirements. All license applications may be downloaded from the Georgia OCI Web site or completed on the Georgia Sircon Portal, access to which may also be found on the OCI's website.

The submission of all filing fees are to be submitted via electronic funds transfer (EFT), effective on any SERFF filing submitted on or after May 1, 2009. To sign up for EFT, contact the SERFF Marketing Team at serffmktg@naic.org or call 816-783-8787. On or after February 1, 2010, the submission of all foreign annual insurance company renewal filings are to be via company portal electronically; this applies also to associated fees. All domestic insurers are still required to file hard copies of their annual insurance company financial statements, renewal forms, and fees.

C. **Appointments:** Each insurer authorized to transact insurance in Georgia shall obtain an agent's certificate of authority for each agent representing such insurer in the selling, soliciting, or negotiating of contracts of insurance in this state. The request for a certificate of authority must be submitted within fifteen days from the date the agency contract is executed or the first insurance application is submitted. (Ga. Code Ann. § 33-23-26).

D. **Licenses Required of Nonresidents:** A nonresident must be licensed to act as an agent, counselor, or adjuster with respect to any insurance activities on property or exposures in Georgia. (Ga. Code Ann. §33-23-4, 16). Georgia accepts the title of "producer" for nonresidents. The nonresident must be appointed in Georgia. Certification of same license types and qualifications in nonresident's home state is required. Nonresident applicants are to complete nonresident uniform application. Applications may be downloaded from the DOI's Web site. (https://www.oci.ga.gov/insurers/home.aspx).

Multi-State Exposures. A license is not required for a nonresident insurance producer who sells, solicits, or negotiates a contract of insurance for commercial property and casualty coverage when risks that are to be insured under that contract are located in more than one state. This exception applies only if the nonresident is licensed to sell, solicit, or negotiate that insurance in the state where the insured maintains its principal place of business and the contract of insurance insures risks located in that state. (Ga. Code Ann. § 33-23-4).

E. **Prelicensing Examination and Education Requirements:**

1. *Residents.*

a. Agents must take forty hours of classroom instruction and pass a qualifying examination, unless otherwise specified. This requirement applies separately for qualification as property/casualty, accident and health, or life agent.

Credit agents require five hours of instruction, but are not required to take a qualifying exam.

b. Limited subagent applicants must take twenty hours of instruction. (Ga. Comp. R. & Regs. r. 120-2-3-.08).
c. Counselor applicants must have five years' experience as agent, subagent, or adjuster in life/accident and health or property/casualty and pass an exam.
d. Applicants for variable products must hold a life agents license and take an eight-hour prelicensing course and pass a qualifying exam.
e. Public adjusters must take a forty-hour course and pass an exam. Crop hail adjusters take an exam only.

Applicants for all other licenses must pass a qualifying examination. (Ga. Code Ann. § 33-23-5). Examination fee: $90 for each examination taken. Examinations are administered by Pearson VUE, 800-274-0488 (still the testing vendor even though the back office vendor has changed.) Holders of the following designations are exempt from these requirements: Chartered Property Casualty Underwriter (CPCU) for property/casualty, Chartered Life Underwriter (CLU) or Fellow, Life Management Institute (FLMI) for life and Certified Insurance Counselor (CIC), Accredited Advisor in Insurance Program (AAI), Registered Employee Benefits Consultant (REBC), CPCU, CLU, or FLMI for counselors.

The following licenses have no education or exam requirements: travel ticket, travel accident and sickness, fraternal agent, and temporary agent.

New Back Office Vendor:

PSI Services LLC is the back office vendor for agents licensing. PSI will handle all agents licensing transactions including initial license applications, temporary license applications, continuing and prelicensing course, provider and instructor approval, license renewals, appointment and terminations, agency License applications, affiliations and renewals. All forms have been updated with their address and contact information.

PSI Services LLC Contact Information:

Telephone: 855-235-5174
Email: GAInslicensing@psionline.com
(https://www.oci.ga.gov/agents//home.aspx).

2. *Nonresidents.* Nonresidents must be appointed in Georgia. Nonresident licenses are renewed annually and require payment of fee and status letter from home state or must be in NAIC's Producer Database. Fees: new and renewal: $100; application: $15. Amendment fee: $115. Applicants may apply online via Sircon

or download the Nonresident Uniform Application for Individual Producer from the OCI's Web site. (Ga. Code Ann. §§ 33-8-1, 33-23-16; https://www.nipr.com/rules_ga_nral.htm).

F. Continuing Education Requirements:

Number of Hours Required: Depends on how long license has been held (also applies to adjusters and counselors). If a licensee holds more than one license type and meets the requirements of the license with the maximum continuing education required, such licensee will also meet the requirements of others:

1. Less than twenty years' experience: twenty-four hours biennially, including three hours of ethics.

2. Twenty years' experience or more: twenty hours biennially, including three hours of ethics each year to be part of the twenty hours.

3. For credit insurance only licensees, ten hours biennially, of self-study, with no ethics requirement.

4. For limited subagent only licensees, ten hours biennially, no ethics requirement.

5. For workers comp adjuster only licensees, twenty hours of CE approved by the Workers Comp Board, no ethics requirement.

   (Ga. Comp. R. & Regs. r. 120-2-3-.15; https://www.oci.ga.gov/Agents/CE%20Requirements.aspx).

CE requirement for agents selling annuities:

1. An agent may not sell, solicit or negotiate an annuity product unless the individual has completed a one-time four hour Annuity Suitability course.

2. Agents who have completed a four-hour Annuity Suitability course in another state shall be deemed to satisfy this state's requirement as long as the course material of that course is similar to this state's requirements. (Ga. Comp. R. & Regs. r. 120-2-3-.15(g)).

   Holders of the following professional designations—CPCU, CLU, FLMI, CIC, CEBS, ChFC, AAI, CFP, CRM, CISR or a major BBA in Risk Management and Insurance—are required to complete only six hours per year with three in ethics. (Terms are now biennial, twelve credits per term with three credits in ethics required).

Excess Hours: A licensee may carry over up to 50 percent of his or her continuing education hours from the previous reporting period. (https://www.oci.ga.gov/Agents/CE%20Requirements.aspx).

Final Exam: Self-study final exams must be monitored.

Reductions and Extensions: Licensees may request reductions or extensions by submitting GID form 101E with the license renewal notice. Form available at https://www.oci.ga.gov/ExternalResources/Forms/AllForms/GID-101E-AL.pdf. Standard reductions are granted for teaching courses in insurance-related topics, legislative or journalistic activities, and projects concerning insurance laws and regulations. Additionally, exemptions may be granted, upon review and approval by GID, for illness and family emergencies that prevent the licensee from completing the requisite CE hours. However, extensions are not considered standard requests and are rarely granted by GID. (Ga. Comp. R. & Regs. r. 120-2-3-.19).

Renewal Procedure for Educational Providers and Instructors:

1. All approved educational providers and instructors must file a renewal application and pay the required fees by October 1, annually. Failure to do so will result in a withdrawal of approval and cancellation of educational providers, courses, and instructors. (Ga. Comp. R. & Regs. r. 120-2-3-.13).

2. PSI Services LLC Contact Information:

   Telephone: 855-235-5174.
   Email: GAInslicensing@psionline.com.

Late filings may be subject to a fee. Nonresidents are exempt from the CE requirement with a letter of certification from the home state.

G. Cancellation of Agency Contracts/Producer Appointments: For termination of an agent's certificate of authority, written notice must be given to the Insurance Department within thirty days of the cancellation and to the agent where reasonably possible, showing the effective date of the termination. (Ga. Code Ann. § 33-23-26).

H. Rules for Risk Retention and Purchasing Groups: A risk retention group must be chartered and licensed as a casualty or liability insurance company and comply with all Georgia laws and requirements that apply to such insurers. Such groups must submit for commissioner's approval a plan of operation or feasibility study. (Ga. Code

Ann. § 33-40-3). Nonresident groups, before entering Georgia, must register with the insurance commissioner and submit reports to the commissioner as described in the law. Purchasing groups must also register with the commissioner and submit reports as required by the law. All groups and all resident and nonresident agents or brokers participating in them must comply with all Georgia insurance laws, including licensing and solicitation requirements or restrictions. (Ga. Code Ann. § 33-40-4). Tax is 4 percent, payable quarterly. (Ga. Code Ann. § 33-40-5). All risk retention group policies must show the following notice in at least ten point type on the front page and on the declarations page of the policy:

NOTICE

> This policy is issued by your risk retention group. Your risk retention group may not be subject to all of the insurance laws and regulations of your state. State insurance insolvency guaranty funds are not available for your risk retention group. (Ga. Code Ann. § 33-40-8).

I. **Other License Rules, Requirements, or Restrictions:** A licensed nonresident may solicit or inspect in Georgia. An unlicensed nonresident may not enter the state for any insurance purpose. Entering the state includes mail or telephone or other electronic communication into the state from the outside, as well as physical presence in the state.

All new resident applicants and active licensees who do not renew their license within six months of expiration shall be required to submit electronic fingerprints through Gemalto Cogent for a criminal background check. The applicant shall bear the cost for electronic fingerprinting. (https:// oci.ga.gov/Agents/Home.aspx).

Every individual, corporation, partnership, or other business entity submitting an application for licensure must submit a Citizenship Affidavit along with the application. (https:// oci.ga.gov/AgencyPortal/). Form GID-276-EN can be found on the Georgia Office of Insurance and Fire Safety Commissioner's website at http://www.oci.ga.gov/ExternalResources/Forms/AllForms/GID-276-EN.pdf.

J. **Policy Countersignature Requirements:** Countersignature only required when in retaliation. (Ga. Code. Ann. § 33-23-32).

K. **Portable Electronics Insurance:** A limited license authorizes any employee of the vendor to sell or offer coverage under a policy of portable electronics insurance to customers at each location where the vendor engages in portable electronic transactions. The sale of portable electronics insurance policies should be limited to sales in connection with the sale by the retail vendor. For more information regarding Portable Electronics Insurance Licensing please see Ga. Code Ann. § 33-23-12(d).

II. Commissions, Fees, Commingling of Funds, and Suitability in Annuity Transactions

A. Commissions: There are no restrictions on division of commissions among Georgia licensed residents or nonresidents. There is no retaliatory provision as to nonresidents. No commission may be paid to an unlicensed resident or nonresident under any circumstances. Rebating of commissions is not allowed. (Ga. Code. Ann. § 33-23-4).

B. Fees: Fees may be charged for certain additional ancillary services as a counselor. Such services include risk identification; loss measurement; gathering and analysis of loss information; verification of workers compensation experience modifiers; setting of risk retention levels; development of retention financing plans; development of insurance specifications; negotiation with insurers regarding coverages, costs, and payment options; implementation of retained and transferred risk programs; monitoring of annual program; and insurance audit services. (Ga. Code Ann. § 33-23-1.1).

C. Disclosure Requirements: If employees of the financial institution that have contact with the general public or financial institution customers with respect to lending, checking, deposit taking, or trust activities are licensed as insurance agents to sell insurance, the employee shall disclose verbally at the time a solicitation is made or an application is taken that the employee is acting as an insurance agent representing one or more specifically identified insurance companies, and that the insurance product is not issued or guaranteed by the financial institution. (Ga. Comp. R. & Regs. r. 120-2-76-.10).

D. Commingling of Funds: All license holders, including nonresidents, must maintain a trust fund for premiums collected for insurers, separate from any other personal funds. (Ga. Code Ann. § 33-23-35).

E. Suitability in Annuity Transactions: In recommending to a consumer the purchase of an annuity or the exchange of an annuity that results in another insurance transaction or series of insurance transactions, the insurance producer, or the insurer where no producer is involved, shall have reasonable grounds for believing that the recommendation is suitable for the consumer on the basis of the facts disclosed by the consumer as to her investments and other insurance products and as to his or her financial situation and needs.

An insurer either must assure that a system to supervise recommendations including, but not limited to, maintaining written procedures and conducting periodic reviews of recommendations. (Ga. Comp. R. & Regs. r. 120-2-94-.06).

Georgia has not adopted the NAIC Suitability in Annuity Transactions Model Regulation.

III. Statutory References: Ga. Code Ann. §§ 33-3-5; 8-1; 23-1.1, 4, 5, 7, 12, 16, 18, 26, 32, 35, 102; 40-3 to 40-5, 8; 49-3. Ga. Comp. R. & Regs. 120-2-3-.06, .08, .13, .15, .18, .19, .25; 120-2-49-.07; 120-2-76-.10; 120-2-94-.06.

GUAM

Department of Revenue and Taxation
1240 Army Drive; Barrigada, GU 96913
P.O. Box 23607 GMF; Barrigada, GU 96921
Telephone: 671-635-1844, -1845
Fax: 671-633-2643;
Email:alice.cruz@revtax.guam.gov
http://www.guamtax.com or http://www.guam.gov/

I. **Licensing Requirements:** Brokers, General Agents, Sub-agents, and Nonresident producers. (22 GCA §15701).

A. **Applicability:** No person, corporation or bank shall act as an agent of any:

1. Local mutual aid association.

2. Local mutual burial association.

3. Statewide mutual assessment corporation.

4. Government mutual insurance company.

5. Casualty company writing accident and health insurance.

6. Health maintenance organization.

7. Any other type of insurance carrier licensed to do business in Guam and which insurance carrier's agents are required to be licensed shall have first procured a license from the department. Unless that individual or entity, and no such insurance carrier shall appoint any person, corporation, or bank shall have obtained a license and no such person, corporation or bank who obtains a license shall engage in business as an agent until that individual or entity shall have been appointed to act as an agent by some duly authorized insurance carrier authorized to do business in Guam. (22 G.C.A. §15704.2).

B. **Licenses Required of Residents:** The following must be licensed in Guam: brokers, general agents, subagents, adjusters, and solicitors. The license expires each year on July 1. A business entity acting as an insurance producer is required to obtain an insurance producer license. Application shall be made using the Uniform Business Entity Application. The annual fees are:

1. Broker: $100.

2. General agent: $100.

3. Subagent: $25.

4. Nonresident producer: $25.

5. Solicitors: $25.

The license term expires annually on July 1. The license must be renewed annually beginning May 1. (22 GCA §15701; https://www.guamtax.com/fees/ISBFees_201303.pdf).

C. **Appointments:** No person, corporation or bank shall engage in business as an agent until that individual or entity has been appointed to act as an agent by some duly authorized insurance carrier authorized to do business in Guam. (22 GCA §15704.2).

The following application forms are used:

1. Appointment of general agent; authority to appoint subagents; authority to accept service of legal process; and authority to countersign policies of insurance. Certificate of Authority, Form I-5. Agreement and Power of Attorney, form I-2.

   In addition to a form I-5 filing for a Certificate of Authority, in order to obtain a general agent's license, the applicant must file an application for a General Agent's License (form I-10). (12 GAR §1102).

   Those who appoint and cancel agents are not required to be certified in advance. However, form I-5 and power of attorney must be filed with the commissioner to advise the department of agent's appointment. The appointment fee for each resident general agent or the renewal thereof every July 1 is $100.

2. NAIC Uniform Application for Individual Insurance Producer License/Registration (https://www.naic.org/documents/committees_ex_pltf_plwg_individual_initial_producer_app_20132015_clean.pdf).

3. Appointment of subagent. Form 1-12. The appointment fee for each subagent is $25.

Form I-13. (12 GAR §1106).

For more clarification on forms and applications, see 12 GAR §1107.

D. Licenses Required of Nonresidents: Guam will license on a reciprocal basis nonresident agents from any state that allows any Guam resident to apply for a nonresident insurance license. Use the NAIC Uniform Application for Nonresident License, Individual or Business Entity. Submit a certificate of good standing issued by the insurance commissioner in the applicant's home state. Submit appointment for Subagent Form, I-12, duly signed by an authorized officer of an insurance company that is licensed in Guam or by a resident general agent licensed in Guam. Licensing fee is $25. (22 GCA §15705.1).

Requirements for Nonresident Brokers: Police clearance issued by the state in which the individual broker is domiciled or FBI background check; proof of existence of a trust account for premiums received by broker from clients; policies can only be placed with insurance companies that are admitted to transact insurance business or licensed in Guam; pay a license fee of $100; and have a statement from the insurance commissioner of the applicant's home state allowing licensing of residents of Guam for nonresident insurance broker's license.

Surplus lines brokers must submit the additional requirements: surety bond in the amount of $2,000; notarized surplus lines broker's statement; Affidavit of Declination; and Agreement and Power of Attorney or other Court Process or Service of Suite Clause. (22 G.C.A. §15802).

Multi-State Exposures. Even when writing a risk with only an incidental exposure in Guam (such as a car on a fleet policy), the nonresident needs a Guam license. (22 GCA §15704.2).

When renewing a nonresident broker license, submit the following additional requirements: 2 percent Assessment (Commercial & Industrial) Liability Premium; and 5 percent Premium Tax (copy of BR20 Stamped "paid"). Tax payment online available at https://pay.guam.gov/pg/HowItWorks.aspx. https://www.guamtax.com/about/regulatory.html . (11 G.C.A. §26202).

E. Prelicensing Examination and Education Requirements: Guam does not require prelicensing education. An insurance exam is required for all insurance licenses. (22 GCA §15704.1). To schedule an exam, contact the Examination Supervisor, alice.cruz@revtax.guam.gov; phone: (671) 635-1844.

F. Continuing Education Requirements: Effective July 1, 2018, agents must complete twelve credit hours plus two hours of ethics, for fourteen total CE hours annually. Brokers must complete six hours of P&C License, six hours of Life and Health, and two hours of Ethics, for fourteen total hours of CE. Adjusters must complete twelve hours of CE in discipline or general credits, plus two hours of ethics, for a total of fourteen hours of CE annually. Any producer who is sixty-five years old or older and who has twenty-five years of insurance experience is eligible for CE Exemption, subject to conditions set by the Commissioner's Office. (https://www.guamtax.com/about/CEPOINTERS-RENEWAL2018-2019.pdf; 22 G.C.A. §15703).

G. **Cancellation of Agency Contracts/Producer Appointments:** When a subagent's or solicitor's appointment is terminated, the Commissioner must be notified immediately, in writing, including proof that the notice of termination was also sent to the subagent or solicitor. The reasons for such cancellation may, but are not required to, be stated on the notice. (12 GAR §1105).

H. **Rules for Risk Retention and Purchasing Groups:** The Territory of Guam has not adopted the Risk Retention Act of 1986. Any contract that falls within the definition of insurance as it is defined in the Insurance Law of Guam is regulated as an insurance activity without regard to the state of domicile of the risk retention or purchasing group.

II. Policy Countersignature Requirements

A. **Applicability:** Countersignature is required on all policies issued on risks in Guam on all lines of insurance and types of insurers. The only exceptions to the countersignature requirement are as follows:

1. Contracts of insurance on transportation and navigation.
2. Contracts of reinsurance between insurance companies or other insurers.
3. Contracts of insurance covering property in interstate or foreign commerce. (22 G.C.A. §18302).

B. **Who Must Countersign:** Only duly authorized resident general agents may countersign policies issued by foreign or alien companies admitted to do business in Guam. (22 G.C.A. §18302).

C. **Other Countersignature Requirements:** Use of countersignature endorsement, signature in blank, and power of attorney is not allowed. A countersigning resident general agent for a property and casualty insurer must keep a copy of the policy or, in lieu thereof, an equivalent document stating: risks covered, endorsements, insurance limits, rates, premiums, percent of coinsurance, and other related information. Guam countersigning law is neither reciprocal nor retaliatory with other states. (22 G.C.A. §18302; 12 GAR §§1135 to 1138).

III. Commissions, Fees, Commingling of Funds, Suitability in Annuity Transactions

A. Commissions: Guam allows the payment of commissions only to licensed brokers or agents. (22 G.C.A. §§15704.2, 15706).

B. Fees: An agent or broker may not charge fees in addition to the commission.

C. Disclosure Requirements: None.

D. Commingling of Funds: Agents and brokers must keep separate accounts for the agency funds and those belonging to insurers.

E. Suitability in Annuity Transactions: Guam has not adopted the suitability in annuity transaction model law.

IV. Statutory References:

11 GCA §	26202
22 GCA §§	15701, 15703, 15704.1, 15704.2, 15705.1, 15706
	15802
	18302
12 GAR §§	1102, 1105 to 1107
	1135 to 1138
12 GAR §§	1102, 1105 to 1107
	1135 to 1138

Web References:

https://www.guamtax.com/fees/ISBFees_201303.pdf.
https://pay.guam.gov/pg/HowItWorks.aspx.
https://www.guamtax.com/about/regulatory.html.

HAWAII

Insurance Division
Department of Commerce and Consumer Affairs
King Kalakaua Building, 335 Merchant Street, Rm. 213, Honolulu, HI 96813;
P.O. Box 3614; Honolulu, HI 96811
Telephone: 808-586-2790; Fax: 808-586-2806
Email: inslic@dcca.hawaii.gov
http://cca.hawaii.gov/ins

I. **Licensing Requirements:** Sales Personnel—Producers, Limited Lines Producers, Surplus Line Brokers, Limited Lines Motor Vehicle Rental Company Producers, Managing General Agents, Limited Lines Portable Electronics Producer., Reinsurance Intermediaries, Life Settlement Brokers/Providers Other Insurance Professionals—Independent Adjusters, Public Adjusters, Independent Bill Reviewers, Crop Adjusters, Workers Compensation Claims Adjusters Limited License. Licenses no longer issued to General Agents, Subagents, and Solicitors.

A. **Applicability:** No person engaging in the business of insurance in Hawaii shall act as, be appointed as, or hold oneself out to be an adjuster or independent bill reviewer unless so licensed by the State of Hawaii. (HRS §431:9-201).

B. **Licenses Required of Residents:** An insurance producer license shall remain in effect so long as the fee is paid and the educational requirements for resident individual producers are met timely. (HRS §431:9A-107). Each of the following must be licensed in Hawaii:

Sales Personnel

1. *Producers.* May be licensed for: life; accident and health or sickness; property; casualty; surety; variable life and variable annuity products; personal lines; limited lines; or any other line of insurance permitted by state law or rule. (HRS §431:9A-103). An appointment must be in place to do business. (HRS §431:9A-114).

    a. License fee: $225 or $300, determined based on birth month and date of the application's receipt (https://cca.hawaii.gov/ins/producers/fees/). Resident issuance fee: $50, service fee: $50 per year; nonresident issuance fee: $75, service fee: $75 per year. (HRS §431:7-101). Business entity renewal–Resident: July 16, odd-numbered years. Nonresident: April 16, even-numbered years. Charts of fees for various licenses and renewal deadlines, including those for business entities, can be found at http://cca.hawaii.gov/ins/producers/fees/.

b. License term: Biennial. Renewal fee: $50 per year (resident), $75 per year (nonresident).
c. Lines of authority:

    (1) Life.
    (2) Accident and health or sickness.
    (3) Property.
    (4) Marine and transportation.
    (5) Vehicle.
    (6) Casualty.
    (7) Surety.
    (8) Title.
    (9) Variable life and variable annuities.
    (10) Personal lines.
    (11) Limited Lines
    (HRS §§431:9A-103, 107).

2. *Limited Lines Producers.*

    a. License fee: $150 or $195, determined based on birth month and date of the application's receipt. Issuance fee: $60; service fee: $45 (annual). (HRS §431:7-101; https://cca.hawaii.gov/ins/producers/fees/).
    b. License term: Biennial. Renewal fee: $45 per year.
    c. Lines of Authority:

        (1) Credit life.
        (2) Credit disability.
        (3) Credit property.
        (4) Credit unemployment.
        (5) Involuntary unemployment.
        (6) Mortgage life.
        (7) Mortgage guaranty.
        (8) Mortgage disability.
        (9) Guaranteed Automobile Protection (GAP) insurance. (HRS §431:9A-103).
        (10) Travel – disability, baggage, and personal effects.
        (11) Vending machines.
        (12) Accident & Sickness as a promotional device to improve circulation of a newspaper. (HRS §431:9A-107.5).

3. *Limited Lines Motor Vehicle Rental Company Producer.*

   a. License fee: Determined based on birth month and date of the applications receipt. See http://cca.hawaii.gov/ins/producers/fees/.
   Issuance fee: $1,000; Service fee $600 per year. (HRS §431:7-101).
   b. Lines of Authority:

      (1) Personal accident.
      (2) Liability insurance, uninsured motorist insurance, or underinsured motorist insurance.
      (3) Personal effects.
      (4) Roadside assistance and emergency sickness.
      (5) Incidental travel or vehicle related coverage. (HRS §431:9A-142).

4. *Managing General Agents.*

   a. License fee: Determined by birth month and date of the applications receipt. (http://cca.hawaii.gov/ins/producers/fees/). $75 issuance fee; $75 service fee per year. (HRS §431:7-101).
   b. License renewal, biennial fee: $75 per year.

5. *Limited Lines Portable Electronics Producer.*

   License fee: Determined by birth month and date of the applications receipt. (http://cca.hawaii.gov/ins/producers/fees/). Issuance fee: $5,000. Biennial renewal fee. $2,500. (HRS §431:31-107).

Hawaii requires a limited lines license for vendors of portable electronic devices such as smartphones, tablet computers, and other similar items to sell insurance policies to cover these devices. The application for a license shall include the location of the vendor's home office and the name, resident address, and email of the designated person who is responsible for the vendor's compliance with the state requirements. The "supervising entity" shall maintain a list of authorized locations of vendors. (HRS §§431:31-101 to 431:31-108).

Other Insurance Professionals

1. *Independent Adjusters.* Fee: Determined by birth month date of the applications receipt. (http://cca.hawaii.gov/ins/producers/fees/).

   Issuance fee: $75; service fee: $45 per year. (HRS §431:7-101).

2. *Public Adjusters.* Must file a $10,000 surety bond. Fee: Determined by birth month date of the application's receipt. See (http://cca.hawaii.gov/ins/producers/fees/). Issuance fee: $75; service fee: $45 per year. (HRS §431:9-223).

3. *Independent Bill Reviewers.* These are independent contractors who review or audit medical bills for insurers. (https://cca.hawaii.gov/ins/producers/instructions_insurance_license/). Fee: Determined by birth month and date of the applications receipt. (http://cca.hawaii.gov/ins/producers/fees).

   Issuance fee: $80; service fee: $60 per year. Although an examination is required by HRS §431:9-206, at the present time, the State of Hawaii does not have an Independent Bill Reviewer examination. Any applicant must hold credentials as a Certified Professional Coder granted by the American Academy of Professional Coders or American Health Information Management Association. (https://cca.hawaii.gov/ins/producers/instructions_insurance_license/resident-independent-bill-reviewer/).

4. *Reinsurance Intermediaries.* Fee: Determined by birth month and date of the applications receipt. Issuance fee: $75. Annual service fee: $75. (HRS §431:7-101). Life Settlement Provider Issuance Fee: $75 renewal fee $1200. Life Settlement Broker Issuance fee: $75. Annual renewal fee: $150. (HRS §431: 7-101. http://cca.hawaii.gov/ins/producers/fees). All resident individuals are required to be fingerprinted prior to submitting a license application for initial license. To obtain fingerprints, schedule an appointment online at http://www.fieldprinthawaii.com.

   If you are submitting applications for two licenses simultaneously (e.g. producer and surplus lines broker), then you will only need to be fingerprinted once. However, if you submit your producer application now and apply for a surplus lines broker license at a later date, you will be required to be fingerprinted again. (files.hawaii.gov/dcca/ins/new-releases/Fingerprints_Required_For_New_Applicants For_Resident_Insurance_License.pdf).

   Instructions and applications for licensure may be found on the Department's Web site at: http://cca.hawaii.gov/ins/producers/instructions_insurance_license/.

C. Appointments:

To appoint a producer as its agent, the insurer shall file a notice of appointment within fifteen days of execution of the contract or the first application is submitted to the insurer. If the commissioner does not receive the form within fifteen days, the appointment shall be effective on the day the commissioner receives the form. Upon receipt of the notice, the commissioner shall, within thirty days, verify the producer's eligibility for appointment. (HRS §431: 9A-114).

Electronic appointments and terminations are being accepted via the National Insurance Producer Registry (NIPR). The Notice of New Appointment Form may be downloaded from the Department's Web site.

D. Licenses Required of Nonresidents: Nonresidents may be licensed on a reciprocal basis. Licensing fees are determined by birth month and date of the applications receipt. (http://cca.hawaii.gov/ins/producers/fees/).

Issuance Fee: $75. Service Fee: $75 annually. Applicants must be licensed in home state. (§431:7-101).

Applications may be downloaded from Department's Web site at: http://cca.hawaii.gov/ins/producers/forms/.

Multi-State Exposures: A license is not required for a nonresident insurance producer who sells, solicits, or negotiates a contract of insurance for commercial property and casualty coverage when risks that are to be insured under that contract are located in more than one state. This exception applies only if the nonresident is licensed to sell, solicit, or negotiate that insurance in the state where the insured maintains its principal place of business and the contract of insurance insures risks located in that state. (HRS §431:9A-104).

E. Prelicensing Examination or Education Requirements:

1. *Residents.* The following licenses require an examination: producer, adjuster (independent, public, and limited), and workers compensation adjuster. Those selling variable contracts must have an NASD registration in the state of Hawaii. The exams are administered by Pearson VUE, 800-274-2608. Exam fee: $75. Fees will not be accepted at the test center. Fees must be paid when making the reservation. (https://cca.hawaii.gov/ins/producers/exam_info/).

   Adjuster applicants must have special experience or education in claims handling. (H.R.S. §431:9-222.5).

   Holders of the CPCU designation are no longer exempt from the exam requirement for any class; holders of the CLU designation are no longer exempt from the exam requirement for life or life/disability.

Prelicensing exam requirements do not apply to the following:

a. Applicants who held an insurance license in this state within the last two-year period.
b. Applicants who hold the same license in good standing in other states or who cancelled the old license less than ninety days ago. (H.R.S. §431:9A-109).

2. *Nonresidents.* An individual who applies for an insurance producer license in this state and who was previously licensed for the same lines of authority in another state shall not be required to complete any prelicensing education or examination, if the person is currently licensed in another state; or the application is received within ninety days of the cancellation of the applicant's previous license and the prior state issues a clearance that:

   a. at the time of cancellation, the applicant was in good standing in that state;
   b. the state's producer database records, as maintained by the National Association of Insurance Commissioners (NAIC) or affiliates or subsidiaries, indicate that the producer is or was licensed in good standing for the lines of authority requested. (H.R.S. §431:9A-109).

F. Continuing Education Requirements:

Number of Hours Required: For licensees authorized to sell only one of the following lines: 1) life or accident and health or sickness, or 2) property, marine and transportation, vehicle, general casualty or surety, twenty-four hours total continuing education hours are required every two years. Twenty-one credit hours shall relate to the specific line of insurance, and three hours shall pertain to the ethics training or the laws and rules relating to insurance. (H.R.S. §431:9A-124(a)).

For those licensed to sell insurance under both lines listed above, twenty-four hours total continuing education hours are required. Ten credit hours pertaining to life or accident and health or sickness, and eleven hours pertaining to property, marine and transportation, vehicle, general casualty, or surety. Three hours shall pertain to the ethics training or the laws and rules relating to insurance. (H.R.S. §431:9A-124(b)).

Excess Hours: May not be carried into the next reporting period. (H.R.S. §431:9A-124(c)).

Requirements ***Not*** *Applicable to the Following:*

1. Limited licensees.

2. Nonresidents on a reciprocal basis. (H.R.S. §431:9A-116).

3. Anyone else granted an exemption by the commissioner. (H.R.S. §431:9A-130).

   Record Keeping: Licensees are responsible for maintaining their own CE records. Licensees shall keep such records for four (4) years after completion of a CE course. (H.R.S. §431-9A:125).

G. **Cancellation of Producer Appointments:** Termination of a producer appointment must be made within thirty days following the effective date of the termination, using the applicable format prescribed by the commissioner. (H.R.S. §431:9A-115).

H. **Rules for Risk Retention and Purchasing Groups:** The Hawaii State Legislature prohibits a purchasing group from purchasing insurance from a risk retention group not chartered in Hawaii or from an insurer not authorized to do business in Hawaii unless the purchase is made through a licensed producer pursuant to the Surplus Lines Law as set forth in Hawaii Revised Statutes §431K-8. (H.R.S. §431K-8).

   For a Risk Retention Group, the following notice must be printed in ten point type on the front of each policy:

   NOTICE

   This policy is issued by your risk retention group. Your risk retention group may not be subject to all of the insurance laws and rules of your state. State insurance insolvency guaranty funds are not available for your risk retention group. (H.R.S. §431K-3(6)).

I. **Other License Rules, Requirements, or Restrictions:** No producer shall not sell, solicit, or negotiate insurance in Hawaii for any class of insurance for which the producer is not licensed and does not hold an appointment from an insurer in this state. (H.R.S. §431:9A-103).

J. **Policy Countersignature Requirements:** None.

K. **Portable Electronics Insurance:** The employees and authorized representatives of vendors may sell portable electronics insurance to customers, and shall not be subject to licensure as an insurance producer under this chapter, provided that the vendor (1) has a limited lines license to authorize employees and authorized representatives are trained to sell or offer portable electronics insurance, (2) the insurer issuing the policy directly supervises or hires another to supervise the administration of such insurance including the development of a training program for employees and authorized representatives of vendors, and (3) no employee or authorized representative holds themselves out as a nonlimited lines producer. (H.R.S. §§431:31-104).

II. Commissions, Fees, Commingling of Funds, and Suitability in Annuity Transactions

A. Commissions: An insurance company or insurance producer must not pay a commission, service fee, brokerage fee, or other valuable consideration to a person for selling, soliciting, or negotiating insurance in Hawaii if that person is required to be licensed and is not so licensed. A person must not accept a commission, service fee, brokerage fee, or other valuable consideration for selling, soliciting, or negotiating insurance in Hawaii if that person is required to be licensed and is not so licensed. Renewal or other deferred commissions may be paid to a person for selling, soliciting, or negotiating insurance in Hawaii if that person was required to be licensed at the time and was so licensed. An insurer or insurance producer may pay or assign commissions, service fees, brokerage fees, or other valuable consideration to an insurance agency or to persons who do not sell, solicit, or negotiate insurance in Hawaii, unless the payment would violate H.R.S. §431:13-103. (H.R.S. §431:9A-113). Rebating of commissions is not allowed. (H.R.S. §431:13-103).

B. Fees: Fees for services may not be charged instead of or in addition to commission for sale of insurance.

C. Disclosure Requirements: Every insurer selling insurance on a mass merchandising basis must, prior to sale, make full and fair disclosures to prospective insureds of all features of the plan, including but not limited to premium rates, claims procedure, benefits, duration of coverage, and policyholder services. (H.R.S. §431:12-106).

D. Commingling of Funds: Licensee must maintain a trust fund in a federally insured Hawaii bank or savings and loan association or financial services loan company for premiums collected for insurers, separate from any other funds of the licensee. In the event the bank, savings and loan association, or financial services loan company account is an interest earning account, such licensee may not retain the interest earned on such funds to the licensee's own use or benefit without the prior written consent of the insurers or person entitled to such funds. (H.R.S. §431:9-230).

E. Suitability in Annuity Transactions: Any insurance producer who is authorized to sell annuity products shall complete, a one-time, four-hour training course approved by the commissioner and conducted by a valid continuing education course provider. Any insurance producer who obtains a life or variable life and variable annuity products line of authority may not engage in the sale of annuities until the training requirements have been met. (H.R.S. §431:10D–626).

Hawaii has adopted the NAIC Suitability in Annuity Transactions Model Regulation. (https://cca.hawaii.gov/ins/files/2014/01/Commissioner_Memorandum_2011-2LIC_REVISED.pdf).

HAWAII

III. References:

H.R.S. §§431:	7-101
	9-201, 206, 222.5, 223, 230
	9A-103, 104, 107, 107.5, 109, 114 to 116, 124, 125, 130, 142
	10D-626
	12-106
	13-103
	31-101 to 108
H.R.S. §§431K-	3, 8

Web References:

https://cca.hawaii.gov/ins/producers/fees/.

https://cca.hawaii.gov/ins/producers/instructions_insurance_license/resident-independent-bill-reviewer/.

http://cca.hawaii.gov/ins/producers/instructions_insurance_license/.

http://cca.hawaii.gov/ins/producers/forms/.

https://cca.hawaii.gov/ins/producers/exam_info/.

files.hawaii.gov/dcca/ins/new-releases/Fingerprints_Required_For_New_Applicants For_Resident_Insurance_License.pdf.

https://cca.hawaii.gov/ins/files/2014/01/Commissioner_Memorandum_2011-2LIC_REVISED.pdf.

IDAHO

Department of Insurance
700 W. State St., 3rd Floor
P.O. Box 83720; Boise, ID 83720-0043
Telephone (general): 208-334-4250;
Telephone (licensing): 208-334-4339;
Fax: 208-334-4398
http://www.doi.idaho.gov
Email: form available at http://www.doi.idaho.gov/about/DOIemail.aspx?did=52

I. Licensing Requirements: Sales Personnel—Producers, Limited Lines Producers, Title Agents, Managing General Agents, Life Settlement Brokers and Providers, Portable Electronics, Entities. Other Insurance Professionals—Independent Adjusters, Public Adjusters, Reinsurance Intermediaries, Third-Party Administrators, Bail Bond Agents, and Independent Review Organizations.

A. Applicability: A person shall not sell, solicit or negotiate insurance in this state for any class or classes of insurance unless the person is licensed as a producer for that line of authority. (Idaho Code § 41-1004).

B. Licenses Required of Residents: Each of the following must be licensed in Idaho. All licenses expire on the last day of the birth month two years from date of issue, however, the initial licensing period may be as little as twenty-one months or as much as thirty-two months.

Sales Personnel

1. *Producers.*

   a. License fee: Initial fee is $80; renewal fee is $80, or $60 if renewal is completed online. (Idaho Admin. Code r. 18.01.02.030). First-time resident applicants must file fingerprint card. Fingerprinting is required for residents only. Bail agents will be required to fingerprint at initial licensing and at each subsequent renewal (see website for special instructions for renewal fingerprints). Fingerprinting is done at PSI testing centers and there is a $70 fingerprinting fee payable to PSI Examination. Fingerprinting fees must be paid separately. Refer to https://doi.idaho.gov/licensing/Fingerprint.
   b. License term: Biennial. Individuals expire at end of birth month after two years. Business entities expire on first day of the following month after two years.

c. Major lines of authority:

(1) Life.
(2) Disability (Health), including accident and health or sickness.
(3) Property.
(4) Casualty (includes surety).
(5) Variable life and variable annuities.
(6) Personal lines.
(7) Any other line permitted under Idaho laws or rules. (Idaho Code § 41-1008).

d. Appointments: Producers acting as agents of an insurer must be appointed within fifteen days of signing the contract or fifteen days from date the first application was submitted. There is no state fee and appointments do not require renewal. (Idaho Code § 41-1018).

Renewal options are available on the Department's Web site at http://www.doi.idaho.gov/licensing/forms/online_licenserenew.aspx.

2. *Limited Lines Producers.*

a. License fee: Initial fee is $80; renewal fee is $80; online renewal is $60. (Idaho Admin. Code r. 18.01. 02. 030).
b. License term: Biennial. End of birth month for individuals.
c. The following lines of authority do not require an exam, but the *Producer Limited Lines Insurance Prelicensing Manual* must be read, and the attestation at the back of the manual must be submitted with the resident application. The Limited Lines manual may be accessed at www.doi.idaho.gov under Study Material in the Resident Producer pages. Lines of authority include, but are not limited to:

(1) Credit (GAP).
(2) Travel.
(3) Pet insurance.
(4) Portable Electronics.
(doi.idaho.gov/Licensing/Individual/LimitedLines).

3. *Bail Agents:* Must be licensed as a Bail Bond Agent. Residents must take the bail surety examination and attach a $15,000 performance bond and surety appointment. License fee: $80; renewal fee: $80; renewal fee reduced to $60 if completed

online. Bail agents must redo fingerprints at the time of renewal. (Idaho Code § 41-1040; doi.idaho.gov/licensing/Bail/Renewal.

4. *Car Rental.* No license required for those selling insurance in connection with car rentals of ninety days or less. (Idaho Code § 41-1005(h)).

5. *Title.* Title agencies must be licensed in each county where policies will be written and physical title plants must be located in Idaho. A surety bond of $10,000 is required for each county in which a title agent is licensed. Application fee: $50 per county. Annual renewal fee: $50. Late fee: $2/day up to $100 total. (Idaho Code § 41-2710; doi.idaho.gov/licensing/TA/Checklist).

6. *Managing General Agents.* Must be licensed as a property & casualty producer, as well as Managing General Agent. License fee: $80. The licensing period for MGA's is one year. All MGA licenses expire at midnight on June 30, annually. (IdahoAdmin. Code r. 18.01.02.30; doi.idaho.gov/Licensing/MGA/Checklist).

   MGA renewals must be done by paper. You can download a form online at this location: doi.idaho.gov/Licensing/MGA/Renewal.

   If renewing on or prior to June 30th, the fee is $80. If renewing on or after July 1st, the fee is $160. MGAs must secure a bond equal to 10 percent of total funds handled in Idaho the previous year (minimum bond of $5,000). The director also requires MGAs to carry an E&O policy with a limit of $250,000 or 25 percent of the gross amount of direct written premiums received by an insurer for the previous year that are attributable to you as their MGA, whichever is greater. (Idaho Code § 41-1503).

7. *Business Entities.* Corporations, partnerships, or limited liability companies that sell, solicit, or negotiate insurance using the name of the agency must be licensed. All individuals in the entity who will be selling insurance must also be licensed and may be registered to the agency; however, a minimum of one registered designated responsible licensed producer is required. Business entities must also be registered with the Idaho Secretary of State at: www.sos.idaho.gov. (Idaho Code § 41-1007).

Other Insurance Professionals

1. *Independent Adjusters.* Initial fee: $80; biennial renewal: $80, general lines. License renewal fee is $60 if renewed electronically. Exam categories for residents include: crop hail; general lines; workers compensation. Exam and fingerprinting is required for residents and those non-resident adjusters

designating Idaho as their home state. (Idaho Admin. Code r. 18.01.02.030; doi.idaho.gov/Licensing/IA/FAQ).

2. *Reinsurance Intermediaries.* Initial fee: $80. Renewal fee: $80. (Idaho Admin. Code r. 18.01.02.030).

3. *Third-Party Administrators.* Administrators must hold a valid certificate of registration. Initial fee: $300; biennial renewal: $80. Biennial renewal is due on or before December 31. Late renewal/reinstatement fees of $160 apply from January 1-31. Late renewals are not accepted after January 31, the administrator must submit new application and fees. (Idaho Admin. Code r. 18.01.02.030; doi.idaho.gov/Company/TPA/Renewal).

The following license types are available online through Sircon or NIPR services: Producer and Limited Lines, Independent and Public Adjuster, Bail Agents, Surplus Lines, Third-Party Administrator, and Life Settlement Broker or Provider. Alternatively, the applications for the following license types must be on paper: Managing General Agent, Reinsurance Intermediary, Independent Review Organization and Title Agency. (doi.idaho.gov/Licensing/default?menu=Types).

If you have been previously licensed in Idaho and if your license has been expired over one year, nonresidents may reapply online; however, residents must apply by paper in this circumstance. If you are adding lines to an existing license there are no fees and this service is available through online services or via paper form.

Note also, if you answered "yes" to any of the background questions, please send the required documents and explanation to the Idaho Department of Insurance via email (agent@doi.idaho.gov) or fax (208-334-4398) or post to the NIPR Attachment Warehouse at www.nipr.com. Please consult with application question for instructions as to required documents.

Noncitizen resident applicants must fax a copy of work authorization or green card to 208-334-4398 or email (agent@doi.idaho.gov) with a note that this is an attachment for an application in-house.

The Idaho Department of Insurance provides the necessary licensing forms at the following Web site: http://www.doi.idaho.gov/licensing/Individual/Forms.aspx.

C. **Appointments:** An insurance producer shall not act as an agent of an insurer unless the insurance producer becomes an appointed agent of that insurer. An insurance producer who is not acting as an agent of an insurer is not required to become appointed. Producers acting as agents of an insurer must be appointed within fifteen days of signing the contract or fifteen days from date the first application was submitted. Appointments should be processed online by companies through appropriate vendors. (Idaho Code § 41-1018).

D. **Licenses Required of Nonresidents:** Nonresidents of Idaho may be licensed as producers, public or independent adjusters, bail agents, life settlement brokers or providers, surplus lines brokers, MGA's, TPA's, IRO's, reinsurance intermediaries or title agencies. (Idaho Code § 41-1009). Entities must be licensed, as well as all individuals in the entity who will be selling insurance. Expiration dates and fees are the same as for residents and are not retaliatory. Nonresidents must be appointed in Idaho with the insurers for whom they write business. Certification from home-state is not required if the home state participates in the NAIC Producer Database (PDB).

Multi-State Exposures: A license is not required for a nonresident insurance producer who sells, solicits, or negotiates a contract of insurance for commercial property and casualty coverage when risks that are to be insured under that contract are located in more than one state. This exception applies only if the nonresident is licensed to sell, solicit, or negotiate that insurance in the state where the insured maintains its principal place of business and the contract of insurance insures risks located in that state. (Idaho Code § 41-1005).

E. **Prelicensing Examination and Education Requirements:**

1. *Residents.* Idaho license applicants (producer bail agents, public and independent adjusters) must pass a qualifying examination to obtain a license. Exams are administered by PSI, 877-526-6833 or http://www.psiexams.com. Exam fee: $60 per exam. The following exams in major lines are available for producers: life, disability (health), property, casualty, personal lines, and bail surety. The limited lines producer licenses noted previously do not require an exam. For all other limited lines, the *Producer Limited Lines Prelicensing Manual* must be read, and the attestation at the back of the manual must be submitted with the resident application. License Candidate Handbooks can be downloaded from the PSI Web site. The manual may be accessed at doi.idaho.gov/Licensing/Fingerprint.

2. *Nonresidents.* Examination requirement is reciprocal with the applicant's home state.

F. Continuing Education Requirements:

Number of Hours Required: Resident producers, bail agents, independent and public adjusters: twenty-four hours with license renewal including three hours of ethics with each biennial renewal period. No exemptions for attaining a certain age or number of years of service. No carryover credit. All insurance producers licensed in property, casualty or personal lines of authority who sell flood insurance through NFIP must complete a one-time course related to the NFIP which will provide three hours of continuing education credit. The NFIP flood insurance course is available through approved continuing education providers in the CE Course Catalog. (doi.idaho.gov/Licensing/CE/GeneralCE).

All licensed producers intending to sell long term care insurance in Idaho must carry the Disability (Health) line of authority and also complete an initial training of eight hours of continuing education in LTC Partnership, which includes the Idaho laws and rules regarding the long term care partnership act. Once the initial course requirement is completed. Each individual who wishes to continue to sell long term care insurance must take a four-hour course every two years. No more than four hours of continuing education credit from courses approved for adjusters shall apply toward the continuation of a producer license.. All licensed producers carrying the life line of authority must take a one-time four credit hour training in annuity suitability. (https://doi.idaho.gov/Licensing/Individual/ContEd).

The penalty for completing the CE requirement after the license renewal date is as follows: One to thirty days: $100 fine; thirty-one to sixty days: $200 fine; sixty-one to ninety days: $300 fine. Failure to comply after ninety days and up to one year from nonrenewal requires retesting and reapplication, along with completion of all twenty-four CE credits. If a license has been expired for one year or longer, the licensee must reapply and retest as a new applicant. (Idaho Code § 41-1013).

Licensee may use classroom instruction or self-study. Courses must be preapproved and listed in the CE Course Catalog and fall within the acceptable subject matter areas for CE credit.

Proof of credit will be downloaded by the Provider within thirty days of completion of the course.

Excess Hours: May not be carried into the next reporting period.

Final Exam: There is no monitoring requirement for the final exam with a self-study course. However, test providers must supply a "written explanation of test security and administration procedures."(doi.idaho.gov/Licensing/CE/GeneralCE; doi.idaho.gov/Licensing/CE/MethodsofInstruction).

Requirements **Not** *Applicable to the Following:*

1. Business entity license.

2. Licensees on active military duty who have formally requested inactive status.

3. Nonresident producer license.

4. Limited Lines only producer license, e.g. credit, Gap.

5. Surplus lines license.

6. License placed on inactive status for reasons of retirement or disability.

   (Idaho Code § 41-1028; doi.idaho.gov/Licensing/CE/ProducerFAQ).

Renewal Procedure:

1. Residents complete CE requirements in advance of expiration. Course provider supplies DOI with credits earned by licensee and sends completion certificate to licensee.

2. Licensee renews license through NIPR or Sircon.

3. Licensee obtains license copy through DOI Web site at: (https://doi.idaho.gov/Licensing/Forms/GenerateLicense).

Nonresidents are exempt from the CE requirement, but follow steps 2 and 3 above.

G. **Cancellation of Agency Contracts/Producer Appointments:** Insurer may backdate terminations up to thirty days. Terminations must be processed online. However, Insurer must give written notice if the termination is for cause to the insurance department, and to the producer. The insurer must file a statement with the Director of Insurance providing the facts relative to the cause of termination. (Idaho Code § 41-1019).

H. **Rules for Risk Retention and Purchasing Groups:** Idaho regulates risk retention and purchasing groups operating or offering coverage on risks in Idaho. Annual fee: $500. (Idaho Admin. Code r. 18.01.02.020). Risk retention groups chartered in

Idaho must be chartered and licensed as a liability company under Idaho insurance laws. Before offering such insurance in any state, each group shall submit a plan of operation to the Director of Insurance. (Idaho Code § 41-4804). Risk retention groups chartered in states other than Idaho must, before transacting insurance business in Idaho, submit to the director the following: (1) a statement identifying the state(s) in which the group is chartered and licensed as a liability company, including the charter date and principal place of business; (2) a copy of the group's plan of operations; (3) a statement of registration designating the director as the group's agent for the purpose of receiving legal documents; (4) a copy of the group's financial statement; (5) a copy of each examination of the group; (6) upon request, a copy of any audit performed on the group; and (7) other information as required to verify the group's continuing qualification as a risk retention group. (Idaho Code § 41-4805). Purchasing groups intending to do business in Idaho shall submit notice to the director, including (1) the state in which the group is domiciled; (2) specific lines of liability insurance the group intends to purchase; (3) the company—and its domicile—from which the group intends to purchase its insurance; (4) the group's principal place of business; and (5) other information as may be necessary for the director to verify the group's qualification. (Idaho Code §§ 41-4808 to 4810). All groups and resident and nonresident agents or brokers participating in them must comply with all Idaho insurance laws, including licensing and solicitation requirements or restrictions. All risk retention group policies must show the following notice in at least ten-point type on the front page and on the declarations page of the policy:

NOTICE

> "This policy has been issued by your risk retention group. Your risk retention group may not be subject to all of the insurance laws and regulations of your state. State insurance insolvency guaranty funds are not available for your risk retention group." (Idaho Code § 41-4805).

I. **Other License Rules, Requirements, or Restrictions:** Unlicensed nonresident may not enter state for any insurance purpose. This includes mail or telephone or other electronic communication into the state from the outside, as well as physical presence in the state. Companies may not accept Idaho business from unlicensed nonresidents. No one may solicit or offer a contract of insurance to any individual or on a property located or domiciled within Idaho without proper licensing as a resident or nonresident. (Idaho Code §§ 41-1004, 1008).

J. **Policy Countersignature Requirements:** Required except for:

1. Life insurance and annuities;

2. Disability Insurance;

3. Title insurance; countersignature of title insurance policies is provided in Idaho Code § 41-2702;

4. Policies covering property in transit while in possession or custody of any common carrier, or the rolling stock or other property of any common carrier used and employed by it as a common carrier of freight or passengers or both;

5. Reinsurance or retrocessions made by or for authorized insurers;

6. Contracts issued by domestic reciprocal insurers writing workmen's compensation for employers commonly known as self-insurers; nor, with respect to countersignature, to policies issued by a reciprocal insurer not using agents compensated by commissions in the general solicitation of business;

7. Bid bonds issued by a surety insurer in connection with any public or private contract; or

8. Ocean marine insurance.

(Idaho Code §§ 41-337, -338.)

K. Portable Electronics Insurance: Any vendor selling portable electronic devices such as wireless phones, smart phones, tablet computers, or other small electronic devices who wishes to sell insurance policies to cover damage or replacement of such devices shall be required to obtain a limited lines license. The license shall authorize any employee or representative of the vendor to offer for sale coverage at each location at which the vendor engages in portable electronics transactions. The supervising entity shall maintain a registry of vendor locations that are authorized to sell or solicit portable electronics insurance coverage in this state. Upon request by the director to the supervising entity, the registry shall be open to inspection and examination by the director during regular business hours of the supervising entity. (Idaho Code § 41-1083). Fees to license depend on number of retail outlets: 1-10 (small) $100; 11 or more (large) $1000. Renewal is biennial; Small vendor renewal is $100, and Large Vendor renewal is $500. (Idaho Code §41-1089).

II. Commissions, Fees, Commingling of Funds, and Suitability in Annuity Transactions

A. Fees: Wholesale and retail producers may charge a fee in addition to or in lieu of commission only after providing a written agreement signed by the client that describes the services that will be performed for the fee charged. Information on the amount of fees charged by a wholesale producer must be disclosed in writing on the face of the policy as separate itemized charges. (Idaho Code § 41-1030).

B. **Disclosure Requirements:** Before charging a fee to a consumer, a retail producer shall provide to the consumer a written statement that describes the services the retail producer will perform and the fees the retail producer will receive as well as whether or not the fees may be negotiated. Acceptance by the consumer of a fee arrangement shall be evidenced by the consumer signing and dating the fee statement. Information regarding the amount of the fees charged by the wholesale producer shall be disclosed in writing on the face of the policy as a separately itemized charge. A producer may charge a fee for those services that are intended to be provided and that are not contingent upon some future event occurring outside of the terms of the insurance contract. A producer may not charge a fee for services in connection with statutorily mandated insurance coverage, such as mandated health plans. (Idaho Code § 41-1030).

C. **Commingling of Funds:** Idaho law states that producers shall not commingle insurer premiums with other agency or personal funds. Premium funds received or collected by producers must be maintained in separate accounts to avoid the commingling of fiduciary funds with personal funds. Idaho law also requires that a bail bond agent maintain a separate account for all collateral received. (Idaho Code § 41-1024, Idaho Admin. Code r. 18.06.02.014).

D. **Suitability in Annuity Transactions:** In recommending to a consumer the purchase of an annuity or the exchange of an annuity that results in an insurance transaction or a series of insurance transactions, the insurance producer, or the insurer where no producer is involved, shall have reasonable grounds for believing that the recommendation is suitable for the consumer on the basis of the facts disclosed by the consumer as to the consumer's investments and other insurance products and as to the consumer's age, financial situation and needs. (Idaho Code § 41-1940, Idaho Admin. Code r. 18.03.01.015).

III. **Statutory References:** Idaho Code §§ 41-337, 338; 41-1004, 1005, 1007 to 1009, 1013, 1018, 1019, 1024, 1028, 1030, 1040, 1089; 41-1503; 41-1940; 41-2702, 2710; 41-4804, 4805, 4808 to 4810. Idaho Admin. Code r. 18.01.02.020, 030; 18.03.01.015; 18.06.02.014.

ILLINOIS

Department of Insurance
320 W. Washington St.; Springfield, IL 62767
Telephone: 217-782-4515; Fax: 217-782-5020
122 S. Michigan Ave., 19th Floor; Chicago 60603
Telephone: 312-814-2420; Fax 312-814-5416
Email: Doi.licensing@illinois.gov
https://insurance.illinois.gov/

I. **Licensing Requirements:** Sales Personnel—Producers, Limited Lines Producers, Car Rental Limited Licensees, Title Insurance Producers, Managing General Agents, Business Entities. Other Insurance Professionals—Public Adjusters, Reinsurance Intermediaries, Third-Party Administrators, Viatical Settlement Providers. An individual applying for a resident insurance producer license must: be at least eighteen years of age; not have committed any act that is a ground for denial, suspension, or revocation of license; complete a prelicensing course of study if required; successfully pass the examinations for the lines of authority for which the person has applied; and pay applicable fees.

A. **Applicability:** A person may not sell, solicit, or negotiate insurance in Illinois for any class or classes of insurance unless the person is licensed for that line of authority. (215 ILCS 5/500-15).

B. **Licenses Required of Residents:** All applications are handled through the State-Based System (SBS) licensing system of the NAIC, which will allow producer licensing functions to be completed electronically through a Web-based system. For more information, please visit http://www.statebasedsystems.com/.

The following must be licensed in Illinois:

Sales Personnel

1. *Producers.*

a. License fee: $50; application fee: $180. Nonresident fee: $250.
b. License term: biennial; renewal fee is $180.
c. Lines of authority:

(1) Life.
(2) Variable life and variable annuity products.
(3) Accident and health or sickness.
(4) Property.

(5) Casualty.
(6) Personal lines P&C.
(7) Any other line of insurance permitted by state law or rules.
(215 ILCS 5/500-35, 500-135)
Fee schedule available at http://insurance.illinois.gov/Producer/producer_fees.pdf.

d. Bond Requirements: Surety bond for the greater of $2,500 or 5 percent of premiums received in previous year up to a maximum of $50,000 total aggregate liability is required for a producer who brokers insurance. The producer or business entity must certify to the DOI that the producer or entity has the bond required. Associations may maintain the bond for their members, but the members are responsible for assuring the bond held for them by the association is in the amount the producer needs, based on the amount of business the producer brokers. Producers are required to tell a person injured under the terms of the bond who the surety is and the bond number. This information must be provided within three working days of the request. (215 ILCS 5/500-130).

e. Other Requirements: A temporary producer license may be issued (fee: $50) for a period of ninety days to an applicant enrolled in a training course and preparing to be licensed. A producer must obtain a signed disclosure from an insured if the producer's compensation exceeds 10 percent of the premium. A temporary insurance producer license for a period not to exceed 180 days and, at the discretion of the director, may renew for an additional 180 without requiring an examination if the Director deems the temporary license is necessary for the servicing of an insurance business in the following cases:

(1) To the surviving spouse or court-appointed personal representative of a licensed insurance producer who dies or becomes mentally or physically disabled to allow adequate time for the same of the insurance business owned by the producer, or the recovery or return of the producer, or to provide for the training and licensing of new personnel to operate the producer's business.
(2) To a member or employee of a business entity licensed as an insurance producer, upon the death or disability of an individual designated in the business entity application or license.
(3) To the designee of a licensed insurance producer entering active services in the armed forces of the United States of America.

The director may limit the authority of any temporary licensee to protect insureds and the public, and may require the temporary licensee to have a suitable sponsor who is a licensed producer or insurer who assumes responsibility for all acts of the temporary licensee. The temporary license may be revoked if the interest of insureds or the public are endangered, and a temporary license may not continue after the owner or personal representative disposes of the business. The license fee is $50, and the applicant must file with the Director a written application by the person desiring the license in the form, with the supplements, and containing the information the Director requires. (215 ILCS 5/500-60).

2. *Limited Lines Producers.*

   a. License fee: $50 annually by December 31, payable by the appointing company. Applicants should contact the limited lines company for licensing information and application. This $50 annual license fee only applies to the eight types of limited lines listed below. If the limited line is not on this list or specified in any other section then the fee is $200 biennially.
   b. License term: Perpetual, as long as the appointing company pays the annual fee.
   c. Limited lines of authority:

      (1) Travel insurance, including baggage or limited travel health, accident, or trip cancellation insurance.
      (2) Industrial life insurance.
      (3) Industrial accident and health insurance.
      (4) Farm mutual insurance.
      (5) Legal expense insurance.
      (6) Enrollment of recipients of public aid or Medicare in a health maintenance organization.
      (7) Limited health care.
      (8) Credit life, credit accident and health, and other credit policies approved by the Director. (215 ILCS 5/500-100, 500-135).

3. *Car Rental Limited Lines Licensee.* Car rental companies must obtain a producer license or obtain the car rental limited license.

   a. License fee: $180 resident, $250 nonresident.
   b. License term: Biennial.
   c. Lines of authority for a car rental limited licensee:

      (1) Personal accident insurance covering the risks of travel.
      (2) Liability insurance, including uninsured and underinsured motorist coverage.
      (3) Personal effects insurance.

(4) Roadside assistance and emergency sickness protection programs.
(5) Any other travel or auto-related coverage that a rental company offers in connection with and incidental to the rental of vehicles.

d. Other requirements: Employees in the car rental location can solicit insurance without a license as long as the car rental company is licensed. If the location is a franchise of a car rental company, the franchise must be licensed. Biennial fee: $50. A car rental limited producer may not advertise, represent, or otherwise hold themselves or any employees out as licensed insurers, insurance producers, insurance agents, or insurance brokers. (215 ILCS 5/500-105, 500-135).

4. Self-Service Storage Facility Limited Lines Licensee. A self-service storage facility must obtain a producer license or obtain a self-service storage facility limited line license before offering or selling insurance in connection with and incidental to the rental of storage space provided by a self-service storage facility. (215 ILCS 5/500-107).

a. License fee: $50.
b. License term: Biennial.
c. The following general categories of coverage may be offered or sold:

(1) insurance that provides hazard insurance coverage to renters for the loss of, or damage to, tangible personal property in storage or in transit during the rental period; or
(2) any other coverage the Director may approve as meaningful and appropriate in connection with the rental of storage space. (215 ILCS 5/500-107, 500-135).

5. *Title Insurance Producers.* Defined as anyone engaged in the "trade, business, occupation or profession of (a) buying or selling interests in real property, (b) making loans secured by interests in real property, or (c) acting as broker, agent, attorney, or representative of natural persons or other legal entities that buy or sell interests in real property or that lend money with such interests as security." (215 ILCS 155/3(4)). This license is handled by the Illinois Department of Financial & Professional Regulation. Visit http://idfpr.com/.

6. *Managing General Agents.* No person shall act as an MGA for risks located in Illinois unless licensed as a producer, registered firm, or licensed third party administrator. An MGA must maintain a surety bond equal to the greater of $100,000 or 5 percent of the gross direct written premium underwritten by

the managing general agent on behalf of the insurer, which shall provide for a discovery period and prior notice of cancellation. Must maintain an E&O policy for the benefit of the insurer with coverage in an amount equal to the greater of $1 million or 5 percent of the gross direct written premium underwritten by the managing general agent on behalf of the insurer. (215 ILCS 5/141a(b)).

7. *Business Entities.* A business entity means corporations, partnerships, or limited liability companies that act as insurance producers. (215 ILCS 5/500-10). Entities may be issued a limited lines producer license for credit life and credit accident and health insurance and other credit insurance policies approved or permitted by the Director. Entities must submit evidence from Secretary of State of approval of use of a fictitious name. If business is brokered in the entity's name, the entity must have a surety bond. Each business entity must appoint at least one licensed individual to be responsible for the entity's compliance with insurance laws. All individuals in the entity who will be selling insurance must also be licensed; form IL446-0153; 7/04. Biennial fee: $150. Must maintain a bond which shall be continuous in form and in the amount of $2,500 or 5 percent of the premiums brokered in the previous calendar year whichever is greater, but not to exceed $50,000 total aggregate liability. Such bond should remain at the place of business; however the producer must provide the information within three working days after receiving a request, should the information be requested. (215 ILCS 5/500-100).

8. *Bail Bonds.* Bail bond licenses are not handled by the Illinois DOI.

Other Insurance Professionals

1. *Public Adjusters.* A person shall not act as a public adjuster unless so licensed in Illinois. Public adjuster's license is renewed annually on the anniversary of original license; fee: $250, biennial. $20,000 surety bond (form PAB) is required. Business entities may also be licensed as public adjusters. Fee: $250, biennial. Application form is IL446-0169 available at http://insurance2.illinois.gov/Producer/Producer_Forms/public_adjuster_lic_app.pdf; registration form for firms is IL446-0149 available at http://insurance.illinois.gov/Producer/Producer_Forms/public_adjuster_firm_reg.pdf. The initial application requires finger prints. Contracts must be approved by the Department before a public adjuster can enter into an agreement with an insured. (215 ILCS 5/1515, 5/1545, 5/1560, 5/1563).

2. *Reinsurance Intermediaries.* Must be licensed as producers. Initial fee: $500; Biennial renewal: $200. The insurance director may require a bond or E&O policy for intermediary managers. (215 ILCS 5/408, 100/10).

3. *Third Party Administrators.* Initial filing fee: $200; Annual renewal: $200. TPA's must have a surety bond (form IL446-0152 06/09 available at https://insurance.illinois.gov/producer/Producer_Forms/ins_prod_bus_entity_bond.pdf) for the larger of $50,000 or 5 percent of the amount of funds handled annually (maximum $1 million). Application form: IL446-0177 available at http://insurance.illinois.gov/producer/Producer_Forms/third_party_adm_lic_app.pdf. (215 ILCS 5/511.104, .105).

4. *Viatical Settlements.* Viatical settlement agents must be appointed by at least one viatical settlement provider; application form revised 05/09 available at http://insurance.illinois.gov/producer/viatical/vs_pl_app.pdf. Provider fees: new, $3,000; annual renewal: $1,500.

   The Illinois Insurance Code does not require separate licenses for either risk managers/risk management consultants or for field/marketing representatives.

   The following application forms are used:

   a. Insurance Producer. Application form from Pearson VUE or Departmental form: Insurance Producer Application/Reinstatement Form. Fee: $500.
   b. Business Entity License. Fee: $500. (215 ILCS 159/10).

C. **Appointments:** Appointments are not required. Producers may also place insurance with companies with whom they do not have an agent's appointment (brokers). A surety bond (Form IL446-0152B 05/09 available at https://insurance.illinois.gov/producer/Producer_Forms/ins_prod_bus_entity_bond.pdf) is required.

D. **Licenses Required of Nonresidents:** Same requirements and fees as apply to residents, unless stated otherwise business entities must be licensed as well as all individuals in the entity who will be selling insurance. Home state licensure will be verified through the Producer Data Base (PDB). Power of attorney naming director for service of suit is required. No appointment is required. Illinois licenses nonresident public adjusters on a reciprocal basis. They must file a verification of good standing as a licensed resident in home state, and the application for a license that was submitted in their home state, or a completed Uniform Application. Nonresidents should submit NAIC Uniform Application for Individual Nonresident License or NAIC Uniform Application for Business Entity Nonresident License/Registration. Nonresident producer application and biennial renewal fee: $250. (215 ILCS 5/500-40, 500-135).

   Applications may be downloaded from the department's Web site at insurance.illinois.gov/Producer/ProducerMain.html#collapse01.

Multi-State Exposures: A license is not required for a nonresident insurance producer who sells, solicits, or negotiates a contract of insurance for commercial property and casualty coverage when risks that are to be insured under that contract are located in more than one state. This exception applies only if the nonresident is licensed to sell, solicit, or negotiate that insurance in the state where the insured maintains its principal place of business and the contract of insurance insures risks located in that state. (215 ILCS 5/500-20(6)).

E. Prelicensing and Education Requirements:

1. *Residents.* Applicants for a producer's license must complete twenty hours of certified study each for life, accident and health, property, fire, or casualty authority and must pass a qualifying examination. Seven and one-half hours of class must be in a classroom setting. Exams are administered by Pearson VUE, 800-274-0402; http://www.pearsonvue.com. Exam fee: $102. Applicants must wait five days after passing an exam to apply for a license.

   Producers who wish to sell long term care must take a special eight-hour course. Failure to complete the required ongoing training of at least four hours prior to renewal will require the producer to complete the eight-hour course again. (insurance.illinois.gov/producer/LTCTrainingRequirement.pdf).

   The motor vehicle line requires twelve and one-half hours of prelicensing education, five of which must be in a classroom setting and an examination.

   There is no education or examination requirement for limited insurance representative's license.

   Public adjusters must pass a qualifying examination.

   Producers who sell flood insurance must complete a one-time, three-hour, certified flood training course.

2. *Nonresidents.* Nonresident examination is reciprocal with applicant's home state.

   (215 ILCS 5/500-30, 500-45).

F. Continuing Education Requirements:

Number of Hours Required: All resident insurance producers are required to complete twenty-four hours for each biennial license renewal period, including three hours of ethics. The licensee must complete certified courses offered by education providers. Courses may be completed by classroom, seminar, webinar, or self-study instruction method. Course instructors receive the same number of credit hours as the students.

Proof of Completion: Submitted by education provider. Students should complete coursework at least one month prior to renewal to allow time for the provider to submit proof of completion to the director.

Excess Hours: Up to twelve hours may be carried into the next renewal period.

Final Exam: The final exam for a self-study course does not have to be monitored. However, the Illinois Code says that a self-study exam cannot be "self-evaluated."

Requirements **Not** *Applicable to the Following:*

1. The following limited licenses: industrial life and health, baggage, limited travel health or trip cancellation, insurance from a local mutual district, county, or township insurance carrier.

2. Temporary licenses.

3. Public adjusters. To renew the license, resident public adjusters must have twenty-four hours of continuing education; three of which must include classroom ethics.

Renewal Procedure:

1. Course provider reports all student course completions to the DOI.

2. Licensee submits renewal application.

Nonresidents are exempt from the CE requirement (except LTC, if applicable) if their home state imposes a CE requirement.

(215 ILCS 5/500-35, 500-90).

G. **Cancellation of Agency Contracts:** Insurers who terminate appointments, employment, contracts, or other insurance business relationships with a producer must notify the Department of Insurance within thirty days of the effective date of termination if the reason is listed in 215 ILCS 5/500-70. The insurer then must notify the producer within fifteen days of notifying the department. The producer may file written comments concerning the substance of the notification with the director within thirty days after receiving the notification and may demand a hearing. Hearings must be held within twenty to thirty days after the mailing of the hearing notice. (215 ILCS 5/500-85).

H. **Rules for Risk Retention and Purchasing Groups:** Illinois regulates risk retention and purchasing groups operating or offering coverage on risks in Illinois. Risk retention groups domiciled in Illinois must be chartered and licensed as liability insurers. Groups not domiciled in Illinois must register with the Director of Insurance and submit reports to the director. Purchasing groups must also register with the director and submit reports. All groups and all resident and nonresident agents or brokers participating in them must comply with all Illinois insurance laws, including licensing and solicitation requirements or restrictions. All risk retention group policies must show the following notice in at least ten point type on the front page and on the declarations page of the policy:

> "This policy is issued by your risk retention group. Your risk retention group is not subject to all of the insurance laws and regulations of your state. State insurance insolvency guaranty fund protection is not available for your risk retention group."

(215 ILCS 5/123B-3 to 123B-9).

I. **Other License Rules, Requirements, or Restrictions:** There are no restrictions on inspecting or servicing in state except unlicensed nonresident may not enter state to solicit. Entering the state includes mail or telephone or other electronic communication into the state from the outside, as well as physical presence in the state.

J. **Policy Countersignature Requirements:** Countersignatures not required (215 ILCS 5/123B-6).

K. **Portable Electronics Insurance:** Employees and authorized representatives of vendors may sell portable electronics insurance to customers and are not subject to licensure so long as the vendor obtains a limited-lines license to authorize its employees to sell portable electronics insurance, the employees are trained to sell portable electronics insurance, and each employee receives basic instruction about portable electronics insurance offered to customers. (215 ILCS 136/20).

II. Commissions, Fees, Commingling of Funds, and Suitability in Annuity Transactions

A. **Commissions:** There are no restrictions on division of commission. Unlicensed individuals may not receive commissions under any circumstances. Rebating of commissions is not allowed. (215 ILCS 5/500-80).

B. **Fees:** Licensed producers may charge service fees separate from commissions but only after providing a written agreement. The agreement must show the amount of the fee and the reason for the charge. A copy of the signed disclosure must be provided to the client and maintained by each producer who collects or receives the service fee or any portion of the service fee for at least seven years. If the combined compensation exceeds 10 percent of attributable premium, the client must sign the agreement. If an insurance policy or contract is cancelled within ninety days of the inception date, the producer must refund a prorated portion of the fee within thirty days after receiving documentation of the cancellation unless the compensation for services covered by the fee agreement were stated to be fully earned at inception of the agreement. (215 ILCS 5/500-80).

C. **Disclosure Requirements:** When an insurance producer or business entity charges any fee or compensation separate from commissions deductible from, or directly attributable to, premiums on insurance policies or contracts, it must comply with all of the following: (215 ILCS 5/500-80).

1. It must provide written disclosure to the consumer or contracting party that clearly specifies the amount or extent of the compensation or fee prior to the delivery of the corresponding policy. A copy of the written disclosure must be maintained by the producer or business entity that collects the compensation or fee for a period of seven years.

2. If the combined compensation or fee exceeds 10 percent of a directly attributable premium amount of a corresponding contract or policy, the disclosure must also include the signature of the consumer or contracting party acknowledging the compensation or fee.

3. If an insurance policy or contract is cancelled for any reason within ninety days following the inception date, the producer or business entity shall refund to the consumer a prorated portion of the fee or compensation within thirty days after the producer or business entity receives proper documentation that the corresponding insurance policy or contract has been cancelled. At no time shall a producer or business entity charge the consumer a fee or compensation for cancellation of any insurance policy or contract.

4. If the policy file contains documentation that the producer performed a service corresponding to the applicable coverage or policy and the written disclosure stated that the fees were fully earned, then those fees shall be fully earned at inception of the disclosure's execution.

D. Commingling of Funds: Collected premiums are trust funds and must be deposited in an account separate from other agency funds. The account must be designated and labeled Premium Fund Trust Account on bank records and on the face of the checks. (50 Ill. Adm. Code 3113.40).

E. Suitability in Annuity Transactions: An insurance producer who engages in the sale of annuity products must obtain a producer license with life line of authority and complete a one-time four credit training course approved by the department and provided by the department approved education provider.

The satisfaction of the training requirements of another state that are substantially similar to the training requirements required by Illinois will satisfy the Illinois training requirement. Producers who sell variable products must also have variable contract line of authority on their license.

Illinois has adopted the NAIC Suitability in Annuity Transactions Model Regulation. (215 ILCS 5/500-35, 5/500-90).

III. Statutory References: 215 ILCS 100/10; 136/20; 155/3; 159/10; 5/123B-3 to 123B-9; 5/141a; 5/408; 5/500-10 to 500-45, 500-60, 500-70, 500-80 to 500-100, 500-105 to 500-107, 500-130 to 500-135; 5/511.104 to 105; 5/1515, 1545, 1560, 1563. 50 Ill. Adm. Code 3113.40.

INDIANA

Insurance Commissioner
311 W. Washington St., #103; Indianapolis, IN 46204
Telephone: 317-232-2385 (Administrative)
317-232-2411; 317-232-2414 (Agency)
317-232-2426 (Consumer)
317-234-5882 (Fax)
http://www.in.gov/idoi
IDOI Resident Licensing Contact – mtapp@idoi.in.gov
Non-Resident Licensing Contact Person – bemiller@idoi.IN.gov

I. **Licensing Requirements:** Sales Personnel—Producers, Limited Lines Credit Producers, Limited Lines Producers, Managing General Agents, Bail Bond Licensees, and Resident Corporations. Other Insurance Professionals—Administrators, Consultants, Public Adjusters, Reinsurance Intermediaries, Utilization Review Agents.

A. **Applicability:** A person shall not sell, solicit, or negotiate insurance in Indiana for any class or classes of insurance unless the person is licensed for that line of authority. (Ind. Code § 27-1-15.6-3).

B. **Licenses Required of Residents:** Indiana residents must be at least eighteen years of age; maintain principal place of residence or principal place of business in Indiana; successfully complete a prelicensing education program and examination when required; not have committed any act that is ground for denial, suspension or revocation of a license; and submit the appropriate forms, application, and nonrefundable fees for the desired license. (Ind. Code Ann. §27-1-28-12). Each of the following must be licensed in Indiana:

Sales Personnel

1. *Producers.* Producer licenses will be issued or renewed for a two-year term, expiring on the last day of the producer's birth month two years from the date of issue or renewal of license.

   a. License fee: $40.
   b. License term: biennial.
   c. Lines of authority:

      (1) Life.
      (2) Health or sickness and accident.
      (3) Personal.

(4) Property.
(5) Casualty.
(6) Surplus lines producer (License fee: $80).
(7) Bail/Recovery Agent.
(9) Variable life and annuity productions.
(10) Title (Ind. Code § 27-1-15.6-7).
(11) Public adjuster (Subject to annual review, Annual fee: $50 due by December 31, and $10,000 surety bond required). (Ind. Code §§ 27-1-15.6-32, 1-27-4; in.gov/idoi/2735.htm).

2. *Limited Lines Producers.*

a. License fee: $40.
b. License term: biennial.
c. Limited lines of authority:

(1) Travel accident.
(2) Travel baggage.
(3) Prearranged funeral insurance.
(4) Multiperil crop and/or crop hail.
(5) Credit.
(6) Industrial fire, mortgage life, guaranty, and disability.
(7) Self-storage.
(8) Portable electronics. (Ind. Code §§ 27-1-15.6-18, 19).

3. *Car Rental Agents.* Not licensed in Indiana. (Ind. Code § 27-1-15.6-4).

4. *Title Insurance Producers:* Must be licensed as limited lines producers. (Ind. Code § 27-1-15.6-19.7).

5. *Managing General Agents.* Annual registration fee: $100. No person or entity may act as an MGA unless the person or entity has a resident producer license. (Ind. Code § 27-1-33-6). A managing general agent has the authority to adjust and pay claims in an amount equal to or exceeding $15,000 per claim. A bond equal to 10 percent of the gross direct written premium (minimum bond, $100,000; maximum, $500,000). An MGA must also maintain an E&O policy with limits of 25 percent of its gross direct written premium (subject to a minimum of $250,000 and a maximum of $10 million whichever is greater). Bond requirements and E&O requirements are adjusted annually on July 1. (760 Ind. Admin. Code 1-52-3 to 5).

6. *Bail Bond and Recovery Agent Licenses.* Indiana licenses bail agents and recovery agents. License expires biennially. Bail Bond Agent initial fee: $650; renewal fee: $600; initial exam fee: $100. Must submit fingerprints and a recent full-face photo with application. Fees for recovery agents: initial and renewal license fee: $300; initial exam fee: $100. Both are subject to a late fee of $100 if renewing past the license expiration date. As of March 31, 2016, new license application and renewal processes and reporting requirements were implemented for Bail and Recovery Agents and Bail/Recovery Class Providers. (http://in.gov/idoi/2491.htm; 760 Ind. Admin. Code 1-6.2-1 to 14). Apply online at either www.sircon.com or http://nipr.com/.

7. *Resident Corporations.* License fee: $40. Must submit a certified copy of the articles of incorporation as on file with the Secretary of State. The lines of authority include Life only; Accident and Health; Life, Accident and Health; Property and Casualty; Title. Note that registering with the Secretary of State is not required prior to submitting the nonresident business entity application. Applicants must designate an individual licensed producer who will be responsible for the business entity's compliance with the insurance laws and administrative rules of Indiana. (Ind. Code Ann. §27-1-15.6-6).

   Renewal applications may be made through Sircon or NIPR, or the uniform NAIC paper application. Paper applications must be accompanied by a check or money order made out to the IDOI at 311 W. Washington St., Indianapolis, Indiana 46204-2787. (in.gov/idoi/2473.htm). The Indiana Department of Insurance emails producer renewal invoices to the email address on file. There is a $100 penalty for failure to report a change of address within thirty days of the change. If a renewal invoice is not received, a producer may go online to renew at either www.Sircon.com/indiana or NIPR.com. Renewal licenses must be printed at www.Sircon.com/Indiana for an electronic processing fee of $5.15. (https://www.in.gov/idoi/2680.htm).

Other Insurance Professionals

1. *Administrators.* Third-Party administrators must have an administrator's license in accordance with Ind. Code § 27-1-25-11.1. Fee: $50. License must be renewed annually by August 31. Every administrator must file and maintain with the commissioner a surety bond, not less than 10 percent of the amount of total funds handled involving Indiana residents or $25,000, whichever is greater, not to exceed $200,000.

   An administrator is not required to hold a license as an administrator in Indiana if:

a. The administrator has its principle place of business in another state.
b. The administrator is not soliciting business as an administrator in Indiana.
c. In the case of any group policy or plan of insurance serviced by the administrator, less than 100 certificate holders reside in this state.

If the applicant holds a valid administrator license in one of the following states, the individual should complete the nonresident initial application: Alaska, Delaware, Florida, Idaho, Missouri, New Hampshire, New Jersey, West Virginia. If the applicant does not hold a valid administrator license in such states, the individual should complete the resident (home state) renewal application. (in.gov/idoi/2352.htm).

Must have a bond if administrator is servicing a governmental or church plan in accordance with Ind. Code § 27-1-25-4(g) equal to the greater of $100,000 or 10 percent of the total funds administered in connection with governmental plans or church plans in Indiana and all other states in which the administrator is authorized to conduct business. The original application and each application for renewal must be accompanied by an audited financial statement that reflects a positive net worth and prepared in accordance with Ind. Code Ann. §27-1-25-11.1-(b)(4).

An entity is not required to hold a license as an administrator in this state if the entity exclusively provides services to one or more bona fide employee benefit plans each of which is established by an employer or an employee organization, or both, and for which the insurance laws of this state are preempted pursuant to the Employee Retirement Income Security Act of 1974, 29 U.S.C. §1001 *et seq*.

Note: Any TPA licensed before June 1 must renew their license before August 31 of the same year. (in.gov/idoi/2352.htm).

2. *Consultants.* Once licensed as a consultant, that person may not continue to hold a producer's license, surplus lines producer's license or limited lines producer's license once licensed as a consultant. Consultant's license expires every twenty-four months. Consulting corporations must also be licensed. The following are not required to be licensed as consultants: attorneys licensed to practice law in Indiana acting in their professional capacity; duly licensed insurance producers or surplus lines insurance producers; trust officers of a bank acting in the normal course of their employment; and actuaries or CPAs who provide information, recommendations, advice, or services in their professional capacity. No one may be simultaneously licensed as producer, limited lines producer, or surplus lines producer and as a consultant. Prior to rendering any service, a consultant must

submit the written agreement for the commissioner's approval not less than thirty days before the form is used. (Ind. Code §27-1-15.6-23).

3. *Independent Adjusters.* Indiana adopted Ind. Code Ann. §27-1-28 governing Independent Adjuster Licensing. The code follows the NAIC independent adjuster model and includes the qualifications and procedures for the licensing of independent adjusters.

   IndependentAdjusters license fee: $40, plus electronic processing charge. License expires biennially. Must complete prelicensing course and pass exam prior to licensing. (Ind. Code §27-1-28-12).

4. *Reinsurance Intermediaries.* Annual fee: $100. Reinsurance intermediary managers must maintain a bond equal to 10 percent of the premium managed (minimum bond, $500,000; maximum, $10 million). They must also submit biographical affidavits on all authorized persons, and maintain an E&O policy with limits equal to 25 percent of the premium managed (minimum limit of liability, $250,000; maximum $10 million). If RM establishes loss reserves, actuarial opinion attesting to the adequacy of loss reserves incurred and outstanding on business produced by RM in accordance with Ind. Code § 27-6-9-23. (760 Indiana Admin. Code 1-51-3 to 5).

   Utilization Review Agents. A Utilization Review Agent may not conduct utilization reviewreviews in Indiana unless the agent holds a certificate of registration issued by the Department. Initial fee: $150; annual renewal, $100. Licenses expire annually on June 30. (Ind. Code § 27-8-17-9; in.gov/idoi/2351.htm).

Applications may be downloaded from the IDOI website at, http://www.in.gov/idoi.

C. **Appointments:** An insurance producer shall not act as an agent of an insurer unless the insurance producer becomes an appointed producer of the insurer. (Ind. Code § 27-1-15.6-14).

D. **Licenses Required of Nonresidents:** Nonresidents wishing to conduct insurance activities in Indiana may be licensed on the same basis as Indiana residents, except for bail bond or recovery agent licenses. Nonresidents whose principal place of business is in Indiana may be licensed as residents but only if they are not licensed as residents other than in Indiana. A nonresident must be currently licensed as a resident and in good standing in the person's home state. In addition, the applicant must submit the proper request for licensure and pay the $80 license fee. A nonresident surplus lines license is $120. The applicant must submit or transmit to the commissioner either the application for licensure that the applicant submitted to their home state or a completed uniform application, and the commissioner may verify the producer's licensing status through the Producer Database maintained by the NAIC and its affiliates or subsidiaries. The applicant's home state must award nonresident producer licenses to residents of Indiana on a reciprocal basis. Nonresidents are not required to take a prelicensing education course or examination. (Ind. Code § 27-1-15.6-32).

Applications may be downloaded from the IDOI website at http://www.in.gov/idoi.

Multi-State Exposures: A license is not required for a nonresident insurance producer who sells, solicits, or negotiates a contract of insurance for commercial property and casualty coverage when risks that are to be insured under that contract are located in more than one state. This exception applies only if the nonresident is licensed to sell, solicit, or negotiate that insurance in the state where the insured maintains its principal place of business and the contract of insurance insures risks located in that state. (Ind. Code § 27-1-15.6-4 (c)(6)).

E. Prelicensing Examination and Education Requirements:

1. *Residents.* Applicants for the following licenses must pass an exam:

   a. Producers. The following licenses require an examination: life; health; life and health or sickness; property and casualty.
   b. Personal lines.
   c. Bail and recovery agents (Exam fee: $100).
   d. Independent and public adjusters.
   e. Surplus lines producers.

   The prelicensing certificate issued upon completion of the course is valid for six months.

   Producer applicants must also obtain the following insurance education-prior to taking the exam. The course must be approved by the commissioner:

   a. Life only or health only – twenty hours.
   b. Personal lines property and casualty – twenty hours.
   c. Life and health – forty hours.
   d. Personal and commercial property and casualty – forty hours.
   e. Title – ten hours. (in.gov/idoi/2479.htm).

Pre-licensing exam content outlines and study materials are available at http://www.in.gov/idoi/2480.htm. Self-study for prelicensing education is approved in Indiana—check with the DOI for more information. (in.gov/idoi/2479.htm). Bail applicants must first apply to the DOI for permission to take the exam and must complete twelve hours of prelicensing education. (Ind. Code § 27-10-3-5). Exams are administered by Sircon, 877-876-4430; http://www.sircon.com. Exam fee: $75.50.

Applicants for insurance producer licenses who have attained a bachelor's degree in insurance are not required to complete prelicensing education and are required to take only the part of the exam pertaining to Indiana laws and rules. (Ind. Code § 27-1-15.6-9(e)).

Applicants for life, health, or variable life and variable annuity products licenses who hold CLU, CFP, or CFC or another nationally recognized designation approved by the commissioner or the National Association of Insurance Commissioners are exempt from prelicensing education and the examination, other than over the sections on Indiana law.

Applicants for property/casualty or personal lines licenses who hold CPCU, CIC, AAI or another nationally recognized designation approved by the commissioner or the National Association of Insurance Commissioners are exempt from prelicensing education and the examination, other than over the sections on Indiana law.

There are no prelicensing examinations for Limited Lines or Title licenses. (in.gov/idoi/2479.htm).

2. *Nonresidents.* Reciprocal with producer's home state. Application fee: $90. (Ind. Code § 27-1-15.6-16, 32).

F. Continuing Education Requirements:

Number of Hours Required: Resident producers must complete at least twenty-four hours of continuing education during the two year license renewal period. Those licensed in life, health, or variable life and variable annuity products must complete at least three of the hours of credit related to ethical practices in marketing and sale of life, health or annuity insurance products. Limited licensees are not required to complete continuing education. Seven hours of CE is required for title insurance licensees, with one hour each concerning ethical practices, title insurance underwriting, escrow issues, and principles of federal real estate settlement procedures. Funeral directors, crop or hail, mortgage, and industrial fire resident limited lines producers must complete at least five hours of continuing education during the two-year license term.

An attorney holding a title license may complete all or any of the required hours in continuing legal education courses related to the business of title insurance or any aspect of real property law. An attorney in good standing admitted to the practice of law and holding a license under Ind. Code § 27-1-15.6 with the exception of a title license, may complete all or any number of hours of continuing education required by completing an equivalent number of hours in continuing legal education courses related to the business of insurance. (Ind. Code § 27-1-15.7-2).

The only course content regulations (other than for limited licensees) are in the long-term care area: Five of the forty hours must be in LTC for producers satisfying the initial eight-hour requirement. Additionally, those who sell LTC under the Indiana LTC program must complete a one-time fifteen-hour course (the fifteen hours counts toward the quadrennial requirement of forty hours). Courses may not cover time management or sales techniques.

The licensee may use classroom instruction or self-study. Any licensee who teaches a course will receive CE credit.

Submit Proof of Completion: With the renewal application.

Excess Hours: May not be carried into next reporting period.

Final Exam: Self-study course exams must be monitored by a licensed agent.

Requirements ***Not*** *Applicable to the Following:*

1. A limited lines producer who is licensed without examination.

2. Limited lines credit producer.

3. Licensees who no longer solicit, but maintain a license in order to collect renewal commissions, who apply for and receive an exception.

4. Public adjusters.

5. An insurance producer who is at least seventy years of age and has been a licensed insurance producer continuously for at least twenty years immediately preceding the license renewal date.

Renewal Procedure:

Indiana does not accept renewals by mail. All renewals must be completed online.

1. Licensee must sign certificate under oath and keep original completion certificate.

2. Renewal form must have course numbers on the back.

3. Licensee pays $40 license renewal fee. ($50 for public adjusters).

4. Licensee must keep completion certificates to respond to the department in the event of an audit. (Ind. Code § 27-1-15.7-2).

Nonresidents are exempt if home state also has a CE requirement and a reciprocal agreement with the Indiana DOI. Nonresidents are also exempt from the LTC requirement but not from the Indiana LTC Program requirement. (Ind. Code § 27-1-15.6-8).

While late renewals are not permitted, individuals whom are unable to comply with license renewal procedures, including completion of continuing education due to military service or other extenuating circumstance such as long-term disability may be eligible for a waiver of those procedures. Such persons should contact the department before the expiration date for instructions as applicable to each individual situation. In order to be granted an extension, individuals will need to pay the renewal fee of $40.00, and submit with the request an extension fee of $25.00. Extensions are granted on a case-by-case basis and may not exceed ninety days (most extensions are for a period of thirty days). Failure to meet the terms of the extension may result in license suspension. If the request for an extension is denied, the licensee must complete continuing education requirements within ninety days after notification of the denial. Renewals received within thirty days of the license expiration date may be accepted without penalty at the discretion of the department. The resident reinstatement fee is $120 plus the $40 renewal fee.

G. **Cancellation of Agency Contracts/Producer Appointments:** The commissioner must promptly notify all appointing insurers and the licensee of any termination, revocation, or suspension of a license made by the commissioner if it is for any of the following reasons:

1. Providing incorrect, misleading, incomplete, or materially untrue information in a license application.

2. Violating:

    a. An insurance law.
    b. A regulation.
    c. A subpoena of an insurance commissioner.
    d. An order of an insurance commissioner of Indiana or of another state.

3. Obtaining or attempting to obtain a license through misrepresentation or fraud.

4. Improperly withholding, misappropriating, or converting any monies or properties received in the course of doing insurance business.

5. Intentionally misrepresenting the terms of an actual or proposed insurance contract or application for insurance.

6. Having been convicted of a felony.

7. Admitting to having committed or being found to have committed any unfair trade practice or fraud in the business of insurance.

8. Using fraudulent, coercive, or dishonest practices, or demonstrating incompetence, untrustworthiness, or financial irresponsibility in the conduct of business in Indiana or elsewhere.

9. Having an insurance producer license, or its equivalent, denied, suspended, or revoked in any other state, province, district, or territory.

10. Forging another's name to an application for insurance or to any document related to an insurance transaction.

11. Improperly using notes or any other reference material to complete an examination for an insurance license.

12. Knowingly accepting insurance business from an individual who is not licensed.

13. Failing to comply with an administrative or court order imposing a child support obligation.

14. Failing to pay state income tax or to comply with any administrative or court order directing payment of state income tax.

15. Failing to satisfy the continuing education requirements established by Ind. Code § 27-1-15.7.

16. Violating Ind. Code § 27-1-15.6-31 by being named as a beneficiary, become an owner of, or receive a collateral assignment of an insurance policy where the insurance producer has no insurable interest in the life of the insured or annuitant.

17. Failing to timely inform the commissioner of a change in legal name or address, in violation of Ind. Code § 27-1-15.6-7(h).

(Ind. Code Ann. § 27-1-15.6-12).

The commissioner must be notified of termination of any appointment, employment, or other insurance business relationship within thirty days. The producer must be notified within fifteen days after notice is sent to the commissioner. (Ind. Code § 27-1-15.6-15).

H. **Rules for Risk Retention and Purchasing Groups:** Indiana regulates risk retention and purchasing groups operating or offering coverage on risks in Indiana. As required under Indiana Code, Chapter 27-7-10, risk retention groups operating in Indiana must register with the commissioner of insurance and submit reports to the commissioner. Purchasing groups must also register with the commissioner and submit reports. All groups and all resident and nonresident agents or brokers participating in them must comply with all Indiana insurance laws, including licensing and solicitation requirements or restrictions. (Ind. Code §§ 27-7-10-13, 14).

All applications and all policies issued by risk retention groups must contain the following notice in ten point type:

NOTICE

"This policy is issued by your risk retention group. Your risk retention group may not be subject to all of the insurance laws and regulations of your state. State insurance insolvency guaranty funds are not available for your risk retention group." (Ind. Code § 27-7-10-18).

I. **Other License Rules, Requirements, or Restrictions:** No unlicensed resident or nonresident may enter the state to engage in any insurance solicitation in Indiana. Solicitation of any form is considered entering the state and requires licensure. Licensed nonresident may solicit, inspect, or service in state on a reciprocal basis with nonresident's home state. (Ind. Code § 27-1-15.6-3).

An individual insurance producer who allows the license to lapse and who has completed all of the required continuing education before the license expired may reinstate the same license without the necessity of passing a written examination within twelve months of the expiration date. A penalty of three times the unpaid renewal fee shall be required for any renewal after the expiration date of the license. However, the Department of Insurance may waive the penalty if the renewal fee is received fewer than thirty days after the expiration date of the license. (Ind. Code § 27-1-15.6-7).

If the commissioner considers the issuance of a temporary license necessary for the servicing of an insurance business, the commissioner, without requiring an examination, may issue a temporary insurance producer license for a period of not more than 180 days to any of the following:

1. To the surviving spouse or court-appointed personal representative of a licensed individual insurance producer who dies or becomes mentally or physically disabled:

    a. To allow adequate time for the sale of the insurance business owned by the producer;
    b. To provide for the servicing of the insurance business until the recovery or return of the producer to the business; or
    c. To provide for the training and licensing of new personnel to operate the producer's business.

2. To a member or employee of a business entity licensed as an insurance producer, upon the death or disability of an individual designated in the business entity application or the license.

3. To the designee of a licensed individual insurance producer entering active service in the armed forces of the United States of America.

4. To an individual in any other circumstance where the commissioner considers the public interest to be best served by the issuance to the individual of a temporary insurance producer license.

    The commissioner may by order limit the authority of a temporary licensee in any way considered necessary to protect insureds and the public, and may require the temporary licensee have a suitable sponsor who is a licensed producer or insurer to assume responsibility for all acts of the temporary licensee. (Ind. Code § 27-1-15.6-11).

Military Service: A licensed insurance producer who is unable to comply with license renewal procedures due to military service or some other extenuating circumstance may request a waiver of the license renewal procedures. The producer may also request a waiver of any examination requirement or any other fine or sanction imposed for failure to comply with the license renewal procedures. (Ind. Code § 27-1-15.6-7(f)).

An individual or corporation shall not engage in the business of an insurance consultant until a consultant license has been issued to the individual or corporation by the commissioner. However, the following people are not required to obtain a consultants license:

1. An attorney licensed to practice law in Indiana acting in the attorney's professional capacity.

2. A duly licensed insurance producer or surplus lines producer.

3. A trust officer of a bank acting in the normal course of the trust officer's employment.

4. An actuary or a certified public accountant who provides information, recommendations, advice, or services in the actuary's or certified public accountants professional capacity.

Consultants must provide their services as outlined in a written agreement, on a form approved by the commissioner. The agreement must (1) outline the nature of the work to be performed by the consultant, and (2) the method of compensation of the consultant. The consultant retains the agreement for not less than two years after completion of the services. A copy of the agreement must be available to the commissioner. In the absence of an agreement on the consultant's fee, the consultant is not entitled to recover a fee in any action at law or in equity. No licensed consultant may employ, be employed by, or be in partnership with, nor receive any remuneration whatsoever, from any licensed insurance agent, surplus lines insurance agent, or limited insurance representative, or insurer. However, a consultant may be compensated by an insurer for providing consulting services to the insurer. (Ind. Code § 27-1-15.6-23(e, f)).

J. **Policy Countersignature Requirements:** Countersignature not required on a policy of insurance issued to a risk retention group or to any member of that group. (Ind. Code § 27-7-10-24).

K. **Portable Electronics Insurance:** Portable electronics means electronic devices that are portable in nature. The term includes accessories, wireless services, and other services related to the use of such a device. Portable electronics insurance means insurance that provides coverage for the repair or replacement of portable electronics, including coverage for loss, theft, inoperability due to mechanical failure, malfunction, damage, or other similar causes of loss. A vendor shall not sell, solicit, or negotiate portable electronics insurance unless the vendor holds a limited lines license. A limited lines license required authorizes each of the following to sell, solicit, or negotiate portable electronics insurance to a customer at each of a vendors locations:

1. The vendor.

2. Each of the vendor's employees or authorized representatives, regardless of whether the employee or authorized representative is individually licensed, if the insurer that issues the portable electronics insurance directly supervises or appoints a supervising entity to supervise: (A) the administration of the portable electronics insurance sold by the vendor; and (B) a training program for the employees and authorized representatives.

The training must provide basic instruction concerning the portable electronics insurance offered to customers of the vendor; and disclosures required by Ind. Code § 27-1-15.9-12. The training must be developed and overseen by employees of the supervising entity who are licensed as insurance producers under Ind. Code § 27-1-15.6 with the Property & Casualty qualification. An employee or authorized representative of a vendor must not advertise, represent, or otherwise profess to be an insurance producer other than a limited lines producer licensed under Ind. Code § 27-1-15.6. (Ind. Code §§ 27-1-15.9-1 to 18; http://www.in.gov/idoi/2761.htm).

II. Commissions, Fees, Commingling of Funds, and Suitability in Annuity Transactions

A. Commissions: There are no restrictions on collection or distribution of commissions to licensed residents or nonresidents except in retaliation with nonresident's home state as to distribution of commission to licensed nonresident. Unlicensed residents or nonresidents who sell, solicit, or negotiate insurance in Indiana may not receive commissions, service fees, brokerage fees, or other valuable consideration. Renewal commissions or other deferred commissions may be paid to a person for selling, soliciting, or negotiating insurance in Indiana if the person was required to be licensed and was licensed at the time of the sale, solicitation, or negotiation. However, unlicensed residents or nonresidents who do not sell, solicit, or negotiate insurance in Indiana may receive such fees as long as payment of the fee does not constitute rebating. (Ind. Code § 27-1-15.6-13).

B. Fees: Producers may not receive compensation for the sale, solicitation, negotiation, or renewal of insurance policies issued to clients for whom the producer, for a fee, acts as a consultant unless the producer provides a written agreement to the client that complies with the requirements for a consultant's agreement which discloses the fact that the producer will receive compensation for the sale of the policy and the method of compensation. Before providing risk management services to an exempt commercial policyholder, risk managers must disclose in writing whether the risk manager will receive commission, fee, or other compensation from an insurer in connection with the purchase of an insurance policy. If the risk manager charges a fee for risk management services, the risk manager must disclose in writing the specific amount of compensation. The disclosure must be acknowledged in writing by the exempt commercial policyholder. (Ind. Code §§ 27-1-15.6-22, 24 (b)).

C. **Disclosure Requirements:** A licensed producer may charge a commercial insured a reasonable fee to reimburse the insurance producer for expenses incurred by the insurance producer at the specific request of the commercial insured, subject to the following requirements:

1. Before incurring any expense, before providing services, the producer must provide written notice to the commercial insured stating that a fee will be charged and setting forth the amount of the fee or the basis for calculating the fee.

2. The amount of a fee and the basis for calculating a fee may not vary among commercial insureds.

3. Any fee that is charged must be identified separately from premium and itemized in any bill provided to the commercial insured. (Ind. Code § 27-1-15.6-24).

D. **Commingling of Funds:** Indiana has no law restricting commingling of insurer premium collections with other agency funds.

E. **Suitability in Annuity Transactions:** A person may not sell, solicit, or negotiate any annuity product unless the person meets the following requirements:

1. The person is licensed as either:

   a. In the case of a fixed annuity, an insurance producer with a life qualification.
   b. In the case of a variable annuity, an insurance producer with a variable annuity product.

2. The person has adequate knowledge of an annuity product to recommend the annuity product.

3. The person complies with the insurer's training standards for annuity products.

4. The person has completed a one-time four-hour annuity-training course. (Ind. Code § 27-1-15.6-19.5).

Insurance producers licensed with a life insurance line of authority who sell annuities must complete a one-time four-hour annuity-training course. Producers who obtain a life qualification must complete the training prior to the sale of an annuity product. The four-hour training course is not in addition to the producer's 24-hour CE requirement for license renewal; it may be used as part of the producer's required CE hours. (Ind. Code § 27-1-15.6-19.5).

Insurers are required to verify that a producer has completed the mandated training before appointing a producer to sell its annuity products, and insurers should have some process in place to ensure their appointed producers are complying with those training standards. (Ind. Code § 27-1-15.6-30).

Indiana has adopted the NAIC Suitability in Annuity Transactions Model Regulation. (IDOI Bulletin 184).

III. **Statutory References:** Ind. Code §§ 27-1-15.6-3, 4, 6 to 9, 11 to 19.7, 22 to 24, 30 to 32; 1-15.7-2; 1-15.9-1 to 18; 1-25-4, 11.1; 1-28-12; 1-33-6; 6-9-23; 7-10-13, 14, 18, 24; 8-17-9; 10-3-5. 760 Ind. Admin. Code 1-6.2-1 to 14; 51-3 to 5; 52-3 to 5.

IOWA

Iowa Insurance Division
601 Locust St, 4th Floor; Des Moines, IA 50309-3738
Telephone: 515-281-5705 or Toll Free: 877-955-1212; Fax: 515-281-3059; https://iid.iowa.gov/

I. Licensing Requirements: Sales Personnel—Producers, Agencies, Managing General Agents, Car Rental Agencies. Other Insurance Professionals—Reinsurance Intermediaries, Third-Party Administrators. A resident agent must be at least eighteen and must have not committed any act that is grounds for denial, suspension or revocation of a license. A resident agent must pay the license fee of $50 and successfully pass the examinations for the lines of authority for which the person has applied.

A. Applicability: A person shall not sell, solicit, or negotiate insurance in this state for any line of insurance unless the person is licensed as an insurance producer for that line of insurance. A person offering to the public, for a fee or commission, to engage in the business of offering any advice, counsel, or service with respect to the benefits, advantages, or disadvantages promised under any policy of insurance must also be licensed as an insurance producer. (Iowa Code § 522B.2).

B. Licenses Required of Residents:

Sales Personnel

1. *Producers.*

   a. License fee: $50.
   b. License term: Three years. A producer must apply for license renewal within sixty days prior to the expiration date of the license.
   c. Lines of authority:

      (1) Crop.
      (2) Surety.
      (3) Accident and health or sickness (insurance coverage for sickness, bodily injury or accidental death and may include benefits for disability income).
      (4) Life (insurance coverage on human lives, including benefits of endowment and annuities and may include benefits in event of death or dismemberment by accident and benefits for disability income).
      (5) Variable life/variable annuity (insurance coverage provided under variable life contracts and variable annuities).

(6) Personal lines property and casualty (insurance sold to individuals or families primarily for noncommercial purposes).

(7) Credit (including credit life, credit disability, credit property, credit unemployment, involuntary unemployment, mortgage life, mortgage guaranty, mortgage disability, guaranteed automobile protection insurance, and any other form of insurance offered in connection with an extension of credit limited to partially or wholly extinguish a credit obligation that that the commissioner determines should be designated a form of credit insurance).

(8) Excess and surplus lines (must be licensed for both property and casualty insurance).

(9) Property (coverage for the direct or consequential loss or damage to property of any kind).

(10) Casualty (coverage against legal liability, including that for death, injury, or disability, or damage to real or personal property).

(11) Reciprocal authority (any other line of insurance issued in another state and for which Iowa grants authority to sell, solicit, or negotiate in Iowa). NIPR application must be submitted by mail with payment and written statement. (Iowa Code § 522B.6).

(12) Portable Sale of Electronic Insurance.

Producer licenses are subject to suspension for providing incorrect, misleading information on application, violating insurance laws obtaining or attempting to obtain a license through misrepresentation or fraud, improperly withholding money received in the course of business, convicted of a felony, nonpayment of child support, a student loan, or state taxes, and failure to cooperate in an investigation by the commissioner. (Iowa Code § 522B.11). Licenses expire for individuals on the last day of the birth month. All nonrenewed licensees can reinstate an expired license up to and including twelve months from the date of the license lapse by meeting the CE requirements and paying the renewal fees plus a late fee of $100 (for all authorities). If the license has been nonrenewed for more than twelve months, it will be processed as a new application and the standard fee ($50 with no penalty fee) will apply. All licenses that have been cancelled, surrendered, or terminated for over thirty days need to apply as a new producer. For licensure of business entities, licenses expire on the last day of incorporation/formation month. (Iowa Code § 522B.6).

2. *Limited Lines Producers.* Credit, crop and surety only.

3. *Cash Bail Bonds.* Not handled by the Iowa DOI.

4. *Title.* Title insurance is prohibited in Iowa. (Iowa Code § 515.48(10)).

5. *Car Rental Agencies.* A limited license for the sale of products offered by car rental companies. Fee: $50 per counter employee with a maximum of $1,000 per calendar year. Term: Three years. (Iowa Code § 522A.5).

6. *Business Entities.* Entities may request to be licensed. The entity must designate one licensed individual to have full responsibility for the conduct of the entity. All entities licenses expire triennially on the last day of the month of the entity incorporation/formation date. (Iowa Code § 522B.5).

7. *Managing General Agents.* Must be licensed as producers. The contract must be filed with the commissioner. The Commissioner may require an E&O policy of $250,000 and a surety bond of $50,000. (Iowa Code Ann. §§ 510.2, .4, 191 IAC 5.43).

Other Insurance Professionals

1. *Reinsurance Intermediaries.* Must meet the licensure requirements of Iowa Code § 521C.3. For example, the commissioner may require the reinsurance intermediary manager to file a bond for the protection of each reinsurer represented by the reinsurance intermediary-manager; or require the individual to maintain an errors and omissions policy in an amount acceptable to the commissioner.

2. *Third-Party Administrators.* Must be certified with the state. License fee: $100. Certificate renews every three years. (Iowa Code § 510.21).

3. *Public Adjusters.* Must be licensed. Post bond, background check/fingerprints required. (Iowa Code § 522C, 191 IAC 55.1 to 5).

The Iowa Division of Insurance does not accept applications via email. The producer's application is located at the NIPR Gateway. Applications may be downloaded from, http://www.nipr.com.

C. **Appointments:** An individual insurance producer who acts as an agent of an insurer must be appointed by that insurer. An insurance producer who is not acting as an agent of an insurer need not be appointed. A business entity is not required to be appointed. Appointment fee: $5, annually for Iowa domiciled companies. Nonresidents: Fee is retaliatory to state of domicile of insurance company. All appointments must be filed electronically. (Iowa Code § 522B.13; 191 IAC 10.15).

D. **Licenses Required of Nonresidents:** Nonresidents must be licensed as an insurance producer in good standing in their home state, and must submit to the commissioner the application submitted to their home state, or in lieu of such application, a completed uniform application. Nonresidents must have a nonresident producer's license to sell, solicit or negotiate insurance on Iowa property or exposures. The division may require any documents reasonably necessary to verify the information contained in the application or to verify the individual making application has the character and competency required to receive a producer license. If the applicant fails to provide the requested information within forty-five days of receipt of the request, the application will expire and the license fee will not be returned. This license expires every three years on the last day of the producer's birth month. A producer must apply for license renewal within sixty days prior to the expiration date of the license. Fee: $50. (Iowa Code § 522B; 191 IAC 10.5).

No bond is required. Nonresidents should apply through the NIPR Gateway at www.nipr.com.

Multi-State Exposures: A license is not required for a nonresident insurance producer who sells, solicits, or negotiates a contract of insurance for commercial property and casualty coverage when risks that are to be insured under that contract are located in more than one state. This exception applies only if the nonresident is licensed to sell, solicit, or negotiate that insurance in the state where the insured maintains its principal place of business and the contract of insurance insures risks located in that state. (Iowa Code 522B.3).

E. **Prelicensing Examination and Education Requirements:** Examination results are valid for ninety days after the date of the test. Failure to apply for licensure within ninety days after the examination is passed will void the examination results.

   1. *Residents.* To obtain a producer's license initially, resident applicants must pass a qualifying examination administered by Pearson VUE. The fee for all individual examinations is $44-$49.

      a. Exam 01. Life Insurance.
      b. Exam 02. Accident and Health or Sickness Insurance.
      c. Exam 55. Personal Lines Insurance.
      d. Exam 44. Commercial Lines Insurance. (Must pass the personal lines exam prior to taking this exam).
      e. Exam 31. Crop Insurance.
      f. Exam 29. Credit.
      g. Exam 46. Surety Insurance.
      h. Exam 82. Excess and Surplus Lines Insurance.
      i. Exam 03. Property Insurance.
      j. Exam 04. Casualty Insurance.
      k. Exam 60. Viatical Settlement Broker.

l. Exam 20. Public Adjusters.
m. Navigator.
n. Variable contracts candidates must have a license for life insurance and pass the Financial Industry Regulatory Authority (FINRA) examinations necessary to obtain an Iowa securities license.
o. Car rental counter employees must pass an exam administered by the car rental provider.

Note: The 05-Life and Accident & Health or Sickness and the 06-Property and Casualty combo exams are no longer being offered. Instead, candidates are now required to schedule both exams together in one order to get the $69 fee. (Pearson Vue Iowa Licensing Candidate Handbook).

2. *Nonresidents.* Examination requirements for nonresident producer's license are reciprocal with nonresident's home state. (Iowa Code § 522B.8).

F. Continuing Education Requirements:

Number of Hours Required: Every licensed resident producer must complete a minimum of thirty-six credits for each CE term in courses approved by the Division. Out of the thirty-six required credits, at least three must be in the subject of ethics. At least eighteen of the thirty-six hours must be approved as classroom method. By the end of the last business day of the producer's CE term, the division must receive from the producer proof of completion of CE courses and payment of the CE fee. A producer may elect to comply with the CE requirements by taking and passing the appropriate licensing examination for each qualification held by the producer.

Producers are required to maintain a record of all CE courses completed by keeping the original certificates of completion for four years after the end of the year of attendance. Producers must request a standard Iowa Certificate of Completion from each provider for each course for which the producer wants to claim Iowa CE credit. (191 IAC 11.1 to 11.4).

These rules do not apply to:

1. A nonresident producer who resides in a state or district having a CE requirement for insurance producers. These producers must file the renewal notice through the NIPR gateway.

2. A resident producer who holds surety or credit insurance.

3. Licensed attorneys who are also insurance producers, who submit proof of completion of continuing legal education for the appropriate calendar years during the CE term, pay the continuing education fee and otherwise comply with the producer license renewal procedures. If the attorney does not have a CE requirement in their home state, they must comply with the Iowa insurance CE requirements.

4. A producer who serves full-time in the armed forces of the United States of America on active duty during a substantial part of the CE term and who submits evidence of such service.

Excess Hours: Excess hours may not be carried into the next reporting period.

Final Exam: Self-study final exams must be monitored by either a CE provider or a disinterested third party. Both the monitor and the producer must sign a statement that the examination was completed by the producer without any outside assistance. A passing grade of 70 percent is required. Only half the producer's credits may be obtained through self-study if they are nondesignation courses.

Any producer holding qualification only for crop insurance line of authority and requesting renewal of a license must be able to demonstrate the following at each renewal:

1. The producer has completed all training and continuing education requirements by the federal Risk Management Association.

2. The producer has competed eighteen credit hours of continuing education, three of which must be in ethics. (191 IAC 11.3(8)).

Nonresidents are exempt from this requirement if they meet their home states' CE requirement. (191 IAC 11.1 to 11.4).

G. **Cancellation of Agency Contracts and Producer Appointments:** When an insurance company terminates its insurance business relationship with an insurance producer the company shall notify the division using NAIC Uniform Appointment/Termination Form or other such form approved by the division. The termination must be filed within thirty days of the date the insurer terminated its agency relationship with the producer. Within fifteen days after notifying the division, the insurer must mail a copy of the notification to the insurance producer at the insurance producer's last known address. (Iowa Code § 522B.14; 191 IAC 10.17).

H. Rules for Risk Retention and Purchasing Groups: Risk Retention Groups must be licensed as liability insurers. Except as provided under the Federal Liability Risk Retention Act of 1986, risk retention and purchasing groups, and all resident and nonresident producers participating in them, must comply with all Iowa insurance laws, including licensing and solicitation requirements or restrictions.

All application forms for insurance from a risk retention agency and all policies issued by risk retention groups must contain the following notice on the first page in ten point type:

NOTICE

"This policy is issued by your risk retention group. Your risk retention group may not be subject to all of the insurance laws and regulations of your state. State insurance insolvency guaranty funds are not available for your risk retention group." (Iowa Code § 515E.4).

I. Other License Rules, Requirements, or Restrictions: Unlicensed nonresidents may enter Iowa to inspect but not to solicit. Mail and telephone or other electronic communication into Iowa from outside Iowa, as well as physical presence in Iowa, is considered entering Iowa. (Iowa Code § 522B.3).

An individual insurance producer who allows the producer's license to lapse, within twelve months from the due date of the renewal fee, may have the same license reinstated without the necessity of passing a written examination by proving CE credits have been met and upon the payment of a $100 reinstatement fee. Such reinstatement fee is in addition to the required renewal fee. (191 IAC 10.9).

Military Service: A licensed insurance producer who is unable to comply with license renewal procedures due to military service or some other extenuating circumstance may request a waiver of those procedures. Such insurance producer may also request a waiver of any examination requirement or any other penalty or sanction imposed for failure to comply with renewal procedures. (Iowa Code § 522B.6(5)).

J. Policy Countersignature Requirements: None.

K. Limitations on Termination of Independent Insurance Producer: An insurance company shall not terminate a contract of an insurance producer who is an independent contractor but who is not an exclusive insurance producer as defined in Iowa Code § 522B.1 without at least 180 days notice, except for loss of license, fraud, nonpayment of company premiums that are due and not in dispute by the producer, or the withdrawal of operations in the state by the insurance company. These requirements do not apply to producers or business entities if there is a written provision expressly granting to the insurance company all rights, title, and interest in the ownership or use of the insurance business written by the producer. (Iowa Code Ann. § 515.106).

II. Commissions, Fees, Commingling of Funds, and Suitability in Annuity Transactions

A. Commissions: An insurer or insurance producer shall not pay a commission, service fee, brokerage, or other valuable consideration to a person for selling, soliciting, or negotiating insurance if that person is required to be licensed and is not so licensed. A person shall not accept any commission, service fee, brokerage or other valuable consideration unless the person performing the service held a valid license for the line of insurance for which the service was rendered at the time the service was performed. (Iowa Code § 522B.12; 191 IAC 10.14).

B. Fees: Iowa-licensed producers may not charge an additional fee for services customarily associated with the solicitation, negotiation or servicing of policies. The prohibition does not apply to assigned risk and commercial property-casualty policies. Any additional fee that a producer intends to charge for assigned risk policies and commercial property and casualty policies must be fully disclosed to the insured. (191 IAC 15.8).

C. Disclosure Requirements: An insurance producer shall not charge fees other than commissions unless such fees are based upon a written agreement signed by the client in advance of the performance of the services under the agreement. A copy of the agreement must be provided to the client at the time the agreement is signed by the client. The agreement must specifically state:

1. The service for which the fee is to be charged.

2. The amount of the fee to be charged or how it will be determined or calculated.

3. That the client is under no obligation to purchase any insurance product through the insurance producer or consultant.

The insurance producer shall retain a copy of the agreement for not less than three years after completion of services, and a copy shall be available to the commissioner upon request. (191 IAC 15.8).

D. Commingling of Funds: Iowa has no restriction on producer commingling of producer and insurer funds. (per IID, 8/12/2020).

E. **Suitability in Annuity Transactions:** An insurance producer shall not solicit the sale of an annuity product unless the insurance producer has adequate knowledge of the product to recommend the annuity and the insurance producer is in compliance with the insurer's standards for product training.

Insurance producers who engage in the sale of annuity products shall complete a one-time, four-credit training course approved by the Iowa insurance division and provided by an education provider approved by the insurance division. Insurance producers may not engage in the sale of annuities until the annuity training course required under this rule has been completed. This requirement applies to resident and nonresident producers alike. A substantially similar course completed in another state will meet this requirement. Note that this requirement is separate from the Indexed Products requirement.

Iowa has adopted the NAIC Suitability in Annuity Transactions Model Regulation.

Insurance producers who engage in the sale of annuity products should note that the Department adopted amendments to Chapter 15, "Unfair Trade Practices," of the Iowa Administrative Code, which establishes certain minimum standards and guidelines of conduct by identifying unfair methods of competition and unfair or deceptive acts or practices in the business of insurance. The adopted amendments are promulgated to conform to the Annuity Disclosure Model Regulation adopted by the National Association of Insurance Commissioners. (191 IAC 15.76).

III. **Statutory References:** Iowa Code §§ 510.2, 4, 21; 515.48, 106; 515E.4; 521C.3; 522A.5; 522B.1 to 3, 5 to 8, 11 to 14; 522C.5. 191 IAC 5.43; 10.5, 9, 14 to 15, 17; 11.1 to 4; 15.8, 76; 55.1 to 5.

KANSAS

Insurance Department
1300 S.W. Arrowhead Rd.; Topeka, KS 66604
Telephone: 785-296-3071
Kansas WATS (outside local area only): 800-432-2484
Fax: 785-296-7805
http://www.ksinsurance.org

Note: Kansas passed its own version of the Producer Licensing Model Act. The state uses the term *agent*, which means the same as *producer* for all intents and purposes. Kansas does not issue a broker license.

I. Licensing Requirements: Sales Personnel—Agents, Entities, Limited Lines Agents, Car Rental Limited Licensees, Managing General Agents. Other Insurance Professionals—Field/ Marketing Representatives, Reinsurance Intermediaries, Risk Managers/Consultants.

A. Applicability: It is unlawful for any person to sell, solicit or negotiate any insurance within Kansas unless such person has been issued a license as an insurance agent in accordance with the laws of Kansas. (KSA §40-4905.)

B. Licenses Required of Residents: Each of the following must be licensed in Kansas.

Sales Personnel

1. *Agents.*

   a. License fee: $90.

   b. License term: Biennial; expires on licensees' date of birth. If the individual licensee's birth year is an odd number, the license will renew on the individual's birthday every odd-numbered year. If the individual licensee's birth year is an even number, the license will renew on the individual's birthday every even-numbered year; on the anniversary of licensing for a firm. Registered resident business entity licenses do not have a renewal requirement.

   c. Lines of authority:

      (1) Life.
      (2) Accident and health or sickness.
      (3) Property and allied lines.
      (4) Casualty and allied lines.
      (5) Variable products.
      (6) Personal lines.

(7) Any other line of insurance permitted under the provisions of chapter 40 of the Kansas Statutes Annotated, and amendments thereto, and any rules and regulations promulgated thereunder.

Note: Kansas passed its own version of the Model Producer Licensing Act. The state does not use the term *producer*, but the term agent means the same as *producer. Agents* may not obtain broker authority. (K.S.A. §40-4903).

2. *Limited Lines Agents.*

   a. Application fee: $90.
   b. License term: Biennial; expires on licensee's date of birth.
   c. Lines of authority:

      (1) Bail bond.
      (2) Crop/hail.
      (3) Prearranged funeral. (pre-need funeral KSA §40-4903).
      (4) Credit products.
      (5) Title.
      (6) Travel.
      (7) Self-service storage.
      (8) Any other line of insurance permitted under the provisions of chapter 40 of the Kansas Statutes Annotated, and amendments thereto, and any rules and regulations promulgated thereunder. (K.S.A. §40-4903.)

3. *Car Rental Limited Line Licensee.* Car rental companies must obtain a business entity license.

   a. Application fee: $30.
   b. Lines of authority for a car rental limited licensee:

      (1) Personal accident insurance covering the risks of travel.
      (2) Motor vehicle liability insurance.
      (3) Personal effects insurance providing coverage to renters and other occupants of the motor vehicle.
      (4) Roadside assistance and emergency sickness protection programs.
      (5) Any other travel or auto-related coverage that a rental company offers in connection with and incidental to the rental of vehicles. (K.S.A. §40-241).

   c. Other Requirements: Employees in the car rental location can solicit insurance without a license as long as the car rental agency location that employs them is licensed. The only insurance that may be solicited is that which is enumerated in 1-5 above per KSA §40-241. No employee or agency can advertise or hold themselves out as licensed insurers, agents or brokers. The car rental agency must provide instruction to each representative on the kinds of insurance coverage offered by the agency.

4. *Entities.* Corporations, associations, partnerships, sole proprietorships, limited liability companies, limited liability partnerships and other legal entities acting as insurance agents and holding a direct agency appointment from an insurance company or companies are required to obtain an insurance agent's license. (K.S.A. §40-4905).

   a. Application fee: $30.
   b. Individuals affiliated with the agency who sell, solicit, or negotiate insurance must be licensed as agents.

5. *Managing General Agents.* Kansas does not issue a separate MGA license. Agent and agency licenses are required. (KSA §40-2129 through 2136).

   a. Application fee: $30.
   b. Commissioner may require a surety bond.

6. *Portable Electronics Limited Lines Licensee.* Portable electronics vendors must obtain a limited lines license to sell or offer coverage under a policy of portable electronics insurance. (K.S.A.40-5601 *et.seq.*)

   a. Application fee $30.
   b. Other requirements: Employees and authorized representatives of vendors can solicit insurance to customers at each location at which the vendor engages in portable electronics transactions without a license as long as the portable electronics vendor that employs them is licensed. The insurer complies with all statutes and regulations. The insurer issuing the portable electronics insurance must either directly supervise or appoint a supervising entity to supervise the administration of the program including development of a training program for employees and authorized representatives of the vendors. The training should be delivered to employees and representatives who directly engages in selling or offering portable electronic' insurance. Training can be in electronic form; however, if electronic then a supplemental education program should be implemented and overseen by a supervising entity. Each employee and authorized representative shall receive basic instruction about the portable electronics insurance offered to the customer and the disclosures required under K.S.A. Supp. 40-5604, and amendments thereto. No employee or authorized representative of a vendor of portable

electronics devices may advertise, represent, or otherwise hold themselves out as a nonlimited limited lines licensed insurance producer.

Other Insurance Professionals

1. *Reinsurance Intermediaries.* Initial fee: $150; annual renewal fee: $100 (due on May 1). Intermediaries may be required to carry a surety bond. Licensed attorneys do not need to be licensed as reinsurance intermediaries. (K.S.A. §40-4503).

2. *Risk Managers or Risk Management Consultants.* These individuals are not required to be licensed provided they stay within the scope of their employer. If they become involved in selling, soliciting, or negotiating insurance business, then they need an agent's license.

3. *Field/Marketing Representatives.* Those responsible for appointing agencies. These individuals must be licensed only if they become involved in selling, soliciting, or negotiating insurance business.

4. *Viatical Settlement Broker License.* Individual that arranges for a viator to sell their policy to a viatical provider. License fee: $100; renewal fee: $50 every anniversary date. No exam or CE necessary. (K.S.A. §40-5001 *et. seq.*).

5. *PublicAdjuster License.* Individual that represents a consumer in a claim that is limited to a first-party and only a commercial lines policy. License fee is $100, renewal fee $100 and due on birthday of either odd year or even year governed by year of birth. CE due is twelve hours of PC approved course including one hour of ethics. (K.S.A. §40-5501 *et. seq.*).

C. **Appointments:** Within thirty days of the date the company appoints such insurance agent, a nonrefundable appointment or certification fee of $2 for each agent certified by a domestic company and $5 for each agent certified by a foreign company shall be billed monthly. (KSA §40-252 and 253).

D. **Licenses Required of Nonresidents:** Licenses that are issued to resident sales personnel and other insurance professionals are also available to nonresidents wishing to conduct insurance activities involving exposures in the state of Kansas. Applicants for a nonresident agent or agency license must submit a $30 application fee in addition to the $50 biennial license fee. Company certification requirements for nonresidents are the same as for Kansas resident license holders; renewed annually.

1. *Agents.* Certificate of resident license is not needed if the home state participates in the Producer Data Base (PDB). In order for a nonresident agent to write business

with any insurer in Kansas, he or she must be appointed with that company in Kansas, not just in the home state. Appointment fees are billed to insurers.

2. *Multi-State Exposures.* A license is not required for a nonresident insurance producer who sells, solicits, or negotiates a contract of insurance for commercial property and casualty coverage when risks that are to be insured under that contract are located in more than one state. This exception applies only if the nonresident is licensed to sell, solicit, or negotiate that insurance in the state where the insured maintains its principal place of business and the contract of insurance insures risks located in that state. (K.S.A. §40-4904).

3. *Entities.* To issue a nonresident agency license, status in the business entity's home state will be verified through PDB. If the home state does not issue an entity license, a Letter of Good Standing issued by the Secretary of State or similar state agency is required. A nonresident agency license consists of a $30 application fee and a $50 license fee, and renews two years from date of licensure and every two years thereafter; $50 biennial license fee.

4. *Applications.* NAIC Uniform Application for Individual Insurance Producer License; NAIC Uniform Application for Business Entity License. Forms may be downloaded from the Department's Web site: http://www.ksinsurance.org.

E. Examination and Age Requirements:

Residents

1. All applicants for licensing must be eighteen years of age and has not committed any act that is grounds for denial or suspension or revocation.

2. Must be fingerprinted for a criminal background check.

3. Applications for the following authorities must pass a qualifying examination administered by Pearson Vue, 888-204-6255: Life, accident and health, property and allied lines, casualty and allied lines, personal lines, title, crop only, and bail bond only.

4. Exams may be taken individually or in the following combinations:

   a. Life can be taken individually or with A&H.
   b. Property and allied lines can be taken individually or with casualty and allied lines.
   c. Personal lines.

5. The following limited lines exams may be taken individually:

    a. Kansas laws and regulations.
    b. Crop.
    c. Title.

6. Bail bond applicants must pass the Kansas laws and regulations examination only.

7. Variable contracts licenses require either FINRA series 6 or series 7 certifications. FINRA registration and a life agent license, but no separate exam is required.

8. Testing fees: $64 for a combined major lines exam; $57 for one major lines exam or one limited line exam.

9. The following licenses do not require an exam: viatical settlement, reinsurance intermediary, excess lines, auto club, self-service storage or travel.

10. Exams must be taken for Public Adjusters (Limited to individuals that represent a consumer in a first-party claim and only on a commercial lines policy).

Nonresidents

1. All applicants must be at least eighteen years of age.

2. Kansas has no examination requirement for nonresident applicants.

F. Continuing Education Requirements for Residents:

Number of Hours Required: Twelve hours, biennially for either P&C or L/A&H; twenty-four hours for those with dual-authority licenses (split 50 percent–50 percent). Two hours biennially for crop. Four hours biennially for title insurance. One hour must be in ethics for L/A&H authority and for P&C authority. Up to three hours may be in agency management. Course instructors receive the same credit as the students. Crop only agents must biennially obtain a minimum of two C.E.C.'s in courses certified as crop under the property and casualty category. Title insurance agents must biennially obtain a minimum of four C.E.C.'s in courses certified title under the property and casualty category. Each licensed insurance agent who is an individual and holds a life insurance license solely for the purpose of selling life insurance or annuity products used to fund a prearranged funeral program must biennially affirm that no other insurance business was transacted during the current biennial renewal period. No C.E.C. shall be applied to satisfy both the biennial property or casualty requirement, or both, and the biennial requirement for life, accident and health or variable contracts, or any combination thereof. (K.S.A. §40-4903).

Excess Hours: May not be carried into the next reporting period.

Final Exam: Self-study courses require a final exam monitored by an independent third-party not related by work or family.

Requirements **Not** *Applicable to the Following:*

1. Inactive agents.

2. New licensees have the remainder of the current term and all of the next biennial term to comply for the first time.

G. Renewal Procedure:

Residents

1. Course provider supplies the licensee with certificate of completion and/or electronic submission through SBS system.

2. Licensee submits certificate of completion to the DOI, at the end of each biennium.

3. Licensee must renew via Kansas Insurance Department Producer Desktop found on our Web site.

Nonresidents

1. No letter of Home State Certification is required. PDB is checked to verify licensing status in home state.

2. Submit the biennial fee ($50) no earlier than three months prior to renewal date.

3. Licensee may renew electronically via NIPR.

H. Licenses Cancelled for Noncompliance:

1. *Residents.* Reinstatement fee of $100 per continuing education category. Proof that CE hours have been completed. If the CE provider does not submit the producer

course information electronically, the producer must submit the KCE-4 or an official grade report from a provider of professional designation courses to the Kansas Insurance Department. Company appointment and/or application forms and fees may be required, dependent upon the length of time that has passed from the producer's renewal due date.

2. *Nonresidents.* Reinstatement fee of $100 per continuing education category. $50 biennial license fee. Certification letter from the producer's home state is not required. License status will be verified through PDB as proof of continuing education compliance (PDB Participating State Report at https://nipr.com/products-and-services/producer-database). Company appointment and/or application forms and fees may be required, dependent upon the length of time that has passed from the producer's renewal due date.

I. **Cancellation/Change of Agency Contracts:** When an agency contract has been effective for more than a year, a notice of 180 days to the agency is necessary to terminate or change the agency contract. The 180-day period may be shortened by mutual agreement or in case of termination for fraud, misrepresentation, or failure to pay the agent account. (K.S.A. §§40-2,106 and 2,107).

J. **Rules for Risk Retention and Purchasing Groups:** KSA §40-4101 *et. seq*.

1. Kansas regulates risk retention and purchasing groups operating or offering coverage on risks in Kansas. Risk retention groups domiciled in Kansas must be chartered and licensed as liability insurance companies and authorized to engage in the business of insurance under the laws of any state. Groups not domiciled in Kansas must register with the insurance commissioner; submit reports to the commissioner as described under K.S.A. §40-4103, and pay a notification fee of $250. Purchasing groups, along with risk retention groups and all resident and nonresident agents participating in them, must comply with all Kansas insurance laws not specifically exempted under the risk retention law, including licensing and solicitation requirements or restrictions.

2. Each risk retention group policy must show the following notice in at least ten-point bold type across the front page and the declarations page:

> This policy is issued by your risk retention group. Your risk retention group may not be subject to all of the insurance laws and regulations of your state. State insurance insolvency guaranty funds are not available for your risk retention group. (K.S.A. §§40-4102 and 40-4103).

K. Other License Rules, Requirements, or Restrictions: None.

L. Cancellation/Change of Agency Contracts: When an agency contract has been effective for more than a year, a notice of 180 days to the agency is necessary to terminate or change the agency contract. The 180-day period may be shortened by mutual agreement or in case of termination for fraud, misrepresentation, or failure to pay the agent account. (K.S.A. §§40-2,106 and 2,107).

M. Licenses Cancelled for Noncompliance:

1. *Residents.* Reinstatement fee of $100 per continuing education category. Proof that CE hours have been completed. If the CE provider does not submit the producer course information electronically, the producer must submit the KCE-4 or an official grade report from a provider of professional designation courses to the Kansas Insurance Department. Company appointment and/or application forms and fees may be required, dependent upon the length of time that has passed from the producer's renewal due date.

2. *Nonresidents.* Reinstatement fee of $100 per continuing education category. $50 biennial license fee. Certification letter from the producer's home state is not required. License status will be verified through PDB as proof of continuing education compliance (PDB Participating State Report at https://nipr.com/products-and-services/producer-database). Company appointment and/or application forms and fees may be required, dependent upon the length of time that has passed from the producer's renewal due date.

N. Forms and Fees: Forms may be downloaded from the Department's Web site, http://www.ksinsurance.org, including:

1. *Agent Application:* NAIC Uniform Application for Individual Insurance Producer License and $90 resident application fee, $80 nonresident application fee.

2. *Business Entity Application:* NAIC Uniform Application for Business Entity Insurance License and $30 resident application fee or $80 nonresident application fee.

3. *Company Appointments:* Appointment fee: $2 for a domestic company; $5 for a foreign company. Submit the Kansas Insurance Department Company Appointment/Cancellation form or electronically through the National Insurance Producer Registry.

4. *MGA appointments*: Appointment reporting form available at ksinsurance.org and $100 appointment notification fee to the Commissioner of Insurance within thirty days.

II. Commissions, Fees, Commingling of Funds, and Suitability in Annuity Transactions

A. **Commissions:** For agents with the same line of authority, there are no restrictions on division of commissions among licensed residents or nonresidents. (K.S.A. §40-4910).

B. **Fees:** Agents may receive fees for services, provided they are supported by a written contract with the client specifying the amount of the fee and the services rendered for the fee and the contract is executed at the beginning of the transaction. (K.S.A. §40-4911).

C. **Disclosure Requirements:** None.

D. **Commingling of Funds:** Kansas has no restriction on agency commingling of agency and insurer funds.

E. **Suitability in Annuity Transactions:** Kansas has adopted the NAIC Suitability in Annuity Transactions Model Regulation which became effective June 1, 2013. The rules were adopted in their entirety with no substantive changes.

III. Statutory References: K.S.A. §§40-214; 40-241; 40-2,106; 40-2,107; 40-2,129 through 40-2,136; 40-4501 through 40-4512; 40-4901 through 40-4918; 40-5001-40-5016; 40-5501 through 40-5519; and Kansas Department of Insurance. With the changes to statutory references, this list may need to be amended. KSA §40-252, KSA §40-4101 *et. seq*.

KENTUCKY

Department of Insurance
215 W. Main St.; P.O. Box 517; Frankfort, KY 40602-0517
Telephone: 502-564-6004; WATS: 800-595-6053
Fax: 502-564-6030
Email: doi.agentlicensingmail@ky.gov
http://insurance.ky.gov

I. **Licensing Requirements:** Sales Personnel—Agents (including Limited Lines), Managing General Agents, Surplus Lines Brokers, Rental Vehicle Agents & Managing Employees, Other Insurance Professionals—Adjusters, Apprentice Adjusters, Consultants, Reinsurance Intermediaries, Administrators, Life Settlement Brokers, and Life Settlement Providers.

A. **Applicability:** An individual or business entity shall not sell, solicit, or negotiate insurance in Kentucky unless duly licensed as the appropriate insurance producer for that line of authority. No individual or business entity shall in this state be, act as, or hold himself, herself, or itself out as an adjuster unless then licensed as an adjuster. No individual or business entity shall act as a consultant with respect to any kind of insurance unless duly licensed as a consultant for that line of authority. No agent shall place, and no insurer shall accept, any insurance with any insurer as to which the agent does not then hold a license and appointment as agent. A rental vehicle agent or rental vehicle managing employee shall not place, and an insurer shall not accept, any insurance with any insurer as to which the licensee does not then hold a license and appointment. A travel retailer, its employee, or its representative shall not offer and disseminate travel insurance, and an insurer shall not accept any travel insurance, for which the limited lines travel insurance producer does not then hold a license and appointment. (KRS §304.9-080).

B. **Licenses Required of Residents:** Each of the following must be licensed in Kentucky.

Individuals and business entities must be licensed for twelve months in order to be subject to license renewal, including continuing education requirements, if applicable.

License renewal for individuals is due by the last day of birth month in even years for individuals born in an even numbered year, and due by last day of birth month in odd years for individuals born in odd numbered years. License renewal for business entities is due by March 31 in even years for business entities licensed in even numbered years, and by March 31 in odd years for business entities licensed in odd numbered years. (KRS §304.9-260).

Sales Personnel

1. *Resident Agents.* (Individuals or business entities).

   a. License fee: $40 plus $40 for each line of authority for individuals; $0 renewal, if one or more active appointments; $40 renewal if no active appointments. For business entities, $100, plus $100 for each line of authority; $0 renewal, if one or more active appointments; $100 renewal, if no active appointments. Individuals may access a summary of fees and applicable deadlines from the department's Web site at: insurance.ky.gov/ppc/Documents/DOI_FeeSchedule122019.pdf.
   b. License term: Biennial; License renewal for individuals is due by the last day of birth month in even years for individuals born in an even numbered year, and due by last day of birth month in odd years for individuals born in odd numbered years. License renewal for business entities is due by March 31 in even years for business entities licensed in even numbered years, and by March 31 in odd years for business entities licensed in odd numbered years. (KRS §304.9-260).
   c. Lines of authority.

      (1) Life.
      (2) Health.
      (3) Property.
      (4) Casualty.
      (5) Variable life and variable annuity products.
      (6) Personal lines.
      (7) Any other line authorized by Kentucky law and deemed appropriate by the Commissioner. (KRS §304.9-030).

   d. Limited lines licenses.

      (1) Limited line credit.
      (2) Travel.
      (3) Surety.
      (4) Crop.
      (5) Rental vehicle.
      (6) Self-service storage space.
      (7) Other lines as specified by the commissioner through administrative regulations. (KRS §304.9-230).

Detailed licensing process instructions and checklists may be found downloaded on the department's Web site at: http://insurance.ky.gov Individuals must complete an application to be submitted to www.nipr.com along with fees.

a. All resident applicants must order a criminal background check report from Administrative Office of the Courts through the Kentucky Court of Justice (https://kycourts.gov/aoc/criminalrecordreports/Pages/default.aspx) and follow the directions given. The nonrefundable cost is $20, payable by credit card or electronic check; failure to complete the steps will result in the Department not receiving the official copy of the background check and applicant will need to reapply for a new report. Report is valid for sixty days and online requests are processed within two business days of being received. Submit any applicable criminal background documents to DOI.
b. If applying for casualty, health, life, personal lines, or property lines of authority, complete a Kentucky approved prelicensing course; and pass the appropriate examination. A list of approved education providers is found on the Web site. (KRS §304.9-105; https://insurance.ky.gov/ppc/CE/Default.aspx).

   If applying for variable life & variable annuity line of authority, list FINRA CRD number on the application.

   Note: You must hold a current registration with a broker, and current life agent license.

   I In order to settle crop claims, a crop agent must obtain an adjusters license. (KRS §§304.9-080, 304.9-230).

Note: Active service members on duty can renew any license or certificate without paying any dues or fees. Additionally, the service member is no longer required to obtain continuing educational credits or meet any other requirement to renew their licenses if circumstances associated with the military duty prevent obtaining training and a waiver request has been submitted or if the active duty military member performs the licensed or certified occupation as part of their military duties. The license or certificate issued is continued as long as the licensee or certificate holder is a member of the Armed Forces of the United States on active duty for a period of at least six months after discharge from active duty. This new law also includes changes that allow spouses to obtain a temporary agent license or certificate without meeting the current requirements in the insurance code. The law allows the department of insurance to issue a temporary or regular license or certificate to the spouse of an active duty member within thirty days if they meet certain conditions: the spouse must prove he or she is married to an active duty service member and hold a valid license or certificate issued by another state, the District of Columbia, or any possession or territory of the United States; and, it has to be shown that the applicant's spouse is assigned to a duty station in Kentucky pursuant to official active duty military orders. The application fee would be capped at the amount required to issue the license. The temporary license will expire after six months and is not renewable. At that point, the licensee must meet the requirements to obtain a permanent license. (KRS §§12.355 to 357).

The fee for business entities is $100, plus $100 for each line of authority. Business entities must submit the following along with a NAIC Uniform Application and fees:

a. List of all individuals designated to act under the business entity's license.
b. For each designated individual: Individual license application or Department of Insurance's identification number for the individual's license (each must be licensed for one or more of the same lines of authority and appointed by at least one insurer; initial designee of nonresident business entity is not required to hold insurer appointment but all subsequent designees must be licensed and appointed).
c. All business entity licensees are advised to contact Kentucky Secretary of State to ensure compliance with Kentucky Corporate Laws.
d. If applying for Variable Life & Variable Annuity line of authority: Provide FINRA CRD number for entity and hold current life line of authority. (KRS §§304.9-130 to 133).

Appointing insurers are responsible for securing background checks on all individuals and business entities appointed. (KRS §304.9-270).

2. *Managing General Agents.* Kentucky's MGA law is substantially similar to the most recent NAIC Model. (KRS §§304.3-500 to 304.3-570). Biennial renewal fee is $40 per the underlying property and casualty license: Licensure fee is $100; renewal fee is $100. MGA's must be licensed and appointed as an agent for property and casualty lines of authority. They may be individuals or entities, and each must provide insurer contracts for review and approval prior to licensure. (KRS §304.3-510; https://insurance.ky.gov/ppc/Documents/DOI_FeeSchedule122019.pdf).

3. *Rental Vehicle.* Persons may use their restricted licenses as rental vehicle agents and managing employees to sell insurance related to vehicle rental transactions at registered locations. At least one licensed managing employee must be assigned to each location at all times, and must be available to answer the unlicensed employees' questions. Each location of the car rental business must be registered with the department before unlicensed employees can sell rental vehicle insurance at that location.

   Prelicensing training and exam, of licensed managing employees is provided by licensed rental vehicle agent. Consumer disclosure instruction and annual education of unlicensed employees, is provided by the licensed rental vehicle agent. There is no longer a requirement to provide proof of CE to the Department.

Rental vehicle agents must submit the following as a package:

a. Form 8301-BE for a business entity; Form 8301 for an individual.
b. Form 8301 for each managing employee.
c. Form 8301-RV registering each business location, identifying the licensed managing employee and certifying compliance with the training and examination of managing employees.
d. Consumer protection disclosures form to be included with the rental vehicle agreement.
e. A business entity applicant must ensure each proposed licensed managing employee has successfully completed a prelicensing course of study and successfully passed a rental vehicle examination.
f. Biennial fees of $100 for the rental vehicle business entity license; $50 per registered business location; and $40 for each managing employee (individual) license.

Rental vehicle agent and managing employee appointment, biennial appointment renewal, and late appointment renewal penalty fees, per insurer, are: $40 for resident individuals, $50 for nonresident individuals, $100 for a resident business entity, and $120 for a nonresident business entity. (KRS §§304.9-505 to 304.9-511; https://insurance.ky.gov/ppc/Documents/FeeSchedule.pdf).

4. *Portable Electronics Insurance.* Application shall be made to the director on the appropriate form; an individual will be designated as the vendor's person responsible for compliance with regulations or if the portable electronics retailer derives more than 50 percent of its revenue from the sale of portable electronics insurance, information must be provided for all officers, directors and shareholder of record who have beneficial ownership of 10 percent or more of any class of securities, who are subject to 15 U.S.C. §78p. There is a $100 fee per location for one to twenty locations in Kentucky or if there are twenty-one or more locations in Kentucky the fee is $2,500. Renewal not required. (KRS §304.9-780; https://insurance.ky.gov/ppc/Documents/FeeSchedule.pdf).

Other Insurance Professionals

1. *Independent, Staff, and Public (P&C Only) Adjusters* (Property and Casualty, Workers Compensation, Crop). Biennial license renewal fee: $50; Licensure fee: $50, plus $50 examination fee; adjusters may not be licensed as both independent or staff (representing insurers) and public (representing insureds). That is, a licensee

shall not represent the interest of both insurer and the insured or claimant. May be individuals or entities. All licensed adjusters must maintain some form of financial responsibility under KRS §304.9-430(3). However, there is no longer a requirement to file proof with the Department.

Business Entity Biennial Renewal Fee $50; Licensure fee: $50; must provide designated individual who is licensed as an adjuster. All individuals, who exercise the business entity's license, must be licensed as an individual adjuster and designated to the entity. (KRS §304.9-433).

2. *Apprentice Adjusters.* Licensure fee $25; a one-year, temporary license as an apprentice adjuster is available to anyone who resides and works in Kentucky and meets the other requirements for an adjuster license for a maximum of twelve months, but does not have the experience or education to pass the adjuster examination. The apprentice adjuster must be sponsored by a licensed adjuster. An individual may hold only one apprentice adjuster license, until the individual is issued an adjuster license in accordance with KRS §304.9-430. Once an individual holds such a license, the individual may again be eligible to hold one apprentice adjuster license. (KRS §304.9-432).

3. *Consultants.* Biennial renewal fee $100; licensure fee $100, for Life & Health **or** Property & Casualty; Examination fee $50. Must be an individual at least age eighteen. Requires five years of actual experience as a licensed agent for the appropriate lines of authority. May be individuals or entities. Business entities may submit a completed NAIC uniform license application at www.nipr.com. It is the published opinion of the Kentucky Department of Insurance that, while it is legal to be licensed as both an agent and a consultant, the individual may not perform both functions for the same transaction. Consultants must maintain an insurance policy or cash surety bond to demonstrate financial responsibility, but there is no longer a requirement to file proof with the Department.

   Business entity biennial renewal fee $100; licensure fee is $100; must provide a designated individual who is licensed as a Consultant Property and Casualty, or Consultant Life and Health producer. All individuals who exercise the business entity's license must be licensed as an individual consultant in this state and designated to the entity's license. (KRS §304.9-350).

4. *Reinsurance Intermediaries.* Broker or Manager. Biennial renewal fee $100; licensure fee $100. Reinsurance intermediary managers are required to be financially responsible but are not required to file proof with the department. May be individual or business entity. A licensed attorney at law of Kentucky, when acting in the professional capacity of an attorney, is not required to be licensed as a

reinsurance intermediary broker or manager. Likewise, the following individuals are not required to be licensed as reinsurance intermediary managers: employee of the reinsurer; U.S. manager of an alien reinsurer; underwriting manager that manages all the reinsurance operations of the reinsurer, is under common control with the reinsurer, and whose compensation is not based on the volume of premiums written; and manager of a joint underwriting or joint reinsurance group which is subject to examination by the insurance regulator at its principal place of business. (KRS §304.9-705; https://insurance.ky.gov/ppc/Documents/FeeSchedule.pdf).

Business Entity Biennial Renewal fee $100; licensure fee is $100; must provide a designated individual who is licensed as a reinsurance intermediary. All individuals who exercise the business entity's license must be licensed as an individual reinsurance intermediary in this state, and be designated by the entity.

5. *Administrators.* Biennial renewal fee $50; licensure fee $50. Must be at least twenty-one years of age and financially responsible. Must be financially responsible, competent, trustworthy, reliable and of good reputation. Applicant must not have had any license issued by the commissioner or application terminated for cause. Applicant must be a resident of Kentucky or is currently licensed and in good standing in his or her home state. May be individuals or entities. Individuals must attain an educational level acceptable to the commissioner. (KRS §§304.9-053, 304.9-371 to 304.9-377). Entities are required to submit Form 8301-TPA–Administrator Applicant Certification and Attestation.

   Business entity biennial renewal fee $100; licensure fee is $100; Form 8301-BE must designate an individual who is licensed as an Administrator in Kentucky. All individuals, who exercise the business entity's license powers, must be licensed as an individual administrator and designated by the entity.

   The following application forms are used:

   a. Individual. NAIC Uniform Application at www.nipr.com.
   b. Individual. Form 8301 BGC (Background Check Report Request is found online at: http://courts.ky.gov/aoc/criminalrecordreports/Pages/default.aspx.)
   c. Business Entity. NAIC Uniform Application at www.nipr.com.
   d. Administrator Applicant Certification and Attestation Form at http://insurance.ky.gov.

6. *Life Settlement Brokers.* Biennial renewal fee: $250 for individuals; licensure fees $250; examination fee $50. Must be at least age twenty-one. NAIC Uniform

Application at www.nipr.com and 8301 Background Check Report Request for an individual (http://courts.ky.gov/aoc/criminalrecordreports/Pages/default.aspx). May be individuals or entities.

Business entity biennial renewal fee $750; licensure fee $750; Form 8301-BE; must designate an individual who is licensed as a Life Settlement Broker. All individuals who exercise the business entity's license must be licensed as Individual Life Settlement Broker and designated by the entity. (KRS §304.15-700; https://insurance.ky.gov/ppc/Documents/FeeSchedule.pdf).

7. Registered Life Settlement Broker: Biennial renewal fee: $250; licensure fees $250. Must hold a life line of authority for twelve full months. NAIC Uniform Application at www.nipr.com, Form 8301 Background Check Report Request at http://courts.ky.gov/aoc/criminalrecordreports/Pages/default.aspx. Individual license only.

8. *Life Settlement Providers.* Biennial renewal fee: $500; licensure fee $500. Must be at least age twenty-one. NAIC Uniform Application at www.nipr.com Form 8301 Background Check Report Request for individual (http://courts.ky.gov/aoc/criminalrecordreports/Pages/default.aspx), May be individual or entities.

   Business entity biennial renewal fee $1,500; licensure fee $1,500 Form 8301-BE; must designate an individual who is licensed as a Life Settlement Broker. All individuals who exercise the business entity's license must be licensed as individual Life Settlement Broker and be designated by the entity. (KRS §304.15-700; https://insurance.ky.gov/ppc/Documents/FeeSchedule.pdf).

Kentucky does not issue a broker's license except for the Surplus Lines Broker License, Life Settlement Broker License, and Reinsurance Broker License. An agent may act as a broker under the agent license, provided that:

A. The agent has held a resident insurance agent with a life line of authority for a minimum of one year;

B. The agent notifies the commissioner of his or her actions as a life settlement broker within 30 days of beginning such operations; and

C. No matter the manner of compensation, the life settlement broker or life insurance agent represents only the owner and owes a fiduciary duty to act according to the owner's instructions and in the owner's best interests. (KRS §304.15-700).

A link to NAIC Uniform Application is available on the Department of Insurance's Web site.

C. **Appointments:** All appointments are biennial, renewable on or before March 31st of odd years for life and health insurers, and nonprofit medical corporations governed by KRS §304.32. All appointments are biennial, renewable on or before March 31 of even years for all other insurers. No agent shall claim to be an agent or representative of, or in any way imply a contractual relationship with, a particular insurer, or place applications for insurance with an insurer unless the agent becomes an appointed agent of the insurer and the agent's appointment has been approved by the commissioner. An agent may act as a representative of and place insurance with an insurer without first obtaining approval of the appointment by the commissioner for a period of fifteen days from the date the first insurance application is executed by the agent. If the agent does not obtain confirmation that the agent's appointment has been approved by the executive director within fifteen days from the date the first insurance application is executed, the agent must immediately discontinue acting as an agent on behalf of the insurer until confirmation is received. (KRS §304.9-270).

Appointment fee: per insurer (when processed at the same time) by agent's lines of authority for individual is $40 for resident licensees, $50 for nonresidents. Appointment fee: per insurer (when processed at the same time) by agent's lines of authority for business entity is $100 for resident entities, $120 for nonresident entities. (https://insurance.ky.gov/ppc/Documents/FeeSchedule.pdf).

D. **Licenses Required of Nonresidents:** Agent, managing general agent, surplus lines broker, life settlement provider and life settlement broker, reinsurance intermediary broker and manager, rental vehicle agent and managing employee, and consultant. If licensed in a reciprocal home state, a substantially similar license may be obtained in Kentucky if:

1. the applicant is currently licensed as a resident and in good standing in the home state;

2. the applicant has paid the required fees;

3. the applicant has submitted the NAIC uniform individual or business entity application;

4. the applicant's home state awards nonresident licenses to Kentucky residents on a reciprocal basis.

Individuals and business entities must be licensed for twelve months in order to be subject to license renewal. (KRS §304.9-140).

License Fee: Agent individual: $50 plus $50 per line of authority; $0 renewal if one or more active appointments; $50 renewal if no active appointments. Agent business entity: $120 plus $120 per line of authority; $0 renewal if one or more active appointments; $120 renewal if no active appointments. Fees for other licenses are the same as for resident individual and business entity.

Appointment Fee: Per insurer (when processed at the same time) by individual agent's lines of authority is $50.

Appointment Fee: Per insurer (when processed at the same time) by agent business entity's lines of authority is $120.

Agent and agent business entity must be licensed for twelve months in order to be subject to license renewal; renewal fees are $50 per individual, $120 per business entity.

Multi-State Exposures: A license is not required for a nonresident insurance producer who sells, solicits, or negotiates a contract of insurance for commercial property and casualty coverage when risks that are to be insured under that contract are located in more than one state. This exception applies only if the nonresident is licensed to sell, solicit, or negotiate that insurance in the state where the insured maintains its principal place of business and the contract of insurance insures risks located in that state. (KRS §304.9-090).

E. Prelicensing Examination and Education Requirements:

1. *Residents.* Prelicensing course training may be either classroom or self-study. All applicants for agent (except variable life and variable annuity, credit, line of authority), consultant, life settlement broker, or adjuster license must pass a qualifying examination initially; examination fee: $50 per line of authority. An applicant who takes an examination required by KRS Chapter 304 shall be permitted to take or retake an examination an unlimited number of times within 120-day timeline once the application has been approved. Each request shall be made on an Examination Retake Form, Form 8304, incorporated by reference in 806 KAR 9:025. Agents must have twenty hours of prelicensing training instruction, per line of authority. Applicants for a life and health or P&C license must complete forty hours of prelicensing education. A life agent, registered as a viatical life settlement broker, must have an agent license with an active life line of

authority for one or more years. Consultants must have five years of experience as an agent.

The following agent licenses with limited lines of authority require an exam only: crop and travel. Motor vehicle physical damage is no longer issued; but agents with these lines of authority may continue to exercise the licenses, as long as they maintain their agent licenses and appropriate appointments. (806 KAR 9:025).

Persons holding professional insurance designations are exempt from the prelicensing training instruction requirements for applicable lines of authority. See KRS §304.9-170 for a list of the professional designations and related lines of authority.

2. *Nonresidents.* If licensed in their home state, agents may receive Kentucky license through reciprocity. Nonresident agents qualifying through reciprocity do not have to provide proof of financial responsibility. (KRS §304.9-140).

F. Continuing Education Requirements:

Number of Hours Required: Agents (other than limited lines): Twenty-four hours, biennially. Must include at least six hours in one or more of the active lines of authority and three hours of ethics. All twenty-four hours may be either self-study or classroom, or a combination of both. Any resident licensee licensed with property and casualty lines of authority selling federal flood insurance must complete a one-time, three-hour course related to the National Flood Insurance Program. Completion of the course will provide the licensee with three hours of continuing education credit. The instructor may also receive CE credit. Life and health agents who sell long-term care partnership products must complete a one-time eight-hour initial training course prior to selling the products, and ongoing training of at least four hours biennially. Individual licensees selling, soliciting, or negotiating the sale of an annuity, as defined by KRS §304.5-030, are required to successfully complete four hours of initial training regarding annuity suitability. Resident independent and public adjusters are required to complete twenty-four hours of CE that includes three hours of ethics. (KRS §304.9-295; 806 KAR 9:025(5)).

Life settlement brokers must have twenty-four hours, with three in life, three in life settlement, and three in ethics.

The following continuing education courses meet the commissioner's standards for continuing education requirements:

1. Any part of the Life Underwriter Training Council life course curriculum.

2. Any part of the Life Underwriter Training Council health course curriculum.

3. Any part of the American College Chartered Life Underwriter diploma curriculum.

4. Any part of the American Institute for Property and Liability Underwriters' Chartered Property and Casualty Underwriter professional designation program.

5. Any part of the Insurance Institute of America's programs.

6. Any part of the Certified Insurance Counselor program.

7. Any insurance-related course taught at an accredited college or university, if the commissioner approves such course.

8. Any course of instruction or seminar developed or sponsored by any authorized insurer, recognized agent association, recognized insurance trade association, or any independent program of instruction, if approved by the commissioner.

9. Any correspondence course approved by the commissioner.

10. Any course in accordance with provisions of reciprocal agreements the commissioner enters with other states. (KRS §304.9-295).

Excess Hours: up to twelve hours (classroom or correspondence) may be carried over into the next reporting period. (806 KAR 9:025).

Requirements **Not** *Applicable to the Following:*

1. Limited lines of authority – surety, travel, limited line credit, crop, rental vehicle, self-storage space, any other limited line as specified by the commissioner.

2. Anyone not licensed for one full year prior to current biennium. Requirement not due until following biennium.

3. Nonresident licensees who satisfy the CE requirements of their home state and whose home state gives the same credit to Kentucky licensees on a reciprocal basis.

4. Those licensed as producers only to receive renewals or deferred commissions, if they are not actively soliciting or writing insurance. Must file notarized affidavit with the Department. (KRS §304.9-295).

CE Credit Procedures:

1. Course provider certifies to Department of Insurance, on prescribed form, the names of all licensees who complete course within thirty days of the completion. Must also provide a certificate to each licensee.

2. Course provider and licensee keep copies of documents for at least five years.

   Approved providers and courses are listed athttps://insurance.ky.gov/PPC/newstatic_info.aspx?static_id=72#read. Courses may be classroom, correspondence, online self-study, or any combination. (806 KAR 9:025).

G. **Cancellation of Agency/Producer Contracts:** An insurer must give written notice to the commissioner within thirty days following the effective date the appointment is cancelled, and the insurer must give notice to the licensee within fifteen days after making notification. Along with the notice, the insurer must file a statement of the facts surrounding the termination of appointment. (KRS §304.9-280).

H. **Rules for Risk Retention and Purchasing Groups:** Risk retention groups are subject to the provisions of KRS §304.45. Persons selling coverage for risk retention groups are required to be licensed as agents. Persons procuring insurance for a purchasing group must be licensed as agents or surplus lines brokers. Persons procuring insurance for a member of a purchasing group under the group's policy must be licensed as agents. The licensing requirement does not apply to salaried employees of an insurer or purchasing group. (KRS §304.45-010).

   The Department of Insurance has issued revised procedures adapting to federal changes. A Kentucky domiciled risk retention group must be chartered and authorized as an insurance company. All other risk retention groups and all purchasing groups must register with the department on forms available from the Department of Insurance. All groups and all resident and nonresident agents or surplus lines brokers participating in them must comply with all Kentucky insurance laws, including licensing requirements or restrictions. They must also pay Kentucky state and applicable local government taxes on insurance for Kentucky risks. All risk retention group policies must show the following notice in at least ten point boldface type across the face of the policy:

NOTICE

"THIS POLICY IS ISSUED BY YOUR RISK RETENTION GROUP. YOUR RISK RETENTION GROUP MAY NOT BE SUBJECT TO ALL OF THE INSURANCE LAWS AND REGULATIONS OF YOUR STATE. STATE INSURANCE INSOLVENCY GUARANTY FUNDS ARE NOT AVAILABLE FOR YOUR RISK RETENTION GROUP." (KRS §304.45-040).

I. **Other License Rules, Requirements, or Restrictions:** Entering the state includes mail or telephone or other electronic communication into the state from the outside, as well as physical presence in the state. See Bulletin 97-5 from the Commissioner. Unlicensed nonresident agent may not enter state for any insurance purpose. Consultants may not recommend purchase of insurance from an insurer in which a member of consultant's immediate family is an executive or majority stockholder. (KRS §304.9-350).

J. **Policy Countersignature Requirements:** Countersignatures are not required of risk retention groups. (KRS §304.45-100).

K. **Portable Electronics Insurance:** A portable electronics insurance retailer license issued under this section shall permit portable electronics retailers to offer and disseminate portable electronics insurance by the licensee, its employees, and authorized representatives at each location at which the portable electronics retailer does business in the state. The supervising entity shall maintain a register of each separate business location where a portable electronics retailer and its employees or authorized representatives offer and disseminate portable electronics insurance. (KRS §304.9-780).

II. Commissions, Fees, Commingling of Funds, and Suitability in Annuity Transactions

A. **Commissions:** An unlicensed individual or business entity may not receive any commission, even if he or she does not perform any services in the state. Rebating of commissions is not allowed. (KRS §304.12-090).

B. **Fees:** Agents may not charge a fee for services provided in connection with the sale of insurance policies, either in addition to, or instead of a commission. A consultant, also licensed as an agent, cannot receive both commission and fees for the same transaction, except as provided in KRS §304.9-350. Consultant's fee must be based on prior written agreement, signed by client, specifying the fee and services to be provided. (KRS §304.9-350).

C. **Disclosure Requirements:** No person licensed as a consultant may receive any fee, commission or thing of value for examining, appraising, reviewing or evaluating any insurance policy, bond, annuity or pension or profit-sharing contract, plan or program or for making recommendation or giving advice with regard to any of the above, unless such compensation is based upon a prior written agreement signed by the party to be charged and specifying or clearly defining the amount or extent of such compensation and the services to be rendered. A copy of every such agreement shall be retained by the licensee for not less than five years after such services have been fully performed. A consultant shall disclose in the agreement to the party to be charged whether he owns an interest in an insurance agency. (KRS §304.9-350).

D. **Commingling of Funds:** Kentucky requires agents to hold insurers' premium funds in a fiduciary capacity. (KRS §304.9-400).

E. **Suitability in Annuity Transactions:** Any individual selling, soliciting or negotiating the sale of an annuity must successfully complete four hours of initial product-specific training.

The training requirements may apply toward a licensee's continuing education requirement as set forth in KRS §§304.9-295 and 304.15-700, if the training has been approved as a continuing education course in accordance with 806 KAR 9:025(5) and proof of completion is made in accordance with 806 KAR 9:025(1). (806 KAR 9:025).

Kentucky has not adopted the NAIC Suitability in Annuity Transactions Model Regulation.

III. Statutory References:

KRS §§12.	355 to 357
KRS §§304.9-	030, 053, 080, 090
	105, 130 to 133, 140
	230, 260, 270, 280, 295
	350, 371 to 377
	400, 430 to 433
	505 to 511
	705, 780
KRS §304.12-	.090.
KRS §304.15-	700
KRS §§304.45	010, 040
	100

806 KAR	9:25

LOUISIANA

Department of Insurance
1702 North 3rd St.; Baton Rouge, LA 70802
PO Box 94214; Baton Rouge, LA 70804
Telephone: 800-259-5300 in LA and 225-342-5900
Fax: 225-342-3754
http://www.ldi.la.gov

I. Licensing Requirements: Licenses are issued for a period of two years, expiring on the last day of the individual's birth month for individual licensees or on March 31 for agencies. Sales Personnel are Producers, Limited Lines Producers, and Managing General Agents. Other Insurance Professionals are Reinsurance Intermediaries, Third-Party Administrators, Surplus Lines Brokers, Professional Employer Organizations, Consultants, Claims, Adjusters, Public Adjusters, and Viatical Settlement Brokers. (http://www.ldi.state.la.us/industry/producer-adjuster/renewals).

A. Applicability: No person shall act as or hold himself out to be an insurance producer unless licensed by the Department of Insurance. No insurance producer shall sell, solicit, make an application for, procure, negotiate for, or place for others any policies for any lines of insurance as to which he is not qualified and licensed in Louisiana. (La. R.S. §22:1543).

B. Licenses Required of Residents: Each of the following must be licensed in Louisiana:

Sales Personnel

1. *Producers.* Producers must be appointed for each insurer represented.

   a. License fee: Initial license application fee for producers, (other than surplus lines brokers): $75. License Amendment fee (adding lines other than surplus lines): $50. Individual producer's biennial renewal fee: $50 (one line) or $55 (multiple lines). Testing for applications requiring an exam now done through testing vendor, PSI Exams. Testing vendor Web site: psiexams.com. Lines that require an exam are life, health and accident, property, casualty, personal lines, industrial fire, bail bond, surplus lines and title and all resident adjuster licenses. Online application for all resident and nonresident producers and adjusters now filed electronically through NIPR at www.NIPR.com. Online applications encouraged. Will accept paper application form 1546A or NAIC Uniform Application. Fingerprints are required for new license applicants. Fingerprinting fee: $39.25. Fingerprinting services also provided through PSI exams. (http://www.ldi.state.la.us/industry/producer-adjuster/license-application) (La. R.S. §22:821).

b. License term: Biennial.

c. Lines of authority:

(1) Life.
(2) Accident and health or sickness.
(3) Variable life and variable annuity.
(4) Property.
(5) Casualty.
(6) Personal lines.
(7) Credit.
(8) Surety.
(9) Bail bonds.
(10) Travel Insurance.
(11) Title.
(12) Industrial Fire.
(13) Limited life, health, and accident.
(14) Surplus Lines.
(15) Portable Electronics.
(16) Self Storage.

Surplus lines. (Fee: $250;Two year renewal $350). Portable Electronics Insurance Limited Lines License (Fee $200, renewal $100). (La. R.S. §22:1547 and 22:821, 22:1550.1).

Individual licenses expire on the last day of the individual's birth month of odd or even years An insurance producer whose license has lapsed may, within two years of expiration, reinstate the license with proof of continuing education requirements and fees paid. If a license has been lapsed more than two years ago the applicant must fulfill the requirements for a new license. (La. R.S. §22:1547).

An individual who applies for an insurance producer license in this state who was previously licensed for the same lines of authority in another state shall not be required to complete any prelicensing education or examination if the individual makes application within ninety days of the cancellation of the previous license. (La. R.S. § 22:1551).

Any applicant for a license covering the same line or lines of insurance for which the applicant was licensed under a similar license in Louisiana within two years of the date of expiration shall be exempt from the requirement of examination. (La. R.S. § 22:1551).

2. *Limited Lines Producers.*

   a. License fee: $75 for first line of authority and $50 for each additional line. Renewal fee: $50; two or more lines $55. (LSA-R.S. §22:821).
   b. License term: Biennial.
   c. Lines of Authority:

      (1) Industrial fire.
      (2) Limited life, health & accident.
      (3) Title.
      (4) Credit lines.
      (5) Surety.
      (6) Bail bonds.
      (7) Surplus lines.
      (8) Travel.
      (La. R.S. §§22:1547, 22:1782.1).

   Lines of authority that do not require an exam have a license fee of $75 for the first line of authority, and $50, $55 for two or more lines. A line that requires an exam may be used as the first line of authority. (La. R.S. §22:821). Lines that do not require an exam:

      (1) Travel.
      (2) Limited life, health, and accident.
      (3) Limited Line Credit.
      (La. R.S. §22:1551).

3. *Entities.* Trade names must be registered with the Secretary of State and the Louisiana Department of Insurance. (La. R.S. §22:1552) All individuals within a corporation or partnership who are transacting business must be licensed and affiliated with the business entity. (La. R.S. §1544).

4. *Managing General Agents.* Must be licensed and appointed as a property and casualty producer prior to filing an MGA application. Initial registration fee: $300. Initial appointment fee: $300. Annual renewal fee: $300. Annual appointment: $300. The commissioner may require a bond in the amount of $250,000 or 10 percent of annual writings (whichever is less). The commissioner may require an E&O policy. (La. R.S. §22:1622, 1623, and 821).

5. *License Renewals*: The Department no longer mails out renewal forms for individual renewals. An electronic online renewal system is available. Individual licensees and officers/employees of resident producer agencies can either go to the DOI

Web site at http://www.ldi.state.la.us/industry/producer-adjuster/renewals and use the online renewal process found therein or may renew online at www.nipr.com. A producer who fails to renew a license before the expiration date is entitled to reinstate that license for a period of two years from the expiration date and will be charged a $50 late fee. Producers are responsible for notifying the insurance company of reinstatement of license and request a new appointment. (La. R.S. §22:821)

Other Insurance Professionals

1. *Third-Party Administrators.* Must be licensed. Initial license fee: $500; annual filing due March 1. Fee: $300. TPAs must post a $100,000 surety bond or deposit $100,000 in trust as security for policyholders and plan participants.

   Most license applications are filed electronically. Applications for other types of licenses may be obtained from the DOI Web site at www.ldi.la.gov along with other types of license applications. (La. R.S. §§22:821 and 22:1651).

2. *Public Adjusters.* First time applicant: $55; Biennial renewal: $50. Fingerprints and examination are required for resident applicants ($39.25 fee). Must post a surety bond of at least $50,000. Information may be downloaded at: http://www.ldi.la.gov. Most applicants file electronically via NIPR. The NAIC uniform application for individual insurance license is also accepted. (La. R.S. §§22:1694-1695 and 22:821).

3. *Claims Adjusters.* Must be licensed. First time applicant: $55, biennial renewal: $50. Fingerprints and examination are required ($39.25 fee). (La. R.S. §§22:821, 1663-1666).

4. *Catastrophe and Emergency Claims Adjuster.* A license is not required for an individual who is employed or retained by an insurer and brought into Louisiana for the purpose of investigating or adjusting losses resulting from a catastrophe or emergency. However, these individuals must be registered. Registration fee: $25 per individual/business entity. Electronic registration form located at: www.ldi.la.gov must be completed by the insurer. (La. R.S. §§22:821 and 1667).

5. *Viatical Settlement Brokers.* Initial fee: $50. Annual renewal: $50. A licensed life insurance producer may operate as a viatical settlement broker without separate licensure by providing a written notice of intent to do so to the Department of Insurance. The notice must include the name and license number of the entity that will be acting as a viatical broker and must be signed by the producer or,

if a corporation, partnership or LLC, signed by an officer or member. (La. R.S. §22:1792, LAC 37:XIII.3905).

C. **Appointments:** An insurance producer shall not act as an agent of an insurer unless the insurance producer becomes an appointed agent of that insurer, except for surplus lines policies placed through licensed surplus lines brokers, surplus lines policies placed with unauthorized insurers by licensed surplus lines brokers, and workers compensation policies placed with the Louisiana Workers' Compensation Corporation. An insurance producer who is not acting as an agent of an authorized insurer is not required to become appointed. (La. R.S. §22:1558). Insurance company must file appointment by electronic means. Fee: $30 per individual appointment; $100 per producer agency appointment. Effective date is the date received by the Insurance Department. If an appointment is disapproved fees will not be refunded. Company appointment renewal fee: $20 for individuals; $100 for producer agencies. Individual appointments expire 12/31 annually. Producer Agency appointments expire 7/31 annually. Insurers must attest that the appointee is trustworthy and competent. The state does not dictate the means by which the insurer makes that determination. An appointment remains in effect until the following date of renewal unless the commissioner revokes the license of the appointed producer, or the insurer cancels via written notice to the producer with a copy filed with a commissioner. (http://www.ldi.state.la.us/industry/producer-adjuster/appointments-affiliations/company-appointment).

D. **Licenses Required of Nonresidents:** The following licenses are available to nonresidents:

Producers. Nonresidents may be licensed as producers.

A nonresident shall receive a producer license if he or she is a licensed resident in good standing in his or her home state; submits the request for licensing and pays the required fees; and provides to the commissioner of insurance the application for licensure submitted to the home state, or a completed Uniform Application; and the nonresident's home state awards such licenses to Louisiana residents on a reciprocal basis. (La. R.S. §22:1548).

Term and expiration of these licenses are the same as for Louisiana resident license. The DOI will obtain confirmation on the status from PDB. A Letter of Certification is required if the information cannot be obtained from PDB. Nonresidents file license applications online through NIPR.

Multi-State Exposures: A license is not required for a nonresident insurance producer who sells, solicits, or negotiates a contract of insurance for commercial property and casualty coverage when risks that are to be insured under that contract are located in more than one state. This exception applies only if the nonresident is licensed to sell, solicit, or negotiate that insurance in the state where the insured maintains its principal place of business and the contract of insurance insures risks located in that state. (La. R.S. §22:1544). Effective January 1, 2020 if a nonresident producer license ceases to be current or in good standing in the producers home state, the nonresident's Louisiana license terminates automatically.

E. Prelicensing Examination and Education Requirements:

1. *Residents.* Prelicensing education requirements are twenty hours per each major line producer authority except bail bond, which requires eight hours. The following candidates for multiple lines of authority must complete forty total hours of prelicensing education: (1) life and accident and health or sickness; (2) property and casualty; (3) life and health and accident. (LAC 37:XI.511). Louisiana producers must pass a qualifying examination initially to obtain a license. Exams are administered by PSI Exams, psiexams.com, 1-800-733-9267. Applicants for some limited licenses are exempt from the examination requirement.

   Exams and fees:

Life:	$40
Health and accident:	$40
Life, health, and accident:	$65
Property:	$40
Casualty:	$40
Property and casualty:	$65
Bail bond:	$15
Surety:	$15
Industrial fire:	$15
Surplus lines:	$15
Title:	$15
Personal lines adjuster:	$15
Personal lines producer:	$15
Automobile adjuster:	$15
Commercial Lines adjuster:	$15
Comprehensive adjuster:	$15
Crop adjuster:	$15
Public adjuster:	$15

   (http://www.ldi.state.la.us/docs/default-source/documents/licensing/producers/licensing-handbook.pdf?sfvrsn=3a877c52_26).

2. *Nonresidents.* Nonresidents are not required to take the Louisiana examination as long as they hold a current license in good standing in their home state. (La. R.S. § 22:1551).

3. *Exemptions.* The following applicants are exempt from the requirement of an examination:

   Limited life, health, and accident insurance. Any applicant for a license to represent a limited life, health and accident, insurer.

   Credit. Any applicant who will be licensed to act only as a producer with respect to life, health, and accident insurance on borrowers or debtors, or with respect to credit property and casualty insurance on collateral and involuntary unemployment commonly known as credit insurance.

   Travel. Any applicant who is a ticket selling agent of a railroad company, carrier by air, or public bus carrier, who acts thereunder as an insurance producer only in reference to the issuance of accident or baggage insurance policies in connection with the transportation that accompanies the transportation ticket. (La. R.S. §22:1551).

A person applying for a license as a producer who has a bachelor's degree or higher from an accredited college or university with major course work in insurance is exempt from prelicensing education requirements. Such person still must take the relevant exam(s). (La. R.S. §22:1545).

F. Continuing Education Requirements:

Number of Hours Required: The number of hours to be completed every two years for license renewal is as follows:

Life – twenty-four hours (must include three hours ethics).

Health and accident – twenty-four hours (must include three hours ethics).

Life, health and accident – twenty-four hours (must include three hours ethics).

Property & casualty – twenty-four hours (must include three hours ethics and three hours flood).

Bail bond – twelve hours (must include minimum six hours on bail enforcement).

Personal lines – twenty-four hours (must include three hours ethics and three hours flood).

Title – twelve hours (must include two hours related to state and federal consumer finance protection laws).

Claims adjuster – twenty-four hours (must include three hours ethics).

Public adjuster – twenty-four hours (must include three hours ethics).

Both life and health with P&C – twenty-four hours (must include three hours ethics).

Both property and casualty with L&H – twenty-four hours (must include three hours ethics and three hours flood).

(La. R.S. §§22:1573, 22:1673, 22:1702). Courses must be approved by the DOI for the lines in which applicant is licensed. Required hours may be obtained through correspondence, verifiable self-study, or classroom courses.

Submit Proof of Completion: Proof of completion is submitted by the CE provider within thirty days of course completion. (LAC 37:XI.727).

Excess Hours: Up to ten hours of P&C and life, accident and health may be carried over to the following renewal period. (La. R.S. §22:1573) .

Final Exam: The exam for a self-study course does not need to be monitored.

Requirements **Not** *Applicable to the Following:*

1. Those holding industrial fire licenses.

2. Those holding licenses in limited lines, which have no exam requirement.

3. Newly licensed producers for their first renewal.

4. The following limited licenses: limited life, health and accident; credit; travel.

5. Licensees over age sixty-five with at least fifteen years experience who are no longer actively engaged in the insurance business and who are receiving Social

Security benefits or who operate through a licensed Louisiana insurer. Form 65A must be completed and approved by the Department. (La. R.S. §22:1573).

Renewal Procedure: Course provider supplies licensee with certificate of completion and reports CE hours to the DOI. (LAC 37:XI.711).

Nonresidents are exempt on a reciprocal basis if home state also has a CE requirement. Send letter of certification from home state with renewal application upon request only if home state license status cannot be verified on the PDB. If home state does not have a CE requirement, the licensee may meet any other state's CE requirement and send letter of confirmation. (LAC 37:XI.705).

Continuing education credits may be granted to individuals participating in a qualified graduate-level national designation program only if the individual passes the test required of such program and earns a certificate of completion. Qualified graduate-level national designation programs include programs in which an individual may be designated as a Chartered Life Underwriter (CLU), Chartered Property and Casualty Underwriter (CPCU), Certified Insurance Counselor (CIC), and other such national professional designations. (La. R.S. §22:1573; LAC 37:XI.711). The number of continuing education credit hours that will be approved for any single program is twenty-four hours.

G. **Cancellation of Agency Contracts/Producer Appointments:** Insurers must report agency contract/producer appointment cancellations to the commissioner of insurance within thirty days. Insurers must substantiate with valid reason and advise the Department in advance of their intention to withdraw. For mass policy cancellations, contemplated when withdrawing from an agency, the insurer is responsible to see that replacement coverage is made without penalty to the insured. Interim policy cancellations or refusal to service existing policies due to agency cancellation should be prompted solely by unfavorable factors of the individual risk not present at inception of the coverage. Insurers are prohibited from rewriting the producer's business on a direct basis or in an affiliated company at higher rate, and must submit valid reasons to the Department if reducing producer's commissions to less than half of traditional commission. (La. R.S. §22:1559).

H. **Rules for Risk Retention and Purchasing Groups:** Louisiana regulates risk retention and purchasing groups operating or offering coverage on risks in Louisiana. Risk retention groups domiciled in Louisiana must be chartered and licensed as liability insurance companies. Groups not domiciled in Louisiana must register with and submit reports to the commissioner as described in the law. (La. R.S. §§22:481-498).

Purchasing groups must also register with the commissioner and submit reports as required by the law. All groups and all resident and nonresident producers participating in them must comply with all Louisiana insurance laws, including licensing and solicitation requirements or restrictions. (La. R.S. § 22:489) All risk retention group policies from groups not chartered in Louisiana must show the following notice in at least ten point type on the front page and on the declarations page of the policy:

NOTICE

> This policy is issued by your risk retention group. Your risk retention group may not be subject to all of the insurance laws and regulations of your state. State insurance insolvency guaranty funds are not available for your risk retention group.

(La. R.S. §22:484).

I. **Other License Rules, Requirements, or Restrictions:** No one may sell or solicit insurance in Louisiana without a license. (La. R.S. §22:1543). Unlicensed nonresidents may not enter Louisiana to solicit, inspect, or service. Entering the state includes mail or telephone or other electronic communication into the state from the outside, as well as physical presence in the state. (La. R.S. §22:1548).

Antifraud Plan: Authorized insurers licensed to operate in Louisiana must file with the Commissioner of Insurance ("Commissioner") an antifraud plan with regard to its operations in the state. The antifraud plans can be submitted electronically at www.ldi.la.gov, which also provides a checklist of the necessary information. (La. R.S. §22:572.1).

J. **Policy Countersignature Requirements:** None

K. **Portable Electronics Insurance:** Vendors selling portable electronic devices such as phones, tablet computers or other portable electronic items that wish to sell insurance policies for those devices must first obtain a limited lines license. The license authorizes any employee or authorized representative of the vendor to sell or offer coverage at each location where the vendor engages in business. (La. R.S. §22:1781.2-.6).

II. Commissions, Fees, Commingling of Funds, and Suitability in Annuity Transactions

A. **Commissions:** An insurer or insurance producer shall not pay any commission, service fee, brokerage, or other valuable consideration to any person or entity for selling, soliciting, or negotiating insurance in this state unless such person or entity holds a valid license as required by law. Rebating of commissions is not allowed. (La. R.S. §22:855).

B. Fees: Licensed producers may charge a fee in addition to commissions only if the fees are prominently disclosed and itemized separately from the premium. Compensation in addition to or in lieu of commissions permitted with certain commercial P&C sales. (La. R.S. §22:855).

C. Disclosure Requirements: Charging fees other than commissions for financial planning by insurance producer are prohibited, unless such fees are based upon a written agreement, signed by the party to be charged in advance of the performance of the services under the agreement. A copy of the agreement shall be provided to the party to be charged at the time the agreement is signed by the party.

1. The services for which the fee is to be charged must be specifically stated in the agreement.

2. The amount of the fee to be charged or how it will be determined or calculated must be specifically stated in the agreement.

3. The agreement must state that the client is under no obligation to purchase any insurance product through the insurance agent, broker, or consultant.

4. The insurance producer must retain a copy of the agreement for not less than three years after completion of services, and a copy must be available to the commissioner upon request. (La. R.S. §22:1964).

D. Commingling of Funds: Third-party administrators are required to maintain a fiduciary account separate from any business or agency accounts. A single account for multiple insurers is acceptable, but records must be kept reflecting where the funds belong. (La. R.S. §22:1647).

E. Suitability in Annuity Transactions: In recommending to a consumer the purchase of an annuity or the exchange of an annuity that results in another insurance transaction or series of insurance transactions, the insurance producer, or the insurer where no producer is involved, must have reasonable grounds for believing that the recommendation is suitable for the consumer on the basis of the facts disclosed by the consumer as to the consumer's financial status; the consumer's tax status; the consumer's investment objectives; and any other information that may be relevant in making recommendations to the consumer. (LAC 37:XIII.11711).

Louisiana requires that any producer who wishes to engage in the sale of annuity products must complete a four-hour training class that is separate from any other prelicensing or continuing education requirement. (La. R.S. §22:1576).

Louisiana has not adopted the NAIC Suitability in Annuity Transactions Model Regulation.

III. Statutory References:

La. R.S. §§22:	481 to 498
	572.1
	821, 855
	1543 to 1545, 1547, 1548, 1550.1 to 1552, 1558, 1559, 1573, 1576
	1622, 1623, 1647, 1651, 1663 to 1667, 1673, 1694, 1695
	1702, 1781.2 to 1782.6, 1782.1, 1792
	1964

LAC 37:XI.	72, 511, 705, 711
LAC 37:XIII.	3905, 11711

Web References:

http://www.ldi.state.la.us/industry/producer-adjuster/renewals.
http://www.ldi.state.la.us/industry/producer-adjuster/license-application.
http://www.ldi.state.la.us/industry/producer-adjuster/renewals.
http://www.ldi.state.la.us/industry/producer-adjuster/appointments-affiliations/company-appointment.
http://www.ldi.state.la.us/docs/default-source/documents/licensing/producers/licensing-handbook.pdf?sfvrsn=3a877c52_26.

MAINE

Superintendent of Insurance
Department of Professional and Financial Regulation
Bureau of Insurance
Physical Address: 76 Northern Ave.;
Gardiner, ME 04345
Mailing Address: 34 State House Station;
Augusta, ME 04333-0034
Telephone: 207-624-8475; Fax: 207-624-8599
http://www.maine.gov/pfr/insurance

I. **Licensing Requirements:** Sales Personnel—Producers, Limited Lines Producers, Entities, Managing General Agents. Other Insurance Professionals—Adjusters, Consultants, Corporations, Third-Party Administrators, Reinsurance Intermediaries, Viatical and Life Settlement Providers and Producers.

A. **Applicability:** A person may not sell, solicit or negotiate insurance in Maine for any class or classes of insurance unless the person is licensed for that line of authority in accordance with the insurance laws of Maine. (24-A M.R.S. §1420-B).

B. **Licenses Required of Residents:** Each of the following must be licensed in Maine:

Sales Personnel

1. *Producers.*

a. Original License fee, including limited lines: $30. Application fee: $15. (24-A M.R.S. §601; https://www.maine.gov/pfr/insurance/regulated/individuals_bus_entities/fee_schedule.html). The NAIC application for residents is available on the BOI Web site.
b. License term: Perpetual, as long as appointment fees are paid and continuing education requirements are met by the due date, unless suspended, revoked, or terminated by the Superintendent of Insurance. (24-A M.R.S. §1416-A).
c. Lines of authority:

(1) Life.
(2) Accident & health or sickness.
(3) Property.
(4) Casualty.
(5) Variable life and variable annuity products.

(6) Personal lines.
(7) Surplus lines.

(24-A M.R.S. §1420-F).

2. *Limited Lines Producers.*

a. License fee: $30. Application fee: $15. https://www.maine.gov/pfr/insurance/regulated/individuals_bus_entities/fee_schedule.html.
b. License term: Perpetual. (24-A M.R.S. §§1416-A).
c. Lines of authority:

(1) Auto rental supplemental liability.
(2) Credit.
(3) Automobile mechanical breakdown.
(4) Title.
(5) Travel, including but not limited to interruption or cancellation, baggage, damages to accommodations, and accident or sickness during travel.

(24-A M.R.S. §1420-F).

3. *Business Entities.* (Includes producer, adjuster, consultant, motor vehicle rental). Any corporation, association, partnership, LLC, LLP, or other legal entity (other than sole proprietors) that operates as an insurance producer, adjuster, or consultant must be licensed in order to authorize individual licensees to act on the entity's behalf or in order to use the name of the business entity in insurance-related advertising in the state of Maine. A business entity has no authority to act on its own without an individual licensee. (24-A M.R.S. §1413). Producer, adjuster, and motor vehicle rental application fee: $15; license fee: $30; consulting firm application fee: $25, license fee: $50; biennial continuation fee: $30; consulting firm continuation fee: $50. (24-A M.R.S. §601; https://www.maine.gov/pfr/insurance/regulated/individuals_bus_entities/fee_schedule.html).

4. *Managing General Agents.* Must be registered with the department. Original registration fee: $100. Annual continuation fee: $100. The superintendent requires a bond in an amount set by the superintendent that is sufficient to protect the insurer. (24-A M.R.S. §§601, 1493).

Other Insurance Professionals

1. *Adjusters (Independent and Public).* License fee: $30 resident; application fee: $15; biennial continuation fee: $30. License term: perpetual. Adjusters may be

individuals or firms. Adjusters who are employees of insurance companies are not required to be licensed. The Maine Revised Statutes define an adjuster as one who "investigates for, settles on behalf of and reports to an insurer, fraternal benefit society, workers' compensation self-insurer, or insured relative to claims arising under the workers' compensation laws or other types of insurance contracts." (24-A M.R.S. §§601, 1402, 1416-A. https://www.maine.gov/pfr/insurance/regulated/individuals_bus_entities/fee_schedule.html).

2. *Consultants.* License fee: $50 per authority, plus $25 initial application fee. License term: perpetual. Biennial continuation fee: $50. Consultants may receive either P&C or life and health authority. $20,000 bond required. Consultants must have a written contract with their clients. May be individuals or firms. Must have no less than five years' experience with the kind of insurance to be covered by the license. Nonresident consultant license: $100 per authority, application fee: $25. (24-A M.R.S. §§601, 1410, 1462, 1464, 1465. https://www.maine.gov/pfr/insurance/regulated/individuals_bus_entities/fee_schedule.html).

3. *Corporations.* Must be licensed as a business entity. (24-A M.R.S. §1413).

4. *Third-Party Administrators.* Must be licensed as such. Must file a bond equal to 5 percent of premiums or claims handled, subject to a minimum amount of $50,000 and a maximum of $1 million. Original license fee: $100; annual continuation fee: $100. (24-A M.R.S. §§601, 1904).

5. *Reinsurance Intermediaries.* Must be licensed as such. Original license fee: $50, annual continuation: $50. Reinsurance intermediary managers may be required to file a surety bond and E&O policy. (24-A M.R.S. §§601, 742).

6. *Viatical and Life Settlements.*

   a. Settlement providers: application and annual renewal, $400. Must provide proof of financial responsibility, which may include evidence of a binding and committed lending facility of at least $1 million with a term of at least one year or a net worth in excess of $100,000. (24-A M.R.S. §§601, 6803).
   b. Settlement producers. Need to apply for an individual producer license with life authority. License fee: $30, application fee: $15. (24-A M.R.S.A. §§601, 6803).

Applications may be downloaded from the Department's Web site at https://www.maine.gov/pfr/insurance/regulated/individuals_bus_entities/producers/index.html.

C. **Appointments:** An insurance producer may not act as an agent of an insurer unless the insurance producer becomes an appointed agent of that insurer. An insurance producer who is not acting as an agent of an insurer is not required to become appointed. Appointments are only to be submitted once the individual or business entity has become licensed. Appointments are not to be submitted with applications for licensure. Both the business entity and the individuals with the entity must be appointed. Branch locations of business entities do not need to be appointed. Insurers may file appointments electronically through the NAIC's National Insurance Producer Registry. To obtain information, contact the NIPR Help Line at 855-674-NIPR (6577), or use the appointment/termination form available on the BOI Web site (http://www.maine.gov/pfr/insurance/regulated/individuals_bus_entities/producers/producer_appoint_terminate_instructions.html) Producer appointment fees: $30 per resident licensee, $70 per nonresident licensee, per company; no longer per line of authority. Biennial renewal fee: $30. There is no fee for business entity appointments. Appointment forms must be filed within fifteen days of the execution of the contract. (24-A M.R.S. §§601, 1420-M).

D. **Licenses Required of Nonresidents:** All nonresident producers, adjusters, consultants, and business entities listed in the sales personnel section are required to be licensed to conduct insurance activities in Maine. Each individual working on behalf of a business entity in Maine must hold an individual nonresident license. The uniform NAIC application for nonresidents is available on the BOI Web site. Nonresidents may also apply electronically through the NAIC's National Insurance Producer Registry at www.nipr.com. Application fee: $15 for producers; license fee: $40; producer appointment fee: $45 per company and biennial renewal fee of $30. Application fee for nonresident business entities: $15; license fee: $70. Appointment required but has no fee. Application fee for nonresident adjuster license: $15; license fee: $60; biennial continuation, $60. Application fee for nonresident consultant license: $25; license fee: $100; biennial continuation: $100. Letters of certification from applicants are not necessary. The BOI uses the NIPR PDB for license verification. (24-A M.R.S. §601, 1420-G; https://www.maine.gov/pfr/insurance/regulated/individuals_bus_entities/fee_schedule.html).

Applications may be downloaded from the BOI Web site at https://www.maine.gov/pfr/insurance/regulated/individuals_bus_entities/producers/index.html.

Multi-State Exposures: A license is not required for a nonresident insurance producer who sells, solicits, or negotiates a contract of insurance for commercial property and casualty coverage when risks that are to be insured under that contract are located in more than one state. This exception applies only if the nonresident is licensed to sell, solicit, or negotiate that insurance in the state where the insured maintains its principal place of business and the contract of insurance insures risks located in that state. (24-A M.R.S. §1420-C).

E. Prelicensing Examination and Education Requirements:

1. *Residents.* Applicants for licenses as producers, consultants, or adjusters must pass a qualifying, written examination. The following exams are administered by Pearson Vue, http:\\www.pearsonvue.com 800-274-4959.

   Major lines:

   Life/health and property/casualty producer.
   Personal lines.

   Limited lines:

   Life and health consultant.
   Credit producer.
   Property and casualty consultant. Note: Maine offers workers compensation authority and P&C authority as separate lines.
   Title producer.
   All lines adjuster.

   Multiple peril crop adjuster.

   Exam fee is $77, payable to Pearson Vue. Consultant applicants must have five years experience prior to taking the exam. Producers selling variable contracts must pass the FINRA exam (formerly, the NASD exam) in addition to passing the exam for a resident producer's license. An individual producer whose license lapses may, within twelve months, reinstate the same license without the necessity of passing a written examination. (24-A M.R.S.A. §§1410, 1411, 1420-F).

2. *Nonresidents.* Evidence of equivalent home state license waives the examination, except those imposed by 24-A M.R.S. §1420-G. (24-A M.R.S. §1420-O).

F. Continuing Education Requirements:

Number of Hours Required, producers and consultants: Twenty-four hours biennially; three hours must be in ethics. This requirement applies to producers and consultants. The BOI does not prescribe the course content, with the exception of the three hour ethics requirement, and the licensee may use classroom instruction or self-study, but all courses must be filed and approved. No credit may be earned for repeating a course previously taken during the same biennium. Home study and classroom instruction may not be combined for credit in a single course.

Proof of Completion: Within thirty days of each session's completion, vendors shall file, in a form acceptable to the superintendent, giving the date and location of the course. Students should be provided a certificate of completion, which they may fax to (207) 624-8599 or email to dawn.kilgore@maine.gov if the course is not reported to the department.

Excess Hours: May not be carried into the next reporting period.

Requirements **Not** *Applicable to the Following:*

1. Anyone licensed less than one year at the time of first compliance.

2. Limited licensees (such as title), except limited annuities.

3. Adjusters.

4. Persons on active military duty.

(CMR 02-031-542).

Continuation procedure:

1. Course provider supplies licensee with certificate of completion and reports the credited hours to the BOI.

2. Licensee keeps the original certificate.

Nonresidents must comply with home state CE requirement.

(24-A M.R.S. §1481-A).

G. **Cancellation of Agency/Producer Contracts:** The insurer must notify the superintendent within thirty days. Insurer must then give written notice of termination to the producer within fifteen days. (24-A M.R.S. §1420-N).

H. **Rules for Risk Retention and Purchasing Groups:** Maine regulates risk retention and purchasing groups operating or offering coverage on risks in Maine. As required under 24-A M.R.S. §6094, risk retention groups domiciled in Maine must be chartered and licensed as liability insurers. At the time of filing, the group must provide the following information in summary form: the identity of the initial members of the group; the identity of those individuals who organized the group or who will provide administrative services or otherwise influence or control the activities of the group; the amount, source, and nature of initial capitalization; the coverages to be afforded; and the states in which the group intends to operate. (24-A M.R.S. §6094).

Groups not domiciled in Maine must register with the superintendent of insurance and submit reports to the superintendent, as described in the law. (24-A M.R.S. §6095). Purchasing groups must also register with the superintendent and submit reports as required by the law. Original registration fee: $100, annual renewal: $100. All groups and all resident and nonresident agents or brokers participating in them must comply with all Maine insurance laws, including licensing and solicitation requirements or restrictions. All risk retention group policies must show the following notice in at least ten point type on the front page and on the declarations page of the policy:

NOTICE

"This policy is issued by your risk retention group. Your risk retention group may not be subject to all of the insurance laws and regulations of your state. State insurance insolvency guaranty funds are not available for your risk retention group."

(24-A M.R.S.A. §§601, 6095).

I. **Other License Rules, Requirements or Restrictions:** None.

J. **Policy Countersignature Requirements:** None.

II. Commissions, Fees, Commingling of Funds, and Suitability in Annuity Transactions

A. **Commissions:** Unlicensed residents or nonresidents may not receive commissions under any circumstance except under 24-A M.R.S. §§1412 or 1420-L. Rebating of commissions is not allowed. (24-A M.R.S. §§ 2160 to 2163-A).

B. **Fees:** Insurance producers may charge a fee for services in addition to or instead of commissions for a large commercial risk (a risk whose aggregate annual premiums for commercial property and casualty insurance sold by a producer totals at least $150,000) after disclosing in writing the amount of the fee. The disclosure also must inform the client that the fee is not part of the premium charge for insurance policies and that it will not be included in the calculation of unearned premium in the event of policy cancellation. (24-A M.R.S. §1450. CMR 02-031-900).

C. **Disclosure Required:** Prior to receiving a fee in lieu of or in combination with commission for the sale of property and casualty insurance policies, the insurance producer must disclose in writing to the insured that the fee is not a part of the premium charge for the insurance policies, and that the fee will not be a part of any calculation of unearned premium owed by the insurer in the event of policy cancellation. In the event that a fee is charged in combination with commission, the amount of the fee and commission must be disclosed separately in writing by the producer to the insured. (CMR 02-031-900).

D. **Commingling of Funds:** Maine has no regulation that explicitly prohibits commingling of funds, but premiums and return premiums are held in trust funds in a fiduciary capacity. (24-A M.R.S. §1449).

E. **Suitability in Annuity Transactions:** In recommending to a consumer the purchase of an annuity or the exchange of an annuity that results in another insurance transaction or series of insurance transactions, the insurance producer, or the insurer where no producer is involved, must have reasonable grounds for believing that the recommendation is suitable for the consumer on the basis of the facts disclosed by the consumer as to his or her investments and other insurance products and as to his or her financial situation and needs. (CMR 02-031-917).

III. References:

24-A M.R.S. §§	601, 742
	1402, 1410, 1411, 1413
	1416-A, 1420-A, 1420-B, 1420-C, 1420-F, 1420-G, 1420-M, 1420-N, 1420-O
	1449, 1450, 1462, 1464, 1465, 1481-A, 1493
	1904, 2160 to 2063-A

CMR	02-031-542
	02-031-900
	02-031-917

Web References:

https://www.maine.gov/pfr/insurance/regulated/individuals_bus_entities/fee_schedule.html.

https://www.maine.gov/pfr/insurance/regulated/individuals_bus_entities/producers/index.html.

MARYLAND

Insurance Administration
Attn: Producer Licensing Unit
200 St. Paul Place Suite 2700
Baltimore, MD 21202-2272
Telephone: 410-468-2000
Licensing Fax: 410-468-2399
Outside Baltimore Metro Area: 800-492-6116
https://insurance.maryland.gov/Pages/default.aspx

I. Licensing Requirements: Sales Personnel—Producers. Other Insurance Professionals—Insurance Advisers, Public Adjusters, Third-Party Administrators, Bail Bondsmen, Adjusters, and Reinsurance Intermediaries.

A. Applicability: An insurance producer may not sell, solicit, or negotiate any insurance on behalf of an insurer for which the insurance producer does not have an appointment. Before a business entity may accept in its own name compensation for acting as an insurance producer, the business entity must obtain a license and an appointment for the kind or subdivision of insurance for which it intends to act as an insurance producer on behalf of an insurer. (Md. INSURANCE Code Ann. §10-103).

B. Licenses Required of Residents: Each of the following must be licensed in Maryland:

Sales Personnel

1. *Producers.*

a. License fee: Initial fee: $54, renewal: $69, which includes a $15 fraud fee.
b. License term: Biennial.
c. Lines of authority:

(1) Life.
(2) Health, accident or sickness.
(3) Property.
(4) Casualty.
(5) Variable life and variable annuities.
(6) Personal lines of property and casualty insurance.
(7) Any other kind of insurance permitted under State law or regulations.

(Md. INSURANCE Code Ann. §§10-112, 2-112).

2. *Limited Lines Producers.*

   a. License fee: Initial fee: $54, biennial renewal: $69 (includes $15 fraud fee and $54 license fee).
   b. Limited lines of authority:

      (1) Automobile. (§10-123).
      (2) Credit products. (§10-112).
      (3) Vehicle rental. (§10-602).
      (4) Title insurance. (§10-125)
      (5) Travel ticket policies of life, accident, or baggage insurance. (§10-122).
      (6) Self-service Storage. (§10-802).
      (7) Peer-to-Peer Car Sharing. (§10-6A-102).
      (8) Portable electronics. (§10-703).

3. *Entities.* A corporation, partnership, or limited liability company must designate a licensed insurance producer to act as the entity's principal contact with the Insurance Administration. Producer firms are required to obtain an appointment with each insurer represented (all fees and requirements for producers apply to firms). Entities (both resident and nonresident) also must register with the Maryland Department of Assessments & Taxation. (Md. INSURANCE Code Ann. §10-106).

4. *Title Producers.* Must be covered by both a $150,000 fidelity bond, and either a $150,000 title surety bond with a concurrently dated power of attorney or letter of credit. A corporation or partnership may obtain one bond to cover all its agents. A Title Insurance Producer Independent Contractor (TIPIC) acting as an agent for a title insurance producer does not need to have a blanket fidelity or surety bond or letter of credit. The TIPIC must be covered under the insurance producer's blanket fidelity bond and blanket surety bond or letter of credit. (Md. INSURANCE Code Ann. §10-121). The title insurance producer is the legal principal of the TIPIC and is liable for all actions of the TIPIC, including unintentional conduct that occurs within the scope of the TIPIC's employment. (Md. INSURANCE Code Ann. §10-121.1).

   An attorney who is associated with any entity other than a law firm (e.g. title agency, insurer, corporation, or partnership) must be covered by a $150,000 fidelity bond as well as either a $150,000 surety bond or letter of credit. The bonding requirements for title insurance producers do not apply to law firms and individual attorneys selling title insurance incidental to the practice of law.

Any person who, for compensation, in any manner solicits, procures, or negotiates title insurance contracts must obtain a title insurance producer's license, but title attorneys admitted to practice before the Court of Appeals of the State of Maryland are exempt from the pre-licensing, examination, and CE requirement.

All controlling persons and all trust money controllers of title insurance agencies must hold a title insurance producer's license.

Non-attorney employees of law firms who, for compensation, in any manner solicit, procure, or negotiate title insurance contracts must obtain a producer's license and meet bond requirements. (Md. INSURANCE Code Ann. §§10-121, 10-125).

5. *Managing General Agents.* Must obtain a certificate of qualification. Initial fee: $30; annual renewal fee: $30. A certificate of qualification expires June 30 after its effective date. Application fee for managing general agent certificate of qualification: $30. (Md. INSURANCE Code Ann. §§8-202, 8-205, 2-112).

Other Insurance Professionals

1. *Insurance Advisers.* Advisers' licenses expire last day of licensee's birth month. Fee: $100 (for initial license within one year of renewal; $200 if over one year from renewal); biennial renewal fee: $215 (includes $15 fraud fee), must pass a written exam. Surety bond of $1,000 is required. Insurance producers may also be licensed as advisers. (Md. INSURANCE Code Ann. §§2-112, 10-203, 10-206, 10-211).

2. *Public Adjusters.* Public adjusters' licenses expire last day of licensee's birth month. Fee: $25 (initial license within one year of renewal) $50 (for initial license over one year from renewal); biennial renewal fee: $65 (includes $15 fraud fee). This license does not apply to adjusters employed by or representing insurers. Must pass a written exam. Requirements also apply to business entities, which must employ one or more individual licensed public adjusters. (Md. INSURANCE Code Ann. §§2-112, 10-402 to 10-404, 10-408). A public adjuster shall complete the required CE no later than thirty days before the expiration date of their public adjuster's license. (Md. INSURANCE Code Ann. §10-408).

3. *Third-Party Administrators.* Must be registered with the insurance commissioner. Only business entities (firms) may be licensed as TPAs. Must carry a surety bond in an amount not less than 10 percent of the average amount of funds that the TPA expects to handle at any one time for all plans administered during the year; minimum, $5,000; maximum, $500,000. If the TPA is a licensed insurer, it is

exempt from the bonding requirement if it has capital and surplus in excess of $1 million. Initial registration fee: $250. Registration expires June 30 of every other year. Biennial renewal fee: $50 plus $15 fraud prevention fee. (Md. INSURANCE Code Ann. §§8-303, 8-305 to 8-308).

4. *Bail Bondsmen.* Are licensed as a property and casualty insurance producer. Each year, a licensed bail bondsman must certify to the commissioner that the majority of his or her income is from providing bail bondsman services. (Md. INSURANCE Code Ann. §§10-304 to 10-308). Bail bondsmen must receive continuing education that directly relates to bail bond insurance.

5. *Motor Vehicle Appraisers and Adjusters.* License not required. (MD Code, Insurance, §§10-501 to 10-504).

6. *Reinsurance Intermediaries.* If not licensed as an insurance producer, must obtain reinsurance intermediary license. Must file a bond and maintain an E&O policy. Expires on July 1 of odd years. (Md. INSURANCE Code Ann. §§8-503, 8-504, 8-509).

7. *Viatical Settlement Providers and Brokers.* Viatical Settlement Provider Registration fee: $1,000. Viatical Settlement Broker must register with the Commissioner. Registration fee: $250; renewal fee: $50. Must be licensed to sell life insurance. Registration fee: $250; renewal fee: $50. Registration expires at the end of every other year on the anniversary of the registration. (Md. INSURANCE Code Ann. §§8-603, 8-604, 8-607).

Maryland does not require licenses or advance certification for risk managers/risk management consultants or field/marketing representatives.

Except for MGAs and reinsurance intermediaries, all Maryland insurance licenses are available online at https://insurance.maryland.gov/Producer/Pages/default.aspx. Various credit cards are accepted as means of payment. Maryland Insurance Administration's producer licensing customer service available at 1-888-204-6198 or by fax at 410-468-2399, or email: producerlicensing.mia@maryland.gov.

Application forms for all license types, excluding managing general agents, may be ordered from the Maryland Insurance Administration by calling 800-492-6116, option 8 between the hours of 8:00 AM and 6:00 PM EST, Monday through Friday. Prometric provices pre-licensing education and insurance licensing examinations to Maryland insurance professionals. Prospective licensees can begin contacting Prometric to schedule examinations on October 1 by calling 1-800-610-1174 or registering online through www.prometric.com.

Applicants may submit initial and renewal applications via NIPR (www.nipr.com). Initial title insurance producer applicants must submit a paper application. Producers may also submit documents via the NIPR's attachment warehouse. Continuing education services are outsourced to Prometric (1-800-324-4592, www.prometric.com).

The forms listed in the next section are to be completed by both resident and nonresident applicants. Letters of certification are not required.

1. *Producers/Individuals.* Maryland uses the NAIC Individual Uniform Application for both residents and nonresidents. For firms (corporations, partnerships, and LLCs), Maryland uses the NAIC Business Entity Uniform Application for both residents and nonresidents. Business entities do not have to submit a letter of good standing from the MD Department of Assessments and Taxation (until after the registration is filed), but entities must attest that they are in good standing in section 8 of the Maryland Supplement.

2. *New/Terminated Producer Appointments.* Each insurer authorized to do business in Maryland must maintain a producer register. Information on new producer appointments must be added to the register within thirty days of the appointment. Written documentation of each appointment must be sent to and maintained by the licensed producer during the term of the appointment and for five years after its termination. (Md. INSURANCE Code Ann. §10-118).

   Terminations must be added to the producer register within thirty days of the termination. Insurers must notify the commissioner of terminations for cause, but terminations for other reasons do not have to be submitted to the commissioner. Terminated producers must be notified within fifteen days after notice to the commissioner. A producer then has thirty days in which to file written comments concerning the substance of the notice of termination. (Md. INSURANCE Code Ann. §10-118).

3. *Temporary Insurance Producer.* Without regard to the education, experience, or examination requirements, the commissioner may issue a temporary license to act as an insurance producer to an individual if the individual is otherwise qualified and is the surviving spouse, next of kin, personal representative, or appointee of the personal representative, of a deceased insurance producer; the spouse, next of kin, employee, or legal guardian of a mentally or physically disabled insurance producer; or an employee of a firm, or an officer or employee of a corporation, of a deceased or disabled insurance producer. The Commissioner shall approve or refuse a temporary license within thirty days of receiving the application. A temporary license expires fifteen months after its effective date. Fee: $27. (Md. INSURANCE Code Ann. §2-112, 10-120).

5. *Motor Club Representative.* Individuals only. The motor club authorization section of the application must be completed by the motor club the applicant wishes to represent. Expires on August 31, annually. Must be appointed. Initial fee: $5; renewal, $2. (Md. INSURANCE Code Ann. §§26-301, 26-305).

C. Appointments: An insurance producer may not act on behalf of an insurer unless the insurance producer has received written documentation of the appointment from the insurer. An insurer may initially accept an application for life insurance, health insurance, or an annuity from an insurance producer who is not appointed by the insurer if, within thirty days of accepting the application, the insurer either rejects the application; or appoints the insurance producer. When there is any termination of the appointment, employment, contract, or other insurance business relationship with an insurance producer, the insurer shall, within thirty days following the effective date of the termination, update the insurer's producer register by entering the effective date of the termination. Appointments are perpetual unless terminated by the insurer. Appointments do not have to be reported to the DOI, but insurers must keep a register for as long as the insurer acts as an insurer in the state. Insurers must provide insurance producers with written documentation of their appointments within thirty days. Producers may not act on behalf of an insurer unless the producer has received written documentation of their appointment from the insurer. Termination of appointments "for cause" must be reported. (Md. INSURANCE Code Ann. §10-118).

D. Licenses Required of Nonresidents: Most nonresidents can be licensed in Maryland by reciprocity. An application for a license needs to be submitted. A producer in good standing in their home state is exempt from the Maryland examination and other education requirements due to reciprocity with the state of residence. Licensing fee: $54. License is biennial, expiring two years from the last day of the licensee's birth month. The same licenses are required of nonresidents that are required of Maryland residents. The same fees are charged. Also, the same applications are used. Nonresidents must be appointed in Maryland with any insurer through whom they will place business in Maryland. Certification of nonresident's home-state license may be verified through the NAIC producer database. Nonresident corporations must register with the Department of Assessments and Taxation. (Md. INSURANCE Code Ann. §10-119).

Multi-State Exposures: A license is not required for a nonresident insurance producer who sells, solicits, or negotiates a contract of insurance for commercial property and casualty coverage when risks that are to be insured under that contract are located in more than one state. This exception applies only if the nonresident is licensed to sell, solicit, or negotiate that insurance in the state where the insured maintains its principal place of business and the contract of insurance insures risks located in that state. (Md. INSURANCE Code Ann. §10-103).

E. Prelicensing Examination and Education Requirements:

Applicants must be at least eighteen years old and meet the character standards of Maryland insurance law. Prelicensing course requirements have changed to twenty hours for life/health, property/casualty, title, personal lines, and automobile examinations. In addition, they must meet the following requirements.

1. *Residents.* Property/casualty applicants must meet the following requirements:

   a. Have at least one year experience in responsible duties as an employee of an insurer, agent, or broker.
   b. Take twenty hours of insurance instruction in a course and school approved by the insurance commissioner.
   c. Pass a qualifying examination.

   Prelicensing education may be waived if the applicant was previously licensed in another state.

   The commissioner may exempt from both the experience and education requirements for a property and casualty license for persons possessing the following designations:

   a. CPCU.
   b. CIC.
   c. AAI.
   d. ARM. (Md. INSURANCE Code Ann. §10-104).

   Prelicensing education is waived if the applicant was licensed previously in another state or jurisdiction.

   Life and accident and health applicants must do the following:

   a. Complete at least twenty hours of approved study.
   b. Have at least one year experience in responsible duties as an employee of an insurer, agent, or broker.
   d. Pass a qualifying examination, administered by Prometric.

e. Prelicensing education may be waived if the applicant was previously licensed in another state. (Md. INSURANCE Code Ann. §10-105).

Exempt from both the experience and education requirements for a life insurance applicant are persons possessing the following designations:

a. CLU.
b. Fellow of the Society of Actuaries.
c. CEBS.
d. ChFC.
e. CIC.
f. CFP.
g. FLMI.
h. LUTCF.

Exempt from both the experience and education requirements for a health insurance applicant are persons who possess the following designations:

a. RHU.
b. CEBS.
c. REBC.
d. HIA. (Md. INSURANCE Code Ann. §10-105).

Title applicants must do the following:

a. Complete at least twenty hours of approved study.
b. Be employed for at least one year by an insurer or producer.
c. Pass a qualifying examination, administered by Prometric.

Public adjuster must both:

a. Pass a qualifying examination administered by PSI. (Md. INSURANCE Code Ann. §10-404).
b. Maryland law no longer requires individual applicants to have been employed regularly by the Administration as an employee or by an insurer, adjuster, insurance producer or public adjuster for a period totaling at least one year. (2016 Md. SB 75).

The following applicants do not have to pass an exam: credit, travel, dental plans, and nonprofit health service; insurance advisers must pass an exam. However, the exam requirement for advisers does not apply to holders of the following designations:

a. CPCU.
b. CLU.
c. CEBS.
d. CFP.
e. CIC.

2. *Nonresidents.* Education and examination requirements for nonresidents are reciprocal with nonresidents' home states. (Md. INSURANCE Code Ann. §10-204).

F. Continuing Education Requirements:

Number of Hours Required: Twenty-four hours, biennially. (COMAR 31.03.02.03; Md. INSURANCE Code Ann. §10-116). Three hours must be in ethics training. This applies to property, casualty, life, health, and public adjuster licenses. The CE program is administered by Prometric, http://www.prometric.com.

Type of Course Required: Licensees shall obtain continuing education credit hours in the kind or subdivision of insurance for which they hold a license. The licensee may earn credit hours through classroom instruction, self-study, or insurer-sponsored courses. Licensee may submit a written request, with documentation, to the commissioner for a waiver of the continuing education requirement due to physical handicap, medical condition, or active military service. Course instructors receive one and one-half times the approved credit hours.

Producers who sell flood insurance are required to obtain two hours out of the total twenty-four required continuing education that directly relates to flood insurance.

1. Licensees with life, health, or a subdivision of life or health: for those who are required to take twenty-four hours of CE, all but three ethics credit hours, must be in life/health courses. For those producers who sell Long Term Care Partnership and are required to take eight hours of initial courses, must take a four-hour refresher course every two years. If a licensee sells long-term care products, two of the credit hours required for the licensee must be from a LTC course.

2. Licensees with property, casualty, or a subdivision of property or casualty: for those required to take twenty-four hours of CE, all credit hours must be in property/casualty courses, except for three hours of ethics. For those licensees who have held a license for 25 or more consecutive years who are required to take eight hours of CE, all credit hours must be in property/casualty courses except for three ethics credits. If a licensee sells flood insurance, a flood

insurance-related course approved for CE must be completed. If a licensee sells bail bonds, four hours of bail bond related courses approved for CE must be completed.

3. Licensees with life/health or a subdivision of life/health and property/casualty or a subdivision of property/casualty: For licensees required to take twenty-four hours of CE, a minimum of six credit hours must be in life/health courses and a minimum of six credit hours must be in property/casualty courses. For licensees required to take eight hours of CE, a minimum of two credit hours must be in life/health courses and a minimum of two credit hours must be in property/casualty courses. If a licensee sells long-term care insurance, two of the life/health credit hours must be from a LTC course. If a licensee sells flood insurance, a flood insurance-related course approved for CE must be completed. If a licensee sells bail bonds, four hours of bail bond related courses approved for CE must be completed. (COMAR 31.03.02.03; MD Code, Insurance §10-116).

Excess Hours: May not be carried into the next reporting period.

Retaking Courses: No credit will be given for taking the same course in a single renewal period. If the same course is taken in consecutive renewal periods, no credit will be given if the course was taken within six months of the time that the previous course was taken.

Final Exam: The final exam for a self-study course does not need to be monitored.

Requirements **Not** *Applicable to the Following:*

1. Attorneys-at-law who are qualified as title insurance agents or brokers and who do not hold any other type of insurance producer license.

2. Holders of a limited lines license who act as insurance producers for limited line credit insurance.

3. Insurance producers who hold only a limited lines license in any type of insurance designated by the commissioner.

4. Any other licensee, at the discretion of the commissioner.

Renewal Procedure: Course providers report credit hours earned by course attendees to Prometric. The licensee does not submit the certificate of course completion with the renewal application but may be asked to submit it if proof of course completion is needed.

Nonresidents: Nonresidents are licensed through reciprocity and are exempt from Maryland continuing education requirements on a reciprocal basis with their resident states. (Md. INSURANCE Code Ann. §10-116; COMAR 31.03.02.03).

G. **Cancellation of Agency/Producer Contracts:** Insurers must maintain information about all terminations. (Md. INSURANCE Code Ann. §10-118).

H. **Rules for Risk Retention and Purchasing Groups:** In Maryland, all risk retention and purchasing groups must comply with the law and registration fees. Domestic groups must be chartered and licensed as casualty insurance companies. (Md. INSURANCE Code Ann. §25-102). Foreign groups must register with the insurance commissioner. Every application form for such a group and every policy issued by a foreign group must contain on the front page and the declaration page the following wording in ten point type:

NOTICE

"This policy is issued by your risk retention group. Your risk retention group may not be subject to all of the insurance laws and regulations of your state. State insurance insolvency guaranty funds are not available for your risk retention group." (Md. INSURANCE Code Ann. §25-103).

I. **Other License Rules, Requirements, or Restrictions:** None.

J. **Policy Countersignature Requirements:** A policy covering a subject of insurance resident, located, or to be performed in this State shall be signed or countersigned by an insurance producer that is a resident of this State if:

(i) the policy is written by an insurance producer that is a resident of another state and is qualified as a nonresident insurance producer in this State; and

(ii) the law of the other state requires a signature or countersignature by an insurance producer that is a resident of that state on a policy written by an insurance producer that is not a resident in that state.

The lack of such a signature does not necessarily render the policy invalid.

This section does not apply to:

(1) reinsurance;

(2) life insurance, health insurance, or annuity contracts;

(3) insurance of:

- (i) rolling stock, vessels, or aircraft of a common carrier used in interstate or foreign commerce;
- (ii) a vehicle principally garaged and used outside the State; or
- (iii) liability or other risks, incident to the ownership, maintenance, or operation of a subject of insurance under item (i) or (ii) of this item;

(4) insurance of property while transported in interstate or in foreign trade, or any liability or risk incident to the transportation;

(5) insurance of wet marine and transportation risks;

(6) bid bonds issued in connection with public or private contracts;

(7) policies or endorsements issued through:

- (i) insurance producers compensated only by salary;
- (ii) insurers not using insurance producers in the general solicitation of business;
- (iii) mutual insurers or other insurers not customarily using insurance producers compensated by commission if no commission is payable to an insurance producer on the policy or endorsement; or
- (iv) insurers or groups of insurers under common management or control that are represented exclusively by insurance producers who represent only the insurers or groups of insurers;

(8) reciprocal insurers; or

(9) insurance written through:

- (i) the Maryland Automobile Insurance Fund; or
- (ii) the Maryland Property Insurance Availability Program.

(Md. INSURANCE Code Ann. §10-128).

II. Commissions, Fees, Commingling of Funds, and Suitability in Annuity Transactions

A. Commissions: No commission, fee, reward, rebate, or other consideration for selling, soliciting, or negotiating insurance may be paid, directly or indirectly, to a person other than a licensed insurance producer. An insurer or insurance producer may pay or assign commissions, service fees, or other valuable consideration to an insurance agency or persons who do not sell, solicit, or negotiate insurance in the State, so long as the payment does not constitute unfair competition, acts, or practices. Rebating of commissions is not allowed. (Md. INSURANCE Code Ann. § 10-130).

B. Fees: A producer licensed to sell health insurance may charge reasonable fees for an administrative service sold by the producer to an employer. A producer may not charge fees for services that are compensated by commissions or other compensation paid to the producer by an insurer, or that the producer performs while acting as an administrator or an adviser.(Md. INSURANCE Code Ann. §27-216).

C. Disclosure Requirements: An agreement between an insurance adviser and another person that relates to the giving of advice or information of the type given by advisers is not enforceable by or for the adviser unless the agreement is in writing; the agreement is executed personally in duplicate by the person to be charged or by the legal representative of the person; a duplicate of the agreement is delivered to and kept by the person when it is signed by that person; the agreement plainly states the amount of the fee paid or to be paid by the person and the services to be performed by the adviser; and the agreement is in the form that the commissioner currently approves. All forms of statements, receipts, and agreements used by licensees must be filed with and approved by the commissioner. (Md. INSURANCE Code Ann. §10-216).

D. Commingling of Funds: An insurance producer acting as such in Maryland may not commingle a premium account with any operating or personal account. An insurance producer so acting in this state may make voluntary deposits into the producers premium account, and, unless prohibited by the carrier or Regulation .04 of COMAR 31.03, chapter .03, commingle premiums paid by a single carrier with the premiums of one or more other carriers into one or more premium accounts.(COMAR 31.03.03.02).

E. Suitability in Annuity Transactions: In recommending to a consumer the purchase of an annuity or the exchange of an annuity that results in another insurance transaction or series of insurance transactions, an insurance producer, or an insurer where no insurance producer is involved, must have reasonable grounds for believing that the recommendation is suitable for the consumer based on the facts disclosed by the consumer as to the consumer's investments and other insurance products and financial situation and needs. A producer who sells annuity products must complete a one-time, four-credit Annuity Suitability training course. (COMAR 31.09.12.04, 31.09.12.08).

III. Statutory References:

Md. INSURANCE Code Ann.	
§2-	212
§§8-	202, 205
	303 to 308
	503, 504, 509
	603, 604, 607
§§10-	103 to 106, 112, 116, 118 to 123, 125, 128, 130
	203, 204, 206, 211
	402 to 404, 408
	501 to 504
	602
	703
	802
§10-6A-	102
§§25-	102, 103
§§26-	301, 305
§27-	216

COMAR	
31.03.	,02.03
	,03.02
31.09.	12.04
	12.08

MASSACHUSETTS

Division of Insurance
1000 Washington St. Suite 810; Boston, MA 02118-6200
Telephone: 617-521-7794;
http://www.mass.gov/doi

I. Licensing Requirements: Licensed Sales Professionals—Producers and Surplus Lines Brokers. Other Insurance Professionals—Public Insurance Adjusters, Advisers, Banks, Motor Clubs and its agents, Motor Vehicle Damage Appraisers, Reinsurance Intermediary Brokers, and Reinsurance Intermediary Managers (Individuals and Business Entities) Life Settlement Brokers and Limitted Lines Portable Electronics.

A. Applicability: A person shall not sell, solicit, or negotiate insurance in the Commonwealth of Massachusetts for any class or classes of insurance unless the person is licensed for that line of authority. (M.G.L. c. 175 §162I).

B. Licenses Required of Residents: Each of the following must be licensed in Massachusetts. These licenses may be issued to individuals and to business entities such as corporations, partnerships, and LLCs. License applications may be made online through NIPR's producer database at www.NIPR.com. All new and renewing individual producers and business entity producers are able to apply and renew online using NIPR's licensing system at www.NIPR.com.

Sales Personnel

1. *Producers.*

a. License fee: triennial initial, $225 (with no property, casualty or personal lines of authority); $300 (with property or casualty line of authority and personal line of authority includes lead paint surcharge). Certain applicants are exempt from paying licensing and lead paint surcharge fees: applicants who are one of the following: 1) Massachusetts residents and as military veteran status and/or 2) legally blind. Massachusetts also offers to the widows/widowers, a member or employee of the business, to a designee of a licensed producer or appointed heir of a deceased licensee, the ability to apply for a one-time temporary license for a period of 180 days; the temporary licenses are also are exempt from fees. (M.G.L. c. 175 §§162Q and 167A).
Individual licenses renew on a triennial basis on the licensee's date of birth, so initial license period may be less than three years. Fees are not refundable or prorated. License renewal applications must be submitted and received on or before the renewal date of such license or the license will be cancelled.

An individual licensee who fails to renew on time will have up to twelve months to reinstate such license, but with a penalty fee imposed. (M.G.L.c. 175 §162M(c).

b. License term: triennial for individuals (renews on birthday) and annual for business entities (from the original date of licensure).
c. Lines of authority (core): life, accident and health or sickness, property, casualty, personal lines and variable life & variable annuity products. A lead paint surcharge of $75 is added to the individual's triennial license fee on any person holding a producer license with the property, casualty or personal lines of authority license. (M.G.L.c. 175 §162G and 162X).

2. *Limited Lines Producers.* Limited lines of authority are available for travel and baggage and credit limited lines insurance. (M.G.L. c 175 §162M (a) (7) and (71/2)). Limited lines Travel Insurance Producer License is available. (M.G,L. c. 175 §162Z).

3. *Managing General Agents.* Must be licensed as producers and maintain E&O insurance (M.G.L. c. 175 §177H).

4. *Business Entities.* Corporations, partnerships, Limited Liability Partnerships (LLPs), and Limited Liability Companies (LLCs) may be licensed as business entity producers. New entities must first submit either Articles of Organization, Foreign Registration Certificate of Organization or LLC/LLP document to the Division of Insurance for the name approval process. Once the name has been approved by the Division of Insurance, the entity can then register with the Massachusetts Secretary of State's Corporate Division. After the name approval process has been completed, a business entity will receive a PIN letter that will enable them to go online to apply for a license via www.nipr.com per the Uniform Application for Resident Business Entity Insurance Producer (either paper or online), such applicants must designate one or more licensed producer(s) (DLRP) who will be responsible for the business entity compliance with relevant laws and regulations. The business entity license must also include those key members who will be covered under the license and who will be selling, soliciting or negotiating on behalf of the business entity. These licenses expire annually. Business entity licensing fees are based upon the number of members of the entity. The fee is $75 per member.

Other Insurance Professionals

1. *Advisers.* Must be at least eighteen years of age. An applicant does not qualify if an insurance license has ever been suspended or revoked. New Adviser applicants must submit a sample of his Adviser's Contract for approval along with the initial application. Adviser's license expires triennially on anniversary of date of issue;

triennial fee: $200. New business entity Advisers must submit a sample contract for approval along with initial application. Business entities renew annually on the anniversary date of issue. Annual fee must be paid per active member. (M.G.L. c. 175 §177A and 177B, https://www.mass.gov/service-details/licensing-requirements-adviser-individual). https://www.mass.gov/service-details/licensing-requirements-adviser-corporate.

2. *Public Insurance Adjusters.* Must be at least twenty-one years of age and have at least two years experience performing services in connection with adjusting of property losses and pass the public insurance adjuster licensing examination. An applicant does not qualify if an insurance license has ever been suspended or revoked. Licenses expire triennially on anniversary of date of issue; a sample contract submission is required with initial application triennial fee: $200. The division only licenses public insurance adjusters (not any other type of adjuster). Business entities renew annually, fee: $66.66 per active member each of whom is also individually licensed as a public insurance adjuster. Contract submission is required with initial application. (M. G. L. c. 175 §172, https://www.mass.gov/service-details/licensing-requirements-public-insurance-adjuster).

3. *Reinsurance Intermediaries.* License expires triennially on anniversary of issue date. Triennial fee: $200. Unlike producer licenses, this license expires three years from date of issue. Intermediary-managers may be required to file a bond and carry E&O insurance. Reinsurance intermediaries must first be licensed as an insurance producer for three years for the lines which business will be transacted as reinsurance intermediaries. The reinsurance intermediary broker must maintain an office in Massachusetts. Business entities renew annually, fee: $66.66 per active member. Application: OTHR008 – Individual Reinsurance Intermediary Application. (M.G.L. c. 175 §177O, and 177S).

4. *Third-Party Administrators.* Massachusetts does not license Third-Party Administrators (TPA) at this time. But, a new division of insurance regulation requires certain entities to register with the division. Entities falling within the definition of TPA as defined in the regulation are required to register with the division in a form and method prescribed by the commissioner. The regulation defines a TPA as a person who, on behalf of a health insurer or purchaser of health benefits, receives or collects charges, contributions or premiums for, or adjusts or settles claims on or for residents of the commonwealth. No such TPA shall do business in the commonwealth prior to registering with the division. (M.G.L. c. 176O §21, 211 CMR 148.01 through 148.04).

   TPA registration must be renewed on an annual basis, no later than April 1 of each year. Any material change(s) to the information contained in a TPA's initial registration or renewal registration must be reported to the division, certified by an officer of the TPA, within thirty days of such changes. All TPAs are required to submit an annual report by April 1 of each year for the year ended, December 31 immediately preceding. A TPA that sells, solicits, or negotiates insurance, as those terms are defined in M.G.L. c. 175, §162H, must be licensed as an insurance producer. (211 CMR 148.01 through 148.06, https://www.mass.gov/info-details/insurance-third-party-administrators).

Applications may be downloaded from the Division's Web site, https://www.mass.gov/files/documents/2019/02/07/tpa-registration-form_2019e.pdf.

C. **Appointments:** An insurance producer shall not act as an agent of an insurer unless the insurance producer becomes an appointed agent of that insurer. An insurance producer who is not acting as an agent of an insurer is not required to become appointed. Insurers must use the Online Producer Appointment Web site (OPRA), https://www.opra.doi.state.ma.us/ to appoint, terminate, and update producer appointments. Appointments renew annually. Appointment fees are paid by the appointing insurer; $75 per year for an individual and per member of a business entity. (M.G.L.c. 175 §162S).

D. **Licenses Required of Nonresidents:** Nonresidents must be licensed in their home states and be in good standing either as insurance producers, advisers, or public insurance adjusters, reinsurance intermediaries, reinsurance intermediary brokers, and reinsurance intermediary managers (individuals and business entities) limited lines portable electronics and life settlement brokers, to conduct insurance activities in Massachusetts. The same renewal term, date, and fee apply to nonresident licenses as to resident licensees. The fee exemption for military veteran status does not apply to nonresidents. Verification of home-state licensure is performed using the NIPR's Producer Database System (PBD). (M.G.L. c. 175 §162N).

Applications may be downloaded from the division's Web site, http://www.mass.gov/doi by clicking on the licensing link.

Multi-State Exposures: A license is not required for nonresident insurance producers who sell, solicit, or negotiate contracts of insurance for commercial property and casualty coverage when risks that are to be insured under contracts are located in more than one state. This exception applies only if the nonresident producer is licensed to sell, solicit, or negotiate insurance in the state where the insured maintains its principal place of business and the contract of insurance insures risks located in that state. (M.G.L.c. 175 §162J).

E. Prelicensing Examination and Education Requirements:

1. *Residents.* Prelicensing course work is not required, but the division of insurance highly recommends that resident applicants take a course prior to taking the exam. Residents applying for the following licenses must pass a qualifying examination administered by Prometric, www.prometric.com, 800-741-9380; fee: please see new examination fees schedule at www.prometric.com.

    a. Producer (life, A&H or sickness, property, casualty, personal lines, limited lines credit and travel).
    b. Adviser (life, A&H or sickness, property and casualty).
    c. Public Insurance Adjuster.
    d. Motor Vehicle Damage Appraiser (written portion only, no fee).

2. *Nonresidents.* Examination is not required for a nonresident producer's insurance license if the nonresident is licensed for the same lines of authority in the home state; examination is required (in states with no reciprocity) for nonresident insurance advisers or public insurance adjuster licenses. (M.G.L.c. 175 §162U).

F. Continuing Education Requirements:

Number of Hours Required: Insurance producers-sixty hours beginning from the original date of licensure three hours of which must be in an approved MA Ethics course; the CE hours are due prior to one's first renewal date of license, which may be less than three years. After the intial licensure period, forty-five hours, are due on a triennial basis prior to one's next license renewal date; these hours are to include three CE hours in ethics. The licensee may use approved classroom instruction or self-study. Public insurance adjusters must complete fifteen hours on a triennial basis prior to renewal of the license. (M.G.L.c. 175 §177E).

Proof of Completion: Producers must retain continuing education completion certification forms, subject to audit by the division. Course providers electronically submit CE credits to the division's vendor, which maintains the Continuing Education Database. Licensees may review their records at www.prometric.com.

Excess Hours: May be carried over into the next thirty-six month period.

Final Exam: The final exam for a self-study course must be monitored by a disinterested third-party.

Public Insurance Adjusters Number of Hours Required: Fifteen hours beginning from the original date of licensure until the completion of the third year of licensure; due on a triennial basis. (M.G.L c175 §172).

Requirements **Not** *Applicable to the Following:*

1. Fraternal organizational agents, travel and baggage producers, licensed insurance advisers, limited line credit insurance producers, auto club agents, and motor vehicle damage appraisers.

2. Anyone licensed prior to April 4, 1983. However, the requirement does apply to such licensees if they have added a new additional line of authority and had to take a licensing exam to do so which would require continuing education hours, since their original license was issued on or before April 4, 1983. If a producer was licensed prior to April 4, 1983, he must still take the mandatory Massachusetts Long-term Care CE requirements if selling long-term care products.

3. Nonresidents who also possess an equivalent resident license or licenses issued by state in which they are resident and which state has continuing educational requirements with respect to such license or licenses, and who are certified by their resident state as being in good standing. If a nonresident producer is going to sell long-term care products to Massachusetts residents, the nonresidents must fulfill the long-term care mandatory Massachusetts long-term care CE hours. (211 CMR 50.03).

Renewal Procedure for Insurance Producers:

Producers must retain continuing education completion certification forms. All CE credits are electronically submitted to Prometric which maintains the Division's CE database. CE hours are due prior to one's license renewal date. All nonproducer renewal applications are due prior to the license renewal dates. Any attempt to subsequently renew an expired insurance or public insurance adjuster license will require the applicant to retake the appropriate licensing exam, pass the exam and apply for a new license. (M.G.L.c. 175 §162M).

Nonresident insurance producers are exempt from Massachusetts CE hours, if the nonresident holds an equivalent license or licenses in home state and has satisfied the home state's continuing education requirements—as long as the home state recognizes the satisfaction of its continuing education requirements imposed upon producers from Massachusetts on the same basis. (M.G.L.c. 175 §162N). Please read #3 above for LTC CE requirements in Massachusetts.

G. **Cancellation of Agency Contracts/Producer Appointments:** The contract of an independent insurance producer for property or casualty insurance, personal lines or both, pursuant to M.G.L.c 175 §163 may not be canceled or modified unless the insurer gives the appointed producer a written notice at least 180 days before the proposed effective date. Any agent receiving such notice may request reference to three referees regarding the question as to whether such cancellation, modification, or expiration will so affect the renewal, continuation, or replacement of policies placed with the company through the efforts of the agent, or the services needed by any policyholder doing business with the company as a result of the efforts of the agent, as to justify renewal or continuation of any policies then in effect having been placed with such company by such agent. In the event the referees find that such cancellation, modification or expiration will affect the renewal, continuation or replacement of any policies placed with the company through the efforts of the agent, or the services needed by any policyholders, the referees shall order continuance or renewal of any policies expiring within a period of thirteen months of the issuance of such notice, at a rate of compensation to such agent equal to that as provided in the agency agreement expiring or being so cancelled or modified, for one additional policy period equal in length to the most recent policy period of such expiring policy, but in no event for more than one year provided that with respect to motor vehicle insurance policies expiring within the thirteen-month period, such policies shall be renewed for policy periods not to exceed one year. Such one-year renewals of all motor vehicle insurance policies shall be provided at expiration of such policies. However, the referees shall not order a continuance or renewal of such policies if they find that the reason for the cancellation or expiration of the agency agreement by the company was legitimately based upon one of the following grounds:

1. The agent was convicted of a dishonest act related to his occupation as an insurance agent.

2. The agent's license to engage as an insurance producer was revoked.

3. The company surrendered its license to do business in the commonwealth. (M.G.L.c. 175 §163).

H. **Rules for Risk Retention and Purchasing Groups:** Massachusetts regulates risk retention and purchasing groups operating or offering coverage on risks in Massachusetts. Risk retention groups domiciled in Massachusetts must be chartered and licensed as liability insurers; while groups chartered or licensed in another state must register with the commissioner of insurance and submit reports to the commissioner. Purchasing groups must also register with the commissioner and submit reports. All risk retention group applications, policies, certificates, contracts or other documents evidencing coverage must contain the following notice in at least ten point type on its front and on the declarations page:

NOTICE

"This policy is issued by your risk retention group. Your risk retention group may not be subject to all of the insurance laws and regulations of your state. State insurance insolvency guaranty funds are not available for your risk retention group." (M.G.L.c. 176L §3).

I. **Other License Rules, Requirements, or Restrictions:** No unlicensed person may engage in sales, solicitation, or negotiation of insurance policies in Massachusetts unless such person is a salaried employee of a producer or an insurer, if such activities are done on the producer's or company's premises and under the immediate direction and general supervision of a duly-licensed producer. This provision applies only to the solicitation and negotiation of property and casualty policies of insurance. (M.G.L.c. 175 §162).

J. **Policy Countersignature Requirements:** None.

II. Commissions, Fees, Commingling of Funds, and Suitability in Annuity Transactions

A. **Commissions:** The entire commission may be paid to a licensed resident or nonresident. Rebating of commissions is not allowed. Unlicensed residents or nonresidents may not receive commissions for acting in Massachusetts as insurance producers.

B. **Fees:** Licensed producers who are designated, in writing, as producer of record to assist an employer in dealing with the Massachusetts Workmen's Compensation Insurance Plan may be paid a fee at a percentage rate comparable to the average commission rate customarily paid by workers compensation insurers that compensate insurance producers for placing business with them. (211 CMR §§45.02 and 45.03; M.G.L.c. 175 §177).

C. **Disclosure Requirements:** None.

D. **Commingling of Funds:** Massachusetts does not prohibit producers' commingling of insurers' premiums with other agency funds. However, the division of insurance recommends that M.G.L.A. 175 §§169 and 176 be reviewed, because a producer who acts in negotiating a policy and who receives any money from the insured shall be deemed to hold the premium in trust for the company and shall be held to be an agent of the company, regardless of any stipulations that may be in the policy or contract.

E. **Suitability in Annuity Transactions:** In recommending to a consumer the purchase of an annuity or the exchange of an annuity that results in another insurance transaction or series of insurance transactions, the insurance producer, or the insurer where no producer is involved, must have reasonable grounds for believing that the recommendation is suitable for the consumer on the basis of the facts disclosed by the consumer as to his or her investments and other insurance products and as to his or her financial situation and needs. (211 CMR 96.05, https://www.mass.gov/files/documents/2017/10/20/211cmr96.pdf).

Massachusetts has not adopted the NAIC Suitability in Annuity Transactions Model Regulation.

III. **Statutory References:** Massachusetts Division of Insurance; M.G.L.c. 175 §§14, 162G, 162I, 162J, 162M, 162N, 162O, 162Q, 162S, 162U, 162X, 162Z 163, 167A, 168, 169, 172, 176, 177, 177A,177B, 177E, 177H, and 177O; M.G.L.c. 176L, §§2, 3, and 6; M.G.L.c. 176O §21(c); and 211 Code Mass. Regs., §§45.02, 45.03, 50.3, 50.04, 96.05, and 148.00.

MICHIGAN

Department of Insurance and Financial Services (DIFS)
Office of Insurance Licensing and Market Conduct
P.O. Box 30220; Lansing, MI 48909-7720
530 W. Allegan Street, Seventh Floor, Lansing MI 48933
Toll Free: 877-999-6442;
Email: DIFS-Licensing@michigan.gov
http://www.michigan.gov/difs

I. Licensing Requirements: Sales Personnel—Producers, Business Entities, Managing General Agents, Solicitors. Other Insurance Professionals—Adjusters, Bail Bondsmen, Counselors, Public Adjusters, Reinsurance Intermediaries, Third-Party Administrators. An appointment by an insurer is no longer required to maintain an active producer license.

A. Applicability: An insurance producer shall not act as an agent of an insurer unless the insurance producer becomes an appointed agent of that insurer. An insurance producer who is not acting as an agent of an insurer is not required to become appointed. (MCLS § 500.1208a).

B. Licenses Required of Residents: Each of the following must be licensed in Michigan:

Sales Personnel

1. *Producers.* File an Electronic Resident License (ERL) application through National Insurance Producer Registry (NIPR). The application/license fee is $10 plus a $5 transaction fee. Initial appointment: $5 if appointed within renewal year; annual appointment renewal fee: $5 billed to each appointing company. (MCLS § 500.240). Licenses are not renewed but are perpetual as long as all continuing education criteria are met (where applicable—see following sections.). The following qualifications are available:

   a. Property only – property, marine.
   b. Casualty only – steam boiler, liability, worker's compensation, auto, plate glass, sprinkler, credit, burglary, livestock, and malpractice. (MCLS § 500.624).
   c. Limited lines property and casualty, which includes: legal expense; livestock, malpractice insurance, marine, surety & fidelity, crop, travel, plate glass. (MCLS § 500.1201(i)).
   d. Personal Lines – personal auto and homeowners insurance.
   f. Life – credit life.
   g. Variable life and variable annuities.

h. Limited Life – may sell only "associated life" (preneed) policies and may not hold any other lines of authority. (MCLS § 500.2080).
i. Accident and health.
j. Credit Products (include credit life, credit disability, credit property, credit unemployment, involuntary unemployment, mortgage life, mortgage guarantee, and mortgage disability).
k. Any other line of insurance permitted under state laws or rules. (MCLS § 500.1206, https://www.michigan.gov/difs/0,5269,7-303-22535_23031---,00.html).

Michigan does not allow insurance brokers.

2. *Managing General Agents (MGAs).* MGAs first must be licensed as producers/business entities, hold the lines of authority being requested for the MGA appointment and be appointed by the insurer for the lines of authority being requested for the MGA appointment. There is no appointment fee. Submit FIS 0242 MGA Appointment/Cancellation. No producer renewal. Annual appointment renewal fee of $5 billed to appointing insurer. The commissioner may require a bond or E&O policy. (MCLS §§ 500.1401, 1403, 500.1405, https://www.michigan.gov/difs/0,5269,7-303-22535_23040---,00.html).

3. *Solicitors.* File an Electronic Resident Licensing (ERL) application through NIPR. The application/license fee is $20 plus a $5 transaction fee. Annual renewal fee of $10 billed to the sponsoring producer or business entity. May be licensed for the following authorities: property, casualty, limited lines property and casualty, crop, surety, travel, personal lines, or title. May not be appointed for life, multiple lines property & casualty, fire & other hazards, workers compensation, variable annuities, or health. Must be sponsored by a currently licensed producer or business entity and may work for only one sponsor at a time and cannot be appointed by the insurance company. A solicitor cannot bind coverage. (MCLS § 500.1214, https://www.michigan.gov/difs/0,5269,7-303-22535_23049---,00.html).

Other Insurance Professionals

1. *Adjusters (Independent and Public).* File an Electronic Resident Licensing (ERL) application through NIPR. The application/license fee is $15 plus a $5 transaction fee. Annual renewal fee is $5. May work independently or in conjunction with an adjusting firm. Independent adjusters represent insurance companies and may be licensed for fire and other hazards, workers compensation, or crop (multiperil crop insurance) authority. Crop insurance adjusters are exempt from examination and are required to provide the name and NAIC number of the company for which the applicant will adjust crop losses. If applying as a nonresident, must hold

that specific line in the home state before receiving this line in Michigan. Public adjusters work for the insured and adjust only fire and other hazards and must have a state approved contract before becoming licensed. Staff adjusters employed by insurance companies do not need to be licensed. Individuals admitted to practice law in Michigan may adjust claims without being licensed but may not represent themselves as adjusters licensed by the State of Michigan. (MCLS § 500.1224, https://www.michigan.gov/difs/0,5269,7-303-22535_60490_23030---,00.html).

2. *Third-Party Administrators.* TPA certification is required if TPA maintains its principal administrative office or principal headquarters in Michigan, solicits a plan or sponsor of a plan or provides administrative services to a plan or sponsor of a plan that is either domiciled in Michigan or has its principal headquarters or principal administrative office in Michigan; or provides substantial administrative services to a carrier for the carrier's business in Michigan. Entities only. Submit $250, which includes $25 certificate fee, $25 financial statement review fee, and $200 application fee, and forms FIS 0849 Application Checklist, FIS 0850 Financial Statement (or an audited financial statement dated within the past twelve months), FIS 0860 Consent to Service, FIS 0861 Application for Certificate of Authority, FIS 0862 Affiliation Statement, and FIS 0863 Fee Processing Card. For annual renewal, a $25 annual financial statement review (FIS 0850 Financial Statement) and FIS-0865-TPA Jurat Page is required. (MCLS §§ 550.910, 550.912, and 550.918, https://www.michigan.gov/difs/0,5269,7-303-22535_22904-70248--,00.html).

3. *Bail Bondsmen.* Bondsmen representing surety and fidelity insurers must be licensed. To become licensed, the applicant must pass the surety and fidelity exam, the limited lines property and casualty exam, or the full property and casualty exam, and hold a Surety, Limited Lines P&C or full P&C line of authority and an active fidelity and surety appointment with each insurer. May employ solicitors who are licensed by the Department of Insurance and Financial Services (DIFS) and sponsored by the bondsman. Must pass the limited lines P&C exam. May not delegate their signature authority to any other person nor delegate the court's prior approval. May use nonlicensed employees (runners) to perform certain services, but such employees cannot solicit the bonds nor take application. (MCLS § 500.410a, https://www.michigan.gov/difs/0,5269,7-303-22535_108217---,00.html).

4. *Counselors.* File an Electronic Resident Licensing (ERL) application through NIPR. The application/license fee is $20 plus a $5 transaction fee. Annual renewal fee is $10. May be licensed for property and casualty or life. Beginning October 2013 may be licensed for accident and health as well. Persons admitted to the practice of law in Michigan may counsel insurance without obtaining a license but cannot represent

themselves as licensed counselors by the State of Michigan. (MCLS § 500.1234, https://www.michigan.gov/difs/0,5269,7-303-22535_60490_23035---,00.html).

5. *Reinsurance Intermediaries.* Submit $100 application fee. FIS 0845 Application, and a copy of proof of bond for $100,000 or a copy of an Errors & Omissions policy for $100,000 for the protection of the reinsurer. Nonresident businesses also complete FIS 0846 Consent to Service. (MCLS § 500.1153).

6. *Business Entities (Agencies).* File an Electronic Resident Licensing (ERL) application through NIPR. The application/license fee is $10 plus a $5 transaction fee. A business entity must be licensed in order to sell, solicit, or negotiate insurance, and to receive commissions in its own name. The appointment renewal fee is billed to each appointing company and is $10 for the first year and $5 annually each year thereafter. For qualifications, see producers section.

   Resident business entities must submit the following with their applications:

   a. Partnerships and Limited Partnerships—partnership agreements.
   b. Sole Proprietorships—DBA filing.
   (MCLS § 500.1205).

Obtaining Applications

All agency or individual license applications may be obtained or linked from the DIFS Web site at http://www.michigan.gov/difs. Select "Forms", click on "Insurance Forms", and scroll down to correct form number. Cash is not accepted.

C. Appointments: An insurance producer shall not act as an agent of an insurer unless the insurance producer becomes an appointed agent of that insurer. An insurance producer who is not acting as an agent of an insurer is not required to become appointed. Insurance companies appoint and cancel producers and business entities electronically. Appointments must be filed within fifteen days from the date the first insurance application is submitted or an agency contract is executed. Appointment cancellations may not take effect more than thirty days prior to the cancellation being filed. Information on obtaining a business partner to provide this service is available at http://www.nipr.com. No fees are sent at the time of appointment. (MCLS § 500.1208a).

D. Licenses Required of Nonresidents: Most of the licenses are available to nonresidents wishing to conduct insurance activities in Michigan, if the individual or business entity is licensed in their home state for the same qualifications. Producers should file an Electronic Nonresident Licensing (ERL) application through NIPR. The application/license fee is $10 plus a $6.18 transaction fee. If they do not hold these qualifications in their home state, they will have to take Michigan's exam. License term, expiration, and fees are the same as for residents. Paper certifications are not needed if the home state participates in the State Producer Licensing Database (PDB). Nonresident producers must have Michigan appointments for all companies with whom they are placing Michigan business. (MCLS § 500.1204e).

1. *Independent Adjusters and Public Adjusters.* File an Electronic Resident Licensing (ERL) application through NIPR. The application/license fee is $15 plus a $6.18 transaction fee. Must be licensed in a state that required successful completion of an examination.

2. *Counselors.* File an Electronic Resident Licensing (ERL) application through NIPR. The application/license fee is $20 plus a $6.18 transaction fee. Must be licensed for this type of license in the home state before receiving a Michigan license or will need to take Michigan examination.

3. *Solicitors.* File an Electronic Resident Licensing (ERL) application through NIPR. The application/license fee is $20 plus a $6.18 transaction fee. Must be licensed for this type of license in the home state before receiving a Michigan license or will need to take Michigan examination.

Nonresident business entities should submit an Electronic Nonresident Licensing (ERL) application through NIPR at http:// www.nipr.com.

Multi-State Exposures: A license is not required for a nonresident insurance producer who sells, solicits, or negotiates a contract of insurance for commercial property and casualty coverage when risks that are to be insured under that contract are located in more than one state. This exception applies only if the nonresident is licensed to sell, solicit, or negotiate that insurance in the state where the insured maintains its principal place of business, and the contract of insurance insures risks located in that state. (MCLS § 500.1202).

E. Prelicensing Examination and Education Requirements:

1. *Residents.* Applicants for a producer or solicitor license must complete one of the following programs of study registered with the Director:

   a. Life: twenty hours.
   b. Accident and health: twenty hours.

c. Life and health: forty hours.
d. Property and casualty producers and solicitors: forty hours.
e. Property only producers and solicitors: twenty hours.
f. Casualty only producers and solicitors: twenty hours.
g. Personal lines producers and solicitors: twenty hours.
(MCLS § 500.1204a).

An applicant shall file a certificate of completion of the registered program of study with the commissioner. The certificate of completion must indicate the course of study was completed by the applicant not more than twelve months before the application for examination is received by the commissioner. An individual who fails to appear for the examination required under this section as scheduled or fails to pass the examination shall reapply for an examination and remit all required examination fees and forms to be rescheduled for another examination. (MCLS § 500.1204). There are no prelicensing education requirements for limited lines property and casualty, credit products, title, adjusters, counselors, or surplus lines.

Applicants must register, schedule and pass a qualifying exam. Michigan's testing vendor is PSI and exam reservation and scheduling can be done at https://candidate.psiexams.com/DIFS. The director may waive the program of study requirements for holders of CPCU, CLU, CIC, AAI, ChFC, CEBS, CFP, FLMI, LUTCF, RHU, REBC, HIA or ARM designations, or for a person who has an Associate's, Bachelor's, or Master's degree with a concentration in insurance from an institution approved by the director. (MCLS § 500.1204).

A license is issued within approximately fourteen days and mailed to the individual at his or her mailing address upon receipt of proof of passing an insurance examination, providing proof of any necessary prelicensing education, submitting an online application and fee for licensure, and passing a background check.

When a licensed individual moves to Michigan from another state, if application is made within ninety days of clearance from their previous home state, the individual does not need to do prelicensing education or examination. (MCLS § 500.1206b). If the individual applies within ninety-one to 365 days after clearance from the home state, the exam is required, but no prelicensing education is necessary. On or after the 366th day, prelicensing education and examination are both required.

When moving from one non-Michigan state to another, a nonresident producer needs to submit an address change within thirty days of the move. Michigan will check the PDB for good standing certification from the new resident state. This will keep the Michigan nonresident license in good standing. If the information is not submitted within thirty days, a new application and fee are required. An insurance producer who has sold or is in the process of selling his or her insurance business and who has not met the continuing education requirements shall not solicit or sell new policies of insurance, bind coverage, or otherwise act as an insurance producer except that the insurance producer may continue to service policies previously sold and may receive commissions on policies previously sold as well as receive partial commissions on policies of insurance sold by a purchasing insurance producer. However the insurance producer may continue to service policies previously sold and may receive commissions on policies previously sold as well as receive partial commissions on policies of insurance sold by a purchasing insurance producer, for a period not to exceed twelve months after the selling insurance producer's license review date. An insurance producer whose license has been cancelled and who wishes to resume soliciting or selling new policies of insurance, bind coverage, or otherwise act as an insurance producer and who has not met the continuing education requirements within the immediately preceding two-year period may reapply for license. (MCLS § 500.1204c).

Exams Available: $40 each.

a. Property Producer/Solicitor only.
b. Casualty Producer/Solicitor only.
c. Limited Lines Property and Casualty Producer/Solicitor: surety; legal expense; livestock mortality; crop; and hail; malpractice and professional liability; and plate glass.
d. Accident & Health Producer: includes accident and health, disability, and long-term care.
e. Life Producer: includes life and limited life.
f. Credit Insurance Producer: products include credit life, credit disability, credit property, credit unemployment, involuntary unemployment, mortgage disability, mortgage guaranty, mortgage life, and Guaranteed Auto Protection [GAP].
g. Personal lines Producer/Solicitor.
h. Public Adjuster (adjuster for the insured).
i. Title Insurance Producer/Solicitor.
j. Independent Adjuster (without workers compensation authority).
k. Independent Adjuster with workers compensation authority.
l. Life Counselor.
m. Property and Casualty Counselor.
n. Surplus Lines Producer.
o. Variable Life and Annuities Producer.
p. Life, Accident & Health Producer.
q. Property and Casualty Producer/Solicitor.
r. Life, Variable Life and Annuities Producer.

2. *Nonresidents.* Must take Michigan examination only if applying for licensure for a qualification not held in their home state. (MCLS § 500.1204e).

F. **Continuing Education (CE) Requirements:** The following requirements are applicable to all Michigan resident producers and solicitors.

Number of Hours Required: A total of twenty-four hours, biennially. Three of those hours must be in approved ethics courses. The licensee may use Michigan-approved classroom instruction or self-study/online as long as a DIFS-approved provider offers it. The same course may not be retaken for credit in the same review period. If an insurance producer has not met his or her continuing education requirements by the review date of his or her license, the producer shall have a ninety-day grace period in which to meet those requirements. During the grace period, the producer may not solicit or sell new policies, bind coverage, or otherwise act as an insurance producer. The license is cancelled if continuing education requirements are not met by the end of the ninety-day grace period. If the license is cancelled, the producer may reapply for licensure upon completion of the CE. Hardship waivers may be granted by the Director. Visit http://www.michigan.gov/difs/0,5269,7-303-13648_60666_77185---,00.html. (MCLS § 500.1204c).

Submit Proof of Completion By: The commissioner shall review an insurance producer's hours of study every two years, in accordance to their review date. The review date is assigned based upon the producer's birth month and year. The first scheduled review date must permit a producer at least twelve months. If it does not, the hours shall be reviewed on the next scheduled review date. CE credits must be entered into the DOI database by the first of the month of the licensee's review date. Providers must report student completions to the DIFS CE Education Roster Entry System within thirty days of course completion. (MCLS § 500.1204c).

Excess Hours: may not be carried over into the next review period.

Final Exam: the final exam for a self-study/online course must be monitored by a disinterested third-party.

Requirements **Not** *Applicable to the Following:*

1. Hardship waivers may be granted by the Director.

2. Counselors.

3. Adjusters.

4. Surplus lines licensees.

5. Travel only licensees.

6. Title only licensees.

7. Crop only licensees.

8. Limited life only licensees.

9. Credit products.

10. Limited lines property & casualty licensees.

Reporting Process:

Course provider sends a completion certificate to the licensee. The licensee keeps the certificate in his or her files for at least two years. Providers supply a course completion roster and $1 per credit hour fee collected from the licensee to the DIFS CE Education Roster Entry System. Providers are allowed up to thirty days to report credits earned. The DIFS strongly suggests that licensees earn CE credits forty-five days prior to their review date. (MCLS § 500.1204c).

Nonresidents are exempt if they remain current with their home state CE requirement. (Michigan is not reciprocal with Guam).

G. Cancellation of Agency Contracts/Producer Appointments: An appointment by an insurer is not required to maintain an active producer license. Appointment cancellations must also be electronically filed. The effective date requested cannot be more than thirty days prior to, or after, the date the cancellation is submitted to DIFS.

Any cancellation for cause must be submitted electronically accompanied by an explanation. Insurer must give immediate notice providing a full disclosure of any acts construable as violations of insurance code or a reflection on the producer's qualification to serve the public interest.

Licenses of those selling auto and homeowners insurance may not be cancelled except for the following reasons:

1. Malfeasance.

2. Breach of fiduciary duty or trust.

3. A violation of Michigan's insurance statutes.

4. Failure to perform as provided by the contract.

5. Submission of less than twenty-five applications for home and auto insurance within the immediately preceding twelve months. (MCLS § 500.1209(2)).

H. Registration for Foreign Risk Retention Groups and Purchasing Groups: The producer (agent/agency) placing business for the foreign risk retention group must be licensed for Surplus Lines. To apply for a Foreign Risk Retention Group Registration, submit the following:

1. FIS 0233 Application for Foreign Risk Retention Group License.

2. FIS 0234 Consent to Service.

3. FIS 0235 Foreign Risk Retention Group Registration Fee Card (along with a $25.00 fee payable to the State of Michigan-Insurance).

4. FIS 0361 Affiliate Statement for each officer, partner, owner, stockholder, member, and Director of the entity.

5. FIS 0364 PG Report of Operation.

6. A copy of the applicant's articles of incorporation.

7. A copy of the applicant's certificate of authority from its chartered state.

8. Submit the most recent domiciliary state examination report or qualifying examination report.

9. A copy of the group's plan of operation/feasibility study.

10. Financial statements for three years or projections for three years.

11. An exhibit of historical or expected loss experience.

12. A financial statement certified by an independent public accountant that contains a statement of opinion by a member of the American Academy of Actuaries or a qualified loss reserve specialist.

13. Copy of reinsurance agreements.

14. Appropriate opinions by a qualified, independent casualty actuary that includes a determination of the minimum premium levels required in order for the RRG to commence operations and prevent hazardous financial conditions.

The forms listed can be found at https://www.michigan.gov/difs/0,5269,7-303-13044_13199---,00.html.

Risk retention groups must also be licensed as a domestic stock or mutual casualty insurer and have an initial capitalization of at least $7.5 million.

Per MCLS § 500.1819, all policies issued by risk retention groups must state on the front and declaration pages of the policy in at least ten point type:

NOTICE

> "This policy is issued by your risk retention group. Your risk retention group may not be subject to all of the insurance laws and regulations of your state. State insurance insolvency guaranty funds are not available for your risk retention group."

A risk retention group that does not have a certificate of authority issued by the director is liable for the payment of 2 percent tax on all direct premiums written less returned may take up to two weeks to complete. (MCLS § 500.1813) premium. Taxes are electronically filed using the NAIC OPTins database. Registration with OPTins is required prior to utilization of the system and

A Purchasing Group is a group that meets all of the following requirements:

1. As one of its purposes, purchases liability insurance on a group basis.

2. Is composed of members whose businesses or activities are similar or related with respect to the liability to which members are exposed by virtue of a related, similar, or common business, trade, product, service, premises, or operation.

3. Purchases insurance only for its group members and only to cover their similar or related liability exposure.

4. Is domiciled in a state.

To apply for a Purchasing Group Registration, submit the following:

1. FIS 0365 Consent to Service (nonresident entities only).

2. FIS 0359 Purchasing Group Application for Registration.

3. FIS 0361 Affiliate Statement for each officer/director.

4. FIS 0364 Purchasing Group Report of Operations.

5. Registration fee: $25 plus $25 per insurer.

If a Purchasing Group is registered to purchase insurance in the surplus lines or nonadmitted market, any surplus lines taxes are to be paid under the purchasing group's name and tax identification number. Electronic reporting and payment are required to be submitted via the NAIC OPTins database. Registration with OPTins is required prior to utilization of the system and may take up to two weeks to complete. (MCLS §§ 500.1801, 500.1827, https://www.michigan.gov/difs/0,5269,7-303-22535_31504---,00.html).

I. **Other License Rules, Requirements, or Restrictions:** Licensed nonresidents may enter Michigan to solicit, inspect, or service, subject to reciprocity provision. Unlicensed nonresidents may not enter the state for any of these purposes. Nonresidents may be licensed as producers only for companies admitted in Michigan. Michigan does not license brokers. Producers, business entities, solicitors, counselors, surplus lines agents/agencies, and adjusters must report any change of mailing address within thirty days. An address change shall be entered electronically on NIPR's Web site at http://www.nipr.com. (MCLS § 500.1206).

J. **Policy Countersignature Requirements:** None.

II. Commissions, Fees, Commingling of Funds, and Suitability in Annuity Transactions

A. **Commissions:** There are no restrictions on distribution of commissions among licensed producers who both represent and are duly appointed by the company paying the commission. Unlicensed individuals may receive commissions or fees from licensed producers if no solicitation, service, or acts of an agent are performed and payment does not violate rebating laws. Rebating of premiums and/or commissions is not allowed. (MCLS § 500.1240).

B. **Fees:** Fees for sale of insurance, in addition to or instead of commissions, are not permitted. A licensed insurance counselor may charge fees only on the basis of a written service agreement. The fee may not be waived if insurance is subsequently written, and the counselor, when acting as producer, will be paid commission by the insurer on any insurance written. The agreement must be executed prior to any services being rendered. The counselor must retain a copy of the agreement for at least two years after completing the services. (MCLS §§ 500.1236, 500.1240 and 500.2024).

C. **Disclosure Requirements:** None.

D. **Commingling of Funds:** Michigan does not prohibit agents' commingling of insurer's premiums with other agency funds. However, the DIFS recommends that commingling of funds not be done. A Michigan producer may not accept a check, made out to that agent, for a Medicare Supplement Policy.

E. **Suitability in Annuity Transactions:** A producer must have reasonable grounds for believing the recommendation is suitable for the consumer. Prior to the execution of a purchase or exchange of an annuity, a producer or insurer must make reasonable efforts to obtain all of the following information. (MCLS § 500.4155).

1. The consumer's financial status.

2. The consumer's tax status.

3. The consumer's and investment objectives.

4. Such other information used or considered to be reasonable by the insurance producer, or the insurer where no producer is involved, in making recommendations to the consumer.

An insurer shall establish a supervision system that is reasonably designed to achieve the insurer's and its producers' compliance with MCLS § 500.4158.

A producer who engages in the sale of annuities shall complete a one-time, four-hour training course. The annuity training course must be submitted by a CE provider and be in compliance with the rules and guidelines applicable to a CE course as provider in Chapter 12 of the MI Insurance Code. The annuity training course may be conducted and completed by classroom or self-study methods in accordance with requirements of Chapter 12 of the MI Insurance Code.

The following topics must be covered in an annuity training course:

1. The types of annuities and various classifications of annuities.

2. Identification of the parties to an annuity.

3. How fixed, variable, and indexed annuity contract provisions affect consumers.

4. The income taxation of qualified and nonqualified annuities.

5. The primary uses of annuities.

6. Appropriate sales practices and replacement and disclosure requirements.

   The annuity training shall cover all topics and shall not present any marketing information or provide training on sales techniques or provide specific information about a particular insurer's products. Additional topics may be offered in conjunction with and in addition to the topics listed. (MCLS § 500.4160).

Variable Annuities:

Resident Producers must be registered with FINRA, have completed FINRA Series 6 or 7 examinations, and must pass the MI Variable Life and Annuities Producer examination.

Nonresident Producers must hold a variable annuities/variable life line of authority in their home state, be registered with FINRA, have completed FINRA Series 6 or 7 examinations, and must pass the Michigan MI Variable Life and Annuities Producer examination. (MCLS § 500.4127).

Fixed Annuities:

To sell fixed annuities one must possess a producer life insurance license in good standing.

III. Statutory References: Mich. Admin. Code. §§ 500.3 and 500.4; Mich. Comp. Laws Service §§ 500.240, 500.410, 500.1153, 500.1201, 500.1203-.1209, 500.1153, 500.1212, 500.1214, 500.1222, 500.1224, 500.1232, 500.1234, 500.1240, 500.1805, 500.1813, 500.1827, 500.1835, 500.1819, 500.2024, 500.2066, 500.2070, 500.2080, 500.3543, 500.1405, 500.4127, 500.4160, 550.910, and 550.912; and the Michigan Department of Insurance and Financial Services.

MINNESOTA

Department of Commerce
85 7th Pl. E., Ste. 280;
St. Paul, MN 55101
Licensing: 651-539-1599; Fax: 651-539-0107
http://mn.gov/commerce/industries/insurance/

I. Licensing Requirements: Sales Personnel—Producers, Limited Lines Producers, Entities, Managing General Agents. Other Insurance Professionals—Adjusters, Catastrophe Adjusters, Field/Marketing Representatives, Public Adjusters, Crop-Hail Adjusters, Reinsurance Intermediaries, Self-Insurance Administrators, Third Party Administrators, Viatical Settlement Brokers and Providers.

A. Applicability: A person shall not sell, solicit, or negotiate insurance in this state for any class or classes of insurance unless the person is licensed for that line of authority. The license itself does not create any authority, actual, apparent, or inherent, in the holder to represent or commit an insurance carrier. (Minn. Stat. Ann. § 60K.32).

B. Licenses Required of Residents: Each of the following must be licensed in Minnesota:

Sales Personnel

1. *Producers.*

   a. License fee: $50 per line new and renewal, plus $40 technology fee; $50 for personal lines new and renewal plus $40 technology fee; $50 for variable products new and $50 renewal plus $40 technology fee per license. Apply through Sircon Licensing. (Minn. Stat. Ann. § 60K.55, https://www.sircon.com/stateInformationCenter/minnesota.jsp).
   b. License term: Two years; expires on the last day of the birth month of the producer in the year that will result in the term of the license being at least twelve months, but no more than twenty-four months.
   c. Lines of authority:

      (1) Life.
      (2) Accident and health.
      (3) Property.
      (4) Casualty.
      (5) Variable life and variable annuity products.
      (6) Personal lines property and casualty.

Producers who take a prelicense examination must also submit fingerprints and an associated fee for background investigations. (Minn. Stat. Ann. §§ 60K.38, 60K.55).

2. *Limited Lines Producers.*

   a. License fee: $50 new and renewal, plus $40 technology fee per license.
   b. License term: Two-year, expires on the last day of the birth month of the producer in the year that will result in the term of the license being at least twelve months, but no more than twenty-four months.
   c. Lines of authority:

      (1) Credit.
      (2) Farm property and liability.
      (3) Title.
      (4) Travel.
      (5) Bail bonds. (Minn. Stat. Ann. §§ 60K.38, 60K.55).

3. *Entities.* Must designate a person as the responsible individual. Fee: $200 initial and renewal. License term: Two years, expires October 31. (Minn. Stat. Ann. § 60K.55).

4. *Managing General Agents.* Same requirements as for agencies. Fee: $200 initial and $200 renewal. The commissioner may require the MGA to post a bond or to carry an E&O policy. The agency must have at least one insurance producer licensed in Minnesota. (Minn. Stat. Ann. § 60H.03).

5. *Portable Electronics Insurance Vendor.* A business entity is required to hold a limited lines license issued under this section to sell or offer coverage under a policy of portable electronics insurance in connection with, and incidental to, a portable electronics transaction with a customer. Portable electronics insurance provides coverage for the repair or replacement of portable electronics, which may cover portable electronics against any one or more of the following causes of loss: loss, theft, mechanical failure, malfunction, damage, or other applicable perils. Fee: ten or fewer locations in Minnesota, $100 per location; more than ten locations in Minnesota, $6,500. License term: two years, expires October 31. (Minn. Stat. Ann. § 60K.381).

6. *Travel Insurance Business Entity Producer.* A business entity or insurer designee is required to hold a limited lines license issued under this section when a travel retailer offers and disseminates travel insurance on its behalf and under its direction. Travel insurance means insurance coverage for personal risks incident to planned travel, including, but not limited to: interruption or cancellation of

trip or event; loss of baggage or personal effects; damages to accommodations or rental vehicles; sickness, accident, disability, or death occurring during travel. It does not include major medical plans, which provide comprehensive medical protection for travelers with trips lasting six months or longer, including those working overseas as an expatriate or military personnel being deployed. Fee: $200 initial and $200 renewal. License term: two years, expires October 31. (Minn. Stat. Ann. §§ 60K.383, 60K.55).

Other Insurance Professionals

1. *Adjusters, Public Adjusters, Crop Hail Adjusters, and Catastrophe Adjusters.* All applications are done online through Sircon.

    a. Independent adjuster: Expires on the last day of the birth month of the producer in the year that will result in the term of the license being at least twelve months, but no more than twenty-four months. Fee: $50 new and renewal plus a $30 technology fee per license.
    b. Public adjuster: Expires on the last day of the birth month of the producer in the year that will result in the term of the license being at least twelve months, but no more than twenty-four months. Fee: $50 new and renewal plus a $30 technology fee per license; must provide $10,000 bond.
    c. Crop hail adjuster: Expires on the last day of the birth month of the producer in the year that will result in the term of the license being at least twelve months, but no more than twenty-four months. Fee: $50 new and renewal.
    d. Catastrophe adjuster: Fee: $20. Must register with the commissioner and provide name of licensed adjuster and insurers with whom the cat adjuster is working. This is a 180-day license; may be extended for 180 days. (Minn. Stat. Ann. § 72B.03).

Independent and public adjusters who take a prelicensing examination must submit fingerprints and an associated fee for background investigations. Licenses will be issued in property and casualty, workers' compensation, and crop lines of business. All current independent and public adjuster licenses were converted to P&C lines of authority effective July 1, 2010. Exemption exists for prelicensing exam for those who are or were licensed in another state for the same lines of authority within the previous ninety days. Having completed all parts of the Insurance Institute of America program in adjusting no longer receives an exemption for the prelicensing exam requirements. (Minn. Stat. Ann. § 60K.56).

Staff adjusters are exempt from the application, licensing, examination, and other requirements.

Continuing education of twenty-four hours is required each licensing period, and three of those hours must be in ethics.

2. *Reinsurance Intermediaries.* Must be licensed in Minnesota. Managers may be required to carry E&O insurance and to file a bond. Initial fee: $200; biennial renewal: $150. (Minn. Stat. Ann. § 60A.71).

3. *Self-Insurance Administrators.* Workers compensation self-insurance administrators must be licensed. (Minn. Stat. Ann. § 79A.21). Applications can be found at http://mn.gov/commerce-stat/pdfs/workers-comp.pdf.

4. *Third-Party Administrators.* Fee: $1,500 new and triennial renewal. Must post a bond. Aside from new applications only, Third-Party Administrator applications are not available through Sircon and cannot be filed electronically. (Minn. Stat. Ann. § 60A.23(8)).

5. *Viatical Settlement Brokers and Providers.* Initial fee: $750; annual renewal: $250. Renewal fee: $250. Brokers and providers must provide a surety bond, evidence of the existence of cash, certificates of deposit, or securities, or any combination thereof in the amount of $250,000 or proof that such financial instruments have been filed with one or more states where the applicant is licensed. Applications and forms can be found at https://mn.gov/commerce/industries/insurance/licensing/ (Minn. Stat. Ann. §§ 60A.9572, 60A.964).

License application forms are available from www.sircon.com.

C. **Appointments:** An appointment is required from the insurer within fifteen days after the first application is submitted to the insurer. Appointments remain in force until voluntarily terminated by the insurer or the producer or until the license of the producer has been terminated for any reason. Fee: $30 for initial appointment per company. (Minn. Stat. Ann. § 60A.14). A licensed insurance producer may not engage in the business of insurance with an insurer unless the producer either has been appointed by that insurer or has the permission of the insurer to transact business on its behalf and obtains an appointment from the insurer within fifteen days after the first application is submitted to the insurer. If the license is not renewed within one year of its expiration, reexamination will be required for licenses that require an examination. (Minn. Stat. Ann. § 60K.49).

D. **Licenses Required of Nonresidents:** Nonresidents must have the same license as residents. Reciprocity will be granted so long as fees are paid, a proper request for licensure is made, and the person submits to the commissioner the application for licensure that the person submitted to their home state or a completed Uniform Application. For adjusters there is also a special registration procedure (in lieu of licensing) for certain catastrophes or emergencies, to be completed within five days of deployment to adjust claims arising from the catastrophe. Nonresidents must secure a Minnesota appointment with the companies for which they will write business. Nonresidents may qualify for resident agent's/producer's license if principal place of business is in Minnesota. Fees: $50 for all lines plus a $40 technology fee per license. (Minn. Stat. Ann. §§ 60K.39, 72B.06).

Multi-State Exposures: A license is not required for a nonresident insurance producer who sells, solicits, or negotiates a contract of insurance for commercial property and casualty coverage when risks that are to be insured under that contract are located in more than one state. This exception applies only if the nonresident is licensed to sell, solicit, or negotiate that insurance in the state where the insured maintains its principal place of business, and the contract of insurance insures risks located in that state. (Minn. Stat. Ann. § 60K.34(2)(7)).

E. Prelicensing Examination and Education Requirements:

1. *Residents.* Applicants for producer's license must complete twenty hours of education per major line of authority, and the commissioner must approve the course. The course must include an introduction to insurance and insurance-related concepts, and must cover a specific major line of authority. (Minn. Stat. Ann. § 60K.361). The education may be classroom, internet, or self-study. Fingerprints are required for a criminal background investigation for new applicants or for adding a new line of business; payment of fee is required. A bona fide professional association of agents not acting on behalf of an insurer may offer such courses but not a school sponsored or offered by, or affiliated with an insurance company or its agents without explanation. Applicants must also pass a PearsonVUE -administered examination www.pearsonvue.com/mncommerce, (833-273-1946). Exam fee: $39.

   The following are exempt from a prelicensing program of studies:

   a. Holder of a two-year Minnesota vocational degree in insurance.
   b. Holder of a four-year college degree in business with an insurance emphasis.
   c. Holders of the following designations: LUTCF (life course only), CEBS (life and health courses only), ChFC (life course only), CIC (life, property, casualty, and personal lines courses only), CFP (Life course only), CLU (life course only), FLMI (life course only), RHU (health course only), REBC (health course only), HIA (health course only), CPCU (property, casualty,

and personal lines courses only), AAI (property, casualty, and personal lines courses only), ARM (property, casualty, and personal lines courses only).

(Minn. Stat. Ann. § 60K.36).

Adjusters (other than crop-hail adjusters) must pass a qualifying examination administered by PSI, 800-733-9267.

No exam is required for Limited Lines Credit Insurance, Title Insurance, Travel Insurance, or Bail Bonds. (Minn. Stat. Ann. § 60K.36).

2. *Nonresidents.* Nonresident applicants for a producer's license must meet the same requirements as residents. Minnesota is reciprocal with nonresident's home state as respects prelicensing requirements only. However, nonresidents are not required to take the examination. (Minn. Stat. Ann. §§ 60K.39, 60K.40).

F. Continuing Education Requirements:

Number of Hours Required: Twenty-four hours, at least three hours in ethics, during each licensing period biennially. Renewals now fall on a birth month basis. Classes may be classroom, self-study, or internet based. Only half of the classes may be obtained through company sponsored courses. Course providers upload course rosters into the Sircon database. Compliance is verified automatically by the Sircon system at the time of license renewal.

Excess Hours: may not be carried into the next reporting period. (Minn. Stat. Ann. §§ 60K.56, 72B.045).

Requirements **Not** *Applicable to the Following:*

a. Credit, title, bail bond, and travel producers, or producers who sell for township mutuals.

Renewal Procedure:

1. Course provider uploads course roster into the Sircon database. Compliance is verified automatically by the Sircon system at the time of renewal.

2. Licensee certifies compliance at the time of renewal. Do not send CE certificates unless requested by the state.

Nonresidents are exempt.

G. **Cancellation of Agency/Producer Contracts:** After an agency/producer contract has been in force for three years, a fire and casualty insurer may not terminate the agency agreement unless it has provided a sixty-day notice, which must include the reason(s) for termination.

An insurance company may not terminate an agency contract based upon any of the following:

1. An adverse loss experience for a single year.

2. The geographic location of the producer's auto and homeowner's insurance business.

3. The performance of obligations required of an insurer under Minnesota Statutes.

During the period of eighteen months after the termination, the insurer must renew all risks for not more than one year unless the risk does not meet current underwriting standards. Then the policy may be nonrenewed with sixty days' notice.

Cancellation or termination is considered to have occurred if a company cancels a line of insurance or a volume of insurance business that equals or exceeds 75 percent of the business placed by that agent with the company.

All company appointments and cancellations must be submitted electronically to the Office of Financial and Insurance Services. (Minn. Stat. Ann. § 60A.171).

H. **Rules for Risk Retention and Purchasing Groups:** Risk Retention Groups (RRG) may be chartered in Minnesota to write liability insurance. Prior to operation, an RRG must submit a plan of operation to the commissioner.

All policies issued by risk retention groups must contain the following notice in ten-point type:

"NOTICE

This policy is issued by your risk retention group. Your risk retention group may not be subject to all of the insurance laws and rules of your state. State insurance insolvency guaranty funds are not available for your risk retention group."

(Minn. Stat. Ann. §§ 60E.03, 60E.04).

I. **Other License Rules, Requirements, or Restrictions:** Unlicensed nonresident may not enter state to solicit, inspect, or service.

J. **Policy Countersignature Requirements:** Countersignatures not required (Minn. Stat. Ann. § 60E.06).

II. Commissions, Fees, Commingling of Funds, and Suitability in Annuity Transactions

A. **Commissions:** Unlicensed individuals may not receive commission, even if no solicitation or service is performed in Minnesota. Rebating of commissions is not allowed. (Minn. Stat. Ann. § 60K.48).

B. **Fees:** Producers may charge a fee for services. (Minn. Stat. Ann. § 60K.46).

C. **Disclosure Requirements:** Before rendering the services, a written statement is provided disclosing:

1. The services for which fees are charged.
2. The amount of the fees.
3. That the fees are charged in addition to premiums.
4. That premiums include a commission.
5. All fees charged are reasonable in relation to the services rendered. (Minn. Stat. Ann. § 60K.46).

D. **Commingling of Funds:** Each agent and agency must keep a separate record for each client or transaction, accounting for all funds that have been deposited in the agent's business account. These records must set forth the information sufficient to identify the transaction and the parties thereto. At a minimum, each record must set forth:

1. The date funds are deposited.
2. The amount deposited.
3. The date of each related disbursement.
4. The check number of each related disbursement.
5. The amount of each related disbursement.
6. A description of each disbursement. (Minn. R. 2795.1400).

E. **Suitability in Annuity Transactions:** An insurance producer must not solicit the sale of an annuity product unless the insurance producer has adequate knowledge of the product to recommend the annuity and the insurance producer is in compliance with the insurer's standards for product training. An insurance producer may rely on insurer-provided product-specific training standards and materials.

An insurance producer who engages in the sale of annuity products must complete a one-time four credit training course approved by the commissioner and provided by a continuing education provider approved by the commissioner. Insurance producers who hold a life insurance line of authority on June 1, 2013 and who desire to sell annuities must complete the training requirements no later than six months after January 1, 2014. Individuals who obtain a life insurance line of authority on or after January 1, 2014, may not engage in the sale of annuities until the annuity training course has been completed. Producers licensed on or after January 1, 2014, have until June 30, 2014, to complete the course. (Minn. Stat. Ann. § 72A.2033).

Minnesota has adopted the NAIC's Suitability in Annuity Transactions Model Regulation. Minn. Stat. Ann. §§ 60K.46 to 60K.56 (2012) (portions of model); §§ 72A.20 to 72A.2036 (2012/2013) (portions of previous version of model); and 61A.021 (tying prohibited).

III. **Statutory References:** Minn. Stat. Ann. §§ 60A.14, .171, .23, .71, .9572, .964; 60E.03, .04, .06; 60H.03; 60K.32, .34, .36 to .40, .46, .49, .55, .56; 72A.2033; 72B.03, .045, .06; 79A.21. Minn. R. 2795.1400.

MISSISSIPPI

Insurance Department
P.O. Box 79; Jackson, MS 39205-0079
Telephone: 601-359-3569, 601-359-3582 (Licensing)
http://www.mid.ms.gov/

I. Licensing Requirements: Sales Personnel—Insurance Producers, Business Entities, Limited Licensees, Managing General Agents, Supervising General Agents. Other Insurance Professionals—Adjusters (Independent, Emergency, Trainee), Adjusting Entities, Professional Bail Agents, Bail Enforcement Agents, Bail Soliciting Agents, Legal Agents, Burial Agents. Automobile Club Agents, Reinsurance Intermediaries, Third-Party Administrators, Viatical Settlement Brokers (Individuals and Business Entities), Viatical Settlement Providers, Viatical Settlement Representatives (Individuals and Business Entities), Public Adjuster (Individual, Trainee, and Emergency), Public Adjusting Entities.

A. Applicability: A person shall not sell, solicit or negotiate insurance in Mississippi for any class or classes of insurance unless the person is licensed for that line of authority. No license shall be issued to a partnership unless all the partners thereof satisfy the same requirements in every respect for an individual producer. (Miss. Code Ann. §83-17-55).

B. Licenses Required of Residents: Each of the following must be licensed in Mississippi:

Sales Personnel

1. *Insurance Producers.*

   a. License fee: $100, renewal: $100 ($50 late fee if after renewal date). May apply electronically through Sircon or NIPR, additional fees may apply. (Miss. Code Ann. §27-15-87).
   b. License term: Biennial (last day of birth month).
   c. Applications: Available from http://www.mid.ms.gov/licensing/producer-individual-licensing.aspx#iplf. Applications printed from the MID web site will not be accepted in place of the renewal invoice. Online applications and renewals are also accepted through www.sircon.com or www.nipr.com.
   d. Lines of authority:
   Insurance Producer license type:

      (1) Life.
      (2) Variable Life and Variable Annuity Products.

(3) Accident and Health.
(4) Personal Lines.
(5) Property.
(6) Casualty.
(7) Credit: Limited Line Credit Insurance Producer license type.
(8) Car rental: Limited Line Insurance Producer license type.
(9) Crop: Limited Lines Insurance Producer license type.
(10) Surety: Limited Lines Insurance Producer license type.
(11) Travel: Limited Lines Insurance Producer license type.
(12) Industrial Fire: Limited Lines Insurance Producer license type.
(13) Industrial Life, Accident and Health, Limited Lines Insurance Producer.
(14) Title: Limited Lines Insurance Producer license type.
(15) Trip Accident and Baggage.
(16) Self-Storage.
(Miss. Code Ann. §83-17-63).

2. *Entities.* A business entity acting as an insurance producer is required to obtain an insurance producer license. Application shall be made using the NAIC uniform business entity application or the MID insurance producer business entity application found at http://www.mid.ms.gov/licensing/producer-individual-licensing.aspx#eplf. Applications printed from the MID web site will not be accepted in place of the renewal invoice. Online applications and renewals are also accepted through www.sircon.com or www.nipr.com.

Each business entity must designate a licensed producer responsible for the business entity's compliance with the insurance laws, rules, and regulations of the State of Mississippi. Mississippi licenses several different types of entities.

Note: A "DBA" is not permitted in Mississippi, unless the entity is licensed as such in the home state and registered as such with the Mississippi Secretary of State's Office.

Insurance Producer Business Entity licenses expire biennially on May 31st. Fee: $200. (Miss. Code Ann. §27-15-85).

Adjuster business entities—submit NAIC uniform application for a Business Entity license, with $400 fee. License expires biennially on May 31st. The following must be submitted for each type of entity:

a. Corporation—articles of incorporation.
b. Limited Liability Company (LLC)—articles of organization.

Most applications for entity licenses can be obtained from the Mississippi Insurance Department Web site at http://www.mid.ms.gov/licensing/producer-individual-licensing.aspx#eplf. Online applications and renewals are also accepted through www.sircon.com or www.nipr.com.

(Miss. Code Ann. §83-17-61).

3. *Limited Licensees.* Limited line licenses are available for Credit, Car Rental, Crop, Surety, Travel, Industrial Fire, Industrial Life, Accident and Health, Title, Trip Accident and Baggage. Fee: $100. (Miss. Code Ann. §§27-15-87, 83-17-63).

4. *Managing General Agents.* Any person, firm, association or corporation who negotiates and binds ceding reinsurance contracts on behalf of an insurer or manages all or part of the insurance business of an insurer (including the management of a separate division, department or underwriting office) and acts as an agent for such insurer whether known as a MGA, manager or other similar term, who—with or without the authority—either separately or together with affiliates, produces, directly or indirectly, and underwrites an amount of gross direct written premium equal to or more than 5 percent of the policyholder surplus as reported in the last annual statement of the insurer in any one quarter or year together with one or more of the following: adjusts or pays claims in excess of an amount determined by the commissioner; or negotiates reinsurance on behalf of the insurer. Managing general agents must be licensed as a producer in Mississippi, whether an individual or entity. The license expires biennially on May 31; annual fee: $100 individual; $100 for corporation. This is an administrative license and does not allow holder to solicit or sell insurance. Application may be done online. (Miss. Code Ann. §83-18-103; https://www.mid.ms.gov/licensing/licensing-forms-fees.aspx#LicenseFees).

5. *Supervising General Agents.* Any person, partnership, association, or corporation having authority to serve as trustees, managers or administrators, except attorneys at law, for such licensed insurance companies or their insureds in the handling of insurance programs underwritten by licensed insurance companies, or in which they may be participating. SGA's must be appointed. Submit form GA-1. Annual fee: $100, corporation; $100, individual. This license does not allow solicitation of the general public. Expires biennially on May 31. (Miss. Code Ann. §§83-53-27, 83-17-1(c); https://www.mid.ms.gov/licensing/licensing-forms-fees.aspx#LicenseFees).

Other Insurance Professionals

1. *Adjusters (Independent, Emergency, Trainee).* Any person who, as an independent contractor, or as an employee of an independent contractor, adjustment bureau,

association, insurance company, or corporation, managing general agent or self-insured, investigates or adjusts losses on behalf of either an insurer, self-insured, or any person who supervises the handling of claims. An application for an independent adjuster license is required. Firm license is $400 and individual license for each adjuster is $100. Licenses expires biennial on the last day of the licensee's birth month.

An adjuster's license is required of independent adjusters but not of salaried employees of insurers or persons who handle claims arising under life, accident and health insurance policies; persons employed only for the purpose of furnishing technical assistance to a licensed adjuster; attorneys who adjust insurance losses from time to time and do not advertise or represent being an adjuster; licensed agents or general agents who process undisputed or uncontested losses under policies they issued; or persons who perform clerical duties with no negotiation with the parties on disputed or contested claims. (Miss. Code Ann. §83-17-401; https://www.mid.ms.gov/licensing/licensing-forms-fees.aspx#LicenseFees).

2. *Public Adjuster Business Entities.* Submit an application for a Public Adjuster Business Entity license with a $400 fee. License expires biennially on May 31. A licensed public adjuster must be designated as a responsible party. (https://www.mid.ms.gov/licensing/licensing-forms-fees.aspx#LicenseFees).

3. *Professional Bail Agents (Personal Surety or Limited Surety).* A limited surety is any individual who is appointed by an insurer by power of attorney to execute or countersign bail bonds in connection with judicial proceedings and who is duly licensed by the commissioner to represent such insurer for the restricted lines of bail, fidelity, and surety, after successfully completing a limited examination by the Department for the restricted lines of business. Submit an application for a professional bail agent license, exam results, and be fingerprinted by the Department $50, along with $100 license fee. Certificate of authority to represent insurer, $25. The professional bail agent must file an annual report before June 1 of each year as required by law. License expires on the last day of September biennially. Renewal fee: $40.

   A personal surety is any individual who, having posted the necessary qualification bond with the commissioner and duly licensed by the commissioner, may execute and sign bail bonds in connection with judicial proceedings. Submit an application for a professional bail agent license, exam results, fingerprints, and photo along with $100 fee. License expires on the last day of September biennially. (Miss. Code Ann. §§83-39-1, 83-39-11).

4. *Bail Enforcement Agents.* Assist the professional bail agent in presenting defendants in court when required, in the apprehension and surrender of defendants to the court, and keeps defendants under necessary surveillance. Submit an application for an enforcement bail agent license, photo, be fingerprinted by the Department for $50, and license fee of $40. License expires on the last day of September biennially. (Miss. Code Ann. §§83-39-1, 83-39-11).

5. *Bail Soliciting Agents.* Agents or employees of a professional bail agent, or independent contractors. They solicit, advertise, or actively seek bail bond business for or on behalf of a professional bail agent. Submit an application for a soliciting bail agent (Form BB-1), photo, be fingerprinted by the Department for $50 and license fee: $40. License expires on the last day of September biennially. (Miss. Code Ann. §§83-39-1, 83-39-11).

6. *Reinsurance Intermediaries.* Submit application (Form RIM-1) and fee of $100 for a corporation or $50 for an individual or unincorporated entity. License expires annually in March. (Miss. Code Ann. §83-19-205; https://www.mid.ms.gov/licensing/licensing-forms-fees.aspx#LicenseFees).

7. *Third-Party Administrators.* A person who directly or indirectly solicits or effects coverage of, underwrites, collects charges or premiums from, or adjusts or settles claims on residents of this state, or residents of another state from offices in this state, in connection with life or health insurance coverage or annuities. There are exemptions listed in Miss. Code Ann. §83-18-1. Submit an application for a TPA license and fee: $200. All TPAs must file an annual report with the commissioner by March 1. License expires annually on date of issuance. (Miss. Code Ann. §§83-18-1, 83-18-3).

8. *Viatical Settlement Representatives or Brokers.* A Viatical Settlement Representative is an individual who is a licensed agent and acts or aids in any manner in the solicitation of a viatical settlement and who is deemed to represent only the viatical settlement provider. Exemptions are listed in Miss. Code Ann. §83-7-203(b). A Viatical Settlement Broker is a licensed agent who acts on behalf of a viator and for a fee, commission or other valuable consideration offers or attempts to negotiate viatical settlements between a viator and one or more viatical settlement providers. An application shall be made for such license along with a $50 fee. The license expires annually on December 31. (Miss. Code Ann. §§83-7-203, 83-7-205).

9. *Viatical Settlement Provider.* (Broker or Representative) Must submit an application for a Viatical Settlement Provider license along with a $200.00 fee. The license expires annually on December 31. A VSP is a person, other than a viator, that enters into a viatical settlement contract. This is also a person that obtains

financing for the purchase, acquisition, transfer or other assignment of one or more viatical settlement contracts, policies or interests or otherwise sells, assigns, transfers, or disposes of one or more viatical settlement contracts. An application shall be made for such license along with a $200 fee. Individuals actually performing the solicitation and/or negotiation must hold a VSR or VSB individual license. (Miss. Code. Ann. §§83-7-203, 83-7-205).

Applications for all licenses are obtained from the Insurance Department. Most may be downloaded from the Web site: http://www.mid.ms.gov/licensing/producer-individual-licensing.aspx#eplf.

Mississippi encourages online application, if available, but not via email. Applications for most license types are available from SIRCON (www.sircon.com/mississippi) or NIPR (www.nipr.com).

C. **Appointments:** An insurance producer shall not act as an agent of an insurer unless the insurance producer becomes an appointed agent of that insurer. An insurance producer who is not acting as an agent of an insurer is not required to become appointed. The Department permits electronic appointments via Sircon (www.sircon.com/mississippi) or NIPR (www.nipr.com). Fee: $25 for agents and general agents. Invoices for renewal appointments of all producers will be sent by the Mississippi Insurance Department and should be paid in full by the annual renewal date, May 31. (Miss. Code Ann. §83-17-75; http://www.mid.ms.gov/licensing/licensing-appointments.aspx#appointments).

D. **Licenses Required of Nonresidents:** Nonresidents may receive a producer license if they currently are licensed as residents and in good standing in their home states, submit the proper application and fee, and if their home state awards nonresident producer licenses to residents of Mississippi on the same basis. A nonresident who moves from one state to another state or a resident producer who moves from this state to another state shall file a change of address and provide certification from the new resident state within thirty days of the change of legal residence (no fee or a license application is required). A person licensed as a surplus lines producer in his or her home state shall receive a nonresident surplus lines producer license upon the filing of the proper application and submission of the license fee (an underlying insurance producer license with property and casualty lines of authority is required). Nonresidents may receive the same licenses as residents except for bail agent license types. The fees are the same as those for residents. A person licensed in this state as a nonresident producer whose license is denied, suspended, or revoked in his or her home state shall also have his or her nonresident license denied, suspended, or revoked in this state without prior notice or hearing. (Miss. Code Ann. §83-17-65).

Multi-State Exposures: A license is not required for a nonresident insurance producer who sells, solicits, or negotiates a contract of insurance for commercial property and casualty coverage when risks that are to be insured under that contract are located in more than one state. This exception applies only if the nonresident is licensed to sell, solicit, or negotiate that insurance in the state where the insured maintains its principal place of business and the contract of insurance insures risks located in that state. (Miss. Code Ann. §83-17-57).

E. Prelicensing Examination or Education Requirements:

1. *Residents.* Educational prerequisites:

   a. Producers: Twenty hours of approved classroom study per line of authority. Prelicensing requirements do not apply to individuals:

      (1) Individual that is exempt from taking the written examination.
      (2) An individual with a bachelor's degree with major coursework in insurance.
      (3) Holding a current and valid CEBS, CHFC, CIC, CFP, CLU, FLMI, LUTCF designation is exempt for the life line of authority.
      (4) Holding current and valid RHU, CEBS, REBC, HIA designation is exempt for accident and health lines of authority.
      (5) Holding current and valid AAI, ARM, CIC, CPCU designation is exempt for the property and casualty lines of authority.
      (6) Limited lines insurance producer or limited lines credit insurance producer.
      (7) Individual seeking a license for variable life and variable annuity product line only.

   b. Independent Adjusters and Public Adjusters: Twenty classroom hours, special experience and training may be substituted subject to approval by the commissioner.
   c. Seeking renewal of producer license: twenty-four classroom hours, three need to be in ethics.
   c. Professional Bail Agent, Soliciting Bail Agent, and Bail Enforcement Agent: Forty classroom hours. (Miss. Code Ann. § 83-17-251; http://www.mid.ms.gov/licensing/pre-licensing-continuing-education.aspx).

   Residents applying for the following licenses must pass a qualifying examination:

   a. Combined life, health & accident or sickness.

b. Life only.
c. Health & accident or sickness.
d. Full lines property & casualty.
e. Property.
f. Casualty.
g. Personal lines.
h. Independent adjuster.
i. Industrial fire.
j. Professional bail agent, soliciting bail agent, and bail enforcement agent.
k. Public adjuster. (http://www.mid.ms.gov/licensing/pre-licensing-continuing-education.aspx).

The tests are administered by Pearson Vue. Web site: http://www.pearsonvue.com; Telephone: 888-293-4222; E-mail Pearsonvuecustomerservice@pearsonvue.com. Neither Miss. Code Ann. §83-17-251 nor the Department website (http://www.mid.ms.gov/licensing/licensing-examinations.aspx) list an exam requirement for managing general agents.

2. *Nonresidents.* Examination and prelicensing education requirements for a nonresident applying for a property and casualty or life/health and accident nonresident producer's license are reciprocal with applicant's home state. (Miss. Code Ann. §83-17-67).

F. Continuing Education Requirements:

Number of Hours Required: All producers and adjusters must complete twelve hours of CE if a license has been in effect for eighteen months or less. If a license has been in effect for more than eighteen months, the licensee must complete a total of twenty-four hours of CE, which must include three hours of ethics on a biennial basis. The licensee must establish whether a CE course is acceptable and whether it meets the CE requirements. (Miss. Code Ann. §§83-17-251, 83-17-257). Bail agents license is a biennial license, but they must complete eight hours of CE on an annual basis. (http://www.mid.ms.gov/licensing/pre-licensing-continuing-education.aspx#ce).

The coursework must be in the line or lines for which licensed. The licensee may use approved self-study courses or classroom instruction. Courses may not be taken for credit more than once in license period. (Miss. Code Ann. §83-17-253).

Submit Proof of Completion by: Providers should submit course completions to MID electronically through SIRCON. (Miss. Code Ann. §83-17-257).

Excess Hours: May not be carried into the next reporting period.

Final Exam: The final exam for a self-study course must be monitored by a disinterested third-party and graded by the course providers.

Renewal Procedure:

1. Course provider supplies licensee with completion certificate.

2. Licensee completes application for renewal and submits electronically through SIRCON or NIPR.

Nonresidents are exempt if the satisfy the CE requirements of their home state. (Miss. Code Ann. §83-17-251).

For more information or clarification on prelicensing and continuing education in Mississippi, please contact the Department or visit http://www.mid.ms.gov/licensing/pdf/prelicenseconteducguidelines.pdf.

G. **Cancellation of Agency/Producer Contracts:** Insurer must notify the MID of the termination within thirty days. If the reason for termination is the violation of any laws of the State of Mississippi or any other governmental entity, the insurer shall indicate as such on the termination notice and provide additional information, documents, records or other data pertaining to the termination or activity of the producer. (Miss. Code Ann. §83-17-77).

H. **Rules for Risk Retention and Purchasing Groups:** Mississippi regulates risk retention and purchasing groups operating or offering coverage on risks in state. As required by Miss. Code Ann. §83-55-1, *et seq*, risk retention groups chartered in Mississippi must be licensed as liability insurers. At the time of filing its application for charter, the risk retention group must provide a summary of the following information: The identity of the initial members of the group; the identity of those individuals who organized the group or who will provide administrative services or influence the activities of the group; the amount and nature of initial capitalization; the coverages to be afforded and the states in which the group intends to operate. Fees: Must file by March 1 of each year a listing of all premiums written on risks in Mississippi. (Miss. Code Ann. §83-55-5).

Groups not domiciled in Mississippi must register with the Insurance Department and submit reports to the commissioner as described in the law. All risk retention group policies must show the following notice in at least ten point type on the front page and on the declarations page of the policy:

> This policy is issued by your risk retention group. Your risk retention group may not be subject to all of the insurance laws and regulations of your state. State insurance insolvency guaranty funds are not available for your risk retention group.

Purchasing groups must also register with the commissioner and submit reports as required by the law. Must file by March 1 of each year a listing of all premiums written on risks in Mississippi. All groups and all resident and nonresident producers participating in them must comply with all Mississippi insurance laws, including licensing and solicitation requirements or restrictions. (Miss. Code Ann. §§83-55-13, 83-55-15).

Risk Retention and Purchasing Groups must submit an annual registration application to renew their authority. The license year runs from March 1 through February 28. (http://www.mid.ms.gov/companies/company-filing-registration.aspx#rrg). (Miss. Code Ann. §§83-55-5, 7).

I. Other License Rules, Requirements, or Restrictions: None

J. Policy Countersignature Requirements: Countersignature not required when insurance policy is issued to a risk retention group. (Miss. Ann. Code §83-55-11).

An agent commissioned and licensed in the state of Mississippi must countersign any contract of insurance or general policy so issued. This does not apply to individual firms and corporations indemnifying themselves through reciprocal contracts and not employing local agents. A facsimile may be used solely in connection with personal accident insurance covering travel, so long as it is not issued for more than seven days. The countersignature may also be in facsimile when authorization is given in writing to an insurer for which the agent is certified to do business. Facsimile authorization may be cancelled by the agent in writing or is automatically cancelled upon death, termination, or nonrenewal of the agent. (Miss. Code Ann. §83-17-21).

Delivery of policies must be through a licensed agent. (Miss. Code Ann. §83-31-37).

II. Commissions, Fees, Commingling of Funds

A. Commissions: An unlicensed resident or nonresident may not receive commissions. However, an unlicensed employee of an agent, agency, or affiliate may receive a one-time, nominal referral fee when that employee refers a prospective insured to the agency, agency, or affiliate. (Miss. Code Ann. §83-17-7).

B. Fees: Licensed producers may charge fees for insurance advisory services but may not also collect a commission. Mississippi law does not permit insurance counseling by anyone not licensed as a producer, attorney, or adjuster, unless employed by an authorized insurer or general agent to an insurer. All fees charged by a producer must be approved by MID in the insurance company's rate filing. (Miss. Code Ann. §83-17-73).

C. **Disclosure Requirements:** None. Must not violate the unfair trade practices act or Mississippi Code.

D. **Commingling of Funds:** Producers may be sanctioned for demonstrating financial irresponsibility in the conduct of business in the state. (Miss. Code Ann. §83-17-71(1)(h)).

Mississippi has not adopted the NAIC model regulation for Suitability in Annuity Transactions.

III. Statutory References:

Miss. Code Ann. §27-	15-87
Miss. Code Ann. §§83-	
7-	203, 205
15-	85, 87
17-	1, 7
	21, 55, 57, 61 to 67, 71 to 77
	251, 153, 257, 401
18-	1, 3, .103
19-	205
31-	37
39-	1, 11
53-	27
55-	5, 11 to 15

Web References:

https://www.mid.ms.gov/licensing/licensing-forms-fees.aspx#LicenseFees.

http://www.mid.ms.gov/licensing/licensing-appointments.aspx#appointments.

http://www.mid.ms.gov/licensing/pre-licensing-continuing-education.aspx.

http://www.mid.ms.gov/licensing/licensing-examinations.aspx.

http://www.mid.ms.gov/companies/company-filing-registration.aspx#rrg.

MISSOURI

Director, Department of Commerce & Insurance
P. O. Box 690; Jefferson City, MO 65102-0690
Telephone: 573-751-3518; Fax: 573-526-3416
Email: licensing@insurance.mo.gov
http://insurance.mo.gov

I. Licensing Requirements: Sales Personnel—Producers and Business Entity Producers. Other Insurance Professionals—Bail Bond Agents, General Bail Bond Agents, Surety Recovery Agents, Public Adjusters, Public Adjuster Solicitors, Reinsurance Intermediaries, Reciprocal and Interinsurance Exchange Representatives, Managing General Agents.

A. Applicability: No person shall sell, solicit or negotiate insurance in Missouri for any class or classes of insurance unless he or she is licensed for that line of authority. (R.S. Mo. §375.014).

B. Licenses Required of Residents: Each of the following must be licensed in Missouri:

Sales Personnel

1. *Producers.* Producer's license is renewed biennially on the producer's birth date. Initial and renewal fee: $100. The following lines of authority are available: life; variable life and variable annuity products; accident and health or sickness; property; casualty; personal lines; title; limited lines credit; limited lines travel; and crop. (R.S. Mo. §§375.015, 375.018).

   No separate license is required for risk managers, risk management consultants, or field/marketing representatives.

2. *Business Entity Producers.* Each business entity producer operated as a sole proprietorship, partnership, corporation, or unincorporated association must be licensed. Each person in the entity that sells, solicits, or negotiates insurance must also be licensed. Individuals transacting business under any name other than their true name must obtain a business entity producer license. Business entity producer licenses expire biennially on the anniversary of date of issue. Initial fee: $100; biennial fee: $100. Business entity producers must notify the commissioner within twenty days of the termination of any business entity producer or of the change in any information provided on the license application. There is no fee for such a change or termination. (R.S. Mo. §375.015). Contact the Missouri Department of Commerce & Insurance for proper documentation of the registered name.

Other Insurance Professionals

1. *Public Adjusters.* Public adjusters (but not adjusters employed by or adjusting claims on behalf of insurers) must be licensed to conduct adjusting activities in Missouri. Bond of $10,000 required. Public adjuster's license expires annually on anniversary date; initial fee: $100; renewal fee: $50. (R.S. Mo. §§325.015 to 325.025).

2. *Public Adjuster Solicitors.* Bond of $10,000 required. Public adjuster solicitor's license expires annually on anniversary date; initial fee: $100; renewal fee: $50. (R.S. Mo. §§325.020, 325.025).

3. *Reinsurance Intermediaries.* Reinsurance intermediaries must be licensed to conduct reinsurance intermediary activities in Missouri. A reinsurance broker must be licensed if it maintains an office in the state of Missouri. A license is not required if the reinsurance broker does not have an office in Missouri and holds a license from a state with reinsurance intermediary laws that are substantially similar to Missouri's. A reinsurance intermediary manager must be licensed in the state if it represents Missouri domiciled insurers whether it has an office in Missouri or not. Initial fee: $100, renewal fee: $50. Application forms may be obtained on the Department's website: http://insurance.mo.gov. (R.S. Mo. §§375.246, 375.1115).

4. *Reciprocal and Interinsurance Exchanges.* Representatives who receive commission must be licensed. (R.S. Mo. §§379.650, 379.670).

5. *Managing General Agents.* Must be licensed as producers. Both a fidelity bond of $100,000, no deductible, and an E&O policy of $100,000 per occurrence and $1 million in the aggregate are required. There also must be a contract between the MGA and insurer. (20 CSR 200-10.200).

6. *General Bail Bond Agents, Bail Bond Agents, Surety Recovery Agents.* Must be licensed. Biennial fee: $150. Biennial renewal: $150. (R.S. Mo. §§374.702, 374.730).

Applications for insurance producer may be filed electronically at www.nipr.com. Paper forms may be obtained on the Department's website: http://insurance.mo.gov.

Applications are not accepted via email.

C. Appointments: Insurers must maintain a register of appointed insurance producers who may sell, solicit, or negotiate insurance contracts for the insurer. The names and license numbers of producers must be entered on the register within thirty days of the appointment. There is no fee. The register must be available for inspection by the

DIFP during normal business hours. Insurers who terminate such relationships for cause must notify the DIFP within thirty days of the effective date of termination. Terminations for other reasons need only be entered in the producer register. No fee shall be charged for adding a producer to or terminating a producer from the register. (R.S. Mo. §375.022).

D. Licenses Required of Nonresidents: The same licenses and fees are required of nonresidents that are required of Missouri residents. Entities must be licensed, as well as all individuals in the entity who will be selling, soliciting, or negotiating insurance. Nonresidents shall receive a nonresident producer license if the nonresident is currently licensed and in good standing in the resident's home state, the nonresident has submitted a request for such licensure and paid the proper fees, the nonresident has submitted a license application to the Director, and the nonresident's home state awards licenses to Missouri residents on a reciprocal basis. The same rules apply to nonresident and resident licenses. Home state insurance department certification (no older than six months) of nonresident's home-state license is required for all residents of states who do not participate in the Producer Database. (R.S. Mo. §375.017). If the applicant is a resident of a state that participates in PDB, no certification letter is required. Application forms may be obtained on the Department's Web site: http://insurance.mo.gov.

Multi-State Exposures: A license is not required for a nonresident insurance producer who sells, solicits, or negotiates a contract of insurance for commercial property and casualty coverage when risks that are to be insured under that contract are located in more than one state. This exception applies only if the nonresident is licensed to sell, solicit, or negotiate that insurance in the state where the insured maintains its principal place of business and the contract of insurance insures risks located in that state. (R.S. Mo. §375.014).

E. Prelicensing Examination and Education Requirements:

1. *Residents.* Applicants for the following insurance licenses must pass a qualifying examination administered by Pearson VUE (http://www.pearsonvue.com/mo/insurance or call 866-274-4740):

    a. Producers: life, accident and health, property, casualty, personal lines, title, and crop. Life producers selling variable contracts require NASD registration. Missouri does not require any prelicensing education prior to taking the exam.
    b. Public adjusters.
    c. Public adjuster solicitors.
    d. Bail bond agents.
    e. Surety recovery agents.

f. Surplus lines.

g. Crop. (R.S. Mo. §375.016; https://insurance.mo.gov/agents/resident/res_agent_licreq.php).

The exam fee: $35 for combined life/accident and health or property/casualty; $29 for life, accident and health, property, casualty, personal lines and navigator; $22 for surplus lines, public adjuster, public adjuster solicitor, crop, title, surety recovery, bail bonds, and title agency qualified principal. (https://home.pearsonvue.com/getattachment/19260121-2726-44db-b3c6-12359f39b339/Missouri%20Insurance%20Licensing%20Candidate%20Handbook.aspx).

The following licenses do not require an examination: restricted to credit, restricted to travel, and business entity producer. (https://insurance.mo.gov/industry/faq/license.php#fees).

Missouri does not have prelicensing education requirements.

2. *Nonresidents.* Nonresident producers are exempt from examination in those lines in which they are currently licensed in their home states, provided they make an application within ninety days of establishing Missouri residence. This exemption applies to residents of those states that award licenses to Missouri residents on the same basis. Nonresident bail bond agents must devote 50 percent of his or her working time to the state of Missouri. (R.S. Mo. §375.016).

3. Bail bond agents, general bail bond agents, and surety recovery agents must complete a twenty-four hour initial basic training prelicensing education requirement. (R.S. Mo. §374.710).

F. Continuing Education Requirements:

Number of Hours Required: Missouri-resident producers licensed for any major line of authority are required to complete sixteen hours of continuing education during any two-year licensure period; eight hours biennially for bail bond, general bail bond, and surety recovery agents. Licensees may use classroom or self-study.

All Missouri-resident licensees licensed in at least one of the major lines of authority seeking to renew their license will need to have completed at least three hours of continuing education in ethics, Missouri laws, and producer duties. These hours may be counted towards the sixteen total continuing education hours required to renew licensure.

Teachers/lecturers of approved courses shall qualify for the same number of CE hours as a person taking the course would receive. (R.S. Mo. §375.020).

Before any licensed producer can sell, solicit, or negotiate a Long-Term Care Partnership product in the state of Missouri, she must complete eight hours of initial training in partnership policies and complete four hours of continuing education in partnership policies every two-year licensure period thereafter. Both the aforementioned hours may be counted towards the sixteen total continuing education hours required to renew licensure. (https://insurance.mo.gov/agents/ce/ce_ltc.php).

Subject to the Director's approval, a producer's active participation as a member, or employee of a business entity producer member, in a local, regional, state, or national professional insurance association may be approved for up to four hours of CE credit per reporting period. Credits received under this provision may not satisfy any CE hours require to be completed in a classroom or classroom equivalent or any CE ethics requirements. (R.S. Mo. §375.029).

Any CE course approved for use to meet professional CE in another Missouri profession, as required by law, that relates to the topic of insurance shall meet the CE requirements under R.S. Mo. §375.020. (R.S. Mo. §375.030).

Submit Proof of Completion: With the biennial renewal application.

Excess Hours: May be carried into the next reporting period.

Final Exam: The final exam for a self-study course must be monitored.

Renewal Procedure:

1. Course provider supplies licensee with certificate of course completion.
2. Licensee copies information onto CE certification summary form for reporting to the DIFP.
3. Licensee mails certification summary form with renewal and $100 renewal fee to DIFP and keeps original certificate. Late fee is $25 per month delayed. (https://insurance.mo.gov/renewin3/).

Nonresident producers are exempt if they satisfy the CE requirements of their home state, and the home state grants the same privilege to Missouri residents. (R.S. Mo. §375.017). The Department website, however, merely states that nonresidents are exempt if their home state has a mandatory CE requirement. (https://insurance.mo.gov/industry/faq/license.php).

G. **Cancellation of Business Entity Producer/Producer Contracts:** Insurers must give agents a ninety-day notice of their intent to cancel a business entity producer contract. The DIFP must be notified within thirty days of terminations for cause. The insurer is required to pay one year of renewal commissions. (R.S. Mo. §§375.033, 375.035).

H. **Rules for Risk Retention and Purchasing Groups:** Risk retention groups and purchasing groups must comply with R.S. Mo. §§375.1080 to 375.1105 and 20 CSR 200-8.100. Risk retention groups chartered and purchasing groups located in states other than Missouri must register with the Missouri Director of Insurance, Financial Institutions and Professional Registration and submit for approval the information prescribed in the laws and regulations. A producer or surplus lines license is required to place insurance with a duly registered purchasing group or risk retention group in the same manner as placing insurance with an authorized insurance company. Annual and renewal registration fee is $100. All risk retention group policies must show the following notice in at least ten-point type on the front page and on the declarations page of the policy:

NOTICE

"This policy is issued by your risk retention group. Your risk retention group may not be subject to all of the insurance laws and regulations of your state. State insurance insolvency guaranty funds are not available for your risk retention group." (R. S. Mo. §§375.1082, 375.1085).

I. **Other License Rules, Requirements, or Restrictions:** Licensing Information Bulletins can be obtained from Pearson VUE (http://pearsonvue.com/). Companies must have on file photocopies of licenses, current Producer Database (PDB) screen print or Missouri Department of Commerce & Insurance screen-print of licensee database of all producers to whom the company pays commission. Unlicensed nonresidents may not solicit insurance in the state. Producers and business entity producers must notify director in writing within thirty days after any change in residence address (business address for business entity producers). License may be revoked for failure to do so if it prevents director from serving a complaint.

Insurers who terminate relationships for cause must notify the DIFP within thirty days of the effective date of termination. Terminations for other reasons need only be entered in the producer register. (R.S. Mo. §375.022).

J. **Policy Countersignature Requirements:** Policies need not be countersigned, unless the state of the non-resident agent or broker imposes a countersignature requirement on policies solicited by residents of Missouri. Foreign companies shall transact business through licensed agents and brokers.

1. Any law requiring that policies be countersigned and delivered through a resident agent shall not apply to any policy of such mutual company on which no commission shall be paid to any local agent.

2. Such mutual company may insert in any form of policy prescribed by the law of this state any provisions or conditions required by its plan of insurance which are not inconsistent or in conflict with any law of this state. (R.S. Mo. §§379.275, 375.901).

II. Commissions, Fees, Commingling of Funds, and Suitability in Annuity Transactions

A. **Commissions:** There are no restrictions on distribution of commissions among licensed resident or nonresident producers of the insurer. No commission may be paid to an unlicensed resident or nonresident under any circumstances. Rebating of commissions is not allowed. (R.S. Mo. §375.076).

B. **Fees:** Producers may charge a fee for services in addition to or instead of commission, provided there is a written agreement with the client to that effect. In addition, insurers or producers may charge additional incidental fees for premium installments, late payments, policy reinstatements, or similar services if the fees are disclosed to the client in writing. (R.S. Mo. §§375.936(12)(c), 379.356).

C. **Disclosure Requirements:** The producer must disclose when a commission will be received in addition to a fee. The written agreement, which must state that the client is under no obligation to purchase any insurance product, must be signed by the client before services are performed. The producer must retain a copy of the agreement for at least three years after services are completed. (20 CSR 700-1.100).

D. **Commingling of Funds:** Missouri does not prohibit producers' commingling of insurer's premiums with other agency funds. (R.S. Mo. §369.249).

E. **Suitability in Annuity Transactions:** In recommending to an individual customer the purchase, sale, or exchange of a variable, indexed or fixed annuity, a producer shall have reasonable grounds for believing that the recommendation is suitable for such customer upon the basis of the facts, if any, disclosed by such customer as to his insurance and investment holdings and as to his current and reasonably anticipated financial situation and needs. Producers recommending annuities must be under a supervisory system. (20 CSR 700-1.146).

III. Statutory References:

R.S. Mo. §§325.	015 to 025
R.S. Mo. §369.	249
R.S. Mo. §§374.	702, 720, 730
R.S. Mo. §§375.	014to018,020,022,029,030, 033, 035, 076, 246, 901, 936
	1082, 1085, 1115
R.S. Mo. §§379.	275, 356, 650, 670

20 CSR	200-10.200
	700-1.100
	700-1.146

Web References:

https://insurance.mo.gov/agents/resident/res_agent_licreq.php.

https://insurance.mo.gov/industry/faq/license.php.

https://insurance.mo.gov/agents/ce/ce_ltc.php.

https://insurance.mo.gov/renewin3.

https://home.pearsonvue.com/getattachment/19260121-2726-44db-b3c6-12359f39b339/Missouri%20Insurance%20Licensing%20Candidate%20Handbook.aspx.

MONTANA

Office of the Commissioner of Securities and Insurance
Montana State Auditor (CSI), 840 Helena Ave., Helena, MT 59601
Telephone: 406-444-2040; Fax: 406-444-3497
http://www.csi.mt.gov/

I. Licensing Requirements: Sales Personnel—Producers, Limited Lines, Managing General Agents. Other Insurance Professionals—Adjusters, Administrators, Consultants, Independent and Public Adjusters, Reinsurance Intermediaries, Viatical Settlement Providers, and Brokers.

A. Applicability: A person may not sell, solicit, or negotiate insurance or act as an insurance producer in Montana unless licensed as an insurance producer. (MCA 33-17-201).

B. Licenses Required of Residents: Each of the following must be licensed in Montana:

Sales Personnel

1. *Producers.*

   a. License fee: no fee for residents. (nipr.com).
   b. License term: producer's license is continuous until cancelled or terminated, as long as continuing education requirements are met.
   c. Lines of authority:

      (1) Life, including benefits of endowment and annuities.
      (2) Property (including marine).
      (3) Casualty.
      (4) Variable life and variable annuity products.
      (5) Personal lines.
      (6) Surety.
      (7) Accident and health or sickness.
      (8) Limited lines credit.
      (9) Any other line of insurance permitted under Montana law. (MCA 33-17-214).

   The commissioner may place an insurance producer on inactive status if the producer enters active service in the Armed Forces of the United States. During the time of inactivity, the producer may not transact business. The commissioner shall waive the continuing education requirements and fees while the producer is on inactive status. In order to be placed on inactive status, the insurance producer must notify the commissioner when called to active service. In order to be taken off inactive status, the insurance producer must notify the commissioner when discharged from active service. (MCA 33-17-219).

Additional points:

a. Producer may present a quote prior to appointment but may not claim to be a representative of the insurer until appointed. (MCA 33-17-236).
b. Montana law requires prelicensing background checks for residents. (MCA 33-17-220).
c. Except as provided by law, the commissioner shall collect a fee of $1,900 from each insurer applying for or annually renewing a certificate of authority to conduct the business of insurance in Montana. (MCA 33-2-708).

2. *Limited Lines Producers.*

   a. License fee: no fee for residents.
   b. Limited lines of authority:

      Credit, which includes: credit life insurance, credit disability insurance, credit property insurance, credit unemployment insurance, involuntary unemployment insurance, mortgage life insurance, mortgage guaranty insurance, mortgage disability insurance, gap insurance, and any other form of insurance offered in connection with an extension of credit. (MCA 33-17-102).

3. *Entities.* Partnerships, corporations, and Limited Liability Companies (LLCs) must obtain a producer's license. The entity must pay the appropriate fee and designate an individual producer to be responsible for compliance with Montana law. Transaction of insurance must be within the entity's organizational documents; respecting a corporation, the secretary of state has issued a certificate of registration or filed the articles of incorporation. (MCA 33-17-211).

4. *Managing General Agents.* Producer license required. MGAs must have an agreement and appointment with the insurer, as required by the NAIC Model Act. (MCA 33-2-1601, 1602).

5. *Car Rental Producers.* Only business entities are eligible. A rental vehicle entity shall designate an individual licensed insurance producer who is responsible

for the rental vehicle entity's compliance with the Montana Insurance Code. (MCA 33-17-1502). Application fee of $100 must be submitted along with a list of customer service personnel. Within fifteen days from the date on which the agency contract is executed, the business entity must hold an appointment with any insurer it represents. (MCA 33-17-236, 33-2-708).

Other Insurance Professionals

1. *Adjusters.* License required. Business entities may be licensed if each individual is licensed, or is named in the business entity license and otherwise qualified for an individual license. Application fee: $50; biennial renewal: $100. (MCA 33-17-301, 33-2-708).

2. *Administrators.* Must have certificate of registration. Annual renewal fee: $100, due July 1. (MCA 33-17-603).

3. *Consultants.* Consultant's license is biennial, based on licensee's birth year. Application fee: $50; biennial renewal, $100. May be licensed as a consultant for the following: life insurance (Disability, Life, Group Contracts, Credit Disability, Credit Life, Group Disability, Blanket Disability), or general insurance (Casualty, Disability, Marine Protection, Wet Marine and Transportation, Property, Surety, Title, Mechanical Breakdown, Prepaid Legal, Involuntary Unemployment, Gap, Mortgage, Credit, Nationwide Inland Marine, Personal Property, Commercial Property). (MCA 33-2-708, 33-17-503, 504).

4. *Independent and Public Adjusters.* Application fee: $50; License is perpetual with biennial renewal: $100. (MCA 33-17-301).

5. *Reinsurance Intermediaries.* Must be licensed as producers. Managers may be required to file a bond and maintain an E&O policy. (MCA 33-2-1701).

6. *Viatical Settlement Providers and Brokers.* Must be licensed. Broker's license fee: $50; biennial renewal, $100. Must file a bond or other mechanism for financial accountability for the provider/broker. Providers: $1,900 license fee. (MCA 33-20-1303, 33-20-1315, 33-2-708).

7. *Managing General Agents.* Must be licensed as a producer. Commissioner may require a bond and an E&O policy. (MCA 33-2-1601).

The following application forms are to be used. They may be downloaded from the CSI's Web site at http://csimt.gov/insurance/licensing/.

1. *Producers.* NAIC Uniform Application for Individual Producers.

2. *Agencies.* NAIC Uniform Business Entity Application.

3. *Adjusters.* Application for adjuster license.

4. *Consultants.* Application for consultant license.

C. **Appointments:** Each insurer appointing an insurance producer in Montana shall file with the commissioner the appointment, specifying the kinds of insurance to be transacted by the insurance producer for the insurer. The appointment may be electronically filed pursuant to rules adopted by the commissioner. Each appointment remains in effect until the insurance producer's license is revoked or otherwise terminated unless written notice of earlier termination of the appointment is filed with the commissioner by the insurer or the insurance producer. The written notice may be electronically filed pursuant to rules adopted by the commissioner. An appointment of which notice is not filed within 15 days of the agency contract is not effective until the date that the insurer filed the notice of appointment with the insurance department. Termination of the insurer's authority in Montana also terminates the appointment. Insurers must submit the appointment request to the commissioner within fifteen days from the date the agency contract is executed. However, the insurer is not required to notify the commissioner of termination of an appointment by affiliation. An appointment by affiliation terminated automatically on termination of the affiliation. (MCA 33-17-236).

D. **Licenses Required of Nonresidents:** Nonresident producer's license initial license fee: $100. Submit individual application. Montana accepts the NAIC Uniform Application for individuals and business entities. Biennial renewal for individual producers: $50. Lapsed license reinstatement fee: $100 (MCA 33-2-708).

Multi-State Exposures. A license is not required for a nonresident insurance producer who sells, solicits, or negotiates a contract of insurance for commercial property and casualty coverage when risks that are to be insured under that contract are located in more than one state. This exception applies only if the nonresident is licensed to sell, solicit, or negotiate that insurance in the state where the insured maintains its principal place of business and the contract of insurance insures risks located in that state. (MCA 33-17-102, 33-17-103).

E. **Prelicensing Examination or Education Requirements:**

1. *Residents.* Applicants for the following licenses must pass a qualifying examination given by Pearson VUE (800-274-8906) to obtain a license initially: life, accident and health, property (including marine), casualty, surety, title, limited lines credit, adjuster, public adjuster, prepaid legal, and consultant.

2. *Nonresidents.* No examination is required for a nonresident, but the applicant must be similarly licensed and in good standing in his or her home state. (MCA 33-17-212).

F. Continuing Education Requirements:

An individual licensed to act as an insurance producer, adjuster or consultant other than an individual licensed only for surety bail bonds or for limited lines credit insurance shall, during each twenty-four-month period, complete at least twenty-four credit hours of approved continuing education, including at least three hours of ethics credits and at least one credit hour on changes in the Montana Insurance Code and the Administrative Rules of Montana.

An individual licensed to act as an insurance producer only for surety bail bonds, prepaid legal, or limited lines credit insurance shall, during each biennium, complete five credit hours of approved continuing education, including at least one credit hour on changes in the Montana Insurance Code and the Administrative Rules of Montana, with the remaining credit hours in the areas of insurance law, ethics, or topics specific to surety bail bonds, prepaid legal, or limited lines credit insurance.

Temporary licensees are exempt from these continuing education requirements. (MCA § 33-17-1203).

Course provider issues completion certificate to the licensee and reports credit to the commissioner. (MCA 33-17-1205).

Nonresidents are exempt from these continuing education requirements on a reciprocal basis if home state has similar CE requirements to Montana. (MCA 33-17-408).

G. Cancellation of Agency/Producer Contracts: Insurers must file notice of termination of appointment with the commissioner within thirty days.

If the termination was for a reason that would require suspension, revocation, or refusal of a license under MCA 33-17-1001 or 33-25-301, the insurer must notify the department immediately of the reason for the termination. (MCA 33-17-237).

H. Rules for Risk Retention and Purchasing Groups: Montana regulates risk retention and purchasing groups operating or offering coverage on risks in Montana. Risk retention groups chartered in Montana must be licensed as casualty insurers. Groups not chartered in Montana must register with the commissioner and submit reports. (MCA 33-11-103, 104). Purchasing groups must register with the commissioner and submit reports. (MCA 33-11-108). All groups and all resident and nonresident agents participating in them must comply with the Code and Administrative Rules of Montana, including licensing and solicitation requirements or restrictions. Any risk retention group in violation of Montana Code Title 33, Chapter 11 is subject to fines and penalties applicable to licensed insurers. All risk retention group policies must show the following notice in at least ten-point type on the front page and on the declarations page of the policy:

NOTICE

"This policy is issued by your risk retention group. Your risk retention group may not be subject to all of the insurance laws and regulations of your state. State insurance insolvency guaranty funds are not available for your risk retention group." (MCA 33-11-103, 104).

I. **Other License Rules, Requirements, or Restrictions:** Unlicensed nonresidents may not enter this state to solicit, inspect, or service. Entering the state includes mail or telephone or other electronic communication into the state from the outside, as well as physical presence in the state. Insurers and producers may not share commissions with a person who must be licensed in Montana and is not so licensed. Insurers may not accept placement of insurance on Montana risks from an unlicensed nonresident. (MCA 33-17-1103). Anyone selling insurance under an assumed or fictitious name must file with the Secretary of State, and furnish the commissioner with a copy of the certificate of assumed name to be shown on license. (MCA 33-17-211).

J. **Policy Countersignature Requirements:** None.

II. Commissions, Fees, Commingling of Funds, and Suitability in Annuity Transactions

A. **Commissions:** An insurer or insurance producer may not pay a commission to a person for services as an insurance producer unless the person performing the service holds a valid license. Sharing commissions with an unlicensed person is also prohibited. (MCA 33-17-1103).

B. **Fees:** Consultants may charge a fee provided there is a written memorandum signed by the party to be charged. The consultant must retain a copy of the memorandum or contract for not less than three years after the services are performed. Licensed consultants are prohibited from charging a fee for services in addition to commission for insurance related activities. (MCA 33-17-511).

C. **Disclosure Requirements:** None.

D. **Commingling of Funds:** All premiums or return premiums received by a producer must be held in a trust account, separate from other agency funds. Nonresidents must also comply, but the trust fund need not be established in Montana. Separate accounts need not be maintained for funds belonging to others, as long as the amounts held for each insured are reasonably ascertainable from the agency records. (MCA 33-17-1102).

E. **Suitability in Annuity Transactions:** In recommending to a consumer the purchase of an annuity or the exchange of an annuity that results in another insurance transaction or series of insurance transactions, the insurance producer or the insurer when an insurance producer is not involved must have reasonable grounds for believing that the recommendation is suitable for the consumer on the basis of the facts disclosed by the consumer as to the consumer's investments, other insurance products, financial situation, and needs.

Prior to the execution of a purchase or exchange of an annuity resulting from a recommendation, an insurance producer or an insurer when an insurance producer is not involved shall make reasonable efforts to obtain the customer's suitability information. (MCA 33-20-805). In this context, "suitability information" includes information reasonably appropriate to determine whether a recommendation is suitable, including the consumer's (1) age; (2) annual income; (3) financial situation and needs, including annuity funding resources; (4) financial experience; (5) financial objectives; (6) intended use of the annuity; (7) financial time horizon; (8) existing assets; (9) liquidity needs; (10) liquid net worth; (11) risk tolerance; (12) tax status; and (13) whether the consumer has a reverse mortgage. (MCA 33-20-804).

III. Statutory References:

MCA 33-2-	708
	1601, 1602
	1701
MCA 33-11-	103, 104, 108
MCA 33-17-	102, 103
	201
	211, 212, 214, 219, 220
	236, 237
	301
	408
	503, 504 , 511

MONTANA

	603
	1102, 1103
	1203, 1205
	1502
MCA 33-20-	804, 805
	1303, 1315

NEBRASKA

Department of Insurance
Terminal Bldg., 941 O St., Ste. 400; Lincoln, NE 68501;
Mailing Address: PO Box 82089
Lincoln, NE 68501-2089
Telephone: 402-471-2201; Fax: 402-471-6559
http://www.doi.nebraska.gov

I. Licensing Requirements: Sales Personnel—Producers, Business Entities, Limited Lines Insurance Reps., Managing General Agents. Other Insurance Professionals—Consultants, Consulting Corporations, Reinsurance Intermediaries, Third-Party Administrators.

A. Applicability: A person shall not sell, solicit, or negotiate insurance in this state for any class or classes of insurance unless the person is licensed for that line of authority in accordance with the Insurance Producers Licensing Act. (Neb. Rev. Stat. Ann. § 44-4050).

B. Licenses Required of Residents: The following must be licensed in Nebraska:

Sales Personnel

1. *Producers.*

   a. License fees (Neb. Rev. Stat. Ann. § 44-4064, https://nipr.com/licensing-center/state-requirements/nebraska-resident-renewal-individual):
      Initial fee: $100.
      Renewal: $50.
      Late Re-issuance fee (within thirty days after expiration): $90.
      Reinstatement fee (after thirty days and up to twelve months): $175.
   b. License term: Biennial, expiring on the last day of the licensee's birth month in which licensee's age is divisible by two. (Neb. Rev. Stat. Ann. § 44-4054).
   c. Lines of authority (Neb. Rev. Stat. Ann. § 44-4054):

      (1) Property.
      (2) Casualty.
      (3) Life and annuities.
      (4) Accident and health or sickness.
      (5) Personal lines.
      (6) Variable life and annuity products.

2. *Limited Lines Producers.*

   a. License fee: Same as producers.
   b. License term: Same as producers.
   c. Limited lines of authority (Neb. Rev. Stat. Ann. § 44-4049):

      (1) Credit (including credit life, credit disability, credit property, credit unemployment, involuntary unemployment, mortgage life, mortgage guaranty, mortgage disability, and Guaranteed Automobile Protection [GAP]).
      (2) Crop/hail.
      (3) Title.
      (4) Prepaid legal.
      (5) Travel insurance.
      (6) Surety.
      (7) Pre-need Funeral insurance.
      (8) Funeral insurance – Director.

3. *Title Insurance Agent* means an authorized person, other than a bona fide employee of the title insurer, who, on behalf of the title insurer, performs the following acts in conjunction with the issuance commitment of title insurance (Neb. Rev. Stat. Ann. § 44-19,108(14)):

   a. Determines insurability and issues title insurance commitments or title insurance policies, or both, based upon the performance or review of a title search or an abstract of title.
   b. Performs one or more of the following functions:

      (1) Collects or disburses premiums, escrow, or security deposits or other funds.
      (2) Handles escrows, settlements, or closings.
      (3) Solicits or negotiates title insurance business.
      (4) Records closing documents.

   Title Agents must file a $100,000 bond if performing escrow closings. (Neb. Rev. Stat. Ann. § 44-19,109(3)).

4. *Car Rental Limited Line Licensee.* Car rental companies must obtain a limited lines producer license.

   a. License fee: $50 new and renewal.
   b. License term: annual.

c. Lines of authority for a car rental limited licensee:

   (1) Personal accident insurance covering the risks of travel.
   (2) MotorVehicle Liability insurance, including uninsured and underinsured motorist coverage.
   (3) Personal property insurance.

d. Other requirements: Trained and supervised employees of a licensed car rental company can solicit insurance without a license as long as the car rental company is licensed. If the location is a franchise of a car rental company, the franchise must be licensed. A limited licensee must provide to the Director an updated list of all rental locations and of all employees of the limited licensee who may act on behalf and under the supervision of the limited licensee. Such listing shall be provided to the Director quarterly. (Neb. Rev. Stat. Ann. § 44-4067).

5. *Business Entities.* Corporations, associations, partnerships, limited liability companies, limited liability partnerships, or other legal entities must also be licensed (brokerage firms must be licensed as agencies), license expires April 30 annually. Fee: $50. Each person who sells insurance must be licensed. (Neb. Rev. Stat. Ann. §§ 44-4054, 44-4064).

6. *Portable Electronic Insurance Agent.* Vendors must obtain a limited line insurance license to sell or offer portable electronic insurance.

   a. License, renewal fee: $50.
   b. License term: Expires annually on April 30.
   c. Other requirements: Trained and supervised employees of a licensed vendor can solicit insurance without a license as long as vendor does not hold itself or employees as authorized insurers. (Neb. Rev. Stat. Ann. § 44-8506).

7. *Managing General Agents.* Must be licensed. License fee: $60. (Neb. Rev. Stat. Ann. §§ 44-4901 to 44-4903).

8. *Self-Storage Facility*

   a. License fee: $50 new and renewal.
   b. License term: Expires annually on the license effective date.
   c. A training program that has been approved by the director.
   d. A certificate from the insurer stating that they are affiliated with the applicant to act as the insurance producer for self-storage insurance.

e. Other requirements: Trained and supervised employees of a licensed self-storage facility can solicit self-storage insurance without a license as long as the self-storage facility is licensed. A limited licensee must provide to the Director an updated list of all self-storage facilities and of all employees of the limited licensee who may act on behalf and under the supervision of the limited licensee. Such listing shall be provided to the Director quarterly. (Neb. Rev. Stat. Ann. § 44-4069).

Other Insurance Professionals

1. *Consultants.* Must have been a licensed producer for at least three years. Fees: $50 initial; biennial renewal: $50; reinstatement fee: $90 + application fee. May be licensed in these authorities: life, health and annuities; and property and casualty. (Neb. Rev. Stat. Ann. § 44-2621).

2. *Consulting Corporations.* Consulting firm license expires annually on June 30, Initial fee: $50; Renewal: $50. (Neb. Rev. St. Ann. § 44-2627).

3. *Reinsurance Intermediaries.* Must be a licensed producer. Managers may be required to file a bond and E&O policy. License expires annually on April 30. License fee: $250.00 Renewal fee: $250. (Neb. Rev. St. Ann. § 44-5603).

4. *Third-Party Administrators.* Application fee: $200.

5. *Viatical Settlements Brokers.*

   a. Application and Renewal fee: $40.
   b. License term: Biennial, expiring on the last day of the licensee's birth month in which licensee's age is divisible by two.
   c. Brokers must maintain an E&O policy of at least $250,000. (Nebraska Admin. Code Title 210, Ch. 76, Section 003).

6. *Viatical Settlements Providers.*

   a. License and Renewal fee: $100.
   b. License term: Expires annually on April 30.
   c. Providers must show evidence of financial responsibility in the amount of $250,000. (Neb. Rev. Stat. Ann. § 44-1103).

7. *Utilization Review Agent.* Application fee: $300. Biennial renewal fee: $100. (Neb. Rev. Stat. Ann. §§ 44-5420, 44-5424).

8. *Surplus Lines.* Application fee: $250.

   Individual License Term: Biennial, expiring on the last day of the licensee's birth month in which licensee's age is divisible by two.

   Corporate License Term: Expires annually on April 30. (Neb. Rev. Stat. Ann. § 44-5504).

9. *Motor Club Representative.*

   a. Application fee: $5.
   b. License term: Perpetual, as long as they maintain at least one active company appointment.
   c. Applicant must either take the motor club exam or get appointed by a company that has a motor club training program approved by the DOI. (Neb. Rev. Stat. Ann. § 44-3716).

All license applications may be downloaded from the Department's Web site: http://www.doi.nebraska.gov/producers/license/.

1. *Producer License.* NAIC Uniform Application for Individual Insurance Producer License.

2. *Producer's Appointment.* All appointments and terminations must be done on-line at www.NIPR.com.

3. *Entity License.* NAIC Uniform Application for Business Entity Insurance License Form.

C. Appointments: An insurance producer shall not act as an agent of an insurer unless the insurance producer becomes an appointed agent of that insurer. An insurance producer who is not acting as an agent of an insurer is not required to become appointed. Fee: $8 (or retaliatory to the domicile of the insurer). Appointments, appointment terminations, and appointment renewals are processed online through the National Insurance Producer Registry (NIPR) at www.nipr.com. Questions concerning renewals may be directed to the Department at 402-471-4913, or DOI.Licensing@Nebraska.gov. (Neb. Rev. Stat. Ann. § 44-4061).

D. Licenses Required of Nonresidents: Nonresidents have the same license fees and term lengths as residents. Nonresident business entities and each person selling insurance must be licensed. Nonresidents must be appointed in Nebraska with the companies for whom they are writing business. Title agents must submit $100,000 bond if they are performing escrow closings. Nonresident licenses for business entities, renewals for business entities or individuals, and nonresident reinstatements can be done through www.nipr.com. (Neb. Rev. Stat. Ann. § 44-4055).

Multi-State Exposures: A license is not required for a nonresident insurance producer who sells, solicits, or negotiates a contract of insurance for commercial property and casualty coverage when risks that are to be insured under that contract are located in more than one state. This exception applies only if the nonresident is licensed to sell, solicit, or negotiate that insurance in the state where the insured maintains its principal place of business and the contract of insurance insures risks located in that state. (Neb. Rev. Stat. Ann. § 44-4051).

Applications may be downloaded from the Department's Web site at: http://www.doi.nebraska.gov.

E. Education Requirements:

1. Applicants for the following licenses must pass qualifying examinations administered by Prometric 800-853-4753 (http://www.prometric.com) or its successor.

   a. Producers.
   b. Insurance consultant licenses: life and annuities, sickness, accident, health; property and casualty.

   Applicants for the following licenses are exempt from the exam requirement: variable contracts, limited line credit, prepaid legal, surety, travel and surplus lines. Motor club only—no exam is required if a training course is taken through the insurer. (Neb. Rev. Stat. Ann. § 44-4068).

   Insurance consultants must have been licensed as producers at least three years or have completed a course of insurance study approved by the Commissioner. (Neb. Rev. Stat. Ann. § 44-2621).

2. *Nonresidents Producers.* Nebraska has reciprocal agreements with all other states waiving examination for nonresidents. (Neb. Rev. Stat. Ann. § 44-4055).

F. Continuing Education Requirements:

Number of Hours Required:

1. Life, accident and health or sickness, property, casualty, or personal lines property and casualty lines: twenty-one hours every two years.

2. Crop only: three hours every two years.

3. Title: six hours per line every two years.

4. Funeral only: six hours every two years.

5. Funeral director, pre-need and embalmer: three hours every two years.

   Licensee is not required to complete more than twenty-four hours every two years.

   In addition to above: three hours of ethics is required every two years. (Neb. Rev. Stat. Ann. §§ 44-3903 to 3905).

   Insurance consultants and brokers must follow the requirements above.

   The following licenses require no continuing education: Limited Lines Credit; Prepaid Legal; Surety; Travel; Surplus Lines; Credit Life; and Credit Accident and Health.

   The licensee may use classroom instruction or self-study.

Excess Hours: may not be carried into the next reporting period.

Renewal Procedure:

1. Course provider uploads completion credits directly to state database.

2. After completing all required hours for a two-year period, licensee is to either complete renewal process through www.NIPR.com or mail in a completed Producer Renewal Form along with their renewal fee. (Nebraska Admin. Code Title 210, Ch. 38, Section 017).

Nonresidents: are exempt from this requirement.

G. **Cancellation of Producer/Agency Contracts:** Insurers must notify the Insurance Department within thirty days after termination of any producer's appointment and the producer electronically through www.nipr.com, stating effective date and cause and circumstances. (Neb. Rev. Stat. Ann. § 44-4062). This information is privileged in any action between the insurer and the terminated producer.

H. Rules for Risk Retention and Purchasing Groups: Nebraska regulates risk retention and purchasing groups operating or offering coverage on risks in Nebraska. Risk retention groups domiciled in Nebraska must be chartered and licensed as liability insurers. Groups not domiciled in Nebraska must register with the Director of Insurance and submit reports to the Director as described in the law under Neb. Rev. Stat. Ann. § 44-4405. Purchasing groups must also register with the Director and submit reports as required by the law. Purchasing groups must pay an initial registration fee of $100, and a $100 fee every October 1st. (Neb. Rev. Stat. Ann. § 44-4417). Risk retention and purchasing groups doing business in Nebraska must use Nebraska licensed producers or Nebraska licensed surplus lines licensee. All risk retention group policies must show the following notice in at least ten-point type on the front page and on the declarations page of the policy:

NOTICE

"THIS POLICY IS ISSUED BYYOUR RISK RETENTION GROUP.YOUR RISK RETENTION GROUP MAY NOT BE SUBJECTTO ALL OFTHE INSURANCE LAWS AND REGULATIONS OF YOUR STATE. STATE INSURANCE INSOLVENCY GUARANTY FUNDS ARE NOT AVAILABLE FORYOUR RISK RETENTION GROUP." (Neb. Rev. St. § 44-4409).

Purchasing groups must include similar language as above if obtaining insurance from a risk retention group or nonadmitted insurer.

I. Other License Rules, Requirements, or Restrictions:

Employees of insurers or organizations employed by insurers who are engaging in the inspection, rating, or classification of risks or in the supervision of the training of insurance producers and who are not individually engaged in the sale, solicitation, or negotiation of insurance do not need to be licensed. (Neb. Rev. Stat. Ann. § 44-4051).

J. Policy Countersignature Requirements: None.

II. Commissions, Fees, Commingling of Funds, and Suitability in Annuity Transactions

A. Commissions: There is no restriction on division of commission among licensed resident or nonresident producers. The retaliatory requirement has been repealed.

Rebating of commissions is not allowed. The Nebraska statute also makes it a crime for an insured to accept a rebate of commission or "any valuable consideration or inducement not specified in the policy." However, if the producer extends interest-free credit for life, liability, or crop hail premiums, such extension of credit is not considered to be a rebate. (Neb. Rev. Stat. Ann. § 44-361).

A licensed agent who has 10 percent or more of his total commissions and fees come from business written upon himself, his relatives, his employer or his employees is presumed to be trying to circumvent the law against rebating. If such business accounts for 30 percent or more of the agent's total commissions or fees, it is conclusively presumed to be an attempt at circumvention. (Neb. Rev. Stat. Ann. § 44-361.01).

B. **Fees:** Consultants can collect a fee or a commission but cannot collect both at the same time. (Neb. Rev. Stat. Ann. § 44-2631). A producer also licensed as a consultant (or any office connected with the producer) may not receive any commission on sale of any insurance within the subject matter of any consulting services for which a fee has already been charged. (Neb. Rev. Stat. Ann. § 44-2616). Contracts for insurance consulting services must be in writing; must state the nature and extent of the services and the fee charged; and a copy must be retained by the consultant for at least five years after completion of the work. (Neb. Rev. Stat. Ann. § 44-2630).

C. **Disclosure Requirements:** None.

D. **Commingling of Funds:** Producer is a fiduciary for insurers' funds and must keep adequate record to account for them at all times. (Neb. Rev. Stat. Ann. § 44-319). Except for funds deposited with a title agent for purposes of escrow or closing, funds shall be deposited in a separate fiduciary trust account or accounts in a qualified institution no. (Neb. Rev. Stat. Ann. § 44-19,116).

E. **Suitability in Annuity Transactions:** The insurance producer, or an insurer if a producer is not involved, shall have reasonable grounds to believe that the recommendation is suitable for the consumer based on the facts disclosed by the consumer before making a recommendation to a consumer under the Nebraska Protection in Annuity Transactions Act. The recommendation shall be based on facts disclosed by the consumer relating to his investments, other insurance products, and the financial situation and needs of the consumer. This information shall include the consumer's suitability information, and, if there is a reasonable basis to believe the information, all of the following:

   1. That the consumer has been reasonably informed of various features of the annuity, such as the potential surrender period and surrender charge, potential tax penalty if the consumer sells, exchanges, surrenders, or annuitizes the annuity, mortality and expense fees, investment advisory fees, potential charges for and features of riders, limitations on interest returns, insurance and investment components, and market risk.

2. That the consumer would benefit from certain features of the annuity, such as tax-deferred growth, annuitization, or death or living benefit.

3. That the particular annuity as a whole, the underlying subaccounts to which funds are allocated at the time of purchase or exchange of the annuity, and riders and similar product enhancements, if any, are suitable, and in the case of an exchange or replacement, the transaction as a whole is suitable for the particular consumer based on his or her suitability information.

4. In the case of an exchange or replacement of an annuity, the exchange or replacement is suitable, including the consideration as to whether:

   a. The consumer will incur a surrender charge, be subject to the commencement of a new surrender period, lose existing benefits, such as death, living, or other contractual benefits, or be subject to increased fees, investment advisory fees, or charges for riders and similar product enhancements.
   b. The consumer would benefit from product enhancements and improvements.
   c. The consumer has had another annuity exchange or replacement and, in particular, an exchange or replacement within the preceding thirty-six months.

   Before the execution of an annuity resulting from a recommendation a producer shall make reasonable efforts to obtain the consumer's suitability. (Neb. Rev. Stat. Ann. § 44-8106).

III. Statutory References: Neb. Rev. St. §§ 44-361, 361.01; 44-1103; 44-2616, 2621, 2627, 2630, 2631; 44-3716, 3901 to 3905; 44-4049 to 4051, 4054, 4055, 4061, 4062, 4064, 4067 to 4069; 44-4405, 4409, 4417; 44-4901 to 4903; 44-5420, 5424, 5504, 5603; 44-8106, 8506; 44-19,108; 44-19,109; 44-19,116. Nebraska Admin. Code Title 210, Ch. 38; Ch. 76.

NEVADA

Department of Business & Industry
Division of Insurance
1818 E. College Parkway, Ste. 103; Carson City, NV 89706
Telephone: 775-687-0700; Fax: 775-687-0787
3300 W. Sahara Ave, Ste. 275; Las Vegas 89102
Telephone: 702-486-4009; Fax: 702-486-4007
http://doi.nv.gov

I. **Licensing Requirements:** Sales Personnel—Producers, Limited Line Producers, Managing General Agents, Entities. Other Insurance Professionals—Associate Adjusters, Consultants, Independent Adjusters, Motor Vehicle Appraisers, Public Adjusters, Reinsurance Intermediaries, Third-Party Administrators, Utilization Review, Viatical Settlements, External Review, Bail Agents, Bail Enforcement Agents, Funeral and Cemetery and Motor Club.

A. **Applicability:** A person shall not sell, solicit or negotiate insurance in this state for any class of insurance unless the person is licensed for that class of insurance. (N.R.S. § 683A.201). A producer of insurance shall not act as an agent unless he is appointed as an agent by the insurer. A producer who is not acting as an agent is a broker who does not need to be appointed. (N.R.S. § 683A.321).

B. **Licenses Required of Residents:**

Sales Personnel

1. *Producers.*

a. License fee:

(1) New and renewal: $125. (N.R.S. §§ 680B.010, 680C.110).
(2) Business entity/agency association or appointment: $50. Renewal of association: $50. Renewal of appointment: $15. (N.R.S. § 680B.010(34)
(3) Modification of existing license: $50.

b. License term: triennial.
c. Lines of authority:

(1) Life.
(2) Accident and Health.

(3) Property.
(4) Casualty, including surety.
(5) Personal lines.
(6) Variable annuities/variable life.
(N.R.S. § 683A.261).

2. *Limited Lines Producers.*

a. License fee: New and renewal: $125. (N.R.S. §§ 680B.010, 680C.110).
b. License term: Triennial.
c. Limited lines of authority:

(1) Credit. Includes the following: life, accident and health, property, involuntary unemployment, and guaranteed asset protection.
(2) Travel and baggage.
(3) Rental car agency.
(4) Portable electronics.
(5) Crop.
(6) Personal property storage insurance.
(N.R.S. § 683A.261).

3. *Fraternal Benefit Societies.* Fraternal Agents: Same fees and terms as producers. (N.R.S. § 695A.330). Initial fee to be paid to Commissioner: $1,000. The society must pay fees based on the amount of outstanding benefit contracts:

600 or less:	$250.
601 to 1,199:	$500.
1,200 or more:	$2,450.

(N.R.S. §§ 680C.110(5)(f), 695A.080).

4. *Managing General Agents.* License and renewal fee: $125. License term: Triennial. Appointment fee: $15 per insurer. Initial and renewal fee to be paid to Commissioner: $60. MGAs must submit a complete set of fingerprints. MGAs must provide a $50,000 surety bond. (N.R.S. §§ 680B.010(7), 680C.110(4)(i), 683A.160; NAC 683A.460).

5. *Title Agents and Escrow Officers.* License and renewal fee: $125. Business entity/agency affiliation or appointment initial fee: $50. License term: Triennial. Association renewal: $50. Renewal of appointment fee: $15 per title insurer. Initial and triennial fee to be paid to Commissioner: $60. Title agencies or title

insurers are required to provide a surety bond or substitute based on the average monthly balance in the trust account or escrow account. Bond amounts:

Balance of $1 million or less: $20,000.
Balance of $1 million to $12.5 million: 2 percent of balance.
Balance of $12.5 million or more: $250,000.

Amounts required may be offset. (N.R.S. §§ 680B.010(25, 34), 680C.110(4)(z, aa), 692A.028, 692A.060, and 692A.1041). Title agent and escrow officers applicants must submit livescan fingerprints or a complete set of fingerprints and applicable fees. (N.R.S. § 683A.251).

6. *Business Entities.* Resident corporations, partnerships, LLCs, and LLPs must submit to the Division of Insurance for purposes of name approval the following ***before*** submission to the Secretary of State:

   a. Corporation—articles of incorporation.
   b. Partnership—partnership agreement (all partners must be licensed).
   c. LLC—articles of organization.
   d. LLP—articles of organization.
   Upon approving the entity's name, the Department of Insurance will stamp the articles for the entity to submit to the Secretary of State.
   The articles must include the following phrase within the entity's purpose clause:
   "To engage in the business of insurance in all lines of authority permitted under the license issued in compliance with Nevada Revised Statutes (NRS) and Nevada Administrative Codes (NAC)." (N.R.S. § 680A.100).

   Business entities should complete the application online through Sircon.

Resident and nonresident business entities:

A producer contracted with an insurer must be appointed within fifteen days after the contract is executed or within fifteen days of the license being issued by the DOI. (N.R.S. § 683A.321).

Any individual selling, soliciting, or negotiating insurance risk on behalf of the business entity in this state must be designated to the business entity's license. Those persons are not required to be officers, directors, or partners in the business entity. Online processing is the preferred method for affiliating and removing affiliations with a business entity. Maintaining associations may be submitted online through the Division's Web site or through Sircon at www.sircon.com/nevada.

Fees: Licensing and Renewal: $125. Modification: $50. Appointment fee: $15.

7. *Bail.*

Bail Agents. Bail agents are appointed by authorized surety insurer. License and renewal fee: $125. Term: triennial. Affiliation fee: $50. Appointment fee per insurer: $15. Must post a $25,000 bond. (N.R.S. §§ 680B.010, 697.040, 697.190).

Bail Solicitors. Bail solicitors work for bail agents. License and renewal fee: $185. Term: triennial. Affiliation fee: $50. Must post a $10,000 bond. (N.R.S. §§ 680B.010, 697.060, and 697.190).

Bail Enforcement Agents. Must submit drug test results to detect the presence of a controlled substance, criminal history and psychological exam. License and renewal fee: $185. Term: triennial. Affiliation fee: $50. Must post a $50,000 bond. (N.R.S. §§ 680B.010, 697.173).

Bail agents, bail solicitors, and bail enforcement agents must all pay a $60 initial and renewal fee to the Commissioner. (N.R.S. § 680C.110(gg to ii)).

8. *Funeral and Burial Services.* Funeral and Cemetery Sellers: Funeral authority allows the licensee to sell services performed by funeral directors and include their sales of supplies and equipment for burial. They must post a $50,000 surety bond and submit fingerprint card. License and renewal fee: $125. Term: triennial, expiring at midnight on April 30 of the third year following the issuance of the license. (N.R.S. §§ 680B.010, 680C.110, 689.150, 689.175, and 689.185).

Cemetery authority allows the licensee to sell preneed contracts or burial merchandise or services for a cemetery. License and renewal fee: $125. Term: triennial. (NRS §§ 680B.010, 680C.110, and 689.480).

Funeral and/or Cemetery Agents work on behalf of a Funeral Seller and/or Cemetery Seller. The agents are affiliated with the applicable Funeral and/or Cemetery Seller. License and renewal fee: $125. Term: triennial. Affiliation fee: $50. (N.R.S. §§ 680B.010, 680C.110, 689.150 to 375, 689.450 to 595).

Funeral and/or Cemetery Agents that sell credit life insurance to fund a preneed contract must also have the appropriate producer license. (N.R.S. §§ 689.295, 689.550).

Other Insurance Professionals

1. *Associate Adjusters.* Employees of licensed adjusters. License and renewal fee: $125; plus the business entity/agency affiliation fee $60. Term: triennial. (N.R.S. §§ 680B.010(8), 680C.110(4)(l), 684A.030).

2. *Insurance Consultants.* License and renewal fee: $125. Term: triennial. May not hold any other insurance license. (N.R.S. §§ 680B.010(33), 680C.110(4)(k), 683C.010, 683C.070).

3. *Independent Adjusters.* License and renewal fee: $125 plus the business entity/agency affiliation fee, $60. Term: triennial. (N.R.S. §§ 680B.010(8), 680C.110(4)(l), 684A.030).

4. *Motor Vehicle Appraisers.* License and renewal fee: $125. Term: triennial. Motor vehicle appraisers must furnish a $2,500 bond. (N.R.S. §§ 680B.010(9), 680C.110(4)(n), 684B.010, 684B.030).

5. *Public Adjusters.* License and renewal fee: $125. Term: triennial. (N.R.S. §§ 680B.010(8), 680C.110(4)(m), 684A.030, 684A.070).

6. *Reinsurance Intermediaries.* License and renewal fee: $185. Term: triennial. Intermediary managers must file a $50,000 surety bond and maintain an E&O policy with limits determined by the commissioner. (N.R.S. §§ 680B.010(28), 680C.110(4)(e, f, g), 681A.330, 681A.420. NAC 681A.080).

7. *Third-Party Administrators.* Must hold a certificate of registration as an administrator. License and renewal fee: $125. Term: triennial. Surety bond of at least $100,000 is required. Refer to NAC 683A.155 for specific bond requirements. (N.R.S. §§ 680B.010(15), 680C.110(4)(h), 683A.025, 683A.085. NAC 683A.155).

8. *Utilization Review.* License and renewal fee: $250. Term: Annual renewal by March 1. Must include a summary of the plan for utilization review. (N.R.S. §§ 683A.376, 683A.378(2), 680C.110(4)(j)).

9. *Viatical Settlements.* Providers and brokers must be licensed. Provider's license and renewal fee: $1060. Term: annual. Broker's license and renewal fee: $560. Term: annual. (N.R.S. §§ 680B.010(32), 680C.110(4)(r, s), 688C.030, 688C.080).

10. *Independent Review Organizations.* Organizations must be registered in Nevada. License fee: $400. License fee for workers compensation reviews: $660. Renewal fee: $160. Term: annual. (N.R.S. §§ 680C.110(4)(c), 683A.3715. NAC 683A.640).

11. *Medical Discount Plans.* Must be registered in Nevada. Registration fee: $500. License and renewal fee: determined by whether it is a standalone plan or is registered by an insurer. Term: annual. (N.R.S. §§ 680C.110(4)(dd), 695H.050, 695H.080, 695H.090).

12. *Exchange Enrollment Facilitator.* License and renewal fee: $185. Term: Triennial. (N.R.S. §§ 680B.010(36), 680C.110(4)(kk), 695J.050). Concurrent producer license prohibited. (N.R.S. § 695J.210).

Application forms may be obtained from Insurance Division or online at: http://doi.nv.gov. Forms may be duplicated.

Fingerprinting:

All individuals applying for a resident license with the Nevada Division of Insurance (Division) must furnish a complete set of fingerprints. Applicants may have their fingerprints taken by a law enforcement agency or authorized vendor. LiveScan Digital Fingerprints services are the method for fingerprint processing. LiveScan Digital Fingerprinting services are also conveniently available through Pearson VUE. Applicants may register to have their fingerprints taken at the same time they register for the state exam. The LiveScan fingerprinting fee is $36.25 plus the vendor's processing fee. Applicants will be provided a receipt which indicates the date the prints were submitted to the Nevada Criminal History Records Repository. The applicants must provide the receipt in place of the physical fingerprint cards when applying for a license and provide the Division with the Civil Applicant Waiver acknowledging authorization of the fingerprint request.

Applicants that utilize hardcopy fingerprint cards may experience delays due to the time required to manually process the paper filing. Applicants utilizing hardcopy cards must provide a money order or cashier's check in the amount of $36.25 made payable to the Department of Public Safety (DPS) must accompany the fingerprint cards.

Hardcopy prints must include the printed name, signature, address, SSN, date of birth, place of birth, weight, height, sex, hair color, citizenship, home and business address of the person being fingerprinted. The Division's ORI number, Miscellaneous NO MNU Number, and the statutory reason for being fingerprinted must also be included on the cards.

Individual applicants are required to submit fingerprints for a criminal history background check. Individuals applicants must also submit the Fingerprint Background Waiver with their application. This waiver authorizes the Division to access the applicant's criminal history from the Federal Bureau of Investigations and State of Nevada and outlines the rights retained by the applicant. To expedite the application process, the Division encourages candidates to get their LiveScan prints done prior to taking their state exam. Pearson VUE contracts with MorphoTrust to offer digital fingerprinting. Candidates can make a fingerprint reservation online or may contact MorphoTrust, USA™ at (866)761-8069 (https://doi.nv.gov/Licensing/Online-Services/).

All licenses remain in effect unless revoked, suspended, or otherwise terminated if a request for a renewal is submitted on or before the date specified in the license. (N.R.S. § 683A.261).

C. **Appointments:** An insurer must appoint and notify the Division within fifteen days after the contract is executed or initial Nevada license is issued. If a producer is licensed in Nevada, the insurer has "fifteen days after the first application for insurance is submitted" to appoint a producer. Nevada generates an Annual Appointment Invoice by July 1 of each year. Fee: $15 per producer per insurer, annually. The invoice is due within sixty days of the invoice print date. Companies that subscribe to SIRCON or National Insurance Producer Registry (NIPR) may obtain a listing of the appointments currently on record with the Division. Appointments that are no longer active may be terminated via SIRCON Compliance Express or the NIPR Company Appointment Reconciliation Report (CARR). For more information contact SIRCON at www.sircon.com or NIPR at www.nipr.com. (N.R.S. § 683A.321).

D. **Licenses Required of Nonresidents:** Nonresidents are licensed on a reciprocal basis as producers. (N.R.S. § 683A.271). Nonresident applicants are encouraged to submit their application electronically at http://www.sircon.com/nevada, or at http://www.nipr.com. Electronic processing fees apply.

Nonresident Producers follow the same fee schedule as Resident Producers.

Resident and nonresident applicants are encouraged to submit their applications electronically utilizing http://doi.nv.gov, www.sircon.com/nevada, or http://www.nipr.com. Electronic processing fees apply. Effective July 1, 2015, Nevada ceased mailing issued and renewal licenses. Once a license is issued or renewed, it is the licensees responsibility to print their license utilizing the Division's licensing portal powered by Vertafore (Sircon) at www.sircon.com/nevada. The licensee must create a Sircon ProducerEdge account in order to print their licenses.

Multi-State Exposures. When writing a risk with even an incidental exposure in Nevada (such as a car on a fleet policy), the nonresident must be licensed in Nevada. (N.R.S. § 683A.271).

E. Prelicensing Examination and Education Requirements:

1. *Residents.*

   a. Producers: Any one of life insurance, accident and health insurance, property insurance, casualty insurance, or personal lines insurance requires fifteen hours. For a course that combines life and health insurance, at least thirty-five hours are required. For a course that combines property and casualty insurance at least thirty-five hours are required. For a course that combines life and health, property, and casualty, at least seventy-five hours are required. For a course that combines life and health, property, casualty, and personal lines, ninety-five hours are required. (NAC 683A.221). Producers are exempt from pre-licensing educational requirements if they hold one or more the following:

      Life insurance: CEBS, CFP, CIC, ChFC, CLU, FLMI, or LUTCF
      Accident and Health insurance: CEBS, HIA, REBC, or RHU
      Property, casualty, or personal lines: AAI, ARM, CIC, or CPCU
      (NAC 683A.170).

   b. Fraternal producers (life and health, qualification): Thirty-five hours of education in the applicable lines of authority; exam in appropriate line(s). (NAC 683A.221; N.R.S. § 695A.330).
   c. Bail agents: one year's residence in Nevada; completion of a six hour bail bonds course; bail exam. (N.R.S. § 697.150).
   d. Bail solicitors: three months' residence in Nevada; six hour bail bonds course; bail exam. (N.R.S. § 697.170).
   e. Bail enforcement agents: eighty hours of training; bail exam. (N.R.S. §§ 697.173, 697.177).
   f. Consultants: Same as Producers (NAC 683A.180, 683A.221).

   Exams are administered by PearsonVue, 800-274-2609; http://www.Pearsonvue.com. Exam fee $61 for vouchers for Life/Health Combo or Property/Casualty Combo exams. $51 for vouchers for Life, Health, Property, Casualty, Bail Bonds, or Personal Lines exams.

2. *Nonresidents.* Are exempt from all prelicensing requirements. (N.R.S. § 683A.271).

F. Continuing Education Requirements:

Number of Hours required: Producers must have thirty hours of continuing education triennially, of which three hours must be in the category of ethics. The course work must be in the licensed line. Bail licensees, three hours triennially. The licensee may use approved classroom instruction or self-study. Submit proof of completion with triennial license renewal. CE course verification and transcript verification are viewable at http://www.sircon.com/nevada. (NAC 683A.330).

Excess Hours: May not be carried into the next reporting period. (NAC 683A.355).

Final Exam: The final exam for a self-study course must be monitored. The monitor may be a training director, manager, supervisor or other professional. It cannot be a relative or subordinate. (NAC 683A.335).

Requirements **Not** *Applicable to the Following:*

1. Licensees with the following designations: CLU, CPCU, CIC, CFP, or ChFC must complete an exemption form for approval.

2. Licensees with twenty years of continuous insurance industry experience as their primary source of income must complete an exemption form for approval.

3. Limited lines licensees (credit insurance, travel, and fixed annuities).

(N.R.S. §§ 683A.242, 683A.291).

Renewal Procedure:

1. Course provider supplies licensee with certificate of completion and must enter completions in SIRCON.

2. Producers may renew online through Sircon at www.sircon.com/Nevada. The original certificate of completion of continuing education need only be provided if the education credits are not reflected in the individual's transcripts at www.sircon.com/nevada. (NAC 683A.330). Once a license is issued or renewed, it is the licensee's responsibility to print their license utilizing the Division's licensing portal powered by Vertafore (Sircon) at www.sircon.com/nevada. The licensee must create a Sircon ProducerEdge account in order to print their licenses at no charge.

Nonresidents: Exempt from this requirement.

G. **Cancellation of Producer Contracts/Producer Appointments:** Appointment terminations for any reason, must be reported to the Division within thirty days after the effective date of the termination. Terminations for cause require the insurer to submit documentation to the Division and notification to the producer within fifteen days after notifying the Division. (N.R.S. § 683A.331).

H. **Rules for Risk Retention and Purchasing Groups:** Nevada regulates risk retention and purchasing groups operating or offering coverage on risks in Nevada.

Risk Retention Groups: Domestic – Captives: Initial registration and Renewal: $250. Term: annual. (N.R.S. §§ 680B.010(30, 31), 680C.110(4)(cc)). Risk retention groups domiciled in Nevada must be chartered and licensed as a liability insurer. (N.R.S. § 695E.140). Groups not domiciled in Nevada must register with the insurance commissioner, pay the Initial Registration: $250. Renewal: $250 and submit reports to the commissioner. (N.R.S. § 695E.150). Risk retention groups registered in Nevada and chartered outside of Nevada must pay a premium tax of two percent. (N.R.S. § 680B.0353). All risk retention groups must comply with all Nevada insurance laws, including licensing and solicitation requirements or restrictions. (N.R.S. § 695E.140). All risk retention group policies must show the following notice in at least ten point type on the front page and on the declarations page of the policy:

NOTICE

> "This policy is issued by your risk retention group. Your risk retention group may not be subject to all of the insurance laws and regulations of your state. State insolvency guaranty funds are not available for your risk retention group." (N.R.S. § 695E.180).

Purchasing Groups: Initial registration and renewal: $100. Term: annual. (N.R.S. §§ 680B.010(35), 680C.110(4)(bb)). Purchasing groups must also register with the commissioner and submit reports as required by the law. (N.R.S. § 695E.120).

I. **Other License Rules, Requirements, or Restrictions:** Licensed nonresidents may solicit in state and maintain a physical location. The license must be made available for public inspection upon request. (N.R.S. § 683A.261).

II. Policy Countersignature Requirements

A. **Applicability:** Countersignature laws apply to all insurers and to all types of insurance on property or exposures in the state of Nevada (regardless of the residence of the insured or place where contract is made), except accident and health insurance, bid bonds issued in connection with any public or private contract, life insurance and annuities, reinsurance or retrocessions made by or for authorized insurers, policies issued to a risk retention group or member of a risk retention group, and policies on property of, or in transit with, common carriers. (N.R.S. § 680A.300).

B. Who Must Countersign: Insurer's duly appointed and licensed resident or nonresident agents must countersign all policies not exempted above, including all amending endorsements and renewal certificates.

C. Other Countersignature Requirements: Countersignature endorsement is prohibited except on multistate accounts. When executing an emergency bond and an authorized agent is not present, power of attorney may be used. When power of attorney is used, the bond must be subsequently countersigned by authorized agent. Countersigning producer maintains records of countersignature transactions, including daily reports, correspondence, names of agents and brokers who wrote the policies, and evidence of fees and commissions charged. The countersigning agent handles normal problems arising between agents and customers. (N.R.S. § 680A.300; NAC 680A.410).

III. Commissions, Fees, Commingling of Funds, and Suitability in Annuity Transactions

A. Commissions: Rebating of commissions is not allowed. A producer who is appointed as an agent may pay a commission or compensation for or on account of the selling, soliciting, procuring or negotiating of insurance in Nevada only to a licensed and appointed producer of insurance of the insurer with whom insurance was placed or to a licensed producer acting as a broker. (N.R.S. §§ 683A.325, 683A.361).

B. Fees: Surplus lines brokers may charge a broker fee. Life and health producers, financial planners, or insurance consultants may charge a consulting fee but only with a written contract. An agent also licensed as a broker of casualty, property, or surety insurance that the agent sells to businesses can enter into an agreement for the agent to receive a fee, a commission paid by the insurer, or a combination of the two for consultation or related advice. A written contract must be signed by the agent and client, and be retained by the agent for not less than five years. (N.R.S. § 686A.230; NAC 686A.335).

C. Disclosure Requirements: A broker who represents a client in an insurance transaction shall disclose to the client:

1. That the broker may receive compensation in some form from an insurer.

2. The name and identity of the source of the compensation and whether the broker has any ownership interest in, or is under common control with, the person providing the compensation.

3. That the compensation received by the broker may differ depending upon the product and insurer.

4. The identity of any other person who will receive compensation from the insurer for assisting the broker in the insurance transaction.

These disclosures must be followed by a documented acknowledgment from the client that clearly indicates the client's understanding of the contents of the disclosure statement before or simultaneously with the consummation of the insurance transaction. In the case of a transaction consummated over the telephone or by electronic means, the client's understanding of the disclosure must be documented by the broker at the time of the transaction and followed by a documented acknowledgment by the client and the broker. (NAC 683A.716).

D. **Commingling of Funds:** Anyone handling insurer premiums must remit received premium, less any commissions, to insurer within fifteen days after receipt; or establish and maintain a trust account in an established financial institution in Nevada for such receipts. This trust account must be separate from any other funds of the individual or firm. However, funds of any insurer that has in advance in writing waived the segregation requirement may be commingled with other funds. (N.R.S. § 683A.400).

E. **Suitability in AnnuityTransactions:** Before an insurer or a producer of insurance recommends to a person the purchase of an annuity, or variable annuity, or the exchange of an annuity or variable annuity that results in the purchase or exchange of an annuity in accordance with the recommendation, the insurer or producer of insurance must make reasonable efforts to obtain:

a. The financial and tax status of the person.

b. The investment objectives of the person.

c. Any other information that the insurer or producer of insurance determines would be useful in making such a recommendation. (NAC 688A.455).

IV. **Statutory References:** Nevada Revised Statutes §§ 680A.100, 300; 680B.010, 0353; 680C.110; 681A.330, 420; 683A.025, 085, 160, 201, 242, 251, 261, 271, 291, 321, 325, 330, 331, 361, 3715, 376, 378, 400; 683C.010, 070; 684A.030, 070; 684B.010; 686A.230; 688A.455; 688C.030, 080; 689.150 to 375, 450 to 595; 692A.028, 060, 1041; 695A.080, 330; 695E.120, 140, 180; 695H.050, 080, 090; 695J.050, 210; 697.040, 060, 150, 170, 173, 177, 190. Nevada Administrative Regulations 680A.410; 681A.080; 683A.155, 170, 180, 221, 330, 335, 355, 460, 640, 716; 686A.335.

NEW HAMPSHIRE

Insurance Department: 21 South Fruit St., Ste. 14; Concord, NH 03301
Telephone: 603-271-2261 – Main; Licensing 603-271-0203
Fax: 603-271-1406 – Main; 603-271-7029 – Licensing
http://www.nh.gov/insurance/

I. **Licensing Requirements:** Producers, Limited Line Insurance Producers, Managing General Agents. Other Insurance Professionals—Adjusters, Public Adjusters, Reinsurance Intermediaries, Third-Party Administrators.

A. **Applicability:** An insurance producer shall not act as an agent of an insurer unless the insurance producer becomes an appointed agent of that insurer. An insurance producer who is not acting as an agent of an insurer is not required to become appointed. (N.H Rev. Stat. Ann. § 402-J:14).

B. **Licenses Required of Residents:** Each of the following must be licensed in New Hampshire:

Sales Personnel

1. *Producers.*

   a. License fee: Application and license fee: $210; Renewal fee: $150; Amendment: $50; Late completion of CE fee: $50; Late renewal fee: $150, plus renewal fee.
   b. License term: biennial.
      (N.H. Rev. Stat. Ann. § 400-A:29).
   c. Major lines of authority:

      (1) Life.
      (2) Accident and health or sickness.
      (3) Variable life and variable annuity products. (must hold life LOA) (residents only).
      (4) Property.
      (5) Casualty.
      (6) Personal lines.
      (N.H. Rev. Stat. Ann. § 402-J:7).

2. *Limited Line Producers.*

    a. Initial license and application fee: Application: $210; Renewal: $150.
    b. License term: Biennial.
    c. Lines of authority:

        (1) Credit. Sells or negotiates the following limited lines: credit life, credit disability, credit property, credit unemployment, involuntary unemployment, mortgage life, mortgage guaranty, mortgage disability, and automobile dealer GAP.
        (2) Travel agent.
        (3) Motor vehicle road service.
        (4) Surplus lines (must hold P&C LOA residents only).
        (5) Title.

        (N.H. Rev. Stat. Ann. § 402-J:2).

3. *Managing General Agents.* Original license: $350, plus $50 application fee; $250 annual renewal. Must first be licensed as producers. The commissioner may require a bond, E&O policy, or financial information and other data. (N.H. Rev. Stat. Ann. §§ 400-A:29(XX), 402-E:2).

Other Insurance Professionals

1. *Adjusters. Residents and nonresidents.* Application and license: $75. $75 biennial renewal on October 1. Late completion of CE fee: $25. License amendment: $50. Late renewal fee: $75, in addition to renewal. (N.H. Rev. Stat. Ann. §§ 400-A:29(XV), 402-B:10-a).

    Lines of authority:

    a. Property and casualty including workers compensation.
    b. Property and casualty excluding workers compensation.
    c. Workers compensation.

2. *Public Adjusters.* Application and license: $100. $100 biennial renewals on October 1. Must have five years of experience. Fee for late renewal: $100, plus renewal. Public adjusters must file a $20,000 bond or letter of credit. (N.H. Rev. Stat. Ann. §§ 400-A29(XVIII), 402-D:5, 402-D:11).

3. *Reinsurance Intermediaries.* Application and license: $350, plus $50 application fee; $250 annual renewal. Must be licensed as a producer. The commissioner may

require intermediary managers to post a bond and carry an E&O policy. (N.H. Rev. Stat. Ann. §§ 400-A:29(XXI), 402-F:2).

4. *Third-Party Administrators.* Application: $1000. Initial certificate: $100. Amendment: $25. Annual renewal: $100. Annual report fee: $100. (N.H. Rev. Stat. Ann. §§ 400-A:29, 402-H:11, 402-H:12).

Resident and nonresident adjusters who have a home state license must apply online via NIPR. Nonresidents without home state license or designated home state can apply online at https://sbs-nh.naic.org/Lion-Web/jsp/ext/login/UserVerification.jsp. See Department's Web site for access to links for online applications. www.nh.gov/insurance.

C. Appointments: An insurance producer shall not act as an agent of an insurer unless the insurance producer becomes an appointed agent of that insurer. An insurance producer who is not acting as an agent of an insurer is not required to become appointed. Lifetime appointment: $25. Appointment termination: $25. Appointments are submitted electronically only via National Insurance Producer Registry (NIPR). (N.H. Rev. Stat. Ann. §§ 400-A:29(X), 402-J:14).

D. Licenses Required of Nonresidents: Granted on a reciprocal basis. New Hampshire has no bond requirements for producers and no retaliatory requirements. Nonresident individual producers are required to apply for original and renewal licenses online with the NAIC at NIPR. (N.H. Rev. Stat. Ann. § 402-J:8).

Multi-State Exposures: A license is not required of a nonresident insurance producer who sells, solicits, or negotiates a contract of insurance for commercial property and casualty coverage when risks that are to be insured under that contract are located in more than one state. This exception applies only if the nonresident is licensed to sell, solicit, or negotiate that insurance in the state where the insured maintains its principal place of business and the contract of insurance insures risks located in that state. (N.H. Rev. Stat. Ann. § 402-J:4).

E. Licensing and Renewal Mode Options:

1. Resident individual producer new licenses and renewals: Residents must apply electronically via www.NIPR.com.

2. Resident business entities: Same as individual.

3. Nonresidents must apply electronically via NIPR.

4. Adjuster. Resident and Nonresidents with a home state adjuster license apply via NIPR. Renewals are electronic via NIPR.

   If a license expires and is renewed within two years of expiration, the reinstatement fee is $300. For expired licenses renewed more than two years after expiration, the rules of the initial application and licensing apply.

(nh.gov/insurance/producers/license.htm#renewal).

F. Prelicensing Examination and Education Requirements:

1. *Residents.* Producer applicants must pass a qualifying examination administered by Prometrics, 800-869-6603 or www.prometric.com/newhampshire, in the class or classes of insurance to be sold and on New Hampshire laws and regulations. Adjusters and public adjusters must pass an exam. CPCUs and CLUs must pass exam on laws and regulations only. The following producer exams are offered: Life, Accident & Health, Life Accident & Health, Property & Casualty, Title, Property, Casualty, Personal Lines, and Credit. The commissioner may impose and collect reasonable application fees in amounts to be determined by the commissioner from sponsoring organizations for submissions of continuing education courses to meet educational requirements established by rule for producers, consultants and adjusters. (N.H. Rev. Stat. Ann. § 400-A:29-a).

2. *Nonresidents.* License in home state or designated home state is required. New Hampshire is reciprocal with all states.

G. Continuing Education Requirements:

Number of Hours Required. Producers: Twenty-four hours, including at least three but not more than ten credit hours in ethics, biennially. Adjusters: twenty-four hours, biennially. Workers compensation adjusters: twenty-four hours (at least ten of which must be in WC). Public adjusters (resident and nonresident): fifteen hours, biennially. The DOI does not prescribe course content. The licensee may use classroom instruction, online, or self-study. (N.H. Rev. Stat. Ann. § 402-B:5-a. N.H. Admin. Rules, Ins. 1302.03) (http://www.gencourt.state.nh.us/rules/state_agencies/ins1300.html.)

The New Hampshire DOI approves courses in house and uses its NAIC partner state-based systems for compliance tracking.

CE completion is required no later than sixty days prior to license expiration date.

Passing the licensing exam satisfies CE requirements for the first renewal period.

Excess Hours: may not be carried into next reporting period.

Final Exam: The final exam for a self-study course does not need to be monitored.

Nonresident Adjusters: If a nonresident licensee has complied with the continuing education requirements of her state of residence or designated home state she will not be required to comply with the requirements of this state (N.H. Rev. St. Ann. § 402-B:5-a).

Nonresident Producers: Exempt from NH CE since all states have a CE requirement for producers in accordance with the Model Producer Licensing Act.

Renewal Procedure: Reminder notices will be emailed with instructions.

H. **Cancellation of Agency Appointments/Producer Contracts:** After termination of a producer's contract, the commissioner must be notified within fifteen days. The insurer must renew all policies that still meet the underwriting requirements for one year. Any risk that does not meet the underwriting requirements must be given sixty days' notice of nonrenewal. Insurer must give the agent a ninety-day notice of its intent to terminate the contract. Fee for termination: $25. (N.H. Rev. Stat. Ann. §§ 400-A:29, 402-J:14, 402-J:15).

I. **Rules for Risk Retention and Purchasing Groups:** Risk retention groups must be licensed and organized as liability insurers. Purchasing groups must be registered with the state. A purchasing group may not purchase insurance on behalf of its New Hampshire members from a risk retention group that is not chartered in a state or from an insurer not admitted in New Hampshire, unless the purchase is effected through a licensed agent or broker acting pursuant to the surplus lines laws and regulations of New Hampshire. (N.H. Rev. Stat. Ann. §§ 405-A:1 to 405-A:13).

Policies issued by risk retention groups must contain the following wording in ten-point type:

NOTICE

This policy is issued by your risk retention group. Your risk retention group may not be subject to all of the insurance laws and regulations of your state. State insurance insolvency guaranty funds are not available for your risk retention group." (N.H. Rev. St. § 405-A:3).

J. **Other License Rules, Requirements, or Restrictions:** An unlicensed nonresident may not enter this state to sell, solicit, or negotiate contracts of insurance. (N.H. Rev. Stat. Ann. § 406-B:3).

K. **Policy Countersignature Requirements:** Foreign insurance or surety companies, although authorized to transact business within the state, shall only make or write policies of insurance which are to be effective in this state through producers who are licensed and properly appointed to transact business in this state. (N.H. Rev. Stat. Ann. § 405:17-b).

L. **Portable Electronics Insurance:** A vendor shall hold a limited lines license to sell or offer coverage under a policy of portable electronics insurance. Portable electronics insurance is coverage for the repair or replacement of portable electronics which may provide coverage for portable electronics against any one or more of the following causes of loss: loss, theft, inoperability due to mechanical failure, malfunction, damage, or other similar causes of loss. Application and License fee: $1,000 ($100 if operating in ten or few locations). Renewal fee: $500 ($100 if operating in ten or few locations). Portable electronics include but are not limited to cell phones, navigation devices, iPods and tablets. (N.H. Rev. Stat. Ann. §§ 402-K:1 to 402-K:7).

II. Commissions, Fees, Commingling of Funds, Suitability in Annuity Transactions

A. **Commissions:** There are no restrictions on distribution of commission between licensed agent and licensed nonresident except the anti-rebating law. (N.H. Rev. Stat. Ann. § 402-J:13).

B. **Fees:** Rebating of premiums is prohibited. Producers may collect either a commission or a service fee, but not both. (N.H. Rev. Stat. Ann. §§ 417:4(IX), 402-J:13).

C. **Disclosure Requirements:** Any contract or agreement with an insurance consultant must be in writing, in duplicate, signed by the person to be charged and plainly specifying the amount of the fee to be paid and the services to be rendered. (N.H. Rev. Stat. Ann. § 405:44-d).

D. **Commingling of Funds:** All insurance producers must establish a premium trust account. The Insurance Department states that the signature card for such an account carry the following statement: "This is an insurance premium trust account maintained under the provisions of Chapter Ins. 4300." Checks drawn on the premium trust account shall bear the notation "Premium Trust Account." (N.H. Admin. Rules, Ins. § 4301.04).

E. **Suitability in Annuity Transactions:** In recommending to a consumer the purchase of an annuity or the exchange of an annuity that results in another insurance transaction or series of insurance transactions, the insurance producer, or the insurer where no producer is involved, shall have reasonable grounds for believing that the recommendation is suitable for the consumer on the basis of the facts disclosed by the consumer as to his or her investments and other insurance products and as to his or her financial situation and needs.

Prior to the execution of a purchase or exchange of an annuity resulting from a recommendation, an insurance producer, or an insurer where no producer is involved, shall make reasonable efforts to obtain information concerning the consumer's financial and tax status, investment objectives, and other information considered to be reasonable in making recommendations to the consumer. (N.H. Admin. Rules, Ins. § 305.05).

III. **Statutory References:** N.H. Rev. Stat. Ann. §§ 400-A:29, A:29-a; 402-B:5-a, B:10-a; 402-D:5, D:11; 402-E:2; 402-F:2; 402-H:11, H:12; 402-J:2, J:4, J:7, J:8, J:13 to J:15; 402-K:1 to K:7; 405:17-b, 44-d; 405-A:1 to A:13; 406-B:3; 417:4. N.H. Admin. Rules, Ins. 305.05; 1302.03; 4301.04.

NEW JERSEY

Commissioner of Banking and Insurance
20 W. State St. 10th Fl.,
P.O. Box 327 325; Trenton, NJ 08625
Telephone: 609-292-7272; Hotline: 1-800-446-7467; Fax: 609-984-5263
Email: inslic@dobi.nj.gov
http://www.state.nj.us/dobi/index.html

I. Licensing Requirements: Sales Personnel—Producers, Limited Line Producers, Consultants, Managing General Agents. Other Insurance Professionals—Public Adjusters, Reinsurance Intermediaries, Viatical Settlements.

A. Applicability: A person shall not sell, solicit or negotiate insurance in New Jersey unless the person is licensed for that line of authority. (N.J. Stat. § 17:22A-29).

B. Licenses Required of Residents: An applicant for a resident license may either be a resident of New Jersey or have his or her principal place of business in New Jersey. Only the following are permitted to conduct insurance sales activity in New Jersey.

Sales Personnel

1. *Producers.* Individuals, partnerships, and corporations that act as insurance agents, brokers, consultants, managing general agents, or the agents of risk retention groups must hold a producer license.

   a. License fees:
   Individual license fee: $150, plus $20 processing fee for online submission or $40 processing fee for paper submission.
   Fingerprinting: $66.05 Live Scan Fee, paid to the vendor at the time of Live Scan.
   Each additional line of authority: $20 for online filing or $40 for paper filing. (N.J.A.C. 11:17-2.12, 2.13).
   Business Entity License Fee: $150, plus $20 processing fee for online submission or $40 processing fee for paper submission for a total of $170 or $190.
   Fingerprinting: $66.05 Live Scan Fee, paid to the vendor at the time of Live Scan. The fingerprinting requirement applies to each officer, partner, director, or owner of more than 10 percent of the entity.
   Renewal Fee: $150 for online. There is an additional $20 processing fee for paper filings. Each additional line of authority: $20 for online filing or $40 for paper filing. (N.J.A.C. 11:17-2.12, 2.13). Late Renewal Fees: $100.
   Additional line of Authority: $20 online; $40 paper application.

N.J. Stat. § 17:22A-44(e) allows the Commissioner to waive the initial licensing fees for disabled US war veterans who have been honorably discharged, or under honorable conditions from a branch of the active or reserve component of the Armed Forces of the United States or the National Guard of any state.

b. License term: Biennial expiring on the last day of the birth month of the producer for individual licensees, and for business entity licensees, biennial on May 31. If the term of the license for new producers would be less than eighteen months, the license will instead expire the following year. (N.J.A.C. 11:17-2.1).
c. Lines of authority:

(1) Life.
(2) Variable life and variable annuity.
(3) Accident and health or sickness.
(4) Property.
(5) Casualty.
(6) Personal lines.
(7) Title.
(8) Surplus lines.
(N.J.A.C. 11:17-2.2).

Organizations licensed as producers must have at least one partner or officer (Designated/responsible licensed producer) who also holds a valid producer's license for the same type(s) of authority.

2. *Limited Lines.*

a. License fees:
Individuals license fee: $75 fee, plus $20 processing fee for online submission or $40 processing fee for paper submission.
Initial processing fee: $20 online; $40 paper application.
Fingerprinting: $66.05 Live Scan fee.
Business entity license fee: $75 license fee plus $20 processing fee for online submission or $40 processing fee for paper submission.
Renewal fee: $75 online, additional $20 for paper processing. Each additional line of authority: $20 for online filing or $40 for paper filing. Each additional line of authority: $20 for online filing or $40 for paper filing. (N.J.A.C. 11:17-2.12, 2.13; N.J. Stat. § 17:22A-44).
Late renewal fee: $50.
Additional line of authority: $20 online; $40 paper application.

Business entities must complete fingerprint forms for each officer, director, partner or owner of 10 percent or more of the applicant business entity. (N.J.A.C. 11:17-2.12).

b. License term: The expiration dates for new and existing individual licensees will be biennial on the last day of the birth month of the producer, and for business entity licensees, biennial on May 31. If the term of the license for new producers or those transitioning to the biennial license would be less than eighteen months if renewed in the second birth month (or May 31 for agencies) following issuance or renewal, the license will instead expire the following birth month (or May 31 for agencies). (N.J.A.C. 11:17-2.1).
c. Lines of authority:

(1) Bail bonds – Requires fingerprinting.
(2) Credit life or health.
(3) Credit involuntary unemployment.
(4) Credit property and casualty.
(5) Ticket life, accident, or property and casualty.
(6) Group mortgage cancellation.
(7) Mortgage guaranty.
(8) Legal expense insurance.
(9) Self-storage personal property insurance.
(10) Car rental insurance.
(11) Travel insurance.
(12) Pet insurance.
(N.J.A.C. 11:17-1.2, 2.2).

Business Entity applicants should submit the following with the application:

a. Corporations—articles of incorporation.
b. Limited Liability Companies (LLCs)—articles of organization.
c. Partnerships—partnership agreements. (N.J.A.C. 11:17-2.3).

Licensing Exception for Fraternal Benefit Societies: Individuals acting as insurance producers with respect to societies shall be licensed in accordance with the provisions of the "New Jersey Insurance Producer Licensing Act of 2001." Notwithstanding the provisions of this section or of any other law to the contrary, a license as an insurance producer is not required of any agent, representative or member of a fraternal benefit society who devotes, or intends to devote, less than 50 percent of his time to the solicitation and procurement of insurance contracts for that fraternal benefit society and who receives, or intends to receive, any commission or other compensation directly dependent on the amount of insurance. Any person who in the preceding calendar year has solicited or procured any of the following contracts of insurance on behalf of a fraternal benefit society shall be presumed to have devoted, or intended to devote, 50 percent of his time to the solicitation or procurement of insurance contracts:

a. Life insurance contracts that, in the aggregate, exceed $200,000 of coverage for all lives insured for the preceding calendar year.
b. A permanent life insurance contract offering more than $10,000 of coverage on an individual life.
c. A term life insurance contract offering more than $50,000 of coverage on an individual life.
d. An insurance contract, other than a life insurance contract, that the fraternal benefit society may write that insures the individual lives of more than twenty-five persons.
e. Any variable life insurance or variable annuity contract.
f. Any funeral insurance policy, as defined in N.J. Stat. § 17B:17-5.1. (N.J. Stat. § 17:44B-32).

Other Insurance Professionals

1. *Public Adjusters.* Must be licensed, pursuant to the Public Adjusters Licensing Act. Initial fee: $50, plus $20 processing fee. In addition, a fee of $66.05 for Live Scan electronic fingerprinting, which is paid to the vendor at the time of Live Scan. Renewal fee: $50. Must post a $10,000 bond. Business entities must complete fingerprint forms for each officer, director, partner or owner of 10 percent or more of the applicant business entity. (N.J.A.C. 11:1-37.9, 11:1-37.18). The licensure period is two years and requires the completion of fifteen hours of continuing education during each subsequent two-year licensure period as a condition of license renewal. The expiration date for new and existing licenses will be biennial on the last day of the birth month of the public adjuster; in the case of a business entity, biennial on May 31. (N.J.A.C. 11:1-37.3, 11:1-37.4).

2. *Reinsurance Intermediaries.* Must be licensed as a producer. Application fee: $20. Intermediary-managers must file a bond and E&O policy of either $100,000 or an amount equal to 25 percent of the gross amount of direct premium, up to $10 million. (N.J.A.C. 11:17-7.3).

3. *Viatical Settlements.* No person or business entity, unless a licensed viatical settlement provider, shall act on behalf of a viator residing in New Jersey unless that person:

   a. Has been licensed as a life producer in the home state for at least one year;

   b. Is a life insurance producer licensed in New Jersey; and

c. Has notified the commissioner and paid the appropriate fees not less than thirty days from the first date of negotiating a viatical settlement on behalf of a viator.

Once processed, the registration remains in effect as long as the New Jersey life producer license is in good standing.

Both individuals and business entities who are involved in the negotiation of viatical settlement transactions must have the life producer license and be registered with the Department. (https://www.nj.gov/dobi/division_insurance/viatical.htm).

Registration and processing fee: $120. (N.J. Stat. § 17B:30B-3).

Viatical settlement providers: A complete copy of the application package appears on the Department's Web site at https://www.state.nj.us/dobi/division_insurance/viatsettprov.htm . Application fee: $1,000.

4. *Managing General Agents.* Must be licensed as an insurance producer for the lines managed. Must maintain a surety bond and an E&O policy equal to either $100,000 or an amount equal to 10 percent of the direct written premium, up to $500,000. (N.J.A.C 11:17-6.3). Form for filing is available on the Departments Web site at https://www.state.nj.us/dobi/insliced/fmmganot.htm.

The New Jersey Insurance Department stopped printing and mailing licenses to insurance producers and public adjusters in August 2010. Insurance producers and public adjusters can print licenses, free of charge, via State Based Systems Connect at www.statebasedsystems.com.

C. **Appointments:** Any insurer authorized to transact business in New Jersey may, by written contract, appoint as its agent, a person that holds a valid insurance producer license. The contract shall authorize the insurance producer to act as an agent for the appointing insurer for all lines of insurance for which the insurer is authorized in New Jersey and the agent holds authority in New Jersey, unless specifically limited. The contract shall contain the duties, responsibilities and limitations of authority between the agent and the appointing insurer, and the agent shall abide by its terms. While the agent is properly licensed, an agency appointment shall continue in effect until termination in accordance with this act. Both the appointing insurer and the appointed agent shall maintain a copy of the agency contract in their office, and shall make the contract available for inspection by the commissioner upon request. (N.J. Stat. § 17:22A-42). Appointment/Termination Fee: electronic submission: $25; paper submission: $35. Renewal Fee: $25. (N.J.A.C. 11:17-2.12, 2.13).

All appointment notifications shall be renewed with the department annually on May 1. An insurer shall utilize the online appointment renewal process available through the National Insurance Producer Registry, located at http://www.nipr.com. The renewal appointment fee of $25 per appointment shall be collected from the insurer. All active appointments on record with the Department as of April 1 of the same year shall be subject to renewal. (N.J.A.C. 11:17-2.10, 2.13).

D. **Licenses Required of Nonresidents:** Nonresidents may be licensed as producers. Certification of valid current license from home state Department and power of attorney to commissioner for service of suit is required. Fees are the same as for residents. Written examination is reciprocal with licensee's home state. Nonresidents may write only lines for which they hold authority in home state. The same application forms are used for nonresidents as for residents. (N.J. Stat. § 17:22A-34).

Multi-State Exposures: A license is not required for a nonresident insurance producer who sells, solicits, or negotiates a contract of insurance for commercial property and casualty coverage when risks that are to be insured under that contract are located in more than one state. This exception applies only if the nonresident is licensed to sell, solicit, or negotiate that insurance in the state where the insured maintains its principal place of business and the contract of insurance insures risks located in that state. (N.J. Stat. § 17:22A-30(b)(6)).

Applications may be downloaded or submitted online at http://www.state.nj.us/dobi/inslic.htm.

E. **Prelicensing Examination and Education Requirements:**

1. *Residents.* New Jersey requires the following prelicensing education. Life: twenty hours. Accident and health or sickness: twenty hours. Property: twenty hours. Casualty: twenty hours. Title: twenty hours. Personal lines: twenty hours. Limited lines bail bonds: ten hours. Public adjusters: none. Viatical settlement: must hold life LOA. Surplus lines: none, but must hold a property and casualty license. (N.J.A.C. 11:17-3.4).

   Applicants for life, health, property, casualty, title, personal lines, bail bonds, surplus lines, and public adjuster licenses must pass a qualifying examination administered by PSI Exams (http://candidate.psiexams.com/index.jsp, or 1-800-733-9267). Exam fee: $47.

   Waiver of prelicensing education requirements may be granted for all authorities if:

   a. The applicant currently holds or has held within the past year a license granted by another state.

b. Applicant is a veteran of the United States armed services and has completed an approved course of veteran's education.
c. Successful completion of insurance subjects at an accredited college or university.

The commissioner may grant a waiver based upon additional professional designation(s) upon finding that the education necessary for the designation(s) satisfies the program of study required for prelicensing education in the applicable line of authority.

a. *Life.* Hold one of the following designations: Certified Employee Benefits Specialist (CEBS), Chartered Financial Consultant (ChFC), Certified Insurance Counselor (CIC), Certified Financial Planner (CFP), Chartered Life Underwriter (CLU), Fellow, Life Management Institute (FLMI), or LUTC Fellow (LUTCF).
b. *Accident and health or sickness.* Hold one of the following designations: Registered Health Underwriter (RHU), CEBS, Registered Employee Benefits Consultant (REBC), or Health Insurance Associate (HIA).
c. *Property, Casualty, or Personal Lines.* Hold one of the following designations: Accredited Adviser in Insurance (AAI), Associate in Risk Management (ARM), CIC, or Chartered Property & Casualty Underwriter (CPCU).
d. *Title.* Currently an attorney at law admitted to practice in New Jersey.

(N.J.A.C. 11:17-3.4(g)).

2. *Nonresidents.* Education and examination requirements for nonresident license applicants are reciprocal with the applicant's home state. (N.J.A.C. 11:17-3.4).

F. Continuing Education Requirements:

Number of Credits Required: Twenty-four credits, biennially. Three credits must be in approved courses related to insurance fraud or professional ethics.

Licensees may use classroom instruction, interactive online courses, and self-study courses. Twelve credits may be obtained each year by fulfilling the continuing education requirements for an approved professional insurance designation.

Excess Credits: Licensees who hold designations that have their own Continuing Education (CE) requirement. In this case, licensee should submit the state's alternative continuing education credit application, along with proof that the designation and required CE have been maintained for the licensing period.

Final Exam: Not applicable.

Requirements **Not** *Applicable to the Following:*

1. Nonresidents (those with business and home addresses outside of New Jersey).

2. Limited lines only.

Renewal Procedure:

1. The approved insurance education provider shall report the names and producer or public adjuster license reference number of those persons completing each continuing education course within fifteen days of course completion or certification of continuing education credits, whichever is later, either in hard copy or through electronic submission.

2. If credit is requested for coursework toward a professional designation or from a college course, licensee is to send the state's alternative continuing education credit application along with proof of passing to the DOI.

Nonresidents are exempt from this requirement. (N.J.A.C. 11:17-3.6).

G. Cancellation of Agency/Producer Contracts: In New Jersey, the term "termination" is synonymous with the term "cancellation." In case of termination of contracts, a ninety-day notice needs to be given to the agent prior to termination. The company shall pay a terminated agent who continues to service policies pursuant to the provisions of N.J. Stat. § 17:22-6.14a a commission that is not less than the amount provided for under the agency contract that was in effect at the time the notice of termination was issued. (N.J.A.C. 11:17-2.10; N.J. Stat. § 17:22-6.14a).

H. Rules for Risk Retention and Purchasing Groups: Risk retention groups must be licensed and chartered as liability insurance companies. All RRG policies contain the following notice in boldface ten point type:

NOTICE

"This policy is issued by your risk retention group. Your risk retention group may not be subject to all of the insurance laws and regulations of your state. State insolvency guaranty funds are not available for your risk retention group." (N.J. Stat. § 17:47A-3).

Purchasing groups must register with the commissioner before doing business in New Jersey. RRG and purchasing groups require a registration fee of $100. (N.J.A.C. 11:2-36.5, Appendices A and C).

I. **Other License Rules, Requirements, or Restrictions:** Unlicensed nonresident may not enter state to solicit, inspect, or service. Entering the state includes mail or telephone or other electronic communication into the state from the outside, as well as physical presence in the state. (N.J.A.C. 11:17A-1.4).

J. **Policy Countersignature Requirements:** No policy of insurance issued by a risk retention group shall be required to be countersigned by an insurance producer residing in New Jersey. (N.J. Stat. § 17:47A-5(b)).

K. **Portable Electronics Insurance:** Insurance providing coverage for the repair or replacement of portable electronics that may provide coverage against any one or more of the following: loss; theft; inoperability due to mechanical failure; malfunction; damage; or other similar causes of loss. (N.J. Stat. § 17:22A-49). A vendor shall not sell, or offer to sell, coverage under a policy of portable electronics insurance unless licensed as a limited lines insurance producer. A license issued to a vendor shall authorize its employees to sell portable electronics insurance. An employee of a vendor of portable electronics shall not advertise, represent or otherwise hold himself out as an insurance producer for any purposes other than as a licensed limited lines insurance producer. Initial application fee: $1,000 ($100 if operating in ten or fewer locations); Renewal fee: $500 ($100 if operation in ten or fewer locations). Portable electronics include but are not limited to cell phones, navigation devices, iPods, and tablets. (N.J. Stat. §§ 17:22A-50, 17:22A-52).

II. Commissions, Fees, Commingling of Funds, Suitability in Annuity Transactions

A. **Commissions:** There are no restrictions on division of commission among licensed resident or nonresident producers. An insurer or insurance producer may pay or assign commissions, service fees, brokerages or other valuable consideration to an insurance agency or to persons who do not sell, solicit or negotiate insurance in this state, unless the payment would violate N.J. Stat. §§ 17:29A-15, 29AA-14, 29B-4, 46A-5, 46B-34, 46B-35, or 17B:30-13, or any other provision of law. Rebating of commissions is not allowed. (N.J.A.C. 11:17A-2.3, 11:17B-2.1).

B. **Fees:** Producers may charge fees for services, but only if fee does not exceed permissible amount under the law. Any fee charged must bear a reasonable relationship to the services provided and shall not be discriminatory. A new written agreement shall be entered into for each fee charged and each time a fee is charged. An initial agreement shall not be used as the sole basis to charge a fee for a renewal policy. No fees may be charged for services not actually performed. The insurance producer may not pay or return, or offer to pay or return, all or part of a fee charged as an inducement to purchase a specific policy, or coverage within a policy, or coverage from a particular insurer. No fees are permitted in connection with life or health insurance. (N.J.A.C. 11:17B-3.1, 3.2).

C. **Fee Disclosure Requirements:** Insurance producers acting as agents for an insurance company shall not charge or receive any fee on a policy to or from a policyholder or insured for services rendered as an insurance producer except for reimbursement of actual out-of-pocket expenses incurred obtaining documents and other materials related to the underwriting process for new automobile applications and subject to the limitations of N.J.A.C. 11:17B-3.2(a)(9).

Any insurance producer charging a fee to an insured or prospective insured shall first obtain a written agreement, which shall be separate and apart from all other agreements and applications, and shall contain the following provisions and no other provisions:

1. A clear statement of the amount of the fee to be charged and the nature of the service to be provided.

2. A statement that such fees are not a part of the premium charged by the insurance company and that such fees can be charged only if the insured consents in writing.

3. A clear statement as to whether a commission will be received from the purchase of insurance.

4. The signature of the insured or prospective insured and the licensed insurance producer and the date of execution of the agreement. (N.J.A.C 11:17B-3.1).

D. **Commingling of Funds:** All premium funds shall be segregated and not in any manner commingled with any other funds of the insurance producer. Producers must maintain a trust fund for premiums collected for insurers separate from any other agency funds. (N.J.A.C. 11:17C-2.1 to 17C-2.3).

E. **Suitability in Annuity Transactions:** A producer, agent, representative of a fraternal benefit society not required to be licensed or an insurer, if no producer, agent, or representative is involved, shall not negotiate or sell an annuity to a consumer unless the producer, representative or insurer has reasonable grounds to believe that the annuity is suitable for the consumer on the basis of the facts disclosed by the consumer as to the consumer's investments, other insurance products, financial situation and objectives.

Reasonable efforts must be made to obtain and record information concerning the consumer's financial and tax status, investment objectives, or any other information considered to be relevant to provide reasonable grounds for believing the annuity is suitable for the consumer. (N.J.A.C. 11:4-59.4, 59.5, 4-59A.3).

III. Statutory References: N.J. Stat. §§ 17:22-6.14a; 17:22A-29, -30, -34; 22A-42, -44, -49; 22A-50, -52; 17:44B-32; 17:47A-3, -5; 17B:17-5.1; 17B:30B-3. N.J.A.C. 11:1-37.3, -37.9, -37.18; 11:2-36.5, -36-Appendices A and C; 11:4-59.4, -59.5; 11:4-59A.3; 11:17-2.1, -2.2, -2.10, -2.12, -2.13; 11:17-3.4, -3.6: 11:17-6.3; 11:17-7.3; 11:17A-1.4, -2.3; 11:17B-2.1, -3.1, -3.2; 11:17C-2.1 to -2.3.

NEW MEXICO

Office of Superintendent of Insurance
1120 Paseo De Peralta
4th Floor,
Santa Fe, NM 87501;
Mailing address: P.O. Box 1689
Santa Fe, NM 87504
Telephone: 505-827-4349, 1-855-427-5674; Fax: 505-827-4373
agents.licensing@state.nm.us
http://www.osi.state.nm.us/

I. Licensing Requirements: Sales Personnel—Insurance Producers, Entities, Limited Licensees, Managing General Agents, Bail Bond, Title, Car Rental, Solicitors. Other Insurance Professionals—Adjusters, Appraisers, Consultants, Motor Club Representatives, Reinsurance Intermediaries, Third-Party Administrators, Viatical Settlements.

A. Applicability: License required: A person shall not sell, solicit or negotiate insurance in this state for any class or classes of insurance unless the person is licensed for that line of insurance in accordance with the Insurance Code.

(N.M. Stat. Ann. §59A–12–4).

B. Licenses Required of Residents: Each of the following must be licensed in New Mexico:

Sales Personnel

1. *Producers*

a. License fee: $30.
b. License term: Biennial.
Biennial renewal fee: $60.
Appointment fee: $20 annually per line of insurance.
Annual continuation of appointment, per type of insurance, per insurer: $20.
Temporary license filing: $30.

(N.M. Stat. Ann. §59A–6–1).

c. Lines of authority:

(1) life insurance coverage on human lives, including benefits of endowment and annuities, and may include benefits in the event of death or dismemberment by accident and benefits for disability income;

(2) accident and health or sickness insurance coverage for sickness, bodily injury or accidental death and may include benefits for disability income;
(3) property insurance coverage for the direct or consequential loss or damage to property of every kind;
(4) casualty insurance coverage against legal liability, including that for death, injury or disability or damage to real or personal property;
(5) variable life and variable annuity products insurance coverage provided under variable life insurance contracts and variable annuities;
(6) personal lines property and casualty insurance coverage sold to individuals and families for primarily noncommercial purposes;
(7) limited line credit insurance; and
(8) any other line of insurance permitted under state laws.

(N.M. Stat. Ann. §59A–12–17).

2. *Limited Lines Producers.*

a. License fee: $30. Renewal fee: $60.
b. License term: Biennial.
c. Lines of authority:

(1) Transportation ticket sellers.
(2) Credit life, health, disability property, or involuntary unemployment insurance.
(3) Portable Electronics. Allowed by statute, but not issued by Superintendent of Insurance.

d. The superintendent may issue a limited insurance producer license to individual applicants employed full time by a vendor of merchandise or other property.

(N.M. Stat. Ann. §§59A-6-1, 59A-12-18, 59A-12-18.1).

3. *Bail Bondsmen Agent; Property Bail Agent.* Must post a surety bond, letter of credit, or certificate of deposit of $25,000. May be licensed for property or surety bail bonds. Initial fee: $30. Biennial continuation of license: $60. Appointment continuation fee: $20. Exam fee: $50. All bail bondsmen are required to file fingerprint impressions. The fee for the fingerprint impressions is $44.00, which consists of an FBI processing fee and DPS processing fee. Register at https://www.aps.gemalto.com/nm/index_NM.htm. (N.M. Stat. Ann. §§59A-6-1, 59A-51-3, 59A-51-8).

4. *Managing General Agents.* No separate license required, but must be licensed as an agent or broker to perform the functions of an MGA. The Superintendent may require a bond or E&O policy. (N.M. Stat. Ann. §59A-12B-3).

5. *Business Entities.* Each individual who will be selling insurance must be listed. A $30 fee per licensee is charged plus $60 biennial license continuation fee, $20 filing of individual affiliation and $20 annual continuation fee of individual affiliation. (N.M. Stat. Ann. §59A-6-1).

6. *Title Producer.* License fee is $30 ($60 biennial renewal), appointment fee is $20 ($20 annual renewal). Must operate or control an abstract plant consisting of a set of records in which an entry has been made of all documents or matters which under law impart constructive notice of matters affecting title to real property or any interest therein or encumbrance thereon, which have been filed or recorded in the county for which such title plant is maintained for a period of not less than twenty years immediately prior to date of application for license. (N.M. Stat. Ann. §59A-6-1, 59A-12-13).

7. *Car Rental Limited Line Licensee.* Car rental companies must obtain the car rental limited license.

   a. License fee: $30. Renewal fee: $60.
   b. License term: Biennial.
   c. Lines of authority for a car rental limited licensee:

      (1) Personal accident insurance covering the risks of travel.
      (2) Liability insurance, including uninsured and underinsured motorist coverage.
      (3) Personal effects insurance.
      (4) Roadside assistance and emergency sickness protection programs.
      (5) Any other travel or auto-related coverage that a rental company offers in connection with and incidental to the rental of vehicles.

   d. Other requirements: Employees in the car rental location can solicit insurance without a license as long as the car rental company is licensed. If the location is a franchise of a car rental company, the franchise must be licensed. (N.M. Stat. Ann. §§59A-6-1, 59A-32A-2, 59A-32A-3).

8. *Insurance vending machine license:*

   (1) filing application for original license and issuance of license, per machine: 25.00.

(2) biennial continuation of license, per machine: 50.00. (N.M. Stat. Ann. §59A-6-1).

Other Insurance Professionals

1. *Adjusters.* Staff adjusters and independent adjusters must be licensed to operate in New Mexico. Application fee: $30. Biennial continuation: $60. All independent adjusters must file at least a $10,000 surety bond, or cash bond in like amount, with the Superintendent. Residents and anyone designating New Mexico as the home state must take an exam and submit fingerprints.

   (N.M. Stat. Ann. §§59A-6-1, 59A-13-2, 59A-13-5).

2. *Insurance Consultants.* License requirement is not applicable to attorneys or public accountants when the individual is acting in that capacity. Application fee: $50; biennial renewal fee: $100. Exam fee: $75. (N.M. Stat. Ann. §§59A-6-1, 59A-11A-2).

3. *Motor Club.* Sales representative application fee: $30. Biennial renewal fee: $60. Motor clubs must have a $200 certificate of authority which renews for $100 annually. (N.M. Stat. Ann. §59A-6-1).

4. *Reinsurance Intermediaries.* Must be licensed producer. Intermediary managers may be required to carry a bond or E&O policy. (N.M. Stat. Ann. §59A-12D-3).

5. *Third-Party Administrators.* Application: $100; biennial continuation $200; exam $75; annual report $50. (N.M. Stat. Ann. §59A-6-1).

6. *Viatical Settlement Brokers.* Application fee: Brokers: $100 with $200 biennial renewal. Providers: $1000 license with $400 biennial renewal. Brokerages: $100 license; $200 biennial renewal; $20 filing of individual affiliation and annual continuation. (N.M. Stat. Ann. §59A-6-1).

   Application forms and instructions for licenses are available at https://www.osi.state.nm.us/index.php/producer-licensing-bureau/.

C. **Appointments:** Each insurer or other principal appointing a producer in this state shall file with the Superintendent a written appointment specifying the name and address of the appointee and the kinds of insurance or business to be transacted by the producer and pay the appointment fee, or license fee. Subject to continuation by the insurer or principal as provided in N.M. Stat. Ann. §59A-11-10, each appointment shall remain in effect until the producer's license is revoked or otherwise terminated, or there is earlier termination of the appointment. Fees: $20 per appointment per year; appointments may be completed and submitted online at www.nipr.com. (N.M. Stat. Ann. §§59A-11-10, 59A-11-12).

D. **Licenses Required of Nonresidents:** Application forms and fees are the same as those used by residents. (N.M. Stat. Ann. §§59A-11-23, 59A-11-24).

Multi-State Exposures: Even when writing a risk with only an incidental exposure in New Mexico (such as a car on a fleet policy), the nonresident needs a New Mexico license. Unlicensed nonresident may not enter state to solicit, inspect, or service. Entry by licensed nonresident is retaliatory with nonresident's home state. (N.M. Stat. Ann. §59A-12-25).

E. **Prelicensing Examination and Education Requirements:**

1. *Residents.* Applicants for the following licenses must pass a qualifying examination:

   a. Life.
   b. Accident and health or sickness.
   c. HMO.
   d. Health care.
   e. Prepaid dental.
   f. Property bail bonds.
   g. Casualty.
   h. Surety bail bonds.
   i. Property.
   j. Crop hail.
   k. Title guaranty.
   m. Property and casualty.
   n. Personal lines.
   o. Independent and staff adjusters.
   p. Public adjuster.

   Exams will be administered by PSI, 1-800-733-9267, https://candidate.psiexams.com/.

   Adjusters require one year of experience or special training. Bail bondsmen must complete ten hours of classroom training and 30 hours of on-the-job training. At the request of the applicant, the exam will be given in Spanish. (N.M. Stat. Ann. §§59A-12-16, 59A-13-4, 59A-51-4.1).

The following are exempt from the examination requirement:

a. CLUs for life and heath, or life or health LOA.
b. CPCUs for property, casualty, surety, marine and transportation, and vehicle LOA.
c. Temporary licensees.
d. Limited licensees.

2. *Nonresidents.* Examination requirement is retaliatory with applicant's home state requirement for nonresident licensees. (N.M. Stat. Ann. §59A-12-16).

F. Continuing Education Requirements:

Number of Hours Required: Twenty-four hours biennially. Ten hours biennially for title licensees. Bail bond solicitors, limited surety agents, property bondsmen, and solicitors, fourteen hours biennially. The course work must be in the area of license and must include three hours of ethics. For title licensees, at least three hours must cover the proper handling of escrow funds, which may satisfy the three hours required for ethics. The remaining hours should be designed to refresh the understanding of basic insurance principles and coverage, laws and insurance rules, and recent or prospective changes to them. A course may utilize any combination of formal classroom instruction, lectures, seminars, panel discussions, question-and-answer periods, correspondence courses, Web Based courses, courses on media disk, audiotapes, and videotapes as long as the provider can assure that a licensee has completed the course. No carry over credit is permitted. No repeating the same course for more credit within a three year period is permitted. Required hours for specialized training must be completed prior to transacting the type of insurance and may be used toward the twenty-four hour general requirement. (NMAC 13.4.7.9, 13.4.7.10).

Reporting Procedure:

Reporting is done by CE providers, who must report completion of CE courses to the superintendent. However, it is the responsibility of the individual licensee to ensure the superintendent's record reflect the completion of the required numbers of CE credits on or before the due date. Any discrepancies must be corrected by the licensee through the CE provider. (NMAC 13.4.7.12).

Requirements **Not** *Applicable to the Following:*

1. Agents of fraternal benefit societies.

2. Limited licensees.

3. Any insurance producer nonresident agent or nonresident broker continuously licensed for twenty-five years or more, without a lapse of ninety days or more.

4. Those holding a license for sole purpose of receiving renewal fee residuals and who do not otherwise transact the business of insurance.

5. Nonresident agents and nonresident brokers who are licensed in another state or country that requires completion of CE credits. (NMAC 13.4.7.2).

G. **Cancellation of Agency Contracts/Producer Appointments:** Insurers must give independent producers 180 days advance notice of termination of appointment with a statement of the reason for termination. The producer has one year after termination to renew existing policies that meet current underwriting standards at standard commission rates. The notice requirement does not apply if termination is for the following reasons:

1. Insolvency.

2. Abandonment.

3. Gross or willful misconduct.

4. Nonpayment to the insurer of money due to the insurer.

5. Fraud or intentional misrepresentation by the agent, either to the insurer or to an insured.

6. If the producer's license is revoked or otherwise terminated by the Superintendent. (N.M. Stat. Ann. §§ 59A-11-13, 59A-11-14).

H. **Rules for Risk Retention and Purchasing Groups:** New Mexico regulates risk retention and purchasing groups operating or offering coverage on risks in New Mexico. Risk retention groups domiciled in New Mexico must be chartered and licensed as liability insurers. Groups not domiciled in New Mexico must provide the following to the Superintendent before engaging in business in New Mexico: (1) notice of operation, including information required by the superintendent; (2) a copy of its plan of operation or feasibility study submitted to the superintendent in the groups state of charter, unless exempted by regulation; (3) a copy of the financial statement prepared by a person acceptable to the superintendent, including any examinations or audits of the group; and (4) a designation of the superintendent as the group's agent for the purpose of serving legal documents or process, with the fee determined by the superintendent. Purchasing groups must also register with the Superintendent and submit reports as required by the law. All groups and all resident and nonresident producers participating in them must comply with all New Mexico insurance laws, including licensing and solicitation requirements or restrictions. The Superintendent has authority to require notice to risk retention group customers that there is limited regulatory oversight and lack of insurance insolvency guaranty fund protection. (N.M. Stat. Ann. §§59A-55-1 to 59A-55-26). **Note**: The statute regarding the taxation of purchasing groups has been repealed.

I. **Other License Rules, Requirements, or Restrictions:** Unlicensed nonresident may not enter state to solicit, inspect, or service. Entry by licensed nonresident is retaliatory with nonresident's home state. (N.M. Stat. Ann. §59A-12-25).

J. **Policy Countersignature Requirements:** None, unless the policy is for health insurance. (N.M. Stat. Ann. §§59A-22-4, 59A-47-24). Purchasing groups and its insurers are exempt from any law that would require that any insurance policy issued to a purchasing group or any of its members be countersigned by an insurance agent or broker residing in New Mexico. (N.M. Stat. Ann. §59A-55-18).

K. **Portable Electronics Insurance:** Insurance covering the loss, theft, mechanical failure or malfunction of or damage to the portable electronics. New Mexico Statute offers a limited producer's license to applicants who are retail vendors or lessors of portable electronics or services. The license authorizes any employee or authorized representative of the vendor to produce such insurance. Currently the superintendent of insurance does not issue portable electronic line of authority. Portable electronics include but are not limited to cell phones, navigation equipment, iPods and tablets. (N.M. Stat. Ann. §§59A-60-1 to 59A-60-7).

II. Commissions, Fees, Commingling of Funds

A. **Commissions:** There are no restrictions on division of commissions among licensed resident producers. Licensees shall not share in commission for a kind of insurance for which the licensee does not hold a license. New Mexico-licensed nonresidents may receive entire commission unless nonresident's home state charges nonresidents a resident countersignature fee: in which case the rules of that state apply. Unlicensed residents or nonresidents may not receive commission on New Mexico business under any circumstances. Rebating of commissions is not allowed. (N.M. Stat. Ann. §§59A-12-24, 59A-16-17, -18).

B. **Fees:** No contract with a consultant for any advice, counsel, recommendation, or other information is enforceable unless the contract or agreement is in writing and duplicated by the person to be charged; the duplicate is delivered to the person to be charged once it is signed; it plainly specifies the amount paid or payable by the person to be charged; and is in a form currently approved by the superintendent. (N.M. Stat. Ann. §59A-11A-5).

C. Disclosure Requirements: None.

D. Commingling of Funds: All premiums a producer collects for insurers are trust funds. They must be remitted to the insurer within fifteen days or deposited in a trust account in an established financial institution, unless insurer has agreed in writing to permit commingling with other agency funds. (N.M. Stat. Ann. §59A-12-22).

III. References:

N.M. Stat. Ann. §§59A-	6-1, 11-10, 11-12 to 11-14, 11-23, 11-24, 11A-2, 11A-5
	12-13, 12-14, 12-16 to 12-18.1, 12-22, 12-25, 12B-3, 12D-3
	13-2, 13-4, 13-5, 16-17, 16-18
	22-4, 32A-2, 32A-3, 47-24
	51-3, 51-4.1, 51-8
	55-1 to 55-26, 60-1 to 60-7

NMAC 13.4.7.	2, 9, 10, 12

Web References:

https://www.osi.state.nm.us/index.php/producer-licensing-bureau/.

https://candidate.psiexams.com/.

NEW YORK

Department of Financial Services
Licensing Services Bureau
One Commerce Plaza, Suite 2003; Albany, NY 12257
Telephone: 800-342-3736
http://www.dfs.ny.gov

I. Licensing Requirements: Sales Personnel—Agents, Brokers, Limited Lines. Other Insurance Professionals—Adjusters (Independent and Public), Bail Bond Agents, Consultants, Mortgage Guaranty Agents, Reinsurance Intermediaries, Life Settlement Brokers.

A. Applicability: No person, firm, association or corporation shall act as an insurance producer, insurance adjuster or life settlement broker in New York without having authority to do so by virtue of a license. Unless licensed as an insurance agent, insurance broker or insurance consultant, no person, firm, association or corporation shall identify or hold himself or itself out to be an insurance advisor, insurance consultant or insurance counselor. (NY CLS Ins. §2102).

B. Licenses Required of Residents: Each of the following must be licensed in New York. License applications may be completed online or downloaded from the department's web site. All licenses may be eligible to renew up to 180 days prior to the expiration of the license. Separate renewal applications must be completed for each license held. An expired license may not be renewed; a relicensing application must be submitted. If an individual license has been expired for a term less than two years, the applicant may file a relicensing application electronically online at www.dfs.ny.gov. If an individual license has been expired for more than two years, the individual must retake the exam and submit a paper application, a passing score report and the appropriate fee; forms may be downloaded from the website.

Fingerprinting is required for the following resident licenses: Adjusters, Bail Bond Agents, Life Settlement Brokers, Life Settlement Providers, and Life Settlement Intermediaries. The New York State Division of Criminal Justice Services will only accept/process fingerprints electronically. The state has entered into a contractual agreement with MorphoTrust USA to provide electronic fingerprint processing services on a statewide basis for all individuals requiring a criminal background check. New York State Department of Financial Services applicants with an address in New York State are required to be electronically fingerprinted by MorphoTrust USA. See https://www.dfs.ny.gov/apps_and_licensing/fingerprinting_procedure.

Sales Personnel

Unless stated otherwise: For individual license holders born in an even numbered year, the license will expire on the license holder's birthday in an even numbered year. For individual license holders born in an odd numbered year, the license will expire on license holder's birthday in an odd numbered year.

1. *Resident Agents.* Application forms: Individuals, Corporations, Partnerships, Limited Liability Companies.

   a. License fee: $80.
   b. License term: biennial. Entity life, accident and health, variable life/variable annuities, and travel accident agent licenses (LA) expire June 30 of odd years; property and casualty, personal lines, and baggage agent licenses (PC) expire June 30 of even years. (NY CLS INS §2103).
   c. Lines of authority:

      (1) Life.
      (2) Accident & health.
      (3) Property & casualty.
      (4) Variable life/variable annuities.
      (5) Personal lines.
      (6) Travel accident.
      (7) Baggage.

2. *Resident Brokers.* Application forms: Individuals, Corporations, Partnerships, Limited Liability Companies.

   a. License fee: $80. Appointments are not required.
   b. License term: biennial. Entity Life, accident & health, variable life/variable annuities and travel accident broker licenses (LB) property & casualty broker licenses (BR) expire October 31 of even years.
   c. Lines of authority:

      (1) Life.
      (2) Accident and health.
      (3) Property and casualty.
      (4) Variable life/variable annuities.
      (5) Personal lines.
      (https://www.dfs.ny.gov/apps_and_licensing/agents_and_brokers/fee_schedules).

3. *Resident Title Insurance Agents.* Application forms: Individuals, Corporations, Partnerships, Limited Liability Companies.

   a. License fee: $80 ($40 if license term is one year or less).
   b. License term: biennial. Entity title insurance agent licenses (TLA) expire June 30 of odd years. There is no line of authority. (NY CLS Ins. §2139).

4. *Limited Lines.* (NY CLS Ins. §§2103(g) and 2131).

   a. License fee: $80 ($40 if license term is one year or less).
   b. License term: biennial.
   c. Lines of authority:

      (1) Fraternal agent.
      (2) Limited rental vehicle insurance.
      (3) Wireless communications equipment vendors.
      (4) Self-service storage personal effects.
      (5) Self-service storage. (NY CLS Ins. §§2103(g), 2131).

5. *Reinsurance Intermediaries.* Application forms: Individuals, Corporations, Partnerships, Limited Liability Companies.

   a. License fee: $1,000 ($500 if license term is one year or less).
   b. License term: biennial. Individual licenses expire on the individual's birthday in odd years if the individual was born in an odd year, and on the individual's birthday in even years if the individual was born in an even year. Entity licenses expire August 31 of even years.

   (NY CLS Ins. §2106).

6. *Managing General Agents.* Managing general agents of insurers must be licensed as agents. (11 NYCRR §33.3).

7. *Bail Bond Agents.* License fee: $50 ($25 if license term is one year or less). License term: biennial. All licenses expire December 31 of even years. Must file a $5,000 bond. Fingerprinting required. (NY CLS Ins. §6802).

8. *Business Entities.* The license authorizes only the members named as sublicensees to act on behalf of the entity.

Other Insurance Professionals

1. *Adjusters.* The following application forms are available for independent and public adjusters: Individuals, Corporations, Partnerships, Limited Liability Companies.

Both independent and public adjusters must be licensed. License fee: $100 ($50 if term one year or less). License term: biennial; all adjuster licenses expire on December 31 of even years. Bond of $1,000 required. Fingerprinting also required. See https://www.dfs.ny.gov/apps_and_licensing/agents_and_brokers/licensing_application_forms_pamornin for instructions. (NY CLS INS §2108).

2. *Consultants.* The following applications are used for general (or life) consultants: Individuals, Corporations, Partnerships, Limited Liability Companies. License fee: $100 ($50 if term one year or less). License term: biennial. For individual license holders born in an even numbered year, license will expire on license holder's birthday in an even numbered year. For individual license holders born in an odd numbered year, license will expire on license holder's birthday in an odd numbered year. Entity licenses for life expire March 31 of odd years. Entity licenses for general expire March 31 of even years. (NY CLS Ins. §2107).

3. *Mortgage Guaranty Agents.* No licensing fee required. License Term: perpetual. (NY CLS Ins. §6505).

4. *Resident Life Settlement Brokers.* Application forms: Individuals, Corporations, Partnerships, Limited Liability Companies. Initial fee: $80 ($40 if term one year or less). License term: biennial. For individual license holders born in an even numbered year, license will expire on license holder's birthday in an even numbered year. For individual license holders born in an odd numbered year, license will expire on license holder's birthday in an odd numbered year. Entity licenses for life expire June 30 of odd years. Fingerprinting also required. See https://www.dfs.ny.gov/apps_and_licensing/agents_and_brokers/licensing_application_forms_lsb for instructions. (NY CLS Ins. §2137).

Some applications may be processed online or downloaded from the Department's Web site at https://www.dfs.ny.gov.

C. Appointments: A notice of appointment within fifteen days from the date the agency contract is executed or the first insurance application is submitted. Certificates of appointment shall be valid until terminated by the appointing insurer after a termination in accordance with the provisions of the agency contract; the license is suspended or revoked by the superintendent; or the license expires and is not renewed. (NY CLS Ins. §2112).

D. Licenses Required of Nonresidents: The same licenses are required of nonresidents. Applicant must be currently licensed and in compliance in their declared home state. License information must be included in the National Producer Database; if not, applicant must submit a currently dated Certification from the state which is declared as the home state and in which applicant's principal place of business or residence is located. The New York Department of Financial Services deems agents and brokers currently licensed in another state and meeting that state's requirements qualified on a reciprocal basis to the extent that the other state extends reciprocity to New York agents and brokers. Nonresident agents must have New York appointments for any insurer with whom they will be placing business in New York. Nonresident fees are retaliatory. (NY CLS Ins. §2101).

Some applications may be processed online or downloaded from the Department's website at https://www.dfs.ny.gov.

Multi-State Exposures: A license is not required for a nonresident insurance producer who sells, solicits, or negotiates a contract of insurance for commercial property and casualty coverage when the majority of the risks that are to be insured under that contract are located in another state. This exception applies only if the nonresident is licensed to sell, solicit, or negotiate that insurance in the state where the insured maintains its principal place of business and the contract of insurance insures risks located in that state. (NY Ins. §2101(a)(9)).

E. Prelicensing Examination and Education Requirements:

1. *Residents.* All license applicants (except excess line broker, limited line agents, reinsurance intermediary, and life settlement broker) must pass a qualifying examination for each line of authority desired. (NY CLS Ins. §2103(f)(1)). Exams are administered by PSI Exams Online. (Phone: 800 733-9267 or https://candidate.psiexams.com).

   Property & casualty agents and brokers and mortgage guaranty agents must have a minimum of ninety hours of instruction in courses approved by the Superintendent of the Department of Financial Services. Personal lines authority requires forty hours. Life/accident and health/variable annuity agents, forty hours. Variable annuity applicants must also present NASD or SECO certificate. (NY CLS Ins. §2103).

   Public adjuster applicants must complete forty hours of prelicensing education prior to taking the exam or submit a "Statement of Employer," which documents at least one year's employment in insurance. At this time, there is no educational requirement for independent adjuster applicants. (NY CLS Ins. §2108).

   Note: Anyone caught impersonating another to take the exam or having another impersonate himself or herself to take the exam can be fined from $500 - $2500 and potentially suffer suspension or revocation of license. (NY CLS Ins. §§ 2126, 2127).

The following exemptions from exam/education requirements apply:

a. CPCUs are exempt from the prelicensing course requirement and a part of the examination for property and casualty agent and broker.
b. CLUs are exempt from the prelicensing course requirement and a part of the examination for life/accident and health agent.
c. Holders of the CLU, FAS, or ASA are exempt from the examination requirement for a life consultant license.
d. Holders of the CPCU, FCAS, or ACAS are exempt from the examination requirement for a general consultant license.
e. Travel accident or baggage agents.
f. Currently licensed agents are exempt from the examination requirement for a broker license. (https://www.dfs.ny.gov/insurance/ogco2005/rg050106.htm).

2. *Nonresidents.* Bail bond agents, consultants and adjusters must pass the New York State qualifying examination. For other licenses, education and examination requirements are reciprocal with nonresident's home state. (NY CLS Ins. § 2136).

F. Continuing Education Requirements:

Number of Hours Required: Fifteen hours, biennially. (Applicable to agents, brokers, consultants, and public adjusters). Courses must be approved for the class licensed. Dual licensees must complete full requirement in both property and casualty and life/accident and health. Classroom instructors receive the same credit as students. Courses may only be taken once in a renewal period.

Renewal Procedure: Continuing education requirement must be met prior to completing the renewal application.

Excess Hours: may not be carried over. (NY CLS Ins. §2132).

Final Exam: must be monitored.

Requirements **Not** *Applicable to the Following:*

1. Licensees where examination is not required.

2. Newly licensed individuals who have held a license for less than two years.

3. Independent adjusters.

4. Reinsurance intermediaries.

5. Limited rental licensees.

6. Service contract registrants.

7. Limited line licensees, bail bond agents, and mortgage guaranty agents.

Nonresidents: Must be compliant with home state's continuing education requirement. Please note that there is no continuing education reciprocity for public adjusters. Thus, all New York licensed public adjusters must complete New York approved CE courses. (NY CLS Ins. §2132).

G. **Cancellation of Agency Contracts/Producer Appointments:** The insurer must file a notice of termination of appointment with the Department of Financial Services and must notify the licensee within fifteen days. (NY CLS Ins. §2112).

H. **Rules for Risk Retention and Purchasing Groups:** Risk retention groups domiciled in New York must be chartered and licensed in the state as a domestic property and casualty insurer. They are subject to all the laws, regulations, and orders applicable to property and casualty insurers organized and licensed in the state. (NY CLS Ins. §5903). Risk retention groups domiciled outside of New York must notify the Superintendent of Financial Services of its intention to do business in the state and must comply with the laws of New York as set forth below:

> "Whenever licensed insurance agents or insurance brokers place business with a risk retention group, such licensee shall report to the superintendent the premiums of direct business for risks resident or located within this state which they have placed with such risk retention group, and such licensee shall keep a complete and separate record of all policies procured from each such risk retention group, which record shall be open to examination by the superintendent…" (NY CLS Ins. §5904(c)(2)).

All risk retention group policies must show the following notice in at least ten point type on the front page and on the declarations page of the policy:

"This policy is issued by your risk retention group. Your risk retention group may not be subject to all of the insurance laws and regulations of your state. State insurance insolvency guaranty funds are not available for your risk retention group." (NY CLS Ins. §5905).

Regulation 134 requires that purchasing groups adhere to applicable state statutes and regulations including excess lines and unauthorized insurer provisions. Authorized insurers dealing with purchasing groups must conform to applicable New York rate and policy form filing and approval requirements, and purchasing groups register with the Department of Financial Services before doing business in the state. According to the regulation, a purchasing group is located in New York if it solicits business or issues a policy in the state.

I. **Other License Rules, Requirements, or Restrictions:** Unlicensed nonresidents may not enter New York to solicit or inspect. Entering the state includes mail or telephone or other electronic communication into the state from the outside, as well as physical presence in the state. (NY CLS Ins. § 1101).

Anyone caught using a false or forged insurance identification card can be fined $1,000 for the first offense, and $5,000 for each subsequent offense. (N.Y. CLS Ins. §2133).

J. **Policy Countersignature Requirements:** None.

II. Commissions, Fees, Commingling of Funds, Suitability of Annuity Transactions

A. **Commissions:** There are no restrictions on distribution of commissions to licensed resident or nonresident agents or brokers. However, insurers may pay commissions for life insurance and variable annuities only to licensed agents appointed to represent that insurer. Nonresidents not licensed in New York may receive commission on insurance on property or other exposures in New York only if no service is performed in state. Department has chosen not to invoke retaliatory commission provision of current law. Rebating of commissions is not allowed. (NY CLS Ins. §2128).

B. **Fees:** Brokers may charge fees for services in connection with negotiation or procurement of insurance contracts if fees are based on written memorandum, signed by the party to be charged showing the amount of fee to be charged. This memorandum must contain the terms of the agreement and the date and the amount of any fees being charged. The basis for charging fees must be fully disclosed prior to the service being rendered. Fees must be segregated from trust funds and accounted for in a manner consistent with sections 20.3(b)(3) and (4) and 20.4(b) of New York

Insurance Regulations. Brokers may not charge fees instead of commission on policies they sell. (NY CLS Ins. §2119).

C. **Disclosure Requirements:** An insurance producer selling an insurance contract must disclose the following information to the purchaser orally or in a prominent writing at or prior to the time of application for the insurance contract:

(1) A description of the role of the insurance producer in the sale.

(2) Whether the insurance producer will receive compensation from the selling insurer or other third party based in whole or in part on the insurance contract the producer sells.

(3) That the compensation paid to the insurance producer may vary depending on a number of factors, including (if applicable) the insurance contract and the insurer that the purchaser selects, the volume of business the producer provides to the insurer or the profitability of the insurance contracts that the producer provides to the insurer.

(4) That the purchaser may obtain information about the compensation expected to be received by the producer based in whole or in part on the sale, and the compensation expected to be received based in whole or in part on any alternative quotes presented by the producer, by requesting such information from the producer. (11 NYCRR § 30.3)

The purchaser may also request additional information which the producer must supply upon request. (11 NYCRR § 30.3(b)).

If an insurance producer is a title insurance agent, then the title insurance agent shall, in lieu of the disclosures required above, provide the written disclosures required by NY CLS Ins §2113(b). As part of such disclosure, the title insurance agent shall provide descriptions of:

(1) the nature of the agent's relationship with the entity referred
(2) that the applicant isn't required to use the title agent's or referred title corporation's services;
(3) Anything of value directly or indirectly paid by the title agent to the referred entity is based on the entity's financial interest in the title agent;
(4) the referring entity isn't required to refer a specific amount of business to the title agent;

(5) the value of compensation the entity expects to receive from the title agent; and

(6) any relevant disclosures required by federal real estate settlement procedures. (NY CLS Ins. §2113(d)).

D. **Commingling of Funds:** Every insurance producer in New York shall be responsible in a fiduciary capacity for all funds received or collected as insurance producer, and shall not, without the express consent of his or its principal, mingle any such funds with his or its own funds or with funds held by him or it in any other capacity. Insurance producers are not required to maintain a separate bank deposit for the funds of each principal, if and as long as the funds so held for each such principal are reasonably ascertainable from the books of account and records of the producer. (NY CLS Ins. §2120).

E. **Suitability of Annuity Transactions:** In recommending to a consumer the purchase or replacement of an annuity contract, the insurance producer, or the insurer where no insurance producer is involved, shall have reasonable grounds for believing that the recommendation is suitable for the consumer on the basis of the facts disclosed by the consumer as to the consumer's investments and other insurance policies or contracts and as to the consumer's financial situation and needs, including the consumer's suitability information, and that there is a reasonable basis to believe all of the following: the consumer has been reasonably informed of various features of the annuity contract, the consumer would benefit from certain features of the annuity contract, the particular annuity is suitable for the particular consumer based on the consumer's suitability information, in case of a replacement of an annuity contract, the replacement is suitable.

Prior to recommending an annuity to a consumer, the producer or insurer shall make reasonable efforts to obtain the consumer's suitability information. (11 NYCRR §224.4).

III. **Statutory References:** NY CLS Ins §§ 1101; 2101 to 2103; 2106 to 2108; 2112; 2113; 2119; 2120; 2126 to 2128; 2131 to 2133; 2136 to 2139; 5903 to 5905; 6505; 6802. 11 NYCRR §§ 30.3; 224.4.

NORTH CAROLINA

Department of Insurance; 325 N. Salisbury St.; Raleigh, NC 27603-5926
Agent Services Division; 1204 Mail Service Center; Raleigh, NC 27699-1204
Telephone: 919-807-6800; Fax: 919-715-3794;
Email: ASD@ncdoi.gov; Web site: http://www.ncdoi.com/

I. **Licensing Requirements:** Sales Personnel—Producers, Limited Representatives, Business Entities, Managing General Agents, Bail Bondsmen & Runners. Other Insurance Professionals—Adjusters (Company or Independent, Self-Employed, Public, Hail), Appraisers, Reinsurance Intermediaries. The North Carolina Department of Insurance requires an electronic application and a criminal background check.

A. **Applicability:** A person shall not sell, solicit, or negotiate insurance in North Carolina unless the person is licensed for that kind of insurance. No individual who holds a valid insurance agent's license issued by the commissioner shall, either directly or for an insurance agency, solicit, negotiate, or otherwise act as an agent for an insurer by which the individual has not been appointed. (N.C. Gen. Stat. §58-33-5).

The North Carolina Licensing Office of Pearson VUE handles the initial review of all new and renewal license applications, responds to applicant inquires on the license process/ application status, and collects all supporting documentation for application review. Applications that need additional regulatory review will be referred to the Agent Services Division for a licensing decision. Additional information on the license administration services provided by Pearson VUE is available on the Department's Web site: www.ncdoi.com.

Insurance and Bail Bond License Administration Vendor: Pearson VUE - 866-265-6329.

Insurance Continuing Education Vendor: Prometric - 866-241-3121.

Insurance and Bail Bond Examination Vendor: Pearson VUE - 800-274-0668.

License application fees collected by North Carolina are listed below; however, there is also a $5 transaction fee for each resident NIPR electronic application submission in addition to below listed fees.

Regarding fingerprint fees below, please note that if a fingerprint fee is indicated, it is only required for the first initial producer license. Subsequent additions to lines of authority generally do not require fingerprint submission and will not incur the $38 fee, unless there are certain lapses of licensure. Please note, if you are submitting multiple applications for Producer LOA, you must wait until the first license requiring fingerprint submission is active on the National Producer database before submitting another application for Producer LOA or the fingerprint fee will be charged again.

B. **Licenses Required of Residents:** Each of the following must be licensed in North Carolina:

Sales Personnel

1. *Producers.* Includes agents, brokers, and limited representatives.

   a. Application and license fee: $82 (includes one-time fingerprinting fee). Amendments: $44, plus $50 per line of authority. Fingerprinting fee: $38. There is a $50 fee for each additional LOA. Appointment Fee: $10 paid by the appointing carrier. In addition NIPR charges a $5 transaction fee. (https://nipr.com/licensing-center/state-requirements/north-carolina-resident-licensing-individual).
   b. License term for producers and limited representatives: Perpetual. Appointments must be renewed annually by the appointing company. The broker's license has an annual renewal, due date 04/01. Broker's licenses expire on 03/31 annually.
   (https://www.ncdoi.gov/licensees/agent-and-adjuster-licensing/renew-your-agent-or-adjuster-license).
   c. Lines of authority:

      (1) Life.
      (2) Accident and health or sickness.
      (3) Variable life and variable annuity products.
      (4) Property.
      (5) Casualty.
      (6) Personal lines.
      (7) Medicare supplement/long-term care.
      (8) Limited lines.
      (N.C. Gen. Stat. §58-33-26).

   An applicant for a resident insurance producer's license must provide a complete set of fingerprints. (N.C. Gen. Stat. §58-33-48).

2. *Limited Representatives.*

    a. Application and License fee: $82, includes one-time fingerprinting fee. Amendments: $44. $50 fee for each additional license. Fingerprinting fee: $38. Appointment Fee: $20 paid by the appointing company. In addition NIPR charges a $5 transaction fee. (https://nipr.com/licensing-center/state-requirements/north-carolina-resident-licensing-individual).
    b. License term: Perpetual. Appointments must be renewed annually.
    c. Lines of authority:

        (1) Motor club.
        (2) Preneed life.
        (3) Dental services.
        (4) Travel, accident and baggage.
        (5) Credit. (11 N.C.A.C. 6A.0402)

3. *Title Agent.* Application and License fee: $132, includes one-time fingerprinting fee. Fingerprinting fee: $38. Appointment Fee: $20. License term: Perpetual. Appointments must be renewed annually paid for the appointing carrier. Each additional line of authority in $50. (https://nipr.com/licensing-center/state-requirements/north-carolina-resident-licensing-individual).

4. *Auto Physical Damage Agent.* Application and License fee: $132, includes one-time fingerprinting fee. Fingerprinting fee: $38. Appointment Fee: $20 paid by the appointing carrier. License term: Perpetual. Appointments must be renewed annually by the appointing carrier. Each additional line of authority: $50. (https://www.ncdoi.gov/licensees/agent-and-adjuster-licensing).

5. *Business Entities.* Application and License fee: $144. Renewal fee is $134. Renews annually on April 1 and expires annually on March 31, with the exception of Surplus Lines Business Entity which renews annually on July 1 and expires annually on August 31. Residents must submit a certificate of good standing from the Secretary of State along with the following:

    a. Corporations—articles of incorporation.
    b. LLCs—articles of organization.
    c. Partnerships—partnership agreements.
    d. Surplus Lines—list of all surplus lines licensed individuals in the agency. Note, this requirement applies to both residents and nonresidents.
    e. Limited Lines Travel—list of all Travel Retailers that sell Limited Lines Travel Coverage for the Limited LinesTravel Producer. Note, this requirement applies to both resident and nonresidents. (N.C. Gen. Stat. §58-33-19; https://nipr.com/licensing-center/state-requirements/north-carolina-resident-renewal-business).

    Nonresidents must be licensed in their home states.

6. *Managing General Agents.* Although no separate license is required for MGAs, an MGA must be licensed as an agent in North Carolina. Their contracts must be approved by the Financial Evaluation Division, 103 Mail Service Center, Raleigh, NC, 27699. MGAs may be required to maintain an E&O policy and file a bond. (N.C. Gen. Stat. §58-34-2).

7. *Bail Bondsmen and Runners.* Initial license fee and Biennial renewal: bondsmen, $200; runners, $120. In addition, there is a $40 processing fee for renewals with Pearson VUE. Renew annually on July 1. Every four years, a bail bondsman or runner seeking to renew a license should provide the commissioner with a renewal application and required documents by June 30. A runner must be appointed by a bondsman and may work for only one bondsman at a time. Must submit a set of fingerprints that have been certified by a law enforcement authority and pay a $38 fingerprinting fee. (N.C. Gen. Stat. §§58-71-51, 58-71-55, 58-71-75(b)). SBS Connect Service for electronic bail bond monthly report filing is now available. Professional bail bond monthly reports are now required to be filed electronically on or before the fifteenth of each month. (11 N.C.A.C. 13.0521; N.C. Gen. Stat. §58-71-165).

   Pursuant to N.C. Gen. Stat. §58-71-200, licensed bail bondsmen and runners may apply for access to North Carolina Administrative Office of the Courts' (NCAOC) Automated Criminal/Infractions System (ACIS) and Civil (VCAP) Systems Access. Instruction for obtaining an ID are available at http://www.ncdoi.com.

   "Each professional bail bondsman, surety bail bondsman, or bail bond runner must apply for and use only their own user ID to perform the free criminal searches. There is no sharing of user IDs permitted under any circumstance. The NCAOC Access Agreement requires attestation from the bondsmen or runner that they will not share their user ID information and North Carolina G.S. 58-71-200(h) specifies that allowing any other person, directly or indirectly, to make use of access granted to the bondsmen of runner pursuant to subsection (a) of N.C. Gen. Stat. § 58-71-200 is a Class H felony." Set up fee: $200. (N.C. Gen. Stat. §58-71-200).

8. *Car Rental Companies and Self-Service Storage Companies.* These companies must obtain a license to sell insurance to their customers. Application and License fee: $144, includes one-time fingerprinting fee. Renewal fee is $134. Renew annually on April 1 (N.C. Gen. Stat. §§58-33-17, 58-33-18; https://nipr.com/licensing-center/state-requirements/north-carolina-resident-licensing-business; https://www.ncdoi.gov/licensees/agent-and-adjuster-licensing/renew-your-agent-or-adjuster-license).

9. *Brokers.* Application and License fee: $94. Renewal fee is $84. Renew annually on April 1. Must be licensed as an agent for the lines of authority to be brokered. Must file a $15,000 surety bond. (N.C. Gen. Stat. §58-33-30(f); https://www.ncdoi.gov/licensees/agent-and-adjuster-licensing/renew-your-agent-or-adjuster-license; https://nipr.com/licensing-center/state-requirements/north-carolina-resident-licensing-individual).

10. *Portable Electronics Business Entity.* Application and License fee: $144. Renewal fee is $134. Renew annually on April 1. Required by vendors to offer portable electronics insurance. This limited license allows employees of vendor to sell portable electronic coverage. Portable Electronic Insurance provides coverage for the repair or replacement of portable electronics which may provide coverage for portable electronics against any one or more of the following causes of loss: loss, theft, and inoperability due to mechanical failure, malfunction, damage, or other similar causes of loss. (N.C. Gen. Stat. §§58-44A-1, 58-44A-5; https://www.ncdoi.gov/licensees/agent-and-adjuster-licensing/renew-your-agent-or-adjuster-license; https://nipr.com/licensing-center/state-requirements/north-carolina-resident-licensing-business).

11. *Limited Lines Travel Business Entity.* Application and License fee: $144. Renewal fee: $134. Renew annually on April 1. This will enable an entity to offer Travel Accident and Baggage through unlicensed Travel Retailers operating under the supervision of the Travel Business Entity and its Designated Responsible License Producer (DRLP). The resident DRLP and any key individuals must meet the fingerprint background check requirement. This licensee must also provide a list of the travel retailers it is marketing through.

    Any person licensed in a major line of authority as an insurance producer is authorized to sell, solicit, and negotiate travel insurance. A property and casualty insurance producer is not required to become appointed by an insurer in order to sell, solicit, or negotiate travel insurance. (N.C. Gen. Stat. §58-33-19; https://nipr.com/licensing-center/state-requirements/north-carolina-resident-licensing-business; https://www.ncdoi.gov/licensees/agent-and-adjuster-licensing/renew-your-agent-or-adjuster-license).

12. *Self-Service Storage Facility Business Entity.* Application and License fee: $144. Renewal fee: $134. Must renew by April 1 annually. (N.C. Gen. Stat. §58-33-18; https://nipr.com/licensing-center/state-requirements/north-carolina-resident-licensing-business; https://www.ncdoi.gov/licensees/agent-and-adjuster-licensing/renew-your-agent-or-adjuster-license).

Other Insurance Professionals

1. *Adjusters, Appraisers.* Public Adjusters and auto damage appraisers must be licensed; licenses expire April 1 of each year. Adjusters are licensed as follows:

    a. Company/independent firm adjuster. Application and License fee: $169. Renewal fee: $109.
    b. Self-employed adjuster. Application and License fee: $169. Renewal fee: $109.
    c. Public adjuster. Application and License fee: $169. Fingerprinting fee: $38. Renewal fee: $109. An additional lapsed license fee of $75 will be charged for late renewals.
    d. Crop-hail adjuster. Application and License fee: $114. Renewal fee: $54.
    e. Motor Vehicle Damage Appraiser. Application and License fee: $169. Renewal fee: $109.
    f. Public Adjuster Business Entity. License and Application fee $144. Renewal fee: $134. $38 fingerprint fee per key person. A key person is an owner, partner, officer, director, member, or manager. (https://www.ncdoi.gov/licensees/agent-and-adjuster-licensing/renew-your-agent-or-adjuster-license; https://nipr.com/licensing-center/state-requirements/north-carolina-resident-licensing-individual; https://nipr.com/licensing-center/state-requirements/north-carolina-resident-licensing-business).

2. *Reinsurance Intermediaries.* Must demonstrate financial responsibility to the Commissioner. Managers may be required to maintain an E&O policy or file a separate fidelity bond. (N.C. Gen. Stat. §58-9-2). For information regarding licensing, reinsurance intermediaries should contact Financial Analysis; 1203 Mail Service Center; Raleigh, NC 27699-1203.

All applicants are encouraged to visit www.ncdoi.com/licensees for more information on how to obtain a resident license.

C. Appointments: No individual who holds a valid insurance agent's license issued by the commissioner shall, either directly or for an insurance agency, solicit, negotiate, or otherwise act as an agent for an insurer by which the individual has not been appointed. The individual shall be authorized to act as an agent for the appointing insurer for all kinds of insurance for which the insurer is authorized in this state and for which the appointed agent is licensed in this state, unless specifically limited. To appoint an individual as its agent, the appointing insurer must file a notice of appointment with the commissioner within fifteen days after the date the first insurance application is submitted. Fee: $10 per-line or type of insurance, annually for agents. Overseas military agents, and limited representatives: $20. (N.C. Gen. Stat. §§58-33-40, 58-33-125).

D. Licenses Required of Nonresidents: Producers from all states may be licensed as North Carolina producers so long as they are currently licensed in good standing in their home state, have submitted the proper application to the Commissioner, and their home state awards North Carolina residents license on a reciprocal basis. Nonresidents must have a North Carolina appointment with the companies for whom they are writing business in North Carolina. Licensee must maintain home state license in good standing or nonresident license is subject to cancellation. Nonresidents who satisfy the CE requirements of their home state are deemed to satisfy the North Carolina CE requirements. (11 N.C.A.C. 6A.0802). Fingerprints are not required for nonresident insurance producer license applicants.

There is also a $5 transaction fee for each nonresident NIPR electronic application submission in addition to below listed fees.

See nonresident application and renewal fees at https://nipr.com/licensing-center/state-requirements/north-carolina-non-resident-licensing-individual, https://nipr.com/licensing-center/state-requirements/north-carolina-non-resident-licensing-business, and https://www.ncdoi.gov/north-carolina-non-resident-renewal-application-fees.

Multi-State Exposures: A license is not required for a nonresident insurance producer who sells, solicits, or negotiates a contract of insurance for commercial property and casualty coverage when risks that are to be insured under that contract are located in more than one state. This exception applies only if the nonresident is licensed to sell, solicit, or negotiate that insurance in the state where the insured maintains its principal place of business and the contract of insurance insures risks located in that state. (N.C. Gen. Stat. §58-33-26(n)(6)).

E. Prelicensing Examination and Education Requirements:

Applicants should submit a resident initial application on NIPR prior to taking any required licensing examinations. Licensing exams cannot be scheduled until a license application is completed online with NIPR and an email authorization from Pearson VUE is received that the applicant is eligible to take an exam. NIPR reserves a National Producer Number (NPN) for applicants when they submit an application.

For additional information, please see the new Insurance Candidate Guide, Resident Licensing Checklist, and Resident License Flow Chart posted on the Department's Web site.

1. *Residents.* Applicants for the following licenses must pass an exam: life, accident and health or sickness, property, casualty, personal lines, auto physical damage agent, surplus lines, Medicare supplement/long-term care, title, company/independent firm adjusters, self-employed adjuster, public adjuster, hail adjuster. Exam fee: $46.00 for each attempt.

   Life, accident and health or sickness, personal lines, property, casualty applicants must complete twenty hours of prelicensing education prior to taking the state examination. Medicare supplement license requires ten hours; bail licenses, twelve hours. Examinations are administered by Pearson Vue, 800-274-0668, or www.pearsonvue.com. (N.C. Gen. Stat. §§58-33-30(d), 58-71-71(a)).

   No prelicensing education is required for the following exams: title, auto physical damage, adjuster, crop hail adjuster, or surplus lines.

   Upon completion of an eligible state examination for insurance agent/producer, adjuster or bail bondsman, veterans may apply for reimbursement through the Veteran Affairs Web site.

2. *Nonresidents.* There is no education or examination requirement for nonresident producers. Nonresident adjusters must have a full-line adjuster's license in their home state and must have qualified with their home state exam. Adjusters whose home state does not license adjusters may qualify by exam from a designated 'home-state' or by taking the North Carolina exam and selecting North Carolina as their "designated home state." (N.C. Gen. Stat. §58-33-32(g)).

   Exemptions. Applicants holding one or more of the following insurance designations are exempt from prelicensing education:

   1. For Accident and Health or Sickness – RHU; CEBS; REBC; and HIA.
   2. For Life – CIC; CEBS; CFP.
   3. For Property – AAI; ARM; CIC.
   4. Casualty – AAI; ARM; CIC.
   5. For Personal Lines – AAI; ARM; CIC.
   6. For Property, Casualty, Personal Lines, Life, Accident and Health or Sickness:

      a. Holds an associate's or bachelor's degree in insurance;
      b. An individual licensed in another state for the same kind of insurance as the lines requested who applies within sixty days of both the cancellation of the prior license and the Division's receipt of the letter of clearance; or

c. An individual licensed in another state for the same kind of insurance as the lines requested.

However, if an applicant who is exempted from prelicensing education as described above fails the exam, that applicant must satisfy North Carolina's mandatory prelicensing education requirement before retaking the exam. (11 N.C.A.C. 6A.0701).

F. Continuing Education Requirements:

Number of Hours Required: Twenty-four hours of insurance continuing education credit (ICECs), biennially. Applies to all agents who hold one or more of the major lines (producers), company/independent, and self-employed adjusters. All licensees subject to CE are required to take three hours of Ethics CE biennially. Property, personal lines and adjuster license holders are required to take three hours of flood every other CE period. (11 N.C.A.C. 6A.0802(a)).

Bail licensees must complete three hours bail bond continuing education credit each year. The continuing education must be completed annually by June 30. (N.C. Gen. Stat. §58-71-71(b)).

Course work must be approved for the lines in which licensed. Licensee may use classroom instruction, self-study, distance learning programs, internet programs or webinar courses. (11 N.C.A.C. 6A.0805). Currently, bail licensees must take classroom courses. (11 N.C.A.C. 13.0523).

Submit Proof of Completion By: The last day of the insurance licensee's birth month in an even numbered year for insurance licensees born in even years. The last day of the insurance licensee's birth month in an odd numbered year for insurance licensees born in odd years. (11 N.C.A.C. 6A.0802(m)).

Excess Hours: Only whole ICECs may be carried forward from one biennial period to the next. (11 N.C.A.C. 6A.0804).

Final Exam: Final exams must be monitored by a disinterested third-party for self-study courses and for classroom courses that provide over eight hours of credit. A secure examination is required for internet programs. (11 N.C.A.C. 6A.0805; 11 N.C.A.C. 6A.0809).

Bail bondsman and runners are exempt from prelicensing and continuing education requirements if they are over sixty-five and licensed for over fifteen years. (N.C. Gen. Stat. §58-71-71).

Renewal Procedure: The license of any person who fails to comply with the continuing education requirements shall lapse except that the Commissioner or administrator may either grant an extension of time for good cause shown or charge an administrative fee of seventy-five dollars ($75.00), or both, in lieu of having the person's license lapse. (N.C. Gen. Stat. §58-33-130(c)).

Nonresidents are exempt if they meet their home state CE requirements. (N.C. Gen. Stat. §58-33-32 (j); 11 N.C.A.C. 6A.0802).

Visit https://www.ncdoi.gov/licensees/agent-and-adjuster-licensing/continuing-education-agents-and-adjusters for more information concerning CE vendors.

G. **Cancellation of Agency Contracts/Producer Appointments:** All company appointments and terminations for insurance companies, motor club companies, and county farm mutual companies are required to be processed electronically through the National Insurance Producer Registry (NIPR). Fee: $10. (N.C. Gen. Stat. §§58-33-125, 58-2-250; 11 N.C.A.C. 6A.0505, 11 N.C.A.C. 6A.0201).

H. **Rules for Risk Retention and Purchasing Groups:** North Carolina regulates risk retention and purchasing groups operating or offering coverage on risks in North Carolina. Risk retention groups chartered in North Carolina must be licensed as liability insurers. (N.C. Gen. Stat. §58-22-15). Groups not chartered in North Carolina must register with and submit reports to the commissioner. (N.C. Gen. Stat. §58-22-20). Purchasing groups must also register with the commissioner and submit reports. (N.C. Gen. Stat. §58-22-40). All groups and all resident and nonresident agents or brokers participating in them must comply with all North Carolina insurance laws, including licensing and solicitation requirements or restrictions, to the extent that they do not conflict with the Federal Liability Risk Retention Act of 1986. All risk retention group policies must show the following notice in at least ten-point type in a contrasting color on the front page and on the declarations page of the policy:

NOTICE

"This policy is issued by your risk retention group. Your risk retention group is not subject to all of the insurance laws and regulations of your state. In the event of the insolvency of your risk retention group, losses under this policy will not be paid by any insurance insolvency or guaranty fund in this State." (N.C. Gen. Stat. § 58-22-20).

I. **Other License Rules, Requirements, or Restrictions:** Nonresident brokers, even if licensed, may not enter North Carolina for solicitation, inspection, or service. Only physical presence is considered entering the state. Nonresident with North

Carolina agent's appointment has same status as resident agent. Unlicensed nonresident may not write insurance on North Carolina properties or exposures, even though no solicitation or service is performed in state. (N.C. Gen. Stat. §58-33-16).

J. **Policy Countersignature Requirements:** Resident agent countersignature of policies is required only on a retaliatory basis for nonresidents whose home state requires resident agent countersignature. (N.C. Gen. Stat. §58-33-60). A policy issued to a risk retention group or a member of that group is not required to be countersigned. (N.C. Gen. Stat. §58-22-30).

II. Commissions, Fees, Commingling of Funds, Suitability in Annuity Transactions

A. **Commissions:** Commissions may only be paid to licensed producers. Rebating of commissions is not allowed. (N.C. Gen. Stat. §§58-33-82, 58-33-85).

B. **Fees:** A producer who deals directly with consumers may charge policy or service fees. (N.C. Gen. Stat. §58-33-82).

C. **Disclosure Requirements:**

1. A sign that informs consumers in large bold print that a fee will be charged, must be displayed in a prominent place so as to be seen and read from any part of the office lobby.

2. The consumer's written consent must be obtained each time a policy fee is charged. The form must be entitled "Policy or Service Fee Consent" and must include the date and amount of the fee.

3. The producer must issue a separate and dated receipt for the policy fee or must indicate the fee separately on the receipt issued for the policy premium. (11 N.C.A.C. 4.0120).

D. **Commingling of Funds:** The accounting records maintained by agents, brokers, and limited representatives shall be separate and apart from any other business records and demonstrate at all times that collected funds due to insurers and return premiums due to policy holders are available at all times. (11 N.C.A.C. 4.0429).

E. **Suitability in Annuity Transactions:** In recommending to a consumer the purchase or exchange of an annuity that results in another insurance transaction or series of insurance transactions, the insurance producer, or insurer if no producer is involved, shall have reasonable grounds for believing that the recommendation is suitable for the consumer on the basis of the facts disclosed by the consumer as to the consumer's investments financial situation and needs.

Before recommending the purchase or exchange of an annuity resulting from a recommendation, the insurance producer, or the insurer where no producer is involved, shall make reasonable efforts to obtain information about the particular consumer's circumstances, including, but not limited to, all of the following; the consumers financial and tax status and the consumer's investment objectives, and any other information used or considered to be reasonable by the insurance producer or insurer in making recommendations to the consumer. (N.C. Gen. Stat. §58-60-170).

Note: Part 4 of Article 60 of Chapter 58 of the General Statutes is subject to a contingent repeal under Session Laws 2017-136, 5. 5. As of August 20, 2021, the repeal is still contingent.

III. Statutory References:

N.C. Gen. Stat. §§58-	
2-	250
9-	2
22-	20, 30, 40
33-	5
	16 to 19, 26, 30, 32, 40, 48, 60, 82, 85
	125, 130
34-	2
44A-	1, 5
60-	170
71-	51, 55, 71, 75
	165, 200

11 N.C.A.C.	
4..	0120, 0429
6A.	0201, 0402, 0505, 0701, 0802, 0804, 0805, 0809
13..	0521, 0523

NORTH CAROLINA

Web References:

https://nipr.com/licensing-center/state-requirements/north-carolina-resident-licensing-individual.
https://nipr.com/licensing-center/state-requirements/north-carolina-resident-renewal-business.
https://nipr.com/licensing-center/state-requirements/north-carolina-resident-licensing-business.
https://www.ncdoi.gov/licensees/agent-and-adjuster-licensing.
https://www.ncdoi.gov/licensees/agent-and-adjuster-licensing/renew-your-agent-or-adjuster-license.

NORTH DAKOTA

Insurance Department;
600 E. Boulevard Avenue
Bismarck, ND 58505-0320
Telephone: 701-328-2440; Fax: 701-328-4880
Email: ndlicensing@nd.gov http://www.nd.gov/ndins/

I. Licensing Requirements: Sales Personnel—Producers, Surplus Lines Producers, Managing General Agents (both individuals and business entities). Other Insurance Professionals—Consultants, Reinsurance Intermediaries, Third Party Administrators, Life Settlement Providers & Brokers.

A. Licenses Required of Residents: No person may act as or hold oneself out to be an insurance producer, insurance consultant, or surplus lines insurance producer unless licensed. A person may not sell, solicit, or negotiate insurance in North Dakota for any class of insurance unless the person is licensed for that line of authority. (N.D. Cent. Code §26.1-26-03).

Sales Personnel

1. *Producers.*

   a. License fee: $100. Submit NAIC uniform application form (electronic applications strongly encouraged and are processed much faster than paper applications). (N.D. Cent. Code §26.1-01-07(l)).
   b. License term: Perpetual with biennial continuation/renewal by last day of birth month. Renewal fee is $25. Department will send reminder postcard sixty days before expiration date. (N.D. Cent. Code §26.1-26-13.4).
   c. No fee to add a line of authority.
   d. Major Lines of Authority:

      (1) Life and annuities.
      (2) Accident and health.
      (3) Property.
      (4) Casualty.
      (5) Variable life and annuity.
      (6) Personal lines.

      (N.D. Cent. Code §26.1-26-11).

e. Limited Lines of Authority:

(1) Credit.
(2) Crop hail.
(3) Legal expense.
(4) Title.
(5) Surety.
(6) Bail bonds.
(7) Travel/baggage.
(8) Portable electronics.

(https://www.nd.gov/ndins/producers/nonresident/addline/)

2. *Managing General Agents.* If the MGA is receiving valuable consideration, he must hold the same line license and be appointed with the company. A bond or an E&O policy or both may be required. Must hold an active insurance producer license and submit a copy of the MGA contract for review. (N.D. Cent. Code §26.1-26.3-01 to -07).

3. *Business Entities.* Must submit NAIC uniform application form with the $100 fee (electronic applications strongly encouraged and are processed much faster than paper applications). Check with the North Dakota Secretary of State to ensure compliance with corporate laws. All individuals in the entity who will be selling insurance must also be licensed. At least one individual who is affiliated with the business entity must hold a North Dakota license for the lines of authority requested. (N.D. Cent. Code §26.1-26-13.3).

Other Insurance Professionals

1. *Consultants.* License fee: $100. Renewal fee is $25 annually, no later than April 30. Written agreement between consultant and client must be approved by the commissioner. Consultants cannot simultaneously hold insurance producer or surplus lines broker and cannot sell, solicit or negotiate insurance in North Dakota; these licenses must be surrendered. A North Dakota consultant license no longer includes the authority to act as a public adjuster. (N.D. Admin. Code 45-02-02-10; https://www.insurance.nd.gov/consultant).

2. *Reinsurance Intermediaries.* Must be licensed as a producer. Intermediary-managers may be required to carry an E&O policy or post a bond or both. (N.D. Cent. Code §26.1-31.1-02).

3. *Third Party Administrators.* License fee: $100. Renewal fee is $50, annually, no later than April 30. Submit NAIC Uniform Application for a Third Party Administrator and must be registered with the North Dakota Secretary of State. Administrators of self-insured plans must maintain a surety bond or proof of insurance satisfactory to the commissioner. The bond must be the greater of $100,000 or 10 percent of the aggregate total amount of administered coverages under the plans handled in North Dakota. Records for all transactions between the administrator, insurers and insured persons must be retained for five years following the end of the contractual relationship. (N.D. Cent. Code §§26.1-27-03.1; https://www.insurance.nd.gov/third-party-administrator).

4. *Life Settlement Providers and Brokers.* Must be licensed. Initial fee for brokers: $100. Annual renewal: $12. Initial fee for providers: $250. Renewal: $100. Brokers must show evidence of financial responsibility through ether a surety bond or a deposit of cash, certificates of deposit or securities in the amount of $150,000. (https://www.insurance.nd.gov/life-settlements).

Applications may be downloaded from www.nd.gov/ndins/producers.

B. Licenses Required of Nonresidents: Nonresidents who hold similar licenses in their home state may obtain each of the above licenses. Business entities must be licensed, as well as all individuals who will be selling insurance. (N.D. Cent. Code §26.1-26-20).

Nonresident must maintain his/her resident license.

1. *Producers.*

   a. License fee: $100. Submit NAIC uniform application form (electronic applications strongly encouraged and are processed mush faster than paper applications). (N.D. Cent. Code §26.1-01-07).
   b. License term: Individual – two years, with biennial continuation/renewal by last day of birth month. Business Entity – Perpetual. Renewal fee is $25. Department will send reminder postcard sixty days before expiration date.
   c. No fee to add a line of authority.

   (https://www.insurance.nd.gov/producers/non-resident-producer).

2. *Third Party Administrators.* Fee is $100. Check with the North Dakota Secretary of State to ensure compliance with corporate laws. Requires a Certificate of Authority. Annual renewal is due by April 30 and the renewal fee is $50. Proof of resident license from home state insurance department is required if resident license

information is not on the National Insurance Producer Registry Producer Data Base (PDB). Administrators of self-insured plans must maintain a surety bond or proof of insurance satisfactory to the commissioner. The bond must be the greater of $100,000 or 10 percent of the aggregate total amount of administered coverages under the plans handled in North Dakota. (N.D. Cent. Code §26.1-27-03.1).

3. *Multi-State Exposures.* A license is not required for a nonresident insurance producer who sells, solicits, or negotiates a contract of insurance for commercial property and casualty coverage when risks that are to be insured under that contract are located in more than one state. This exception applies only if the nonresident is licensed to sell, solicit, or negotiate that insurance in the state where the insured maintains its principal place of business and the contract of insurance insures risks located in that state. (N.D. Cent. Code §26.1-26-09(f)).

C. **Appointments:** Insurance producers, both individuals and business entities, may not act as an agent of an insurer unless the insurance producer becomes an appointed agent of that insurer. An insurance producer who is not acting as an agent of an insurer is not required to become appointed. To appoint an insurance producer as its agent, the appointing insurer shall file a notice of appointment within thirty days from the later of the date the agency contract is executed or the first insurance application is submitted. Initial and renewal fee is $10, renewed annually on April 30. Report appointments electronically or on form SFN 50291 (11/02). Must be renewed electronically through NIPR. (N.D. Cent. Code §26.1-26-13.1).

D. **Prelicensing Examination Requirements:**

1. *Residents.* Applicants for producer or consultant license must pass an exam administered by PSI to qualify for license. PSI Web site: https://candidate.psiexams.com/. PSI phone: call PSI at 1-800-733-9267. There is a fee for exams, prices vary see PSI for information. Applicants who wish to sell variable products must have an active ND Securities license. (N.D. Cent. Code §26.1-26-13.2; N.D. Admin. Code 45-02-02-11). For test center locations, see http://www.nd.gov/ndins/producers/resident/apply/.

   Applicants for travel are exempt from the exam requirement. Applicants for title are exempt from examination, but must be a licensed abstractor or attorney or complete at least eighty hours of training by an insurer licensed in title. (N.D. Admin. Code §45-02-02-04). Fingerprints are collected at the test site following passage of the licensing exam.

2. *Nonresidents.* Must be licensed and in good standing in resident state for the lines of authority requested. (N.D. Cent. Code §26.1-26-25).

E. Continuing Education Requirements:

Number of Hours Required: Twenty-four hours, biennially, of which three must be in ethics. Courses must be approved by DOI for credit. Licensees may use classroom instruction or self-study. Course instructors receive the same number of credit hours. Out-of-state courses are subject to approval by the Commissioner. (N.D. Cent. Code §§26.1-26-31.1, 26.1-26-31.6, 26.1-26-31.7).

Excess Hours: Up to twelve hours may be carried into the next reporting period. Ethics credits cannot be carried forward as ethics credits.

Final Exam: Final exams for self-study courses do not need to be monitored.

Requirements **Not** *Applicable to the Following:*

1. Those producers who sell only surety, bail bonds, title insurance, legal expense, credit, or travel/baggage insurance. (N.D. Admin. Code 45-02-04-09.3).

   Note: The CE exemption for producers who were sixty-two or older and whose age plus years of experience equaled eighty-five or more was repealed in 2009. However, producers who were sixty-two or older and whose age plus years of experience equaled eighty-five before January 1, 2010 may be grandfathered in under this provision. (N.D. Cent. Code §26.1-26-31.1; https://www.insurance.nd.gov/continuing-education-faq-producer).

Renewal Procedure:

1. Submit the uniform continuation/renewal application with twenty-five dollar fee due biennially by last day of birth month (electronic applications strongly encouraged and are processed much faster than paper applications).

2. Producer must be in compliance with CE before submitting renewal application.

Nonresidents who satisfy the continuing education requirements of their home state and are in good standing in their home state are deemed to have satisfied the continuing education hours for North Dakota. They must maintain their resident license, complete the electronic continuation/renewal process, and pay a twenty-five dollar continuation fee biennially by birth month. (N.D. Cent. Code §26.1-26-47.1; N.D. Admin. Code 45-02-04-11).

F. Cancellation of Agency Contracts/Producer Appointments: The DOI must be notified of termination within thirty days on form SFN 50291. The producer must be notified within fifteen days of notice being sent to the DOI. (N.D. Cent. Code 26.1-26-34). Unless there are compelling reasons to submit on paper, companies should file agent terminations electronically through the National Insurance Producer Registry (NIPR). (https://www.insurance.nd.gov/producers/appointments).

G. **Rules for Risk Retention and Purchasing Groups:** North Dakota regulates risk retention and purchasing groups operating or offering coverage on risks in North Dakota. Risk retention groups chartered in North Dakota must be licensed as liability insurers. Groups not chartered in North Dakota must register with the insurance commissioner and submit reports to the commissioner as required by law. (N.D. Cent. Code §§26.1-46-02, 26.1-46-03). Purchasing groups must also register with the commissioner and submit reports as required by the law. (N.D. Cent. Code §26.1-46-07). All groups and all resident and nonresident producers participating in them must comply with all North Dakota insurance laws, including licensing and solicitation requirements or restrictions. All risk retention group policies must show the following notice in at least ten-point type on the front page and on the declarations page of the policy:

NOTICE

"This policy is issued by your risk retention group. Your risk retention group may not be subject to all of the insurance laws and regulations of your state. State insurance insolvency guaranty funds are not available for your risk retention group." (N.D. Cent. Code §26.1-46-03).

H. **Other License Rules, Requirements, or Restrictions:** Unlicensed nonresidents may not enter North Dakota for any insurance purpose. Consultants may not be concurrently licensed as producers or surplus lines producers. (N.D. Cent. Code §§26.1-26-03, 26.1-26-41).

I. **Policy Countersignature Requirements:** North Dakota's countersignature requirement applies only on a retaliatory basis with nonresident's home state. No requirement that an insurance producer resident in North Dakota sign or countersign an insurance policy covering a subject of insurance resident, located, or to be performed in this state. However, if the laws of another state require a countersignature by an insurance producer resident in that state on an insurance policy written by a nonresident insurance producer of that state, then any policy written by a nonresident insurance producer of that state must be countersigned by an insurance producer resident in North Dakota.

Excess loss reinsurance contract must be written only by a company authorized to do business in ND. The contract must be countersigned by a licensed ND resident insurance producer. (N.D. Cent. Code §§26.1-11-07, 26.1-22-21).

II. Commissions, Fees, Commingling of Funds, and Suitability of Annuity Transactions

A. Commissions: There is no restriction on distribution of commission among licensed residents or nonresidents. No commission may be paid to anyone who is not licensed. Anyone receiving valuable consideration must be licensed and appointed. Rebating of commissions is not allowed. (N.D. Cent. Code §§26.1-26-04, 26.1-04-03).

B. Fees: Producers may not charge fees for services instead of or in addition to commission for sale of insurance. Consultants and administrators may charge fees for services. (N.D. Cent. Code §26.1-26-04).

C. Disclosure Requirements: In advance of rendering any service as a consultant, such consultant or producer shall prepare a form of written agreement which shall substantially comply with the model form available on request from the department of insurance. The form prepared by the consultant shall be submitted to the department for the commissioner's approval or disapproval. If the commissioner disapproves the form, the consultant shall not use that form.

In advance of rendering any services as an insurance consultant, a written agreement on the form which has been approved by the department shall be signed by both consultant and client. The consultant shall retain a copy of the agreement for not less than two years after completion of the services. A copy of the agreement shall be available to the department upon request. (N.D. Cent. Code §26.1-26-35).

D. Commingling of Funds: North Dakota does not prohibit agents' commingling of insurer's premiums with other agency funds. However, North Dakota does not allow a producer to misappropriate or convert to one's own use premium moneys. (N.D. Cent. Code §26.1-26-42(10)).

E. Suitability in Annuity Transactions: An insurance producer who engages in the sale of annuity products shall complete a one-time, four-hour training course. In recommending to a consumer the purchase of an annuity or the exchange of an annuity that results in another insurance transaction or series of insurance transactions, the insurance producer, or the insurer when no producer is involved, must have reasonable grounds for believing that the recommendation is suitable for the consumer on the basis of the facts disclosed by the consumer as to the consumer's investments and other insurance products and as to the consumer's financial situation and needs, including the consumer's suitability information, and that there is a reasonable basis to believe all of the following:

1. The consumer has been reasonably informed of various features of the annuity, such as the potential surrender period and surrender charge; potential tax penalty

if the consumer sells, exchanges, surrenders or annuitizes the annuity; mortality and expense fees; investment advisory fees; potential charges for and features of riders; limitations on interest returns; insurance and investment components; and market risk.

2. The consumer would benefit from certain features of the annuity, such as tax-deferred growth, annuitization, or death or living benefit.

3. The particular annuity as a whole, the underlying subaccounts to which funds are allocated at the time of purchase or exchange of the annuity, and riders and similar product enhancements, if any, are suitable, and in the case of an exchange or replacement, the transaction as a whole is suitable, for the particular consumer based on the consumer's suitability information.

4. In the case of an exchange or replacement of an annuity, the exchange or replacement is suitable, including taking into consideration whether:

   a. The consumer will incur a surrender charge; be subject to the commencement of a new surrender period; lose existing benefits, such as death, living, or other contractual benefits; or be subject to increased fees, investment advisory fees, or charges for riders and similar product enhancements.
   b. The consumer would benefit from product enhancements and improvements.
   c. The consumer has had another annuity exchange or replacement and, in particular, an exchange or replacement within the preceding thirty-six months.

   Before the execution of a purchase, replacement, or exchange of an annuity resulting from a recommendation, an insurance producer, or an insurer when no producer is involved, shall make reasonable efforts to obtain the consumer's suitability information. (N D. Cent. Code §§26.1-34.2-03*, 26.1-34.2-03.1*). *Both of these statutes are updating on January 1, 2022.

III. Statutory References:

N.D. Cent. Code §26.1-01-	07,
N.D. Cent. Code §26.1-11-	07,
N.D. Cent. Code §26.1-22-	21
N.D. Cent. Code §§26.1-26-	03, 04, 09
	11, 13.1 to 13.4
	20, 25

	31.1, 31.6, 31.7, 34, 35
	41, 42, 47.1
N.D. Cent. Code §§26.1-26.3-	01 to 07
N.D. Cent. Code §26.1-27-	03.1,
N.D. Cent. Code §26.1-31.1-	02,
N.D. Cent. Code §§26.1-34.2-	03, 03.1
N.D. Cent. Code §§26.1-46-	02, 03, 07.

N.D. Admin. Code 45-02-02-	04, 10, 11
N.D. Admin. Code 45-02-04-	09.3, 11

Web References:

https://www.nd.gov/ndins/producers/nonresident/addline/.
https://www.insurance.nd.gov/third-party-administrator.
https://www.insurance.nd.gov/life-settlements.
https://www.insurance.nd.gov/producers/non-resident-producer.
https://www.insurance.nd.gov/continuing-education-faq-producer.
https://www.insurance.nd.gov/producers/appointments.

OHIO

Department of Insurance
50 West Town St.; Third Floor – Suite 300
Columbus, OH 43215
Telephone: 614-644-2658
Licensing: 614-644-2665; Fax: 614-644-3475
http://www.insurance.ohio.gov
Email: licensing@insurance.ohio.gov

I. **Licensing Requirements:** Sales Personnel—Major Lines, Limited Line and Managing General Agents—Public Insurance Adjusters, Public Adjuster Agents, Reinsurance Intermediaries, Third Party Administrators. Surety Bail Bond, Title, Viatical Settlement Brokers.

A. **Applicability:** No person shall sell, solicit, or negotiate insurance in Ohio unless the person is licensed for that line of authority. (ORC Ann. §3905.02). Business entities are required to be licensed if they are collecting commissions through their FEIN.

B. **Licenses Required of Residents:** Each of the following must be licensed in Ohio. Obtain all license applications from Department of Insurance.

Sales Personnel

1. *Agents.*

a. License fee: $10 per line of authority. Renewal Fee: $25. Renewal fee waived for resident individuals who are compliant with their CE requirements. The Uniform Agent Application may be used. The form may be downloaded from the Department Web site:
https://pdb.nipr.com/my-nipr/main/identifyLicensee.htm?execution=e1s1. View the state of Ohio's individual application checklist at: https://insurance.ohio.gov/static/Forms/Documents/INS3010.pdf

b. License term: An individual seeking to renew a resident insurance agent license shall apply biennially for a renewal of the license on or before the last day of the licensee's birth month. The initial license period must be greater than eighteen months but less than twenty-nine months. This provision is not applicable to surety bail bond, surplus lines, third party administrators, managing general agents, reinsurance intermediaries, public insurance adjusters, viatical settlement providers, and viatical settlement broker licenses. (ORC Ann. §3905.06 and OAC Ann. 3901-5-09).

c. Lines of authority:

   (1) Life.
   (2) Accident & health.
   (3) Property.
   (4) Casualty.
   (5) Personal lines.
   (6) Variable products.
   (7) Surety bail bonds renew annually on or before February 28th. Application and renewal fee: $150 plus criminal background check and $25 for wallet photo card.
   (8) Title. (ORC Ann. 3905.06)

2. *Limited Lines Agents.*

   a. License Fee: $10 per line of authority.
   b. License term: Renews biennially on or before the last day of the licensee's birth month. The initial license period must be greater than eighteen months but less than twenty-nine months. Renewal fee: $25. (OAC Ann. 3901-5-09 subsection J).
   c. Limited lines of authority:

      (1) Credit.
      (2) Car rental.
      (3) Crop.
      (4) Funeral expense. (Must be a Licensed Funeral Director).
      (5) Portable Electronics.
      (6) Travel.
      (7) Title insurance marketing representative.
      (8) Limited Lines Self Storage. (ORC Ann. 3905.06)

3. *Business Entities (Partnerships, Corporations, Limited Liability Companies).* Agency partnerships, LLCs, and corporations must be licensed by the Insurance Department. License fee: $10 per line of authority. License term: Renews biennially on September 30. Resident business renews on even numbered years and nonresident business renews on odd numbered years. (OAC Ann. 3901-5-09 subsection J). Renewal fee: $25. Changes in agency principals or ownership share must be reported to Insurance Department within thirty days after date of change, on forms provided by Insurance Department. Business entities must have at least one licensed agent affiliated with the entity in order to maintain the Ohio license. (OAC Ann. 3901-5-09). Resident business

entity applicants must register with the Ohio Secretary of State as a license prerequisite. Nonresident business entity applicants must contact the Ohio Secretary of State to verify if registration is required to do business in Ohio. (OAC Ann. 3901-5-09). Any changes in name, address, licensed agents, additions of trade or fictitious names must be reported within thirty days.

4. *Managing General Agents.* Must be licensed; annual fee: $20. Must maintain a bond of at least $50,000 and an E&O policy. License expires on the last day of February. (ORC Ann. §3905.72). Official checklist is located at https://insurance.ohio.gov/static/Forms/Documents/INS3028.pdf

Other Insurance Professionals

1. *Public Insurance Adjusters.* Public adjuster's license expires December 31. New: $100. Renewal: $50 annually. If the applicant is a business entity, the fee is $100 for each person named on the application. A $1,000 bond is required. (ORC Ann. §3951.03 and §3951.06). Official checklist is located at: https://insurance.ohio.gov/static/Forms/Documents/INS3025.pdf.

2. *Public Insurance Adjuster Agents.* Employees of public adjusters. New license: $100. Annual fee: $50. A $1,000 bond is required. (ORC Ann. §3951.03 and §3951.06).

3. *Reinsurance Intermediaries.* Must be licensed. Annual fee: $500. Expires on December 31. (ORC Ann. §3905.81).

4. *Third Party Administrators.* Must be licensed in the manner prescribed by the Administrators Review Board. Filing fee: $200. Renewal (June 30 annually): $300. Must also post a fidelity bond and must carry any type of professional liability and/or E&O insurance required by ERISA. (OAC Ann. 3901-8-05). Must be registered with the SOS.

5. *Viatical Settlements.* Brokers: new, $200. Annual Renewal: $100. Providers, new: $1,000. Annual Renewal: $500. License expires March 31. (OAC Ann. 3901-9-01). Official checklist for an individual broker is located at https://insurance.ohio.gov/static/Forms/Documents/INS3042.pdf, for an entity is located at https://insurance.ohio.gov/static/Forms/Documents/INS3044.pdf.

6. *Portable Electronics Vendors.* "Portable electronics insurance" means insurance providing coverage for the repair or replacement of portable electronics, which may be offered on a month-to-month or other periodic basis as a group or master commercial inland marine policy issued to a vendor by an insurer, and may cover portable electronics against loss, theft, inoperability due to mechanical failure, malfunction, damage, or other applicable perils. (ORC Ann. §3905.062).

Application fee: Ten stores or less, $100; eleven or more, $1000. Renewal Fee: Ten stores or less, $100; eleven or more, $500. License Term: Renews biennially on September 30 on even numbered years. (OAC Ann. 3901-5-09).

The following application forms are used:

1. *Agent License.* NAIC Uniform Producer Application for Individual Resident/ Nonresident License (2014).

2. *Corporate Agency License.* NAIC Uniform Application for Business Entity Nonresident License/Registration (2014).

3. *Public Adjusters.* Must file the Individual Public Insurance Adjuster, form INS3214 as a Public Insurance Adjuster/Public Insurance Adjuster Agent.

   Electronic applications should be submitted through the National Insurance Producer Registry at www.nipr.com.

   The Ohio Department of Insurance accepts initial applications and renewal applications via the Internet for resident and nonresident agents (Individuals and Business Entity).

C. **Appointments:** An insurance agent shall not act as an agent of an insurer unless the insurance agent is appointed as an agent of the insurer. An insurance agent who does not act as an agent of an insurer shall not be required to be appointed as an agent of the insurer. Fees: $15, first issue and annual renewal. (ORC Ann. §3905.20) (https://insurance.ohio.gov/wps/portal/gov/odi/agents-and-agencies/appointments/agent-appointment-termination-fees).

D. **Licenses Required of Nonresidents:** Nonresidents have the same fees as residents for all of the various license types listed above. For Major Lines, Limited Lines and Title: Nonresident agents must be appointed in Ohio with the companies for whom they are writing business. Certification of resident license (less than ninety days old) from home state is not required if state is on NIPR Producer data base. Appointing company will be billed $15 for each appointment. Producer data base lookup is available. Uniform nonresident producer application can be used.

   Applications may be submitted through the National Insurance Producer Registry, www.nipr.com. License fee: $10 per line of authority for individual and business entity major line nonresident applicants. License term: An individual seeking to renew a nonresident insurance agent license shall apply biennially for a renewal of the license on or before the last day of the licensee's birth month. Renewal fee: $25. (ORC Ann. §3905.40).

Multi-State Exposures: A license is not required for a nonresident insurance producer who sells, solicits, or negotiates a contract of insurance for commercial property and casualty coverage when risks that are to be insured under that contract are located in more than one state. This exception applies only if the nonresident is licensed to sell, solicit, or negotiate that insurance in the state where the insured maintains its principal place of business and the contract of insurance insures risks located in that state. (ORC Ann. §3905.03).

E. **Prelicensing Examination and Education Requirements:** Ohio requires all resident applicants to pass a criminal background check conducted by the Ohio Bureau of Criminal Investigation and Identification (BCI) and the Federal Bureau of Investigations (FBI) (ORC Ann. §3905.051). Criminal background check fee: $46 ($22 for State BCI and $24 for FBI) plus any vendor fees. Ohio has signed an agreement with the vendors listed on its site that the vendors will not charge more than $71 total. Applicants must use WebCheck, a Web-based fingerprinting technology that processes background checks within two business days. See Ohio's Web site for WebCheck locations. (https://insurance.ohio.gov/static/Forms/Documents/INS3044.pdf) The use of other background investigations services is not permitted. The results of the background check must be directly submitted to the Ohio Department of Insurance from BCI or the results will be returned.

1. *Residents.* Ohio resident applicants must successfully pass an exam prior to submitting an application for licensing. Any application received before the passage of an exam will be returned when an exam is required. Exam required for: Agent (all lines of authority), title, public insurance adjuster, and surety bail bonds. No examination is required for public adjuster agents. (ORC Ann. §3905.04).

   Prelicensing education required for: Life, Accident & Health; Property, Casualty, Personal Lines and Surety Bail Bonds. Applicants for these lines must have successfully completed twenty hours of a program of insurance for each line. The applicant must be at least eighteen years old.

   Prelicensing education is waived for the following:

   a. Life applicants who hold CLU, CEBS, ChFC, CIC, CFP, FLMI, or LUTCF designations. (OAC Ann. 3901-5-07(D)(3)).
   b. Property/casualty applicants who hold CPCU, AAI, ARM, or CIC designations. (OAC Ann. 3901-5-07(D)(2)).

c. Accident and health who hold RHU, CEBS, REBC, or HIA designations. (OAC Ann. 3901-5-07(D)(4)).
d. Applicants with an Associate or Bachelor's degree with a major in insurance.
e. Title applicants.
f. Public insurance adjuster applicants. (OAC Ann. 3901-5-07).

The exams are administered by Prometric. Schedule by phone: 877-346-4014, fax: 877-341-9469; TDD User: 800.790.3926 or on the Web: https://www.prometric.com/test-takers/search/ce-1. Examination fee: $49.50. Duplicate score report: $15. Practice tests are free.

Prometric
Attn: Ohio Continuing Education
7941 Corporate Drive, Nottingham, MD 21236; Email: CESupportTeam@Prometric.com.
(https://www.prometric.com/test-takers/search/ohceprod).

Applicants not required to take an exam must apply directly to the Department of Insurance for a license. Applicants required to take the exam must apply directly to the Department of Insurance for a license only after passing the required exam.

2. *Nonresidents.* Examination is not required of nonresidents applying for a nonresident agent's license, but they must be currently licensed in state of residence.

F. Continuing Education Requirements:

Number of Hours Required: Twenty-four hours (three in ethics), biennially (applicable to all major LOA licensed agents). Licensees who hold only a title license must complete twelve hours (ten title-specific and two ethics) biennially. Licensees who hold both a title and a resident major line must complete twenty-four hours (ten title specific and three ethics). Surety bail bond agents must complete seven hours (six surety bail bond specific & one ethics). Licensees who hold both surety bail bond license and a resident major line can only count ethics hours towards both. (OAC Ann. 3901-5-01). The DOI does not prescribe course content. Viatical/life settlement broker license must complete fifteen hours of approved continuing education specifically related to viatical/life settlements and viatical/life transactions. (OAC Ann. 3901-9-03). Licensee may use classroom instruction, self-study or distance learning. Program is administered by Prometric, 800-532-2170. Can view continuing education at https://insurance.ohio.gov/wps/portal/gov/odi/agents-and-agencies/agent-education/agent-license-education-law-changes.

Licensees who publish books or articles on insurance may receive up to ten hours of CE credit upon request (seven hours for viatical/life settlement CE). Those who write material for use in a CE course may receive the same number of hours as students in the course. Course instructors receive double the number of hours as students in the course. An agent may earn up to four CE credits per renewal cycle for membership and active participation in local, regional, state or national professional insurance associations if qualified under OAC Ann. 3901-5-01(F)(5). (OAC Ann. 3901-5-01).

All licensees (resident & nonresident) who shall sell, solicit, or negotiate long-term care insurance must complete an initial eight-hour partnership program training course. Any licensee that sells, solicits or negotiates any long-term care insurance shall complete at least four hours of continuing education in every renewal cycle thereafter. (ORC Ann. §3923.443).

Submit Proof of Completion by: the initial renewal period for newly licensed individuals shall not be less than eighteen months nor more than twenty-nine months from license issuance date. (OAC Ann. 3901-5-09).

Excess Hours: may not be carried into the next reporting period.

CE Requirements **Not** *Applicable to the Following:*

1. Those granted inactive status. These persons do not need to file a CE report but must maintain proof of their inactive status.

2. Limited Lines licensees.

3. Nonresident agents in compliance with the continuing education requirements of their home state. (OAC Ann. 3901-5-01).

Renewal Procedure:

1. The course provider sends CE credit to the Ohio Insurance Department, who then records the attendance in the licensee's file.

2. A licensee may check on his or her status at the Department's Web site at http://www.insurance.ohio.gov.

3. The agent shall submit a renewal application to the Department. The application must be accompanied by a biennial license renewal fee of $25. The following agents are not required to pay the license renewal fee: (a) Individual resident agents who hold a major line of authority or title license and have met their continuing

education requirements; (b) Surety bail bond agents; or (c) Surplus line brokers. (OAC Ann. 3901-5-01).

Nonresidents are exempt on a reciprocal basis if home state also requires CE.

G. **Cancellation of Agency Contracts/Producer Appointments:** Appointments and terminations must be processed electronically. The Department must be notified within thirty days. (ORC Ann. §3905.20).

H. **Rules for Risk Retention and Purchasing Groups:** Prior to operating in Ohio, risk retention groups and purchasing groups must register with the Department of Insurance and provide other information about the group required by ORC Ann. §3960.02. Agent licensing, administrative enforcement, operating requirements and the applicability of other general insurance laws to risk retention groups and purchasing groups operating in Ohio are located in ORC Ann. §3960.06

All risk retention group policies must contain the following wording in ten point type on both the declarations and the front page:

"This policy is issued by your risk retention group. Your risk retention group may not be subject to all of the insurance laws and regulations of your state. State insurance insolvency guaranty funds are not available for your risk retention group." (ORC Ann. §3960.04).

I. **Other License Rules, Requirements, or Restrictions:** Every licensed agent must notify the Superintendent of Insurance of any change in name or residential, mailing, email, or business address within thirty days of the change. (ORC Ann. §3905.061).

J. **Policy Countersignature Requirements:** Ohio has eliminated its countersignature requirement except that when the laws of any other jurisdiction require countersignature and payment of a fee or commission for Ohio agents the same requirements apply to nonresidents from that jurisdiction placing coverage in Ohio. Purchasing groups are exempted from countersignature requirements. (ORC Ann. §§3901.86 and 3960.06).

II. Commissions, Fees, Commingling of Funds, and Suitability in Annuity Transactions

A. **Commissions:** Ohio has no restrictions on distribution of commissions between individuals and/or business entities that are licensed for the same line of authority. No unlicensed resident or nonresident may be paid a commission under any circumstances. Rebating of commissions is not allowed. (OAC Ann. 3901-5-09(N)).

B. **Fees:** Agents in Ohio can now charge fees in lieu of or in addition to earning a commission, but only in limited circumstances and subject to several conditions. An agent cannot charge a fee for taking or submitting an application or for processing a change, cancellation, claim, or renewal in connection with any personal lines policy or coverage. (ORC Ann. §3905.55).

C. **Disclosure Requirements:** Any fees must be disclosed in a manner that identifies the fee and the premium; fees cannot be calculated as a percentage of premium; and cannot be refunded, forgiven, waived, offset, or reduced by any commission. The amount of the fee and the obligation to pay it cannot be conditioned upon the occurrence of a future event, such as purchase of insurance. The agent must disclose that the fee is *not* required by the insurer or the state and that the agent is not required by the insurer to charge the fee. The insured must accept the fee. Failure to comply with the restrictions is an unfair and deceptive practice. (ORC Ann. §3905.55).

D. **Commingling of Funds:** In general, Ohio does not prohibit agent's commingling of insurer's premiums with other agency funds. However, surplus lines brokers must maintain a separate trust account for the premium tax on surplus lines placements, and title agents must maintain a separate trust account for all escrow funds. Please refer to the online Surplus Lines Chart for additional information regarding surplus lines reports.

E. **Suitability in Annuity Transactions:** An insurance agent shall not solicit the sale of an annuity product unless the insurance agent has adequate knowledge of the product to recommend the annuity and the insurance agent is in compliance with the insurer's standards for product training. An insurance agent may rely on insurer-provided product-specific training standards and materials to comply with this paragraph. The insurance agent must have a minimum of four hours of continuing education relating to the sale of annuities.

In recommending to a consumer the purchase, exchange or replacement of an annuity that results in another insurance transaction or series of insurance transactions, the insurance agent, or the insurer where no agent is involved, shall have reasonable grounds for believing that the recommendation is suitable for the consumer on the basis of the facts disclosed by the consumer as to the consumer's investments and other insurance products and as to the consumer's financial situation and needs, including the consumer's suitability information, and that there is a reasonable basis to believe all of the following: the consumer has been reasonably informed of various features of the annuity, the consumer would benefit from certain features of the annuity, the particular annuity as a whole, including underlying subaccounts to which funds are allocated and riders are suitable for the particular consumer based on the consumer's suitability information, and in the case of an exchange or replacement of an annuity, the exchange or replacement is suitable. (OAC Ann. 3901-6-13).

III. Statutory References: ORC Ann. §§3905.01; 3905.02 through 3905.081; 3905.55, 3905.71 through 3905.79; 3951.02 through 3951.10; 3953.01, 3953.21, 3953.22, 3953.24; 3959.01 through 3959.99; 3960.01 through 3960.13; OAC Ann 3901-5-07 through 3901-5-09; 3901-6-13.

OKLAHOMA

Oklahoma Insurance Department
Five Corporate Plaza
400 NE 50th St.
Oklahoma City, OK 73105-1816
Telephone: 405-521-2828; Fax: 405-521-6635
Licensing: 405-521-3916; Fax: 405-522-3642
Web site: www.ok.gov/oid
Email: licensing@oid.ok.gov

I. Licensing Requirements: Sales Personnel—Producers, Customer Service Representatives, Business Entities, Limited Lines Producers, Managing General Agents. Other Insurance Professionals—Adjusters, Bail Bondsmen, Insurance Consultants, Title, Aircraft Title, Motor Service Club, Surplus Lines Broker, Public Adjusters, Reinsurance Intermediaries, Third Party Administrators, Viatical Settlement Providers & Brokers, Temporary Agents, Life Settlement Providers and Brokers.

A. Applicability: A person shall not sell, solicit, or negotiate insurance in this state for any class or classes of insurance unless the person is licensed for that line of authority. (36 Okla. Stat. §1435.4). An insurance producer shall not act as an agent of an insurer unless the insurance producer becomes an appointed agent of that insurer. An insurance producer who is not acting as an agent of an insurer is not required to become appointed. (36 Okla. Stat. §1435.15).

B. Licenses Required of Residents: Each of the following must be licensed in Oklahoma. Most licenses are biennial, expiring on last day of birth month. Fee is doubled for late reinstatement. Applications must be processed electronically at www.nipr.com. All licenses apply to all lines for which licensee has qualified.

Sales Personnel

General Note about License Terms:

Unless stated otherwise, the license term expires on the last day of birth month. Initial biennial license terms are at least eighteen months but not more than thirty months. Initial license fee prorated based on term length.

1. *Insurance Agent/Producers.*

   a. License and Renewal fee: Resident: $60. Nonresident: $100.
   b. License Term: Biennial. Late reinstatement fee: Double renewal fee.

Agencies Producer (all license types) – Nonresident: $20.00 for Designation for Service of Process plus $20.00 Review of Paperwork Fee.
Agencies Producer (all license types) – Resident: Review of Articles $20.00.

c. Lines of authority:

(1) Life.
(2) Accident and health or sickness.
(3) Property.
(4) Casualty.
(5) P&C Personal Lines.
(6) Commercial lines.
(7) Variable life and variable annuity products. (36 Okla. Stat. §1435.23 and 1435.8).

2. *Title Insurance Agent/Producers.*

a. License and renewal fee: Resident: $60. Nonresident: $100.
b. License term: Biennial. Late reinstatement fee: Double renewal fee.
c. Lines of authority:

(1) Title insurance.
(2) Aircraft title insurance. (36 Okla. Stat. §1435.23 and 1435.8).

3. *Limited Lines Producers.*

a. License and renewal fee: Resident: $40. Nonresident: $100.
b. License term: Biennial. Late reinstatement fee: Double renewal fee.
c. Limited lines of authority:

(1) Credit.
(2) Car rental: License fee based on number of locations. License fee one or two locations: $40. License fee three or more locations: $500.
(3) Crop.
(4) Travel.
(5) Surety.
(6) Prepaid legal liability insurance.
(7) Self-Service Storage Insurance (effective November 1, 2019) (36 Okla. Stat. §1435.23 and 1435.20).

4. *Motor Service Club Representative.* License and Renewal fee: $40. Term: Biennial. Late reinstatement fee: Double renewal fee. New application must be submitted.

5. *Life and Health Insurance Brokers.* The Oklahoma Life, Accident and Health Insurance Broker Act was repealed during the 2018 Oklahoma legislative session with a repeal effective date of November 1, 2018.

6. *Customer Service Reps.* License and renewal fee: $40. Term: Biennial. Late reinstatement fee: Double renewal fee. Must be a salaried employee. Compensation must not include commissions; however, up to 49 percent of such compensation may be based on production or volume of business. Must be appointed by the producer, broker, or agency. Cannot be appointed by more than one appointing insurance producer, broker, or agency at any one time (36 Okla. Stat. §1435.31).

7. *Business Entities.* A business entity acting as an insurance producer is required to obtain an insurance producer license with a separate $60 fee. All agency renewal applications must be processed electronically via NIPR. A domestic business entity must be organized pursuant to the provisions of the laws of Oklahoma and maintain its principal place of business in Oklahoma. The agency must designate an Oklahoma licensed producer responsible for the business entity's compliance with the insurance laws, rules and regulations of Oklahoma. Designated producer changes, address changes within the same state, phone, and email changes must all be processed at www.nipr.com. (36 Okla. Stat. §1435.7).

8. *Managing General Agents.* License and renewal fee: Resident: $60. Nonresident: $100. Term: Biennial. Late reinstatement fee: Double renewal fee. Must be licensed as a producer. The commissioner may require a bond and/or an E&O policy. (36 Okla. Stat. §1473).

Other Insurance Professionals

General Note about License Terms:

Unless stated otherwise, license term expires on last day of birth month. Initial biennial license terms are at least eighteen months but not more than thirty months. Initial license fee prorated based on term length.

1. *Adjusters.* Adjusters are licensed as follows:

    a. Insurance Adjuster: License and renewal fee: One line of authority: $30; two or more lines of authority: $50. Term: Biennial. Late reinstatement fee: Double renewal fee. Lines of authority available: Property; Casualty; Workers' compensation; Crime and fidelity bonds; Crop/Hail; or Multi-peril. (36 Okla. Stat. §6209 and 6212).
    b. Public Adjuster: License and Renewal fee: $30. Term: Biennial. Late reinstatement fee: Double renewal fee. Bond of $25,000 required. Lines of authority available: Property only. (36 Okla. Stat. §6202, 6212 and 6214).

c. Catastrophic/Emergency Adjuster: License fee: $15. Term: ninety days. (36 Okla. Stat. §6212 and 6218).
d. Apprentice/Trainee Adjuster: License fee: $20. Term: Six months after issue. (36 Okla. Stat. §6204.1, 6212 and 6218).
Must apply for licenses electronically at www.nipr.com.

2. *Bail Bondsmen.* License fee: $250. Initial investigation fee: $100. Term: Biennial. Renewal: $200. An applicant for a multi-county agent bondsman license must pay a $750 license fee. Late reinstatement fee: Double license fee. Professional, surety, cash, and property authorities are available. An applicant's business address and mailing address must be in the same county. (59 Okla. Stat. §1305 and 1309).

3. *Insurance Consultants.* No individual may concurrently hold a consultant's license and a license as an insurance producer, surplus lines insurance broker, or limited lines producer. An insurance consultant is an individual or legal entity who, for a fee, is held out to the public as engaged in the business of offering any advice, counsel, opinion or service with respect to the benefits, advantages, or disadvantages promised under any policy of insurance that could be issued or delivered in Oklahoma. This license is required of anyone serving as an insurance consultant, except:

    a. Attorneys licensed to practice in Oklahoma acting in their professional capacity;
    b. Duly licensed insurance producers;
    c. Surplus lines producers;
    d. Bank trust officers acting in the normal course of employment; or
    e. Certified public accountants acting in their professional capacity.
    License and renewal fee: $100. Term: Biennial. A $5,000 to $40,000 bond (based on volume of business) is required. (36 Okla. Stat. §1435.2, 1435.23, and 1435.30).

4. *Reinsurance Intermediaries.* License and renewal fee: $100. Term: Biennial. Intermediary managers must provide evidence of a bond and an E&O policy. (36 Okla. Stat. §5103).

5. *Third Party Administrators.* Individuals are not required to be licensed except where the individual is a general partner in a partnership licensed as a TPA. License and renewal fee: $100. Term: Annual. Minimum of a $10,000 bond protecting the insurer or trust is required. Administrators must have a written contract with an insurer or trust. Corporations must report list of companies for whom they serve as a TPA. Submit Forms TPA-1 and TPA-2. A copy of the home state TPA license is required at renewal. (36 Okla. Stat. §1442, 1448, and 1450).

6. *Viatical Settlement Providers/Brokers.* License and renewal fee: $500. Term: Annual. A service process fee of $20 is required for first time nonresident applicants. Providers and brokers must file evidence of financial responsibility. This may be provided by surety bonds; E&O policies; deposit of cash, certificates of deposit, securities, or any combination thereof in the amount of $50,000. (36 Okla. Stat. §4055.3).

   Applicants must apply electronically through www.nipr.com.

7. *Temporary Agent's License.* License Fee: $20; Term: 180 days. This type of license is issued for the following reasons:

   a. To the surviving spouse or court-appointed personal representative of a licensed insurance producer who dies or becomes mentally or physically disabled to allow adequate time for the sale of the business, or the return of the producer to the business or to provide training and licensing of new personnel.
   b. To a member or employee of a business entity upon the death or disability of an individual designated in the business entity license or application.
   c. To the designee of a licensed insurance producer who enters active military service in the United States Armed Forces.
   d. In any other circumstances the commissioner deems in the public interest. (36 Okla. Stat. §1435.12).

C. **Appointments:** An insurance producer shall not act as an agent of an insurer unless the insurance producer becomes an appointed agent of that insurer. An insurance producer who is not acting as an agent of an insurer is not required to become appointed. Appointments are required within fifteen days from the date the agent contract is executed. Appointment fee: $30. Annual renewal fee: $30. All company appointments must be processed electronically. (36 Okla. Stat. §1435.15 and 1435.23; Okla. Admin. Code 365:1-13-1).

D. **Licenses Required of Nonresidents:** Nonresidents may hold each of the previously listed licenses. Entities must be licensed as well as all individuals in the entity who will be selling insurance. NAIC Uniform Application is to be submitted. Nonresident adjuster applicants should consult the insurance Department's Website for instructions on examination requirements. Generally, a nonresident adjuster may receive a license without examination if the applicant is licensed and has passed an examination in their home state. Applicants may designate another state as their home state if the resident state does not license or examine adjusters. (36 Okla. Stat. §6208).

   Multi-State Exposures: A license is not required for a nonresident insurance producer who sells, solicits, or negotiates a contract of insurance for commercial property and casualty coverage when risks that are to be insured under that contract are located in more than one state. This exception applies only if the nonresident is licensed to sell, solicit, or negotiate that insurance in the state where the insured maintains its principal place of business and the contract of insurance insures risks located in that state. (36 Okla. Stat. §1435.5).

E. Prelicensing Examination and Education Requirements:

1. *Residents.*

   Producer and CSR applicants must pass exams for the following major lines: Life, Accident and Health; Property; Casualty; P&C Personal lines; P&C Commercial lines, Title, and Aircraft title. Exam fee: Cannot exceed $100 (36 Okla. Stat. §1435.23(A)(3)).

   Adjusters must pass exams for the following lines: Property and Casualty (Exam Fee doubled), Casualty, Crop/Hail, Crime & Fidelity bonds, Motor Vehicle Physical Damage, Fire and Allied lines (Property), Workers Compensation. (36 Okla. Stat. §6208, 6212).

   An applicant who has failed the license examination may retake the exam. The exams are administered by Prometric. Examinations may be scheduled through www.prometric.com.

   Bail bond applicants must complete sixteen hours of prelicensing education sponsored by the Oklahoma Bondsman Association and pass an exam. Exam fee: $100. (59 Okla. Stat. §1308).

2. *Nonresidents.* Examination requirement is reciprocal with nonresident's home state. (36 Okla. Stat. §1435.10 and 6208).

F. Continuing Education Requirements:

Number of Hours Required:

1. Agent/Producers: Not less than twenty-one hours biennially, including three hours in ethics, two hours in legislative updates and one hour in flood insurance.

2. Title Agent/Producers: Not less than sixteen hours biennially, including two hours in ethics, two hours in legislative updates and one hour in flood insurance.

3. Adjusters: Not less than twenty-four hours biennially, including three hours of ethics, two hours in legislative updates and one hour in flood insurance.

4. Customer Service Reps.: Not less than ten hours biennially, including three in ethics, two hours in legislative updates and one hour in flood insurance.

5. Bail Bondsmen: Not less than sixteen hours biennially. Continuing education requirements shall be provided and are required each year to accumulate sixteen hours to renew license biennially. (59 Okla. Stat. §1308.1; Okla. Admin. Code 365:25-5-3).

The licensee may use classroom instruction or a self-study course approved by the Department. Participants in an approved professional designation program exceeding twenty-four hours are deemed to have met the biennial requirement for continuing education. (36 Okla. Stat. §1435.29 and 6217; Okla. Admin. Code 365:25-3-1 and 365:25-3-14).

Proof of Completion: Submitted by CE provider.

Excess Hours: Producers and Adjusters may carry six hours into the next reporting period. (Okla. Admin. Code 365:25-3-1 and 365:25-3-14).

Final Exam: All self-study courses require an exam.

CE Requirements ***Not*** *Applicable to the Following:*

1. Limited lines licensees.

O.A.C. § 365:25-3-1(c) & 36 O.S. § 1435.29

Renewal Procedure:

1. Course provider supplies licensee with completion certificate and electronically uploads CE credit to the DOI. The licensee should verify that the license number shown on the certificate is correct.

2. Licensee should keep certificate for three to four years.

   Nonresidents are exempt on a reciprocal basis if home state has substantially similar requirements to those of Oklahoma. If home state is not reciprocal with Oklahoma, licensee may meet the CE requirements of any state that has CE requirements where licensee has an active license and that state is reciprocal with Oklahoma.

G. **Cancellation of Agency/Producer Contracts:** Insurers must notify insurance commissioner within thirty days following the effective date of termination and within fifteen days after notification to the commissioner, must mail a copy of notification to the producer. (36 Okla. Stat. §1435.16).

H. Rules for Risk Retention and Purchasing Groups: A risk retention group to be chartered in Oklahoma must be licensed as a liability insurer and comply with all Oklahoma laws and requirements that apply to such insurers. The RRG must submit a plan of operation or feasibility study for the commissioner's approval. RRGs and PGs must pay an annual fee of $400. Nonresident groups, before entering Oklahoma, must register with the insurance commissioner and submit reports to the commissioner as described in the law. All risk retention group policies must show the following notice in at least ten-point type on the front page and on the declarations page of the policy:

NOTICE

"This policy is issued by your risk retention group. Your risk retention group may not be subject to all of the insurance laws and regulations of your state. State insurance insolvency guaranty funds are not available for your risk retention group." (36 Okla. Stat. §6451 through 6468).

I. Other License Rules, Requirements, or Restrictions: Unlicensed nonresidents may not enter state to solicit or inspect. Entering the state includes mail or telephone into the state from the outside, as well as physical presence in the state.

J. Policy Countersignature Requirements: No insurance contract which is otherwise valid shall be rendered invalid by reason of the apparent execution on behalf of the insurer by the signature of an individual not authorized to execute as of the date of the policy if the policy is countersigned by an individual who is authorized. Every commitment and policy of title insurance issued by an insurance company in Oklahoma must be countersigned by a title insurance producer for a title insurance company. Purchasing groups are exempt from countersignature laws. (36 Okla. Stat. §3618, 5001 (effective November 1, 2018) and 6457).

II. Commissions, Fees, Commingling of Funds, and Suitability in Annuity Transactions

A. Commissions: An insurer or insurance producer may pay or assign commissions, service fees, brokerages, or other valuable consideration to an insurance agency or to persons who do not sell, solicit, or negotiate insurance unless the payment is an unfair trade practice such as a rebate or inducement. Override commissions may be accepted from unlicensed persons. (36 Okla. Stat. §1435.14).

B. Fees: Fees may be charged for insurance consulting services only if based on prior written agreement on a form approved by the commissioner and signed by the producer or consultant and client. The agreement is to be retained at least three years after the services are completed. Producers acting as consultants may offset all or part of fees by commissions received for any insurance written. (36 Okla. Stat. §1435.30).

Fees may be charged to the consumer. However, the fee passed on to the consumer must be the actual expense incurred by the insurance company, insurance agency, or insurance producer. A duplicate fee cannot be charged. (36 Okla. Stat. §3623.1).

C. **Disclosure Requirements:** None.

D. **Commingling of Funds:** Property and casualty producers shall not commingle premiums belonging to insurers and returned premiums belonging to insureds with the personal funds of the producer or with any other funds except those directly connected with the producer licensee's insurance business. (36 Okla. Stat. § 1435.13a).

E. **Suitability in Annuity Transactions:** In recommending to a consumer the purchase of an annuity or the exchange of an annuity that results in another insurance transaction or series of insurance transactions, the insurance producer, or the insurer where no producer is involved, shall have reasonable grounds for believing that the recommendation is suitable for the consumer on the basis of the facts disclosed by the consumer as to his or her investments and other insurance products and as to his or her financial situation and needs.

Prior to the execution of a purchase or exchange of an annuity resulting from a recommendation, the producer or an insurer if no producer is involved shall make reasonable efforts to obtain information concerning the consumer's financial and tax status, investment objectives, and other information as to be considered reasonable by the insurance producer or insurer if no producer is involved. (Okla. Admin. Code 365:25-17-7).

III. **Statutory References: 36** Okla. Stat. §1435.1 through 1435.41; 1441 through 1452; 1471 through 1478; 5101 through 5113; 6202 through 6221; 59 Okla. Stat. §1301 through 1340; Okla. Admin. Code 365:1-13-1, 365:25-3-1 and 365:25-17-7.

OREGON

Dept. of Consumer & Business Services
Insurance Division
350 Winter St. N.E., Room 410; Salem, OR 97301-3883
Mailing address: Oregon Ins. Division, P.O. Box 14480, Salem, OR 97309-0405
Telephone: 503-947-7981; Fax: 503-378-4351;
Website: www.oregon.gov/dcbs/insurance/pages/index.aspx ;
Email: web.insagent@oregon.gov

I. Licensing Requirements: Sales Personnel—Producers, Limited Class Producers, Car Rental Limited Line Licensees, Entities, Managing General Agents. Other Insurance Professionals—Adjusters, Consultants, Life Settlement Providers/Brokers, Public Adjusters, Reinsurance Intermediaries, Third-Party Administrators, Self-Service Storage.

A. Applicability: A person may not sell, solicit or negotiate insurance in Oregon for any class or classes of insurance unless the person is licensed as an insurance producer for that class or those classes of business. An insurance producer shall not act as an agent of an insurer unless the insurance producer is an appointed agent of that insurer or the insurance producer transacts insurance on behalf of another insurance producer who is an appointed agent of that insurer according to department conditions and limitations. (O.R.S. §§744.053 and 744.078).

B. Licenses Required of Residents: Each of the following must be licensed in Oregon:

Sales Personnel

1. *Producers.*

   a. License fee: $30. Application; $45, license. Fingerprint and background check fee: $56.25.00. Fingerprints are taken at PSI locations. For more details, visit PSI's Web site at http://www.psionline.com/PROGRAMS/Fingerprint%20 hours.pdf. Personal checks are not accepted. (Or. Admin. R. 836-009-0007).
   b. License term: biennial. Renewal fee: $45, plus processing. The license expires biennially at the end of the month of the individual's birthday anniversary. All renewals are processed through NIPR. (Or. Admin. R. 836-009-0007).
   c. Lines of authority (Note: Oregon refers to classes of insurance):

      (1) Life.
      (2) Health.
      (3) Property.
      (4) Casualty.

(5) Variable products.
(6) Property and casualty sold to individuals and families. (Personal Lines) (O.R.S. §744.062).

2. *Limited Class (Lines) Producers.*

a. License fee: $75. Fingerprint and background check fee: $50. Fingerprints are taken at PSI locations. Personal checks are not accepted. (Or. Admin. R. 836-009-0007).
b. License term: biennial. Renewal fee: $45, plus processing fee.
c. Limited lines of authority:

(1) Credit.
(2) Crop.
(3) Surety.
(4) Title.
(5) Travel.
(6) Mechanical Breakdown.

3. *Car Rental Limited Line Licensee.* Car rental companies must obtain a limited license.

a. License fee: $200.
b. License term: biennial. Renewal fee: $200, plus processing fee.
c. Lines of authority for a car rental limited licensee:

(1) Personal accident insurance covering the risks of travel.
(2) Liability insurance, including uninsured and underinsured motorist coverage.
(3) Personal effects insurance.
(4) Roadside assistance and emergency sickness protection programs.

d. Other Requirements: Employees or designated agents in the car rental location can solicit insurance without a license as long as the car rental company is licensed. The rental company must provide the same training and oversight to a designated agent as it provides for employees. The syllabus for the training program shall be filed annually with the Director of the Department of Consumer and Business Services by the rental company and is subject to approval by the director. The rental company shall certify annually to the director that all employees involved in the sale or offer of coverage to members of the public have completed or will complete the training program prior to conducting such sales or offers. The rental company shall also certify annually to the director that all such employees will receive continuing education on a regular basis concerning the topics covered in the training program. If the location is a franchise of a car rental company, the franchise must be licensed. Designated Agents: A rental company that obtains a limited license must conduct a training program for the rental company's employees and designated agents concerning the types of coverage the company offers. The company must file the syllabus for the training program annually with the Director of the Department of Consumer and Business Services and obtain the director's approval. The company must also annually certify to the director that all of the company's employees and designated agents who are involved in selling or offering coverage to members of the public have completed or will complete the training program before making sales or offers. Additionally, the company has to certify that the employees and designated agents will receive continuing education on a regular basis concerning the topics covered in the training program. (O.R.S. §§744.852 – 744.856).

4. *Travel Retailer Registration.* A travel retailer may offer travel insurance on behalf of and at the direction of a limited travel producer and may receive compensation for doing so. Under such an arrangement information distributed to customers must contain the name, license number, and contact information of the producer. In addition, the producer must supply the retailer with an affidavit stating that the retailer is not guilty of any offense under 18 USC 1033. In addition, the producer must designate an employee who is a limited travel insurance producer as responsible for ensuring the compliance with the laws. Every employee of the retailer who offers such insurance must receive a program of instruction. Information distributed to customers must state that the retailer itself is not the producer and is not authorized to answer technical questions. It must also explain that purchase of insurance is not required to purchase any other product sold by the retailer. (O.R.S. § 744).

5. *Business Entities.* Must have an agent license and must have at least one DRLP, Designated Responsible Licensed Producer, and list licensed individuals as affiliates of the agency. (O.R.S. §744).

6. *Managing General Agents.* Managing general agents must have a producer license, with an endorsement to that license as an MGA. MGAs must maintain an E&O policy with limits not less than $500,000. (O.R.S. §§744.300 to 744.316).

The Oregon Insurance Division will not issue printed initial, renewal, or replacement licenses. All license information for active licensees will be available on the department's Web site.

Fingerprinting: Beginning in 2011, all fingerprinting will be performed at the testing centers via "live scan" technology. Fingerprinting is not required for resident licensees adding a line of authority to an existing license.

Other Insurance Professionals

All of the following are required to attest to a statement acknowledging no conviction of a misdemeanor or felony in the last two years for renewal or any past convictions for application. Otherwise, they must provide details with the license renewal request or application.

1. *Adjusters*. Operative January 1, 2020 a person may not engage in business as an adjuster unless the person has obtained a license in accordance with section 6 of the 2019 Insurance Act found at 2019 Ore. ALS 151, 2019 Ore. Laws 151, 2019 Ore. SB 251 unless exempted by O.R.S. §744.515. Adjusters must have an adjuster's license, which expires biennially on the last day of the month of the individual's birthday anniversary: initial fee: $75, plus processing fee. Fingerprint/background check fee: $50. Renewal fee: $45, plus processing fee. May be licensed for general lines or for health. (O.R.S. §§744.505 to 744.535, Or. Admin. R. 836-009-0007).

   Operative January 1, 2020, O.R.S. §744.535 has been repealed. Now nonresident adjusters must apply for the license as provided in section 5 of the new insurance Act, found at 2019 Ore. ALS 151, 2019 Ore. Laws 151, 2019 Ore. SB 251, and pass an examination set by the director. (2019 Ore. ALS 151, 2019 Ore. Laws 151, 2019 Ore. SB 251, operative January 1, 2020).

2. *Consultants.* Persons selling insurance advice or holding themselves out to be insurance consultants must be licensed; nonresidents must have similar license type in their resident state; must have five years insurance experience or equivalent educational qualifications; may be licensed for these lines: life, health, property and casualty. Consultants must maintain an E&O policy with limits not less than $500,000. Initial fee: $75, plus processing fee. Fingerprint/background check fee: $55. The consultant license expires biennially on the last day of the month of the individual's birthday anniversary. Renewal fee: $45, plus processing fee. (O.R.S. §§744.605 – 744.665).

3. *Life Settlement Providers/Brokers.* Also known as viatical settlement providers/brokers. Life settlement brokers must be licensed; life settlement providers must be registered with the insurance division. Fees: Providers, new: $400. Renewal: $200. Brokers, new: $45, plus processing fee, renewal: $45 plus processing fee. Background check: $50. (O.R.S. §§744.318 – 744.338, Or. Admin. R. 836-014-0210).

4. *Public Adjusters.* Operative January 1, 2020 a person may not engage in business as an adjuster unless the person has obtained a license in accordance with

section 6 of the 2019 Insurance Act found at 2019 Ore. ALS 151, 2019 Ore. Laws 151, 2019 Ore. SB 251 unless exempted by O.R.S. §744.515. Oregon licenses general lines adjusters which includes both public and independent adjusters. Must have an adjuster's license, which renews every two years. An individual's license expires biennially in the month of the individual's birthday anniversary. The license of a person other than an individual expires on the last day of the month in which the second anniversary of the initial issuance date occurs. Initial fee: $75 plus processing fee. Renewal fee: $45 plus processing fee. Fingerprint/background check fee: $55. (O.R.S. §§744.505 – 744.575, Or. Admin. R. 836-071-0130).

5. *Reinsurance Intermediaries.* Persons holding an insurance producer license may have their license endorsed with the designation of reinsurance intermediary. To obtain and maintain the endorsement of reinsurance intermediary manager, a resident reinsurance intermediary must maintain an E&O policy of at least $500,000. Initial fee: $75, plus processing fee. Renewal fee: $45, plus processing fee (O.R.S. §§744.800 – 744.820).

6. *Third-Party Administrators.* Must be licensed. Initial and biennial fee: $45 plus processing fee. Renewal $45, plus processing fee. Must maintain an E&O policy with a $500,00 limit. Entity applicants must submit articles of incorporation, articles of organization, or partnership agreements as well as a list of individuals responsible for conduct of affairs. Biographical affidavits for each owner, partner, director and officer must be provided. (O.R.S. §§744.700 – 744.740, Or. Admin. R. 836-075-0000).

   All license applications are submitted through NIPR.

   1. *Individuals.* All licenses are submitted through NIPR.
   2. *Firms or Corporations.* All licenses are submitted through NIPR.
   3. *Agency.* Affiliations Form 440-2139 (7/13) is located on the Oregon Insurance Division Web site (www.insurance.oregon.gov) and must be emailed to web.insagent@oregon.gov or faxed to 503-378-4351.

7. *Portable Electronics Vendor.* Limited license available only to a business entity that sells portable electronics devices. License fee: $200, plus processing fee; biennial. Application is to be submitted through NIPR.com. Portable electronics include but are not limited to cell phones, tablets, navigation devices.

8. *Self-Service Storage.* Limited license available only to a business entity who issues, sells or offers for sale insurance coverage to occupants at a self-service storage facility. License fee: $200 plus processing fee; biennial. Application is to be submitted through NIPR.com.

C. **Appointments:** An insurance producer shall not act as an agent of an insurer unless the insurance producer is an appointed agent of that insurer; or the insurance producer transacts insurance on behalf of another insurance producer who is an appointed agent of that insurer according to conditions and limitations established by the Director of the Department of Consumer and Business Services by rule. There is no fee for appointment. (O.R.S. §744.078).

D. **Licenses Required of Nonresidents:** The same license requirements apply to nonresidents. Nonresidents must have Oregon appointments for the companies with whom they place business in Oregon. Initial fee: $75 plus processing fee. Renewal fee: $45 plus processing fee. Renewals are processed through NIPR. (Or. Admin. R. 836-009-0007).

Multi-State Exposures. A license is not required for a nonresident insurance producer who sells, solicits, or negotiates a contract of insurance for commercial property and casualty coverage when risks that are to be insured under that contract are located in more than one state. This exception applies only if the nonresident is licensed to sell, solicit, or negotiate that insurance in the state where the insured maintains its principal place of business and the contract of insurance insures risks located in that state. (O.R.S. §744.056).

E. **Prelicensing Examination and Education Requirements:**

1. *Residents.* All resident applicants must complete authorized prelicensing education as follows: property insurance, twenty hours; casualty insurance, twenty hours; personal lines insurance, twenty hours; life insurance, twenty hours; health insurance, twenty hours. Agent applicants must also pass an exam. Exams are given in the following areas: Property and casualty; property; casualty; life; health; life and health; surplus lines; personal lines. A grade of 70 percent or higher is required to pass.

   All licensing courses require twenty hours focusing on the basic principles for the line of business, the duties and responsibilities of an insurance producer and Oregon related laws for authority to transact business.

   An applicant may satisfy the experience requirements for the examination by obtaining an insurance degree from an accredited college or university or may substitute successful completion of coursework required for obtaining an industry recognized designation described in this section for all or a part of the number of years of experience as follows:

   a. AAI, ARM, CEBS, ChFC, CIC, CPCU, HIA, LOMA, LUTCF, REBC, RHU – three years.

b. ACSR, CPIW, CPSR – two years.
c. Proof of three years of licensure in another state or Canada, if within two years of date of application for licensing in Oregon.
d. Three years verifiable proof of experience as an unlicensed person performing duties and activities described in Or. Admin. R. 836-071-0280, if within two years of date of application for licensing. (Or. Admin. R. 836-071-0180).

Life agents who wish to sell variable annuities must also pass an NASD exam and be registered to an Oregon securities dealer.

Applicants for an adjuster license must pass a qualifying examination.

Applicants for a consultant license must pass a qualifying examination and have five years' experience. Exam is waived for licensed producers with five years experience. Applicants must hold a substantially similar license type in their resident state.

Consultant exams are given in the following areas: general lines; life; health; life and health.

All examinations are administered by PSI 800-733-9267. Holders of the CPCU or CLU designation are exempt from these requirements for the respective licenses.

Examination fees are as follows:

Property and casualty (includes law)	$55
Property (includes law)	$45
Casualty (includes law)	$45
Personal lines (includes law)	$45
Surplus lines	$45
Life and health (includes law)	$55
Life (includes law)	$45
Health (includes law)	$45
Adjuster general lines or life and health	$45
Adjuster health or single line	$45
Consultant general lines or life and health	$55
Consultant life or health only, or single line	$45
Oregon law portion	$55

(Or. Admin. R. 836-009-0007).

2. *Nonresidents.* The education and examination requirements for nonresidents apply on a reciprocal basis.

F. Continuing Education Requirements:

Number of Hours Required: Every insurance producer must complete twelve hours of continuing education annually or twenty-four hours in each two-year renewal period including at least three credit hours on the subject of Oregon statutes and administrative rules, including recent changes and at least three credit hours on the subject of professional ethics for insurance producers. A maximum of four hours in approved agency management courses is allowed at each renewal. (Or. Admin. R. 836-071-0215). The maximum credit for one day is eight hours.

Flood Insurance Education: Applicants for new and renewal resident producer licenses to sell property insurance who also want to sell flood insurance shall demonstrate that they have completed a one-time minimum three-hour continuing education course about the federal flood insurance program. If this course has been approved for Oregon CE credit, it may be submitted with the renewal and counted toward the total twenty-four hour obligation necessary to renew the license.

Agents are required to take courses that meet their professional needs. However, the law no longer mandates a certain percentage in the areas licensed.

The licensee may use classroom instruction or self-study.

Submit Proof of Completion by: CE providers download CE credits directly into producer records. By Oregon law, they have fifteen days to do so. A producer may not renew until all CE is complete, visible in their Oregon record and downloaded to NIPR.

Excess Hours: May not be carried into the next reporting period.

Final Exam: All home study courses, except for certain Internet courses, require monitoring by a registered proctor or librarian, licensed accountant, lawyer, or state or community college representative. Contact course provider for details.

Requirements **Not** *Applicable to the Following:*

1. Limited licensees who did not have to take an exam according to O.R.S. §744.067(5).

Renewal Procedure:

1. Course provider downloads CE credits directly into producer record within fifteen days of completion. Updates take at least twenty-four hours to register with NIPR.

2. Renewals must be done electronically and can be done through NIPR.com.

Nonresidents are exempt from the CE requirement. (O.R.S. §744.072).

G. **Cancellation of Agency Contracts/Producer Appointments:** Insurer must give ninety-day notice to insurance producer prior to effective date of termination. Insurer need not provide notice if one of the reasons listed in O.R.S. §744.081(2) is met, including but not limited to the producer's license being denied or producer's insolvency. A producer may terminate an agency appointment at any time provided notice is given to the insurer. The director may require reasonable proof from the insurance producer that the insurance producer has given such notice to the insurer. The director must be notified no later than the 30th day after the effective date of termination. (O.R.S. §744.081).

H. **Rules for Risk Retention and Purchasing Groups:** Oregon regulates risk retention and purchasing groups operating or offering coverage on risks in Oregon. As required under O.R.S. §§735.300 through 735.365, risk retention groups domiciled in Oregon must be chartered and licensed as liability insurers. Domestic risk retention groups must submit a plan of operation or feasibility study for the director's approval. Risk retention groups not domiciled in Oregon must submit to the department of insurance a statement identifying its chartering information in compliance with O.R.S. §735.315(1)(a). Risk retention groups not domiciled in Oregon must submit a copy of the plan of operation or feasibility study, along with revisions, that was submitted in the home state to the Oregon director for approval. They must also submit reports to the director, as described in the law, and a statement designating the director as its agent for the purpose of receiving service of legal documents or process. Purchasing groups must also register with the director in compliance with O.R.S. §735.330 and submit reports as required by the law. All groups and all resident and nonresident agents or brokers participating in them must comply with all Oregon insurance laws, including licensing and solicitation requirements or restrictions. RRG fees, new and renewal: $350; RPG fees, new and renewal: $100. All risk retention group policies must show the following notice in at least ten point type on the front page and on the declarations page of the policy:

NOTICE

"This policy is issued by your risk retention group. Your risk retention group may not be subject to all of the insurance laws and regulations of your state. State insurance insolvency guaranty funds are not available for your risk retention group." (O.R.S. §735.315(6)).

I. **Other License Rules, Requirements, or Restrictions:** No unlicensed nonresident may enter Oregon to sell, solicit, or negotiate to Oregon businesses. Licensed nonresidents may enter the state for any of these purposes. Insurers may not accept Oregon business from unlicensed nonresidents. Entering the state includes mail or telephone or other electronic communication into the state from the outside, as well as physical presence in the state. All licensees must report business and home address changes and telephone numbers within thirty days of change. Insurers and agencies must report terminations of agents within thirty days of termination date. (Or. Admin. R. 836-071-0328).

J. **Policy Countersignature Requirements:** None.

II. Commissions, Fees, Commingling of Funds, Suitability in Annuity Transactions

A. **Commissions:** There are no restrictions on the division of commissions among licensed residents or nonresidents and no retaliatory provision as to nonresidents. Unlicensed residents or nonresidents may receive commission as long as they did not sell, solicit, or negotiate insurance to obtain the commission. Rebating of commissions is not allowed. (O.R.S. §§746.045 and 744.076).

B. **Fees:** The Oregon Insurance Division defines "service fee" as a charge made by an insurance producer with respect to an insurance transaction to a party other than the insurer, which is not a part of the insurer's rate filing. "Service fee" does not include finance or service charges.

Unless authorized in O.R.S. §§744.091 and 744.093, a service fee may be charged only in those instances where the insurance producer has provided service additional to what is the usual and customary practice of insurance producers under similar circumstances. The insurance producer must give a written explanation of the charge and the reason for it to the person charged.

A service fee may not be charged with respect to arranging the financing of premium payments. This does not preclude finance charges by insurance producers on their own accounts, or service charges by premium finance companies. (Or. Admin. R. 836-071-0277).

C. **Disclosure Requirements:** When an insurance producer receives compensation from an insured, they may not also accept or receive any compensation from an insurer or other third-party for the placement of insurance for the prospective insured unless the insurance producer, prior to the prospective insured's purchase of insurance, has:

1. Obtained the prospective insured's documented acknowledgment that the compensation will be received.

2. Disclosed the amount of compensation from the insurer or other third party for the placement. If the amount of compensation is not known at the time of disclosure, the insurance producer shall disclose the specific method for calculating the compensation and, if possible, a reasonable estimate of the amount.

3. Disclosed the nature of the work that the insurance producer or affiliate will perform on behalf of the prospective insured.

"Compensation from a prospective insured" does not include any fee or amount collected by or paid to the insurance producer that does not exceed an amount established by the director.

When an insurance producer receives any compensation from a prospective insured for transacting insurance and receives no compensation from an insurer or other third party for placement of insurance for the prospective insured, the insurance producer must obtain the prospective insured's documented acknowledgement that the compensation will be received and must disclose the nature of the work that the insurance producer will perform on behalf of the prospective insured. (Or. Admin. R. 836-071-0260).

D. **Commingling of Funds:** Producers, including nonresidents collecting Oregon premiums, must maintain a trust fund for premiums collected for insurers separate from any other agency or personal funds. (O.R.S. §744.083).

E. **Suitability in Annuity Transactions:** The insurance producer, or the insurer where no insurance producer is involved, shall have reasonable grounds for believing that the recommendation is suitable for the consumer on the basis of the facts disclosed by the consumer as to his or her investments and other insurance products and as to his or her financial situation and needs, including the consumer's suitability information, and that there is a reasonable basis to believe the consumer has been reasonably informed of various features of the annuity, the consumer would benefit from certain features of the annuity, the particular annuity as a whole and the underlying subaccounts and riders are suitable for the particular consumer based on his suitability information, and in the case of an exchange or replacement of an annuity the exchanges or replacement is suitable for the consumer. (Or. Admin. R. 836-080-0180).

III. **Statutory References:** Oregon Revised Statutes Title 56, §§735.300 through 735.360; 744.052 through 744.089; 744.650; Oregon Administrative Rules 836-009-0007; 836-071-0146 – 836-071-0272; 836-075-0000; 836-080-0180.

PENNSYLVANIA

Insurance Department
1236 Strawberry Sq.; Harrisburg, PA 17120
Telephone: 717-787-3840, Fax: 717-787-8553
http://www.insurance.pa.gov

I. Licensing Requirements: Insurance Producers, Managing General Agents, and Title Insurance Agents, Other Insurance Professionals—Motor Vehicle Damage Appraisers, Public Adjusters, Professional Bondsman, Reinsurance Intermediaries, Third Party Administrators, Viatical Settlement Brokers, business entities as defined in applicable statutes.

A. Applicability: Anyone who sells, solicits, negotiates, or receives commission from these activities in Pennsylvania must obtain a license as an insurance producer. An insurance producer shall not act on behalf of or as a representative of the insurer unless the insurance producer is appointed by the insurer. An insurance producer not acting as a representative of an insurer is not required to be appointed. (40 P.S. §§310.3 and 310.71).

B. Licenses Required of Residents: Each of the following must be licensed in Pennsylvania. Applications for all licenses are obtained from Department of Insurance's Web site at www.insurance.pa.gov. Applicants are encouraged to use electronic services to apply. See the DOI's Web site for information.

Sales Personnel

1. *Producers.*

   a. Resident License fee: $55, new and renewal. Adding line of authority, $25. (40 P.S. §310.5).
   b. License term: biennial expiring on last day of birth month for individuals.
   c. Lines of authority:

      (1) Variable authority (includes variable life/variable annuity).
      (2) Life & annuity.
      (3) Accident & health.
      (4) Property & allied lines.
      (5) Casualty & allied lines.
      (6) Title.
      (7) Personal lines property/casualty.
      (8) Credit life, accident and health and credit unemployment.
      (9) Public adjuster or public adjuster solicitor (31 Pa. Code §37.39).

Business entity applicants for a resident entity producer license must submit the following along with an application:

a. Corporations—articles of incorporation.
b. Limited Liability Companies (LLCs)—articles of organization.
c. Limited Partnerships (LLP).
Entity licenses expire biennially on date of license issuance.
Nonresident entities need to submit these documents only upon request. (40 P.S. §310.5).

Other Insurance Professionals

1. *Motor Vehicle Damage Appraisers.* Motor vehicle damage appraiser's license expires June 30 annually. Initial fee: $55. Annual renewal fee: $55. No bond is required. Licenses are issued to individuals only.

2. *Public Adjusters.* Initial fee and renewal fee: $200. Bond of $20,000. (63 P.S. §1604).

3. *Professional Bondsman.* Initial and renewal fee: $100.

4. *Reinsurance Intermediaries.* Must be licensed as reinsurance intermediary broker or manager. Managers may be required to have a bond and an E&O policy, both in the amount acceptable to the department. Written contract including the minimum provisions set forth in the statute is required for all reinsurance intermediaries. Broker license is valid for two years; manager license for two years or until contract renewal date, whichever time is less. (40 P.S. §321.2 and 321.6).

5. *Third Party Administrators.* Initial fee: $100. Must maintain an E&O policy. Must also post a fidelity bond equal to 50 percent of the funds handled; bond penalty not to exceed $500,000. (40 P.S. §324.4).

6. *Viatical Settlement Brokers.* New and renewal: $100. (40 P.S. §626.3).

Applications should be submitted electronically; however, paper applications may be downloaded for use but will require longer cycle time. To submit electronically or obtain a paper application, visit the department Web site at www.insurance.pa.gov, or go directly to the form/application page located at http://www.insurance.pa.gov/Licensees/MaintainYourLicense/Documents/VIATICAL%20INDIVIDUAL%20APP.pdf.

C. Appointments: An insurance producer shall not act on behalf of or as a representative of the insurer unless the insurance producer is appointed by the insurer. An insurance producer not acting as a representative of an insurer is not required to be appointed. Fee: $18.00 per year. (40 P.S. §310.71 and 31 Pa. Code §37.72).

D. **Licenses Required of Nonresidents:** All of the above licenses are required of nonresidents to conduct insurance activities in Pennsylvania. Producer fees: $110, $110 renewal. The nonresident application for both individuals and business entities is available online only. Visit the DOI Web site for more information on submitting application. (40 P.S. §§310.5 and 310.10).

Multi-State Exposures: A license is not required for a nonresident insurance producer who sells, solicits, or negotiates a contract of insurance for commercial property and casualty coverage when risks that are to be insured under that contract are located in more than one state. This exception applies only if the nonresident is licensed to sell, solicit, or negotiate that insurance in the state where the insured maintains its principal place of business and the contract of insurance insures risks located in that state. (40 P.S. §310.3).

E. **Prelicensing Examination and Education Requirements:**

1. *Residents.* Applicants for producer licenses must complete twenty-four hours of prelicensing education (minimum of three in ethics) and pass an exam. Exams are administered by Prometric (https://www.prometric.com/Pennsylvania). Application fee is $55. Public adjuster, physical damage appraisers, and viatical broker applicants must also pass an exam. All new applicants for resident insurance producer license must be fingerprinted and all title agent applicants must be fingerprinted. Fee is $22.60. See department Web site at: http://www.insurance.pa.gov/Licensees/Documents/Fingerprinting%20Process%20Changes%20November%202017.pdf for instructions. (40 P.S. §310.4). Preexamination education credits shall be valid for one year from the date the course is successfully completed.

The following exams are given.

Combined exams:

Life, accident and health.
Property and casualty.

Surplus lines:

Producer.

Other:

Life Insurance and annuities.
Accident and health.
Property.
Casualty.

Public insurance adjuster.

Motor vehicle physical damage appraiser.
Personal lines.
Viatical settlement broker.
Title insurance.

No exam is required for the following authorities:

a. Variable products—however, applicant must have active FINRA registration (CRD Number).
b. Fire and allied lines for domestic mutual fire insurers.
c. Restricted fraternal authority.
d. All limited line producer licenses.

The prelicensing examination and education requirements are not required if the person is:

a. A business entity.
b. Possesses CLU designation and is applying for life or accident and health.
c. Possesses CPCU designation and is applying for property, casualty, or accident and health.
d. Possesses CIC designation and is applying for life, accident and health or property and casualty.
e. Possesses any other professional designation which the requirements are waived by the commissioner.
f. A person who has a line of authority limited to limited line credit insurance.
g. A person who has a line of authority limited to a limited line. (40 P.S. §310.4).
h. An individual whose line of authority will be restricted to domestic mutual fire insurance and will be with an insurer writing only coverage other than insurance upon automobiles as authorized by section 202(b)(1) through (3) of the act of May 17, 1921 (P.L.682, No.284), known asThe Insurance Company Law of 1921.

i. The individual whose line of authority will be restricted fraternal pursuant to section 609 of the act of December 14, 1992 (P.L. 835, No. 134), known as the Fraternal Benefit Societies Code. (40 P.S. §310.4(d)(9) and (10)).

2. *Nonresidents.* Must pass the exam for title authority. Other examination requirements are reciprocal with nonresident's home state.

F. Continuing Education Requirements:

Number of Credit Hours Required: All resident insurance producers except limited lines; twenty-four hours, biennially. Pennsylvania's CE program is administered by Prometric. Note: Title agents must complete twenty-four credit hours unless they are an attorney who meets continuing legal education, then only three credits are required. (40 P.S. §910-26). The licensee may use classroom instruction or self-study. A course instructor receives double credit for the course taught, but the instructor may not earn credit for instructing a subsequent offering of the same course within the same licensing period. Failure to comply with continuing education requirements by the expiration date of the license shall be deemed a voluntary termination of the insurance producer's license. (31 Pa. Code §39a.10).

Excess Hour Carry Over: Up to twenty-four credit hours may be carried into the next licensing period. (40 P.S. §310.8).

For prelicensing and continuing education requirements see www.prometric.com. For individual continuing education transcripts see www.sircon.com/pennsylvania.

Requirements **Not** *Applicable to the Following:*

1. An insurance producer who was licensed prior to January 1, 1971, and has been continuously licensed for no additional lines of authority.

2. A licensee which is a business entity.

3. A licensee who has only a limited line of authority.

4. Insurance producers whose only line of authority on their license is restricted fraternal.

5. A licensee who has a line of authority limited to limited line credit insurance if the insurer provided a course of instruction to each individual whose duties will include selling, soliciting or negotiating the insurance.

6. A nonresident licensee who has satisfied the continuing education requirements of the home state.

7. Insurance producers whose only line of authority on their license is domestic mutual fire (restricted).

   (40 P.S. §310.8).

Renewal Procedure:

1. Course provider must file course completion with insurance department, or CE administrator if directed, within fifteen days of course completion and supply licensee with certificate of completion within thirty days.

2. Licensee is to keep the original certificate at least six years.

   For online renewal see https://www.sircon.com/stateInformationCenter/pennsylvania.jsp and http://www.nipr.com/index.htm.

G. Cancellation of Agency/Producer Contracts: Insurers must notify the DOI within thirty days of termination and notify the producer within the next fifteen days. (40 P.S. §310.71a).

H. Rules for Risk Retention and Purchasing Groups: A Pennsylvania domestic risk retention group must be licensed as an insurer and also submit for approval to the department a plan of operation or a feasibility study. A foreign risk retention group must register prior to doing business. Every application form for insurance from a risk retention group and every policy issued by a risk retention group must contain the following notice in ten-point type on the front page and declarations page:

NOTICE

"This policy is issued by your risk retention group. Your risk retention group may not be subject to all of the insurance laws and regulations of your state. State insurance insolvency guaranty funds are not available for your risk retention group." (40 P.S. §991.1505).

I. Other License Rules, Requirements, or Restrictions: Solicitation, inspection, or service in state by licensed nonresident, retaliatory with licensee's home state; by unlicensed nonresident, prohibited. Entering the state includes mail or telephone or other electronic communication into the state from the outside, as well as physical presence in the state. All new license candidates must first register online via the IdentoGO website at https://uenroll.identogo.com or by telephone to be fingerprinted (https://www.insurance.pa.gov/Licensees/MaintainYourLicense/Pages/Fingerprinting-Information.aspx), unless a nonresident applying under reciprocity (40 P.S. §310.10). The fee for submitting fingerprints with an initial producer license is $22.60.

J. **Policy Countersignature Requirements:** None.

II. Commissions, Fees, Commingling of Funds, and Suitability in Annuity Transactions

A. **Commissions:** There are no restrictions on distribution of commissions among licensed residents or nonresidents that hold the same lines of authority. Commission payment to unlicensed resident or nonresident or a licensed producer without the appropriate line of authority is prohibited. Rebating of commissions is not allowed. (40 P.S. §§310.72 and 310.73).

B. **Fees:** Insurance producers may charge fees for services beyond those normal to the sale of insurance. The basis for the fees must be disclosed in writing, and the fees must be reasonable for the services performed. No fees are permitted for placing business in the Fair Plan or Assigned Risk Plan. (40 P.S. §§310.71(b) and 310.74).

C. **Disclosure Requirements:** An insurance producer acting on behalf of or representing an insurance consumer shall execute a written agreement with the insurance consumer prior to representing or acting on their behalf that delineates the services to be provided; and provides full and complete disclosure of the fee to be paid to the insurance producer by the insurance consumer. (40 P.S. §310.71(b)).

D. **Commingling of Funds:** Pennsylvania prohibits agents from commingling insurer's premiums with other agency funds without the express consent of the insurer. (31 Pa. Code §37.81).

E. **Suitability in Annuity Transactions:** In making a recommendation to a consumer for the purchase of an annuity or the exchange of an annuity that results in another insurance transaction or series of insurance transactions, the insurance producer, or the insurer where no insurance producer is involved, shall have reasonable grounds for believing that:

1. The recommendation is suitable for the consumer on the basis of the facts disclosed by the consumer as to the consumer's investments and other insurance products and as to the consumer's suitability information.

2. The consumer has been reasonably informed of various features of the annuity, including the potential surrender period and surrender charge, potential tax penalty if the consumer sells, replaces, surrenders or annuitizes the annuity, morality and expense fees, investment advisory fees, potential charges for and features of riders, limitations on interest returns, insurance and investment components and market risk.

3. The consumer would benefit from certain features of the annuity, including tax-deferred growth, annuitization or death or living benefit.

4. The particular annuity as a whole, the underlying subaccounts to which funds are allocated at the time of purchase or replacement of the annuity, and riders and similar product enhancements, if any, are suitable and, in the case of a replacement, the transaction as a whole is suitable for the consumer based on the consumer's suitability information.

5. In the case of a replacement of an annuity, the replacement is suitable and shall take into consideration whether the consumer will take on a surrender charge, be subject to a new surrender period, lose existing benefits, or be subject to increased fees; if the consumer would benefit from product enhancements and improvements; and if the consumer has had another annuity replacement.

   Prior to the execution of a purchase or exchange of an annuity resulting from a recommendation, an insurance producer, or an insurer where no insurance producer is involved, shall make reasonable efforts to obtain the consumer's suitability information. (40 P.S. §627-3) (Effective December 25, 2018).

III. Statutory References: 40 Pennsylvania Statutes, §§310.1 through 310.14; 310.31 through 310.35; 310.41 through 310.51; 310.71 through 310.74; 321.1 through 321.10; 322.1 through 322.7; 324.1 through 324.13; 627-3; 991.1501 through 991.1516. 71 Pennsylvania Statutes §240.12A. 31 Pennsylvania Administrative Code §§37.72 and 39.840.

PUERTO RICO

Office of the Commissioner of Insurance
World Plaza Building, 268 Luis Munoz Rivera Ave., San Juan, PR 00918
Telephone: 787-304-8686; Fax: 787-273-6082
http://ocs.pr.gov/enocspr/

I. Licensing Requirements: Sales Personnel—Authorized Representatives, Producers, General Agents, Solicitors. Other Insurance Professionals—Advisory Organizations, Consultants, Independent Adjusters, Public Adjusters, Rating Organizations. Puerto Rico recently replaced the terms Agent and Broker with Authorized Representative and Producer respectively.

A. Applicability: No person in Puerto Rico shall act as or pretend to be an insurance producer, authorized representative, general agent, solicitor, adjuster or consultant unless she holds a license. No producer or solicitor may transact or accept applications for any kind of insurance for which she does not hold a license or procure or place said application for others. No producer may act or state that she acts as authorized representative of an insurer unless there is a written contract subscribed to those effects between the latter and the insurer. No person may be issued a license in more than one of the following classifications: producer, authorized representative, general agent, solicitor, adjuster, or consultant, except that a person holding an authorized representative license may obtain a license as a general agent and proxy, and a producer may obtain a license of consultant. A person who holds both a producer and consultant license at the same time may not receive commissions or other valuable consideration for both under the same insurance or insurable object. (26 L.P.R.A. §949i).

B. Licenses Required of Residents: License terms are now biennial. Initial licenses may be issued for up to thirty months. Initial license fees are prorated based on term length. Fees are collected through NIPR to cover the full license period. (26 L.P.R.A. §953b).

Each of the following must be licensed in Puerto Rico:

Sales Personnel

The Puerto Rico DOI issues only one license to each agent—the universal license. The agent has to procure the official appointment directly from the insurer. Appointments and terminations have to be submitted through NIPR for authorized representatives. For temporary/provisional, newly authorized representatives, and general agents, the appointments have to be submitted in paper.

1. *Authorized Representatives.* License fees: Individuals: $157 annually. Corporations: $315 annually. (26 L.P.R.A. §701).

2. *General Agents.* License fees: One or two appointments: $1,051 annually. Two or more appointments: $5,257 annually. (26 L.P.R.A. §701).

3. *Producers/Brokers.* License fees: Individuals: $525 annually. Corporations: less than $1 million in premiums, $1,051 annually. $1 million or more in premiums: $2,103 annually. (26 L.P.R.A. §701). Must post a bond of at least $10,000 for each licensed individual. A professional liability policy may replace the bond. (26 L.P.R.A. §951).

4. *Solicitors.* License fee: $52 annually. (26 L.P.R.A. §701).

5. *Limited Licenses.* License fee: $1,051 if representing two or fewer insurers; $5,257 if representing more than two insurers. (26 L.P.R.A. §701). Lines of Authority: Automobile rental, travel, and critical illness. (26 L.P.R.A. §950e). For further information or clarification, please visit the department website at https://ocs.pr.gov/.Pages/default.aspx and contact the department.

Other Insurance Professionals

1. *Consultants.* Must have five years of experience as a producer or an adjuster. (26 L.P.R.A. §951g). May be licensed for property, casualty, surety, transportation and marine, title, and life and disability. (26 L.P.R.A. §949g). License fee: $420 annually. (26 L.P.R.A. §701). Must post $25,000 bond. A professional liability policy may be filed in lieu of the bond. (26 L.P.R.A. §951j).

2. *Public Adjusters.* License fee: $210 annually. (26 L.P.R.A. §701). Must post $10,000 bond. A professional liability policy may be filed in lieu of the bond; if multiple people are listed on the license, the bond is multiplied by number of people listed. (26 L.P.R.A. §952a).

3. *Independent Adjusters.* License fee: Annually $210. (26 L.P.R.A. §701).

4. *Rating Organizations.* Annually on June 30, $2,103 for each kind of insurance authorized. (26 L.P.R.A. §701).

5. *Advisory Organizations.* License fee: $525 annually on June 30. (26 L.P.R.A. §701).

6. *Surplus Lines Brokers.* License fee: $525 annually. A $25,000 bond is required. (26 L.P.R.A. §§701, 1011).

Each insurer or general agent procures agents' licenses on renewal. License applications are obtained from the commissioner. Applications are available online at https://ocs.pr.gov/English/Licensees/Pages/default.aspx. Renewals are completed electronically at www.nipr.com. One year residency is no longer required.

C. **Licenses Required of Nonresidents:** A nonresident producer must meet the following requirements: (a) the state or jurisdiction of the United States where the producer comes from has adopted the provisions of the Model Act for Licensing Producers approved by the National Association of Insurance Commissioners and that grants to a resident producer in Puerto Rico a similar privilege; (b) holds a license as producer duly issued by the insurance commissioner of the state or jurisdiction from whence he comes and presents a copy of the license application to the Commissioner; (c) in addition, businesses must be organized under the laws of a state or jurisdiction of the United States; provide evidence about being duly registered and authorized according to the laws of Puerto Rico to engage in business in Puerto Rico; and designate a person residing in Puerto Rico to be in charge of those matters that involve insurance transactions in Puerto Rico. (26 L.P.R.A. §951m). License fee: $841 annually. Nonresident license applications and renewals are available through NIPR at www.nipr.com. (26 L.P.R.A. §701).

No license as nonresident producer shall be issued to any person who has a direct or indirect economic or financial interest in a general agent or resident producer or in the business of a solicitor authorized as resident in Puerto Rico. (26 L.P.R.A. §951m).

Multi-State Exposures. Even when writing a risk with only an incidental exposure in Puerto Rico (such as a car on a fleet policy), the nonresident needs a Puerto Rico license. (26 L.P.R.A. §951m).

D. **Examination and Education Requirements:**

1. *Residents.* Solicitors and adjusters must hold a high school diploma or equivalent. (26 L.P.R.A. §§951d and 951p). Law No. 63-2013 of July 19, 2013 requires a high school diploma for producers. Consultants must have five years' experience as a producer or adjuster. (26 L.P.R.A. §951g). Written examination is required for producers, solicitors, adjusters and consultants. Education requirements do not apply to general agents.

2. *Nonresidents.* At the discretion of the insurance commissioner, nonresidents are exempt from the examination requirement if they have fulfilled qualification requirements of their home state.

Annual Examination Fees

Authorized Representatives	$150.00
Adjusters	$150.00
Solicitors	$150.00
Producers	$150.00
Consultants	$150.00
Brokers	$150.00
Limited Licenses	$150.00
Intermediary and Reinsurance Producer	$150.00
Intermediary Reinsurance Manager	$150.00

(26 L.P.R.A. §701).

E. **Continuing Education Requirements:** During the compliance period, all licensees shall take and pass a total of no less than twenty-four hours of continuing education courses within each renewal period, of which at least three hours will be devoted to the topic of professional ethics.

Of the total twenty-four hours that are required, viatical agreements brokers and the viatical agreements agents will take in addition at least seven hours in matters related to viatical agreements.

Of the total twenty-four hours that are required, intermediary reinsurance producers and intermediary reinsurance managers will take in addition at least seven hours in matters related to reinsurance.

All nonresident licensees, in whose state of residence there are continuing education requirements, shall provide, on applying for a renewal of their license, evidence of having complied with the continuing education requirements of their state of residence. Compliance requirements is verified through NIPR.

All nonresident licensees, in whose state of residence there is no continuing education requirement, shall comply with the continuing education requirements that are applicable in Puerto Rico.

If a licensee on one or more occasion accumulates hours in excess of the total required for accreditation under the continuing education requirement, such excess may be accredited to subsequent renewals, according to the requirements for general hours, professional ethics, viatical agreements, and reinsurance.

Licensees aged sixty years old with twenty-five years of experience are exempt.

These CE rules may be found under Reglamentos de Puerto Rico, Oficina Del Comisionado De Seguros, 7811 Regla Num. 52. Be aware that the document is only available in Spanish.

F. **Cancellation of Agency Contracts/Producer Appointments:** When a producer is canceling a license, it must mail notice to the Commissioner; proof of mailing is required. If a producer's license is being cancelled for nonsatisfaction of the reasons in 26 L.P.R.A. §950i, the Commissioner shall notify the producer at least fifteen days before the effective date of cancellation, subject to the producer's right to be heard. (26 L.P.R.A. §953c).

The cancellation of the appointment of a solicitor at the request of the producer shall be effective ten days after the date on which the producer has provided the evidence to the commissioner attesting that he sent the solicitor the notice of cancellation of his appointment. Any information regarding the cancellation that is furnished to the commissioner is privileged information. (26 L.P.R.A. §951e).

The cancellation of the contract subscribed between the insurer and the producer for the negotiation of insurance shall be notified to the commissioner in the manner prescribed by the latter within the fifteen days following the date on which the contract was cancelled. Authorized representative appointments and terminations have to be processed through NIPR (26 L.P.R.A. §949l).

G. **Rules for Risk Retention and Purchasing Groups:** Puerto Rico has no law regulating risk retention or purchasing groups, but general restrictions on agency licensing and practices apply.

H. **Other License Rules, Requirements, or Restrictions:** Soliciting is now allowed for licensed nonresident producers. (26 L.P.R.A. §951n).

II. Countersignature Requirements

A. **Applicability:** Laws apply to all insurers and all types of insurance, regardless of residence of insured, including contracts made outside of Puerto Rico covering property or exposures in Puerto Rico except surplus lines insurance, reinsurance, group life or group disability, insurance sold through vending machines licensed by commissioner, ocean marine insurance, or insurance in connection with property in course of transportation in trade by sea or air. (26 L.P.R.A. §329).

B. **Who Must Countersign:** Policies not exempted above must be countersigned by insurer's manager, general agent, or authorized representative residing in Puerto Rico. (26 L.P.R.A. §329).

C. Other Countersignature Requirements: Countersignature endorsement is not permitted, nor is signature in blank. Facsimile signature is permitted. Countersigning agent must keep records of all details of all insurance transactions, including name of nonresident. (26 L.P.R.A. §329).

III. Commissions, Fees, Commingling of Funds, Suitability in Annuity Transactions

A. Commissions: The commission to be paid to any producer for negotiating insurance shall be circumscribed to the maximum amount fixed in the schedule of types approved by the commissioner for the corresponding kind or subdivision of insurance. (26 L.P.R.A. §949k). No insurer, general agent, manager or producer shall pay any commission or compensation whatsoever for transacting insurance unless by the date the same is due the person entitled to the same holds a license issued pursuant to this Code for the kind of insurance transacted. Rebating of commissions is not allowed. (26 L.P.R.A. §949j).

B. Fees: Fee for service may not be charged instead of or in addition to commission for the sale of insurance. (26 L.P.R.A. §949k).

C. Disclosure Requirements: None.

D. Commingling of Funds: Commingling of insurer's premiums with agency funds is prohibited by law. (26 L.P.R.A. §952h).

E. Suitability in Annuity Transactions: Puerto Rico has taken no action on this so far.

IV. Statutory References:

Reglamentos de Puerto Rico, Oficina Del Comisionado De Seguros, 7811 Regla Num. 52.

26 L.P.R.A. §§	329
	701
	949g, 949i to 949l
	950e
	951, 951d, 951e, 951g, 951j, 951m, 951n, 951p
	952a, 952h
	953b, 953c
	1011

RHODE ISLAND

Department of Business Regulation, Insurance Division,
1511 Pontiac Ave.; Building 69-2, Cranston, RI 02920
Telephone: 401- 462-9520; Fax: 401- 462-9602
http://www.dbr.ri.gov/divisions/insurance/ Email: DBR.Insurance@dbr.ri.gov

I. Licensing Requirements: Sales Personnel—Producers and Limited Lines Producers. Other Insurance Professionals—Claim Adjusters (Personal, Commercial, and Workers Compensation), Motor Vehicle Damage Appraisers, Third Party Administrators, Managing General Agents, and Reinsurance Intermediary Brokers and Managers.

A. Applicability: A person shall not sell, solicit, or negotiate insurance in Rhode Island for any class or classes of insurance unless the person is licensed for that line of authority. (R.I. Gen. Laws §27-2.4-3).

B. Licenses Required of Residents:

Sales Personnel

1. *Producers.*

   a. License and renewal fee: $120. Reinstatement thirty days after expiration and within one year of expiration: $50 fee plus $120 annual license fee – total $170. Adding additional line of authority: $50. (230 RICR 020-50-5).
   b. License term: biennial, based on birth month.
   c. Lines of authority:

      (1) Life.
      (2) Accident and health or sickness.
      (3) Property.
      (4) Casualty.
      (5) Personal lines property and casualty.
      (6) Variable life and variable annuity products.
      (7) Limited lines credit.
      (8) Limited Lines Travel (R.I. Gen. Laws § 27-79.1-4).
      (9) Portable Electronics (R.I. Gen. Laws § 27-2.7-4).
      (10) Any other line permitted under state laws or regulations. (R.I. Gen. Laws §27-2.4-9).

   Individual applicants must submit an NAIC Uniform Application. All residents are required to obtain a criminal background report generated by the Office of the Rhode Island Attorney General which must be submitted at the time of original application. All background questions answered "yes" require a written explanation and supporting documentation, if applicable.

Rhode Island residents are required to carry and maintain errors and omissions (E&O) insurance in an amount no less than $250,000 per claim and $500,000 annual aggregate limit. Licensees shall maintain records and keep copies of all such E&O policies.

2. *Limited Lines Producers.*

   a. License and Renewal fee: $120. Reinstatement thirty days after expiration and within one year of expiration: $50 fee plus $120 annual license fee – total $170. Adding additional line of authority: $50. See "Producers" for additional licensing requirements. (230 RICR 020-50-5).
   b. License term: Biennial.
   c. Limited lines of authority—car rental, credit products, crop insurance, surety and travel.

   To apply or renew online, visit the National Producer Registry (NIPR) Web site at www.NIPR.com.

C. Appointments: Rhode Island is a nonappointing state. Insurance companies are required to comply with the Annual Contracted Producer Report and pay a fee for each individual and/or business entity that have paid in excess of $100 or more in commission for the prior calendar year by March 1. The Contracted Producer Report requirement is part of the Annual Filing Statement. (RI Gen. Laws §27-2.4-2). There is no reporting requirement for the producer. (https://dbr.ri.gov/documents/divisions/insurance/ACPR_FAQs.pdf).

D. Licenses Required of Nonresidents:

1. *Producers.*

   License and Renewal fee: $130. Reinstatement thirty days after expiration and within one year of expiration: $50 fee plus $130 annual license fee – total $180. Adding additional line of authority: $50. Term: Biennial. (230 RICR 020-50-5).

   Nonresident individual applicants are required to submit a current NAIC Uniform Application. Nonresident applicants must have an active producer license in their home state that can be verified on the State Producer Licensing

Database. A letter of certification is not required. Nonresident producer license applicants are not required to pass an examination. All producer licenses are available to nonresident individuals. (RI Gen. Laws §27-2.4-10).

To apply or renew online, visit the National Producer Registry (NIPR) Web site at www.NIPR.com.

2. *Limited Lines Producers.*

License and Renewal fee: $130. Reinstatement thirty days after expiration and within one year of expiration: $50 fee plus $130 annual license fee – total $180. Adding additional line of authority: $50. Term: Biennial. (230 RICR 020-50-5).

Multi-State Exposures: A license is not required for a nonresident insurance producer who sells, solicits, or negotiates a contract of insurance for commercial property and casualty coverage when risks that are to be insured under that contract are located in more than one state. This exception applies only if the nonresident is licensed to sell, solicit, or negotiate that insurance in the state where the insured maintains its principal place of business and the contract of insurance insures risks located in that state. (RI Gen. Laws §27-2.4-5).

E. Other Insurance License Types:

1. *Claims Adjusters (residents and nonresidents):*

Rhode Island no longer offers Claims Adjuster as a license class. (http://www.dbr.ri.gov/documents/news/insurance/InsuranceBulletin2014-8.pdf).

Application fee (company, public, or independent adjuster): $250. Renewal fee: $250. Reinstatement thirty days after expiration and within one year of expiration: $50 fee plus $250 annual license fee – total $300. Adding additional line of authority: $50. Term: Biennial. (230 RICR 020-50-5 and R.I. Gen. Laws § 27-10-3).

Examination and Criminal Background Reports Requirements

Rhode Island Residents: Both required.

Nonresidents in a Reciprocal State: Neither required if applicant can show proof of active license. Non-resident adjuster licenses are reciprocal with all states.

Other Nonresidents: Both required. Special criminal background requirements for New York and Massachusetts residents.

To apply or renew online, visit the National Producer Registry (NIPR) Web site at www.NIPR.com.

2. *Motor Vehicle Damage Appraisers (residents and nonresidents):*

Application fee: $150. Renewal fee: $150. Reinstatement thirty days after expiration and within one year of expiration: $50 fee plus $150 annual license fee – total $200. Adding additional line of authority: $50. Term: Biennial. (230 RICR 020-50-5).

Examination and Criminal Background Reports Requirements:

Rhode Island Residents: Both required.

Nonresidents: Both required. Special criminal background requirements for New York and Massachusetts residents.

To apply or renew online, visit the National Producer Registry (NIPR) Web site at www.NIPR.com.

3. *Third Party Administrators (TPAs):*

Submit application for Certificate of Authority. Fee: $250. Annual report submission fee: $250, due on March 1. (230 RICR 020-50-5 and R.I. Gen. Laws §27-20.7-4 and 14).

All initial licenses and renewals are to be made through NIPR.

For initial licenses, licensee must submit by email: Copies of all organizational documents—such as articles of incorporation, articles of association, and partnership agreements—must be submitted, as well as copies of all bylaws, rules, regulations, or other documents relating to the administrator's internal affairs. An independently verified NAIC Biographical Affidavit or Business Character Report must also be submitted. The most recent two years' annual financial statements or reports are required. A business plan must be submitted. (R.I. Gen. Laws §27-20.7-12).

Lines of business covered under the TPA license:

a. Life.
b. Health.
c. Annuities.

Activities that require a TPA Certificate of Authority:

a. Soliciting or effecting coverage.
b. Underwriting.
c. Collecting premiums or charges.
d. Adjusting or settling claims for Rhode Island residents or if the TPA's office is in Rhode Island.

4. *Reinsurance Intermediary Brokers and Managers (resident and nonresident):*

License and renewal fee: $200. Term: Biennial. (230 RICR 020-50-5).

Applicants must be licensed producers in Rhode Island or in states with similar laws to Rhode Island's reinsurance intermediary laws. Rhode Island resident applicants are required to obtain a criminal background report generated by the Office of the Rhode Island Attorney General. (RI Gen. Laws §27-52-3).

5. *Portable Electronic Vendor:*

License and renewal fee: $200. Term: Biennial, expires May 31. (230 RICR 020-50-5 and R.I. Gen. Laws § 27-2.7-7).

"Portable electronics insurance" means insurance providing coverage for the repair or replacement of portable electronics which may provide coverage for portable electronics against any one or more of the following causes of loss: loss, theft, inoperability due to mechanical failure, malfunction, damage or other similar causes of loss. (RI Gen. Laws §27-2.7-1). A vendor is required to hold a portable electronics insurance vendor license to sell or offer coverage under a policy of portable electronics insurance. (RI Gen. Laws §27-2.7-2).

6. *Limited Lines Travel:*

License and renewal fee: $120 for residents; $130 for nonresidents. Biennial. Any person licensed as a producer in a major line of authority is authorized to sell, solicit, and negotiate travel insurance. A P&C producer is not required to be appointed by an insurer. (230 RICR 020-50-5; R.I. Gen. Laws §27-79.1-4).

Application must be made via NIPR.

7. *Managing General Agent:*

License and renewal fee: $120 for residents; $130 for nonresidents. (R.I. Gen. Laws §27-51-3; 230 RICR 020-50-5).

Must apply for a producer business entity license through NIPR and select Managing General Agent as Line of Authority.

F. Examination Requirements:

Resident individuals applying for a producer license shall pass a written examination unless exempt. (R.I. Gen. Laws §27-2.4-7). Applicants should register for examination by calling Pearson Vue (test administrator) at 800-274-3739 or visit their Web site at https://home.pearsonvue.com/ri/insurance. The reservation must be made at least twenty-four hours before the desired examination date and the $80 examination fee must be paid at the time of registration.

2. *Nonresidents.* Requirements are reciprocal with the applicant's home state. (R.I. Gen. Laws §27-2.4-11).

G. Continuing Education Requirements

(Producer—Residents only):

Number of Hours Required: Twenty-four hours during each two-year renewal, including three hours in ethics. All courses must be approved by the division. Course instructors receive the same credit as students. Credit will not be given if the producer repeats the same course within the two-year renewal cycle. (230 RICR 020-50-2).

Course providers will upload proof of course completion into licensee's electronic record.

Excess Hours: Up to twelve hours may be carried over through the end of the next renewal period. Excess ethics credits carry over as general credits. (230 RICR 020-50-2).

Final Exam: A monitored exam is not required for self-study courses.

Requirements **Not** *Applicable to the Following:*

1. Residents licensed to sell insurance for which an examination is not required.

2. Persons holding licenses limited to credit, crop, travel, surety, car rental or title insurance.

3. Nonresident licensees who meet continuing education requirements established by the insurance department in their home state if the home state is reciprocal with Rhode Island.

4. Residents holding a license continuously without a lapse of licensure for twenty-five years and who are age fifty-five at the time of renewal.

    a. A lapse has occurred if the producer's license expired and was not reinstated.
    b. A producer's license may be reinstated if the producer submits an Application of License Reinstatement and pays the renewal fee and reinstatement fee if the application is submitted more than thirty days after expiration of the license. If a license is reinstated it is not considered to have lapsed. Licenses cannot be reinstated more than one year after expiration.
    c. A producer who reinstates must complete continuing education in exactly the same manner as they would have been required if the license was renewed prior to the expiration date.

5. Any exemption granted by the department. (230 RICR 020-50-2).

Renewal Procedure:

1. Licensee must complete the NAIC Uniform Individual Producer Renewal process (paper or online at www.nipr.com). Licensees have the ability to renew online sixty days prior to the expiration date.

2. Each individual and/or business entity must issue a separate check for each biennial renewal license. Licenses must be renewed and a new license is not generated for each renewal.

3 Licenses can be printed by accessing the following link: https://sbs.naic.org/solar-external-lookup/license-manager.

4. Nonresidents are exempt from continuing education on a reciprocal basis. (230 RICR 020-50-2).

H. Cancellation of Agency Contracts: An insurer that terminates the employment contract or other insurance business relationship with an insurance producer must notify the insurance commissioner within thirty days following the effective date of the termination. Upon the written request of the insurance commissioner, the insurer shall provide additional information, documents, records, or other data pertaining to the termination or activity of the insurance producer.

Within fifteen days after making the notification, the insurer must mail a copy of the notification to the insurance producer. Within thirty days of receipt of such notice, the producer may file written comments concerning the substance of the notice with the commissioner. (R.I. Gen. Laws §27-2.4-16).

See R.I. Gen. Laws §§27-2.4-20 to 20.1 for special rules for terminating certain insurance producer contracts.

I. **Rules for Risk Retention and Purchasing Groups:** Rhode Island requires all risk retention groups seeking to do business in the state to submit a plan of operation or feasibility study for the commissioner's approval. RRGs must also submit reports to the commissioner as described in the Risk Retention Group Filing Requirements. A policy issued to an RRG does not require countersignature. (R.I. Gen. Laws §§27-46-3, 27-46-6).

All RRG policies must show the following notice in at least ten point type and in all capital letters on the front page and on the declarations page of the policy:

NOTICE

"This policy is issued by your risk retention group. Your risk retention group may not be subject to all of the insurance laws and regulations of your state. State insurance insolvency guaranty funds are not available for your risk retention group." (R.I. Gen. Laws §27-46-4).

II. Policy Countersignature Requirements

A. **Applicability:** Rhode Island's countersignature law applies on a reciprocal basis. There is no requirement that an insurance producer resident in Rhode Island sign or countersign an insurance policy covering a subject of insurance resident, located, or to be performed in this state. However, if the laws of another state require a countersignature by an insurance producer resident in that state on an insurance policy written by a nonresident insurance producer of that state, then any policy written by a nonresident insurance producer of that state must be countersigned by an insurance producer resident in Rhode Island.

B. **Who Must Countersign:** Retaliatory with other states. (R.I. Gen. Laws §27-2-17).

III. Commissions, Fees, Commingling of Funds and Suitability in Annuity Transactions

A. **Commissions:** There are no restrictions on distribution of commissions among licensed agents or brokers except that distribution to a nonresident is reciprocal with nonresident's home state. No unlicensed resident or nonresident may receive commissions under any circumstances. Rebating of commissions is not allowed. (R.I. Gen. Laws §27-2.4-15).

B. **Fees:** Rhode Island insurance law does not allow producers (other than surplus lines producers) to charge fees for services that are customarily associated with the solicitation, negotiation or servicing of policies. (R.I. Gen. Laws §27-2.4-15).

C. **Commingling of Funds:** Rhode Island does not prohibit commingling of insurer's premiums with other agency funds.

D. **Suitability in Annuity Transactions:** In recommending to a consumer the purchase of an annuity or the exchange of an annuity that results in another insurance transaction or series of insurance transactions, the insurance producer, or the insurer where no producer is involved, shall have reasonable grounds for believing that the recommendation is suitable for the consumer on the basis of the facts disclosed by the consumer as to his or her investments and other insurance products and as to his or her financial situation and needs, including the consumer's suitability information, and that there is a reasonable basis to believe the consumer has been reasonably informed of various features of the annuity, the consumer would benefit from certain features of the annuity, the particular annuity as a whole, including the underlying subaccounts and riders are suitable for the consumer, and in case of an exchange or replacement of an annuity, the exchange or replacement is suitable for the consumer. (230 RICR 020-25-1).

IV. Independently Procured Insurance

A. **Rules:** Insureds who procure, continue, or renew insurance with an insurer not licensed to do insurance business in Rhode Island on properties, risks, or exposures located or to be performed in whole or in part in Rhode Island, other than insurance procured through a surplus lines licensee, shall, within thirty days after the date the insurance was so procured, continued, or renewed, file a written report with the tax administrator on forms prescribed by the tax administrator, showing the insured's name and address, insurer's name and address, the subject of the insurance, a general description of the coverage, the amount of premium currently charged and additional pertinent information reasonably requested by the tax administrator. The gross premiums charged for the insurance are subject to a 4 percent tax, which is due when filing the report. (R.I. Gen. Laws §27-3-38.1).

B. **Industrial Insured Exemption:** To qualify as an industrial insured, a company must use the services of a full-time employee acting as insurance manager or buyer or use the services of a continuously qualified insurance consultant. The firm must also employ at least twenty-five full-time employees and have aggregate annual premiums, excluding workers' comp, of at least $25,000. (R.I. Gen. Laws §27-16-1.2).

V. **Statutory References: Licensing and Countersignature:** R.I. Gen. Laws §§27-2.4-1 through 27-2.4-22; 27-3.2-1 through 27-3.2-10; 27-10-1 through 27-10-14; 27-10.1-1 through 27-10.1-10; 27-46-1 through 27-46-15; 27-51-1 through 27-51-9; 27-52-1 through 27-52-13; RI ADC 11-5-12:6; 11-5-36:7; 11-5-36:10; 11-5-36-40:5 through 12; 11-36-103:4; Insurance Regulations 36 and 40.

SOUTH CAROLINA

Department of Insurance
Capitol Center, 1201 Main St., Suite 1000;
Columbia, SC 29201
Telephone: 803-737-6160; 803-737-6095 (Individual Licensing); and 803-737-6160 (Other Matters)
Fax: 803-737-6231
agntmail@doi.sc.gov
http://www.doi.sc.gov

I. **Licensing Requirements:** Sales Personnel—Producers, Limited Lines Producers, Entities, Professional Bondsmen, Surety Bondsmen, Bail Bond Runners, Managing General Agents, Brokers, Motor Vehicle Physical Damage Appraisers, Rental Car Companies. Other Insurance Professionals—Adjusters, Appraisers, Premium Service Companies, Private Review Agents, Public Adjusters, Reinsurance Intermediaries, Special Agents, Third Party Administrators, Benefit Plan Administrators.

A. **Applicability:** South Carolina licensing laws apply to any person who:

1. Sells, solicits, or negotiates insurance on behalf of an insurer.

2. Takes or transmits other than for himself an application for insurance or a policy of insurance to or from an insurer.

3. Advertises or otherwise gives notice that he will receive or transmit insurance applications or policies.

4. Receives or delivers a policy of insurance of an insurer.

5. Receives, collects, or transmits any premium of insurance.

6. Performs any other act in the making of an insurance contract for or with an insurer, other than for himself; whether these acts are done by an employee of an insurer or at the instance or request of an insurer, must be an appointed producer of the insurer for which the act is done or the risk is taken. (S.C. Code Ann. §38-43-10).

B. **Licenses Required of Residents:** Each of the following must be licensed in South Carolina. Application forms for producer's licenses are obtained from the Insurance Department's Web site. Residents and nonresidents may also now apply online at NIPR; see the link located at https://doi.sc.gov/354/Licensing-CE. As of January 1, 2017 fingerprints are now required for new and existing resident and limited lines producers. You do not need to re-fingerprint with future license renewals once your fingerprints have been successfully submitted and processed. The fingerprinting fee is $50.50. See http://doi.sc.gov/879/Fingerprinting and bulletin 2016-10 (https://doi.sc.gov/DocumentCenter/View/9639/Bulletin-2016-10-Fingerprinting-and-Criminal-History-Background-Check?bidId=).

Link to renew online through the department web site: https://online.doi.sc.gov/Eng/Public/Individuals/IndvdlLicRnwlAppTerms.aspx.

Sales Personnel

1. *Producers.*

   a. License fee: $25 plus $25 for criminal history report paid to South Carolina State Law Enforcement Division (SLED).
   Instructions for applications at http://doi.sc.gov/481/Producer. Salaried sales employees of direct writing insurers must be licensed as producers.
   b. Biennial Renewal fee: $25. License term: Continuous, subject to compliance with license renewal requirements and continuing education biennially by the end of the producer's birth year birth month. Appointments must be renewed on September 1 of even years.
   c. Lines of authority:
      (1) Life.
      (2) Accident and health.
      (3) Property.
      (4) Casualty.
      (5) Variable life and variable annuity products.
      (6) Personal lines property and casualty.
      (7) Limited line.
      (8) Any other line permitted under state laws or regulations.
      (S.C. Code Ann. §§38-43-75).

2. *Limited Lines Producers.*

   a. License fee: $25 plus $25 for criminal history report paid to South Carolina State Law Enforcement Division (SLED).
   See "Producers" above for instructions.
   b. Biennial Renewal fee: $25. License term: Continuous as long as the limited lines producer renews the license by the end of producer's birth month. Appointments must be renewed by September 30 of even numbered years. (S.C. Code Ann. §§38-43-80).

c. Limited lines of authority:
   (1) Crop/hail.
   (2) Title.
   (3) Travel Baggage. Appointment fee: $20.
   (4) Preneed.
   (5) Surety.
   (S.C. Code Ann. §§38-43-80).

3. *Entities/Agencies.* License and renewal fee: $40, term biennial. Corporations, partnerships, or limited liability companies that act as insurance producers. The entities must have at least one South Carolina licensed producer. Paper applications for residents should include Agency Application, Form Number 3511. (S.C. Code Ann. §§38-43-80).

4. *Bondsman.* License and renewal fee: $400. Expires annually on June 30. Must submit passport sized full-face photo and two fingerprint cards when applying for license. Must submit SLED background report when renewing. Must submit $150 annually to clerk of court for bondsman's home county. Must also submit $100 annually to clerk of court for any other county where she is doing business. Application Form BB1100. (S.C. Code Ann. §§38-53-90 and 38-53-100). South Carolina Department of Insurance contact info for Bail Bondsmen: 803-737-6134 or wseawright@doi.sc.gov.

5. *Surety Bondsman.* License fee: $200. Renewal fee: $0. Expires annually on June 30. Complete application form BB1100, with photo attached, and submit to Department of Insurance. Must obtain a producer license and be able to obtain an appointment from a licensed insurance carrier to become licensed as a surety bail agent. A surety bondsman shall also pay $150 annually to the clerk of court of her home county. No surety bondsman may become a surety on an undertaking unless he or she has registered his current license with the office of the clerk of the circuit court in the county in which he or she resides and registers a certified copy of the license with the clerk of the circuit court in any other county in which he or she writes bail bonds. (S.C. Code Ann. §38-53-100, 38-53-260).

6. *Bail Bond Runner.* License and renewal fee: $200. Expires annually on June 30. Complete application BB1100 with photo and two fingerprint cards attached. Must also submit $100 annually to clerk of court for any other county where she is doing business. Can represent only one Professional Bondsman—appointment Form BB1102. Runner may be authorized to execute bail bonds by a Professional Bondsman—submit Power of Attorney-Bail Bond Runner, form BB1104. (S.C. Code Ann. §§38-53-100 and 38-53-120).

7. *Rental Car.* Licensing and renewal fee is $40, renewed biennially in December of even numbered years. (https://doi.sc.gov/DocumentCenter/View/2344/Rental-Car-Company-Renewal-Memo). Application (SCID 3700 and appointment Form SCID 3705). The rental car company must submit its application package to the licensing and appointing insurer. (S.C. Code Ann. §38-43-500).

8. *Brokers.* Licensing fee: $200, renewed biennially. An insurance broker as defined by South Carolina may place insurance with either an eligible surplus lines insurer or with a licensed insurance agent in an insurance carrier licensed in South Carolina. No resident shall be licensed as an insurance broker unless such person, at the time the initial or renewal application is made for an insurance broker's license, possesses a valid, current insurance producer's property and casualty license. Individuals applying for a resident surplus lines broker license must pass the state surplus lines broker license examination. Nonresidents must hold a surplus lines broker license in the home state. Every broker's license issued is restricted to those lines of business for which specific application is made and must be supported by record of prior issuance of producer's license for such lines of business. (S.C. Code Ann. §38-45-20 and S.C. Code Regs. 69-6).

Other Insurance Professionals

1. *Adjusters.* License fee and renewal fee: $80 biennially in August of odd numbered years. Resident applicants must submit a current domestic SLED Report and $25 fee, and certification of passage of adjuster examination.

   Staff adjusters for insurers and independent adjusters must be licensed. Only individuals may be licensed as adjusters. Residents may apply for an adjuster license online, or download the paper application, at https://doi.sc.gov/355/Adjuster. Resident applicants must submit a current domestic SLED Report and $25 fee, and certification of passage of adjuster examination. (S.C. Code Ann. §38-47-10 and 38-47-30; (https://doi.sc.gov/355/Adjuster).

2. *Motor Vehicle Physical Damage Appraisers.* License fee: $80, biennially in October of odd numbered years. Resident applicants may apply online at www.doi.sc.gov. Resident applicants submit a SLED report, form 3515 (if applying on paper), $80 fee, and proof of passage of motor vehicle physical damage appraiser examination. (S.C. Code Ann. §38-49-20; https://doi.sc.gov/373/Appraiser).

3. *Public Adjusters.* License and renewal fee is $80, payable biennially on October 1 of even numbered years. Public adjusters are permitted to be licensed in South Carolina. Only individuals may be licensed as adjusters. Residents may apply online at www.doi.sc.gov. Resident applicants must submit a current domestic

SLED Report and $25 fee. (S.C. Code Ann. §38-48-50; https://doi.sc.gov/437/Public-Adjuster).

4. *Reinsurance Intermediaries.* License and renewal fee: $100; Term: Annual, expires December 31. Must be a licensed producer in South Carolina. Reinsurance intermediary brokers may only work for a corporation or reinsurance intermediary manager if that corporation or intermediary manager is also a licensed as a producer in South Carolina. Intermediary managers must post a bond of $50,000. (S.C. Code Ann. §38-46-30; https://doi.sc.gov/550/Licensing).

6. *Third Party Administrators.* License and renewal fee: $100. Must complete application online at https://www.doi.sc.gov/572/Third-Party-Administrators-TPAs.Term: Annual, expires March 1. Bond or other acceptable securities in the amount of not less than $75,000 and not more than $500,000 is required. (S.C. Code Ann. §§38-51-20 and 38-51-30).

C. **Appointments:** A license issued by the director gives the insurer the right to appoint any number of producers to take risks or transact any business of insurance in South Carolina. The notification to the director must give both the business address and residence addresses of the producer. Appointment fees must be paid by the insurer and may not be passed on to the producer. The local appointment initial and biennial fee is $40. Special and general appointment initial and biennial fee is $100. Additionally, the appointment fee applicable to a producer of a common carrier who sells only transportation ticket policies on accident and health insurance or baggage insurance on personal effects is $20.The initial appointment fee must be paid in advance by the insurer. Appointment renewal fees are due on a biennial basis and must be paid by September 30 of an even numbered year, otherwise the appointment must be canceled. An insurer may reactivate an appointment that was canceled due to the insurer's nonrenewal by December first of the same year and must pay a $250 penalty. Insurers appointing ten or more producers each year must appoint electronically. (S.C. Code Ann. §§38-43-50 and 38-43-80). Questions regarding the appointment process should be directed to South Carolina Department of Insurance agentmail@doi.sc.gov or 803-737-6095.

D. **Licenses Required of Nonresidents:** The same licenses are required of residents and nonresidents to conduct insurance activities in South Carolina. (S.C. Code Ann. §38-43-70). If licensing information cannot be obtained from the NAIC Producer Database, a current Home State Letter of Certification must be submitted. Nonresident applicants can find more information at https://www.doi.sc.gov/354/Licensing-CE.

All applications, new or renewal, must be made online through NIPR. All paper applications and checks will be returned to the applicant without being processed. (https://www.doi.sc.gov/354/Licensing-CE).

Nonresident adjusters are licensed on a reciprocal basis. Fees are retaliatory. Corporations, firms, and partnerships cannot be licensed as adjusters. (S.C. Code Ann. §38-47-20; https://www.doi.sc.gov/354/Licensing-CE).

Multi-State Exposures: A license is not required for a nonresident insurance producer who sells, solicits, or negotiates a contract of insurance for commercial property and casualty coverage when risks that are to be insured under that contract are located in more than one state. This exception applies only if the nonresident is licensed to sell, solicit, or negotiate that insurance in the state where the insured maintains its principal place of business and the contract of insurance insures risks located in that state. (S.C. Code Ann. §38-43-20).

E. Examination and Education Requirements:

South Carolina Department of Insurance contact information for questions about continuing education and prelicensing education: 803-737-6223 or kwilson@doi.sc.gov.

1. *Residents.* Applicants for a producer license must pass a qualifying examination, as well as the following:

    a. Adjusters for Property, casualty, surety, and marine lines.
    b. Appraisers.
    c. Crop hail adjusters.
    d. Professional bondsmen and runners.
    e. Public adjusters.
    f. Brokers.

    Bail bond applicants must complete the following prelicensing education and pass an exam:

    a. Professional Bondsmen: twenty hour bail bond course.
    b. Surety Bondsmen: twenty hour bail bond course.
    c. Runners: twenty hour bail bond course.

    South Carolina has contracted with PSI Services LLC to provide the licensing examination for the department. Please contact PSI Services LLC directly to register for an exam, pay the exam fee, and schedule an appointment. You can view South Carolina-specific information at http://candidate.psiexams.com/ or contact PSI directly at 800-733-9267. Exam Fee: $45. (S.C. Code Ann. §38-43-100; https://www.doi.sc.gov/354/Licensing-CE).

2. *Nonresidents.* An examination is not required of nonresident producers who are licensed for the same lines of authority in their home states. (S.C. Code Ann. §38-43-101).

F. Continuing Education Requirements:

Number of Hours Required: Twenty-four hours biennially, with a minimum of eight hours in each line of authority, with at least three hours of ethics. Licensee may use classroom instruction or self-study. Classroom course instructors receive the same credit as students. (S.C. Code Ann. §38-43-106).

Bail bond licensees must complete eight hours of CE, annually. (S.C. Code Ann. §38-53-85).

A licensed resident producer who has obtained one of the following designations may use the credit hours earned to maintain the designation toward the fulfillment of the twenty-four hour requirement: CLU, FLMI, CFP, LUTCF, RHU, REBC, or CHFC for a life, accident, and health license; or CPCU or CIC for a property and casualty license. (S.C. Code §38-43-106).

Submit Proof of Completion by: the last day of the producer's birth month.

Excess Hours: A maximum of eighteen hours may be carried into the next reporting period. A course may be repeated, but licensees may not receive credit for a course more than once in a single reporting period.

Final Exam: A final exam is required for a self-study course. (S.C. Code Regs. 69-50).

Requirements **Not** *Applicable to the Following:*

1. Limited lines producers.

2. Limited line credit producers.

3. Nonresident producers who have satisfied the CE requirements of their home state.

4. Professional and surety bondsmen and runners who are at least sixty years old and have been continuously licensed for at least twenty years.

   (S.C. Code Ann. §§38-43-106, 38-53-85; S.C. Code Regs. 69-50).

CE Records and Course Renewal:

1. Course provider electronically submits class roster to the continuing education administrator.

2. Licensee keeps course completion certificate for records.

3. Reporting agency informs insurance companies of agent status.

4. Reporting agency notifies the licensee ninety days prior to renewal of producer license.

5. Insurance companies are given the opportunity to renew in September of even numbered years any agent who has complied with CE requirements.

6. Licensee remits appropriate fee to continuing education administrator.

7. A biennial fee is due by the last day of the producer's birth month of their renewal year.

(S.C. Code Ann. §38-43-106; S.C. Code Regs. 69-50).

G. **Cancellation of Agency Contracts/Producer Appointments:** When an insurer terminates the appointment, employment, contract, or other insurance business relationship with a producer, the Director of Insurance must be notified within thirty days following the effective date of the termination. Upon written request of the director, the insurer must provide additional information, documents, records, or other data pertaining to the termination. (https://doi.sc.gov/513/Appointments).

Within fifteen days after making the notification of termination, the insurer must mail a copy of the notification to the producer. If the producer is terminated for cause for any of the reasons listed in §38-43-130 the insurer shall provide a copy of the notification to the producer by certified mail, return receipt requested, postage prepaid, or by overnight delivery using a nationally recognized carrier. (S.C. Code Ann. §38-43-55).

H. **Rules for Risk Retention and Purchasing Groups:** A risk retention group must be registered as a liability insurance company. All policies issued by risk retention groups must contain the following wording in ten-point type on the front and declaration pages:

NOTICE

"This policy is issued by your risk retention group. Your risk retention group may not be subject to all of the insurance laws and regulations of your state. State insurance insolvency guaranty funds are not available for your risk retention group." (S.C. Code Ann. §38-87-40).

I. **Other License Rules, Requirements, or Restrictions:** Licensed nonresident agents may enter the state to solicit, inspect, or service insurance policies (retaliatory with nonresident's home state limitations) but must be licensed in the state. A nonresident not licensed as an agent may not enter the state for any of these purposes. Entering the state includes: mail, telephone, or other electronic communication into the state from the outside—including the Internet—as well as physical presence in the state. (S.C. Code Ann. §§38-43-20, 38-43-70).

J. **Policy Countersignature Requirements:** None.

II. Commissions, Fees, Commingling of Funds, Suitability of Annuity Transactions

A. **Commissions:** An insurance company or insurance producer may not pay a commission, service fee, brokerage, or other valuable consideration to a person for selling, soliciting, or negotiating insurance in South Carolina if that person is required to be licensed pursuant to the provisions of this chapter and is not licensed.

An insurer or insurance producer may pay or assign service fees or other valuable consideration to an insurance agency or to a person who does not sell, solicit, or negotiate insurance in South Carolina, unless the payment violates another provision of Title 38. A payment made pursuant to the provisions of this subsection must not be based on completion of the sale of the insurance policy. (S.C. Code Ann. §38-43-200).

B. **Fees:** Fees may be charged for services not related to the sale and normal servicing of insurance policies. These fees must be approved by the Forms and Rates Division of the Department.

No policy fee may be charged by a broker unless it is a reasonable fee, it is made part of the contract, and the six percent broker's premium tax is paid upon the policy fee. If for any reason the director disapproves the placement or the insurer ultimately refuses to write the risk, the broker shall immediately refund the full policy fee to the policyholder. (S.C. Code Ann. §38-45-160).

C. **Disclosure Requirements:** Fees for uninsured motorist related transactions may be charged only to consumers who have had a lapse in their automobile coverage. Notice of these fees must be posted prominently in the agent's or broker's office. (S.C. Code Ann. §38-55-50).

No title insurer or agent may accept an order for, issue a title insurance policy to, or provide services to an applicant if it knows or has reason to believe that the applicant was referred to it by any producer of title business or associate where the producer, the associate, or both, have a financial interest in the title insurer or title agent to which business is referred unless the producer has disclosed the financial interest. The disclosure must be made in writing on forms prescribed by the director. The title insurer or agent shall maintain the disclosure forms for a period of three years. (S.C. Code Ann. §38-75-960).

D. Commingling of Funds: South Carolina does not prohibit agent's commingling of insurer's premiums with other agency (producer/entity) funds. (S.C. Code Ann. §38-43-670).

E. Suitability in Annuity Transactions: In recommending to a consumer the purchase of an annuity or the exchange of an annuity that results in another insurance transaction or series of insurance transactions, the insurance producer, or the insurer where no producer is involved, shall have reasonable grounds for believing that the recommendation is suitable for the consumer on the basis of the facts disclosed by the consumer as to his or her investments and other insurance products and as to his or her financial situation and needs, including the consumer's suitability information, and that there is a reasonable basis to believe the consumer has been reasonably informed of various features of the annuity, the consumer would benefit from certain features of the annuity, that the annuity as a whole and the subaccounts and riders are suitable, and in case of an exchange or replacement of an annuity, the exchange or replacement is suitable. (S.C. Code Regs. 69-29).

III. South Carolina Insurance Data Security Act:

A. In an attempt to develop standards for the investigation and notification to state insurance commissioners when a cybersecurity event has happened to a licensee, NAIC has developed the Insurance Data Security Model Law. (https://www.nuco.com/fcs/2018/04/19/naic-cybersecurity-model-law-analysis/).

B. South Carolina signed into law the South Carolina Insurance Data Security Act and the Act became effective on January 1, 2019. Modeled after the NAIC Insurance Data Security Model Law, the Act defines the requirements applicable to a "licensee." In addition, the Act establishes standards for data security, as well as standards for the investigation of and notification to the Director of a cybersecurity event. (https://www.doi.sc.gov/918/Cybersecurity). The Act is contained in Title 38, chapter 99 of the South Carolina Code of Laws.

SOUTH CAROLINA

IV. References:

S.C. Code Ann. §§38-	43-10, 20, 50, 55, 70, 75, 80, 100, 101, 106, 200, 500, 670	S.C. Code Regs. 69-	6, 29, 50
	45-20, 160		
	46-30, 47-10 to 47-30		
	48-50, 49-20		
	51-20, 30		
	53-85, 90, 100, 120, 260		
	55-50, 75-960, 87-40		

Web References:

https://doi.sc.gov/354/Licensing-CE.

http://doi.sc.gov/481/Producer.

https://doi.sc.gov/355/Adjuster.

https://doi.sc.gov/373/Appraiser.

https://doi.sc.gov/437/Public-Adjuster.

https://doi.sc.gov/550/Licensing.

https://www.doi.sc.gov/572/Third-Party-Administrators-TPAs.

https://doi.sc.gov/513/Appointments.

https://www.doi.sc.gov/918/Cybersecurity.

https://online.doi.sc.gov/Eng/Public/Individuals/IndvdlLicRnwlAppTerms.aspx.

https://doi.sc.gov/DocumentCenter/View/2344/Rental-Car-Company-Renewal-Memo.

https://www.nuco.com/fcs/2018/04/19/naic-cybersecurity-model-law-analysis/.

https://doi.sc.gov/DocumentCenter/View/9639/Bulletin-2016-10-Fingerprinting-and-Criminal-History-Background-Check?bidId=.

SOUTH DAKOTA

Division of Insurance
124 S. Euclid Ave. 2nd Floor, Pierre, SD 57501
Telephone: 605-773-3563; Fax: 605-773-5369
http://dlr.sd.gov/insurance/
Email: sdinsurance@state.sd.us

I. Licensing Requirements: Sales Personnel—Producers, Car Rental Limited Licensees, Managing General Agents, Business Entities. Other Insurance Professionals—Bail Bondspersons.

A. Applicability: No person may sell, solicit, or negotiate insurance in this state for any line of insurance unless the person is licensed for that line of authority. (SDCL §58-30-143).

B. Licenses Required of Residents: Each of the following must be licensed in South Dakota. Applications for all licenses are obtained from Sircon or NIPR. The following lines of authority are available:

Sales Personnel

1. *Producers.* (May be agents of the insurer or of the insured).

    a. License fee: $25. Renewal fee: $25 for resident. (SDCL §58-2-29).
    b. License term: Appointment renewals are due annually on April 30th. License renewal fee is due biennially by end of birth month. (SDCL §§58-30-74 and 58-30-121). Resident producers are subject to continuing education requirements for all lines but limited lines travel and credit insurance. Only renewal fee is due for those only having a limited lines travel credit insurance license. Failure to complete any part of continuing education or to pay fee will result in termination of license.
    c. Lines of authority:

        (1) Property.
        (2) Casualty.
        (3) Life.
        (4) Accident and health or sickness.
        (5) Variable life and annuity.
        (6) Personal lines.
        (7) Limited lines.
        (8) Any other line of insurance permitted under state laws or rules (SDCL §58-30-152).

2. *Car Rental Limited Line Licensee.* Car rental companies must obtain a producer license.

   a. License fee: $25.
   b. License term: Perpetual.
   c. Lines of authority for a car rental limited licensee:

      (1) Personal accident insurance covering the risks of travel.
      (2) Liability insurance, including uninsured and underinsured motorist coverage.
      (3) Personal effects insurance.
      (4) Roadside assistance and emergency sickness protection programs.
      (5) Any other travel or auto-related coverage that a rental company offers in connection with and incidental to the rental of vehicles.

   d. Other requirements: Employees in the car rental location can solicit insurance without a license as long as the car rental company is licensed. If the location is a franchise of a car rental company, the franchise must be licensed. (SDCL §§58-30-197 to 58-30-208).

3. *Managing General Agents.* Must be currently licensed as a resident or nonresident producer. Application fee: $25 for residents, $30 for nonresidents. Must have a written contract that sets forth the responsibility of each party. The contract between the insurer and the MGA must be filed with and approved by the Director of Insurance. The director may require a bond or E&O policy. (SDCL §58-30-126).

4. *Business Entities.* Any legal entity acting as an insurance producer must be licensed in addition to individual producers. License fee: $25 for residents; $30 for nonresidents. The annual appointment fee must be paid by April 30 for each insurer represented; $10 for residents and $20 for nonresidents. (SDCL §58-30-29 and SDCL §58-30-149).

5. *Third Party Administrators.* An administrator is not required to hold a license as an administrator in South Dakota if all of the following conditions are met:

   a. The administrator has its principal place of business in another state.
   b. The administrator is not soliciting business as an administrator in this state.
   c. In the case of any group policy or plan of insurance serviced by the administrator and less than one hundred certificate holders reside in South Dakota.

   A person is not required to hold a license as an administrator in South Dakota if the person exclusively provides services to one or more bona fide employee benefit plans each of which is established by an employer or an employee organization, or both and for which the insurance laws of South Dakota are preempted pursuant to the Employee Retirement Income Security Act (ERISA) of 1974. Such persons shall register with the director annually, verifying their status as described within this section. Each administrator licensed or registered in this state shall file an annual report for the preceding calendar year with the director on or before July 1 of each year. Nonresident TPAs must submit a copy of Certificate of Authority or License of state of domicile. Filing Fee: $500. Renewal Fee: $250. (SDCL §§58-29D-22, 58-29D-26 and 58-29D-27).

6. *Pharmacy Benefit Managers.*

   Pharmacy Benefits Managers are required to be licensed as a Third Party Administrator. The PBM status is a qualification type under the TPA license. A PBM must renew on or before July 1 of each year. (SDCL §58-29E-2).

   License Fee: $500. Renewal Fee: $250.

7. *Discount Medical Plan Organization* (DMPO). A Discount Medical Plan Organization (DMPO) is required to obtain registration and shall file an annual renewal on or before July first of each year. (SDCL §58-17E-9).

   A discount medical plan organization that is a health carrier registered pursuant to Title 58:

   1. Is not required to register as a discount medical plan organization. However, any of its affiliates that operate as a discount medical plan organization in this state shall comply with all provisions of this chapter and shall register as a discount medical plan organization.
   2. Is required to comply with SDCL §§58-17E-24 to 58-17E-38, inclusive, 58-17E-40, and 58-17E-42 to 58-17E-44, inclusive.

   Filing Fee: Each registered DMPO shall maintain in force a surety bond in its own name in an amount not less than $20,000 and shall be in favor of any person and the director of the Division of Insurance; or deposit in lieu of surety bond. In lieu of the bond required, a registered DMPO may deposit and maintain deposited at all times, and have a market value of not less than $35,000. (SDCL §§58-17E-20 and 58-17E-21).

8. *Managed Care Contractor.* Managed Care Contractors (MCC's) are required to register with the director prior to engaging in any managed care business in the

state of South Dakota. MCC's must renew on or before July 1 of each year. The director shall consult with the secretary if possible. (SDCL §§58-17F-16 and 58-17F-20).

Registration Fee: $250. Renewal Fee: $250.

9. *Utilization Review Organization.*

Utilization Review Organization (URO) shall register with the Division of Insurance prior to conducting business in the State of South Dakota. URO's must renew on or before July 1 of each year. (SDCL §§58-17H-35 and 58-17H-39).

Registration Fee: $250. Renewal Fee: $250.

10. *Independent Review Organizations.*

Independent Review Organizations (IRO's) are required to obtain certification by the Division of Insurance. An IRO certification is good for two years and must be renewed through the Division of Insurance. Certification Fee: None. Renewal Fee: None. (S.D. Admin. R. 20:06:53).

11. *Portable Electronics License.*

A vendor must have a portable electronics license to sell or offer coverage under a policy of portable electronics insurance. Portable electronics insurance is insurance providing coverage for the repair or replacement of portable electronics which may provide coverage for portable electronics against any one or more of the following causes of loss: loss, theft, inoperability due to mechanical failure, malfunction, damage, or other similar causes of loss. (SDCL §58-47-2 and SDCL §58-47-3).

License fee: $25. Renewal fee: $20. Term: Annual.

Other Insurance Professionals

Bail Bondspersons. Must submit a completed application with $30 fee, state and federal fingerprint cards, photograph, and $43.25 fee to the South Dakota Department of Criminal Investigation. (SDCL §58-22-7). Background checks must now be federal criminal background checks as opposed to state background checks. Bail bondspersons must report felony prosecutions to the Division. They may not use their own license to bail themselves out. (SB 38). The following types of bail licenses are available: professional bondsperson, property bondsperson, runner, and surety bondsperson.

All bail bond applicants must be residents of South Dakota for at least one year. (SDCL §58-22-6).

Surety bondspersons must also be appointed by an insurer and submit a $10 appointment fee. A $10 renewal fee is due prior to May 1 annually. (SDCL §58-22-8).

Professional bondspersons must also submit detailed financial statements by March 1st annually. Must file a sworn statement listing all bond forfeitures and their dates and amounts, as well as the name of the courts where the forfeitures were made. A $10,000 deposit also must be made. (SDCL §58-22-24).

Property bondspersons must have property to pledge as security.

All application forms can be found on the Division of Insurance Web site, http://dlr.sd.gov/insurance.

C. **Appointments:** To appoint an insurance producer or business entity as its agent, the appointing insurer shall file a notice of appointment within fifteen days from the date the agency contract is executed or the first insurance application is submitted. The insurer is responsible for the acts of its representatives and insurance producers, including those acts where the insurance producer has solicited, sold, or negotiated insurance on behalf of that insurer prior to the date of appointment. (SDCL §58-30-176). All appointments are done electronically. Original appointment for residents $10; annual renewal for nonresidents $20 with annual renewal fee. (SDCL §58-2-29).

D. **Licenses Required of Nonresidents:** Nonresidents may be licensed as producers in South Dakota. The appointment fee for a nonresident producer license and portable electronic license is $20 per company, plus $30 application fee for initial license. Nonresidents may also be appointed as managing general agents if licensed as a South Dakota nonresident producer. Annual fee: $30. Nonresident licenses must be renewed biennially by the end of birth month. The renewal fee is $50. However, this fee is subject to retaliatory law. All appointments/terminations are done electronically. Partnership or corporation license is also required for a nonresident firm or corporation, on the same basis as for residents, except appointment fee is $20 annually. (SDCL §58-30-159).

Multi-State Exposures: A license is not required for a nonresident insurance producer who sells, solicits, or negotiates a contract of insurance for commercial property and casualty coverage when risks that are to be insured under that contract are located in more than one state. This exception applies only if the nonresident is licensed to sell, solicit, or negotiate that insurance in the state where the insured maintains its principal place of business and the contract of insurance insures risks located in that state. (SDCL §58-30-144).

E. **Prelicensing Examination and Education Requirements:**

1. *Residents.* All licenses require passing an exam ($10 fee plus an exam fee charged by Prometric), except the following lines: restricted to credit life and credit health; surplus lines broker; and limited licenses. Exams are administered by Prometric, 800-864-8373.

   Title applicants should contact the South Dakota Board of Abstractors. Applicants for variable life/variable annuity authority must be registered with the South Dakota Division of Securities and pass NASD series 6, 7, 63, or 66.

2. *Nonresidents.* Lines of insurance are based on the lines licensed for in the home state, as indicated on the NAIC Producer Data Base.

F. **Continuing Education Requirements:** Only resident producers are required to comply with South Dakota's CE laws. (SDCL §§58-30-114 through 121).

Number of Hours Required (Biennially):

Life/Health alone – ten hours.

Property/Casualty alone – ten hours.

Life/Health and Property/Casualty – twenty hours.

Crop alone – four hours.

Crop and Life/Health – two hours Crop and eight hours Life/Health.

Crop and Property/Casualty – two hours Crop and eight hours Property/Casualty.

Crop, Property/Casualty and Life/Health – two hours crop, eight hours Property/Casualty and ten hours Life/Health (S.D. Admin. R. 20:06:18:03).

Courses must be approved for the particular line. Certain courses for particular designations are approved for CE credit. (See S.D. Admin. R. 20:06:18:08 for specifics). The licensee may use classroom instruction or self-study. The CE period will be waived for any new qualification added during the two-year CE period of an existing producer's license until the first renewal. (S.D. Admin. R. 20:06:18:03.01). No more than 50 percent of required hours may be earned from any one insurance company-sponsored courses. (S.D. Admin. R. 20:06:18:09). A course may be taken only once in a two year reporting period. (S.D. Admin. R. 20:06:18:20).

Excess Hours: may not be carried into the next reporting period.

Final Exam: the final exam for a self-study course does not need to be monitored.

Requirements **Not** *Applicable to the Following:*

1. A licensee holding a limited license to sell only credit life and credit health insurance.

2. A licensee outside the United Sales or its territories.

3. A licensee who is a resident attorney licensed to practice law in the state.

4. A licensee who is a transportation ticket agent of common carriers holding a limited license to sell only travel accident and baggage insurance.

5. A licensee who is an employee of a trade association holding a limited license to sell only surety bonds to its association members.

6. A licensee who is licensed to sell only bail bonds. (S.D. Admin. R. 20:06:18:02).

Renewal Procedure:

1. Course provider submits completion data to Sircon.

2. Licensee submits $20 fee to the Division of Insurance by end of birth month biennially.

Nonresidents are exempt from this requirement. If a nonresident producer fails to comply with home state CE requirements resulting in termination of license, then nonresident South Dakota license will also be terminated immediately. (S.D. Admin. R. 20:06:18:03).

G. **Cancellation of Agency Contracts/Producer Appointments:** An insurer or authorized representative of the insurer that terminates the appointment, employment, contract, or other insurance business relationship with an insurance producer shall notify the director within thirty days following the effective date of the termination. Upon the written request of the director, the insurer shall provide additional information, documents, records, or other data pertaining to the termination or activity of the insurance producer. Within fifteen days after making the notification, the insurer shall mail, or if acceptable, send by electronic means, a copy of the notification to the insurance producer. The insurer shall promptly notify the director in a written or electronic format if, upon further review or investigation, the insurer discovers additional information that would have been reportable had the insurer then known of its existence. (SDCL §§58-30-180 to 58-30-183).

H. **Risk Retention and Purchasing Groups:** South Dakota regulates risk retention and purchasing groups operating or offering coverage on risks in South Dakota.

1. Risk retention groups must be chartered and licensed as liability insurers in South Dakota, and submit plans of operation and feasibility studies as required by the law. All groups and all resident and nonresident producers participating in them must comply with all South Dakota insurance laws, including licensing and solicitation requirements or restrictions.

2. All policies issued by a Risk Retention Group must show the following notice in at least ten point type on the front page and on the declarations page of the policy:

NOTICE

"This policy is issued by your risk retention group. Your risk retention group may not be subject to all of the insurance laws and regulations of your state. State insurance solvency guaranty funds are not available for your risk retention group." (SDCL §58-6A-9).

3. Insurance policies issued to RRGs do not require countersignature.

I. **Other License Rules, Requirements, or Restrictions:** Licensed producers may write only lines of insurance for which they are personally licensed even though the corporation or partnership license covers additional lines of insurance. Unlicensed nonresident may not sell, solicit, or negotiate insurance in this state. Entering the state includes mail or telephone calls or other electronic communication into the state from the outside, as well as physical presence in the state.

J. **Policy Countersignature Requirements:** None. (SDCL §58-30-175).

II. Commissions, Fees, Commingling of Funds, and Suitability in Annuity Transactions

A. **Commissions:** No unlicensed resident or nonresident may be paid commission under any circumstances. Rebating of commissions is not allowed. (SDCL 58-30-171).

B. **Fees:** Fees in any way related to an insurance contract are construed as premium ("the consideration for insurance, by whatever name called") and as such must conform to the nondiscriminatory and anti-rebating provisions of the insurance code. South Dakota law does not permit a producer to charge fees in addition to premium. Therefore, no producer may act as both agent of the insured and charge the consumer consultant fees in addition to commissions earned on policies. (SDCL §§58-11-1 and 58-33-36).

A commission, service fee, brokerage fee, or any other valuable consideration for a referral paid to a person not appropriately licensed, paid, or assigned by an insurer or producer must be a fixed dollar amount that is not related to the amount of commission or premium for an insurance transaction and is not dependent upon whether the referral results in a transaction. (SDCL §58-30-174).

C. **Disclosure Requirements:** None.

D. **Commingling of Funds:** South Dakota does not prohibit producers' commingling of insurer's premiums with other agency funds, although funds must still be held in trust and reasonably ascertainable. (SDCL §58-30-90).

E. **Suitability in Annuity Transactions:** In recommending to a consumer the purchase of an annuity or the exchange of an annuity that results in another insurance transaction or series of insurance transactions, the insurance producer, or the insurer if no producer is involved, shall have reasonable grounds for believing that the recommendation is suitable for the consumer on the basis of the facts disclosed by the consumer as to the consumer's investments and other insurance products and as to the consumer's financial situation and needs, and there is a reasonable basis for believing that:

1. The consumer has been reasonably informed of various features of the annuity.

2. The consumer would benefit from certain features of the annuity.

3. The particular annuity as a whole is suitable for the particular consumer based on the consumer's suitability information.

4. In the case of an exchange or replacement of an annuity, the exchange or replacement is suitable. (SDCL §58-33A-16).

III. **Statutory References:** S.D. Codified Laws §§58-2-29; 58-6A-1 through 58-6A-24; 58-22-7; 58-29D-22 through 58-29D-26; 58-30-90 through 58-30-195; 58-33A-16; S.D. Admin. R. 20:06:18:03.

TENNESSEE

Department of Commerce and Insurance
500 James Robertson Pkwy., Nashville, TN 37243-0565
Telephone: 615-741-2693; Fax: 615-532-2862
https://tn.gov/commerce/
Email: ce.agent.licensing@tn.gov

I. Licensing Requirements: Sales Personnel—Producers, Limited Insurance Representatives, Managing General Agents. Other Insurance Professionals—Administrators, Reinsurance Intermediaries.

A. Applicability: A person shall not sell, solicit, or negotiate insurance in Tennessee for any class or classes of insurance unless the person is licensed for that line of authority in accordance with this part. (Tenn. Code Ann. §56-6-103).

B. Licenses Required of Residents:

Sales Personnel

1. *Producers.*

   a. Application fee: $50. Renewal fee: $60 biennially. File electronically through NIPR. (Tenn. Code Ann. §56-6-121).
   b. License term: Two years. Licenses remain in effect for twenty-four months following the last day of the licensee's birth month. (Tenn. Code Ann. §56-6-107).
   c. Lines of authority:

      (1) Life.
      (2) Accident and Health or Sickness. All HMOs must license their representatives as accident and health insurance agents.
      (3) Property.
      (4) Casualty.
      (5) Personal lines.
      (6) Limited line credit
      (7) Variable life and annuity.
      (8) Any other line of insurance permitted under Tennessee law. (Tenn. Code Ann. §56-6-107).

2. *Limited Insurance Representatives.*

   a. Application fee: $50. Renewal fee: $30 biennially. Submit the NAIC Uniform Application. (Tenn. Code Ann. §56-6-121).

b. License term: Two years. Licenses remain in effect for twenty-four months following the last day of the licensee's birth month. (Tenn. Code Ann. §56-6-107).

c. Lines of authority:

   (1) Baggage or limited travel accident.
   (2) Bail bond.
   (3) Credit life, credit accident and health, involuntary unemployment credit insurance, mortgage guaranty insurance, and personal property insurance (sold to a debtor under a master group policy issued to a creditor).
   (4) Crop.
   (5) Title. Licensed attorneys who act as title insurance agents, as an ancillary part of the practice of law must file a $25,000 surety bond within thirty days of license issuance. If not an attorney, must pass title examination.
   (6) Portable electronics.
   (7) Self-service storage. (Tenn. Code Ann. § 56-6-110).

3. *Managing General Agents.* Must be licensed as an insurance agent in Tennessee. The DOI may require a bond or E&O policy. Separate licenses are not required for risk managers/consultants. Field/marketing representatives are not required to be certified in advance. Licenses are renewed annually. A single license applies for all lines for which applicant is qualified. (Tenn. Code Ann. §56-6-503).

4. *Business Entity.* May obtain a producer's license but only an individual licensed producer may sell, solicit, or negotiate an insurance contract. Uniform Business Entity Application must be submitted with a $50 filing fee. Licenses expire biennially on March 1. (Tenn. Code Ann. §56-6-106).

Other Insurance Professionals

Reinsurance Intermediaries. Must be licensed as producers. Intermediary managers may be required to carry a bond and E&O insurance. (Tenn. Code Ann. §56-6-803).

Public Adjusters. Filing and Renewal Fee: $100. Term: Biennial. Business entities must designate a licensed individual public adjuster to be responsible for the business entity's compliance with the insurance laws, rules, and regulations. Required to carry a bond ($50,000) and E&O insurance ($500,000). (Tenn. Code Ann. §56-6-903).

Crop Insurance Adjusters. Filing and Renewal Fee: $100. (Tenn. Code Ann. §56-6-1002).

C. **Appointments:** An insurance producer may not act as an agent of an insurer unless the producer is an appointed agent of that insurer. An insurance producer who is not acting as an agent of an insurer is not required to become appointed. A $15 company appointment fee must be issued for each insurer with whom the agent does business. (Tenn. Code Ann. §§56-6-115 and 56-6-121). Fees associated with company appointments of insurance producers will be collected through the NIPR. Appointment fees will be collected electronically simultaneously with the filing of the notice of appointment.

D. **Licenses Required of Nonresidents:** Nonresidents must also be licensed as agents to do business in Tennessee. A $50 filing fee must accompany application (nonresident fee subject to retaliatory). Application and filing fees submitted electronically through NIPR. Written license examination may be waived upon certification of resident license from the home state insurance department, including written exam requirement in the home state. Nonresidents must be appointed in Tennessee by the companies for whom they are writing business. (Tenn. Code Ann. §§56-6-108 and 56-6-109).

Multi-State Exposures: A license is not required for a person who is not a resident of Tennessee who sells, solicits, or negotiates a contract of insurance for commercial property and casualty risks to an insured with risks located in more than one state insured under that contract. The exception applies only if the nonresident is licensed as an insurance producer to sell, solicit, or negotiate that insurance in the state where the insured maintains its principal place of business, and the contract of insurance insures risks located in that state. (Tenn. Code Ann. §56-6-104).

E. **Prelicensing Examination and Education Requirements:**

1. *Residents.* An insurance producer is required to complete the following prelicensing hours prior to taking the examination (Tenn. Comp. R. & Regs. 0780-01-56-.06):

Lines of Insurance	Number of Hours
Title	Twenty
Life	Twenty
Accident and Health	Twenty
Property	Twenty
Casualty	Twenty
Personal Lines	Twenty

The following are exempt from prelicensing education:

a. Persons holding an insurance degree from an accredited college or university.
b. For Life line of authority, persons holding the following designations: CLU, CIC, CEBS, ChFC, CFP, FLMI, and LUTCF.

c. For Health line of authority: CIC, RHU, CEBS, REBC, and HIA.
d. For property, personal lines, and casualty lines of authority: CPCU, CIC, AAI and ARM.

After taking the course, the applicant must pass a qualifying examination administered by Pearson Vue, 800-274-4957.

Exam fees (Tenn. Comp. R. & Regs. 0780-01-56-.07):

a. Life or accident and health or property or casualty: $59.
b. Life and accident and health combination: $59.
c. Property and casualty combination: $59.
d. Single limited line title: $59.
e Public Adjuster: $59.
f. Personal Lines: $59.
Fees are nontransferable and nonrefundable. (TN Licensing Candidate Handbook).

2. *Nonresidents.* Examination requirement may be waived in Tennessee upon certification that nonresident's home state license was issued under similar requirements to Tennessee's.

F. Continuing Education Requirements:

1. *Number of Hours Required:* All lines license: twenty-four hours biennially; three hours shall have course concentration in ethics during each continuing education biennium. The DOI must approve all courses. The licensee may use classroom instruction or self-study. Instructors earn credit for courses they teach. (Tenn. Comp. R. & Regs. 0780-01-56-.08).

   Any producer not licensed to sell long-term care insurance prior to July 1, 2008, must complete a one-time eight-hour training course in long-term care insurance. For those licensed before July 1, 2008, the course must have been completed by July 1, 2009. An additional four hours of CE must be completed every twenty-four months unless the producer is exempt from CE requirements. The long-term care CE course counts towards the producers twenty-four hour CE requirement. (Tenn. Code Ann. §56-42-109).

2. *Submit Proof of Completion by:* License renewal. Note: Education providers submit proof of completion electronically.

3. *Excess Hours:* Twelve hours; however, no ethics credit shall carryover. (Tenn. Comp. R. & Regs. 0780-01-56-.08).

4. *Final Exam:* The final exam for a self-study course does not need to be monitored.

5. *Requirements* **Not** *Applicable to the Following:*

   a. Insurance producers who have been continuously licensed since January 1, 1994. Producers whose licenses went inactive any time since this date will not be exempt. (Tenn. Code Ann. §56-6-107).
   b. An insurance producer that is a business entity. (Tenn. Code Ann. §56-6-107).
   c. Limited lines licensees (credit products, mortgage guaranty, crop, travel accident and baggage, legal, title-licensed attorney). (Tenn. Code Ann. §56-6-110).

6. *Renewal Procedure:*

   a. Course provider sends certificate of completion to licensee and submits electronically to State Based Systems.
   b. Licensee should keep copy of the certification for verification, if needed.

7. *Nonresidents* are exempt from this requirement on a reciprocal basis.

G. Cancellation of Agency/Producer Contracts: An insurer or authorized representative of the insurer that terminates the appointment, employment, contract or other insurance business relationship with a producer shall notify the commissioner within thirty days following the effective date of the termination. A fee of $15 per producer cancellation applies. If commissioner requests details, there is no liability on the part of the commissioner, the insurer, or their representative for any information.

Within fifteen days after making the notification, the insurer shall mail a copy of the notification to the producer. If the producer is terminated for cause for any of the reasons listed in §56-6-112, the insurer shall provide a copy of the notification by certified mail, return receipt requested, postage prepaid or by overnight delivery using a nationally recognized carrier. (Tenn. Code Ann. §56-6-117).

H. Rules for Risk Retention and Purchasing Groups: Risk retention groups must be licensed as liability insurers, and must submit a feasibility study or plan of operation to the commissioner for approval. (Tenn. Code Ann. §56-45-103). The following must be stamped on the declarations of risk retention group policies in ten-point type:

NOTICE

"This policy is issued by your risk retention group. Your risk retention group may not be subject to all of the insurance laws and regulations of your state. State insurance insolvency guaranty funds are not available for your risk retention group." (Tenn. Code Ann. §56-45-104).

I. **Other License Rules, Requirements, or Restrictions:** Unlicensed nonresident may not enter Tennessee to solicit, inspect, or service. Entering the state includes mail, telephone, or other electronic communication into the state from the outside, as well as physical presence in the state. Entry into Tennessee by licensed nonresidents is retaliatory with nonresident's home state.

J. **Policy Countersignature Requirements:** It is unlawful for the corporation to write a policy except through licensed resident agents who shall countersign and receive the full commission usually paid. Any law requiring that policies be countersigned and delivered through a resident agent shall not apply to any policy of the mutual company on which no commission shall be paid to any local agent. (Tenn. Code Ann. §§56-15-108).

II. Commissions, Fees, Commingling of Funds, Suitability in Annuity Transactions

A. **Commissions:** There are no restrictions on distribution of commissions among licensed producers. In no event may an unlicensed resident or nonresident receive commission on insurance covering risks in Tennessee. Rebating of commissions is not allowed. (Tenn. Code Ann. §56-2-412).

B. **Fees:** Agents may not charge a fee for service provided in connection with the sale, solicitation, negotiation, or servicing of insurance policies, either in addition to or instead of a commission, unless fees are charged pursuant to a written agreement. (Tenn. Code Ann. §56-2-412).

C. **Disclosure Requirements:** A fee agreement must contain a statement of the services for which the fee is being charged, the amount of the fee and how it is calculated, and a disclosure stating that the client is under no obligation to purchase any insurance product through the insurance producer or consultant. The agreement must be kept for at least three years. (Tenn. Code Ann. §56-6-125).

D. **Commingling of Funds:** Tennessee law states that money collected by a producer must be held in a fiduciary capacity, and shall not be misappropriated, converted, or improperly withheld. (Tenn. Code Ann. §56-6-116).

E. **Suitability in Annuity Transactions:** In recommending to a consumer the purchase of an annuity or the exchange of an annuity that results in another insurance transaction or series of insurance transactions, the insurance producer, or the insurer where no producer is involved, shall have reasonable grounds for believing that the recommendation is suitable for the consumer on the basis of the facts disclosed by the consumer as to his or her investments and other insurance products and as to his or her financial situation and needs.

Before executing a purchase or exchange of an annuity resulting from a recommendation, a producer or insurer if no producer is involved shall make reasonable efforts to obtain information concerning the consumer's financial and tax status, investment objectives, and other reasonable information. (Tenn. Comp. R. & Regs. 0780-01-86-.06).

III. **Statutory References:** Tenn. Code Ann. §§56-6-101 to 56-6-126; 56-6-401 to 56-6-510; 56-6-801 to 56-6-812; and 56-45-101 to 56-45-114; Tenn. Comp. R. & Regs. 0780-01-86-.06 to 0780-01-86-.08.

TEXAS

Texas Department of Insurance;
333 Guadalupe; Austin, TX 78701
P.O. Box 12030; Austin TX 78711
Telephone: 512-676-6000; Fax: 512-490-1029
https://www.tdi.texas.gov

I. Licensing Requirements: Sales Personnel—Agents, Company Employees, Managing General Agents, Limited Lines, Specialty. Other Insurance Professionals—Adjusters; Agricultural Agents; Life Insurance Counselors, Risk Management Consultants, Reinsurance Intermediaries, Escrow Officer.

A. Applicability: Unless the person holds a license or certificate of authority issued by the Texas Department of Insurance, a person may not solicit or receive an application for insurance in Texas or aid in the transaction of the business of an insurer. Texas law does not allow an employee or agent of a corporation or partnership to perform an act of an agent without obtaining a license. (Tex. Ins. Code §4001.101).

B. Licenses Required of Residents: Each of the following must be licensed in Texas:

Sales Personnel

1. *General Lines.* Life, accident, and health and HMO. License fee: $50. Biennial renewal $50. Temporary (ninety days) license fee: $150. (28 Tex. Admin. Code §19.802).

2. *Funeral Prearrangement Life.* License fee: $50. Biennial renewal: $50. Temporary (ninety days) license fee: $150. (28 Tex. Admin. Code §19.802).

3. *Life Insurance* not exceeding $25,000. License fee: $50. Biennial renewal: $50. Temporary (ninety days) license fee: $150. (https://tdi.texas.gov/agent/life-agent-apply.html).

4. *Life Agent.* License fee: $50. Biennial renewal: $50. Temporary (ninety days) license fee: $150. (28 Tex. Admin. Code §19.802).

5. *Limited Lines.* License fee: $50. Biennial renewal: $50. Temporary license fee: $150. (28 Tex. Admin. Code §19.802).

6. *General Lines Property and Casualty.* License fee: $50. Biennial renewal: $50. Temporary (ninety days) license fee: $150. (28 Tex. Admin. Code §19.802).

7. *General Lines Property and Casualty (Emergency).* Ninety-day license. License fee: $50. (28 Tex. Admin. Code §19.802).

8. *Personal Lines Property & Casualty.* License fee: $50. Biennial renewal: $50. Temporary (ninety days) license fee: $150. (28 Tex. Admin. Code §19.802).

9. *County Mutual (selling property & casualty insurance).* License fee: $50. Biennial renewal: $50. Temporary (ninety days) license fee: $150. (28 Tex. Admin. Code §19.802).

10. *Managing General Agent (MGA)—Property and Casualty.* License fee: $50. Biennial renewal: $50. (28 Tex. Admin. Code §19.802).

11. *Emergency MGA—Property and Casualty.* Issued for six months. Fee: $50. (28 Tex. Admin. Code §19.802).

12. *Specialty—Credit.* This authority permits the sale of both individual and group credit insurance. License fee: $50. Biennial renewal: $50. (28 Tex. Admin. Code §19.802).

13. *Specialty—Travel.* License fee: $50. Biennial renewal: $50. (28 Tex. Admin. Code §19.802).

14. *Specialty—Rental Car Company.* Authorizes any properly trained salaried employee of rental vehicle companies or franchisees of rental vehicle companies to sell excess liability, accident and health, and personal effects insurance, in connection with the rental of vehicles or vehicle equipment. License fee: $50. Biennial renewal: $50. (28 Tex. Admin. Code §19.802).

15. *Specialty—Self-Service Storage Facility.* Issued to a self-service storage facility or to the franchisee of a self-service storage facility to sell insurance that provides hazard insurance coverage and any other coverage in connection with the rental of storage space. License fee: $50. Biennial renewal: $50. (28 Tex. Admin. Code §19.802).

16. *Specialty—Telecommunications Equipment Vendor.* Issued to a retail vendor of telecommunications equipment to sell insurance that provides coverage to customers for the loss of, the malfunction of, or damage to telecommunications equipment. License fee: $50. Biennial renewal: $50. (28 Tex. Admin. Code §19.802).

17. *Title Insurance Agent.* License fee: $50. Biennial renewal: $35.

18. *Escrow Officer.* License fee: $35. Biennial renewal: $35.

19. *Title Insurance—Direct Operation License.* License fee: $50. Biennial renewal: $35.

Applications for most license types can be found online at https://www.sircon.com/products/apply.jsp. Paper applications are no longer accepted.

Applicants for temporary licenses, risk managers and public insurance adjusters must use the paper Application for Individual Agent License, found at https://www.tdi.texas.gov/forms/finagentlicense/fin506.pdf.

The expiration date for all licenses will be changed to the last day of the licensee's birth month starting April 17, 2018.

Other Insurance Professionals

1. *Risk Manager.* License fee: $50. Biennial renewal: $50.

2. *Reinsurance/Broker.* Places reinsurance on behalf of insurer. Has no authority to bind. License fee: $500. Biennial renewal: $500.

3. *Reinsurance/Manager.* Places reinsurance on behalf of insurer. Has authority to bind. License fee: $500. Biennial renewal: $500.

4. *Adjuster—All Lines.* License fee: $50. Biennial renewal: $50. (28 Tex. Admin. Code §19.802).

5. *Adjuster—Property & Casualty.* License fee: $50. Biennial renewal: $50. (28 Tex. Admin. Code §19.802).

6. *Adjuster—Workers Compensation.* License fee: $50. Biennial renewal: $50. (28 Tex. Admin. Code §19.802).

7. *Emergency Adjuster.* Ninety-day license. License fee: $20. (28 Tex. Admin. Code §19.802). Apply online at https://www.sircon.com/resource/layout.jsp?page=texasLps&type=texas.

8. *Adjuster Trainee.* Up to twelve month license. $50 Application Fee. (http://tdi.texas.gov/agent/adjuster-trainee-apply.html).

9. *Public Insurance Adjusters.* License fee: $50. Biennial renewal: $50. (28 Tex. Admin. Code §19.802).

10. *Public Insurance Adjuster Trainees.* License fee 180-day license, $50. Biennial renewal: $50. May be renewed only once within an eighteen month period. (28 Tex. Admin. Code §19.802).

Applications for most license types can be found online at https://www.sircon.com/products/apply.jsp. Paper applications are no longer accepted.

Applicants for temporary licenses, risk managers and public insurance adjusters must use the paper Application for Individual Agent License, found at https://www.tdi.texas.gov/forms/finagentlicense/fin506.pdf.

Business Entities: Partnerships, corporations, depository institutions, and farm credit administrators may apply for a Texas insurance license. Agency applicants must show financial responsibility by bond or E&O policy, file evidence of authority to do business in the state of Texas from the secretary of state, and a current franchise tax certificate of good standing from the Texas state comptroller. Agency applicants must register each assumed name and Texas location from which the entity will conduct insurance business by filing separate department of insurance Form LDTL and $50 registration fee. (Tex. Ins. Code §4001.106).

Electronic Fingerprinting: Before attempting to schedule for fingerprinting, print and complete the FAST Pass form from the Texas Department of Insurance Website: http://www.tdi.texas.gov/forms/form11.html. You will need information from the FAST Pass form to make your electronic fingerprinting appointment. Print and complete the FAST Pass form from TDI's Website at http://www.tdi.texas.gov/forms/. You will need the information from the FAST Pass form when making your electronic fingerprint appointment. Then schedule an appointment to be electronic fingerprinted. You must schedule a fingerprint appointment by visiting http://www.identogo.com or by calling 1-888-467-2080. Pursuant to DPS requirements on the vendor, you will be photographed as part of the fingerprint process. You must pay the $41.45 fee to the vendor in a manner that is acceptable to the vendor. All electronic fingerprint appointments must be made by DPS' vendor, MorphoTrust USA (formerly known as L1 Enrollment). The vendor has over ninety Texas fingerprint locations, including the Pearson VUE testing centers which administer the TDI agent/adjuster licensing examinations.

C. **Appointments:** A person who obtains a license may not engage in business as an agent unless the person has been appointed to act as an agent by an insurer designated and authorized to engage in business in Texas. An authorizing appointment continues in effect without the necessity of renewal until the appointment is terminated or withdrawn by the insurer or the agent. (Tex. Ins. Code §4001.201-.203). A $10 appointment fee is now required for each notice of appointment submitted to TDI.

D. Licenses Required of Nonresidents: Nonresidents may be licensed as agents with the same provisions as resident agents if the department can verify status in the National Producer Database (PDB) system. If not currently listed in the PDB, must obtain and attach a certificate of good standing from resident state that is not more than ninety days old. Nonresidents are not required to submit a fingerprint card. However, nonresidents must submit a copy of the applicant's criminal history records if applying without reciprocity (Tex. I(ns. Code §4102.114).

Applications for most license types can be found online at https://www.sircon.com/products/apply.jsp. Paper applications are no longer accepted.

Applicants for temporary licenses, risk managers and public insurance adjusters must use the paper Application for Individual Agent License, found at https://www.tdi.texas.gov/forms/finagentlicense/fin506.pdf.

Multi-State Exposures. Even when writing a risk with only an incidental exposure in Texas (such as a car on a fleet policy), the nonresident needs a Texas license. (Tex. Ins. Code § 4102.114).

E. Prelicensing Examination and Education Requirements: (If the license type requires an exam, the candidate must have passed the exam 12 months prior to applying for the license. Holders of temporary licenses may get a full license if they take and pass the exam while the temporary license is active.)

1. *Residents.* These are the prerequisites for licensing in Texas:

    a. General Lines. Life, accident and health. Must pass exam administered by PearsonVUE, http://www.pearsonvue.com/tx/insurance/. Exam fee: $62. Holders of the CLU designation are exempt from the exam requirement.
    b. Temporary General Lines—Life, Accident and Health. Must complete forty hours of training within fourteen days of application. (Tex. Ins. Code §4001.160).
    c. Life Agent. Must pass exam administered by Pearson VUE, http://www.pearsonvue.com/tx/insurance/ Exam fee: $62.
    d. Funeral Prearrangement Life. Must complete five hours of training offered by appointing insurer. Must pass exam approved by Department of Insurance and administered by insurer.
    e. Temporary Funeral Prearrangement Life. Must complete forty hours of training within fourteen days of application.
    f. Life Insurance not exceeding $25,000. Must complete five hours of training offered by appointing insurer. Must pass exam approved by Department of Insurance and administered by insurer.

g. Temporary Life Insurance not exceeding $25,000. Must complete forty hours of training within fourteen days of application.
h. Limited Lines. Must pass exam administered by Pearson VUE. Exam fee: $48.
i. Temporary Limited Lines. Forty hours of prelicensing education within fourteen days of application.
j. General Lines Property and Casualty. Must pass exam administered by Pearson VUE. Exam fee: $62. Holders of the CPCU are exempt from the exam requirement.
k. Temporary General Lines Property and Casualty. Forty hours of training within fourteen days of application.
l. Personal Lines Property & Casualty. Must pass exam administered by Pearson VUE, http://www.pearsonvue.com/tx/insurance/. Exam fee: $62.
m. General Lines Property and Casualty (Emergency). No prelicensing requirements.
n. County Mutual (selling property & casualty insurance). Must complete five hours of training offered by appointing insurer. Must pass exam approved by Department of Insurance and administered by insurer.
o. Temporary County Mutual (selling property & casualty insurance). Forty hours of training within fourteen days of application.
p. Managing General Agent (MGA)—Property and Casualty. Must pass exam administered by Pearson VUE. Exam fee: $62.
q. Emergency Managing General Agent (MGA)—Property and Casualty. No prelicensing requirements.
r. Risk Manager. Must pass exam administered by Pearson VUE. Exam fee: $48. Holders of CPCU, CIC, or ARM designations are exempt from exam requirement.
s. Reinsurance Broker. No prelicensing requirements.
t. Reinsurance Manager. Must have at least three years of experience in insurance or reinsurance.
u. Adjuster—All Lines. Must pass exam administered by Pearson VUE or by successfully completing a TDI-approved course. Exam fee: $62. Holders of the CPCU or AIC designations are exempt from the exam requirement.
v. Adjuster—Property, Casualty, and Surety. Must pass exam administered by Pearson VUE or by successfully completing a TDI-approved course. Exam fee: $62. Holders of the CPCU or AIC designations are exempt from the exam requirement.
w. Adjuster—Workers Compensation. Must pass exam administered by Pearson VUE or by successfully completing a TDI-approved course. Exam fee: $48. Holders of the CPCU or AIC designations are exempt from the exam requirement.

aa. Emergency Adjuster. No prelicensing requirements.

bb. Public Insurance Adjuster. Must pass exam administered by Pearson VUE. Exam fee: $48.

cc. Public Insurance Adjuster Trainee. The trainee may practice only under the direction and sponsorship of a licensed sponsoring public insurance adjuster.

dd. Adjuster Trainee. The trainee is required to undergo education and training as an adjuster under the direction and supervision of the licensed sponsoring adjuster or insurer.

ee. Specialty—Credit. Each individual who will act as an agent under the specialty insurance license must successfully complete an approved training program before selling any insurance. The licensee must train its employees who actually will be offering insurance in connection with an associated consumer transaction.

ff. Specialty—Travel. Each individual who will act as an agent under the specialty insurance license must successfully complete an approved training program before selling any insurance. The licensee must train its employees who actually will be offering insurance in connection with an associated consumer transaction.

gg. Specialty—Rental Car Company. Each individual who will act as an agent under the specialty insurance license must successfully complete an approved training program before selling any insurance. The licensee must train its employees who actually will be offering insurance in connection with an associated consumer transaction.

hh. Specialty—Self-Service Storage Facility. Each individual who will act as an agent under the specialty insurance license must successfully complete an approved training program before selling any insurance. The licensee must train its employees who actually will be offering insurance in connection with an associated consumer transaction.

ii. Specialty—Telecommunications Equipment Vendor. Each individual who will act as an agent under the specialty insurance license must successfully complete an approved training program before selling any insurance. The licensee must train its employees who actually will be offering insurance in connection with an associated consumer transaction.

jj. Title Insurance Agent. Must own or lease a twenty-five year abstract plant.

kk. Escrow Officer. Must be a Texas resident.

ll. Title Insurance—Direct Operation License. Must hold Texas certificate of authority to operate as a title insurance company and own or lease a twenty-five year abstract plant.

Licensees called to active military may apply to the department for an exemption from or an extension of time for meeting the continuing education requirements or extending their license renewal. The licensee must request the exemption or extension prior to the end of the reporting period for which it applies and must include:

(1) A copy of the order to active duty status, service in a combat theater, or other positive documentation of military service that shall prevent the licensee from compliance;
(2) A clear request for either an extension or exemption, or both;
(3) The expected duration of the assignment; and
(4) Any other information the licensee believes may assist the department or that the department requests on a case by case basis. (28 Tex. Admin. Code §19.1004).

Any individual who qualifies is exempt from the continuing education requirements.

2. *Nonresidents.* Education and examination requirements for nonresident agents are reciprocal with nonresident's home state certification. (28 Tex. Admin. Code §19.1004).

F. Continuing Education Requirements:

Number of Hours Required: The following licensees are required to complete twenty-four hours, biennially within licensing period, including three hours of ethics or two hours of consumer protection (28 Tex. Admin. Code §19.1003)(Tex. Ins. Code § 4004.054):

1. General Lines. Life, accident and health, HMO. Hours must include three hours in ethics. 50 percent of hours must be classroom/classroom equivalent.

2. Life Agent. Hours must include three hours in ethics. 50 percent of hours must be classroom/classroom equivalent.

3. General Lines Property and Casualty. Hours must include three hours in ethics. 50 percent of hours must be classroom/classroom equivalent.

4. Personal Lines Property & Casualty. Hours must include three hours in ethics. 50 percent of hours must be classroom/classroom equivalent.

5. Adjuster—All Lines. Two hours must be in consumer protection. 50 percent of hours must be classroom/classroom equivalent.

6. Adjuster—Property, Casualty, and Surety. Two hours must be in consumer protection. 50 percent of hours must be classroom/classroom equivalent.

7. Adjuster—Workers Compensation. Two hours must be in consumer protection. 50 percent of hours must be classroom/classroom equivalent.

8. Managing General Agents. Hours must include three hours in ethics. 50 percent of hours must be classroom/classroom equivalent.

9. Public Insurance Adjuster. Two hours must be in consumer protection. 50percent of hours must be classroom/classroom equivalent.

The following licensees are required to complete ten hours, biennially within the licensing period, including three hours of ethics or two hours of consumer protection:

1. Life Insurance not exceeding $25,000. Hours must include three hours in ethics. 50 percent of hours must be classroom/classroom equivalent.

2. Limited Lines. Hours must include three hours in ethics. 50 percent of hours must be classroom/classroom equivalent.

3. County Mutual. Hours must include three hours in ethics. 50 percent of hours must be classroom/classroom equivalent. (28 Tex. Admin. Code §19.1003).

The following licensees are required to complete ten hours, biennially within the licensing period:

1. Title Insurance Agent. Applicable to sole proprietors and individual partners only.

2. Escrow Officer License.

Submit Proof of Completion by: When requested by the Department of Insurance.

Excess Hours: May not be carried into next reporting period. (28 Tex. Admin. Code §19.1003).

Final Exam: The final exam for a self-study course does not require monitoring by a disinterested third party.

*Requirements **Not** Applicable to the Following:*

1. Temporary general lines—life, accident and health.

2. Funeral prearrangement life.

3. Temporary funeral prearrangement life.
4. Temporary life insurance not exceeding $25,000.
5. Temporary limited lines.
6. Temporary general lines—property and casualty.
7. General lines property and casualty (emergency).
8. Temporary county mutual.
9. Emergency managing general agents.
10. Risk managers.
11. Reinsurance brokers/managers.
12. Adjuster trainees.
13. Public insurance adjuster trainees.
14. Emergency adjusters.
15. Specialty credit.
16. Specialty travel.
17. Specialty rental car company.
18. Specialty self-storage facility.
19. Specialty telecommunications equipment vendor.
20. Title insurance—direct operation.

Renewal Procedure:

1. Course provider sends certificate of completion to licensee.
2. Licensee is to keep evidence of CE completion for a minimum of five years. This evidence must be available to the TDI at any time.

Nonresidents are exempt on a reciprocal basis, if they meet their home state's CE requirement.

Exemptions:

A producer who has held a license continually for twenty years is exempt from the continuing education requirements.

G. Cancellation of Agency Contracts/Producer Appointments: Agency contracts for fire and casualty insurance in effect for at least two years are protected. They may not be terminated by the insurance company (except for cause—such as insolvency, misconduct, or license revocation) without a six-month prior notice. Then, insurers must continue to offer renewals for six months after the termination of the contract. Agency commissions and premium remittances to insurer will be conducted as if the agent's appointment continued. Violation of these provisions subject an insurer to a fine of $1,000 to $10,000 and the agent may enter a civil suit for damages. (Tex. Ins. Code §§4051.351 through 4051.362).

H. Rules for Risk Retention and Purchasing Groups: Risk retention groups chartered in Texas must be chartered and licensed in the state as a domestic insurer and must comply with all the laws, regulations, and orders applicable to insurers chartered and licensed in the state. Risk retention groups domiciled outside of Texas must notify the commissioner of its intention to do business in the state and must comply with specifics set forth in §2201 of the Texas Insurance Code. All risk retention group policies must show the following notice in at least ten point type on the front page and on the declarations page of the policy:

> "This policy is issued by your risk retention group. Your risk retention group may not be subject to all of the insurance laws and regulations of your state. State insurance insolvency guaranty funds are not available for your risk retention group."

Purchasing groups that meet the criteria of the Federal Liability Risk Retention Act of 1986 are exempt from Texas law relating to the creation of groups for the purchase of insurance, or the prohibition of group purchasing or any law that would discriminate against a purchasing group or its members. A notice to the commissioner accompanied by a filing fee not to exceed $100 is required. Current rules and regulations adopted by the Texas Department of Insurance have set the filing fee at $50. (Tex. Ins. Code §2201.256).

I. Policy Countersignature Requirements: Countersignature requirements don't apply to an agent acting on behalf of a risk retention group or a purchasing group located in Texas. A purchasing group is exempt from any law of Texas that requires countersignatures. (Tex. Ins. Code §§2201.005 and 2201.254).

II. Commissions, Fees, Commingling of Funds, Suitability in Annuity Transactions

A. **Commissions:** There are no restrictions on division of commission between licensed residents and nonresidents. Rebating of commissions is prohibited. (Tex. Ins. Code §4005.053).

B. **Fees:** Property and casualty agents may charge a fee to reimburse for obtaining motor vehicle record or photograph of property to be insured. Property and casualty agents may also charge a reasonable fee for services to a client that may include special delivery or postal services, printing and reproduction services, electronic mail service and telephone transmission costs, and similar costs that the agent incurs on the client's behalf. For a property and casualty agent to receive an allowable fee, they must inform the client of the fee and obtain written consent for each fee to be charged. (Tex. Ins. Code §4005.003). No application fee is required for military personnel, veteran, or family member that has a license in another state. This does not however apply to license renewals. Military identification along a request for a fee waiver should be presented when they apply.

C. **Disclosure Requirements:** Other than a service fee described above, an agent or the affiliate may not accept or receive any compensation from an insurer or other third party for that placement or renewal unless the agent has, before the customer's purchase of insurance (1) obtained the customer's documented acknowledgment that the compensation will be received by the agent or affiliate, and; (2) provided a description of the method and factors used to compute the compensation to be received from the insurer or other third party for that placement. This does not apply to agents acting as intermediaries, reinsurance intermediaries, surplus lines agents, or agents whose sole compensation is derived from commissions, salaries, and other remuneration paid by the insurer. (Tex. Ins. Code §4005.004).

D. **Commingling of Funds:** Not prohibited. However, a separate trust account is required for surplus lines premium taxes. (Tex. Ins. Code §225.007).

E. **Suitability in Annuity Transactions:** In recommending to a consumer the purchase of an annuity or the exchange of an annuity that results in another insurance transaction or series of insurance transactions, the agent, or the insurer if an agent is not involved, must have a reasonable basis to believe that the recommendation is suitable for the consumer based on the consumer's investments, financial situation and needs, and suitability information; the consumer has reasonably been informed of various features of the annuity, the consumer would benefit from various features of the annuity, the annuity as a whole is suitable for the consumer. (Tex. Ins. Code §1115.051).

III. Statutory References: Texas Insurance Code §§4001.001 through 4153.153; 28 Texas Administrative Code §19.

UTAH

Insurance Department
4315 S. 2700 W., Suite 2300, Taylorsville, UT 84129
Telephone: 801-957-9200; Fax: 385-465-6055
Email: licensing.uid@utah.gov
https://insurance.utah.gov

I. Licensing Requirements: Sales Personnel—Producers, Limited Lines, Entities, Managing General Agents. Other Insurance Professionals—Consultants, Independent Adjusters, Public Adjusters, Reinsurance Intermediaries, Third Party Administrators, Title Agents.

Applicants are encouraged to visit Utah's Licensing Information Bulletin to obtain detailed descriptions on how to prepare for licensing exams, apply for a license, schedule/register for an exam, and what to do after taking it. The Licensing Information Bulletin can be obtained through the Web site.

A. Applicability: Licensing laws apply to all insurers and types of insurance. (U.C.A. §31A-23a-103).

B. Licenses Required of Residents: Each of the following must be licensed in Utah. All licenses expire every two years at the end of the licensee's birth month.

Sales Personnel

1. *Producers.*

   a. License fee: $75, new. $75, renewal.
   b. License term: Biennial.
   c. Lines of authority:

      (1) Life.
      (2) Variable contracts (must hold a life insurance license and be FINRA qualified and registered with Utah Securities Division).
      (3) Accident and health.
      (4) Property.
      (5) Casualty.
      (6) Title (residents only).

         (A) Search.
         (B) Marketing representative's title (residents only).
         (C) Escrow (residents only).

(7) Personal lines. (U.C.A. §§31a-23a-104 to 106).

2. *Limited Lines.*

a. License fee: $50, new and renewal.
b. License term: Biennial.
c. Lines of authority.
Limited line insurance:

(1) Limited line credit insurance.
(2) Bail bond (Residents only).
(3) Rental car.
(4) Legal expense insurance.
(5) Motor club insurance.
(6) Travel insurance.
(7) Self-service storage insurance.
(8) Guaranteed asset protection waiver.
(9) Crop.
(10) Portable Electronics. (U.C.A. §§31a-23a-104 to 106).

3. *Entities.* Corporations, LLCs, partnerships, or firms conducting their business as organizations must also be licensed. Fee: $85. (U.C.A. §31A-23a-104).

4. *Managing General Agents.* Must file an E&O policy and be licensed as a producer. Fee: $75. (U.C.A. §§31a-23a-104 to 106, 601).

Adding a line of authority incurs an additional fee of $25.

The Utah Insurance Department accepts only electronic filings. Paper filings will be rejected. The Utah Insurance Department licenses both individuals and organizations as Managing General Agents/Agencies.

All new resident applicants are required to be fingerprinted. Fingerprints are submitted via LiveScan and must be completed at an authorized PSI Testing Center located in Utah. A $28.25 BCI/FBI fingerprinting submission fee plus a $20 PSI fee must be paid by credit card at the time of application. Check with the department or PSI for current BCI/FBI fees. Fingerprint submissions are not required for renewals.

Other Insurance Professionals

1. *Consultants.* Biennial fee: $75. Must also be licensed as an agent for three of the past four years. May qualify in either Life, Variable Contracts, A&H, Property and/or Casualty. (U.C.A. §§31a-23a-104 to 106).

2. *Independent Adjusters.* Biennial fee: $75. May qualify in property and casualty or A&H.

3. *Public Adjusters.* Biennial fee: $75.

4. *Reinsurance Intermediaries.* Bond may be required. Must first be licensed as a producer before a reinsurance intermediary license will be issued. The Utah Insurance Department licenses both individuals and organizations as Reinsurance Intermediaries. (U.C.A. §§31a-23a-104 to 106).

5. *Third Party Administrators.* Biennial fee: $75. TPAs are required to carry a bond, E&O policy, or employee dishonesty policy equal to 10 percent of funds handled (minimum $5,000, maximum $500,000). After completing the application, fax a copy of the bond to the Department at 801-538-3830 or email to licensing.uid@utah.gov. (U.C.A. §§31a-25-201 and 205).

6. *Title.* Individual title producers are charged a $75 fee (Resident only) and a $15 fee at the time of initial and renewal application. Title agencies are required to provide a professional liability policy or bond in excess of $50,000. A title insurance agency, shall at the time of licensure be owned or managed by one or more natural persons who are licensed with both title search and escrow for at least three of the five years immediately preceding the date on which the title insurance agency applies for a license. Those applying for an initial title insurance agency license must pay an assessment of $1,000 at the time of application. (U.C.A. §31A-23a-204).

If a licensee fails to renew a license, he or she has up to one year to reinstate the license, subject to the following conditions:

1. All current and past due fees are paid.

2. Penalty of $125 from one day up to twelve months.

3. All continuing education requirements have been completed-limited and nonresident licenses do not need to fulfill this requirement as one does not require CE, and the other is expected to comply with home state CE standards.

If the licensee does not apply for reinstatement within one year of the lapse date, he or she will be required to apply for a license as a new applicant. Organizations whose licenses have lapsed may not be reinstated more than one year from the renewal date. (U.C.A. §31A-23a-113).

The following application forms are used:

1. *All Resident.* Licensees are required to take qualifying exam. Utah Licensing Information Bulletins may be obtained from https://insurance.utah.gov/agent/producers/exam/bulletin.php. Applications for license are submitted electronically via www.sircon.com/utah or NIPR. The Department no longer accepts paper applications.

2. *Organizations.* Application for licenses are submitted electronically via www.sircon.com/utah.

Utah has mandated that all resident applications for individuals and agencies must be sent electronically via http://www.sircon.com/utah or http://nipr.com.

Utah does not accept applications via email. Applications may be downloaded from the Department's Web site, www.insurance.utah.gov.

C. Appointments: To appoint a person, an insurer shall identify the date the appointment is to be effective and submit the electronic appointment to the commissioner no later than fifteen days after the identified effective date of appointment. If an insurer appoints an agency, the insurer need not appoint, report, or pay appointment reporting fees for an individual designated on the agency's license. (U.C.A. §31A-23a-115).

An agency shall report to the commissioner all new and all terminated designations. (U.C.A. §31A-23a-302).

D. Licenses Required of Nonresidents: All of the above, including corporations or firms, must be licensed to conduct insurance activities in Utah. The licensing fees are $50 for limited agents; $75 for agents; $85 for firms.

The following individuals are exempt from nonresident licensure (U.C.A. § 4-1-111, as amended by 2018 Ut. SB 227), and from paying a license fee:

1. An individual who is serving in the Armed Forces of the United States while the individual is stationed within this state, if: (i) the individual holds a valid license to practice the regulated occupation or profession issued by any other state or

jurisdiction recognized by the department; and (ii) the license is current and the individual is in good standing in the state or jurisdiction of licensure; and

2. The spouse of an individual serving in the Armed Forces of the United States while the individual is stationed within this state, if: (i) the spouse holds a valid license to practice the regulated occupation or profession issued by any other state or jurisdiction recognized by the department; and (ii) the license is current and the individual is in good standing in the state or jurisdiction of licensure. (U.C.A. §31A-23a-104, as amended by 2018 Ut. SB 227).

As Utah is an electronically-mandated state, individuals or organizations must submit an application for a nonresident license electronically. See www.nipr.com or www.sircon.com for electronic application and instructions.

Utah Insurance Department no longer accepts paper applications. Paper applications will be rejected and returned.

Multi-State Exposures: A license is not required for a nonresident insurance producer who sells, solicits, or negotiates a contract of insurance for commercial property and casualty coverage when risks that are to be insured under that contract are located in more than one state. This exception applies only if the nonresident is licensed to sell, solicit, or negotiate that insurance in the state where the insured maintains its principal place of business and the contract of insurance insures risks located in that state. (U.C.A. §31A-23a-201).

E. Education Requirements:

1. *Residents.* Obtain application bulletins from https://insurance.utah.gov/wp-content/uploads/LicensingBulletin.pdf. Applicants for the following licenses must pass a qualifying examination:

   a. Producer's Life: $59.
   b. Producer's Accident/Health: $59.
   c. Producer's Life and Accident/Health: $74.
   d. Producer's Property: $59.
   e. Producer's Casualty: $59.
   f. Producer's Property and Casualty: $74.
   g. Personal Lines: $59.
   h. Surplus Lines Producer: $59.
   i. Consultant's Life: $59.
   j. Consultant's Accident/Health: $59.

k. Consultant's Life and Accident/Health: $74.
l. Consultant's Property and Casualty and Personal Lines: $74.
m. Adjuster's Property and Casualty (Public or Independent): $59.
n. Adjuster's Accident/Health: $59.
o. Adjuster's Workers Compensation: $59.
p. Adjuster's Crop: $59.
q. Adjuster's Property & Casualty: $59.
r. Utah Laws and Regulations: $59. (U.C.A. §31A-23a-202).

Those agents selling variable contracts must have NASD licensing and be registered with the Securities Division of the Utah Commerce Department. Attorneys who are members of the Utah Bar are exempt from the adjuster examination. Adjuster applicants who have passed the Associate in Claims (AIC) coursework are exempt from the adjuster exam.

2. *Nonresidents* are exempt from the examination requirement if licensed in their state of residence.

F. Continuing Education Requirements:

Number of Hours Required: Twenty-four hours required; twelve hours must be in the classroom; three hours must be in ethics training, the remaining may be in any line of insurance. The CE requirement applies to producers (except title producers who are required to complete twelve hours, three of which are ethics) and adjusters. If continuously licensed for twenty or more years, six hours, three of which are ethics, are required. No more than twelve hours may be from courses provided by insurers. All twenty-four hours must be from courses approved by the Utah Insurance Department.

Proof of completion of continuing education hours must be kept on file with the producer. The Department may conduct random audits of producers by mail to verify their C.E. hours.

Certify Completion on renewal application. Submit Proof of Completion upon request by DOI.

Excess Hours may not be carried into the next reporting period.

Final Exam: The final exam for a self-study course does not need to be monitored.

Requirements not applicable to licensees first licensed before April 1, 1978 and who have applied to the commissioner for a grandfathering waiver.

Renewal Procedure:

1. Course provider supplies copy of completion certificate to the licensee and notifies DOI of completion.

2. Licensee retains copy in licensee's files of certificate along with application for renewal, in case of CE audit.

Producers holding and maintaining a CLU, ChFC, RHU with completion of PACE program, CPCU with completion of CPD program, CFP, REBC, CIC, CPSR, ACSR, CISR, CRM, SOFE, or IRES with completion of their CE requirements are exempt.

Nonresidents are exempt if their home state has substantially comparable requirements to those of Utah.

(https://insurance.utah.gov/licensee/producers/ce).

G. Cancellation of Agency Contracts/Producer Appointments: When terminating an appointment, an insurer must notify DOI electronically unless terminating for cause. Termination for cause must be submitted with a written explanation and any supporting documents. (U.C.A. §31A-23a-115).

H. Rules for Risk Retention and Purchasing Groups: RRGs may be chartered and licensed to write liability insurance. The following notice must appear in ten-point type on the declarations page:

NOTICE

"This policy is issued by your risk retention group. Your risk retention group may not be subject to all of the insurance laws and regulations of your state. State insurance insolvency guaranty funds are not available for your risk retention group." (U.C.A. §31A-15-204).

I. Other License Rules, Requirements, or Restrictions: Unlicensed nonresidents may not enter Utah for any insurance purpose that necessitates licensure. Entering the state includes mail or telephone or other electronic communication into the state from the outside, as well as physical presence in the state.

J. Policy Countersignature Requirements: Insurers domiciled in any state that requires a fixed fee or commission to be paid its resident agents for policy countersignature must pay the same fee or commission to a Utah resident agent for countersignature of Utah policies. Utah exempts purchasing groups and their insurers from countersignature requirements. A policy issued to a risk retention group may not be required to be countersigned. (U.C.A. § §31A-15-206.5 and 31A-15-207).

II. Commissions, Fees, Commingling of Funds, Suitability in Annuity Transactions

A. **Commissions:** There are no restrictions on distribution of commissions to licensed residents or nonresidents who are the appointed agents of the commission payer—except that Utah is retaliatory with home state requirements of nonresidents. An unlicensed resident or nonresident may not receive any commission under any circumstances. Rebating of commissions is not allowed.

B. **Fees:** Licensed consultants may, with proper disclosure, charge a fee for insurance-related services. Licensed producers may receive noncommission compensation subject to requirements outlined in U.C.A. §31A-23a-501(3).

C. **Disclosure Requirements:** Prior to performing the consulting services, the producer for the insured or consultant discloses to the client, prominently, in writing, the relationship to an insurer or other producer, and that as a result of those interests the consultant's recommendations should be given appropriate scrutiny. The producer for the insured's or consultant's fee is agreed upon, in writing, prior to performing the requested services. (U.C.A. §31A-23a-401).

D. **Commingling of Funds:** Utah agents must maintain a separate account for funds payable to insurers.

E. **Suitability in Annuity Transactions:** In recommending to a consumer the purchase of an annuity or the exchange of an annuity that results in another insurance transaction or series of insurance transactions, the insurance producer, or the insurer where no producer is involved, shall have reasonable grounds for believing that the recommendation is suitable for the consumer on the basis of the facts disclosed by the consumer as to his or her investments and other insurance products, financial situation, tax status, investment objectives, and any other information considered reasonable. An insurer either shall assure that a system to supervise recommendations that is reasonably designed to achieve compliance with this rule is established, or shall establish and maintain such a system, including: maintaining written procedures, and conducting periodic reviews of its records that are reasonably designed to assist in detecting and preventing violations of this rule. (U.A.C. R590-230-5).

III. Statutory References: U.C.A. §§31A-23a-101 through 31A-23a-809; 31A-15-201 through 31A-15-214.

VERMONT

Department of Banking, Insurance, Securities & Health Care Administration
Producer Licensing Division
89 Main St., Montpelier, VT 05620-3101
Telephone: 802-828-3301(Main), 802-828-3303(Producer); Fax: 802-828-1633;
Email: dfr.insuranceinfo@vermont.gov
https://dfr.vermont.gov/industry/insurance

I. Licensing Requirements: Sales Personnel—Producers, Limited Lines Producers, Managing General Agents, Business Entities. Surplus Lines Brokers, Other Insurance Professionals—Adjusters, Auto Damage Appraisers, Consultants, Public Adjusters, Reinsurance Intermediaries, Viatical Settlement Providers/Brokers.

A. Applicability: A person shall not sell, solicit or negotiate insurance in Vermont for any class or classes of insurance unless the person is licensed for that line of authority. Appointments are required. (8 V.S.A. §4813b).

B. Licenses Required of Residents: Each of the following must be licensed in Vermont. All licenses expire March 31, biennially. License applications can be obtained from the Department's Website at: https://dfr.vermont.gov/industry/insurance/producer-and-individual-licensing/apply-and-renew-your-license/producer-license. Initial application fee: $30, charged for each license shown below, with biennial license renewal fee shown. Vermont does not have a grace period for license renewal, and a license cannot be reactivated. A licensee, whose license has lapsed, must reapply for a new license. (8 V.S.A. §§4798).

Sales Personnel

1. *Producers.*

   a. Application fee: $30. License fee: $30, new and renewal plus a $30.00 application fee.
   b. License term: Biennial.
   c. Lines of authority:

      (1) Life.
      (2) Accident and health or sickness.
      (3) Property.
      (4) Casualty.
      (5) Personal lines.
      (6) Variable life/variable annuity products.
      (7) Any other line permitted under Vermont laws or regulations. (8 V.S.A. §4813g).

2. *Limited Lines Producers.*

   a. Application fee: $30. License fee: $30, new and renewal for individuals. $150, new and renewal for business entity limited lines producers. (8 V.S.A. § 4800).
   b. License term: Biennial, odd years.
   c. Limited lines of authority:

      (1) Travel accident.
      (2) Travel baggage.
      (3) Credit.
      (4) Rental.
      (5) Crop.
      (6) Surety.
      (http://www.dfr.vermont.gov/reg-bul-ord/limited-lines-producer-licenses).

3. *Managing General Agents.* Must be licensed and appointed as a producer or reinsurance intermediary. Application fee: $30; initial and renewal fee: $300. Must acquire a bond in the amount of $20,000.00. Must carry an E&O policy in the amount of $250,000. (8 V.S.A. §§4800 and 4817, https://dfr.vermont.gov/industry/insurance/producer-and-individual-licensing/apply-and-renew-your-license/managing-general).

4. *Business Entities.*

   a. Business entities must submit the NAIC Uniform Resident Business Entity application. Application fee: $30. License fee: $30. The business entity must have a designated licensed producer. $150, new and renewal for business entity limited lines producers. (8 V.S.A. § 4800).
   b. Business entity limited lines producer license for rental car insurance. A limited lines license is available to rental car agencies. (CVR 21-020-054).
   c. Business entity limited lines producer license for credit insurance. A limited lines license is available to business entities. (CVR 21-020-060).
   d. Business entity limited lines producer license for portable electronics insurance. A limited lines license is available to business entities. (CVR 21-020-065).

Other Insurance Professionals

1. *Adjusters.* All adjusters must be licensed for either property and casualty, or workers compensation. Application fee: $30. Initial fee and biennial renewal fee: $120. Requires two years of experience. License renews even years. (8 V.S.A. §4800).

2. *Auto Damage Appraisers.* Application fee: $30. Initial fee and biennial renewal fee: $120. Requires two years of experience. License renews even years. https://dfr.vermont.gov/industry/insurance/producer-and-individual-licensing/apply-and-renew-your-license/auto-damage).

3. *Consultants.* Application fee: $30. Insurance consultant's fee: $200. Must post a bond of $5,000. Consultants may not also be licensed as producers, surplus lines insurance broker, or limited lines producer in any line. License renews even years. (8 V.S.A. §4800, 4802).

4. *Public Adjusters.* Application fee: $30. Initial fee and biennial renewal fee: $200. Requires two years' experience. License renews even years. (8 V.S.A. §4800).

5. *Reinsurance Intermediaries.* Application fee: $30. Initial fee and biennial renewal: $200. License renews even years. Must be currently licensed as a producer. (8 V.S.A. §4800, 4817).

6. *Viatical Settlement Providers/Brokers.* Initial fee and annual renewal: $100 for Brokers. $50 initial fee and $400 renewal fee for Providers. Providers must post a $50,000 bond. Brokers must carry E&O policy of $250,000. License renews even years.

   (8 V.S.A. §4800, CVR 21-020-047).

Partnerships and corporations may not be licensed for any of these.

The following application forms are used. Applications may be downloaded from the Department's Web site, https://dfr.vermont.gov/industry/insurance. Producer licenses and adjuster licenses may be submitted and processed electronically by going to the Department's link at https://dfr.vermont.gov/industry/insurance/producer-and-individual-licensing. Nonresident PC Adjuster, DHS adjuster, WC Adjuster, Crop Adjuster, Public Adjuster, Appraiser, Title Agent, Limited Lines Producer, and Limited Lines Business Entity license applications, as well as Non Resident Producer, Business Entity and Surplus Broker License applications, must now be submitted electronically to the Department.

a. NAIC Uniform Application—completed by the applicant.
b. The NAIC Uniform Application is also used for all other license types.
c. Commercial Licenses: Commercial line filings that do not contain a signed certification and completed checklist will be rejected and the filer will be required to resubmit the filing with a new filing fee. The certification and checklist must be submitted for a rate, rule, form (or any combination) filing. These documents are posted on the agency's Web site.

d. Checklists concerning property, casualty, life, and annuity filings are posted on the agency's Web site. They are intended to help the filing process by listing the necessary elements of the filing packet. In order to pass to the next stage of review by an analyst, a submission must comply with the checklist instructions for inclusions and compliance.

C. **Appointments:** An insurance producer or limited lines producer may not act as an agent of an insurer unless the producer becomes an appointed agent of that insurer. A producer who is not acting as an agent of an insurer is not required to become appointed. An insurer shall make an appointment for each line of insurance for which an insurance producer or limited lines producer will be acting as an agent of the insurer. Appointment fee: $60 ($120 beginning June 1, 2021) biennially, billed monthly to company. Use the NAIC Uniform Appointment/Termination Form. Appointments expire on June 1 of odd years. (8 V.S.A. §4813 l). Effective July 1, 2012, appointment and appointment termination requests will only be accepted electronically. (8 V.S.A. §4813 l).

D. **Licenses Required of Nonresidents:** The license requirements for nonresidents are the same as for residents, except that license fees are retaliatory with nonresident's home state (sponsoring insurer's state of domicile for appointments). Business entities are not required to be licensed. If a nonresident business entity wishes to be licensed in Vermont, it must submit an NAIC uniform business entity application for nonresident business entity insurance license, a $30 application fee, and the appropriate fee retaliatory with the entity's home state. The same application form is used for nonresidents as for residents. Nonresidents must be appointed in Vermont with the companies for whom they write business. Certification (no older than ninety days) of nonresident by home state insurance department is required unless the home state insurance department reports license information to the Producer Database (PDB).

Applications can be found on the Vermont Department of Financial Regulation's website at https://dfr.vermont.gov/industry/insurance/producer-and-individual-licensing/apply-and-renew-your-license/producer-license. (8V.S.A. §§4813h and 4813n).

Multi-State Exposures: A license is not required for a nonresident insurance producer who sells, solicits, or negotiates a contract of insurance for commercial property and casualty coverage when risks that are to be insured under that contract are located in more than one state. This exception applies only if the nonresident is licensed to sell, solicit, or negotiate that insurance in the state where the insured maintains its principal place of business and the contract of insurance insures risks located in that state. (8 V.S.A §4813d).

E. Prelicensing Examination and Education Requirements

1. *Residents.* The following licenses require an exam:

    a. Insurance Producer Licenses: Life—accident, health, and HMO; property and casualty; personal lines; bail bond; title; and variable life and annuity.
    b. Insurance Adjuster Licenses: Property, casualty, and workers compensation.
    c. Other Licenses: Motor vehicle damage appraiser and public adjuster. Variable products authority requires NASD certification.

    Accident, health, and HMO producer applicants must pass the accident and health, and HMO examination. The casualty examination does not qualify applicants to sell accident, health, and HMO insurance.

    Variable annuity applicants must have passed the life insurance examination. They must also show that they have passed FINRA examination Series 6, 63, or 7. (https://www.nipr.com/rules_vt_nrl.htm).

    Adjuster and appraiser applicants must have two years' experience in insurance claims handling or loss appraising.

    Workers compensation resident and nonresident adjusters must complete educational and training programs designated by the commissioner. They must attend and satisfactorily participate in seminars administered by the Department of Labor and Industry in order to renew a license. Contact the Department of Labor and Industry at 802-828-2286.

    Limited lines insurance producer applicants do not need to pass an exam for travel baggage, travel accident, rental, or credit.

    For producer exam only: Holders of the CPCU and CLU designations are exempt from all but the part of the exam dealing with Vermont insurance laws and regulations.

    For information about examinations visit http://www.prometric.com.

    Exam fees are payable to Prometric.

2. *Nonresidents.* Examination requirements for nonresident applicants are reciprocal with nonresident's home state as long as home state has an examination requirement. However, nonresidents applying for license as workers compensation adjusters must take the Vermont exam. (8 V.S.A. §4800(3)(B)(iv) - (v)).

F. **Continuing Education Requirements:** Producers: twenty-four hours, biennially. The CE term expires on March 31 of odd years. The continuing education requirements do not apply until after the producer's first renewal of the license. There is a maximum of six CE credit hours relating to insurance agency management in any one review period. A producer must have at least three CE credit hours in ethics each renewal. Additionally, a producer licensed to sell property and casualty insurance must complete a one-time three hour CE course related to the National Flood Insurance Program. Instructors earn the same number of hours for a course as students. Workers compensation adjusters must take one seminar each year, conducted by the Department of Labor and Industry, before licenses can be renewed. Nonresident producers satisfy CE requirements by maintaining good standing in their state of residence. Producers may request up to a six month extension to satisfy CE requirements. Extra hours do not carry over to the next period. (8 V.S.A., §4800a, CVR 21-020-052).

G. **Cancellation of Agency Contracts/Producer Appointments:** In general, a cancelled property and casualty producer (except an exclusive producer) may renew any policy with the terminating insurer for a one-year term following the termination. This is subject to timely payment of renewal premium, the insurer's statutory right to cancel under certain circumstances, and the producer's continued good standing in the insurance community. The insurer may be relieved of the renewal obligation by the commissioner. The insurer must furnish to the commissioner convincing proof that, because of financial insecurity or other reason, compliance will represent a potential hazard to Vermont policyholders in general. The insurer must provide prompt notice to the commissioner. (8 V.S.A. §3884).

H. **Rules for Risk Retention and Purchasing Groups:** RRGs are licensed to write liability insurance. All such groups must submit a plan of operation and a feasibility study to be approved by the commissioner. The group must also provide information regarding the individuals who organized the group and its capitalization. All policies issued by risk retention groups must contain the following wording in ten-point type:

> "This policy is issued by your risk retention group. Your risk retention group may not be subject to all of the insurance laws and regulations of your State. State insurance insolvency guaranty funds are not available for your risk retention group." (https://recreationrrg.com/what-is-rrg).

I. **Other License Rules, Requirements, or Restrictions:** A nonresident may not enter Vermont to solicit, inspect, or service unless licensed in Vermont. Entering the state includes mail, telephone, or other electronic communication into the state from the outside, as well as physical presence in the state.

J. **Policy Countersignature Requirements:** None. (Vt. Stat. Ann. tit. 8, §4809).

II. Commissions, Fees, Commingling of Funds

A. Commissions: There are no restrictions on distribution of commissions to licensed residents or nonresidents producers. Unlicensed resident or nonresident persons may not receive commission or other fees for selling, soliciting or negotiating insurance if that person was required to be licensed. Vermont law is not retaliatory with respect to commissions. Rebating of commissions is not allowed. (8 V.S.A. §4796).

B. Fees: Producers may charge a fee for services.

C. Disclosure Requirements: Producers must obtain a prior written agreement with a client, policyholder or other member of the public concerning fees or charges made by that producer directly to the client, policyholder, or member of the public for that producer procuring, servicing, or providing advice on insurance contracts. (8 V.S.A. §4724).

In advance of rendering any service as a consultant, a written agreement on a form approved by the Commissioner must be prepared by the consultant and signed by the consultant and the client. The agreement must outline the nature of the work to be performed by the consultant and state his fee for the work. The consultant must retain a copy of the agreement for at least two years after completion of the services. The copy must be available to the commissioner. (8 V.S.A. §4802).

D. Commingling of Funds: Producers are fiduciaries for the premiums received. All premiums received must be immediately remitted to the insurer or deposited in a trust account. The producer must show no intent to inappropriately use or commingle premiums with the producer's operating account.

III. Statutory References: Vermont Statutes Annotated, tit. 8, §§4724, 4796 through 4798; 4800; 4800a; 4802 through 4809; 4813b through 4813o; 4815 through 4824; 6050 through 6061. Code of Vermont Rules 21-020-047, 21-020-054, 21-020-052, 21-020-060 and 21-020-065.

VIRGIN ISLANDS

Office of the Lieutenant Governor
Division of Banking and Insurance
No. 5049 Kongens Gade, St. Thomas, VI 00802
Telephone: 340-774-2991; Fax: 340-774-9458
1131 King Street, Suite 101
Christiansted, St Croix, VI 00820
Telephone: (340) 773-6449; Fax: (340) 719-3801
https://ltg.gov.vi/departments/banking-insurance-and-financial-regualtion/

I. Licensing Requirements: Sales Personnel—Agents, Brokers, Managing General Agents, Solicitors. Other Insurance Professionals—Independent and Public Adjusters.

A. Applicability: No agent, broker, or solicitor shall solicit or take applications for, procure or place for others any kind of insurance for which he is not then licensed. (22 V.I.C. §752).

B. Licenses Required of Residents: An agent is required to have but one license inclusive of all kinds or combination of kinds of insurance he is licensed to handle, regardless of the number of insurers for whom he is appointed as agent for such insurances or any of them. All licenses expire December 31 annually. Applicants may obtain license applications from the Division of Banking and Insurance. (22 V.I.C. §759).

Each of the following must be licensed:

Sales Personnel

1. *Agents.* A single license is issued for all lines for which agent has qualified; the Insurance Division web site lists the initial fee as $850 and $450 for renewal, as well as $50 for appointment. (22 V.I.C. §759; https://ltg.gov.vi/departments/banking-insurance-and-financial-regulation/#1546768965413-8a2ec2a6-3e58).

2. *Brokers.* Brokers must be licensed under 22 V.I.C. §760. However, the website does not list licensing fees for general brokers.

3. *Managing General Agents.* Must be licensed. Must maintain a bond $50,000 or 10 percent of the MGA's total annual written premium from the preceding calendar year. (22 V.I.C. §771).

4. *Solicitors.* Solicitor's license, initial fee: $400. Annual renewal: $200. (https://ltg.gov.vi/departments/banking-insurance-and-financial-regulation/#1546768965413-8a2ec2a6-3e58).

Other Insurance Professionals

Adjusters. Independent and public adjusters, but not insurers' staff adjusters, must be licensed. Initial fee: $500. Annual renewal: $250 according to the Insurance Division web site. Public adjusters must have a $5,000 bond. Separate licenses are issued for independent and public adjusters. An individual may hold both licenses; the full licensing fee must be paid for each license. The license fee for an emergency independent adjuster is $300. (22 V.I.C. §§767, 768, 779; https://ltg.gov.vi/departments/banking-insurance-and-financial-regulation/#1546768965413-8a2ec2a6-3e58).

C. **Licenses Required of Nonresidents:** Nonresident applicants must be in good standing in their home state, currently hold a license for the lines of authority requested in the Virgin Islands, and the applicant's home state must award Virgin Islands residents the same license on a reciprocal basis. Satisfactory proof that the applicant is licensed in his home state is required. Initial producer fee: $700. Renewal: $400. Application for renewal of a nonresident license for individuals and business entities must be made by December 31 each year; late fee: $800. (22 V.I.C. §763; https://ltg.gov.vi/departments/banking-insurance-and-financial-regulation/#1546768965413-8a2ec2a6-3e58).

Multi-State Exposures. Even when writing a risk with only an incidental exposure in Virgin Islands (such as a car on a fleet policy), the nonresident needs a Virgin Islands license. (22 V.I.C. §763).

D. **Prelicensing Examination and Education Requirements:**

1. *Residents.* Applicants for all licenses must pass a qualifying examination covering all insurance lines to which the license applies. (22 V.I.C. §757).

2. *Nonresidents.* Applicants for license as nonresident agent or as nonresident broker who have fulfilled the qualification requirements in their state of residence and who are deemed by the commissioner to be fully qualified and competent do not need to pass an examination. (22 V.I.C. §757).

E. **Continuing Education Requirements:** Producers are required to complete 24 credits of continuing education for each biennial compliance period. Three of the 24 credits must be in ethics. The Commissioner shall by regulations establish minimum continuing education requirements for the renewal or reissuance of a license to an insurance producer. (22 V.I.C. §770).

If a nonresident satisfies the CE requirements of his or her home state, it shall constitute satisfaction of the CE requirements for the Virgin Islands, provided that the nonresident's home state recognizes the satisfication of CE requirements of Virgin Islands residents on a reciprocal basis. (22 V.I.C. §764).

F. **Cancellation of Agency Contracts/Producer Appointments:** The Virgin Islands has no laws or regulations in this area.

G. **Rules for Risk Retention and Purchasing Groups:** The Virgin Islands has no laws or regulations in this area.

H. **Other License Rules, Requirements, or Restrictions:** A nonresident licensee is subject to the same obligation and duties, including the Commissioner's supervision, as a resident licensee, except for the requirement of maintaining an office in the Virgin Islands. (22 V.I.C. §763).

II. Policy Countersignature Requirements

A. **Applicability:** No insurer shall issue an insurance contract covering a subject of insurance resident, located, or to be performed in this territory unless the insurance contract is countersigned by its licensed agent, or manager or general agent. The territory's countersigning law applies to all insurers except surplus lines insurers, and to insurance on all property and operations within the Virgin Islands (except life or disability insurance, reinsurance, and insurance on rolling stock, vessels or aircraft of common carriers in interstate or foreign commerce, and vehicles principally garaged outside the Virgin Islands), regardless of residence of insured. (22 V.I.C. §§220, 221).

B. **Who Must Countersign:** All policies must be countersigned by the insurer's licensed resident agent, general agent, or manager. (22 V.I.C. §220).

C. **Other Countersignature Requirements:** Neither signatures nor countersignatures are permitted in blank. (22 V.I.C. §220).

III. Commissions, Fees, Commingling of Funds, Suitability in Annuity Transactions

A. *Commissions:* Unlicensed persons, resident or nonresident, may not receive commission under any circumstances. Rebating of commissions is not allowed. (22 V.I.C. §§778, 779).

B. *Fees:* The premium stated in the policy shall be inclusive of all fees, charges, premiums, or other consideration chargeed for the insurance. No insurer or its officer, employee, agent, solicitor, or other representative shall charge or receive any fee, compensation, or consideration for insurance that is not included in the premium specified in the policy. However, any amount due with respect to gross receipts taxes may be stated separately in the policy or on an invoice for such policy. (22 V.I.C. §818).

C. *Disclosure Requirements:* None.

D. **Commingling of Funds:** The Virgin Islands does not have laws or regulations in this area.

E. **Suitability in Annuity Transactions:** The Virgin Islands has not taken action to date in this area.

IV. Statutory References:

22 V.I.C. §§	220, 221
	752, 757, 759
	760, 763, 764, 767, 768
	770, 771, 779
	818

VIRGINIA

State Corporation Commission, Bureau of Insurance
Tyler Building, 6th floor, 1300 E. Main St.
Richmond, Virginia 23219
Mailing: P.O. Box 1157; Richmond, VA 23218-1157
Telephone: 804-371-9741; Fax: 804-371-9290
Email: AgentLicensing@scc.virginia.gov www.scc.virginia.gov/boi

I. Licensing Requirements: Sales Personnel—Agents, Managing General Agents. Other Insurance Professionals—Consultants, Public Adjusters, Reinsurance Intermediaries, Viatical Settlement Brokers, Viatical Settlement Providers.

A. Applicability: No person shall sell, solicit, or negotiate contracts of insurance or annuity on behalf of an insurer, or share, commission, or other valuable consideration arising from the sale, solicitation, or negotiation of any such contract unless the person holds a valid license to transact the class of insurance involved. No person shall submit business to any joint underwriting association or any plan for the equitable distribution of risks among insurers unless the person holds a valid license to transact the class of insurance involved. Appointments are required. (Va. Code Ann. §38.2-1822).

B. Licenses Required of Residents: The following must be licensed and appointed:

Sales Personnel

1. *Agents.* Virginia has a producer license with five major classifications: life and annuities, health, personal lines, property and casualty and title. They have many subclasses, listed below.

Life and Annuities Qualification (Va. Code Ann. §38.2-1815).

Annuities (except variable).
Burial.
Credit life.
Industrial life.
Life.
Mortgage redemption.
Mutual assessment life.
Modified guaranteed annuities.
Modified guaranteed life. (http://www.scc.virginia.gov/boi/pro/appfee.aspx).

Health Qualification (Va. Code Ann. §38.2-1815.1).

Accident and sickness.
Credit accident and sickness.
Dental benefit contracts.
Dental service plans.
Dental Plan Organizations
HMOs.
Health services plan.
Long-term care.
Medicare supplement
Mortgage accident and sickness.
Mutual assessment health.
Optometric services plans. (http://www.scc.virginia.gov/boi/pro/appfee.aspx).

Personal Lines Qualification (Va. Code Ann. §38.2-1814).

Aircraft.
Animal.
Burglary and theft.
Credit involuntary unemployment.
Credit property.
Farm-owners.
Fire.
Glass.
Home protection.
Homeowners.
Legal services.
Marine.
Miscellaneous property.
Mortgage guaranty.
Motor vehicle.
Mutual assessment property and casualty.
Personal injury liability.
Pet accident, sickness, and hospitalization.
Property damage liability.
Travel.
Water damage. (http://www.scc.virginia.gov/boi/pro/appfee.aspx).

Property and Casualty Qualification
(Includes the Personal Lines Classes, above) (Va. Code Ann. §38.2-1814).

Boiler and machinery.
Commercial multi-peril.
Credit.
Fidelity.
Surety.
Workers compensation and employers liability. (http://www.scc.virginia.gov/boi/pro/appfee.aspx).

Individuals and agencies must be appointed with insurer. Licenses are continuous unless surrendered, terminated, canceled, suspended, or revoked; $15 nonrefundable processing fee per line of authority. Appointments must be renewed annually by June 30.

Applicant must obtain the appropriate license within 183 calendar days from the date the applicant passes the examination. If not, the examination date becomes invalid. Companies handle appointment of agents, for which a $10 fee is payable by the company. Appointment fees are billed to companies on a quarterly basis and are not payable at time of submission of appointment notification. Companies are billed as of June 30 of each year, $10 for each appointment renewal. Appointment renewal fees are due on August 10. Failure to pay any quarterly or renewal fees by the due date will result in a penalty of $50 per day for each day between the date due and the date full payment is received. Restricted licenses are available for a number of kinds of insurance sold as incidental to other business activities. Agents may be individuals, partnerships, corporations, limited partnerships, or limited liability companies. Virginia does not license sole proprietorships. Residents must submit criminal history record report (no older than ninety days) from the Virginia State Police with application. (Va. Code Ann. §§38.2-1817, 38.2-1834 https://www.scc.virginia.gov/boi/pro/renew.aspx).

2. *Managing General Agents.* Must be licensed as MGAs. Insurers utilizing MGAs must notify the Bureau of Insurance. The application form is available by calling 804-371-9063. The application fee is $500; biennial renewal, $500. License expires on June 30. Renewal applications must be received and fee paid prior to June 1 of the renewal year. The MGA must have a fidelity bond equal to 10 percent of its annual gross direct written premium. It must also maintain errors and omissions insurance with limits of $1 million or 25 percent of its written premium, whichever is greater. (Va. Code Ann. §38.2-1359, https://scc.virginia.gov/getattachment/5ea26aa5-66dd-4427-b5d4-efba4f03e7cd//mga.pdf).

3. *Limited Lines Agents.* Fee: $15. An individual may obtain a license as a limited lines credit insurance agent, a limited lines life and health agent, a limited lines property and casualty agent, a motor vehicle rental contract insurance agent, or other type

of license of restricted authority without taking such examination. (Va. Code Ann. §§38.2-1814 and 38.2-1815, https://www.scc.virginia.gov/boi/pro/appfee.aspx).

4. *Public Adjuster.* Fee: $250. No person shall engage in the business of public adjusting, on or after January 1, 2013, without first applying for and obtaining a license from the commission. Residents must maintain a bond in the amount of $50,000. Biennial renewal based from the date of issuance. Must complete twenty-four hours of continuing education, three of which must be in ethics. (Va. Code Ann. §§38.2-1845.1 through 38.2-1845.23, https://scc.virginia.gov/pages/Application-Fees).

5. *Portable Electronics.* Vendors are required to hold a limited lines property and casualty insurance agent license to sell or offer a policy covering portable electronics. Portable electronics are devices that are portable in nature such as cell phones, GPS devices, hands free communication devices along with accessories and related services. (Va. Code Ann. §§38.2-1875 through 38.2-1880).

6. *Self-Storage.* A lessor is required to hold a limited lines property and casualty insurance agent license to sell or offer coverage under a policy of self-storage insurance. The license shall authorize any employee or authorized representative of a licensed lessor to sell or offer self-storage insurance coverage under a policy of self-storage insurance to a customer at each location at which the lessor engages in self-storage unit transactions. (Va. Code Ann. §§38.2-1881 through 38.2-1886).

7. *Travel.* All individual producers who are selling travel insurance are required to hold a limited lines property & casualty license unless they are already licensed as a property & casualty or personal lines producer. All business entities who are selling travel insurance are required to hold a limited lines firm license unless they already are licensed as a property & casualty producer. The license authorizes producers to sell insurance coverage for personal risks incident to planned travel, including (i) interruption or cancellation of trip or event; (ii) loss of baggage or personal effects; (iii) damages to accommodations or rental vehicles; or (iv) sickness, accident, or death occurring during travel. "Travel insurance" does not include major medical plans that provide comprehensive medical protection for travelers with trips lasting six months or longer, including those working overseas as an expatriate or deployed overseas as military personnel. (Va. Code Ann. *§§38.2-1887 through 38.2-1890).*

Other Insurance Professionals

1. *Consultants.* Consultants are those who—for a fee—advise on matters regarding life, health, property, or casualty insurance, except attorneys acting in their professional

capacities, trust officers acting in the normal course of employment, actuaries or certified public accountants consulting during the normal course of business, and any persons employed as risk managers who consult for their employers only. If a partnership, corporation, or limited liability company renders insurance advice, an insurance consultant's license must be obtained for each active member who will be consulting. To be licensed as an insurance consultant, the individual must first satisfy all prelicensing requirements for insurance producers in the field of insurance in which he or she wishes to consult. Beginning January 1, 2021, each insurance consultant shall submit biennially to the Commission a renewal application in a form and manner prescribed by the Commission, along with a nonrefundable renewal application processing fee prescribed by the Commission, for the renewal of the license. Effective July 1, 2016, insurance agencies are required to maintain a Designated Licensed Producer ("DLP") responsible for the agency's compliance with insurance laws and regulations. The license authority of any business entity licensed as a consultant shall terminate immediately if the designated licensed producer responsible for the business entity's compliance with the insurance laws is removed for any reason and a new responsible producer has not been designated and the Commission notified within thirty calendar days of such removal and of the new designated responsible producer.

(2016 Virginia Laws Ch. 552 (H.B. 393), Va. Code Ann. §§38.2-1837 through 38.2-1845, https://www.scc.virginia.gov/boi/pro/enf.aspx).

2. *Reinsurance Intermediaries.* Insurers or reinsurers who utilize reinsurance intermediaries must notify each of its intermediaries to request a license application packet from the Bureau of Insurance. The application fee is $500; biennial renewal, $500. License expires on June 30. Renewal applications must be received and fee paid prior to June first. In addition to the application, the applicant must submit a plan of operation, a completed biographical affidavit, and a certified financial statement. Application form for licensing is available by calling 804-371-9546. A reinsurance intermediary manager must also maintain a fidelity bond and an E&O policy in limits acceptable to the Bureau and must submit a copy of its contract to the Bureau. (Va. Code Ann. §38.2-1348).

3. *Viatical Settlement Brokers.* Viatical Settlement Broker means any person who, for another and for a fee, commission or other valuable consideration, offers or advertises the availability of viatical settlements, introduces viators to viatical settlement providers, or offers or attempts to negotiate viatical settlements between a viator and one or more viatical settlement providers. "Viatical Settlement Broker" does not include an attorney, accountant or financial planner who is not paid by the viatical settlement provider or viatical settlement purchaser and who is retained to represent the viator. Persons offering life settlements must

be licensed as a Viatical Settlement Broker. A business entity acting as a Viatical Settlement Broker is required to obtain a Viatical Settlement Broker's license. Fee: $50. Beginning January 1, 2021, each individual settlement broker shall submit biennially to the Commission a renewal application in the form and manner prescribed by the Commission, along with a nonrefundable renewal application processing fee prescribed by the Commission for the renewal of the license. The original application must include a Criminal History Record Report obtained from the Virginia State Police 804-674-2000. (Va. Code Ann. §38.2-1865.1, http://www.scc.virginia.gov/boi/pro/appfee.aspx).

4. *Viatical Settlement Providers.* License renews annually on July 1, expires on June 30. Renewal applications must be received and fee paid prior to March 1. Fees: new, $500; renewal, $300. Must post either a surety bond in the amount of $100,000 or an E&O policy in the sum of not less than $100,000 per occurrence and $1 million for all occurrences within one year; or make and maintain a deposit of not less than $100,000 with the Treasurer of Virginia, and provide an antifraud plan. (Va. Code Ann. §38.2-6002).

5. *Title Settlement Agents.* Must first be licensed as a title insurance agent and be appointed by an insurer in Virginia. Must also file an E&O policy of at least $250,000, a blanket fidelity bond, or employee dishonesty policy of at least $100,000, and an original surety bond of $200,000. Business entity registration and renewal fee is $100. Agent registration and renewal fee is $35. (14 Va. Admin. Code §5-395-40).

   Applicants may apply online at https://scc.virginia.gov/boi/online.aspx. Forms for MGAs, reinsurance intermediaries, and viatical settlement providers may be downloaded from https://scc.virginia.gov/pages/Licensing-Registration-Forms.

   a. MGAs. Please call 804-371-9063.
   b. Reinsurance Intermediaries. Application for licensing form is available by calling 804-371-9546.

C. **Appointments:** The insurer shall, within thirty calendar days of the date of execution of the first insurance application or policy submitted by a licensed but not yet appointed agent, either reject such application or policy or file with the commission a notice of appointment in a form acceptable to the commission. The insurer shall provide to the licensed agent, within the same thirty day period, verification that the notice of appointment has been filed with the commission. The company must notify the agent if the commission notifies the company that the attempt to appoint the agent was invalid. The company's notice must be provided within five business days of receipt of the invalid appointment notice from the commission. Any agent who sells or solicits insurance on behalf of the insurer after being notified of an invalid appointment shall be in violation of Virginia law. (Va. Code Ann. §38.2-1833).

D. Licenses Required of Nonresidents: Nonresidents may obtain any Virginia license that is available to residents on a reciprocal basis, provided the nonresident holds equivalent license or authority in his or her home state. Nonrefundable license processing fee: $15 per line of authority. Nonresident agent must appoint the Clerk of the Virginia State Corporation Commission for service of process in order to obtain a nonresident license. There is no bond requirement for agents. Nonresident individuals may apply online at https://scc.virginia.gov/boi/online.aspx. For more information visit https://www.nipr.com/rules_va_nrl.htm.

A nonresident corporation, LLC, or partnership seeking an agency license in Virginia may apply online at http://scc.virginia.gov/boi/online.aspx. Virginia does not license sole proprietorships. A business entity is not required to first obtain a certificate of authority, including a certificate of registration, certificate of organization, certificate of limited partnership, or charter, from the commission prior to being eligible to obtain a license as an insurance agent, consultant, public adjuster, surplus lines broker, or viatical settlement broker. However, the business entity must still obtain the necessary certificate of authority within ninety days of the issuance of the license. A failure to obtain that certificate of authority may result in the Bureau of Insurance terminating the producer license.

Multi-State Exposures: A license is not required for a nonresident insurance producer who sells, solicits, or negotiates a contract of insurance for commercial property and casualty coverage when risks that are to be insured under that contract are located in more than one state. This exception applies only if the nonresident is licensed to sell, solicit, or negotiate that insurance in the state where the insured maintains its principal place of business and the contract of insurance insures risks located in that state. (Va. Code Ann. §38.2-1821.1).

E. Prelicensing Examination and Education Requirements:

1. *Residents.* Applicants must pass an exam for life and annuities, health, personal lines, property and casualty, public adjuster, title, or the consultant's license. A producer license with a title qualification requires the completion of a prelicensing study course prior to scheduling the examination. For more information, visit www.pearsonvue.com/va/insurance or contact Pearson VUE at 888-204-6272. CLUs and CPCUs are exempt from all prelicensing requirements unless the agent's license is terminated for not meeting CE requirements.

   Resident applicants for a variable life and annuity license must first be licensed for life and annuities, and must have passed FINRA series 6 or series 7 examinations.

Applicants for various restricted or temporary licenses are exempt from the examination requirements.

If an applicant does not obtain a license within 183 calendar days of taking the exam, the applicant will be required to retake the exam. (Va. Code Ann. §38.2-1817).

2. *Nonresidents.* Nonresidents have no examination requirements, but must be fully qualified in their home state for the lines of insurance they are applying for in Virginia. Florida and Pennsylvania title agents applying for a Virginia nonresident producer license with a title qualification must pass Virginia's title exam prior to applying for the license. Virginia statutes do not require nonresident applicants to take Virginia's prelicensing study course prior to taking the Title exam.

F. Continuing Education Requirements:

Residents—Number of Hours Required: Sixteen hours, biennially; twenty-four hours of continuing education credit is required if the agent holds more than one category of license. Applicable to life and annuities agents, health agents, personal lines agents, property and casualty agents, title agents, life and health consultants, and property and casualty consultants. At least eight hours must be in each line licensed and three of the required hours must be in ethics, which may include Virginia insurance law and regulations. Licensees may use classroom instruction or self-study. A maximum of 75 percent of the credits may come from courses provided by insurance companies or insurance agencies. (Va. Code Ann. §38.2-1866). Public adjusters must complete twenty-four hours of continuing education, three of which must be in ethics. (Va. Code Ann. §38.2-1845.9). Pearson VUE administers Virginia's CE program, http://www.pearsonvue.com/va/insurance/ce/index.asp, 877-234-2366, or www.VirginiaInsuranceCE.com.

Nonresidents. Nonresidents are only required to pay the nonrefundable continuance fee.

Complete Courses and Pay Continuance Fee by November 30 of even years.

Excess Hours: May be forwarded to the next reporting period only.

Final Exam: The final exam for a self-study course must be proctored. The regulations dictate that the proctor cannot be a relative, friend, or an acquaintance. The proctor must be a disinterested party over the age of eighteen years and unrelated to the student. Visit www.virginiainsurancece.com to view a list of approved proctors.

Requirements **Not** *Applicable to the Following: (Effective January 1, 2019).*

1. Resident and nonresident licensees whose licenses were issued in the second year of the biennium and who are not otherwise exempt from the continuing education requirements for that license.

2. The following licenses are exempt from fulfilling the continuing education requirements.

   a. Life and health insurance consultants who are also licensed both as life and annuities insurance agents and as health agents and who satisfy the continuing education requirements needed for continuation of their life and annuities and health agent licenses.
   b. Property and casualty insurance consultants who are also licensed as property and casualty agents and who satisfy the continuing education requirements needed for continuation of their property and casualty agent license.
   c. Nonresident agents who furnish evidence that they are currently in good standing in their home state, provided that the agents home state will grant similar exemptions to Virginia agents.
   d. Agents who have applied for and received a permanent exemption from the continuing education requirements set forth in Va. Code Ann. §§38.2-1871.

C.E. Filing Procedure:

1. Course provider supplies licensee with a Certificate of Course Completion.

2. Course provider submits course completion rosters to Pearson VUE.

3. Licensee must pay $22 continuance fee at www.VirginiaInsuranceCE.com.

4. Licensee keeps a copy of the Certificate of Course Completion and receipt of $22 continuance fee payment.

5. Nonresidents are not required to take Virginia CE courses. Nonresidents must pay the $20 continuance fee, and Pearson VUE will verify agent's home state licensure on the NAIC's Producer Database. The fee can be paid at www.VirginiaInsuranceCE.com.

G. Cancellation of Agency Contracts/Producer Appointments: Upon termination of an agent/agency by an insurer, the insurer must notify the agent within five calendar days. The insurer must also file (electronically) with the Bureau of Insurance the appointment cancellation within thirty calendar days. (Va. Code Ann. §38.2-1834).

H. **Rules for Risk Retention and Purchasing Groups:** Virginia regulates risk retention and purchasing groups operating or offering coverage on risks in Virginia as required under Virginia Code §§38.2-5100 to 38.2-5115. Risk retention groups domiciled in Virginia must be chartered and licensed as liability insurers. Groups not domiciled in Virginia must register with the commissioner of insurance and submit reports to the commissioner as described in the law. Purchasing groups must also register with the commissioner and submit reports as required by the law. All groups domiciled in Virginia and all resident and nonresident agents or brokers participating in them must comply with all Virginia insurance laws, including licensing and solicitation requirements or restrictions. All risk retention group applications and policies must show the following notice in at least ten point type on the front page and on the declarations page of the policy:

NOTICE

"This policy is issued by your risk retention group. Your risk retention group may not be subject to all of the insurance laws and regulations of your state. State insurance insolvency guaranty funds are not available for your risk retention group." (Va. Code Ann. §38.2-5103).

I. **Other License Rules, Requirements, or Restrictions:** Licensed nonresidents may act as an agent in Virginia and conduct insurance business. Virginia is reciprocal with the nonresident's home state. Unlicensed nonresidents may not enter the state for any insurance purpose. Entering the state includes mail or telephone or other electronic communication into the state from the outside, as well as physical presence in the state. All licensees must report in writing to the Bureau of Insurance within thirty calendar days any change of name or residence, administrative actions, and felony convictions. (https://www.scc.virginia.gov/boi/pro/enf.aspx).

J. **Policy Countersignature Requirements:** None.

III. Commissions, Fees, Commingling of Funds, Suitability in Annuity Transactions

A. **Commissions:** There are no restrictions on distribution of commissions. An unlicensed resident or nonresident may not receive commission under any circumstance. Rebating of commissions is not allowed. (Va. Code Ann. §38.2-1812).

B. **Fees:** Agents may charge fees in addition to commissions for services performed in connection with the sale of insurance provided they are disclosed properly. (Va. Code Ann. §38.2-1812.2).

C. **Disclosure Requirements:** Agent may not charge, demand, or receive any consideration in return for rendering services associated with a contract of insurance, when the consideration is in addition to the premium for such contract, unless:

1. The applicant or policyholder consents in writing before any services are rendered, on a form that includes the applicant's or policyholder's signature, the duration of services and amount of fees to be charged, the services for which the fees are charged, and a statement that the agent is entitled to receive a commission from the insurer for selling, soliciting, or negotiating the insurance.

2. A schedule of fees and documentation for services rendered is maintained in the agent's office and is made available to applicants or policyholders upon request. (Va. Code Ann. §38.2-1812.2).

D. **Commingling of Funds:** Agents must maintain a separate fiduciary account for certain premiums and may not commingle these premiums with personal or nonbusiness funds and shall be reasonably ascertainable from the agent's records. (Va. Code Ann. §38.2-1813).

E. **Suitability in Annuity Transactions:** In recommending to a consumer the purchase of an annuity or the exchange of an annuity that results in another insurance transaction or series of insurance transactions, the agent, or the insurer where no agent is involved, shall have reasonable grounds for believing that the recommendation is suitable for the consumer on the basis of the facts disclosed by the consumer as to his investments and other insurance products and as to his financial situation and needs. An insurer either shall assure that a system to supervise recommendations that is reasonably designed to achieve compliance with this requirement is established, or shall establish and maintain such a system, including, but not limited to: maintaining written procedures and conducting periodic reviews of its records that are reasonably designed to assist in detecting and preventing violations. (14 Va. Admin. Code §5-45-40).

IV. **Statutory References:** Virginia Code §§38.2-1800 through 38.2-1890; 38.2-5100 through 38.2-5115; 38.2-6000 through 38.2-6016; 38.2-1346 through 38.2-1364.

WASHINGTON

Office of Insurance Commissioner; Licensing & Education
5000 Capitol Blvd., SE Tumwater, WA 98501;
Mailing: P.O. Box 40255, Olympia, WA 98504-0255;
Telephone: 360-725-7000; Fax: 360-586-2019
Email: licinfo@oic.wa.gov;
https://insurance.wa.gov/producers

I. **Licensing Requirements:** Sales Personnel—Producers, Limited Lines Producers, Business Entities. Other Insurance Professionals—Independent Adjusters, Crop Adjusters, Public Adjusters, Reinsurance Intermediaries, Life Settlement Brokers, Rental Car Agents, Specialty Producers, Self-Service Storage.

A. **Applicability:** Licensing laws apply to all insurers in the general solicitation of business and to all insurance and surety bonds except credit life and disability, bid bonds, insurance on property in course of transportation in interstate or foreign commerce, title insurance, and insurance on vehicles principally garaged and used outside the state.

B. **Licenses Required of Residents:** Each of the following must be licensed in the state. As of December 17, 2018, licenses expire biennially on the last day of the licensee's birth month (for firms or corporations, two years from issue date and every two years thereafter) (https://www.insurance.wa.gov/expiration-date-and-renewal-period-changes). Renewal dates for appointments are biennially assigned by the Office of the Insurance Commissioner. Must submit applications electronically. (Rev. Code Wash. § 48.17.060)

All applications for licenses, renewals, appointments, and affiliations, must be submitted electronically through the Commissioner's website or through a third-party licensing provider. The Commissioner will no longer print or mail any document generated as part of a licensing process which the Commissioner has determined to be an exclusive online licensing process. Specific instructions for applying for a license may be found on the Commissioner's website at https://www.insurance.wa.gov/get-licensed.

Sales Personnel

1. *Producers.*

a. License fee: $55 plus initial $5 filing fee. Biennial renewal fee: $55. Fingerprint Processing Fee (Resident fingerprints must be submitted electronically): All resident applicants must do the electronic fingerprints scheduled through

IDEMIA (formerly MorphoTrust) at 1-888 771-5097 or visit their website at https://www.identogo.com/. This fee is $49.25, which reflects the combined cost of the background check fee and IDEMIA IdentoGO's additional charge for providing the service, also known as a rolling fee. (https://www.insurance.wa.gov/individual-license-fees and https://www.insurance.wa.gov/fingerprint-requirements).

b. License term: Biennial. Initial license will expire on the last day of the individual's next birth month plus one year, and every two years thereafter.
c. Lines of authority:

(1) Life.
(2) Disability.
(3) Property.
(4) Casualty.
(5) Personal lines.
(6) Surety only.
(7) Limited line credit.
(8) Travel.
(9) Variable lines.
(10) Portable electronics.
(11) Rental car.
(12) Self-service storage.
(13) Any other line permitted under state laws or rules.
(Rev. Code Wash. §§48.14.010(1)(e) and 48.17.170).

Sales employees of insurers, if compensated by commissions, must be licensed producers. PLE certificates, exam score reports, and other supporting documents may be uploaded into the electronic application.

Every resident producer who places insurance with an insurer with which he is not appointed must maintain a bond in favor of the people of the state of Washington of at least $2,500 or 5 percent of brokered premiums. (Rev. Code Wash. § 48.17.250).

2. *Limited Lines Agents.*

a. License fee: $20 plus initial $5 filing fee. $20 biennial renewal fee. Fingerprint processing fee (Resident fingerprints must be submitted electronically). All resident applicants must do the electronic fingerprints scheduled through IDEMIA (formerly MorphoTrust) at 1-888 771-5097 or visit their website at https://www.identogo.com/. This fee is $49.25, which reflects the combined cost of the background check fee and IDEMIA IdentoGO's additional charge for providing the service, also known as a rolling fee.

b. License term: biennial.
c. Lines of authority:

    (1) Surety.
    (2) Travel.
    (3) Credit.

All fees may be combined into one credit card, e-check or check payable to Washington Insurance Commissioner. The fingerprint fee is paid directly to the fingerprint vendor; it is not included with the license fees.

(Rev. Code Wash. §§48.14.010(1)(e) and 48.17.170).

3. *Business Entities.* Business entities must submit an electronic application. The appointment notice must be submitted electronically by the carrier within fifteen days of the business entity's first piece of business or at the time of agency contract, whichever comes earlier; residents must submit articles of incorporation or formation and letter of good standing from the Secretary of State. Licenses are biennial and expire two years from issue date. License fee: $55 for each location plus $5 filing fee, and $20 affiliation fee for each affiliated licensee. The business entity must also name a Designated Licensed Responsible Person (DLRP). All individuals selling insurance in an entity must also be licensed and affiliated. (Wash. Rev. Code Ann. §48.17.090).

4. *Variable life and annuity producers.* Must have producers license with life line of authority and a securities license. Submit an online request to add variable life line of authority. Fingerprint processing fee: All resident applicants must do the electronic fingerprints scheduled through IDEMIA (formerly MorphoTrust) at 1-888 771-5097 or visit their website at https://www.identogo.com/. This fee is $49.25, which reflects the combined cost of the background check fee and IDEMIA IdentoGO's additional charge for providing the service, also known as a rolling fee. (Wash. Admin. Code 284-17-015). Fingerprinting is not required on nonresident licensees.

5. *Title Insurance Agents.* Title Insurance licenses are only issued to agencies not to individuals. License application: $50. Filing fee: $5. Each additional location: $50. Biennial renewal: $50. Fingerprinting not required. (Rev. Code Wash. §48.14.010).

Other Insurance Professionals

1. *Independent Adjusters.* Adjuster's license fee: $50 plus initial $5 filing fee with $50 biennial renewal fee. Individual resident applicants must submit fingerprints electronically. Submit an online application, exam score, application fees, and fingerprint processing fee. All resident applicants must do the electronic fingerprints scheduled through IDEMIA (formerly MorphoTrust) at 1-888 771-5097 or visit their website at https://www.identogo.com/ for $49.25 which covers the prints and the background check fees. Fingerprinting is not required of nonresident licensees. Corporations or LLCs must submit articles of incorporation or formation; firms must file their trade names with the Department of Licensing. (Rev. Code Wash. §48.14.010(i)).

2. *Public Adjusters.* Biennial fee: $50 plus initial $5 filing fee with $50 biennial renewal fee. Public adjusters must provide a $5,000 surety bond form. Individual resident applicants must submit fingerprints electronically. Submit an online application, exam score, and fingerprint processing fee. All resident applicants must do the electronic fingerprints scheduled through IDEMIA (formerly MorphoTrust) at 1-888 771-5097 or visit their website at https://www.identogo.com/. The fee is $49.25. Fingerprinting is not required of nonresident licensees. Resident Corporations or LLCs must submit articles of incorporation or formation; firms must file their trade names with the Department of Licensing. All fees may be combined into one check payable to Washington Insurance Commissioner. (Rev. Code Wash. §§48.14.010(i) & 48.17.430).

3. *Crop Adjusters.* Effective June 27, 2011, Washington offers crop adjuster licenses. License application $50 plus initial $5 filing fee. Renewal every two years: $50. Individual resident applicants must submit fingerprints electronically. Fingerprint processing fee for residents: All resident applicants must do the electronic fingerprints scheduled through IDEMIA (formerly MorphoTrust) at 1-888 771-5097 or visit their website at https://www.identogo.com. The fee is $49.25. This fee reflects the combined cost of the background check fee and IDEMIA IdentoGO's additional charge for providing the service, also known as a rolling fee. Nonresidents are not required to be fingerprinted. (Rev. Code Wash. §§ 48.17.010, 48.17.390 and 48.17.420).

3. *Reinsurance Intermediaries.* Brokers: $50 each year. Managers: $100 each year. Managers may be required to post a bond and carry an E&O policy. (Rev. Code Wash. §48.14.010(g)). Producer Licensing & Oversight Division does not license reinsurance intermediaries. Company Supervision Division does.

4. *Life Settlement Brokers.* Must be qualified as a life agent. License fee $100. Biennial renewal fee: $100. Individual resident applicants must submit

fingerprints electronically. Submit application form, verification of life agent qualification, and fingerprint processing fee. All resident applicants must do the electronic fingerprints scheduled through IDEMIA (formerly MorphoTrust) at 1-888 771-5097 or visit their website at https://www.identogo.com. The fee is $49.25. This fee reflects the combined cost of the background check fee and IDEMIA IdentoGO's additional charge for providing the service, also known as a rolling fee. Fingerprinting is not required of nonresidents. All fees may be combined into one check payable to Washington Insurance Commissioner.

5. *Rental Car Agents.* Only issued to business entities. Corporations or LLCs must submit a paper uniform application, copy of articles of incorporation or formation and letter of good standing from the Secretary of State. Firms, including partnerships and sole proprietorships, must file their trade names with the Department of Licensing and must submit Insurer Certificate for Rental Car Agent (RCA1, Rental Car Agent Authorized Endorsees, RCA2, Rental Car Agent Premium Handling Authority, RCA3) copies of the brochure or other written materials available where car rental insurance is sold, and copies of training and education program materials. License fee for two years: with forty-nine or fewer employees—$130; with fifty or more employees—$375. Appointment fee: $20 each underwriting insurer. Location fee: $35 each additional location. (Wash. Rev. Code Ann. § 48.17.170 and https://www.insurance.wa.gov/rental-car-agent-business-entity-resident).

6. *Self-Service Storage.* License fee for two years: with forty-nine or fewer employees—$130; with fifty or more employees—$375. One location: no additional fee. Two or more locations: $35 for each additional location. Complete the uniform application for business-entity insurance license and forms SSS1 and SSS2. The training program must meet the minimum standards established by Rev. Code Wash. § 48.170.070. A copy of the training program must be submitted to the office of the Commissioner.

C. **Appointments/Affiliations:** An insurance producer or title agent may not act as an agent of an insurer unless the insurance producer or title agent becomes an appointed agent of that insurer. An insurance producer who is not acting as an agent of that insurer is not required to become appointed. The appointment notice is electronically filed within fifteen days from the date the agency contract is executed or the first insurance application is submitted, whichever is earlier. Appointments and affiliations are continuous and expire only when the producer's license is revoked, terminated, nonrenewed, or when fees are not paid. Fee: $20—file all appointment and/or affiliation notices electronically. (Rev. Code Wash. §48.17.160). (All company appointments including new, renewal, and terminations must be submitted electronically.) A business entity may terminate an affiliation of an insurance producer or surplus lines broker through the Commissioner's website; the effective date of the termination is the date of receipt by the Commissioner. (Wash. Admin. Code 284-17-445).

D. **Licenses Required of Nonresidents:** Nonresidents may obtain producer licenses on a reciprocal basis. All applicants pay Washington fees. If the state of domicile does not participate in the Producer Data Base (PDB), a letter of certification is required from home state insurance department (ninety days), appointment of Commissioner for service of process. Applications must be submitted online at the Department's website, https://www.insurance.wa.gov, or through NIPR.

A license as an insurance producer is not required of a person who is not a resident of this state who sells, solicits, or negotiates a contract of insurance for commercial property and casualty risks to an insured with risks located in more than one state insured under that contract, provided that the person is otherwise licensed as an insurance producer to sell, solicit, or negotiate the insurance in the state where the insured maintains its principal place of business and the contract of insurance insures risks located in that state. (Rev. Code Wash. §48.17.062).

Nonresidents applicants are no longer required to submit a fingerprint card when applying for any Washington license.

E. **Prelicensing Examination and Education Requirements:**

1. *Residents.* Applicants for agent's license must satisfy the following requirements:

    a. Complete twenty hours for each major line of authority sought (life, disability, property, or casualty), including four hours on Washington's general statutes and regulations of approved instruction. Rules and laws specific to each line apply. Nonresidents moving into Washington are exempt if they were licensed in their home state within ninety days of the date of the home state license being cancelled. (Wash. Admin. Code 284-17-510).
    b. Certificate of completion is issued by the approved prelicensing education provider and must be presented by the exam candidate at the exam test center prior to sitting for the insurance exam.
    c. Must pass a qualifying examination administered by PSI Services. Visit PSI's web site (www.psiexams.com) or call them at 800-733-9267 to register for an exam. Pearson VUE, no longer provides testing for Washington. Call 800-274-8949, to retrieve a copy of your previous score reports from Pearson Vue if needed. The examinations required for each line of authority are identified on the Commissioner's website at www.insurance.wa.gov.
    d. Applicants who are not licensed within 180 days of passing the examination must retake the test.

e. Approved methods of instruction for prelicensing exams are lecture and home self-study.

f. Single-line exam fees are $45. Combination exams are $62. Fingerprinting is scheduled and fees are collected through IDEMIA (formerly MorphoTrust) at 1-888 771-5097 or visit their website at https://www.identogo.com. The fee is $49.25. This fee reflects the combined cost of the background check fee and IDEMIA IdentoGO's additional charge for providing the service, also known as a rolling fee. Fingerprinting is not required of nonresident licensees.
Persons who have completed the CEBS, ChFC, CIC, CFP, CLU, FLMI, LUTCF, RHU, REBC, HIA, AAF, ARM, and CPCU designation programs in the last twelve months are exempted from the prelicensing requirements for the respective lines of business. (Wash. Admin. Code 284-17-515).

2. *Nonresidents.* Examination is reciprocal with nonresident home state.

F. Continuing Education Requirements (Residents Only):

Number of Hours Required: Twenty-four hours, with three of those hours required to be ethics, biennially. Licensee may use classroom instruction or self-study. CE instructors no longer get double credit for courses taught. (Wash. Admin. Code 284-17-224).

Resident and nonresident licensees who sell long-term care insurance, long term care partnership insurance or both, are required to take an approved eight hour course on long-term care, long-term partnership, or both initially and a four hour refresher course every two years. The Commissioner will prescribe the content of the course. Course materials must be submitted electronically or via electronic media to the Commissioner and approved prior to use. The insurer, not the licensee must certify to the Commissioner, that its appointees complied with this requirement. The approved eight-hour course may also count towards the required continuing education credit hours, if it is approved for that purpose.

Resident and nonresident licensees who sell annuities after March 29, 2012, must complete a one-time four-hour annuity suitability course. (Wash. Admin. Code 284-17-265).

Submit proof of completion by: Biennial renewal.

Excess Hours: May not be carried into the next reporting period. (Wash. Admin. Code 284-17-252).

Final Exam: The final exam for a self-study course does not need to be monitored.

Requirements **Not** *Applicable to the Following:*

1. Licensees who are called to active military service may request a continuing education waiver from the DOI.

2. A medical waiver may be requested from the DOI by licensees who have a medical condition. The request must be accompanied by a statement from the treating provider describing the illness or injury. (Wash. Admin. Code 284-17-254).

3. Individuals holding travel, surety, and credit licenses.

4. Adjusters. (Wash. Admin. Code 284-17-222).

Renewal Procedure:

1. Course provider sends certificate of completion to licensee and reports the licensee's completed continuing education credits to the Office of the Insurance Commissioner.

2. Licensee submits renewal application and verifies that all courses completed are included in the online renewal; licensee may input completion certificate information for any courses which have not been automatically loaded into the licensees' renewal application. For courses manually input by the licensee, copies of the course completion certificates must be sent to the Office of the Insurance Commissioner for verification prior to the renewal being processed.

3. Licensee keeps original certificates.

   Renewal must be completed online through the office of the insurance Commissioner's website at http://www.insurance.wa.gov/ or National Insurance Producer Registry (NIPR) at http://www.nipr.com. (Wash. Admin. Code 284-17-443).

Nonresidents are exempt from this requirement.

G. Cancellation of Agency Contracts/Producer Appointments: No insurer may terminate for reasons that are arbitrary or discriminatory. If the contract is terminated for one of the reasons specified in Rev. Code Wash. §§48.17.530 and 48.17.595, it must be reported to the commissioner within thirty days. The terminated party must be given the reasons in writing upon request. For any other reason, the insurer must give written notice of intent to cancel within 120 days. During this

120-day period, the insurer may not amend its contract with the agent, nor may the agent bind any new business on behalf of the terminating company. Insurer must then accept renewals up to one year following the date of the notice and conduct this business with the agent as if the agent continued on contract. After the one year renewal period—if the insurer does not have a valid reason for nonrenewing a policy and if the policyholder wishes to remain with the same company—the insurer is to assign the policy to the nearest agent willing to accept the assignment. The regulation does not apply to life, disability, surety, ocean marine, foreign trade, or title insurance. It also does not apply to policies of an insurer if the business is not owned by the agent, to general agents, to the extent they are acting as general agents, nor to termination resulting from the insolvency of the insurer. The effective date of termination is the date of receipt by the commissioner. (Rev. Code Wash. §48.17.591).

H. **Rules for Risk Retention and Purchasing Groups:** Anyone acting or offering to act as an agent or broker for a risk retention or purchasing group covering risks in Washington is subject to state laws pertaining to licensing before commencing such activities. A risk retention group may be chartered in Washington as a liability insurance company under Revised Code of Washington Chapters 48.05, 48.06, and 48.92. A risk retention group chartered in another state may apply to the commissioner for registration in the state. Risk retention groups may not join in the guaranty solvency fund, but they must participate in joint underwriting associations and mandatory pools or plans of the commissioners. Purchasing groups must also register with the commissioner and submit reports as required by Revised Code of Washington §48.92.080. All groups and all resident and nonresident agents or brokers participating in them must comply with all state of Washington laws to the extent that they do not conflict with the Federal Liability Risk Retention Act of 1986, including licensing and solicitation requirements or restrictions. All risk retention group policies must show the following notice in at least ten-point type on the front page and on the declarations page of the policy:

NOTICE

"This policy is issued by your risk retention group. Your risk retention group may not be subject to all of the insurance laws and regulations of your state. State insurance insolvency guaranty funds are not available for your risk retention group." (Rev. Code Wash. §48.92.040(7)).

I. **Other License Rules, Requirements, or Restrictions:** Unlicensed nonresidents may not enter Washington to solicit, inspect, or service. Entering the state includes mail, telephone, or other electronic communication into the state from the outside, as well as physical presence in the state. (Rev. Code Wash. §48.92.120).

J. **Policy Countersignature Requirements:** No insurance contract which is otherwise valid shall be rendered invalid by reason of the apparent execution of the insurer by the signature of an individual not authorized to execute as of the date of the policy if the policy is countersigned by an individual who is authorized.

A policy written to a risk retention group shall not be required to be countersigned. (Rev. Code Wash. § 48.18.210 and 48.92.060).

II. Commissions, Fees, Commingling of Funds, Suitability in Annuity Transactions

A. **Commissions:** There are no restrictions on distribution of commissions as to licensed nonresidents. It is no longer required that producers must be licensed in the same lines of insurance in order to share commissions. Additionally, commissions can be shared with unlicensed persons as long as the payment is a result of a referral leading to an insurance sale, AND the referring person is not an insured client of the producer and the referring person did not sell, solicit, or negotiate the transaction. Per Rev. Code Wash. §§ 48.30.133 (4) and 48.17.490. Rebating of commissions is not allowed. (Rev. Code Wash. § 48.17.490).

B. **Fees:** Producers may charge fees in accordance with Rev. Code Wash. §48.17.270 (see below).

C. **Disclosure Requirements:** An insurance agent producer may receive a commission paid by the insurer, a fee paid by the insured; or a combination of commission paid by the insurer and a fee paid by the insured from which a producer may offset or reimburse the insured for all or part of the fee. If the compensation received by a producer who deals directly with the insured includes a fee, the insurance producer must disclose in writing to the insured:

1. The full amount of the fee paid by the insured.

2. The full amount of any commission paid to the insurance producer by the insurer, if one is received.

3. An explanation of any offset or reimbursement of fees or commissions.

4. The name of the insurer that may pay commission to the producer.

5. When the insurance producer may receive additional compensation, notice that states the producer:

a. May receive additional commission in the form of future incentive compensation from the insurer, including contingent commissions and other awards and bonuses based on factors that typically include the total sales volume, growth, profitability, and retention of business placed by the insurance producer with the insurer, and incentive compensation is only paid if the performance criteria established in the agency-insurer agreement is met by the insurance producer or the business entity with which the insurance producer is affiliated.
b. Will furnish to the insured or prospective insured specific information relating to additional commission upon request.
The written disclosure of compensation must be provided prior to the sale of the policy, signed by the insurer and insured, and retained by the producer for five years. (Rev. Code Wash. §48.17.270).

D. **Commingling of Funds:** All producers must keep insurer premiums separate from other funds except they may include funds for advance payments and those needed to cover the cost of handling the transactions. Title insurance agents and brokers whose average daily balance of premiums for Washington business is at least $1 million are exempt. (Rev. Code Wash. §48.17.600).

E. **Suitability in Annuity Transactions:** In recommending the purchase of an annuity or the exchange of an annuity that results in another insurance transaction or series of insurance transactions to a consumer, the insurance producer, or the insurer when no producer is involved, must have reasonable grounds for believing that the recommendation is suitable for the consumer on the basis of the facts disclosed by the consumer about their financial status and tax status, investment objectives, and other information considered to be reasonable when making a recommendation to the consumer. An insurer must assure that a system to supervise recommendations, reasonably designed to achieve compliance with this section, is established and maintained. The system must include, but is not limited to, written procedures and conducting periodic review of its records that are reasonably designed to assist in detecting and preventing violations of this section. (Wash. Rev. Code Ann. §48.23.015).

III. **Statutory References:** Revised Code of Washington §§48.14.010; 48.17.010; 48.17.060 through 48.17.067; 48.17.090; 48.17.110; 48.17.160 through 48.17.180; 48.17.250; 48.17.270; 48.17.380 through 48.17.390; 48.17.430; 48.17.480 through 48.17.490; 48.17.600; 48.92.040 through 48.92.080; 48.94.010; Washington Administrative Code 284-17-015; 284-17-224 through 284-17-226; 248-17-244 through 284-17-246; 248-17-250 through 284-17-252; 284-17-443.

WEST VIRGINIA

Insurance Commissioner
P.O. Box 50540
900 Pennsylvania Ave
Charleston, WV 25302
Telephone: 304-558-0610;
Fax: 304-558-4965;
Email: OICAgentLicensing@wv.gov;
http://www.wvinsurance.gov

I. Licensing Requirements: Sales Personnel—Producers, Limited Licensees, Managing General Agents. Other Insurance Professionals—Adjusters, Reinsurance Intermediaries.

A. Applicability: Licensing laws apply to all insurers except:

1. Hospital service corporations and medical service corporations.

2. Fraternal benefit societies.

3. Farmers' mutual fire insurance companies.

4. Warranties.

5. Service contracts.

6. Maintenance agreements. (W. Va. Code §33-4-2).

B. Licenses Required of Residents: Each of the following must be licensed in West Virginia:

Sales Personnel

1. *Producers* (representing either insurer or insured).

   a. License fee: $50 submitted with Uniform Application. Renewal fee: $50.
   b. License term: Biennial; expires on the last day of the producer's birth month.
   c. Lines of Authority:

      (1) Life.
      (2) Accident and health or sickness.
      (3) Property

(4) Casualty.
(5) Variable products (requires NASD registration).
(6) Personal lines.
(7) Credit – limited line credit insurance.
(8) Any other line of insurance permitted under West Virginia's state laws or regulations. (W. Va. Code § 33-12-9)

2. *Limited Licensees.*

a. License and renewal fee: $50.
b. License term: Biennial; expires on the last day of the licensee's birth month.
c. Limited Lines of Authority:

(1) Car rental.
(2) Limited lines credit.
(3) Title.
(4) Travel.

3. *Managing General Agents.* Must submit agency producer license form (MGA-1) or individual producer license form (MGA-2) along with $500 nonrefundable application fee. Renews annually; renewal fee is $200. Renewals are due between May 1 and June 1. Copy of bond or E&O policy requirements must also be submitted. The following must also be submitted: evidence of each insurer's bond and E&O coverages; a list of names and addresses of all insurers doing business in the state with which the producer has a contract to act or for whom the producer acts as an MGA; a copy of the written contract in force with each insurer doing business in the state with which the producer has a contract to act or for whom the producer acts as an MGA; and a completed MGA Contract Review Form for each contract submitted. (W. Va. Code, §33-37-2).

4. *Business Entities.* Submit the Uniform Business Entity application. The licensing fee is $200. Renewal is annually between March 1 and June 1. (http://www.wvinsurance.gov/Portals/0/pdf/webforms-licensing/Apply%20for%20a%20BE%20license.pdf?ver=2017-08-18-112808-117). The application and instructions may be found on the DOI Web site or apply electronically at www.nipr.com.

Other Insurance Professionals

1. *Adjusters.* Adjuster's license expires May 31; annual fee $25. They may be licensed as any one, or combination of a company adjuster (which includes independent adjusters), a public adjuster, or crop adjuster, but cannot serve in multiple

capacities on the same claim. (W. Va. Code §33-12B-3 and -8). There is no charge for emergency licenses for adjusters. (W. Va. Code §33-12B-4).

2. *Field/Marketing Representatives.* Marketing representatives for health maintenance organizations must be licensed as accident and health producers.

3. *Reinsurance Intermediaries.* Managers may be required to carry a bond or E&O policy. (W. Va. Code §33-38-3).

   Residents are not licensed as brokers. Application forms for all licenses are obtained from the insurance commissioner. Applications may also be downloaded from the department's Web site, http://www.wvinsurance.gov.

   a. Producer application, for all lines, is NAIC Uniform Individual application.
   b. Producer application for only credit insurance (life and sickness and health) is NAIC Uniform Application.
   c. Producer appointments are to be submitted electronically through NIPR or on form WVAT. Fee: $25 per company represented.
   d. Adjusters' application form has no form number.

4. *Third Party Administrators.* A $200 fee is due annually on the first day of July. License remains valid, unless surrendered, suspended or revoked by the commissioner, for as long as the administrator continues in business in West Virginia and remains in compliance. (W. Va. Code, §33-46-15).

5. *Viatical Settlement Providers.* Initial application fee: $600. $300 annual renewal fee due on or before May 31. Must provide evidence of a minimum equity of not less than $250,000 or through a surety bond in the amount of $250,000. Must complete a Viatical Settlement Provider Licensing Application (VSP-2). (W. Va. Code §33-13C-3).

6. *Viatical Settlement Brokers.* Fifty dollar initial fee for individuals and $200 initial fee for entities. Licenses are renewed biannually on the last day of the broker's birth month. Business entities will continue to renew the Viatical Settlement Broker license annually by June 30. Must provide evidence of a minimum equity of not less than $250,000 or through a surety bond in the amount of $250,000. Must complete a Viatical Settlement Broker Application (VSB-1, individuals; and VSB-BE, entities). (W. Va. Code §33-13C-3).

C. **Appointments:** An individual insurance producer may not act as an agent of an insurer unless the individual insurance producer becomes an appointed agent of that insurer. An individual insurance producer who is not acting as an agent of an insurer is not required to become appointed. To appoint an individual insurance producer as its agent, the appointing insurer shall file, in a format approved by the insurance commissioner, a notice of appointment within fifteen days from the date the agency contract is executed or the first insurance application is submitted. An insurer may also elect to appoint an individual insurance producer to all or some insurers within the insurer's holding company system or group by the filing of a single appointment request. (W. Va. Code, §33-12-18).

D. **Licenses Required of Nonresidents:** Nonresidents must be licensed as producers and adjusters to conduct insurance activities in West Virginia.

Producers must be appointed to each insurance company for whom the nonresident intends to solicit business in West Virginia. License fee: $50. License term: Biennial; expires on the last day of the producer's birth month—insurance companies are responsible for renewing appointments and paying $25 per producer renewal fee. Nonresidents can no longer obtain a broker's license in the state.

The following application forms are used for nonresidents:

a. Producer application for all lines for new producers or to add company appointments to an existing license, NAIC Uniform Application.

b. Producer application for credit insurance (life and accident and health or sickness), NAIC Uniform Application only (not available electronically).

c. Adjuster's application form has no form number.

Applications may also be downloaded from the Department's Web site, http://www.wvinsurance.gov or submitted electronically through NIPR.

Multi-State Exposures: A license is not required for a nonresident insurance producer who sells, solicits, or negotiates a contract of insurance for commercial property and casualty coverage when risks that are to be insured under that contract are located in more than one state. This exception applies only if the nonresident is licensed to sell, solicit, or negotiate that insurance in the state where the insured maintains its principal place of business and the contract of insurance insures risks located in that state. (W. Va. Code, §33-12-4).

E. Prelicensing Examination and Education Requirements:

1. *Residents.* Applicants for the following licenses must pass a qualifying examination administered by Pearson VUE, 800-274-2614: life; accident and sickness; property and casualty; adjusters; personal lines; and surplus lines brokers. Exam fee: $88. Newly licensed producers or producers adding a new power to their license are required to pass twenty hours of approved education for life or accident and sickness only, forty hours for life and accident and sickness or property and casualty, prior to taking the license examination. Prelicensing education is not required for adjusters. Applicants for variable annuity license must pass NASD series 6 or 7. Waiver of examination: An examination is not required as proof of competency for those persons applying to this office for a resident individual insurance producer's license if such person holds one or more of the following professional designations or degrees.

   a. Certified Employee Benefits Specialist (CEBS), Chartered Financial Consultant (ChFC), Certified Insurance Counselor (CIC), Certified Financial Planner (CFP), Chartered Life Underwriter (CLU), Fellow Life Management Institute (FLMI), Life Underwriting Training Counsel Fellow (LUTCF) for Life Line of Authority.
   b. Registered Health Underwriter (RHU), Certified Employee Benefits Specialist (CEBS), Registered Employee Benefits Consultant (REBC), Health Information Administration (HIA) for Health Line of Authority.
   c. Accredited Advisor in Insurance (AAI), Associate in Risk Management (ARM), Certified Insurance Counselor (CIC), Chartered Property Casualty Underwriter (CPCU) for Property and Casualty Lines of Authority.
   d. College insurance degree for all lines of authority. (W. Va. CSR §114-2-2).

2. *Nonresidents.* West Virginia is reciprocal with nonresident's home state as to examination requirements. Nonresident adjusters who are not licensed as adjusters in their home state must take the West Virginia adjuster exam prior to applying for a license. (W. Va. CSR §114-2-2).

F. Continuing Education Requirements:

Number of Hours Required: Twenty-four hours, biennially, for producers including three hours of approved ethics courses. Producers selling long-term care insurance must complete a one-time training course prior to July 1, 2010. The training must be at least eight hours. Beginning July 1, 2010, producers who sell long-term care insurance must complete four hours of CE in long-term care insurance for each twenty-four month period. A producer's annual active membership in an organization or association approved by the commissioner as a state, regional, or national insurance organization or association may be approved for up to two hours of continuing education credits, provided only two hours are awarded for such membership per biennial reporting period. This credit applies only to producers who are required to take more than six hours of CE biennially. The CE requirement applies to those licensed to sell the following types of insurance:

1. Life insurance, annuity contracts, variable annuity contracts, and variable life insurance.

2. Accident and health or sickness insurance.

3. All lines of property and casualty insurance.

4. All other lines of insurance that require an exam for licensing.

5. Preneed burial insurance contract.

6. Individual insurance producers appointed on behalf of a licensed health maintenance organization.

7. Individual insurance producers engaged in telemarketing insurance products. (W. Va. CSR §114-42-3).

Individuals licensed as a viatical settlement broker who are not also licensed as a life insurance producer are required to complete on a biennial basis fifteen hours of training related to viatical settlements and viatical settlement transactions. Of the fifteen hours required, twelve hours must be in viatical settlements and three hours must be in ethics. If a viatical settlement broker is also licensed as a producer, the three hour ethics course can be used towards both licenses. (W. Va. Code, §33-13C-3).

The DOI does not prescribe course content. The licensee may use approved classroom instruction or self-study. Course instructors earn the same number of credit hours as the students. The following licensees need six hours of CE biennially:

1. Producers who sell only preneed burial insurance contracts.

2. Producers who telemarket insurance products by a scripted presentation that has been filed with and approved by the commissioner.

The West Virginia Department of Insurance has converted to the NAIC's State Based System (SBS), a Web based licensing system offering faster issuance of licenses and renewals. Effective September 20, 2011, the original West Virginia license number will no longer be used and the NPN number will be used for all identification purposes.

Effective September 20, 2011, all provider, course, agent transcripts, and roster information will be migrated to a Web based system and will be available through Sircon's online services.

Submit Proof of Completion by: June 30 of biennial reporting year.

Excess Hours: For those producers who must complete more than six hours of continuing education, a maximum carryover of six hours may be allowed. (W.Va. CSR §114-42-6).

Final Exam: The final exam for a self-study course must be monitored by someone with no business or family relationship to the licensee.

*Requirements **Not** Applicable to the Following:*

1. Adjusters.

2. Limited licenses for which no exam was required.

3. Licensees who sell only credit life/accident and sickness or other insurance associated with credit transactions.

4. New licensees in the second half of a biennium.

5. Any limited or restricted licenses, as the commissioner deems appropriate.

6. Nonresident insurance producers.

7. Individual insurance producers who have voluntarily cancelled their licenses. (W. Va. CSR §114-42-4).

Compliance Procedure:

1. Course provider sends notification of course completers to Thomson Prometric.

2. Course provider sends completion certificate to the licensee who keeps certificates in his or her records.

Nonresidents are exempt from this requirement.

G. **Cancellation of Agency Contracts/Producer Appointments:** An insurer that terminates the appointment, employment, contract or other insurance business relationship with a producer shall notify the insurance commissioner within thirty days following the effective date of the termination. Additional information, documents, records, or other data pertaining to the termination must be provided upon written request of the insurance commissioner.

At the time of making the notification, the insurer shall simultaneously mail a copy of the notification to the producer. If the producer is terminated for cause for any of the reasons listed in section 24 of the West Virginia Code, the insurer shall provide a copy of the notification to the producer by certified mail, return receipt requested, postage prepaid or by overnight delivery using a nationally recognized carrier. (W. Va. Code §§ 33-12-25).

H. **Rules for Risk Retention and Purchasing Groups:** Regulates risk retention and purchasing groups operating or offering coverage on risks in West Virginia. As required under W. Va. Code §§33-32-1 through 33-32-24, risk retention groups domiciled in West Virginia must be chartered and licensed as liability insurers, while groups not domiciled in West Virginia must register with the insurance commissioner and submit reports to the commissioner as described in the law. Purchasing groups must also register with the commissioner and submit reports as required by the law. All groups and all resident and nonresident producers participating in them must comply with all West Virginia insurance laws, including licensing and solicitation requirements or restrictions. All risk retention group policies must show the following notice in at least ten point type on the front page and on the declarations page of the policy:

NOTICE

"This policy is issued by your risk retention group. Your risk retention group may not be subject to all of the insurance laws and rules of your state. State insurance insolvency guaranty funds are not available for your risk retention group." (W. Va. Code §33-32-9).

Purchasing groups which obtain liability insurance from an insurer not admitted in West Virginia or a risk retention group must give the following notice to each member on each group certificate or evidence of insurance:

"This Insurer is not licensed to do business in West Virginia, and is not subject to the West Virginia Insurance Guaranty Act or to all of the protections of the insurance laws and rules of this state." (W. Va. Code §33-32-18).

I. Policy Countersignature Requirements:

A countersignature endorsement is necessary if there is an interstate risk. Must be signed by a licensed resident agent of the insurer. This section does not apply to:

1. Reinsurance.
2. Credit insurance.
3. Any contract of insurance covering the rolling stock of any railroad or covering any vessel, aircraft, or motor carrier used in interstate or foreign commerce or covering any liability or other risks incident to the ownership, maintenance, or operation thereof;
4. Any contract of insurance covering any property or interstate or foreign commerce, or any liability or risks incident thereto.
   The entire commission payable by an insured licensed to transact insurance in this state on any insurance policy shall be paid directly to the licensed individual insurance producer who countersigns the policy. (W. Va. Code §33-12-11 and 33-12-23).

II. Commissions, Fees, Commingling of Funds, Suitability in Annuity Transactions

A. Commissions: Under no circumstances may an unlicensed or unappointed resident or nonresident receive commission on any insurance policy. Rebating of commissions is not allowed. (W. Va. Code § 33-11-4).

B. Fees: Fees may not be charged in addition to or instead of commission on any transaction involving or relating to the sale of insurance.

C. Disclosure Requirements: According to the Insurance Sales Consumer Protection Act: "A financial institution soliciting the purchase of or selling insurance, and any person soliciting the purchase of or selling insurance on the premises of, in connection with a product offering of, or using a name identifiable with, a financial institution, shall prominently disclose to customers, in writing, in clear and concise language, including in any advertisement or promotional material, and orally during any customer contact, that insurance offered, recommended, sponsored, or sold: (1) Is not a deposit; (2) Is not insured by the federal deposit insurance corporation or, where applicable, the National Credit Union Share Insurance Fund; (3) Is not guaranteed by any insured depository institution; and (4) Where appropriate, involves investment risk, including potential loss of principal." (W. Va. Code §33-11A-9).

D. **Commingling of Funds:** West Virginia does not prohibit producers from commingling insurer's premiums with other agency funds.

E. **Suitability in Annuity Transactions:** In recommending to a consumer the purchase of an annuity or the exchange of an annuity that results in another insurance transaction or series of insurance transactions, the insurance producer, or the insurer where no producer is involved, must have reasonable grounds for believing that the recommendation is suitable for the consumer on the basis of the facts disclosed by the consumer as to his or her investments and other insurance products and his or her financial situation and needs, including the consumer's suitability information, and that there is a reasonable basis to believe:

1. That the consumer has been reasonably informed of various features of the annuity, such as the potential surrender period and surrender charge, potential tax penalty if the consumer sells, exchanges, surrenders or annuitizes the annuity, mortality and expense fees, investment advisory fees, potential charges for and features of riders, limitations on interest returns, insurance and investment components and market risk.

2. The consumer would benefit from certain features of the annuity.

3. The particular annuity as a whole is suitable for the particular consumer. (WV CSR § 114-11B-5).

III. **Statutory References:** W. Va. Code §§33-12-1 through 33-12-37; 33-12B-1 through 33-12B-14; 33-32-1 through 33-32-24; W. Va. CSR §§114-42-1 through 114-42-8.

WISCONSIN

Office of the Commissioner of Insurance
P.O. Box 7872; Madison, WI 53707-7872;
125 South Webster St. Madison, WI 53703
Telephone: (General) 608-266-3585, (Licensing) 608-266-8699;
Fax: 608-267-9451
Email: ociagentlicensing@wisconsin.gov
http://oci.wi.gov

I. Licensing Requirements: Resident and nonresident intermediary (Sales Personnel, Agents, Brokers, Producers Limited Line Agents), Managing General Agents—Employee Benefit Plan Administrators (Individuals), Reinsurance Intermediaries, Life Settlement Brokers.

For exemption of licensing individuals as intermediaries, refer to Wis. Adm. Code Ins 6.595 (2),

A. Applicability: Licensing laws apply to all insurers and to all types of insurance including surplus lines resident and nonresident agents.

B. Licenses Required: Anyone negotiating, soliciting, or selling insurance in Wisconsin must be licensed.

Agents (Intermediaries)

1. *Agents.*

   a. License fee: $75 per line of authority plus Application fee: $10 (residents only).
   b. License term: Individual intermediary license renewed biennially. License expires at the end of the agent's birth month in odd or even year depending on original issue. Renewal fee: $35 resident and $70 nonresident agent. (Wis. Stat. § 601.31).
   c. Major lines of authority:

      (1) Life.
      (2) Accident and health.
      (3) Property.
      (4) Casualty.
      (5) Personal lines P&C.
      (6) Variable Life/Variable Annuity. (Wis. Adm. Code Ins 6.50).

In order to sell auto or homeowners insurance, the agent must obtain authority in both property and casualty.

All resident license candidates are required to complete a digital fingerprint, which costs $39.25. Reservations can be made online on Fieldprint at http://www.fieldprintwisconsin.com. At the time of reservation must enter the Fieldprint code: FPWIOCIInsurance. Fingerprint information is valid for 180 days.

2. *Limited Lines Agents.*

    a. License fee: $75 per line of authority plus Application fee: $10 (residents only).
    b. License term: Individual intermediary renewed biennially. License expires at the end of the agent's birth month in odd or even year depending on original issue. Renewal fee: $35 resident or $70 nonresident agents.
    c. Limited Lines of authority:

        (1) Credit.
        (2) Title.
        (3) Legal expense.
        (4) Surety.
        (5) Crop.
        (6) Travel. (Wis. Adm. Code Ins 6.50).

3. *Business Entities (Firms).*

    Corporate licensing is available but is not required. However, all individuals in the firm selling insurance must be licensed and appointed. Wisconsin provides insurance intermediary firm license to resident and nonresident entities. Firms can apply online at NIPR at www.nipr.com or at an NIPR authorized business partner. The license fee is $100. The renewal fees are $35 for resident firms and $75 for nonresident firms. The entity does not have the authority to act as an agent.

4. *Managing General Agents.* MGAs and MGA firms are required to hold a license. Current law defines a managing general agent as a person who manages all or part of the insurance business of an insurer or manages a separate division, department, or underwriting office; acts as an agent for the insurer; and with or without the authority, either separately or together with affiliates, directly or indirectly:

    a. Produces and underwrites in any one quarter or year an amount of gross direct written premium equal to or more than 5 percent of the policyholder surplus as reported in the last annual statement of the insurer.

b. Adjusts or pays claims in any one quarter or year in excess of 3 percent of the policy holder surplus as reported in the last annual statement of the insurer, or negotiates reinsurance on behalf of the insurer, or both. (Wis. Adm. Code Ins 42.01).

Residents or nonresidents can apply via NIPR at www.nipr.com or through an authorized business partner. For agents: $75 initial license fee. $35 resident biennial renewal fee. $70 nonresident biennial renewal fee. For firms: $100 initial license fee. $35 resident biennial renewal fee. $70 nonresident biennial renewal fee. There is no exam requirement for resident agents. MGA individual must hold license before applying for MGA firm license.

Other Insurance Professionals

1. *Employee Benefit Plan Administrators (Individuals & Firms).* Licensing laws apply to administrators who administer insured or wholly or partially self-insured employee benefit plans to one or more employees who are residents of Wisconsin. Anyone directly or indirectly soliciting, collecting premiums or charges, otherwise effecting coverage, or adjusting and settling claims for a plan must be licensed as an employee benefit plan administrator. Applications can apply online on NIPR at www.nipr.com or through an authorized business partner of NIPR. There is $100 application fee. The applicant must also submit financial statements and a signed and sealed original performance bond. This license is renewed annually. An annual regulation fee of $100 is due August 1st. Individuals or firms performing these responsibilities may contact OCI Licensing Section at ociagentlicensing@wisconsin.gov.

2. *Reinsurance Intermediaries.* Reinsurance intermediary-brokers, reinsurance intermediary-managers, and reinsurance intermediary firms are required to hold a license. Individuals are not required to be licensed if they are included under the license of a reinsurance intermediary firm. Reinsurance intermediaries are required to obtain authorization or enter into a contract with insurers that must meet certain standards. (Wis. Stat. §628.04).

   Resident reinsurance individual intermediary can apply online at NIPR at www.nipr.com or at an authorized business partner. There is a $75 application fee, a $35 annual renewal fee for brokers and a $35 biennial renewal fee for managers. There is no exam requirement for resident agents.

   Resident reinsurance intermediary firms can apply online via NIPR at www.nipr.com. There is a $100 application fee, a $35 resident biennial renewal fee and a $70 nonresident biennial renewal fee.

3. *Variable Contracts.* Resident agents must hold valid a life license, and provide proof of FINRA registration for series 6 or 7.

4. *Life Settlement Brokers.* Individuals negotiating settlements between a life insurance policyholder and a life settlement provider must be licensed as a life settlement broker. Resident and nonresident life settlement brokers can apply online at www.nipr.com or an authorized business partner and pay a $750 application fee and a $250 regulation fee annually by July 1. Applicant must submit an original endorsement from a licensed insurer identifying professional liability insurance held in an amount not less than $1 million, submit a list of approved life settlement providers they will be representing and complete required training. (Wis. Stat. § 601.31).

5. *Agent Appointments.* The appointment fees are made available to the company annually. Appointments and terminations must be provided electronically by the insurer.

C. Appointments: An insurer shall report to the commissioner all appointments, including renewals of appointments, and all terminations of appointments of insurance agents in Wisconsin, and shall pay the $16 annual fee for each resident agent and $30 annual for each nonresident agent. (Wis. Stat.§628.11).

"Effective January 2016, the Wisconsin Office of the Commissioner of Insurance (OCI) will process all company appointments electronically through the National Insurance Producer Registry (NIPR). The appointment renewal invoice will include all initial appointments submitted by the companies on or before November 23, 2015, as well as all resident/nonresident appointment renewals...... Companies who had previously qualified for OCI exemption from the electronic appointment process will need to set up an account directly with NIPR or one of their Authorized Business Partners to submit their appointment transactions. All appointments will need to be submitted electronically as OCI stopped accepting appointment and termination paper forms on November 23, 2015." In addition, paper checks will no longer be accepted. (December 16, 2015 Bulletin available at http://oci.wi.gov/bulletin/1215annbilling.htm).

D. Prelicensing Examination and Education Requirements:

1. *Residents.* All candidates applying for a major line resident license must have completed eight hours of ethics and law education, plus twelve hours of product knowledge for each major line, at a school approved by the commissioner. Applicants for an intermediary-agent's license must pass a qualifying examination for each line of insurance to be sold. The exam fees are $75 per line of authority.

Late arrivers are not allowed to sit for the test. Those who do not cancel their appointment two days before the scheduled exam date will forfeit their exam fee (https://home.psiexams.com/api/tests/YTLQVU5M/bulletins). Exams are administered by PSI Exams. Exams can be scheduled online at https://home.psiexams.com/#/home.

Candidates applying for the following limited lines are exempt from the education requirement: title, credit, and legal expense. Candidates who have completed a two-year Wisconsin vocational school degree in insurance or a four-year college degree in business with an insurance emphasis and those holding the specific designations identified in the law are also exempt.

a. An applicant applying for an original resident license for the life line of authority who provides satisfactory evidence of currently holding any of the following professional designations or successor designations: Certified Employee Benefit Specialist (CEBS), Chartered Financial Consultant (ChFC), Certified Insurance Counselor (CIC), Certified Financial Planner (CFP), Chartered Life Underwriter (CLU), Fellow of the Life Management Institute (FLMI), or Life Underwriter Training Council Fellow (LUTCF).
b. An applicant applying for an original resident license for the accident & health line of authority who provides satisfactory evidence of currently holding any of the following professional designations or successor designations: Registered Health Underwriter (RHU), Certified Employee Benefit Specialist (CEBS), Registered Employee Benefits Counselor (REBC), or Health Insurance Associate (HIA).
c. An applicant applying for an original resident license for the property, casualty, or personal lines P&C lines of authority who provides satisfactory evidence of currently holding any of the following professional designations or successor designations: Accredited Advisor in Insurance (AAI), Associate in Risk Management (ARM), Certified Insurance Counselor (CIC), or Chartered Property and Casualty Underwriter (CPCU). (Wis. Adm. Code Ins 26.04).

2. *Nonresidents* are exempt from these requirements.

E. Continuing Education Requirements:

Agents are encouraged to complete CE courses online to avoid delays in renewing their insurance licenses. The following link contains information regarding online CE options: sbs.naic.org/solar-external-lookup.

Number of Hours Required: Licensees in the five major lines (property, casualty, life, accident and health, or personal lines) and the limited line of auto must complete twenty-four hours each biennium, three of which must be in ethics in insurance. The licensee must complete certified courses offered by approved education providers. Course instructors receive the same number of credit hours as the students. (Wis. Adm. Code Ins 28.04).

Proof of Completion is electronically banked by the provider and sent through State Based Systems (SBS) within ten days of completion. Agents are advised to maintain course completion certificates in the event that a discrepancy occurs.

Excess Hours may not be carried into the next renewal period.

Final Exam: Self-study and internet based courses must include an exam.

Requirements **Not** *Applicable to the Following:*

Resident limited line credit, legal expense, and title insurance agents. A nonresident intermediary whose state of residence grants similar exemptions to Wisconsin residents. (Wis. Adm. Code Ins 28.04).

Renewal Procedure:

1. The provider reports all student course completions to the DOI through SBS.

2. Agent must pay the renewal fee online on NIPR at www.nipr.com or an authorized NIPR business partner before the deadline.

3. Those in compliance can print a copy of their license at oci.wi.gov.

Nonresidents are exempt from the CE requirement but must pay the renewal fee.

F. **Cancellation of Producer Appointments:** Insurers must report agent appointments and invoices are made available annually for such appointments. (Wis. Stat. §628.11).

G. **Rules for Risk Retention and Purchasing Groups:** Wisconsin's risk retention and purchasing groups are subject to the state's surplus lines statutes and rules. Effective July 1, 2015, surplus lines agents, direct placement policyholders, and risk retention groups should no longer report multistate surplus lines policies to the Surplus Lines Clearinghouse, but should continue reporting policies to OCI. Bulletin 6-25-2015 at https://oci.wi.gov/Pages/Regulation/Bulletin20150625SurplusLines.aspx.

H. Policy Countersignature Requirements: None.

II. Commissions, Fees, Commingling of Funds, Suitability in Annuity Transactions:

A. Commissions: There are no restrictions on distribution of commissions among licensed resident or nonresident intermediary-agents. An unlicensed resident or nonresident may not receive commission. Rebating of commissions is not allowed. (Wis. Stat. §628.61).

B. Fees: An intermediary may not accept compensation due to an insured's purchase of insurance from the intermediary-agent and another source unless the intermediary, before the insured incurs an obligation to pay compensation, clearly and conspicuously and in writing discloses to the insured that the intermediary will also receive compensation from the other source. Intermediaries may charge a consulting fee on new business if there is a prior written agreement with the insured. The payment of the consulting fee cannot be waived if the insured purchases insurance from the agent because that could be considered a rebate. A separate service fee may not be charged on renewal business because that would have to be included in the premium filed by the company. (Wis. Stat. §628.32).

C. Disclosure Requirements: An agent may not accept compensation from an insured or from both an insured and another source due to the insured's purchase of insurance or for advice regarding the insured's insurance needs or coverage unless the agent, before the insured incurs an obligation to pay compensation, clearly and conspicuously and in writing discloses to the insured all of the following:

1. The amount of compensation to be paid by the insured, excluding commissions paid by the insurer to the intermediary.

2. If compensation will be paid by another source, the fact that the intermediary will also receive compensation from the other source. (Wis. Stat. §628.32).

D. Commingling of Funds: Wisconsin does not prohibit agents' commingling of insurer's premiums with other agency funds.

E. Suitability in Annuity Transactions:

An insurance intermediary may not solicit the sale of an annuity product unless the insurance intermediary has adequate knowledge of the product to recommend the annuity and the insurance intermediary is in compliance with the insurer's standards for product training. An insurance intermediary may rely on insurer-provided product-specific training standards and materials to comply with this paragraph.

An insurance intermediary who engages in the sale of annuity products shall complete a one-time four hour training course approved by the commissioner and provided by an education provider approved by the commissioner. (Wis. Stat. §628.347).

III. Statutory References: Wisconsin Statutes §§601.31 628.03 through 628.12, 628.32, 628.347; Wis. Admin. Code Ins 6.595(2), 6.50, 26.04, 28.04, 42.01.

WYOMING

Wyoming Insurance Department
106 East 6th Avenue; Cheyenne, WY 82001
Telephone: (Main): 307-777-7401; (800) 438-5768
(Licensing); 307-777-7319
Email: insurancelicensing@wyo.gov
http://doi.wyo.gov/

I. Licensing Requirements:—Producers, Limited Line Producers, Managing General Agents, Surplus Lines Brokers. Other Insurance Professionals—Adjusters, Consultants, Rental Car Agents, Travel, Preneed Funeral Agents, Reinsurance Intermediary Managers and Brokers.

A. Applicability: A person shall not sell, solicit or negotiate insurance in Wyoming for any class or classes of insurance unless the person is licensed for that line of authority. (Wyo. Stat. §26-9-203).

B. Licenses Required of Residents: Anyone negotiating, soliciting, placing insurance or annuities, or advising on insurance needs and coverage must be licensed in Wyoming.

Sales Personnel

1. *Producers.*

   a. License fee: The biennial fee is $100 with a $30 continuing education reporting fee for any one or combination of property, casualty and personal lines (https://doi.wyo.gov/licensing/ce). The biennial fee is $100 for any one or combination of life, health, and variable life/variable annuities. The biennial fee is $100 for credit. The biennial fee for limited lines crop and pre-need funeral is $20. There is a $39 fee for criminal record history check. Fingerprinting is required. (Wyo. Stat. §§26-4-101, 26-9-206, 26-9-231). The Wyoming Department of Insurance web site has noted that it may take four to six weeks to complete a criminal history background check due to a large volume of fingerprinting requirements. Because licenses are not processed until the department receives the criminal history, the time frame to obtain a resident license may be delayed, and applicants should plan accordingly.
   b. License term: The license term is two years and expires on the last day of the licensee's birth month in the second year following license issuance or renewal. (Wyo. Stat. §26-9-207).
   c. Lines of authority:

      (1) Life.

(2) Accident, health, sickness, or disability.
(3) Variable life and variable annuities.
(4) Limited line credit.
(5) Property.
(6) Casualty.
(7) Personal lines.
(8) Any other line permitted under state laws or regulations.
(9) Specialty Limited Lines – Travel, Portable Electronics and Rental Car. (Wyo. Stat. §§26-9-207 and 26-9-234).
(10) Limited Lines License – Crop and Pre-need.

2. *Business Entities:* Required to obtain a license if acting as an insurance producer. (Wyo. Stat. §26-9-206). A business entity license is a two-year license that expires the last day of the license issue month. Law change effective July 1, 2019. So long as the license is not revoked or suspended and as long as fees are paid, continuing education requirements are met by the due date, a written request for continuation is submitted to the commissioner on the appropriate forms, and the entity complies with all other code provisions. The entity must pay the fee, and submit the written request on the appropriate forms before the last day of the month the license became effective in the second year following the issuance or renewal of that license. If a business entity allows a license to lapse, they may reinstate the same license for a penalty fee within twelve months from the due date of the initial continuation fee. Continuation fee is $100, and the late fee is also $100. The business entity must designate a licensed producer responsible for the business entity's compliance with the insurance laws, rules and regulations of Wyoming. (Wyo. Stat. §26-4-101)

   Lines of authority:

   a. Life.
   b. Accident, health, sickness, or disability.
   c. Variable life and variable annuities.
   d. Limited line credit.
   e. Property.
   f. Casualty.
   g. Personal lines only (noncommercial property and casualty).
   h. Specialty limited lines – rental car, portable electronics, and travel.

3. *Managing General Agents.* Managing general agents must register with the department. A managing general agent may also be licensed as an insurance producer. A managing general agent may be required to carry a bond and an errors and omissions policy. (Wyo. Stat. §26-46-102). A copy of the written contract between the managing

general agent and the insurer must be submitted, and an appointment must be held with the same insurance company as the contract. (WCWR 044-0002-29(6)).

Other Insurance Professionals

1. *Adjusters.* Licenses are issued for general lines and crop/hail. Licenses are issued to independent and staff/company adjusters. The license term is two years, and licenses renew on the second anniversary of the last day of the month of the licensee's birthday. The licensing fee is $100 with a $39 fingerprinting fee. The renewal fee is $100 with a $30 continuing education filing fee. (Wyo. Stat. §§26-9-219, 26-4-101, 26-9-206. https://doi.wyo.gov/licensing/ce). Attorneys licensed to practice law in Wyoming and a licensed producer who adjusts or assists in adjustment of losses arising under policies issued through that producer are exempt from resident licensing. An individual may be licensed as both an adjuster and a producer, but a producer is not required to be licensed as an adjuster to adjust claims on policies the producer has written.

2. *Consultants (Including Public Adjusters).* A consultant license is issued to public adjusters and to individuals compensated by the insured for advice. The application fee is $100 for the original license and $100 biennial continuation fee. Public Adjusters licensed as consultants take the general lines adjuster exam. May be licensed as life, annuities, and health consultants or as property and casualty consultants. A producer licensed as a consultant may not act in the dual capacity of an insurance producer and a consultant in the same insurance transaction. (Wyo. Stat. §§26-9-220 and 26-4-101).

3. *Reinsurance Intermediaries.* Reinsurance intermediary managers and brokers must register with the department and may be required to post a bond or carry an errors and omissions policy. The reinsurance intermediary must also be licensed as a producer. (Wyo. Stat. §26-47-103(c)(i)).

4. *Third Party Administrators.* Third party administrators must register with the department and are required to post a bond. Registration fee $200. There is also a $200 biennial fee. Registrations renew on March 31. Renewal is biennial. (WCWR 044-0002-4).

5. *Preneed Funeral Agents.* Individuals accepting and holding funds in trust for the benefit of the contract holder for purposes of funding a preneed funeral service plan must be licensed as a preneed funeral agent. The NAIC Uniform Application is accepted for licensing, the application fee is $20, and the license is a two-year term and a $39 fingerprinting fee. The license is a two-year term. (https://doi.wyo.gov/licensing/limited-lines).

6. *Bail Bonds.* Individuals and firms issuing bail bonds underwritten by an insurance company are required to obtain an insurance producer license with a casualty line of authority. (https://doi.wyo.gov/licensing/bail-bonds).

C. **Appointments:** All individual and business entity producers must become appointed by the represented insurer. The appointment must be received and filed fifteen days after the first insurance application is submitted or the agency contract is executed. The filing fee for an appointment is $15 per producer for each insurer represented. Appointment/termination form is to be used. All appointments renew annually on March 31. Insurance companies must file an NAIC form UCAA Expansion Application to designate the representatives authorized to appoint producers. Electronic appointments are encouraged, and can be completed through Sircon or NIPR. An insurer must notify the department of a termination of an appointment within thirty days, see more below on cancelling agent contracts/appointments. (Wyo. Stat. §§26-4-101 and 26-9-213).

D. **Licenses Required of Nonresidents:** Nonresidents may be licensed as producers, consultants, adjusters, or surplus lines brokers if the applicant has a current license in good standing in the home state and if the home state awards nonresident licenses on a reciprocal basis.

Producers: The NAIC Uniform Application is accepted. Individual producers licensed in their resident states may apply online through Sircon or NIPR. Nonresident producer licensing fees are $150 for any one or combination of life, accident, health, and any variable life/variable annuity. Nonresident producer licensing fees are $150 for any one or combination of property, casualty, or personal lines. The nonresident licensing fee is $150 for limited line credit.

Nonresident business entities may be licensed as producer firms by submitting the Uniform Application for Business Entity License/Registration. The licensing fee is $150. Business entity licenses are two-year licenses, expiring the last day of the issue month. (Wyo. Stat. §§26-4-101, 26-9-208).

Adjusters: A state-specific application is accepted for adjuster licensing. If the state in which the adjuster maintains his principal place of residence or principal place of business does not license adjusters for the line of authority being applied for, individuals are required to have a designated home state. A list of the states that Wyoming will accept as designated home states can be found at http://www.wyo.gov/. The licensing fee is $100. For nonresident adjusters designating Wyoming as the home state, the licensing fee is $100, along with a $39 criminal history record check fee. The license term is two years. If the adjuster is not licensed in the adjuster's home state, the adjuster must pass a qualifying examination and provide background information. Applications may be downloaded from the Insurance Department's Website at http://doi.wyo.gov/. The renewal fee is $150. An individual may be licensed as both an adjuster and a producer, but a producer is not required to be licensed as an adjuster to adjust claims on policies the producer has written. (https://doi.wyo.gov/licensing/adjusters; Wyo. Stat. §26-4-101).

Consultants (includes public adjusters): The NAIC Uniform Application is accepted for consultant licensing. The application fee is $100. Licenses renew every two years; renewal fee is $150. Consultants are licensed for life, health, and annuities or property and casualty. A producer licensed as a consultant may not act in the dual capacity of an insurance producer and a consultant in the same insurance transaction. (Wyo. Stat. §26-9-220; Wyo. Stat. §26-4-101).

Reinsurance Intermediaries: Reinsurance intermediary managers and brokers must register with the department and may be required to post a bond or carry an errors and omissions policy. The reinsurance intermediary must be licensed as a producer. (Wyo. Stat. §26-47-103).

Third Party Administrators: Third party administrators must register with the department and are required to post a bond in an amount no less than $1,000 and no more than $500,000, depending on the actual or expected premium written in Wyoming. This must include power of attorney to execute the bond. There is a nonrefundable registration fee of $200. There is no filing fee for the application for registration. Forms may be downloaded from the insurance department's Website at http://doi.wyo.gov/. Registrations renew biennially on March 31; renewal fee: $200. (https://doi.wyo.gov/companies/tpa).

Preneed Funeral Agents: Individuals accepting and holding funds in trust for the benefit of the contract holder for purposes of funding a preneed funeral service plan must be licensed as a preneed funeral agent. The NAIC Uniform Application is accepted for licensing and the application fee is $20 and the license is a two-year term. (https://doi.wyo.gov/licensing/limited-lines).

Multi-State Exposures: A license is not required for a nonresident insurance producer who sells, solicits, or negotiates a contract of insurance for commercial property and casualty coverage when risks that are to be insured under that contract are located in more than one state. This exception applies only if the nonresident is licensed to sell, solicit, or negotiate that insurance in the state where the insured maintains its principal place of business and the contract of insurance insures risks located in that state. (Wyo. Stat. §26-9-204).

E. Prelicensing Examination and Education Requirements:

1. *Residents.* The following exams are offered:

   Insurance Producer Licenses

   Life.
   Accident/health/sickness/disability.
   Variable life and variable annuities.
   Limited line credit.
   Property and casualty.
   Property.
   Casualty.
   Personal lines.
   Title.

   Other Licenses

   Surplus lines.
   Crop hail adjuster.
   General lines adjuster.
   Life/Disability consultant.
   Property/Liability consultant.
   Prearranged Funeral Agent.

   Applicants for all Wyoming resident licenses must pass a qualifying examination. All examinations are currently administered by Pearson VUE, 866-936-7786. (Wyo. Stat. §26-9-205; https://doi.wyo.gov/licensing). Applicants for the following are not required to take an exam: motor club, rental car, portable electronic devices or travel Insurance licenses. (https://doi.wyo.gov/licensing/limited-lines).

2. *Nonresidents.* No examination is required for a nonresident producer to obtain any line of authority previously held in another state. A person licensed as an insurance producer in another state who moves to this state shall apply within ninety days of establishing legal residence to become a resident licensee. (Wyo. Stat. §26-9-209).

F. Continuing Education Requirements:

All resident producers, other than some limited lines producers, all adjusters, including nonresident adjusters designating Wyoming as their home state, and consultants must complete and report twenty-four hours of continuing education, including three hours of ethics, prior to the license expiration or renewal date. The continuing education requirement is in addition to the license renewal application and fee. Continuing education must be completed and reported online through Sircon with a $30 filing fee. This is paid with the license renewal. Course participants must present a written certification of completed courses. The Continuing Education provider must provide a course participant with certification within fifteen days of the date of successful completion of a course. Any person teaching any approved continuing education course or lecturing at any approved seminar qualifies for the same number of classroom hours granted to the person taking the course or seminar. (Wyo. Stat. §26-9-231 and WCWR 044-0002-20).

Continuing education credits must be completed during the two-year licensing period and may not be carried forward to future periods. (Wyo. Stat. §26-9-231).

Continuing Education Requirements **Not** Applicable to the Following:

1. Credit producers.
2. Preneed funeral agents.
3. Motor club agents.
4. Travel/baggage producers.
5. Rental car representatives.

Nonresident producers are exempt from the CE requirement. (https://doi.wyo.gov/licensing/ce; https://doi.wyo.gov/licensing/limited-lines).

G. Cancellation of Agency Contracts/Producer Appointments: Wyoming requires an insurer to give a thirty-day notice to the insurance department and a written notice to the producer of appointment terminations within fifteen days of the effective date of termination of a company appointment. There is an appointment termination filing fee of $15. An insurer terminating an appointment for cause must complete the termination for cause reporting form and submit supporting documentation to the insurance department. (Wyo. Stat. §§26-4-101, 26-9-214).

H. Rules for Risk Retention and Purchasing Groups: Risk retention groups domiciled in Wyoming must be chartered and licensed as casualty insurers. Groups not domiciled in Wyoming must register with the commissioner and submit reports to the commissioner as described in the law. Purchasing groups must also register with the commissioner and submit reports as required by the law. Producers and surplus lines brokers representing risk retention or risk-purchasing groups must comply with all Wyoming insurance laws, including licensing. (Wyo. Stat. §26-36-104).

Each risk retention group or risk-purchasing group seeking to do business in the state of Wyoming shall pay a registration fee of $200, which shall accompany the required registration application. Additionally, each risk retention group or risk-purchasing group shall be required to pay an annual fee of $200 payable on or before March 1 of each year to renew its registration. (https://doi.wyo.gov/companies/risk-retention-groups; https://doi.wyo.gov/companies/risk-purchasing-groups).

All risk retention group policies must show the following notice in at least ten-point type on the front page and on the declarations page of the policy:

NOTICE

"This policy is issued by your risk retention group. Your risk retention group may not be subject to all of the insurance laws and regulations of your state. State insurance insolvency guaranty funds are not available for your risk retention group." (Wyo. Stat. §26-36-105).

I. **Policy Countersignature Requirements:** None.

II. Commissions, Fees, Commingling of Funds, Suitability in Annuity Transactions

A. **Commissions:** An insurer or insurance producer may pay or assign commissions, brokerages, or other valuable consideration to an insurance agency or to persons who do not sell, solicit, or negotiate insurance in this state, unless the payment would violate Wyoming Statute §§26-13-110 or 26-13-112. Rebating of commissions is not allowed. (Wyo. Stat. §26-9-212).

B. **Fees:** No person may collect any premium or charge for insurance in excess of the premium or charge applicable to the insurance specified in the policy in accordance with the applicable classifications and rates as filed with and approved by the commissioner. (Wyo. Stat. §26-13-121).

C. **Disclosure Requirements:** None.

D. **Commingling of Funds:** All premiums or return premiums received by a producer must be held in a trust account, separate from other agency funds. (Wyo. Stat. §26-9-229).

E. Suitability in Annuity Transactions: Insurers and producers shall have reasonable grounds for believing that the recommendation is suitable for the consumer on the basis of the facts disclosed by the consumer as to his or her investments and other insurance products and as to his or her financial situation and needs. (WCWR 044-0002-64).

III. Statutory References:

Wyo. Stat. §26-4-	101
Wyo. Stat. §26-9-	203 to 209
	212 to 214, 219
	220, 229
	231, 234
Wyo. Stat. §§26-36-	104, 105
Wyo. Stat. §26-46-	102
Wyo. Stat. §26-47-	103

WCWR 044-0002-	4
	20, 29
	64

Web References:

https://doi.wyo.gov/licensing.
https://doi.wyo.gov/licensing/ce.
https://doi.wyo.gov/licensing/limited-lines.
https://doi.wyo.gov/licensing/adjusters.
https://doi.wyo.gov/companies/tpa.
https://doi.wyo.gov/companies/risk-retention-groups.
https://doi.wyo.gov/companies/risk-purchasing-groups.

ALABAMA

A. **Resident Licensing:** Residents who are licensed as property and casualty producers, and who are deemed to have had sufficient experience in the insurance business may be licensed to place insurance with nonadmitted insurers. A high school diploma and three years of recent full-time experience is required to be licensed in the property, casualty, or surety fields. The surplus lines broker's license expires annually on December 31. Individual initial fee: $230 ($30 application fee; $200 license fee); Individual annual renewal fee: $200. Business entities initial fee: $530 ($30 application fee; $500 license fee). Business entities annual renewal fee: $500. Application process is mandatory online at www.nipr.com. The applicant must file a $50,000 bond (form AL-SLB-13 available at https://www.aldoi.gov/PDF/Licensing/FormALSLB13.pdf). Courtesy filings are not accepted. No state other than an insured's Home State may require a surplus lines broker to be licensed in order to sell, solicit, or negotiate nonadmitted insurance with respect to such insured. (Ala. Code §§27-10-24, 27-4-2).

B. **Nonresident Licensing:** Nonresidents licensed in their home state for surplus lines may be licensed for this purpose in Alabama, on a reciprocal basis. Nonresident individuals and business entities must submit a copy of the application for licensure that was submitted to the home state. Each will need to submit form AL-SLB-13 and be in good standing in their home state. (Ala. Admin. Code r. 482-1-036-.03(2)).

C. **Diligent Effort:** Insurance may be procured through a licensed surplus lines broker if: the full amount of insurance is not procurable after diligent effort from among insurers authorized to transact and actually transacting that kind and class of insurance in this state or has been procured to the full extent such insurers are willing to insure; the insurance must not be procured for the purpose of securing advantages as to a lower premium rate than would be accepted by an authorized insurer. This section and surplus lines law do not apply as to life or disability insurance. (Ala. Code § 27-10-20).

   The diligent effort requirement of Ala. Code §27-10-20(1)(b) is satisfied in those circumstances meeting both of the following criteria without the need for contacting or obtaining declinations from authorized insurers:

   1. The prospective insured requires personal or commercial property insurance coverage against destruction of, or damage to, property caused by wind or wind events and hail.

   2. The property to be insured is located within an area in Baldwin County or Mobile County south of the southern right-of-way line of Interstate 10. (https://www.aldoi.gov/PDF/Legal/2010-01%20-%20Surplus%20Lines.pdf).

In instances meeting both criteria above, a producer or surplus lines broker is not required to contact authorized insurers or document such efforts in the form of three declinations or otherwise, and the coverage may be bound through an unauthorized insurer if the other requirements in Ala. Code §27-10-20(1) are satisfied.

Commercial Purchaser Exemption. Surplus lines brokers seeking to procure or place nonadmitted insurance on behalf of an "exempt commercial purchaser" pursuant to the NRRA are not required to perform a diligent search if:

1. The broker has disclosed to the exempt commercial purchaser that insurance may or may not be available from the admitted market that may provide greater protection with more regulatory oversight; and

2. The exempt commercial purchaser has subsequently requested in writing for the broker to procure or place such insurance from a nonadmitted insurer.

D. Tax: Six percent of direct premiums less return premiums and exclusive of sums collected to cover state or federal taxes, on surplus lines insurance subject to tax transacted by the broker during the preceding calendar year as shown by the annual statement filed with the commissioner; due annually on March 1 as a tax imposed for the privilege of transacting business as a surplus lines broker in Alabama. (Ala. Code §27-10-31).

In compliance with NRRA, no state other than the Home State of an insured may require any premium tax payment for nonadmitted insurance.

Multi-State Premium Tax Allocation. Legislation was passed to allow Alabama to join Surplus Lines Insurance Multi-State Compliance Compact (SLIMPACT), which does not yet have the ten member states required to establish a clearinghouse. Until SLIMPACT is operational, if Alabama is deemed the home state of a multi-state policy, 100 percent of the premium is taxed at the 6 percent tax rate and 100 percent of the tax is remitted to Alabama. (https://aldoi.gov/SurplusLineWeb/MultiStateInfo.aspx; Ala. Code §27-10-31).

Premium Defined. "Premium Tax" means, with respect to nonadmitted insurance, any tax, fee, assessment, or other charge imposed by a government entity directly or indirectly based on any payment made as consideration for such insurance, including premium deposits, assessments, registration fees, and any other compensation given in consideration for a contract of insurance. (Ala. Code §27-61-1).

E. Stamping Fee: None.

F. Surplus Lines Association: None.

G. Other Requirements or Restrictions:

Exemptions. The surplus lines insurance law does not apply to the following when placed by licensed agents or brokers of this state:

1. Reinsurance.

2. Wet marine and transportation insurance.

3. Insurance on subjects located, resident or to be performed wholly outside of this state or on vehicles or aircraft owned and principally garaged outside this state.

4. Insurance on property or operation of railroads engaged in interstate commerce.

5. Insurance of aircraft owned or operated by manufacturers of aircraft or aircraft operated in scheduled interstate flight, or cargo of such aircraft or against liability, other than workmen's compensation and the employer's liability, arising out of the ownership, maintenance or use of such aircraft.

6. The property and operations of the shipbuilding and ship repair industry engaged in interstate or foreign commerce and vessels, cargoes, watercraft, piers, wharves, graving docks, dry docks, marine railways and building ways, commonly known as wet marine. (Ala. Code §27-10-34).

Eligibility. A licensed surplus lines broker may accept and place surplus lines business for any insurance producer licensed in this state for the kind and class of insurance involved and may compensate the producer therefor. (Ala. Code §27-10-25).

At appropriate times the Department will publish lists of certain unauthorized insurers known by the Department to be ineligible to either financial requirements or claim practices. No lists of approved insurers will be published by the Department. The responsibility of ascertaining eligibility of insurers is that of the broker. The NAIC can furnish a listing of alien nonadmitted insurers who have filed financial data with one or more states or with a surplus lines association cooperating with a state. (Ala. Admin. Code r. 482-1-036-.05). Surplus lines brokers must ascertain financial condition of unauthorized insurers and may not use any that do not have capital and surplus of at least $5 million. Life and disability insurance may not be placed with nonadmitted insurers. A surplus lines broker must not knowingly place surplus lines insurance with an insurer that is unsound financially, or ineligible under Ala. Code §27-10-22. The broker must ascertain the financial condition of the unauthorized insurer before placing insurance, and shall not insure with any of the following:

1. With any insurer not authorized in at least one state of the United States for the kind of insurance involved, and with capital or surplus, or both, amounting to at least $5 million; or guaranteed trust fund amounting to at least $5 million.

2. With an alien insurer not authorized to transact insurance in at least one state of the United States, unless the insurer establishes an effective trust fund of at least $2.5 million within the United States administered by a recognized financial institution and held for the benefit of all its policyholders or policyholders and creditors in the United States, and with capital or surplus, or both, amounting to at least $15 million.

3. With a foreign or alien insurer who has transacted insurance as an authorized insurer in its state or country of domicile for less than five years, unless it is a wholly owned subsidiary of an insurer authorized to transact insurance in this state or unless it makes a deposit in this state as may be permitted under subsection (c).

4. With an insurer the voting control of which is held in whole or substantial part by any government or governmental agency.

5. In any insurer made ineligible as a surplus lines insurer by order of the commissioner received by or known to the broker. The commissioner may issue an order of ineligibility if he or she finds the insurer does not meet the financial requirements of this section, has without just cause refused to pay valid claims arising under its contracts in this state or otherwise conducted its affairs in a manner as to result in injury or loss to the insuring public of this state; or has conducted its affairs in a manner as to result in the avoidance of the required payment of tax.

When it appears that any particular risk eligible to be placed in accordance with the surplus lines law but on which insurance coverage in whole or in part is not procurable from foreign or alien insurers meeting all of the requirements above except for paragraph (3), then the surplus lines broker may file a supplemental signed statement setting forth the facts and advising the department that the part of the risk is being placed with named unauthorized insurers which meet all of the requirements except for paragraph (3), in the amounts and percentages in the statement. These named unauthorized insurers, before accepting any risk in this state, must deposit with the department cash or securities acceptable to the commissioner and with a market value of not less than $1 million, to be held by the department for the benefit of Alabama policyholders only. (Ala. Code §27-10-26).

Notice. The surplus lines contract must be initialed by, or bear the name and license number of, the surplus lines broker who procured it and must have stamped upon it the following:

"This contract is registered and delivered as a surplus lines coverage under the Alabama Surplus Lines Insurance Law." (Ala. Code §27-10-22).

Evidence of Coverage. Upon placing a surplus lines coverage, the broker must promptly issue and deliver to the insured evidence of the insurance consisting either of the policy as issued by the insurer or, if such policy is not available, the surplus lines broker's certificate. Such certificate must be executed by the broker and must show the description and location of the subject of the insurance, coverage, conditions and term of the insurance, the premium and rate charged and taxes collected from the insured and the name and address of the insured and insurer. If the direct risk is assumed by more than one insurer, the certificate must show the name and address and proportion of the entire direct risk assumed by each insurer. If after the issuance and delivery of the certificate there is any change to the identity of the insurers, or the proportion of the direct risk assumed by an insurer or any other material respect as to the insurance coverage evidenced by the certificate, the broker must promptly issue and deliver to the insured a substitute certificate showing the accurate current status of the coverage and the insurers responsible. If the policy is not available upon placement, the broker and the certificate has been issued and provided, upon request from the insured the broker must as soon as reasonably possible procure the policy evidencing the insurance and deliver the policy to the insured in replacement of the broker's certificate. Any broker who knowingly or negligently issues a false certificate or who fails promptly to notify the insured of any material change with respect to the insurance by delivery of a substitute certificate will be subject to penalties. (Ala. Code §27-10-27).

Records. Each surplus lines broker must keep in his office in the state a full and true record of each surplus lines contract procured by him, including a copy of the policy, certificate, cover note or other confirmation of insurance and of the daily report, if any, and showing such of the following items as may be applicable:

1. Amount of the insurance and risks insured against.

2. Gross premium charged.

3. Return premium paid, if any.

4. Rate of premium charged upon the several items of property.

5. Effective date of the contract and the terms thereof.

6. Name and address of the insurer.

7. Name and address of the insured.

8. Brief general description of property insured and where located.

9. Amount of tax and other sums collected from the insured.

10. Other information as may be required by the commissioner.

The record must be open at all times to examination by the commissioner for a period of five years following the issuance of the contract. (Ala. Code §27-10-29).

Reports. Within thirty days of the effective date of the insurance policy, the surplus lines broker must file a written report under Form ID-12 (Certificate of Surplus Lines Broker), which validates that coverage was written through the unauthorized market. The report must be filed online at https://aldoi.gov/SurplusLineWeb/SLInfo.aspx. If so required by the commissioner, the report must be in the form of a broker's affidavit. If so required by the commissioner, the report must be accompanied by a written statement signed by the insured to the effect that the coverage was placed in an unauthorized insurer with the insured's knowledge and consent.(Ala. Code § 27-10-21). A written statement signed by the insured acknowledging that he understands that the insurance coverage is provided by an insurer that is not licensed in Alabama is required for certain personal lines policies-private passenger automobile, homeowners (owner-occupied), renters/tenants, farm-owner policies, condominium (unit owner), dwelling fire, and mobile home/manufactured housing property. The written statement must be retained by the surplus lines broker. Certain mistakes made on the Form ID-12 filing, can be corrected by the broker using the website (https://aldoi.gov/SurplusLineWeb/PDF/SLProcessInstructions.pdf). The report of a full and true record of each surplus lines contract must be kept and made available to the commissioner for five years next following the issuance of the contract. (Ala. Code §§ 27-10-3)

Annual Statements. On or before March 1 every year, each surplus lines broker must file with the commissioner a verified statement of all surplus lines insurance transacted by him during the preceding calendar year. The statement must be **on** forms as prescribed and furnished by the commissioner and must show:

1. Gross amount of each kind of insurance transacted.

2. Aggregate gross premiums charged, exclusive of sums collected to cover state or federal taxes.

3. Aggregate of returned premiums and taxes paid to insureds.

4. Aggregate of net premiums.

5. Additional information as required by the commissioner. (Ala. Code §27-10-30).

H. Independently Procured Insurance:

1. *Rules.* Anyone who may desire to place his insurance in a foreign insurer not authorized to do business in Alabama may do so, and any insured who procures, or causes to be procured, or continues or renews insurance in an unauthorized foreign insurer or any self-insurer who so procures or continues excess loss, catastrophe or other insurance within Alabama, other than insurance procured through a surplus lines broker pursuant to the surplus lines law shall, within ninety days after the date such insurance was so procured, continued or renewed, file a written report of the same with the commissioner on forms designated by the commissioner and furnished to such an insured upon request. The report shall show the name and address of the insured or insureds, name and address of the insurer, the subject of the insurance, a general description of the coverage, the amount of premium currently charged, and such additional pertinent information as is reasonably requested by the commissioner. The insured is responsible for payment of a 4 percent tax. (Ala. Code §27-10-35).

2. *Industrial Insured Exemption.* Industrial insureds in Alabama may purchase insurance directly from surplus lines insurers without the use of a broker if certain insurance coverages cannot be procured on terms acceptable to the insureds from authorized insurers. Such coverages, designated "surplus lines," may be procured from unauthorized insurers. The insured must have a full-time employee acting as insurance manager or buyer or must retain the services of a regularly and continuously retained, qualified insurance consultant. The annual premium for all risks (other than workers compensation and group insurance) must be at least $25,000 and the firm must have at least twenty-five employees. (Ala. Code §27-10-20).

NRRA Implementation

Alabama Legislature 2011-537

I. Compact: SLIMPACT.

J. Home State Definition:

1. **In General.** Except as provided in subparagraph (b), the term "home state" means, with respect to an insured:

   a. The state in which an insured maintains its principal place of business or, in the case of an individual, the individual's principal residence.

   b. If 100 percent of the insured risk is located out of the state referred to in subparagraph 1a the state to which the greatest percentage of the insured's taxable premium for that insurance contract is allocated.

2. **Affiliated Groups.** If more than one insured from an affiliated group are named insureds on a single nonadmitted insurance contract, the term "home state" means the home state, as determined pursuant to subparagraph (a), of the member of the affiliated group that has the largest percentage of premium attributed to it under such insurance contract.

3. "Principal Place of Business" means, with respect to determining the home state of the insured, the state where the insured maintains its headquarters and where the insured's high-level officers direct, control, and coordinate the business activities of the insured.

4. "Affiliate" means, with respect to an insured, any entity that controls, is controlled by, or is under common control with the insured.

5 "Control" means an entity has "control" over another entity if:

   a The entity directly or indirectly or acting through one or more other persons owns, controls, or has the power to vote 25 percent or more of any class of voting securities of the other entity; or
   b The entity controls in any manner the election of a majority of the directors or trustees of the other entity. (Ala. Code §27-61-1).

Statutory References: Ala. Code §§ 27-4-2; 27-10-20 to -22, -24 to -27, -29 to -31, -35; 27-61-1. Ala. Admin. Code r. 482-1-036-.03

ALASKA

A. Resident Licensing: Fees for surplus lines broker's/producer's license are: initially, individual or firm, resident or nonresident (including one compliance officer): $300. Surplus lines licenses are renewable on a biennial basis. (3 Alaska Admin. Code 31.040). If renewal applications are submitted less than sixty days after a license has expired, a $100 late fee will be assessed. If renewal applications are submitted more than sixty days but less than two years after a license has expired, a $200 late fee will be assessed. (3 Alaska Admin. Code 31.060). Renewal applications will not be accepted two years or more after a license has expired. Fingerprint cards are required to be submitted with the initial license application and require an additional fee of $48.25 for individuals. Fingerprint card and fee are not required if currently Alaska licensed. To qualify, applicants must first be licensed as either an insurance producer or managing general agent for property and casualty lines of authority; pass the surplus lines broker examination; and maintain an E&O policy if required. (https://www.commerce.alaska.gov/web/ins/SurplusLines.aspx).

Additionally, please note that applications not completed within 120 days from the date of filing will be considered withdrawn and a new application and application fee will be required pursuant to Alaska Stat. §21.27.040(f). Per department policy, if an applicant submits a paper application when the application may be filed electronically, an additional processing fee of $50 is required in addition to the application fee. (https://www.commerce.alaska.gov/web/ins/Producers/ResidentLicense.aspx).

B. Nonresident Licensing: The initial and renewal licensing fees for nonresident surplus lines brokers and firms is $300. Nonresident surplus lines licenses are renewable on a biennial basis. If renewal applications are submitted less than sixty days after a license has expired, a $100 late fee will be assessed. If renewal applications are submitted more than sixty days but less than two years after a license has expired, a $200 late fee will be assessed. (3 Alaska Admin. Code 31.040, 060).

C. Diligent Effort: Insurance may be procured through a surplus lines broker from an eligible nonadmitted insurer only if the producing broker:

1. Determines through a diligent search that the full amount, kind, or class of insurance cannot be obtained from an insurer that is admitted to do business in Alaska and is actually writing the particular kind or class of insurance required by the client in Alaska.

2. Completes the search before the surplus lines broker binds the insurance contract.

3. Provides documentation of the search to the surplus lines broker no later than fifteen days after the binding of the insurance contract. (3 Alaska Admin. Code 25.010).

This search must be documented and retained in the producing and surplus lines broker's files. Acceptable documentation includes the following:

1. Documentation of declinations from admitted insurers writing the particular kind or class of insurance required by the client in Alaska.

   An oral declination is acceptable if documented in writing and includes the name, office location, and phone number of the insurer (not the wholesaler or insurance group but the actual company providing the declination), the name and position of the person contacted, the date of contact, and the reason for the declination.

2. Evidence that the full amount, kind, or class of insurance could not be obtained from all admitted insurers the producing broker can access.

3. Affirmation that the coverage is on the director's current surplus lines placement list under 3 Alaska Admin. Code § 25.040. Business recognized as generally unavailable in the admitted market is on the division's surplus lines placement list found at: https://www.commerce.alaska.gov/web/Portals/11/Pub/SurplusLines/sl-placement-list.pdf. New lists, as they are available, will be at https://www.commerce.alaska.gov/web/ins/resources/orders/regulatory.aspx.

4. An exception from the director under Alaska Stat. §21.34.020(a)(4).

5. Documentation that the broker procuring or placing the surplus policy has disclosed to an exempt commercial purchaser that insurance may be available from the admitted market that may provider greater protection with more regulatory oversight and the exempt commercial purchaser has requested in writing that the broker procure or place the insurance from a nonadmitted insurer. (3 Alaska Admin Code. 25.035).

D. Reports, Tax and Fees: Tax is 2.7 percent on the net premium, which is the total gross premiums less any return premiums, for the surplus lines insurance. The premium tax is due at the time of filing the quarterly reports for transactions occurring during the period covered by the report. The tax must be paid by the Automated Clearing House (ACH) Tax Payment debit or credit method. (Alaska Stat. § 21.34.180; 3 Alaska Admin Code 21.570). The fee for filing the quarterly report is 1 percent on gross premiums charged less any return premiums as reported and must be paid at the time the report is filed by the Automated Clearing House (ACH) Tax Payment debit or credit method. (Alaska Stat. §21.34.190; 3 Alaska Admin Code 21.570). The ACH payments must be made through the Online Premium Tax for insurance (OPTins) application located at: https://www.optins.org. (https://www.commerce.alaska.gov/web/Portals/11/Pub/Consumers/Orders/Regulatory/2017/R17-08.pdf).

Where the insurance covers properties, risks, or exposures located or to be performed both in and out of this state and the home state of the insured is Alaska, the tax payable shall be computed based on an amount equal to 2.7 percent on 100 percent of the premium. (Alaska Stat. §21.34.180).

Quarterly Reports. Surplus lines brokers must file with the director, on forms prescribed by the director, a report of all surplus lines insurance, by type of insurance as required to be reported in the annual statement that must be filed with the director by admitted insurers. The report must include all surplus lines transactions during the preceding period showing the aggregate gross premiums written, the aggregate return premiums, the amount of aggregate tax remitted to this state, and the amount of aggregate tax allocated to each other state for which an allocation is made. The forms are to be filed quarterly on March 1, June 1, September 1, and December 1 of each year. If the due date falls on a weekend or holiday, the next business day is the due date. The reports must be filed through the Online Premium Tax for insurance (OPTins) application located at: https://www.optins.org. (https://www.commerce.alaska.gov/web/Portals/11/Pub/Consumers/Orders/Regulatory/2017/R17-08.pdf).

Report of Surplus Lines Transaction. This form is attached to the Quarterly Report and must include the following:

1. The name and address of the insured.

2. The identity of each insurer including the NAIC number and percent of coverage provided by each.

3. A complete description of the subject and location of the risk (at a minimum each state in which the risk covers).

4. The policy term and policy number.

5. Identification of the type of insurance.

6. The gross premium written for each type of insurance identified in 5.

7. The name and firm license number of the producing broker if working for a firm.

8. The name and firm license number of the surplus lines broker if working for a firm. (3 Alaska Admin. Code 25.090).

Quarterly Reports. Such reports must be filed electronically in a location specified by the Director, on or before March 1, June 1, September 1, and December 1. The report must include the following: the name of the surplus lines broker; the broker's license number; and the quarter's total gross premiums written, less any return or exempt premium, and the quarter's total taxes and fees for all coverage where the insured's home state is Alaska. The report must be signed, physically or electronically, by the surplus lines broker.

Late Filing Fees. Surplus lines brokers must pay a penalty for late filing of a quarterly report or filing of a new transaction not previously reported if filed after the due date of the quarterly report according to the following rate schedule:

(1) One to thirty days late, $100.

(2) Thirty-one to sixty days late, $200.

(3) More than sixty days late, $300.

These late fees do not apply to the filing of the amended reports under 3 Alaska Admin Code 25.105, except for filing a new transaction not previously reported.

(3 Alaska Admin. Code 25.100).

Late Fees. Surplus lines brokers must pay a late fee of $50 per month plus 5 percent of the tax due each calendar month or part of a month during which a broker fails to pay the full amount of tax or a portion of the tax and interest of 1 percent of the tax due each calendar month or part of a month for the period the broker fails to pay the tax. The late payment fee, not including interest, may not exceed $250 plus 25 percent of the tax due. The tax payment must be made in the form required by the director, or a penalty will be added to the tax equal to 25 percent of the tax due, not to exceed $2,000, with a minimum penalty of $100. (Alaska Stat. §21.34.180).

If the filing fee is not paid when due, an additional late payment fee of $250 plus 2 percent of the fee due per month, or part of a month, shall become due and payable by the surplus lines broker. (Alaska Stat. §21.34.190).

E. **Stamping Fee:** None. Alaska does not have a surplus lines stamping office.

F. Surplus Lines Association: Alaska does not have a surplus lines association. A surplus lines association of surplus lines brokers may be formed to promote compliance by its members with the laws of Alaska, encourage attendance to NAIC meetings, facilitate communication with organizations of admitted insurers with regard to the surplus lines market, streamline information received by its members relative to surplus lines coverage, and verify taxes and fees for surplus lines insurance for each surplus lines broker. Each surplus lines association is required to file the following documents with the director:

(1) A copy of its constituition, articles of agreement, or certificate of incorporation;

(2) A copy of its governing bylaws and regulations;

(3) A list of current members;

(4) The name of the Alaska resident upon whom notices, orders of the director, or processes issued at the director's instruction may be served;

(5) An agreement that the director may examine the association under Alaska Stat. §21.34.090; and

(6) A schedule of membership fees and assessments. (Alaska Stat. §21.34.090)

G. Other Requirements or Restrictions:

Restrictions. Reinsurance, wet marine and transportation insurance, insurance independently procured, life insurance, health insurance except as provided in Alaska Stat. §21.34.035, and annuity contracts may not be procured through a surplus lines broker. (Alaska Stat. §21.34.020).

A subscription policy that includes a combination of admitted and nonadmitted insurers is a surplus lines insurance placement in its entirety and is subject to Alaska surplus lines law. The surplus lines broker is not required to collect any tax that would constitute double taxation of the admitted company portion of the insurance. The filing fee is required on the entire subscription policy, admitted insurer premiums included. Losses or claims are not covered by the Alaska Insurance Guaranty Association Act. (Alaska Stat. §21.34.025).

Life and accident and health insurance may not be placed with nonadmitted insurers. Workers compensation insurance may be placed with nonadmitted insurers if the director considers it in the best interest of the public and issues an order to that effect, the insurance is written in accordance with surplus lines statutes, and all conditions for writing workers compensation insurance in a nonadmitted market receive compliance. The minimum capital and surplus amounts required is two times that normally required. (Alaska Stat. §21.34.030).

Eligibility. Use of nonadmitted insurers not on the division's eligible surplus lines insurer list is permitted only when the full amount of coverage needed is not procurable from an eligible surplus lines insurer. However, the company must still meet the capital and surplus requirements of Alaska Stat. §21.34.040. The surplus lines broker must fulfill the additional requirements in 3 Alaska Admin. Code 25.010. Such a transaction must be reported in writing to the division of insurance and additional written notice given to the insured and the producing broker (if different from the surplus lines broker) within thirty days of placement.

For nonadmitted insurers domiciled outside the United States, a broker may place business with such insurers, provided the insurer is listed on the Quarterly Listing of Alien Insurers maintained by the International Insurers Department of the National Association of Insurance Commissioners (NAIC). Alien insurers that are not on the quarterly listing and want to write business in Alaska must apply for approval to be listed on the eligible surplus lines insurer list. The director may approve an alien insurer's request for eligibility if the nonadmitted insurer:

1. Establishes satisfactory evidence of good report and financial integrity.

2. Maintains capital and surplus of $15 million.

3. Maintains a trust of $2.5 million deposited in a U.S. financial institution. (Alaska Stat. §21.34.040).

4. Submits an application at https://www.commerce.alaska.gov/web/ins/SurplusLines.aspx, the required fee of $1,000, and consents to service of process and forwarding designation (https://www.commerce.alaska.gov/web/ins/Insurers/Amendments.aspx).

5. Submits designation of persons to contact (Alaska Stat. §21.34.040).

Notice. Every evidence of insurance negotiated, placed, or procured must bear the name of the surplus lines broker, and must contain the following wording, exactly word for word, in at least ten point type (Alaska Stat. §21.34.100):

> "This is evidence of insurance procured and developed under the Alaska Surplus Lines Law, AS 21.34. It is not covered by the Alaska Insurance Guaranty Association Act, AS. 21.80."

Endorsements of the original and company audits related to a policy are considered evidence of insurance. (3 Alaska Admin Code 25.060).

Notification: A contract of insurance placed by a surplus lines broker is not binding upon the insured and a premium charged is not due and payable until:

1. The surplus lines broker has notified the insured in writing, that the insurer with whom the surplus lines broker places the insurance does not hold a certificate of authority issued by Alaska and is not subject to its supervision, and, in the event of the insolvency of the surplus lines insurer, losses will not be covered under the Alaska Insurance Guaranty Association Act. A copy of said notice shall be maintained by the surplus lines broker with the records of the contract, available for examination; or

2. The producing broker has notified the insured and the surplus lines broker in writing that the insurer with whom the surplus lines is placed does not hold a certificate of authority issued by Alaska and is not subject to Alaska's supervision, and, in the event of the insolvency of the surplus lines insurer, losses will not be covered under the Alaska Insurance Guaranty Association Act. A copy of said notice shall be maintained by the producing broker and the surplus lines broker with the records of the contract, available for examination.

An eligible surplus lines insurer shall include in each policy an Alaska Policyholder Notice regarding nonrenewal and premium increase, in a format approved by the director. The surplus lines broker shall ensure the required notice is part of each policy. The most current approved format is in Bulletin 08-06 https://www.commerce.alaska.gov/web/portals/11/pub/Bulletins/B08-06.pdf (3 Alaska Admin. Code 25.050).

H. Independently Procured Insurance:

1. *Rules.* Insureds in Alaska may purchase insurance directly from insurers without the use of an agent or a broker. The transaction may be made with an unauthorized or nonadmitted insurer and must be reported by the insured to the Division of Insurance within thirty days after the date the insurance is procured, continued, or renewed, in writing and in a form prescribed by the director. The report must show the name and address of the insured, name and address of the insurer, the subject of the insurance, a general description of the coverage, the amount of premium currently charged, and additional information required by the director. (Alaska Stat. §21.33.061(a)).

2. *Premium Tax.* For purposes of this section, "premium" includes all premiums, membership fees, assessments, dues, and any other consideration for insurance. Where the insured's home state is Alaska, the insured must pay to the director, on or before

March 1 following the calendar year in which the insurance was procured, continued, or renewed, a tax of 3.7 percent of the gross premiums paid for the insurance other than wet marine and transportation insurance, less any return premiums. For wet marine and transportation insurance, where the insured's home state is Alaska, the insured must pay to the director a tax of 0.75 percent of the gross premiums paid for the wet marine and transportation insurance. If the independently procured insurance covers properties, risks, or exposures located or to be performed both in and out of Alaska and the home state of the insured is Alaska, the tax payable shall be computed based on an amount equal to 3.7 percent or 0.75 percent on that portion of the net premiums allocated to Alaska plus an amount equal to the portions of the premium allocated to other remitting states or territories based on the tax rates and fees applicable to the other states or territories plus 3.7 percent or 0.75 percent of the portions of the premium allocated to other states that have failed to enter into an agreement with Alaska. In the event of cancellation and rewriting of the insurance contract, the additional premium for tax purposes is the premium in excess of the unearned premium of the canceled insurance contract. (Alaska Stat. §21.33.061(c)).

3. *Late Payment Fee.* If the premium tax described above is not paid by the prescribed deadline, the tax may be increased by a late payment fee of $1,000 or 10 percent of the tax due, whichever is greater; interest at the rate of 1 percent a month or part of a month from the date the payment was due to the date paid; and a penalty not to exceed $100 a day or 25 percent of the tax due, whichever is greater, from the date the payment was due to the date paid. (Alaska Stat. §21.33.061(j)).

NRRA Implementation

2011 Alaska House Bill No. 164 (Amending Alaska Stat. §§ 21.03.021 to 21.96.030)

Agreement: Alaska signed the NIMA Agreement on July 21, 2011, but withdrew from NIMA effective June 25, 2012. The director is authorized to participate in an agreement with another state or territory for the purposes of collecting and disbursing to the other state or territory any premium tax collected and payable to the other state or territory and for receiving from the other state or territory premium tax it has collected and is owed to Alaska. To the extent that another state or territory where a portion of the properties, risks, or exposures reside has failed to enter into an agreement with Alaska, the director will retain all of the net premium tax collected by Alaska.

I. Definition:

1. "Home State," for purposes of determining the home state of an insured in a multistate placement of nonadmitted insurance, is defined as follows:

a. Except as provided in (2) of this paragraph, "home state" means, with respect to an insured:

   (1) The state in which an insured maintains its principal place of business or, in the case of an individual, the individual's principal residence.

   (2) If 100 percent of the insured risk is located out of the state referred to in (1) of this subparagraph, the state to which the greatest percentage of the insured's taxable premium for that insurance contract is allocated.

b. If two or more insureds from an affiliated group are named insureds on a single policy, "home state" under (a) of this paragraph is based on the member of the affiliated group that has the largest percentage of premium attributed to it under the insurance contract.

c. For purposes of (a) of this paragraph, the principal place of business of an insured is the state where the insured maintains its headquarters and where the insured's high-level officers direct control and coordinate the business activities of the insured.

For surplus lines transactions, a license is not required unless the home state of the insured is Alaska.

J. References:

Alaska Stat. §§21.	33.061
	34.020, 025, 030, 040, 090, 100, 180, 190

3 Alaska Admin. Code	21.57
	25.010, 035, 050, 060, 090, 100
	31.040, 060

Web References:

https://www.commerce.alaska.gov/web/ins/SurplusLines.aspx.

https://www.commerce.alaska.gov/web/ins/Producers/ResidentLicense.aspx.

https://www.commerce.alaska.gov/web/Portals/11/Pub/Consumers/Orders/Regulatory/2017/R17-08.pdf.

ARIZONA

A. Resident Licensing: A person (individual or business entity) cannot act as a surplus lines broker in Arizona on behalf of an insured whose home state is Arizona unless the person has a current surplus lines broker license. (A.R.S. §20-411(a)). An individual who is a resident of Arizona, who is licensed as a resident insurance producer authorized for property or casualty insurance and who passes Arizona's surplus lines insurance broker examination may also apply for a surplus lines broker license (Form L-152). (A.R.S. §20-411(b), (c)). Forms available at https://insurance.az.gov/producers/surplus-lines-broker/surplus-lines-broker-license-application-individual. A business entity organized in Arizona that is licensed in Arizona as a resident property or casualty insurance producer may apply for a surplus lines broker license (Form L-176). Surplus lines broker authority added to an existing Arizona insurance license (whether for an individual or business entity) expires at the same time as the other authority on the Arizona insurance license. A newly issued Arizona insurance license expires for a business entity four years after the last day of the month in which the license was issued; and, for an individual, at least three years but not more than four years after the last day of the month of the licensee's birthday. (A.R.S. §20-411(d)). A licensee adding surplus lines broker authority to an existing insurance license will be charged $600 for a license with a remaining term of less than two years or $1,000 for a license with a remaining term of two years or more. (A.R.S. §20-167(A)(10)(a)). A fingerprint card and a $22 fingerprint card processing fee are required for a resident who does not already hold a resident insurance license and for each new officer, member, or director of a business entity. (A.R.S. §20-285(E)).

At least one individual must be licensed as a surplus lines broker at each location where surplus lines insurance is transacted in Arizona. (A.R.S. §20-411(E)).

The director shall participate in the national insurance producer database of the National Association of Insurance Commissioners or any other equivalent national database for the licensure and license renewal of surplus lines brokers. (A.R.S. §20-411(H)).

Only the insured's home state may require a surplus line broker to be licensed to sell, solicit or negotiate nonadmitted insurance with respect to a particular placement. If Arizona is the insured's home state, the surplus lines broker must be licensed in Arizona. (A.R.S. §20-411).

B. Nonresident Licensing: A person whose principal place of residence or business is outside Arizona must hold a nonresident license in Arizona in order to procure insurance on behalf of an insured whose home state is in Arizona. A nonresident may be licensed as an Arizona surplus lines broker if licensed as a surplus lines broker in the nonresident's home state. A nonresident is subject to the same requirements as a resident except a nonresident is not required to pass a prelicensing exam, furnish fingerprints or complete insurance continuing education. (A.R.S. §§20-287; 20-411.02).

Mexican Insurance Surplus Lines Licensing. Any resident or nonresident licensed insurance producer that maintains an office in Arizona may apply for a Mexican insurance surplus lines broker license (Form L-152 and Form L-FPVfor an individual; Form L-176 for a business entity), and upon licensure, may solicit and accept insurance applications for coverage provided by alien insurers that are not licensed in Arizona to be effective within Mexico and not effective anywhere within Arizona; and may collect commission arising from those policies. The applicant is subject to the same requirements as other surplus lines brokers except that no exam is required for a Mexican insurance surplus lines broker license. (A.R.S. §20-411.01).

C. Diligent Effort: Insurance coverage is recognized as surplus lines when either the Arizona Department of Insurance, after a hearing, determines that a particular insurance coverage is not readily procurable from authorized insurers; or the surplus lines broker finds that insurance coverage is not readily procurable from authorized insurers, after making a diligent effort to procure coverage, or the coverage has been procured to the full extent the insurers are willing to insure. (A.R.S. §§20-407, 20-409). Insurance can only be procured from unauthorized insurers that the Arizona Department of Insurance has verified meets the requirements of A.R.S. §20-413. (A.R.S. §20-413. https://insurance.az.gov/producers/surplus-lines-broker). Surplus lines brokers no longer need to annually recertify surplus lines insurers for Arizona's List of Qualified Unauthorized Insurers (the "White List"). (Bulletin 2016-05).

Commercial Purchaser Exemption. A surplus broker seeking to procure or place nonadmitted insurance on behalf of an "exempt commercial purchaser" is not required to perform a diligent search if:

1. The broker has disclosed to the exempt commercial purchaser that insurance may or may not be available from the admitted market that may provide greater protection with more regulatory oversight.

2. The exempt commercial purchaser has subsequently requested in writing for the broker to procure or place such insurance from a nonadmitted insurer. (Bulletin 2011-06).

Arizona uses the term "industrial insured," rather than "exempt commercial purchaser." "Industrial insured" is defined in A.R.S. §20-401.07(C), and that definition is the same as "exempt commercial purchaser" under the Federal Nonadmitted and Reinsurance Reform Act (NRRA). (Bulletin 2011-06).

D. Tax: 3 percent of gross premiums, including policy fees other than the association stamping fees and exclusive of returned premiums due to policy cancellation or returned premiums. For transactions for Arizona home-state insureds, a surplus lines broker must file transaction data to the Surplus Lines Association of Arizona using the Association's Website (http://www.sla-az.org), must use the Website to produce a tax report and must remit the tax due with the tax report to the Arizona Department of Insurance. As of July 21, 2011, the NRRA permits only the insured's home state to require the payment of premium tax for nonadmitted insurance. Therefore, for transactions for which the insured is located outside Arizona, reporting is made to the insured's home state and not to Arizona. The tax for Arizona single-state risks is due semiannually on or before February 15 of each year for the preceding July through December and on or before August 15 of each year for the preceding January through June. Each surplus lines broker must use the Surplus Lines Association of Arizona Website to produce the tax report, and then must remit the tax with the report to the Arizona Department of Insurance. Beginning December 21, 2019, the director may require that reports and payments under A.R.S. §§ 20-415, -416, 416.01, and -417 be submitted electronically. (A.R.S. §§20-415, 20-416).

Multi-State Placements. Arizona no longer requires quarterly filings for multi-state risks. Multi-state risks are filed and reported the same as Arizona only risks. (Affirmed by S. Wede, 4/10/2020). Arizona has not entered into a multi-state compact or multi-state agreement; therefore, the entirety of tax due for transactions involving insureds whose home state is Arizona is payable to the State of Arizona, regardless of other portions that would otherwise be allocable to other states. The Arizona Department of Insurance intends to issue a regulatory bulletin if and when Arizona begins participating in tax-sharing agreement. Until such a bulletin is issued, the Arizona tax rate must be applied to new and renewal policies that have an effective date on or after July 21, 2011, when Arizona is the insured's home state.

By the date given on the Surplus Lines Association website (https://www.sla-az.org), you must report transactions to the Surplus Lines Association and file reports and pay premium tax to the Department of Insurance, as follows: Only file, report and pay tax on transactions for which Arizona is the "home state" and file transactions and download the 2018A report for insurance procured between January 1 and June 30, 2018.

Restrictions. The tax applied to gross premiums, including policy fees other than stamping fees, is not applicable to premiums returned on account of cancellation or reduction of premium and is not applicable to gross premiums and returned premiums on business exempted from surplus lines provisions. The surplus lines broker must collect the tax from the insured in addition to the full amount of the gross premium charged by the insurer for the insurance. The surplus lines broker must return the tax on any portion of the premium unearned at the termination of the insurance policy to the policyholder. The surplus lines broker is prohibited from absorbing the tax and from rebating, for any reason, any part of the tax or commission. (A.R.S. §20-416(C)).

E. Stamping Fee: 0.2 percent. Upon reporting a transaction, the Surplus Lines Association of Arizona will invoice the surplus lines broker. (https://www.sla-az.org).

F. Surplus Lines Association:

Scott Wede
The Surplus Lines Association of Arizona
14747 N. Northsight Blvd., Ste. 111-449
Scottsdale, AZ 85260
Phone: 602-279-6344
Email: swede@sla-az.org
Website: http://www.sla-az.org/

G. Other Requirements or Restrictions:

Exemptions. The surplus lines laws do not apply to reinsurance or to the following classes of insurance placed by licensed insurance producers of Arizona:

1. Ocean marine and foreign trade insurance.

2. Insurance on subjects located, resident or to be performed wholly outside Arizona, or on vehicles or aircraft owned and principally garaged outside of Arizona.

3. Insurance for an insured that is a federally recognized Indian tribe or who is a member of a federally recognized Indian tribe on subjects of insurance that are located, resident, or to be performed wholly within the boundaries of a federally recognized Indian reservation.

4. Insurance on property or operations of railroads engaged in interstate commerce. (A.R.S. §20-420).

5. Mexican insurance (as described in A.R.S §20-422).

6. State of Arizona property and liability insurance.

7. Surplus line insurance purchased by federally recognized Indian tribes and tribal members to cover risks on its own reservation.

Any insurance producer that places any of the above classes of insurance with an unauthorized insurer shall keep a record of each coverage in detail. Specific requirements for such records are described below in "Records." The producer shall retain the record for at least three years after the expiration or cancellation of the policy and shall make the record available in Arizona and open to examination. All "exempt class" policies must be reported and filed using the "X" code.

Eligibility. Placing insurance with an unauthorized insurer cannot be for the purpose of securing advantages either as to premium rate or terms of the insurance contract.

A surplus lines broker must not knowingly place any surplus lines coverage on behalf of an insured whose home state is Arizona with an unauthorized insurer that does not meet the minimum financial requirements of this section or is declared by the director to be in a hazardous financial condition, improperly managed or unreliable in insurance transactions.

An unauthorized foreign insurer authorized to transact insurance on a surplus lines basis in at least one other state must possess a minimum capital and surplus that equals the greater of either the minimum capital and surplus requirements imposed by article 1 of this chapter or $15 million.

An unauthorized alien insurer other than a title insurer must possess minimum capital and surplus of at least $15 million and must maintain within the United States in public depositories or trust institutions approved by the director assets in the amount of $2.5 million. The director may require the association to maintain a larger fund if the public interest reasonably requires a larger fund.

An unauthorized insurance exchange authorized to transact insurance on a surplus lines basis in at least one other state must possess minimum aggregate capital and surplus of at least $50 million. (A.R.S. §20-413).

Notice. Insurance contracts procured as surplus lines coverage are fully valid and enforceable as to all parties and will be recognized in all matters in the same manner as like contracts issued by authorized insurers.

Any policy and any evidence of surplus lines coverage from an unauthorized insurer that is issued for delivery to the insured must contain a conspicuously stamped or written notice in bold-faced type that states one of the following:

1. If the surplus lines policy or evidence of coverage is issued by a surplus lines insurer that is not a domestic surplus lines insurer:

    "Pursuant to §20-401.01, subsection B, paragraph 1, Arizona Revised Statutes, this policy is issued by an insurer that does not possess a certificate of authority from the director of the Arizona Department of Insurance. If the insurer that issued this policy becomes insolvent, insureds or claimants will not be eligible for insurance guaranty fund protection pursuant to title 20 Arizona Revised Statutes."

2. If the surplus lines policy or evidence of coverage is issued by a domestic surplus lines insurer:

   "If the insurer that issued this policy becomes insolvent, insureds or claimants will not be eligible for insurance guaranty fund protection pursuant to title 20, Arizona Revised Statutes."

A surplus lines broker may charge and receive a fee in addition to the premium for services provided in the transaction of surplus lines insurance if, before effecting any coverage, both of the following conditions are met:

1. The service fees and the specific services for which the fees are charged are disclosed to the insured or the insured's representative and are agreed in writing by the insured or the insured's representative.

2. The taxes are paid on any fees charged to the insured. (A.R.S. §20-410).

Records. Each surplus lines broker must keep in its principal place of business a full and true record of each surplus lines contract procured by the broker under the surplus lines license. The director may examine the record at any time within three years after the expiration or cancellation date of the policy. The record shall include:

1. The name and address of the insurer.

2. The name and address of the insured.

3. The amount of insurance.

4. The gross premium charged.

5. The return premium paid, if any.

6. The rate of premium charged on the several items of coverage.

7. The effective date and terms of the contract.

8. A brief general description of the risks insured against and the property insured. (A.R.S. §20-414).

Statements. Each surplus lines broker must file with the director a semiannual statement of all surplus lines insurance business covering Arizona single state risks transacted by the broker during the period for which the statement is being filed. The statement must show:

1. The gross amount of each kind of insurance transacted.

2. The aggregate gross premiums charged.

3. The aggregate of return premiums paid to insureds.

4. The aggregate of net premiums.

5. Such additional information as may reasonably be required by the director.

The statement is due on or before February 15 of each year for the preceding July through December and on or before August 15 of each year for the preceding January through June for business covering Arizona single state risks.

Each surplus lines broker must file with the clearinghouse a quarterly notarized statement of all surplus lines business covering multi-state risks transacted by the broker on behalf of insureds whose home state is Arizona during the calendar quarter for which the statement is being filed. A facsimile of the original notarized statement may be submitted in lieu of the original notarized statement, which must be maintained by the broker for six years after the calendar year in which the statement was filed. The statement is due on February 15 for the quarter ending the preceding December 31, May 15 for the quarter ending the preceding March 31, August 15 for the quarter ending the preceding June 30 and November 15 for the quarter ending the preceding September 30. Surplus lines brokers are not responsible for reporting any fees or remitting any premium taxes or stamping fees due on fees charged by an insurance producer in connection with the transaction of surplus lines insurance. (A.R.S. §20-415).

NRRA Implementation

H. Compact: Arizona has not entered into a compact. The director is permitted to enter a compact or multi-state agreement for the reporting, payment, collection and allocation of premium taxes on unauthorized surplus lines coverage of multi-state risks, following a hearing to determine whether such action would be "in the best interests of the state." (A.R.S. §20-416.01).

I. Definitions: Arizona is the insured's home state if the insured maintains its principal place of business in Arizona or, in the case of an individual, the individual's principal residence is within Arizona, and if any of the insured risk is located within Arizona. If all of the insured risks are located outside of Arizona, then the insured's home state is the state to which the greatest percentage of the insured's taxable premium for that insurance contract is located. If more than one insured from an affiliate group are named insureds on a single nonadmitted insurance placement, Arizona will be considered the home state for that placement if Arizona is the home state of the member of the affiliated group that has the largest percentage of premium attributed to it under the insurance contract. If Arizona is considered the insured's home state, only Arizona's requirements apply to the surplus lines insurance transaction. "Domestic surplus lines insurer" means an insurer that is domiciled in and authorized to transact insurance in this state and that has received approval from the department pursuant to section 20–407.01 to write surplus lines insurance coverage in this state. (A.R.S. §20-401).

J. References:

A.R.S. §§20-	167, 285, 287
	401, 401.07, 407
	409 to 411.02, 414 to 416.01
	420, 422

DIFI Bulletins	2011-06
	2016-05

Web References:

https://insurance.az.gov/producers/surplus-lines-broker

https://www.sla-az.org

ARKANSAS

A. **Resident Licensing:** If an insured's home state is Arkansas, a person cannot procure a contract of surplus lines insurance with a nonadmitted insurer unless the insurer possesses a current surplus lines broker's license issued by the insurance commissioner. A person, while licensed as a resident insurance producer of Arkansas as to property, casualty, surety, and marine insurance, who has held the license in Arkansas or another state, or both, for three years before application for a surplus lines broker's license, and who is deemed by the commissioner to be competent and trustworthy, may be licensed as a surplus lines broker. The surplus lines producer license expires annually January 1. Original license fee, per NIPR: $1,035; each additional individual: $100. Annual Renewal fee: $25. (A.C.A. §§ 23-65-308; 23-61-401; https://www.nipr.com/rules_ar_rl.htm). The applicant must submit an application through the National Insurance Producer Registry at www.NIPR.com. A resident applicant must file a $50,000 surety bond, and must pass an examination prior to licensing. The applicant must also complete the Arkansas State Police Form ASP-122 online and pay the $24 background check fee.

   Contact PSI services, 888-204-259, for more information. Resident exam and license fee: $1,085 (includes $1035 license and $50 exam fee). First time test taker fee: $50. Retake fee: $50. Filing and payment take place through OPTins.

   Any corporation or partnership which provides a facility for transacting business on a surplus lines basis must apply for and obtain a surplus lines broker's license in the name of the corporation or partnership. Each individual to act as a surplus lines broker under the license must qualify individually for a surplus lines broker's license and upon doing so will be added to the license of the corporate or partnership broker. (054 00 CARR 024-8).

B. **Nonresident Licensing:** Nonresidents licensed in their home state for surplus lines may also be licensed in Arkansas. Bonds are not required of nonresidents. No exam is required for nonresidents. (A.C.A. § 23-65-308).

C. **Diligent Effort:** If certain insurance coverages cannot be procured from authorized insurers, surplus lines coverage may be procured from unauthorized insurers subject to the following conditions:

   1. The insurance must be procured through a licensed surplus lines broker.

   2. If Arkansas is the home state of the insured, the full amount of insurance required must not be procurable, after diligent effort has been made, from among authorized insurers who are actually marketing that kind or class of insurance in Arkansas. The

amount of insurance placed in an unauthorized insurer is only the balance over the amount procurable from authorized insurers and the agent or broker will maintain written documentation of compliance with A.C.A. § 23-65-305.

3. If Arkansas is the home state of the insured, the amount of insurance placed in an unauthorized insurer is only the balance over the amount procurable from authorized insurers.

   The originating producer or broker must attempt to place the business with those admitted insurers which he or she has reason to believe are actually marketing in Arkansas the kind or class of insurance sought to be placed before business may be placed in surplus lines insurers. The surplus lines broker may rely on the diligent effort made by the originating producer or broker. If the surplus lines broker also serves as the originating producer or broker, the surplus lines broker must make diligent effort to secure coverage through the admitted market. The originating agent or broker and the surplus lines broker may consider to be a "declination" any offer of similar coverage by an admitted insurer wherein such insurer would require a gross premium of 20 percent or more higher than the total gross premium and charges for insurance (including taxes and expense of underwriting) applicable to the procurable surplus lines coverage. (A.C.A. § 23-65-305; 00 CARR 024-5).

Commercial Purchaser Exemption. A surplus lines broker seeking to procure or place nonadmitted insurance in Arkansas for an "exempt commercial purchaser," as defined by A.C.A. § 23-65-304, is not required to perform a diligent search if both:

1. The surplus lines broker has disclosed to the exempt commercial purchaser that insurance may or may not be available from the admitted market that may provide greater protection with more regulatory oversight.

2. The exempt commercial purchaser has subsequently requested in writing for the broker to procure or place such insurance from a nonadmitted insurer. (Ark. Code Ann. § 23-65-305).

D. Tax: 4 percent of total monthly written direct premiums, including expense of underwriting, less returns and taxes collected must be submitted with Form SL-2 and SL-2A. Tax must be paid within sixty days following the end of the month in which the policy is written. (A.C.A.§ 23-65-315). The surplus lines broker will remit to the Treasurer of the State through the insurance commissioner a tax of 4 percent on the direct premiums written less return premiums and exclusive sums collected to cover state or federal taxes. Form SL-4 is due March 1 annually and must be accompanied by full payment of the balance of taxes due for surplus lines insurance procured during the preceding calendar year. (054 00 CARR 024-11). Forms available at https://insurance.

arkansas.gov/pages/industry-regulation/accounting/surplus-lines-brokers-filing/.

Late Payment Fees. If a surplus lines broker fails to remit the tax by the due date, the surplus lines broker shall be liable for a fine $50 for each day of delinquency commencing with the sixty-first day after the end of the month in which surplus lines insurance was procured. (A.C.A. § 23-65-316). The Department does not accept post mark dates as evidence of filing.

Multi-State Premium Tax Allocation. The commissioner may participate in a multi-state agreement or enter into a compact for the purpose of reporting, collecting, and apportioning surplus lines insurance premium taxes. If a surplus lines insurance policy covers risks or exposures only partially in this state and the commissioner has entered into an agreement with other states for the apportionment of premium taxes for multi-state risks, the tax payable by the surplus lines broker shall be computed and paid on the proportion of the premium that is properly allocable to the risks or exposures located in this state according to the terms of the agreement. (A.C.A.§ 23-65-315).

Premium Defined. "Premium" means any payment made as consideration for an insurance contract for the insurance, including premium deposits, assessments, registration fees, and any other compensation given in consideration for a contract of insurance (A.C.A. § 23-65-304).

E. **Stamping Fee:** None. Arkansas has no stamping office.

F. **Other Requirements or Restrictions:**

Exemptions. The surplus lines subchapter does not apply to reinsurance; wet marine and foreign trade insurance; insurance on subjects that are located, resident, or to be performed outside Arkansas; insurance on subjects that are on vehicles or aircraft principally garaged outside Arkansas; insurance on property or operation of railroads engaged in interstate commerce; and insurance on aircraft. (A.C.A. § 23-65-302).

Eligibility. A surplus lines broker may place surplus lines insurance if the nonadmitted insurer is authorized to write the type of insurance in its domiciliary jurisdiction, has capital and surplus that equals the greater of the minimum capital and surplus requirements of the state or $15 million, and is a nonadmitted insurer domiciled outside the United States that is listed on the quarterly listing of alien insurers. (A.C.A. § 23-65-305).

Only insurers on commissioner's approved list shall be used (includes the NAIC list of alien surplus lines insurers). (A.C.A. § 23-65-310).

Notice. All insurance contracts procured and delivered as surplus lines coverage must be initiated by, or bear the name of, the surplus lines broker who procured it. The contract must contain a conspicuous statement substantially similar to the following:

> "This contract is registered and delivered as a surplus lines coverage under the Surplus Lines Insurance Law, and it may in some respects be different from contracts issued by insurers in the admitted markets, and, accordingly, it may, depending upon the circumstances, be more or less favorable to an insured than a contract from an admitted carrier might be. The protection of the Arkansas Property and Casualty Guaranty Act does not apply to this contract. A tax of 4 percent is required to be collected from the insured on all surplus lines premiums." (A.C.A. § 23-65-307; 054 00 CARR 024-6).

Form SL-3, Disclosure to Surplus Lines Insured, must be signed by the insured and retained by the originating producer or broker. (054 00 CARR 024-7).

Quarterly Statements. On or before March 1, June 1, September 1, and December 1 of each year a surplus lines broker must file with the insurance commissioner a statement for the preceding period of the surplus lines insurance transactions of an insured whose home state is the state of Arkansas. The statement must be on forms as prescribed and furnished by the commissioner and must show:

1. The gross amount of each kind of insurance transacted.

2. The aggregate gross premiums charged, exclusive of sums collected to cover state or federal taxes.

3. The aggregate of returned premiums and taxes paid to insureds.

4. The aggregate of net premiums.

5. Additional information as required by the commissioner. (A.C.A. § 23-65-314).

If a surplus lines broker fails to file his quarterly statement by the due dates, he will be liable for a fine of $50 for each day of delinquency commencing with the due date. (A.C.A. § 23-65-316).

Annual Statements. On or before March 1 of each year, all licensed surplus lines brokers must complete and submit Form SL-4, even if the broker did not write any Arkansas business on a surplus lines basis during the preceding calendar year. (054 00 CARR 024 -11).

Brokers' Affidavits. At the time of the procuring of surplus lines insurance in Arkansas, when it is the home state of the insured, the surplus lines broker must execute an affidavit on a form (SL-2) prescribed by the insurance commissioner; provide any information that the commissioner requires; state required facts; and file the affidavit with the commissioner within sixty days following the end of the month in which the insurance was procured. (A.C.A. §23-65-306; 054 00 CARR 024-5).

Brokers' Records. A surplus lines broker must maintain complete records as to expenses of underwriting and the amount of such expense collected from insureds. It is sufficient for the records to be maintained as a total for each surplus lines insurer; it is not necessary to maintain records on an individual risk basis. The records must include a copy of the daily report, if any, and show:

1. Amount of the insurance.
2. Gross premium charged.
3. Return premium paid, if any.
4. Rate of premium charged upon the several items of property.
5. Effective date of the contract and the contract terms.
6. Name and address of the insurer.
7. Name and address of the insured.
8. A brief general description of the property insured and where located.
9. Other information as required by the insurance commissioner. The records must be open to examination by the commissioner and must be kept available and open to inspection for the next five years following the termination of the contracts. (A.C.A. § 23-65-313; 054 00 CARR 024-10).

G. Surplus Lines Association:

Arkansas Professional Surplus Lines Association
c/o Argenia, Inc
PO Box 17370
Little Rock, AR 72222
Phone: 501-227-9670
Fax: 501-227-8105
Website: www.argenia.com

H. Independently Procured Insurance:

1. *Rule.* An insured whose home state is Arkansas who directly procures, causes to be procured, continues, or renews insurance in an unauthorized insurer, including surplus lines insurance when procured without the use of a surplus lines broker, must file a written report with the insurance commissioner on forms designated by the Commissioner and furnished to the insured upon request. The report must show:

   a. The name and address of each named insured.

   b. The name and address of the insurer.

   c. The subject of the insurance.

   d. A general description of coverage.

   e. The amount of premium currently charged.

   f. Additional pertinent information reasonably requested by the commissioner. (A.C.A. § 23-65-103).

2. *Premium Tax.* The insured must withhold 2 percent from the amount of premium charged by and otherwise payable to the insurer for the insurance, and within thirty days after the insurance was so procured, continued, or renewed, and coincidentally with the filing of the report with the commissioner, the insured must pay the amount of the tax to the Treasurer of State through the commissioner. The tax is 4 percent if procured from an approved surplus lines carrier. If the tax is delinquent, it will bear interest at the rate of 6 percent per year, compounded annually. (A.C.A. § 23-65-103).

NRRA Implementation

2011 Arkansas House Bill No. 2143; Act 1055

I. Compact: Arkansas has not entered into a compact at this point. However, the insurance commissioner may enter into written multi-state agreements or compacts with other state jurisdictions on behalf of the State of Arkansas to provide for cooperation and assistance among member jurisdictions in the administration and collection of taxes imposed on multi-state surplus lines insurance. (A.C.A. § 23-65-401).

J. Definitions:

1. "Home State" means, with respect to an insured:

   a. The state in which an insured maintains its principal place of business; or the state that is an individual's principal residence.

   b. "Principal place of business" means the state in which the insured maintains its headquarters and where the insured's high-level officers direct, control, and coordinate the business activities of the insured.

   c. If 100 percent of the insured risk is located out-of-state, the state to which the greatest percentage of the insured's taxable premium for the insurance contract is allocated.

2. If more than one insured from an affiliated group are named insureds on a single nonadmitted insurance contract, "home state" means the home state of the member of the affiliated group that has the largest percentage of premium attributed to it under the insurance. (A.C.A. § 23-65-304).

K. Statutory References: 054 00 CARR 024; A.C.A. §§ 23-61-401; 23-65-103; 23-65-302; 23-65-304 to 308; 23-65-310; 23-65-313 to 316; 23-65-401

CALIFORNIA

A. Resident Licensing: Residents may be licensed to place business with nonadmitted insurers. Applicants must hold an active California resident property and casualty broker-agent license to be eligible for an individual surplus lines license.

Individuals: Complete the qualifying licensing examination, (for property and casualty broker-agent license combined, $55 at CDI sites and $88 at PSI sites); on CDI's online application service, mark surplus lines broker box. Submit an application through Sircon's Apply for a license and select the Property Broker-Agent and Casualty Broker-Agent boxes. License renewals are required to be filed electronically https://www.sircon.com/products/renew.jsp. Must also submit fingerprints through live scan; Fee: $59 at CDI examination sites and $68.95 at PSI test centers. The unlicensed surplus lines broker applicant will need to apply for both a property and casualty broker-agent license and a surplus lines broker license. When submitting the original application for a surplus lines license, the applicant must submit the $188 property and casualty broker-agent license fee and the appropriate license fee with the application. Fee is $646 for a surplus lines broker only transacting on behalf of a surplus lines business entity broker; surplus lines broker not only transacting on behalf of a business entity $1,296. (insurance.ca.gov/0200-industry/).

Surplus lines broker's licenses may be issued to an individual, a corporation, partnership, or limited liability company. The surplus lines broker's license applies to lines other than navigation/transportation (marine, air, railroads). A bond of $50,000, Form LIC 447-31, executed in California, by a California admitted surety and accompanied by a jurat and power of attorney for attorney-in-fact executing bond; completed in the name of and signed by the applicant is required. For all applicants except individuals who will transact only on behalf of a licensed business entity must file a Business Entity Endorsement, form LIC 411-8A; such individuals are not required to submit a bond. Business entity licensees must provide two hours of training using a curriculum to be developed by the Surplus Lines Association of California to each of its employees who solicit, negotiate, or effect insurance coverage placed with a nonadmitted insurer every five years. The surplus lines broker license will be cancelled if the property and casualty broker-agent license is inactivated due to a late renewal or other circumstances.

For organizations and those individuals who do not transact only on behalf of a business entity, there is a biennial license filing fee of $1,296 for an ontime renewal, and $1,944 if renewed within one year after the license expiration date. For individuals who only transact on behalf of a licensed business entity, the biennial licensing fee is $646 for an on time renewal, and $969 if renewed within one year after the license expiration date. Organizations shall provide the names of all persons who may exercise the power and perform the duties under the license. The named persons must be individually licensed as surplus lines brokers. Whenever an organization licensed as a surplus lines broker desires to change, remove, or add to the natural person or persons who are to transact insurance under authority of its license, it shall immediately file an electronic form with the commissioner for an endorsement changing its license accordingly, on form 411-8A. The fee for adding or removing, from any surplus lines broker's license issued to an organization, the name of any natural person named thereon is $29. (Cal. Ins. Code §1765(d)).

Any surplus lines broker organization for which the broker will be transacting on their behalf will need to submit a Business Entity Endorsement, form LIC 411-8A or file through CDI's endorsement and termination online service. When terminating a surplus lines broker, the surplus lines broker organization will need to submit a Business Entity Endorsement termination, Form LIC 411-8T or file through CDI's endorsement and termination online service. The fee for submitting either of these forms is $29. You may access CDI's endorsement and termination online service at http://www.insurance.ca.gov/0200-industry/0010-producer-online-services/0450-bus-entity-endorse/index.cfm.

The following types of coverage may be placed with a nonadmitted insurer for a home state insured only by and through a special lines' surplus broker:

1. Reinsurance of the liability of an admitted insurer.

2. Insurance against perils of navigation, transit, or transportation upon hulls, freights, or disbursements, or other ship-owner interests; upon goods, wares, merchandise, and all other personal property and interests therein, in course of exportation from or importation into any country, or transportation coastwise, including transportation by land or water from point of origin to final destination and including war risks; and marine builder's risks, dry docks, and marine railways, including insurance of ship repairer's liability, and protection and indemnity insurance, but excluding insurance covering bridges or tunnels.

3. Aircraft or spacecraft insurance.

4. Insurance on property or operations of railroads engaged in interstate commerce. (Cal. Ins. Code §1760.5).

The same requirements apply as those for a surplus lines license. Application for a special lines' surplus lines broker license is online. Individuals must file form LIC-050 for certification; business entities, LIC 441-11. Both must file a $50,000 bond by a California admitted surety and accompanied by a jurat and power of attorney for attorney-in-fact executing bond; completed in the name of the applicant and signed by the applicant on

Form LIC-447-31. Individuals transacting only on behalf of a licensed business entity are not required to submit a bond. See above for special requirements and licensing fees for individuals and business entities. If applying for a special lines' surplus lines license at the same time as applying for a surplus lines license, the applicant need only pay one fee.

B. Nonresident Licensing: A nonresident must hold an individual nonresident surplus lines broker license in California and a license for property and casualty in his or her resident state. New and renewal biennial fees: $646 for individuals who only transact on behalf of a licensed business entity, $1,296 for business entities and individuals who do not transact only on behalf of a licensed business entity. Must post a bond of $50,000 by a California admitted surety and accompanied by a jurat and power of attorney for attorney-in-fact executing bond, completed in the name of the applicant and signed by the applicant on Form LIC-447-31. Nonresident business entities must apply on paper form LIC 441-11. (insurance.ca.gov/0200-industry/0050-renew-license/0200-requirements/surplus-line.cfm).

C. Diligent Effort: Business must be placed through a licensed surplus lines broker. Broker must certify to the commissioner that three admitted insurers that actually write the particular type of insurance for the class of business seeking it have declined the risk; or fewer than three admitted insurers actually write the particular type of insurance for the class of business seeking it. These declinations must be in writing.

Records of surplus lines transactions shall be maintained by every surplus lines broker in a file pertaining to a particular insured for a period of eighteen months after the transaction. (http://www.insurance.ca.gov/01-consumers/105-type/95-guides/09-comm/commercialguide.cfm#surpluslineinsurance).

The records required by Cal. Ins. Code §1764.1 must be kept for a period of five years.

A diligent search is not required for coverages appearing on the commissioner's export list. The Diligent Search Report may be downloaded from: http://www.slacal.org/brokers/broker-filing-forms/sl2-form1.

Mandatory reports do not apply to the following lines of business: reinsurance of an admitted insurer; air craft or space craft insurance; insurance on the property of railroads engaged in interstate commerce; insurance against perils of navigation, transit or transportation upon hulls, freights or disbursements, or other shipowner interests; upon goods, wares, merchandise and all other personal property and interests therein, in the course of exportation from or importation into any country, or transportation coastwise, including transportation by land or water from point of origin to final destination and including war risks; and marine builder's risks, dry docks and marine railways, including insurance of ship repairer's liability, and protection and indemnity insurance, but excluding insurance covering bridges or tunnels.

Confidential Report of Surplus Lines Placement (Form SL-1) must be filed within sixty days of placement. Form SL-2, "Diligent Search Report," (see above) is to be filed at the same time—filing is to be made with the Surplus Lines Association of California. Three declinations from admitted insurers that actually write the particular type of insurance are evidence of a diligent search. Also considered as such evidence is the fact that fewer than three admitted insurers write a particular line in California. (Cal. Ins. Code §1763).

Commercial Purchaser Exemption. The diligent search requirement does not apply to a commercial insured as defined in Cal. Ins. Code §1760.1 when both of the following occur:

1. The surplus lines broker procuring or placing the surplus lines insurance has disclosed in writing to the commercial insured that surplus insurance may or may not be available from the admitted market that may provide greater protection with more regulatory oversight.

2. The commercial insured has subsequently requested in writing that the surplus lines broker procure or place surplus insurance from a nonadmitted insurer.

The surplus lines broker is responsible to ensure that the applicant is a commercial insured. A surplus lines broker who reasonably relies on information provided in good faith by the applicant, whether directly or through a producer, shall be deemed to be in compliance with this requirement. (Cal. Ins. Code §1763).

A "commercial insured" means any person purchasing commercial insurance that, at the time of placement:

1. Employs or retains a qualified risk manager to negotiate insurance coverage.

2. Has paid aggregate nationwide commercial property and casualty insurance premiums in excess of $100,000 in the immediately preceding twelve months.

3. Meets at least one of the following criteria:

    i. Possesses a net worth in excess of $20 million, as adjusted under § 1760.1(b)(3)(B).

    ii. Generates annual revenues in excess of $50 million, as adjusted under § 1760.1(b)(3)(B)

    iii. Employs more than 500 full-time employees per individual insured or is a member of an affiliated group employing more than 1,000 employees in the aggregate.

iv. Is a non-profit organization or public entity generating annual budgeted expenditures of at least $30 million as adjusted under § 1760.1(b)(3)(B).

v. Is a municipality with a population in excess of 50,000 persons.

(Cal. Ins. Code §1760.1).

D. Tax: 3 percent. Every surplus lines broker shall annually, on or before the first day of March each year, pay to the insurance commissioner for the use of the State of California a tax of 3 percent of the gross premiums charged less return premiums upon business done by him under authority of his license during the preceding year, excluding any portions of premiums upon business done involving the risk finance portion of any blended finite risk product used in the financing element of state or federal Superfund environmental settlements involving remediation of soil or groundwater contamination or by the provisions of Cal. Ins. Code § 1760.5.

If during any calendar year 3 percent of the return premiums upon business done by a surplus lines broker exceed 3 percent of gross premiums of the gross premiums upon that business done by him in that year, then he may either carry forward excess to the next succeeding year and apply it as a credit against 3 percent of gross premiums on the business done by him in the succeeding year, or he may elect to receive, and thereupon be paid a refund equal to the amount of taxes theretofore paid by him on that excess of return premiums paid over gross premiums received.

For the purpose of determining that tax, the total gross premium charged for all that nonadmitted insurance placed in a single transaction with one underwriter or group of underwriters, whether in one or more policies, shall be the entire premium charged on all nonadmitted insurance for the California home state insured.This provision shall not apply to interstate motor transit operations conducted between this and other states.

A penalty of 10 percent of the amount due pursuant to this section shall be levied upon and paid by any surplus lines broker who fails to make the necessary payment within the time required, plus interest at the rate of 1 percent per calendar month or fraction thereof, from March 1, the due date of the annual tax, until the date the payment is received by the commissioner.

Any surplus lines broker to whom an extension is granted shall, in addition to the tax, pay interest at the rate of 1 percent per month or fraction thereof from March 1, until the date of payment. If your annual tax is more than $20,000 you must make monthly installments through the EFT system. (Cal. Ins. Code §1775.5).

E. Stamping Fee: 0.25 percent.

The commissioner may delegate certain duties to an advisory organization under this section. Said advisory organizations shall have the authority to assess a stamping fee for each premium-bearing document submitted to the organization. This fee may be periodically established by the organization and shall reflect all reasonable costs associated with the advisory organization's services and be subject to review by the commissioner. Except as otherwise provided, the stamping fee may not exceed three-fourths of 1 percent of the premium for the insurance. (Cal. Ins. Code § 1780.56(b)).

F. Surplus Lines Association:

Surplus Lines Association of California
12667 Alcosta Boulevard
Suite 450
San Ramon, CA 94583
Phone: (415) 434-4900
Fax: (415) 434-3117
www.slacal.com

G. Other Requirements or Restrictions:

Eligibility. Use of nonadmitted insurers solely to obtain lower rate is prohibited. In 2011, the List of Eligible Surplus Line Insurers, (LESLI) was replaced by the List of Approved Surplus Line Insurers (LASLI).The LASLI is a voluntary list of nonadmitted insurers that the California Department of Insurance (CDI) has approved for use by surplus line brokers. As a result, there may be nonadmitted insurers that are not on LASLI but pursuant to the NRRA and Cal. Ins. Code §1765.1 are nonetheless eligible for use by surplus line brokers, as long as the broker has determined at the time of placement that the insurer meets specific eligibility criteria. Check http://www.insurance.ca.gov/01-consumers/120-company/07-lasli/ for additional information about Surplus Lines Insurers and Nonadmitted Insurer Eligibility.

Notice. All surplus lines contracts must carry the following notice to the insured (Form D-2) — in bold face, sixteen-point type (Note: this is not sixteen-point type):

NOTICE

1. THE INSURANCE POLICY THAT YOU [HAVE PURCHASED] [ARE APPLYING TO PURCHASE] IS BEING ISSUED BY AN INSURER THAT IS NOT LICENSED BY THE STATE OF CALIFORNIA. THESE COMPANIES ARE CALLED "NONADMITTED" OR "SURPLUS LINES" INSURERS.

2. THE INSURER IS NOT SUBJECT TO THE FINANCIAL SOLVENCY REGULATION AND ENFORCEMENT WHICH APPLIES TO CALIFORNIA LICENSED INSURERS.

3. THE INSURER DOES NOT PARTICIPATE IN ANY OF THE INSURANCE GUARANTEE FUNDS CREATED BY CALIFORNIA LAW. THEREFORE, THESE FUNDS WILL NOT PAY YOUR CLAIMS OR PROTECT YOUR ASSETS IF THE INSURER BECOMES INSOLVENT AND IS UNABLE TO MAKE PAYMENTS AS PROMISED.

4. THE INSURER SHOULD BE LICENSED EITHER AS A FOREIGN INSURER IN ANOTHER STATE IN THE UNITED STATES OR AS A NON-UNITED STATES (ALIEN) INSURER. YOU SHOULD ASK QUESTIONS OF YOUR INSURANCE AGENT, BROKER, OR "SURPLUS LINES" BROKER OR CONTACT THE CALIFORNIA DEPARTMENT OF INSURANCE AT THE TOLL-FREE NUMBER 1-800-927-4357 OR INTERNET WEBSITE WWW.INSURANCE.CA.GOV. ASK WHETHER OR NOT THE INSURER IS LICENSED AS A FOREIGN OR NON-UNITED STATES (ALIEN) INSURER AND FOR ADDITIONAL INFORMATION ABOUT THE INSURER. YOU MAY ALSO CONTACT THE NAIC'S INTERNET WEBSITE AT WWW.NAIC.ORG.

5. FOREIGN INSURERS SHOULD BE LICENSED BY A STATE IN THE UNITED STATES AND YOU MAY CONTACT THAT STATE'S DEPARTMENT OF INSURANCE TO OBTAIN MORE INFORMATION ABOUT THAT INSURER. YOU CAN FIND A LINK TO EACH STATE FROM THIS NAIC INTERNET WEBSITE: HTTPS://NAIC.ORG/STATEWEBMAP.HTM.

6. FOR NON-UNITED STATES (ALIEN) INSURERS, THE INSURER SHOULD BE LICENSED BY A COUNTRY OUTSIDE OF THE UNITED STATES AND SHOULD BE ON THE NAIC'S INTERNATIONAL INSURERS DEPARTMENT (IID) LISTING OF APPROVED NONADMITTED NON-UNITED STATES INSURERS. ASK YOUR AGENT, BROKER, OR "SURPLUS LINES" BROKER TO OBTAIN MORE INFORMATION ABOUT THAT INSURER.

7. CALIFORNIA MAINTAINS A LIST OF APPROVED SURPLUS LINES INSURERS APPROVED BY THE INSURANCE COMMISSIONER. ASK YOUR AGENT OR BROKER IF THE INSURER IS ON THAT LIST, OR VIEW THAT LIST AT THE INTERNET WEBSITE OF THE CALIFORNIA DEPARTMENT OF INSURANCE: WWW.INSURANCE.CA.GOV/01-CONSUMERS/120-COMPANY/07-LASLI/LASLI.CFM.

8. IF YOU, AS THE APPLICANT, REQUIRED THAT THE INSURANCE POLICY YOU HAVE PURCHASED BE BOUND IMMEDIATELY, EITHER BECAUSE EXISTING COVERAGE WAS GOING TO LAPSE WITHIN TWO BUSINESS DAYS OR BECAUSE YOU WERE REQUIRED TO HAVE COVERAGE WITHIN TWO BUSINESS DAYS, AND YOU DID NOT RECEIVE THIS DISCLOSURE FORM AND A REQUEST FOR

YOUR SIGNATURE UNTIL AFTER COVERAGE BECAME EFFECTIVE, YOU HAVE THE RIGHT TO CANCEL THIS POLICY WITHIN FIVE DAYS OF RECEIVING THIS DISCLOSURE. IF YOU CANCEL COVERAGE, THE PREMIUM WILL BE PRORATED AND ANY BROKER FEE CHARGED FOR THIS INSURANCE WILL BE RETURNED TO YOU. (Cal. Ins. Code §1764.1(b)).

The notice is required only on new business. If a policy is renewed with a new policy number, the notice is not required, if the carrier remains the same.

A signed copy of the disclosure (form D-1) must be obtained from the applicant prior to placement, with specified exceptions.

If delivery of the policy is not made within thirty days after the date of the issuance of the certificate or upon which the risk has been bound or the home state insured or the home state insured applicant has been advised that coverage has been or will be obtained, the surplus lines broker shall deliver to the insured either of the following:

a. A photostatic copy of evidence that the insurance has been bound.

b. If the nonadmitted insurer is located outside the United States, a cover note, placing slip or similar document evidencing coverage issued or certified to by any broker located outside the United States who actually placed that insurance with the nonadmitted insurer. (Cal. Ins. Code §1764.3).

State-mandated private passenger auto coverages are not exportable.

Courtesy filings of taxes and nonavailability certificates are not allowed in California.

Surplus lines brokers are permitted to advertise in all media using the names of nonadmitted insurers and describing specific nonadmitted insurance products, provided that:

1. the insurer is authorized to accept placements from the surplus lines broker under § 1765.1;
2. a nonadmitted insurer's name does not appear in connection with any nonadmitted insurance product of that insurer;
3. the insurer's unlicensed status is disclosed in type no smaller than any telephone or fax number or address in the ad;
4. the ad contains no false statements or information about premium rates;

5. the ad contains no information about a nonadmitted insurer's premiums or rates. (Cal. Ins. Code §1773).

Annual Statements. On or before March 1 of each year the surplus lines broker, placing business for a home state insured, must file with the commissioner a sworn statement of all business transacted under his or her surplus lines license during the last preceding calendar year.

The statement must contain an account of the business done by the surplus lines broker placing business for a home state insured for the prior year, and must include (A) the total amount of gross premium, (B) the total gross premium for single state risks where 100 percent of the premium is attributable to risks in California, and (C) for multi-state risks, the percentage of gross premium allocated to California and each other state. The commissioner may waive or modify any of the forgoing requirements by issuance of a notice published on the department's website. (Cal. Ins. Code §1774).

Reports. Each surplus lines broker must file with the commissioner, within sixty days of placing any insurance for a home state insured with a nonadmitted insurer, a written report that shall be kept confidential, regarding the insurance. This report shall contain:

1. the name and address of the insured;

2. verification that the insured is a home state insured;

3. the identity of the insurer(s);

4. a description of the subject and location of the risk;

5. the amount of premium charged for the insurance;

6. a copy of the declarations page of the policy or a copy of the certificate or binder evidencing the placement of insurance;

7. other information that the commissioner may reasonably require. (Cal. Ins. Code §1763).

H. Independently Procured Insurance:

1. *Rules.* Every California home state insured who effects insurance to protect himself, herself, or itself against loss, damage, or liability with any nonadmitted insurer must pay a gross premium tax of 3 percent charged for the use of the state, less 3 percent

of returned premiums that were subject to the tax received by reason of cancellation or reduction of premium.

If during any calendar quarter 3 percent of the returned premiums received that were subject to the tax imposed by this part exceed 3 percent of the gross premiums paid or to be paid by that person on contracts that took effect or were renewed in that calendar quarter, then that person may either carry forward the excess to a succeeding calendar quarter and apply it as a credit against the 3 percent of gross premiums paid or to be paid by that person in the succeeding calendar quarter, or the person may elect to receive, and be paid a refund equal to the amount of taxes paid by the person on the excess of returned premiums received over gross premiums paid or to be paid. (Cal. Rev. & Tax Code §13210(a)).

California home state insureds subject to the tax on returned premiums must file a return on or before the first day of the third month following the close of the calendar quarter during which a taxable insurance contract took effect or was renewed. A penalty of 10 percent of the amount of the payment due will be imposed upon any person who fails to make the necessary payment within the time period. (Cal. Rev. & Tax Code §13220).

2. *Industrial Insured Exemption.* An industrial insured is an insured in California who does all of the following:

    a. Employs at least twenty-five employees on average during the prior twelve months; and

    b. Has aggregate annual premiums for insurance for all risks other than workers compensation and health coverage totaling no less than $25,000; or

    c. Obtains insurance through the services of a full-time employee acting as an insurance manager or a continuously retained insurance consultant. A "continuously retained insurance consultant" does not include:

        (i) Any agent or broker through whom the insurance is being placed.
        (ii) Any subagent or subproducer involved in the transaction.
        (iii) Any agent or broker which is a business organization employing or contracting with any person mentioned in clauses (i) and (ii). Industrial insureds are exempt from the requirement to sign the disclosure form set forth in Cal. Ins. Code § 1764.1.The surplus lines broker shall be responsible to ensure that the applicant is an industrial insured. (Cal. Ins. Code §1764.1(c)).

NRRA Implementation

I. Compact: California has not entered into a compact at this point.

J. Definitions:

1. "Home State" means any of the following with respect to an insured or applicant, except as provided in paragraphs 2 and 4:

   a. The state in which the insured maintains its principal place of business or, in the case of an individual, the individual's principal residence.

   b. If 100 percent of the insured risk is located outside the state referred to in subparagraph (a), the state to which the greatest percentage of the insured's taxable premium for that insurance contract is allocated.

2. "Principal Place of Business" means, with respect to subparagraph (a) of paragraph 1 determining the home state of the insured:

   a. The state where the insured maintains its headquarters and where the insured's high-level officers direct, control, and coordinate the business activities;

   b. If the insured's high-level officers direct, control, and coordinate the business activities in more than one state, the state in which the greatest percentage of the insured's taxable premium for that insurance contract is allocated; or

   c. If the insured maintains its headquarters or the insured's high-level officers direct, control, and coordinate the business activities outside any state, the state to which the greatest percentage of the insured's taxable premium for that insurance contract is allocated.

3. "Principal Residence" means, with respect to determining the home state of the insured:

   a. The state where the insured resides for the greatest number of days during a calendar year; or

   b. If the insured's principal residence is located outside any state, the state to which the greatest percentage of the insured's taxable premium for that insurance contract is allocated.

4. "Affiliated Groups". If more than one insured from an affiliated group are named insureds on a single nonadmitted insurance contract, the term "home state" means the

home state, as determined pursuant to subparagraph 1(a) of this subdivision, of the member of the affiliated group that has the largest percentage of premium attributed to it under such insurance contract. (Cal. Ins. Code § 1760.1(e)(4)).

The surplus lines broker is responsible for determining whether an applicant for nonadmitted insurance is a California home state insured. A surplus lines broker who reasonably relies on information provided in good faith by the applicant, whether directly or through the producer, is deemed to be in compliance with this requirement. (Cal. Ins. Code §1760.2).

K. **Statutory References:** Cal. Ins. Code §§ 1760.1, -.2, -.5; 1763; 1764.1, -.3; 1765; 1765.1; 1773; 1774; 1775.5; 1780.56. Cal. Rev. & Tax Code §§ 13210; 13220.

Insurance.ca.gov/0200-industry/

COLORADO

A. Resident Licensing: A resident individual applying for a surplus lines license shall pass a written examination. Find more information at https://www.pearsonvue.com/co/insurance/ or call 1-800-274-2616. (There is no prelicensing class requirement for a surplus lines license). The examination shall reasonably test the individual applicant's minimum acceptable level of competence as to the particular line or lines of authority for which the individual applicant seeks qualification, unless an individual applicant has been licensed as an insurance producer for the same line or lines of authority in another state within the twelve months immediately preceding the date of receipt of application. There shall be a separate portion of the examination required for each line of insurance which the applicant proposes to transact under the license. (C.R.S. § 10-2-402). Exam fee: fee for licensing examination at test center is $41 and $31 via OnVUE. Fee is due at time of reservation. Fees are not accepted at the test center. To change or cancel a reservation call (800) 274-2616 at least forty-eight hours prior to the exam or you will forfeit any chance of a refund. After you have passed the exam go to www.Sircon.com/Colorado. The authority to write surplus lines expires on the licensee's birthday, as part of the producer license. Fees: New, $144 and renewal, $134. (Candidate Handbook, p. 13, available at https://home.pearsonvue.com/getattachment/9df8c6db-f2e3-4d14-a674-f07ba560388c/Colorado%20Division%20of%20Insurance%20Licensing%20Candidate%20Handbook.aspx).

B. Nonresident Licensing: Nonresidents may be licensed for surplus lines in Colorado. Any person holding a nonresident surplus lines license, or the equivalent issued by another state or territory that offers Colorado surplus lines producers a nonresident license on a reciprocal basis can be licensed as a surplus lines producer so long as the resident producer conducts business in accordance with the provisions of Colorado's statutes and the resident or nonresident surplus lines producer promptly remits the taxes required by C.R.S. §10-5-111. They must produce a letter showing that they are authorized to sell surplus lines in their home state. The nonresident must maintain a license in the home state in good standing. In order to hold a Colorado surplus lines license, the nonresident must also secure a nonresident producer license. (C.R.S. § 10-2-502). If you hold a valid surplus lines license in another state, go to: http://www.Sircon.com/Colorado to apply for a Colorado license. Fees: New $294 and renewal, $284. A $6.18 nonrefundable NIPR transaction fee will be charged for each nonresident license, state and license type to which you apply.

C. Diligent Effort: A diligent effort must be made to procure coverage with an admitted insurer before placing coverage with an approved nonadmitted insurer. Due diligence shall be satisfied by documentation prepared by the producer, office of the producer or broker. The documentation must demonstrate that the coverage required was not procurable after a comprehensive search was made from a minimum of three admitted insurers authorized to and currently transacting that line of business in this state. If there are fewer than three admitted insurers in this state which are authorized and currently transacting the line of business needed, such diligent effort shall be met by searching this lesser market. A written record documenting diligent search efforts shall be maintained by the broker or producer for a period of not less than three years from the effective date of the coverage. The broker may rely upon representations made by a producer with regard to search efforts made by the producer. The determination of placement and evidence of diligent search efforts must be made each policy period prior to placement of coverage with an approved nonadmitted insurer. (3 CCR 702-2:2-4-1). Diligent search forms are available on the Surplus Lines Association of Colorado website at https://colosla.org/wp-content/uploads/2013/03/Diligent-Effort-Affidavit-10-25-2016-2-fillable.docx.

Commercial Purchaser Exemption. The diligent effort requirements do not apply to transactions with exempt commercial policyholders, as defined pursuant to C.R.S. §10-4-401(3)(b) excluding purchasers of title insurance. (C.R.S. § 10-4-1402).

D. Tax: 3 percent. On or before the first day of March of each year, each surplus lines broker shall remit to the Division of Insurance a tax of 3 percent on the net premiums, including fees paid by the insured. Fees include broker fees charged in lieu of, or in addition to commissions but do not include sums collected to cover federal and other state taxes and examination fees. (C.R.S. §§10-5-111.5 and 10-6-128). Effective August 20, 2014 the Division of Insurance has rules that risks or exposures located on Indian reservations are not subject to surplus lines tax. This applies to all transactions, including endorsements that are effective after this date.

The commissioner may participate in tax-sharing agreements to collect and disburse the entire amount of tax payable at a rate of 3 percent on the net premiums, if the purposes of the tax-sharing agreement are limited to:

1. Facilitating the payment and allocation of premium taxes on nonadmitted insurance for multi-state risks among states participating in the agreement.

2. Adopting uniform requirements, forms, and procedures that facilitate the reporting, payment, collection, and allocation of premium taxes for nonadmitted insurance for multi-state risks.

3. Coordinating the reporting of premium taxes and transaction data of multi-state risks among the states participating in the agreement.

4. Establishing a mechanism to facilitate the receipt and distribution of premium taxes and transaction data-related to nonadmitted insurance of multi-state risks. (C.R.S. § 10-5-111.5).

The policy's premium tax will be based upon the Home State of the insured. If an insured has a Home state status and exposures in Colorado 100 percent of the tax will be paid to Colorado. If an insured has a home state of Colorado but no exposures in the state no tax will be paid. If the insured has a home state elsewhere but without exposures in that state the majority of exposures are located in Colorado 100 percent of the tax will be paid to Colorado. The surplus lines tax is applicable to any fees levied by the insurer and/or surplus lines broker. The monthly and annual filings are both required to be filed online with the Colorado Division of Insurance Surplus Lines Tax System. (C.R.S. §10-5-111).

Note: Any fees charged by a broker that are the subject of a contract independent of an insurance policy and not appearing on the policy are not subject to surplus lines tax.

E. **Stamping Fee:** None. No stamping fee is currently in force.

F. **Surplus Lines Association:** Jon Wethey, Executive Director. Surplus Lines Association of Colorado, mailing address: P.O. Box 799, Golden, CO 80402-0799. Phone: (303) 681-4924. Website: www.colosla.org. Email: surplusline@earthlink.net.

G. **Other Requirements or Restrictions:** Placement of insurance with a nonadmitted insurer shall not be for the purpose of securing a lower premium rate than that which would be accepted by an admitted insurer unless the premium rate quoted by the admitted insurer is more than 10 percent higher than that quoted by the nonadmitted insurer.

Eligibility. No broker shall place any coverage with a nonadmitted insurer unless, at the time of placement, such nonadmitted insurer is an eligible nonadmitted insurer.

Notice. All surplus lines contracts must have initials or name of surplus lines broker and be stamped with the following message, found in C.R.S. §10-5-104:

> "This contract is delivered as surplus line coverage under the 'Nonadmitted Insurance Act'. The insurer issuing this contract is not licensed in Colorado but is an eligible nonadmitted insurer. There is no protection under the provisions of the 'Colorado Insurance Guaranty Association Act'." (3 CCR 702-2:2-4-1).

A policy issued by an insurer that is not eligible in Colorado must contain the following additional disclosure:

> "This policy is issued by an insurance company that is not regulated by the Colorado Division of Insurance. The insurance company may not provide claims service and may not be subject to service of process in Colorado. If the

> insurance company becomes insolvent, insureds or claimants will not be eligible for protection under Colorado insurance law." (3 CCR 702-2:2-4-1).

Claims-made policies must be endorsed as follows:

> "This policy is a claims-made policy which provides liability coverage only if a claim is made during the policy period or any applicable extended reporting period."

(C.R.S. §10-5-104; 3 CCR 702-2:2-4-1).

If an auto policy does not provide the basic complying policy coverages in C.R.S. §10-4-620, the following must appear on the policy:

> "This policy does not meet the statutory requirements of this State's financial responsibility laws. It does not provide liability coverage for bodily injury and property damage." (3 CCR 702-2:2-4-1).

The law is not applicable to reinsurance.

If the surplus lines broker charges a fee, the following disclosure must be given to the retail producer in writing. There is no requirement that it appear on the policy:

> "The cost of the insurance coverage provided herein includes a fee to a wholesale intermediary in addition to the premium charges." (3 CCR 702-1:1-2-9).

Reports. Each broker shall, no later than the fifteenth of each month for the prior month, submit a report to the Division of Insurance showing each policy written including those accepted from licensed producers. The report must include:

1. The name of the insured.
2. The line of business.
3. The name of the nonadmitted insurer.
4. The surplus lines premium.
5. The policy fees charged.
6. The surplus lines taxes due. (3 CCR 702-2:2-4:1).

A producer should file a $0 premium report if no transactions take place. Effective July 21, 2011, for an insured whose home state is not Colorado but the insurance policy covers risks or exposures located in Colorado, the broker should not include a surplus lines policy on their monthly report, unless:

1. The insured's home state is Colorado.

2. The insured's home state is not Colorado, but the insurance policy covers risks or exposures located in Colorado, and 100 percent of the insured risk is located outside the insured's home state, and the greatest percentage of the taxable premium for that policy is payable to Colorado. (per https://drive.google.com/file/d/0B7EeY5Lrg3_qVHBaQ3VIUW5ZY1E/view?resourcekey=0-kiu2IViWX0axiGZmxC4QrQ).

H. Independently Procured Insurance:

1. *Rules.* Colorado allows transactions involving contracts of insurance independently procured through negotiations occurring entirely outside of the state which are reported and on which a premium tax of 2.25 percent is paid annually, before March 1, in the next succeeding the calendar year in which the insurance was effectuated, continued, or renewed of the net premiums charged for such insurance. Late tax includes a 25 percent penalty. (C.R.S. §§ 10-3-903, and -909).

2. *Industrial Insured Exemption.* To qualify as an industrial insured, the company must:

   a. Utilize a full-time employee acting as an insurance manager or buyer; or the services of a qualified insurance consultant who does not receive a commission for placing the risk.

   b. Have aggregate annual premiums for insurance on all risks totaling at least $100,000.

   c. Have at least 100 full-time employees. (C.R.S. §10-3-910).

NRRA Implementation

House Bill 1215, which was signed into law in April 2012, incorporated several provisions of the NRRA. http://www.legispeak.com/bill/2012/hb12-1215.

I. Compact: None.

J. Home State Definition: NRRA definition.

K. Statutory References: C.R.S. §§ 10-2-402; 10-2-502; 20-3-903, -909, -910; 10-4-620, -1402;; 10-4-10, -111, -111.5; 10-6-128. 3 CRR 702-1:1-2-9; 702-2:2-4-1. Candidate Handbook p. 13. 0

CONNECTICUT

A. **Resident Licensing:** Both individuals and business entities applying for a surplus lines broker license must be currently licensed and in good standing as a Connecticut property and casualty producer. There is an examination requirement for individuals. If the surplus lines individual broker will be transacting surplus lines business through or for a business entity, that business entity must also hold a surplus lines license. Likewise, a business entity licensed for surplus lines must designate at least one individual holding a Connecticut surplus lines license who is responsible for the entity's compliance with the insurance laws and rules of Connecticut. Initial and reinstatement fees are $675. The renewal fee is $625. Surplus lines licenses expire September 30 of even numbered years. Individuals and business entities may apply online at cidonline.ct.gov/lit/CTLicensingTask.jsp or www.nipr.com. (Conn. Gen. Stat. §§ 38a-11 and 38a-794).

   Only the insured's home state may require a surplus lines broker to be licensed to sell, solicit or negotiate nonadmitted insurance with respect to a particular placement. If Connecticut is the insured's home state, the surplus lines broker must be licensed in Connecticut. The NRRA provides that Connecticut may not collect licensing fees for surplus lines brokers as of July 12, 2012, unless Connecticut participates in the NAIC's national insurance producer database or any other equivalent uniform national database. (15 U.S.C. 8203). Connecticut participates in the National Insurance Producer Registry (NIPR), which provides such a database, thus satisfying the NRRA requirement. (Conn. Gen. Stat. §§ 38a-277 and 38a-743).

B. **Nonresident Licensing:** Both nonresident individuals and nonresident business entities applying for a surplus lines license must be similarly licensed in good standing in the home state or any other state. It is not a requirement to hold an underlying Connecticut property and casualty producer license. (Conn. Gen. Stat. § 38a-794).

C. **Diligent Effort:** Diligent effort is defined as declination by three licensed insurers which customarily write the kind of business requested, or the line or class of business is not generally available as established by the insurance commissioner. The records supporting the three declinations must be maintained by the broker throughout the policy period and must include: the specific reason, the date declined, and the name and title of the insurance company underwriter. (Conn. Gen. Stat. §38a-741).

   Commercial Purchaser Exemption. On or after July 21, 2011, the NRRA provides that a surplus lines broker seeking to procure or place nonadmitted insurance on behalf of an "exempt commercial purchaser" is not required to perform a diligent search if:

1. The broker has disclosed to the exempt commercial purchaser that insurance may or may not be available from the admitted market that may provide greater protection with more regulatory oversight.

2. The exempt commercial purchaser has subsequently requested in writing for the broker to procure or place such insurance from a nonadmitted insurer.

Connecticut has adopted the NRRA definition of "exempt commercial purchaser." (Conn. Gen. Stat. § 38a-271(b)(6)).

Exportable List. The Insurance Department maintains a list of those lines of insurance or their components for which coverages are believed by the commissioner to be generally unavailable from licensed insurers, commonly known as "the exportable list." The exportable list is found on the Insurance Department Website at the following address: https://portal.ct.gov/CID/Financial-Division/Exportable-List. (Conn. Gen. Stat. § 38a-741).

Brokers' Statements. When any insurance policy is procured under the authority of a surplus lines broker for a line of insurance or its component that does not appear on the exportable list, both the surplus lines broker and the insured are to execute a statement setting forth facts showing that the surplus lines broker and insured were unable, after diligent effort, to procure the full amount of insurance necessary to protect the interests of the insured from any authorized insurer or insurers. In the event that a portion of the coverage is obtained from an authorized insurer, such a statement is further required to show that the portion of insurance procured from unauthorized insurer(s) is excess over that procured from authorized insurer(s). Such licensee shall file such statements with the commissioner with the quarterly tax filing. (Conn. Gen. Stat. § 38a-741(b)(1)).

D. Tax: Four percent of gross premiums, less returns, payable quarterly. (Conn. Gen. Stat. §38a-743). Insurance Department shall impose interest payments (minimum of 1 percent per month late) and 10 percent penalty of the whole or such part of the principal of the premium tax, which is unpaid, for delinquent tax payments. Surplus lines brokers may charge service fees in accordance with Regs., Conn. State Agencies §§ 38a-707-1 and 38a-707-9; the surplus lines tax is not applicable to such fees. All licensees (individuals and business entities) are required to file a tax return electronically via OPTins (www.optins.org). Tax returns must be posted on or before the quarterly due date. Due dates are: May 15, August 15, November 15, and February 15. (https://portal.ct.gov/CID/Licensing---Producers/Surplus-Lines-Broker-FAQs--Individual-and-Business-Entities).

Late Payment Penalty. There is a penalty of 10 percent of the premium tax due and interest of 1 percent of the penalty per month or fraction of a month. The department will invoice licensees via OPTins for penalty and interest assessments. (Conn. Gen. Stat. §38a-743).

E. Stamping Fee: None. Connecticut does not have a stamping office.

F. Surplus Lines Association: Julie Sonier, New England Surplus Lines Assn, Inc., c/o A.I.I. Insurance Brokerage, P.O. Box 1139, East Douglas, MA 01516. Phone: 508-476-1990 Fax: 508-476-1991. Email: jsonier@agencyint.com.

G. Other Requirements or Restrictions: Usage of surplus lines market which may be obtained through a residual marketing mechanism such as assigned risk auto or fair plan property risks, to obtain better rates or for workers compensation is prohibited. Eligible surplus lines insurers are included on the Connecticut Insurance Department's ("CID") list of Licensed Insurance Companies, Approved Reinsurers and Surplus Lines Insurers found on the CID website at www.ct.gov/cid. Service fees may not be charged without a written memorandum, signed by the party to be charged and specifying and clearly defining the premium applicable to the policy and the amount of any service fees assessed. A producer and surplus lines broker involved in the same transaction may each charge a flat fee per policy for business placed in the surplus lines market, provided that the sum of the fee charged shall not exceed $250 in the aggregate. In the alternative, such producer and surplus lines broker may charge a fee of up to 5 percent of the applicable premium, not to exceed $500 in the aggregate. Service fees are not permitted for renewals handled in the usual and customary manner, except that such fees may be charged on renewal business where a reunderwriting of the risk is necessary. (Regs., Conn. State Agencies § 38a-707-7).

Record. Each licensee must keep a complete and separate record of all policies procured from surplus lines insurers, which must show:

1. The exact amount of each kind of insurance permitted, and that has been procured for each insured.
2. The gross premiums charged by the insurers for each kind of insurance permitted.
3. The amount of each kind of premiums of insurance which were returned to each insured.
4. The name of the insurer or insurers which issued each policy.
5. The effective dates of the policies.
6. The terms of the policies. (Conn. Gen. Stat. § 38a-742).

Annual Statements. Each surplus lines insurer must file an annual statement with the department, and this includes both domiciled and nondomiciled companies. All eligible surplus lines insurers will be required to report their financial condition on a quarterly basis. These reports are to include a breakdown of the company's Connecticut business showing premiums and losses by line. Quarterly filings are to be made as follows: period ending March 31 to be filed on or before May 15; period ending June 30 to be filed on or before August 15; period ending September 30 to be filed on or before November 15. (Conn. Gen. Stat. § 38a-743). A Connecticut-licensed property/casualty producer must submit surplus lines business through a Connecticut-licensed surplus lines broker.

The cover of the policy shall bear the following in no less than twelve point, boldface type in capital letters:

NOTICE

"THIS IS A SURPLUS LINES POLICY AND IS NOT PROTECTED BY THE CONNECTICUT INSURANCE GUARANTY ASSOCIATION OR SUBJECT TO REVIEW BY THE CONNECTICUT INSURANCE DEPARTMENT. IT IS IMPORTANT THAT YOU READ AND UNDERSTAND THIS POLICY." (Conn. Gen. Stat. §38a-745).

H. Independently Procured Insurance:

1. *Rules.* Industrial insureds may procure their own insurance through a surplus lines carrier. They must report the transaction to the Commissioner of Revenue Services within sixty days. The insured is responsible for paying the tax, currently 4 percent of gross premiums. The term "premium" includes all premiums, membership fees, assessments, dues and any other consideration for insurance. After January 1, 2012, the insured must pay quarterly premium taxes: on or before May 15 for the period from January 1 to March 31; on or before August 15 for the period from April 1 to June 30; on or before November 15 for the period from July 1 to September 20; and on or before February 15 for the period from October 1 to December 31. The late payment penalty is 10 percent and interest of 1 percent per month or fraction of such month from the date the tax was due to the date paid. (Conn. Gen. Stat. §38a-277).

2. *Industrial Insured Exemption.* An industrial insured may procure insurance by the use of the services of a full-time employee acting as an insurance manager or buyer, or the services of a regularly and continuously retained qualified insurance consultant; and whose aggregate annual premiums for insurance, excluding life, accident and health insurance, total at least $50,000 in the aggregate. (Conn. Gen. Stat. § 38a-271(b)(6)).

NRRA Implementation

I. Compact: None. Connecticut withdrew from NIMA in May, 2012.

J. Definitions:

1. *Home State.* Connecticut is the insured's home state if the insured maintains its principal place of business here; or in the case of an individual, the individual's principal residence is Connecticut. If Connecticut is considered the insured's home state, only Connecticut's requirements regarding the placement of such business will apply. If 100 percent of the insured risk is located outside of Connecticut, then the insured's home state is the state to which the greatest percentage of the insured's taxable premium for that insurance contract is allocated. (Conn. Gen. Stat. § 38a-277).

K. Statutory References: Conn. Gen. Stat. §§ 38a-11, 271, 277, 741 to 743, 745, 792. Regs., Conn. State Agencies §§ 38a-707-1, 7, 9.

L. Web References: https://portal.ct.gov/CID/Licensing---Producers/Surplus-Lines-Broker-FAQs--Individual-and-Business-Entities.

DELAWARE

A. **Resident Licensing:** Residents licensed as producers may be licensed to place insurance with unauthorized insurers that meet the eligibility requirements of the Nonadmitted and Reinsurance Reform Act of 2010 (NRRA). Any individual, while licensed in Delaware as a resident or nonresident producer, who is deemed by the commissioner to be competent and trustworthy with respect to the handling of surplus lines may be licensed as a surplus lines broker. Applications to be made to the Commissioner on a form prescribed by the same. (18 Del. C. §1920). Initial fee: $150, renewal: $150. Surplus lines brokers must satisfy the Delaware continuing education requirement for biennial license continuation due by February 28 in even numbered years. Any producer licensed in Delaware may place business with a surplus lines broker and receive commission. (18 Del. C. §§ 701, 1922).

B. **Nonresident Licensing:** Nonresidents may be licensed for this purpose, on a reciprocal basis. Initial fee: $250. Renewal fee: $200. Nonresident licenses renew biennially by February 28 of odd numbered years. Non-resident adjusters whose home states do not have examination requirements for adjusters shall be required to satisfy this State's examination requirements prior to licensure. (18 Del. C. §§ 701, 1708).

C. **Diligent Effort:** Each broker is responsible for ensuring a diligent effort among insurers authorized to transact and write the particular type of insurance in Delaware before obtaining a policy from a nonadmitted insurer for a home-state insured. A diligent search may only be performed by a surplus lines broker licensed in Delaware who also holds a property and casualty producer license. (18 Del. C. § 1912(c)).

Surplus lines broker must retain Statement of Diligent Effort, (Form SL-1923) and file Notice of Insurance Transaction (Form SL-1905) electronically via email attachment within thirty days after effective date for all lines, except those designated by commissioner as recognized surplus lines. At this time the commissioner has not so declared any lines. Due to changes in the surplus lines law, all surplus lines brokers should watch the Department's Website at www.delawareinsurance.gov for updates of required filings. Form SL-1923 and Form SL-1905 are available at insurance.delaware.gov/information/surpluslines/#SL_forms.

Commercial Purchaser Exemption. A surplus lines broker seeking to procure or place nonadmitted insurance in Delaware for an exempt commercial purchaser whose home state is this state is not to be required to satisfy any requirement to make a diligent effort to determine whether the full amount or type of insurance sought by such exempt commercial purchaser can be obtained from admitted insurers if both:

1. The broker procuring or placing the surplus lines insurance has disclosed to the exempt commercial purchaser that such insurance may or may not be available from the admitted market that may provide greater protection with more regulatory oversight.

2. The exempt commercial purchaser has subsequently requested in writing the broker to procure or place such insurance from a nonadmitted insurer.

An exempt commercial purchaser is any person purchasing commercial insurance who, at the time of placement, meets the following requirements:

1. The person employs or retains a qualified risk manager to negotiate insurance coverage.

2. The person has paid aggregate nationwide commercial property and casualty insurance premiums in excess of $100,000 in the immediately preceding twelve months.

3. The person meets at least one of the following criteria:

   a. The person possesses a net worth in excess of $20 million; as adjusted.

   b. The person generates annual revenues in excess of $50 million; as adjusted.

   c. The person employs more than 500 full-time or full-time equivalent employees per individual insured or is a member of an affiliated group employing more than 1,000 employees in the aggregate.

   d. The person is a not-for-profit organization or public entity generating annual budgeted expenditures of at least $30 million; as adjusted.

   e. The person is a municipality with a population in excess of 50,000 persons.

Note: Effective January 1, 2016, and each fifth January 1 occurring thereafter, the amounts in paragraphs 3(a), (b), and (d), above, shall be adjusted to reflect the percentage change for such five year period in the Consumer Price Index for All Urban Consumers published by the Bureau of Labor Statistics of the Department of Labor. (18 Del. C. § 1914).

D. Tax: Three percent. Every surplus lines broker must collect and pay to the state treasurer through the commissioner a 3 percent tax on the gross premiums charged, less any return premiums and exclusive of sum collected to cover federal and state taxes and examination fees, for insurance placed or procured under his or her surplus lines license in which Delaware is the home state of the insured. Fees associated with the policy are considered part of the premium and are taxable. The premium tax is due annually on or before March 1. (18 Del. C. § 1925).

If any broker fails to file his or her annual statement or fails to remit the tax prior to or on the date the tax is due, he or she will be liable for a fine of $25 for each day of delinquency commencing with the first day after the tax is due. (18 Del. C. § 1927(a)).

Multi-State Premium Tax Allocation. If a surplus lines policy procured through a surplus lines broker covers properties, risks, or exposures only partially located or to be performed in Delaware, but Delaware is the home state of the insured, all premium for the policy will be considered written on properties, risks, or exposures located, or to be performed in Delaware. (18 Del. C. § 1925(c)).

Premium Defined. The term "premium tax" means, with respect to surplus lines, any tax, fee, assessment, or other charge imposed by a government entity directly or indirectly based on any payment made as consideration for an insurance contract for such insurance, including premium deposits, assessments, registration fees, and any other compensation given in consideration for a contract of insurance. (18 Del. C. § 1904(17)).

E. **Stamping Fee:** None. Delaware has no stamping office.

F. **Surplus Lines Association:** None.

G. **Other Requirements or Restrictions:**

Exclusions. License is for all lines except life, health, reinsurance, wet marine and transportation insurance; insurance on subjects located, resident or to be performed wholly outside Delaware or on vehicles or aircraft owned and principally garaged outside of Delaware; insurance on operations of railroads engaged in transportation in interstate commerce and their property used in such operations; insurance of aircraft owned or operated by manufacturers of aircraft or of aircraft operated in commercial interstate flight or cargo of such aircraft or against liability, other than worker's compensation and employer's liability, arising out of the ownership, maintenance or use of such aircraft; and transactions for which a certificate of authority to do business is not required of an insurer under the insurance laws of this State. (18 Del. C. § 1905).

Eligibility. Surplus lines may not be used in order to procure advantageous rate or terms. The insurance department provides the "Registered Eligible Nonadmitted Insurers List" for informational purposes only. Exclusive use of the companies on this list is no longer mandatory. It is a list of companies that have presented the commissioner with evidence of their qualifications as an eligible nonadmitted insurer under the Nonadmitted and

Reinsurance Act of 2010 (NRRA) requirements and have voluntarily registered with the department to be included on the list. The list is not all-inclusive. Any nonadmitted insurer that meets the eligibility standards set forth in the NRRA and Title 18 Delaware Code, Chapter 19, is eligible to transact insurance in this state even if they are not included in this listing.

A broker shall not knowingly place surplus lines insurance with an insurer that is unsound financially or that does not meet the eligibility requirements. (18 Del. C. § 1913(b)).

The commissioner may consider a surplus lines insurer to be eligible if the nonadmitted insurer:

1. Is a United States domestic insurer with capital and surplus or its equivalent under the laws of its domiciliary jurisdiction which equals the greater of:

    a. The minimum capital and surplus requirements under the law of this state; or

    b. $15 million.

    The requirements of paragraph (1)(a) may be satisfied if an insurer possesses less than the minimum capital and surplus upon an affirmative finding of acceptability by the commissioner. The finding may be based on such factors as: quality of management; capital and surplus of any parent company; company underwriting profit and investment income trends; market availability; and company record and reputation within the industry. The commissioner may not make an affirmative finding of acceptability when the nonadmitted insurer's capital and surplus is less than $4.5 million.

2. Is listed on the Quarterly Listing of Alien Insurers maintained by the International Insurers Department of the NAIC if the insurer is not domiciled in the United States or its territories. (18 Del. C. § 1931(a)).

NOTICE

Every surplus lines contract shall have stamped upon it, initialed by or bearing the name of the surplus line broker who procured it, the following:

> "This insurance contract is issued pursuant to the Delaware Insurance Laws by an insurer neither licensed by nor under the jurisdiction of the Delaware Insurance Department. This insurer does not participate in insurance guaranty funds created by state law. In the event of the insolvency of the surplus lines insurer, losses will not be paid by the state insurance guaranty fund." (18 Del. C. § 1917(b)).

Courtesy filing of taxes and certificates of nonavailability are not allowed in Delaware.

Evidence of Coverage. Upon placing a surplus lines coverage for a home state insured, the broker must promptly issue and deliver to the insured evidence of the insurance consisting either of the policy as issued by the insurer or, if such policy is not then available, the surplus line brokers certificate. Such a certificate must be executed by the broker and must show the name and license number of the individual surplus lines broker, the description and location of the subject of the insurance, coverage, conditions and term of the insurance, the premium and rate charged, taxes collected from the insured, and the name and address of the insured and insurer. If the risk is assumed by more than one insurer, the certificate must state the name and address and proportion of the entire risk assumed by each such insurer. (18 Del. C. § 1916(a)).

Records. Each broker must keep in his or her office a full and true record of each surplus lines coverage procured for a home state insured, including a copy of each daily report, if any, a copy of each certificate of insurance issued, and such of the following items as may be applicable:

1. Verification that the insured is a Delaware home state insured.

2. Whether or not a policy is a single-state or multi-state policy.

3. Verification that a commercial insured qualifies under 18 Del. C. § 1914.

4. Amount of the insurance.

5. Gross premium charged.

6. Return premium paid, if any.

7. Rate of premium charged upon the several items of property.

8. Effective date of the contract and the terms thereof.

9. Name and address of each insurer on the direct risk and the proportion of the entire risk assumed by such insurer if less than the entire risk.

10. Name and address of the insured.

11. Brief general description of the property or risk insured and where located or to be performed.

12. A tax allocation spreadsheet detailing the portion of premium attributable to properties, risks, or exposures located in each state.

13. Other information as required by the Commissioner.

14. A written statement on a form prescribed by the commissioner as to the diligent effort to place the coverage with admitted insurers under 18 Del. C. §1912 and the result of that effort. The written statement must be open to public inspection and must affirm that the insured was expressly advised in writing prior to placement of the insurance that:

    a. The surplus lines insurer with whom the insurance was to be placed is not licensed in Delaware and is not subject to Delaware's supervision; and

    b. In the event of the insolvency of the surplus lines insurer, losses will not be paid by the State Insurance Guaranty Fund. The broker's record must be open to examination at all times within five years after issuance of the coverage to which it relates. (18 Del. C. § 1923).

Annual Statements. Licensed surplus lines brokers must file an annual statement with the Commissioner of surplus lines business written. Annual reports are required even if no business was written. Unless the commissioner determines that more frequent reporting is necessary, each broker shall on or before March 1 of each year file with the commissioner a statement verified by the broker of all surplus lines insurance transacted by him or her during the preceding calendar year. (18 Del. C. § 1924).

H. Independently Procured Insurance:

1. *Rules.* Any person whose home state is Delaware may directly procure or directly renew insurance with a nonadmitted insurer without the involvement of a surplus lines licensee, on a risk located or to be performed, in whole or in part, in Delaware.

   Each insured whose home state is Delaware that independently procures or continues or renews insurance with a nonadmitted insurer on properties, risks, or exposures located or to be performed in whole or in part in Delaware, other than insurance procured through a surplus lines broker, is subject to 2 percent tax on the gross premiums charged.

   On or before March 1 each year, the insured that independently procures insurance must file a written report with the commissioner, upon forms prescribed by the commissioner, showing the name and address of the insured or insured's, name and address of the insurer, the subject of the insurance, a general description of the coverage, the amount of premium currently charged, and additional pertinent information reasonably requested by the commissioner.

At the time of filing the report the insured shall pay to the state treasurer through the commissioner a 3 percent tax on the gross premiums charged. (18 Del. C. § 1926).

If any insured who independently procured insurance fails to file the report and remit the tax prior to or on the date the tax is due, he or she will be liable for a fine of $25 for each day of delinquency commencing with the first day after the tax is due. (18 Del. C. § 1927).

2. *Industrial Insured Exemption*. Delaware defines an "industrial insured" as an insured:

   a. Who procures the insurance of any risk or risks by use of the services of a full-time employee acting as an insurance manager or buyer.

   b. Whose aggregate annual premiums for insurance on all risks total at least $25,000.

   c. Who has at least twenty-five full-time employees.

   (18 Del. C. § 6902(20)).

Note: The industrial insured exemption applies to rate and form filings only. Premiums for this coverage are not tax exempt.

NRRA Implementation

I. Compact: The commissioner is authorized to enter into an interstate cooperative agreement, reciprocal agreement, or compact, hereafter Agreement, for the purpose of carrying out the NRRA and to facilitate the collection, allocation, and disbursement of premium taxes attributable to the placement of nonadmitted insurance, to provide for uniform methods of allocation and reporting among nonadmitted insurance risk classifications, and share information among states relating to nonadmitted insurance premium taxes. (18 Del. C. § 1903(a)).

J. Definitions:

1. *Home State.* In general, except as provided under the definition of "Affiliated Groups" below, means, with respect to an insured:

   (a) The state in which an insured maintains its principal place of business or, in the case of an individual, the individuals principal residence.

(b) If 100 percent of the insured risk is located outside of Delaware, the state to which the greatest percentage of the insured's taxable premium for that insurance contract is allocated. (18 Del. C. § 1904(9)(a))

2. *Affiliated Groups.* If more than one insured from an affiliated group are named insured's on a single nonadmitted insurance contract, the term home state means the home state, as determined pursuant to the definition above, of the member of the affiliated group that has the largest percentage of premium attributed to it under such insurance contract. (18 Del. C. § 1904(9)(b)).

   The surplus lines broker is responsible for determining whether an applicant for nonadmitted insurance is a Delaware home state insured. A surplus lines broker who reasonably relies on information provided in good faith by the applicant, whether directly or through the producer, shall be deemed to be in compliance with this requirement. A broker with reasonable doubt as to this is under duty to inform the Commissioner and immediately cease placing business with this insurer. (18 Del. C. § 1913).

K. Statutory References: 18 Del. C. §§ 701; 1708; 1903 to 1905; 1912 to 1914; 1916, 1917; 1920; 1922 to 1927; 1931; 6902.

DISTRICT OF COLUMBIA

A. **Resident and Nonresident Licensing:** Any person may be licensed as a surplus lines insurance producer to procure policies from companies which are not authorized to do business in the District of Columbia. An individual cannot be issued a license unless the person holds, or is simultaneously issued, a license in the property or casualty line of insurance. (D.C. Code § 31-1131.07). The license to procure lines in unauthorized companies expires biennially on April 30; license fee: $200. (D.C. Code § 31-4302).

B. **Diligent Effort:** Any person licensed as a surplus lines insurance producer may procure policies from companies which are not authorized to do business in the District of Columbia where such person is, after diligent effort, unable to procure policies to cover the kind or kinds of business required from companies duly authorized to transact business in the District of Columbia.

Commercial Purchaser Exemption. Surplus lines producers seeking to procure or place nonadmitted insurance on behalf of an "exempt commercial purchaser" are not required to perform a diligent search if:

1. The broker has disclosed to the exempt commercial purchaser that insurance may or may not be available from the admitted market that may provide greater protection with more regulatory oversight.

2. The exempt commercial purchaser has subsequently requested in writing for the broker to procure or place such insurance from a nonadmitted insurer. (15 USCS § 8205).

"Exempt Commercial Purchaser" means a person buying commercial insurance who, at the time of placement, satisfies the following:

(1) The person retains a qualified risk manager to negotiate insurance coverage.

(2) The person has paid aggregate, nationwide commercial property and casualty premiums greater than $100,000 in the immediately preceding year.

(3) The person satisfies at least one of the following:

(a) The person's net worth is greater than $20 million, as adjusted.

(b) The person generates annual revenues greater that $50 million, as adjusted.

(c) The person employs more than 500 full-time or equivalent employees per insured or is a member of an affiliated group employing more than 1,000 individuals in the aggregate.

(d) The person is a nonprofit organization generating annual budgeted expenditures greater than $30 million, as adjusted.

(e) The person is a municipality with a population greater than 50,000 individuals. (15 U.S.C. § 8206).

C. Tax: 2 percent. Each agent or broker licensed to procure policies from unauthorized companies is required to pay to the Collector of Taxes, through the commissioner, on February 1 and August 1 of each year, a sum equal to 2 percent of the amount of the gross premiums upon all kinds of policies procured by him during the immediately preceding six months' period ending December 31 and June 30, respectively, and, in default of such payment, the commissioner, through the Corporation Counsel, may bring suit to recover the same. The tax does not apply to fees levied by the producer. Agents and brokers engaged to procure insurance on behalf of the D.C. government are exempt from the two percent tax on gross premiums. (DC Code § 31-2502.40(a)). Additional instructions and forms can be found at disb.dc.gov/publication/surplus-lines-tax-form .Monthly affidavit and semi-annual premium tax filing instructions can be found at: http://disb.dc.gov/node/322362.

D. Stamping Fee: None. The District of Columbia does not have a stamping office.

E. Surplus Lines Association: None.

F. Other Requirements or Restrictions:

Eligibility. Surplus lines producers cannot procure policies from unauthorized companies whose standards of solvency and management do not meet the requirements necessary for the protection of the policyholders. Surplus lines producers cannot place with any unauthorized company any risk which could be placed with an authorized company except for abnormal provisions of the policy. Surplus lines producers cannot procure from an unauthorized company any policy which covers a risk of a class generally covered in the District by authorized companies and which authorized companies would cover at a rate not higher than that charged by authorized companies on other District risks of the same class. (DC Code §31-2502.40(b)).

Affidavits. Each agent or broker licensed to procure policies from unauthorized companies must execute and file with the department on or before the tenth day of each month an affidavit covering the transactions of the previous calendar month, setting forth:

1. The description and location of the insured property or risk, and the name of the insured.

2. The amount insured in the policy or contract.

3. The gross premiums charged thereon.

4. The name of the company whose policy or contract is issued, and the kind or kinds of business effected.

5. That said agent or broker after diligent effort was unable to procure the policies or contracts required to protect the property or risk described in the affidavit from companies duly authorized to transact business in the District. (DC Code §31-2502.40(a)).

   Surplus lines producers are not required to file an affidavit for those months in which no reportable transactions occurred. The Department of Insurance, Securities and Banking may impose a penalty or take other regulatory action against a surplus lines producer for failing to remit an affidavit within thirty days of a previous calendar month in which reportable transactions occurred.

Records. Each agent or broker so licensed to procure policies from unauthorized companies shall keep a separate account of the business transacted thereunder, which shall be open at all times to the inspection of the commissioner. (DC Code §31-2502.40(b)).

G. Independently Procured Insurance:

1. The District of Columbia has no provision for independently procured insurance.

2. The District of Columbia does not have an industrial insured exemption.

NRRA Implementation

H. Compact: The District of Columbia is not currently a part to a compact agreement.

I. Home State Definition: The NRRA home state definition applies to the District of Columbia: The District of Columbia is considered the home state if the insured maintains its principal place of business or, in the case of an individual, the individual's principal residence here. The District of Columbia's requirements regarding the placement of such business will apply if the District of Columbia is considered the home state. However, if 100 percent of the insured risk is located outside of the District, then the home state is the state to which the greatest percentage of the insured's taxable premium for that insurance contract is allocated. With respect to an affiliated group, if more than one insured from the affiliated group is a named insured on a single nonadmitted insurance contract, the home state is that of the member of the affiliated group that has the largest percentage of premium attributed to the member under the insurance contract. See the Nonadmitted and Reinsurance Reform Act of 2010 (NRRA), 15 U.S.C. § 8201, for more information.

J. **Surplus Lines Notice:** The insurance policy that you have purchased is being issued by an insurer that is not licensed by the District of Columbia, Department of Insurance Securities and Banking. It is issued by a nonadmitted carrier and is therefore not protected by the District of Columbia Insurance Guaranty Association. (per DISB, 7/16/2020)

K. **Statutory References:** D.C. Code §§ 31-1131.07, 2502.40, 4302. 15 U.S.C. §§ 8201, 8206.

FLORIDA

A. **Resident Licensing:** Applicants for a surplus lines license must be a natural person, at least eighteen years of age, be a United States citizen or legal alien who possesses a work authorization from the United States Bureau of Citizenship and Immigration Services, be a bona fide resident of Florida, and who must within four years prior to the application date meet the prelicensing education/experience requirements by fulfilling one of the following:

1. A minimum of one year's experience working for a licensed and appointed Florida surplus lines agent.

2. Complete sixty class hours in surplus and excess lines from a course approved by the Department.

3. Obtain and submit a Letter of Clearance indicating that applicant held a surplus lines or property and casualty line of authority license for at least one year in applicant's previous home state and apply for a Florida surplus lines license within ninety days of requesting the Letter of Clearance. (Fla. Stat. Ann. § 626.927).

   All applicants must successfully pass a written examination given by the Florida Department, unless exempted by §626.221. (Fla. Stat. Ann. §626.221).

   The applicant must be licensed and appointed as a Florida resident general lines (property, casualty, surety, marine, health and miscellaneous lines, Type & Class: 2-20) insurance agent.

Note: As of October 1, 2012, surplus lines agents are no longer required to file a Surplus Lines Agent Bond. (2012 Fla. Sess. Law Serv. Ch. 2012-209, House Bill No. 725) and (Fla. Stat. Ann. §626.927).

The application for licensure shall be made through the Florida Department of Financial Services Website at the online "MyProfile" portal, which may be accessed at: https://dice.fldfs.com/public/pb_index.aspx.

Applicants are required to submit their fingerprints prior to licensure. For resident applicants, fingerprints must be taken by LiveScan method at one of the Department's fingerprint sites. The fingerprinting fee is $45.80 (plus local Florida county sales tax). Fingerprinting is completed through the vendor IdentoGO by Idemia. You can register, find locations, and pay for fingerprinting by visiting https://fl.ibtfingerprint.com/.

Florida surplus lines agents must appoint themselves after getting licensed. To do this, access the Department's Website and then follow the instructions below:

1. Log in to your MyProfile account.

2. Select the "Access eAppoint" link.

3. If a new user, applicant must first register by selecting "Register to become an appointing entity".

4. Then, select "New Appointment" in the eAppoint Workbench. Once "New Appointment" has been selected, follow the on screen instructions to complete your self-appointment.

The original and renewal appointment fee is $150. A 3 percent convenience fee applies if paying with a credit card. Surplus lines agent's appointments are subject to renewal in the agent's birth month. All initial appointments are valid for a period of twenty-four months in order to bring the appointment date up to the next renewal birth month. Once the appointment has been renewed, unless cancelled by the agent, the appointment is subject to renewal thereafter every twenty-four months. A surplus lines agent must be licensed and appointed as a general lines agent. Any general lines agent licensed in Florida may place business through licensed and appointed surplus lines agents and receive a commission. (Fla. Stat. Ann. §§626.381, 624.501(11) and 626.927).

Note the following regarding appointments:

1. *Invalid Address.* If a licensee/appointee has an invalid address on file with the Department, then no appointing entity will be able to renew the licensee's appointment. (This process is already in place for initiating original appointments and is now incorporated into the appointment renewal process). In order that the licensee is able to have their appointment(s) renewed, the licensee shall update their address(es) at the "MyProfile" online portal for the Florida Department of Financial Services' Bureau of Licensing. The addresses included in this process are email, home, business and mailing.

2. *Late Fees.* The Department shall assess the surplus lines agent late fees. Late fee for initial/original appointment is $250. Late fee for renewals is $25. These late fees are in addition to the statutory $150 appointment fee. A late original appointment is any initial/original appointment that has a requested effective date more than forty-five days before the submittal date. A late renewal appointment is one that is paid after the renewal month. (Fla. Stat. Ann. §§626.371 and 626.381).

3. *Renewal Timeline and Notifications.* The Department shall send an email notification to the surplus lines agent thirty days before his or her appointment is up for renewal, in addition to posting the renewal invoice in their eAppoint account.

   The renewal invoice will become available for payment on the first day of the renewal month and can be paid through the last day of the renewal month without late fees being assessed.

   Additionally, on the first day of the month following the expiration date of an appointment, an email notification will be sent to the surplus lines agent advising payment was not received, late fees have been assessed, and the invoice will continue to be available for forty-five more days for payment, including late fees, otherwise the appointment will be cancelled. If the appointment is not renewed after this forty-five-day period, the appointment will be cancelled for nonrenewal and an email notification will be sent to the surplus lines agent and the licensee notifying them of the appointment cancellation along with information on the process for reappointment and the late fee.

   If the surplus lines agent wishes to reinstate an appointment after it has been cancelled for nonrenewal, and no lapse in appointment coverage is desired, the surplus lines agent will be required to process an initial/original appointment submission and enter the requested effective date. If the initial/original appointment's requested effective date is more than forty-five days from the submittal date, then the late fee for an initial/original appointment described above will be assessed. (https://myfloridacfo.com/Division/Agents/Industry/News/AppointChanges_Jan2012.htm#:~:text=The%20renewal%20invoice%20will%20become%20available%20for%20payment,the%20renewal%20month%20without%20late%20fees%20being%20assessed).

4. *FSLSO Membership.* Anyone licensed as a surplus line agent is deemed to be a member of the Florida Surplus Lines Service Office. You must complete a new agent membership form by visiting: https://slip.fslso.com and selecting "Register".

B. Nonresident Licensing: A nonresident individual must be a natural person, at least eighteen years of age, licensed in his or her home state as a resident surplus lines agent and otherwise qualified under the laws of this state may be licensed as a nonresident surplus lines agent. The applicant for a nonresident surplus lines agent license must meet the same licensing requirements as a resident surplus lines agent (except the pre-licensing education requirement), which includes passing the Florida surplus lines examination, unless they already took and passed a surplus lines license examination in their home state, which is reciprocal with Florida (states that meet Florida surplus lines examination exemption can be found at: https://www.myfloridacfo.com/Division/Agents/Licensure/Agents-Adjusters/recip_surplus.htm). The authority of the nonresident license is limited to the specific lines of authority granted in the license issued by the agent's home state and the lines authorized by the nonresident state. (Fla. Stat. Ann. §626.9272). To qualify for a nonresident surplus lines agent license in Florida, an agent must:

1. Be licensed and appointed as a Florida nonresident general lines agent (Type & Class 9-20); and

2 Hold a license as a resident surplus lines agent licensed in the state of residence.

Nonresident applicants must submit their fingerprints. Fingerprint cards will be sent to the applicants mailing address after payment of $46.80 (plus local Florida county sales tax is received by IdentoGO by Idemia at https://fl.ibtfingerprint.com). Fingerprints must be taken by a technician within a law enforcement agency or an entity approved by the Florida Department of Financial Services. Both completed cards must be mailed to the address found at https://www.myfloridacfo.com/division/agents/licensure/agents-adjusters/fingerprinting.htm.

Nonresidents placing Florida insurance for a risk purchasing group with a Florida-eligible surplus lines insurer must:

1. If a resident of Florida, be licensed and appointed as a general lines agent and a surplus lines agent.

2. If not a resident of Florida, be licensed and appointed as a nonresident general lines agent and a nonresident surplus lines agent in Florida.

C. **Diligent Effort:** The full amount of insurance required must not be procurable, after a diligent effort has been made by the producing agent to do so, from among the insurers authorized to transact and actually writing that kind and class of insurance in this state, and the amount of insurance exported shall be only the excess over the amount so procurable from authorized insurers. A statement of diligent effort must be maintained in the surplus lines agent's file on a risk-by-risk basis. The statement can be obtained at https://www.fslso.com/BusinessForms/DiligentEffort. The policy or contract form under which the insurance is exported shall not be more favorable to the insured as to the coverage or rate than under similar contracts on file and in actual current use in this state by the majority of authorized insurers actually writing similar coverages on similar risks. (Fla. Stat. Ann. §626.916). Three declinations are required. However, if a residential structure has a dwelling replacement cost of $700,000 or more, the application must have been rejected by at least one authorized insurer currently writing this type of coverage and documenting this rejection. (Fla. Stat. Ann. §626.914). The surplus lines agent may charge a reasonable policy fee for each policy exported. A diligent effort must be made by the producing agent in accordance with Fla. Stat. Ann. section 626.916(1)(a). Surplus lines agents must verify that the diligent effort has been made by requiring a properly documented statement of diligent effort from the retail or producing agent. (Fla. Stat. Ann. §626.916(1)(a)).

In addition, each surplus lines agent must keep in their Florida office, or in the agent's state of residence for a nonresident who does not have an office in Florida, a full and true record for a period of five years following the expiration or cancellation of each surplus lines contract. Each surplus lines agent shall maintain all surplus lines business records in his or her general lines agency office, or managing general agency office. The record shall at all times be open to examination by the Department or the Florida Surplus Lines Service Office without notice and shall be so kept available and open for five years next following expiration or cancellation of the contract.

A surplus lines agent's record shall include applications and all certificates, cover notes, and other forms of confirmation of insurance coverage and any substitutions thereof or endorsements thereto relative to said contract procured by the agent and showing such of the following items as may be applicable: amount of the insurance and perils insured against; a brief general description of property insured and where located; the gross premium charged; the return premium paid, if any; rate of premium charged upon the several items of property; effective date of the contract, and the terms thereof; name and Post Office address of the insured and name and home-office address of insurer; the amount collected from the insured; and any other information required from the Department. (Fla. Stat. Ann. §626.930).

Commercial Purchaser Exemption. Surplus lines agents seeking to procure or place nonadmitted insurance on behalf of an "exempt commercial purchaser" are not required to perform a diligent search if:

1. The agent has disclosed to the exempt commercial purchaser that such insurance may or may not be available from the admitted market that may provide greater protection with more regulatory oversight.

2. The exempt commercial purchaser has subsequently requested in writing for the agent to procure or place such insurance from a nonadmitted insurer.

   Certain lines of coverages may be exempt from the diligent effort search requirements as specified in Florida Stat. §§626.916(3)(b) and 627.062(3)(d)(1). Additional guidance regarding compliance with the diligent effort and the disclosure requirements are included in the Florida Agent Procedures Manual located at www.fslso.com under the main menu's Comply section.

D. Tax: 4.95 percent. All new and renewal policies with an effective date on or after July 1, 2020 will incur a tax of 4.95 percent of the total gross premium and paid quarterly. The tax does not apply to certain wet marine and transportation risks, aviation, hangar keepers' liability coverage, airport incidental products liability, and risks of state government and its agencies. In addition, the surplus lines office will collect a service fee of up to .3 percent of the total gross premium of each policy, to be paid by the insured. Risks of state government and its agencies are exempted from the service fee. The surplus lines tax and service fee is also applicable to any fees, such as policy fees and, inspection fees levied by the surplus lines agent, or the surplus lines insurer. The surplus lines agent is prohibited from absorbing the tax or, as an inducement for insurance or for any other reason, rebating all or any part of such tax or of his or her commission. A 9 percent interest rate will be charged on delinquent fees. Agents may also be fined up to $500/day for delinquent taxes. (Fla. Stat. Ann. §§626.9325, 626.932, 626.936, 626.921).

Definition of Premium. For the purpose of calculating the premium receipts tax due pursuant to Section 626.932 of the Florida Statute, the term "premium" means the consideration for insurance by whatever name called and includes any assessment, or any membership, policy, survey, inspection, service, or similar fee or charge in consideration for an insurance contract, which items are deemed to be a part of the premium. The per-policy fee authorized by Section 626.916(4) of the Florida Statute is specifically included within the meaning of the term "premium." However, the service fee imposed pursuant to Section 626.9325 of the Florida Statute is excluded from the meaning of the term "premium."

Multi-State Premium Tax Allocation. If a surplus lines policy covers risks or exposures only partially in Florida, and the state is the home state as defined in the federal Nonadmitted and Reinsurance Reform Act of 2010 (NRRA) the tax payable shall be computed on the gross premium. Multi-state risks will also be taxed at 4.94 percent on the entire premium, eliminating the requirement to charge the tax rate of the state where the risk or exposure is located. This is applicable to all new and renewal policies with an effective date on or after July 1, 2020.

Tax payments are due on or before the forty-fifth day following each calendar quarter in accordance with the invoice provided by the FSLSO. Checks should be made payable and mailed to:

Florida Department of Financial Services
P.O. Box 864593, Orlando, FL 32886-4593
or overnight to Wells Fargo Bank
FSLSO, Lockbox #864593
11050 Lake Underhill Road
Orlando, FL 32825
(Fla. Stat. Ann. §626.932).

Payments may also be made electronically through the surplus lines information portal at https://slip.fslso.com/portal/.

Specific Due Dates:

- 4th quarter invoices issued in January are due by February 14th.
- 1st quarter invoices issued in April are due by May 15th.
- 2nd quarter invoices issued in July are due by August 14th.
- 3rd quarter invoices issued in October are due by November 14th. (https://www.fslso.com/Invoicing-Refunds/Accounting).

E. **Stamping Fee:** All new and renewal policies with an effective date on or after April 1, 2020 will incur a service fee of 0.06 percent of the total gross premium as defined in Florida Statute 626.9325. A fee of 0.1 percent for policies with an effective date between April 1, 2007 and March 31, 2013; 0.2 percent for policies with an effective date between April 1, 2013 and March 31, 2014; 0.175 percent for policies with an effective date between April 1, 2014 and March 31, 2016; 0.15 percent for policies with an effective date between April 1, 2016 and March 31, 2017; .1 percent for policies with an effective date on or after April 1, 2017. (Referred to as Service Fee in Florida). See additional rules below for more details.

The surplus lines agent must pay on or before the forty-fifth day following each calendar quarter to the FSLSO the service fees related to all policies reported during the previous calendar quarter in accordance with the plan of operation of the FSLSO. Interest will be charged on the amount of any delinquent service fee due at the rate of 9 percent per-year compounded annually, beginning the date the service fee becomes delinquent. Checks should be made payable and mailed to: Florida Surplus Lines Service Office, P.O. Box 864593, Orlando, FL 32886-4593; or overnight to Wells Fargo Bank, FSLSO, Lockbox #864593, 11050 Lake Underhill Road, Orlando, FL 32825. Payments may also be made electronically through the surplus lines information portal at https://slip.fslso.com/portal/Common/login.aspx?ReturnUrl=%2fportal%2f. (Fla. Stat. Ann. §626.9325).

F. **Surplus Lines Service Office:** Florida Surplus Lines Service Office, 1441 Maclay Commerce Drive, Suite 200, Tallahassee 32312. 800-562-4496. FAX: 850-513-9624. Website: www.fslso.com.

G. **Surplus Lines Association:** Florida Surplus Lines Association, 325 John Knox Rd #L103, Tallahassee, FL 32303. Phone: 850.224.0711. Fax: 850.222.3019. Website: www.myfsla.com.

H. Other Requirements or Restrictions:

Exemptions. Separate lists of rules apply to commercial aviation and ocean marine insurance. (Fla. Stat. Ann. §626.917). The surplus lines law applies to accident and health to the extent that these products can be written by a property-casualty insurer. Other accident and health, and primary workers compensation and basic private passenger auto liability insurance may not be placed with nonadmitted insurers.

Eligibility. Generally, insurers not on the eligibility list or federally authorized may not be used. Use of surplus lines is not allowed for better rates or forms. There are limited circumstances that require prior approval by the Office of Insurance Regulation (OIR). Surplus lines agents and general lines agents placing the business may be liable for loss if an unapproved insurer is used.

An unauthorized insurer must be made eligible to become a surplus lines insurer by the Office of Insurance Regulation (OIR). The insurer must be currently authorized in the state or country of its domicile as to the kind or kinds of insurance proposed to be placed and must have been such an insurer for no less than the three years next preceding or must be the wholly owned subsidiary of such authorized insurer or must be the wholly owned subsidiary of an already eligible surplus lines insurer as to the kind or kinds of insurance proposed for a period of not less than the three years next preceding. The Office of Insurance Regulation (OIR) may waive the three-year requirement if the insurer provides a product or service not readily available to the consumers of Florida or has operated successfully for a period of at least one year next preceding and has capital and surplus of not less than $25 million. The requesting surplus lines agent or the insurer must furnish the Office of Insurance Regulation (OIR) with a duly authenticated copy of its current annual financial statement in English and with all monetary values expressed in United States dollars at an exchange rate then-current and shown in the statement, and additional relevant information may be requested by the Office of Insurance Regulation (OIR). (Fla. Stat. Ann. §626.918).

Notice. All surplus lines contracts, policies, certificates, cover notes or confirmation of coverage must carry the following wording:

> "This insurance is issued pursuant to the Florida Surplus Lines Law. Persons insured by surplus lines carriers do not have the protection of the Florida Insurance Guaranty Act to the extent of any right of recovery for the obligation of an insolvent unlicensed insurer." (Fla. Stat. Ann. §626.924).

Additional information required on the contract includes: name, address and identification number of the Florida licensed and appointed surplus lines agent; name and address of the producing agent, not agency, through whom the business originated; Florida surplus lines agent's countersignature; full name and address of the insurer(s) and the percentage of participation, if more than one insurer is participating on the risk; policy term, effective, and expiration date; issue date or countersign date; total policy premium, including all fees, such as the policy and inspection fees; total amount of tax charged; total amount of service fee charged; total amount of Citizens' assessment; total amount of CAT Fund assessment, and the $2/$4 EMPA Surcharge. Surplus lines policies issued on or after October 1, 2009, shall have stamped or printed on the face of the policy in at least fourteen-point, boldface type, the following statement: "Surplus lines insurers' policy rates and forms are not approved by any Florida regulatory agency." (Fla. Stat. Ann. §626.924). The FSLSO provides a Sample Face Page to ensure all the required information is included at https://www.fslso.com/BusinessForms/SampleFacePage.

As a condition of holding a license, all licensed and appointed surplus lines agents are deemed to be members of Florida Surplus Lines Service Office (FSLSO): 1441 Maclay Commerce Drive, Suite 200, Tallahassee, FL 32312. Telephone: 800-562-4496. FAX: 850-513-9624.

Reports. All licensed surplus lines agents are required to electronically submit all premium bearing transactions placed with an eligible surplus lines insurer to the Florida Surplus Lines Service Office (FSLSO) within thirty days from the effective date of the transaction.

Records. All licensed surplus lines agents must keep and maintain a full and accurate record of each surplus lines policy and all attachments for a period of five years. (Fla. Stat. Ann. §626.930)

Quarterly Affidavits. Each surplus lines agent shall on or before the forty-fifth day following each calendar quarter file with the FSLSO an affidavit, on forms as prescribed and furnished by the FSLSO, stating that all surplus lines insurance transacted by him during such calendar quarter has been submitted to the FSLSO as required. If there is no surplus lines business transacted in the reporting quarter, an affidavit is not required to be submitted to the FSLSO. The Quarterly Report Affidavit should be submitted electronically via the Surplus Lines Information Portal (SLIP). Form available at: https://www.fslso.com/BusinessForms/QuarterlyAffidavit (Fla. Stat. Ann. §626.931)

In addition, licensed surplus lines agents are required to:

1. Maintain a record of policy records required by Florida Law.

2. Notify the FSLSO and the Florida Department of Financial Services within thirty days after a change of principal business street address, mailing address, or email address.

3. Notify the FSLSO in writing of a transfer of previously filed policies to another agent. The accepting agent should also notify the FSLSO in writing of acceptance of responsibility for the files.

   (Fla. Stat. Ann. §§ 626.930, 626.931).

I. Additional Rules:

Late Tax and Service Fee Penalties. Taxes and service fees not paid when due are recoverable through legal action by the Florida Department of Financial Services.

Any agent who neglects to pay the taxes or service fees as required by law and within the time due may be fined up to $500 per day for each day the payment is late; beginning the day after the tax is due. Interest shall be charged on the amount of any delinquent tax due at the rate of 9 percent per-year, compounded annually, beginning the date the tax becomes delinquent. (Fla. Stat. Ann. §626.936).

Notice of Nonrenewal. Any agent wishing to nonrenew or surrender a surplus lines license must notify the FSLSO and the Florida Department of Financial Services in writing of their intent to do so.

Failure to File a Quarterly Affidavit Penalty. Any agent who neglects to file a quarterly report affidavit within the time required by law may be fined up to $50 per day for each day the report is late, beginning the day after the quarterly report affidavit was due until the report is received by the FSLSO. Note, an affidavit is no longer required if you have not transacted business during the reporting time-frame for the quarter beginning July 1, 2016. (Fla. Stat. Ann. §626.936 and 626.931 as amended by House Bill 651).

Florida Hurricane Catastrophe Fund (FHCF). FHCF Assessments are due on or before the forty-fifth day following each calendar quarter in accordance with the invoice provided by the FSLSO. Checks should be made payable to Florida Hurricane Catastrophe Fund, and mailed to: FSLSO, P.O. Box 864593, Orlando, FL 32886-4593, or overnight to Wells Fargo Bank, Lockbox #864593, 11050 Lake Underhill Road, Orlando, FL 32825. The Florida Office of Insurance Regulation (OIR) has directed the Florida Surplus Lines Service Office (FSLSO), by order, to discontinue assessing the Florida Hurricane Catastrophe Fund (FHCF) emergency assessment on applicable surplus lines policies issued or renewed with an effective date on or after January 1, 2015. For policies issued or renewed with an effective date on or after January 1, 2015, the Florida Hurricane Catastrophe Fund assessment will no longer be assessed. For policies issued or renewed with an effective date between January 1, 2011 - December 31, 2014, and all subsequent endorsements to those policies, the Florida Hurricane Catastrophe Fund assessment will continue to be charged at 1.3 percent. For policies issued or renewed with an effective date between

January 1, 2007 - December 31, 2010, and all subsequent endorsements to those policies, the Florida Hurricane Catastrophe Fund assessment will continue to be charged at 1.0 percent. (https://www.floir.com/siteDocuments/2014CATFundEmergAssessmentSurplusLines156729-14-O.pdf).

EMPA Surcharges. EMPA Surcharges are due on or before the forty-fifth day following each calendar quarter in accordance with the invoice provided by the FSLSO. Checks should be made payable to Florida Division of Emergency Management and mailed to: FSLSO, P.O. Box 864593, Orlando, FL, 32886-4593, or overnight to Wells Fargo Bank, FSLSO, Lockbox #864593, 11050 Lake Underhill Road, Orlando FL 32825. (http://www.fslso.com/docs/default-source/procedure-manuals/AgentProceduresManual.pdf (See pages 10-11)).

Citizens Assessments. Citizens assessments are due on or before the end of the forty-fifth day following each calendar quarter in accordance with the invoice provided by the FSLSO. Checks should be made payable to Citizens Property Insurance Corp. and mailed to FSLSO, P.O. Box 864593, Orlando, FL 32886-4593, or overnight to Wells Fargo Bank, FSLSO, Lockbox #864593, 11050 Lake Underhill Road, Orlando, FL 32825.

Citizens 2005 Emergency Assessment. The Florida Office of Insurance Regulation has directed the Florida Surplus Lines Service Office (FSLSO) to discontinue assessing the Citizens Property Insurance Corporation (CPIC) emergency assessment on applicable surplus lines policies issued or renewed with an effective date on or after July 1, 2015.

For policies issued or renewed with an effective date on or after July 1, 2015, the CPIC assessment will no longer be assessed.

Pursuant to Order #156458-10 issued on January 22, 2020 by Florida's Office of Insurance Regulation, effective April 1, 2020, surplus lines issued or renewed prior to July 1, 2015 and all related transactions reported to FSLSO will not have the CPIC assessment charged or credited. As a result of this subsequent resolution and Order, the last day to report surplus lines policy data through the FSLSO system (SLIP or XML Batch) where the CPIC assessment will be charged or credited was March 31, 2020.

J. Independently Procured Insurance:

1. *Rules.* Insureds in Florida may purchase insurance directly from unauthorized insurers without the use of a licensed and appointed surplus lines agent or broker. Insurance may be placed with an unlicensed insurer or with an unauthorized surplus lines carrier. The insured must withhold 5 percent tax plus up to a 0.3 percent service fee, as well as any applicable assessments levied by the state of Florida, from the amount of premium charged by and otherwise payable to the insurer for such insurance. On

or before the forty-fifth day following each calendar quarter after the insurance is procured, continued, or renewed, the insured must make payable to the Department the amount of tax. The insured must remit the tax and the service fee to the Florida Surplus Lines Service Office, who is then required to forward to the Department the taxes within ten days after receipt. The insured is responsible if the IPC policy is not filed with the FSLSO and/or if the taxes, service fees, and applicable assessments are not paid. This section does not authorize independent procurement of workers' compensation insurance, life insurance, or health insurance. (Fla. Stat. Ann. §626.938).

2. *Industrial Insured Exemption.* Florida does not have an industrial insured exemption.

Multistate Policies

K. Home State Definition: Florida uses the NRRA home state definition for premium tax allocation purposes:

> Florida is the Home State if the insured maintains its principal place of business or, in the case of an individual, the individual's principal residence in Florida. If Florida is the principal place of business, but if 100 percent of the risk is located outside of Florida, then the home state is the state to which the greatest percentage of the insured's taxable premium is allocated.

Pursuant to Florida Statute 626.932, multistate risks will also be taxed at 4.94 percent on the entire premium, eliminating the requirement to charge the tax rate of the state where the risk or exposure is located. This is applicable to all new and renewal policies with an effective date on or after July 1, 2020.

> For further information contact the FSLSO at 1800-562-4496, email them at agent.services@fslso.com or visit their website at www.FSLSO.com.

L. Statutory References: Florida Statutes Annotated §§626.913 through 626.939, 626.381.

GEORGIA

A. Resident and Nonresident Licensing: A licensed resident property, casualty, surety agent may be licensed to place insurance with nonadmitted insurers. Surplus lines brokers must also hold or apply for a property and casualty agent license. Georgia is transitioning from an annual renewal to a biennial renewal of licenses: biennial fee will be $600; examination, $90. A bond of $20,000 is required on form GID-114 (https://ociga.seamlessdocs.com/f/surpluslinesbrokerbond). Applicants must also pass the surplus lines broker exam. Agents licensed in Georgia may place business through licensed surplus lines brokers and receive commission. Nonresidents may be licensed for this purpose, if licensed in their home state. (Ga. Code Ann. § 33-23-37; Ga. Comp. R. & Regs. r. 120-2-2-.60).

All new resident applicants, excluding active licensees and individuals that apply for reinstatement within six months of expiration date, shall be required to submit electronic fingerprints through a vendor selected by the department for a criminal background check. The applicant shall bear the cost for electronic fingerprinting. (Ga. Comp. R. & Regs. r. 120-2-3-.07).

Furthermore, beginning January 1, 2012, every individual, corporation, partnership, or other business entity submitting an application for licensure must submit a Citizenship Affidavit along with the application. Form GID-276-EN can be found on the Georgia Office of Insurance and Fire Safety Commissioner's website at: https://oci.georgia.gov/citizenship-affidavit.

B. Diligent Effort: The insured or the insured's agent has made an effort to procure the desired insurance coverage or benefits from authorized insurers, but such effort has been unsuccessful in obtaining insurance coverage or benefits which are satisfactory to the insured; and the insurance shall not be procured under this chapter for personal passenger motor vehicle coverage or residential dwelling property coverage unless such insurance cannot be obtained from an authorized insurer. Surplus lines broker must file a quarterly affidavit with the commissioner. (Ga. Code Ann. § 33-5-21).

Commercial Purchaser Exemption. Brokers are not required to make a due diligence search to determine whether the full amount or type of insurance can be obtained from authorized insurers when the surplus lines broker is seeking to procure or place nonadmitted insurance for an exempt commercial purchaser, provided that the broker procuring or placing the surplus lines insurance has disclosed to the exempt commercial purchaser that such insurance may be available from the admitted market that may provide greater protection with more regulatory oversight; and the exempt commercial purchaser has subsequently requested in writing for the broker to procure or place such insurance from a nonadmitted insurer. (Ga. Code Ann. § 33-5-21).

C. Tax: 4 percent of gross premiums less returns; filed quarterly. Surplus lines brokers are required to remit to the commissioner, on or before April 15, July 15, October 15, and January 15, at the time his quarterly affidavit is submitted, as a tax imposed for the privilege of doing business as a surplus lines broker in Georgia, a tax of 4 percent on all premiums paid to the surplus lines broker during the preceding quarter, less return premiums and exclusive amount of sums collected to cover state or federal taxes, on surplus lines insurance subject to tax transacted by him during the preceding quarter as shown by his affidavit filed with the commissioner. Exempt from the tax and from the surplus lines law are reinsurance; insurance on property or operations of railroads in interstate commerce; vehicles or aircraft owned and principally garaged or hangared outside the state; aircraft owned or operated by aircraft manufacturers or operated in scheduled interstate flight, and their cargo or liability (other than workers compensation or employers liability). (Ga. Code Ann. §§ 33-5-29, -31).

Multi-State Premium Tax Allocation. If a surplus lines policy covers risks or exposures located or to be performed both in and out of this state, the sum payable must be computed based on an amount equal to 4 percent of that portion of the gross premiums allocated to Georgia plus an amount equal to the portion of premiums allocated to other states or territories on the basis of the tax rates and fees applicable to properties, risks, or exposures located or to be performed outside this state. (Ga. Code Ann. § 33-5-31).

If Georgia participates in a cooperative agreement, compact, or reciprocal agreement with other states pursuant to code Sections 33-5-40 to 33-5-44 and a surplus lines policy covers risks or exposures located or to be performed both in and out of this state, the sum payable shall be computed based on an amount equal to 4 percent of that portion of the gross premiums allocated to this state plus an amount equal to the portion of premiums allocated to other states or territories on the basis of the tax rates and fees applicable to properties, risks, or exposures located or to be performed outside this state. (Ga. Code Ann. § 33-5-33).

Late Tax Payment Penalty. If any surplus lines broker fails to remit the tax within thirty days after the tax is due, he or she will be liable for a penalty of either $25 for each day of delinquency commencing after the expiration of the thirty day period or an amount equal to 100 percent of the tax, whichever is less, except that for good cause shown, the commissioner may grant a reasonable extension of time within which the affidavit may be filed and the tax may be paid. The tax may be recovered by distraint and the penalty and tax may be recovered by an action instituted by the commissioner in any court of competent jurisdiction. The commissioner shall pay to the Office of the State Treasurer any penalty so collected. (Ga. Code Ann. § 33-5-32).

D. Stamping Fee: None. Georgia does not have a surplus lines stamping office.

E. Other Requirements or Restrictions:

Eligibility. Georgia requires that brokers insure only with an insurance company domiciled in a United States jurisdiction that is authorized to write the type of insurance in its domiciliary jurisdiction and has a capital and surplus or its equivalent under the laws of its domiciliary jurisdiction which equals the greater of a minimum capital and surplus requirements ofTitle 33 of the Georgia Code Annotated; or $15 million.The requirements may be satisfied by an insurer that possesses less than the minimum capital and surplus upon an affirmative finding of acceptability by the commissioner.The finding shall be based upon such factors as quality of management, capital, and surplus of any parent company, company underwriting profit and investment income trends, market availability, and company record and reputation within the industry. In no event shall the commissioner make an affirmative finding of acceptability when the unauthorized insurer's capital and surplus is less than $4.5 million. (Ga. Code Ann. § 33-5-25).

Brokers must ascertain the financial condition of the unauthorized insurer before placing insurance with the unauthorized insurer. Furthermore, brokers cannot not place surplus lines insurance with any insurer who does not meet the threshold requirements based on currently available, reliable financial information. A broker's license may be suspended or revoked for any violation.The insurer providing the surplus lines coverage is required to annually furnish the broker a copy of its current annual financial statement and, in the case of a group of foreign individual underwriters, evidence of compliance with required trust or security fund deposits. No list of approved nonadmitted insurers is published but the surplus lines broker must file financial data on any new insurer used, for approval by commissioner before use. All surplus lines contracts must bear the name of, or be initialed by, the surplus lines broker and must show on their face the following surplus lines warning language:

> "This contract is registered and delivered as a surplus lines coverage under the Surplus lines Insurance Law O.C.G.A. Chapter 33-5."

Life insurance may not be placed with nonadmitted insurers.

Products liability, insurers must also comply with reporting requirements of 120-2-18-.09 using form GID-42 available at https://oci.georgia.gov/.

Courtesy filings of taxes and certificates of nonavailability are not allowed in Georgia.

(Ga. Code Ann. §§ 33-5-25 to 26; Ga. Comp. R. & Regs. 120-2-18-.09).

Records. Each licensed surplus lines broker shall keep in his office a separate account of each policy written or renewed showing the exact amount of insurance placed, the name and post office address of the insured, the name and home address of the insurer, the location of the insured property, the gross premium charged therefor, the amount of premium tax paid thereon, the nature of the risk, the number, date, and term of the policy, and any other information as the commissioner may require. The record must at all times be open to examination by the commissioner. (Ga. Code Ann. § 33-5-28).

Reports. Each surplus lines broker must file with the commissioner, on a quarterly basis, an affidavit executed by the surplus lines broker. Such affidavit must furnish certificate or cover note number, name of insured, the amount of the premium, the tax paid thereon, and any other information as the commissioner may require for all surplus lines transactions in which premiums were paid to the surplus lines broker during the previous quarter. The quarterly affidavit shall be filed with the commissioner on or before the 15th of April, July, October, and January. (Ga. Code Ann. § 33-5-29).

Failure to File Quarterly Affidavit Penalty. If any surplus lines broker fails to file his or her quarterly affidavit within thirty days after it is due, he or she shall be liable for a penalty $25 for each day of delinquency commencing after the expiration of the thirty days, except that for good cause shown, the commissioner may grant a reasonable extension of time within which the affidavit may be filed. (Ga. Code Ann. § 33-5-32).

F. Surplus Lines Association:

Georgia Surplus Lines Association, Inc.
3805 Crestwood Parkway NW
Duluth, GA 30096
Phone: (770) 921-0488
Website: https://georgiasurpluslinesassociation.org/

GSLA Voting Membership: $150. GSLA Associate Membership – Individual: $150. GSLA Associate Membership – Market, Company, or Organization: $1,000. Renews annually.

G. Independently Procured Insurance:

1. *Rules.* Insureds in Georgia may purchase insurance directly from surplus lines insurers without the use of a broker. The transaction may be made with an unlicensed insurer or with an unapproved surplus lines insurer. Every insured who in this state procures or causes to be procured or continues or renews insurance with an unauthorized insurer upon a subject of insurance resident, located, or to be performed both within and outside this state, must within thirty days after the date such insurance was so procured, continued, or renewed file a report of the same with the commissioner in writing and upon forms designated by the commissioner and furnished to such

an insured upon request. The report must state the name and address of the insured or insureds, name and address of the insurer, the subject of the insurance, a general description of the coverage, and the amount of premium. The insured is responsible for payment of the 4 percent tax. (Ga. Code Ann § 33-5-33).

2. *Industrial Insured.* In Georgia, "industrial insured" means an insured who procures the insurance of any risk or risks through the use of the services of a full-time employee who acts as an insurance manager, risk manager, or insurance buyer or through the services of a person licensed as a property and casualty agent, broker, or counselor in such person's state of domicile whose aggregate annual premiums for insurance on all risks total at least $25,000; and either has at least twenty-five full-time employees, gross assets in excess of $3 million, or annual gross revenues in excess of $5 million. (Ga. Code Ann. § 33-41-2).

NRRA Implementation

H. Compact: The Governor, on behalf of the state, advised by and in consultation with the Commissioner of Insurance, is authorized to enter into a cooperative agreement, compact, or reciprocal agreement with another state or states for the purpose of the collection of insurance premium taxes.

In the event the Governor enters into a cooperative agreement, compact, or reciprocal agreement with another state or states as authorized under this part, notice of such action will be communicated to the chairperson of the House Committee on Insurance and the chairperson of the Senate Insurance and Labor Committee. The commissioner shall thereafter annually issue a report to such committees that assesses whether, in his or her opinion, the agreement continues to be in the best financial interest of the state. (Ga. Code Ann. § 33-5-41).

The cooperative agreement, compact, or reciprocal agreement for the purpose of the collection of insurance premiums imposed shall substantially follow the form of the model Surplus Lines Insurance Multi-State Compliance Compact, also known as SLIMPACT-lite, created by the National Conference of Insurance Legislators or the model Nonadmitted Insurance Multi-State Agreement, also known as NIMA, created by the National Association of Insurance Commissioners, as such documents exist on July 1, 2011. (Ga. Code Ann. § 33-5-42).

I. Definitions:

1. Home State means.

   a. The state in which an insured maintains its principal place of business or, in the case of an individual, the individual's principal residence; or

b. If 100 percent of the insured risk is located outside the state referred to in subparagraph a. of this paragraph, the state to which the greatest percentage of the insured's taxable premium for that insurance contract is allocated.

2. Affiliated Groups. If more than one insured from an affiliated group are named insureds on a single nonadmitted insurance contract, the term 'home state' means the home state, as determined according to subparagraph a. of this paragraph, of the member of the affiliated group that has the largest percentage of premium attributed to it under such insurance contract.

3. Principal Place of Business. The state where the insured maintains its headquarters and where the insured's high-level officers direct, control, and coordinate the business's activities. (Ga. Code Ann. §33-5-20.1).

J. Statutory References: Ga. Code Ann. §§ 33-5-20.1 to 21; 5-21; 5-25 to 26; 5-28 to 29; 5-31 to 33; 5-41 to 42; 23-37; 41-2. Ga. Comp. R. & Regs. 120-2-2-.60; 120-2-18-.09.

GUAM

A. **Resident and Nonresident Licensing:** Must be licensed as a broker or general agent, pay a fee of $100, secure an agency agreement with other brokers, agents, or insurers, post a bond of $2,000, submit a notarized Surplus Lines Broker's Statement, Affidavit of Declination, and Agreement and Power of Attorney or other court process or service of suit clause. The license shall expire on the first day of July next following the date of issue. (22 GCA §§15801, 15802).

When renewing a nonresident broker license, submit the following additional requirements: Two percent Assessment (Commercial & Industrial) Liability Premium; and four percent Premium Tax (copy of BR20 Stamped "paid"). Online tax paying is available at https://pay.guam.gov/pg/HowItWorks.aspx. (11 GCA §26202; https://www.guamtax.com/about/regulatory.html).

B. **Diligent Effort:** Before the person named in such license shall procure, effect or issue any such insurance policy or indemnity contract or surety bond, he or she shall in every case execute and file with the commissioner his or her affidavit in acceptable form. The affidavit will state that the insured is unable to procure, in any company or companies or insurers admitted to do business in Guam, the amount or kind of insurance necessary to protect the property or undertakings of the insured described in such affidavit at rates not less than the minimum rates on such property promulgated by an authorized rating bureau or other bureau or conference whose rates have been accepted by the commissioner of banking and insurance, and filed in the insurance department as the fair and equitable rate. (22 GCA §15803).

C. **Tax:** 5 percent of the premium paid by the insured to the surplus lines broker. The tax applies to all lines of insurance. No other fees may be levied by the surplus lines broker; thus, the surplus lines tax does not apply to such fees. Every broker or agent who fails or refuses to file an annual statement and pay taxes by July 1, will be liable for a daily fine of $25 and immediate license revocation for a minimum of one year and until taxes are paid. (22 GCA §15807, 11 GCA §26202).

D. **Stamping Fee:** None. Guam does not have a surplus lines stamping office.

E. **Other Requirements or Restrictions:** There is no list of approved surplus lines insurers. Every policy issued by surplus lines brokers must be endorsed:

> ISSUED IN AN UNAUTHORIZED COMPANY, UNDER AGENT'S (OR BROKER'S) LICENSE NO. ________

The endorsement must be properly filled in and signed by the broker or agent. (22 GCA §15804).

Only lines or risks that are not available or that cannot be procured in Guam may be placed with surplus lines insurers. A risk cannot be placed with a surplus lines company for a better rate or form. (22 GCA §§15201, 15202 to 15204).

Records. Every surplus lines broker or agent must keep a separate account of the business done under his surplus line license and on or before July 1 each year, must file with the commissioner a statement for the calendar year preceding, giving:

1. The name of the insured to whom such policy or indemnity contract granting such unauthorized insurance has been issued.

2. The name and home office of each company issuing any such policy or contract.

3. The amount of such insurance.

4. The great premiums charged therein or therefore.

5. The date and term of the policy.

6. The amount of premium returned on each policy canceled or not taken.

7. Other information required by the commissioner. (22 G.C.A. §15805).

F. Surplus Lines Association: None.

G. Independently Procured Insurance:

1. *Rules.* Insureds may purchase their own coverage in Guam. However, it may be purchased only from an admitted domestic insurer. The insurer is responsible for payment of the 5 percent tax. (22 GCA §§15101, 15102; 15316).

2. *Industrial Insured Exemption.* In Guam, "industrial insured" is defined as an insured who:

   a. Procures the insurance of any risk or risks by use of the services of an employee acting as an insurance manager or buyer.

   b. Whose aggregate annual premiums for insurance on all risks total at least $15,000.

   c. Who has at least ten full-time employees. (22 G.C.A. §23101).

GUAM

NRRA Implementation

Guam has not implemented any NRRA legislation.

H. Statutory References:

11 GCA §	26202
22 GCA §§	15101, 15102
	15201, 15202 to 15204
	15316
	15801 to 15805, 15807
	23101

Web References:

https://pay.guam.gov/pg/HowItWorks.aspx.

https://www.guamtax.com/about/regulatory.html.

HAWAII

A. **Resident Licensing:** Residents may be licensed to place insurance with nonadmitted insurers. Issuance fee: $150 service fee: $45 per year. Application fee varies by birth month and application date. For the most up to date complete table for individual initial application fees see the licensing fees link available at http://cca.hawaii.gov/ins/producers/instructions_insurance_license/resident-surplus-lines-broker/#R_SLB_II. Applicants must be licensed as a Hawaii resident producer or submit a resident producer application at the same time as the surplus lines application. Resident surplus lines broker licenses expire on licensee's birth month, even or odd year. Resident business entity license types are renewable biennially on July 16 of each odd year. (H.R.S. §§431:7-101, 8-310). Licensees may also be required to secure a General Excise Tax License; check with the Department of Taxation. Everyone licensed as a producer under Chapter 431 must pay a tax of 0.15 percent of commissions. (H.R.S. §237-13(7)).

   Individuals may apply for licensure online at NIPR's Web site at www.nipr.com. Instructions and applications for licensure may be found on the Department's Website at http://cca.hawaii.gov/ins/producers/instructions_insurance_license/.

   Paper applications for an initial surplus lines license are no longer accepted.

   Applicants for a surplus lines broker license shall pass a written examination, which shall test the applicant's knowledge in property, marine and transportation, vehicle, general casualty, and surety insurance, the duties and responsibilities of a surplus lines broker, and finally, the insurance laws and rules of Hawaii. An applicant who fails to appear for the examination as scheduled or fails to pass the examination shall reapply for an examination and remit all required fees and forms before being scheduled for another examination. Examination scores shall be valid for a period of two years. (H.R.S. §431:8–324).

B. **Nonresident Licensing:** Nonresidents may be licensed, on a reciprocal basis, for this purpose if licensed as a surplus lines producer in their home state. Issuance fee: $150; $45 service fee per year. Nonresident surplus lines broker licenses expire on licensee's birth month, even or odd year. Nonresident business entity license types are renewable biennially on April 16 of each even year. Application fee varies by birth month and application date. For the complete table for individual initial application fees see the licensing fees link available at https://cca.hawaii.gov/ins/producers/instructions_insurance_license/nonresident-surplus-lines-broker/. Applicants must be licensed as a Hawaii nonresident producer or submit a resident producer application at the same time as the surplus lines application. (H.R.S. §§431:7-101, 8-321, 322). Licensees may be required to secure a General Excise Tax License, check with the Department of Taxation. (H.R.S. §237-13(7)).

Individuals may apply for licensure on NIPR's Web site at http://nipr.com/license_form.htm or by submitting a paper application and fees to the mailing address above.

Exempt from the surplus lines broker examination are the following:

1. An individual who applies for a nonresident surplus lines broker license in Hawaii who was previously licensed to sell surplus lines insurance in another state. However, note that this exemption is only available if the person is currently licensed in that state or if the application is received within ninety days of the cancellation of the applicant's previous license and if the prior state issues a certification that, at the time of cancellation, the applicant was licensed in good standing in that state, or the state's producer database records, maintained by the National Association of Insurance Commissioners, its affiliates, or its subsidiaries, indicate that the surplus lines broker's license is or was in good standing.

2. A person licensed as a surplus lines broker in another state who moves to Hawaii and makes application within ninety days of establishing legal residence to become a resident licensee. (H.R.S. §431:8-323).

C. **Diligent Effort:** Surplus lines brokers must verify that a diligent effort was completed prior to placing the risk. The following must be maintained in the broker's office:

1. Broker's diligent efforts to place insurance with authorized insurers.

2. Notice to insured that insurer is not authorized and that claims are not covered by the guaranty fund. (H.R.S. §§431:8-307, 312).

Commercial Purchaser Exception. A surplus lines broker is not required to make a due diligence search to determine whether the full amount or type of insurance can be obtained from authorized insurers when the broker is seeking to procure or place unauthorized insurance for an exempt commercial purchaser provided both:

1. The broker procuring or placing the surplus lines insurance has disclosed to the exempt commercial purchaser that such insurance may or may not be available from the admitted market that may provide greater protection with more regulatory oversight.

2. The exempt commercial purchaser has subsequently requested in writing for the broker to procure or place the insurance from an unauthorized insurer. (H.R.S. §431:8-301).

D. **Tax:** 4.68 percent. Within forty-five days after the end of each calendar quarter, each surplus lines broker must pay to the director of finance, through the commissioner, a premium tax on surplus lines insurance transacted by the broker during the calendar quarter for insurance for which Hawaii is the home state of the insured. The tax rate is 4.68 percent of gross premiums, less return premiums, on surplus lines insurance allocated to Hawaii. The tax rate and fees of other states shall be applied to the gross premiums, less return premiums, allocated to those states.

As used in this subsection, "gross premiums" mean the amount of the policy or coverage premium charged by the insurer in consideration for the insurance contract. Any charges for policy, survey, inspection, service, or similar fees or other charges added by the broker shall not be considered part of gross premiums. (H.R.S. §431:8-315).

Multi-State Premium Tax Allocation. The tax of the states shall be computed upon the portion of the premium which is properly allocable to the risks and exposures for which the home state is Hawaii. Note: Effective October 1, 2019, Hawaii has eliminated the need to apply out-of-state tax rates to risk located in other states on a home state policy. All home state policies will be taxed entirely at the Hawaii rate of 4.68 percent. The change also eliminated the requirement to report premium allocated by risk among the states and eliminated regulator authority to join a tax sharing compact.

The tax on any portion of the premium unearned at the termination of the insurance contract must be returned to the policyholder. (H.R.S. §431:8-315).

If any surplus lines broker fails to pay the premium tax when it is due, the surplus lines broker may be liable for a fine of up to $25 for each day of delinquency. The commissioner may collect the premium tax by distraint and recover the fine by instituting an action in any court of competent jurisdiction. (H.R.S. §431:8-316).

The Division extends OPTins implementation to Surplus Lines Licensees. The Hawaii Insurance Division will no longer process paper checks. Tax forms and the corresponding payment will be immediately received by the Hawaii Insurance Department upon submission. To register for OPTins, please contact the OPTins Marketing Team at optinsmktg@naic.org or call (816)783-8787. For further questions please visit the OPTins FAQ page at http://www.optins.org/faq.htm.

E. **Stamping Fee:** None. Hawaii does not have a stamping office.

F. **Other Requirements or Restrictions:** All resident individuals are required to be fingerprinted prior to submitting a license application for initial license or license reactivation. To obtain fingerprints, schedule an appointment online at: www.fieldprinthawaii.com.

If you are submitting applications for two licenses simultaneously (e.g. producer and surplus lines broker), then you will only need to be fingerprinted once. However, if you submit your producer application now and apply for a surplus lines broker license at a later date, you will be required to be fingerprinted again.

No surplus lines broker shall, either knowingly or without reasonable investigation of the financial condition and general reputation of the insurer, place insurance with a financially unsound insurer or with an insurer engaging in an unfair practice. Surplus lines brokers may place surplus lines insurance only with insurers who are authorized to write that type of insurance in the insurer's domiciliary state. (H.R.S. §431:8-302).

Eligibility. A surplus lines broker shall not place coverage with an unauthorized insurer unless, at the time of placement, the surplus lines broker has determined that the unauthorized insurer has capital and surplus or its equivalent under the laws of its domiciliary state that equal the greater of the minimum capital requirement of this state or a minimum of $15 million. These requirements may be satisfied by the insurer's possessing less than the minimum capital and surplus upon an affirmative finding of acceptability by the commissioner. The finding shall be based upon such factors as quality of management, capital, and surplus of any parent company, company underwriting profit and investment income trends, market availability, and company record and reputation within the industry. In no event shall the commissioner make an affirmative finding of acceptability when the unauthorized insurer's capital and surplus is less than $4.5 million. The broker must have on file a certificate affirming that the insurer's capital and surplus which equals the minimum capital and surplus requirements of Hawaii for that kind of insurer as specified by this section. (H.R.S. §431:8-302).

Notice. All insurance contracts procured and delivered must bear the surplus lines broker's name and address and have stamped conspicuously upon the first page of the contract as follows:

> "This insurance contract is issued by an insurer which is not licensed by the State of Hawaii and is not subject to its regulation or examination. If the insurer is found insolvent, claims under this contract are not covered by any guaranty fund of the State of Hawaii." (H.R.S. §431:8-306).

Regarding courtesy filing of taxes, the Hawaii Insurance Division says: "Hawaii Revised Statutes Chapter 431 Article 8, Unauthorized Insurers and Surplus Lines, does not address this issue and is, therefore, not permitted."

Quarterly Statements. Each surplus lines broker must file with the commissioner within forty-five days of the end of each calendar quarter a verified statement of all surplus lines insurance transacted during the calendar quarter. First quarter statements are due on or before May 15; second quarter, on or before August 15; third quarter, on or before November 15; and fourth quarter, on or before February 15. The statement must be on forms as prescribed and furnished by the commissioner and must show the gross amount of premiums for each kind of insurance transacted: the gross premiums charged and itemized by state; the returned premiums paid to insureds; the net premiums and; the amount of remitted taxes and fees; and additional information as required by the commissioner. (H.R.S. §431:8-313).

If any surplus lines broker fails to file a quarterly statement, the surplus lines broker may be liable for a fine of up to $25 for each day of delinquency. The commissioner may recover the fine for failure to file the statement by instituting an action in any court of competent jurisdiction. (H.R.S. §431:8-316).

G. Surplus Lines Association: None.

H. Independently Procured Insurance:

1. *Rules.* Insureds may purchase, continue or renew coverage directly from an insurer which is not authorized to transact business in Hawaii. Each insured, if Hawaii is the home state of the insured, who procures or continues or renews insurance from an unauthorized insurer on a risk located in Hawaii, other than insurance procured through a surplus lines broker must file within forty-five days after the end of the calendar quarter in which the insurance was so procured, continued or renewed, file a written report with the commissioner. The following lines may not be procured independently: life, accident and health or sickness, or annuities. (H.R.S. §431:8-205).

2. *Tax.* The insured is responsible for paying the tax of 4.68 percent on gross premiums charged for the unauthorized insurance allocable to Hawaii, less any return premiums at the time of filing. Gross premiums, less any return premiums, charged for the insurance allocable to other states, are subject to the taxes and fees of those other states. However, at the time of filing the report, the insured must pay the tax and fees of Hawaii and all other states to the director of finance, through the commissioner, for insurance for which Hawaii is the home state of the insured. Delinquent taxes bear an interest rate penalty of ten percent per year. "Gross premiums" mean the amount of the policy or coverage premium charged by the insurer in consideration for the insurance contract. Any charges for policy, survey, inspection, service, or similar fees or other charges added by the broker are not considered part of gross premiums. (H.R.S. §431:8-205).

3. *Industrial Insured Exemption.* Hawaii has no industrial insured exemption.

NRRA Implementation

I. Compact: Within forty-five days after the end of each calendar quarter, each surplus lines broker shall pay the director of finance through the commissioner, a premium tax on surplus lines insurance transacted by the broker during the calendar quarter for all home state policies. A tax rate of 4.68 percent of gross premiums, less return premiums, applies on surplus lines insurance for home state policies. Any unearned portion of the premium shall be returned to the policyholder at the end of the insurance contract. (H.R.S. §431:8-315).

J. Definitions:

1. "Home State," with respect to an insured, means the state in which an insured maintains the insured's principal place of business or, in the case of an individual, the state in which the individual maintains the individual's principal residence; except that if 100 percent of the insured risk is located out of the state where the insured maintains the insured's principal place of business or the state where the individual maintains the principal residence, the home state is the state where the greatest percentage of the insured's taxable premium for that insurance contract is allocated.

2. "Home state of affiliated group" means the home state of the member of the affiliated group that has the largest percentage of premium attributed to it under an insurance contract, which has more than one insured from the affiliated group listed as named insureds on a single unauthorized insurance contract.

3. "Principal place of business" means, with respect to determining the home state of the insured:

    a. The state where the insured maintains the insured's headquarters and where the insured's high-level officers direct, control, and coordinate the business activities.

    b. If the insured's high-level officers direct, control, and coordinate the business activities in more than one state, the state in which the greatest percentage of the insured's taxable premium for that insurance contract is allocated.

    c. If the insured maintains the insured's headquarters or the insured's high-level officers direct, control, and coordinate the business activities outside any state, the state in which the greatest percentage of the insured's taxable premium for that insurance contract is allocated.

4. "Principal residence" means with respect to determining the home state of the individual insured:

    a. The state where the individual insured resides for the greatest number of days during a calendar year.

b. If the insured's principal residence is located outside any state, the state in which the greatest percentage of the insured's taxable premium for that insurance contract is allocated. (H.R.S. §431:8-102).

K. Statutory References:

H.R.S. §237	13
H.R.S. §431:7-	101
H.R.S. §§431:8-	102, 205
	301, 302, 306, 307, 310, 312, 313, 315, 316
	321 to 324

Web References:

http://www.optins.org/faq.htm.

http://cca.hawaii.gov/ins/producers/instructions_insurance_license/resident-surplus-lines-broker/#R_SLB_II.

http://cca.hawaii.gov/ins/producers/instructions_insurance_license/.

https://cca.hawaii.gov/ins/producers/instructions_insurance_license/nonresident-surplus-lines-broker/.

IDAHO

A. **Resident and Nonresident Licensing:** Resident applicants must first be licensed as a property or casualty producer with at least two years' experience as a licensed producer. Idaho does not license agencies as surplus lines brokers. A surplus lines broker must be a member of the Surplus Lines Association. Licenses are issued for a term of two years. The surplus lines broker's license expires on same date as their producer P&C, at end of birth month biennially. Individuals have an option to renew both the surplus lines and the P&C license online for $60 or by paper renewal form for $80. Initial fee: $80. Renewal: $60 (online) or $80 (paper). (Idaho Code §§ 41-1214, -1223). (doi.idaho.gov/Licensing/Surplus/Default).

   First-time resident applicants for producer licenses must file a fingerprint card at the time of testing through the test vendor, PSI EXAMS Examination and fingerprinting fees are paid separately. Fingerprinting fees are $70, which includes the FBI processing fee. Personal checks and cash are not accepted. Exam fees are $60 each exam. Candidates who wish to register for an exam can contact PSI at 800-733-9267 or register online at: www.psiexams.com. Registration fees are nonrefundable.

B. **Nonresident Licensing:** Nonresidents may be licensed as surplus lines brokers so long as such person is licensed in their home state as a surplus lines broker and has a producer license for property and casualty, and the applicant's home state awards nonresident licenses to residents of this state on the same basis. Verification for surplus lines and P&C licensing is checked via PDB (Producer Database) for nonresident applications. The resident surplus lines broker's license expires on same date as their producer P&C, at end of birth month. Individuals have an option to renew both the surplus lines and the P&C license online for $60 or by paper renewal form for $80. Initial fee: $80. Renewal: $60 (online) or $80 (paper). (Idaho Code §§ 41-1214, - 1223). Nonresidents may apply for a Surplus Lines license without the underlying P&C producer license, but must use a licensed producer to conduct the diligent search in order to obtain the required declinations before placing the surplus lines business—except where exempted—such as with items listed on the export list. (doi.idaho.gov/Licensing/Surplus/Default).

C. **Diligent Effort:** Diligent search or effort by the surplus lines producer will be deemed to have been exercised if at least three authorized companies, which are engaged in writing in Idaho the type of coverage sought, or if there are no companies actually engaged in writing such coverage, the risk shall be submitted to at least three companies which, in the surplus line producer's or the insurance producer's professional judgment, are the most likely to accept the risk. If these three companies decline the risk, then the coverage may be placed with an eligible surplus lines carrier. (Idaho Code § 41-1214).

Commercial Purchaser Exemption. A surplus lines broker seeking to procure from or place insurance with an unauthorized insurer for an exempt commercial purchaser is not required to satisfy the diligent search requirement when:

1. The surplus lines broker or referring insurance producer procuring or placing the surplus lines insurance has disclosed to the exempt commercial purchaser that such insurance may or may not be available from the admitted market that may provide greater protection with more regulatory oversight.

2. The exempt commercial purchaser has subsequently requested in writing the surplus lines broker or referring insurance producer to procure or place such insurance from an unauthorized insurer. (Idaho Code § 41-1214).

   An exempt commercial purchaser means any person purchasing commercial insurance who, at the time of placement, meets the following requirements:

   (i) The person employs or retains a qualified risk manager to negotiate insurance coverage.

   (ii) The person has paid aggregate nationwide commercial property and casualty insurance premiums in excess of $100,000 in the immediately preceding twelve months.

   (iii) The person meets at least one of the following criteria (Note: amounts subject to adjustment based on the consumer price index):

      (1) Possesses a net worth in excess of $20 million.
      (2) Generates annual revenues in excess of $50 million.
      (3) Employs more than 500 full-time or full-time equivalent employees per individual insured or is a member of an affiliated group employing more than 1,000 employees in the aggregate.
      (4) A nonprofit organization or public entity generating annual budgeted expenditures of at least $30 million.
      (5) A municipality with a population in excess of 50,000 persons.

   (Idaho Code § 41-1213).

D. Tax: 1.5 percent. On or before March 1 of each year, each broker must remit to the director a tax on the premiums, exclusive of sums collected to cover federal and state taxes and examination fees, on surplus lines insurance subject to tax transacted by him or her with unauthorized insurers during the preceding calendar year as shown by his or her annual statement filed with the director, and at the rate of 1.5 percent. Such tax shall be in lieu of all other taxes upon such insurers with respect to the business so reported. In some cases, brokers may levy fees, policy fees, services fees and other like fees, and such fees are a part of the premium and subject to premium tax where such fees are in consideration for coverage under insurance contract. (Idaho Code § 41-1229).

Multi-State Premium Allocation. For property and casualty insurance other than worker's compensation insurance, if Idaho is the insured's home state, then the tax so payable must be computed upon the entire premium described above, without regard to whether the policy covers risks or exposures that are located in Idaho. For all other lines of insurance, if a surplus lines policy covers risks or exposures only partially in Idaho, the tax so payable must be computed upon the proportion of the premium that is properly allocable to the risks or exposures located in Idaho. Each broker must round amounts to the nearest whole dollar on documents submitted to the director. Documents prepared or maintained by the director will express dollar amounts rounded to the nearest whole dollar. (Idaho Code § 41-1229).

Nonpayment Penalty. If any broker fails to file his annual report, or fails to remit the tax described, by section 41-1229, prior to April 1 after the tax is due, he or she is liable for a fine of $25 for each day of delinquency commencing with April 1. Delinquent tax will be charged 6 percent interest per annum, compounded annually. The tax may be collected by distraint, or the tax and fine may be recovered by an action instituted by the director in any court of competent jurisdiction. Any fine collected by the director shall be paid to the state treasurer and credited to the general fund. (Idaho Code § 41-1230).

All tax and fee filings must be submitted electronically. Instructions and more information can be found at doi.idaho.gov/company/PremiumTax/.

E. **Stamping Fee:** To be paid by the insured to the surplus lines association within thirty days of receipt of the policy. (Idaho Code § 41-1233(3)).

F. **Surplus Lines Association:** Surplus Lines Association of Idaho, Inc., 595 South 14th St., Boise, ID 83702. Phone: 208- 336-2901. Website: http://www.idahosurplusline.org Email: wendy@idahosurplusline.org.

G. **Other Requirements or Restrictions:**

Exemptions. The surplus lines premium tax and insurance laws do not apply to the following when placed by licensed agents or surplus lines brokers of this state:

(1) Ocean marine and foreign trade insurance.

(2) Insurance on subjects located, resident, or to be performed wholly outside of Idaho, or on vehicles or aircraft owned and principally garaged outside of Idaho.

(3) Insurance on operations of railroads engaged in transportation in interstate commerce and their property used in such operations.

(4) Insurance of aircraft owned or operated by manufacturers of aircraft, or of aircraft operated in commercial scheduled interstate flight, or cargo of such aircraft, or against liability, other than worker's compensation and employer's liability, arising out of the ownership, maintenance or use of such aircraft.

(Idaho Code § 41-1212).

Eligibility. A licensed surplus lines broker may accept and place a surplus lines business for any insurance agent licensed in the state for the kind of insurance involved and may compensate the agent. If surplus lines insurance cannot be procured from authorized insurers, it may be procured from unauthorized insurers, subject to the following conditions:

1. The insurance must be procured through a licensed surplus lines broker who is a member of a Surplus Lines Association approved by the director.

2. The full amount or kind of insurance required must not be procurable from insurers who are authorized to do business in this state. The amount of insurance exported must be only the excess over the amount procurable from authorized insurers unless the excess is not available without support of other coverages, provided that a diligent search is made among the insurers authorized to transact and actually writing that particular kind and class of insurance in this state.

3. The insurance must not be so exported for the purpose of securing advantages either as to:

   a. A lower premium rate than would be accepted by an authorized insurer.

   b. Terms of the insurance contract.

A surplus lines broker may not knowingly place surplus lines insurance with insurers that are financially unsound or ineligible for listing. The department reviews the financial condition of surplus lines insurers only upon application for listing and upon notification from other sources of possible adverse conditions leading to removal from the list of eligible surplus lines insurers. A listing indicates only that the insurer appears to the department to be sound financially as of the time of listing and to have satisfactory claims practices, and the department has no credible evidence to the contrary. The director may suspend or revoke the license of any surplus lines broker who knowingly places coverage with an insurer that is in unsound financial condition. (Idaho Code §§ 41-1217, -1224).

The surplus lines broker may only so insure with the following:

> Any foreign insurer authorized to write the kind of insurance in its domiciliary jurisdiction and has capital and surplus or its equivalent under the laws of its domiciliary jurisdiction that equals the greater of the minimum capital and surplus requirements under the laws of Idaho or $15 million; or any alien insurer that is listed on the quarterly listing of alien insurers maintained by the international insurers department of the National Association of Insurance Commissioners. These requirements may be satisfied by an insurer that possesses less than the minimum capital and surplus upon an affirmative finding of acceptability by the director. Such finding shall be based upon factors such as quality of management, capital and surplus of any parent company, company underwriting profit and investment income trends, market availability and company record and reputation within the industry. The director is prohibited from making an affirmative finding of acceptability when the foreign insurer's capital and surplus is less than $4.5 million. (Idaho Code § 41-1214).
>
> "For any violation of the provisions of this section, a surplus line broker may be subject to a fine of not less than $100 and not more than $5,000, or the surplus line broker's license may be revoked, suspended or nonrenewed, or both such fine and license revocation, suspension or nonrenewal." If a broker's surplus lines license is suspended or revoked, the director shall suspend or revoke all other licenses of the same individual issued under title 41, Idaho Code. (Idaho Code §§ 41-1214, -1224).
>
> *Notice*. Every insurance contract procured and delivered must have the following notice stamped on it in red ink, at least ten-point bold type or in black ink in at least twelve-point bold type, with the name of the surplus lines broker who procured it:
>
>> "This surplus lines contract is issued pursuant to the Idaho insurance laws by an insurer not licensed by the Idaho Department of Insurance. There is no coverage provided for surplus lines insurance by either the Idaho Insurance Guaranty Association or by the Idaho Life and Health Insurance Guaranty Association." (Idaho Code § 41-1220).

Evidence of Insurance. Upon placing a surplus lines coverage, the broker must promptly issue and deliver to the insured evidence of the insurance consisting either of the policy as issued by the insurer or, if such policy is not then available, a certificate showing the description and location of the subject of the insurance, coverage, conditions and term of the insurance, the premium and rate charged and taxes collected from the insured, and the name and address of the insured and insurer. If the direct risk is assumed by more than one insurer, the certificate shall state the name and address and proportion of the entire direct risk assumed by each such insurer. If after issuance and delivery of the certificate there is a change as to the identity of the insurers, or the proportion of the direct risk assumed by an insurer as stated in the broker's original certificate, or in any other material respect as to the insurance coverage evidenced by the certificate, the broker must promptly issue and deliver to the insured a substitute certificate showing the current status of the coverage and the responsible insurers. Upon request by the insured, the broker must procure from the insurer and deliver as soon as reasonably possible the policy to the insured in replacement of the broker's certificate. (Idaho Code §41-1219).

Records. Each broker shall keep in his office a full and true record of each surplus lines coverage procured by him, including a copy of each daily report, if any, a copy of each certificate of insurance issued by him, and such of the following items as may be applicable:

1. The amount of the insurance.
2. The gross premium charged.
3. The return premium paid, if any.
4. The rate of premium charged upon the several items of property.
5. The effective date of the contract, and the terms thereof.
6. The name and address of each insurer on the direct risk and the proportion of the entire risk assumed by such insurer if less than the entire risk.
7. The name and address of the insured.
8. A brief general description of the property of risk injured and where located or to be performed.
9. Other information as may be required by the director.

Records must at all times within five years after issuance of the coverage to which it relates be open to examination in this state by the director. (Idaho Code § 41-1227).

Reports. Within thirty days of receipt of the policy by the surplus line broker, the broker must execute and file with the director an affidavit setting forth facts on whether the insurance was eligible for export. A binder is acceptable until the policy is issued. (Idaho Code §41-1215).

Annual Report: Each broker must on or before March 1 of each year file with the director a verified report of all surplus lines insurance transacted by him during the preceding calendar year. The statement shall be filed electronically as prescribed and furnished by the director and shall show:

1. The gross amount of each kind of insurance transacted.

2. Aggregate gross premiums charged.

3. Aggregate of returned premiums paid to insureds.

4. Aggregate of net premiums.

5. Additional information as required by the director.

(Idaho Code § 41-1228).

If any broker fails to file his annual report prior to April 1 after the report is due, he or she is liable for a fine of $25 for each day of delinquency commencing with the first day of April. The fine may be recovered by an action instituted by the director in any court of competent jurisdiction. Any fine collected by the director shall be paid to the state treasurer and credited to the general fund. (Idaho Code § 41-1230).

Courtesy filings of taxes and certificates of nonavailability are not allowed in Idaho.

H. Independently Procured Insurance:

1. *Rules.* Every insured who independently procures insurance pursuant to Idaho Code § 41-1233 must file a written report with the Surplus Lines Association on forms designated by the director (and posted by the Surplus Lines Association) within thirty days after the date such insurance policy was received by the insured, continued or renewed. The report must show the name and address of the insured or insureds, name and address of the insurer, the subject of the insurance, a general description of the coverage, the amount of premium currently charged, and such additional pertinent information as the director reasonably requests. If the insurance covers also a subject of insurance resident, located or to be performed outside this state a proper pro rata portion of the entire premium payable for all such insurance must be allocated to this state for the purposes of this section.

   Any insurance in an unauthorized insurer procured through negotiations or an application in whole or in part occurring or made within or from within this state, or for which premiums in whole or in part are remitted directly or indirectly from within this state, shall be deemed to be insurance procured or continued or renewed in this state within the intent described above. (Idaho Code § 41-1233).

2. *Tax.* The insured is subject to a premium tax of 1.5 percent, payable within thirty days after the insurance policy was so received by the insured, continued or renewed, at the same time the report is filed with the surplus line association. The insured must pay the amount of the tax to the director in addition to a stamping fee to the Surplus Lines Association. (Idaho Code § 41-1229).

   If the tax is delinquent, it will bear interest at the rate of 6 percent per year, compounded annually. (Idaho Code § 41-1233(4).

3. *Industrial Insured Exemption.* Idaho has no industrial insured exemption.

NRRA Implementation

I. Compact: Idaho is not currently a part to a compact or agreement. See Bulletin No. 11-08 at https://doi.idaho.gov/DisplayPDF?Id=2026 for an explanation of Idaho amendments written in response to the NRRA. These amendments were signed into law in April of 2011 and are already reflected in the rest of our Idaho section.

J. Definitions:

1. "Home State" *means:*

   a. The state in which an insured maintains its principal place of business or, in the case of an individual, the individual's principal residence.

   b. If 100 percent of the insured risk is located out of state, the state to which the greatest percentage of the insured's taxable premium for that insurance contract is allocated.

2. "Affiliated Groups": If more than one insured from an affiliated group are named insureds on a single nonadmitted insurance contract, then "home state" means the home state of the member of the affiliated group that has the largest percentage of premium attributed to it under such insurance contract. "Affiliated Group" means any group of entities that are all affiliated. "Affiliated" means, with respect to an insured, any entity that controls, is controlled by or is under common control with the insured.

   a. "Principal place of business" means the state where the insured maintains its headquarters and where the insured's high level officers direct, control and coordinate the business activities of the insured.

b. "Control" means:

(1) An entity directly or indirectly, or acting through one or more persons, owns or controls another entity or has the power to vote 25 percent or more of any class of voting securities of another entity.
(2) An entity controls in any manner the election of a majority of the directors or trustees of another entity. (Idaho Code § 41-1213).

K. **Statutory References:** Idaho Code §§ 41-1212 to 1215, 1217, 1219 to 1220; 1223 to 1224; 1227 to 1230; 1233.

ILLINOIS

A. Resident Licensing: Any licensed producer who is a resident of Illinois may be licensed as a surplus lines producer. The surplus lines producer's license expires one year from date of issue. Annual fee: $400. Applicant must maintain membership in Surplus Line Association of Illinois; there is no fee for membership in the Surplus Line Association of Illinois. Producers licensed in Illinois may place business through licensed surplus lines producers and receive commission. (215 ILCS 5/445). Illinois Surplus Lines Licensing is done through the NIPR Web site at www.nipr.com. Illinois only licenses individuals for surplus line licenses, not corporations or business entities. (https://slai.org/licenses/_licenses.html).

B. Nonresident Licensing: Nonresidents may be licensed as surplus lines producers if licensed as a resident and in good standing in their home state and currently hold an Illinois nonresident producer license. Nonresident licensing is also done through the NIPR Web site at www.nipr.com and the requirements for licensure of residents listed above apply equally to nonresident licensees and applicants. (215 ILCS 5/500-40).

C. Diligent Effort: The surplus lines producer must exert diligent effort to procure the policies or contracts required by the insureds from insurers which are authorized to transact business in Illinois. Diligent effort by the surplus lines producer shall be deemed to have been exercised if the surplus lines producer or the referring insurance producer shall submit a risk to three or more authorized insurers that are engaged in writing in Illinois the type of coverage sought, or if there are no insurers actually engaged in writing such coverage, the risk shall be submitted to insurers which, in the surplus lines producer's or the insurance producer's professional judgment, are the most likely to accept the risk. (50 Ill. Adm. Code 2701.50(a)).

Submission of insuring contracts to the Surplus Line Association of Illinois constitutes a certification by the surplus lines producer or by the insurance producer who presented the risk to the surplus lines producer for placement as a surplus lines risk that after diligent effort the required insurance could not be procured from insurers that are authorized to transact business in Illinois and that such procurement was otherwise in accordance with the surplus lines law. (50 Ill. Adm. Code 2701.50(b)).

The surplus lines producer must maintain a record of its diligent effort with a copy of the insurance that was placed. The record must state the name of the authorized insurers and the individuals contacted at each insurer who declined the risk. If the diligent effort was made by an insurance producer, the surplus lines producer must maintain a written record signed by the insurance producer that the insurance producer made such diligent effort, and the insurance producer must maintain a record that states the name of the authorized insurer and the individuals contacted at each insurer who declined the risk. (50 Ill. Adm. Code 2701.60). All policies must be submitted to the Surplus Line Association of Illinois for countersignature and recording.

Commercial Purchaser Exemption. Licensed surplus line producers may procure surplus line insurance from an unauthorized insurer for an exempt commercial purchaser without making the required diligent effort to procure the insurance from authorized insurers if:

1. The producer has disclosed to the exempt commercial purchaser that insurance may or may not be available from the authorized insurers that may provide greater protection with more regulatory oversight; and

2. The exempt commercial purchaser has subsequently requested in writing for the broker to procure or place such insurance from an unauthorized insurer. (50 Ill. Adm. Code 2701.50(c)).

   An exempt commercial purchaser is any person purchasing commercial insurance that, at the time of placement, meets the following requirements:

   (A) The person employs or retains a qualified risk manager to negotiate insurance coverage.

   (B) The person has paid aggregate nationwide commercial property and casualty insurance premiums in excess of $100,000 in the immediately preceding twelve months.

   (C) The person meets at least one of the following:

   (1) The person possesses a net worth in excess of $20 million, as adjusted.
   (2) The person generates annual revenues in excess of $50 million, as adjusted.
   (3) The person employs more than 500 full-time or full-time equivalent employees per individual insured or is a member of an affiliated group employing more than 1,000 employees in the aggregate.
   (4) The person is a not-for-profit organization or public entity generating annual budgeted expenditures of at least $30 million, as adjusted.
   (5) The person is a municipality with a population in excess of 50,000 persons. (215 ILCS 5/445).

D. Tax: 3.5 percent rounded to the nearest whole dollar. A surplus lines producer must pay the director a sum equal to 3.5 percent of the gross premiums less returned premiums upon all surplus lines insurance submitted to the Surplus Line Association of Illinois during the preceding six months. The tax is collected semi-annually on August 1 and February 1. In addition, surplus lines producers must pay a fire marshal tax of 1 percent of gross premiums less returned premiums on all surplus lines insurance subject to fire marshal tax (see the Surplus Line Association Web site at www.slai.org for information about insurance subject to the fire marshal tax) during the preceding year on or before March 31 of each year. The surplus lines laws, taxes and filing requirements are not applicable to insurance on property or operations of railroads or aircraft engaged in interstate or foreign commerce, and wet marine insurance, including marine builder's risk and protection and indemnity insurance. The surplus lines tax, fire marshal tax and stamping fee are levied on the licensed surplus lines producer, who is permitted to pass these costs on to the insured, and if they are charged to the insured, they must each be shown as separate line items on the declarations page. The surplus lines premium tax, fire marshal tax and stamping fees do not apply to any fees levied by the surplus lines producer. Taxes are rounded to the nearest whole dollar. (215 ILCS 5/445(3); slai.org/info/procnew_ch06.asp).

Late Tax Payment Penalty. Penalties for failure to pay the full amount due will be calculated based on how late the payment is. Penalties for being one-seven days late are 10 percent of tax, not to exceed $1,000. Penalties for being eight-fourteen days late are 10 percent of tax, not to exceed $1,500. Penalties for being fifteen-twenty-one days late are 10 percent of tax, not to exceed $2,000. Penalties for being more than twenty-one days late are 10 percent of tax with no limit. In addition to the above penalties, penalties for failure to file a tax return or required report will be calculated based on how late the return or report is filed. Penalties for being one-seven days late are 10 percent of tax or $400 (whichever is greater), not to exceed $1,000. Penalties for being eight-fourteen days late are 10 percent of tax or $400 (whichever is greater) not to exceed $1,500. Penalties for being fifteen-twenty-one days late are 10 percent of tax or $400 (whichever is greater), not to exceed $2,000. Penalties for being more than twenty-one days late are 10 percent of tax or $400 (whichever is greater)) for each month are partial month, the entire penalty being limited to 50 percent of the tax or $2,000 whichever is greater). The director, through the attorney general, may institute an action in the name of the People of the State of Illinois, in any court of competent jurisdiction, for the recovery of the amount of such taxes and penalties due, and prosecute the same to final judgment, and take such steps as are necessary to collect the same. (215 ILCS 5/412).

E. **Stamping Fee:** Currently 0.075 percent, rounded to the nearest whole dollar. (slai.org/info/procnew_ch06.asp).

F. **Surplus Lines Association:** Surplus Line Association of Illinois, 222 S. Riverside Plaza, Suite 2220, Chicago, IL 60606-6101. Telephone: 312-263-1993. Website: http://www.slai.org; Email: info@slai.org for general inquiries.

G. Other Requirements or Restrictions:

Exemptions. The Illinois surplus lines law does not apply to the following lines of business: reinsurance, property and operations of railroads or aircraft engaged in interstate or foreign commerce; insurance of vessels, crafts, or hulls; cargoes; marine builder's risks; marine protection and indemnity, or other risks including strikes and war risks insured under ocean or wet marine forms of policies. (215 ILCS 5/445(11)). Surplus lines insurance may not be placed on a risk where there is an Illinois law requiring the insurance be placed with an authorized insurer; for any primary workers' comp risk; or for any personal lines risk where the coverage is available in a residual market. (215 ILCS 5/445(1.5(d))).

Eligibility. Licensed surplus lines producers may procure surplus lines insurance from an unauthorized insurer domiciled in the United States only if the insurer:

1. Is permitted in its domiciliary jurisdiction to write the type of insurance involved; and

2. Has, based upon information available to the surplus lines producer has a policyholders surplus of not less than $15 million determined in accordance with the laws of its domiciliary jurisdiction; and

3. Has standards of solvency and management that are adequate for the protection of policyholders.

   Licensed surplus line producers may procure surplus line insurance from an unauthorized insurer domiciled outside of the United States only if the insurer meets the standards for unauthorized insurers described above or is listed on the Quarterly Listing of Alien Insurers maintained by the International Insurers Department of the NAIC. (50 Ill. Adm. Code 2701.30).

It is unlawful to deliver a surplus lines policy to the insured unless it has been countersigned by the Surplus Line Association of Illinois.

Insurance cannot be placed with an unauthorized company to achieve a difference in premium or rate quoted by an authorized company.

Notice. Where an unauthorized insurer does not meet the standards set forth in above, a surplus lines producer may, if necessary, procure insurance from that insurer only if prior written warning of such fact or condition is given to the insured by the insurance producer or surplus lines producer:

In accordance with Section 445 of the Illinois Insurance Code, I hereby provide you with a written WARNING that the above-captioned unauthorized company with which

I propose to place the captioned coverage does not, or I am unable to verify that it does (checked as applicable):

______Have a policyholder surplus of $15 million or more.

______Meet minimal standards of solvency and management which are adequate for your protection. (50 Ill. Adm. Code 2701 ILL. A).

For policies placed with an Illinois domestic surplus lines insurer, the following notice must be stamped on the face of each policy in twelve-point bold-face type:

> **"Notice to Policyholder: This contract is issued, by a domestic surplus lines insurer, as defined in Section 445a, pursuant to Section 445 and as such is not covered by the Illinois Insurance Guaranty Fund."** (215 ILCS 5/445(10.5)).

For all other surplus lines insurers the stamping notice is the following:

> **"Notice to Policyholder: This contract is issued, pursuant to Section 445 of the Illinois Insurance Code, by a company not authorized and licensed to transact business in Illinois and as such is not covered by the Illinois Insurance Guaranty Fund."** (50 Ill. Adm. Code 2701.120(a)).

Records. Surplus lines producers must keep separate accounts and records of the business transacted under their surplus line license, to be kept for seven years from the policy effective date and to be open at all times to the inspection of the director or his representative. This includes complete copies of surplus lines insurance contracts maintained on paper or by electronic means, and a record of declinations for each surplus policy written, as well as records of diligent efforts made by producers. (215 ILCS 5/445, 50 Ill. Adm. Code 2701.60).

Reports. A surplus lines producer shall submit every insurance contract issued under his or her license to the Surplus Line Association of Illinois for recording and countersignature.

The submission and countersignature may be effected through electronic means. The submission shall set forth the name of the insured, the description and location of the insured property or risk, the amount insured, the gross premiums charged or returned, the name of the unauthorized insurer from whom coverage has been procured, the kind or kinds of insurance procured, and the amount of premium subject to tax required by §12 of the Fire Investigation Act.

Tax forms and payments are due twice a year, and tax forms must be filed even if no tax is due. Failure to file by the due dates subjects the licensee to an automatic minimum penalty of $400. (215 ILCS 5/412).

H. Independently Procured Insurance:

1. *Rules.* Industrial insureds may independently procure insurance. Policies must be filed within ninety days of the effective date. Endorsements must be filed with ninety days of the issue date of the endorsement. Filings are made electronically at https://www.slai.org/ipfile. Overview, instructions and user manual are available at the Surplus Line Association Web site (www.slai.org).

   Independent procurement tax is 3.5 percent, fire marshal tax is 1 percent of the fire premium as described in the schedule on the Surplus Line Association Web site, and filing fee is 0.075 percent for policies effective 01/01/2019 and later, 0.125 percent for policies effective from 01/01/2018 through 12/31/2018. Taxes and fees are rounded to the nearest whole dollar and must be paid within thirty days of the filing. (https://www.slai.org/info/info_ipfile_taxfee.asp).

2. *Industrial Insured Exemption.* An industrial insured is an "exempt commercial purchaser" as described under "Commercial Purchaser Exemption" in Section C, above, whose home state is Illinois. (215 ILCS 5/121-2.08).

NRRA Implementation

I. Compact: Illinois is not currently a party to a compact or an agreement.

J. Definitions: Home State. (A) Illinois is the insured's home state if the insured maintains its principal place of business in Illinois or—in the case of an individual—the individual's principal residence is in Illinois. If Illinois is considered the insured's home state, only Illinois' requirements regarding the placement of such business will apply. If 100 percent of the insured risk is located outside of Illinois, then the insured's home state is the state to which the greatest percentage of the insured's taxable premium for that insurance contract is allocated. If more than one insured from an affiliate group are named insureds on a single surplus lines insurance contract, Illinois will be considered the home state for that placement if Illinois is the home state of the member of the affiliated group that has the largest percentage of premium attributed to it under such insurance contract. (215 ILCS 5/445).

(B) If more than one insured from a group that is not affiliated are named insureds on a single surplus lines insurance contract, then: (1) If individual group members pay 100 percent of the premium for the insurance from their own funds, "home state" means the home state, as determined pursuant to item (A) of the statutory definition, of each individual group member; each individual group member's coverage under the surplus lines insurance contract shall be treated as a separate surplus lines contract for the purposes of this Section; (2) otherwise, "home state" means the home state, as determined pursuant to item (A) of the statutory definition described in the paragraph above, of the group. Nothing in this definition shall be construed to alter the terms of the surplus lines insurance contract. (215 ILCS 5/445).

Affiliate means, with respect to an insured, any entity that controls, is controlled by, or is under common control with the insured. (215 ILCS 5/445). For the purpose of this definition, an entity has control over another entity if: (1) the entity directly or indirectly or acting through one or more persons owns, controls, or has the power to vote 25 percent or more of any class of voting securities of the other entity; or (2) the entity controls in any manner the election of a majority of the directors or trustees of the other entity. (215 ILCS 5/445).

K. Statutory References: 215 ILCS 5/121-2.08; 5/412; 5/445; 5/500-40. 50 Ill. Adm. Code 2701.30, 50, 60, 120; 2701 ILL. A.

INDIANA

Note: After years of deliberation, Indiana has repealed the law providing for a multistate surplus lines insurance compact, SLIMPACT, due to a lack of participation by other states.

A. **Resident Licensing:** License fee: $80. Surplus lines producers may be individuals, firms, or corporations licensed under the law of the home state to place surplus lines insurance. A surplus lines producer must be licensed in Indiana as an insurance producer qualified as to the line or lines of insurance to be written. Any licensed resident or nonresident producer may place surplus lines business with any licensed surplus lines producer. Residents must hold an Indiana property & casualty producer license before applying for a surplus lines license, and the property & casualty license must be provided at the test site in lieu of a prelicensing certificate. Residents must pass the surplus lines exam and submit the original passing score report with their application. Exam fee: $75.50. Residents do not have to post bond. The surplus lines producer's license is for a term of two years, and license renewal date's are the same as the applicant's birth month. Renewals must be completed online. The biennial renewal fee is $80. Electronic application and renewal are available online through Vertafore (formerly known as Sircon) at www.sircon.com/indiana. Individuals choosing to submit the application in hardcopy may download the requisite forms at the department's Web site. Completed hardcopy applications should be mailed to the department's surplus lines coordinator at the address listed on the bottom of the application. (Ind. Code § 27-1-15.8-2 to 4; 27-1-15.6-32).).

   Business entities must identify at least one licensed surplus lines producer before the entity can be licensed for surplus lines. If more than one individual is named, each individual must be licensed in Indiana as a surplus lines producer. License application and renewal cost is $80. (Ind. Code § 27-1-15.6-6).

B. **Nonresident Licensing:** Nonresidents may be licensed for this purpose, if they hold an Indiana property and casualty producer licensed and have a current license for surplus lines authority in their home state. Business entities must identify at least one licensed surplus lines producer before the entity can be licensed for surplus lines. If more than one individual is named, each individual must be licensed in Indiana as a surplus lines producer. License and renewal fee: $120. Retaliatory fees can be viewed through links under nonresident requirements at http://www.in.gov/idoi/2484.htm. Nonresidents do not have to post bond.

   Notwithstanding any other provision of this chapter, a nonresident producer who receives a nonresident producer license under this section must maintain licensure in good standing in the nonresident producer's home state. (Ind. Code § 27-1-15.6-8).

C. Diligent Effort: Diligent effort, as determined to the satisfaction of the department, requires the licensee to be unable to procure the amount of insurance desired from insurers authorized and licensed to do business in Indiana. The department advises that coverage is not considered unavailable if it could be obtained in the admitted market but at a higher premium. As described below in more detail, an affidavit of nonavailability through admitted insurers for all placements each month must be filed by the 20th of the following month. Zero reports are not required. (Ind. Code § 27-1-15.8-3, 4; https://www.in.gov/idoi/2487.htm).

Commercial Purchaser Exemption. Surplus lines brokers seeking to procure or place nonadmitted insurance on behalf of an "exempt commercial purchaser" are not required to perform a diligent search if both:

1. The broker has disclosed to the exempt commercial purchaser that insurance may or may not be available from the admitted market that may provide greater protection with more regulatory oversight.

2. The exempt commercial purchaser has subsequently requested in writing for the broker to procure or place such insurance from a nonadmitted insurer. (https://www.wsia.org/wcm/Legislative_Advocacy___PAC/State_Info/Indiana.aspx).

D. Tax: Taxes are 2.5 percent of gross premiums, including any inspection or policy writing fees. Taxes are due on or before February 1 on all gross premiums upon all policies and contracts procured by the surplus lines producer during the preceding twelve month period ending December 31. Semi-annual premium tax filings are required even if no placements were made during the preceding six months. (Ind. Code § 27-1-15.8-4).

Multi-State Premium Tax Allocation: Indiana is still collecting 100 percent of surplus lines premium tax on multistate risks.

Late Premium Tax Penalty. If a surplus lines producer does not remit the tax due to the department within the time prescribed, the commissioner will assess the surplus lines producer a penalty 10 percent of the amount due. The commissioner will assess a further penalty of an additional 1 percent of the amount due for each month or portion of a month that any amount due remains unpaid after the first month. Penalties assessed are payable by the surplus lines producer and are not collectible from an insured. (Ind. Code § 27-1-15.8-4).

Premium Defined. "Premium" means money or any other thing of value paid or given in consideration to an insurer, insurance producer, or solicitor on account of or in connection with a contract of insurance and must include as a part but not in limitation of the above, policy fees, admission fees, membership fees and regular or special assessments and payments made on account of annuities. (Ind. Code § 27-1-2-3(w)).

E. **Stamping Fee:** None.

F. **Surplus Lines Association:** None.

G. **Other Requirements or Restrictions:**

Eligibility. Only nonadmitted insurers on commissioner's authorized list may be used. Insurer may charge inspection or policy writing fee, but agent's service fee is prohibited. Surplus Lines application, instructions, and other forms are available at www.in.gov/idoi/2483.

Records. A licensed surplus lines producer must keep a separate account of all business transacted under this section. The account may be inspected at any time by the commissioner or the commissioner's deputy or examiner. (Ind. Code § 27-1-15.8-4(d)).

Monthly Affidavits. Licensed surplus lines producers must execute and file with the department of insurance on or before the twentieth day of each month an affidavit that specifies all transactions, policies, and contracts procured during the preceding calendar month, including:

1. The description and location of the insured property or risk and the name of the insured.

2. The gross premiums charged in the policy or contract.

3. The name and home office address of the insurer whose policy or contract is issued, and the kind of insurance effected.

4. A statement that:

    a. The licensee, after diligent effort, was unable to procure from any insurer authorized to transact the particular class of insurance business in Indiana the full amount of insurance required to protect the insured.

    b. The insurance placed under this chapter is not placed for the purpose of procuring it at a premium rate lower than would be accepted by an insurer authorized and licensed to transact insurance business in Indiana.

Monthly affidavit forms may be downloaded from the Department's Web site at: http://www.in.gov/idoi/2487.htm.

Surplus line producers are no longer required to submit monthly reports and affidavits if no business is written for that particular month. (Ind. Code § 27-1-15.8-4(b)).

Annual Statements. Licensed surplus lines producers must file with the department, not later than March 31 of each year, the financial statement, dated as of December 31 of the preceding year, of each unauthorized insurer from whom the surplus lines producer has procured a policy or contract. The insurance commissioner may, in the commissioner's discretion, after reviewing the financial statement of the unauthorized insurer, order the surplus lines producer to cancel an unauthorized insurer's policies and contracts if the commissioner is of the opinion that the financial statement or condition of the unauthorized insurer does not warrant continuance of the risk. (Ind. Code § 27-1-15.8-4(c)).

Licensed surplus lines producers must keep a separate account of all business transacted under this section. The account may be inspected at any time by the commissioner or the commissioner's deputy or examiner.

Surplus lines producers may accept and place policies or contracts authorized under this section for an insurance producer duly licensed in Indiana, and may compensate the insurance producer even though the insurance producer is not licensed under this chapter. (Ind. Code § 27-1-15.8-4(g))

Commission Fees. The commission shall collect a fee, payable by the insured directly or through a surplus lines licensee, on each transaction processed through the compact clearinghouse, to cover the cost of the operations and activities of the commission and the commission's staff.

H. Independently Procured Insurance:

1. *Rules.* Industrial insureds in Indiana may purchase insurance that is not readily available in the insurance marketplace directly from unauthorized insurers without the use of an agent or a broker. An industrial insured that purchases insurance directly from an unauthorized insurer should provide an affidavit to the department, along with a statement noting it was unable to procure the insurance from an authorized insurer. In addition, the industrial insureds must file an affidavit specifying all transactions undertaken and policies and contracts procured during the preceding calendar year, including: the description and location of the insured property or risk and the name of the insured; the gross premiums charged for the policy or contract; the name and home office address of the insurer that issues the policy or contract and the kind of insurance affected; and a statement that the insured, after diligent effort, was unable to procure from any insurer authorized to transact the particular kind of business in Indiana the full amount of insurance coverage required to protect the insured. This affidavit is submitted with the premium tax. (Ind. Code § 27-4-5-2(8)).

2. *Tax.* Taxes of 2.5 percent of gross premiums are due on or before February 1 on all gross premiums upon all policies and contract procured by the insured during the preceding twelve month period ending December 31. Premium tax filings are required even if no placements were made during the preceding six months. In addition, in the event the premium tax is not remitted in compliance with the above section, an additional 10 percent of the amount due will be added for the first month after the dates above, and an additional 1 percent of the amount due will be added for each additional month the taxes are unpaid. (Ind. Code § 27-1-15.8-4).

3. *Industrial Insured Exemption.* The firm must:

   a. Have a full-time employee acting as an insurance manager or buyer or use the services of a consultant.

   b. Have aggregate annual premium for insurance on all risks that total at least $25,000.

   c. Have at least twenty-five full-time employees.

   d. Remits to department 2.5 percent of all gross premiums.

   e. Files an affidavit with all transactions undertaken and policies and contracts procured during the calendar year. (Ind. Code § 27-4-5-2).

NRRA Implementation

I. Compact: None.

J. Definitions:

1. "Home State" means:

   a. With respect to an insured:

      (i) The state in which the insured maintains:
         (a) The insured's principal place of business.
         (b) If the insured is an individual, the insured's principal residence.
      (ii) If 100 percent of the insured risk is located outside the state described in clause (a), the state to which the greatest percentage of the insured's taxable premium for the insurance contract is allocated.

   b. With respect to an affiliated group, if more than one insured from the affiliated group is a named insured on a single nonadmitted insurance contract, the home state determined under subdivision (1) of the member of the affiliated group that has the largest percentage of premium attributed to the member under the insurance contract.

2. "Principal Place of Business" means, with respect to determining the home state of an insured, the state where the:

   a. Insured maintains the insured's headquarters.

   b. Insured's officers direct, control, and coordinate the business activities of the insured.

3. "Affiliate" means, with respect to an insured, an entity that controls, is controlled by, or is under common control with the insured.

4. "Control" means ownership or power to vote at least 25 percent of any class of voting securities; or power to determine the election of a majority of the directors or trustees; of an entity.

(Ind. Code §27-1-15.8-1).

K. Statutory References: Ind. Code §§ 27-1-2-3; 1-15.6-6, 8, 32; 1-15.8-1 to 4; 4-5-2.

IOWA

A. Resident Licensing: To apply for a surplus lines license, resident applicants must hold an active property & casualty license in Iowa, pass the Surplus Lines exam, then submit their application via NIPR unless otherwise directed by the Division. Applicants must be at least eighteen years of age, pay the license fee, and must have the requisite character and competence to receive a license as an insurance producer. License fee: $50. Renewal fee: $50. Producer licenses are valid for three years. (Iowa Code §§ 522B.5).

Business Entities. License/renewal fee: $50. Business entities must designate a licensed producer responsible for the business entity's compliance with the insurance laws and rules of the state. The application form is the uniform business entity application. (Iowa Code §§ 522B.5).

B. Nonresident Licensing: Nonresidents may be licensed for surplus lines authority in Iowa. License/renewal fee is $50. In order to receive a surplus lines license, all of the following must apply:

1. The person is currently licensed as an insurance producer and is in good standing in the person's home state with the surplus/excess line of authority.

2. The person has submitted the proper request for licensure and has paid the required fees.

3. The person has submitted or transmitted to the commissioner the application for licensure that the person submitted to the person's home state, or in lieu of such application, a completed uniform application.

4. The person's home state awards nonresident insurance producer licenses to residents of this state on the same basis. (Iowa Code § 522B.7).

C. Diligent Effort: The diligent effort certification is completed with each electronic record submitted.

Commercial Purchaser Exemption. Surplus lines brokers seeking to procure or place nonadmitted insurance on behalf of an "exempt commercial purchaser" are not required to perform a diligent search if:

1. The broker has disclosed to the exempt commercial purchaser that insurance may or may not be available from the admitted market that may provide greater protection with more regulatory oversight.

2. The exempt commercial purchaser has subsequently requested in writing for the broker to procure or place such insurance from a nonadmitted insurer. (Iowa Code § 515I.9).

   The exempt commercial purchaser must meet all of the following requirements:

   a. The person employs or retains a qualified risk manager to negotiate insurance coverage.

   b. The person has paid aggregate, nationwide commercial property and casualty insurance premiums in excess of $100,000 in the immediately preceding twelve months.

   c. The person meets at least one of the following criteria:

      (1) The person possesses a net worth in excess of $20 million, as adjusted.
      (2) The person generates annual revenues in excess of $50 million, as adjusted.
      (3) The person employs more than 500 full time or full time equivalent employees per individual insured or is a member of an affiliated group employing more than 1,000 employees in the aggregate.
      (4) The person is a nonprofit organization or public entity generating annual budgeted expenditures of at least $30 million, as adjusted.
      (5) The person is a municipality with a population in excess of 50,000 persons. (Iowa Code § 515I.2(8)).

D. Tax: 1 percent. For all premiums collected during the calendar year, every unauthorized insurer is required to pay a premium tax of 1 percent to the commissioner of insurance before March 1, next succeeding the calendar year in which the insurance was so effectuated, continued, or renewed. If the premium tax is not paid before March 1, the tax will be increased by a penalty of 25 percent and by the amount of an additional penalty computed at the rate of 1 percent per month or any part thereof from the date such payment was due to the date paid. (Iowa Code Ann. §432.1).

A bulletin will be sent sixty days prior to all nonadmitted surplus lines companies, purchasing groups, and risk retention groups. No invoices will be sent. All premium tax submissions must be submitted electronically at OPTins.org. The Excel workbooks used for the recording and reporting of taxes due can be found at https://iid.iowa.gov/premtax and https://iid.iowa.gov/slapp. You can also access the spread-sheets at www.optins.org. Receipt for Payment of Taxes are due on or before March 1 to avoid any penalties.

The late penalty fee is automatically calculated and charged in the premium tax workbook. (Iowa Code § 515I.10).

Multi-State Premium Tax Allocation. In determining the amount of premiums taxable in the state, all premiums written, procured, or received in the state and all premiums on policies negotiated in the state will be deemed written on property or risks located or resident in the state, except such premiums are as properly allocated or apportioned and reported as taxable premiums of any other state or states. See below.

On multi-state risks where Iowa is not the home state, Iowa will not collect any premium tax. On a multistate risk where Iowa is the home state, Iowa will collect 100 percent of the tax. On a single state policy where Iowa is the home state, Iowa will collect 100 percent of the premium tax. (Iowa Code § 515I.10).

Premium Defined. The term "premium" includes all premiums, membership fees, assessments, dues, and any other consideration for insurance. Any fees are passed on to the insured.

E. **Stamping Fee:** None.

F. **Surplus Lines Association:** Not active at this time.

G. **Other Requirements or Restrictions:**

Exemptions. The surplus lines insurance law does not apply to the following:

1. Reinsurance.

2. Attorneys acting in the ordinary relation of attorney and client in the adjustment of claims or losses.

3. Transactions in Iowa involving a policy lawfully solicited, written and delivered outside of the state, covering subjects not located or expressly to be performed in Iowa at the time of issue, and which transactions are subsequent to the issuance of the policy.

4. Transactions in this state involving group or blanket insurance and group annuities where the master policy of such groups was lawfully issued and delivered in a state the company was authorized to do an insurance transaction in.

5. Transactions involving any insurance policy issued prior to July 1, 1967.

6. Insurance on vessels, crafts or hulls, cargoes, marine builder's risk, marine protection and indemnity on other risk including strikes and war risks commonly insured under ocean or wet marine forms of policy.

7. Transactions involving risks located in the state where the policy or contract of insurance for such risk was principally negotiated and delivered outside of Iowa and was lawfully issued in a state or foreign country where the insurer was authorized, and had no contact with Iowa except in connection with inspections or losses required by the contract or policy covering the risk located in Iowa.

8. Transactions involving a multiple employer welfare arrangement meeting the conditions in Iowa Code §507A.4(9).

9. A self-funded health benefit plan sponsored by an employer in Iowa under the federal Employee Retirement Security Act of 1974 if the plan is granted a waiver by the commissioner and meets the conditions in Iowa Code Ann. §507A.4(10). (Iowa Code § 507A.4).

Eligibility. Surplus lines insurance may be placed by a surplus lines insurance producer with a nonadmitted insurer or domestic surplus lines insurer only if all of the following requirements are met:

1. The proposed nonadmitted insurer or domestic surplus lines insurer is an eligible surplus lines insurer approved by the commissioner.

2. The proposed nonadmitted insurer or domestic surplus lines insurer is authorized to write the type of insurance sought in Iowa.

3. Unless otherwise exempt from this requirement, after a diligent search the full amount or type of insurance cannot be obtained from an admitted insurer.

4. All other requirements of the surplus lines chapter are met. (Iowa Code § 515I.3).

A nonadmitted insurer seeking to qualify as an eligible surplus lines insurer must submit a request to qualify in a form and format as directed by the commissioner. (Iowa Code § 515I.4).

Notice. A producer who places coverage with a qualified surplus lines carrier must deliver to the insured, within thirty days of the date the policy is issued, the notice below. Compliance can be achieved by stamping a verbatim copy of this language in a clear and conspicuous place on the policy:

> "This policy is issued, pursuant to Iowa Code chapter 515I, by an eligible surplus lines insurer in Iowa and as such is not covered by the Iowa Insurance Guaranty Association." (191 IAC 21.4).

Evidence of Coverage. Upon placement of surplus lines insurance, the surplus lines producer must deliver to the insured the policy or contract, or if the policy or contract is not available at that time, then a certificate, cover note, binder, or other evidence of insurance.

As soon as reasonably possible after placement, the producer must deliver a copy of the policy or contract, or if not available, a certificate of insurance to the insured to replace any evidence of insurance previously issued. Each policy or contract or certificate of insurance must contain or have attached a complete record of all policy or contract insuring agreements, conditions, exclusions, clauses, endorsements, or any other material facts that would regularly be included in the policy or contract.

If, after delivery or any evidence of insurance, there is a change in the identity of any eligible surplus lines insurer, or the proportion of the risk assumed by such insurer, or any other material change in coverage as stated or evidenced, the producer must promptly issue and deliver to the insurer an appropriate substitute for, or endorsement of the original document, showing the current status of coverage and the surplus lines insurer responsible for the coverage. (Iowa Code § 515I.5(104)).

Records. Each surplus lines producer must keep a full and true record of each surplus lines policy or contract placed by an eligible surplus lines insurer and issued or delivered by that person which covers risks wholly or partly located or to be performed in the state. These records must be made available to the commissioner for examination upon request, and must be maintained for a period of not less than five years following termination of the surplus lines insurance policy or contract. (Iowa Code Ann. §515I.5(5)).

Reports. A surplus lines insurance producer must file a report and remit all premium taxes due to Iowa for all surplus lines insurance placed by an eligible surplus lines insurer and issued or delivered to that person during the reported period established by the commissioner. (Iowa Code Ann. § 515I.5). A producer who places insurance with a qualified surplus lines carrier must file an annual report on or before March 1 when the policies have been issued during the preceding calendar year. Failure to file an annual return or pay the taxes will be deemed grounds for the revocation of a producer's license by the insurance division, and failure to file within the time requirements will subject the producer to further penalties. The annual report is not required to be filed if no business was written in the preceding year. (191 IAC 21.3).

H. Independently Procured Insurance:

1. *Rules.* When Iowa is the home state of the insured, a person who directly procured, continues, or renews a surplus lines insurance policy or contract independently and without using a surplus lines producer on properties, risks, or exposures

located or to be performed in whole or in part in Iowa must file a written report regarding the transaction with the commissioner. Each person who independently procures a surplus lines insurance policy or contract must pay a premium tax of 1 percent or the premium amount. The commissioner may assess a penalty of one percent of the delinquent amount of taxes owed per month. (Iowa Code § 515I.10).

2. *Industrial Insured Exemption.* Iowa does not have an industrial insured exemption.

NRRA Implementation

I. Compact: Iowa has not entered into a compact or agreement at this time.

J. Definitions:

1. *Home State.* Iowa is the home state if the insured maintains its principal place of business or, in the case of an individual, the individual's principal residence here. This state's requirements regarding the placement of such business will apply in Iowa if this state is considered the home state. However, if 100 percent of the insured risk is located outside of this state, then the home state is the state to which the greatest percentage of the insured's taxable premium for that insurance contract is allocated. With respect to an affiliated group, if more than one insured from the affiliated group is a named insured on a single nonadmitted insurance contract, the home state is that of the member of the affiliated group that has the largest percentage of premium attributed to the member under the insurance contract. (Iowa Code § 515I.2(9)).

2. *Principal Place of Business.* The principal place of business is the state where the named insured conducts the majority of his business. (Iowa Code § 515I.2(9)).

3. *Affiliate.* Affiliate means, with respect to an insurer, any entity that controls, is controlled by, or is under common control with the insurer. "Affiliated Group" means any group of entities that are affiliates. (Iowa Code § 515I.2(2, 3)).

4. *Control.* Control means either of the following: (a) an entity that directly or indirectly, or acting through one or more persons, owns, controls, or has the power to vote 25 percent or more of any class of voting securities of another entity; or (b) an entity controls in any manner the election of a majority of the directors or trustees of another entity. (Iowa Code § 515.2(6)).

K. Statutory References: Iowa Code §§ 432.1; 507A.4; 515I2 to 5, 9, 10; 522B.5 to 7. 191 IAC 21.3, 4.

KANSAS

Note: Surplus Lines is termed "Excess Coverage" in the State of Kansas.

A. Resident and Nonresident Licensing: Upon receipt of a proper application, the commissioner of insurance may issue an excess lines coverage license to any licensed property and casualty agent of Kansas or any other state. Before any such license will be issued, the applicant must submit proper application (NAIC Uniform Application) and submit a fee of $50. Excess lines coverage licenses are renewable each year on May 1 upon the payment of a $50 renewal fee. (KSA § 40-246b). Applications and renewals can be completed online at www.nipr.com or through the mail. Renewal is contingent upon receipt of all required tax forms.

B. Nonresident Licensing: Licensing for nonresidents is the same as the licensing for residents. The certification of insurance authority in the applicant's state of residence is verified through the National Association of Insurance Commissioners Producer Database (PDB). (KSA § 40-4906(d)).

C. Diligent Effort: Diligent effort is where a licensed excess lines coverage agent is unable to secure the amount of insurance required to protect the property, person, or firm described in such agent's affidavit or statement from loss or damage in regularly admitted companies during the preceding year. See Other Requirements or Restrictions below for more details. (KSA §40-246b).

Commercial Purchaser Exemption. Surplus lines brokers seeking to procure or place nonadmitted insurance on behalf of an "exempt commercial purchaser" are not required to perform a diligent search if both:

1. the broker has disclosed to the exempt commercial purchaser that insurance may or may not be available from the admitted market that may provide greater protection with more regulatory oversight; and

2. the exempt commercial purchaser has subsequently requested in writing for the broker to procure or place such insurance from a nonadmitted insurer. (KSA § 40-246g).

The definition of 'exempt commercial purchaser' can be found in KSA § 40-246i.

D. Tax: 6 percent. On March 1 of each year, each licensed agent must collect and pay to the commissioner a sum based on the total gross premiums charged, less any return premiums, for surplus lines insurance provided by the licensee pursuant to the license. (KSA § 40-246c).

Multi-State Premium Tax Allocation. The multistate tax system was repealed in 2015.

The tax on any portion of the premium unearned at termination of insurance, if any, having been credited by the state to the licensee must be returned to the policyholder directly by the surplus lines licensee or through the producing broker. The surplus lines licensee is prohibited from rebating any part of the tax for any reason. (KSA § 40-246c).

Late Tax Payment Penalty. The commissioner of insurance will collect double the amount of tax from any licensee or other responsible individual who fails to pay the tax to the commissioner within the period stated above. (KSA §§ 40-246c, 40-246a.).

Premium Defined. "Gross premium" means the amount charged to the insured for the insurance procured. When an audit or gross receipts contract requires a deposit premium, the amount collected during the calendar year either as a deposit or partial payment must be reported on the affidavit and annual statement reporting forms as gross premium for that calendar year. Gross premium must not include the tax due on the premium nor will the tax be charged to the insured unless specifically identified and provided for in the policy. (K. A. R. § 40-8-7).

E. **Stamping Fee:** None. Kansas does not have a stamping office.

F. **Surplus Lines Association:** None.

G. **Other Requirements or Restrictions:** (KSA §40-246b).

Eligibility. Any licensed excess lines coverage agent may negotiate for insureds whose home state is Kansas or to effect insurance or reinsurance for persons or corporations other than such agent, with insurers not authorized to do business in Kansas. Life insurance may not be placed with nonadmitted insurers. (KSA § 40-214).

No excess lines agent can place insurance on a Kansas domiciled risk with an insurer whose name does not appear on the list of insurers not authorized to do business in Kansas pursuant to KSA § 40–246e. Only those insurers who have filed a certified copy of their most recent annual statement with the commissioner may appear on the list. No company will appear on the list whose capital or surplus as shown on the annual statement does not equal or exceed $4.5 million. Insurance exchanges that issue contracts on behalf of their members and pay the filing fee described below may appear on the list if their individual members have a capital or surplus equal to or in excess of $1.5 million and the aggregate capital or surplus of all members of the exchange is at least $15 million. A nonrefundable filing fee of $200 is required of any insurer submitting its annual statement for review by the commissioner for inclusion on the list. (KSA § 40-246e).

If business is placed with a nonadmitted company that is subsequently determined to be insolvent, the excess lines agent placing such business with such company is relieved of any responsibility to the insured as it relates to such insolvency, if the excess lines agent has satisfactorily complied with all requirements pertaining to notification of the insured, has properly obtained the written consent of the insured and has used due diligence in selecting the insurer. It is presumed that due diligence was used in selecting the insurer if such insurer was on the list compiled pursuant to KSA § 40–246e at the time coverage first became effective. (KSA § 40-246b).

Notice. Each insurance contract procured and delivered as excess coverage must bear the signature of the agent who placed the coverage with a nonadmitted insurer. (K.A.R. § 40-8-8). The following notice must be stamped in a prominent manner on the declarations page:

> "This policy is issued by an insurer not authorized to do business in Kansas and, as such, the form, financial condition, and rates are not subject to review by the Commissioner of Insurance and the insured is not protected by any guaranty fund." (KSA 40-246b).

Evidence of Coverage. The licensed excess coverage agent must, prior to placing insurance with an insurer not authorized to do business in this state, obtain the written consent of the prospective named insured and provide such insured the following information in a form promulgated by the commissioner:

1. A statement that the coverage will be obtained from an insurer not authorized to do business in Kansas.

2. A statement that the insurer's name appears on the list of companies maintained by the commissioner.

3. A notice that the insurer's financial condition, policy forms, rates and trade practices are not subject to the review or jurisdiction of the commissioner.

4. A statement that the protection of the guaranty associations is not afforded to policyholders of the insurer.

5. A statement or notice with respect to any other information deemed necessary by the commissioner pertinent to insuring with an insurer not authorized to do business in Kansas.

In the event the insured desires that coverage be bound with an insurer not admitted to Kansas and it is not possible to obtain the written consent of the insured prior to binding the coverage, the excess lines agent may bind the coverage after advising the insured of the information set out above and must obtain written confirmation that the insured desires that coverage be placed with an insurer not admitted to this state within thirty days after binding coverage. (KSA § 40-246b).

When business comes to a licensed excess lines agent in which Kansas is the home state for placement with an insurer not authorized to do business in Kansas from an agent not licensed as an excess lines agent, it is the responsibility of the licensed excess lines agent to ascertain that the insured has been provided the above information and has consented to being insured with an insurer not authorized to do business in Kansas.

Records. Each excess lines agent must keep a separate record book in such agent's office showing the transactions of fire and casualty insurance and reinsurance placed in companies not authorized to do business in Kansas, the amount of gross premiums charged thereon, the insurer with which the policy was placed, the date, term and number of the policy, the location and nature of the risk, the name of the insured and such other information as the commissioner may require and such record shall be available at all times for inspection by the commissioner of insurance or the commissioner's authorized representatives. (KSA § 40-246b).

The record to be maintained by each excess lines agent must include the following:

1. A duplicate copy of the combined affidavit annual statement.

2. The exact amount of each kind of insurance permitted under this act which has been procured for each assured.

3. The home address of the insurer and the kind or kinds of insurance effected.

4. The address of the insured, and a brief description of the property insured.

5. The insurance cancelled or added, and its premiums.

6. A duplicate of the policy with each rider, endorsement, and attachment.

7. Evidence that the information and consent of the insured required by KSA § 40-246b was provided and obtained. (K.A.R. § 40-8-11).

Annual Affidavits. On or before March 1 of each year, licensed excess lines coverage agents must file with the insurance department of Kansas a sworn affidavit or statement to the effect that, after diligent effort, the agent has been unable to secure the amount of insurance required to protect the property, person, or firm described in such agent's affidavit or statement from loss or damage in regularly admitted companies during the preceding year. Mere rate differential shall not be grounds for placing a particular risk in a nonadmitted carrier when an admitted carrier would accept such risk at a different rate. (KSA § 40-246b).

H. Independently Procured Insurance:

1. Kansas permits independently procured coverage, provided the policyholder reports the coverage and pays the applicable taxes using the department's Self-Procured Insurance Tax Report form on the department's website.

2. *Industrial Insured Exemption*. In Kansas, an exemption is allowed in the licensing law for industrial insureds:

    a. Who procure the insurance of any risk or risks by use of the services of a full-time employee acting as an insurance manager or buyer.

    b. Whose aggregate annual premiums for the kinds of insurance total at least $50,000.

    c. Who have at least twenty-five full-time employees.

    d. Whose principal activity consists of the manufacture of a product or products.

    e. Who contribute not less than $10,000 to the capital or surplus of the industrial insured captive insurance company that insures its risks. Such contribution shall be in the form of cash which may be returned at such time as the risks of the industrial insured cease to be insured by the captive insurance company. (KSA § 40-4301, 5701).

NRRA Implementation

I. Compact:

I. Compact: KSA §§ 40-5701, 40-5702 and 40-5703, which was SLIMPACT, were repealed. Kansas is no longer a SLIMPACT state.

J. Definitions:

1. *Home State*. Except as provided in subparagraph b., the term "Home State" means, with respect to an insured:

    a. The state in which an insured maintains its principal place of business or, in the case of an individual, the individual's state of principal residence.

b. If 100 percent of the insured risk is located out of the state referred to in subparagraph (1)(a), the state to which the greatest percentage of the insured's taxable premium for that insurance contract is allocated.

2. *Home State, Affiliated Groups.* If more than one insured from an affiliated group are named insureds on a single nonadmitted insurance contract, the term "home state" means the home state, as determined pursuant to subparagraph a., of the member of the affiliated group that has the largest percentage of premium attributed to it under such insurance contract.

3. "Principal Place of Business" means with respect to determining the Home State of the insured, the state where the insured maintains its headquarters and where the insured's high-level officers direct, control and coordinate the business activities of the insured. (KSA 40-246i).

K. Statutory References: KSA §§ 40-214; 246a to 246c; 246e; 246g; 246i; 4301; 4906; 5701. K.A.R. §§ 40-8-7, 8-8, 8-11.

KENTUCKY

A. Resident Licensing: Any Kentucky-licensed agent may submit business through licensed surplus lines brokers and receive commission on that business. Individuals licensed by Kentucky as resident agents with property and casualty lines of authority may be licensed to place insurance with nonadmitted insurers. Initial application and biennial renewal fee: $100. (KRS §304.10-120; 806 KAR 4:010).

NRRA provides that no state, other than an insured's home state, may require a surplus lines broker to be licensed in order to sell, solicit, or negotiate nonadmitted insurance with respect to such insured.

The following forms are used for surplus lines broker license applicants:

1. The Electronic Application may be submitted through the National Insurance Producer Registry (NIPR) at www.nipr.com or via Paper Application—Form 8301.

2. Electronic AOC Background Check Report at http://courts.ky.gov.

The following forms are used for business entity applicants:

1. Electronic Application submitted through the National Insurance Producer Registry (NIPR) at www.nipr.com or Paper Application – Form 8301-BE.

2. Resident business entities must provide a designated agent who holds both property-casualty and surplus lines broker licenses.

A licensed resident surplus lines broker must keep in force:

(a) Evidence of financial responsibility in the sum of not less than $1 million per occurrence and the sum of $2 million in the aggregate, for all occurrences within one year, either in the form of an errors and omissions insurance policy issued by an authorized insurer, a bond issued by an authorized corporate surety, a deposit, or a combination of a bond and deposit; and

(b) A bond in favor of the State of Kentucky in the sum of $50,000 with an authorized corporate surety. (KRS §304.10-140).

B. Nonresident Licensing: An applicant licensed as a surplus lines broker and in good standing in the applicant's home state may be issued a nonresident surplus lines broker's license in Kentucky if the applicant's home state issues surplus lines broker licenses to Kentucky residents on the same basis. (KRS §304.10-120).

Exceptions: An applicant shall be qualified to list Kentucky as their home state in order to obtain a license under KRS §304.9-230 if:

1. the applicant has a home state that does not issue a license to sell, solicit, and negotiate travel insurance; and

2. the applicant has otherwise met the requirements for the license in accordance with the applicable statutes.

The commissioner shall offer the applicant the opportunity to complete any prelicensing courses and exams that are required online and the applicant shall not hold resident licenses for more than one state.

Courtesy filings by a licensed surplus lines broker on behalf of someone who does not hold a Kentucky surplus lines license are considered a violation of KRS §§304.9-080(1) and 304.10-040(1). (KRS §304.9-120).

C. **Diligent Effort:** Surplus lines coverage may be procured from unauthorized insurers if the insurance is procured through a licensed surplus lines broker and, after diligent effort, the licensed agent has been unable to get the full amount of insurance from an insurance authorized to transact, and that actually writes, that kind and class of insurance in Kentucky. If the licensed agent is able to procure an amount of insurance less than the full amount, only the excess amount needed to procure the full amount shall be exported. The insurance shall not be exported for the purpose of securing either a lower premium rate than would be accepted by an authorized insurer or more advantageous terms of the insurance contract. (KRS §304.10-040).

Commercial Purchaser Exemption. The requirements related to a diligent effort shall not be required for coverage procured or placed for an exempt commercial purchaser if:

1. The broker procuring or placing the surplus lines insurance has disclosed to the exempt commercial purchaser that insurance may or may not be available from the admitted market that may provide greater protection with more regulatory oversight; and

2. The exempt commercial purchaser has subsequently requested in writing that the broker procure or place insurance from a nonadmitted insurer. (KRS § 304.10-040).

"Exempt commercial purchaser" means any person purchasing commercial insurance that, at the time of placement, meets the following requirements:

1. The person employs or retains a qualified risk manager to negotiate insurance coverage.

2. The person has paid aggregate nationwide commercial property and casualty insurance premium in excess of $100,000 in the immediately preceding twelve months.

3. The person meets at least one of the following criteria:

   a. The person possesses a net worth in excess of $20 million, as adjusted.

   b. The person generates annual revenues in excess of $50 million, as adjusted.

   c. The person employs more than 500 full-time or full-time equivalent employees per individual insured or is a member of an affiliated group employing more than 1,000 employees in the aggregate.

   d. The person is a not-for-profit organization or public entity generating annual budgeted expenditures of at least $30 million, as adjusted.

   e. The person is a municipality with a population in excess of 50,000 persons.

   The amounts in subparagraphs 3.a., b., and d. will be adjusted every fifth January 1 to reflect the percentage change for the five year period in the consumer price index for all urban consumers published by the Bureau of Labor Statistics of the Department of Labor. (KRS §304.10-030).

D. Taxes: 3 percent. Each broker must pay a tax at the rate of 3 percent on the premiums, assessments, fees, charges, or other consideration deemed part of the premium, on surplus lines insurance subject to tax transacted by him or her with unauthorized insurers during the preceding calendar quarter as shown by his or her quarterly statement filed with the commissioner in accordance with KRS §304.10-170.The tax is not assessed on the premium surcharge tax, the local government premium tax, or any other state or federal tax. The tax must be remitted to the commissioner within thirty days of the end of each calendar quarter. When collected, the tax will be credited to the insurance regulatory trust fund.

In addition, brokers are responsible for collecting and paying a Kentucky Premium Surcharge of $1.80 on every $100 to be reported and remitted monthly to the Kentucky Department of Revenue. (KRS §304.10-180; DOI Bulletin 2010-02).

Many Kentucky cities and counties tax property and casualty insurance premiums. As such, brokers are responsible for collecting and paying any applicable local government premium taxes directly to the taxing entity on an annual basis.

1. If Kentucky is the Home State of the insured:

   a. The 3 percent Kentucky Surplus Lines Tax is applied to premiums for all locations.

   b. The Kentucky Premium Surcharge is applied to premiums for Kentucky locations only.

   c. Local Government Premium Taxes are applied to those premiums generated by risks located within Kentucky taxing authorities only.

2. If Kentucky is not the Home State of the insured, no Kentucky taxes are applied to the policy premiums, and no Affidavit should be filed for the policy. (KRS §304.10-030; 806 KAR 10:030).

Premium Defined. "Premium" is the consideration for insurance, by whatever name called. Any "assessment," or any "membership," "policy," "survey," "inspection," "service," or similar fee or other charge in consideration for an insurance contract is deemed part of the premium. (KRS §304.14-030).

E. Stamping Fee: None. Kentucky does not have a surplus lines stamping office.

F. Surplus Lines Association:

527 Wellington Way

Suite 180 & 350

Lexington, KY 40503

Phone: (859) 245-2500

Fax: (859) 245-2550

Website: rpsins.com/locations/rps-lexington/

NOTE: The Kentucky DOI does not maintain updated contact information for this association. The contact information for Surplus Lines at the Kentucky DOI is as follows:

Phone – (502) 782-5138

Fax – (502) 564-5922

Email – DOI.SurplusLines@ky.gov

(https://insurance.ky.gov/ppc/staff.aspx?menuid=96)

G. Other Requirements or Restrictions:

Exemptions. Kentucky surplus lines laws do not apply to the following: ocean marine and foreign trade insurance; insurance on subjects located, resident or on operations wholly located outside Kentucky, or on vehicles or aircraft garaged or hangared outside the state; insurance on property or operations of railroads engaged in interstate commerce; aircraft owned or operated by aircraft manufacturers or operated in scheduled interstate flight; and their cargo or liability (other than workers compensation and employer's liability arising out of the ownership, maintenance, or use of aircraft); or reinsurance. (KRS §304.10-020).

Eligibility. Life and accident and health insurance may not be placed with nonadmitted insurers. Courtesy filings of taxes and certificates of nonavailability are not allowed in Kentucky. A broker shall place surplus lines insurance only with an insurer that he or she knows, or in the exercise of reasonable diligence could know:

1. Is authorized to write the type of insurance in its domiciliary jurisdiction.

2. Has capital and surplus or its equivalent under the laws of its domiciliary jurisdiction that equals the greater of:

    a. The minimum capital and surplus requirements set forth in KRS §304.3-120; or

    b. $15 million.

3. Is listed on the quarterly listing of alien insurers maintained by the National Association of Insurance Commissioners, if the insurer is a nonadmitted insurer domiciled outside of the United States.

A broker may place insurance covering certificates of investment with an insurance company or guarantee fund which is financially sound and has capital funds and reserves in excess of $15 million; and place insurance with a United States insurance exchange which the commissioner, in his or her discretion, may designate for use by surplus lines brokers licensed by the Commonwealth of Kentucky. (KRS §304.10-070).

Evidence of Insurance. Upon placing a surplus lines coverage, a broker must promptly issue and deliver to the insured evidence of the insurance consisting either of the policy as issued by the insurer, or, if such policy is not then available, the surplus lines broker's certificate. Such a certificate must be executed by the broker and shall show the description and location of the subject of the insurance, coverage, conditions, and term of the insurance, the premium, and rate charged and taxes collected from the insured, and the name and address of the insured and insurer. If the direct risk is assumed by more than one insurer, the certificate must state the name and address and proportion of the entire direct risk assumed by each such insurer.

No broker may issue a certificate or cover note or purport to insure or represent that insurance will be or has been granted by any unauthorized insurer, unless he has prior written authority from the insurer for the insurance or has received information from the insurer in the regular course of business that such insurance has been granted, or an insurance policy providing the insurance actually has been issued by the insurer and delivered to the insured.

If after the issuance and delivery of such certificate there is any change as to the identity of the insurers, of the proportion of the direct risk assumed by an insurer as stated in the broker's original certificate, or in any other material respect as to the insurance evidenced by the certificate, the broker must promptly issue and deliver to the insured a substitute certificate accurately showing the current status of the coverage and the insurers responsible thereunder.

If a policy issued by the insurer is not available upon placement of the insurance and the broker has issued and delivered his certificate upon request by the insurer the broker must as soon as reasonably possible procure from the insurer its policy evidencing such insurance and deliver the policy to the insured in replacement of the issued broker's certificate. (KRS §304.10-080).

Notice. The following notice must be stamped on the front page of all surplus lines policies, initialed by or bearing the name of the surplus lines broker who procured it:

> "This insurance has been placed with an insurer not licensed to transact business in the Commonwealth of Kentucky but eligible as a surplus lines insurer. The insurer is not a member of the Kentucky Insurance Guaranty Association. Should the insurer become insolvent, the protection and benefits of the Kentucky Insurance Guaranty Association are not available." (KRS §304.10-090).

Records. Each broker shall keep in his or her office a full and true record of each surplus lines coverage procured by him, including a copy of each daily report, if any, a copy of each certificate of insurance issued by him, and of the following items as may be applicable:

1. The amount of the insurance.

2. The gross premium charged.

3. The return premium paid, if any.

4. The rate of premium charged upon the several items of property.

5. The effective date of the contract, and the terms thereof.

6. The name and address of each insurer on the direct risk and the proportion of the entire risk assumed by the insurer if less than the entire risk.

7. The name and address of the insured.

8. The brief general description of the property or risk insured and where located or to be performed.

9. Other information as may be required by the commissioner.

The record must be open to examination by the commissioner at all times within five years after issuance of the coverage to which it relates. (KRS §304.10-160).

Quarterly Statements. Each broker shall, within thirty days of the end of each calendar quarter, file with the commissioner a verified statement of all surplus lines insurance transacted by him during the preceding calendar quarter. The statement must be on forms as prescribed by the commissioner and must show:

1. The gross amount of each kind of insurance transacted.

2. The aggregate of gross premiums charged.

3. The aggregate of returned premiums paid insureds.

4. The aggregate of net premiums.

5. Any additional information as required by the commissioner. (KRS §304.10-170).

The department will generate a quarterly report of all surplus lines transactions for a preceding calendar quarter, for each surplus lines broker based on the affidavits filed in accordance with 806 KAR 10:030. Each licensed surplus broker must retrieve his or her quarterly report from the department's secure website at https://insurance.ky.gov/doieservices/default.aspx and remit a signed copy of the quarterly report, along with the surplus lines premium tax and any applicable penalties in accordance with KRS §304.99-085, within thirty days of the end of each calendar quarter.

The quarterly report must be submitted by all licensed brokers even if no insurance transactions were completed during the period. (806 KAR 10:030).

Reports. At the time of effecting any surplus lines insurance, the broker must execute an affidavit setting forth facts from which it can be determined whether such insurance was eligible for export. This affidavit must be filed within fifteen days of the invoice date or effective date of each surplus lines transaction, whichever is later. Affidavits must be filed electronically via eServices. (KRS §304:10-050; 806 KAR 10:030; confirmed by KDOI 8/16/2021).

H. Independently Procured Insurance:

1. *Rules.* Only insureds who meet the definition of Industrial Insured and Government Entity Insured may transact insurance business in Kentucky with insurance companies which do not hold a certificate of authority issued by the commissioner without the services of a licensed surplus lines broker. The insurance carrier must report the transaction to the Kentucky Revenue Cabinet and pay a tax of 2 percent, as well as 2 percent to the Kentucky Revenue Cabinet Kentucky Premium and any applicable local government premium taxes; under KRS §304.11-050, the unauthorized insurer is to pay the tax, not the insured. Within the Kentucky Department of Insurance, the term "exempt entity" refers to all three categories. It is important to note that the Exempt Entities discussed in this section are NOT the same as an Exempt Commercial Purchaser as defined in KRS §304.10-040 (KRS §304.11-050).

2. *Industrial Insured Exemption.* To qualify as an industrial insured, the insured must be:

    a. An insured who procures the insurance of any risk or risks other than life and annuity contracts by use of the services of a full-time employee acting as an insurance manager or buyer or the services of a regularly and continuously retained qualified insurance consultant.

    b. An insured whose aggregate annual premiums for insurance on all risks total at least $25,000.

    c. An insured having at least twenty-five full-time employees.

    d. All entities that have qualified as industrial insureds as of July 1, 1999 are included. (KRS §304.11-020(2)(a)).

3. *Government Entity Insured.* To qualify as a government entity insured, the insured must:

    a. Be a government entity, municipal corporation, or public agency located in a city or county having a population of less than 50,000.

b. Procure insurance (other than life or annuity contracts) through a full-time employee functioning as risk manager or insurance buyer, or have continuously retained services of a qualified insurance consultant.

c. Have aggregate annual premiums of at least $100,000, exclusive of life, health, medical, or annuity premiums.

d. Have at least fifty full-time employees.

e. That satisfies the criteria the commissioner promulgates by administrative regulation. (KRS §304.11-020(2)(b)).

4. *Exempt Commercial Policyholder.* Means an insured that employs the services of an insurance agent or broker, procures commercial insurance with the services of a full-time risk manager, or a licensed insurance consultant and:

a. Is a city, county, or urban-county with a population of at least 50,000 persons, or the Commonwealth, or a not-for-profit organization or a public entity with an annual budget of at least $25 million or assets of at least $25 million in the preceding fiscal year; or

b. Certifies that it meets all four of the following criteria:

(1) Possesses a net worth of more than $25 million at the time the policy of insurance is issued.
(2) Generated net revenue or sales of more than $50 million in the preceding fiscal year.
(3) Employs more than 100 employees per individual company or 200 employees per holding company aggregate at the time the policy of insurance is issued.
(4) Paid annual aggregate insurance premiums of more than $500,000 in the preceding fiscal year.

All industrial insureds, government entity insureds, and exempt commercial policyholders must reapply to the commission for their respective insured status every three years on a form proscribed by the commissioner. (KRS §304.11-020(2)(c)).

NRRA Implementation

I. Compact: No longer a SLIMPACT state.

J. Home State Definition:

1. "Home State" means:

   a. The state in which an insured maintains its principal place of business or, in the case of an individual, the individual's principal residence; or

   b. If 100 percent of the insured risk is located out of the state referred to in this paragraph, the state to which the greatest percentage of the insured's taxable premium for that insurance contract is allocated; or

   c. If more than one insured from an affiliated group are named insureds on a single nonadmitted insurance contract, the home state, as determined pursuant to paragraph (a) of this section, of the member of the affiliated group that has the largest percentage of premium attributed to it under the insurance contract. (KRS §304.10-030).

K. Statutory References:

KRS §304.9-	120
KRS §§304.10-	020 to 050
	070 to 090
	120
	140
	160 to 180
KRS §§304.11-	020, 050
KRS §304.14-	30

806 KAR	4:010.
	10:030.

Kentucky DOI Bulletin 2010-02.

LOUISIANA

A. **Resident Licensing:** Licensed producers with at least two years insurance experience may be licensed to place business with nonadmitted insurers after passing a surplus lines examination. An individual resident of Louisiana may take a qualifying examination through PSI Exams (psiexams.com, 1-800-733-9267). A partnership or corporation may obtain a surplus lines brokers license. A business entity (resident or nonresident) may submit an application for an insurance producer license for the line of surplus lines at www.nipr.com. However, all individuals listed as countersigning individuals must qualify by passing the surplus lines examination. Exam Fee: $15; a score of 70 percent or better is required to pass. License fee for first-time applicant: $250. Biennial renewal fee: $350. (La. R.S. §§22:821, 1545; LAC 37:XI.503).

   Only the insured's home state may require a surplus lines broker to possess license to sell, solicit, or negotiate surplus lines insurance with respect to a particular policy.

B. **Nonresident Licensing:** An individual nonresident may apply for an insurance producer license for the line of surplus lines at www.nipr.com. A nonresident shall receive a producer license if:

   1. The person is currently licensed as a resident and in good standing in his or her home state.

   2. The person has submitted the proper request for licensure and has paid the fees required. Exam fee: $15. License fee for first-time applicant: $250. Biennial renewal fee: $350.

   3. The person has submitted or transmitted to the Commissioner of Insurance the application for licensure that the person submitted to his or her home state, or in lieu of the same, a completed Uniform Application.

   4. The person's home state awards nonresident producer licenses to residents of this state on the same basis. (La. R.S. §22:1548).

      Note: A nonresident producer who moves from one state to another state or a resident producer who moves from Louisiana to another state shall file a change of address and provide certification from the new resident state within thirty days of legal change of residence. The change of address shall include the producer's current and prior addresses. And if a nonresident producer license ceases to be current or in good standing in Louisiana if the home state license ceases to be current or in good standing. (La. R.S. 22:1548).

C. **Diligent Effort:** Any licensed surplus lines broker that procures a personal lines policy with an approved unauthorized insurer or eligible unauthorized insurer shall obtain from the applicant for insurance no later than the date of binding coverage, an acknowledgment on a standardized form promulgated by the Commissioner of Insurance which shall be maintained by the licensed surplus lines broker. The acknowledgment shall verify that:

1. The applicant was expressly advised prior to placement of the surplus lines insurance.

2. The insurance may be placed with a surplus lines insurer.

3. In the event of insolvency of the insurer, losses shall not be paid by the Louisiana Insurance Guaranty Association or the Louisiana Life and Health Insurance Guaranty Association.

4. The applicant for insurance expressly authorizes the procurement of surplus lines insurance coverage.

5. The coverage is being procured through a duly licensed surplus lines broker.

Acknowledgment is not needed at renewal as long as the policy is renewed with the same insurer. (La. R.S. §22:438).

"Surplus lines" insurance may be procured from a surplus lines insurer who must be a licensed surplus lines broker. It may also be procured without regard to the availability of coverage from authorized insurers. (La. R.S. §22:432).

Commercial Purchaser Exemption: A surplus lines broker seeking to procure surplus lines insurance on behalf of an exempt commercial purchaser is not required to perform a diligent search if the broker has disclosed to the exempt commercial purchaser that insurance may or may not be available from the admitted market that may provide greater protection with more regulatory oversight; and the exempt commercial purchaser has subsequently requested in writing for the surplus lines broker to procure insurance from a surplus lines insurer. The tax is 5 percent. (From the Louisiana Insurance Dept.)

D. **Tax:** 4.85 percent. On or before March 1, June 1, September 1, and December 1 of each year, each surplus lines broker must remit to the Commissioner of Insurance a tax on the premiums on surplus lines insurance reported in the surplus lines tax report, described below. (La. R.S. §22:439).

Multi-State Risk Premium Tax: Louisiana has withdrawn from the Nonadmitted Insurance Multistate Agreement (NIMA) and will no longer share surplus lines taxes with NIMA states. However, new and renewal multistate policies dated prior to October 1, 2015 are still subject to NIMA rules and reporting to the Surplus Lines Clearinghouse. (Bulletin 2015-06).

Premium Defined: "Premium" means all sums charged, received, or deposited as consideration for the purchase or continuance of insurance for a definitely stated term, and includes any assessment, membership, policy, survey, inspection, service or similar fee made by an insurer. (La. R.S. §22:46(13)).

E. **Stamping Fee:** None. Louisiana does not have a Surplus Lines Stamping Office.

F. **Surplus Lines Association:** Louisiana Surplus Lines Association, PO Box 2781, Baton Rouge, LA 70821. Phone: (225) 343-2776. FAX: (225) 344-1132. Email: info@lasurpluslines.com. Website: www.lasurpluslines.com.

G. **Other Requirements or Restrictions:** Surplus lines coverage may only be procured by licensed Louisiana surplus lines brokers and placed with insurers on the list of approved unauthorized insurers as maintained by the Commissioner of Insurance. To obtain and maintain placement on the list, foreign and alien insurers must be financially sound and authorized in their own jurisdiction to write the type of insurance placed, and one of the following must be satisfied: the foreign insurer has capital or surplus under the laws of its home jurisdiction that meets the greater of the minimum requirements of the laws of Louisiana or $15 million; or an insurer not domiciled in the United States or its territories must be listed by the International Insurers Department of the NAIC. (La. R.S. §22:435). The list of approved unauthorized foreign and alien insurers, or white list is prepared as needed by the commissioner.

Exemptions. The surplus lines provisions do not apply to reinsurance or to the following types of insurance when placed by licensed surplus lines brokers:

1. Insurance on property or operation of railroads engaged in interstate commerce.

2. Insurance on aircraft owned or operated by manufacturers of aircraft, or of aircraft operated in scheduled interstate flight, or cargo of such aircraft; or against liability, other than workers compensation and employer's liability, arising out of the ownership, maintenance, or use of such aircraft.

3. Ocean marine and foreign trade insurance. (La. R.S. 22:443).

   The broker must place the coverage with insurers with the financial strength outlined in the statute and prior listing on the National Association of Insurance Commissioners Nonadmitted Insurer Information Office for alien insurers. (La. R.S. §22:436).

The broker must show on any document issued by and/or delivered by them evidencing such insurance for not less than five years from the effective date, all of the insurers must clearly stamp on any such documents that, on the demand of the assured or its representative, the latest financial statements of any such insurers are available at its office for inspection. (La. R.S. §22:443).

Eligibility Requirements. A surplus lines broker cannot insure with any insurer unless it has capital and surplus of not less than $15 million. This requirement may be satisfied by an insurer's possessing less than the minimum capital and surplus upon an affirmative finding by the commissioner. Acceptability will be based on factors such as quality of management, capital, and surplus of any parent company, company underwriting profit and investment income trends, market availability; and company record and reputation within the industry. The commissioner cannot make an affirmative finding of acceptability where the unauthorized insurer's capital and surplus is less than $4.5 million. (La. R.S. §22:435).

All surplus lines contracts must indicate the name of the Louisiana surplus lines broker who procured it. Because the countersignature law was repealed, all surplus lines policies must now be signed by the broker as opposed to countersigned. These policies must be stamped or printed with the following notice in either red or prominently offset by a black border, in bold type that is uniform, appropriately spaced, and not less than ten point in type size:

NOTICE

> "This insurance policy is delivered as surplus lines coverage under the Louisiana Insurance Code.
>
> In the event of insolvency of the company issuing this contract, the policyholder or claimant is not covered by the Louisiana Insurance Guaranty Association or the Louisiana Life and Health Guaranty Association which guarantees only specific types of policies issued by insurance companies authorized to do business in Louisiana.
>
> This surplus lines policy has been procured by the following licensed Louisiana surplus lines broker:..."
>
> Both the signature and the printed name of the Louisiana-licensed surplus lines broker shall be recorded beneath this statement. (La. R.S. §22:433).

Each policy delivered to the insured as a surplus lines placement shall have the full and accurate dollar amount of the premium disclosed on the policy, which shall be inclusive of all fees, charges, premiums, surplus lines tax, or other consideration charged for the insurance, and must note the name of the licensed Louisiana surplus lines broker that procured the policy. In a subsequent modification of the policy, the insurer may require evidence of insurability procured at the insured's expense. The premium and premium tax must be separately stated on the declarations page. (La. R.S. §22:855).

Records. Each licensed surplus lines broker shall keep a full and true record of each surplus lines contract, procured by him including a copy of the daily report, if any, showing such of the following items as may be applicable: (1) amount of the insurance; (2) gross premiums charged; (3) return premium paid, if any; (4) rate of premium charged upon the several items of property; (5) effective date of the contract, and the terms thereof; (6) name and address of the insurer; (7) name and address of the insured; (8) brief general description of property insured and where located; and (9) other information as may be required by the Commissioner of Insurance. The record shall at all times be open to examination by the Commissioner of Insurance. (La. R.S. 22:437).

Acknowledgments. Any licensed surplus lines broker that procures a personal lines policy with an approved unauthorized insurer or eligible unauthorized insurer shall obtain from the applicant for insurance no later than the date of binding coverage, an acknowledgment on a standardized form promulgated by the Commissioner of Insurance which shall be maintained by the licensed surplus lines broker. The acknowledgment shall verify that:

1. The applicant was expressly advised prior to placement of the surplus lines insurance.

2. The insurance may be placed with an approved surplus lines insurer.

3. In the event of insolvency of the insurer, losses shall not be paid by the Louisiana Insurance Guaranty Association.

4. The applicant for insurance expressly authorizes the procurement of surplus lines insurance coverage.

5. The coverage is being procured through a duly licensed surplus lines broker.

Acknowledgment is not needed at renewal as long as the policy is renewed with the same insurer. (La. R.S. 22:438).

Reports. On or before March 1, June 1, September 1, and December 1 of each year, each surplus lines broker shall transmit to the Commissioner of Insurance a surplus lines tax report for the prior calendar quarter for single-state, Louisiana properties, risks, or exposures. The report shall be in a manner and format prescribed by the commissioner and include any additional information as required. (La. R.S. 22:439).

Unauthorized insurers must annually file: (1) a copy of the insurer's annual statement as of the preceding December 31; (2) evidence that, if the insurer issues workers compensation insurance in Louisiana, it has established and maintained a workers' compensation claims office or has retained a licensed claims adjuster; (3) a copy of the producer production report by April 15 of each year, listing all business placed by licensed surplus lines brokers; and (4) evidence from the insurer's state of domicile showing the types of insurance the insurer may write in that state. (La. R.S. §22:436).

H. Independently Procured Insurance:

1. *Rules.* Any person who obtains an insurance coverage for single-state, Louisiana properties, risks, or exposures from an unauthorized insurer without going through a licensed Louisiana producer or placed in accordance with the statutory surplus lines provisions is required to pay a 5 percent tax on the gross premium. The tax is due on the same dates and conditions as levied on licensed surplus lines producers and is payable to the Commissioner of Insurance.

2. *Industrial Insured Exemption.* Louisiana allows an exemption in its licensing law for an "industrial insured", defined as:

    a. An insured who procures the insurance policy by use of the services of a full-time employee acting as an insurance manager or buyer.

    b. An insured whose aggregate annual premium for insurance on all risks totals at least twenty-five thousand dollars.

    c. An insured having at least twenty-five full-time employees. (La. R.S. §23:1161).

NRRA Implementation

I. Compact: Louisiana is no longer in NIMA (dissolved)

J. Definitions:

1. Home State. Louisiana is the insured's home state if the insured's principal place of business is in Louisiana, or, in the case of a natural person, the insured's principal residence is in Louisiana. If Louisiana is the insured's home state, only Louisiana's requirements regarding the procurement of surplus lines insurance will apply. If Louisiana is the principal place of business or residence and 100 percent of the insured properties, risks, or exposures are outside of Louisiana, the insured's home state is the state that receives the greatest allocation of the insured's taxable premium for that surplus lines insurance contract. (La. R.S. §22:46(8.1)).

2. "Principal place of business" means, with respect to determining the home state of the insured, (a) the state where the insured maintains its headquarters and where the

insured's high-level officers direct, control and coordinate the business activities; or (b) if the insured's high-level officers direct, control and coordinate the business activities in more than one state, the state in which the greatest percentage of the insured's taxable premium for that insurance contract is allocated; or (c) if the insured maintains its headquarters or the insured's high level officers direct, control and coordinate the business activities outside any state, the state to which the greatest percentage of the insured's taxable premium for that insurance contract is allocated.

3. Principal residence means, with respect to determining the home state of the insured, the state where the insured resides for the greatest number of days during a calendar year; or if the insured's principal residence is located outside any state, the state to which the greatest percentage of the insured's taxable premium for that insurance contract is allocated.

   If more than one insured from an affiliated group are the named insureds on a single surplus lines insurance contract, Louisiana will be the home state for that contract if Louisiana is the principal place of business of the member of the affiliated group that has the largest percentage of premium attributed to it under such surplus lines insurance contract. (La. R.S. §22:46(8.1).

4. Affiliate, with respect to an insured, means an entity that controls, is controlled by, or is under common control with the insured. (15 U.S.C. §8206(2)).

5. Control, relative to ownership, means ownership representing or the authority to represent over 50 percent of the total 100 percent ownership. (La. R.S. §22:46(5)).

K. Statutory References:

La. R.S. §§22:	46
	432 to 439
	443
	821, 855
	1545, 1548
La. R.S. §23:	1161

LAC 37:XI.	503
LDI Bulletin	2015-06
15 U.S.C. §	8206

MAINE

A. **Resident Licensing:** Resident producers may be licensed to place insurance with nonadmitted insurers. Application fee: $15. License fee: $150. Biennial appointment fee: $30. (24-A M.R.S. §601). Applicant must file $20,000 bond. (24-A M.R.S. §2020). Licensed producers may do business through producers with surplus lines authority and receive commission. (24-A M.R.S. §2012).

B. **Nonresident Licensing:** Nonresident producers who are considered by the Superintendent to be competent in regard to the handling of surplus lines may apply for surplus lines authority and be issued a license on a reciprocal basis if they hold a similar license in their home state. They may apply for surplus lines authority on other than a reciprocal basis, if they maintain a business location within Maine and transact only liability business on behalf of a purchasing group registered with the Superintendent. (24-A M.R.S. §2012). Application fee: $15. License fee: $150. Biennial appointment renewal fee: $70. (24-A M.R.S. §601).

C. **Diligent Effort:** Maine does not require a certain number of declinations before the surplus lines market may be used. If certain insurance coverages cannot be procured from authorized insurers, then the coverage may be procured from unauthorized insurers, subject to the following:

1. The insurance must be procured through a licensed producer with surplus lines authority.

2. The desired coverage is necessary for the adequate protection of a risk in Maine.

3. It may be written under the laws of Maine by an authorized insurer.

4. The insurance is not available after diligent effort has been made to place the coverage with authroized insurers. (24-A M.R.S. §2004).

The diligent effort requirement does not apply to the following lines:

1. Wet marine and transportation insurance.

2. Insurance on subjects located, resident or to be performed wholly outside of Maine, or on vehicles or aircraft owned and principally garaged outside Maine.

3. Insurance on operations of railroads engaged in transportation in interstate commerce and their property is used in such operations.

4. Insurance on aircraft owned or operated by manufacturers of aircraft or of aircraft operated in commercial interstate flight or cargo of such aircraft; or against liability, other than workers compensation and employers liability, arising out of the ownership, maintenance, or use of such aircraft. (24-A M.R.S. §2002-A).

Commercial Purchaser Exemption. Insurance placed by a producer with surplus lines authority for an exempt commercial purchaser is exempt from the due diligence requirement if both:

1. The producer has disclosed to the exempt commercial purchaser that such insurance may or may not be available from the admitted market that provides greater protection with more regulatory oversight.

2. The exempt commercial purchaser has subsequently requested in writing for the producer to procure or place such insurance from a nonadmitted insurer. (24-A M.R.S. §2002-A(3)(E)).

D. Tax: 3 percent. All gross direct insurance premiums paid to insurers that do not have certificates of authority to do business in Maine are subject to taxation if Maine is the insured's home state, as defined in the federal Nonadmitted and Reinsurance Reform Act of 2010. The tax rate is 3 percent of the premiums subject to tax, payable quarterly to the Bureau of Revenue Services. The surplus lines tax applies to all fees, such as membership, policy, survey, inspection, service and finance fees that are assessed by and paid to an insurance company in consideration for an insurance policy. Except as otherwise provided in accordance with a multi-state agreement, every producer holding surplus lines authority in Maine must pay the tax due and every insured subject to tax must file a return and pay the tax due. An insurance agency may elect to collect and pay the tax on surplus lines premiums on behalf of all of its employees who are surplus lines producers and file a single return. (36 M.R.S. §2531).

If any producer fails to remit the tax within thirty days after the tax is due, the Superintendent may, following an adjudicatory hearing, assess a penalty of not less than $25 for each day of delinquency. Any fine collected by the Superintendent must be paid to the Treasurer of State and credited to the Insurance Regulatory Fund. (24-A M.R.S. §2018).

Multi-State Premium Tax Allocation: For any nonadmitted insurance premiums that are subject to taxation by Maine and interstate allocation of taxes in accordance with the federal Nonadmitted and Reinsurance Reform Act of 2010, Public Law 111-203, Section 521, the rate of taxation on each participating state's share of the premium must be that state's applicable nonadmitted insurance premium tax rate. (36 M.R.S. §2532).

Premium Defined: Premium is the consideration for insurance, including any assessment, membership, policy, survey, inspection, service, similar fee, or other charge. (24-A M.R.S. §2403).

E. **Stamping Fee:** None. Maine does not have a Surplus Lines Stamping Office.

F. **Surplus Lines Association:** None.

G. **Other Requirements or Restrictions:** Use of the surplus lines market solely to obtain a better rate is prohibited. The Superintendent occasionally publishes a list of approved surplus lines insurers. Producers must adhere to the list when it is in effect. (https://www.maine.gov/pfr/insurance/legal/bulletins/pdf/457.pdf?utm_content=&utm_medium=email&utm_name=&utm_source=govdelivery&utm_term=).

Eligibility. Insurers are eligible if the insurer is authorized to write such insurance in its domiciliary jurisdiction; has established satisfactory evidence of good repute and financial integrity; and maintains capital and surplus, or its equivalent under the laws of its state of domicile, in an amount at least equal to the greater of the minimum capital and surplus that would be required if the insurer were licensed in Maine and $15 million.

The Superintendent may list an insurer as eligible if it does not meet the minimum capital and surplus requirements upon an affirmative finding of acceptability by the Superintendent. The finding must be based upon such factors as quality of management, capital and surplus of any parent company, company underwriting profit and investment income trends, market availability and company record and reputation within the industry. The Superintendent may not make an affirmative finding of acceptability if the nonadmitted insurer's capital and surplus is less than $4.5 million.

A non-United States insurer is considered eligible to write insurance on an unauthorized basis in this state if it is listed on the quarterly listing of alien insurers maintained by the National Association of Insurance Commissioners. (24-A M.R.S. §2007).

Notice. All surplus lines contracts must identify the producer with surplus lines authority who procured it, and contain the following wording:

> "This insurance contract is issued pursuant to the Maine Insurance Laws by an insurer neither licensed by nor under the jurisdiction of the Maine Bureau of Insurance." (24-A M.R.S. §2009).

Records. Each producer must keep in the producer's office a full and true record of each surplus lines coverage procured by the producer, including a copy of each daily report, if any, a copy of each certificate of insurance issued, books of account in which financial entries are recorded respecting these transactions and such of the following items as may be applicable: (1) the amount of the insurance; (2) the gross premium charged; (3) the return premium paid, if any; (4) the rate of premium charged upon the several items of property; (5) the effective date and the terms of the contract; (6) the name and address of each insurer on the direct risk and the proportion of the entire risk assumed by such insurer, if less than the entire risk; (7) the name and address of the insured; (8) a brief general description of the property or risk insured and where located or to be performed; and (9) any other information as may be required by the Superintendent. The record must be open to examination by the Superintendent at all times within five years after issuance of the coverage to which it relates. Records may be maintained in electronic form. Reports are not required to be routinely made to the Superintendent, but records must be produced upon request. (24-A M.R.S. §2015).

Life, health, employee benefit excess, and workers compensation insurance may not be placed with nonadmitted insurers. The surplus lines law may not be used to place reinsurance. (24-A M.R.S. §2002-A).

H. Independently Procured Insurance:

1. *Rules.* For all coverage placed in accordance with Title 24-A, chapter 19, the tax must be paid by the surplus lines producer. For all other nonadmitted insurance, the tax must be paid by the insured. (24-A M.R.S. §2006).

2. *Industrial Insured Exemption.* Maine defines an "industrial insured" as an insured:

    a. Who procures the insurance of any risk or risks by use of the services of a full-time employee acting as an insurance manager or buyer.

    b. Whose aggregate annual premium for insurance on all risks totals at least $25,000.

    c. Who has at least twenty-five full-time employees. (24-A M.R.S. §6701).

NRRA Implementation

I. Compact: None. However, Maine's tax assessor may, after consultation with the Department of Professional and Financial Regulation, Bureau of Insurance, enter into a multi-state agreement, in accordance with the federal Nonadmitted and Reinsurance Reform Act of 2010, for the reporting of nonadmitted insurance premiums and the collection and allocation of nonadmitted insurance taxes. For any nonadmitted insurance premiums that are subject to taxation by Maine and interstate allocation of taxes in accordance with the federal Nonadmitted and Reinsurance Reform Act of 2010, the rate of taxation on each participating state's share of the premium must be that state's applicable nonadmitted insurance premium tax rate. (36 M.R.S. §2532).

J. Definitions:

1. Home State means, with respect to an insured:

   a. The state in which an insured maintains its principal place of business or, in the case of an individual, the individual's principal residence.

   b. If 100 percent of the insured risk is located out of the state referred to in subparagraph 1, the state to which the greatest percentage of the insured's taxable premium for that insurance contract is allocated.

   c. With respect to an affiliated group, if more than one of the insureds from an affiliated group are named insureds on a single nonadmitted insurance contract, the home state, as determined pursuant to paragraph a, of the member of the affiliated group that has the largest percentage of premium attributed to it under that insurance contract. (24-A M.R.S. § 2003).

2. Principal place of business means the single state in which the natural persons who establish policy for the direction, control and coordination of the operations of the entity as a whole primarily exercise that function, determined by the association in its reasonable judgment by considering: (1) the state in which the primary executive and administrative headquarters of the entity is located; (2) the state in which the principal office of the chief executive officer of the entity is located; (3) the state in which the board of directors or similar governing body of the entity conducts the majority of its meetings; (4) the state in which the executive or management committee of the board of directors or similar governing body of the entity conducts the majority of its meetings; (5) the state from which management of the overall operations of the entity is directed; and (6) if a benefit plan sponsored by affiliated companies comprising a consolidated corporation, the state in which the company has its principal place of business is determined using factors (1)-(5). However, in the case of a plan sponsor, if more than 50 percent of the participants in the benefit plan are employed in a single area, that state is the principal place of business of the plan sponsor. In lieu of a specific designation of a principal place of business of a plan sponsor of a benefit plan, the principal place of business is that of the employer or employee organization that has the largest investment in the benefit plan in question. (24-A M.R.S. §4605-A).

3. Affiliate means, with respect to an insured, any entity that controls, is controlled by or is under common control with the insured. (24-A M.R.S. §2003).

4. Control means the possession, direct or indirect, of the power to direct the management and policies of a person, whether through the ownership of voting securities, by contract other than a commercial contract for goods or nonmanagement services, or otherwise, unless the power is solely the result of an official position with or a corporate office held by the person. Control is presumed to exist if any person is the beneficial owner of 10 percent or more of the voting securities or guaranty capital shares, or the right to cast 10 percent or more of the votes in the election of directors or other governing body of any other person. (24-A M.R.S. §222).

K. References:

24-A M.R.S. §§	601, 742
	1402, 1410, 1411, 1413
	1416-A, 1420-A, 1420-B, 1420-C, 1420-F, 1420-G, 1420-M, 1420-N, 1420-O
	1449, 1450, 1462, 1464, 1465, 1481-A, 1493
	1904, 2160 to 2063-A

CMR	02-031-542
	02-031-900
	02-031-917

Web References:

(https://www.maine.gov/pfr/insurance/legal/bulletins/pdf/457.pdf?utm_content=&utm_medium=email&utm_name=&utm_source=govdelivery&utm_term=).

https://www.maine.gov/pfr/insurance/legal/bulletins/pdf/457.pdf?utm_content=&utm_medium=email&utm_name=&utm_source=govdelivery&utm_term=.

MARYLAND

A. Resident Licensing: Residents must be qualified as an insurance producer, hold a producer's license for the type of insurance being sold, and be found competent and trustworthy as determined by the commissioner before applying for a certificate of qualification to act as a surplus lines broker. (Md. INSURANCE Code Ann. §3-311). The surplus lines broker's license is issued for a term expiring on June 30 of the next odd-numbered year following the date of issuance and may be renewed biennially thereafter. Initial Certificate Fee: $100 over one year from renewal; $100 within one year of renewal. Biennial renewal fee: $200. A $10,000 surety bond is required. Any Maryland licensed agent or broker may place business through surplus lines brokers and receive commissions. (Md. INSURANCE Code Ann. §§2-112, 3-310 to 316; COMAR 31.03.06.02).

An insurer seeking to do business as a surplus lines insurer must file the following documents with the Commissioner: (1) a written request for approval to write the type of insurance sought; (2) a certified copy of the insurer's annual statement, on convention form, showing the amount of surplus business by line written on in-state risks during the period of the annual statement; and (3) a certificate of compliance issued by the insurance department of the insurer's state of domicile. (Md. INSURANCE Code Ann. §3-318(a)).

A person is not required to obtain a certificate of qualification to act as a surplus lines broker in Maryland if: (1) Maryland is not the home state of the insured; and (2) the surplus lines broker has obtained a license or other authorization from the home state of the insured.(Md. INSURANCE Code Ann. §3-310).

B. Nonresident Licensing: Nonresidents licensed for surplus lines in their home state may obtain Maryland surplus lines authority if their home state does the same for Maryland licensees. The same forms and fees are required for nonresident applications as for resident applications. (Md. INSURANCE Code Ann. §10-119).

C. Diligent Effort: A diligent search will be deemed completed if the surplus lines broker or insurance producer obtains declinations of a risk from three authorized insurers that are writing the particular kind and class of insurance in Maryland and the declinations are included in the affidavit (see Other Requirements and Restrictions for details). In addition, an insurance producer must obtain a declination from each insurer for which the insurance producer has been appointed that the insurance producer knows, or should know, is actually writing on a broad basis the particular kind and class of insurance sought. A diligent search is required for all personal lines renewals.

A diligent search is not necessary for any coverage on a list of eligible surplus lines coverages compiled by the commissioner; or if the diligent search is waived by a commercial insured in accordance with the process determined by the commissioner. (Md. INSURANCE Code Ann. §§3-306, 306.1; COMAR 31.03.06.11). Coverage of a type listed under the Surplus Lines Exportable List may be placed without conducting a diligent search. The originating producer must file an affidavit as described in Md. INSURANCE Code Ann. §3-307 within forty-five days after the last day of the quarter in which the surplus lines insurance is placed. (COMAR 31.03.06.10).

Commercial Purchaser Exemption. Notwithstanding the aforementioned exemptions, a surplus lines broker is not required to perform a diligent search to determine whether the full amount or type of insurance can be obtained from admitted insurers when the surplus lines broker is seeking to procure or place nonadmitted insurance for an exempt commercial purchaser if both:

1. The surplus lines broker has disclosed to the exempt commercial purchaser that the insurance may or may not be available from admitted insurers that may be subject to greater protection and regulatory oversight.

2. The exempt commercial purchaser subsequently has requested the surplus lines broker in writing to procure nonadmitted insurance from or place the nonadmitted insurance with a nonadmitted insurer. (Md. INSURANCE Code Ann. §3-306.1).

To qualify as an exempt commercial purchaser, the insured must meet the following requirements at the time of placement:

1. Employ or retain a qualified risk manager to negotiate coverage;

2. Have paid aggregate nationwide commercial property and casualty insurance premiums in excess of $100,000 in the immediately preceding twelve months; and

3. Satisfy at least one of the following criteria:

    a. Possess a net worth in excess of $20 million.

    b. Generate revenues in excess of $50 million.

    c. Employ more than 500 full-time employees per individual insured or is a member of an affiliated group employing more than 1,000 employees in the aggregate.

d. Is a nonprofit or public entity generating annual budgeted expenditures of at least $30 million.

e. Is a municipality with a population in excess of 50,000 persons. (COMAR 31.03.06.11).

D. Tax: 3 percent. The premiums charged for surplus lines insurance are subject to a premium receipts tax of 3 percent on all gross premiums, less any returned premiums, charged for surplus lines insurance, due semiannually on or before March 15 and September 15 of each year. The surplus lines tax does not apply to fees levied by the broker. (Md. INSURANCE Code Ann. §3-324; COMAR 31.03.06.05, 31.03.06.06).

For policies effective **before** July 21, 2011, if the policy covers property, risks, or exposures located or to be performed entirely in Maryland, the premium receipts tax must be computed on the entire premium at a rate of 3 percent. If the policy covers property, risks, or exposures located or to be performed both in and outside the state, the premium receipts tax shall be computed at the 3 percent rate only on that portion of the premium that is properly allocable to the risks located in Maryland. (Md. INSURANCE Code Ann. §3-324).

For policies effective **on or after** July 21, 2011, if Maryland is the insured's home state, the premium receipts tax shall be computed on the entire premium at 3 percent. Only the home state of an insured may receive premium receipts tax payments and reports for nonadmitted insurance. (Md. INSURANCE Code Ann. §3-324).

On delivery of the cover note, certificate of insurance, policy, or other initial confirmation of insurance, a surplus lines broker shall charge the insured the amount of the premium receipts tax in addition to the full amount of the gross premium charged by the insurer for the surplus lines insurance.

The surplus lines broker must return to the insured the premium receipts tax on any unearned part of the premium.

The surplus lines broker may not absorb the premium receipts tax; or rebate all or part of the premium receipts tax or the surplus lines broker's commission. (Md. INSURANCE Code Ann. §3-324).

Premium Defined. "Premium" means consideration for insurance. "Premium" includes: an assessment and a membership fee, policy fee, survey fee, inspection fee, service fee, or other similar fee in consideration for an insurance contract.

"Premium" does not include: an assessment of members of domestic mutual or reciprocal insurers or an assessment made under any State law that provides for insolvency protection or insurance availability. (Md. INSURANCE Code Ann. §1-101(ff)).

E. **Stamping Fee:** None. Maryland does not have a surplus lines stamping office.

F. **Surplus Lines Association:** Maryland Excess & Specialty Lines Brokers Association, PO Box 4072, Salisbury, MD 21803. Phone: 410-546-1255. (https://www.claimspages.com/tools/insurance-associations/maryland/maryland-excess-specialty-lines-brokers-association/410-546-1255/).

Contact: David Riffert, Phone: (301) 439-4700 (https://surplusmanual.lockelord.com/eligibility/maryland/#).

G. **Other Requirements or Restrictions:** A surplus lines broker may not place surplus lines insurance with an unauthorized insurer that has been determined to be insolvent or financially unsafe or if the commissioner has determined that the insurer has refused to pay just claims. Use of surplus lines expressly to gain rate or form advantage is prohibited, but there is no restriction once risk is rejected by admitted markets. (Md. INSURANCE Code Ann. §§3-306, 3-319).

Exemptions. Life, health, annuities, reinsurance, certain types of wet marine insurance, private passenger auto, workers compensation, and railroad insurance may not be placed with nonadmitted insurers. (Md. INSURANCE Code Ann. §3-302).

Eligibility. The commissioner may not approve an insurer as a surplus lines insurer unless the insurer is authorized in its domiciliary jurisdiction to write the type of insurance it seeks to write; has capital and surplus, or their equivalent under the laws of its domiciliary jurisdiction, equal to the greater of the minimum capital and surplus required under the laws of its domiciliary jurisdiction or $15 million. For a foreign insurer, the requirements of eligibility may be satisfied by the insurer's possessing less than the minimum capital and surplus if the commissioner makes an affirmative finding of acceptability. The finding is based on the following or similar factors: the quality of management; the capital and surplus of any parent company; the company underwriting profit and investment income trends; the market availability; and the company record and reputation of the foreign insurer in the industry. The commissioner may not make an affirmative finding of acceptability if the foreign insurer's capital and surplus is less than $4.5 million. (Md. INSURANCE Code §3-318).

Notice. Each insurance contract or confirmation procured and delivered must be endorsed or stamped conspicuously in boldface type on the first page of the insurance contract or confirmation as follows:

> "This insurance is issued by a nonadmitted insurer not under the jurisdiction of the Maryland Insurance Commissioner."

In addition, each insurance contract or confirmation must be accompanied by a written disclosure (see below), as prescribed by the commissioner that is written in clear, plain English; explains that the insurer does not possess a certificate of authority from the commissioner to engage in the insurance business in Maryland; and includes any other information that the commissioner requires. (Md. INSURANCE Code Ann. §3-308).

The written disclosure required by Md. INSURANCE Code Ann. §3-308 shall be on a separate piece of paper, in the form prescribed by COMAR 31.03.06.09(B), containing only the disclosure and be attached to the contract or binder that shall be provided to the insured at the time of initial purchase or delivery.

(COMAR 31.03.06.09).

Records. Each surplus lines broker shall keep separate records and accounts of all business transacted under the surplus lines broker's certificate of qualification, including copies of: (1) any daily report made by the surplus lines broker; and (2) each binder or cover note delivered by the surplus lines broker. The records described shall be kept by the surplus lines broker for three years after the issuance of the coverage to which the record relates and shall be available at any reasonable time during that period for examination by the commissioner. Every surplus lines broker shall maintain an adequate record of all return or additional premiums resulting from cancellations, adjustments made on deposit or minimum premiums, audit premiums, additional or return premiums as a result of endorsement to existing policies, additional or return premiums resulting from changes in the amount or type of coverage, and other changes resulting from any other cause. (Md. INSURANCE Code §3-322; COMAR 31.03.06.07).

Affidavits. Affidavits of nonavailability with admitted insurers—after a diligent search—must be filed with commissioner within forty-five days after the last day of the calendar quarter in which the surplus lines insurance was placed. The affidavits must set forth the facts referred to in Md. INSURANCE Code Ann. §3-306 and any other facts required by the commissioner. Affidavits must be personally executed by the surplus lines broker or the originating insurance producer at the time the surplus lines insurance is placed. (Md. INSURANCE Code Ann. §3-307; COMAR 31.03.06.03).

Reports. On or before March 15 and September 15 each surplus lines broker must file with the commissioner a report of the gross premiums charged less premiums returned for business subject to tax during the preceding half calendar year (1/1–6/30 for the September 15 report, and 7/1–12/31 for the March 15 report). Reports must be verified in a manner prescribed by the commissioner and contain that information required by the commissioner. The reports shall be open to the public and must include the gross amount of each kind of insurance business transacted and the total gross premiums charged, the total returned premiums and taxes repaid to insureds, the total net premiums, and any additional information required by the commissioner. (COMAR 31.03.06.05).

H. Independently Procured Insurance:

1. *Rules.* Each insured that procures or causes to be procured insurance with an unauthorized insurer, or an insured or self-insured that procures or continues excess loss, catastrophe, or other insurance with an unauthorized insurer, on a subject of insurance resident, located, or to be performed in Maryland, other than surplus lines insurance, shall file with the Commissioner a report on or before March 15 and September 15. The relevant forms can be found at http://insurance.maryland.gov/Producer/Pages/SurplusLinesBrokers.aspx.

   Premium receipts tax of 3 percent of the gross premiums charged must be paid to the commissioner before March 1 of the next calendar year after the insurance was procured. (Md. INSURANCE Code Ann. §§4-209 to 211).

2. *Industrial Insured Exemption.* Industrial insured is defined as an insured that procures the insurance of a risk by the services of a full-time employee acting as an insurance manager or buyer or a regularly and continuously retained qualified insurance consultant; has an aggregate annual premium for all risks totaling at least $100,000; or has at least twenty-five full-time employees. (Md. INSURANCE Code Ann. §4-201).

NRRA Implementation

I. Compact: None. Maryland adopted the NRRA via Chapters 520 and 521, Acts 2011, which took effect July 1, 2011. (MIA Financial Regulation Bulletin 11-26.).

J. Definitions:

1. Maryland defines "Home State" in terms of the NRRA. Maryland is the home state if the insured maintains its principal place of business or, in the case of an individual, the individual's principal residence here. Maryland's requirements regarding the placement of such business will apply if Maryland is considered the home state. However, if 100 percent of the insured risk is located outside of Maryland, then the home state is the state to which the greatest percentage of the insured's taxable premium for that insurance contract is allocated. With respect to an affiliated group, if more than one insured from the affiliated group is a named insured on a single nonadmitted insurance contract, the home state

is that of the member of the affiliated group that has the largest percentage of premium attributed to the member under the insurance contract. (NRRA §527(6), 15 U.S.C.S. §8206(6)).

2. Principal Place of Business. For a plan sponsor or person other than an individual, its principal place of business is the single state in which the individuals who establish policy for the direction, control, and coordination of the operations of the entity, as a whole, primarily exercise that function, as determined by the corporation in its reasonable judgment by considering the following factors: (i) the state in which the primary executive and administrative headquarters of the entity is located; (ii) the state in which the principal office of the chief executive officer of the entity is located; (iii) the state in which the board of directors, or similar governing person or persons, of the entity conducts the majority of its meetings; (iv) the state in which the executive or management committee of the board of directors, or similar governing person or persons, of the entity conducts the majority of its meetings; (v) the state from which the management of the overall operations of the entity is directed; and (vi) for a benefit plan sponsored by affiliated companies comprising a consolidated corporation, the state in which the holding company or controlling affiliate has its principal place of business, as determined under the factors in this paragraph. (Md. INSURANCE Code Ann. §9-404).

   For a plan sponsor, if more than 50 percent of the participants in the benefit plan are employed in a single state, that state is deemed to be the principal place of business of the plan sponsor. (Md. INSURANCE Code Ann. §9-404).

   For an association, a committee, a joint board of trustees, or any other similar group of representatives of the parties who establish or maintain a benefit plan when there is no specific or clear designation of a principal place of business, the principal place of business is the principal place of business of the employer or employee organization that has the largest investment in the benefit plan in question. (Md. INSURANCE Code Ann. §9-404).

3. "Affiliate" is a person that directly or indirectly, through one or more intermediaries, controls, is controlled by, or is under common control with another person. (Md. INSURANCE Code Ann. §7-101).

4. Control. "Control", "controlling", "controlled by", or "under common control with" means the direct or indirect possession of the power to direct or cause the direction of the management and policies of a person, through ownership of voting securities or of securities convertible into voting securities, by contract other than a commercial contract for goods or nonmanagement services, or otherwise, whether or not the

power is exercised or sought to be exercised unless the power is the result of an official position with or corporate office held by the person. (Md. INSURANCE Code Ann. §7-101).

K. Statutory References:

Md. INSURANCE Code Ann. §§	
1-	101
2-	112
3-	302, 306 to 308, 310 to 316, 318, 322, 324
4-	201, 209 to 211
7-	101
9-	404
10-	119

COMAR 31.03.06.	02, 05 to 07, 09 to 11

MIA Financial Regulation Bulletin	11-26

15 U.S.C.S. §	8206

MASSACHUSETTS

A. Resident Licensing: Applicants must file an online application with NIPR; paper applications are no longer accepted at the division. Resident licensees are required to first be licensed as a producer with the property and casualty lines of authority. If the commissioner finds that the applicant is trustworthy and competent, a special insurance broker's license (Surplus Lines Broker) will be issued to the applicant. Special insurance brokers' licenses are renewable annually and expire each year on the day which they were originally issued. Initial and renewal fee is $150. Use the online licensing procedures provided by National Insurance Producer Registry (NIPR) at www.nipr.com.

B. Nonresident Licensing: Nonresidents may be licensed as special insurance brokers in Massachusetts if licensed in their home state. (M.G.L.A. 175 §168).

C. Diligent Effort: Affidavit of nonavailability through admitted insurers must be filed with the commissioner for each line within twenty days after procurement. Affidavits are not required for transactions involving exempt commercial risks or those defined as large commercial policyholders if the commercial risk or policyholder acknowledges in writing that it understands that the insurance company is not admitted to transact insurance in Massachusetts and that, in the event of insolvency, losses will not be picked up by the Massachusetts Insurers Insolvency Fund. Special insurance brokers must maintain a copy of the written acknowledgment. (M.G.L.A. 175 §168).

The Affidavit by Assured may be downloaded from the DOI Website:
http://www.mass.gov/ocabr/docs/doi/producer/surpaffidavit.pdf

Commercial Purchaser Exemption. The affidavit is not required in connection with a transaction with an exempt commercial risk or policyholder as defined in M.G.L.A. 175 §224, if the commercial risk or policy holder acknowledges in writing its understanding, that: (1) the company from which insurance is procured is not admitted to transact insurance in the commonwealth; and (2) in the event of the insolvency of the company, a loss will not be paid by the Massachusetts Insurers Insolvency Fund under chapter 175D. (M.G.L.A. 175 §§168, 224).

D. Tax: 4 percent of gross premium less returns payable annually in January at the time the annual statement is filed. (M.G.L.A. 175 §168(d). The surplus lines tax does not apply to any fees levied by the surplus lines broker. (M.G.L.A. 175 §168).

Multi-State Premium Tax Allocation. If the insurance covers properties, risks or exposures located or to be performed both in and outside of Massachusetts: (i) an amount equal to 4 percent of such gross premiums allocated to Massachusetts; plus (ii) an amount equal to the portion of the premiums allocated to other states or territories on the basis of the tax rates and fees applicable to properties, risks or exposures located or to be performed outside of Massachusetts; to the extent that other states where portions of the insured properties, risks or exposures are located have failed to enter into a compact or reciprocal allocation procedure with Massachusetts, the net premium tax collected shall be retained by Massachusetts. (M.G.L.A. 175 §168).

E. **Stamping Fee:** None. Massachusetts does not have a surplus lines stamping office.

F. **Surplus Lines Association:** New England Surplus Lines Association, Inc. c/o A.I.I. Insurance Brokerage PO Box 1139, East Douglas, MA 01516. Phone: 508-476-1990. Fax: 508-476-1990. Contact name: Julie Sonier. (https://www.slai.org/links/associations.html#NG). (Although Massachusetts does not have a Surplus Lines Association, New England Surplus Lines Association, Inc. serves Massachusetts in this capacity).

G. **Other Requirements or Restrictions:** Use of nonadmitted insurers not on commissioner's approved list is prohibited. Life, accident and health, compulsory motor vehicle, and workers compensation insurance may not be placed with nonadmitted insurers.

Eligibility. No company will be determined to be an eligible alien unauthorized insurer unless it has provided satisfactory evidence to the commissioner of its good reputation and financial integrity; has capital and surplus or its equivalent under the laws of its domiciliary jurisdiction in an amount of at least $20 million; has in force a United States trust fund of not less than the greater of $5.4 million or a percentage of its United States surplus lines gross liabilities arising from business written after January 1, 1998 excluding certain lines; and has submitted to the commissioner an application evidencing the company's compliance with the requirements that has been approved by the commissioner. (M.G.L.A. 175 §168A(c)). The requirements of the application are covered in M.G.L.A. 175 §168A(d).

Notice. Surplus lines policies must contain the following disclosure notice to the policyholder:

> "This policy is insured by a company which is not admitted to transact insurance in the commonwealth, is not supervised by the commissioner of insurance and, in the event of an insolvency of such company, a loss shall not be paid by the Massachusetts Insurers Insolvency Fund under chapter 175D." (M.G.L.A. 175 §168(c)).

Annual Statements. Each licensed special broker must keep a separate account of the business done under the license, a certified copy of which account he must file with the commissioner, showing the exact amount of such insurance placed for each person, the gross premium charged thereon, the companies in which the same is placed, the date of the policies and the term thereof, and also a report in the same detail of all such policies cancelled, with the gross return premiums thereon, and will annually, in January, file with the state treasurer a sworn statement of the gross premiums charged for insurance procured or placed and the gross return premiums on such insurance cancelled under such license during the year ending on December 31 last preceding. (M.G.L.A. 175 §168(d)).

H. Independently Procured Insurance:

1. *Rules.* Massachusetts has no laws governing the independent procurement of insurance.

2. *Industrial Insured Exemption.* Massachusetts has no industrial insured exemption.

NRRA Implementation

I. Compact: None. However, the commissioner is authorized to enter into a cooperative agreement, reciprocal agreement or compact with another state or states. Prior to entering into such an agreement or compact, the commissioner will provide public notice and an opportunity for comment thereon. (M.G.L.A. 175 §168(e)).

J. Definitions:

1. "Home State" means: Massachusetts is the home state if the insured maintains its principal place of business or, in the case of an individual, the individual's principal residence here. This state's requirements regarding the placement of such business will apply if this state is considered the home state. However, if 100 percent of the insured risk is located outside of Massachusetts, then the home state is the state to which the greatest percentage of the insured's taxable premium for that insurance contract is allocated. (15 U.S.C. §8206(6)(A); M.G.L.A. 175 §168(a)). With respect to an affiliated group, if more than one (1) insured from the affiliated group is a named insured on a single nonadmitted insurance contract, the home state is that of the member of the affiliated group that has the largest percentage of premium attributed to the member under the insurance contract. (15 U.S.C. §8206(6)(B)).

2. "Affiliate" means, with respect to an insured, an entity that controls, is controlled by, or is under common control with the insured. (15 U.S.C. §8026(2)).

3. "Control." An entity has "control" over another entity if: (1) The entity directly or indirectly or acting through one or more other persons owns, controls, or has the power to vote 25 percent or more of any class of voting securities of any other entity; or (2) the entity controls in any manner the election of a majority of the directors or trustees of the other entity. (15 U.S.C. §8206(4)).

K. Statutory References: M.G.L.A. 175 §§168, 168A, 224. 15 U.S.C. §8026.

MICHIGAN

A. **Resident Licensing:** Resident individual and agency producers must be initially licensed for property & casualty. A resident individual producer must pass a surplus lines exam to qualify for licensure. If examination is not passed within six months, the applicant must submit a new license application, fee, and reschedule the exam. The current Michigan testing contractor is PSI and all testing fees are charged by and paid to the contractor. Agencies must have an affiliated licensed surplus lines producer in good standing in order to obtain a surplus lines license. Individual and agency applicants must electronically apply via NIPR at www.nipr.com. Initial state application and license fees are $110 each plus a $5 NIPR transaction fee. Both individual and agency surplus lines licenses renewal fees are $100. Licenses expire annually on March 31. A Michigan licensed property and casualty producer may place business through a Michigan licensed surplus lines producer and negotiate a split of the commission. (MCLS § 500.1905, MCLS § 500.240(1)(i) and https://www.michigan.gov/difs/0,5269,7-303-22535_26607-346402--,00.html).

B. **Nonresident Licensing:** A nonresident individual shall receive a nonresident surplus lines insurance producer license if he or she meets all of the following:

1. Is currently licensed for surplus lines in his home state as well as holding a property & casualty license as the prerequisite license for surplus lines and is in good standing in his or her home state; must submit a home state letter of certification if the home state does not participate in the NAIC PDB.

2. The electronic nonresident licensing and application fee of $110 fee and the NIPR transaction fee is paid and received.

3. The person's home state awards nonresident producer licenses to residents of this state on the same basis. (MCLS § 500.1206a, https://www.nipr.com/rules_mi_nrl.htm).

Agencies must have an affiliated Michigan licensed surplus lines individual producer in good standing affiliated with them prior to applying for a surplus lines license. Initial application and license fees are $110 each plus a NIPR transaction fee. Agency applicants must electronically apply via NIPR at http://www.nipr.com. Both individual and agency producer surplus lines licenses renewal fees are $100 each. Licenses expire annually on March 31.

C. **Diligent Effort:** Surplus lines taxes and supporting documentation must be filed in the form and manner prescribed by the Department of Insurance and Financial Services (DIFS) Director. The director shall maintain, on a current basis, a list of those lines of insurance for which coverages are determined to be generally unavailable in the authorized insurance market. Any person may request in writing that a coverage be added or removed from the current list, which shall be granted or denied within thirty days after receiving the written request. The director shall encourage dissemination of information regarding the availability of coverages, for which the public interest necessitates additions to or deletions from the list. The list shall be published at least quarterly and shall be revised as required and is available to all licensees and other members of the public. (MCLS § 500.1910).

Coverage may be placed with an unauthorized insurer domiciled in a U.S. jurisdiction or listed on the NAIC Quarterly Alien Listing. However, coverage placed with an insurer not recognized by the NAIC shall only be at the insistence of the insured or after diligent efforts to place the business with NAIC approved insurers have failed. For policies issued with an unauthorized insurer not NAIC recognized, the tax filing must be accompanied by a completed affidavit, Report of Transaction with an Unauthorized Insurer not Recognized as Eligible. The affidavit must be signed by the surplus lines producer indicating the reason for issuing the policy with an unauthorized insurer not NAIC recognized. (MCLS § 500.1910, http://www.quakerma.com/FaF/State%20Affidavits/Michigan%20Affidavit.pdf)

Commercial Purchaser Exemption: Under the Nonadmitted and Reinsurance Reform Act, surplus lines brokers seeking to procure or place nonadmitted insurance on behalf of an "exempt commercial purchaser" are not required to perform a diligent search if the licensee has disclosed to the exempt commercial purchaser that insurance may or may not be available from the admitted market that may provide greater protection with more regulatory oversight; and the exempt commercial purchaser has subsequently requested in writing for the broker to procure or place such insurance from a nonadmitted insurer.

D. Required Tax and Regulatory Fee: Electronic reporting and tax payments are required to be submitted via NAIC OPTins. Registration at http://www.optins.org/ may take up to two weeks. One-time filers may use FIS 0255. A combined 2 percent tax and 0.5 percent regulatory fee are due on the aggregate total premium written for all policies written during the previous six month period less any returned premium amounts. The semi-annual report is due on August 15 and February 15 accompanied by the surplus lines tax payment. Direct placement filers may use the Michigan Form FIS 0255 found at https://www.michigan.gov/documents/cis_ofis_fis_0255_24151_7.pdf. (MCLS § 500.1905, https://www.michigan.gov/difs/0,5269,7-303-22535_26607-76219--,00.html).

Premium Defined. Premiums mean amounts received on covered policies or contracts less returned premiums, considerations, deposits and less dividends and experience credits. The term does not include an amount received for a policy or contract or a portion of a policy or contract for which coverage is not provided under MCLS § 500.7704. However, accessible premiums shall not be reduced on account of sections MCLS § 500.7704(5)(c) relating to interest limitations and MCLS § 500.7704(6)(b), (c), and (e) relating to any one individual, participant, or contract holder. (MCLS § 500.7705(p)).

E. **Stamping Fee:** None. Michigan does not have a stamping office.

F. **Surplus Lines Association:** None.

G. **Other Requirements or Restrictions:**

In addition to commissions, licensed surplus lines producers may add a fee to cover costs incurred. The fee may be higher if approved by the director. Currently, the approved fee stands at $62 per Director Bulletin 2013-14-INS. Any additional fees may be charged only to the extent that actual additional costs are incurred for services performed by persons or entities unrelated to the licensee exceed that amount. Fees shall not be included as part of the policy premium in computation of premium taxes.

Before placement of insurance with an eligible unauthorized insurer, a licensee shall inform an insured or the insured's representative that coverage is being placed with an insurer not licensed in Michigan and that payment of loss may not be guaranteed in the event of insolvency of the unauthorized insurer. Within thirty days after the date on which the risk was bound or the insured or applicant was advised that coverage has been or will be obtained, the agent or broker shall deliver a policy, a written binder, a certificate, or other written evidence of the insurance, to the insured or the insured's representative. (MCLS § 500.1905 and 500.1912).

Exemptions. The director maintains a list of coverages unavailable through admitted insurers. Coverages generally unavailable or problematic in obtaining coverage in the authorized market may be placed with surplus lines insurers under specific conditions as specified in Section 500.1910. The list of unavailable coverages is:

1. Animal mortality.

2. Environmental impairment.

3. Kidnap and ransom or extortion insurance.

4. Liability for entertainment, recreational, or sporting events or facilities written to include injury to participants.

5. Personal injury and/or assault and battery when not written with bodily injury and property damage liability.

6. Products recall insurance.

7. Property and liability insurance on mobile, traveling, or fixed recreational or amusement businesses.

8. Property insurance on vacant buildings not insurable through the Michigan Basic Property Insurance Association.

9. Rain or pluvious insurance.

10. Products liability when written alone.

11. Railroad liability.

12. Flood insurance not provided under the federal flood insurance program.

13. High hazard cargo insurance.

(https://www.michigan.gov/documents/lara/quarterly_surplus_lines_list_4252011_351537_7.pdf)

Coverage may be placed with an unauthorized insurer not recognized by the NAIC only at the insistence of the insured or after diligent efforts have failed. (MCLS § 500.1950).

Eligibility. Licensee must offer surplus lines insurance only to insurers that are in a stable and unimpaired financial condition. The commissioner will not recognize an insurer as an eligible surplus lines insurer unless the insurer continuously maintains capital and surplus of at least $1.5 million, and is approved to write such business in its state of domicile. (Nonadmitted and Reinsurance Reform Act of 2010 and Non-Admitted Insurance Model Act). (MCLS § 500.1920).

Notice. Section 500.1922 of the Michigan insurance code states that all policies placed in the surplus lines market must contain the following statement and must be printed, typed or stamped in red ink on its face, in not less than ten point type, and not covered over or concealed in any manner:

> "This insurance has been placed with an insurer that is not licensed by the State of Michigan. In case of insolvency, payment of claims may not be guaranteed."

Evidence of Coverage. Only a licensee shall issue evidence of placement of insurance with an eligible unauthorized insurer. A licensee must not issue that evidence, cause any risk to be insured by an eligible unauthorized insurer, or advise any insured or applicant for insurance that insurance has been or will be obtained from an eligible unauthorized insurer unless one of the following conditions is met:

1. The licensee has prior written authority from the eligible unauthorized insurer to cause the risk to be insured.

2. The licensee has received a written or oral communication in the ordinary course of business that the coverage has been obtained.

3. A policy of insurance covering the insured for the risk has actually been issued by the eligible unauthorized insurer and has been delivered to the insured or the insured's representative. (MCLS § 500.1911).

If the surplus lines licensee acts in reliance on prior written authority from an eligible unauthorized insurer, the licensee, within thirty days after the date on which the risk was bound or the insured or applicant was advised that coverage has been or will be obtained, must deliver a policy or other written evidence of the insurance to the insured or the insured's representative. (MCLS § 500.1912).

Records. Each surplus lines licensee must keep a separate account of each transaction entered into and must periodically file certified evidence of these transactions in the form and manner prescribed by the commissioner. (MCLS § 500.1913).

Each surplus lines licensee shall allow the commissioner free access at reasonable times to all of the books and records relating to surplus lines transactions. If the commissioner considers it necessary, he or she may examine the books and records. (MCLS § 500.1906).

H. Independently Procured Insurance:

1. *Rules.* An insured may purchase coverage directly, without the assistance of an individual or agency producer from unauthorized insurers. The policyholder must submit the required 2.5 percent tax and regulatory fee on the premium written less returned premium and a written report thirty days after the date the insurance was procured, continued, or renewed. The report must show the name and address of the insured or insureds; the name and address of the insurer; the subject of the insurance; a general description of the coverage; the amount of premium currently charged for the insurance; and any additional pertinent information, reasonably requested by the commissioner. Taxes are filed on the Michigan Form FIS 0255 when independently procured.

2. *Industrial Insured Exemption.* Industrial Insured means an insured that meets all of the following:

   a. That procures insurance by use of the services of a full-time employee acting as a risk manager or insurance manager or utilizing the services of a regularly and continuously qualified insurance consultant.

   b. Whose aggregate annual premiums for insurance on all risks total at least $25,000.

   c. That has at least twenty-five full-time employees. (MCLS § 500.4601(m)).

NRRA Implementation

I. Compact: None.

J. Definitions:

1. "Home State" means: Under the NRRA, Michigan is the home state if the insured maintains its principal place of business or, in the case of an individual, the individual's principal residence. This state's requirements regarding the placement of such business will apply if Michigan is considered the home state. However, if 100 percent of the insured risk is located outside of Michigan, then the home state is the state to which the greatest percentage of the insured's taxable premium for that insurance contract is allocated. (15 U.S.C. §8206(6)(A)).

2. "Affiliated Group." With respect to an affiliated group, if more than one (1) insured from the affiliated group is a named insured on a single nonadmitted insurance contract, the home state is that of the member of the affiliated group that has the largest percentage of premium attributed to the member under the insurance contract. (15 U.S.C. §8206(6)(B)).

3. "Principal place of business" means the state in which the natural persons who establish policy for the direction, control, and coordination of the entity as a whole primarily exercise that function. The association considers all of the following factors in making this determination in its reasonable judgment: (1) the state in which the primary executive and adminstrative headquarters of the entity is located; (2) the state in which the principal office of the chief executive officer of the entity is located; (3) the state in which the Board of Directors or similar governing persons conducts the majority of its meetings; (4) the state in which the executive or management committee of the Board of Directors or similar governing persons conducts the majority of its meetings; (5) the state from which the management of the overall operations of the entity is directed; (6) for a benefit plan sponsored by affiliated companies comprising

a consolidated corporation, the state in which the holding company or controlling affiliate has its principal place of business. For a plan sponsor, however, if more than 50 percent of the participants in the benefit plan are employed in a single state, that state is the principal place of business of the plan sponsor. (MCLS § §500.7705(q)).

4. "Affiliate" means, with respect to an insured, an entity that controls, is controlled by, or is under common control with the insured. (15 U.S.C. §8206(2)).

5. "Control." An entity has "control" over another entity if: the entity directly or indirectly or acting through one or more persons owns, controls, or has the power to vote 25 percent or more of any class of voting securities of the other entity; or the entity controls in any manner the election of a majority of the directors or trustees of the other entity. (15 U.S.C. §8206(4)).

K. Statutory References: Michigan Compiled Laws Service, Chapters 12, 19, 46, and 77; Nonadmitted and Reinsurance Reform Act of 2010 and 15 U.S.C. §8206.

MINNESOTA

A. **Resident Licensing:** Residents who hold a property and casualty license may be licensed to place insurance with ineligible or eligible surplus lines insurers. Initial surplus lines license: $500 plus $40 technology fee, and $500 for each renewal. (Minn. Stat. Ann. § 60K.55). Licenses expire on the last day of the birth month of the producer in the year that will result in the term of the license being at least twelve months, but no more than twenty-four months. A bond is no longer required. Producers licensed for property and casualty lines in Minnesota may place business with surplus lines brokers and receive commission. (Minn. Stat. Ann. § 60A.204).

For the purposes of carrying out the provisions of the NRRA, the Commissioner is authorized to utilize the National Insurance Producer Database of the National Association of Insurance Commissioners, or any other equivalent uniform national database, for the licensure of surplus lines brokers and for renewal of the licenses.

B. **Nonresident Licensing:** Nonresidents may be licensed to place surplus lines insurance, if so licensed in his or her home state. (Minn. Stat. Ann. § 60A.198).

All surplus lines licenses in Minnesota are members of the Surplus Lines Association of Minnesota and shall register on the Association Web site: https://www.mnsla.com/

C. **Diligent Effort:** Affidavit of nonavailability through admitted insurers must be kept on file by the broker after procurement, other than for the exceptions permitted by law. A diligent search is required. If the producer can show three declinations, coverage is considered non-available.

Commercial Purchaser Exemption. A surplus lines broker is not required to make a diligent search to determine whether the full amount or type of insurance can be obtained from licensed insurers when the broker is seeking to procure or place nonadmitted insurance for an exempt commercial purchaser provided:

1. The broker procuring or placing the nonadmitted insurance has disclosed to the exempt commercial purchaser that the insurance may or may not be available from a licensed insurer that may provide greater protection with more regulatory oversight.

2. The exempt commercial purchaser has subsequently requested in writing for the broker to procure or place the insurance from a nonadmitted insurer. (Minn. Stat. Ann. § 60A.201).

D. Tax: 3 percent for placement by surplus lines brokers with nonadmitted insurers. (Minn. Stat. Ann. § 297I.30).

2 percent for independently procured insurance with nonadmitted insurers. Tax is due annually on March 1 for independently procured insurance. (Minn. Stat. Ann. § 297I.05).

Multistate Premium Tax Allocation. If taxable surplus lines insurance placed by a surplus lines licensee covers a subject of insurance residing, located, or to be performed outside this state, a proper pro rata portion of the entire premium payable for all of that insurance must be allocated according to the subjects of insurance residing, located, or to be performed in this state. For policies that become effective on or after July 21, 2011, when Minnesota is the home state of the insured, 100 percent of the gross premiums are taxable in Minnesota with no allocation to other states. (Minn. Stat. Ann. § 297I.05; revenue.state.mn.us/surplus-lines-insurance-tax).

E. Stamping Fee: The fee is 0.0004 percent effective 10/1/16. For policies effective on or after 1/1/2018, all policy premium and fees are subject to stamping fees. All premium bearing surplus lines transactions shall be electronically filed with the stamping office prior to delivery of the policy or contract to the insured. Stamping fee is paid to the Surplus Lines Association of Minnesota, 600 Clark St., PO box 86, Mora, MN. 55051. Stamping fees are to be reported and payable semi-annually in August and February using the Stamping Fee Form found on the Association Web site at https://www.mnsla.com/Documents/2Stamping%20Fee%20Report%202019.pdf.

Any insurance agent, or surplus lines broker who delivers in this state any insurance policy or contract that has not been stamped by the association shall be subject to a penalty payable to the commissioner as follows: $50 for delivery of the first unstamped policy; $250 for delivery of a second unstamped policy; and $1,000 per policy for delivery of any additional unstamped policies. (Minn. Stat. Ann. § 60A.2086).

F. Surplus Lines Association: The website for the new stamping office is: www.mnsla.com. Executive Director: Nicholas Schroeder. Additional information will be made available in our online edition as it becomes available. Surplus Lines Association of Minnesota, 600 Clark St, PO Box 86, Mora, MN 55051. Phone: (320) 679-4244. Fax: (320) 679-8230. Email: nschroeder@mnsla.com.

G. Other Requirements or Restrictions:

Eligibility. A surplus lines broker must place nonadmitted insurance only with insurers which are in a stable and unimpaired financial condition. The commissioner will recognize an insurer as an eligible surplus lines insurer when satisfied that the insurer is in a stable, unimpaired financial condition and that the insurer is qualified to provide coverage in compliance with Minnesota surplus lines law. If filed with full supporting documentation before July 1 of any year, applications will be acted upon by the commissioner before December 31 of the year of submission.

The commissioner cannot authorize a foreign insurer as an eligible surplus lines insurer unless it is domiciled within a United States jurisdiction, is authorized to write the type of insurance in its domiciliary jurisdiction, and it has capital and surplus (or its equivalent under the laws of its domiciliary jurisdiction) which equals the greater of either the minimum capital and surplus requirements under the laws of Minnesota or $15 million. These requirements may be satisfied by an insurer's possessing less than the minimum capital and surplus upon an affirmative finding of acceptability by the commissioner. The finding will be based upon factors such as quality of management, capital, and surplus of any parent company, company underwriting profit and investment income trends, market availability, and company record and reputation within the industry. In no event will the commissioner make an affirmative finding of acceptability when the surplus lines insurer's capital and surplus is less than $4.5 million. (Minn. Stat. Ann. § 60A.206).

Notice. Policies with eligible surplus lines carriers must contain the following notice, which is not to be covered or concealed in any manner and which must be printed in not less than ten point type:

> "THIS INSURANCE IS ISSUED PURSUANT TO THE MINNESOTA SURPLUS LINES INSURANCE ACT. THE INSURER IS AN ELIGIBLE SURPLUS LINES INSURER BUT IS NOT OTHERWISE LICENSED BY THE STATE OF MINNESOTA. IN CASE OF INSOLVENCY, PAYMENT OF CLAIMS IS NOT GUARANTEED." (Minn. Stat. Ann. § 60A.207).

Before an ineligible surplus lines insurer can be used, the producer must first attempt to place the insurance with a licensed insurer, or if that is not possible, with an eligible surplus lines insurer. If coverage is not obtainable from a licensed insurer or an eligible surplus lines insurer, the producer must certify to the commissioner, on a form prescribed by the commissioner, that these attempts were made. Risks may be placed with ineligible surplus lines carriers, if the surplus lines licensee can demonstrate that coverage was not available from eligible surplus lines carriers. Policies with ineligible surplus lines carriers must contain the following notice, printed in all capital letters, in red ink and not less than ten point type:

> "THIS INSURANCE IS ISSUED PURSUANT TO THE MINNESOTA SURPLUS LINES INSURANCE ACT. THIS INSURANCE IS PLACED WITH AN INSURER THAT IS NOT LICENSED BY THE STATE NOR RECOGNIZED BY THE COMMISSIONER OF COMMERCE AS AN ELIGIBLE SURPLUS LINES INSURER. IN CASE OF ANY DISPUTE RELATIVE TO THE TERMS OR

> CONDITIONS OF THE POLICY OR THE PRACTICES OF THE INSURER, THE COMMISSIONER OF COMMERCE WILL NOT BE ABLE TO ASSIST IN THE DISPUTE. IN CASE OF INSOLVENCY, PAYMENT OF CLAIMS IS NOT GUARANTEED."

This notice shall not be covered or concealed in any manner. (Minn. Stat. Ann. § 60A.209).

There shall be a rebuttable presumption that the following coverages are available from a licensed insurer: mandatory auto coverage under Minn. Stat. Ann. § 65B, private passenger auto, workers compensation, and homeowners insurance below $500,000 of coverage. There shall also be a rebuttable presumption that the following coverages are not available from a licensed insurer: coverage where only a part of a certain risk is acceptable to licensed insurers and not other parts, and any coverage the broker cannot procure after a diligent search. An entire coverage may be placed with an eligible surplus line insurer if such insurer will accept the entire coverage but not the rejected portion alone. (Minn. Stat. Ann. § 60A.201).

Placement Fees. A surplus lines licensee may charge a fee charged pursuant to subdivision 1 and commission, in addition to the premium, that is not excessive or discriminatory; the licensee shall maintain complete documentation of all fees and commissions charged. (Minn. Stat. Ann. § 60A.204).

The producing surplus lines licensee is responsible for filing taxes and certificates of nonavailability. However, the nonresident may request permission from the Department of Revenue to have a Minnesota resident make the filing for the nonresident. If such permission is not received, the nonresident must make the filing. (Minn. Stat. Ann. § 60A.206).

Evidence of Coverage. A broker shall, within seven working days after the date on which a risk was bound or the insured or applicant was advised that coverage has been or will be obtained, deliver to the insured or the insured's representative a policy, a written binder, a certificate or other written evidence of insurance placed with a nonadmitted insurer. The written communication showing that insurance has been obtained must identify all known nonadmitted insurers directly assuming any risk of loss. If there is more than one nonadmitted insurer, any document issued or certified by the broker must specify, to the extent known by the broker, whether the obligation is joint or several, and if the obligation is several, the proportion of the obligation assumed by each insurer. (Minn. Stat. Ann. § 60A.202).

Records. Each surplus lines broker must keep a separate account of each transaction entered into. Evidence of these transactions must be documented in the form and manner designated by the commissioner and retained by the broker for a minimum of five years. The forms must be readily available for review and audit by the commissioner. (Minn. Stat. Ann. § 60A.203).

Annual Statements. Eligible surplus lines insurers domiciled within the United States must file an annual statement and an annual financial audit by March 1. Eligible surplus lines insurers domiciled outside the United States shall file an annual statement on the standard nonadmitted insurers information office financial reporting form as prescribed by the National Association of Insurance Commissioners and an annual financial audit performed by an independent accounting firm. The commissioner must not prohibit a surplus lines broker from placing nonadmitted insurance with, or procuring nonadmitted insurance from, an alien insurer that is included on the Quarterly Listing of Alien Insurers maintained by the National Association of Insurance Commissioners International Insurers Department. (Minn. Stat. Ann. §§ 60A.13, 60A.206).

Surplus lines brokers must submit every insurance policy or contract issued under the broker's license to the Surplus Lines Association of Minnesota for recording and stamping. The submission and stamping must be effected through electronic means. The submission must include the name of the insured; a description and location of the insured property or risk; the amount insured; the gross premiums charged or returned; the name of the nonadmitted insurer from whom coverage has been procured; the kind or kinds of insurance procured; and the amount of premium subject to tax. (Minn. Stat. Ann. § 60A.2086).

H. Independently Procured Insurance:

1. *Rules.* Any person, firm, or corporation may secure coverage upon any property, interests, or risks of any nature other than life insurance in Minnesota in companies not authorized to do business in Minnesota. The insured must agree to file with the Commissioner of Revenue all returns required and pay to the Commissioner of Revenue any taxes required to be paid. Upon that agreement, the Commissioner of Commerce shall issue a license, good for one year. Insurance procured under the license is valid and the provisions of the policies are considered to be in accordance, and construed as if identical in effect, with the standard policy prescribed by the laws of this state. Such insurance may only be obtained from an unlicensed foreign insurer. The transaction must be reported to the insurance department and the insured must pay 2 percent tax on gross premiums. (Minn. Stat. Ann. §§ 60A.19, 60A.198, 297I.05).

2. *Industrial Insured Exemption.* Minnesota has no industrial insured exemption.

NRRA Implementation

I. Compact: None.

J. Definitions:

"Home State" means the state in which an insured maintains its principal place of business, or in the case of an individual, the individual's principal residence. If 100 percent of the insured risk is located out of the state, the term means the state to which the greatest percentage of the insured's taxable premium for that insurance contract is allocated. If more than one insured from an affiliated group are named insureds on a single nonadmitted insurance contract, the term means the home state of the member of the affiliated group that has the largest percentage of premium attributed to it under that insurance contract. (Minn. Stat. Ann. § 60A.196).

"Affiliate" means, with respect to an insured, any entity that controls, is controlled by, or is under common control with the insured. (15 U.S.C. § 8206).

An entity has "control" over another entity if the entity either: 1) directly or indirectly or acting through one or more other persons owns, controls, or has the power to vote 25 percent or more of any class of voting securities of the other entity, or 2) controls in any manner the election of a majority of the directors or trustees of the other entity. (15 U.S.C. § 8206).

K. Statutory References: Minn. Stat. Ann. §§ 60A.13, .19, .196, .198, .201 to .204, .206 to .209; 60K.55; 297I.05, .30. 15 USC § 8206.

MISSISSIPPI

A. Resident Licensing: Surplus lines insurance producers licenses are issued to qualified holders of resident insurance producer license with property, casualty and/or personal lines of authority upon the biennial payment fee of $100 and the submission of a completed Surplus Lines Insurance Producer License Application (available on the Mississippi Insurance Department Web site). The privilege license will continue from the date of issuance until the last day of the month of the licensee's birthday in the second year following issuance or renewal of the license, with a minimum term of twelve months. Applicants must be regularly commissioned to represent a fire and casualty insurance company to do business in Mississippi. All licensed surplus lines agents are automatically deemed to be members of the Mississippi Surplus Lines Association. A person must have a surplus lines license in order to receive any commissions or other valuable consideration on the placement of insurance coverage in the eligible surplus lines market. Resident surplus lines licensees who move from Mississippi to another state must file a change of address and provide certification from the new resident state within thirty days of the change of legal residence. No fee or license application is required. (Miss. Code Ann. §83-21-19).

B. Nonresident Licensing: A nonresident applicant is eligible to receive a surplus lines insurance producer license if the applicant is currently licensed as a surplus lines insurance producer or the equivalent and is in good standing in his or her home state. Nonresident applicants must submit the proper request for licensure and pay the biennial fee of $100. (Miss. Code Ann. §83-21-19). In addition, the nonresident applicant's home state must award nonresident surplus lines licenses to residents of Mississippi on the same basis. Nonresident applicants are not required to hold an insurance producer license with a property, casualty and/or personal lines line of authority if the person is not required to perform a diligent search of admitted insurers. A nonresident surplus lines insurance producer licensee who moves from one state to another state must file a change of address and provide certification from the new resident state within thirty days of the change of legal residence. No fee or license application is required.

The commissioner may verify a person's licensing status through the National Producer Database maintained by the National Association of Insurance Commissioners, its affiliates or subsidiaries.

If the commissioner decides to nonrenew, suspend, revoke or to deny an application for a license, the commissioner must notify the applicant or licensee and advise, in writing, the applicant or licensee of the reason for the denial or nonrenewal of the applicant's or licensee's license. The applicant or licensee may make written demand upon the commissioner within ten days for a hearing before the commissioner to determine the reasonableness of the commissioner's action. The hearing shall be held within thirty days. (Miss. Code Ann. §83-21-19).

C. **Diligent Effort:**

The Mississippi Insurance Code does not list a diligent search requirement for surplus lines brokers. (Miss. Code Ann. §83-21-23).

Commercial Purchaser Exemption. As amended, Miss. Code Ann. §83-21-23 does not define an exempt commercial purchaser.

D. **Tax:** 4 percent. Surplus lines insurance producers are required to pay a tax of 4 percent on the amount of gross premiums received for insurance in nonadmitted insurers to the Commissioner of Insurance within thirty days from January 1 and July 1 of each year by electronic payment through the online reporting system, SLIP. MSLA no longer accepts checks. The term "gross premiums" means the total gross amount of premiums received (including policy fees) on each and every surplus lines insurance contract, less cancellations and returned premiums. (Miss. Code Ann. §83-21-25). Please visit https://www.msla.org/producers/producer-faqs/ for more information on filings.

Multi-State Premium Tax Allocation. Mississippi has withdrawn from Nonadmitted Insurance Multi-State Agreement (NIMA) and now follows the "home state rule". If Mississippi is the home state in a multi-state nonadmitted insurance policy placement, the entire risk will be considered a Mississippi risk and subject to the nonadmitted policy fee. (Miss. Code Ann. §83-21-18).

E. **Policy Fee (MWUA Fee):** 3 percent. All surplus lines insurance producers placing insurance through nonadmitted insurers must collect from the insured and remit to the Mississippi Surplus Lines Association a nonadmitted policy fee on all premiums collected for all insurance written by such surplus lines insurance producers for policies from nonadmitted insurers for any and all risks in Mississippi. The nonadmitted policy fee is a percentage of the total policy premium but the nonadmitted policy fee is not to be considered a premium and is not subject to premium taxes or commissions. However, failure to pay the nonadmitted policy fee will be treated the same as failure to pay the premium. Within twenty days of the end of the quarter, surplus lines insurance producers placing insurance through nonadmitted insurers must remit all nonadmitted policy fees collected in the preceding quarter by electronic payment through the online reporting system, SLIP. MSLA no longer accepts checks. (Miss. Code Ann. §83-34-4. This statute will be repealed effective July 1, 2022).

F. **Stamping Fee:** The stamping fee is 0.25 percent. The 0.25 percent stamping fee is due semi-annually and must be paid by electronic payment through the online reporting system, SLIP. MSLA no longer accepts checks. (http://www.msla.org/producers/e-pay/).

The tax and stamping fee are applicable to any fees levied by the surplus lines insurer or agent. MSLA is paperless. All required documentation: a copy of policy declaration page or binder, and a copy of any endorsements, cancellations, or audit can now be uploaded directly into the reporting system online. The Monthly Transaction Report/Monthly Tax Report can also be certified online. Visit www.msla.org for more information. (Miss. Code Ann. §83-21-21).

G. **Surplus Lines Association:** Mississippi Surplus Lines Association, 504 Keywood Circle, Suite B. Flowood, MS, 39232; Phone 601-713-1111; Fax: 601-713-1122; Website: www.msla.org.

H. **Other Requirements or Restrictions:** Surplus lines insurance may be placed by a surplus lines insurance producer if each insurer is an eligible surplus lines insurer; each insurer is authorized to write the line of insurance in its domiciliary jurisdiction; and the full amount or type of insurance cannot be obtained from insurers who are admitted to do business in this state. The full amount or type of insurance may be procured from eligible surplus lines insurers. (Miss. Code Ann. §83-21-19).

Eligibility. The Commissioner of Insurance will annually promulgate a list of nonadmitted insurers found eligible for writing business in the state of Mississippi, provided each such insurer has capital and surplus or its equivalent under the laws of its domiciliary jurisdiction, which is the greater of the same requirements as to capital and surplus as is required of a company licensed to do business in the State of Mississippi or $15 million. This requirement may be satisfied by an insurer's possessing of less than the minimum capital and surplus upon an affirmative finding of acceptability by the commissioner. The finding shall be based upon such factors as quality of management, capital, and surplus of any parent company, company underwriting profit and investment income trends, market availability and company record and reputation within the industry. In no event will the commissioner make an affirmative finding of acceptability when the nonadmitted insurer's capital and surplus is less than $4.5 million. (Miss. Code Ann. §83-21-17).

Life insurance and accident and health insurance written by life insurance companies may not be placed with nonadmitted insurers. Workers compensation insurance may not be placed with nonadmitted insurers.

Courtesy filings are not allowed in Mississippi. All laws and restrictions must be followed.

Each nonadmitted insurer shall annually pay a filing fee of $500 in order to be eligible for certification as a nonadmitted insurer. (Miss. Code Ann. §83-21-17).

Notice. Every surplus lines contract must bear the name of the agent who procured it. Every surplus lines insurance contract shall have stamped upon it in bold ten point type the following notice:

> "**Note:** This insurance policy is issued pursuant to Mississippi law covering surplus lines insurance. The company issuing the policy is not licensed by

the State of Mississippi, but is authorized to do business in Mississippi as a nonadmitted company. The policy is not protected by the Mississippi Insurance Guaranty Association in the event of the insurer's insolvency." (Miss. Code Ann. §83-21-19).

I. Independently Procured Insurance:

1. *Rules.* "Independently procured insurance" means any property and casualty insurance permitted in a state to be placed directly with a nonadmitted insurer eligible to accept such business. All corporations, firms, persons, or individuals obtaining insurance on property situated in Mississippi owned by corporations, firms, or individuals resident therein, against fire, lightning, or tornado from companies, associations, firms, or corporations not authorized to transact business in Mississippi, must file with the insurance commissioner a sworn statement or declaration, setting forth the name of the company, number of policy, amount of insurance rate, premium, and description. An insured who does not purchase insurance through a surplus lines insurance producer and directly or independently procures or renews coverage from a nonadmitted carrier is subject to the 4 percent premium tax and 5 percent nonadmitted policy fee (3 percent for risks beginning on or after July 1, 2012). Policies that cover residential earthquake or flood risks that are not written through the National Flood Insurance Program shall be exempt from the nonadmitted policy fee. The insured is responsible for payment of these taxes and fees. (Miss. Code Ann. §83-34-4. This statute will be repealed effective July 1, 2022).

2. *Industrial Insured Exemption.* A surplus lines insurance producer is not required to perform a due diligence search when the surplus lines insurance producer is seeking to procure or place nonadmitted insurance for an exempt commercial purchaser. (Miss. Code Ann. §83-21-23).

NRRA Implementation

J. Compact: None.

K. Definitions:

1. "Home State" means:

   In general, except as provided in subparagraph b., the term "home state" means, with respect to an insured:

   a. The state in which an insured maintains its principal place of business or, in the case of an individual, the individual's principal residence.

b. If 100 percent of the insured risk is located outside the state referred to in subparagraph 1(a), the state to which the greatest percentage of the insured's taxable premium for that insurance contract is allocated.

2. If more than one insured from an affiliated group are named insureds on a single nonadmitted insurance contract, the term "home state" means the home state, as determined according to subparagraph 1.a of this paragraph, of the member of the affiliated group that the largest percentage of premium attributed to it under such insurance contract. (Miss. Code Ann. §83-21-18).

3. "Principal place of business" means, with respect to determining the home state of the insured, the state where the insured maintains its headquarters and where the insured's high-level officers direct, control and coordinate the business activities. (Miss. Code Ann. §83-21-18).

4. "Principal residence" means, with respect to determining the home state of the individual, the state where the individual resides for the greatest number of days during a calendar year. (Miss. Code Ann. §83-21-18).

L. Statutory References:

Miss. Code Ann. §§83-21-	17 to 25
*Miss. Code Ann. §83-34-	4
	*This statute will be repealed as of July 1, 2022.

Web References:

http://www.msla.org/producers/e-pay/.

MISSOURI

A. **Resident and Nonresident Licensing:** Resident and nonresident property and casualty producers may be licensed for surplus lines and may place insurance with nonadmitted insurers by passing a qualifying examination. Surplus lines licenses expire every two years on the licensee's birth date. Initial fee: $100; Renewal fee: $100. (R.S. Mo. §384.043).

Licensed producers may deal with surplus lines licensees and receive commission. (R.S. Mo. §384.045).

The Director may promulgate and amend rules relating to domestice surplus lines insurers as are necessary to enable the Director to carry out the provisions of Chapter 384. (R.S. Mo. §384.018).

A person selling, soliciting, or negotiating nonadmitted insurance with respect to an insured is required to obtain or possess a current surplus lines insurance license issued by the director only if Missouri is such insured's home state. (R.S. Mo. §384.043).

B. **Records of Surplus Lines Licensee:** Each surplus lines licensee shall keep in his/her Missouri office a full and true record of each surplus lines contract placed by the licensee, including a copy of the policy, certificate, cover note, or other evidence of insurance showing as many of the following as are applicable:

1. Amount of the insurance and perils insured;
2. A brief description of the property insured and its location;
3. The gross premium charged;
4. Any return premium paid;
5. Rate of premium charged upon the several items of property;
6. Effective date of the contract, and the terms thereof;
7. Name and address of the insured;
8. Name and address of the insurer;
9. Amount of tax and other sums to be collected from the insured; and
10. Identity of the producing broker, any confirming correspondence from the insurer or its representative and the application.

These records shall be kept open to the Director at all reasonable times for examination, without notice, for a period of no less than three years following the termination of the contract. Any costs of examination incurred by the Director in examining the records of a nonresident surplus lines licensee shall be paid by the nonresident surplus lines licensee. (R.S. Mo. §384.048).

Commercial Purchaser Exemption. A surplus lines licensee seeking to procure or place nonadmitted insurance in Missouri for an exempt commercial purchaser is not required to satisfy any requirement to make a due diligence search to determine whether the full amount or type of insurance sought by such exempt commercial purchaser can be obtained from nonadmitted insurers if:

1. The surplus lines licensee procuring or placing the surplus lines insurance has disclosed to the exempt commercial purchaser that such insurance may or may not be available from the admitted market that may provide greater protection with more regulatory oversight.

2. The exempt commercial purchaser has subsequently requested in writing the surplus lines licensee to procure or place such insurance from a nonadmitted insurer. (R.S. Mo. §384.021).

An exempt commercial purchaser must:

1. Employ or retain a qualified risk manager.

2. Pay aggregate property and casualty premiums in excess of $100,000 in the immediately preceding twelve months.

They must also meet at least **one** of the following requirements:

1. Possess a net worth in excess of $22,040 million.

2. Generate annual revenues in excess of $55,100 million.

3. Employ more than 500 full-time employees per individual insured.

4. Is a nonprofit or public entity generating annual budgeted expenditures of at least $36,060 million.

5. Is a municipality with a population in excess of 50,000 persons (R.S. Mo. §384.015).

C. Tax: 5 percent of Missouri net premium due annually, before April 16, payable to the Missouri Department of Revenue. The Missouri surplus lines tax is applicable to any fees levied by the surplus lines licensee. Premium means the gross amount of charges for surplus lines insurance for risks within Missouri less federal, state, and local taxes and returned premiums.

The 5 percent tax on net premiums is levied upon and only upon the entire gross premium for nonadmitted or surplus lines insurance policies for which the home state of the insured is Missouri. (R.S. Mo. §384.051).

Net Premiums Defined. The gross amount of charges for surplus lines insurance, exclusive of sums collected for the payment of federal, state and local taxes, less returned premiums. (R.S. Mo. §384.057).

D. **Stamping Fee:** None. Missouri does not have a surplus lines stamping office.

E. **Surplus Lines Association:** Surplus Lines Association of Missouri, c/o Ann Monaco Warren, General Counsel, Inglish & Monaco, P.C., 237 East High Street, Jefferson City, MO 65102 . Phone: 573-634-2522. Email: awarren@inglishmonaco.com, or surpluslines@insurance.mo.gov. (https://surplusmanual.lockelord.com/eligibility/missouri/).

F. **Other Requirements or Restrictions:** Surplus lines insurance means any insurance of risks resident, located, or to be performed in this state, permitted to be placed through a surplus lines licensee with a nonadmitted insurer eligible to accept such insurance, other than reinsurance, and life and health insurance and annuities. (R.S. Mo. §384.015).

Eligibility. A surplus lines licensee cannot place coverage with a nonadmitted insurer, unless, at the time of placement, the surplus lines licensee has determined that the nonadmitted insurer is authorized to write the kind of insurance in its domiciliary jurisdiction and either:

1. Has capital and surplus or its equivalent under the laws of its domiciliary jurisdiction, which equals the greater of the minimum capital and surplus requirements under the laws of Missouri or $15 million. These requirements may be satisfied by an insurer's possessing less than the minimum capital and surplus upon an affirmative finding of acceptability by the director provided that the finding shall be based upon such factors as quality of management, capital and surplus of any parent company, company underwriting profit and investment income trends, market availability and company record and reputation within the industry, and in no event will the director make an affirmative finding of acceptability when the nonadmitted insurer's capital and surplus is less than $4,500,000; or

2. The nonadmitted insurer appears on the most recent list of eligible surplus lines insurers published by the director from time to time but at least semiannually or on the most recent quarterly listing of alien insurers maintained by the international insurers department of the National Association of Insurance Commissioners. (R.S. Mo. §384.021).

Notice. Each policy or other evidence of surplus lines insurance must bear the name of the surplus lines licensee and the following legend in ten-point type:

> "This is evidence of insurance procured and developed under the Missouri Surplus Lines Laws. It is NOT covered by the Missouri Insurance Guaranty Association. The insurer is not licensed by the state of Missouri and is not subject to its supervision." (R.S. Mo. §384.036).

Annual Statements. Before March 2 of each year, each surplus lines broker must report a statement showing, with respect to the year ending the immediately preceding December 31 for nonadmitted insurance where the home state of the insured is this state, the gross amounts charged for surplus lines insurance, exclusive of sums collected for the payment of federal, state or local taxes; and the amount of net premiums with respect to the insurance. (R.S. Mo. §384.057).

An annual report shall be made under oath and presented, before March 2 of each year, to the director on the specified forms and shall include:

1. The name and address of the insured;
2. The identity of the insurer or insurers;
3. A description of the subject and location of the risk;
4. A general description of the coverage;
5. The amount of premium charged for the insurance;
6. Such other pertinent information as the director may reasonably require. (R.S. Mo. §384.051).

Quarterly Statements. No later than within forty-five days after the end of each calendar quarter ending March 31, June 30, September 30, and December 31, each surplus lines broker must report a statement showing, with respect to each calendar quarter for nonadmitted insurance where the home state of the insured is this state, the gross amounts charged for surplus lines insurance, exclusive of sums collected for the payment of federal, state, or local taxes; and the amount of net premiums with respect to the insurance. (R.S. Mo. §384.057).

The placement of nonadmitted insurance is subject to the statutory and regulatory requirements of Missouri surplus lines law only if Missouri is the insured's home state. (https://insurance.mo.gov/Contribute%20Documents/Carrier-Notice.pdf).

G. Independently Procured Insurance:

Every insured or self-insurer in Missouri who procures, causes to be procured, or continues or renews insurance with any surplus lines insurer, excess of loss, catastrophe or other insurance, upon a subject of insurance resident, located or to be performed within Missouri must file a written report of the insurance procured, continued or renewed in the year previous to the director before March 2 of each year. (R.S. Mo. §384.051).

NRRA Implementation

H. Compact: None.

I. Definitions:

1. "Home State": Except as provided in paragraph 2 of this subdivision, the term "home state" means, with respect to an insured:

   a. The state in which an insured maintains its principal place of business or, in the case of an individual, the individual's principal residence.

   b. If 100 percent of the insured risk is located out of the state referred to in subparagraph a of this paragraph, the state to which the greatest percentage of the insured's taxable premium for that insurance contract is allocated.

2. If more than one insured from an affiliated group are named insureds on a single nonadmitted insurance contract, the term "home state" means the home state, as determined under paragraph 1.a of this subdivision, of the member of the affiliated group that has the largest percentage of premium attributed to it under such insurance contract.

3. The principal place of business is the state where the insured maintains its headquarters and where the insured's high-level officers direct, control and coordinate the business activities of the insured. (R.S. Mo. §384.015

J. Statutory References:

R.S. Mo. §§384.	015, 018, 021, 036, 043, 045 to 051, 057

Web References:

https://surplusmanual.lockelord.com/eligibility/missouri/.

https://insurance.mo.gov/Contribute%20Documents/Carrier-Notice.pdf.

MONTANA

A. Resident Licensing: If Montana is the home state of the insured, the person placing a contract of surplus lines insurance with an unauthorized insurer must possess a current surplus lines insurance producer's license issued by the commissioner. To be eligible for a resident surplus lines insurance producer license, the person must hold a current property and casualty insurance producer license. Persons applying for a resident surplus lines insurance producer license must remit to the commissioner an initial fee of $50 and a completed license application. Licenses are renewable every two years at a renewal fee of $100. Lapsed license reinstatement fee: $200. (MCA 33-2-305, 708).

The commissioner may participate in the National Association of Insurance Commissioners' producer licensing database regarding surplus lines insurance producer licensing. (MCA 33-2-305).

B. Nonresident Licensing: To be eligible for a surplus lines insurance producer license in Montana, nonresident applicants must hold a current surplus lines insurance producer license in their home state. In addition, nonresident applicants must remit to the commissioner an initial fee of $100 and a completed application. Licenses are renewable every two years at a renewal fee of $50. Lapsed license reinstatement fee: $200. (MCA 33-2-708). The home state of a nonresident applicant must award nonresident surplus lines insurance producers' licenses to residents of Montana on the same basis. (MCA 33-17-401).

C. Business Entity Licensing: A business entity is eligible to be licensed as a surplus lines insurance producer in Montana if the business entity license lists the individuals within the business entity who have satisfied the requirements of this part to become surplus lines insurance producers and only those individuals listed on the business entity license transact surplus lines insurance. (MCA 33-2-305).

D. Diligent Effort: To place a contract of insurance with an unauthorized insurer, surplus lines insurance producers are required to first make a diligent effort to place the business with a minimum of three insurers authorized and actually transacting that line of business in Montana. If fewer than three insurers are authorized and actually transacting the line of business in Montana, diligent effort must be met by searching this lesser market. (MCA 33-2-302).

Exempt Commercial Purchaser. A surplus lines insurance producer placing coverage with an eligible surplus lines insurer for an exempt commercial purchaser is not required to satisfy the diligent effort requirements if both:

1. The producing insurance producer placing the coverage has disclosed to the exempt commercial purchaser that the insurance may or may not be available from an authorized insurer that may provide greater protection with more regulatory oversight; and

2. The exempt commercial purchaser has subsequently requested in writing to the surplus lines insurance producer that the coverage be placed with the surplus lines insurer. (MCA 33-2-302).

E. **Tax:** The premium tax is 2.75 percent, and the fire premium tax is 2.5 percent. When Montana is the home state of the insured, the surplus lines producer must collect from the insured and pay to the commissioner a tax of 2.75 percent on net premiums collected for surplus lines insurance transacted in Montana during the preceding period on or before April 1 of each year. The surplus lines producer must also collect from the insured a 2.50 percent tax on the fire premium associated with a surplus lines insurance policy. (MCA 33-2-311, 33-2-705).

If Montana is not the home state of the insured, the commissioner may not collect any tax or stamping fee regardless of whether the coverage includes risks or exposures partially located or to be performed in this state. (MCA 33-2-311).

A surplus lines insurance producer who fails to pay the required taxes is liable for a penalty of $25 for each day of delinquency, commencing thirty calendar days after the due date. (MCA 33-2-312).

If the commissioner enters an agreement for multistate risks, and the agreement requires participating states to develop a single, blended tax for multistate risks, the provisions of MCA 50-3-109 do not apply to the collection of premium taxes. In this state, the blended tax must be 3.3 percent on premiums and calculated in the same manner as authorized premium taxes under MCA 33-2-705, except that amounts collected specifically for applicable state and federal taxes and in excess of the premium otherwise required are not considered part of the premium in calculating the tax. (MCA 33-2-323).

F. **Stamping Fee:** The stamping fee is 0.25 percent if the policy is mailed. There is no stamping fee if the policy is filed electronically through the surplus lines portal on the department website at https://csimt.gov/insurance/. (ARM 6.6.2804).

If a surplus lines producer does not pay the stamping fee, the commissioner may impose a penalty of 25 percent of the stamping fee plus 1.5 percent a month from the date of delinquency until the stamping fee is paid. (MCA 33-2-312).

G. **Clearinghouse Processing Fee:** If the commissioner has entered an agreement with a clearinghouse to process multistate risks and allocate and distribute taxes and fees collected, the clearinghouse may collect a processing fee from the surplus lines insurance producer. The processing fee may be a flat fee per submission, a percentage of the premium payable for surplus lines insurance, or a combination of a flat fee and a percentage of premium payable. When a percentage of premium payable is used in calculating the processing fee, the charge may not exceed 1 percent of the premium payable for surplus lines insurance. The commissioner will establish the processing fee by rule to be commensurate with the clearinghouse's charges to process multistate risks and allocate and distribute taxes and fees collected to the participating states.

If applicable, the surplus lines insurance producer shall collect the stamping fee and clearinghouse processing fee from the insured in addition to the premium payable for the insurance contract and any taxes and fees. (MCA 33-2-321).

H. **Surplus Lines Association:** The primary contact for surplus lines is the Montana Department of Insurance, 840 Helena Ave., Helena, MT 59601. Phone: (406) 444-2040 or (800) 322-6148. Fax: (406) 444-3497 or (406) 444-3413. Website: www.csimt.gov.

I. **Other Requirements or Restrictions:** Pursuant to the NRRA, the transaction of surplus lines insurance is subject to the statutory and regulatory requirements of the home state of the insured, regardless of whether a multistate risk is covered. If, at the time of the surplus lines insurance transaction, the home state is Montana, the surplus lines insurance transaction is subject to the applicable statutory and regulatory requirements in Montana. If the home state is not Montana, the Montana statutory and regulatory requirements regarding the surplus lines insurance transaction are preempted by the statutory and regulatory requirements of the home state. (MCA 33-2-302).

Requirements. When Montana is the home state at the time of the surplus lines insurance transaction, certain criteria apply. A producing insurance producer may request a surplus lines insurance producer to place a contract of insurance with an unauthorized insurer if the insurer is an eligible surplus lines insurer; the line of insurance or the full amount of the line of insurance cannot be obtained from authorized insurers or, in the case of a renewal, the line of insurance has not become available from an authorized insurer. If the insurance producer making a diligent effort to place the business with a minimum of three insurers authorized and transacting business in Montana and if fewer than three insurers are authorized and transacting the line of business in Montana, diligent effort must be met by searching the lesser market. The insurance cannot be procured for the purpose of securing a lower premium rate than would be accepted by an authorized insurer unless the premium rate quoted by the authorized insurer is at least 10 percent higher and at least $1,500 greater than the premium rate quoted by the unauthorized insurer or an advantage in terms of the insurance contract. (MCA 33-2-302).

Submissions. Each insurance contract, cover note, or certificate of insurance procured and delivered as surplus lines insurance must be filed with: the commissioner, if Montana is the home state of the insured and the coverage is for a single-state risk or the commissioner has not entered an agreement for multistate risks or the clearinghouse, if in operation and if the commissioner has entered an agreement for multistate risks. The commissioner will establish by rule a submission form for reporting surplus lines transactions. The form may be different for insureds than for independently procured insurance, surplus line producers, single-state risks, or multistate risks. The submission form for surplus lines insurance producers must include information regarding the producing producer's diligent efforts to place the coverage with authorized insurers and the results of the efforts and the producing insurance producer's affirmation that the producer has expressly advised the insured prior to placing the insurance that the surplus lines insurer with whom the insurance is placed is not authorized in this state and is not subject to the same supervision as an authorized insurer and in the event of the insolvency of the surplus lines insurer, the property and casualty guaranty fund of the state will not pay losses under the surplus lines coverage. (MCA 33-2-303).

Endorsements. The commissioner may establish by rule an endorsement to be made on each contract, cover note, or certificate of surplus lines insurance procured and delivered by a surplus lines insurance producer under this part advising the insured that the coverage is issued by an unauthorized insurer that is not covered by the property and casualty guaranty fund of this state if the unauthorized insurer becomes insolvent. The surplus lines insurance producer shall properly fill in and sign the endorsement. (MCA 33-2-303).

Eligibility. If an unauthorized insurer is domiciled in any state, a surplus lines insurance producer may not place insurance with that unauthorized insurer unless, at the time of placement, the unauthorized insurer is authorized to issue the same kind of property or casualty insurance in its domiciliary jurisdiction, and maintains capital and surplus or its equivalent under the laws of its state of domicile, which equals the greater of the minimum capital and surplus requirements of MCA 33-2-109 and 33-2-110, or $15 million. An insurer possessing less than $15 million capital and surplus may satisfy the requirements of this subsection upon an affirmative finding of acceptability by the commissioner. If the commissioner makes an exception to the $15 million capital and surplus requirement, the commissioner's finding must be based upon such factors as the quality of management, capital, and surplus of a parent company; company underwriting profit and investment income trends; market availability; and company record and reputation within the industry. The commissioner may not make an affirmative finding of acceptability when the surplus lines insurer's capital and surplus is less than $4.5 million. (MCA 33-2-307).

Foreign surplus lines insurers must submit an application on a form approved by the commissioner. The foreign surplus lines insurer can place surplus lines insurance in Montana after the surplus lines insurer is added to the Montana Eligible Surplus Lines Companies list.

If an unauthorized insurer is an alien insurer, a surplus lines insurance producer may not place insurance with that unauthorized insurer unless, at the time of placement, the unauthorized insurer appears on the National Association of Insurance Commissioners' Nonadmitted Insurers Quarterly Listing. (MCA 33-2-307).

Evidence of Insurance. Upon placing surplus lines insurance, the surplus lines insurance producer shall promptly issue or deliver to the insured or the insuring producer evidence of the insurance, consisting either of the policy as issued by the insurer or, if the policy is not then available, a cover note or certificate of insurance signed or countersigned by the insurance producer. The cover note or certificate must show the subject, coverage, conditions, and term of the insurance, the premium charged and taxes collected from the insured, and the name and address of the insurer. If a direct risk is assumed by more than one insurer, the cover note or certificate must state the name and address and proportion of the entire direct risk assumed by each insurer. (MCA 33-2-308).

Records. Each surplus lines insurance producer shall keep a separate record and account of all business transacted under the producer's license, including a copy of each daily report, if any, or of each policy, certificate of insurance, cover note, or other evidence of insurance issued or delivered by the producer. The records must be available for examination by the commissioner at any reasonable time within five years after the issuance of the surplus lines insurance to which it relates. (MCA 33-2-310).

Reports. By the reporting date established by the commissioner, the surplus lines insurance producer must file with the commissioner or with the clearinghouse if requested by the commissioner a tax and fee statement for the preceding reporting period. The commissioner will establish by rule the content and form of the tax and fee statement that must include, but is not limited to:

(1) the name and principal residence of the insured or the address at which the insured maintains its principal place of business;

(2) a brief and general description of the risk or exposure insured and where located;

(3) the name and home office address of each insurer providing the surplus lines insurance;

(4) the amount of each surplus lines insurance policy, the premium rate, and the gross premium charged for the policy;

(5) the date and term of the policy;

(6) the amount of premium returned on each policy cancelled or not taken;

(7) the amount of tax and other sums to be collected from the insured;

(8) the identity of the producing insurance producer; and

(9) any additional information that the commissioner may reasonably require. (MCA 33-2-310).

J. Independently Procured Insurance: Insureds in Montana may purchase coverage directly either from licensed insurers or eligible surplus lines carriers. The insured is responsible for reporting the transaction to the Department of Insurance and for paying the premium tax of 2.75 percent and the fire premium tax of 2.50 percent. The insured is also responsible for paying any associated stamping fee. (MCA 33-2-705, 33-2-310, 33-2-311, 33-2-321).

NRRA Implementation

K. Compact: None. However, as described in Part E above the commissioner is authorized by law to enter into a cooperative or reciprocal agreement with other states, individually or collectively, for the purposes of collecting, allocating, and disbursing premium taxes and fees attributable to multistate risks. (MCA 33-2-323).

L. Definitions:

1. "Home State" means, with respect to an insured:

   a. The state in which the insured maintains its principal place of business or, in the case of an individual, the individual's principal residence.

   b. If 100 percent of the insured risk is located outside the state referred to in paragraph (1), the state with the greatest allocated percentage of the insured's taxable premium for that surplus lines insurance contract.

   c. If more than one insured from an affiliated group are named insureds on a single surplus lines insurance contract, the home state as determined under paragraph a or paragraph b for the member of the affiliated group that has the largest percentage of premium attributed to it under the surplus lines insurance contract.

   d. If a group policyholder pays 100 percent of the premium from its own funds, the home state of the group policyholder as determined under paragraph a, or if a group policyholder does not pay 100 percent of the premiums from its own funds, the home state of the group member as determined under paragraph a.

2. "Principal place of business" means the state where the insured business maintains its headquarters and where the insured's high-level officers direct, control, and coordinate the business activities of the insured.

3. "Independently procured insurance" means surplus lines insurance procured directly by an insured from an eligible surplus lines insurer. (MCA 33-2-301).

M. Statutory References:

MCA 33-2-	301 to 303, 305, 307, 308
	310 to 312
	321, 323
	708
MCA 33-17-	401

ARM 6.6.	2804

NEBRASKA

A. **Resident Licensing:** No person, other than an exempt commercial purchaser, can place, procure, or effect insurance for or on behalf of an insured whose home state is Nebraska in any nonadmitted insurer until such person has first been issued a surplus lines license. Applications are available for download at the Nebraska Department of Insurance Web site. Applications must include the applicant's Social Security number. Initial and biennial renewal fee: $250. Individual surplus lines expire on the licensee's birthday in the first year after issuance in which his or her age is divisible by two. Licenses may be renewed within ninety days of expiration or within thirty days after expiration as long as a late renewal fee of an additional $100 is paid. (Neb. Rev. Stat. Ann. § 44-5504).

The director may use the National Insurance Producer Database of the National Association of Insurance Commissioners, or any other equivalent uniform national data base, for the licensure of an individual or an entity as a surplus lines producer and for renewal of such license.

Surplus lines licenses may be issued to foreign or domestic corporations. The corporate surplus lines license is required to list all officers or employees of the corporation who currently hold an insurance producer license or meet the requirements for an individual surplus lines license and who have authority to transact surplus lines business on behalf of the corporation. Only individuals listed on the corporate surplus lines license can transact surplus lines business on behalf of the corporate licensee. (Neb. Rev. Stat. Ann. § 44-5503). Initial and annual fee: $250. All corporate surplus lines licenses expire on April 30 of each year. (Neb. Rev. Stat. Ann. § 44-5504).

B. **Nonresident Licensing:** A person licensed as a surplus lines producer in his or her home state shall receive a nonresident surplus lines producer license if: the person is currently licensed as a resident and in good standing in his or her home state; the person has submitted the proper request for licensure and has paid the fees required; the person has submitted to the director the application for licensure that the person submitted to his or her home state, or in lieu of the same, a completed uniform application; the person's home state must award nonresident producer licenses to residents of Nebraska on the same basis. (Neb. Rev. Stat. Ann. § 44-4055).

C. **Diligent Effort:** Reports must be filed on or before March 1 for the quarter ending the preceding December 31, June 1 for the quarter ending the preceding March 31, September 1 for the quarter ending the preceding June 30, and December 1 for the quarter ending the preceding September 30 of each year; every surplus lines licensee must file a report containing required information, including: (1) the name of the nonadmitted insurer; (2) the name of the licensee; (3) the number of policies issued by each nonadmitted insurer; (4) except for insurance placed or procured on behalf of an exempt commercial purchaser, a sworn statement by the licensee with regard to the coverages described in the quarterly report that, to the best of the licensee's knowledge and belief, the licensee could not reasonably procure such coverages from an admitted insurer; and (5) the premium volume for each nonadmitted insurer by line of business. (Neb. Rev. Stat. Ann. § 44-5511). An affidavit of nonavailability is not required, but producer must obtain and retain a form signed by insured permitting use of the nonadmitted insurer, and must file quarterly reports listing all nonadmitted business written, even if the amount is $0.00. (Neb. Rev. Stat. Ann. § 44-5510).

Commercial Purchaser Exemption. A surplus lines licensee seeking to procure or place nonadmitted insurance for an exempt commercial purchaser whose home state is Nebraska is not required to make a due diligence search to determine whether the full amount or type of insurance sought by such exempt commercial purchaser can be obtained from admitted insurers if:

1. The surplus lines licensee procuring or placing the insurance has disclosed to the exempt commercial purchaser that such insurance may or may not be available from the admitted market that may provide greater protection with more regulatory oversight.

2. The exempt commercial purchaser has subsequently requested in writing the surplus lines licensee to procure or place such insurance for a nonadmitted insurer. (Neb. Rev. Stat. Ann. § 44-5510).

D. Tax: Flat, 3 percent. Every surplus lines licensee transacting business under the Surplus Lines Insurance Act must collect and pay to the Director on or before March 1 for the quarter ending the preceding December 31, June 1 for the quarter ending the preceding March 31, September 1 for the quarter ending the preceding June 30, and December 1 for the quarter ending the preceding September 30 a sum based on the total gross premiums charged, less any return premiums, for surplus lines insurance provided by the licensee pursuant to the license. Taxes cannot be determined on a retaliatory basis.

In-State Risks. For purposes of the portion that is attributable to in-state risks, an amount and rate equal to 3 percent of the total gross premiums charged, less any return premiums.

Multi-State Risks. For purposes of the portion that is attributable to out-of-state risks, an amount equal to the portion of the premiums allocated to each of the other states or territories and at a rate as established by each state or territory as being applicable to the properties, risks, or exposures located or performed outside of this state. The tax on any portion of the premium unearned at termination of insurance having been credited by the state to the licensee will be returned to the policyholder directly by the surplus lines licensee or through the producing broker, if any. The surplus lines licensee is prohibited from rebating, for any reason, any portion of the tax.

The director may utilize or adopt the allocation schedule included in the Nonadmitted Insurance Multi-State Agreement (NIMA) for the purpose of allocating risk and computing the tax due on the portion of premium attributable to each risk classification and to each state in which properties, risks, or exposures are located. (Neb. Rev. Stat. Ann. § 44-5506).

Commercial Purchaser Exemption. A surplus lines licensee seeking to procure or place nonadmitted insurance for an exempt commercial purchaser whose home state is Nebraska shall not be required to make a due diligence search to determine whether the full amount or type of insurance sought by such exempt commercial purchaser can be obtained from admitted insurers if the surplus lines licensee has disclosed to the exempt commercial purchaser that such insurance may or may not be available from the admitted market that may provide greater protection with more regulatory oversight, and the exempt commercial purchaser subsequently requested in writing the surplus lines licensee to procure or place such insurance for a nonadmitted insurer. (Neb. Rev. Stat. Ann. §§44-5506, 44-5510).

E. **Stamping Fee:** None. Nebraska does not have a stamping office.

F. **Surplus Lines Association:** None. Questions regarding Surplus Lines can be directed to the DOI.

Nebraska Dept. of Insurance

P.O. Box 82089

Lincoln, NE 68501-2089

P: (402) 471-4646

F: (402) 471-4610

DOI.SurplusLines@Nebraska.gov

G. **Other Requirements or Restrictions:**

Eligibility. A surplus lines licensee shall not place coverage with a nonadmitted insurer unless, at the time of placement, the surplus lines licensee has determined that the nonadmitted insurer: is authorized to write such insurance in its domiciliary jurisdiction; has established satisfactory evidence of good repute and financial integrity; and possesses capital and surplus or its equivalent under the laws of its domiciliary jurisdiction that equals the greater of the minimum capital and surplus requirements under the laws of this state or $15,000,000; or if minimum capital and surplus does not meet the requirements of set forth above, then upon an affirmative finding of acceptability by the director. The finding will be based upon such factors as quality of management, capital and surplus of any parent company, company underwriting profit and investment income trends, market availability, and company record and reputation within the industry. The director will not make an affirmative finding of acceptability if the nonadmitted insurer's capital and surplus is less than $4,500,000.

No surplus lines licensee shall place nonadmitted insurance with or procure nonadmitted insurance from a nonadmitted insurer domiciled outside the United States unless the insurer is listed on the Quarterly Listing of Alien Insurers maintained by the International Insurers Department of the National Association of Insurance Commissioners. (Neb. Rev. Stat. Ann. § 44-5508).

NOTICE

All surplus lines contracts must have the following stamped on the declarations page: (1) The licensee's name, business address, and surplus lines license number; (2) the licensee's business transaction name, if different from the licensee's name; and (3) the following warning:

> "This policy is issued by a nonadmitted insurer, and in the event of the insolvency of such insurer, this policy will not be covered by the Nebraska Property and Liability Insurance Guaranty Association." (Neb. Rev. Stat. Ann. § 44-5509).

Records. Each surplus lines licensee must keep in the licensee's office a true and complete record of the business transacted by the licensee showing:

1. The exact amount of insurance or limits of exposure.

2. The gross premiums charged therefore.

3. The return premium paid thereon.

4. The rate of premium charged for such insurance.

5. The date of such insurance and terms thereof.

6. The name and address of the nonadmitted insurer writing such insurance.

7. A copy of the declaration page of each policy and a copy of each policy form issued by the licensee.

8. A copy of the written statement described in subdivision (1)(c) of Neb. Rev. Stat. Ann. § 44-5510 or, in lieu thereof, a copy of the application containing such written statement.

9. The name of the insured.

10. The address of the principal residence of the insured or the address at which the insured maintains its principal place of business.

11. A brief and general description of the risk or exposure insured and where located.

12. Documentation showing that the nonadmitted insurer writing such insurance complies with the requirements of Neb. Rev. Stat. Ann. § 44-5508.

13. Such other facts and information as the Department may direct and require.

    Such records shall be kept by the licensee in the licensee's office within the state for not less than five years and shall at all times be open and subject to the inspection and examination of the Department or its officers. (Neb. Rev. Stat. Ann. § 44-5505).

Statements. Every surplus lines licensee transacting business under the Surplus Lines Insurance Act must, on or before March 1 for the quarter ending the preceding December 31, June 1 for the quarter ending the preceding March 31, September 1 for the quarter ending the preceding June 30, and December 1 for the quarter ending the preceding September 30 of each year, make and file with the Department a verified statement upon a form prescribed by the Department or a designee of the director which must exhibit the true amount of all such business transacted during that period and must be filed in conjunction with the tax amount prescribed above. (Neb. Rev.Stat. Ann. § 44-5506).

Reports. On or before March 1 for the quarter ending the preceding December 31, June 1 for the quarter ending the preceding March 31, September 1 for the quarter ending the preceding June 30, and December 1 for the quarter ending the preceding September 30 of each year, every surplus lines licensee must file with the Department a report containing such information as the Department may require, including: (1) the name of the nonadmitted insurer; (2) the name of the licensee; (3) the number of policies issued by each nonadmitted insurer; (4) except for insurance placed or procured on behalf of an exempt commercial purchaser, a sworn statement by the licensee with regard to the coverages described in the quarterly report that, to the best of the licensee's knowledge and belief, the licensee could not reasonably procure such coverages from an admitted insurer; and (5) the premium volume for each nonadmitted insurer by line of business. (Neb. Rev. Stat. Ann. § 44-5511).

H. Independently Procured Insurance: Nebraska does not have an industrial insured exemption but the NRRA's Commercial Purchaser Exemption is in effect.

Rules. Exempt commercial purchaser means any person purchasing commercial insurance that, at the time of placement, meets the following requirements:

(a) The person employs or retains a qualified risk manager to negotiate insurance coverage.

(b) The person has paid aggregate nationwide commercial property and casualty insurance premiums in excess of one hundred thousand dollars in the immediately preceding twelve months.

(c) The person meets at least one of the following criteria:

(i) The person possesses a net worth in excess of twenty million dollars, as such amount is adjusted pursuant to subdivision (5)(b) of this section.

(ii) The person generates annual revenue in excess of fifty million dollars, as such amount is adjusted pursuant to subdivision (5)(b) of this section.

(iii) The person employs more than five hundred full-time or full-time equivalent employees per individual insured or is a member of an affiliated group employing more than one thousand employees in the aggregate.

(iv) The person is a not-for-profit organization or public entity generating annual budgeted expenditures of at least thirty million dollars, as such amount is adjusted pursuant to subdivision (5)(b) of this section.

(v) The person is a municipality with a population in excess of fifty thousand inhabitants.

(Neb. Rev. Stat. Ann. § 44-5502).

Commercial Purchaser Exemption. Every exempt commercial purchaser whose home state is Nebraska must, on or before March 1 for the quarter ending the preceding December 31, June 1 for the quarter ending the preceding March 31, September 1 for the quarter ending the preceding June 30, and December 1 for the quarter ending the preceding September 30 of each year, pay to the Department a tax in the amount described above for in-state and out-of-state risks. The calculation of the taxes due is based only on those premiums remitted for the placement or procurement of insurance by an exempt commercial purchaser whose home state is Nebraska. Forms are available on the Nebraska Department of Insurance Web site for an exempt commercial purchaser tax filing. (Neb. Rev. Stat. Ann. §44-5515).

NRRA Implementation

I. Compact: None. Nebraska withdrew from NIMA on March 5, 2012.

J. Definitions:

1. Home State means, with respect to an insured:

   a. The state in which an insured maintains its principal place of business or, in the case of an individual, the individual's principal residence; or

   b. If 100 percent of the insured risk is located out of the state, the state to which the greatest percentage of the insured's taxable premium for that insurance contract is allocated.

2. If more than one insured from an affiliated group are named insureds on a single nonadmitted insurance contract, home state means the home state, as described above, of the member of the affiliated group that has the largest percentage of premium attributed to it under such insurance contract.

3. When determining the home state of the insured, the principal place of business is the state in which the insured maintains its headquarters and where the insured's high-level officers direct, control, and coordinate the business activities of the insured.

4. Affiliated group means a group of entities in which each entity, with respect to an insured, controls, is controlled by or is under common control with the insured.

5. Control means to own, control, or have the power of an entity directly, indirectly, or acting through one or more other persons to vote 25 percent or more of any class of voting securities of another entity; or to direct, by an entity, in any manner, the election of a majority of directors or trustees of another entity.

(Neb. Rev. Stat. Ann. § 44-5502).

K. Statutory References: Neb. Rev. Stat. Ann. §§ 44-4055, 5502 to 5506, 5508 to 5511, 55154.

NEVADA

A. **Resident and Nonresident Licensing:** Any person who has been licensed by Nevada as a producer of insurance for general lines for at least six months, or has been licensed in another state as a surplus lines broker and continues to be licensed in that state, may be licensed as a surplus lines broker. Applicants must file an application for a license and pay an initial application fee of $125. Licenses are renewable every three years upon the payment of a renewal fee of $125. Individuals transacting on behalf of a business entity must pay an additional $60 affiliation fee. In addition, applicants must pass any examination prescribed by the Commissioner on the subject of surplus lines. A surplus lines broker's license may not be issued or renewed by the Commissioner if the applicant fails to submit a completed and signed statement prescribed by the Division of Welfare and Supportive Services pursuant to N.R.S. § 425.520 or if the applicant indicates on the required statement that the applicant is subject to a court order for the support of a child and is not in compliance with that order. (N.R.S. §§ 680B.010, 680C.110, 685A.120).

Late Renewal. A license which is not renewed expires at midnight on the last day specified for its renewal. The Commissioner may accept a request for renewal received by the Commissioner within thirty days after the expiration of the license if the request is accompanied by the statement made pursuant to N.R.S. § 685.127, all applicable fees for renewal, and a penalty of 50 percent of all applicable fees. (N.R.S. § 685A.120).

All resident and nonresident brokers must be a member of the Nevada Surplus Lines Association as a condition of continued licensure. (N.R.S. § 685A.075).

B. **Diligent Effort:** If Nevada is the insured's home state and certain insurance coverages cannot be procured from authorized insurers, nonadmitted insurance may be procured from unauthorized insurers so long as the full amount of insurance required is not procurable from an insurer authorized to engage in the business of insurance in Nevada, after diligent effort has been made to do so. (N.R.S. § 685A.040).

Commercial Purchaser Exemption. A broker is not required to make a diligent effort to determine whether the full amount or type of insurance can be obtained from admitted insurers when the broker is seeking to procure or place nonadmitted insurance for an exempt commercial purchaser if (N.R.S. § 685A.040):

1. The broker procuring or placing the nonadmitted insurance has disclosed to the exempt commercial purchaser that such insurance may or may not be available from the admitted market that may provide greater protection with more regulatory oversight.

2. The exempt commercial purchaser has subsequently requested in writing for the broker to procure or place such insurance from a nonadmitted insurer.

   To qualify as an exempt commercial purchaser, the purchaser must:

   a. Employ or retain a qualified risk manager.

   b. Have paid aggregate nationwide commercial property and casualty insurance premiums of more than $100,000 in the last twelve months.

   c. Meet one of the following conditions:

      (1) Have a net worth of more than $20 million.
      (2) Generate annual revenues of more than $50 million.
      (3) Employ more than 500 full-time or full-time equivalent employees.
      (4) Is a member of an affiliated group that employs more than 1,000 employees.
      (5) Is a nonprofit organization or a public entity with an annual budget of $30 million or more.
      (6) Is a city whose population is 25,000 or more.
      (7) Is a county whose population is 20,000 or more. (N.R.S. § 685A.032).

C. **Tax:** 3.5 percent. A broker who has written coverage for which Nevada is the insured's home state must pay a tax of 3.5 percent on net direct premiums and net direct considerations, by February 15 for the calendar quarter ending the preceding December 31; May 15 for the calendar quarter ending the preceding March 31; August 15 for the calendar quarter ending the preceding June 30; November 15 for the calendar quarter ending the preceding September 30. (N.R.S. §§ 680B.027 (updating January 1, 2021), 685A.175, 685A.180).

   A broker who receives a credit for tax paid must refund to each insured the amount of the credit attributable to the insured when the insurer pays a return premium or within thirty days, whichever is earlier. (N.R.S. § 685A.180).

   Premium Defined. Premium means the consideration for insurance. The term includes any "assessment," "membership," "policy," "survey," "inspection," "service," or similar fee or other charge assessed or collected by the insurer or an agent of the insurer in consideration for an insurance contract or its procurement. (N.R.S. § 679A.115).

   Multi-State Premium Tax. Nevada has withdrawn from the Nonadmitted Insurance Multi-State Agreement (NIMA). Instead the requirement of exclusive home state taxation, pursuant to the Nonadmitted and Reinsurance Reform Act (NRRA) of 2010 will apply. If the Home State of the insured risk is Nevada, then Nevada shall collect

100 percent of the nonadmitted insurance premium tax pertaining to that risk. Where Nevada is not the home state, no premium tax filing in Nevada is needed. Surplus lines brokers should continue to submit all premium tax filings to the Nevada Surplus Lines Association (NSLA). Visit doi.nv.gov/News_Notices/Bulletins/2012_Bulletins/ for more information.

Late Premium Tax Payment Penalties. A broker who fails to pay the tax is liable for either:

1. If the aggregate amount of the tax owed by the broker is more than $50, for a penalty in the first year of delinquency in the amount of $1,000 or 125 percent of the delinquent tax, whichever is larger.

2. If the aggregate amount of the tax owed by the broker is $50 or less, for a penalty in the first year of delinquency in an amount equal to the amount of the delinquent tax. (N.R.S. § 685A.190).

   Interest. Interest must be charged on all penalties imposed in an amount equal to the prime rate at the largest bank in the State of Nevada, as ascertained by the Commissioner of Financial Institutions on January 1 of the year in which the tax became due, plus 2 percent. The rate must be adjusted on July 1 and January 1 thereafter. The interest charged must be compounded monthly and must continue to accrue until the penalty and interest are paid in full. (N.R.S. § 685A.190).

Collection. The tax may be collected by distraint, or the tax and penalty may be recovered by an action instituted by the Commissioner, in the name of the state, the Attorney General representing the Commissioner, in any court of competent jurisdiction. (N.R.S. § 685A.190).

Notice. No proceeding to recover taxes, penalties, or fines may be maintained unless it is commenced by the giving of notice to the person against whom the proceeding is brought within five years after the occurrence of the charged act or omission. This limitation does not apply if the Commissioner finds fraudulent or willful evasion of taxes. (N.R.S. § 685A.190).

D. Stamping Fee: 0.4 percent. Must be paid within thirty days of receipt of invoice. (NAC 685A.370).

E. Surplus Lines Association: Nevada Surplus Lines Association, 6490 S. McCarran Blvd, #39, Reno, NV 89509-5317. Phone: (775) 826-7898. Fax: (775) 826-7003. Email: info@nsla.org. Web site: http://www.nsla.org. All surplus lines brokers are automatically members of the association.

F. Other Requirements or Restrictions:

Exemptions. The Nonadmitted Insurance Law of Nevada does not apply to:

1. Reinsurance;

2. Wet marine and transportation insurance;

3. Insurance of subjects located, resident or to be performed wholly outside of Nevada, or on vehicles or aircraft owned and principally garaged outside Nevada;

4. Insurance of property and operations of railroads engaged in interstate commerce;

5. Insurance of aircraft of common carriers, or cargo of such aircraft, or against liability, other than employer's liability, arising out of the ownership, maintenance or use of such aircraft; or

6. Insurance of automobile bodily injury and property damage liability risks when written by Mexican insurers and covering in Mexico and not in the United States of America. (N.R.S. § 685A.020).

Eligibility. A broker shall not knowingly place surplus lines insurance with an insurer which is unsound financially or ineligible pursuant to this section. The insurance must not be so exported for the purpose of procuring it at a premium rate lower than would be accepted by any authorized insurer; difference in rates alone will not support the export of the insurance if any authorized insurer is able and willing to carry the risk. Differences, bearing directly upon the cost of insurance, in the terms of policies which otherwise provide substantially the same coverage will not support the export of the insurance. (N.R.S. §§ 685A.070, 685A.040).

For nonadmitted insurers domiciled in a U.S. jurisdiction, a surplus lines broker is permitted to place nonadmitted insurance with such insurers provided they are authorized to write such business in their state of domicile and maintain minimum capital and surplus of $15 million or the minimum capital and surplus requirements pursuant to N.R.S. § 680A.120, whichever is greater. (N.R.S. § 685A.070).

An insurer possessing less than the minimum required capital and surplus may still be eligible for placement of nonadmitted insurance if there has been an affirmative finding of acceptability by the Commissioner. The finding must be based upon such factors as the quality of management, capital and surplus of any parent company, company underwriting profit and investment income trends, market availability, and company record and reputation within the industry. The Commissioner may not make an affirmative finding of acceptability when the nonadmitted insurer's combined capital and surplus is less than $4.5 million. (N.R.S. § 685A.070).

Notice. All surplus lines contracts must bear the following wording in a conspicuous manner:

> "This insurance contract is issued pursuant to the Nevada insurance laws by an insurer neither licensed by nor under the supervision of the Division of Insurance of the Department of Business and Industry of the State of Nevada. If the insurer is found insolvent, a claim under this contract is not covered by the Nevada Insurance Guaranty Association Act." (N.R.S. § 685A.090).

Foreign Eligibility. For admitted insurers domiciled outside of the United States, a surplus lines broker may place nonadmitted insurance business with such insurers provided the insurer is listed on the Quarterly Listing of Alien Insurers maintained by the International Insurers Department of the National Association of Insurance Commissioners (NAIC). If an alien insurer is not included on the NAIC list, the previously existing eligibility standards as set forth in N.R.S. § 685A.070 continue to apply.

Report. At the time of effecting any surplus lines insurance for which Nevada is the home state, the broker must, within ninety days after such insurance is so effected, submit a report, in the form prescribed or accepted by the Commissioner, setting forth facts from which it can be determined whether such insurance is eligible for export under N.R.S. § 685A.040. The broker must keep in his or her office the report prepared along with the report of coverage and any other information the Commissioner requires. The report prepared must not be removed from the office of the broker and must be open to examination by the Commissioner or a representative of the Commissioner at all times within five years after issuance of the coverage to which it relates. (N.R.S. § 685A.050).

The licensed surplus lines broker who is first engaged by or on behalf of an applicant for insurance may charge a fee for procuring surplus lines coverage. Except as otherwise provided by agreement between the insurer and that broker, the sum of the fee and any other commissions, fees and charges payable to that broker must not exceed 20 percent of the premium paid by the insured. (N.R.S. § 685A.155).

Records. Each broker shall keep in his or her office a full and true record of each surplus lines coverage procured by the broker for which Nevada is the insured's home state, including a copy of each daily report, if any, a copy of each certificate of insurance issued by the broker, and the following, as applicable: (1) the amount of the insurance; (2) the gross premium charged; (3) the return premium paid, if any; (4) the rate of premium charged upon the several items of property; (5) the effective date of the contract, and the terms thereof; (6) the name and address of each insurer on the direct risk and the proportion of the entire risk assumed by that insurer if less than the entire risk; (7) the name and address of the insured; (8) a brief general description of the property or risk insured and where located or to be performed; and (9) any other information as may be required by the Commissioner. The record must not be removed from the office of the broker and must be open to examination by the Commissioner or a representative of the Commissioner at all times within five years after issuance of the coverage to which it relates. (N.R.S. § 685A.160).

Quarterly Statements. Each broker who has written coverage for which Nevada is the insured's home state must submit a copy of a quarterly statement by February 15 for the calendar quarter ending the preceding December 31; May 15 for the calendar quarter ending the preceding March 31; August 15 for the calendar quarter ending the preceding June 30; November 15 for the calendar quarter ending the preceding September 30. The statement must include an accounting of the aggregate gross premiums for the quarter; the aggregate of the return premiums received; and the amount of tax remitted to the Commissioner. The report must be on a form approved by the Commissioner. A broker who fails to make and file the quarterly statement is liable for a penalty of $500. (N.R.S. §§ 685A.175, 685A.190).

G. Independently Procured Insurance:

1. *Rules.* Certain Nevada insureds may procure coverage directly from insurers. Any coverage procured from an unauthorized insurer, for which an insured for whom Nevada is the home state must pay premium, is subject to a premium tax of 3.5 percent. The tax is payable by February 15 for the calendar quarter ending the preceding December 31; May 15 for the calendar quarter ending the preceding March 31; August 15 for the calendar quarter ending the preceding June 30; November 15 for the calendar quarter ending the preceding September 30. In addition, the transaction must be reported to the state within forty-five days. (N.R.S. §§ 680B.040, 685A.175).

2. *Industrial Insured Exemption.* Transactions, other than for workers' compensation insurance involving the procurement of excess liability insurance above underlying liability coverage or self-insured retention of at least $25 million, if procured from an unauthorized alien or foreign insurer who does not solicit, negotiate or enter into such transactions in this state by any means. To qualify for this exemption, the firm must employ 250 or more people and have total property and casualty premiums (excluding workers' compensation) of $1 million or more. (N.R.S. § 680A.070(9)).

NRRA Implementation

H. Compact: None.

NEVADA

I. Definitions:

1. "Home State" means:

   a. For an insured:

      (1) The state in which the insured maintains its principal place of business or, in the case of an individual, the individual's principal residence; or
      (2) If 100 percent of the insured risk is located outside of the state determined pursuant to paragraph (a), the state to which the greatest percentage of the insured's taxable premium for that insurance contract is allocated.

      If more than one insured from an affiliated group is a named insured on a single nonadmitted insurance contract, the state determined pursuant to paragraph (a) of subsection 1 for the member of the affiliated group that has the largest percentage of premium attributed to it under the nonadmitted insurance contract.

   b. For a policy of group insurance:

      (1) If the group policyholder pays 100 percent of the premium from its own funds, the state determined pursuant to paragraph (a) of subsection 1 for the group policyholder.
      (2) If the group policyholder does not pay 100 percent of the premium from its own funds, the state determined pursuant to paragraph (a) of subsection 1 for the group member. (N.R.S. § 685A.034).

2. "Principal place of business" means, for the purpose of determining the home state of the insured:

   a. The state where the insured maintains its headquarters and where the insured's high-level officers direct, control and coordinate its business activities.

   b. If the insured's high-level officers direct, control and coordinate its business activities in more than one state, the state in which the greatest percentage of the insured's taxable premium for that insurance contract is allocated.

   c. If the insured's high-level officers direct, control and coordinate its business activities outside of any state, the state to which the greatest percentage of the insured's taxable premium for that insurance contract is allocated. (N.R.S. § 685A.038).

3. "Principal residence" means, for the purpose of determining the home state of the insured:

   a. The state where the insured resides for the greatest number of days during a calendar year.

   b. If the insured's principal residence is located outside of any state, the state to which the greatest percentage of the insured's taxable premium for that insurance contract is allocated. (N.R.S. § 685A.0385).

J. Statutory References: Nevada Revised Statutes §§ 679A.115; 680A.070; 680B.010, 027, 040; 680C.110; 685A.020 to 090, 120, 155, 160, 175 to 190, 370.

NEW HAMPSHIRE

(Called Excess Insurance in New Hampshire)

A. Resident Licensing: Residents may be licensed to place insurance with nonadmitted insurers. A resident individual shall pass a written examination testing the knowledge of the individual concerning the lines of authority for which application is made, the duties and responsibilities of an insurance producer and the insurance laws and regulations of this state. Bond is not required. Producers licensed in New Hampshire may do business with licensed surplus lines agents and receive commission. Application and license fee $210; biennial renewal $150; $50 amendment fee. (N.H. Rev. Stat. Ann. §§ 402-J:5, 405:17-b, 400-A:29). Monthly reporting (N.H. Rev. Stat. Ann. § 405:25), annual tax statement forms (N.H. Rev. Stat. Ann. § 405:29), and payments are to be submitted using the OPTins (Online Premium Tax for Insurance); this is an online product launched by the NAIC.

Only the insured's home state may require a surplus lines broker to be licensed to sell, solicit or negotiate nonadmitted insurance with respect to a particular placement. New Hampshire participates in the National Insurance Producer Registry (NIPR) for licensing purposes, in accordance to the NRRA licensing mandate.

B. Nonresident Licensing: A nonresident shall receive a nonresident producer license if:

1. The person is currently licensed as a resident in good standing in his or her home state.

2. The person has submitted the proper request for licensure and has paid the fees required: $210, same as for residents.

3. The person has submitted or transmitted to the commissioner the application for licensure that the person submitted to his or her home state, or in lieu of same, a completed uniform application.

4. The person's home state awards nonresident producer licenses to residents of this state on the same basis. (N.H. Rev. Stat. Ann. § 402-J:8).

C. Diligent Effort: Every such licensee shall, on or before the tenth day of each month, execute and file with the commissioner, a statement under oath covering all insurance policies and contracts of insurance or suretyship procured by him under his said license during the calendar month preceding, giving the name of the company issuing each of said policies, the name and residence of the insured and the amount, term and premium of each policy and contract and the kind of property or risk insured thereby, and that he was unable to procure in companies admitted to do business in the state the amount of insurance necessary to protect said property or risk. (N.H. Rev. Stat. Ann. § 405:25).

Commercial Purchaser Exemption. A surplus lines broker seeking to procure or place nonadmitted insurance on behalf of a "large commercial policyholder" is required to perform a diligent search. (N.H. Rev. Stat. Ann. §§ 412:7, 405:24).

D. Tax: 3 percent. Every person who procures or causes to be procured or continues or renews insurance with a surplus lines company shall collect and pay to the commissioner a sum of 3 percent based on the total gross premiums charged, less any return premiums, for surplus insurance provided by the licensee pursuant to the license. Where the insurance covers properties, risks, or exposures located or to be performed both in and out of this state, the sum payable shall be computed based on an amount equal to 3 percent on that portion of the gross premiums allocated to New Hampshire, plus an amount equal to the portion of the premiums allocated to other states or territories on the basis of the tax rates and fees applicable to properties, risks or exposures located or to be performed outside New Hampshire, less the amount of gross premiums allocated to New Hampshire and returned to the insured.

Taxes are to be paid each January for the previous year. Any producer failing to file the report or failing to remit the proper tax within the time period of filing shall pay a penalty proportionate to the lateness of the payment: 1-30 days after the due date, 3 percent of the tax due; thirty-one to sixty days after the due date, 6 percent of the tax due; more than sixty days late, 12 percent of the tax due. The surplus lines tax does not apply to fees levied by the surplus lines broker. (N.H. Rev. Stat. Ann. § 405:29).

Premium Defined. The term "premium" includes all premiums, membership fees, assessments, dues, and any other consideration for insurance. (N.H. Rev. Stat. Ann. § 406-B:11).

Multi-State Premium Tax Allocation. For premiums on unlicensed insurance independently procured with tax liability for multi-state risks, the provisions of N.H. Rev. Stat. Ann. § 405-B apply. (N.H. Rev. Stat. § 406-B:17-a). If a policy covers risks or exposures only partially in New Hampshire, the tax payable shall be computed on the portions of the premium which are properly allocable to the risks or exposures located in New Hampshire. In determining the amount of premiums taxable in this state, all premiums written, procured, or received in this state and all premiums on policies negotiated in this state shall be deemed written on property or risks located or resident in New Hampshire, except such premiums as are properly allocated or apportioned and reported as taxable premiums of any other state or states. (N.H. Rev. Stat. Ann. § 406-B:11).

E. Stamping Fee: None. New Hampshire does not have a surplus lines stamping office.

F. Other Requirements or Restrictions:

Notice. Only nonadmitted companies on the commissioner's approved list may be used. Before delivering to the insured a policy or binder of insurance written under the provisions of this section, every producer shall have stamped in a form approved by the commissioner on the face of the binder or policy the following:

> "The company issuing this policy is an eligible surplus lines insurer in the state of New Hampshire and the rates charged and policy forms used have not been approved by the commissioner of insurance. If the company issuing this policy becomes insolvent, the New Hampshire insurance guaranty fund shall not be liable for any claims made against the policy." (N.H. Rev. Stat. Ann. § 405:24).

Courtesy filings of taxes and certificates of nonavailability are allowed in New Hampshire.

Eligibility. Surplus lines insurance may be placed by a surplus lines licensee if the insurer is authorized to write the type of insurance in its domiciliary jurisdiction, and either meets the criteria established through a multi-state agreement pursuant to N.H. Rev. Stat. Ann. § 405-B:3 or the insurer has capital and surplus or its equivalent under the laws of its domiciliary jurisdiction which equals the greater of the minimum capital and surplus requirements under N.H. Rev. Stat. Ann. §§ 401:4 or 402:13 or $15 million or the insurer is a nonadmitted insurer domiciled outside the United States that is listed on the Quarterly Listing of Alien Insurers maintained by the International Insurers Department of the National Association of Insurance Commissioners.

G. Surplus Lines Association:

Surplus Lines Association: New England Surplus Lines Association, Inc. c/o A.I.I. Insurance Brokerage, P.O. Box 1139, East Douglas, MA 01516. Phone: (508) 476-1990. Fax: (508) 476-1991.

(https://www.slai.org/links/associations.html#NG).

H. Independently Procured Insurance:

1. *Rules.* Where the insurance covers properties, risks, or exposures located or to be performed both in and out of New Hampshire, the sum payable shall be computed based on an amount equal to 4 percent on such insurance other than marine insurance and a premium tax of 2 percent of gross premium charged for such marine insurance, the portion of the gross premiums allocated to New Hampshire, plus an amount equal to the portion of the premiums allocated to other states or territories on the basis of the tax rates and fees applicable to properties, risks or exposures located or to be performed outside this state, less the amount of gross premiums allocated to New Hampshire and returned to the insured. The insured must report the transaction to

the insurance department and must pay the appropriate premium tax within sixty days. If it is late, the tax will be increased with a penalty contingent on the number of days that have passed since the due date. If a payment is received one to thirty days late, the penalty will be 3 percent of the tax due, if payment is thirty to sixty days late, the penalty is 6 percent of the tax due. For payments more than sixty days late, the penalty is 12 percent of the tax due. (N.H. Rev. Stat. Ann. §§ 406-B:11, 406-B:17).

2. *Industrial Insured Exemption.* In order to qualify as an "industrial insured", the insured must:

   a. Procure the insurance of any risk or risks other than life and annuity contracts and health insurance contracts by use of the services of a full-time employee acting as an insurance manager or buyer or the services of a regularly and continuously retained qualified insurance consultant.

   b. Have aggregate annual premiums for insurance on all risks total at least $15,000.

   c. Have at least twenty-five full-time employees. (N.H. Rev. Stat. Ann. § 406-B:16).

NRRA Implementation

I. Compact: None. However, the commissioner is authorized to enter into a cooperative or reciprocal agreement, or compact with another state in order to facilitate the collection, allocation, and disbursement of premium taxes attributable to the placement of nonadmitted insurance, provide for uniform methods of allocation and reporting among nonadmitted insurance risk classifications, and share information among states relating to nonadmitted insurance premium taxes. (N.H. Rev. Stat. Ann. § 405-B:3).

J. Definitions:

1. "Home State" means:

   a. New Hampshire is the insured's home state if the insured maintains its principle place of business here or, in the case of an individual; the individual's principal residence is here. If New Hampshire is considered the insured's home state, only New Hampshire's requirements regarding the placement of such business will apply. If 100 percent of the insured risk is located outside New Hampshire, then the insured's home state is the state to which the greatest percentage of the insured's taxable premium for that insurance contract is allocated.

(N.H. Rev. Stat. Ann. §§ 405-B:2).

K. Statutory References: New Hampshire Revised Statutes Annotated §§ 400-A:29; 402-J:5, J:8; 405-B:2, B:3; 405:17-b, 24, 25, 29; 406-B:11, B:16 to B:17-a; 412:7.

NEW JERSEY

A. **Resident Licensing:** Resident producers may hold surplus lines authority if they also hold property and casualty authority and pass the surplus lines examination administered by PSI Testing Authorities (http://candidate.psiexams.com/). Producers holding property and casualty authority may place business with licensed surplus lines producers and receive commission. No surplus lines producer shall charge any fee to an originating broker in connection with the negotiation or procurement of any contract of surplus lines insurance that shall exceed an amount set forth by the Commissioner pursuant to regulation, plus the actual costs incurred for any services performed by a person that is not associated with the surplus lines producer, such as inspection services. (N.J. Stat. § 17:22A-38). Please note the following fee limitations:

1. For personal lines, a fee not to exceed $50.

2. For commercial lines, a fee equal to the greater of 2 percent of the premium for the applicable policy period or $100, but in no event in excess of $250. (N.J.A.C. 11:17B-3.2(b)).

Only the insured's home state may require a surplus lines producer to be licensed to sell, solicit, or negotiate nonadmitted insurance with respect to a particular placement. If New Jersey is the insured's home state, the surplus lines producer must be licensed in New Jersey. New Jersey participates in the National Insurance Producer Registry (NIPR) in accordance with the Nonadmitted and Reinsurance Reform Act (NRRA) mandate.

B. **Nonresident Licensing:** A nonresident shall receive a nonresident producer license if:

1. The person is currently licensed as a resident insurance producer in good standing in his or her home state.

2. The person has submitted the proper request for licensure and has paid the fees required.

3. The person has submitted or transmitted to the Commissioner the application for licensure that the person submitted to his home state, or in lieu of the same, a completed uniform application.

4. The person's home state awards nonresident producer licenses to residents of this state on the same basis. (N.J. Stat. § 17:22A-34).

C. **Diligent Effort:** "Diligent Effort" means a process by which a licensed New Jersey insurance producer places coverage on behalf of a New Jersey insured with a surplus lines insurer after the risk has been declined by three authorized insurers, each of which is authorized in New Jersey to write insurance of the kind requested and is an insurer that the producer has a good faith reason to believe might consider writing the type of coverage or class of insurance involved. An affidavit or certificate of nonavailability through admitted insurers no longer needs to be filed with the Commissioner. Rather, the originating broker must submit an affidavit or certification (form SLPS-6-CERT-1 https://www.state.nj.us/dobi/division_insurance/pdfs/slps6cert1.pdf) to the surplus lines agent documenting the efforts made to place the coverage with authorized insurers. A copy of the affidavit must be kept by both the originating broker and the surplus lines agent for five years. (N.J.A.C. 11:1-33.2, 33.3).

Commercial Purchaser Exemption. A surplus lines producer seeking to procure or place nonadmitted insurance on behalf of an "exempt commercial purchaser" is not required to perform a diligent search if both:

1. The broker has disclosed to the exempt commercial purchaser that insurance may or may not be available from the admitted market that may provide greater protection with more regulatory oversight.

2. The exempt commercial purchaser has subsequently requested in writing that the broker procure from or place such insurance with a nonadmitted insurer. (N.J.A.C 11:1-33.3).

D. **Tax:** 5 percent of gross premiums less returns. Tax must be paid by the surplus lines agent within forty-five days after the end of each calendar quarter. Exempt from the tax and application of the surplus lines law are railroad or aviation risks engaged in interstate or international commerce, insurance commonly written under ocean or wet marine policies, and risks of state government, its agencies, any county or municipality or any agency thereof. The surplus lines tax does not apply to any fees levied by the surplus lines broker. If a surplus lines policy covers risks or exposures in this state and other states, where New Jersey is the home state, as defined in N.J. Stat. § 17:22-6.41, the tax payable pursuant to this section shall be based on the total United States premium for the applicable policy. (N.J. Stat. § 17:22-6.59).

E. **Stamping Fee:** None. New Jersey does not have a surplus lines stamping office.

F. **Other Requirements or Restrictions:** The Commissioner publishes a list of currently eligible nonadmitted insurers (see "white list,"https://www.state.nj.us/dobi/division_insurance/sleo.htm) that may accept business on a surplus lines basis. The premium rate for a surplus lines policy must not be lower than the lowest rate filed by any authorized insurer in the state; however, lower rate may apply if coverage or limits are reduced. The New Jersey code requires that all surplus lines policies in New Jersey must be executed or countersigned by a licensed producer with surplus lines authority. (N.J. Stat. § 17:22-6.50).

Eligibility. For nonadmitted insurers domiciled in a U.S. jurisdiction, a producer is permitted to place nonadmitted insurance with such insurers provided they are authorized to write such business in their state of domicile and maintain minimum capital and surplus of $15 million (or the minimum capital and surplus amount required in New Jersey pursuant to N.J. Stat. § 17:17-1, whichever is greater). (N.J. Stat. § 17:22-6.45). For nonadmitted insurers domiciled outside the U.S., a producer may place business with such insurers provided the insurer is listed on the Quarterly Listing of Alien Insurers maintained by the International Insurers Department of the NAIC. (N.J.A.C 11:1-31.3).

No surplus lines agent shall exercise binding authority in New Jersey on behalf of any insurer unless the agent has first filed electronically with the Commissioner for informational purposes and not for the purpose of approval or disapproval the written agreement between the agent and the insurer setting forth the terms, conditions and limitations governing the exercise of the binding authority by the agent. A copy of any amendments to the agreement and of any notice of cancellation or termination of the agreement shall be filed by the agent with the Commissioner no later than ten days after adoption thereof. The agreement shall include the following items:

1. A description of the classes of insurance for which the agent holds binding authority.
2. The geographical limits upon the exercise of binding authority by the agent.
3. The maximum dollar limitation on the binding authority of the agent for any one risk for each class of insurance written by the agent.
4. The maximum policy period for which the agent may bind a risk.
5. If the binding authority is delegable by the agent, a prohibition against the delegation without the prior written approval of the insurer. (N.J. Stat. § 17:22-6.42).

G. Required Notices:

1. At the time of quotation, the originating producer must provide the following statement on the form:

   "The undersigned applicant has been advised by the undersigned originating insurance producer and understands that an insurance policy written by a surplus lines insurer is not subject to the filing or approval requirements of the

New Jersey Department of Banking and Insurance. Such a policy may contain conditions, limitations and different terms than a policy issued by an insurer granted a Certificate of Authority by the New Jersey Department of Banking and Insurance."

This notice must be signed and dated by both agent and insured. (N.J.A.C.11:1-33.3, Appendix, Exhibit A).

2. At the time of issuing or delivering a surplus lines policy, evidence of coverage, or a renewal policy, the surplus lines producer must place on the policy, or provide as a stand-alone notice:

   "This policy is written by a surplus lines insurer and is not subject to the filing or approval requirements of the New Jersey Department of Banking and Insurance. Such a policy may contain conditions, limitations, exclusions and different terms than a policy issued by an insurer granted a Certificate of Authority by the New Jersey Department of Banking and Insurance. The insurer has been approved by the Department as an eligible surplus lines insurer, but the policy is not covered by the New Jersey Insurance Guaranty Fund, and only a policy of medical malpractice liability insurance as defined in N.J.S.A. 17:30D-3d or a policy of property insurance covering owner-occupied dwellings of less than four dwelling units are covered by the New Jersey Surplus Lines Guaranty Fund." (N.J.A.C. 11:1-33.3, Appendix, Exhibit A-2).

3. New Jersey licensed surplus lines agents may place coverage with an ineligible, unauthorized insurer only when coverage is not otherwise procurable from admitted insurer or authorized surplus lines insurer. The following must be completed:

   1. The surplus lines agent must complete forms SLPS-6-Cert1 and SLPS-8-AFF3 prior to each renewal.

   2. The most recent certified annual statement of the insurer's financial condition must be filed with the Surplus Lines Examining Office.

   3. The policy, binder or cover note shall be clearly stamped in boldface type with the following notice:

      "All or some of the insurers participating in this risk have not been admitted to transact business in the State of New Jersey, nor have they been approved as surplus lines insurers by the Commissioner of Banking and Insurance of New Jersey. The placing of such insurance by a duly licensed surplus lines

> agent in this State shall not be construed as approval of such insurer by the Commissioner of Banking and Insurance of the State of New Jersey and insurance coverage provided by such insurer is not protected by either the New Jersey Guaranty Fund or by the New Jersey Surplus Lines Insurance Guaranty Fund." (N.J.A.C 11:1-33.3).

Surplus lines producers are required to execute or countersign evidence of insurance to be promptly issued and delivered to the insured upon placing surplus lines coverage. (N.J. Stat. § 17:22-6.50).

H. Surplus Lines Association: NJSLA, 30 Montgomery St. Suite 900, Jersey City, NJ 07302. Phone: (732) 599-1057. Email: https://njsla.org/contact/. Website: https://njsla.org/.

I. Independently Procured Insurance:

1. *Rules.* The transaction must be reported to the New Jersey Department of Banking and Insurance within thirty days and the insured is responsible for paying the 5 percent tax on the gross premium amount. (N.J. Stat. § 17:22-6.64).

2. *Industrial Insured Exemption.* New Jersey does not have an industrial insured exemption.

NRRA Implementation

J. Compact: None.

K. Definitions: "Home State." New Jersey is the insured's home state if the insured maintains its principal place of business here or, in the case of an individual, the individual's principal residence is here. If New Jersey is considered the insured's home state, only New Jersey's requirements regarding the placement of such business will apply. However, if 100 percent of the insured risk is located outside of New Jersey, then the insured's home state is the state to which the greatest percentage of the insured's taxable premium for that insurance contract is allocated.

If more than one insured from an affiliated group are named insureds on a single nonadmitted insurance placement, New Jersey will be considered the home state for that placement if New Jersey is the home state of the member of the affiliated group that has the largest percentage of premium attributed to it under such insurance contract. (N.J. Stat. § 17:22-6.41).

L. Statutory References: N.J. Stat. §§ 17:22-6.41, -6.42, -6.45, -6.50, -6.59, -6.64; 17:22A-34, -38. N.J.A.C. 11:1-31.3, -33.2, -33.3. N.J.A.C. 11:1-33.3 Appendix, Exhibit A.

NEW MEXICO

A. Resident Licensing: No person shall act as a surplus lines broker, or place insurance of risks resident, located or to be performed in New Mexico in any unauthorized insurer on behalf of others, for compensation, as an independent contractor in any form, unless licensed as a surplus lines broker. Residents must be currently licensed as an insurance agent in this state as to the kinds of insurance to be exported under the surplus lines broker license applied for. In addition, residents need have had experience or special training or education sufficient in duration and character as such an agent as to render the applicant, in the opinion of the superintendent, reasonably competent to engage in business as a surplus lines broker. The surplus lines broker's license expires annually March 1. Filing fee for qualification as an eligible surplus lines insurer: $1,000. License Fee for original license and issuance: $100. Biennial renewal: $200. Filing of individual affiliation per kind of insurance: $20. Annual renewal of individual affiliation: $20. A bond is no longer required. A New Mexico-licensed general lines agent may place business through licensed surplus lines brokers and receive commission. (N.M. Stat. Ann. §§59A-6-1, 59A-14-4, 59A-14-7, 59A-14-9).

B. Nonresident Licensing: A licensed nonresident may be licensed as a surplus lines broker in order to place exportable surplus lines coverage with a risk retention group or on behalf of a risk purchasing group. A nonresident surplus lines broker is subject to the same requirements as residents. (NMAC 13.19.2.11).

C. Diligent Effort: New Mexico has an approved surplus lines export list that requires no affidavit. Unless the risk is listed on the approved New Mexico surplus lines export list, within fifteen days of the issuance of the policy, the producing broker must complete the Producing Broker Affidavit and certify to the Superintendent that at least four insurers authorized in New Mexico, including insurers by whom the surplus lines broker is not appointed, will not write the coverage and that the broker knows from substantial recent experience that the coverage cannot be obtained from any authorized insurer in New Mexico. The form must show the following information:

1. The names of the insurer and insured.

2. The expiration date.

3. The subject and location of the risk.

4. Type and amount of coverage.

5. Amount of deductible and premium.

6. Any other information required by the superintendent of insurance. (NMAC 13.19.2.19).

The affidavit shall affirm that the insured was expressly advised prior to the placement of the insurance and in the insurance policy that both:

1. The surplus lines insurer with which the insurance was to be placed is not an authorized insurer in this state and is not subject to the superintendent's supervision.

2. In the event the surplus lines insurer becomes insolvent, claims will not be paid nor will unearned premiums be returned by any New Mexico insurance guaranty fund.

In addition to the above, the producing broker must also provide to the surplus lines broker a sworn, affidavit describing the diligent efforts to place the coverage with authorized insurers and the results thereof.

Within sixty days after the end of each calendar quarter, the surplus lines broker must file, with the Superintendent of Insurance, copies of all reports and affidavits described above as well as a copy of the policy declarations page of all surplus lines insurance business transacted during the calendar quarter. The surplus lines broker shall preserve the original producing broker affidavits in compliance. The declarations pages shall be confidential and shall not be subject to public inspection. The superintendent's copy of the affidavits shall be open to public inspection. If the producing broker has failed to provide the producing broker affidavit, the surplus lines broker shall at the time of quarterly filing, notify the superintendent of the producing broker's failure to comply. (N.M. Stat. Ann. §59A-14-11).

Commercial Purchaser Exemption: Surplus lines brokers seeking to procure or place nonadmitted insurance on behalf of an "exempt commercial purchaser" are not required to perform a diligent search if:

1. The broker has disclosed to the exempt commercial purchaser that insurance may or may not be available from the admitted market that may provide greater protection with more regulatory oversight; and

2. The exempt commercial purchaser has subsequently requested in writing for the broker to procure or place such insurance from an eligible surplus lines insurer. (N.M. Stat. Ann. §59A-14-3).

D. Tax: 3.003 percent of net premiums less returns, due within sixty days of the end of each quarter. The surplus lines tax is applicable to any additional amount charged to the insured, including fees levied by the surplus lines broker, purchasing group or for inspection.

Premium defined. "Premium" includes any additional amount charged the insured, including policy fees, risk purchasing group fees and inspection fees. "Premium" does not include any additional amount charged the insured for local, state or federal tax, regulatory authority fee, or examination fee, if any. (N.M. Stat. Ann. §7-40-3).

E. **Stamping Fee:** None. New Mexico does not have a stamping office.

F. **Surplus Lines Association:** New Mexico does not have a surplus lines association. However information can be found here Surplus Lines Brokers Association c/o Independent Insurance Agents of New Mexico; 1511 University Boulevard N.E., Albuquerque, New Mexico 87102. Phone: 505-843-7231. Fax: 505-243-3367. Email: info@iianm.org. Website: iianm.org.

G. **Other Requirements or Restrictions:**

Exemptions. New Mexico surplus lines laws do not apply to reinsurance; wet marine and transportation insurance; insurance on vehicles or aircraft owned and principally garaged outside New Mexico; insurance of property and operations of railroads engaged in interstate commerce; insurance of aircraft carriers, or cargo of such aircraft, or against liability, other than employer's liability, arising out of ownership, maintenance or use of such aircraft; insurance of automobile bodily injury and property damage liability risks when written in Mexican insurers and covering in Mexico and not in the United States; or independently procured insurance. (N.M. Stat. Ann. §59A-14-1).

Eligibility. Surplus lines brokers may only utilize surplus lines insurers who are listed on the DOI's eligibility listing or who are listed on the current NAIC Quarterly Listing of Alien Insurers. To qualify as an eligible surplus lines insurer, a nonadmitted insurer must file information with the superintendent demonstrating that the insurer has capital and surplus equaling the greater of $15 million or the minimum capital and surplus required in New Mexico for that particular line of business. Alternatively, the superintendent may affirmatively find that the insurer is acceptable when the insurer's capital and surplus is greater than $4.5 million and based upon factors such as quality of management, capital and surplus of any parent company, company underwriting profit and investment income trends and company record and reputation within the industry. If the insurer is a member of an insurance exchange, the insurer must maintain capital and surplus of not less than $50 million in the aggregate. For insurance exchanges that maintain funds for the protection of all insurance exchange policyholders, each individual syndicate shall maintain minimum capital and surplus, or the equivalent thereof, of not less than $5 million. If the insurer is an alien insurer, it must be listed on the quarterly listing of alien insurers maintained by the international insurers department of the association or in compliance with nationwide uniform eligibility requirements adopted through the compact commission. A list of nonadmitted insurers that qualify as an eligible surplus lines insurer must be maintained. To appear on the list, a nonadmitted insurer must provide to the superintendent a copy of its most current annual statement certified and sworn to. The statement must be provided when it is provided to the insurer's domicile, but never more than nine months after the close of the period reported upon. The statement shall either be filed with and approved by the regulatory authority in the insurer's domicile or certified as correct and in accordance with applicable accounting principles by a public accounting firm licensed in the insurer's domicile. (N.M. Stat. Ann. §59A-14-4).

Notice. All surplus lines contracts must contain the name, address, and signature of the producing surplus lines broker printed prominently in boldface ten point or larger type on the declarations page. The following message must also be printed on the policy, either on the declarations page or attached as an endorsement, in boldface ten-point or larger type:

> "This policy provides surplus lines insurance by an insurer not otherwise authorized to transact business in New Mexico. This policy is not subject to supervision, review or approval by the superintendent of insurance. The insurance so provided is not within the protection of any guaranty fund law of New Mexico designed to protect the public in the event of the insurer's insolvency." (N.M. Stat. Ann. §59A-14-5).

Records. Each surplus lines broker must keep in its office complete records of business transaction, including, but not limited to: income and disbursements; copies of all policies, endorsements, cancellations, filing documents, reports and other related records. The records must be available for examination by the superintendent at all times within seven years after issuance of coverage. The surplus lines broker must immediately notify the superintendent in writing of any change of office address. Failure to do so within twenty days will result in a $50 fine. (N.M. Stat. Ann. §59A-14-10).

Life, accident and health, private passenger auto for military excluded in New Mexico, and workers compensation insurance may not be placed with nonadmitted insurers.

New Mexico does not allow courtesy filings.

H. Independently Procured Insurance:

1. *Rules.* Each insured in New Mexico who procures or continues or renews insurance with a nonadmitted insurer on a risk located or to be performed in whole or in part in New Mexico, other than insurance procured through a surplus lines licensee shall, within ninety days after the date such insurance was so procured, continued or renewed, file a written report of the same with the Superintendent of Insurance, showing the name and address of the insured or insureds, name and address of the insurer, the subject of the insurance, a general description of the coverage, the amount

of premium currently charged therefore and such additional pertinent information as is reasonably requested by the Superintendent. (N.M. Stat. Ann. §59A-15-4).

2. *Industrial Insured Exemption.* An industrial insured may procure the insurance of any risk by using the services of a full-time employee acting as a risk manager or insurance manager (or by utilizing the services of a regularly and continuously qualified insurance consultant). Additionally, the industrial insured must have aggregate annual premiums in excess of $25,000, and have at least twenty-five full-time employees. (N.M. Stat. Ann. §59A-15-2).

NRRA Implementation

I. Compact: New Mexico enacted Legislation in 2017 that eliminated SLIMPACT authorization.

J. Definitions:

1. "Home State" means: New Mexico is the insured's Home State if the insured maintains its principal place of business here or, in the case of an individual, only New Mexico's requirements regarding the placement of such business will apply. If 100 percent of the insured risk is located outside of New Mexico, then the insured's Home State is the state to which the greatest percentage of the insured's taxable premium for that insurance contract is allocated. If more than one insured from an affiliate group are named insureds on a single nonadmitted insurance placement, New Mexico will be considered the Home State for that placement if New Mexico is the Home State of the Member of the affiliated group that has the largest percentage of premium attributed to it under such insurance contract. For an affiliated group of insured entities, the "Home State" is the principal place of business of the group member to which the largest percentage of premium is allocated.

2. "Affiliated Group" means, with respect to an insured, any group of entities that are all "affiliated".

3. "Affiliate" means, with respect to an insured, any entity that controls, is controlled by, or is under common control with the insured.

4. "Control" means an entity directly or indirectly or acting through one or more other persons owns, controls or has the power to vote 25 percent or more of any class of voting securities of another entity; or an entity controls in any manner the election of a majority of the directors or trustees of another entity.

5. "Principal Place of Business" means where the insured maintains its headquarters and where the insured's high-level officers direct, control and coordinate the business activities of the insured. (N.M. Stat. Ann. §59A-14-2).

K. References:

N.M. Stat. Ann. §	7-40-3
N.M. Stat. Ann. §§59A-	6-1
	14-1 to 14-5, 14-7, 14-9 to 14-11
	15-2, 15-4

NMAC 13.19.	2.11, 2.19

NEW YORK

(Called Excess Lines in New York)

A. **Resident Licensing:** Individual licenses are effective from the date issued to date of birth expiration. This date may be in odd or even years based on the licensee's birth year. For business entities (corporations, LLCs, and partnerships), the excess line license expires October 31 of even years. Fees: $400 or $200. In counties with a population of less than 100,000, $50 or $25. (NY CLS Ins. §2105, effective Feb. 15, 2021). Full fees are charged during the first year of the licensing period and half fees are charged during the second year. Make checks payable to "Superintendent of Financial Services." Excess line brokers may charge additional fees when agreed to in writing by the insured. Brokers may do business with licensed excess line brokers and receive commission. The following application forms are to be submitted: individuals, corporations, partnerships, limited liability companies. (NY CLS Ins. §2104)

B. **Nonresident Licensing:** Nonresidents may also be licensed as excess line brokers, if so licensed in their home state, provided the applicant's home state will license New York licensees in the same manner. If California is the home state, a $50,000 bond is required. (NY CLS Ins. §2136).

C. **Diligent Effort:** No excess line broker shall place coverage for a risk with any unauthorized insurer, when the insured's home state is New York, unless the risk has been declined by at least three authorized insurers, each of which is authorized in New York to write the kind of insurance requested and is an insurer that the excess line broker has reason to believe might consider writing the type of coverage or class of insurance involved. Declinations obtained from authorized insurers which are affiliates of, or under common control with, each other or the unauthorized insurer, do not meet the diligent efforts requirements unless such related insurers operate as distinct and autonomous entities, and for underwriting purposes, compete with each other for the same type of coverage or class of insurance. (NY CLS Ins. §2118).

Unauthorized insurers must be solvent, financially stable, and have surplus of not less than $45 million as of January 1, 2016. Every three years thereafter, the minimum policyholders' surplus shall be increased by $1,000,000. (11 NYCRR §27.13).

Exemption. Three declinations from licensed insurers are not required if the Superintendent, after an on-the-record hearing, determines another number is appropriate. (NY CLS Ins. §2118(4)).

Commercial Purchaser Exemption. Diligent effort requirements do not apply to excess line brokers seeking to procure or place insurance in New York for an exempt commercial purchaser if the broker discloses to the exempt commercial purchaser that the insurance may or may not be available from the authorized market that may provide greater protection with more regulatory oversight, and the exempt commercial purchaser has subsequently requested in writing that the licensee procure or place the insurance from an unauthorized insurer. (NY CLS Ins. §2118(b)(3)(F)).

D. **Tax:** New York taxes 100 percent of each excess line policy's written premium when New York is the "home state of the insured" except for non-US exposures. Every excess line broker must pay to the superintendent a sum equal to 3.6 percent of the total gross premium charged the insured, less the amount of premiums returned to the insured. Checks or electronic payment of the premium tax must be payable to the order of the Superintendent of Financial Services and accompany an annual premium tax statement. The tax and annual premium tax statement are due by March 15 of each year. The annual premium tax statement must include excess line premiums on a written basis (not on a cash received basis) and all additional premiums charged including all return premiums paid to an insured, or indicate that there are no excess line premiums written. A licensed excess line broker shall execute and electronically file an annual premium tax statement. An excess line broker may make a paper filing by requesting an exemption from the Superintendent of Financial Services (NY Ins. NS §2118(d); 11 NYCRR §§27.8, 27.21).

Premium Tax Allocation. For insurance contracts that have an effective date on or after July 21, 2011, where the property or risk is located both inside the United States and outside the United States, an excess line broker shall determine the taxable portion of the premium by using the method of allocation prescribed by the allocation schedule in 11 NYCRR Appx. 5 pertaining to the appropriate classification for the property or risk; in case of policies covering multiple classifications, brokers shall follow the procedures found in 11 NYCRR §27.9. (11 NYCRR §27.9; 11 NYCRR Appx. 5).

Premium Defined. "Premium" includes all amounts received as consideration for insurance contracts or reinsurance contracts, other than for annuity contracts, and includes premium deposits, assessments, policy fees, membership fees, and every other compensation for such contract. (NY CLS Ins. §9101).

E. **Stamping Fee:** .17 percent starting January 1, 2017 ((NY Ins. §2130).

Table of Stamping Fees

a) 0.4 percent of New York Excess Line Premium for policies incepting before 1 July 2004.

b) 0.3 percent of NYELP for policies incepting on or after 1 July 2004 and before 1 July 2005.

c) 0.2 percent of NYELP for policies incepting on or after 1 July 2005.

d) 0.18 percent of NYELP for policies incepting one or after 1 July 2015.

e) $25 for each item submitted more than forty-five days after inception date.

f) $25 for each item suspended and returned to the member (https://www.elany.org/manual.aspx?d=1213&bk=3#bk).

F. **Surplus Lines Association:** Excess Line Association of New York, 120 Wall Street, 24th Floor, New York, NY 10005. Phone: 646-292-5500. Email: elany@elany.org. Web site: elany.org.

G. **Other Requirements or Restrictions:**

Users of nonadmitted insurers must adhere strictly to the provisions of 11 NYCRR §§27.0 to 27.22.

1. The broker must keep all records five years after policy expiration. (11 NYCRR §27.19).

2. The broker must use only nonadmitted insurers that have appointed the Superintendent for service of suit, meet minimum financial and claims practice requirements of Regulation 41, and are not controlled by any foreign government or its subdivision, which provide such insurer certain unfair competitive advantages. (11 NYCRR §27.13).

3. The following notice must appear on all excess line policies, binders, memorandum, or other certificate evidencing coverage, in no smaller than ten-point type:

   "THE INSURER(S) NAMED HEREIN IS (ARE) NOT LICENSED BY THE STATE OF NEW YORK, NOT SUBJECT TO ITS SUPERVISION, AND IN THE EVENT OF THE INSOLVENCY OF THE INSURER(S), NOT PROTECTED BY THE NEW YORK STATE SECURITY FUNDS. THE POLICY MAY NOT BE SUBJECT TO ALL OF THE REGULATIONS OF THE DEPARTMENT OF FINANCIAL SERVICES PERTAINING TO POLICY FORMS." (11 NYCRR §27.15).

4. Excess line broker must report status of coverage requests within ten days. (11 NYCRR §27.15).

5. Advertising of nonadmitted insurers is prohibited. (11 NYCRR §27.11).

6. Life, accident and health, annuities, workers compensation, mortgage guaranty, financial guaranty, GAP, title, primary medical malpractice coverage for doctors, dentists and general hospitals, and private passenger auto liability eligible for New York Auto Plan may not be placed with nonadmitted insurers. (11 NYCRR §27.11).

7. Courtesy filings are not allowed in New York. (https://www.elany.org/elany-says)

Exemptions. Excess line insurance law does not apply to: reinsurance; insurance against loss of or damage to property having a permanent situs outside of New York; ocean marine insurance; marine insurance against the perils of navigation in course of exportation from or importation into any country, or transportation coastwise; marine insurance in connection with ocean going vessels. (NY CLS Ins. §§2105, 2117(b, c)).

H. Independently Procured Insurance:

1. *Rules.* New York insureds may purchase coverage directly from an unauthorized insurer. The tax of 3.6 percent is due within sixty days at the end of the quarter in which the policy became effective and is payable to the Department of Taxation and Finance. (NY CLS Tax§§1551, 1554).

2. *Industrial Insured Exemption.* (With respect to captive insurers only) New York defines "Industrial Insured" as an insured:

   a. Whose net worth exceeds $100 million.

   b. Who is a member of a holding company system whose net worth exceeds $100 million.

   c. Who is the metropolitan transportation authority and its statutory subsidiaries. When filing an application to form a pure captive insurance company the metropolitan transportation authority shall submit written notice of such filing to the governor, the temporary president of the senate, and the speaker of the assembly.

   d. Who is a city with a population of one million or more. When filing an application to form a pure captive insurance company, a city with a population of one million or more shall submit written notice of such filing to the governor, the temporary president of the senate, and the speaker of the assembly. (NY CLS Ins. §7002(e)).

NRRA Implementation

I. Compact: None.

J. Definitions:

1. "Home State." New York is the home state if the insured maintains its principal place of business or, in the case of an individual, the individual's principal residence in New York. New York's requirements regarding the placement of unauthorized insurance will apply if New York is considered the home state. If 100 percent of the insured risk is located outside of New York, then the home state is the state to which the greatest percentage of the insured's taxable premium for that insurance contract is allocated. If more than one insured from an affiliated group are named insureds on a single nonadmitted insurance contract, the term "home state" means the home state of the member of the affiliated group that has the largest percentage of premium attributed to it under the insurance contract.

2. "Affiliated group" means any group of entities that are all affiliated.

3. "Affiliate" means any entity that controls, is controlled by, or is under common control with the Insured.

4. "Control." An entity controls another entity if the entity either directly or indirectly or acting through one or more persons owns, controls, or has the power to vote 25 percent or more of any class of voting securities of the other entity; or controls in any manner the election of a majority of the directors or trustees of the other entity.

5. "Principal place of business" means, with respect to determining the home state of the insured, the state where the insured maintains its headquarters and where the high-level officers direct, control, and coordinate the business activities. If the insured's high-level officers direct, control, and coordinate the business activities in more than one state, or if the insured's principal place of business is located outside any state, then the principal place of business refers to the state to which the greatest percentage of the insured's taxable premium for that insurance contract is allocated.

6. "Principal residence" means, with respect to determining the home state of the individual insured, the state where the individual insured resides for the greatest number of days during a calendar year. (NY CLS Ins. §2101).

K. Statutory References: NY CLS Ins §§ 2101; 2104; 2105; 2117; 2118; 2130; 2136; 7002; 9101. NY CLS Tax §§ 1551; 1554. 11 NYCRR §§27.1 to 27.22; 11 NYCRR Appx. 5.

NORTH CAROLINA

A. **Resident Licensing:** North Carolina surplus lines licenses are only issued to qualified holders of current property agent licenses. Applicants must pay an initial licensing fee of $100 ($50 license, $50 application processing), submit a completed license application online via www.nipr.com, and pass a qualifying examination to be considered for a surplus lines license. There is also a $5 transaction fee for using NIPR. All North Carolina Surplus Lines licenses expire annually on August 31 each year and require completion of the NIPR renewal application and payment of renewal fee of $90 ($50 license and $40 transaction) due by August 31. Failure to complete the renewal application and pay the renewal fee through NIPR will result in the surplus lines license expiring effective August 31.

   Note: On the NCDOI website, the surplus lines license fee is $94 annually ($50 license, $44 processing). Please contact the NCDOI for clarification.

   Licensees must submit an application for renewal no later than thirty days before the August 31 expiration date and must pay an annual renewal fee of $90 ($50 license and $40 transaction processing). There is also a $5 transaction fee for using NIPR. Any person who does not renew a surplus lines license and applies for another surplus lines license more than two years after the expiration date of the previous license is required to satisfy every condition for initial licensing as described above. (N.C. Gen. Stat. §58-21-65; https://www.ncdoi.gov/licensees/surplus-lines-licensing).

   The North Carolina Licensing Office of Pearson VUE provides administrative services on behalf of the Agent Services Division of the North Carolina Department of Insurance. These services include, but are not limited to, renewal license application and new license application review/processing. PearsonVUE charges a processing fee for their services that is included in the surplus lines license renewal application fees in addition to all other current license fees. PHONE (Toll Free): 866-265-6329, E-MAIL: NorthCarolinaLicensingOffice@pearson.com.

   Each resident and nonresident surplus lines licensee must maintain an active membership in the North Carolina Surplus Lines Association as a condition of continued licensure. Any person who places surplus lines insurance without a valid surplus lines license in effect shall pay a penalty of $1,000 and be subject to such other penalties as provided by law. (N.C. Gen. Stat. §§58-21-40(d), 58-21-65(d); https://www.ncsla.com/membership/requirements).

B. **Nonresident Licensing:** Individuals licensed as surplus lines producers in their home state are permitted to receive a nonresident surplus lines license provided that they are currently licensed as a resident and in good standing in their home state, and their home state awards licenses to North Carolina residents on a reciprocal basis. Initial licensing fee: $94 for individuals; $144 for business entities. Renewal fee: $84 for individuals; $134 for business entities. There is also a $5 transaction fee for using NIPR. (N.C. Gen. Stat. §§58-33-32; 58-33-125; https://nipr.com/licensing-center/state-requirements/north-carolina-non-resident-licensing-individual; https://nipr.com/licensing-center/state-requirements/north-carolina-non-resident-licensing-business).

C. **Corporate Licensing:** Corporations are eligible to be resident surplus lines licensees only if the corporate licensee lists individuals within the corporation who have satisfied the resident surplus lines licensing requirements described above; and only those individuals listed on the corporate license and who are surplus lines licensees are permitted to transact surplus lines business. (N.C. Gen. Stat. §58-21-65).

D. **Diligent Effort:** Insurance may be procured through a surplus lines licensee from nonadmitted insurers if the full amount or kind of insurance cannot be obtained from insurers who are admitted to do business in North Carolina. Such full amount or kind of insurance may be procured from eligible surplus lines insurers, provided that a diligent search is made among the insurers who are admitted to transact and are actually writing the particular kind and class of insurance. (N.C. Gen. Stat. §58-21-15(2)).

The diligent search requirements for the placement of surplus lines insurance in North Carolina are governed by N.C. Gen. Stat. §58-21-15. The statute is broadly worded and does not require a specified number of declinations from admitted insurers before insurance is placed with an authorized surplus lines insurer. NCDOI has maintained the position that the producing agent is responsible for conducting a diligent search for the placement of insurance with admitted insurers in NC. In the event that insurance cannot be placed with an admitted insurer in NC, it is the responsibility of the surplus lines licensee to confirm that the diligent search was conducted by the producing agent. North Carolina insurance laws, including the Surplus Lines Act, are silent as to the type of documentation that the surplus lines licensee may use as confirmation of the diligent search by the producing agent. This decision regarding acceptable documentation confirming the diligent search can be determined by the surplus lines licensee.

Applicants must complete the online "Compliance Acknowledgement", which verifies that the surplus lines licensee has complied with all requirements of the Surplus Lines Act, found in Article 21 of Chapter 58 of the North Carolina General Statutes.

- Licensees will no longer be required to obtain a signed Form F from the insured and the producing broker.

- This compliance agreement verifies that a diligent search has been made by the producing agent or the surplus lines licensee. In either case, it is the responsibility of the surplus lines licensee to verify that the diligent search has been performed. The form may be found at https://www.ncdoi.gov/insurance-industry/form-and-rate-filings/property-and-casualty-pc/surplus-lines#placing-business.

- The original form must be retained in the files of the surplus lines licensee and available for inspection by the Commissioner for a period of at least five (5) years.

Commercial Purchaser Exemption. A surplus lines licensee seeking to procure or place nonadmitted insurance in this state for an exempt commercial purchaser shall not be required to make a due diligence search to determine whether the full amount or type of insurance sought by such exempt commercial purchaser can be obtained from admitted insurers if all of the following apply:

1. The licensee procuring or placing the surplus lines insurance has disclosed to the exempt commercial purchaser that such insurance may or may not be available from the admitted market that may provide greater protection with more regulatory oversight.
2. The exempt commercial purchaser has subsequently requested in writing the licensee to procure or place such insurance from a nonadmitted insurer. (N.C. Gen. Stat. §58-21-16).

E. **Tax:** 5 percent. Gross premiums charged, plus any insurer charged fees, less any return premiums, for surplus lines insurance on insureds for whom North Carolina is the home state are subject to a premium receipts tax of 5 percent, which must be collected by the surplus lines licensee as specified by the commissioner, in addition to the full amount of the gross premium charged by the insurer for the insurance. The tax on any portion of the premium unearned at termination of insurance having been credited by the state to the licensee must be returned to the policyholder directly by the surplus lines licensee or through the producing broker, if any. The surplus lines licensee is prohibited from absorbing such tax and from rebating for any reason any part of such tax. To the extent that other states in which portions of the properties, risks, or exposures reside have failed to enter into a compact or reciprocal allocation procedure with North Carolina, the premium tax collected shall be retained by this state. (N.C. Gen. Stat. §58-21-85).

F. **Stamping Fee:** 0.4 percent on all new policies and renewals and endorsements on these filings.

The NC Surplus Lines Stamping Office processes all surplus lines premium tax transactions.

NCDOI still processes surplus lines premium tax transactions for policies with effective dates prior to January 1, 2017 and for Risk Purchasing Groups and Independent Procurement. (https://www.ncdoi.gov/insurance-industry/form-and-rate-filings/property-and-casualty-pc/surplus-lines#placing-business).

G. Other Requirements or Restrictions: Surplus lines may be placed by a surplus lines licensee if each insurer is an eligible surplus lines insurer; each insurer is authorized to write the kind of insurance in its domiciliary jurisdiction; the full amount or kind of insurance cannot be obtained from insurers who are admitted to do business in North Carolina. Such full amount or kind of insurance may be procured from eligible surplus lines insurers, provided that a diligent search is made among the insurers who are admitted to transact and are actually writing the particular kind and class of insurance in North Carolina. (N.C. Gen. Stat. §58-21-15).

Eligibility. A surplus lines licensee is not permitted to place coverage with a nonadmitted insurer unless at the time of placement, the surplus lines licensee has determined that the nonadmitted insurer has capital and surplus or its equivalent under the laws of its domiciliary jurisdiction, which equals the greater of either North Carolina's minimum capital and surplus requirements under N.C. Gen. Stat. §58-7-75, or $15 million. These requirements may be satisfied by an insurer's possessing less than the minimum capital and surplus upon an affirmative finding of acceptability by the commissioner. The finding will be based upon such factors as quality of management, capital, and surplus of any parent company, company underwriting profit and investment income trends, market availability, and company record and reputation within the industry. In no event will the commissioner make an affirmative finding of acceptability when the nonadmitted insurer's capital and surplus is less than $4.5 million. (N.C. Gen. Stat. §58-21-20).

All surplus lines contracts issued must bear the name of the licensee and the following legend in twelve-point type and in contrasting color or in twelve point type and underlined and in bold print:

> *For nonadmitted insurers:* "The insurance company with which this coverage has been placed is not licensed by the State of North Carolina and is not subject to its supervision. In the event of the insolvency of the insurance company, losses under this policy will not be paid by any State Insurance Guaranty or Solvency Fund."
>
> *For nonadmitted domestic surplus lines insurers:* "The insurance company with which this coverage has been placed is domiciled and authorized by the State of North Carolina and is subject to its supervision. However, in the event of the insolvency of the insurance company, losses under this policy will not be paid by any State insurance guaranty or solvency fund."

(N.C. Gen. Stat. §58-21-45).

The Department of Insurance has determined that N.C. Gen. Stat. §58-33-82(a) prohibits courtesy filings in North Carolina.

Reports. Within thirty days after the placing of any surplus lines insurance, the surplus lines licensee must file with the commissioner a report with the Commissioner or the stamping office, in a form prescribed by the Commissioner, regarding the insurance and including the name of the insured; the identity of the insurer or insurers; a description of the subject and location of the risk; the amount of premium charged for the insurance; the amount of premium tax for the insurance; the policy period; the policy number; an acknowledged statement that the surplus lines licensee has complied with all relevant surplus lines laws; the name, address, telephone number, and electronic mail address of the licensee, as applicable; and any other relevant information the commissioner may reasonably require. These filings must be made with the North Carolina Surplus Lines Association, found online at nclsa.com. (N.C. Gen. Stat. §58-21-35; https://www.ncdoi.gov/insurance-industry/form-and-rate-filings/property-and-casualty-pc/surplus-lines#placing-business).

North Carolina does not require any quarterly or annual re-ports on business that was entered in the NCSLA SLIP system. The quarterly invoice is considered the report.

No reports are required for "0" premium filings in a quarter. If no filings are entered into SLIP, then no invoice will be generated.

Records. Each surplus lines licensee must keep in his or her office a full and true record of each surplus lines insurance contract placed by or through the licensee, including a copy of the policy, certificate, cover note, or other evidence of insurance, as well as a copy of the report described above. (N.C. Gen. Stat. §58-21-35).

The record of each contract must be kept open at all reasonable times to examination by the commissioner without notice for a period not less than five years following termination of the contract.

H. Surplus Lines Association:

North Carolina Surplus Lines Association,
8412 Falls of Neuse, Suite 206
Raleigh, NC 27615.
Phone: (919) 746-8415
Email: CONTACT@NCSLA.COM
Website: http://www.ncsla.com/.

I. Independently Procured Insurance:

1. *Rules.* Any person in North Carolina may directly procure or renew insurance with an eligible surplus lines insurer, without the involvement of an agent, broker, or surplus lines licensee, on a risk located or to be performed, in whole or in part, in North Carolina. Within thirty days, the insured must report the transaction to the Insurance Department and must pay the 5 percent tax. The report must contain a description of the insured's "diligent effort" to place the risk in the admitted market. (N.C. Gen. Stat. §58-28-5(b)).

2. *Industrial Insured Exemption.* North Carolina does not have an industrial insured exemption.

NRRA Implementation

J. Compact: None.

K. Definitions:

1. Home State. Except as regarding affiliated groups, the term "home state" means, with respect to an insured, either of the following:

   a. The state in which an insured maintains its principal place of business or, in the case of an individual, the individual's principal residence.

   b. If 100 percent of the insured risk is located out of the state referred to in section (1) above, the state to which the greatest percentage of the insured's taxable premium for that insurance contract is allocated.

2. Affiliate, Affiliated Groups. With respect to an insured, an affiliate is any entity that controls, is controlled by, or is under common control with the insured. An affiliated group means any group of entities that are all affiliated.

   If two or more insureds from an affiliated group are named insureds on a single nonadmitted insurance contract, the term "home state" means the home state, as determined above, of the member of the affiliated group that has the largest percentage of premium attributed to it under that insurance contract. (N.C. Gen. Stat. §§58-21-10, 58-21-11).

3. *Exempt commercial purchaser* mean any person purchasing commercial insurance that, at the time of placement, meets all of the following requirements:

   a. The person employs or retains a qualified risk manager to negotiate insurance coverage;

b. The person has paid aggregate nationwide commercial property and casualty insurance premiums in excess of $100,000 in the immediately preceding twelve months; and

c. The person satisfies at least one of the following criteria:

(1) The person possesses a net worth in excess of $20 million*;
(2) The person generates annual revenues in excess of $50 million*;
(3) The person employs more than 500 full-time or full-time equivalent employees per insured or is a member of an affiliated group employing more than 1,000 employees in the aggregate;
(4) The person is a nonprofit organization or public entity generating annual budgeted expenditures of at least $30 million*; or
(5) The person is a municipality with a population in excess of 50,000 persons.

*Every five years, the dollar amounts in sections 1, 2, and 4 above are subject to adjustment according to the Consumer Price Index published by the Bureau of Labor Statistics. (N.C. Gen. Stat. §58-21-16).

L. Statutory References:

N.C. Gen. Stat. §§58-	
21-	10, 11, 15, 16, 20, 35 to 45, 65, 85
28-	5
33-	32
	125

M. Web References:

https://www.ncdoi.gov/licensees/surplus-lines-licensing.
https://www.ncsla.com/membership/requirements.
https://nipr.com/licensing-center/state-requirements/north-carolina-non-resident-licensing-individual.
https://nipr.com/licensing-center/state-requirements/north-carolina-non-resident-licensing-business.
https://www.ncdoi.gov/insurance-industry/form-and-rate-filings/property-and-casualty-pc/surplus-lines#placing-business.

NORTH DAKOTA

A. **Resident Licensing:** North Dakota surplus lines producer applicants must first be licensed as producers for the appropriate line of authority. Licensed surplus lines producers are permitted to place insurance with nonadmitted insurers. Initial licensing fee: $100. The North Dakota surplus lines license is renewable annually on April 30. Annual renewal fee: $25. If the applicant is a business entity, it must designate an individual principal insurance producer who holds a North Dakota surplus lines license, and this individual will be responsible for the filing of the annual report and payment of the premium tax. (N.D. Cent. Code §§26.1-01-07, 26.1-26-17).

B. **Nonresident Licensing:** Nonresidents may be licensed in North Dakota as surplus lines producers if they hold the same authority in their home state. North Dakota producers may place business through licensed surplus lines brokers and receive commission. (N.D. Cent. Code §26.1-26-20). Initial fee: $100. Annual renewal fee: $25.

C. **Diligent Effort:** After placing any surplus lines insurance, the surplus lines producer is required to execute and file a report of placement no later than March 1st for the quarter ending the preceding December 31st, June first for the quarter ending the preceding March 31st, September 1st for the quarter ending the preceding June 30th, and December 1st for the quarter ending the preceding September 30 of each year. The Surplus Lines Report of Placement supplied by the North Dakota Insurance Department (SFN 59883) can be found at https://www.insurance.nd.gov/surplus-lines. It must be signed by the licensed producer (or designated responsible producer if the licensed producer is a business entity). Business may not be placed with surplus lines carrier for the sole purpose of obtaining a lower premium. The report of placement must include the name and address of the insured, a description of the subject and location of the risk, the identity of the insurer or insurers, the amount of premium charged for the insurance, a tax allocation spreadsheet detailing the portion of the premium attributable to properties, risks, or exposures located in each state, any other pertinent information as the commissioner may require, and an affidavit as to the diligent efforts to place coverage with admitted insurers. (N.D. Cent. Code §26.1-44-02; N.D. Admin. Code 45-09-01-03; 2019 N.D. HB 1075).

Commercial Purchaser Exemption. A surplus lines producer seeking to place nonadmitted insurance for an exempt commercial purchaser is not required to make a due diligence search or to file the affidavit described above if the surplus lines producer has disclosed to the exempt commercial purchaser that such insurance may or may not be available from the admitted market that may provide greater protection with more regulatory oversight and the exempt commercial purchaser has subsequently requested in writing the surplus lines producer to procure or place such insurance from a nonadmitted insurer. (N.D.

Cent. Code §26.1-44-02). An exempt commercial purchaser is any person purchasing commercial insurance that meets the following requirements at the time of placement:

1. The person employs or retains a qualified risk manager to negotiate insurance coverage.

2. The person has paid nationwide commercial property and casualty insurance premiums in excess of $100,000 in the immediately preceding twelve months.

3. The person meets at least one of the following (dollar amounts are subject to adjustment):

   a. Net worth in excess of $20 million.

   b. Annual revenues in excess of $50 million.

   c. Employs more than 500 full-time or full-time equivalent employees per individual insured or is a member of an affiliated group employing more than 1,000 employees in the aggregate.

   d. A not-for-profit organization or public entity generating annual budgeted expenditures of at least $30 million.

   e. A municipality with a population in excess of 50,000 persons. (N.D. Cent. Code §26.1-44-01.1).

   Each fifth January first occurring after July 21, 2010, and ongoing thereafter, these amounts will be adjusted to reflect the percentage change for such five-year period in the consumer price index for all urban consumers published by the bureau of labor statistics of the department of labor. (N.D. Cent. Code § 26.1-44-01.1).

D. Tax: 1.75 percent. If the insured's home state is North Dakota, in addition to the full amount of gross premiums charged by the insurer for the insurance on properties, risks, or exposures located or to be performed in this state or another state, every surplus lines producer must collect and pay to the commissioner an annual tax equal to 1.75 percent of the gross premiums charged, assessments, membership fees, subscriber fees, policy fees, and service fees, less any return premiums, for surplus lines insurance provided by the surplus lines producer on or before March 1 of each year.

The tax on any portion of the premium unearned at termination of insurance having been credited by the state to the surplus lines producer must be returned to the policyholder directly by the surplus lines producer. The surplus lines producer is prohibited from rebating, for any reason, any part of the tax.

At the time of filing the verified report as described below, each surplus lines producer must pay the premium tax due for the policies written during the period covered by the report. (N.D. Cent. Code § 26.1-44-03.1)

Multi-State Tax. If a multi-state policy is effective prior to June 1, 2015, the tax rate on non-North Dakota risks is the particular tax rate of the state of the risk. Policy endorsements are not considered policy "placements," and policy endorsements made on or after June 1, 2015, do not change the tax rate.

A penalty of $25 a day will be charged for late filing of annual statements, reports of placements and diligent search statements. The penalty will be charged daily but will be capped at $500 per late item. (https://www.insurance.nd.gov/surplus-lines).

E. **Stamping Fee:** None. North Dakota does not have a surplus lines stamping office.

F. **Surplus Lines Association:** None.

G. **Other Requirements or Restrictions:**

Eligibility. Surplus lines insurance may be placed by a surplus lines producer if each insurer is an eligible surplus lines insurer, each insurer is authorized to write the kind of insurance in its domiciliary jurisdiction, and the full amount or type of insurance cannot be obtained from insurers who are admitted to do business in North Dakota. (N.D. Cent. Code §26.1-44-03). Eligible surplus lines insurers, including any insurer listed on the NAIC Quarterly Listing of Alien insurers, must register with the insurance department. Coverage can only be placed in the nonadmitted market if one of the following is true:

1. A diligent search has determined the inability to procure the insurance from an insurer authorized to do business in North Dakota. A licensed surplus lines producer must conduct the search, unless the licensed surplus lines producer deems a search done by a licensed producer or the insured was sufficient.

2. If the coverage is listed in Appendix I of N.D. Admin. Code 45-09-01, there is a presumption that the insured is unable, after diligent search, to procure the insurance, indemnity contract or surety bond desired from a company authorized to do business in North Dakota.

3. The insured is an exempt commercial purchaser.

(https://www.insurance.nd.gov/surplus-lines).

At the time of placement the surplus lines producer must have determined that the nonadmitted insurer has established satisfactory evidence of good repute and financial integrity and has capital and surplus or its equivalent under the laws of its domiciliary jurisdiction which equals the greater of the minimum capital and surplus requirements under the law of this state or $15 million. These requirements may be satisfied by an insurer possessing less than the minimum capital and surplus upon an affirmative finding of acceptability by the commissioner. The finding must be based upon such factors as quality of management, capital and surplus of any parent company, company underwriting profit and investment income trends, market availability, and company record and reputation within the industry. The commissioner may not make an affirmative finding of acceptability when the nonadmitted insurer's capital and surplus is less than $4.5 million. (N.D. Cent. Code §26.1-44-03).

Notice. If the insured's home state is North Dakota, the surplus lines producer must give the following consumer notice to every person applying for insurance with a nonadmitted insurer. The notice must be printed in sixteen point type on a separate document affixed to the application. The applicant must sign and date a copy of the notice to acknowledge receiving it. The surplus lines producer must maintain the signed notice in its file for a period of five years from expiration of the policy. The surplus lines producer must tender a copy of the signed notice to the insured at the time of delivery of each policy the producer transacts with a nonadmitted insurer. The copy must be a separate document affixed to the policy.

NOTICE:

1. An insurer that is not licensed in this state is issuing the insurance policy that you have applied to purchase. These companies are called "nonadmitted" or "surplus lines" insurers.

2. The insurer is not subject to the financial solvency regulation and enforcement that applies to licensed insurers in this state.

3. These insurers generally do not participate in insurance guaranty funds created by state law. These guaranty funds will not pay your claims or protect your assets if the insurer becomes insolvent and is unable to make payments as promised.

4. Some states maintain lists of approved or eligible surplus lines insurers and surplus lines producers may use only insurers on the lists. Some states issue orders that particular surplus lines insurers cannot be used.

5. For additional information about the above matters and about the insurer, you should ask questions of your insurance producer or surplus lines producer. You may also contact your insurance department consumer help line.

(N.D. Cent. Code §26.1-44-05).

Reports. Each surplus lines producer, within sixty days after the placing of any surplus lines insurance where the insured's home state is North Dakota, must execute and file a written report regarding the insurance which must be kept confidential by the commissioner. The report must include:

1. The name and address of the insured.

2. The identity of the insurer or insurers.

3. A description of the subject and location of the risk.

4. The amount of premium charged for the insurance.

5. A tax allocation spreadsheet detailing the portion of premium attributable to properties, risks, or exposures located in each state.

6. Any other pertinent information as the commissioner may reasonably require.

7. An affidavit on a form prescribed by the commissioner as to the diligent efforts to place the coverage with admitted insurers and the results of that effort. The affidavit must be open to public inspection. The affidavit must affirm that the insured was expressly advised in writing prior to placement of the insurance that the surplus lines insurer with whom the insurance was to be placed is not licensed in North Dakota and is not subject to the state's supervision. The affidavit must also include affirmation that the insured was advised in writing that in the event of the insolvency of the surplus lines insurer, losses will not be paid by the state insurance guaranty fund. (N.D. Cent. Code §26.1-44-02).

The Report of Placement of Surplus Lines Insurance (Form SFN 59883) and the Surplus Lines Affidavit (Form SFN 4818) can be downloaded online at https://www.insurance.nd.gov/surplus-lines. The report form and affidavit should be mailed to: North Dakota Insurance Department, 600 E. Boulevard Ave., Dept. 401, Bismarck, ND 58505-0320. Reporting can also be done online at apps.nd.gov/NDINS/surpluslines/Login.

Annual Report: If the insured's home state is North Dakota, on or before March 2 of each year, each surplus lines producer shall file with the commissioner on forms prescribed by the commissioner a verified report of all surplus lines insurance transacted during the preceding calendar year, including:

1. The aggregate gross premiums written.

2. The aggregate return premiums.

3. The amount of aggregate tax remitted on risks located or to be performed in this state.

4. The amount of aggregate tax remitted on risks located or to be performed in another state.

An annual tax statement is not required to be filed when a surplus lines producer has transacted no surplus lines insurance during the preceding calendar year. (N.D. Cent. Code §26.1-44-06.1).

Records. If the insured's home state is North Dakota, each surplus lines producer must keep a full and true record of each surplus lines insurance contract placed by or through the producer, including a copy of the policy, certificate, cover note, or other evidence of insurance showing each of the following applicable items:

1. The amount of the insurance, risks, and perils insured.
2. A brief description of the property insured and its location.
3. The gross premium charged.
4. Any return premium paid.
5. The rate of premium charged upon the several items of property.
6. The effective date and terms of the contract.
7. The name and address of the insured.
8. The name and address of the insurer.
9. The amount of tax and other sums to be collected from the insured.
10. The allocation of taxes by state.
11. The identity of the producer of record.
12. Any confirming correspondence from the insurer or its representative.
13. The application.

Records of each contract must be kept within North Dakota and open at all reasonable times to examination by the commissioner without notice for a period not less than five years following termination of the contract. In lieu of maintaining offices in this state, each nonresident surplus lines producer must make available to the commissioner any and all records that the commissioner deems necessary for examination. (N.D. Cent. Code §26.1-44-06).

Penalties. Every surplus lines producer who fails or refuses to make and file the verified report required by described above, or fails or refuses to file the endorsement, audit, or cancellation required under N.D. Cent. Code §26.1-44-06.1, or fails or refuses to pay the taxes required to be paid prior to the March 2 after such tax is due, is liable for a fine of $25 for each day of delinquency, not to exceed $500 for each failure or refusal to file. (N.D. Cent. Code § 26.1-44-08).

Revocation of License. If the license of a surplus lines producer is revoked, whether by the action of the Commissioner or by judicial proceedings, another license may not be issued to that surplus lines producer until two years have elapsed from the effective date of the revocation, nor until all taxes and fines are paid, nor until the commissioner is satisfied that full compliance with the surplus lines law of North Dakota will be had. (N.D. Cent. Code § 26.1-44-08).

H. Independently Procured Insurance:

1. *Rules.* If the insured's home state is North Dakota, each insured in North Dakota who independently procures or continues or renews insurance with a nonadmitted insurer on properties, risks, or exposures located or to be performed in whole or in part in this state, other than insurance procured through a surplus lines producer, is subject to the same requirements and restrictions as apply to a surplus lines producer. (N.D. Cent. Code §26.1-44-10).

2. *Industrial Insured Exemption.* Though the prohibition on unauthorized insurance does not apply to transactions involving insurance contracts issued to one or more industrial insureds, an industrial insured is not exempted from taxation on independently procured insurance. An industrial insured is an insured who procures the insurance of any risk or risks other than life and annuity contracts by use of the services of a full-time employee acting as an insurance manager or buyer or the services of a regularly and continuously retained qualified insurance consultant; has aggregate annual premiums for insurance on all risks total at least $25,000; and has at least twenty-five full-time employees. (N.D. Cent. Code §26.1-02-05).

NORTH DAKOTA

NRRA Implementation

I. Compact: House Bill 1146 repeals North Dakota's participation in the Surplus Lines Insurance Multi-State Compliance Compact (SLIMPACT) and changes premium tax on all out of state risks to North Dakota's premium tax rate of 1.75 percent. The placement of surplus lines coverage and reporting of premium tax is still governed by the "Home State" definition, but as was effective June 1, 2015, on multi-state policies where North Dakota is the Home State the tax rate on both North Dakota and non-North Dakota risks is 1.75 percent. (https://www.insurance.nd.gov/sites/www/files/documents/Communications/Summary%20of%20Insurance%20Legislation/2015legislationsummary.pdf).

J. Definitions:

1. "Home State" means:

   a. Except as provided in subdivision b, "home state" means, with respect to an insured:

      (1) The state in which an insured maintains its principal place of business or, in the case of an individual, the individual's principal residence.
      (2) If 100 percent of the insured risk is located out of the state referred to in paragraph 1, the state to which the greatest percentage of the insured's taxable premium for that insurance contract is allocated.

   b. If more than one insured from an affiliated group are named insureds on a single nonadmitted insurance contract, the term "home state" means the home state, as determined pursuant to subdivision a, of the member of the affiliated group that has the largest percentage of premium attributed to it under such insurance contract. (N.D. Cent. Code §26.1-44-01.1).

2. "Affiliate" means with respect to an insured, any entity that controls, is controlled by, or is under common control with the insured.

3. "Control." An entity has "control" over another entity if:

   a. The entity directly or indirectly or acting through one or more other persons owns, controls, or has the power to vote 25 percent or more of any class of voting securities of the other entity; or

   b. The entity controls in any manner the election of a majority of the directors or trustees of the other entity. (N.D. Cent. Code §26.1-10-01).

K. Statutory References:

N.D. Cent. Code §26.1-01-	07,
N.D. Cent. Code §26.1-02-	05,
N.D. Cent. Code §261.-10-	01,
N.D. Cent. Code §§26.1-26-	17, 20
N.D. Cent. Code §§26.1-44-	01.1 to 03.1, 05 to 06.1
	08, 10

N.D. Admin. Code 45-09-01-	3
	Appx I

Web References:

https://www.insurance.nd.gov/surplus-lines.

https://www.insurance.nd.gov/sites/www/files/documents/Communications/Summary%20of%20Insurance%20Legislation/2015legislationsummary.pdf.

OHIO

A. **Resident Licensing:** To be eligible for a surplus line broker's license, a person must have both a property license and a casualty license. The surplus lines broker license expires annually on January 31. The application form for an individual surplus lines broker's license is INS3245 (3/14). Initial and Annual Renewal Fee: $100. In addition, applicants must file a $25,000 bond, using form INS 3245 (3/14). All forms are available at http://insurance.ohio.gov/agent/pages/surplines.aspx. Note that which form to use depends on whether you are an individual or business entity and whether you are applying or renewing. Ohio-licensed property and casualty agents may do business with surplus lines brokers and receive commission. Business entities may also be licensed as surplus lines producers. (ORC Ann. §§3905.30, 3905.32, 3905.35).

B. **Nonresident Licensing:** To be eligible for a nonresident surplus line broker's license, a person must hold an active surplus line broker license in the person's home state. A nonresident surplus line broker must obtain a nonresident license with a property and casualty line of authority in this state if the broker is or will be personally performing the due diligence requirements under §3905.33 of the Revised Code. The insurer can also be designated as a domestic surplus lines insurer pursuant to section 3905.332 of the Revised Code. (ORC Ann. §§3905.30, 3905.33).

C. **Diligent Effort:** No surplus lines broker is permitted to solicit, procure, place, or renew any insurance with an unauthorized insurer unless an agent or surplus lines broker is unable to procure the requested insurance from an authorized insurer. Due diligence requires an agent to contact at least five of the authorized insurers the agent represents, or as many insurers as the agent represents, that customarily write the kind of insurance required by the insured. Due diligence is presumed if declinations are received from each authorized insurer contacted. If any authorized insurer fails to respond within ten days after the initial contact, the agent or surplus line broker may assume the insurer has declined to accept the risk. Due diligence shall only be performed by an agent licensed in this state that holds an active property and casualty insurance license. (ORC Ann. §3905.33).

   Commercial Purchaser Exemption. An insurance agent or surplus lines broker is exempt from the due diligence requirements if the agent or surplus lines broker is seeking to procure or place unauthorized insurance for a person that qualifies as an exempt commercial purchaser and both of the following are true:

   a. The surplus lines broker procuring or placing the surplus lines insurance has disclosed to the exempt commercial purchaser that the insurance may or may not be available from the authorized market that may provide greater protection with more regulatory oversight.

b. After receipt of the disclosure, the exempt commercial purchaser has requested in writing that the insurance agent or broker procure or place the insurance from an unauthorized insurer.

To qualify as an exempt commercial purchaser, (1) the person employs or retains a qualified risk manager, (2) the person has paid aggregate nationwide commercial property and casualty insurance premiums in excess of one hundred thousand dollars in the immediately preceding twelve months, and (3) the person meets one of the other conditions set forth in §3905.331(A)(3) of the Revised Code. (ORC Ann. §3905.331).

A domestic insurer may be designated a domestic surplus line insurer if the domestic insurer possesses capital and surplus of at least 15 million dollars, the insurer is seeking to become a domestic surplus lines insurer pursuant to a resolution adopted by its board of directors, and the superintendent has authorized the designation in writing. A domestic insurer shall only write surplus lines insurance in Ohio in accordance with the requirements of ORC Ann. §3905.332. (ORC Ann. §3905.332).

D. Tax: 5 percent. Each surplus lines broker is required to pay to the treasurer of state, on or before March 31 of each year, 5 percent of the balance of the gross premiums charged for insurance placed or procured under the license after a deduction for return premiums in the prescribed format or in compliance with any requirements of a multistate agreement or compact entered into by the superintendent. The Surplus Lines Premium Tax Summary form INS 4001 should accompany each tax payment. The tax will be collected from the insured by the surplus lines broker who placed or procured the policy of insurance at the time the policy is delivered to the insured.

Late Premium Tax Payment Penalties. Surplus lines broker licenses will not be renewed until payment is made. If the tax is not paid when due, the tax shall be increased by a penalty of 25 percent. An interest charge will be made on the entire sum of the tax plus penalty, which interest will be computed from the date the tax is due until it is paid. Payment is considered made when it is received, irrespective of any United States postal service marking or other stamp or mark indicating the date on which the payment may have been mailed.

The superintendent, in the superintendent's sole discretion, may waive the 25 percent penalty and interest charge thereon for a first-time, inadvertent nonpayment of the tax when due if the nonpayment is reported immediately upon discovery and the outstanding tax is thereafter immediately paid to the superintendent. (ORC Ann. §3905.36).

E. Stamping Fee: None. Ohio does not have a stamping office.

F. **Surplus Lines Association:** Ohio Association of Professional Specialty Lines. Mailing address:

OAPSLO
175 S. 3rd St.
Suite 940
Columbus, OH 43215

If you have any questions, please contact: oapslo@oapslo.org. Website: www.oapslo.org.

G. **Other Requirements or Restrictions:**

Exemptions. The surplus lines law does not apply to ocean marine insurance when placed by licensed agents of the state. (ORC Ann. §3905.38).

Eligibility. No surplus lines broker is permitted to solicit, procure an application for, bind, issue, renew, or deliver a policy with any insurer that is not eligible to write insurance on an unauthorized basis in Ohio. (ORC Ann. §3905.33).

Pursuant to the "Nonadmitted and Reinsurance Reform Act of 2010," 15 U.S.C. §8201 *et seq.*, 124 Stat. 1589, or any successor or replacement law, where this state is the home state of the insured, an insurer shall be considered eligible to write insurance on an unauthorized basis in this state if either of the following are true:

1. The insurer meets the requirements and criteria in sections 5A(2) and 5C(2)(a) of the nonadmitted insurance model act adopted by the national association of insurance commissioners, or alternative nationwide uniform eligibility requirements adopted by this state through participation in a compact or other nationwide system pursuant to 15 U.S.C. §8201 *et seq.*, 124 Stat. 1589.

2. For unauthorized insurance placed with, or procured from an unauthorized insurer domiciled outside the United States, the insurer is listed on the quarterly listing of alien insurers maintained by the international insurers department of the national association of insurance commissioners. (ORC Ann. §3905.33).

   Life, accident and health, and workers compensation insurance may not be placed with nonadmitted insurers.

   Ohio recommends all surplus lines contracts have this wording in ten point or larger and boldface type:

> "The insurance hereby evidenced is written by an approved nonlicensed insurer in the State of Ohio and is not covered in case of insolvency by the Ohio Insurance Guaranty Association."

Signed statement from the insured. Except when exempt from due diligence requirements, an insurance agent who procures or places insurance through a surplus lines broker must obtain a signed statement from the insured acknowledging that the insurance policy is to be placed with a company or insurer not authorized to do business in Ohio and acknowledging that, in the event of the insolvency of the insurer, the insured is not entitled to any benefits or proceeds from the Ohio Insurance Guaranty Association. The statement must be on a form prescribed by the superintendent and need not be notarized. The agent shall submit the original signed statement to the surplus lines broker within thirty days after the effective date of the policy. If no other agent is involved, the surplus lines broker must obtain the statement from the insured. The statement must be on Form INS 4024 (available at https://insurance.ohio.gov/static/Forms/Documents/INS4024.pdf) as prescribed by the superintendent. (ORC Ann. §3905.33).

The surplus lines broker must maintain the original signed statement or a copy of the statement, and the originating agent must keep a copy of the statement, for at least five years after the effective date of the policy to which the signed statement pertains. A copy of the signed statement must be given to the insured at the time the insurance is bound or a policy is delivered. Statements are not to be sent to the Insurance Department. (ORC Ann. §3905.33).

Business Reports. Each surplus lines broker must keep a separate account of the business done under the person's license. On or before March 31 or when required under a multistate agreement or compact entered into by the superintendent of insurance, each surplus lines broker must file details of the business done during the preceding calendar year. Surplus lines brokers are to report their business using the Online Surplus Lines, Risk Retention and Purchasing Group application. Instructions for using the secure application can be found on the Web site www.insurance.ohio.gov. New brokers are mailed user IDs and passwords when their license is issued. Only brokers with valid licenses will be able to use the application. This application allows transactions to be entered at any time throughout the year. (ORC Ann. §3905.34).

H. Independently Procured Insurance: Every insured that enters into an independent procurement or direct placement agreement with any insurance company not authorized to do business in Ohio for which there is a gross premium shall file the details of the transaction annually, on or before March 31. At the time of filing, the insured must pay to the treasurer of state a tax of 5 percent of gross premiums, after a deduction for return premium, if any, as calculated in the prescribed format or in compliance with any requirements of a multi-state agreement or compact entered into by the superintendent. The Statement of

Premium Taxes for Unauthorized Insurers form INS 4023 should accompany each tax payment. An insurer may submit the required details of the transaction and remit the tax payment on behalf of an insured. (ORC Ann. §3905.36).

If the tax is not paid when due, the tax will be increased by a penalty of 25 percent. An interest charge must be made on the entire sum of the tax plus penalty, computed from the date the tax is due until it is paid. Payment is considered made when it is received, irrespective of any United States postal service marking or other stamp or mark indicating the date on which the payment may have been mailed. (ORC Ann. §3905.36).

The superintendent, in the superintendent's sole discretion, may waive the 25 percent penalty and interest charge thereon for a first-time, inadvertent nonpayment of the tax when due if the nonpayment is reported immediately upon discovery and the outstanding tax is thereafter immediately paid to the superintendent. (ORC Ann. §3905.36).

NRRA Implementation

I. Compact: None at this time. However, the superintendent is authorized to enter into SLIMPACT or a different multi-state agreement or compact if it is in Ohio's financial best interest. (ORC Ann. §3905.33).

J. Definitions:

1. "Home State" means the state in which an insured maintains its principal place of business or, in the case of an individual, the individual's principal residence except in the case of either of the following:

    a. If 100 percent of the insured risk is located out of the state in which an insured maintains its principal place of business or principle residence, "home state" means the state to which the greatest percentage of the insured's taxable premium for that insurance contract is allocated.

    b. If more than one insured from an affiliated group are named insureds on a single unauthorized insurance contract, "home state" means the state in which the member of the affiliated group that has the largest percentage of premium attributed to it under such insurance contract.

2. "Principal place of business" means the state where the insured maintains the insured's headquarters and where the insured's high-level officers direct, control, and coordinate the business activities of the insured. (ORC Ann. §3905.30).

K. Statutory References: ORC Ann. §§3905.30 to 3905.38.

OKLAHOMA

A. Resident Licensing: Resident licensed producers may be licensed as surplus lines producers. Applicants must have passed the P&C examination. Biennial license expires on last day of the producer's birth month; biennial license fee: $100. A bond is required for resident surplus lines brokers. The amount of the bond is based on the gross premium amount or gross fees received. The bond ranges from $5,000 for gross premiums or fees less than $25,000 to $40,000 for gross premiums or fees in excess of $1 million. See Okla. Admin. Code §365:25-3-12 for complete bond amounts. Residents licensed for the line of insurance offered may do business with licensed surplus lines producers and receive commission. An Oklahoma surplus lines license is only required where Oklahoma is the home state of the insured. (Okla. Stat. Ann. tit. 36, §§1435.6, 1106(2), and 1111).

B. Nonresident Licensing: Nonresident licensed producers may be licensed as surplus lines producers without an examination if licensed as surplus lines producer in home state. A bond is not required for nonresident surplus lines brokers. The home state must award nonresident producer licenses to Oklahoma residents on the same basis. (Okla. Stat. Ann. tit. 36, §1435.9).

C. Diligent Effort: If a particular insurance coverage or type, class, or kind of coverage is not readily procurable from authorized insurers in Oklahoma, a surplus lines licensee or broker may place the coverage with a nonadmitted insurer or surplus lines insurer as defined in the Unauthorized Insurers and Surplus Lines Insurance Act. Surplus lines brokers are required to make a due diligence search to determine whether the full amount or type of insurance can be obtained from admitted insurers when the broker is seeking to procure or place nonadmitted insurance. (Okla. Stat. Ann. tit. 36, §§1106, 1106.1, and 1108).

Commercial Purchaser Exemption. A due diligence search is not required when a surplus lines broker is seeking to procure or place nonadmitted insurance for an exempt commercial purchaser, provided both:

1. The broker procuring or placing the surplus lines insurance has disclosed to the exempt commercial purchaser that such insurance may or may not be available from the admitted market that may provide greater protection with more regulatory oversight.

2. The exempt commercial purchaser has subsequently requested in writing for the broker to procure or place such insurance from a nonadmitted insurer. (Okla. Stat. Ann. tit. 36, §1106.1).

D. Tax: 6 percent. Where Oklahoma is the home state of the insured, every surplus lines licensee or broker must collect and pay to the insurance commissioner a sum based on the total gross premiums, less any return premiums, for surplus lines insurance provided by the licensee pursuant to the license. Any such unearned gross premium credited by the state to the surplus broker or licensee must be returned to the policyholder by the broker or licensee. The surplus lines licensee is prohibited from rebating, for any reason, any part of the tax. (Okla. Stat. Ann. tit. 36, §1115).

When Oklahoma is the home state, the surplus lines licensee or broker must make the tax filings and payments to the insurance commissioner in a quarterly manner, by January 31 for the quarter ending the preceding December 31; by April 30 for the quarter ending the preceding March 31; by July 31 for the quarter ending the preceding June 30; and by October 31 for the quarter ending the preceding September 30 (this is what is noted on the website, but the statute on Lexis states something different). The surplus lines broker quarterly summary includes forms that detail the types of coverages written, the aggregate amount of insurance issued, the gross premiums charged, and the gross return premium. Form SL-3a must be signed by the broker with an original or live signature, notarized, and filed on or before the last day of the month following the close of a calendar quarter. The specific forms which may be filed electronically with OPTins are:

1. SL-3a Affidavit of a true and correct report. File in one part.

2. SL-3b Spreadsheet to accumulate premium and tax data by the company number and company name of the surplus line carrier. File in one part only.

3. SL- 3c Affidavit of coverage. File in one part.

4. SL-3d Affidavit for return of premiums and the credit or refund of premium taxes.

   Any surplus lines licensee or broker who fails to remit the surplus line tax for more than sixty days after it is due will be liable to a civil penalty of not to exceed $25 for each additional day of delinquency. (Okla. Stat. Ann. tit. 36, §1116; Okla. Admin. Code 365:1-9-5).

Multi-State Premium Tax Allocation. Until the insurance commissioner decides to join the Nonadmitted Insurance Multi-State Agreement or any other multi-state agreement, if Oklahoma is the home state of the insured and the insurance covers properties, risks or exposures located or to be performed in and out of Oklahoma, the sum payable must be computed based on an amount equal to 6 percent of the total gross premiums whether the properties, risks or exposures are located or to be performed inside or outside Oklahoma. (Okla. Stat. Ann. tit. 36, §1115).

E. Stamping Fee: None. Oklahoma does not have a stamping office.

F. Other Requirements or Restrictions:

Eligibility. When insurance that is required to protect the interest of the assured cannot be procured from authorized insurers after direct inquiry to authorized insurers, insurance may be procured from surplus lines insurers if the insurer has capital and surplus or its equivalent under the laws of its domiciliary jurisdiction which equals the greater of the minimum capital and surplus requirements under the laws of this state for nonadmitted insurers, or $15 million. This requirement may be satisfied by an insurer possessing less than the minimum capital and surplus upon an affirmative finding of acceptability by the insurance commissioner. The finding will be based upon such factors as quality of management, capital and surplus of any parent company, company underwriting profit and investment income trends, market availability and company record and reputation within the industry. In no event will the insurance commissioner make an affirmative finding of acceptability when the nonadmitted insurer's capital and surplus is less than $4.5 million. The insurer, if an alien insurer, must be listed on the National Association of Insurance Commissioners Nonadmitted Insurers Quarterly Listing; and the insurance shall be procured through a licensed surplus lines licensee or broker licensed in the insurer's home state. (Okla. Stat. Ann. tit. 36, §1106).

A surplus lines licensee or broker may accept and place surplus lines insurance from any insurance agent or broker licensed in Oklahoma for the kind of insurance involved, and may compensate such agent or broker therefore. The insurance agent or broker has the right to receive from the surplus lines insurer the customary commission. (Okla. Stat. Ann. tit. 36, §1111).

Notice. Insurance contracts procured as surplus line coverage must contain in bold-face type a notification stamped by the surplus lines licensee or broker or surplus lines insurer on the declaration page of the policy that the contracts are not subject to the protection of any guaranty association in the event of liquidation or receivership of the surplus lines insurer. The notification shall be stamped by either the unauthorized insurer or the broker. (Okla. Stat. Ann. tit. 36, §1109).

Annual Statements. Each surplus lines licensee or broker must file with the insurance commissioner a verified statement of all surplus lines insurance transacted by the broker during the preceding calendar year on or before April 1 of each year where Oklahoma is the state of the insured. The statement must be on a form prescribed and furnished by the insurance commissioner and must show such information required to be submitted to the insurance commissioner. (Okla. Stat. Ann. tit. 36, §1114).

Records. Each surplus lines licensee or broker must keep a full and true record of each surplus lines contract procured by the surplus lines broker, and such record may be examined at any time within three years thereafter by the insurance commissioner. (Okla. Stat. Ann. tit. 36, §1113).

G. Surplus Lines Association: None.

H. Independently Procured Insurance:

Tax Reports and Filing Dates. After procuring any surplus line insurance where Oklahoma is the home state and the insurance involves a multi-state risk, the surplus lines licensee and broker shall submit such information relating to the transaction as may be established by the insurance commissioner. The insured procuring independently procured insurance must make the tax filings and payments to the Oklahoma insurance commissioner in a quarterly manner, by January 31 for the quarter ending the preceding December 31; by April 30 for the quarter ending the preceding March 31; by July 31 for the quarter ending the preceding June 30; and by October 31 for the quarter ending the preceding September 30 (this is what is noted on the website, but the statute on Lexis states something different).

Tax. Where Oklahoma is the home state of the insured, gross premiums charged for independently procured insurance, less any return premiums, are subject to a premium tax at the rate of 6 percent payable to the Oklahoma insurance commissioner, whether the properties, risks or exposures are located or to be performed inside or outside Oklahoma. (Okla. Stat. Ann. tit. 36, §1115).

Forms. The direct placement by an insured summary includes forms that detail the types of coverages written, the aggregate amount of insurance issued, the gross premiums charged, the gross return premium, and the tax due. Form DSL-3a must be signed by the affiant, generally the individual responsible for procuring risk coverage, with an original signature, notarized and filed within thirty (30) days next succeeding the issuance of evidence of coverage. The specific forms are:

1. DSL-3a Affidavit of a true and correct report. File in one part.

2. DSL-3b Spreadsheet to accumulate premium and tax data by the company number and company name of the surplus lines carrier. File in one part only.

3. DSL-3c Affidavit of coverage. File in one part.

4. DSL-3d Affidavit for return of premiums and the credit or refund of premium taxes. (Okla. Admin. Code 365:1-9-5).

NRRA Implementation

I. Compact: None.

J. Home State Definition:

1. "Home State" means:

   a. Except as provided in subparagraphs b through e of this paragraph, with respect to an insured:

      (1) The state in which an insured maintains its principal place of business or, in the case of an individual, the individual's principal residence.

      (2) If 100 percent of the insured risk is located out of the state referred to in division (1) of this subparagraph, the state to which the greatest percentage of the insured's taxable premium for the insurance contract is allocated.

   b. With respect to determining the home state of the insured, "principal place of business" means:

      (1) The state where the insured maintains its headquarters and where the insured's high-level officers direct, control and coordinate the business activities; or

      (2) If the insured maintains its headquarters or the insured's high-level officers direct, control and coordinate business activities outside Oklahoma, the state in which the greatest percentage of the insured's taxable premium for the insurance contract is allocated.

   c. With respect to determining the home state of the insured "principal residence" means:

      (1) The state where the insured resides for the greatest number of days during the calendar year; or

      (2) If the insured's principal residence is located outside any state, the state to which the greatest percentage of the insured's taxable premium for that insurance is allocated.

   d. If more than one insured from an affiliated group are named insureds on a single nonadmitted insurance contract, the term "home state" means the home state, as determined pursuant to division (1) of subparagraph a of this paragraph, of the member affiliated group that has the largest percentage of premium attributed to it under such insurance contract; or

e. When the group policyholder pays 100 percent of the premium from its own funds, the term "home state" means the home state, as determined pursuant to division (1) of subparagraph a of this paragraph, of the group policyholder. When the group policyholder does not pay 100 percent of the premium from its own funds, the term home state means the home state, as determined pursuant to division (1) of subparagraph a of this paragraph, or of the group member. (Okla. Stat. Ann. tit. 36, §1100.1).

K. Statutory References: Okla. Stat. Ann. tit. 36 §§1100 through 1120; 1435.6 and 1435.9; Okla. Admin. Code 365:1-9-5.

OREGON

A. Resident Licensing: Applicants must have a property and casualty insurance producer's license and pass a surplus lines exam to qualify for a surplus lines agent license in Oregon. A grade of 70 percent or higher is required to pass. Cost of exam: \$45. Application fee: \$30; License fee: \$45 plus a processing fee. There is no separate renewal fee. Upon renewal, the surplus lines producer must provide a signed renewal notice or signed statement acknowledging that the producer has had no conviction of a misdemeanor or felony in the last two years. Otherwise, details of a conviction or misdemeanor must be provided with the renewal request. Oregon licensed agents may place business through surplus lines licensees and receive commission. (O.R.S. §744.058).

B. Nonresident Licensing: Nonresidents may be licensed for surplus lines in Oregon. A nonresident person shall receive a nonresident insurance producer license if:

1. The person is currently licensed as a resident insurance producer and is in good standing in the person's home state.

2. The person has submitted the proper request for a nonresident insurance producer license and has paid the applicable fees.

3. The person has submitted or transmitted to the director the resident insurance producer license application that the person submitted to the person's home state, or in lieu of that application, a completed uniform application.

4. The person's home state grants nonresident insurance producer licenses to residents of this state on the same basis. (O.R.S. §744.063).

C. Diligent Effort: Insurance may be procured through a surplus lines licensee from a nonadmitted insurer if:

1. The insurer is an eligible surplus lines insurer.

2. A diligent search has first been made among the insurers who are authorized to transact and are actually writing the particular kind and class of insurance in this state.

3. It is determined that the full amount or kind of insurance cannot be obtained from those insurers. (O.R.S. §735.410).

Commercial Purchaser Exemption. Diligent effort requirements do not apply to a surplus lines licensee seeking to procure or place nonadmitted insurance in Oregon for an exempt commercial purchaser if both:

1. The surplus lines licensee procuring or placing the surplus lines insurance has disclosed to the exempt commercial purchaser that such insurance may or may not be available from the admitted market that may provide greater protection with more regulatory oversight.

2. The exempt commercial purchaser has subsequently requested in writing that the surplus lines licensee procure or place such insurance from a nonadmitted insurer. (O.R.S. §735.410).

D. **Tax:** 2 percent. Each surplus lines licensee must pay a surplus lines premium tax of 2 percent of the gross amount of premiums and other fees, excluding the Surplus Lines Service Charge, received on Oregon home state risk. The taxes must be collected by the surplus lines licensee as specified by the director, in addition to the gross amount of premiums charged by the insurer or the insurer's insurance producer and other intermediaries for the insurance. Taxes on any portion of the premium unearned at termination of insurance having been credited by the state to the licensee must be returned to the policyholder directly by the surplus lines licensee or through the insurance producer, if any. Surplus lines licensees are prohibited from absorbing the taxes, and from rebating for any reason, any part of the taxes. Surplus lines taxes are due quarterly on the forty-fifth day following the calendar quarter in which the premium is collected. The taxes must be paid to and reported on forms prescribed by the director or upon the director's order paid to and reported on forms prescribed by the Surplus Line Association of Oregon. If a surplus lines license is terminated or nonrenewed for any reason, the taxes described in this section are due on the thirtieth day after the termination or nonrenewal. (ORS §735.470).

Note: The Surplus Lines Service Charge is $10 for both new and renewal policies. There is also a 0.3% Fire Marshal's tax on all premiums and other fees, excluding the Surplus Lines Service Charge. (http://www.oregonsla.org/resources/tax-calculator).

Multi-State Policies. For the purposes of carrying out the NRRA, the director may collect taxes on 100 percent of the gross amount of premiums on Oregon home state risks. If the director enters into a compact or otherwise establishes procedures with other states, the director by rule will establish procedures to facilitate the reporting, collection, payment, allocation and disbursement of premium taxes on Oregon home state risks that also include risks allocable to other states. (O.R.S. §735.470).

E. **Stamping Fee:** $10 flat charge on new or renewal transactions, no charge on endorsements.

F. **Surplus Lines Association:** Surplus Lines Association of Oregon; 7360 SW Hunziker Street, Suite 105, Portland, OR 97223. Phone: 503-718-6700. Fax: 503-718-6702. Web site: http://www.oregonsla.org. Email: info@oregonsla.org.

Regarding courtesy filings of taxes and certificates of nonavailability, the Oregon Insurance Division says: "The term 'courtesy filing' is not a recognized term in our statutes. If an Oregon surplus line licensee does this type of transaction, that licensee—'in essence'—takes on the responsibility, filing, and tax remittance requirement as if written by that licensee."

G. **Other Requirements or Restrictions:** A surplus lines licensee may not place any coverage with a nonadmitted insurer unless at the time of placement the nonadmitted insurer has obtained authorization to write the kind of insurance to be placed by the surplus lines licensee by the insurance supervisory official in the insurer's domiciliary jurisdiction. The licensee must meet the eligibility requirements below, and must file with the director no more than six months after the close of the period reported upon a certified copy of its current annual statement that is:

1. Filed with and approved by the regulatory authority in the domicile of the nonadmitted insurer.

2. Certified by an accounting or auditing firm licensed in the jurisdiction of the insurer's domicile.

3. In the case of an insurance exchange, an aggregate combined statement of all underwriting syndicates operating during the period reported. (O.R.S. §735.415).

Exemptions. Reinsurance, wet marine, transportation insurance, independently procured insurance, life insurance, health insurance and annuities may not be written by nonadmitted insurers. (O.R.S. §731.144).

Eligibility. Nonadmitted insurers must meet one of the following:

1. Have capital and surplus or its equivalent under the laws of its domiciliary jurisdiction that equals the greater of either the minimum capital and surplus requirements under the laws of this state of its domiciliary jurisdiction or $15 million, except that the requirements of this subparagraph may be satisfied by an insurer possessing less than $15 million the minimum capital and surplus upon an affirmative finding of acceptability by the Director of the Department of Consumer and Business Services. The finding will be based upon such factors as quality of management, capital and surplus of any parent company, company underwriting profit and investment income

trends, market availability and company record and reputation within the industry. In no event shall the director make an affirmative finding of acceptability when the surplus lines nonadmitted insurer's capital and surplus is less than $4.5 million.

2. If an alien insurer, must maintain the requirements of 1. and additionally, must maintain with the United States an irrevocable trust fund in either a national bank or a member of the Federal Reserve System, in an amount not less than $5.4 million.

3. In the case of a group of insurers that includes incorporated and individual unincorporated underwriters, maintains a trust fund of not less than $100 million as security to the full amount thereof for all policyholders and creditors in the United States of each member of the group, and such trust shall likewise comply with the terms and conditions established in subsection 2. For alien insurers, except that the incorporated members of the group may not be engaged in any business other than underwriting as a member of the group and shall be subject to the same level of solvency regulation and control by the group's domiciliary regulators as are the unincorporated members.

4. In the case of an insurance exchange created by the laws of individual states, maintains capital and surplus, or the substantial equivalent thereof, of not less than $75 million in the aggregate. For insurance exchanges that maintain funds for the protection of all insurance exchange policyholders, each individual syndicate shall maintain minimum capital and surplus, or the substantial equivalent thereof, of not less than $5 million. If the insurance exchange does not maintain funds for the protection of all insurance exchange policyholders, each individual syndicate maintain the requirements in 1.

5. Is listed on the NAIC Quarterly Listing of Alien Insurers maintained by the National Association of Insurance Commissioners and meets additional requirements regarding the use of the list established by rule of the director. (O.R.S. §735.415).

Notice. All surplus lines contracts must bear the name of the licensee and the following legend in bold typeface:

> "This insurance was procured and developed under the Oregon Surplus Lines laws. It is not covered by the provisions of ORS 734.510 to 734.710 relating to the Oregon Insurance Guaranty Association. If the insurer issuing this insurance becomes insolvent, the Oregon Insurance Guaranty Association has no obligation to pay claims under this evidence of insurance." (O.R.S. §735.435).

Evidence of Coverage. Upon placing surplus lines insurance on an Oregon home state risk the surplus lines licensee must promptly deliver to the insured or the producing insurance producer the policy, or if such policy is not then available, a certificate, cover note or binder. The certificate, cover note or binder must be executed by the surplus lines licensee and must show the description and location of the subject of the insurance, coverages including any material limitations other than those in standard forms, a general description of the coverages of the insurance, the premium and rate charged and taxes to be collected from the insured, and the name and address of the insured and surplus lines insurer or insurers and proportion of the entire risk assumed by each, and the name of the surplus lines licensee and the licensee's license number. (O.R.S. §735.435(1)).

Records. Each surplus lines licensee is required to keep a full and true record of each surplus lines insurance contract placed on an Oregon home state risk, including a copy of the policy, certificate, cover note or other evidence of insurance showing the amount of the insurance and perils insured; a brief description of the property insured and its location; the gross premium charged; any return premium paid; the rate of premium charged upon the several items of property; the effective date of the contract and the terms thereof; the name and address of the insured; the name and address of the insurer; the amount of tax and other sums to be collected from the insured; and the identity of the producing insurance producer, any confirming correspondence from the insurer or its representative and the application.

The record of each contract must be kept open at all reasonable times to examination by the Director of the Department of Consumer and Business Services without notice for a period not less than five years following termination of the contract. (O.R.S. §735.460).

Individual Policy Reports. Within ninety days after the placing of any surplus lines insurance in Oregon on an Oregon home state risk, each surplus lines licensee must file with the Director of the Department of Consumer and Business Services a statement signed by the licensee regarding the insurance, which must be kept confidential, including the name and address of the insured; the identity of the insurer or insurers; a description of the subject and location of the risk; the amount of premium charged for the insurance; and such other pertinent information as the director may reasonably require. (O.R.S. §735.425).

Monthly Reports. On or before the end of each month, each surplus lines licensee must file with the Director of the Department of Consumer and Business Services, as prescribed by the director, a verified report of all surplus lines insurance transacted on Oregon home state risks during the preceding ninety days. The report need not show transacted surplus lines insurance that was reported in an earlier report. The report must show the aggregate gross premiums written; the aggregate return premiums; and the amount of aggregate tax. (ORS §735.465 (1)).

Diligent Effort Statements. Surplus lines producers are required to file a statement on a standardized form as to the diligent efforts made to place coverage with admitted insurers and the results thereof. The statement must be signed by the producing surplus lines insurance producer and must affirm that the insured was expressly advised prior to placement of the insurance that the surplus lines insurer with whom the insurance was to be placed is not licensed in this state and is not subject to its supervision; and in the event of the insolvency of the surplus lines insurer, losses will not be paid by the state insurance guaranty fund. The necessary form is available on the Oregon Surplus Lines Association Website at http://www.oregonsla.org/. (O.R.S. §735.425(1)(b)).

H. Independently Procured Insurance: Each insured in this state who obtains independently procured insurance, or continues or renews independently procured insurance on Oregon home state risks, other than insurance procured through a surplus lines licensee, must file, within thirty days after the date the insurance was procured, continued or renewed, a written report with the Director of the Department of Consumer and Business Services showing the name and address of the insurer; the subject of the insurance; the amount of premium currently charged; and any additional pertinent information reasonably requested by the director.

Taxes. At the time of filing the report, each independently insured must pay the director an amount equal to 2 percent of the gross premiums reported. The filing of the report and payment of the taxes may be made by a person authorized by the insured to act on the insured's behalf. (O.R.S. §735.417).

NRRA Implementation

I. Compact: None.

J. Definitions:

1. "Home State" means, with respect to an insured:

    a. The state in which an insured maintains the insured's principal place of business or, in the case of an individual, the individual's principal residence.

    b. If 100 percent of the insured risk is located out of the state described in paragraph (a) of this subsection, the state to which the greatest percentage of the insured's taxable premium for that insurance contract is allocated.

    c. If two or more insureds from an affiliated group are named as insureds on a single nonadmitted insurance contract, the state, as determined pursuant to paragraph (a) or (b) of this subsection, of the member of the affiliated group that has the greatest percentage of premium attributed to it under the insurance contract. (O.R.S. §735.405 (8)).

K. Statutory References: Oregon Revised Statutes §§735.400 through 735.495; 744.058 through 744.072; Oregon Administrative Code 836-071-0260 through 836-071-0277.

PENNSYLVANIA

A. Resident Licensing: Resident surplus lines license applicants must first be licensed as property and casualty producers to place surplus lines insurance with nonadmitted insurers. Applicants must submit a properly completed license application on a form supplied by the Department and pass the Pennsylvania surplus lines examination. In addition, applicants must pay an initial licensing fee of $200. Surplus lines licenses expire every two years on the last day of the birth month of the licensee. The biennial renewal fee is $200. Failure to renew license prior to the expiration date will result in $400 penalty. (40 P.S. §991.1615).

B. Nonresident Licensing: Nonresident surplus lines license applicants must first be licensed as property and casualty producers to place surplus lines insurance with nonadmitted insurers. Nonresidents must also be licensed in good standing as surplus lines producers in their home state, which must offer Pennsylvania resident surplus lines producers the ability to be licensed as surplus lines producers in that state on a reciprocal basis. (https://www.insurance.pa.gov/Licensees/MaintainYourLicense/Pages/Insurance-Producer-Non-Resident-Individual.aspx).

C. Business Licensing: To be eligible as a surplus lines licensee in Pennsylvania, business entities must designate officers or partners who hold surplus lines licenses to be responsible for compliance; provide a list of surplus lines licensees placing business through the entity; and submit a $200 fee. Business entity surplus lines licenses expire biennially on the last day of the month in which it was originally issued. The biennial renewal fee is $200. (40 P.S. §991.1615).

D. Diligent Effort: Within thirty days after the surplus lines licensee has placed insurance with an eligible surplus lines insurer, the producer must execute and forward to the surplus lines licensee a written statement on form 1609-PR (REV. 08/12) (Declaration by the Producer) declaring that a diligent effort to procure the desired coverage from admitted insurers was made. The surplus lines licensee must file this form, along with the surplus lines affidavit form 1609-SLL, with the Insurance Department within forty-five days after the insurance has been placed in an eligible surplus lines insurer. Forms may be downloaded from the Surplus Lines Association's Website at http://www.pasla.org (40 P.S. §991.1609).

Commercial Purchaser Exemption. The diligent search, the 25 percent limitation and reporting requirements do not apply to placements of insurance with nonadmitted insurers for an exempt commercial purchaser if both:

1. The surplus lines licensee procuring or placing the surplus lines insurance has disclosed to the exempt commercial purchaser that the insurance may be available from the admitted market that may provide greater protection with more regulatory oversight.

2. The exempt commercial purchaser has subsequently requested in writing the surplus lines licensee to procure or place the insurance from a nonadmitted insurer. (40 P.S. §991.1610).

E. **Tax:** A tax of 3 percent is levied on all premiums charged for insurance which is placed with either an eligible surplus lines insurer, other than a risk retention group, or other nonadmitted insurer. The tax is based on the gross premiums charged less any return premiums and is in addition to the full amount of the gross premiums charged by the insurer for the insurance. The tax on any unearned portion of the premium must be returned to the insured. Neither the surplus lines licensee nor the writing producer is permitted to pay directly or indirectly the tax or any portion thereof, either as an inducement to the insured to purchase the insurance or for any other reason. (40 P.S. §991.1621).

Multi-State Premium Tax Allocation. In the event that a placement of insurance involves insurance resident, located or to be performed in one or more states other than Pennsylvania, then the premium taxes provided for in this section will be levied according to the following:

1. For policies placed before July 1, 2011, only on that portion of the premium reasonably ascribable to that portion of the risk situated in Pennsylvania.

2. For policies placed after June 30, 2011, upon the gross premium charged less any return premiums where Pennsylvania is the home state of the insured. (40 P.S. §991.1621).

F. **Stamping Fee:** Stamping fees for filings received within forty-five days before the effective date of the placement will carry a stamping fee of $20 per filing. The fee is payable by the insured and remitted by the surplus lines licensee to the Pennsylvania Surplus Lines Association (PSLA). Stamping fees for filings received after forty-five days of the effective date of the placement will carry a stamping fee of $45 per filing. $20 of the fee is to be payable by the insured with the remaining $25 payable by the surplus lines licensee. The entire fee is to be remitted by the surplus lines licensee to PSLA. See PLSA Bulletins 2007-10-26, 2010-10-13 and 2016-14-10 at http://www.pasla.org/psla_bulletins_date.htm. (http://www.pasla.org/stampingfee_faq.htm).

G. **Other Requirements or Restrictions:** Surplus lines insurance must be placed through a Pennsylvania licensed surplus lines agent. The Pennsylvania Insurance Department does not permit courtesy or accommodation filings. The department maintains a list of eligible surplus lines insurers.

Eligibility. Surplus lines licensees may place nonadmitted insurance with foreign insurers that are eligible in Pennsylvania provided that the insurer is authorized to write the type of insurance in its domiciliary jurisdiction and has capital and surplus or its equivalent under the laws of its domiciliary jurisdiction which is greater than or equal to $15 million. The requirement of this subparagraph may be satisfied by an insurer possessing less than the minimum capital and surplus upon an affirmative finding of acceptability by the commissioner. The finding will be based upon such factors as quality of management, capital and surplus of any parent company, company underwriting profit and investment income trends, market availability and company record and reputation within the industry. In no event will the commissioner make an affirmative finding of acceptability when the nonadmitted insurer's capital and surplus is less than $4.5 million. (40 P.S. §991.1605).

Notice. All surplus lines contracts shall bear the name of the surplus lines licensee and the following legend in ten point type:

> "The insurer which has issued this insurance is not licensed by the Pennsylvania Insurance Department and is subject to limited regulation. This insurance is not covered by the Pennsylvania Property and Casualty Insurance Guaranty Association." (40 P.S. §991.1612(d)).

Annual Reports. Each surplus lines licensee must file a Gross Premium Tax Report (RCT-123) with the Department of Revenue and electronically in PSLA's Electronic Filing System. RCT-123 must report all premiums transacted from the placement of insurance with either an eligible surplus lines insurer or other nonadmitted insurers during the previous calendar year on or before January 31 of each year. The following requirements apply:

1. A remittance of the taxes due must accompany the report.

2. Reports must be made on forms prescribed by the Department of Revenue.

3. The report must set forth the name of the insured, the home state of the insured, if required by the department, identification of the insurer, the type of insurance, gross premiums charged less any return premiums allowed, the tax due as provided in this section and any other information as required by the Department of Revenue.

4. A surplus lines business entity licensee that files the annual premium tax return with the Department of Revenue is required to include in its return the premium taxes generated during the year subject to reporting by all licensees associated with said business entity during the reporting period.

5. Neither the surplus lines licensee nor the writing producer is permitted to pay directly or indirectly the tax or any portion of the tax, either as an inducement to the insured to purchase the insurance or for any other reason.

6. The surplus lines licensee must collect from the insured or the writing producer the amount of the tax at the time of delivery of the initial policy, cover note or other evidence of insurance or at the time thereafter as is reasonably consistent with normal credit terms customary in the business.

7. A penalty will be imposed for failure to file the report required under this subsection on or before the due date. (40 P.S. §991.1621).

   Record Keeping Requirements. Each surplus lines licensee shall keep in its office a full and true record of each surplus lines insurance contract placed by or through it, including a copy of the policy, certificate, cover note or other evidence of insurance. The record of each contract shall be kept open at all reasonable times to examination by the department without notice for a period of not less than five (5) years following termination of the contract. (40 P.S. § 991.1619).

H. **Surplus Lines Association:** Pennsylvania Surplus Lines Association (PSLA) 180 Sheree Boulevard, Suite 3100; Exton, PA 19341. Phone: 610-594-1340. Fax: 610-594-7623. Web site: www.pasla.org.

   The department has contracted with the PSLA to function as a stamping office.

I. **Independently Procured Insurance:**

   1. *Rules.* Independently procured insurance is any insurance directly procured by an insured from a nonadmitted insurer. The insured must report the transaction on forms prescribed by the Department of Revenue within thirty days after the last day of the month in which such insurance was independently procured, continued, or renewed. The tax of 3 percent must be paid on the date the report is due. (40 P.S. §§991.1602 and 991.1622).

NRRA Implementation

J. **Compact:** None.

K. **Definitions:**

   1. Except as provided under paragraph (2), with respect to an insured, "home state" means:

      a. The state in which an insured maintains its principal place of business or, in the case of an individual, the individual's principal residence.

b. If 100 percent of the insured risk is located out of the state referred to under subparagraph (a), the state to which the greatest percentage of the insured's taxable premium for that insurance contract is allocated.

2. If more than one insured from an affiliated group are named insureds on a single nonadmitted insurance contract, the term means the home state, as determined under paragraph (1), of the member of the affiliated group that has the largest percentage of premium attributed to it under the insurance contract. (40 P.S. §991.1602).

L. Statutory References: 40 Pennsylvania Statutes §§991.1601 through 991.1626.

PUERTO RICO

A. **Resident Licensing:** Any licensed resident broker or agent may be licensed to place insurance with nonadmitted insurers. The surplus lines broker's license expires biennially on the birth month of the license holder. Fee: $1,050. Applicant must file bond in the amount specified by the commissioner but not exceeding $25,000. Agents or brokers licensed in Puerto Rico may place business through licensed surplus lines brokers and receive commission. (26 L.P.R.A. §§1011, 1012).

B. **Nonresident Licensing:** Nonresidents may be licensed in Puerto Rico with the same fee and requirements as residents. (26 L.P.R.A. §§951m, 1011).

C. **Diligent Effort:** Affidavit of nonavailability must be filed with the Commissioner for each line at time of procurement using forms designed by the Office of the Commissioner to determine satisfaction of the requirements of 26 L.P.R.A. §1007. The affidavit must also include the following:

(1) Name and address of the insurer and the person to whom the Commissioner may send copies of legal documents;

(2) Number of the policy issued;

(3) Exact name and address of the insured;

(4) Nature and amount of liability assumed by the insurer;

(5) Premium rate charged;

(6) Amount of total premium; and

(7) Any other information required by the Commissioner. (26 L.P.R.A. §1008).

D. **Tax:** 9 percent of gross premium exclusive of tax to be reported and paid by the surplus lines broker within sixty days after procurement. The surplus lines tax is also applicable to any fees levied by the surplus lines broker. The surplus lines broker and the premium charged shall not be subject to taxes under L.P.R.A. Title 26 other than as described in this section. (26 L.P.R.A. §1013).

E. **Stamping Fee:** None. Puerto Rico does not have a surplus lines stamping office.

F. **Other Requirements or Restrictions:** Surplus lines insurance may not be used to obtain better rate or terms (26 L.P.R.A. §1007). Only nonadmitted insurers approved by the commissioner may be used, except the commissioner may approve other insurers based on supplementary affidavit when coverage from the approved list is exhausted or unavailable (26 L.P.R.A. §1007a). Aircraft and marine insurance are not exempt from the surplus lines laws (26 L.P.R.A. §1001).

Notice. All surplus lines contracts must provide for service of legal process as required in 26 L.P.R.A. §1018, bear the name of or be initialed by the surplus lines broker, and be stamped with the following message:

> "This contract is registered and delivered as a surplus line coverage under the Insurance Code of the Commonwealth of Puerto Rico." (26 L.P.R.A. §1009).

Records. Upon the commissioner's order, any person in Puerto Rico who is the insured under any policy issued by an unauthorized insurer upon a subject of insurance resident, located, or to be performed in Puerto Rico at the time the policy was issued, shall produce for examination all policies and other documents evidencing and relating to the insurance, and shall disclose the amount of the gross premiums paid or agreed to be paid for the insurance, through whom the insurance was procured, and such other information relative to the placing of such insurance as may reasonably be required. (26 L.P.R.A. §1017). Producers must keep a full record of the circumstances and details of each surplus line contract procured and of related subsequent matters for at least five years from the date of the contract. (26 L.P.R.A. §1007a).

Reports. Any insured, residing in Puerto Rico, who transacts or causes to transact insurance relative to a subject of insurance, residing, located or to be performed in Puerto Rico with an unauthorized insurer, except unauthorized insurers eligible pursuant to 26 L.P.R.A. §1007a, must, within thirty days after having transacted such insurance, file with the commissioner a report containing the following: (a) name and address of the insured; (b) name and address of the insurer; (c) subject of the insurance; (d) description of the coverage; (e) total amount of the premium charged; (f) aliquot part of the premium corresponding to a subject of insurance resident, located or to be performed in Puerto Rico, if it also covers subjects of insurance residing, located or to be performed outside Puerto Rico; (g) Any additional information required by the commissioner. (26 L.P.R.A. §1020).

Within sixty days after a surplus line coverage has been procured, the producer shall file with the commissioner a report thereof for tax purposes, stating the names and addresses of the insurer and the insured, the policy number and date of issue, the amount of premium received, and the computation and amount of tax due. (26 L.P.R.A. §1013). For those who choose the option to make a lump payment within sixty days of the end of the year, instead of within sixty days of coverage, a guarantee bond or certificate of deposit with the Secretary of the Treasury of the greater between 10 percent of the total surplus lines insurance during the previous calendar year and $25,000 is required. "It is important to emphasize that this bond does not substitute nor is it equivalent to the bond required for obtaining the Surplus Lines Broker license." The Commissioner requires that, from the date of the ruling letter (5/26/2016), brokers pay the additional bond at the time of filing the annual report with this Office. (Ruling Letter CN-2016-201-AG).

G. Surplus Lines Association: None.

H. Independently Procured Insurance:

1. *Rules.* Such insurance is allowed in Puerto Rico. The insured may be placed with an unlicensed insurer or an unauthorized surplus lines carrier, the transaction must be reported to the Department of Insurance, and the insured is responsible for the declaration of the coverage and the payment of the 15 percent tax on the total premium, within thirty days of the effective date. The payment must be through a certified check to the Secretary of the Treasury. A surplus lines broker may not take part in this placement. The rules described herein are not applicable to disability or life insurance. (26 L.P.R.A. §1020).

2. *Industrial Insured Exemption.* Puerto Rico has no industrial insured exemption.

NRRA Implementation

Puerto Rico was a member of NIMA, which dissolved in December of 2017. Please check with the Department of Insurance regarding changes in procedures during this process.

I. Statutory References:

26 L.P.R.A. §§	951m
	1001, 1007 to 1009
	1011 to 1013, 1017
	1020

Ruling Letter	CN-2016-201-AG

RHODE ISLAND

A. **Resident Licensing:** The insurance commissioner may issue a surplus lines broker's license to any resident person actively licensed in Rhode Island as a property and casualty insurance producer, except life and health and accident. (R.I. Gen. Laws §27-3-38). The initial licensing and biennial fee is $100. (230 RICR 020-50-1). Rhode Island resident applicants must complete and hold a bond of $25,000. (R.I. Gen. Laws §27-3-39). Rhode Island surplus lines broker's licenses are issued for a term of two years and expire on the same date as the active Rhode Island property and casualty insurance producer license. The biennial license renewal fee is $100, comprised of $50 per license year. (R.I. Gen. Laws §27-3-42). Licensees may renew the license up to thirty days past the expiration date at $100; renewal more than thirty days late requires $150. Resident applicants may apply for and renew Rhode Island surplus lines broker's licenses online at http://www.nipr.com.

A Rhode Island business entity acting as a surplus lines broker may elect to obtain a surplus lines broker license. Application must be made using the uniform business entity application. Prior to approving the application, the commissioner must find that the business entity applicant has paid the appropriate initial licensing fees and that it has designated a licensed surplus lines broker responsible for the business entity's compliance with the insurance laws and rules of Rhode Island. (R.I. Gen. Laws §27-3-38). To apply for or renew a license see http://www.nipr.com/.

B. **Nonresident Licensing:** The insurance commissioner may issue a surplus lines broker's license to any nonresident person actively licensed in Rhode Island as a property and casualty insurance producer. The initial licensing fee is $100. Nonresident applicants residing in California must complete and hold a surplus lines broker bond of $25,000. All other nonresident applicants are not required to file a surplus lines broker bond. Rhode Island surplus lines broker's licenses are issued for a term of two years and expire on the same date as the active Rhode Island property and casualty insurance producer license. The biennial license renewal fee is $100, comprised of $50 per license year (R.I. Gen. Laws §27-3-42). Licensees may renew the license up to thirty days past the expiration date at $100; renewal more than thirty days late requires $150. Nonresident applicants may apply for and renew Rhode Island surplus lines broker's licenses online at www.nipr.com.

C. **Diligent Effort:** When any surplus lines policy of insurance is procured under the authority of a surplus lines broker's license, there must be executed, both by the licensee and by the insured, affidavits setting forth facts showing that the insured or a licensed Rhode Island producer were unable, after diligent effort, to procure from no less than three admitted insurers the full amount of insurance required to protect the property owned or controlled by the insured or the risks insured. The aforementioned affidavit shall not be required when insuring the following interests: amusement parks and devices, environmental improvement and/or remediation sites, vacant property or property under renovation, demolition operations, event cancellation due to weather, railroad liability, discontinued products, fireworks and pyrotechnics, warehouseman's legal liability, excess property coverage, private flood, and contingent liability. (R.I. Gen. Laws §27-3-38).

Commercial Purchaser Exemption. Surplus lines brokers seeking to procure or place nonadmitted insurance on behalf of an "exempt commercial purchaser" are not required to perform a diligent search or file an affidavit if both:

1. The broker has disclosed to the exempt commercial purchaser that insurance may or may not be available from the admitted market that may provide greater protection with more regulatory oversight.

2. The exempt commercial purchaser has subsequently requested in writing for the broker to procure or place such insurance from a nonadmitted insurer. (R.I. Gen. Laws §27-3-38).

D. Tax: 4 percent. Gross premiums charged for surplus lines insurance, less any return premiums, are subject to a tax at the rate of 4 percent, payable annually on April 1. (R.I. Gen. Laws §27-3-38).

Multi-state Insurance Premium Tax: Where the insurance covers properties, risks or exposures located or to be performed both in and out of this state, the sum payable must be computed based on:

1. An amount equal to 4 percent on that portion of the gross premiums allocated to this state; plus

2. An amount equal to the portion of the premiums allocated to other states or territories on the basis of the tax rates and fees applicable to properties, risks or exposures located or to be performed outside of this state.

   The commissioner is authorized to participate in a multi-state surplus lines agreement for the purpose of collecting and disbursing to reciprocal states any funds collected applicable to other properties, risks or exposures located or to be performed outside of Rhode Island. To the extent that other states where portions of the properties, risks or exposures reside have failed to enter into compact or reciprocal allocation procedure with Rhode Island, the net premium tax collected will be retained by this state. (R.I. Gen. Laws §27-3-38.1).

E. **Stamping Fee:** None.

F. **Other Requirements or Restrictions:** The use of surplus lines to obtain a better rate or more favorable terms of coverage is not permitted. Only nonadmitted insurers on the commissioner's approved list are permitted to be used. Surplus lines laws are not applicable to life insurance, disability, accident, or health insurance.

Eligibility. Surplus lines insurance may be placed by a surplus lines broker if each insurer is authorized to write the type of insurance in its domiciliary jurisdiction. A surplus lines licensee is not permitted to place coverage with a nonadmitted insurer, unless, at the time of placement, the nonadmitted insurer has established satisfactory evidence of good repute and financial integrity and has capital and surplus, or its equivalent under the laws of its domiciliary jurisdiction, which equals the greater of the minimum capital and surplus requirements under the law of Rhode Island or $15 million. The capital and surplus requirements above may be satisfied by an insurer possessing less than the minimum capital and surplus upon an affirmative finding of acceptability by the commissioner. The finding will be based upon such factors as quality of management, capital and surplus of any parent company, company underwriting profit and investment income trends, market availability and company record and reputation within the industry. In no event shall the commissioner make an affirmative finding of acceptability when the nonadmitted insurer's capital and surplus is less than $4.5 million. (R.I. Gen. Laws §27-3-40).

Notice. Every application form for insurance from a surplus lines insurer, every affidavit form executed by the insured, and every policy (on its front and declaration pages) issued by the surplus lines insurer, must contain in ten-point type the following notice:

> "THIS INSURANCE CONTRACT HAS BEEN PLACED WITH AN INSURER NOT LICENSED TO DO BUSINESS IN THE STATE OF RHODE ISLAND BUT APPROVED AS A SURPLUS LINES INSURER. THE INSURER IS NOT A MEMBER OF THE RHODE ISLAND INSURERS INSOLVENCY FUND. SHOULD THE INSURER BECOME INSOLVENT, THE PROTECTION AND BENEFITS OF THE RHODE ISLAND INSURANCE INSOLVENCY FUND ARE NOT AVAILABLE." (R.I. Gen. Laws §27-3-38).

Courtesy filings are not accepted in Rhode Island.

Additional Fees. Surplus lines producers may charge fees in addition to commissions only when such fees are not included in the premium and are reasonably appropriate to cover underwriting expenses that are unique to a surplus lines agency. Additional fees must be fully disclosed to the insured in writing prior to the sale. The disclosure information must be retained by the producer for a period of three years following the expiration of the policy. (230 RICR 020-50-1).

Records. Licensees must keep a complete and separate record of all policies procured from approved surplus lines insurers under the license. These records must be kept open to the examination of both the insurance commissioner and tax administrator at all reasonable times and must show: the exact amount of each kind of insurance permitted under this section which has been procured for each insured; the gross premiums and fees charged by the insurers or brokers for each kind of insurance permitted under this section which were returned to each insured; the name of the insurer or insurers which issued each of these policies, the effective dates of these policies; and the terms for which these policies were issued. (R.I. Gen. Laws §27-3-38).

Annual Reports. Licensees are required to file two separate reports with the insurance commissioner: Reports must be filed electronically to dbr.specialreports@dbr.ri.gov. (R.I. Gen. Laws §27-3-38).

1. *Surplus Line Broker Annual Report.* On a form prescribed by the insurance commissioner showing the business procured under the surplus line license for the preceding calendar year, and the report is due annually on or before April 1 (when surplus line premium taxes are due). (230 RICR 020-50-1).

2. *Lead Liability Coverage Report.* Surplus Line Brokers shall file an annual lead liability coverage report on an individual licensee basis utilizing the respective form provided in Insurance Regulation 11, Section 7, Exhibit B.

(R.I. Gen. Laws §27-3-38; 230 RICR 020-50-1).

G. Surplus Lines Association: None.

I. Independently Procured Insurance:

Each insured in Rhode Island who procures, continues, or renews insurance with an insurer not licensed to do any insurance business in Rhode Island on properties, risks, or exposures located or to be performed in whole or in part in Rhode Island, other than insurance procured through a surplus lines licensee, must, within thirty days after the date the insurance was so procured, continued, or renewed, file a written report with the tax administrator, on forms prescribed by the tax administrator, showing the insured's name and address, the insurer's name and address, the subject of the insurance, a general description of the coverage, the amount of premium currently charged, and additional pertinent information reasonably requested by the tax administrator. The gross premiums charged for the insurance are subject to a 4 percent tax, which is due when filing the report. (RI Gen. Laws §27-3-38.1).

If an independently procured policy covers properties, risks or exposures only partially located or to be performed in Rhode Island, the tax payable by the insured will be computed on the portion of the premium properly attributable to the properties, risks or exposures located or to be performed in Rhode Island based on:

1. An amount equal to 4 percent on that portion of the gross premiums allocated to this state; plus

2. An amount equal to the portion of the premiums allocated to other states or territories on the basis of the tax rates and fees applicable to properties, risks or exposures located or to be performed outside of this state. (RI Gen. Laws §27-3-38.1).

NRRA Implementation

J. Compact: SLIMPACT

K. Definitions:

1. With respect to an insured, "home state" means:

   a. The state in which an insured maintains its principal place of business or, in the case of an individual, the individual's principal residence; or

   b. If 100 percent of the insured risk is located out of the state referred to in (1)(a), the state to which the greatest percentage of the insured's taxable premium for that insurance contract is allocated.

2. "Principal place of business" means, with respect to determining the home state of the insured:

   a. The state where the insured maintains its headquarters and where the insured's high level officers direct, control and coordinate the business activities; or

   b. If the insured's high-level officers direct, control and coordinate the business activities in more than one state, the state in which the greatest percentage of the insured's taxable premium for that insurance contract is allocated; or

   c. If the insured maintains its headquarters or the insured's high-level officers direct, control and coordinate the business activities outside any state, the state to which the greatest percentage of the insured's taxable premium for that insurance contract is allocated.

3. "Principal residence" means, with respect to determining the home state of the insured, (i) the state where the insured resides for the greatest number of days during a calendar years; or (ii) if the insured's principal residence is located outside any state, the state to which the greatest percentage of the insured's taxable premium for that insurance contract is allocated.

4. "Affiliated groups." If more than one insured from an affiliated group are named insureds on a single nonadmitted insurance contract, the term "home state" means the home state, as determined above, of the member of the affiliated group that has the largest percentage of premium attributed to it under such insurance contract. (R.I. Gen. Laws §27-3-38.2).

L. **Statutory References:** Rhode Island Gen. Laws §§27-3-38 through 27-3-42; 27-75; Code of Rhode Island Rules 02 030 011 and 02 030 103; and Insurance Regulations 11, 103 and 110.

SOUTH CAROLINA

A. Resident Licensing: Any licensed resident surplus lines broker may do business with nonadmitted insurers on the department's approved list. The applicant must pass a state broker licensing examination, file a $10,000 bond, available at https://doi.sc.gov/575/Surplus-Lines-Broker, and pay the $200 biennial fee, due in May of even numbered years. (https://doi.sc.gov/575/Surplus-Lines-Broker). Surplus lines brokers may place surplus lines for other brokers and pay commission. Residents can apply online at www.doi.sc.gov. Renewal is in May of even numbered years. Brokers may renew online at http://doi.sc.gov or www.nipr.com. (S.C. Code Ann. §38-45-20).

Fingerprinting is not required at every renewal. If a resident producer was fingerprinted at initial licensure or for the most recent compliance period, fingerprints are not required again so long as the license remains active. (https://doi.sc.gov/354/Licensing-CE).

B. Nonresident Licensing: In order for an applicant to qualify for a nonresident surplus lines broker's license in South Carolina, the applicant must be licensed as a surplus lines broker in the home state or have the excess or surplus line of authority. Nonresidents may apply online at www.nipr.com. (S.C. Code Ann. §38-45-30; https://doi.sc.gov/575/Surplus-Lines-Broker).

C. Diligent Effort: Every insurance broker who sells an insurance policy written or issued by an insurer not licensed to do business in South Carolina is personally liable for the limits of the coverage provided for in the policy if the broker fails to comply with the provisions of the surplus lines insurance law relating to policies issued by insurers not licensed to do business in South Carolina. (S.C. Code Ann. §38-45-120).

Commercial Purchaser Exemption. Surplus lines brokers seeking to procure or place nonadmitted insurance on behalf of an "exempt commercial purchaser" are not required to perform a diligent search if both:

1. The broker has disclosed to the exempt commercial purchaser that insurance may or may not be available from the admitted market that may provide greater protection with more regulatory oversight.

2. The exempt commercial purchaser has subsequently requested in writing for the broker to procure or place such insurance from a nonadmitted insurer. (S.C. Code Ann. §38-45-90).

D. Tax: Six percent; South Carolina is collecting a 6 percent blended tax rate. This 6 percent blended tax rate includes the 4 percent state tax and the 2 percent municipality tax.

Surplus lines brokers will no longer have to pay two separate entities. (S.C. Code Ann. §38-45-10(13)).

The South Carolina Department of Insurance will collect 100 percent of the blended tax rate of 6 percent on premiums written and policy fees paid if South Carolina is the home state of the insured. Payment must be made within thirty days after March 31, June 30, September 30, and December 31 each year. (S.C. Code Ann. §38-45-20(5)).

Questions regarding premium and tax returns should be addressed to Sharon Waddell at swaddell@doi.sc.gov or 803-737-4910, or Angela Davis at adavis@doi.sc.gov or 803-737-6279.

E. **Stamping Fee:** None. South Carolina does not have a stamping office.

F. **Other Requirements or Restrictions:** All brokers doing any kind of insurance business in South Carolina must make and keep a full and correct record of the business done by them, showing the number, date, term, amount insured, premiums, and the person to whom issued of every policy or certificate of renewal. The information from these records must be furnished to the director or his designee on demand and the original books or records are open to the inspection of the director or his designee on demand. These records must be kept for a minimum of five years. The director or his designee may examine broker records, with the costs of such examination to be borne by the broker. (S.C. Code. Ann. §38-45-80).

No policy fee may be charged by a broker unless it is a reasonable fee, it is made part of the contract, and the 4 percent broker's premium tax is paid upon the policy fee. If for any reason the director disapproves the placement or the insurer ultimately refuses to write the risk, the broker shall immediately refund the full policy fee to the policyholder. (S.C. Code Ann. §38-45-160).

The following must be written or stamped on the face of each surplus lines contract:

> "This company has been approved by the director or his designee of the South Carolina Department of Insurance to write business in this state as an eligible surplus lines insurer, but it is not afforded guaranty fund protection." (S.C. Code Ann. §38-45-110).

Life and health (except stop-loss coverage in connection with self-insured programs), private passenger auto liability, and workers compensation insurance may not be placed with nonadmitted insurers.

Eligibility. South Carolina has no eligibility requirements, therefore under NRRA brokers are permitted to place nonadmitted insurance with U.S. domestic insurers that are eligible in South Carolina provided they are authorized to write such business in their state of domicile and maintain minimum capital and surplus of $15 million or the minimum capital and surplus amount required in the state, whichever is greater. NRRA allows brokers to place business with non-U.S. carriers that are included on the NAIC's Quarterly Listing of Alien Insurers.

G. Surplus Lines Association: No association.

H. Independently Procured Insurance:

1. *Rules.* South Carolina has no statutes regarding independently procured insurance.

2. *Industrial Insured Exemption.* Must have a full-time employee acting as an insurance/risk manager or utilize the services of a regularly and continuously qualified insurance consultant, must have at least twenty-five full-time employees, and annual aggregate premiums for insurance on all risks total at least $25,000. (S.C. Code Ann. §38-25-150(8)).

NRRA Implementation

I. Compact: None.

J. Definitions: Home State. Under the NRRA, South Carolina is the "home state" if the insured maintains its principal place of business or, in the case of an individual, the individual's principal residence here. South Carolina's requirements regarding the placement of such business will apply if South Carolina is considered the home state. However, if 100 percent of the insured risk is located outside of South Carolina, then the home state is the state to which the greatest percentage of the insured's taxable premium for that insurance contract is allocated. With respect to an affiliated group, if more than one insured from the affiliated group is a named insured on a single nonadmitted insurance contract, the home state is that of the member of the affiliated group that has the largest percentage of premium attributed to the member under the insurance contract.

K. References:

S.C. Code Ann. §§38-	25-150
	45-10 to 45-30, 80, 90, 110, 120, 160

Web References:

https://doi.sc.gov/575/Surplus-Lines-Broker.

https://doi.sc.gov/354/Licensing-CE.

SOUTH DAKOTA

A. **Resident Licensing:** Only licensed insurance producers are eligible to be licensed as surplus lines brokers. (SDCL §58-32-7). Resident producers, licensed as surplus lines brokers, may be authorized to place P&C insurance with non-admitted insurers. The surplus lines broker's license expires by end of birth month biennially. (SDCL §58-30-121). License fee is $50 and renewal fee is $100. (SDCL §58-2-29). Resident applicants must file $2,000 bond within thirty days of license being issued. (SDCL §58-32-10.1). Any South Dakota licensed producer may place business through licensed surplus lines brokers and receive commission. (SDCL §58-32-15).

B. **Nonresident Licensing:** Only licensed insurance producers are eligible to be licensed as surplus lines brokers. Nonresident producers, licensed as surplus lines brokers, may be authorized to place P&C insurance with non-admitted insurers. The surplus lines broker's license expires by end of birth month biennially. (SDCL §58-30-121). License fee is $50 and renewal fee is $100. (SDCL §58-2-29). Any South Dakota licensed producer may place business through licensed surplus lines brokers and receive commission. (SDCL §58-2-29).

C. **Diligent Effort:** At the time of procuring, effecting, and issuing surplus line insurance, the broker must execute an affidavit, setting forth facts from which it can be determined whether such insurance was eligible for export. The broker must file this affidavit with the director within thirty days after the insurance was procured. This is subject to change for multistate risks due to multi-state agreement reporting requirements. (SDCL §58-32-20 and SDCL §58-32-17).

   Surplus lines broker reports business written due to non-availability through an admitted insurer on the surplus lines broker's affidavit, available only to licensed surplus lines brokers upon licensure or on request from the Producer Licensing Section of the Division of Insurance. Available online at http://dlr.sd.gov/insurance.

   Commercial Purchaser Exemption. Diligent efforts requirements do not apply to exempt commercial lines policyholders if both:

   1. The broker procuring or placing the surplus lines insurance has disclosed to the exempt commercial purchaser that the insurance may or may not be available from the admitted market that may provide greater protection with more regulatory oversight.

   2. The exempt commercial purchaser has subsequently requested in writing the broker to procure or place the insurance from a non-admitted insurer. (SDCL §58-32-16).

D. **Tax:** Tax is 2.5 percent of gross premiums, except fire, and 3 percent for fire premiums collected. See the Premium Tax Report for specifics on how to calculate the fire premium tax. Taxes are normally due on April 1 each year. However, if in any prior calendar year, a broker collects and remits in excess of $5,000 of surplus lines premium tax, the broker must in the following year remit surplus line taxes on a quarterly basis. (SDCL §58-32-44).

Multi-State Surplus Lines Policies. After the passage of the Non-admitted and Reinsurance Reform Act (NRRA), South Dakota enacted enabling legislation to join multistate agreements concerning surplus lines insurance and became a signatory to the Non-admitted Insurance Multi-State Agreement (NIMA). NIMA functions to provide uniform filing and allocation of surplus lines premium tax when a NIMA participating state is the "Home State" under the provisions of the NRRA and the policy includes premium for an exposure in more than one state/territory, regardless of NIMA participation status.

For multi-state surplus lines policies, the affidavit requirement in South Dakota is satisfied by accurately supplying the required information at the SLAS Clearinghouse at www.slasclearinghouse.com.

The SLAS Clearinghouse Website contains information, training opportunities, filing instructions and contact information.

South Dakota brokers need to complete the Clearinghouse Registration Form and submit this to the Clearinghouse to file policies.

Additional information can be found in Bulletin 12-03 and 12-06.

Premium Defined. South Dakota law defines "premium" as "the consideration for insurance by whatever name called." Any assessment, or any membership, policy, survey, inspection, service, or similar fee or other charge in consideration for an insurance contract is deemed part of the premium. (SDCL §58-11-1).

Single State Surplus Lines Policies. The division requires all surplus lines premium tax filings to be filed with the Florida Surplus Lines Service Office Clearinghouse. All South Dakota surplus lines tax reporting and remittance will take place through the SLAS Clearinghouse website. Brokers are no longer required to file affidavits or surplus lines broker premium tax reports with the division on surplus lines policies. This requirement is met by accurately supplying the required information at the SLAS Clearinghouse website. Brokers must report surplus lines business to the Clearinghouse within thirty days of the effective date of the policy. In order to file policies, South Dakota brokers need to register with the Clearinghouse at its website. The Clearinghouse Website is http://www.slasclearinghouse.com. Due to NIMA dissolution, reporting of multi-state surplus lines risks will cease effective 9/30/16. Endorsements and cancellations can be reported until September 30, 2017. South Dakota will continue to utilize the clearinghouse operated by the Florida Surplus

Lines Service Office for all surplus lines filings where South Dakota is the Home State. More information can also be found on the department Web site at http://dlr.sd.gov/insurance.

The SLAS Clearinghouse will prepare invoices the first business day after a quarter ends; they have forty-five days to pay the invoices. The Clearinghouse will email an invoice with payment instructions to the producer. The division will no longer accept checks. Filing with the Clearinghouse fulfills the requirements of the tax reports.

Additional information can be found in Bulletins 12-06 and 16-05.

Insurance companies will continue to file with the division using the designated forms.

E. **Stamping Fee:** None.

F. **Other Requirements or Restrictions:** Use of non-admitted insurers not meeting the eligibility requirements described below is prohibited. Books and records must be kept for five years and are subject to audit by the division.

Notice. All surplus lines contracts must be initialed by or bear the name of procuring surplus lines broker and be stamped with the following in at least ten point or larger boldface type:

> "THIS INSURANCE CONTRACT IS ISSUED BY A NONADMITTED INSURER WHICH IS NOT LICENSED BY NOR UNDER THE JURISDICTION OF THE SOUTH DAKOTA INSURANCE DIRECTOR." (SDCL §58-32-32).

Life and health insurance, annuities, worker's compensation, or reinsurance may not be written by non-admitted insurers.

Annual Statements. A non-admitted insurer writing business in South Dakota is required to file an annual statement of business written on a form approved by the director called the Unauthorized Insurer Business Written & Premium Tax Report, along with a copy of Schedule T and the state page from the Annual Statement. (SDCL §58-32-41).

A foreign company is required to submit schedule T or state page.

Exemptions. South Dakota surplus line law does not apply to ocean marine, foreign trade insurance, insurance on railroads engaged in interstate commerce, insurance on aircraft owned by aircraft manufacturers, aircraft operated in commercial interstate flight, cargo on such aircraft, or liability—other than workers compensation or employers liability—arising out of ownership, maintenance, or use of such aircraft. (SDCL §58-32-5).

An alien company is required to submit NAIC/NAIIO annual statement or similar information as submitted to domicile country regulatory agency, written in English with U.S. dollar conversion factors.

Eligibility. Surplus lines insurance may be placed by a surplus lines licensee if the insurer is authorized to write the type of insurance in its domiciliary jurisdiction, and either meets the criteria established through a multi-state agreement or meets one of the following criteria.

1. The insurer has capital and surplus or its equivalent under the laws of its domiciliary jurisdiction which equals the greater of:

    a. The minimum capital and surplus requirements in South Dakota. (SDCL §58-6-23).

    b. $15 million.

    These requirements may be satisfied by an insurer's possessing less than the minimum capital and surplus upon an affirmative finding of acceptability by the director. The finding will be based upon such factors as quality of management, capital and surplus of any parent company, company underwriting profit and investment income trends, market availability, and company record and reputation within the industry. The director may not make an affirmative finding of acceptability if the nonadmitted insurer's capital and surplus is less than $4.5 million. (SDCL §58-32-22).

G. Surplus Lines Association: None.

H. Independently Procured Insurance:

1. *Rules.* Insurance may be procured independently in South Dakota with the insured being responsible for payment of the premium tax of 2.5 percent of the gross premium amount. (SDCL §58-32-50). Beginning January 1, 2013, all new and renewal policies with the effective date of January 1, 2013 need to go through the SLAS Clearinghouse. The SLAS Clearinghouse Web site is: http://www.slasclearinghouse.com. More information can also be found on the Department Website at http://dlr.sd.gov/insurance.

All filings to the Clearinghouse need to still be made within thirty days of the effective date of the policy.

Additional information can be found in Bulletin 12-06.

I. Home State Definition:

1. "Home State" means, with respect to an insured:

   a. The state in which an insured maintains its principal place of business or, in the case of an individual, the individual's principal residence.

   b. If 100 percent of the insured risk is located out of the state referred to in subdivision a of this section, the state to which the greatest percentage of the insured's taxable premium for the insurance contract is allocated.

   If more than one insured from an affiliated group are named insureds on a single non-admitted insurance contract, the term means the home state as determined under subdivision (1) of this section of the member of the affiliated group that has the largest percentage of premium attributable to it under the contract. (SDCL §58-32-3.1).

J. Statutory References: SDCL §§10-44-2; 58-2-29; 58-32-1 through 58-32-58, 58-6A-1.

TENNESSEE

A. Resident Licensing: Applicant must hold a current license in Tennessee. Authorized resident property and casualty producers of admitted companies may be licensed to write surplus lines business through approved nonadmitted insurers. The surplus lines producer's license shall be for a twenty-four month period. New licenses issued on or after January 1, 2012, may be renewed for ensuing periods of twenty-four months expiring on the last day of the producer's birth month. Biannual fee: $120. There is no bond requirement. Forms are available for download at www.nipr.com. (Tenn. Code Ann. §56-14-104).

B. Nonresident Licensing: Nonresidents may be licensed for surplus lines for a twenty-four month period if they hold a nonresident license for Tennessee. Biannual fee of $120 is subject to retaliation. (Tenn. Code Ann. §56-14-104).

C. Diligent Effort: No insurance coverage shall be eligible for surplus lines unless the full amount of insurance required is not procurable, after a diligent effort among the insurers licensed to transact and actually writing that kind and class of insurance in this state, and the amount of insurance eligible for surplus lines shall be only the amount in excess of the amount so procurable from licensed insurers. (Tenn. Code Ann. §56-14-105). Within thirty days of the end of each calendar month, the surplus lines agent shall make an affidavit of nonavailability verifying that the insurance could not be placed in the admitted market after a diligent search. The affidavit shall include an affirmation that the agent is, after diligent effort, unable to procure from an admitted company or admitted companies the full amount of insurance required to protect the interest of the insured for each surplus lines insurance transaction. (Tenn. Code Ann. §56-14-106).

Commercial Purchaser Exemption. A broker is not required to make a diligent effort to determine whether the full amount or type of insurance can be obtained from admitted insurers when the broker has disclosed to the exempt commercial purchaser that such insurance may or may not be available from admitted companies that may provide greater protection with more regulatory oversight, and the exempt commercial purchaser has subsequently requested in writing that the surplus lines agent procure or place such insurance from a nonadmitted company. (Tenn. Code Ann. §56-14-105).

D. Tax: For policies and additional premium endorsements, the tax rate is a flat 5 percent for all types of premiums. "Premium" includes all premiums, membership fees, assessments, dues or any other consideration for insurance. On or before February 15 for the quarter ending the preceding December 31, on or before May 15 for the quarter ending the preceding March 31, on or before August 15 for the quarter ending the preceding June 30, and on or before November 15 for the quarter ending the preceding September 30, at the time of filing the reports each surplus lines licensee shall pay the premium tax due for the policies written during the period covered by the report in the manner prescribed by the commissioner. In addition, agents will receive an invoice for a Clearinghouse Transactions fee (0.175% of gross premium) for all policies beginning with effectives on or after October 1, 2016. The surplus lines tax is applicable to any fees levied by the surplus lines agent. (Tenn. Code Ann. §56-14-113).

E. **Stamping Fee:** None. Tennessee does not have a stamping office.

F. **Other Requirements or Restrictions:** Only nonadmitted foreign surplus lines companies approved by the commissioner or alien surplus lines companies listed on the NAIC International Insurers Department may be used.

Exemptions. Primary personal automobile liability, surety, and workers compensation, except as provided in Tennessee Code §56-14-105(a), may not be placed with nonadmitted insurers. (Tenn. Code Ann. §56-14-105).

Eligibility. For nonadmitted insurers, a surplus lines broker is permitted to place nonadmitted insurance with such insurers provided they are domiciled in the United States, are authorized to write the type of insurance in their domiciliary jurisdiction, and maintains either the greater of the minimum capital and surplus under the laws of the state or $15 million each. If the unauthorized insurer does not satisfy the requirements of subdivision (b)(1)(A), the commissioner may make an affirmative finding that the unauthorized insurer is acceptable. The commissioner's finding shall be based upon such facts as quality of management, capital and surplus of any parent company, company underwriting profit and investment income trends, market availability and company record and reputation within the industry. In no event shall the commissioner make an affirmative finding of acceptability when the unauthorized insurer's capital and surplus is less than $4.5 million; or the unauthorized insurer is not a United States domiciled insurer but is listed by the NAIC International Insurers Department. (Tenn. Code Ann. §56-14-109).

Records. Each surplus lines agent is required to keep a record of each surplus lines contract procured by such agent, including a copy of the daily report, and showing the following items as may be applicable:

1. Amount of the insurance and perils insured against.

2. Brief general description of property insured and where located.

3. Gross premium charged.

4. Return premium paid, if any.

5. Rate of premium charged upon the several items of property.

6. Effective date of the contract, and its terms.

7. Name and post office address of the insured.

8. Name and home office address of the insurer.

9. Amount collected from the insured.

10. Other information as may be required by the commissioner.

The record must be open to examination by the commissioner without notice, and kept available and open to the commissioner for three years following expiration or cancellation of the contract. (Tenn. Code Ann. §56-14-116).

Notice. All surplus lines policies must be stamped with the following wording:

> "This insurance contract is with an insurer not licensed to transact insurance in this state and is issued and delivered as a surplus lines coverage pursuant to the Tennessee insurance statutes." (Tenn. Code Ann. §56-14-107).

Reports. Quarterly reports are due on or before February 15 for the quarter ending the preceding December 31, on or before May 15 for the quarter ending the preceding March 31, on or before August 15 for the quarter ending the preceding June 30, and on or before November 15 for the quarter ending the preceding September 30, and must show: the aggregate gross premiums written, aggregate return premiums, and the amount of tax remitted. An affidavit for any new or renewal surplus lines contacts or endorsements is due within thirty days of its placing. The affidavit must be promptly filed and must include a confirmation that the agent is unable to procure from an admitted company the full amount of insurance required to protect the interest of the insured for each transaction except exempt commercial purchasers. (Amended April 6, 2015) (Tenn. Code Ann. §56-14-106).

G. Surplus Lines Association: None.

H. Independently Procured Insurance:

1. *Rules.* Tennessee appears to have no statutes regarding independently procured insurance.

2. *Industrial Insured Exemption.* An industrial insured employs a full-time employee acting as an insurance manager or buyer, has aggregate annual insurance premiums for all risks totaling at least $25,000, and has at least twenty-five full-time employees. (Tenn. Code Ann. §56-2-105).

NRRA Implementation

I. Compact: None. Slimpact was repealed effective April 4, 2014. Tennessee is an associate member of NIMA and requires agents/brokers to utilize their electronic services for filing affidavits for policies, but not for payment of taxes. As of December 2017 NIMA will have completed the process of dissolving and concluding operations. Check with the department of insurance regarding changes in procedures during this process. http://www.magnetmail.net/actions/email_web_version.cfm?recipient_id=1262088409&message_id=14448228&user_id=NAPSLO&jobid=37952939). Tennessee is also in the process of making OPTins available for reporting and paying surplus lines taxes electronically.

J. Definitions:

1. "Home State" means, with respect to an insured:

    a. The state in which an insured maintains its principal place of business or, in the case of an individual, the individual's principal residence; or

    b. If 100 percent of the insured risk is located out of the state referred to in subdivision (1)(a), the state to which the greatest percentage of the insured's taxable premium for that insurance contract is allocated.

2. Affiliated groups: If more than one (1) insured from an affiliated group are named insureds on a single nonadmitted insurance contract, the term "home state" means the home state, as determined pursuant to subdivision (a), of the member of the affiliated group that has the largest percentage of premium attributed to it under such insurance contract.

3. When determining the home state of the insured, the principal place of business is the state in which the insured maintains its headquarters and where the insured's high-level officers direct, control, and coordinate the business activities of the insured. (Tenn. Code Ann. §56-14-102).

K. Statutory References: Tenn. Code Ann. §§56-14-101 through 56-14-117.

TEXAS

A. Resident and Nonresident Licensing: Anyone holding a general lines property and casualty license or a managing general agent's license may be licensed to place insurance with eligible nonadmitted insurers. The surplus lines agent's license expires biennially. Original fee: $50. Biennial renewal: $50. Qualifying examination: $50. Applicant must pass an examination. Licensed Texas P&C agents may place business through licensed surplus lines agents and receive commission. There is no CE requirement. (http://tdi.texas.gov/agent/surplus-lines-apply.html).

B. Diligent Effort: All surplus lines agents shall file with the Surplus Lines Stamping Office of Texas a true and correct copy of each surplus lines insurance contract within sixty days after the effective date or issue date, whichever is later. Filings may be done electronically. However, copies of contracts issued through a surplus lines agent to a purchasing group or its members do not need to be filed with the stamping office or the Texas Department of Insurance. Agents must demonstrate a diligent effort to place the risk in the admitted market. An eligible surplus lines insurer may provide surplus lines insurance only in the amount that exceeds the amount of insurance obtainable from authorized insurers. (28 Tex. Admin. Code §15.106).

Commercial Purchaser Exemption. The agent must first disclose to the purchaser that the coverage may or may not be available from the admitted market that may provide greater protection with more regulatory oversight. After receiving this disclosure, the exempt commercial purchaser must request in writing that the agent procure the coverage in the surplus lines market. (Tex. Ins. Code §981.004). Under the NRRA, a buyer must also meet the following requirements to qualify as an exempt commercial purchaser:

1. Employ or retain a qualified risk manager.

2. Pay aggregate nationwide commercial property and casualty insurance premium in excess of $100,000 in the immediately preceding twelve months.

3. Satisfy at least one of the following:

   a. Possess a net worth in excess of $20 million.

   b. Generate annual revenues in excess of $50 million.

   c. Employ more than 500 full-time employees per individual insured or be a member of an affiliated group employing more than 1,000 employees in the aggregate.

d. Be a nonprofit organization or public entity generating annual expenses of at least $30 million.

e. Be a municipality with a population in excess of 50,000 persons.

TDI may adopt regulations to impose reporting and record-keeping requirements on an agent for exempt commercial purchaser procurements. SLSOT will notify you of any necessary procedures resulting from the future adoption of new TDI regulations relating to exempt commercial purchasers. (Tex. Ins. Code §981.0031).

C. **Tax:** Tax of 4.85 percent of gross premiums, payable annually, by March 1. The surplus lines tax is also applicable to any fees levied by the surplus lines agent. (Tex. Ins. Code §225.004).

D. **Stamping Fee:** Stamping fee of .06 percent on policies effective on or before Dec. 31, 2015, and 0.15 percent on policies effective on or after January 1, 2016. The Texas Surplus Lines Stamping Office is located at 805 Las Cimas Parkway, #300; Austin, TX 78746. Telephone: 512-531-1880. Web site: http://www.sltx.org (28 Tex. Admin. Code §15.103 and § 15.106).

E. **Surplus Lines Association:** Great Hills Corporate Center, 9020-I Capital of TX Hwy N., Suite 370, Austin, TX 78759. Phone: 512-343-9058. Fax: 512-343-2896. Email: jptsla@tsla.org. Web site: http://www.tsla.org.

F. **Other Requirements or Restrictions:** An eligible surplus lines insurer may provide surplus lines insurance only if the full amount of required insurance cannot be obtained, after a diligent effort, from an insurer authorized to write and actually writing that kind and class of insurance in this state; the insurance is placed through a surplus lines agent; and the insurer meets eligibility requirements as of the inception date and annual anniversary date of each insurance contract, cover note, or other confirmation of insurance. An eligible surplus lines insurer may provide surplus lines insurance only in the amount that exceeds the amount of insurance obtainable from authorized insurers. Use of surplus lines to avoid Texas Motor Vehicle Assigned Risk Plan is prohibited. TDI maintains a list of eligible surplus lines insurers in accordance with Chapter 28, Section 15.8 (j) Texas Administrative code. However the Texas surplus lines agent is responsible for compliance with Tex. Insurance Code Sec. 981.211 as to insurer's solvency, financial security, and premium tax payment. Premiums on risks or exposures that are properly allocated to federal waters, international waters, or under the jurisdiction of a foreign government shall not be taxable. All surplus lines contracts must have stamped or affixed the wording prescribed in Tex. Insurance Code Sec. 981.101. Purchasing groups with insurers not admitted in Texas must operate through surplus lines agents, who must pay the tax on the group premiums for Texas exposures annually with their surplus lines tax. Any agent placing business with a purchasing group or risk retention group must report to the commissioner annually by March 1 the activities and scope of services being provided to the group. Purchasing groups in Texas who do not have taxes reported by a surplus lines agent must pay the tax on the group premiums for Texas exposures annually by March 1.

Policies must contain the Notice of Policyholder Complaint Procedures and information regarding service of process.

Courtesy filing of taxes and surplus lines policies is not allowed in Texas.

Eligibility. An eligible surplus lines insurer must maintain capital and surplus in an amount of at least $15 million. If an eligible surplus lines insurer is an insurance exchange created by the laws of another state, the syndicates of the exchange must maintain acceptable capital and surplus, or the equivalent under the laws of the exchange's domiciliary function in at least $75 million in the aggregate; 50 percent of the surplus must be accessible to the exchange or the exchange's domiciliary commissioner in event of insolvency or impairment; and an individual syndicate must maintain at least $5 million for the exchange of all policyholders or the greater of the minimum capital and surplus of the exchange's domiciliary jurisdiction or $15 million. (Tex. Ins. Code §981.057).

Notice. A surplus lines document must state, in eleven point type, the following:

> "This insurance contract is with an insurer not licensed to transact insurance in this state and is issued and delivered as surplus line coverage under the Texas insurance statutes. The Texas Department of Insurance does not audit the finances or review the solvency of the surplus lines insurer providing this coverage, and the insurer is not a member of the property and casualty insurance guaranty association created under Chapter 462, Insurance Code. Chapter 225, Insurance Code, requires payment of a ______________ (insert appropriate tax rate) percent tax on gross premium." (Tex. Ins. Code §981.101).

Records. Each surplus lines agent shall maintain a contract file which shall contain a complete and true record of each individual surplus lines contract, including a copy of the daily report or other evidence of insurance, and showing the following items as applicable: (1) amount of insurance and perils insured against; (2) brief general description of the property insured and the location of the property; (3) gross premium paid; (4) return premium paid, if any; (5) rate(s) of premium charged; (6) effective date(s) of the contract, and the terms; (7) name and mailing address of the insured; (8) name and home office address of the insurer, underwriting syndicate or other risk bearing entity; (9) amount collected from the insured; (10) record of losses or claims filed and payments made; (11) a true and correct copy of the insurance policy, contract and other detailed evidences of coverage, as issued to the insured; and (12) all correspondence relating to the specific insurance coverage of that contract file. (28 Tex. Admin. Code §15.110).

Reports. Not later than the sixtieth day after the later of the effective date or the issue date of new or renewal surplus lines insurance, a surplus lines agent responsible under Section 225.006 for the filing, reporting, collection, payment and other requirements imposed by Chapter 225 shall file with the stamping office: (1) a copy of the policy issued; or (2) if the policy has not been issued, a copy of the certificate, cover note, or other confirmation of insurance delivered to the insured; (3) a copy of each substitute certificate, cover note, or other confirmation of insurance delivered to an insured; (4) a copy of each endorsement of an original policy, certificate, cover note, or other confirmation of insurance delivered to an insured; and (5) a memorandum from the agent informing the stamping office of the substance of any change represented as compared with the original coverage. (Tex. Ins. Code §981.105).

G. Independently Procured Insurance:

1. *Rules.* Texas does not regulate the placement of independently procured insurance. Texas defines independently procured insurance as insurance placed with an unlicensed company when all the transactions involved in the negotiation and procurement of the coverage occur entirely outside of Texas, up to and including delivery of the policy and payment of the premium. Insureds may purchase coverage directly from insurers only if they leave Texas and procure coverage from the insurer or out of state broker. Coverage may be placed with an unlicensed insurer or unauthorized surplus lines carrier. If the insured purchases independently procured coverage, he or she must report the transaction to the Comptroller of Public Accounts and pay the prescribed tax; payable annually, by March 1. The insured may designate a third party to pay the tax. Policies are subject to a tax of 4.85 percent. Premiums on risks or exposures which are properly allocated to federal waters, international waters, or under the jurisdiction of a foreign government shall not be taxable. Due to recent court decisions, Texas no longer enforces the tax on independently procured insurance if the only connection with the state is that some or all of the risk is located in Texas. The state continues to enforce the tax only when policyholders are domiciled or headquartered in Texas. (Texas Insurance Tax Procedures Manual, Chapter 17).

2. *Industrial Insured Exemption.* Texas has no industrial insured exemption. (Tex. Ins. Code §226.053; *Dow Chemical Co. v. Rylander*, 38 S.W.3d 741 (Tex. App. 2001)).

NRRA Implementation

H. Compact: NIMA.

I. Definitions:

1. "Home State" means:

   a. For a business, the state in which the insured maintains its principal place of business is the home state.

   b. For an individual, the state in which the insured maintains its principal residence is the home state.

   c. If 100 percent of the insured risk is located outside of the state identified in a or b above, the state to which the greatest percentage of the insured's taxable premium is allocated becomes the home state for that policy. However, if a tiny portion of the insured risk is located in the state identified in a or b above, that state is the home state—even if another state has the vast majority of the risk insured.

   d. If more than one insured from an affiliated group are named insureds on a single policy, the home state of the member of the group that has the largest percentage of premium attributed to it is the home state for that policy. (Tex. Ins. Code §981.002).

J. Statutory References: Texas Insurance Code, §§981.001 through 981.009; 981.051 through 981.065; 981.101 through 981.105; 981.151 through 981.160; 981.201 through 981.222; 28 TAC §§ 15.101 through 15.115.

UTAH

A. **Resident Licensing:** Upon satisfying the additional requirements—e.g., having held a producer property/casualty license for three of the last four years and taken the surplus lines exam—a resident holder of a producer's license may obtain the authority to act as a surplus lines producer. This license authorizes the holder to arrange insurance contracts with unauthorized insurers under Utah Code §31A-15-103 but only as to the types of insurance under Subsection (1) to which producer's license applies. Register for an exam by going to https://candidate.psiexams.com/ or calling 800-733-9267. Exam fees, fingerprinting fees, and fingerprint processing fees should be paid to PSI. Fingerprinting must be done at the PSI test center. Payment must be made by credit card at the test center. After passing the exam candidates should remain at the test center to complete an application via Sircon or NIPR on a test center kiosk. Print and show the certificate to the test center as proof of payment. Examination fee: $59. Fingerprint Submission Fee: $28.25 (plus $20 PSI processing fee). Individual license fee: $75. Agency license fee: $85. Individual renewal: $75. Individual reinstatement: $125. (https://insurance.utah.gov/licensee/producers/fees).

B. **Nonresident Licensing:** In order to place surplus lines policies, nonresidents must be licensed as surplus lines brokers/producers in good standing in the applicant's home state, and complete a Uniform Application. Individual license fee $75. Organization license fee: $85. Residents and nonresidents may apply online at Sircon or NIPR. Paper applications will be rejected and returned. Individual renewal: $75. Individual reinstatement: $125. (https://insurance.utah.gov/licensee/producers/fees).

C. **Diligent Effort:** A good faith effort must be made to place the insurance with admitted insurers the producer has reason to believe will consider writing the type of coverage or class of insurance involved. The producing agent must document his or her efforts to place coverage with admitted insurers. Both the producing agent and surplus lines broker/producer must keep evidence of this good faith effort for three years from the inception date of coverage or renewal. Within sixty days of the effective date, the surplus lines broker/producer must file a copy of the policy and justification for placement with the Surplus Line Association of Utah. (U.A.C. R590-171-6).

   Exempt Commercial Purchaser. A diligent search is not required of a broker if the broker has disclosed to the exempt commercial purchaser that insurance may or may not be available from the admitted market that may provide greater protection with more regulatory oversight, and the exempt commercial purchaser has subsequently requested in writing for the broker to procure from or place such insurance with a nonadmitted insurer. (U.A.C. R590-171-6).

D. **Tax:** Tax is 4.25 percent of gross premiums less return premiums due to cancellations or premium reductions. Gross premium means the monetary consideration for an insurance policy including all fees charged to the insured, however designated. Gross premiums do not include separately negotiated broker fees that are not listed on the policy. Failure to pay taxes in accordance with the deadlines will result in a penalty of 25 percent of the tax due, plus 1.5 percent per month from the time of default until full payment of the tax. The insurer, all producers involved in the transaction, and the policyholder are jointly and severally liable for the payment of the surplus lines tax. It is unlawful for the producer to pay the tax for the insured. (U.A.C. R590-157-3).

Premium Defined. Premium means the monetary consideration for an insurance policy. "Premium" includes an assessment, membership fee, required contribution, or monetary consideration. "Premium" does not include consideration paid to a third party administrator for the third party administrator's services. "Premium" includes an amount paid by a third party administrator to an insurer for insurance on the risks administered by the third party administrator. (U.C.A. §31A-1-301).

E. **Stamping Fee:** A stamping fee of 0.18 percent of all gross premiums and fees. If the stamping fee is not paid when due, the commissioner or advisory organization may impose a penalty of an additional 25 percent of the stamping fee due, plus one and one half percent per month from the time of default until full payment of the stamping fee. (U.C.A. §31A-15-103 and U.A.C. R590-157-4).

F. **Surplus Lines Association:** Surplus Lines Association of Utah, 6711 South 1300 East, Salt Lake City, UT 84121; this is a stamping office. Phone: 801-944-0114. Fax: 801-944-0116. Email: sbruno@slaut.org. Web site: www.slaut.org.

G. **Other Requirements or Restrictions:** Placement with the surplus lines insurer solely to obtain a better price does not constitute good faith unless the producer demonstrates that the price quoted by the admitted market is excessive as defined in UCA §31A-19a-201(2). (U.A.C. R590-171-6).

Before a surplus line producer may place insurance with an unauthorized insurer, the surplus line producer must give the applicant written notice of the known deficiencies of the insurer or the limitations on the surplus line producer's investigation; and explain the need to place the business with that insurer. A copy of this notice shall be kept in the office of the surplus line producer for at least five years. (U.C.A. §31A-15-103).

Use of nonadmitted insurers not on the commissioner's recognized list is prohibited. The commissioner has ruled that each surplus lines producer must be a member of the Utah Surplus Lines Association. All surplus lines contracts must bear surplus lines brokers/producer's name or initials and have attached the following statement:

> "The insurer issuing this policy does not hold a certificate of authority to do business in this state and thus is not fully subject to regulation by the Utah insurance

commissioner. This policy receives no protection from any of the guaranty associations created under Title 31A, Chapter 28 (U.C.A. §31A-15-103 [8])."

Eligibility. A nonadmitted insurer must be authorized to write in their state of domicile and maintain minimum capital and surplus of $15 million. The Surplus Lines Association of Utah maintains a list of authorized nonadmitted insurers.

All surplus line filings, submissions, and endorsements must be filed electronically. Accounts may be set up through http://slaut.org under "Login" under the Quick Links. Any filings received through the mail will be charged $50 per filing.

Courtesy filings of taxes and certificates of nonavailability are not allowed in Utah.

Records. When the commissioner has reason to believe that insurance has been effectuated by or for any person in Utah with an unauthorized insurer, the commissioner may, in writing, order the person to produce for examination all insurance contracts and other documents evidencing insurance with both authorized and unauthorized insurers and to disclose to the commissioner the amount of insurance, the name and address of each insurer, the gross amount of premium, and the name and address of any person who has assisted in effecting the insurance. (U.C.A. §31A-15-109).

Reports. Within sixty days of the effective date of a surplus lines transaction, the surplus lines producer must file with the SLA a copy of the policy, binder, certificate, endorsement or other documentation sufficient to identify the subject of the insurance; the coverage, conditions and terms of insurance; the type of transaction; the effective date; the premium charged; the premium taxes payable; the name and address of the policyholder and insurer. (U.A.C. R590-157-6).

H. Independently Procured Insurance:

1. *Rules.* Any person seeking insurance may obtain it from an unauthorized insurer if no producer resident doing business in Utah is involved and if negotiations occur primarily outside Utah. Insurance may be procured independently only on a surplus lines basis, from authorized or unauthorized surplus lines carriers. The transaction must be reported to the Surplus Line Association within sixty days on prescribed forms. The insured must pay the tax of 4.25 percent. (U.C.A. §§31A-15-104 and 31A-3-301).

2. *Industrial Insured Exemption.* Must utilize a full-time insurance manager or risk manager; or the services of a regularly and continuously qualified insurance consultant; must have total P&C premiums (excluding workers comp) of $25,000 or more; and have at least twenty-five full time employees. (U.C.A. §31A-37-102).

NRRA Implementation

I. **Compact:** NIMA. As of December 2017 NIMA will have completed the process of dissolving and concluding operations. Check with the department of insurance regarding changes in procedures during this process. (https://www.napslo.org/docs/PDF/Legislative/NIMA%20Board%20Votes%20to%20Dissolve.pdf).

J. **Definitions:** Utah is the insured's home state if the insured maintains its principal place of business here or, in the case of an individual, if the individual's principal place of residence is here. If Utah is the insured's home state, only Utah's requirements regarding the placement of such business applies. If 100 percent of the insured risk is located outside of Utah, then the insured's home state is the state to which the greatest percentage of the insured's taxable premium for that insurance contract is allocated.

If more than one insured from an affiliate group are named insureds on a single nonadmitted insurance placement, Utah will be considered the home state for that placement if Utah is the home state of the member of the affiliated group that has the largest percentage of premium attributed to it under such insured contract.

"Principal place of business," means the state where the insured maintains its headquarters, and where the insured's high-level officers direct, control, and coordinate the business activities. If such activities are conducted in more than one state, the state in which the greatest percentage of the insured's taxable premium for that insurance contract is allocated. If the insured maintains its headquarters or such activities are conducted outside any state, the state to which the greatest percentage of the insured's taxable premium for that insurance contract is allocated. (15 USC §8206(6)).

K. **Statutory References**: Utah Code §§31A-15-101 through 31A-15-111; 31A-3-301.

VERMONT

A. Resident Licensing: Residents who are licensed as producers may be licensed to place insurance with nonadmitted insurers. Applicant must have at least one year experience and submit the NAIC Uniform Application for Individual Licenses and Attachment #3, Affidavit of Experience. The surplus lines producer's license expires March 31, biennially on even years. Application fee: $30; initial and renewal fee: $400. (8 V.S.A. §§4800(2)(A)(vi) and 4807).

B. Nonresident Licensing: Nonresidents may be licensed for surplus lines in Vermont if also licensed in their home states. Nonresident applicants must submit the NAIC Uniform Application for Individual Licenses and Attachment #3, Affidavit of Experience, and a home state certification (no more than ninety days old) if that state does not report surplus lines license information to the PDB. Application fee: $30; biennial license fee is determined by state of residence but at least $400. (8 V.S.A. §4807(c)).

C. Diligent Effort: Use of nonadmitted insurers not on commissioner's approved list is prohibited. Insurance coverage must not be placed with a nonadmitted insurer unless the full amount of insurance required is not reasonably procurable from admitted insurers actually transacting that kind and class of insurance in this state. The amount of insurance exported must be only the excess over the amount procurable from admitted insurers actually transacting and insuring that kind and class of insurance. (8 V.S.A. §5024).

Commercial Purchaser Exemption. A broker is not required to make a diligent effort to determine whether reasonably procurable insurance is available if the broker procuring or placing the insurance has disclosed to the exempt purchaser that such insurance may be available from an admitted insurer and may provide greater protection with more regulatory oversight, and the purchaser has subsequently requested in writing the broker to procure such insurance from a nonadmitted insurer. (8 V.S.A. §5024).

D. Tax: 3 percent of gross premiums less returns. The tax must be paid to the Commissioner of Taxes each quarter with a duplicate copy of the quarterly report even if no business was written. If no business was written, the L104B form must still be completed. The original must be sent to the Commissioner of Insurance with a copy to the Commissioner of Taxes along with a check for the tax.

Where the insurance covers properties, risks, or exposures located or to be performed both in and out of this state, the sum payable shall be calculated based on gross premiums charged less any return premiums as follows: an amount equal to 3 percent on that portion of the premiums applicable to risks or properties located or to be performed in Vermont, plus an amount equal to a percentage on that portion of the premiums applicable to properties, risks, or exposures located or to be performed outside Vermont. (8 V.S.A. §5035).

E. **Stamping Fee:** None. Vermont has no stamping office.

F. **Surplus Lines Association:** Vermont does not have a surplus lines association.

G. **Other Requirements or Restrictions:**

Exemptions. Life and accident and health insurance; annuities; reinsurance; property or operations of railroads or aircraft engaged in interstate commerce; and ocean or wet marine covering vessels, cargo, protection and indemnity are exempt from provisions pertaining to placement with nonadmitted insurers. (8 V.S.A. §§5025 and 5028).

Eligibility. For nonadmitted insurers domiciled in a U.S. jurisdiction, a surplus lines broker is permitted to place nonadmitted insurance with such insurers provided they maintain capital and surplus or its equivalent under the laws of its domiciliary jurisdiction which equals the greater of the minimum capital and surplus requirements under the law of the state or $15 million and if an alien insurer is listed on the quarterly listing of alien insurers maintained by the NAIC international insurers department. (8 V.S.A. §5026).

A nonadmitted insurer may receive approval upon an affirmative finding of acceptability by the commissioner. The finding shall be based upon such factors as quality of management, capital and surplus of any parent company, company underwriting profit and investment-income trends, market availability, and company record and reputation within the industry. In no event, however, shall the commissioner make an affirmative finding of acceptability when the surplus lines insurer's capital and surplus is less than $4.5 million. (8 V.S.A. §5026).

Notice. All surplus lines contracts must show the following stamped or written conspicuously in no smaller than ten point boldface type of a contrasting color upon the first page of the policy and the confirmation of insurance, if any:

> "The company issuing this policy has not been licensed by the State of Vermont and the rates charged have not been approved by the Commissioner of Financial Regulation. Any default on the part of the insurer is not covered by the Vermont Insurance Guaranty Association." (8 V.S.A. §5028).

Records. Each surplus lines broker shall keep a full and true record of each contract covering a domestic risk placed with a surplus lines insurer, including a copy of the daily report, and the following: (1) Amount of the insurance and perils insured; (2) Description of property insured and its locations; (3) Gross premium charged; (4) Return premium paid, if any; (5) Rate of premium charged upon the items of property; (6) Effective date of the contract, and its terms; (7) Name and post office address of the insured; (8) Name and post office address of the insurer; (9) Name and post office address of brokerage house, and name of licensed individual producer with whom business was placed; (10) Amount collected from the insured; and (11) Other information required by the commissioner. The record shall be kept until three years following termination of the contract. (8 V.S.A. § 5033).

Reports. Quarterly report of all surplus lines business placed must be filed with the commissioner within thirty days after the close of each calendar quarter. (8 V.S.A. §5034).

H. Independently Procured Insurance:

1. *Rules.* Insureds may purchase coverage directly from insurers or surplus lines carriers. If the contract is made in Vermont, it may not be with an unlicensed insurer or unauthorized surplus lines carrier. If the insured purchases surplus lines coverage, he must report, before March 1 of the year following purchase and each year thereafter, the transaction to the Department of Taxes and pay the 3 percent tax. (8 V.S.A. §5036).

2. *Validity and Enforceability.* Insurance contracts procured as surplus lines insurance from nonadmitted insurers, in accordance with Vermont law, are valid and enforceable to the same extent as insurance contracts procured from admitted insurers. (8 V.S.A. §5029).

3. *Industrial Insured Exemption.* The insured must use a full-time employee acting as an insurance manager or buyer to purchase insurance. The insured's aggregate annual premiums must be in excess of $25,000 and it must have at least twenty-five full-time employees. (8 V.S.A. §3368).

NRRA Implementation

I. Compact: SLIMPACT. (Insurance Bulletin 169, https://dfr.vermont.gov/sites/finreg/files/regbul/dfr-bulletin-insurance-169.pdf).

J. Definitions: Home State. Vermont is the insured's home state if the insured maintains its principal place of business here or, in the case of an individual, the individual's principal residence is here. If Vermont is considered the insured's home state, only Vermont's requirements regarding the placement of such business will apply. If 100 percent of the insured risk is located outside of Vermont, then the insured's home state is the state to which the greatest percentage of the insured's taxable premium for that insurance contract is allocated.

If more than one insured from an affiliate group are named insureds on a single nonadmitted insurance placement, Vermont will be considered the home state for that placement if Vermont is the home state of the member of the affiliated group that has the largest percentage of premium attributed to it under such insurance contract. (8 V.S.A. §5022).

K. Statutory References: Vermont Statues Annotated, tit. 8, §§3368, 4800, 4807, 5022, 5024, 5026, 5028, 5034 through 5036.

VIRGIN ISLANDS

A. Resident Licensing: Any person maintaining an office in the Virgin Islands, whom the commissioner deems competent and trustworthy, may be licensed as a surplus lines broker. The surplus lines broker's license expires annually on December 31. Initial application and renewal fee: $300 according to statute. Applicant must file $10,000 bond with an authorized corporate surety approved by the commissioner. Any insurance agent or broker licensed in the territory for the kind of insurance involved may place business with a licensed surplus lines broker and receive commission. (22 V.I.C. §656). Note, the Division website lists different fees, so contact the Division for clarification. According to the website, license and renewal are $500. In addition, the Division lists the initial certificate of authority/registration fee as $1,100, with a $600 renewal fee. (https://ltg.gov.vi/departments/banking-insurance-and-financial-regulation/#1546768965413-8a2ec2a6-3e58).

B. Nonresident Licensing: Licensed nonresident agents or brokers may facilitate resident licensed surplus lines brokers in seeking surplus lines coverage. However, it is the responsibility of the licensed surplus lines broker for the placement of surplus lines through eligible surplus lines carriers. (22 V.I.C. §§653, 763)

C. Diligent Effort: The insurance must not be procurable, after diligent effort has been made to do so from among a majority of the insurers authorized to transact that kind of insurance in this territory and placing the insurance in an unauthorized insurer must not be for the purpose of securing a lower premium rate than would be accepted by any authorized insurer.

Within thirty days after the procuring of any surplus line insurance, the surplus line broker must execute and shall file with the Commissioner a written report which shall include the name and address of the insured; the identity of the insurer or insurers; a description of the subject and location of the risk; the amount of premium charged for the insurance; and such other pertinent information as the Commissioner may reasonably require. The broker must also file an affidavit setting forth the facts of the broker's diligent effort. (22 V.I.C. §653)

D. Tax: 5 percent of quarterly gross premiums less returns, payable on or before the first day of February, May, August, and November of each year to the commissioner of insurance. (22 V.I.C. §662). Filing fee: $50. Even if no business is written, the quarterly report must be filed and accompanied by the $50 fee. (https://ltg.gov.vi/departments/banking-insurance-and-financial-regulation/#1546768965413-8a2ec2a6-3e58).

Premium defined. "Premium" means all sums charged, received or deposited as consideration for an insurance contract. Any assessment, membership, policy, survey, inspection, service or similar fee or charge made in consideration for an insurance contract is deemed part of the premium. (22 V.I.C. §817).

E. Stamping Fee: None. The Virgin Islands does not have a surplus lines stamping office.

F. Surplus Lines Association: None.

G. Other Requirements or Restrictions:

Eligibility. Use of nonadmitted insurers not meeting financial requirements of the Virgin Islands and use of surplus lines to obtain lower premium rate are prohibited.

Notice. Surplus lines policies must contain the following wording:

"This contract is registered and delivered as surplus line coverage under the Insurance Code of the Virgin Islands. It is not covered by the Guaranty Fund established pursuant to Title 33, §3061, V.I.C." (22 V.I.C. §654).

Records. During the five years next following the date of completion of such transaction, each surplus lines broker must keep available a full and true record of each surplus line contract procured including a copy of the daily report showing such of the following items as may be applicable:

(1) Amount of the insurance.

(2) Gross premiums charged.

(3) Return premium paid, if any.

(4) Rate of premium charged upon the several items of property.

(5) Effective date of the contract and terms thereof.

(6) Name and address of the insurer.

(7) Name and address of the insured.

(8) Brief general description of property insured and where located.

(9) Other information required by the commissioner. (22 V.I.C. §660).

Annual Statements: Each surplus line broker shall on or before the first day of March of each year file with the commissioner a verified statement of all surplus line insurance transacted by the broker during the preceding calendar year. (22 V.I.C. §661).

Courtesy filings of taxes and certificates of nonavailability are not allowed in the Virgin Islands.

Exemptions: The surplus lines provisions shall not apply to the following: reinsurance; ocean marine and foreign trade insurance; insurance on objects located, resident, or wholly performed outside the Virgin Islands; insurance on vehicles or aircraft owned and principally garaged outside the Virgin Islands; and insurance of aircraft owned or operated by aircraft manufacturers, or of aircraft or aircraft cargo used in interstate flight, or against liability, other than employer's liability aristing out of the ownership, maintenance, or use of such aircraft. (22 V.I.C. 666).

H. Independently Procured Insurance:

1. *Rules.* The Virgin Islands have no statutes regarding independently procured insurance.

NRRA Implementation

The Virgin Islands have not addressed NRRA at this time.

I. Statutory References:

22 V.I.C. §§	653, 654, 656
	660 to 662, 666
	763
	817

Web References:

https://ltg.gov.vi/departments/banking-insurance-and-financial-regulation/#1546768965413-8a2ec2a6-3e58.

VIRGINIA

A. **Resident Licensing:** Resident applicants are required to be licensed as Virginia property and casualty insurance agents prior to being licensed as surplus lines brokers. Applicants must file a certification of attestation (Form SLB-2, https://scc.virginia.gov/pages/Licensing-Registration-Forms) with the commission that the applicant has in force a $25,000 surety bond in favor of Virginia. The surety bond is not permitted to be terminated unless the licensee provides at least thirty days' prior written notice of the termination to the commission. The nonrefundable application processing fee is $50. Virginia surplus lines broker licenses are issued on an annual basis and expire on June 30 of each year. On or before June 1 of each year, licensees must apply for license renewal and pay a nonrefundable renewal application processing fee of $50.

Note: The cost of the processing fee will likely change, to an amount and to be paid in a manner prescribed by the Commission effective January 1, 2021. All renewals will take effect on July 1. Any license not renewed by June 30 of each year will terminate effective July 1 of that year. Licenses may be renewed via Sircon or NIPR. Each licensed surplus lines broker is required to report any change in his or her residence or name to the commission within thirty calendar days. In addition, each surplus lines broker convicted of a felony must report the facts and circumstances regarding the criminal conviction to the commission within thirty calendar days. Any resident surplus lines licensee who has moved his or her residence from Virginia will have all licenses immediately terminated by the commission, regardless of whether the commission is notified prior to the move. However, nothing will prevent such a surplus lines broker from applying for a license as a nonresident surplus lines broker. (Va. Code Ann. §§38.2-1857.1, 38.2-1857.2, and 38.2-1857.5.)

Note: Effective January 1, 2021, applicants for a surplus broker license must be fingerprinted and submit to a criminal history record check. The cost of fingerprinting and the record check shall be paid by the applicant. (2018 Virginia SB 1222, and VA. Code Ann. §38.2-1857.2).

B. **Nonresident Licensing:** Nonresident applicants must submit proof that he or she is currently licensed or otherwise authorized as a resident surplus lines broker and is in good standing in his or her home state. A nonresident applicant's home state must issue nonresident surplus lines broker licenses to residents of Virginia on the same basis. Nonresident applicants must submit a Virginia surplus lines broker license application and pay a nonrefundable application processing fee of $50. Virginia nonresident surplus lines broker licenses are issued on an annual basis and expire on June 30 of each year. On or before June 1 of each year, nonresident licensees must apply for license renewal and pay a nonrefundable renewal application processing fee of $50. All renewals will take effect on July 1. Any nonresident license not renewed by June 30 of each year will terminate effective July 1 of that year. Each licensed surplus lines broker is required to report any change to his or her name to the commission within thirty calendar days. In addition, each surplus lines broker convicted of a felony must report the facts and circumstances regarding the criminal conviction to the commission within thirty calendar days. Any nonresident surplus lines broker who moves from one state to another state must file a change of address with the commission within thirty days of the change of legal residence. Any licenses issued to nonresidents will be terminated at any time that the nonresident's equivalent authority in his or her home state is terminated, suspended, or revoked. (Va. Code Ann. §§38.2-1857.2, 38.2-1857.3, 38.2-1857.5 and 38.2-1857.9).

Note: Effective January 1, 2021, applicants for a surplus broker license must be fingerprinted and submit to a criminal history record check. The cost of fingerprinting and the record check shall be paid by the applicant. (2018 Virginia SB 1222, and VA. Code Ann. §38.2-1857.2).

C. **Diligent Effort:** Not required.

D. **Tax:** Tax is 2.25 percent. Every licensed surplus lines broker, or any person required to be licensed as a surplus lines broker, is subject to annual taxes of 2.25 percent on the gross amount of all premiums, assessments, dues and fees collected, received or derived, or obligations taken during the calendar year; adjusted for the amount of premiums written for additional insurance coverage and premiums returned as a result of an insurance rider, policy cancellation, rate adjustment or an excess of advance premium over actual premium on each policy of insurance procured with an eligible nonadmitted insurer. For policies effective on or after July 1, 2011, such payments are required to be made based on the direct gross premium income from policies for insureds whose home state is the Commonwealth of Virginia. (Va. Code Ann. §38.2-4809 & 58.1-2501).

Filing Deadlines. A surplus lines broker is required to file a quarterly tax report and make payment if its annual Insurance Premiums License Tax liability can reasonably be expected to exceed $1,500 and, during the quarter, it derived direct gross premium income from policies for insured parties whose home state is the Commonwealth of Virginia. A surplus lines broker is not required to file the quarterly tax report if its annual tax liability is not expected to exceed $1,500, or if it did not have a tax liability for the current period. No report is required for a quarter if there is a credit from a prior period or returned premiums within the same taxable year that equals or exceeds the amount of the tax liability for the current period. Surplus Lines Brokers Quarterly Tax Reports, Form 801, are due on the 30th day of April, July, October and January. Surplus Lines Brokers should submit quarterly tax reports and payments online with eforms at http://www.tax.virginia.gov/site.cfm?alias=eforms. In addition to their quarterly reports, surplus lines brokers also file an annual reconciliation tax report, due on or before March 1 following the close of the previous calendar year. The Virginia Surplus Lines Broker's Annual Reconciliation Tax Report, Form 802, must be filed even if no insurance premiums license tax is owed. (Va. Code Ann. §38.2-4809 and https://tax.virginia.gov/insurance-premiums-license-tax).

If you are unable to submit your quarterly tax report and annual reconciliation report electronically, you may file paper returns. Form 801 and Form 802 are available to download and print for paper submission.

Penalties. Any surplus lines broker that fails to file with the department their annual report, Form 802, Surplus Lines Brokers Annual Reconciliation Tax Report (due March 1 following the close of the previous calendar year), will be subject to a late filing fine of $50 per day for each day's failure to submit the report. Any surplus lines broker that fails to pay its insurance premiums license tax by the March 1 due date is subject to a 10 percent penalty that shall be added to the amount of the unpaid tax liability. In the event that a surplus lines broker fails to pay its insurance premiums license tax, the commission may suspend or revoke the license to conduct business in the Commonwealth of Virginia pursuant to Code of Virginia §38.2-1857.7 upon notification from the department. All surplus lines brokers are required to file an annual report by March 1 reporting the direct gross premium income derived from policies for insured parties whose home state is Virginia during the preceding year ending December 31. Upon the failure of any surplus lines broker to pay the annual insurance premiums license tax due with the annual report, interest is assessed at the rate of interest established pursuant to Code of Virginia §58.1-15 for the period between the due date of the annual report and the date of full payment. (Va. Code Ann. §38.2-4809, https://www.tax.virginia.gov/forms/search?search=&year=All&category=4.).

Annual Maintenance Fund Assessment. Every licensed surplus lines broker, or any person required to be licensed as a surplus lines broker, is to be subject to an annual maintenance fund assessment (currently one tenth of one percent of premiums received, with a $300 minimum annual assessment for each licensee) due annually by March 1. If a new assessment order is made changing this rate it will be viewable at http://www.scc.virginia.gov/boi/pro/slb.aspx. Late payments are subject to a 10 percent late payment penalty plus a $50 per day penalty. Go to http://www.scc.virginia.gov/boi/co/assess/files/slb_instruct.pdf for detailed instructions on how to file assessments. (Va. Code Ann. §38.2-400 and §38.2-4809.1).

Overestimates. If any person overestimates and overpays the assessment, the commission shall order a refund of the amount of the overpayment to the person. If any person overestimates and overpays the insurance premiums license tax, the department shall order a refund of the amount of the overpayment. (Va. Code Ann. §38.2-4809).

Fiduciary Duty. If any licensed surplus lines broker or any person required to be licensed as a surplus lines broker charges and collects from the insured the taxes and assessments required by this section, such person shall be a fiduciary to Virginia for any taxes and assessments owed to Virginia. (Va. Code Ann. §38.2-4809).

Fraudulent Filings. In addition to other penalties provided by law, any licensed surplus lines broker or any person required to be licensed as a surplus lines broker who willfully fails or refuses to pay the full amount of the tax or assessment required by this chapter, either by himself or through his agents or employees, or who makes a false or fraudulent return with intent to evade the tax or assessment hereby levied, or who makes a false or fraudulent claim for refund will be guilty of a Class 1 misdemeanor. (Va. Code Ann. §§38.2-4809 and 58.1-2501).

E. **Stamping Fee:** None. Virginia does not have a stamping office.

F. **Surplus Lines Association:** Virginia Surplus Lines Association, c/o Atlantic Specialty Lines, Inc., 9020 Stony Point Parkway, Suite 450, Richmond, VA 23235. Phone: 804-320-9500. Fax: 804-320-7280. Email: Greg Provenzo – GregProv@AtlanticSpecial.com.

G. **Other Requirements or Restrictions:** Surplus lines brokers are not permitted to accept surplus lines business from any person, other than an applicant for insurance or a duly licensed property or casualty insurance agent. Surplus lines brokers may not compensate any person, other than a duly licensed property or casualty insurance agent, for surplus lines business. No person, other than an applicant for insurance or a duly licensed property or casualty insurance agent, is permitted to place surplus lines business with a surplus lines broker, nor may any person, other than a duly licensed property or casualty insurance agent, accept compensation for such business. (Va. Code Ann. §38.2-1857.6).

Eligibility. Any unlicensed foreign insurer wishing to be approved by the commission to issue surplus lines coverage may receive such approval upon providing evidence that it is authorized to write the type of insurance in its domiciliary jurisdiction; and proof that it has capital and surplus or its equivalent under the laws of its domiciliary jurisdiction, which equal the greater of (i) the minimum capital and surplus requirements under Virginia surplus lines law, or (ii) $15 million. Notwithstanding the capital and surplus requirements, an unlicensed foreign insurer may receive approval upon an affirmative finding of acceptability by the commission. The finding shall be based upon such factors as quality of management, capital and surplus of any parent company, company underwriting profit and investment income trends, market availability, and company record and reputation within the industry. In no event shall the commission make an affirmative finding of acceptability when the surplus lines insurer's capital and surplus is less than $4.5 million. (Va. Code Ann. §38.2-4811).

Use of surplus lines to obtain a better rate or form is no longer prohibited. Only those insurers may be used that are listed on the Bureau of Insurance letter of approval of an unlicensed insurer for the type of insurance written. Interstate railroad property, and liability or other risks incidental thereto are exempt from surplus lines regulations. All surplus lines contracts must be signed by, and show license number and mailing address of the surplus lines broker and contain the following statement:

NOTICE TO THE INSURED

> "The insurance policy that you have applied for has been placed with or is being obtained from an insurer approved by the State Corporation Commission as an eligible nonadmitted insurer of the Commonwealth of Virginia. Therefore, you, the policyholder, and persons filing a claim against you are not protected under the Virginia Property and Casualty Insurance Guaranty Association Act (§§38.2-1600 et seq.) of the Code of Virginia against default of the company due to insolvency. In the event of insurance company insolvency, you may be unable to collect any amount owed to you by the company regardless of the terms of this insurance policy, and you may have to pay for any claims made against you. [Virginia Form SLB-9 (Rev. 9/96) https://scc.virginia.gov/getattachment/32e8a02c-b7a5-4dd2-90dd-ece667aa6549/slb-9.pdf]." (Va. Code Ann. §38.2-4806).

Records. Every licensed surplus lines broker is required to keep in his or her office a complete record of (i) each policy of insurance procured by him under this chapter during the previous calendar year; (ii) the name and address of the insurer or insurers; (iii) the inception and expiration dates of each policy; (iv) the perils insured against; (v) the location of each risk so insured and the premium rate and the gross premium charged for each such policy of insurance; (vi) the amount of premium returned; and (vii) any other information the commission requires. The record of each policy of insurance must be kept open at all reasonable times to examination by the commission without notice for a period of not less than five years following termination of the policy. (Va. Code Ann. §38.2-4807).

Evidence. Each policy or other written evidence of insurance procured pursuant to this chapter must be delivered promptly to the named insured shown on the policy's declarations page. No surplus lines broker may issue or deliver any policy or other written evidence of insurance or represent that insurance will be or has been granted by an eligible nonadmitted insurer unless (i) he has prior written authority from such insurer for the insurance, (ii) he has received information from the insurer in the regular course of business that the insurance has been granted, or (iii) an insurance policy providing the insurance actually has been issued by the insurer and delivered to the named insured shown on the policy's declarations page. (Va. Code Ann. §38.2-4810).

Prior Approval. No surplus lines broker may procure a policy of insurance with any nonadmitted insurer unless such nonadmitted insurer has prior approval of the commission to issue surplus lines insurance. (Va. Code Ann. §38.2-4811).

Pre-Payment Acceptance. No surplus lines broker may accept a payment of premium for issuance of surplus lines insurance before placing the insurance with an eligible nonadmitted insurer. (Va. Code Ann. §38.2-4808).

Courtesy Filings. Courtesy filings of taxes and certificates of nonavailability are not allowed in Virginia.

H. Independently Procured Insurance:

1. *Rules.* The Virginia statutes do not prohibit any person from obtaining insurance upon his own life or property from an unlicensed insurer. (Va. Code Ann. §38.2-1802).

2. *Industrial Insured Exemption.* An industrial insured is an insured (i) who procures the insurance of any risk or risks other than life and annuity contracts by use of the services of a full-time employee acting as an insurance manager or buyer or the services of a regularly and continuously retained licensed insurance consultant, (ii) whose aggregate annual premiums for insurance on all risks, except for life, annuity, and accident and sickness insurance, total at least $100,000, (iii) who has at least twenty-five full-time employees, and (iv) either has gross assets in excess of $3 million or has annual gross revenues in excess of $5 million. (Va. Code Ann. §38.2-1039).

NRRA Implementation

I. Compact: None.

J. Definitions:

1. "Home State" means:

   a. The state in which an insured maintains its principal place of business or, in the case of an individual, the individual's principal residence.

   b. If 100 percent of the insured risk is located out of the state referred to in clause (a) of this definition, "home state" means the state to which the greatest percentage of the insured's taxable premium for that insurance contract is allocated. When more than one insured from an affiliated group are named insureds on a single insurance contract, "home state" means the state of the member of the affiliated group that has the largest percentage of premium attributed to it under such insurance contract.

2. "Principal place of business" means the state where the insured maintains its headquarters and where the insured's high-level officers direct, control, and coordinate the business activities of the insured. (Va. Code Ann. §38.2-4805.2).

K. Statutory References: Virginia Code §§38.2-1857.1 through 38.2-1857.9 and 38.2-4806 through 38.2-4815.

WASHINGTON

A. **Resident Licensing:** Resident applicants are required to pay an initial application fee of $200, plus a $5 filing fee and a $20 affiliation fee (this only applies if the surplus lines broker is affiliating to a licensed surplus lines business entity license). Resident surplus lines broker licenses expire every two years on the licensee's date of birth. Licensees are required to pay a biennial renewal fee of $200. Fingerprinting is required of all resident surplus lines broker license applicants. The fingerprint fee is done through IDEMIA (formerly MorphoTrust) at 1-888 771-5097 or visit their website at https://www.identogo.com/. This fee is $49.25, which reflects the combined cost of the background check fee and IDEMIA IdentoGO's additional charge for providing the service, also known as a rolling fee. All applications and renewals are required to be completed and paid for online http://www.insurance.wa.gov/. (Rev. Code Wash. §48.14.010(1)(h)).

Prerequisites. Resident surplus lines broker applicants must first be licensed as a producer for both property and casualty lines of authority to qualify for a surplus lines broker license. In addition, applicants must take and pass the required examination prior to being issued a surplus lines license. (Rev. Code Wash. §48.15.070(1)).

Bond. Every resident surplus lines broker must maintain two bonds: one for $2,500 or five percent of premiums from placement of coverage with surplus line insurers in the previous calendar year, whichever is greater, up to $100,000 total aggregate liability, and a separate $20,000 bond. The bond must be made in favor of the people of the State of Washington or a named insured so that the people of Washington are covered. The bond may be continuous, and total aggregate liability on the bond may be limited to the required amount stated of the bond. (Rev. Code Wash. §48.15.070(5)).

Business Entity Licensing. Business entity applicants are required to pay an initial license fee of $200, plus a $5 filing fee and a $20 affiliation fee. Business entity surplus lines licenses expire every two years on the date the license was originally issued. The biennial renewal fee is $200. In addition, business entity licensees must file an online completed affiliation notice at the time of application, and pay a $20 affiliation fee, and name a designated responsible licensed person (DRLP). Business entities may affiliate a licensee electronically through the office of the insurance commissioner's web site at http://www.insurance.wa.gov. Fingerprinting is required of all resident surplus lines brokers affiliated with a business entity. The fingerprint fee is $49.25.

B. **Nonresident Licensing:** Nonresidents holding a surplus lines broker license in their home state meet the minimum requirements for licensing in Washington. The nonresident surplus line broker's license expires and is subject to the same renewal and fee requirements for renewal as the resident surplus lines broker license. However, nonresident surplus lines applicants are not required to submit fingerprints or maintain surety bonds. The commissioner will waive the Washington surplus line broker's examination for a person who has and maintains a current resident surplus line broker's license, or the equivalent, in the applicant's home state. (Rev. Code Wash. §48.15.073(2) and Wash. Admin. Code 284-15-010). Beginning in January 2018 the Office of the Insurance Commissioner will: 1) license non-resident applicants for surplus line broker licenses if their resident state issues non-resident surplus line broker licenses to residents of this state, and 2) waive the examination requirement if a licensed non-resident surplus line broker moves to Washington and wishes to become licensed as a resident surplus line broker and their application is received by the OIC within ninety days of the cancellation of the broker's resident license in the other state. (Rev. Code Wash. § 48.15.070(3)).

Licensed nonresident surplus line brokers must appoint the commissioner as the surplus line broker's attorney to receive service of legal process issued against the surplus line broker in Washington upon causes of action arising within Washington. The appointment is irrevocable for as long as there could be any cause of action against the surplus lines broker arising out of insurance transactions in Washington. (Wash. Rev. Code Ann. §48.15.073).

All applications for resident, business entity, and nonresident surplus lines broker licenses must be submitted electronically through the commissioner's Web site at https://www.insurance.wa.gov/surplus-line-broker-business-entity-non-resident.

C. **Diligent Effort:** If surplus lines insurance coverages cannot be procured from authorized insurers, then such coverages may be procured from unauthorized insurers, subject to the following conditions:

1. *Requirements.* The insurance must be procured through a licensed surplus lines broker licensed in accordance with the licensing requirements described above. If the insurance is property and casualty insurance, except industrial insurance, then the insurance must be procured under the laws and rules of the insured's home state.

2. *Diligent Effort.* The insurance must not be procurable, after diligent effort has been made to do so from among a majority of the insurers authorized to transact that kind of insurance in this state.

3. *Restrictions.* Coverage may not be procured from an unauthorized insurer for the purpose of securing a lower premium rate than would be accepted by any authorized insurer nor to secure any other competitive advantage.

4. *Certification.* At the time of procuring the insurance, the surplus line broker must certify to the accuracy of the facts supporting the surplus line broker's diligent effort required in (2) and (3) of this paragraph. The certification must set forth the facts supporting the

surplus line broker's diligent effort; the certification must state that under the penalty of suspension or revocation of the surplus line broker's license the facts contained in the certification are true and correct; the certification may be in electronic, digital, or another format as designated by the commissioner; the certification must be filed with the commissioner within sixty days after the insurance is procured. (Rev. Code Wash. §48.15.040 and Wash. Admin. Code 284-15-030).

5. *Commercial Purchaser Exemption.* Surplus lines brokers seeking to procure from or place insurance with an unauthorized insurer for an exempt commercial purchaser are not required to satisfy the diligent effort requirements described above when:

   a. The surplus line broker or referring insurance producer procuring or placing the surplus line insurance has disclosed to the exempt commercial purchaser that such insurance may or may not be available from the admitted market that may provide greater protection with more regulatory oversight.

   b. The exempt commercial purchaser has subsequently requested in writing the surplus line broker or referring insurance producer to procure or place such insurance from an unauthorized insurer. (Rev. Code Wash. §48.15.043).

D. Tax: 2 percent. On or before March first of each year, each surplus lines broker must remit electronically to the treasurer of the State of Washington through the commissioner, a tax of 2 percent on the premiums, exclusive of sums collected to cover federal and state taxes and examination fees, on surplus lines insurance transacted by him or her during the preceding calendar year as shown by his or her annual statement filed with the commissioner. (Rev. Code Wash. §48.14.020).

Multi-State Premium Tax Allocation. For property and casualty insurance, other than industrial insurance, if Washington is the insured's home state and the insurance covers risks in the United States or its territories, the tax must be computed upon the entire premium, without regard to whether the policy covers risks or exposures that are located in Washington. If Washington is the insured's home state and the insurance covers risks outside the United States, no tax on the non-US portion of the premium is due. This does not mean that it is exempt from all other taxes. For all other lines of insurance, if a surplus line policy covers risks or exposures only partially in Washington, the tax so payable must be computed upon the proportion of the premium that is properly allocable to the risks or exposures located in Washington. (Rev. Code Wash. §48.15.120 amended by 2015 Wash. Legis. Serv. Ch. 132 (H.B. 1308)).

E. Stamping Fee: The stamping fee is 0.10 percent for policies with inception dates of July 1 or later; 0.25 percent for policies with inception dates between July 1 2006 and

June 30, 2011; .4 percent for policies with inception dates of June 30, 2006 and earlier. (http://www.surpluslines.org/filing-information/taxes-and-fees/)

F. **Surplus Lines Association:** Surplus Line Association of Washington, 600 University Street, Suite 1710 Seattle, WA 98101. Phone: 206-682-3409. Fax: 206-623-3326. Website: http://www.surpluslines.org.

G. **Other Requirements or Restrictions:** Surplus lines brokers are restricted from knowingly placing surplus lines insurance with insurers that are financially unsound. Surplus lines brokers are required to ascertain the financial condition of the unauthorized insurer, and maintain written evidence thereof, before placing insurance therewith. A surplus line broker may place insurance with an alien unauthorized insurer shown on the National Association of Insurance Commissioners (NAIC) Quarterly Listing of Alien Insurers. The financial condition of an insurer named on the listing is deemed to be adequately documented. (Wash. Rev. Code Ann. §48.15.090 and Wash. Admin. Code 284-15-020).

Exemptions. The surplus lines provisions do not apply to reinsurance or the following types of insurance when placed by licensed insurance producers of Washington:

1. Ocean marine and foreign trade insurances.

2. Insurance on subjects located, resident or to be performed wholly outside of Washington, or on vehicles or aircraft owned and principally garaged outside of Washington.

3. Insurance on property or operations of railroads engaged in interstate commerce.

4. Insurance of aircraft owned or operated by manufacturers of aircraft, or of aircraft operated in scheduled interstate flight, or cargo of such aircraft, or against liability, other than workers' compensation and employer's liability, arising out of the ownership, maintenance or use of such aircraft. (Rev. Code Wash. §48.15.160).

Eligibility. The surplus line broker may only insure with any foreign insurer that is authorized to write the kind of insurance in its domiciliary jurisdiction and has capital and surplus, or its equivalent under the laws of its domiciliary jurisdiction, which equals the greater of the minimum capital and surplus requirements under the laws of Washington or $15 million. The eligibility requirements may be satisfied by an insurer possessing less than the minimum capital and surplus upon an affirmative finding of acceptability by the commissioner. The finding must be based upon factors such as quality of management, capital and surplus of any parent company, company underwriting profit and investment income trends, market availability, and company record and reputation within the industry. The commissioner is prohibited from making an affirmative finding of acceptability when the foreign insurer's capital and surplus is less than $4.5 million. (Rev. Code Wash. §48.15.090 and Wash. Admin. Code 284-15-050).

Annual Tax Statements. Each surplus line broker must, on or before March first of each year, file with the commissioner a verified statement of all surplus lines insurance transacted by him or her during the preceding calendar year. The statement must be in a form and format as prescribed by the commissioner and must show the aggregate of net premiums. The commissioner may require additional information. Annual tax statements are not required to be filed by surplus lines brokers who procure property and casualty insurance when the insured's home state is a state other than Washington. (Rev. Code Wash. §48.15.110).

Notice. All surplus lines contracts must be initialed by or bear the name of the surplus lines broker and be stamped as follows (Wash. Admin. Code 284-15-030):

> "This contract is registered and delivered as a surplus line coverage under the insurance code of the state of Washington, Title 48 RCW. It is not protected by any Washington state guaranty association law."

Records. Each licensed surplus lines broker must keep a full and true record of each surplus line contract procured by him or her (including a copy of the daily report, if any) showing the amount of the insurance; the gross premiums charged; the return premium paid, if any; the rate of premium charged upon the several items of property; the effective date of the contract, and the terms thereof; the name and address of the insurer; the name and address of the insured; a brief general description of property insured and where located; and any other information as may be required by the commissioner. All records as to any particular transaction must be kept available and open to the inspection of the commissioner at any business time for five years. In addition, the Surplus Line Association of Washington requires the following be submitted monthly: Declarations Sheet, any supplemental Declarations Sheets. Service of Suit, and Forms List. Electronic filing through SLIP at https://www.surpluslines.org/filing-information/electronic-filing/ or https://slip.surpluslines.org/Common/login.aspx?ReturnUrl=%2f is preferred, but not required. (Rev. Code Wash. §48.15.100).

Courtesy Filings. Courtesy filing of taxes and affidavits is allowed in Washington.

H. Independently Procured Insurance: Washington statutes allow direct procurement of insurance from a licensed, authorized insurer only. Direct procurement on a surplus lines basis is not allowed but must be obtained only through a Washington-licensed surplus lines broker. According to the Revised Code of Washington, "A person, other than a duly licensed surplus lines broker acting in good faith under her license, who makes a contract of insurance in this state, directly or indirectly, on behalf of an unauthorized insurer, without complying with the provisions of this chapter, is personally liable for the performance of such contract." (Rev. Code Wash. §48.15.020).

I. Industrial Insured Exemption: Washington has no industrial insured exemption. See Wash. Rev. Code Ann. Title 51 for more details.

NRRA Implementation

J. Compact: None.

K. Definitions:

1. Except for affiliated groups, "home state" means, with respect to an insured:

   a. The state in which an insured maintains its principal place of business or, in the case of an individual, the individual's principal residence; or

   b. If 100 percent of the insured risk is located out of the state referred to in this subsection, the state to which the greatest percentage of the insured's taxable premium for that insurance contract is allocated.

Affiliated Groups. If more than one insured from an affiliated group are named insureds on a single insurance contract issued by an unauthorized insurer, the term "home state" means the insured's home state, as determined pursuant to (a) of this paragraph, of the member of the affiliated group that has the largest percentage of premium attributed to it under the insurance contract.

Principal Place of Business. To determine the home state of the insured, the principal place of business is the state where the insured maintains its headquarters and where the insured's high-level officers direct, control, and coordinate the business activities of the insured. (Rev. Code Wash. §48.15.010).

L. Statutory References: Revised Code of Washington §§48.14.10; 48.15.020 through 48.15.170; Washington Administrative Code 284-15-010 through 284-15-110.

WEST VIRGINIA

A. **Resident Licensing:** The West Virginia surplus lines broker license expires annually at midnight on May 31. The initial and annual renewal fee is $200. Failure to apply for renewal by May 1 will result in a $100 penalty.

Resident applicants are required to have held a valid individual insurance producer license for the type or types of insurance an applicant expects and intends to export to the surplus lines market for at least three consecutive years immediately preceding the date of application. Of the three consecutive years required for qualification, applicants are required to have held a valid West Virginia resident or nonresident insurance producer license for at least one year, or to hold a valid excess or surplus line broker license issued by another state. Additionally, applicants are required to pass a qualifying examination. The examination fee is $88. Scheduling and payment of exams is done online through Pearson VUE, at https://home.pearsonvue.com/getattachment/f12f2b28-d842-45ab-bc92-d1650e9f9165/West%20Virginia%20Insurance%20Licensing%20Candidate%20Handbook.aspx. Residents must have established and continue to maintain an office in West Virginia.

West Virginia licensed producers may place business with surplus lines brokers and receive commission. (W. Va. Code, §33-12C-8; W. Va. CSR §114-20-3).

Letters of certification: $5; letters of clearance: $10; duplicate license: $5. (W. Va. Code §33-12C-25).

B. **Nonresident Licensing:** The West Virginia surplus lines broker license expires annually on May 31. The initial and annual renewal fee is $200. Failure to renew by May 1 will result in a $100 penalty.

If the Commissioner determines that a surplus lines licensee of another state is competent, trustworthy and meets the licensing requirements of West Virginia, the Commissioner may, in his or her discretion, issue a nonresident surplus lines license. A license shall not be issued unless the prospective licensee furnishes the Commissioner with the name and address of a resident of West Virginia upon whom notices or orders of the Commissioner or persons affecting the nonresident surplus lines licensee may be served.

Nonresident applicants are required to have held a valid individual insurance producer license for the type or types of insurance an applicant expects and intends to export to the surplus lines market for at least three consecutive years immediately preceding the date of application. Of the three consecutive years required for qualification, applicants are required to have held a valid West Virginia resident or nonresident insurance producer license for at least one year, or to hold a valid excess or surplus line broker license issued by another state. Nonresidents are not required to pass the qualifying examination if duly licensed as a surplus lines broker in their home state. (W. Va. Code §33-12C-8; W. Va. CSR. §114-20-3).

Letters of certification: $5; letters of clearance: $10; duplicate license: $5. (W. Va. Code § 33-12C-25).

C. **Diligent Effort:** Insurance coverage written by a surplus lines insurer and placed by a surplus lines licensee for an insured whose home state is West Virginia may not be procured until a diligent search has been made by the individual insurance producer to place the risk with an admitted insurer. The surplus lines licensee must submit to the commissioner a sworn notarized affidavit that a diligent search has been made by the individual insurance producer to place the risk with licensed insurers authorized to write and actually writing the particular risk sought to be placed in the excess lines market. (W. Va. CSR §114-20-4).

Commercial Purchaser Exemption. A licensee is not required to perform a diligent search in accordance with section 4 of this rule when seeking to procure or place nonadmitted insurance for an exempt commercial purchaser whose home state is West Virginia if the prospective purchaser has signed a document prior to the placement of such insurance that provides that the licensee has disclosed that such insurance may or may not be available from an admitted insurer that might provide greater protection and more regulatory oversight and that the purchaser has nonetheless requested that the licensee procure or place with a nonadmitted carrier. (W. Va. CSR. §114-20-4A).

D. **Tax:** 4.55 percent. On and after the date on which NIMA is made effective in West Virginia, each surplus lines licensee, with respect to those policies where West Virginia is the home state and for which the payment of premium taxes is due, must forward such payments and related information as required by NIMA to the Clearinghouse for deposit in the Clearinghouse account and must send any additional information to the commissioner as may be required by him as set forth on the agency Website.

Surplus lines licensees are required to make a quarterly tax filing on or before February 15 for the quarter ending the preceding December 31, May 15 for the quarter ending the preceding March 31, August 15 for the quarter ending the preceding June 30, and November 15 for the quarter ending the preceding September 30 and pay such fees as may be established by the Clearinghouse.

On and after the date on which NIMA is made effective in West Virginia, the taxes required to be paid where West Virginia is the home state, are as follows:

1. On the portion of premium allocated to West Virginia, as determined by the Commissioner based on Annex A and Annex B of NIMA: 4.55 percent.

2. On the portion of the premium allocated to each signatory state, as determined by the commissioner based on Annex A and Annex B of NIMA: the rate specified by that state, as listed in allocation tables published by the Clearinghouse.

3. On the portion deemed to be allocated to states not participating in NIMA: 4.55 percent. (W. Va. CSR § 114-20-5).

The method of tax allocation for multistate risks must follow what is set forth in Annex A and Annex B of NIMA. (W. Va. Code, §33-12C-7).

E. **Stamping Fee:** None. West Virginia does not have a stamping office.

F. **Surplus Lines Association:** Rusty Ellis, CPCU West Virginia Surplus Lines Assn, c/o DVUA of West Virginia, Inc., 3857 Teays Valley Road, Suite 1, Hurricane, WV 25526. Phone: 304-757-1175. Fax: 304-757-1182.

G. **Other Requirements or Restrictions:** Each licensed surplus lines licensee who participates directly or indirectly in effecting any insurance contract on a surplus lines basis on behalf of any insured whose home state is West Virginia may not knowingly place any coverage in an insolvent insurer. (W. Va. Code, §33-12C-26). Licensees may accept and place authorized surplus lines business from any individual insurance producer licensed in West Virginia for the kind of insurance involved, and may compensate the individual insurance producer. The surplus lines licensee has the right to receive from the surplus lines insurer the customary commission. In those instances in which surplus lines business is produced to a surplus lines licensee by an individual insurance producer licensed in this state for the kind of insurance involved, it is the surplus lines licensee's responsibility to include the necessary information in the mandatory Annual Report of Written Surplus Lines and Annual Surplus Lines Tax Return Reconciliation Form.

Workers compensation insurance may not be placed with nonadmitted insurers.

Eligibility. Brokers are permitted to place nonadmitted insurance with U.S. domestic insurers that are eligible in this state provided they are authorized to write such business in their State of Domicile and maintain minimum capital and surplus of $15 million or the minimum capital and surplus amount required in the state, whichever is greater. Under the NRRA, brokers are permitted to place business with non-U.S. carriers that are included on the NAIC's Quarterly Listing of Alien Insurers. (W. Va. Code, §33-12C-5).

Disclosures. Once negotiations over the available terms and conditions for specific coverages begin, at least the following facts must be disclosed in writing to the potential insured: that the insurance will be placed through a surplus lines insurer and the name of the insurer; that the producer is not an agent of the potential insurer because surplus lines insurers are not permitted to appoint individual insurance producers; that the surplus lines market is a specialty market that has limited regulatory oversight by the commissioner, and specifically, there is no regulation of policy coverage forms or rates; and that no protection is afforded under any West Virginia guaranty fund mechanism. (W. Va. CSR 114-20-8).

Notice. Each surplus lines insurance policy or evidence of insurance shall have printed or stamped in contrasting color on the front page the following statement:

> "THIS COMPANY IS NOT LICENSED TO DO BUSINESS IN WEST VIRGINIA, AND IS NOT SUBJECT TO THE WEST VIRGINIA INSURANCE GUARANTY ACT." (W. Va. CSR 114-20-4).

Records. Each surplus lines licensee must keep in his or her office a full and true record of each surplus lines contract procured by him or her on behalf of any insured whose home state is West Virginia, and the records may be examined at any time thereafter by the commissioner. The records must include the name and address of the surplus lines insurer; the names and addresses of the insureds; the amount of insurance; the gross premium charged; the return premium paid, if any; the rate of premium charged on the several items of coverages; the effective date of the contract and the terms of the contract; a brief general description of the risks insured against and the property insured; the policy number; the written due diligence declaration of the individual insurance producer (unless the due diligence requirement is not applicable); and any additional information the commissioner may require to effectuate the provisions the NRRA and NIMA. (W. Va. Code, §33-12C-16; W. Va. CSR 114-20-4).

Advertising. Surplus lines licensees may advertise their services and product lines to other producers. Such advertisements must identify the fact that the insurance will be placed with a surplus lines insurer. The advertisements may not identify the insurer by name nor act as a solicitation on behalf of any surplus lines insurer. The advertisements may not identify specific rates or specific policy provisions.

Referrals. A surplus lines licensee may originate surplus lines insurance or accept applications for surplus lines insurance from any other producer duly licensed as to the kinds of insurance involved. The surplus lines licensee may compensate the producer. (W. Va. CSR 114-20-8).

Reports. On or before May 1, the end of the month following each year, each surplus lines licensee shall file with the commissioner, on forms prescribed by the commissioner, a verified report in duplicate of all surplus lines insurance transacted during the preceding period. The report shall show the following:

1. Aggregate gross premiums written.

2. Aggregate return premiums.

3. Amount of aggregate tax remitted to this state.

4. Amount of aggregate tax due or remitted to each other state for which an allocation is made. (W. Va. Code, §33-12C-17).

NRRA Implementation

H. Compact: West Virginia has authorized admittance to the Nonadmitted Insurance Multi-State Agreement (NIMA) but has not yet done so.

As of December 2017 NIMA will have completed the process of dissolving and concluding operations. Check with the department of insurance regarding changes in procedures during this process. (https://www.napslo.org/docs/PDF/Legislative/NIMA%20Board%20Votes%20to%20Dissolve.pdf).

I. Statutory References: W. Va. Code, §§33-12C-1 through 33-12C-15; 33-3-33.

WISCONSIN

A. **Resident Licensing:** Residents may be licensed to place business with nonadmitted insurers. Residents must hold a property and casualty license before applying for a surplus line agent. Applications can be submitted online at www.sircon.com or www.nipr.com with payment of a $100 application fee. Annual renewal fee is $100.

B. **Nonresident Licensing:** Nonresidents may be licensed for surplus lines on the same basis as residents. Nonresidents must submit an electronic application at www.sircon.com or www.nipr.com. Application fee is $100, annual renewal fee is $100. (Wis. Admin. Code Ins 6.59).

C. **Diligent Effort:** No affidavit of nonavailability is required.

D. **Tax:** 3 percent of gross premiums for all lines. The surplus lines tax is applicable to any fees charged by the surplus lines broker. The tax is due to the state annually on or before March 1. (Wis. Stat. §618.43 and Wis. Admin. Code Ins 6.17).

E. **Stamping Fee:** None. Wisconsin does not have a stamping office.

F. **Surplus Lines Association:** No Association.

G. **Other Requirements or Restrictions:**

Exemptions. Only classes of insurance approved by the commissioner may be placed, excluding title, workers compensation, and mortgage guarantee insurance. No agent or broker shall, either knowingly or without adequate investigation of the financial condition and general reputation of the insurer, place insurance under this section with financially unsound insurers or with insurers engaging in unfair practices, or with otherwise substandard insurers, without giving the applicant notice in writing of the deficiencies of the insurer; notice that the insurer has not obtained a certificate of authority in Wisconsin and is not regulated in Wisconsin; and notice that the risk is not protected by the Wisconsin insurance security fund. To be financially sound, an insurer must be able to satisfy standards comparable to those applied under the laws of this state to authorized insurers. (Wis. Stat. §618.41). Surplus lines agents, direct placement policyholders, and risk retention groups should no longer report multistate surplus lines policies to the Surplus Lines Clearinghouse, but should continue reporting policies to OCI Bulletin 6-25-2015 at https://oci.wi.gov/Pages/Regulation/Bulletin20150625SurplusLines.aspx.

Eligibility. Brokers are permitted to place nonadmitted insurance with U.S. domestic insurers that are eligible in this state provided they are authorized to write such business in their State of Domicile and maintain minimum capital and surplus of $15 million or the minimum capital and surplus amount required in the state, whichever is greater. Alternatively, the commission can find the unauthorized insurers capital and surplus are acceptable based on factors including the quality of management, capital and surplus of any parent company, company underwriting profit and investment income trends, market availability, and company record and reputation within the industry. The minimum required capital and surplus is $4.5 million. NRRA allows brokers to place business with non-U.S. carriers that are included on the NAIC's Quarterly Listing of Alien Insurers. (Wis. Stat. §618.416).

Notice. Every new or renewal insurance policy must contain the name and address of the insurance agent or broker who procured it, and shall have stamped or affixed upon it the following:

> "This insurance contract is with an insurer which has not obtained a certificate of authority to transact a regular insurance business in the state of Wisconsin, and is issued and delivered as a surplus lines coverage pursuant to s. 618.41 of the Wisconsin Statutes. Section 618.43(1), Wisconsin Statutes, requires payment by the policyholder of 3 percent tax on gross premium."

In addition, the policy must include a description of the subject of the insurance, and indicate the coverage, conditions and term of the insurance, the premium charged and premium taxes to be collected from the policyholder, and the name and address of the policyholder and insurer. If the direct risk is assumed by more than one insurer, the policy must state the names and addresses of all insurers and the portion of the entire direct risk each has assumed. (Wis. Stat. §618.41).

Evidence of Insurance. Upon placing new or renewal coverage, the agent or broker must promptly deliver to the policyholder or her agent evidence of the insurance consisting either of the policy as issued by the insurer or, if the policy is not then available, a certificate, cover note or other confirmation of insurance. (Wis. Stat. §618.41).

Records. An agent or broker must keep in his or her office for a period of five years any notice given to application regarding deficiencies of insurer. (Wis. Stat. §618.41).

H. Independently Procured Insurance:

1. *Rules.* Insureds in Wisconsin may purchase insurance directly from insurers without the use of an agent or a broker if no agent or broker doing business in Wisconsin is involved or if negotiations occur primarily outside of the state. Policyholders are

liable for a premium tax of 3 percent of gross premiums within sixty days after the insurance procured or renewed. (Wis. Stat. §§618.42 and 618.43).

2. *Industrial Insured Exemption*. Wisconsin has no industrial insured exemption.

NRRA Implementation

I. Compact: None.

J. Definitions: Home State. This state is the home state if the insured maintains its principal place of business or, in the case of an individual, the individual's principal residence here. This state's requirements regarding the placement of such business will apply if this state is considered the home state. However, if 100 percent of the insured risk is located outside of this state, then the home state is the state to which the greatest percentage of the insured's taxable premium for that insurance contract is allocated. With respect to an affiliated group, if more than one insured from the affiliated group is a named insured on a single nonadmitted insurance contract, the home state is that of the member of the affiliated group that has the largest percentage of premium attributed to the member under the insurance contract.

"Principal Place of Business" means, with respect to determining the home state of an Insured, the state where the Insured maintains its headquarters and where the Insured's high-level officers direct, control, and coordinate the business activities of the insured.

"Principal residence" means, with respect to determining the home state of an insured who is an individual, the state where the individual resides for the greatest number of days during a calendar year. (Wis. Stat. §618.40).

K. Statutory References: Wisconsin Statutes §§601.31 and 618.39 through 618.61.

WYOMING

A. **Resident Licensing:** Licensed property and casualty producers may be licensed to place insurance with nonadmitted insurers after successfully passing a required examination and submitting the uniform application, surplus lines bond and licensing fees to the department. Exam registration and payment can be made online through Pearson VUE at http://www.pearsonvue.com/wy/insurance/, or through the phone at 866-936-7786. The exam fee is $113 for combination major lines and $96 for single line or limited line examinations. Initial and renewal applications can be submitted online through Sircon or NIPR or by mail; electronic submission is preferred. The initial or renewal license fee: $100. The individual surplus lines broker's license expires every two years on the last day of the birth month. A firm surplus lines broker's license expires every two years on March 31. Applicant must file a $10,000 bond. The bond must be issued by an authorized insurer. The bond must not be terminated unless at least thirty days prior written notice is given to the licensee and filed with the commissioner. (Wyo. Stat. §§26-4-101, 26-11-112, and 26-11-114).

Only the insured's home state may require a surplus lines broker to be licensed to sell, solicit, or negotiate nonadmitted insurance with respect to a particular placement. If Wyoming is the insured's home state, the surplus lines broker must be licensed in Wyoming.

A Wyoming licensed surplus line broker may accept and place surplus line business for any insurance agent licensed in Wyoming for the kind of insurance involved and may compensate the agent accordingly. (Wyo. Stat. §26-11-115).

B. **Nonresident Licensing:** Nonresidents may be licensed as surplus lines brokers if identically licensed in their home state. A property and casualty license is needed only if the licensee will be accessing the admitted market in Wyoming. No bond is required for nonresidents. The initial licensing fee is $100; renewal license fee is $150. Fees are the same for individuals and business entities. Renewal timeline is the same as resident licensing. Nonresident firms must designate a responsible producer, who must hold a Wyoming surplus lines license. (Wyo. Stat. §§26-4-101, 26-11-112).

C. **Diligent Effort:** The surplus lines broker shall verify that a properly conducted diligent effort search was performed and documented as prescribed by the commissioner. The report must certify that the full amount of insurance required is not procurable, after diligent effort has been made to do so, from among the insurers authorized to transact and actually write that kind and class of insurance in this state, and the amount of insurance exported shall be only the excess over the amount procurable from authorized insurers. Use of surplus lines to obtain better rate or terms is prohibited. Within forty-five days after placing any surplus lines insurance for an insured whose home state is Wyoming, each surplus lines broker shall report policy transaction data with the SLAS Clearinghouse.

Commercial Purchaser Exemption. A surplus lines broker seeking to procure or place nonadmitted insurance on behalf of an "exempt commercial purchaser" is not required to perform a diligent search if the broker has disclosed that insurance may or may not be available from the admitted market that may provide greater protection with more regulatory oversight and the exempt commercial purchaser has subsequently requested in writing for the broker to procure or place such insurance from a nonadmitted insurer. (Wyo. Stat. §26-11-104).

D. Tax: 3 percent of gross premiums, less the amount of any return premium, payable quarterly by the surplus lines broker. There is a $25 per day fine for each day the tax is late from the due date to the date of receipt. The surplus lines broker must pay interest on the amount of any delinquent tax due, at the rate of 9 percent per year, compounded annually; beginning the day the amount becomes delinquent. The surplus lines tax is also applicable to any fees levied on the policy. (Wyo. Stat. §§26-11-118 and 26-11-119).

E. Stamping Fee: None. Wyoming does not have a stamping office.

F. Surplus Lines Association: None.

G. Other Requirements or Restrictions:

Exemptions. Wyoming surplus lines law does not apply to wet marine and transportation insurance; insurance on vehicles or aircraft owned and principally garaged outside of Wyoming; insurance on railroad operations engaged in interstate commerce and their property used in those operations; insurance on aircraft owned or operated by manufacturers or operated in commercial interstate flight; or against liability, other than workers compensation and employers liability, arising out of the ownership, maintenance, or use of that aircraft. No countersignature is required on surplus lines policies. Wyoming does not allow courtesy filings of taxes or certificates of nonavailability. (Wyo. Stat. §26-11-102).

Eligibility. Brokers are permitted to place nonadmitted insurance with U.S. domestic insurers that are eligible in this state provided they are authorized to write such business in their state of domicile and maintain minimum capital and surplus of $15 million or the minimum capital and surplus amount required in the state, whichever is greater. These requirements may be satisfied by an insurer's possessing less than the minimum capital and surplus upon an affirmative finding of acceptability by the commissioner; however in no event shall the commissioner make an affirmative finding of acceptability when the nonadmitted insurer's capital and surplus is less than $4.5 million. For brokers to place business with non-U.S. carriers they must be included on the NAIC's Quarterly Listing of Alien Insurers. The commissioner may from time to time publish a list of all surplus lines insurers he deems eligible currently and mail a copy of the list to each broker, but the commissioner is not obligated to determine the actual financial condition or claims practices of any nonadmitted insurer. (Wyo. Stat. §26-11-107).

Notice. All surplus line insurance contracts must have stamped or printed upon it, in at least ten point bold font, the name and address of the surplus line broker who procured the coverage, and the following statement:

> "This insurance contract is issued pursuant to the Wyoming Nonadmitted Insurance Laws by an insurer neither licensed by nor under the jurisdiction of the Wyoming Insurance Department. In the event of insolvency of the surplus lines insurer, losses will not be paid by the Wyoming Insurance Guaranty Association or the Wyoming Life and Health Insurance Guaranty Association." (Wyo. Stat. §26-11-109).

A surplus lines broker is required to notify the insured in writing of the disclosures in Wyoming Statutes §26-11-109(b). The applicant must sign a copy of the notice acknowledging its receipt.

A signed copy of this notice must be in the insured's file that is maintained by the surplus lines broker. A contract of insurance is not binding and no premium charged is due and payable until the insured receives this notification. The notification can be a separate document or included in a quotation, proposal, letter, or other similar document.

Evidence of Insurance Coverage. Upon placing surplus lines insurance, the surplus lines broker shall promptly issue and deliver to the insured or the producer the policy, or if the policy is not available, a certificate, cover note, binder or other evidence of the insurance. A certificate if issued and delivered must contain or have attached a complete record of all policy insuring agreements, conditions, exclusions, clauses endorsements or any other material facts that would regularly be included in the policy. The certificate, cover note, binder, or other evidence of insurance must be executed by the broker and must show: the description and location of the subject of the insurance; coverages including any material limitations other than those in standard forms; a general description of the insured; the name and address of the insured and surplus lines insurer or insurers; and the proportion of the entire risk assumed by each and the name and license number of the surplus lines broker. If after issuance and delivery of evidence of insurance there is any change to the insurer's identity, or the proportion of the risk assumed by any insurer or any other material change in coverage, the surplus lines broker must promptly issue and deliver to the insured or the original producer an appropriate substitute for, or endorsement of the original document, accurately showing the current status of the coverage and the insurers responsible for the coverage. (Wyo. Stat. §26-11-108).

Records. Each surplus lines broker shall keep in his or her office a full and true record of each surplus lines insurance contract placed by or through the broker, including a copy of the policy, certificate, cover note or other evidence of insurance showing each of the following:

(i) amount of the insurance, risks, and perils insured;

(ii) gross premium charged;

(iii) return premium paid, if any;

(iv) rate of premium charged upon the several items of property;

(v) effective date of contract and the terms thereof;

(vi) name and address of each insurer on the direct risk and the proportion of the entire risk assumed by each insurer if less than the entire risk;

(vii) name and address of the insured;

(viii) brief general description of the property or risk insured and where located or to be performed;

(ix) amount of tax and other sums to be collected from the insured;

(x) allocation of surplus lines taxes by state;

(xi) identity of the producer, any confirming correspondence from the insurer or its representative, and the application; and

(xii) any other information the commissioner requires.

The record of each contract must be kept for at least five years following termination of the contract, and must be kept open at all reasonable times to examination by the commissioner without notice. Nonresident surplus lines brokers must make available to the commissioner any and all records deemed necessary for examination, in lieu of maintaining an office in Wyoming. (Wyo. Stat. §26-11-116).

Quarterly Affidavit Report. Each surplus lines broker must file with the SLAS Clearinghouse a verified report of all surplus line insurance transactions for the previous quarter. Failing to file the quarterly report may result in a fine up to $25 per day for each day the delinquency continues and required to pay 9 percent interest on any delinquent tax due, beginning the day after the report was due until the date the report is received. The report must include the affidavit as to the diligent effort to place coverages with admitted insurers and the results of that effort. (Wyo. Stat. §§26-11-117 and 26-11-119).

H. Independently Procured Insurance:

1. *Rules.* Each insured in this state who procures, continues or renews insurance with a nonadmitted insurer on properties, risks or exposures located or to be performed in whole or in part in this state, other than insurance procured through a surplus lines broker, shall, within forty-five days after the date the insurance was so procured, continued or renewed, file policy transaction data with the SLAS Clearinghouse, showing the name and address of the insured or insureds, name and address of the insurer, the subject of insurance, a general description of the coverage, the amount of premium currently charged and additional pertinent information requested by the commissioner. The insured is subject to the same tax payment requirements as apply to a surplus lines broker. (Wyo. Stat. §26-11-124).

2. *Industrial Insured Exemption.* An industrial insured obtains insurance of any risk other than life and annuity contracts through the services of a full-time employee acting as an insurance manager or buyer or through the services of a continuously retained qualified insurance consultant, has aggregate premiums total at least $25,000, and has at least twenty-five full-time employees. (Wyo. Stat. §26-12-101).

NRRA Implementation

J. Compact: Wyoming adopted NIMA (HB 242); however, the Board of Directors of NIMA voted on April 28, 2016 to discontinue operations and dissolve the NIMA, Inc. organization. The SLAS Clearinghouse will continue to accept surplus lines filings and payments for Wyoming policies effective October 1, 2016 and after. The Florida Surplus Lines Service Office serves as the Department's vendor for all surplus lines policy reporting and premium tax payments. Beginning October 1, 2016, all new and renewal multistate policies for Wyoming will be reported as single state policies through the SLAS Clearinghouse single state reporting platform in SLIP, with 100 percent of the premium being reported to and taxed by the respective home state. See Memorandum 01-2016. (https://doi.wyo.gov/legal/memorandum).

K. Definitions:

1. *Home State.* Wyoming is the insured's home state if the insured maintains its principal place of business here or, in the case of an individual, the individual's principal place of residence is here. If Wyoming is considered the home state, only Wyoming's requirements regarding placement of such business will apply. If 100 percent of the risk is located outside of Wyoming, then the insured's home state is the state to which

the greatest percentage of the insured's taxable premium for that insurance contract is allocated.

If more than one insured from an affiliated group are named insureds on a single nonadmitted insurance placement, Wyoming is considered the home state for that placement if Wyoming is the home state of the member of the affiliated group that has the largest percentage of premium attributed to it under such insurance contracts. (Wyo. Stat. §26-11-103).

2. *Principal Place of Business.* With respect to determining the home state of the insured, the state where the insured maintains its headquarters and where the insured's high-level officers direct, control, and coordinate the business activities; or if the insured's high-level officers direct, control and coordinate the business activities is more than one state, the state in which the greatest percentage of the insured's taxable premium for that insurance contract is allocated; or if headquarters are outside any state, the state to which the greatest percentage of the insured's taxable premium for that insurance contract is allocated. (Wyo. Stat. §26-11-103).

3. *Principal Residence.* With respect to determining the home state of the insured, the state where the insured resides for the greatest number of days during the calendar year, or if the residence is located outside of any state, the state to which the greatest percentage of the insured's taxable premium for that insurance contract is allocated. (Wyo. Stat. §26-11-103).

L. Statutory References:

Wyo. Stat. §26-4-	101
Wyo. Stat. §§26-11-	102 to 104, 107 to 109
	112, 114 to 119
	124
Wyo. Stat. §26-12-	101

Web References:

https://doi.wyo.gov/legal/memorandum.